AFIPS

CONFERENCE PROCEEDINGS

VOLUME 56

1987

NATIONAL COMPUTER CONFERENCE

June 15–18, 1987
Chicago, Illinois

MARGARET K. BUTLER
Program Chair

JOHN M. BROWN
Conference Chair

Sponsored by

AMERICAN FEDERATION OF INFORMATION PROCESSING SOCIETIES, INC.
ASSOCIATION FOR COMPUTING MACHINERY
DATA PROCESSING MANAGEMENT ASSOCIATION
IEEE COMPUTER SOCIETY
SOCIETY FOR COMPUTER SIMULATION

AFIPS PRESS

1899 PRESTON WHITE DRIVE
RESTON, VIRGINIA 22091

Library of Congress Catalog Card Number 80-649583
ISSN 0095-6880
ISBN 0-88283-051-1

AFIPS PRESS
1899 Preston White Drive
Reston, Virginia 22091

The National Computer Conference
sponsored by

AMERICAN FEDERATION OF INFORMATION PROCESSING SOCIETIES, INC.
ASSOCIATION FOR COMPUTING MACHINERY
DATA PROCESSING MANAGEMENT ASSOCIATION
IEEE COMPUTER SOCIETY
SOCIETY FOR COMPUTER SIMULATION

Printed in the United States of America

Preface

JOHN M. BROWN
1987 NCC Chair

No industry has ever seen changes occur as rapidly as data processing. In 1987, we find ourselves smack-dab in the middle of some of the most profound changes to date, with no indication that the rate of change will ever slow. Even the name "data processing" is bring replaced with new ones like "Information Management and Movement." We are surrounded by an ever increasing ubiquity of distributed computing brought about by powerful microprocessors, with an ever increasing need to network microcomputers together and to mini and mainframe computers. The 1987 National Computer Conference recognizes the needs of the data professionals to stay current with these changes and to understand the trends for the future. In NCC '87, we challenge you to "Discover the Power of Information."

The planning and execution of a conference with the size and scope of NCC requires a large number of dedicated people. The volunteers who were part of the 1987 Conference Steering Committee and the various subcommittees are an especially hardworking and professional set. They organized an extremely timely and relevant conference—from the insightful technical program to the Professional Development seminars to the many special activities. They participated with enthusiasm because NCC is a special kind of conference sponsored by industry professionals for industry professionals. They in turn received invaluable assistance from the AFIPS staff and the NCC Board, who all put in efforts well beyond the call of duty.

As you read through these Proceedings, whether it is for the first time or as a refresher for what you heard and saw at the conference, I am sure you will find it to be a useful and valuable reference source for what is happening in computing.

Introduction

MARGARET BUTLER
1987 NCC Program Chair

The technical program is designed to afford you, the Conference attendee, the opportunity to "Discover the Power of Information" for yourself. National Computer Conference attendees come from all segments of the information industry; they are a mixed lot, difficult to characterize simply on the basis of educational background, profession or career, or special interest. Consequently, in planning for NCC '87, the Program Committee attempted to produce a balanced program which would permit you either to focus on acquiring in-depth knowledge in your particular specialty or to broaden your perspective by exploring what is going on in other parts of the computing world.

To cover the ever-widening scope of the industry, the program consists of some 90 sessions organized in ten major topic areas (or tracks). Featured sessions in the various topic areas are scattered throughout the four-day program. In these, technical experts and industry leaders describe recent developments, discuss issues of critical and timely importance, and present their views of the industry's future. Featured sessions are scheduled so as not to conflict with one another to allow you to attend all of them should you so desire.

In addition to the topic area sessions, the NCC '87 Program includes a number of special sessions and the Small Business Day seminar series. Also offered is a preview of plans for the Smithsonian's major new exhibition on the development of information technologies, centering on computers and communications and a pair of Pioneer Day sessions on Early Operating Systems. You may also find the program dealing with software aspects of SDI meets your fancy.

This volume is intended as a true Conference Proceedings, insofar as possible. Use it to get the most from NCC '87 while in Chicago and as a valuable reference in your library afterward. It contains the 62 percent of the submitted papers selected for presentation with the assistance of this year's staff of referees, topic area descriptions, and position papers contributed by session organizers, program participants, or members of the NCC '87 Program Committee. I speak for the entire Program Committee in saying we believe we have succeeded in putting together an exciting and educational menu of program sessions designed to meet your needs and interests. Enjoy.

CONTENTS

ARTIFICIAL INTELLIGENCE

MARTHA EVENS
Illinois Institute of Technology
Chicago, Illinois
and
HAL BERGHEL
University of Arkansas
Fayetteville, Arkansas
and
SANDRA TAYLOR
Britton Lee, Inc.
Los Gatos, California

Artificial intelligence (AI) is probably the most controversial area of computer science. Historically, the domain of AI was at best loosely formulated, as were the underlying principles upon which this new field was constructed. As a result, the early days of artificial intelligence were more concerned with characterizing the problems than with formulating their solutions.

Because of the limited success achieved in developing systems which can purport to have even a minimum level of intelligence, researchers lowered their expectations. Consequently, there now exist many special-purpose AI systems with enormous practical benefits, albeit with less than earthshaking significance. For example, research in natural language processing has advanced to the point where in some instances man-machine interfaces can be tailored to the human rather than to the machine. Although you may not be able to strike up a conversation with a computer, you can rely upon a question-answer system to simplify the interface with a database management system, and while it is not useful to discuss your health problems with a machine, knowledge-based systems may assist a physician in making a differential diagnosis.

Other areas in which rapid progress is evident include expert systems, logic programming, knowledge representation, rule-based systems, theorem proving, scene analysis, and pattern classification. Each of these areas is at a stage in which real applications can be envisioned to follow from current research. As a result, many businesses and industries are developing these resources.

The sessions in this track focus on some of the recent advances. Areas with great promise include logic programming, speech synthesis, automated reasoning and intelligent learning environments, natural language front-ends for databases, expert systems, and office automation. These topics and more are covered.

Is your business ready for AI? The Artificial Intelligence sessions are designed to present some of the most promising technological advances and show how they relate to real-world problems. There may be an AI system today capable of solving one of your problems!

Preparing your company for artificial intelligence

by JOHN BOWYER, JUDITH MARKOWITZ, and JAY YUSKO
Navistar International
Oakbrook Terrace, Illinois

ABSTRACT

We have identified four critical facets of preparing a company for artificial intelligence (AI):

1. Support from upper management
2. Education and promotion
3. Initial project selection
4. Project development methodology.

The support of upper management should include both a positive attitude and financial support. Educational and promotional programs must involve all parts of a company, including the AI group. Both programs set a positive tone within the entire company and help to separate unrealistic expectations and fear from reality. However, initial AI projects must be selected carefully to ensure long term acceptance of AI technology within a company.

Initial project selection must be based on a constellation of factors including appropriateness to business philosophy, return on investment, delivery, likelihood of technical success, and user acceptance. Proper project selection should be followed by a highly people-oriented project development methodology which involves experts and users from the onset of the project until completion.

INTRODUCTION

Preparing a company for artificial intelligence (AI) is a multifaceted effort. We have identified four areas that must be addressed: (1) support from upper management, (2) education and promotion, (3) initial project selection, and (4) project development methodology. This paper discusses each of them in turn.

SUPPORT FROM UPPER MANAGEMENT

Support from upper management is critical to the success of an AI program. This support must include more than a positive attitude toward the use of AI technology within a company; upper management must make an actual commitment to using AI represented by adequate budget and personnel. Such a commitment is the basis upon which a successful AI program can be developed.

Support from upper management can establish an initial positive attitude in a company which will act as a model for other levels of management within the company. It also will facilitate crossing departmental boundaries when that is required for developing AI projects.

EDUCATION AND PROMOTION

To sustain the momentum begun by upper management, a strong company-wide educational and promotional program must be instituted. Different types of educational programs are necessary for different levels and groups within the company.

Management

One of the greatest problems in the AI industry is hype. It is essential that management understands the difference between hype and reality about what can be delivered using AI technology. Otherwise, expectations will be unrealistic and AI projects will be doomed from the start.

Non-AI Technical Personnel

There is no need for conventional data processing people to become proficient in the technical aspects of AI. When a problem can be solved using conventional data processing methods, it should be solved that way. However, non-AI technical personnel need to be educated to recognize when AI technology fits a specific problem.

AI Technical Personnel

Just as non-AI technical personnel need to understand AI, AI technical people need to understand conventional data processing. They have to realize that AI cannot and should not be used to solve all the problems within a company.

Users

Users include both the experts whose knowledge is used to build an AI system and the people who will use the system in their everyday work. Users need to be educated in the basic concepts of an AI system. Those who will use the system need to view the system as a tool to help them in their jobs and understand it will not replace them.

INITIAL PROJECT SELECTION

Because the first few AI projects selected can make or break the AI initiative within a company, the projects must be selected to ensure success. The aspects to consider when selecting an AI project are:

1. Technical success
2. Return on investment
3. Visibility
4. Business success
5. Cooperative experts
6. User acceptance

None of these criteria stand alone; all must be considered to ensure company-wide success. For example, a project can be technically successful and perform as designed yet it may not be successful within the company. An AI system's return on investment, visibility throughout a company, and how it will fit into the total business plan of the company must all be evaluated when selecting initial projects. Further, cooperative experts must produce the knowledge needed in the system. Finally, the system must be accepted by the users; if the users do not use the system in their work environment, the AI initiative will fail.

PROJECT DEVELOPMENT METHODOLOGY

AI project development is highly people-oriented. An AI system is built around the knowledge of experts within the company. These experts are providing more than specifications; they are imparting their many years of knowledge and experience. Because the system will incorporate their personal and hard won knowledge, the company experts need to be involved from start to end.

As mentioned earlier, the experts have to be educated in the basic concepts of AI so that they fully understand what knowledge is needed and how it will be used in the system. Prototypes have to be developed very early, not only to show proof of concept, but to show the experts their knowledge at work. Prototypes give the experts a chance to critique the system and be involved in the total system development process. Such prototypes should include only features that will be delivered in the final system. False expectations, future disappointment, and failure can result from unrealistic prototyping.

Another important aspect of AI project development is the early involvement of the people who will use the system. In particular, the method of delivery must be developed during the early prototype stages with input from the people who will use the system. User involvement helps to guarantee that the system can be delivered and will be used.

Finally, support and maintenance of the AI system must be part of the project development. The users and experts need to know that they will be able to add new knowledge and make changes to the AI system when necessary. They also have to know that the AI group will support user requirements if any complex problems arise.

CONCLUSION

We have discussed what we believe are the four major areas that should be addressed to prepare a company for AI: (1) support from upper management, (2) education and promotion, (3) initial project selection, and (4) project development methodology. Although we believe the one unifying factor is education, all four areas have to be addressed to make AI a lasting endeavor within a company.

A methodology for building expert systems

by HOWARD HILL
Knowledge Based Systems, Inc.
Oakbrook Terrace, Illinois

ABSTRACT

This paper provides a methodology, or process, that can be used to construct expert systems. The methodology is suited primarily for building troubleshooting, advisory, and diagnostic expert systems; however, it also can be useful for building other types of systems.

INTRODUCTION

This paper defines a methodology, or process, that can be used to build expert systems. This rather informal paper is intended for managers or engineers and programmers unfamiliar with expert systems. Therefore, the methodology described is practical, not theoretical. The thesis of this paper is that it is possible to build working expert systems in significantly less time and for less money than is generally recognized, and this paper explains how it can be done.

Generally, most of the effort required to build an expert system is in gathering and organizing knowledge from the domain expert. Existing knowledge engineering approaches are costly, time-consuming processes; they require much effort by both the domain expert and the knowledge engineer.

Most of the time in building an expert system is consumed by the itertative process of traditional knowledge engineering. A prototype system is built, tested, found to be wanting, and discarded. Information gleaned from this process is used to build yet another prototype which in turn is tested, found to be wanting, and ultimately discarded. This process continues until a system is developed that seems to work.

The traditional process of knowledge engineering can be improved by applying a concept software engineers have known for some time: it is much easier to do the job right the first time than to do it over and over. The cost of fixing bugs during the requirements phase of a software project is orders of magnitude less than the cost of fixing the same bugs after a product has been released to customers. The same principle applies to building expert systems. The development process can be reduced to only one iteration by first defining what the system should do, collecting all knowledge at one time, choosing the best knowledge representation from the start, and knowing what performance values the system must achieve to be accepted.

Many of the conventional problems often present in knowledge engineering vanish when this one-iteration approach is applied. For example, the problem of paradigm shift occurs when acquired knowledge exceeds the limits of a chosen representation. This problem is eliminated by selecting a knowledge representation paradigm after all knowledge has been collected.

Another cost present in building expert systems is the cost of the domain expert's time. Good domain experts are expensive; they have little time at best. Any good knowledge engineering methodology must minimize the use of their time.

FOUNDATIONS

There are a few key principles we use to construct this new methodology: problem decomposition, target system decomposition, and locality.

First, all people know far more than they can tell. People do not have complete access to the processes they use to solve problems. Indeed, as people acquire more expertise, they typically find it harder to state the reasoning and knowledge they used to solve problems. Further, if they attempt to do so, the offered reasoning model and knowledge often is incomplete. This situation is called the paradox of expertise.[1] Consequently, some authors advise prospective knowledge engineers to be wary of a domain expert's advice, and perhaps to seek less experienced domain experts.

Thus, much of the difficulty in knowledge engineering is caused by the difficulty of experienced domain experts to elucidate the methods and knowledge they use to solve problems. If a knowledge engineer can help with this problem, the cost of building an expert system will be reduced.

Although most expert systems work by modeling a domain expert's reasoning process and knowledge, this does not have to be the case. Commonly used knowledge representations, for example, do not mimic human thought processes. No expert I know thinks in terms of production rules, yet this is one of the most popular and successful knowledge representations used in expert systems today.

Second, the solution strategy used in an expert system also does not have to be one that matches a domain expert's problem solving technique. Once the requirement for an emulative solution strategy is relaxed, a rather mechanical knowledge acquisition process can be used to develop a solution strategy that will be used by the expert system. This will speed up the early stages of the development process.

The strategy of "divide and conquer" is well known in computer science. Using this strategy, problems are decomposed into separate subproblems, and the solution of the complete problem is obtained by combining the solutions to the subproblems. This process is useful for some problems because it can be much easier to solve many small subproblems than it is to solve an original problem.

Diagnosis, advisory, and troubleshooting problems usually can be decomposed using this technique. In such cases, the divide and conquer principle is applied recursively to a problem until the problem is broken down into atomic subproblems. These atomic subproblems represent the lowest level of problem that an expert system is designed to solve.

For example, an expert system designed to give advice about loans could have a problem decomposed into giving advice about commercial loans and retail loans. These two subproblems would be further decomposed into giving advice about various specific types of commercial and retail loans (e.g., asset-based commercial loans). The decomposition process would stop when the loan types being considered were the basic, or fundamental, types that a system's user would reasonably consider.

Further, not only can the expert system problem be decomposed using divide and conquer, the target system that the expert system is designed to troubleshoot, diagnose, or give advice about, can also be decomposed into many atomic subsystems.

An automobile can be considered to be a collection of subsystems such as an engine, wheels, drive train, body, and frame. Each of these subsystems also can be decomposed into subsystems. For example, some subsystems of a drive train would be the transmission, drive shaft, differential, and rear axles. This process would be repeated until a complete hierarchy consisting of the smallest meaningful subsystems for an automobile was obtained.

The third principle on which the methodology is based is the principle of locality. That is, if a target system has been properly decomposed, then separate atomic subproblems will be associated with each atomic subsystem. As a result, it should be possible to recursively decompose large target systems into hierarchies of atomic subsystems with one or more atomic subproblems associated with each atomic subsystem.

For diagnosis, advisory, and troubleshooting expert systems, the process of recursive decomposition of both the target system and the problem usually can be done by a knowledge engineer with only a minimal amount of help from the domain expert.

If presented with the complete decomposition of a target system, a domain expert will find it easy to elucidate the methods he or she used to solve the subproblem. Given a complete hierarchical decomposition of the target system and the problem, it is possible for a domain expert and knowledge engineer to elucidate the methods, that is, the knowledge and reasoning strategies, needed to solve every atomic subproblem. Therefore, since the solution to a problem is the sum of the solutions to all its atomic subproblems, it follows that the domain expert and knowledge engineer can obtain through target system and problem decomposition, the knowledge and reasoning strategies necessary to solve the complete problem.

METHODOLOGY

This section describes a methodology that can be used to build troubleshooting, advisory, and diagnostic expert systems.

Define System Objectives

First, it is necessary to determine what a proposed system will do. The system's function should be specified in a one- or two-page document that clearly states the objectives of the finished system. Documenting a system's objectives requires the cooperation of the system's end users, the domain expert, and the knowledge engineer.

Define Subsystems

After the problem that the expert system must solve is stated, the knowledge engineer uses the divide and conquer strategy to decompose both the target system and the problem into atomic subsystems. Each subsystem is then broken down to the lowest level that the expert system should address. An automobile-mechanic advisory system, for example, would not need to address the theory of condensed matter to advise a mechanic about changing a power-steering unit. Often, existing documentation can be used as a knowledge source for such a step.

Next, a knowledge engineer and the domain expert should identify every possible subproblem that can occur in each atomic subsystem. This step requires a series of interviews with the domain expert. At the end of this step, the problem should be completely decomposed into atomic subproblems, and each subproblem related to an atomic subsystem. Typically, every atomic subsystem will have several different subproblems associated with it.

Create Cause Tables

The domain expert must identify the causes of each atomic subproblem and the symptoms associated with each cause. Symptoms fall into two categories: those that increase the confidence that the cause is present, and those that rule out the cause. The end result of this step is a series of tables, one for each cause. Each table should list the subproblem to which a cause is connected, the subsystem to which the subproblem relates, and the symptoms that are associated with the cause. If more than one domain expert is available, then a Delphi technique can be used to increase the accuracy of the cause tables.

Write Knowledge Engineering Document

Next, the knowledge engineer writes a knowledge engineering document. This document contains the cause tables, the complete hierarchical decomposition of the target system, and a complete list of subproblems together with their relationship to the subsystems.

Perform Parretto Analysis

The knowledge engineering document contains all the domain knowledge needed for the system. However, because many of the possible subproblems and their causes stated in the tables actually may never occur, Parretto analysis is used to screen the data for plausibility. The basic idea behind Parretto's principle is that only a few of the potential causes account for most problems encountered. This is the basis for the 80/20 rule which states the 80 percent of the problems occur due to about only 20 percent of the causes.

In some systems (e.g., medical expert systems), it is necessary to include all potential causes, however unlikely. In such cases, a Parretto analysis is not needed.[2]

The Parretto analysis is accomplished best by analyzing historical problem records and using the data to weed out possible causes that (1) have never resulted in a problem and (2) are expected never to result in a problem. The assistance of a domain expert is necessary for this analysis.[1]

However, in most situations a reliable set of historical problem records will not exist. Therefore, it usually is necessary for a domain expert to estimate the likelihood of problems occurring as a result of each cause identified. Because people typically are not accurate at estimating probability, the domain expert should rank each cause according to the following estimates:

1. Almost always causes problems.
2. Commonly causes problems.
3. Occasionally causes problems.
4. Rarely causes problems.
5. Possibly can cause problems but there is no evidence of problems related to this cause.
6. Problems related to this cause will never occur.

After each cause has been analyzed, the Parretto analysis proceeds by plotting the ranked list of causes versus the likelihood of each cause resulting in a problem. The plot will take the form of a monotone decreasing curve. If the curve has a definite knee, and the knee occurs low enough, then causes below the knee can be eliminated safely from the knowledge engineering document. If no knee is found, then causes with a zero likelihood of resulting in problems can be eliminated safely.

The outcome of the Parretto analysis is a ranking of the problem-likelihood related to all possible causes in the knowledge engineering document together with a cutoff point that specifies the problem-likelihood limit for causes that will be included in the system. Only data associated with causes above the cutoff will be included in the system.

Build Control Flow Model

Next, it is necessary to build a control flow model. Although the strategy the expert system will use does not closely mimic the strategy the domain expert uses, the overall strategy used by the domain expert is best to use in the expert system. The flow model is a high-level description of the steps the domain expert uses to solve the specified problem. The flow model will form the basis for the control-rule meta-knowledge the expert system will need. A typical flow model consists of a flowchart or an equivalent design language specification of the steps the domain expert takes to solve the problem.

Verify Knowledge Engineering Document

After the flow model is constructed, it is necessary to verify and inspect the knowledge that will reside in the finished system. This step consists of carefully inspecting, on a line-by-line basis, each piece of information in the knowledge engineering document. Four issues must be considered. First, the knowledge engineer should verify that the proper decomposition into atomic subsystems and atomic subproblems has been achieved. Second, the engineer must ensure that the causes and the symptoms for each cause within each subproblem have been identified correctly. Third, the problem-likelihood for every cause within the document must be verified. Finally, the consultation flow model must be reviewed for correctness.

The inspected knowledge engineering document is a valuable asset. It documents exactly what knowledge will be included in the finished system, completely specifies the behavior of the system, and acts as a reference guide for maintainers of the system.

Define Shell Parameters

The next step is to decide which expert system shell parameters to use. This step consists of choosing a knowledge representation, an inferencing strategy, a user interface design, the knowledge debugging parameters, and deciding on the nature and strategy behind the system's explanations. Many good books exist that can help knowledge engineers choose shell parameters. Since all knowledge required in the system has been collected prior to this step, the process should be straightforward.

Code Knowledge Base

Once a shell[3] has been acquired, the engineer codes the knowledge contained in the knowledge engineering document into a knowledge base the shell can use. Generally, the cause table knowledge will be simple to code into either production rules or frames and will form the bulk of the knowledge base. The control flow-model knowledge will encode into meta-knowledge that controls the order in which rules or frames are invoked.

Establish Test Cases

While the knowledge base is being coded, a set of test cases can be collected or constructed from scratch with the help of the domain expert. The test cases should be selected to reflect actual problems the system should be able to solve. Remember, the purpose of testing is to find errors—not prove correctness. Each test case, therefore, should be included because it has the potential to find an error in the knowledge base.

Building an expert system using the methodology described in this paper, only a few possible types of bugs can occur. The primary type of bug that could be found is the "insufficiency bug," an error caused by missing knowledge. Insufficient knowledge usually is results from using too high a threshold in the Parretto analysis. Another type of bug could occur due to incorrect partitioning of the target system into atomic subsystems. Incorrect partitioning causes interactions between the subsystems that the causes tables do not address. As a result, the system will not be able to solve some problems correctly. Insufficiency bugs are also a consequence of incorrect partitioning.

Many of the problems frequently encountered in traditional expert system development will not occur, or will rarely occur when this methodology is used. Such bugs include paradigm shift, contradiction, subsumption, incorrect knowledge, and bugs due to the inability to access knowledge, (i.e., a missing relation in a frame, or a rule conclusion that is neither a goal nor subgoal).

Test and Validate

After the system is coded, testing must be done. This consists of running the test suite through the system and observing the system's behavior. Because no human activity is perfect, bugs will exist in any non-trivial knowledge base. Testing and fixing these bugs is a necessary part of knowledge engineering.

When testing is complete, validation can be performed. Validation consists of comparing the accuracy of the expert system against a known "gold standard" for accuracy.

Several levels of gold standards can be used. One of the best is to build a validation test suite of cases by selecting cases from actual problems that have occurred in the past. Accuracy is established by giving these cases to a panel of human domain experts and measuring its solution accuracy as well as the extent to which it agrees on the solutions to each case. These numbers form a baseline against which the expert system's accuracy is measured.

Actual validation is done by running the calibrated validation test suite through the expert system and comparing the system's accuracy to the accuracy of the domain-expert panel. Although systems vary in accuracy, generally it is possible to achieve the same level of accuracy as the domain expert panel.

Once the system is finished, the knowledge engineering document and the system should be placed under change control. All changes to the system must be reflected in the knowledge engineering document.

CONCLUSION

I have used the methodology described in this paper to build several systems, and found it superior to the methods generally discussed in the literature. By concentrating on doing the knowledge engineering only once, and doing it right the first time, it is possible to build expert systems much more rapidly than is commonly supposed.

REFERENCES

1. Waterman, D. A. *A Guide to Expert Systems.* Reading, MA: Addison-Wesley, 1985.
2. Buchanan, B. and E. Shortliffe. *Rule-Based Expert Systems.* Reading, MA: Addison-Wesley, 1985.
3. Hayes-Roth, F., D. Waterman, and D. Lenat. *Building Expert Systems.* Reading, MA: Addison-Wesley, 1985.

A framework for expert modelbase systems

by ROBERT W. BLANNING
Vanderbilt University
Nashville, Tennessee

ABSTRACT

The growing integration of database management systems with expert systems to produce what are coming to be called expert database systems suggests that there may also be a productive integration of causal decision models with expert systems. We examine in this paper three possible areas of integration: (1) the use of expert systems in helping end users to construct decision models and to interpret their outputs, (2) the incorporation of knowledge bases into decision support systems (DSS), and (3) the use of expert systems in interfacing models with their users. The latter case consists of (1) natural language query processing for decision models, and (2) the use of expert systems technology in integrating the appropriate models in a model base to respond to a user query.

INTRODUCTION

An important theoretical and practical issue in decision support systems (DSS) is managing decision models. Such decision models include linear programming models of production and distribution processes and simulations of the financial structure of a firm. For this reason a discipline of model management,[1,2,3] along with a few commercially implemented model management systems,[4] is being developed within DSS. The purpose of a model management system is to insulate its users from the physical operations of model storage and processing, just as the purpose of a database management system is to insulate its users from the physical operations of data storage and processing. The principal areas of concern in the model management literature are (1) the organization of model bases (both network and relational frameworks have been developed), (2) the design of model base query languages, and (3) the efficient implementation and operation of model management systems.

During the past few years increasing attention has been paid to the application of artificial intelligence (AI)—especially expert systems and, to a lesser extent, natural language query processing—to model management. This development parallels a similar area of interest in database management—the synthesis of database management systems with expert systems to produce what are coming to be called expert database systems.[5,6] An expert database system has been defined as "a system for developing applications requiring knowledge-based processing of shared information."[7] Implicit in this definition is the assumption that the information under consideration is stored data. We examine here a case in which the reformation is a decision model in the form of a stored algorithm, and we call such a system an *expert modelbase system.*

There are three areas in which AI may be applied to the management of decision models. First, expert systems may be developed to help end users to construct models and to interpret their results. Second, a DSS may contain an expert system along with or in place of a causal decision model. Third, certain AI techniques (including expert system techniques) may be useful in translating and executing user queries to a model management system. These three topics are examined in the following three sections of this paper.

INTELLIGENT MODEL CONSTRUCTION AND INTERPRETATION

We begin by defining a model base as a set of one or more models. We expect there will be some commonality among the models' input and output attributes, which means that the outputs of some models will be inputs to other models. For example, the output of a sales forecasting model may be the input to a production planning model, and the output of the production planning model may be the input to a distribution scheduling model. Such a linking of models corresponds to a relational join in database management, in which the models are viewed as virtual relations. Tuples in virtual relations do not exist in stored form, they are generated on demand by a stored algorithm.[8] In this section we are concerned only with individual models. Later we will be concerned with the integration of models in a model base.

Models are similar to data files in that they contain functional dependencies. For example, the output of a model is functionally dependent on its input, just as the content attributes of a file are funtionally dependent on the key attributes.* However, there are additional functional dependencies in model management. For example, the output of a model is also functionally dependent on any parameters in the model, and assignment statements in imperative programming languages (and for that matter, *let* and *where* statements in functional programming languages) are examples of functional dependencies. Since the dependency structures of decision models are in many cases quite complex, it often requires substantial expertise to construct these models and to interpret their outputs.

There are two ways in which expert systems can be applied to model construction. If the model solution technique has been programmed and the software is available to the model builder, as is usually the case in linear programming, then the expertise required is to identify the components of the model from a description of the problem. For example, in linear programming models, the components would be the decision variables, the objective function, and the constraints. Expert systems are now being developed to help users formulate linear programming models in certain restricted problem domains (e.g., determining optimal product mixes or transportation schedules).[9,10] On the other hand, if the tool is a programming language (such as a simulation language), then the problem is one of automatic programming. An example is a system used for generating GPSS programs from natural language descriptions of queueing problems.[11]

Since most expert systems provide explanations of their reasoning processes, it seems reasonable that expert systems

*There are two possible departures from determinism in decision modeling, neither of which presents a problem in practice. First, certain constrained optimization models can have multiple global optima, but this seldom arises in practice. Second, Monte Carlo simulations can produce different outputs from the same input, depending on the sequence of random numbers used, but for most applications the sample size is sufficiently large (and variance reduction techniques may be used) that the differences in output are small.

should be developed to help a user to interpret the outputs of causal models and to evaluate the inputs to and the assumptions in the models. Two such systems have been developed, one for linear programming models[12] and the other for spreadsheet generators.[13,14] The former system accesses the output of a linear programming model (i.e., the optimal tableau or a tableau demonstrating that there is no feasible solution or that the solution is unbounded) and answers questions about causal chains of events (e.g., from resources through facilities to end products). The latter system uses the algebraic expressions in a spreadsheet generator to answer questions about why particular outputs are unusually high or low or why certain outputs have changed very little although some of the inputs have changed significantly (e.g., certain changes may have cancelled each other out).

A problem domain closely related to the construction and interpretation of decision models is (1) the selection of statistical procedures that help an analyst draw inferences from a set of data and (2) the interpretation of the outputs of these procedures. This is also an active area of AI research, and expert systems are being developed for this purpose.[15] Thus, we may expect to see a growing number of software systems that allow end users to construct, solve, and interpret decision support algorithms without having to know details of the algorithmic techniques.[16]

INTELLIGENT MODELS

A second approach to intelligent model management is to capture in the models some of a manager's knowledge of the real world. This has been done in the development of knowledge-based DSS (i.e., expert systems as applied to management).[17] Expert systems of this type have been developed in the following problem domains:

1. *Finance and accounting*. Examples are expert systems for portfolio selection,[18] auditing accounts receivable,[19] and analyzing corporate financial statements.[20]
2. *Operations*. Examples are systems for configuring customer orders,[21] scheduling production,[22] and servicing equipment.[23]
3. *Marketing*. There are a large number of models, called decision calculus models, in use in marketing that have some of the properties of expert systems.[24,25,26] The models contain a certain amount of expertise in a general area (e.g., advertising budgeting), but they require substantial expertise on the part of the user that is specific to the product line under consideration.

Incorporating expertise into DSS gives rise to such issues as the proper way to incorporate knowledge-based DSS into existing corporate planning and other decision-making processes, the integration of knowledge-based DSS with data-based and model-based DSS, and the possible use of knowledge-based DSS in helping researchers and managers to understand and possibly improve managerial decision processes.[27,28] These and other similar issues will almost certainly be investigated thoroughly as more knowledge-based DSS are implemented.

INTELLIGENT MODEL EXECUTION

Once a model base has been constructed, its users will present queries that must be translated and executed. Two types of intelligence may be required here. First, if the query is presented in a "natural" language (i.e., in a sufficiently large subset of the user's language that the user appears to be conversing with the model base or, more exactly, with the model management system), then the system must translate the query into an unambiguous form for execution. This is currently accomplished in some database systems by natural language query processors,[29] and there are indications that similar processors can be constructed for decision models.[30,31,32]

Second, after a model management system has interpreted a query (whether it was presented in a natural language or in a structured model query language), the model management system must (1) select the model or models needed to prepare a response and then (2) execute the models. When only one model is required, this is usually not difficult. If there is more than one model, it will be necessary to identify the appropriate models and to construct a sequence of operations (i.e., model executions) needed to respond to the query. It has been suggested that models be represented as statements in first order logic and that a query be viewed as a statement to be inferred from the model statements by means of resolution programming,[33,34] connection graphs,[35] or, more generally, logic programming.[36,37]

A more flexible model base may be constructed by using more powerful AI techniques, such as semantic nets and frames.[37,38,39] Using such techniques would allow several processing functions (e.g., matrix generation and optimization in liner programming) to be combined in one information structure. It also would allow integrity constraints and other rules relevant to model base processing to be conveniently stored and accessed. Several recent software development efforts suggest that these more complex knowledge structures can be usefully applied to model management.[40,41]

CONCLUSION

Until recently, three important sources of information for decision support—stored data, decision models, and expert knowledge—have been regarded as largely separate, but we are beginning to find interesting relationships among them. Some of the literature on model management emphasizes the relationships between data and models, and the ongoing research on expert database systems is focused on the relationships between data and knowledge. In addition, we have seen a growing interest in the relationships between models and knowledge. Such interest suggests that it may be productive to view a DSS as a system that provides convenient user access to a variety of information sources—especially data, models, and knowledge[42]—that are useful in decision support.

ACKNOWLEDGEMENT

This research was supported by the Dean's Fund for Faculty Research of the Owen Graduate School of Management of Vanderbilt University.

REFERENCES

1. Bonczek, R. H., C. W. Holsapple, and A. B. Whinston. "The Evolution from MIS to DSS: Extension of Data Management to Model Management." In M. J. Ginzberg, W. R. Reitman, and E. A. Stohr. Amsterdam: North-Holland, 1982, pp. 61–78.
2. Dolk, D. R. and B. R. Konsynski. "Model Management in Organizations." *Information & Management,* 9(1985), 1, pp. 35–47.
3. Blanning, R. W. "Issues in the Design of Relational Model Management Systems." *AFIPS, Proceedings of the National Computer Conference,* (Vol. 52) 1983, pp. 395–401.
4. Palmer, K. H., N. K. Boudwin, H. A. Patton, A. J. Rowland, J. D. Sammes, and D. M. Smith. *A Model-Management Framework for Mathematical Programming.* New York: Wiley, 1984.
5. Kerschberg, L. (ed.) *Proceedings of the First International Workshop on Expert Database Systems* (Vols. I and II) 1984.
6. Kerschberg, L. (ed.) *Proceedings of the First International Conference on Expert Database Systems.* 1986.
7. Smith, J. M. "Expert Database Systems: A Database Perspective." *Proceedings of the First International Workshop on Expert Database Systems* (Vol. I) 1984, pp. K-1–K-22.
8. Blanning, R. W. "A Relational Framework for Join Implementation in Model Management Systems." *Decision Support Systems,* 1 (1985), 1, pp. 69–81.
9. Binbasioglu, M. and M. Jarke. "Domain-Specific DSS Tools for Knowledge-Based Model Building." *Proceedings of the Nineteenth Annual Hawaii International Conference on System Sciences,* (Vol. 1A) 1986, pp. 503–514.
10. Murphy, F. H. and E. A. Stohr. "An Intelligent System for Formulating Linear Programs." *Decision Support Systems,* 2 (1986), 1, pp. 39–47.
11. Heidorn, G. E. "Simulation Programming Through Natural Language Dialogue." In M. A. Geisler (ed.) *Logistics.* Amsterdam: North-Holland, 1975, 71–83.
12. Greenberg, H. J. "A Functional Description of ANALYZE: A Computer-Assisted Analysis System for Linear Programming Models." *ACM Transactions on Mathematical Software,* 9 (1983), 1, pp. 18–56.
13. Kosy, D. W. and B. P. Wise. "Self-Explanatory Financial Planning Models" *Proceedings of the National Conference on Artificial Intelligence,* 1984, pp. 176–181.
14. Kosy, D. W. and B. P. Wise. "Overview of ROME: A Reason-Oriented Modeling Environment." In L. F. Pau (ed.) *Artificial Intelligence in Economics and Management.* Amsterdam: North-Holland, 1986, pp. 21–30.
15. Gale, W. A. and D. Pregibon. "Artificial Intelligence Research in Statistics." *AI Magazine,* 5 (1985), 4, pp. 72–75.
16. Hwang, S. "Automtic Model Building Systems: A Survey." In J. J. Elam, (ed.) *DDS-85 Transactions,* 1985, pp. 22–32.
17. Blanning, R. W. "Management Applications of Expert Systems." *Information & Management,* 7 (1984), 6, pp. 311–316.
18. Clarkson, G. P. E. *Portfolio Selection: A Simulation of Trust Investment.* Englewood Cliffs, NJ: Prentice-Hall, 1962.
19. Dungan, C. W. and J. S. Chandler. "AUDITOR: A Microcomputer-Based Expert System to Support Auditors in the Field." *Expert Systems,* 2 (1986), 4, pp. 210–221.
20. Bouwman, M. J. "Human Diagnostic Reasoning by Computer: An Illustration from Financial Analysis." *Management Science,* 29 (1983), 6, pp. 653–672.
21. Scown, S. J. *The Artificial Intelligence Experience: An Introduction.* Digital Equipment Corporation, 1985 pp. 110–145.
22. Fox, M. S. and S. F. Smith. "ISIS—A Knowledge-Based System for Factory Scheduling." *Expert Systems,* 1 (1984), 1, pp. 25–49.
23. Richardson, J. J. (ed.) *Artificial Intelligence in Maintenance.* Park Ridge, IL: Noyes Publications, 1985, pp. 391–405.
24. Little, J. D. C. "Models and Managers: The Concept of a Decision Calculus." *Management Science,* 16 (1970), 8, pp. B-466–B-485.
25. Chakravarti, D., A. Mitchell, and R. Staelin. "Judgement Based Marketing Decision Models: Problems and Possible Solutions." *Journal of Marketing,* 45 (1981), 4, pp. 13–23.
26. Little, J. D. C., and L. M. Lodish. "Commentary on 'Judgement Based Market Decision Models.'" *Journal of Marketing,* 45 (1981), 4, 24–29.
27. Blanning, R. W. "Issues in the Design of Expert Systems for Management." *AFIPS Proceedings of the National Computer Conference* (Vol. 53) 1984, pp. 489–495.
28. Dhar, V. "On the Plausibility and Scope of Expert Systems in Management." *Proceedings of the Nineteenth Annual Hawaii International Conference on System Sciences* (Vol. 1) 1986, pp. 328–338.
29. Tennant, H. *Natural Language Processing.* New York: Petrocelli, 1981.
30. Blanning, R. W. "Conversing with Management Information Systems in Natural Language." *Communications of the ACM,* 27 (1984), 3, pp. 201–207.
31. Blanning, R. W., "A System for Natural Language Communication Between a Decision Model and Its Users." In L. F. Pau (ed.) *Artificial Intelligence in Economics and Management.* Amsterdam: North-Holland, 1986, pp. 77–85.
32. Blanning, R. W. "A Framework for Structured/Natural Language Model Query Processing." *Proceedings of the Nineteenth Annual Hawaii International Conference on System Sciences* (Vol. 1A) 1986, pp. 487–493.
33. Bonczek, R. A., C. W. Holsapple, and A. B. Whinston. *Foundations of Decision Support Systems.* New York: Academic Press, 1981.
34. Dutta, A. and A. Basu. "An Artificial Intelligence Approach to Model Management in Decision Support Systems." *IEEE Computer,* 17 (1984), 9, pp. 89–97.
35. Chen, M. C., J. E. Fedorowicz, and L. J. Henschen. "Deductive Processes in Databases and Decision Support Systems." *Proceedings of the North Central ACM 82 Conference,* 1982, pp. 81–100.
36. Blanning, R. W. "A PROLOG-Based Framework for Model Management." *Proceedings of the First International Workshop on Expert Database Systems* (Vol. II) 1984, pp. 633–642.
37. Lee, R. M. and L. W. Miller. "A Logic Programming Framework for Planning and Simulation." *Decision Support Systems,* 2 (1986), 1, pp. 15–25.
38. Dolk, D. R. and B. R. Konsynski. "Knowledge Representation for Model Management Systems." *IEEE Transactions on Software Engineering,* SE-10 (1984), 6, pp. 619–628.
39. Fedorowicz, J. and G. B. Williams. "Representing Modeling Knowledge in Decision Support Systems." *Decision Support Systems,* 2 (1986), 1, pp. 3–14.
40. McIntyre, S. C., B. R. Konsynski, and J. F. Nunamaker, Jr. "Automating Planning Environments: Knowledge Integration and Model Scripting." *Journal of Management Information Systems,* II (1986), 4, pp. 49–69.
41. Applegate, L. M., B. R. Konsynski, and J. F. Nunamaker. "Model Management Systems: Design for Decision Support." *Decision Support Systems,* 2 (1986), 1, pp. 81–91.
42. Blanning, R. W. "Expert Systems for Management: Research and Applications." *Journal of Information Science,* 9 (1985), 2, pp. 153–162.

A concept space for experiments in artificial intelligence

by RICHARD D. AMORI
East Stroudsburg University
East Stroudsburg, Pennsylvania

ABSTRACT

Describing phenomena in terms of coordinate systems and vector spaces has been beneficial in traditional science. Describing robotics experiments as points or vectors in a "space" of concepts taken from applied artificial intelligence has been equally beneficial. Such a perspective has benefits for both robotics and artificial intelligence. The five concepts, each of which constitutes an ordered axis or dimension, are: (1) task specification/directions, (2) perception (sensing) and other input/output (I/0), (3) world modeling, (4) reasoning, and (5) activity planning/execution. The implemented projects, which involve digital vision, natural language processing, tool manipulation, and a robot under expert system control, are discussed as points in this space. Additional experiments underway are described in the same context.

INTRODUCTION

In a recent paper Hopcroft[1] argued persuasively that we should take a more general view of robotics as the study of representing, manipulating, and reasoning about objects using a computer. Such a view raises issues in programming languages and representations, which are traditional computer science concerns. He argues that not only will computer science contribute greatly to robotics, but that robotics and other application areas will contribute greatly to computer science. We agree, and wish to point out that such a mutually beneficial relationship is especially fruitful for general artificial intelligence. We argue that, just as artificial intelligence has contributed greatly to the development of robotics, robotics can contribute greatly to, and permit systematic investigation of, more broadly-based artificial intelligence concerns. We have held this position for several years and have used it to develop a research program based on robotics but which addresses several, more widely applicable, themes of artificial intelligence.

This paper (and an accompanying videotape[2]) describes a set of seven robotics projects and experiments conducted at East Stroudsburg University. The robotics efforts are discussed in the context of a five dimensional "space" of concepts from artificial intelligence. The dimensions of this space are concepts from artificial intelligence which permit us to talk conveniently about the ordering of experiments in the sense of complexity of the experiment, location of an experiment in the space, and future directions for experiments. Each concept is a dimension or axis, each project may be considered a five tuple in this space and each can be discussed component by component.

First we consider each concept dimension or axis and then we discuss each robotics project, component by component.

CONCEPT DIMENSIONS OR AXES

The seven robotics projects are discussed in the context of the following "space" of concepts: task specification/direction, perception, sensing and other input/output (I/0), world modeling, reasoning, and activity planning and execution. The space may be represented as shown in Figure 1.

Task Specification/Directions

The task specification/directions axis describes the manner in which a problem is posed to a robot, and the amount, type, and source of directions provided to the robot. Such specifications and directions can range from highly explicit to highly implicit. An example of highly explicit task specification is traditional rote training: teach-by-guiding or teach-by-showing. A less explicit, and more flexible specification would be the use of a high-level robot programming language to provide the direction. An implicit task specification would correspond to specify the task in a natural language, such as English.

Perception (Sensing) and Other I/0

The perception (sensing) and other I/0 axis describes the manner in which the robot interacts with its environment—how it senses its environment and how it changes its environment. Sensory devices along this axis can range from no external sensors (dead reckoning) and perhaps some simple internal sensors such as limit switches; to a few sensors such as sonic range finders, force/torque or digital vision; to a rich coordinated array of sensors such as combinations of range finders, multiple cameras, and lasers. Robots with no sensors are non-adaptive whereas those with sensors can become adaptive. A variety of end effectors can permit interactions on this axis ranging from very simple pick and place interactions to those capable of substantial environment changes perhaps achieved by using a multi-fingered gripper with an assortment of tools.

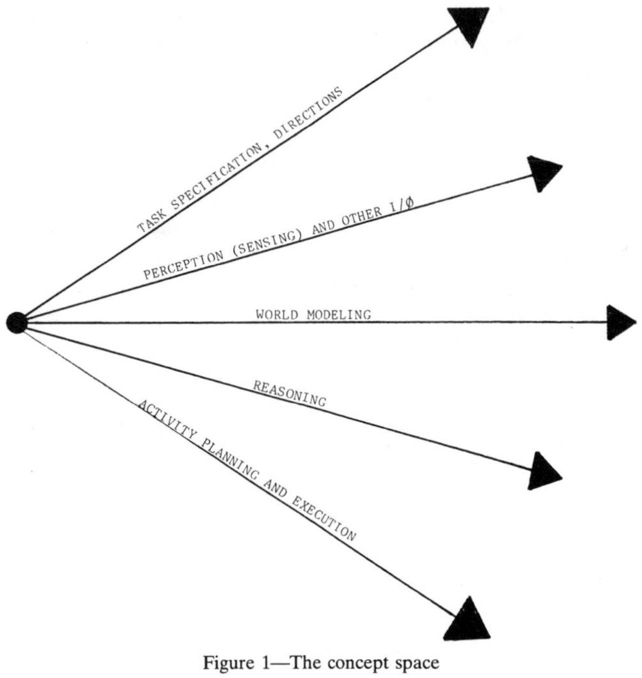

Figure 1—The concept space

World Modeling

The world modeling dimension describes the model of the world obtained from sensors and the location of model. For most traditional robotics applications, the world model is created and maintained by a human operator; that is, no world model is maintained by the robot. Some elementary world modeling can be performed by robots programmed in robot programming languages. Such programs maintain such model information as coordinate system data, force/torque data, and gripper open/closed data. Complex world models are mandatory for experiments involving natural language processing, vision scene analysis, or expert system control of a robot.

Reasoning

The reasoning axis describes the amount of reasoning performed and whether a robot or human performs the inferencing. Traditional industrial robotics applications do not involve reasoning by the robot. All inferencing is done by the human operator. Thus, at the left end of the reasoning axis we might attach the label "none." Elementary, on-board robot reasoning is required for applications involving semantic analysis for natural language but sophisticated inferencing is required when an expert system is used for robot control or when a complex visual scene must be analyzed.

Activity Planning and Execution

The activity planning and execution axis describes the type of plan formulated and carried out, and whether planning is done by the human operator or by the robot. Most traditional robotics planning is performed by a human operator during the training phase and robot execution is merely a direct playback of previously stored activity sequences. Some planning can be done on-board when a robot is directed by a robot programming language. More sophisticated on-board planning must be done if a robot is driven by natural language or controlled by an expert system.

Advantages of Concept Space

Labeled appropriately, axes descriptions provide a richer space within which we can place and discuss our robotics projects, as seen in Figure 2. Further, when activities are described within these dimensions, it is easy to see the demarcation between traditional robotics (i.e., industrial, non-intelligent) and advanced robotics, which requires artificial intelligence techniques.

Using this space of concepts, robotics experiments can be carried out which achieve robotics goals and at the same time permit us to explore broader artificial intelligence issues. We discuss a set of such projects and experiments next.

PROJECTS DISCUSSION

Let us consider the seven robotics projects and their locations in this concept space. The first three projects—alphabet, coffee, and piano worlds—involve no autonomous intelligent behavior by the robots. The last four projects—egg harvesting, blocks, workbench, and bagger worlds—involve increasingly autonomous robotic behavior.

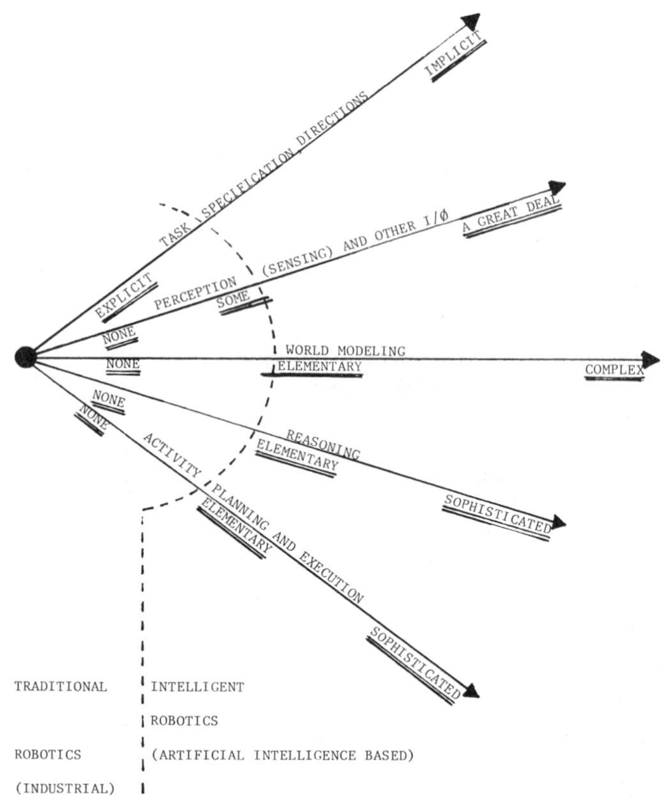

Figure 2—The concept space with some orderings on the axes

Alphabet World

In the alphabet world project, a robot picks up alphabet cubes and spells out "ESU-ROBOTICS." The robot's end effector is a magnetic finger, and each letter cube has a metal strip attached to its top surface. This project is representative of many simple industrial level tasks known as pick-and-place operations.

Location in the concept space

Alphabet world is a traditional robotics application and is located at the leftmost, or non-intelligent, end of each of the concept dimensions. The task specification/direction is explicitly provided by a human operator during training. Alphabet world is also at the leftmost end of the perception axis because there is no external perception. As do many current industrial robots, the alphabet world robot operates by dead reckoning. Knowledge of the world is entirely resident in the human operator and world modeling and reasoning are performed entirely by the operator. Activity planning is also performed by the operator who provides it to the robot. Subsequent robotic execution is a straightforward playback of the previously stored, operator determined, set of moves.

Coffee World

In the second project, the robot prepares a cup of coffee. The world objects are geometrically more complex (e.g., coffee pot and sugar container) than in the alphabet project, and a more general purpose, 3-finger end effector is used. The coffee application illustrates a popular way in which robots are trained or guided to perform a task: the human navigator uses his senses to inform another human operator, the pilot, about how close the end effector is to the desired pickup point of an object (e.g., the handle on the coffee pot). By means of entries on a computer keyboard the pilot manipulates the robot's movements. The computer records the moves for later playback.

Location in the concept space

As is the alphabet world, coffee world is a traditional robotics exercise that can be plotted at the leftmost, or non-intelligent, end of each of the concept dimensions. Task specification/direction, perception, world modeling, reasoning, and activity planning all are provided by a human operator. Execution is simply the playback of a sequence of moves previously stored on disk.

Piano World

In the piano world project, a teach pendant is used to train the robot to "play" a tune on a toy piano. A complete training videotape exists for this traditional style of robotics.[3]

Location in the concept space

Piano world falls into the same traditional robotics region as alphabet and coffee worlds. Extensive human involvement is required and the robot is used as a straightforward playback device.

Egg Harvesting World

Egg harvesting world is a prototype project for the real-world application of harvesting vaccines that are grown in eggs. A digital vision system, robot, and conveyor belt operate together. The egg sack (simulated by a cardboard cutout) travels down the conveyor and is detected by the vision system. A robot then positions its vacuum gripper over the egg sack and transfers it to a petri dish for the next processing step.

Location in the concept space

Egg harvesting world is the first project to take us out of the region of traditional industrial robotics. Task specification/direction is not provided directly by a human operator who guides the robot using a teach pendant or keyboard. No advance guiding is done. We plot this project further to the right on the task specification axis than the first three projects because task specification is provided by program code in Pascal on the robot host and by code in the vision system programming language.[4] We also plot the project further right on the perception axis since blob (i.e., the egg) acquisition and location are computed by the vision system. In the first three examples, knowledge of the world resided in a human and the necessary world modeling was performed by the human. In the egg harvesting project, the world model—consisting of several distinct physical coordinate systems—is housed in the computer. The robot's actions depend on the on-board model of its environment. Reasoning is still provided by a human operator and the result is reflected in the design of the robot's Pascal control program. In effect, the final product of the human reasoning process is "hardwired" into Pascal program code. Although "hardwired" into code, the use of a high-level programming language still provides considerably more robotic flexibility than what is provided by the simpler teach pendant guiding. In contrast with the earlier examples, activity planning is no longer done by an operator. Rather, the robot determines the necessary trajectory plans using the world model and the Pascal control program. Further, the robot synchronizes its own operation with the conveyor during execution.

Egg harvesting world illustrates reassignment of many of the problem solving functions from a human operator to a robot. Outward movement is observed on all axes, and the robot is more autonomous than in the previous examples.

Blocks World

In the blocks world experiment, a robot is directed by English sentences. Sentences such as "Move the yellow block to the green workspace," and "Pick up the yellow block and place it on the red area," are provided as input. The robot then performs the task based on the natural language input. In effect, the robot is "programmed" in natural language.

Location in the concept space

Because a number of techniques from artificial intelligence are used, the blocks world project is plotted squarely in the region of intelligent (i.e., non-traditional) robotics. It is plotted to the right end of the task specification/directions axis. Tasks are not explicitly and rigidly specified by guiding or using a teach pendant; or even less rigidly, but still explicitly, by using a formal computer programming language. Rather, task specification/direction is given implicitly using a very high-level language—English—in the same manner as humans specify tasks.

In blocks world, the relatively simple domain and the emphasis on processing natural language do not require much perception (dead reckoning is sufficient). However, by requiring natural language interpretation, the project is plotted farther right than egg harvesting on the world modeling, reasoning and activity planning, and execution axes. The blocks world robot must world model both physical level models (coordinate systems) and semantic level models (for natural language processing). The robot is also required to perform some elementary linguistic reasoning as it extracts meaning from a sentence. Activity planning likewise becomes more sophisticated since analysis of natural language is required to formulate a plan of action. Execution complexity is at about the same level as in egg harvesting world.

Overall in blocks world, we observe robot behavior which is yet more autonomous than that found in the previous worlds.

Workbench World

In the workbench world experiment, a robot is again directed by English sentences, but the language and the domain are more complicated than in blocks world. The world is a child's toy workbench. Tasks are more complex than in previous projects. The robot must select a proper tool (e.g., hammer, screwdriver) and mate it to a proper fastener (e.g., nail, screw). The robot understands and carries out instructions of such sentences as "Drive a nail into the top hole in the first column," and "Screw a screw into the first hole on the left side."

The language understood by the robot is more descriptive and complex. For example, multiple prepositional phrases are used and screw is used as both a noun and a verb.

Location in the concept space

As was the case for blocks world, the utilization of many techniques from artificial intelligence places workbench squarely in the region of advanced, intelligent robotics, yet farther right on the axes. Tasks are not specified explicitly using guiding or even at a higher level using a robot programming language. Rather, tasks are specified implicitly using natural language even more complex than that used in blocks world. Placement along the perception axis is the same as in blocks world (i.e., dead reckoning). However, because of the broader scope of the natural language accepted and the richer domain (i.e., tool and fastener choices), the project is plotted farther right along the world modeling, reasoning and activity planning, and execution axes.

The methods used in the two natural language robotics experiments are interesting in their own right, but are beyond the scope of this paper. More extensive treatment of blocks world and workbench world is available on videotape[5] and in a paper.[6]

Bagger World

Bagger world is the most complicated project. It illustrates integration of a digital vision system, a robot, a voice synthesizer, and an expert system. The coordinating computer is a Burroughs XE550 running under Centix (a UNIX V variant). Six computers and six programming languages are required. About 100 modules make up the bagger system.

The problem posed in this experiment and discussed by Winston,[7] is to illustrate a forward-chaining expert system; in this case, a system which automates the activities of a person who bags supermarket groceries. The expert system models the decision-making process of the expert human bagger. A human bagger considers what groceries must be bagged and determines the best way to bag those groceries based on experience and reason. For example, the human bagger knows that a bottle of Coke will crush a bag of potato chips and therefore would not place the bottle on top of the bag based on that knowledge. The human also reasons that bags cost money and therefore bag space should be used efficiently. Thus, a human bagger uses such knowledge and experience to determine the best way to bag a set of groceries.

Input to the automated system is provided by a digital vision system which views simulated grocery items (colored blocks of wood with various geometric shapes). Scene analysis is performed by the vision system and the result is passed to the expert system. The expert system "reasons" to determine a bagging solution, and directs the robot to carry out the solution; that is, to place the grocery items into the proper large or small bag. The bags are colored cardboard cutouts in the robot's workspace. As the robot carries out its actions, a voice synthesizer verbalizes what the robot is doing. Also, the robot can be interrupted during execution and can explain its line of reasoning. That is, the robot can explain why it is performing certain selected activities.

Location in the concept space

Bagger's extensive use of artificial intelligence techniques also places it in the region of advanced, intelligent robotics but in a region different than blocks world and workbench world.

Bagger world tasks are not specified directly by guiding; they are obtained by reasoning about a perceived visual scene. The use of digital vision for individual object identification and scene analysis move the project far to the right on the perception axis. The use of several types of models, both physical and conceptual, move the project farther to the right along the world model axis. A separate inferencing subsystem, the expert system, provides sophisticated decision making and moves bagger world farther right along the reasoning axis. Activity planning is the result of activating the separate inferencing subsystem which handles various grocery item choices and bag selections. Execution is similar to the other projects with the exception that the plan is verbalized by the voice synthesizer which is synchronized with the actions being carried out.

Discussion of how bagger is constructed is beyond the scope of this paper but additional technical information may be found in a paper by Brands, Peters, Shafer, and Snyder.[8] The expert system tool used is commercially available RULEMASTER,[9] described by Michie, Muggleton, Riese, and Zubrick.[10] The voice synthesizer is from Microvox, Incorporated.[11]

WORK UNDERWAY

Several additional robotics experiments have been completed recently or are now underway that extend the work described in this paper and which can be plotted even farther right along one or more dimensions in the concept space.

TODUS is a task-oriented discourse-understanding system which has just been completed.[12] TODUS is a natural language front end to a multi-agent robot domain that uses an augmented transition network of utterance grammars to process task-oriented English text. Well formed sentences, sentence fragments, and pronominal and elliptical references are handled. This project extends to the right along the task specification/directions and world modeling axes.

MAPS is a multi-agent planning system under construction which accepts directions from TODUS and must plan activities for up to four robots. Robot cooperation is required to perform some of the tasks. MAPS is plotted to the right along the world modeling and the activity planning and execution axes.

KNOVIS is a knowledge-based vision system under construction which uses a knowledge-based approach to improve the robustness of digital vision systems for scene analysis in an industrial setting. This project extends to the right along the perception/sensing axis.

HITAS is a hierarchical target-assessment system under construction which will incorporate dynamic recovery planning (changing a plan due to a change in the world and formulating a new plan) and elementary qualitative geometric reasoning about the domain. This project will extend to the right along the activity planning and execution, world modeling, and reasoning axes.

Each of these experiments uses robotics to investigate issues of broad artificial intelligence interest: natural language interfaces, multiple cooperating intelligent agents, vision, dynamic planning, and qualitative reasoning.

CONCLUSION

The robotics projects presented in this paper illustrate the utility of the notion of a concept space for experiments in artificial intelligence. The concept space provides a unifying framework for a variety of robotics activities and permits systematic experimentation and development. Experiments have been conducted and are now underway which are conveniently expressed and discussed using the concept-space taxonomy.

The limited robot domains chosen have resulted in steady progress in robotics as well, by permitting the orderly investigation of broader artificial intelligence topics not usually associated with robotics, such as natural language interfaces and embedded expert systems.

The mutually beneficial relationship between robotics and more broadly based artificial intelligence concerns is particularly clear when placed in the context of robotics experiments in the concept space.

ACKNOWLEDGEMENTS

Thanks are due to all of the East Stroudsburg University students who worked on the projects during the past several years as part of their class work or internship experience; John Peters, Ray Shafer, Sheldon Snyder, Kathy Brands and Kevin Lysek merit special recognition for exemplary service.

Portions of this research were supported by a grant from the Ben Franklin Partnership, Commonwealth of Pennsylvania.

REFERENCES

1. Hopcroft, J. "The Impact of Robotics on Computer Science." *Communications of the ACM,* 29 (1986), 6.
2. Amori, R. *A Concept Space for Experiments in Artificial Intelligence* (Videotape). East Stroudsburg, Pennsylvania: East Stroudsburg University Communication Center, 1986.
3. Becker, R. and S. Shackleford. *Training the Rhino* (Videotape). East Stroudsburg, Pennsylvania: East Stroudsburg University Communication Center, 1985.
4. Control Automation Inc. Intervision V-1000, Digital Vision System. Princeton, New Jersey, 1985.
5. Amori, R. *Natural Language Robotics-II* (Videotape). East Stroudsburg Pennsylvania: East Stroudsburg University Communication Center, 1984.
6. Amori, R. "NL/TEMPLATE: An Approach and Tool for Building Practical Natural Language Interfaces." *Proceedings of the Annual Conference of the Association for Computing Machinery—ACM85,* held in Denver, Colorado, October 1985.
7. Winston, P. *Artificial Intelligence* (2nd ed.). Reading, Massachusetts: Addison-Wesley, 1984.
8. Brands, K., J. Peters, R. Shafer, and S. Snyder. *East Stroudsburg University Bagger System,* Design Documents, Computer Science Dept., East Stroudsburg University, Pennsylvania, 1986.
9. RULEMASTER, Expert System Tool. Available from Radian Corp., 8501 Mo-Pac Boulevard, Austin, Texas 78766.
10. Michie, D., S. Muggleton, C. Riese, and S. Zubrick. "RULEMASTER: A Second Generation Knowledge Engineering Facility." *Proceedings of the First Conference on Artificial Intelligence Applications,* (IEEE/AAAI), held in Denver, Colorado, December 1984.
11. Micromint, Inc. Microvox. Text to Speech Synthesizer. Cedarhurst, New York.
12. Percey, D. and C. Taylor. *TODUS: A Knowledge Based Approach to a Task Oriented Discourse Understanding System.* M.Sc. Thesis, Computer Science Department, East Stroudsburg University, Pennsylvania, 1986.

Microcomputer PROLOG implementations: The state-of-the-art

by HAL BERGHEL and RICHARD RANKIN
University of Arkansas
Fayetteville, Arkansas

ABSTRACT

In this paper we discuss several characteristics of microcomputer PROLOG implementations including an overview of current products, a comparison of the range of built-in predicates, a description of the environment, and benchmark results.

INTRODUCTION

Although logic programming has a relatively short history in computer science, its impact has been significant. After the announcement that the Japanese Fifth Generation Project would standardize Japan's 1990s machines around the logic programming approach,[1] industry leaders and researchers began to devote considerable attention to this area. What follows is a general description of the various implementations of the logic programming language PROLOG that are available for microcomputers. These implementations are of considerable importance, for they allow virtually every interested person to enter the world of logic programming with minimal expense. It is our intention to acquaint interested readers with the current state-of-the-art.

PROLOG, as a logic programming language, developed from the early work of Kowalski[2,3,4] and Colmerauer[5,6] in the 1970s. As this work circulated, prototypes of the language appeared in France, England, Hungary, and Canada, and each was injected with some of its own design philosophy. As a result, there are at least three different models, each relying upon its own distinctive syntax, and each appealing to a particular subset of the research/development community. To standardize our treatment of a non-standardized language, we employ the Edinburgh nomenclature[7] in the following discussion.

One of the most significant aspects of PROLOG is that, at least in the ideal, it supports a clear distinction between the *logic* of the program and the mechanism of *control.*[8] This means that the programming is oriented toward the logic of the problem, leaving the control mechanism to the system. The important implication of this strategy is that the range of built-in predicates affects the convenience and speed of software development. However, since the various software houses have different design objectives, the predicates are not uniformly distributed over the entire range. Thus, some products may be better suited for certain applications than others. We provide a detailed classification of these predicates together with an analysis by product.

Of course, since the control mechanism is largely left to the implementation, differing strategies will have different effects upon performance. We also provide a series of benchmark results which shed light on the relative performance characteristics.

The products reviewed here are, alphabetically, Arity PROLOG, version 4.0 (Arity Corporation); micro-PROLOG professional (Logic Programming Associates); MPROLOG, version 2.1 (Logicware); PROLOG 2, version 1.2 (Expert Systems International); PROLOG-86 + , version 1.0 (Solution Systems); Turbo PROLOG, version 1.0 (Borland International) and VML PROLOG, version 1.9m (Automata Design Associates). We believe these are the most current versions. Only one of the MS-DOS implementations that we know of, PROLOG-V, was not included (at the request of the manufacturer). One product from Applied Logic Systems was announced but not released as of this writing. This paper updates and integrates the results presented in earlier publications and reports.[9,10,11]

GENERAL DESCRIPTION OF THE IMPLEMENTATIONS

A general summary of the implementations appears in Table 1. As the table shows, two of the products provide compilers, and all but one provide interpreters. The lack of an interpreter for Turbo PROLOG is intended; the designers have developed a compiler that behaves as if it were incremental (!), therefore they believe the interpreter is not needed.

Three of the products support virtual memory (up to one gigabyte in some cases), and all but one provide shell support

TABLE I—Overview

Product:	P2	AR	LPA	MP	P86	VML	TUR
Version:	1.2	4.0	PRO	2.1	1.0	1.9	1.0
Interpreter	+	+	+	+	+	+	–
Compiler	+	+	–	–	–	–	+
Virtual Memory	+	+	–	–	–	+	–
Shell Support	+	+	+	+	–	+	+
DOS Services							
Time/Date	+	+	+	–	+	+	+
Interrupt Facilities	–	+	+	–	–	+	+
Directory Facilities	+	+	+	–	+	+	+
Keyboard Facilities	+	+	+	+	–	+	+
Internal Clock Timing	–	–	–	–	–	+	–
Editor	+	–	+	+	+	–	+
Interactive	+	+	+	+	+	–	+
Multiple Windowing	+	–	+	–	+	–	+
Screen Control	+	+	+	+	+	+	+
Modularization	+	+	+	+	+	+	–
Module Privacy	+	+	+	+	+	+	–
Export/Import	+	–	+	+	–	+	–
Multiple Worlds	–	+	–	–	–	+	–
Multiple Theories	–	–	–	–	–	+	–
Database Indexing	+	+	–	–	–	+	–
Clause Indexing	–	+	–	–	–	+	–
Hashing	–	+	–	–	–	–	–
B-Trees	–	+	–	–	–	–	–
Optimization							
Cyclic Structure Checking	–	–	–	–	–	+	–
Garbage Collection Control	+	+	–	+	–	–	–
TRO	+	+	–	+	–	–	+
Stack Control	–	+	–	+	–	–	–
System Information							
LIPS count	–	–	–	–	–	+	–
Heap Used/Remaining	+/+	+/–	–/+	–/–	–/+	–/+	–/+
CPU Time	+	–	–	+	–	–	–
DCG	+	+	–	+	+	+	–
Structured Programming	–	+	+	–	+	–	–
# b-i preds (approx.)	255	170	90	150	155	210	90

which allows users to suspend PROLOG and execute independent object modules without altering the state of the interpreter (see the Built-In Predicates section). Among the DOS services supported are those concerning the time/date information in the control information area, the BIOS/DOS interrupt facilities, directory-related function calls (e.g., DIR, MKDIR, CHDIR, RENAME, and COPY), and keyboard facilities for retrieving scan codes and information from the keyboard status byte. In addition, some products allow the use of a programmable timer.

By *interactive editor,* we refer to an automatic re-invocation of the editor upon determination of compiler/run-time error. *Multiple windowing* refers to the ability to define different screen functions for the available window partitions. Screen control allows the user to configure the system for the desired video attributes beyond the DOS specification for video mode.

Six products support modularization of procedures. Module privacy is a technique whereby predicates are hidden from users, frequently to prevent name conflicts between modules. Worlds and theories are similar entities that are used to accomplish roughly the same thing. Technically, a world is a region within a database. One normally would use individual worlds to avoid backtracking through the larger database of which the world is a part. A theory is a database region which may involve the physical separation of the clauses into separate files.

Database indexing refers to the way in which the clauses are indexed and accessed. Clause indexing involves addressing a clause by its internal reference number. Hashing and B-trees increase the efficiency of searching. All of these features are extremely important for large clause sets.

The sub-category entitled *optimization* is a grab-bag of features which in one way or another relate to the efficiency of the implementation. A cyclic structure is created when a variable is unified with a term which contains that variable. The result is the generation of an infinite term as the unification repeatedly instantiates the term's variable with itself. It is not at all clear that the procedural interpretation of this phenomenon is consistent with the semantics of first order logic. Occur checks anticipate this behavior, but do so at considerable cost in efficiency. As a result, occur checking is not supported (as far as we know). A compromise is cyclic structure checking. In this case, the variable responsible for the infinite loop is returned in lieu of the infinite term. This surrogate does not appreciably decrease performance. Garbage collection control and stack control allow a programmer greater latitude in speed/space trade-offs. TRO stands for tail recursion optimization.

The system information features are useful for benchmarking and program development. DCG refers to the mechanism for translating definite clause grammars into PROLOG clauses. Finally, a ' + ' for structured programming indicates that such control structures as "if then . . . else . . . ," "case," and so forth, are available.

We note that the number of built-in predicates specifically excludes a count of logical and arithmetic operators. Further, the numeric tally of the built-in predicates should be interpreted as an estimate of the number of substantially different predicates, rather than the total number. For example, since the distinction between "get0(term)" and "get0(handle,term)" is one of input type rather than functionality, both would be subsumed under one predicate. However, the capabilities of redirecting the standard input would be noted in the feature tables. Other cases of essentially duplicate functionality include predicates related to I/O, clause handling, formatting, string manipulation, and so forth. We believe that this "selective tally" approach provides a more reasonable first glance estimate of overall functionality than those which overlook the fact that some predicates are extremely narrow in scope, and that predicates are not distributed uniformly over the range covered in our classification.

One general consideration does not appear in the table. This concerns the issue of whether one of the products is a legitimate PROLOG. We do not enter into the controversy here beyond mentioning that Turbo PROLOG is a strongly typed language that does not support general unification. Further, it lacks the metalogical facilities normally associated with PROLOG environments. For further details on this issue, see Weeks and Berghel[10] and Pereira.[12] Additional discussion of Turbo PROLOG can be found in Rubin[13, 14] and Shammas.[15]

BUILT-IN PREDICATES

The classification of predicates used here is an emendation of the taxonomy employed in Weeks and Berghel.[9] The scheme is somewhat arbitrary and is simply the approach to the classification we find convenient. We call attention to the fact that the categorization is intended only for ease of use. For example, creating a separate category for strings does not imply that strings are separate data structures. No predicate was counted unless it appeared in the documentation for the product. Since the tables are self-explanatory, we make only very general comments regarding anomalies within the classification.

LPA's micro-PROLOG is distinctively different in terms of built-in predicates. In this case, there are multiple program environments, each of which has its own set of predicates. The environments are SIMPLE, micro-PROLOG, and DECsystem-10. Both SIMPLE and micro-PROLOG use syntax based upon the Marseilles implementation, whereas DECsystem-10 is essentially the Edinburgh syntax. Further, as a simplified interactive version of micro-PROLOG, SIMPLE has its own character: it supports infix notation. This makes the classification difficult because the range of built-in predicates depends upon the environment.

Although SIMPLE and micro-PROLOG are compatible to the extent that any module written in SIMPLE can be included in micro-PROLOG, neither is completely compatible with the DECsystem-10 environment. To illustrate, one can access micro-PROLOG clauses from the DECsystem-10 mode, but not the converse. As a result, such features as DCG's, which are supported in the DECsystem-10 environment, are not available under micro-PROLOG. Thus, the question becomes one of which environment should be compared. Since the DECsystem-10 predicates are only a subset

TABLE II—I/O predicates

Product:	P2	AR	LPA	MP	P86	VML	TUR
PROGRAM/CLAUSE I/O							
save ws by predicate(s)	–	+	+	–	–	–	–
delete ws by file	–	–	–	–	+	+	–
replace ws w/file	–	–	–	–	+	–	–
update file from ws	–	+	–	–	–	+	–
load/save binary image	+	+	+	–	–	–	–
load/save state	+	–	–	–	–	–	–
CHARACTER I/O							
get char from stream/file	+/+	+/+	–/–	+/+	+/+	+/+	+/+
get pr char (stream)	+	+	–	+	+	–	–
get w/o echo (stream)	+	+	–	–	–	+	–
skip to char (stream/file)	+/+	+/+	–/–	–/–	+/+	+/+	–/–
skip w/o echo (stream)	–	–	–	–	+	+	–
put char to stream/file	+/+	+/+	–/–	+/+	+/+	+/+	+/+
newline (stream/file)	+/+	+/+	–/–	+/+	+/+	+/+	+/+
newpage (stream)	–	–	–	+	–	+	–
write spaces (stream/file)	+/+	+/+	–/–	+/+	+/+	+/+	+/+
STRING I/O							
get string from stream/file	+/+	+/+	–/–	+/+	+/–	+/+	+/+
put string to stream	+	+	–	+	+	+	+
TERM I/O							
read term from stream/file	+/+	+/+	+/+	+/+	+/+	+/+	+/+
read token from str/file	+/+	–/–	+/+	+/+	+/+	+/+	–/–
read number from str/file	+/+	–/–	–/–	–/–	–/–	+/+	+/+
write to stream/file	+/+	+/+	+/+	+/+	+/+	+/+	+/+
write quoted to str/file	+/+	+/+	+/+	+/+	+/+	+/+	+/+
write ops prefix str/file	+/+	+/+	–/–	–/–	–/–	+/+	–/–
write formatted	+	+	+	+	+	+	+
declare operator	+	+	–	+	+	+	–
remove operator	+	+	–	+	–	+	–
get info about operator	+	+	–	+	–	–	–
define a prompt for I/O	+	–	–	–	+	–	–
direct file access position	+	+	+	–	+	+	+
fixed length file access	–	–	+	–	–	–	–
report on output environment	+	–	+	+	+	–	–

of Clocksin/Mellish, we evaluated micro-PROLOG. We emphasize that without complete compatibility, representing the product by an "inclusive-or" tally of each of the three environments would be misleading.

In a similar vein, M PROLOG has a distinctive way of supporting predicates. Some predicates, such as those for program/clause I/O and debugging and tracing, are supported only within the professional editor, PDSS. As a result, the tally of predicates refers only to those predicates in the language, although the features supported include those supported in PDSS as well. We believe this is the most reasonable way to describe M PROLOG.

With regard to program/clause I/O (see Table 2), the kernel is the pair of predicates which loads and stores a file (variations of consult and reconsult). However, the enhancements mentioned in Table 2 can save an enormous amount of work. One must remember that only consult and reconsult were present in the original PROLOG specification, so the variation between products is quite wide. For example, some products offer load options that are not cumulative and others use buffered I/O which is user-transparent.

Since the control predicates for success and failure are part of the language standard (such that it is), they are not included in the comparison (see Table 3). We note, however, that Turbo lacks the success predicate. Further, it is now quite common for products to include limited cuts (e.g., "snips"), which are useful but not part of the original language. In

TABLE III—Control predicates

Product:	P2	AR	LPA	MP	P86	VML	TUR
STREAM/FILE CONTROL							
create a file	+	+	+	+	+	+	+
open a stream/file	+/+	+/+	+/+	+/+	+/+	+/+	+/+
close a stream/file	+/+	+/+	+/+	+/+	+/+	+/+	+/+
temporary redir stdin	+	+	+	+	+	+	+
temporary redir stdout	+	+	+	+	+	+	+
turn on/off error calls	–	+	–	+	–	–	–
BACKTRACKING							
cut	+	+	+	+	+	+	+
repeat	+	+	–	+	+	+	–
logical set	+	+	+	+	+	+	–
explicit procedure call	+	+	–	+	+	+	–
special termination	+	+	+	+	+	–	+
number of solutions	+	–	+	–	+	+	–

Table 5, *full relational set* refers to the set of operators $\{<, >, <=, =>\}$ or their notational equivalents.

Structure manipulation (see Table 7) is important if one is to take full advantage of symbolic programming. Particularly important are such predicates as the ability to unify on arbitrary tree structures, decompose, compose, and convert between structures.

We also wish to note that, in contrast to earlier reports,[9, 10, 11] the present comparison indicates that a great deal of attention is being paid to extensions to the language. We believe that this reflects a desire on the part of the developers to establish PROLOG as a complete language environment rather than simply an experimental tool. To illustrate, the number of built-in predicates in the products under study that are not directly related to PROLOG typically constitute between 25 percent to 35 percent of the total.

PERFORMANCE CHARACTERISTICS

Traditionally, performance assessments fall into two categories. In some cases, the analysis is based upon an abstract model of the environment. Simulation and stochastic modeling illustrate this sort of evaluation. In other cases, the actual performance of the system in use is measured. These are usually called "benchmarks" or "workload models." In either case, one seeks to extract from the analysis some estimate of

TABLE IV—Term predicates

Product:	P2	AR	LPA	MP	P86	VML	TUR
CLASSIFICATION/CONVERSION							
is a variable	+	+	+	+	+	+	–
is a non variable	+	+	–	+	+	+	–
is an atom	+	+	+	+	+	+	–
is a number	+	+	+	+	+	+	–
is either atom or number	+	+	–	+	+	+	–
is a list	+	–	+	+	+	–	–
is quoted	–	–	–	+	+	+	–
is name	–	+	–	–	+	–	+
COMPARISON							
matching plus unification	+	+	+	+	+	+	+
does not match	+	+	–	+	+	+	+
equivalent	+	+	+	+	+	+	+
not equivalent	+	+	–	+	+	+	+
relational inequalities	+	+	–	+	+	+	+

TABLE V—Arithmetic evaluation predicates and operators

Product:	P2	AR	LPA	MP	P86	VML	TUR
PREDICATES							
evaluate and unify	+	+	+	+	+	+	+
arithmetically equal	+	+	+	+	+	+	+
not arithmetically equal	+	+	+	+	+	+	+
full relational set	+	+	–	+	+	+	+
OPERATORS							
arithmetic operators	+	+	+	+	+	+	+
X**n	+	+	–	+	+	+	+
int(f or n)	+	–	–	–	+	+	–
float(f or n)	+	–	–	–	+	+	–
log2(X)	+	+	–	–	+	+	–
log10(X)	–	–	–	–	+	+	+
lognat(X)	–	+	–	–	–	–	+
abs(X)	–	+	–	+	+	+	+
round(X,N)	+	+	–	–	–	–	–
sqrt(X)	+	+	–	–	+	+	+
sin(X)	+	+	–	–	+	+	+
cos(X)	+	+	–	–	+	+	+
tan(X)	+	+	–	–	+	+	+
asin(X)	+	+	–	–	+	+	–
acos(X)	+	+	–	–	+	+	–
atan(X)	+	+	–	–	+	+	+
floor(X)	–	–	–	–	+	+	–
greatest integer	+	+	+	+	–	+	–
atoi(<ascii>,<int>)	+	–	–	+	+	+	+
stof(<ascii>,<flt>)	+	–	–	+	+	+	+
bitwise AND	+	+	–	+	+	+	+
logical AND	–	–	–	–	+	+	–
bitwise OR	+	+	–	+	+	+	+
logical OR	–	–	–	–	–	+	–
bitwise EXCL-OR	–	–	–	–	+	+	+
logical EXCL-OR	–	–	–	–	–	+	–
bitwise NEGATION	+	+	–	+	+	+	+
arithmetic NEGATION	+	+	–	+	+	+	+
n-bit shift(left)	+	+	–	+	+	+	+
n-bit shift(right)	+	+	–	+	+	+	+
random number	–	+	–	+	+	+	+
random seed	–	–	–	+	+	+	–
counter	–	+	–	–	–	–	–

TABLE VI—Database control predicates

Product:	P2	AR	LPA	MP	P86	VML	TUR
CLAUSE CONTROL							
list all clauses	+	+	+	+	+	+	–
list specified clauses	+	+	+	+	+	+	–
assemble/disassemble clause	+	+	+	+	+	+	–
add a clause to the database	+	+	+	+	+	+	+
remove:							
first clause for predicate	+	+	+	+	+	+	+
all clauses for predicate	+	+	+	+	+	+	–
report presence of predicate	+	+	–	+	–	+	–
TERM CONTROL							
record term	+	+	–	–	–	–	–
erase term	–	+	–	–	–	–	–
report term	–	+	–	–	–	–	–
replace term	–	+	–	–	–	–	–
manipulate reference #	–	+	–	–	–	–	–

TABLE VII—Structure manipulation predicates

Product:	P2	AR	LPA	MP	P86	VML	TUR
structure unification pred	+	+	–	+	+	+	–
get the Nth argument	+	+	–	+	+	+	–
convert list/structure	–	+	–	+	+	+	–
convert list/atom	+	+	–	+	+	+	–
convert list/string	+	–	+	+	+	–	–
length of a list	+	+	–	+	+	+	–
sort list	+	+	–	+	–	–	–
append	+	–	–	+	–	+	–

TABLE VIII—Set predicates

Product:	P2	AR	LPA	MP	P86	VML	TUR
set unification	+	+	–	+	+	+	–
findall/bagof	+	+	+	+	+	+	+
membership	–	–	–	–	–	+	–
intersection	–	–	–	–	–	–	–
union	–	–	–	–	–	–	–

TABLE IX—String predicates

Product:	P2	AR	LPA	MP	P86	VML	TUR
search for substring	+	+	–	+	+	–	–
get substring	+	+	–	+	+	–	–
get position of substring	+	+	–	+	+	–	–
get length of substring	–	+	–	+	–	–	–
get length of string	+	+	–	+	+	–	+
concatenate strings	+	+	–	+	+	+	+

TABLE X—Debugging and trace predicates

Product:	P2	AR	LPA	MP	P86	VML	TUR
trace program execution	+	+	+	+	+	+	+
trace single goal	+	+	+	+	+	+	–
trace multiple goals	+	+	+	–	+	–	–
report goals to be traced	+	+	+	+	+	+	–
goal ancestry	+	–	–	+	+	+	–

TABLE XI—Shell support predicates

Product:	P2	AR	LPA	MP	P86	VML	TUR
EXEC	+	+	+	+	+	+	+
report file existence	+	–	–	–	–	–	+
rename a file	+	+	+	–	+	–	+
erase a file	+	+	+	–	+	+	+
link files	–	+	–	–	–	–	–

system performance in terms of responsiveness, throughput, and cost.[16]

Ideally, the programs used in benchmarking are known *a priori* to be relevant to the intended application of the computer resource. From our experience, this ideal is seldom realized. Instead, general-purpose and "home-grown" programs which anticipate patterns of usage are used. Of course, if the anticipated patterns are unrealized, the benchmark results are likely to be unreliable. We mention this because we believe benchmarks are very coarse measurements; and, consequently, we encourage readers to take our results with a large grain of salt.

Benchmarks are not without value as long as their results are not misused. Misuse can result from misrepresenting the relevance of the test or by misinterpreting the results.[17] We propose a modest objective: we try to gain some general understanding of the performance of the PROLOG products by running rather typical sorts of procedures, in fact, those procedures we use most often. As a result, our findings are biased toward our own interests in computational linguistics[18, 19] and approximate string matching.[20, 21] However, because the routines we used are mainstream, our results may be of interest to others.

In the interest of completeness, we refer the reader to the work of Wilk at Edinburgh.[22, 23] Wilk's approach is completely different. His intention is to develop standard benchmark techniques for PROLOG environments, carefully selecting benchmarks so that the entire breadth of PROLOG functionality is measured. This is an ambitious project and worthy of continued attention, although we suspect no general agreement will be reached regarding the confidence level to assign to his tests.

We also call your attention to other PROLOG benchmark results appearing in the trade press,[15, 24] which occasionally are at odds with our own.

BENCHMARK RESULTS

We begin the results discussion with an analysis of recursion limits. Because PROLOG is an ideal environment for recursion, it is natural to determine the cost of implementation. In microcomputer environments, memory consumption usually is more critical than processing speed. The part of memory most affected is the stack. Unless some optimization takes place, recursion may fill the stack with unnecessary latent calls. To reduce this problem, software developers implement such functions as structure sharing, garbage collection, and last call optimization. Because users typically have no way of knowing whether and to what extent optimization is present, empirical tests are useful.

We performed two separate recursion tests on each product. The tests were adapted from Covington.[25] The number of full recursions before failure (stack space exceeded) is presented in Figure 1. When possible, we defined the largest stack space possible in the environment file. Otherwise, default values were used.

Tail recursion (see Figure 2) should be more efficient because the recursion is invoked at the end of a goal set. For

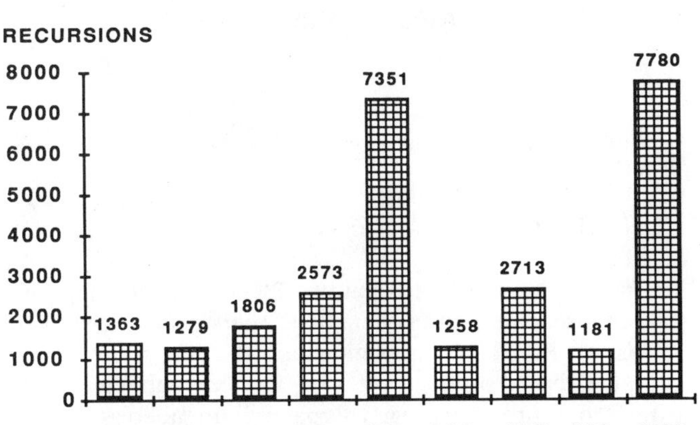

Figure 1—Recursions before failure (normal recursions)

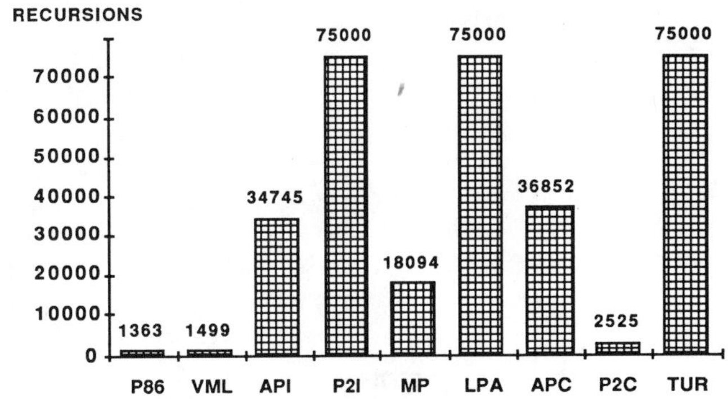

Figure 2—Recursions before failure (tail recursion)

interpreted PROLOG 2, micro-PROLOG, and Turbo, the tests were terminated at 75,000 recursions. Since these products claim optimized tail recursion, additional testing seemed unnecessary. In the case of Arity PROLOG, the failure was not a result of non-optimization; it was a result of the way that the counter represents large integers. Because there is no way of determining the upper bound on recursions without a counter, Figure 2 provides the actual results without adjustment.

The next benchmarks deal with string operations, and are, for the most part, standard procedures defined in Clocksin and Mellish.[7] The values are presented in terms of run times. The results of all tests appear in Figures 3 and 4. Naive reverse is a variation on the *de facto* standard benchmark for PROLOG. Despite its frequent use, it has shortcomings: it can overstate the efficiency of the implementation.

The last test (see Figure 5) is a general benchmark which is supposed to have its origins in ICOT. The code fragment is as follows:

```
tak(X,Y,Z,Z):-X=<Y,!.
tak(X,Y,Z,R):-
    tak1(X,Y,Z,R1),!,
    tak1(Y,Z,X,R2),!,
```

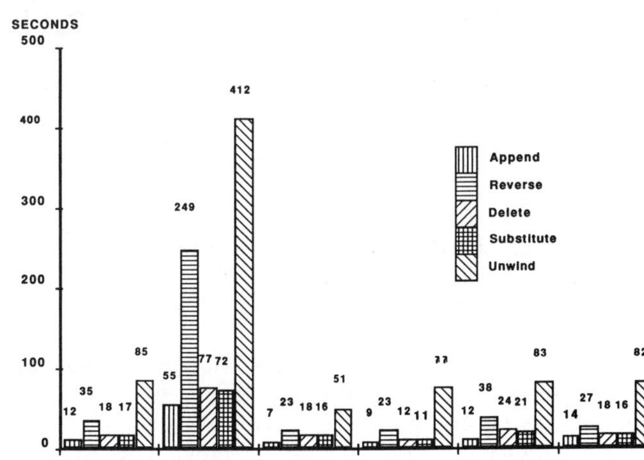

Figure 3—String functions (interpreters)

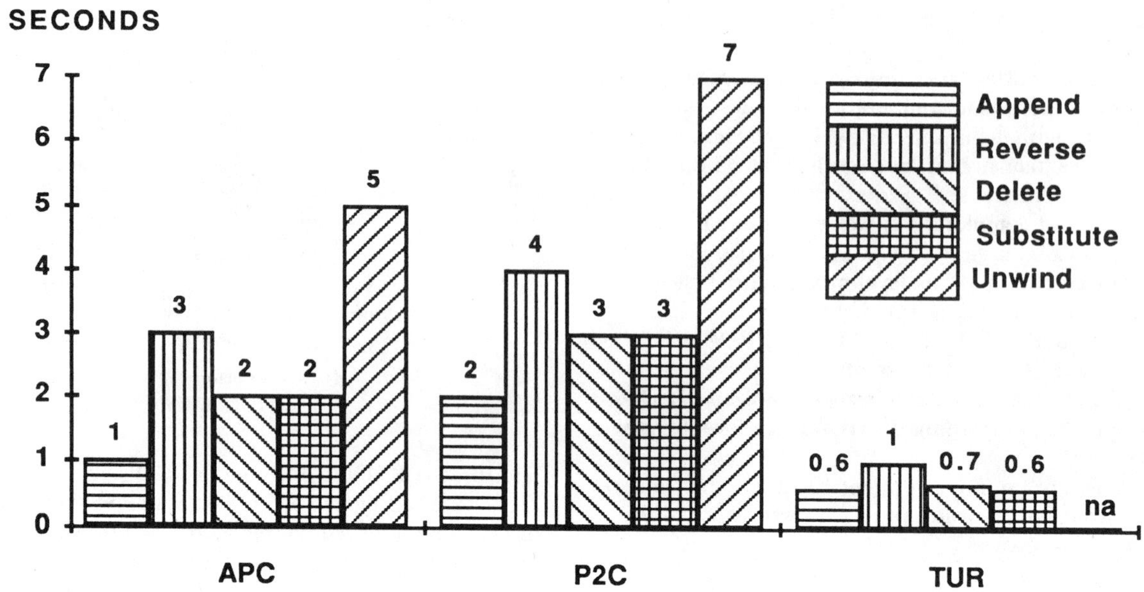

Figure 4—String functions (compilers)

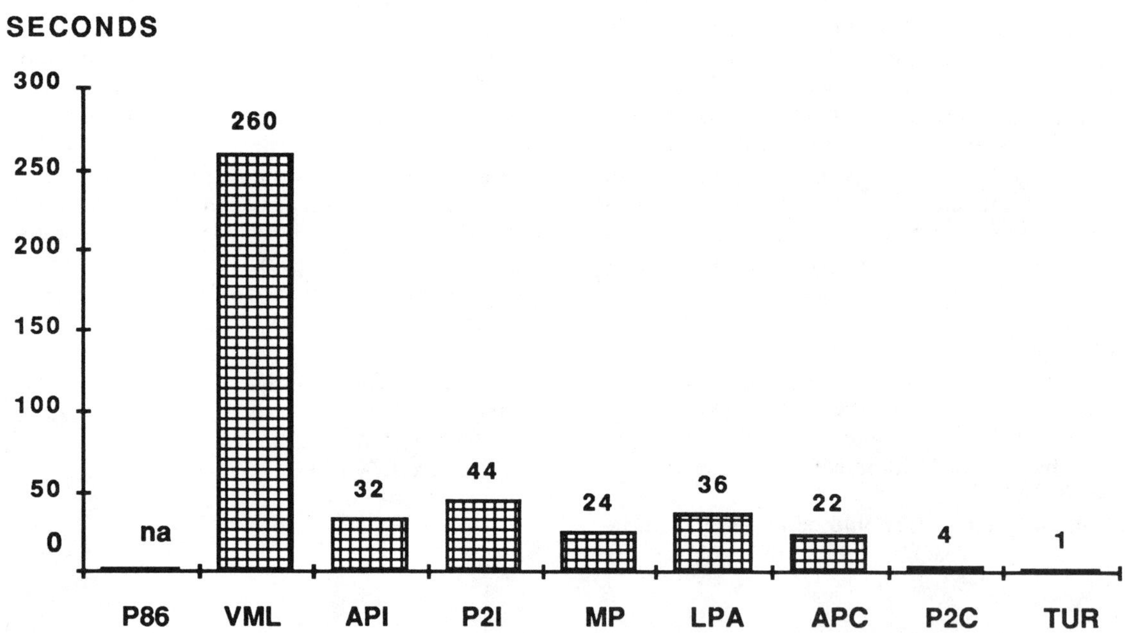

Figure 5—Agglomerative benchmark

```
    tak1(Z,X,Y,R3),!,
    tak(R1,R2,R3,R),!.
tak1(X,Y,Z,R):-X1 is X-1,
    tak(X1,Y,Z,R).
?-tak(12,8,4,N).
```

The test was provided by Robert Morein of Automata Design Associates. It is an agglomerative measure which attempts to assess the overall strengths of the products. We note that PROLOG 86+ would not run the program, presumably due to inefficient memory reclamation.

For additional details on these and other benchmarks, including a listing of the clause sets, see Berghel, Stubbendieck, Traudt.[11]

CONCLUSION

As increasing attention is paid to PROLOG, growing numbers of researchers and system developers wish to avail themselves of PROLOG implementations. For many, microcomputer-based products offer the most cost-effective way to exploit logic programming. This paper is intended as a general overview of these products so that interested parties may select the product most consistent with their needs.

ACKNOWLEDGEMENTS

The classification scheme used in this paper is a result of collaboration with J. Weeks. The benchmark results are taken from earlier work with G. Stubbendieck and E. Traudt. We wish to thank L. Baxter, P. Gabel, J. Grayson, and R. Morein for many useful comments and criticisms.

REFERENCES

1. Mota-Oka, T. (ed.) *Fifth Generation Computer Systems* (Proceedings of the International Conference on Fifth Generation Computer Systems). Amsterdam: North Holland, 1982.
2. Kowalski, R. "Search Strategies for Theorem Proving." In B. Meltzer and D. Michie (eds.) *Machine Intelligence* (Vol. 5). New York: Edinburgh University Press, 1969.
3. Kowalski, R. "And-Or Graphs, Theorem Proving Graphs and Bi-directional Search." In B. Meltzer and D. Michie (eds.) *Machine Intelligence* (Vol. 7). New York: Edinburgh University Press, 1972.
4. Kowalski, R. "Predicate Logic as a Programming Language." *Proceedings of IFIP 74,* 1974, pp. 569–574.
5. Colmerauer, A., H. Kanoui, R. Pasero, and P. Roussel. "Un Systeme de Communication Homme-Machine en Français." Report, Group Intelligence Artificielle, University d'Aix Marseilles, 1973.
6. Colmerauer, A. "Les Systèmes-Q ou un Formalisme pour Analyzer et Synthesiser des Phrases sur Ordinateur." Report #43, Department d'Informatique, Universite de Montreal, 1973.
7. Clocksin, W. and C. Mellish. *Programming in PROLOG.* New York: Springer-Verlag, 1981.
8. Kowalski, R. "Algorithm = Logic + Control." *Communications of the ACM,* 22 (1979), 7, pp. 424–436.
9. Weeks, J. and H. Berghel. "A Comparative Feature-Analysis of Microcomputer PROLOG Implementations." *SIGPLAN Notices,* 21 (1986), 2, pp. 46–61.
10. Weeks, J. and H. Berghel. "Turbo + PROLOG." *Bulletin of the IEEE Computer Society Technical Committee on Personal Computing* (October 1986), pp. 1–7.
11. Berghel, H., G. Stubbendieck, and E. Traudt. "Performance Characteristics of Microcomputer PROLOG Implementations." *Proceedings of the 1986 ACM Sigsmall/PC Symposium on Small Systems,* 1986, pp. 64–71.
12. Pereira, F., Bix Communication: ask.experts, message #17 (Electronic Mail). McGraw Hill/Byte Information Exchange, June 8, 1986.
13. Rubin, D. "Turbo PROLOG: A PROLOG Compiler for the PC Programmer." *AI Expert,* Premier Issue (1986), pp. 87–98.
14. Rubin, D. "Inside Turbo PROLOG." *Computer Language* (July 1986), pp. 23–28.
15. Shammas, N. "Turbo Prolog." *Byte* (September 1986), pp. 293–295.
16. Muntz, R. "Performance Measure and Evaluation." In A. Ralston and E. Reilly, Jr., *Encyclopedia of Computer Science and Engineering.* New York: van Nostrand Reinhold, 1983.
17. Fleming, P. and J. Wallace. "How Not to Lie with Statistics: the Correct Way to Summarize Benchmark Results." *Communications of the ACM,* 29 (1986), 3, pp. 218–221.
18. Berghel, H. and J. Weeks. "On Implementing Elementary Movement Transformations with Definite Clause Grammars." *Proceedings of the Fifth Phoenix Conference on Computers and Communications,* 1986, pp. 366–370.
19. Berghel, H. "Extending the Capabilities of Word Processing Software through Horn Clause Lexical Databases." *AFIPS Proceedings of the National Computer Conference* (Vol. 55) 1986, pp. 251–257.
20. Berghel, H. "Crossword Compilation with Horn Clauses." *The Computer Journal* [in press].
21. Berghel, H. "A Logical Framework for the Correction of Spelling Errors in Electronic Documents." *Information Processing and Management* [in press].
22. Wilk, P. "The Production and Evaluation of a Set of PROLOG Benchmarks," Artificial Intelligence Applications Institute Report #AIAI-PSG51, University of Edinburgh, 1986.
23. Wilk, P. "PROLOG Benchmarking," Artificial Intelligence Applications Institute Report #AIAI-TR-14, University of Edinburgh, 1986.
24. Wong, W. "PROLOG—A Language for Artificial Intelligence." *PC Magazine* (October 14, 1986), pp. 247–263.
25. Covington, M. "Programming in Logic—Part 2." *PC Tech Journal* (January 1986), pp. 145–155.

Speech synthesis: System design and applications

by JARED BERNSTEIN
SRI International
Menlo Park, California

ABSTRACT

This paper introduces speech synthesis. Included are: a review of current synthesis technologies, an examination of the component algorithms and control structures needed for text-to-speech synthesis, and a discussion of current and future research topics.

INTRODUCTION

The purpose of this tutorial is to introduce speech synthesis. Included are: a review of current synthesis technologies, an examination of the component algorithms and control structures needed for text-to-speech synthesis, and a discussion of current and future research topics.

Current Synthesis Systems

Speech synthesis refers to two kinds of processes: (1) encoding, transmission or storage, and decoding of natural speech that might better be called "re-synthesis"; and (2) synthesis of speech by rule from linguistic input such as written text. One common method of encoding/decoding speech at low bit rates is Linear Predictive Coding (LPC) which is an efficient method of de-convolving the fundamental frequency from the spectral envelope based on the assumption that the speech spectrum can be adequately modeled as an all-pole linear filter that is excited by an impulse train. Fundamental work on LPC is presented in Markel and Gray,[1] Makhoul,[2] and Atal and Hanauer.[3] Encoding speech for later resynthesis is reviewed by Flanagan.[4]

The focus of this tutorial is speech synthesis by rule and, in particular, synthesis from text.

A paper by Kaplan and Lerner[5] reviews commercial offerings in synthesis, and includes an overview of the component processes in the Prose 2000 product. Other system-level descriptions of text-to-speech systems can be found in Allen,[6] Allen, Hunnicutt and Klatt,[7] Hertz,[8] and Umeda.[9] An early Bell Laboratories systems is clearly presented in the text of patent 3,704,345.[10]

Text to Speech Components

A text-to-speech system can be implemented as a set of processes connected in series. The first linguistically interesting process of a text-to-speech converter is the system for translating words (as written in standard spellings) into phonemic forms that describe pronunciations. This is usually called *letter-to-sound* (LTS) conversion. The classic sources that provide complete descriptions with complete rule sets are McIlroy;[11] Hunnicutt;[12] and Elovitz, Johnson, McHugh, and Shore.[13] A comparison of Hunnicutt's and Elovitz's rules is presented by Bernstein and Nessly.[14] A more recent approach to LTS is explained in Hertz.[8] Related morphological and lexical issues are covered in Allen,[7] Umeda,[9] and Church.[15]

The next process in series is allophonics. Allophones are contextually conditioned variants of phonemes. Rules for selecting the appropriate allophonic form for a phoneme in a given context are important in synthesizing natural-sounding and intelligible speech. Rule sets are given in Klatt[16] and Allen[6] for synthesis; computational allophonics are discussed with recognition applications in mind by Oshika, Weeks, Nue, and Auerbach;[17] Woods et al.[18] and Church.[19]

After the text to be spoken is in allophonic form, a subsequent prosodic process is required to assign a rhythm and melody to the string of allophones. Conventionally, the rhythm of the sentence is taken to be the result of segment-level durations. The best duration rules in the literature probably are Klatt's.[16,20] A general problem with the rhythm of synthetic speech used in text-to-speech systems results because the systems do not "understand" what they are saying, and conventional punctuation is less than complete (following the "when in doubt, leave it out" school of commas). One might gain some speech quality by implementing some of the processes studied by Cooper and Paccia-Cooper.[21]

The melody of English sentences is encoded in the fundamental frequency (f0) of the voiced portions and the way that the f0 patterns are aligned in time. Most text to speech systems use some version of a "hat and declination" f0 pattern[22] as, for instance, parameterized by Maeda.[23] This f0 rule provides a humdrum rendition of most neutral declarative sentences of the kind on which the hat and declination studies were based, but it becomes wearing in connected text. Other sources on f0 patterns are Cooper and Sorensen[24] Bernstein's review[25] of Cooper and Sorensen, and a recent collection edited by Cutler and Ladd.[26] The most promising recent development is Pierrehumbert's PhD. thesis,[27] but her 1981 paper[28] suggests a meaning-blind application of her theory which reduces it almost to a variation of Maeda.[23]

The next process used in text-to-speech systems converting a linguistic transcription of allophones with durations and f0 values into a parametric description suitable to drive a signal synthesizer. An excellent and clear introduction to this aspect of synthesis is Chapter 6 of Flanagan.[4] The somewhat standard approach now is Klatt's[29] synthesis by rule logic that is used in DECTalk, the Prose 2000, and new products from Texas Instruments and IBM. Klatt presented his approach in more detail in Allen, Hunnicutt, and Klatt.[7] Some alternative approaches to phonetic synthesis are discussed in the "Phonetic Synthesis by Concatenation" section of this paper.

FAST LETTER-TO-SOUND CONVERSION

Introduction

The usual practice in letter-to-sound conversion[8,12,13] involves checking substrings of letters and right and left contexts for each of several rules, then replacing the letter string with a phoneme string. Movement is from left to right through the word, with stress assignment and vowel reduction handled in a second pass through the word (usually from right to left). Unfortunately, the resulting software has been Byzantine, or the phonemic output is inaccurate, or both. Within this general framework, there also have been several attempts to automatically train letter-to-sound rules for optimal accuracy or size.[11,30,31] These optimizing approaches have not resulted in high accuracy systems for several reasons but at least in part because they assumed an overly restricted algorithm structure.

Linguistic Content

This section describes elements of an algorithm and its associated data structures that allow fast and accurate letter-to-sound conversion in English. The description ignores affix stripping. The structure of the algorithm is based on three generalizations about the linguistic content of the rules of English spelling and phonology:

1. The rules of English phonology (and the published rule-sets for letter-to-sound conversion) may have more different left environments but many more rules have right environments than have left environments.
2. Stress assignment (inside the stress-neutral suffixes; e.g., -ed and -ing) is much more simply handled from the right end of the word than from the left end.
3. There are orthographic cues for certain letter-sound correspondences that are not phonological. Such cues are either morphological or reflect changes in spelling conventions.

Design Consequences

Taking advantage of the historical and linguistic nature of English spelling, a system can perform high accuracy letter-to-sound conversion, stress assignment, and vowel reduction in one right to left pass, starting inside the stress-neutral suffixes (e.g., "-ing" or "-ly"). Thus, a right-environment semaphore can be set by the operation of the previous rule and checked with a single instruction. Furthermore, stress assignment can be accomplished by using three bits of the semaphore and a pointer to the last vowel phoneme, if any. The principal advantage of this approach is increased speed. The increased speed results because the largest portion of the processing time in most implementations of context-sensitive rules is spent context matching (some 80 percent or more of which is trivialized in this approach). The rest of the summary describes the rule structure and semaphore flags used and gives an example of how they work.

Details

A rule example is:
  (e.g., for ⟨ian⟩ as in "Armenian") :
Right environment semaphore:
  (Boundary)
Letter string:
  IAN
Left environment:
  (or (N (sequence TH) (sequence PH)))
Phoneme string:
  EaN
Semaphore Set:
  (Tense Vowel & I-Short)

This example means check for the boundary bit in the semaphore. If set, check the letter string, and if it matches, check the left environment which could be N or TH or PH. If right, replace the "ian" with /EaN/. Then, the phonological flags (like voiced, vowel, high) are set from the /E/, and the tense vowel and I-short flags are set out of the rule. The other consequence of this rule would be to increment the syllable count by two.

The semaphore has three kinds of flags: (1) logical bits, like negative and disjunctive, that control the interpretation of the remaining flags; (2) the usual phonological flags such as voiced, nasal, stop, sonorant, and labial, that are set based on the leftmost phoneme inserted; and (3) morphological/orthographic flags such as soft, palatalize, irreducible, and latin, that are explicitly carried in the rule.

PHONETIC SYNTHESIS BY CONCATENATION

Designs for Phoneme-input Unlimited LPC Synthesis

Phonemic synthesis is the transformation of a transcribed pronunciation, like that found in a dictionary, into a speech signal. Sivertsen[32] is the classic reference on inventories for synthetic speech by concatenation. Units that have been tried with known results include phonemes, allophones, diphones, syllables, demisyllables, and words. Any of these units may be the internal unit in a phoneme-input synthesizer because the map from phonemic input into any of these units is straightforward. The issue is: Which unit can give the highest quality at a reasonable memory size? In the following sections we describe allophones, diphones, and demisyllables with reference to synthesis.

Allophones

Allophones are contextually determined variants of phonemes; so they are the same "size" as phonemes except there are more of them. Though linguists rarely identify more than 60 allophones in English, for reasonable synthesis one might need as many as 300 vowel allophones and 100 consonant allophones (assuming consonant voicing by rule.) For instance, a system might need a "labial-velar /e/" as in "beg", and also use it in any of the contexts with {p,b,f,v,m} on the left and {k,g,ng} on the right. A description of Texas Instruments' allophonic synthesizer can be found in *Electronic Design,* June 25, 1981. With 128 allophones, the resulting speech is poor. C. Harris' early report[33] on the possibility of splicing phoneme length units is discouraging. Some of the reasons for the failure of phoneme concatenation are discussed by Wang.[34]

Diphones

Diphones are stored lengths of speech that extend from near the target of one phoneme to near the target of the next. The diphone is an appropriate unit for synthesis because co-articulation is mainly restricted to the immediate phonemic context. In speech, the path between phoneme targets often is non-linear and even non-monotonic within any usual acoustic parameter space (e.g., track the formants or LPC coefficients in the word "joy"). Thus, the primary advantage of diphones over allophones is that they include exactly the transition from one target to the next. The first diphone system was described by Dixon and Maxey;[35] more recent diphone work has been reported by Olive[36] and by Schwartz, Klovstad, Makhoul, Klatt, and Zue.[37] Although there are only about 40 phonemes in English and thus, ideally, about 1600 diphones, Schwartz suggests that about 2000 diphones would be needed for high quality diphone synthesis because some diphones are not really context-free, and the vowel dipthongs in English should be treated as pseudo-diphones.

Demisyllables

Demisyllables are initial or final portions of syllables that can be concatenated to form syllable sequences. Syllabic synthesis should be a very natural way to synthesize by concatenation, because (it is claimed) allophonic and coarticulatory variations rarely cross syllable boundaries. A method for cutting and joining demisyllables for synthesis by concatenation has been outlined by Fujimura, Macchi, and Lovins.[38] They estimate between 1000 and 1200 demisyllables would be needed for a high quality unlimited synthesis system.

Hybrid

A hybrid concatenation system may be necessary to fix apparent problems with any of the three concatenation methods. In particular, LPC-based concatenative synthesis methods have trouble with sequences like ⟨vowel⟩ {l,r,y,w} ⟨vowel⟩. These "vowel-medial semi-vowels" can be handled by what Sivertsen calls "syllable dyads." to synthesize these sounds by concatenation, about 300 vowel-medial semi-vowels would have to be added to any of the inventories. A system that actually reaches production may need to include several types of units reflecting solutions to various detailed problems encountered in development.

System Requirements for These Designs

Assuming 42 bits per frame, an average speech rate of 150 words per minute, and a microprocessor that is fast enough to interpolate every other 20 msec frame, we can calculate a nominal memory size for each of the concatenation methods outlined. It probably is best to generate prosodic information by rule within the synthesizer system rather than try to store and adjust pitch, amplitudes, and gains as appropriate to current context. The "overhead" code (including the map from phonemes to internal units and the prosodics) would be less than 20k bytes.

1. *Allophones.* Full length vowels average 180 msec and consonants average 80 msec. Sampling every other 20 msec frame yields 4.5 frames per vowel and 2 frames per consonant. 300 vowels and 100 consonants, therefore, can be stored as 1550 frames at 6 bytes/frame for an allophone table of 10k bytes.
2. *Diphones.* Inter-phoneme transitions average about 100 msec. Sampling every other 20 msec frame of 2000 diphones that average 100 msec in length requires 5000 frames to be stored in 30k bytes.
3. *Demisyllables.* The average length of a demisyllable is 260 msec. 1200 demisyllables of 6.5 frames each would require storing 7800 6-byte frames in 48k bytes.

Reasonable quality synthetic speech should be possible with a total memory size between 40 kbytes and 70 kbytes, an LPC chip, and a microprocessor. Methods such as vector quantization for compressing LPC data could reduce the nominal table sizes given here by 10 percent to 40 percent.

VOICE INSTRUMENTATION

One could use vocal cues to direct user attention and to code the source and urgency of information within a voice interactive command/control environment. Voice output has several particular advantages in a user interface, especially when integrated with a voice recognition capability. A voice message reaches users regardless of their visual orientation and, like a flashing display or a red warning light, it can notify users that the system designers believe some aspect of the current situation requires user attention.

Also, voice response or verification are needed to maintain the advantages of voice input during "hands-busy eyes-busy" operation. Note, however, that just as an all-red instrument panel would decrease the advantage of bright red warning lights, routine or needless use of voice output could nullify its real advantages—especially if the same or a similar voice recites all the messages in a similar way. Therefore, there is a need to think carefully and design voice into complex displays in ways that use the distinctive communicative value of voice to best advantage.

In contrast to a written message, a spoken message carries several kinds of indexical information (for instance, the gender, size, and age of the speaker) as well as paralinguistic signals that express the speaker's attitude toward the message (for instance, the message is routine, or surprizing, or urgent). By understanding and modeling the indexical properties of speech, we can develop separate vocal identities for different information sources. Through control of the paralinguistic aspects of a synthetic speech signal, we can use conventional modes of speaking to command a user's attention or reinforce the intent of the message by speaking it in a manner consistent with its content.

For example, differences in speech might be observed as message content changes from routine (e.g., "Fuel level at 80 percent") to urgent (e.g., "Fuel level reading inconsistent"). At each level of linguistic description, and at every stage in the synthesis process, there can be changes that reflect urgency. From the research literature we can guess that both voice pitch and amplitude may increase and that voice pitch may become more dynamic. Furthermore, the timing of the message and its enunciation may change, although these changes are less well understood. One course of action is to identify and test hypotheses about these changes by studying human speech; then decide the correct level at which to implement these changes in the message-generation subsystem of the command/control system.

The currently available text-to-speech devices (in particular, the Prose 2000 and DECTalk) are limited in the range of control that the host processor has over the indexical and paralinguistic properties of the synthetic speech. The Prose 2000 allows considerable control of speech parameters related to paralinguistic meaning, but supports a limited range of voice identities. DECTalk, in contrast, features six different voice identities, although host control of paralinguistic aspects is limited. Neither device offers the host a full set of appropriate controls for selecting voices and for encoding apparent attitude into the speech signal.

Steps needed for incorporating multiple voices into the command/control environment would involve: (1) understanding the acoustic-phonetic bases of indexical and paralinguistic information, (2) formulating that information in a way consistent with the message-generation logic of the command/control system, and (3) adapting (i.e. simplifying) the voice output control specification to the limitations of the available synthesis devices for demonstration and user evaluation, or (4) attempting to implement a special-purpose synthesis system to support the full range of indexical and paralinguistic cues identified in (1).

REFERENCES

1. Markel, J. D. and A. H. Gray, Jr. *Linear Prediction of Speech*. New York: Springer-Verlag, 1976.
2. Makhoul, J. "Liner Prediction: A Tutorial Review." IEEE, 63 (1975) pp. 561–580.
3. Atal, B. S. and S. L. Hanauer. "Speech Analysis and Synthesis by Linear Prediction of the Speech Wave," *Journal of the Acoustical Society of America,* 50 (1971) pp. 637–655.
4. Flanagan, J. L. *Speech Analysis Synthesis and Perception*. New York: Springer-Verlag, 1972.
5. Kaplan, G. and E. J. Lerner. "Realism in Synthetic Speech," *IEEE Spectrum,* April 1985, pp. 32–37.
6. Allen, J. "Synthesis of Speech from Unrestricted Text," *Proceedings of the IEEE,* 64 (1976) 4, pp. 433–442.
7. Allen, J., S. Hunnicutt, and D. Klatt. *From Text to Speech: The MITalk System*. Cambridge, UK: Cambridge University Press, 1986.
8. Hertz, S. R. "From Text to Speech with SRS," *Journal of the Acoustical Society of America,* 72 (1982) 4, pp. 1155–1170.
9. Umeda, N. "Linguistic Rules for Text-to-Speech Synthesis," *Proceedings of the IEEE,* 64 (1976) 4, pp. 443–451.
10. Coker, C. H. "Conversion of Printed Text into Synthetic Speech." U.S. Patent No. 3,704,345, November 1972.
11. McElroy, D. "Synthetic English Speech by Rule." Memorandum, Bell Telephone Laboratories, Murray Hill, New Jersey, 1974.
12. Hunnicutt, S. "Phonological Rules for a Text-to-Speech System." *Am. J. Computational Linguistics,* 1976, Microfiche 57.
13. Elovitz, H. S., R. W. Johnson, R. W. McHugh, and J. E. Shore. "Letter-to-Sound Rules for Automatic Translation of English Text to Phonetics," *IEEE Transactions: Acoustics, Speech, Signal Processing,* 24 (1976) pp. 446–459.
14. Bernstein, J. and L. Nessly. "Performance Comparison of Component Algorithms for the Phonemicization of Orthography," *Proceedings of the 19th Annual Conference of the Association for Computational Linguistics,* 1981, pp. 19–22.
15. Church, K. "Morphological Decomposition and Stress Assignment for Speech Synthesis," *Proceedings of the 24th Annual Conference of the Association for Computational Linguistics,* 1986, pp. 156–164.
16. Klatt, D. "Structure of a Phonological Rule Component for a Synthesis-by-Rule Program," *IEEE Transactions: Acoustics, Speech, Signal Processing,* 24 (1976) pp. 391–398.
17. Oshika, B. T., V. W. Zue, R. V. Weeks, H. Neu, and I. Auerbach. "The Role of Phonological Rules in Speech Understanding Research," *IEEE Transactions: Acoustics, Speech, Signal Processing,* 23 (1975) pp. 104–112.
18. Woods, W., et al. "Speech Understanding Systems, Vol. III." Final Technical Program Report No. 3438, ONR Department of the Navy Contract No. N00014-75-C-0533, 10-30-74 to 10-29-76. Bolt, Beranek, and Newman, Inc., Cambridge, Massachusetts, 02138.
19. Church, K. W. "Phrase-Structure Parsing: A Method for Taking Advantage of Allophonic Constraints." Indiana University Linguistics Club, Bloomington, Indiana 47405. June 1983.
20. Klatt, D. "Synthesis by Rule of Segmental Durations in English Sentences," in B. Lindblom and S. Ohman (eds.), *Frontiers of Speech Communication Research*. New York: Academic Press, 1979, p. 287.
21. Cooper, W. E. and J. Paccia-Cooper. *Syntax and Speech*. Cambridge, Massachusetts: Harvard University Press, 1980, pp. 180–193.
22. t'Hart, J. and A. Cohen. "Intonation by Rule: A Perceptual Quest," *Journal of Phon.,* 1(1973) pp. 309–327.
23. Maeda, S. A. "A Characterization of American English Intonation." Unpublished Ph.D. thesis, Massachusetts Institute of Technology, 1976.
24. Cooper, W. E. and J. M. Sorensen. *Fundamental Frequency in Sentence Production*. New York: Springer-Verlag, 1981.
25. Bernstein, J. Review in *IEEE Transactions: Acoustics, Speech, Signal Processing,* 31 (1983) p. 515.
26. Cutler, A. and D. R. Ladd (eds.). *Prosody: Models and Measurements*. New York: Springer-Verlag, 1983.
27. Pierrehumbert, J. "The Phonology and Phonetics of English Intonation." Ph.D. dissertation, Cambridge, Massachusetts: MIT Press, 1980.
28. Pierrehumbert, J. "Synthesizing Intonation," *Journal of the Acoustical Society of America,* 70 (1981) 4, pp. 985–995.
29. Klatt, D. H. "Software for a Cascade/Parallel Formant Synthesizer," *Journal of the Acoustical Society of America,* 67 (1980) 3, pp. 971–995.
30. Klatt, D. and D. Shipman. "Letter-to-Phoneme Rules: A Semi-automatic Discovery Procedure." Paper CC2 presented at the 104th Meeting of the Acoustical Society of America, Fall 1982.
31. Lucassen, J. and R. Mercer. "An Information Theoretic Approach to the Automatic Determination of Phonemic Baseforms." Paper 42.5 presented at the IEEE ICASSP, 1984.
32. Sivertsen, E. "Segment Inventories for Speech Synthesis," *Language and Speech,* 4 (1961) p. 27.
33. Harris, C. "A Study of the Building Blocks of Speech," *Journal of the Acoustical Society of America,* 25 (1953) p. 962.
34. Wang, W. S.-Y. "Transition and Release as Perceptual Cues for Final Plosives," *Journal of Speech and Hearing Research,* 2 (1959) p. 66.
35. Dixon, R. and H. Maxey. "Terminal Analogue Synthesis of Continuous Speech Using the Diphone Method of Segment Assembly," *IEEE Transactions on Audio and Electroacoustics,* 16 (1968) 1, p. 40.
36. Olive, J. "Rule Synthesis of Speech from Dyadic Units," *Proceedings of the IEEE ICASSP,* 1977, pp. 568–570.
37. Schwartz, R., J. Klovstad, J. Makhoul, D. Klatt, and V. Zue. "Diphone Synthesis for Phonetic Vocoding," *Proceedings of the IEEE ICASSP,* 1979, p. 891.
38. Fujimura, O., M. Macchi, and J. Lovins. "Demisyllables and Affixes for Speech Synthesis." Paper given at the Ninth International Congress of Acoustics, 1977.

Voice mail and office automation

by DOUGLAS L. HOGAN
SPARTA, Incorporated
McLean, Virginia

ABSTRACT

Contrary to expectations of a few years ago, voice mail or voice messaging technology has rapidly outpaced speech recognition and speech synthesis in applications for office automation. This growth is a result of rapid technological advances in such areas as computing technology and digital telephony. The falling cost of voice message storage, the power of computer control of messaging, and user comfort with voice information all contribute to making voice mail desirable.

This paper reviews voice mail technology, including coding and storage. Also, three office automation areas are discussed. Finally, lack of standards for voice mail is discussed.

INTRODUCTION

As recently as seven years ago in a survey of the speech technology market[1] there were predictions of rapid advances in the use of speech recognition and speech response for computer input and output. However, in the same report there was no mention of voice mail! Today we find that voice mail (also called voice store-and-forward or voice messaging) and its supporting technology have become the major market in speech technology and are becoming an intimate part of office automation.

The major economic/technological reasons for the rapid growth of voice mail have risen out of the advances in computing technology. These advances have led to extensive use of computers in office automation and to advances in digital communications including digital telephony. Speech signal processing for data compression has become economical; storage of digital information has become even more economical. With speech in digital form, computer control can provide maximum flexibility in supporting applications involving storage and retrieval of audio information. Additionally, the telephone is still the ubiquitous terminal; it is everywhere.

The other major reason for the growth of voice mail is a matter of human factors. Speech is the natural means for human communication and individuals like to use it when it is convenient to do so. The importance of this last point cannot be overemphasized; applications must fit user needs.[2]

In the following sections, the technology of voice coding and storage, applications including office automation, and a standards issue are discussed.

VOICE CODING

Data and Information Rate

Telephone-quality speech signals may be simply encoded at a sampling rate of 8,000 samples per second. These samples may then be converted to digital representation using an analog to digital (A/D) converter; 11 bits per sample, or a rate of 88,000 bits per second, maintains telephone quality. However, if we examine the information rate in such a signal we conclude that it is well under 100 bits per second. This conclusion is obtained by assuming a speaking rate of four words per second, a generous estimate of 15 bits per word, and an allowance of 40 bits per second to account for ancillary information such as the speaker's identity and perhaps some indication of the speaker's physical and mental state. Voice coding methods are used to reduce the gap between the data rates of simply digitized speech and the true information rate.

Removal of Redundancy

The step following simple digitization consists of encoding the samples in a way that tries to eliminate some of the redundancy in the signal. Encoding may be minimal or extensive; with extensive encoding, speech intelligibility and quality is reduced and increased computational requirements are incurred. Some encoding methods attempt to extract parameters that are directly related to modeling speech signal generation as a vocal tract excited by an appropriate source. A comprehensive discussion of voice coding is contained in the treatise by Jayant and Noll.[3]

Waveform coding

Waveform coding methods deal directly with digitized voice signals. The simplest waveform coding uses only those signals as quantized by the A/D converter; more complex waveform coding methods remove some or much of the inherent redundancy by methods that do not take into account information about generative constraints in the voice signal. There are two significantly different types of waveform coding. The first type of coding, framed signals, represents each time sample with a fixed number of bits that must remain in frame synchronization. The second type of coding, unframed signals, uses only one bit per sample and; achieving frame synchronization is not a problem.

Framed signals. The simplest framed signal is an 11-bit linear quantization of the speech samples often called pulse code modulation (PCM). It also has been determined that logarithmic companding (compressing followed by expanding) of a speech signal will provide the same perceived fidelity with the logarithmic samples described as 7-bit quantities. This log-PCM at 56,000 bits per second has been the standard for most digital telephony. Other forms of waveform digitization based on PCM include differential PCM (DPCM) and adaptive differential PCM (ADPCM). These variations attempt to exploit some of the redundancy remaining in the PCM quantized sequence. The difference in DPCM between successive samples can be encoded with fewer bits. In ADPCM, a certain amount of past history is retained and used to determine whether the quantization step size should be changed. In differentially coded systems, such as DPCM and ADPCM, any bias results in a gradual drift of the signal. This is countered by introducing a less-than-unity feedback in the reconstruction feedback loop. Currently, a 32 kbit/sec ADPCM standard is being implemented for digital telephone circuits. It will eventually replace the present log-PCM standard by providing telephone quality speech at 32,000 bits per second instead of 56,000 bits per second.

Another way of reducing the data rate of a PCM signal is called "block PCM". Because speech signals usually remain in high or low amplitude for a considerable number of milliseconds, blocks of PCM values having fewer steps can be accompanied by a block multiplier. Still another PCM derivative is sub-band coding. This method takes advantage of signal redundancy in a different manner: the spectrum is filtered into two or more frequency bands, each of these "sub-bands" is downshifted to baseband, sampled at an appropriate rate, then digitized and encoded. Since the upper frequency sub-bands contain less information than low frequency sub-bands, coding efficiency is improved by using appropriate and possibly different coding methods for each sub-band.

Unframed signals. Unframed signal waveform coding of speech uses one-bit frames thus, frame synchronization can never be lost. This coding method is known as delta modulation. Delta modulation is accomplished by sampling the speech waveform considerably faster than required by the sampling theorem and by performing a reconstruction of the waveform with unit steps between successive samples. Analysis is actually performed by comparing the sampled signal with the reconstruction. The sign of the difference of these two signals is encoded as a 1 or a 0. If the reconstructed signal lags behind the true signal for too many samples, a condition known as "slope overload" is said to exist. Slope overload is countered by increasing the complexity of the coding to vary the slope of the reconstructed signal; such a process is called continuously variable slope deltamodulation (CVSD) or adaptive deltamodulation (ADM).

Source/tract coding (vocoders)

The source/tract class of speech coding techniques often is referred to as narrow band systems, most of which have data rates of 4800 bits per second or less. Source/tract coding is accomplished by modeling the speech generation process to some degree of fidelity. Such modeling is done in two parts: (1) modeling of the excitation and (2) modeling of the vocal tract. That is, narrow band coding systems extract the excitation and vocal tract descriptions separately and describe them efficiently. Systems using these techniques are also called vocoders. The two most common forms are the channel vocoder and the linear predictive vocoder. Both vocoder forms require extraction of the excitation.

Modeling excitation. Excitation of the vocal tract can be considered (to a first approximation) as either "voiced" or "unvoiced". Voiced refers to excitation due to periodic pulses of air from the glottis (vocal cords). Unvoiced refers to excitation due to turbulent air flow or release of puffs of air by aperiodic openings and closures of the vocal tract. Thus, the analysis consists of making an excitation decision; and, if the excitation is voiced, to measure the distance between the excitation pulses (pitch period) or the frequency of those pulses (pitch frequency). The excitation decision generally can be made on the basis of energy concentration in the spectrum. Determining pitch may be done in many ways: (1) the fundamental (first) harmonic may be followed with a tracking filter; (2) when the fundamental is not present, an autocorrelation process or an approximation to such a process may be used; (3) alternatively, some form of observing peaks in the time domain waveform may also be used. Information about the excitation can be coded at a relatively low bit rate; in most vocoders a rate of about 120 bits per second is used for this purpose.

Modeling the vocal tract. The channel vocoder was an early (1937) attempt to remove some of the redundant information from the speech signal; in fact, it was an attempt to model speech in terms of source and tract. This vocoder obtains the spectral description of vocal tract shapes using a set of contiguous band-pass filters spanning the speech spectrum. The output of these filters is rectified, low-pass filtered (because the vocal tract shape is expected to change slowly), sampled, and quantized. Thus, the speech signal spectrum is described in from 10 to 16 channels, sampled 40 or 50 times per second, and quantized in a few bits per sample. A total data rate of approximately 2400 bits per second, encoded in fixed format frames every 20 or 25 msec, usually is sufficient to describe such a vocoder.

The time behavior of the vocal tract also can be modeled as a predictor which is formed as a weighted function of a moderate number of past samples of the tract output. This linear predictor is based on obtaining the best fit between a predicted signal and the true signal using a least-squares error criterion. Typically, the predictor is based on analysis of 100 to 200 samples; the predictor can regenerate the analyzed segment of speech with about 10 to 14 coefficients operating recursively on an initial set of that many samples. The predictor is calculated by forming autocorrelations of sections of the speech signal over the period for which near stationarity of the signal is expected. This is approximately 20 msec for voiced speech. The set of autocorrelation equations is solved for its eigenvalues; these become the predictors.

A number of variations of the linear prediction method are in use. One variation describes the prediction function in terms of the complex roots of the linear equation; this can be construed as approximating the vocal tract with an all-pole model. Another form describes the tract shape as though it were a lattice filter and the filter coefficients are derived iteratively by removing correlation effects of each coefficient successively. This method is known in the literature as the partial correlation or PARCOR method.

Linear prediction methods are treated exhaustively in the book by Markel and Gray.[4] Linear prediction vocoders are normally encoded in fixed size frames of about 50 bits every 20 or 25 msec. Thus, including excitation, a 2400 bit/sec vocoder can be achieved. A variation on these methods is the residual excited linear prediction (RELP) vocoder. With this method, the excitation signal is taken as the error signal between the predicted and actual signal. This signal may be encoded by a waveform coding method in from 2400 to 7200 bits per second with a resulting RELP vocoder rate of from 4800 to 9600 bits per second.

Adaptive predictive coding

Another form of coding called adaptive predictive coding (APC) is, in effect, a hybrid of waveform coding and LPC vocoding. In one such system a fourth order spectrum predictor is combined with a pitch predictor and the error signal between these two predicted signals and the true signal is coded by a waveform coding method. The spectrum predictor is optimized by adaptation instead of direct computation as in the LPC vocoder.

Technology

A few years ago, real-time performance of the more complex voice coding algorithms would have required a significant investment in equipment. In the past three years, significant advances have been made in programmable signal processing devices.[5] Today, any of the algorithms described in this paper can be carried out in real time using a single signal-processing chip. For this reason, selection of the speech coding algorithm essentially has no economic impact on a voice mail system and the criteria for selection involve only data rate versus quality, and algorithm differences versus standardization. The latter point is discussed in the last section of this paper.

VOICE STORAGE

One primary feature of voice mail is important for storage: access to the information is inherently sequential. Thus, disk technology is totally appropriate for voice test storage. Given the assumption of a certain amount of random access memory for buffering, there are no bars to input and output of voice information from any rotating media. Further, the cost of disk technology is reduced by a factor of two about every two years; thus, capacious storage is quite economical.

Additional economy can be achieved by not recording silence intervals. It is only necessary to delineate the beginnings and ends of speech segments and their time of occurrence relative to a baseline (e.g., the beginning of the message). In this way, it is possible to reproduce the original input speech with its correct timing including all of the pauses. Voice detector circuits are available; some are available on the same device as speech encoders and decoders.[6]

Given digital storage of voice messages, many manipulations are possible. One possible manipulation is the ability to scan or review messages at speeds faster than real time. This is readily accomplished by deleting segments of the speech data of from 20 to 40 msec long, and playing out the undeleted parts of the speech data at their normal speeds. The result is an overall reduction in playback time without the pitch distortion associated with speeded speech. A number of voice mail systems provide some version of speeded voice message review.

APPLICATIONS

The net result of having digitized speech signals in a computer controlled memory is that any desired application can be built around that speech database. The success or failure of a system will take place at the applications stage. Applications functions must be both useful and convenient. In the simplest application, the telephone instrument must be a data entry device as well. In such a case, the speech compression signal processor can easily decode the dual tone multifrequency (DTMF) signals generated at telephone keypads. These signals then can be used for any desired control functions. Three application areas for voice messaging are discussed briefly in the following sections.

Telephone

Voice messaging applications range from simple, such as an answering machine or the voice analog of electronic mail to complex, such as using data input with tone signals from the telephone keypad, forwarding calls, and automatic distribution. Voice mail can be used to respond with computer generated voice messages (either from text-to-speech systems or concatenations of prerecorded words/phrases in simple dialogs). In this way there can be interaction between a user with a telephone and a computer system. Applications of such interaction range from order entry to college class selection and scheduling.

In the past, many voice mail systems have relied on using the conventional analog telephone plant for access to a central site containing the voice mail control and all of the voice mail files. Now the trend is to replace much of that plant with a local digital telephone system; this permits local data networks to be integrated with the local telephone network. Thus, the switchboard becomes both a voice and data resource in office automation. In addition, movement to the Integrated Services Digital Network (ISDN) in the telecommunications industry will accelerate the decline of the analog telephone network. For digital networks that do not have to differentiate between voice and data, it will become cost effective to handle voice mail similar to electronic mail—using the same sort of store-and-forward capabilities provided by interconnection of digital data networks.

Text/Data

Conversely, we may think of integrating text and data into the office telephone system. From either point of view, it is desirable to have voice mail and electronic (text) mail integrated within the same system. Text systems can facilitate telephone directory service and dialing, and can display information about voice messages that are waiting or have been previously heard and stored.

Voice messages can be used to annotate text information and messages. This is useful to both an originator of text information and a recipient who is commenting on or reviewing the information.

Finally, voice messaging can be used to access text messages or text databases when a data terminal is not available. Text-to-speech systems can be used to access text messages and databases. A more complex control structure would be required for formatted or non-text databases; as an example, consider the problem of reading a table to a listener and the extra words required to describe column and other structures.

Pictorial Information

Just as with text information, voice message annotation can be helpful in describing pictorial information (i.e., graphics or images) displayed in an office automation system. For example, annotation can be used to explain and point out features of the pictorial information.

Although voice messaging usually is thought of as a non-real-time (delayed time) service, its technology can be used to support records of real time multi-media remote conferencing. This kind of conferencing normally involves pictorial information displays and voice discussions among participants located at two or more sites. An example of a potential application would be using voice messaging technology to support a record of a remote conference enabling review or later re-enactment of part or all of the conference.

STANDARDS

The major outstanding issue of concern for voice mail is the lack of standardization. Many vendors use a proprietary voice compression method; others use a variety of standard algorithms or standard implementations of algorithms that are available at the device level. Data rates in use range from 32,000 bits per second down to 2400 bits per second. In addition, there is no standard way in which voice data and associated time information are stored. Consequently, it is not possible to transfer digital voice message files between differing systems; voice information must first be converted to analog form. Bridging disparate mail systems in analog form leads to another problem. A speech signal that has been encoded and decoded with one algorithm will sound fine to a listener. However, if the speech signal is encoded with a second algorithm artifacts of the first algorithm may be left which can have an adverse effect on the quality of the speech produced by the second algorithm.

In addition to the coding standardization issue, the usual standards issues of using electronic mail across organizations including naming and addressing, directories, and routing information, also must be addressed. These issues together with the problems of compatible voice coding, will be taken up at a future time by a standards organization.* In the meantime, the voice mail vendors continue to go their separate ways.

ACKNOWLEDGEMENTS

I would like to acknowledge the assistance of my colleague, Dr. Beatrice T. Oshika, in helping to shape this paper. I also would like to acknowledge the discussion I had with Ms. Nancy M. Dinicola of Voice Computer Technologies Corporation regarding the real world of voice mail.

REFERENCES

1. Kolbus, D. I. "Computer Speech Communication," Research Report No. 623, SRI International Business Intelligence Program, Menlo Park, California: SRI International, 1979.
2. Gould, J. D. and S. J. Boies. "Speech Filing—An Office System for Principals." *IBM Systems Journal,* 23 (1984) 1, pp. 65–81.
3. Jayant, N. S. and P. Noll. *Digital Coding of Waveforms.* Englewood Cliffs, New Jersey: Prentice Hall, 1984.
4. Markel, J. D. and A. R. Gray, Jr. *Linear Prediction of Speech.* New York: Springer-Verlag, 1976.
5. Bursky, D. "Algorithms and Chips Cooperate to Squeeze More Speech Signals into Less Bandwidth," *Electronic Design,* October 3, 1985, pp. 90–100.
6. "New Chip Integrates Codec Functions," *Voice News,* October 1986, p. 3.
7. *Data Communication Networks: Message Handling Systems Recommendations X.400–X.430.* Red Book, Volume VIII—Fascile VIII.7, Geneva: CCITT, 1985.

---

* The most recent version of these standards is the X.400 series[7] of the International Telegraph and Telephone Consultative Committee (CCITT) which reserves the voice coding problem as one for future study. Although these standards have begun to address many aspects of electronic mail, it will be some time before they become specific enough to be useful for voice mail.

Artificial intelligence in office information systems

by PETER COOK and CLARENCE A. ELLIS
MCC
Austin, Texas
BIPIN C. DESAI
Concordia University
Montreal, Quebec, Canada
CLAUDE FRASSON
Université de Montréal
Montreal, Quebec, Canada
JOHN MYLOPOULOS
Unversity of Toronto
Toronto, Ontario, Canada
NAJAH NAFFAH
Bull-Transac
Massy, France

INTRODUCTION

The recent interest in the application of artificial intelligence (AI) to office problems through the vehicle of automated office systems is due both to the "pull" of those interested in office problems and the "push" of the AI community. The pull from within the body of manufacturers and users of office systems comes from the lessons learned during the last decade while observing the rise of management information systems and their problems. The push from the AI community is due to a widely held view within that group that many of their systems have matured to an extent that these can earn, and are earning, their keep in the commercial sector.

Artificial intelligence, which has been confined largely to research and development laboratories, is finally moving to the office. One sees increasing evidence of AI technology that is being merged with existing products; this marriage of AI with the traditional product renders the union more powerful and easier to use. The goal of AI in the early days was to recreate the working of the human mind in a machine (and hence the oxymoronic term): this goal has evolved over the years into a more attainable one, namely, that of making computer systems easier to use by humans whatever their training and understanding.

The current efforts of the AI community, as related to applications in OIS, is to merge AI smoothly into existing software and systems, making them easier to use. Thus expert systems, the most prodigious product of the AI research, are mated with existing systems like the Automatic Teller Machine to make the latter more expert in allowing a withdrawal or an advance without the intervention of a human banker. Speech recognition and natural language interfaces allow additional ease in interacting with existing software systems.

USER INTERFACE

The evolution of user interfaces is based on several converging forces and components which have been the subject of recent research.

The first step in this evolution involved relational query languages with non-procedural aproaches such as SQL[1] or example-based systems such as QBE.[2] The main problems with this type of language are that the users must be aware of the database structure such as the relations and their attributes. The users, particularly the untrained end-users, have difficulties in building the request using the database manipulation language. Furthermore, they generally have imprecise ideas about what they are searching for.

A natural language interface allows the user of a database to input a query in a natural language such as English or French rather than in the formal query language; the goal being to permit the user to express his/her information needs in his/her own language, and in conceptual terms particular to his/her understanding of the database application domain. The user is also freed from knowing about database management systems, data models, or database schemes. Allowing the user to access a database using natural language shifts onto the computer system the burden of mediating between the two views of data: the way in which the data is stored and the way in which an end-user thinks about it. A DBMS, particularly a relational one, accomplishes part of this task. What the user interface must do is reconcile the user's view with the DBMS's view.

In order to achieve this data independence, the interface must incorporate a considerable amount of knowledge. This includes knowledge about natural languages, the domain database application, and DBMS's and their query languages.

THE USER PROFILE

All the above approaches are means to facilitate the accessing of data, however, they do not identify the user. There is presently an increasing need for improving the user interface, but the effort should be directed toward considering the type of user for which the system is intended.

The present systems do not distinguish between users, who, in fact, are different according to their knowledge and experience in the use of the system, their interests in the database, the kind and the form of the reponse that they require from the database. These aspects should be considered in order to fit the users' needs. The introduction of artificial intelligence components able to recognize a wide variety of users, should greatly enhance the interaction in database systems. The benefits are characterized by an individualized dialogue, personally tailored help, simplification of the interactive process, and responses which are given according to the views and interests of the user.

To achieve these objectives, the user profile should constitute an important part of an intelligent interface. A user profile can be composed of various types of information such as: (1) information on customs, level of experience and qualifications of the user in his/her environment, (2) familiarity of the user with the system, (3) information objectives and interests of the user in the database, and (4) a recording of the transactions (history).

The important fact is that this knowledge must be dynamic. It is updated after each transaction in order ot obtain a precise image of the user, who will then be identified automatically. With a classical system, the user is more or less able to query a database and extract pertinent data from the flow of the elements produced as output. An intelligent interface should be able to recognize the user and dynamically adapt the dialogue. The desired results should then be deduced by the interface.

Applications of the user profile are numerous. The most important concern information retrieval systems and intelligent tutoring systems. In this last domain, other aspects such as the psychological reactions and performance factor of the user must be included in the profile.

KNOWLEDGE REPRESENTATION

Artificial Intelligence can be of value in the development of the "office of the future" in at least two ways. First, by adding to the functionality of office information systems with natural language front-ends, problem solving and planning submodules, expert system front-ends that add some subjective "judgment" to the system's capabilities. Fikes,[3] Barber,[4] and Woo,[5] provide good examples of this type of application of AI. Second, and perhaps more important, AI can be used to facilitate the development of office information systems. One way to do this is to build "automatic programming" environments. Another way is to adopt knowledge representation ideas in the development of new classes of languages for requirements analysis and design. It is this last area of AI influence on Office Automation that will be the focus of the rest of the section.

To construct a requirements or design specification for an office information system demands the representation and integration of disparate knowledge into a coherent knowledge base. Thus, a requirements specification for an office information system needs to capture the knowledge that exists within the office, and which prescribes the patterns of behavior of the system to be built and its environment. For instance, to build a student information system one needs to describe students, their associated attributes—such as address, field of study, courses and supervisor—the activities they participate in (such as registering in courses) if certain rules are satisfied (such as pre-requisites for the courses have been completed successfully)—and the like. One needs also to describe the activities to be carried out by the intended system, the information it will handle, and how that information is obtained from the environment. In addition, for an office information system to be useful, there must exist a framework for the interpretation of its contents with respect to the intended application. Such interpretation is only possible if the system and/or its users "know" how accurate, complete, and precise the information handled by the system is. For the student registration system, for example, it must be known how often student records are updated in order to determine how the contents of the system "match" reality for a query such as "Who is taking course csc324?". If updating of the system is instantaneous, its contents fully reflect the current state of the environment. If, on the other hand, it is updated once a week, one can only answer the above question with something like "As of date X, the following students: . . . ".

It follows from these observations that knowledge bases built during the early phases of office information system construction will need to have a number of features. First, they must provide an account of the structure, static, and dynamic, of the environment within which the system must function. Second, they must provide an account of how the contents of the system to be built relate to the environment. Additionally, one can expect that such knowledge bases will, in general, be large, involving thousands of concepts, which must be described and organized in a way that renders the knowledge base comprehensible. Moreover, the knowledge bases will be dynamic in the sense that the rules and procedures that determine the behavior of the environment will change frequently.

What kind of a knowledge representation framework can accommodate these requirements? First, the framework must provide support for the representation of time to facilitate the modeling of the dynamics of the intended system and its environment. Second, the framework must draw a distinction between the contents of the information system and the state of the environment, so that one can make statements about the accuracy and completeness of the information handled by the intended office information system. Third, the framework must offer structuring mechanisms since, as was said before, this is a knowledge engineering in-the-large activity. The requirements modeling language RML,[6] and its successor CML[7] exemplify the kinds of linguistic tools one can develop taking these considerations into account. Both languages treat a requirements specification as a history of the world being modeled. CML, however, goes further in treating a requirements specification as a history of our knowledge of the world. This feature makes CML powerful enough to talk about the completeness, accuracy, and precision of the information handled by the intended system.

Applying knowledge representation techniques to the development of design specification languages is slightly more problematic. One might argue (and many have!) that design specifications should be independent of the environment within which the system under development will eventually function, and should simply provide an account of the system's behavior. Consider, however, a system which maintains information about, say, students at a University. A formal specification of such a system which merely describes its behavior but doesn't try to provide an account of what the information handled by the system means in the first place (i.e., how it relates to reality), seems incomplete. It tells us how symbols will eventually be pushed around inside a machine. It doesn't give us any guidelines on how to interpret these symbols. This observation suggests that, at least for information systems, a design specification should come with an account of how mechanism behavior corresponds to the world being modeled. For design specifications of this sort we need linguistic tools that on the one hand, allow for the description of system components, their state, and I/O behavior; and on the other, come with a rich semantic theory that allows one to relate system states and functions to the world being modeled. The so-called semantic data models (attempt to) do just that. (See Brodie[8] and Borgida.[9]) An example of a semantic office model is described in Gibbs.[10]

We have discussed how and why knowledge representation techniques can influence the features of requirements and design languages for office information systems. Implicit in our arguments is the assumption that building such systems requires several linguistic levels: some for requirements modeling, others for design, and still others for implementation. What implications does such an influence have for the environments offered for building such systems? To start with, each linguistic level used needs an environment. Those for the more procedural levels can offer typical facilities such as special purposes editors, interpreters, tracing and debugging packages, version control, and the like. The environments for the less procedural levels need reasoning facilities so that a user can probe a knowledge base to see if it is consistent with his/her expectations. A second type of facility needed for such an environment is intended to make it possible to generate lower level (and more procedural) specifications from higher level (and more declarative) ones. Depending on the nature of the two levels, it may be possible to have a compiler that handles this job. Alternatively, the environment may provide facilities for the interactive generation of the lower level specification from the higher level one. These facilities could include expert system features so that the environment plays the role of an active assistant rather than a passive bookkeeper in the generation of a specification. A third desirable facility involves the maintenance and management of multiple specifications for a particular software system corresponding to the different linguistic levels supported by the environment. Such a facility would allow a user to maintain a requirements specification, a design specification, and an implementation specification of his/her software, along with information on how parts of one specification relate to parts of others. With such a setup, it is possible to determine how changes of the specification at one level affect the specifications at other levels. The research project outlined in Jarke, Mylopoulos, Schmidt, and Vassiliou[11] focuses on an environment intended to provide all three facilities mentioned above. It is fair to add that there are scores of research issues to be addressed in realizing an environment of the type advocated here and that a research program addressing such issues can only be described as long term.

OTHER OIS AIDS

Meetings constitute an important part of the communication and coordination work of organizations. They are used to disseminate information, explore ideas, resolve disagreements, and enhance teamwork to achieve organizational goals. The large amount of manager time consumed by meetings has been documented and reported in the literature.

The task of organizing and executing an effective meeting can, however, be both time consuming and difficult. After this time consuming preparation, there are no guarantees that the meeting will proceed smoothly, and evaluation of the "goodness" of a meeting is quite elusive. Unsuccessful or wasteful meetings are experienced frequently, but the exact causes of these failures are largely undocumented and not well understood. One of the reasons for this lack of understanding is that the results and effects of a meeting can be quite diverse, ranging from meeting minutes and action items to feelings of wasted time and latent disdain for certain people and tasks: these can be very difficult to capture and quantify. Another reason is related to the sometimes surprising and unpredictable nature of participant behavior. A further reason is the lack of formal models of meetings, and lack of a "theory of meetings" within which researchers can work and relevant results can be interpreted. The thrust of Project Nick at MCC is to perform interdisciplinary research into the analysis of content, structure, and protocols of meetings. Our group has been performing research in the areas of meeting analysis and meeting augmentation. In this ongoing effort, we are theorizing on a large set of ideas; assembling and implementing a subset of these ideas; and performing experiments to validate those ideas which appear most promising and applicable. We believe that new technology may present the opportunity for new and better meeting styles and organizations.

The meetings research is based on a two pronged approach with both aspects proceeding in parallel and complementing each other. The two prongs are building theories and building systems.

Building Theories—This aspect of our work began with a careful definition of our basic notions (meeting, exploration, design) and proceeds by creating intuitions, wild ideas, assertions, and hypotheses. The hypotheses, in turn, suggest certain systems which we can build to confirm these hypotheses. This work has tried to pinpoint aspects of meetings which frequently go wrong, and to develop measures of goodness of meetings; all of this interdisciplinary work is clearly dependent upon factors such as the type and intent of the meeting.

Building Systems—This includes the construction, test, and usage of electronic meeting aids. Our meeting aid equipment includes an electronic blackboard and interconnected personal computers for all meeting participants.

In the future, we envision analyses of information derived during the meeting, and used to enhance the meeting in real time.

HARDWARE FOR OIS USING AI

Current work in office information systems has demonstrated the applicability of various techniques of artificial intelligence to the office environment. The main hardware components of an office information system must be developed specifically to support artificial intelligence programming in order to achieve maximum utilization. This is particularly true for a workstation, the site of interaction with a user which demands the highest degree of intelligence. Three characteristics of the workstation can be identified; emphasis on AI techniques, application to the office environment, and inclusion of multimedia and natural language processing (NLP) capabilities. Workstations for future office information systems must combine these features if they are to achieve any degree of success.

In addition to the fairly standard hardware, the workstation requires a number of less common components that are required to fulfill the software objectives of the projects.[12] These components include:

1. A telephone interface.
2. Audio hardware. Specialized devices are to be used for the recognition and generation of human speech and possibly for sampling and compressing audio signals. This hardware is necessary for the multimedia user interface.
3. A data filtering device. To perform pattern-oriented retrieval from the disk at high speed, a special processor known as the Schuss filter[13] will be integrated with the workstation hardware. The use of a hardware filter on the intelligent workstation is one of the most novel aspects of the system.

The main requirements for the operating system used by the intelligent workstation are support for: (1) distributed processing, (2) Real-time processing, and (3) Knowledge-based applications.

Since office applications are inherently distributed, the operating system must provide facilities for networking and interprocess communication. The data handled in the office include audio and image data in addition to the traditional numeric and character data types. To perform such functions as acquisition and storage of audio data, the operating system must have real-time processing capabilities. Finally, knowledge-based applications can benefit from operating system support. For example, many intelligent applications for the office will make use of large, shared knowledge bases in which case adding and retrieving knowledge becomes crucial. It is expected that the Schuss filter can be used to improve the efficiency of knowledge retrieval.

CONCLUSION

We have examined the various areas of application of AI technology in office information systems and the office of the future. The use of more convenient user interfaces in the form of natural languages and the convenience of individualized interface require, the maintenance of a wide variety of knowledge by the interface system. In addition, the system must be able to interpret the contents of the information system. Such interpretation requires that the system know the dynamic environment within which the system operates, as well as the accuracy of the information contained in the system.

Support for other office functions like meetings, which constitute an important part of the communication and coordination work of an organization, is also essential. The use of modern technology, including AI, to improve meetings is thus vital.

The need of an intelligent workstation which supports AI programming is obvious. Such a workstation must have the capability to support AI programming, multimedia and natural language processing.

REFERENCES

1. Chamberlin, D.D. et al. "SEQUEL 2: A Unified Approach to Data Definition, Manipulation, and Control." IBM *J. R&D,* 20 (1976) 6, pp. 560–575.
2. Zlooff, M.M. "Query-by-example: A Data Base Language." *IBM Systems Journal,* 16, 4, pp. 324–343.
3. Fikes, R. "Odyssey: A Knowledge-Based Assistant." *Artificial Intelligence,* Vol. 16, 1981, pp. 331–361.
4. Barber, G. "Supporting Organizational Problem Solving with a Workstation." *ACM Transactions on Office Information Systems,* 1 (1983) 1.
5. Woo, C. and F. Lochovsky. "Supporting Distributed Office Problem Solving in Organizations." *ACM Transactions on Office Information Systems,* 4 (1986) 3.
6. Greenspan, S. "Requirements Modeling: A Knowledge Representation Approach to Requirements Definition." Ph.D. thesis, Department of Computer Science, University of Toronto, 1984.
7. Stanley, M."A Formal Semantics for CML." M.Sc. thesis, Department of Computer Science, University of Toronto, 1986.
8. Brodie, M.L. "On the Development of Data Models." in M., Brodie, J. Mylopoulos, and J. Schmidt. (eds.) *On Conceptual Modeling: Perspectives from Artificial Intelligence, Databases and Programming Languages,* New York: Springer Verlag, 1984.
9. Borgida, A. "Features of Languages for the Development of Information Systems at the Conceptual Level." *IEEE Software,* January, 1985, pp. 63–73.
10. Gibbs, S. and D. Tsichritzis. "A Data Modeling Approach for Office Information Systems." *ACM Transactions on Office Information Systems,* 1, (1983) 4.
11. Jarke, M., J. Mylopoulos, J. Schmidt, and Y. Vassiliou. "Towards a Knowledge Based Software Development Environment." in J. Schmidt, and C. Thanos, (eds.) *Foundations for Knowledge Base Management,* Proceedings of Workshop on Foundations on Knowledge Base Management, Chania, June 1986.
12. Naffah, N. et al. "Design Issues of an Intelligent Workstation for the Office." *AFIPS, Proceedings of the National Computer Conference* (Vol. 55) 1986, pp. 153–159.
13. Gonzales, Rubio R. et al. "The Schuss Filter; A Processor for Non-numerical Data Processing." *Proc. of IEEE Annual Symposium on Computer Architecture,* Ann Arbor, 1984.

A portable natural language interface*

by BIPIN C. DESAI, JOHN McMANUS, and PHILIP J. VINCENT
Concordia University
Montreal, Quebec

ABSTRACT

A natural language interface allows database system users to input a query in a natural language such as English or French rather than in a formal query language. Such interfaces could also provide for natural language updates, but this paper deals only with queries.

The goal of a natural language interface is to permit users to express their information needs in their own language and in conceptual terms particular to their understanding of the database application domain. Users also are freed from knowing about database management systems (DBMS), data models and database schemas.

Allowing a user to access a database using natural language shifts onto the computer system (the interface and the DBMS) the burden of mediating between two views of data: the way in which the data is stored (the database view) and the way in which an end user thinks about it (the user's view). A DBMS, particularly a relational one, accomplishes part of this task. The interface must reconcile the user's view with the DBMS' view.

To achieve such data independence, the interface must incorporate a considerable amount of knowledge including knowledge about natural language, the domain database application, and DBMSs and their query languages.

*This work was supported in part by a contract from the Canadian Workplace Automation Research Center of the Department of Communication, Government of Canada.

INTRODUCTION

A natural language interface is portable if it can be transferred with minimum effort from the database for which it was designed to a new database. The degree of portability is reflected in the amount of effort required to transfer the interface. If an interface is handtailored to a particular database, major reprogramming is required to convert it to a new database. In the extreme case, the effort will be equal to the task of programming the interface to the original database. On the other hand, an interface that requires no effort to transfer is beyond the capabilities of current research. Such an interface would have to learn by itself the characteristics of a new database and adapt its linguistic and computational abilities accordingly.

The general design structure for an interface that allows a moderate degree of portability is presented in the next section of this paper. The goal of the design structure is to minimize the amount of reprogramming necessary for three types of database transfer: (1) change of DBMS, (2) change of application domain, and (3) conceptual reorganization of the database.

The key to achieving some degree of portability is modularity. Early natural language systems[1] were handtailored for particular applications. In their data structures and procedures, they intermixed knowledge about language with knowledge about the domain application. They also conflated user request with how to obtain the information requested. The early systems were inherently not portable because they were not modular.

Natural language interfaces can be modularized in three dimensions. The first dimension keeps distinct the three main types of knowledge required; that is, knowledge about language, the application domain, and databases. The second separates procedural knowledge from declarative knowledge. The ability to parse an English sentence is inherently procedural whereas the vocabulary a parser accepts is naturally declarative. A parser and its lexicon should therefore be kept separate. The third dimension distinguishes between general knowledge and domain-specific knowledge. This dimension is crucial for portability. As much of the interface as possible should be designed using only general knowledge. A transfer to a different DBMS or application thus would not require changing modules that incorporate general knowledge only.

GENERAL DESIGN STRUCTURE

Figure 1 graphically illustrates a possible design of a portable natural language interface. The design includes three procedural modules and three declarative modules. The procedural modules are the parser, the semantic analyzer, and the query generator. The declarative modules are the lexicon, the

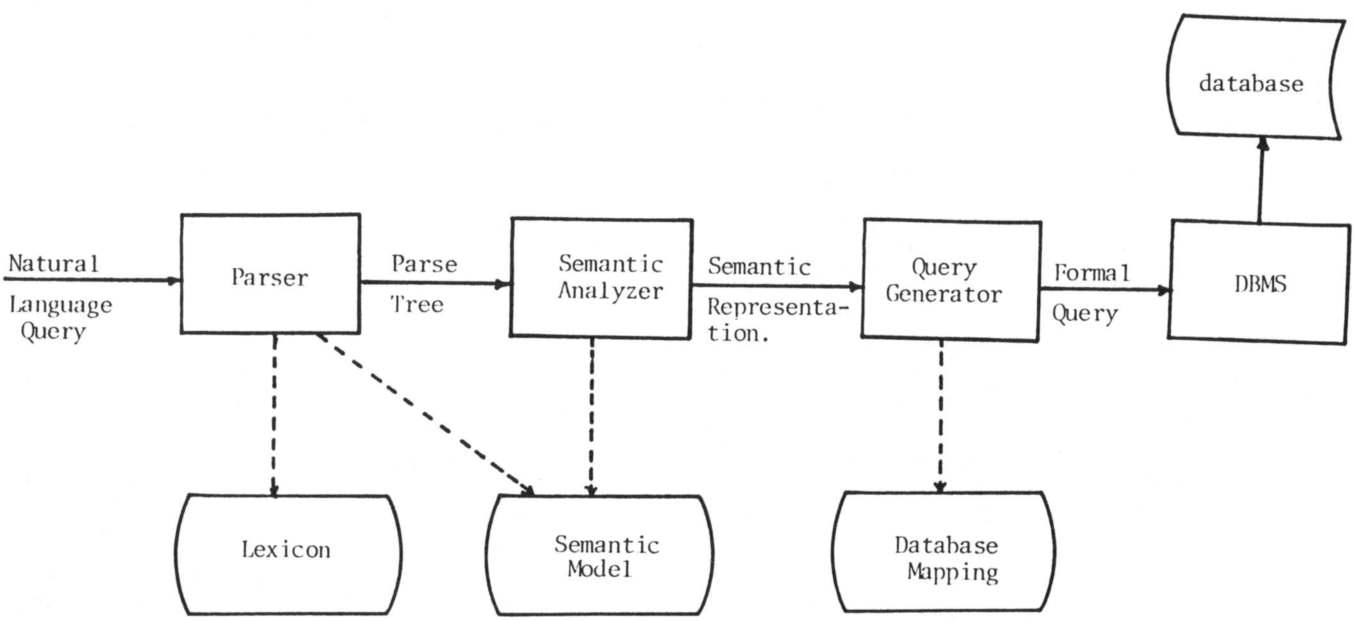

Figure 1—A general design structure for a portable natural language interface to a DBMS

semantic model, and the DB mapping. The DBMS and database also are shown in Figure 1, but they are not part of the interface.

A natural language query is input to the interface and the interface's final output is a formal DBMS query. The procedural modules, each using knowledge in the declarative modules, successively transform the natural language query. Using the lexicon and the semantic model, the parser outputs a parse tree representation of the query. Using the semantic model, the semantic analyzer transforms the parse tree into a semantic representation of the query. Finally, using information in the DB mapping, the query generator in turn transforms this semantic representation into a formal DBMS query.

The procedural modules are written as generally as possible, incorporating domain-independent knowledge only. The domain-specific knowledge is isolated in the declarative modules. The lexicon contains the words users may use in their queries. The semantic model is a formal representation of the application domain. It should not be confused with the DBMS conceptual schema; rather, it corresponds to a DBMS enterprise schema. The DB mapping contains the mapping between the concepts of the semantic model and the corresponding structures of the database.

Following is a description of the portability achieved by the design. If the application domain is changed, only the lexicon, the semantic model, and the DB mapping have to be modified. If the DBMS is changed, only the query generator is modified. If the database is reorganized without semantic change, only the DB mapping is changed. The parser and the semantic analyzer are perfectly portable; immune to any domain, DBMS, or database transfer.

THE IMPORTANCE OF THE SEMANTIC MODEL

Language can be described as the encoding of thought for the purpose of communication. Communication is between a sender and a receiver. The sender formulates a thought, encodes it into language, and sends it to the receiver. The receiver receives the sender's language and decodes it, attempting to recreate the sender's original thought. An act of communication is deemed more or less successful according to how perfectly the original and recreated thoughts match. A match is possible only if a model of mutual comprehension exists. Culture provides such a model for normal human communication.

The basic process of communication occurs analogously in a natural language database system. A user formulates his or her information need according to his or her understanding of the application domain. Then the user encodes this need into language and sends it to the interface. The interface (i.e., the parser and semantic analyzer modules) decodes the language and recreates the user's original information need. A model of mutual comprehension is necessary, and is provided by the semantic model which is the interface's representation of the application domain and, to complete the analogy, the common culture of the user and the interface.

The semantic model is therefore crucial to the interface. Each natural language question is translated, or decoded, into a query on and in the terms of the semantic model. Its exact form depends upon the formalism of the semantic model. There is no general consensus about which formalism should be used in implementing the semantic model. Examples include object-based data models[2] and artificial intelligence knowledge representation schemes.[3,4] The other declarative knowledge in the system is defined with reference to the semantic model. Each word in the lexicon is associated with a particular concept in the semantic model. The DB mapping relates the concepts of the semantic model to the database structures.

Is the semantic model necessary? In other words: Could there be a mapping directly between the words of the lexicon and the database structures? The argument against this direct mapping is that a database schema does not adequately represent the domain semantics and fails to provide a model of mutual comprehension. Without a separate semantic model, the burden of handling the domain-specific semantics devolves onto the semantic analysis procedure. This procedure, as outlined in the previous section, is meant to be domain independent and portable. Eschewing a semantic model therefore results in a handtailored non-portable interface.

THE PROBLEM OF AMBIGUITY

A natural language interface has to cope with the inherent ambiguity of natural language. Ambiguity serves a useful purpose in human communication by reducing the verbiage necessary to express an idea. The ambiguity is resolved by context or by interaction.[5]

There are two main types of ambiguity: syntactic and semantic. Syntactic ambiguities arise when there are multiple valid parses of the same query. For example, "Which course has the largest enrollment of students in computer science?" may be parsed with "in computer science" modifying either the course or the students, with different interpretations resulting. Semantic ambiguities occur when the parsed constituents have several possible meanings. For example, "Where is the Netherlands?" may request the position of a ship or a country, though syntactically it is unambiguous.[5]

Many ambiguities can be resolved with recourse to the semantic model. However, complete automatic resolution of all ambiguities is not possible. The system must echo back paraphrases of the possible meanings of the query and thereby allow a user to choose the intended interpretation.

PARSING

To parse a query, it is necessary to use a grammar that describes the structure of strings accepted by the interface. Given such a grammar, the parser assigns a structure, or parse tree, to each grammatical query it processes. The grammar, which should allow a user wide linguistic variation, is incorporated within the parser module. The domain-specific knowledge the parser requires is in the lexicon or dictionary.

The lexicon contains all the words accepted by the parser. Associated with each word is its syntactic category and its association to the semantic model. The entry for *red* would include *adjective* as its syntactic category and *instance-of-color* as its conceptual association. The entry for *part* would indicate that it is a noun and that it is associated with the entity type "part" assuming an entity-based semantic model. The entry for *who* would indicate that it is an interrogative personal pronoun and indicate the set of entity types that it might refer to. The entry for *supply* would have *verb* as its syntactic category and the relationship or aggregation "supply" as its associated concept.

Assuming such a lexicon and the simplified grammar of Figure 2, a parse of: "Who supplies red parts?" would produce the tree of Figure 3.

In addition to the parse tree in Figure 3, the parse would pass to the semantic analyzer: (1) pointers to the appropriate concepts, (2) the morphological information that the input string contains the third person singular form of *supply* and the plural form of *part,* and (3) the further syntactic information that *who* is the subject and *part* is the object of *supply*. The semantic analyzer would access the semantic model and disambiguate *who* by checking which entities can serve in the role of subject to the concept "supply." The morphological information of third person singular indicates that *who* refers to the specific entities. If entity types were desired, the phrase would have been: "Who supplies red parts?"

This description represents one extreme of the use of semantics in parsing: a completely syntactic parse followed by semantic analysis.[2] However, pure syntactic parsing can cause problems. Natural language viewed syntactically has many ambiguities. The major type of syntactic ambiguity arises from the fact that modifying phrases and clauses can be physically separated from the constituents they modify. For example, the question "Who drove down the street in the car?" has a syntactically valid reading of: "the street is in the car."[5] A simple semantic intervention would rule out this possible parsing. Indeed, when the length of the query and the number of modifiers increases the number of parses grows exponentially.[4]

The other extreme of the use of semantics in parsing is a semantic grammar[2] in which semantic and syntactic categories are intermixed in the constituent structures the grammar uses to describe the language. The problem with this approach is that it introduces domain-specific semantics within the parser and makes the interface less portable. It also makes it much more difficult to provide wide linguistic coverage. In a syntactic parser, the passive form of all verbs can be allowed with the introduction of one general transformation rule. In a semantic grammar, on the other hand, the passive transformation would have to be added for every verb.

There seems to be a general consensus[2,4,6,7] that the best approach is a syntactically based parser with general semantic checks or routines. The syntactic base permits portability and wide linguistic coverage. With semantic intervention many ambiguities can be resolved early in the parsing process. Syntactic and semantic disambiguation proceed together. Modifier placement is determined by seeing which concepts are linked in the semantic model. Semantic or lexical ambiguity caused by words having multiple meanings is resolved by maintaining a set of candidate meanings for each word during parsing and restricting the set as the syntactic structure provides a context. Often not all ambiguities will be resolved and the interface should present the multiple interpretations to the user as described in the previous section.

S → NP VP
NP → PRON
NP → ADJS N
ADJS → ∅ / ADJ / ADJS
VP → V
VP → V NP

Figure 2—A simplifed grammar

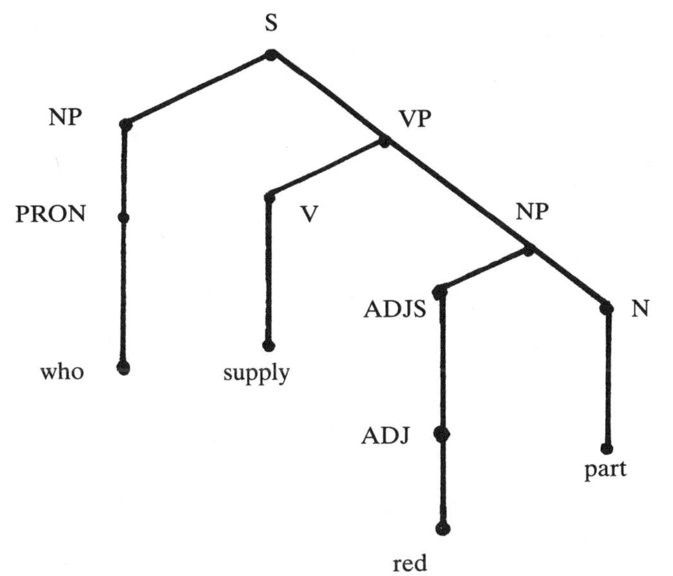

Figure 3—A parse tree representation

Semantic checking may also reveal meaningless queries. It may not be possible to associate a modifying phrase with any head noun phrase. For example, "Who supplies red projects?" is a meaningless query if projects do not have the attribute color. Similarly, the restriction of candidate meanings for words can lead to recognizing a meaningless query when the set of candidate meanings becomes null. This would occur in the following question: "Which projects supply red parts?" The word *projects* originally has one candidate meaning. However, the verb *supply* does not allow that candidate meaning as its subject, thereby rendering the query meaningless.

Adding semantics to the parsing process allows the output of the parse to be more than just a syntactic parse tree. An incipient semantic representation can be created. It would be based on the association of concepts implied by modifying phrases and clauses and by verb–noun phrase relationships.

THE LEXICON

Kaplan[5] defines three types of lexical entries: general, structural, and volatile. General entries are those that apply in practically any domain. These include closed classes of words such as auxiliary verbs, prepositions, and conjunctions. General entries constitute a permanent part of the interface. Structural entries are those that make reference to aspects of the semantic model and must be changed for each new application. These are the nouns, verbs, adjectives and their many synonyms that typically are used in a particular domain. The impossibility of predicting during system design all the various synonyms that may be used argues for an interactive synonym generator that enables the user himself to extend the vocabulary accepted by the interface. Volatile entries are those which refer to specific values in the database. They also are the most problematic. Keeping each value in the lexicon is too expensive because doing so essentially entails a duplication of the database. Searching the database is not a feasible solution because the interface may not know where the unknown lexical item is located in the database and because possible but not actual values can be used. One proposed solution[8] is to represent values from limited domains or those used frequently and to disallow the user of other values in queries. However, a better solution is for the interface to ask a user for clarification when it is confronted with unknown lexical items.

SEMANTIC ANALYSIS

The semantic model encodes the user's view of the domain. In its simplest form, a semantic model must represent a user's knowledge of the objects in the domain, the properties of those objects, and the relationships among them. Various representation formalisms such as semantic data models,[2] semantic networks,[3] and case grammar frames[7] are used. The common point among them is that they are richer semantically than database schemas and are able to provide a data independence that DB schemas alone cannot provide.

The semantic analysis must recognize the propositional content in a user's query. The basic proposition in a query is determined by the main verb and the noun phrases to which it relates. This verb–noun phrase relationship is similar to the way a predicate relates its arguments and the way aggregation relates entities and attributes. The main verb of a query can thus be seen as defining its main predicate. Additional propositions or predicates are defined by modifying phrases and clauses. These predicates are, in effect, nested within the main predicate. Adjectival and prepositional phrases have very simple predicate realizations. For example, *green* becomes color *(x,green)* and *in London* becomes *in(x,London)*. Clausal modifiers add another level to the nesting because the verbs within the clauses also represent predicates. Therefore, the semantic analyzer must unnest all the predicates and relate the resulting separated predicates through common variables.

This propositional content of the query must be transformed into a conceptual calculus form analogous to relational calculus. That is, the propositional content must be transformed into a declarative description of the information desired in terms of the users' concepts rather than the relations of a relational database.

QUERY GENERATION

The task of the query generator is to take a conceptual calculus query and transform it into a query of the underlying DBMS. First it must map the concepts of the semantic model into the underlying database structures and then translate the query. If the back-end DBMS is relational, mapping and translating may be relatively straightforward. However, if the DBMS is a hierarchical or network system, the task is complicated by an extra burden of having to physically navigate through the files and records of the database.

CONCLUSIONS

The basic framework for a portable natural interface to a DBMS is presented in this paper. The purpose of the interface is to make a database more user-friendly. To achieve portability, modularity and separation of general and domain-specific knowledge are necessary. The procedural modules are the parser, the semantic analyzer, and the query generator. The declarative modules, in which all the domain-specific knowledge is isolated, are the lexicon, the semantic model, and DB mapping. The semantic model, more semantically expressive than a DB schema, is necessary to provide portability and data independence.

REFERENCES

1. Hendrix, G.G., E. Sacerdoti, D. Sagalowicz, and J. Slocum. "Developing a Natural Language Interface to Complex Data. *ACM Transactions on Database Systems,* 3 (1978) 2, pp. 105–147.
2. Ishikawa, H. "A Knowledge-Based Approach to Designing a Portable Natural Language Interface to Database Systems." *Proceedings of the 1986 International Conference on Data Engineering,* IEEE Computer Society, 1986, pp. 134–143.
3. Ginsparg, J.M. "A Robust Portable Natural Language Data Base Interface." *Proceedings of the 1983 Conference on Applied Natural Language Processing,* 1983, pp. 25–30.
4. Konolidge, K. "A Framework for a Portable Natural Language Interface to Large Data Bases." Technical Note 197, Artificial Intelligence Center, SRI International, 1979.
5. Kaplan, S.J. "Designing a Portable Natural Language Database Query System." *ACM Transactions on Database Systems* 9 (1984) 1, pp. 1–19.
6. Boguraev, B.K. and K. Sparck Jones. "How to Drive a Database Front-End Using General Semantic Information." *Proceedings of the 1983 Conference on Applied Natural Language Processing,* 1983, pp. 81–88.
7. Grishman, R., L. Hirschman, and C. Friedman. "Isolating Domain Dependencies in Natural Language Interfaces." *Proceedings of the 1983 Conference on Applied Natural Language Processing,* 1983, pp. 46–53.
8. Templeton, M. and J. Burger. "Problems in Natural-Language Interface with Examples from EUFID." *Proceedings of the 1983 Conference on Applied Natural Language Processing,* 1983, pp. 3–16.

A method for increasing software productivity called object-oriented design—with applications for AI

by DAVID C. RINE
George Mason University
Fairfax, Virginia

ABSTRACT

Object-oriented design language research has suggested some basic concepts that object-oriented programming and languages should support. These are: (1) information hiding, (2) data abstraction, (3) dynamic binding, and (4) inheritance. Object-oriented languages are receiving extensive use in artificial intelligence. Although the Ada language possesses the information hiding and data abstraction concepts, it does not possess the dynamic binding and inheritance concepts. These and other limiting factors in developing AI software using object-oriented methods are discussed in this paper. Object-oriented design is becoming an important method for establishing database and knowledge base systems software as productivity issues rely more on tools for reconfiguring existing software and rapidly prototyping software under development. We present some features of object-oriented design pertaining to the development of such databases and knowledge bases including data modeling, data sublanguages, and distribution techniques.

INTRODUCTION: OBJECT-ORIENTED DESIGN LANGUAGES

Software development studies generally have confirmed that software development costs increase and software productivity decreases in more than a linear relationship as the size of the entire project increases.[1] Software productivity also seems to depend upon such things as:

a. The amount of code.
b. The number of concepts that must be understood to make one programmer's subsystem interact properly with another's.

Software metrics have been developed in an attempt to measure software productivity that includes (a) and (b). Further, (b) is influenced by such concepts as:

c. Information hiding.
d. Data abstraction.

It has been observed that, consequently, one can reduce the amount of code written in some projects by acquiring most of the code parts from libraries containing pre-packaged code.

Therefore, in this paper we do not think of databases or knowledge bases in the usual logical record-oriented fashion. We think of data banks of machine components—potentially live data banks that can be thought of as organized nests or hives of clones. These machine component banks, which we identify with logical entities termed *objects,* can be thought of as being managed in ways that are both similar and different from the ways logical records are managed. Ideally, the objects themselves should be able to adapt, similar to self-adaptive automata, depending on the context in which they are placed. Adaptation makes such banks ideally suited for rapid prototyping and simulating of artificial intelligence (AI) software systems. With a little effort, one can see that a language supporting the definition and manipulation of such banks, or bases, goes far beyond the generic language properties of Ada and into languages that possess powerful dynamic binding, inheritance, and adaptive properties.

Pascoe[3] has suggested some basic concepts of object-oriented programming and languages. These are: (1) information hiding, (2) data abstraction, (3) dynamic binding, and (4) inheritance. OOLs are used a great deal in AI. Although the Ada language possesses concepts (1) and (2), it does not possess (3) and (4). Therefore, it may be asked to what extent do these concepts limit development of AI software?

In *Artificial Intelligence,*[20] Winston suggests three approaches to answering the question: "Where is knowledge about procedures stored?" and later suggests that any of the three can be used in controlling a robot. Let us repeat these three approaches:

- A system exhibits action-centered control when the system's procedures know what subproceedures to use to perform actions.
- A system exhibits object-centered control when the system's class descriptions specify how to deal with objects in their own class.
- A system exhibits request-centered control when the system's procedures know their own purpose so that they may respond to requests.[20]

In this paper, we address the second AI approach, object-centered control.

NEEDS: OBJECT-ORIENTED DESIGN METHODS IN AI

Rapid prototyping, simulating, and reconfigurating of systems are important to the development of AI software. In the past, managers of large organizations were only infrequently able to get answers to "what-if" questions. The reasons for this included:

- Rapid prototyping of such systems was non-productive.
- Simulatings of such organizations were too costly to develop.
- Reconfigurating existing systems was not well-supported.

Also, management would attempt to take advantage of the experience of a systems analyst who had worked on similar cases to gain answers to "what-if" questions. More recently, however, we have begun to see the emergence of AI techniques[5] to model large organizations. Such techniques are used to automatically generate the necessary scenarios for a particular business environment through rapid prototyping that supports rapid reconfigurability of potential systems.

Object-oriented programming is both a packaging technology and a software engineering method that addresses these software productivity issues. The kind of packaging approaches used will influence:

e. Software reconfigurability.
f. Ability to prototype rapidly.
g. The types of applications that may be developed.

Issues of object-oriented languages (OOL) began with the Small-talk-80 system (trademark of Xerox Corporation).[2] The Smalltalk language offers a uniform and powerful metaphor whereby procedures and data that belong together are packaged in an object. An object is a package of data and procedures that belong together, and Smalltalk procedures are called *methods*. An object can be thought of in many ways; for example, it can be casually thought of as a considerably expanded version of the Pascal record. Smalltalk does computation by sending messages to objects.

METHODS: DESIGN AND LANGUAGE

Abstract reasoning has played an important role in designing modern software. On the one hand, the role of structured systems analysis has made such tools as data flow diagrams and structure/HIPO charts common in the top-down approach to procedure-oriented design. On the other hand, a bottom-up approach has been introduced by using existing packages and object-oriented designs. Shooman[1] has suggested that certain applications are better developed through the top-down approaches, while other applications are more suited to bottom-up approaches. One factor, of course, is the amount of interaction anticipated between individual processes or modules. It has been suggested, for example, that the top-down approach is appropriate when there is a great deal of anticipated process/module interaction, and the bottom-up approach is more suitable when there is little, if any, interaction.

Booch[6] has suggested an object-oriented design (OOD) method that includes: (1) defining the software engineering problem, (2) developing an informal strategy, (3) formalizing the strategy, and (4) implementing the solution. Formalizing the strategy includes: (a) identifying objects of interest by choosing them as nouns, pronouns, and noun clauses from the problem's text and (b) identifying operations of interest by choosing them as verbs, verb phrases, and predicates from the problem's text. Moreover, it is pointed out that some objects identify classes of objects. Further, operations are identified to manipulate or act upon certain objects. It also is pointed out that only proper nouns and nouns of direct reference will represent objects at the code level, while other objects identify classes of objects. The method, therefore, implies an inheritance concept through the introduction of such classes.

It has been suggested that Ada is an OOL,[7] but by our accepted definition, using concepts (1) through (4) described in the Introduction section, this is not the case. On the other hand, the OOD notation introduced in Booch's method, along with Ada, does imply the concepts of information hiding, data abstraction, and inheritance.

In summary, we are faced with a problem of mapping or transforming an OOD notation that has three of the properties of an OOL into a language, namely Ada, that has only two of the properties of an OOL. This problem may be severe because there is a possibility of losing information in the transformation.

The problem of losing information is similar to that faced by database designers when mapping entity-relationship (E-R) model diagrams, which clearly distinguish entities from attributes, into a relational model which may not. Lossless transformations are those for which it is guaranteed that information will not be lost. Identifying lossless transformations between design notations (language syntax) is a fundamental problem in systems analysis. Automating these transformations is somewhat like developing a language parser or reverse parser that will transform language "programs" into a lossless equivalent representation in object form (for example, where the object form is a relation, relation of relations, tree, or tree of trees).

Recent general research about AI software design using graphics support based upon hierarchies of data flow diagrams and knowledge base support using dictionaries of data definitions can be found in Harandi and Lubars.[11]

DATABASE SUPPORT: SCHEMAS

AI software engineers develop material in high level "chunks" which may be thought of as software design schemas. Often such schemas are developed in an arbitrary manner and so the software designer must recall many rather detailed design "objects." This further suggests a need for organized libraries of reusable code in software development tasks. In our framework, the high-level chunks are like database schemas. Design success may depend on the availability of schemas that logically locate desired library components and allow the software engineer to fit the components into the partially completed design.

Thus a library of these stored design schemas, which can be thought of as objects, and a system for schema manipulation are needed. These schemas, or objects, would be combined into an integrated knowledge base for use by a software engineer or program development expert system.

At the lowest logical level of detail in these schemas, one may casually think of certain objects as being like database records, each record being comprised of procedures, functions (modules), and data items; a notion similar to the most general kind of Ada record. These database records may also be thought of in terms of E-R relationships or relations in a relational model, but such that the entities can be like procedures and functions (modules) as well as data items. On the other hand, higher level objects evolve by use of superclasses from lower level classes, permitting the inheritance characteristics of object-oriented design.

Such schemas can be generated using object-oriented dictionaries as tools in the requirements gathering stage.

Moreover, messages and methods afford a means for generalizing the notion of data manipulation languages used in standard database management systems (DBMS).

Objects and messages in this context may be termed *object sublanguages* (borrowing from the notion of data sublanguage of DBMSs). An object base may also be managed in a distributed fashion. Tools for designing such systems essentially are the same as the partitioning algorithms used in setting up distributed databases.

Recent research has been carried out in this regard at a somewhat lower level of design abstraction that includes program structure as well as objects. In particular, Young[12] has used the idea of a design template as an abstract and generic problem solution, which is applicable to a large number of such situations as we have mentioned here. Templates include a generic procedural structure as well as an abstract defining ability of data objects. Other results on relationships between object-oriented design and database systems also have been published.[13]

AI: OBJECT-ORIENTED DESIGN

An early foundational work by P.J. Landin[8] describes how some of the semantics of Algol can be formalized by establishing a correspondence between expressions of Algol and expressions in a modified form of Church's lambda notation, an important formalism of LISP. Landin describes a model for computer languages and computer behavior that is based on the notions of functional application and functional abstraction. That model then is used as an abstract object language into which Algol is mapped. The second part of Landin's paper gives a formal description realizing an abstract compiler into the abstract object language. Such mappings between languages are an important part of system design.

The notion of "object" mentioned in this early paper is similar to the modern notion of "object" mentioned herein, since they are packaged parts of programs which can further be built-up into classes, which in turn are objects.

Much AI software has been developed using LISP. Moreover, relationships between Ada and LISP were reported at the 1985 AI-Ada Conference at George Mason University. For example, there has been some work in developing LISP translators in Ada, and LISP has been viewed as a higher-level design tool for software that eventually will be coded in Ada.

The language ExperCommonLISP is one of the most comprehensive OOLs for the Apple Macintosh because it implements all the features of OOLs described in this paper except unique instance methods.[9] Classes, superclasses, and subclasses, for example, are nicely implemented in this expansion of CommonLISP. Another version of object-oriented LISP, Zeta LISP, is available on the Symbolics AI workstations.

Therefore, from the computer language point of view, ExperCommonLISP incorporates more of the features of a true OOL than does Ada. Hence, because of the need for lossless transformations from design notation to computer language, ExperCommonLISP may be a more desirable initial target than Ada. This suggests a modification of the method of OOD, geared toward Ada, introduced earlier.

The use of OOD also has appeared in PROLOG (another popular AI language) language programming. Shapiro and Takeuchi[10] have observed that Concurrent PROLOG is capable of expressing object-oriented language concepts, achieving the property of inheritance (i.e., the class-superclass hierarchy). In this approach certain goals can be thought of as objects which accept messages. Presumably this observation could be applied to (non-concurrent) PROLOG as well. There is a correspondence between PROLOG goals and Ada (also Pascal for that matter) procedures.

Advantages of an object-oriented approach to database systems design are described by Maier and Stein.[14] They state that such an approach may result in a system that offers reductions in application development efforts beyond those achieveable by traditional DBS approaches. Gem-Stone[14] is such an object-oriented DBMS that affords packaging of both system behavior and structure.

With data sublanguages and models of traditional DBMSs such as those using the relational approach, a data model is analogous to a fixed abstract data type which cannot change over time as additional operators, for example, become important to the application. Even when designing and implementing such a DBMS with a language having powerful data abstraction and encapsulation capabilities (such as Ada) and including the use of generics, it is not easy to change types and expand the model (e.g., beyond the given relational model implemented through Ada packaging). Therefore, the management of changing types in an object-oriented database is an important problem area.[15]

DISTRIBUTION OF OBJECTS: PARTITIONING ALGORITHMS

Previously, partitioning in database design has been a procedure used to assign a logical object (e.g., relation in a relational model) from a conceptual or external schema of the database to one or more physical objects identified in internal schemas (stored database). Further, in the design of a geographically distributed database such logical objects (often termed *fragments*) are assigned, with possible replication, to the various geographical sites.

With such traditional databases Navathe, Ceri, Wiederhold, and Dou[16] extended the work of Hoffer and Severance[17] by defining an algorithm in which attributes of an object are permuted in such a way that attributes with "high affinity" are clustered together. Further, information about the use of attributes by transactions is initially converted into a square matrix, termed the attribute affinity matrix, a symmetric square matrix u defined as follows:

$$u_{k_i} = \begin{cases} 1 \text{ if transaction } k \text{ uses attribute } a_i \\ 0 \text{ otherwise} \end{cases}$$

Their algorithm[16] is a specialization of general algorithms that permute rows and columns of a square matrix to obtain a semiblock diagonal form, applied to partition a set of interacting variables into subsets which interact minimally.

In our context, the logical objects are objects as previously defined, and transactions from users may be replaced by messages from users or other objects.

Suppose that $M1$, $M2$, $M3$, $M4$ are messages or users which refer to objects 01, 02, 03, 04, 05, 06. Then this can be represented by the following incidence matrix MO =

		Objects					
		01	02	03	04	05	06
Messages	$M1$	1	1	0	0	1	0
	$M2$	1	0	1	0	0	0
	$M3$	0	1	1	0	1	0
	$M4$	0	0	0	1	1	1

Then if we break up the objects into the following groups it is possible to process the messages in parallel:

$P1$	$P2$	$P3$	$P4$
01	03	05	02
04			06

Another possible grouping follows, involving some duplication with fewer groups (it is no longer a partition):

$P1$	$P2$	$P3$
01	03	02
04	05	06
05		

Once the grouping is carried out, it is possible to assign each group of objects to a segment of external storage—much like traditional program segmentation but at a higher level of abstraction—or to a node in a distributed system with its own processor and memory. Note that the processors may be non-von Neumann such as data flow processors.

In summary, the following factors must be considered:

1. Assignment of objects (and methods) to storage segments and nodes as well as the segment or node arrangement
2. Location of objects at storage segments or nodes and determination of all relevant addresses from user-supplied information and from information contained in a segment or node
3. Assumptions about whether all instances of an object are to be stored on a single storage segment or node (similar to horizontal partitioning[16]).

DATA FLOW: OBJECT-ORIENTED MODELING

From the Introduction of this paper, recall that we referenced three ways of controlling a robot[20] and have emphasized object-centered control. Each component in a computer-integrated manufacturing system may be a self-contained robot. The robots are therefore components of a distributed system. Bruno and Balsamo[18] have described an object-oriented approach for modeling such systems using data flow concepts.

In this section, we take the position that data represents the internal states of an object and that data flow is the general means of describing connections between objects. Included are data flow diagrams between classes. Moreover, as a possible application each object may comprise the logical behavior characteristics of a robot or automaton.

Tools that support the design of such systems may include a database or knowledge base of such object descriptions. Such support would be helfpul in the rapid prototyping of potential distributed systems.

Target implementation languages may differ and depend upon their ability to capture object-oriented and data flow designs, but Bruno and Balsama have used Ada.

Let us now turn to further details used to represent an object. Because of our interest in capturing the behavior and control characteristics of each object, robot or automaton, we will use the concept of a finite state machine (or process).

A finite state machine (fsm) is defined as a six-tuple $\langle S0, S, I, O, \text{delta}, \text{lambda}\rangle$, $S0$ in S, S, I, O are finite sets, delta and lambda are functions, and they are related as follows:

$S0$—the initial state of the fsm
S—finite set of states (different data in memory)
I—set of inputs
O—set of outputs
delta: $S \times I \rightarrow S$—an input causes a state change
lambda: $S \times I \rightarrow O$—an input causes an output

With respect to the object-orientedness of the model, when a message m is sent to such an object an attempt is made to match the message with a selector i in I corresponding to a method of the object. If a match occurs, then the method is executed changing the internal state of the object and producing some output. If no match occurs, then the object does not change its state non-trivially.

It is also possible to consider another alternative when no match occurs. If message m does match with a selector corresponding to a method of the object, then a search may be made of those selectors in a fsm containing the given fsm as a subsystem, thereby allowing the object-oriented concept of superclassing and inheritance.

THEORY: CATEGORIES

A category K comprises a collection $OBJ(K)$, called the set of objects of K, together with for each pair A, B of objects of K a distinct set $K(A, B)$ called the set of morphisms from A to B subject to two conditions.[19]

In the object-oriented design sense, an object A can be thought of as a "package" $\langle S, P\rangle$ pair of states (data) and processes (procedures) P that can receive messages f and send messages g. When $A - \langle S, P\rangle$ receives a message corresponding to one of its methods associated with P it can change its internal state (manipulate its data accordingly). And data manipulation may include the sending of a message to another object B.

An object category, OC can be formed from this object-oriented design concept by calling pairs $\langle S, P\rangle$ category objects, which are members of $OBJ(OC)$, and by calling messages f $\langle S1, P1\rangle \rightarrow \langle S2, P2\rangle$ category morphisms, which are members of $MORPH(OC)$. It can be shown that this definition of OC satisfies the properties of a category.[19]

An example of a pair $\langle S, P\rangle$ is an Ada package. However, since the Ada language does not possess the inheritance property of OOLs, subclasses and superclasses are not part of the language. Further in this respect, subobjects and superobjects do not occur naturally. Therefore, inclusion morphisms[19] would not be a natural part of the corresponding category.

NATURAL LANGUAGES: FUZZY SETS AND OBJECTS

An object, we recall, is a package of data and method (operation) definitions. Associated with an object is its class, similar to the idea of instance of a class. For example, to say that "Pussy is a cat" is an abbreviated way of saying that "Pussy is an instance of class cat." Thus, "Pussy" is a member of the class "cat." Hence, we also have the idea of membership.

Using natural language, class instances can be purposefully quite abstract, often intentionally vague. For example, instead of saying "John is tall," i.e., "John is a tall person," we may say that "John is quite tall" or "John is very tall." Quite tall and very tall are imprecise. Moreover, a fuzzy set[21] in natural languages is a mapping from a set U into the closed unit interval of reals $[0, 1]$. For example: $tall: U \rightarrow [0, 1]$ is a fuzzy set. The range of tall determines the various grades or degrees of membership. Two attributes such as very tall or quite tall can be identified as similar or synonomous if there is sufficient overlap of their membership, as in common usage.

While fuzzy sets afford some measure of similarity, in the past it has been common in database design to consolidate these attributes as identical when they are sufficiently synonomous, sometimes creating a standardized word, such as *tall,* in order to remove any undesirable logical redundancies.

This concept of fuzzy sets allows us to add the idea of degree of membership of an instance in a class, as well as the interesting notion of imprecise inheritance. Moreover, earlier we had interpreted an object as a stand-alone automaton that is capable of receiving and sending messages, as well as changing its internal states (data). In the context of this section a fuzzy object would be like a fuzzy automaton.

Fuzziness is an intrinsic property of natural language. This is one of many ways by which user-friendliness of software may be increased, including:

- Sentences
- Menus
- Levels of abstraction
- Mix of the above
- Approximate reasoning
- Syntax and semantics

In the second major step of database design[22] and in the second step in knowledge base design, different initial user views are consolidated into a conceptual schema using the rules of identity, aggregation, and generalization. These rules can be thought of as class rules that rely upon "is a" to perform generalization and "is part of" to perform aggregation with identity classes that are synonomous, have similar semantic meaning, and have overlapping grades of membership such that their intersection is a basis for the identity. Moreover, aggregation and generalization allow for subclasses and superclasses based upon membership grades.

One of the important system components used to maintain fuzzy objects is a piece of software, known as a defuzzifier, between the user interface and knowledge base.

TABLE I—Differences between Smalltalk-80 and Ada

	Smalltalk-80	Ada
Binding time	late	early
Operator overloading	yes	yes
Inheritance	yes	no
Multiple inheritance	yes	no
Classes	yes	no
Information hiding	yes	yes
Data abstraction	yes	yes

SUMMARY: OBJECT-ORIENTEDNESS AND AI

Object-oriented programming is more a code packaging technique than it is a coding technique; and it is therefore a means by which software developers can encapsulate functional designs in a manageable fashion. While languages such as Smalltalk-80, LISP, PROLOG and Ada are very different languages, they do have certain object-oriented language properties in common which make each of them viable candidates for work in developing software for AI applications.

Table I summarizes some of the differences between Smalltalk-80 and Ada.

A class is sometimes referred to as a software integrated circuit in order to draw a comparison with the packaging of hardware silicon chips.

Further basic concepts of object-oriented programming may be found in Cox.[4]

REFERENCES

1. Shooman, M. *Software Engineering: Design, Reliability and Management,* New York: McGraw-Hill, 1983.
2. Goldberg, A. and D. Robson. *Smalltalk-80: The Language and its Implementation,* Reading, Massachusetts: Addison-Wesley, 1983.
3. Pascoe, G. "Elements of Object-oriented Programming." *BYTE,* 11 (1986) 8.
4. Cox, B. *Object Oriented Programming: An Evolutionary Approach,* Reading, Massachusetts: Addison-Wesley, 1986.
5. Klahr, P. and W. Fought. "Knowledge-based Simulation." *Proceedings of the First Conference AAAI,* Stanford, California, 1980.
6. Booch, G. In *An Object Oriented Design Handbook for Ada Software,* Frederick, Maryland: EVB Software Engineering, 1985.
7. Booch, G. "Object Oriented Design." *ADA LETTERS,* 1 (1982) 3.
8. Landin, P. "A Correspondence Between Algol 60 and Church's Lambda-notation: Part I, Part II." *CACM,* 8 (1965) 2.
9. Schmucker, K. "Object-oriented Languages for the Macintosh." *BYTE,* 11 (1986) 8.
10. Shapiro, E. and A. Takeuchi. "Object Oriented Programming in Concurrent PROLOG." ICOT Technical Report TR-004, Institute for New Generation Computer Technology, Japan, April, 1983.
11. Harandi, M. and M. Lubars. "A Knowledge Based Design for Software Systems." ACM 0-89791-173-3. Univ. of Illinois Computer Science Department, 1985.
12. Young, F. and M. Harandi. "Template Based Specification and Design." IEEE CH2138-6, Computer Science Department, Univ. of Illinois—Urbana, 1985.
13. *Proceedings of the 1986 International Workshop on Object-Oriented Data-*

base Systems. IEEE Computer Society, ISBN 0-8186-0734-1, September 1986.
14. Maier, D. and J. Stein. "Development of an Object-oriented DBMS," *Proceedings of the OOPSLA Conf.,* ACM 548861, September, 1986 (SIGPLAN Notices, Nov., 1986).
15. Skarra, A. and S. Zdonik. "The Management of Changing Types in an Object-oriented Database." *Proceedings of the 1986 OOPSLA Conference.* ACM 548861, September, 1986.
16. Navathe, S., S. Ceri, G. Wiederhold, J. Dou. "Vertical Partitioning Algorithms for Database Design." *ACM Transactions on Database Systems,* 19 (1984) December.
17. Hoffer, J. and J. Froscher. "The Use of Cluster Analysis in Physical Database Design." *Proceedings of the International Conference on Very Large Databases,* Framingham, Massachusetts, 1975.
18. Bruno, G. and A. Balsamo. "Petri Net-based Object-oriented Modelling of Distributed Systems." *Proceedings of OOPSLA '86,* ACM (SIGPLAN vol. 21, no. 11), 1986.
19. Mitchell, B. *Theory of Categories,* Academic Press, New York, 1965.
20. Winston, P. *Artificial Intelligence* (2nd ed.) Reading, Massachusetts: Addison-Wesley, 1984.
21. Zadeh, L. "A Computational Approach to Fuzzy Quantifiers in Natural Languages." *Comp. and Maths. with Applications,* 9 (1983) 1.
22. Teory, T. and J. Fry. *Design of Database Structures,* Prentice-Hall,1982.

The Ada–AI interface

by JORGE L. DIAZ-HERRERA
George Mason University
Fairfax, Virginia

ABSTRACT

In this paper we investigate the interactions between artificial intelligence and Ada. The Ada language has been mandated for use in all U.S. Department of Defense mission critical embedded systems. Artificial intelligence has become an important ingredient in such systems. Currently, LISP is the language of choice among DoD AI implementors, and its continued use may retard the expected widespread use of Ada. However, many algorithms used in typical AI applications are procedural in nature, and thus are better suited to languages like Ada. Key pivotal questions addressed here are: What are the specific linguistic needs of AI applications software development? What has Ada to offer? Is there a missing link between AI and Ada? One main conclusion drawn is that Ada provides adequate support for the conventional techniques used in AI (which represent 75 percent to 80 percent of typical AI code); the other non-conventional techniques may not be directly supported by the language itself but through the programming environment (APSE), the program library, and the run-time system.

Ada® is a registered trademark of US DoD, AJPO

INTRODUCTION

Several factors motivate this discussion about artificial intelligence (AI) and the programming language Ada. The most important is the fact that Ada has become the standard computer programming language for the U.S. Department of Defense (DoD) and recently it has been mandated for use in all information systems, and in particular for mission critical embedded software. The language may eventually dominate the software world, since it has a high level of standardization and it is expected to have a wide dissemination.

The Ada language is intended to be used in a great variety of applications; however, there may be some application areas for which the language may not be suitable. One of these areas is AI. Although no standard language exists, almost all AI programming within DoD is done in LISP. If this trend continues, Ada's expected usage and acceptance may be hampered.

Another important aspect indicates that most AI techniques do not seem incompatible with Ada. It has been reported that only about 20 percent to 25 percent of the code written for a typical AI application is "pure" AI code;[1] in other words, 75 percent to 80 percent of AI code is inherently procedural (i.e., not appropriate for LISP or PROLOG but ideally suited to a language like Ada).

In this paper we discuss some of these factors, paying particular attention to the needs of AI and the features offered by Ada in this area. We do not intend to compare programming languages or discuss the benefits and pitfalls of AI, the Ada language, or their methods for software development. Instead, we provide a positive view about their coexistence. First of all, we explore the interrelations between these two radically different approaches to problem solving. We analyze AI and Ada approaches to software development within the framework of modern software engineering and current system complexity problems and reliability needs. We then identify the general requirements of typical AI applications and present the relevant aspects concerning the use of Ada for AI applications.

SOFTWARE ENGINEERING, ADA AND AI

For several years there has been considerable general discontent with the process of designing and producing software and the quality of the software produced. Efforts are underway to find ways for greatly increasing programmer productivity and for enhancing the quality of the products.

Two main research directions have been proposed. On the one hand, a popular *evolutionary* (or transformational) approach strives to develop a refined "programming environment" that provides full automation of the software production process and which is centered around one standard language and a standard set of interfaces.[2] On the other hand, a less widespread but more *revolutionary* (or breakthrough seeking) approach tries to devise a new programming paradigm by adopting "knowledge based" tools into the software production environment.[3] Both approaches are centered around the idea of sophisticated software engineering environments (SEE).

Ada

The Ada language is the cornerstone of many efforts within the evolutionary approach.[4,5] The language is the result of an international competition for a new standard higher-order language specially designed for programming large real-time embedded applications.[6] The effort came as a response to the increasing cost of software mainly caused by the difficulties of software maintenance and the huge number of languages and dialects in use.

Ada is basically a block-structured language, with excellent information hiding capabilities and system-level structuring features. The language provides a unified set of concurrent programming constructs and a well-defined program library and configuration management system. Ada is a design and implementation language, supporting both bottom-up and top-down incremental programming in which programs are made up of one or more (typically many) separately compiled units.

The Ada language defines a standard multi-layered open-ended programming support environment (APSE) as an integral part of the solution.[7,8,9] The environment includes all facilities and tools that a software designer requires throughout the software life cycle, including methodology-specific, language-specific, and applications-specific tools.

AI

The revolutionary approach to the software problem is based on AI research, seeking ways out of the "von Neumann bottleneck" through newer computational formalisms for the software process. However, AI researchers have rarely concerned themselves with software reliability and maintainability. Software engineering techniques must be used during development,[10] although various AI techniques can add new power to existing development tools.[11] In AI, open-ended "knowledge representation systems" are the paradigms for programming in the future.

AI has made progress towards the development of concepts, linguistic tools, and techniques for knowledge representation. Different computational paradigms have been put forward and some of the most widely known are: functional programming, logic or predicate programming, rule-based and knowledge based systems, object-oriented or message passing systems, networks, and frame-based and production systems.[12] In fact, the sheer number of programming paradigms may prevent the development of a standard environment. Recent developments call for more consolidated environments combining features originally found only in individual paradigm environments.[13]

It is clear that programming is a problem solving activity. Thus it is expected that future programming environments will include "intelligent" tools. From an AI point of view, programming should be made as easy as possible by shifting the burden from the programmer to the machine through the construction of programming environments.

ADA SUPPORT FOR AI APPLICATIONS DEVELOPMENT

AI languages focus on symbol manipulation and list processing, supporting dynamically changing representations and flexible (non-procedural) control flow.[14] The linguistic and computational needs of AI can be grouped into two broad categories; namely, traditional and non-traditional requirements.

Ada Support for Traditional AI Requirements

Traditional AI requirements include basic features such as dynamic data structures, recursion, symbol manipulation, pattern matching, data as objects, reusable functions, and relaxed typing. Ada certainly is capable of handling traditional AI techniques.

All these basic requirements are satisfied by Ada's clear and up-to-date control and data structuring facilities, powerful data abstraction mechanisms, and comprehensive support for modularity.

Dynamic data structuring

Ada defines a rich basic set of data primitives as well as novel facilities for specifying programmer-defined new data types. Dynamic data structuring; that is, defining and constructing data structures at run-time, is done in Ada as it is done in LISP.[15,16] Automatic storage management is not required in Ada, although the Language Reference Manual does not preclude garbage collection (an implementation-dependent feature).

Recursion

Ada provides good recursive programming facilities.

Symbol processing and pattern matching

Ada library packages[15] are the means for providing LISP-like list processing and pattern-directed computation on list structures.

Data as objects

Ada provides specific language mechanisms which unify the representation and operations of programmer defined data types. This is achieved by using private types in packages, one of the unique features of the Ada language. Although not a "complete" object-oriented language, Ada possesses many of the required features.[17]

Relaxed type checking

Even though Ada is a strongly typed language, it allows for the creation of "type-less" programs by using generic program units.

Reusable functions

Reusability is one of Ada's strong points. It also is achieved through library units—an intrinsic concept in Ada—in the form of self-contained (generic) packages.

Ada Support for Non-traditional AI Requirements

Non-traditional requirements are AI techniques not usually found in procedural programming. These include functional programming and programs as data, logic and predicate programming, incremental (and interactive) compilation, and rapid prototyping. These requirements are not directly supported by Ada at the language level, but can conveniently be satisfied by the Ada environment, its library system, and the Ada run-time system.

Non-traditional AI requirements can be satisfied by the Ada programming system at the programming environment level and at the standard libraries level. The environment level incorporates special AI tools. The set of standard libraries provides interoperability among the tools for supporting specific AI applications.

Functional programming and programs as data

Functional programming refers to elementary forms of function definition (no side effects). The idea is to use factor-forming operations combining primitive functions into more complex functions, and so on. This approach also eliminates the need for variables and "procedural" descriptions. In general mappings define applicative operators in which a function takes another function as input.[18]

Ada satisfies the requirements for functional programming by providing a rich set of objects and primitive functions, data abstraction facilities for defining new types of objects and new primitive operations, and a mechanism for defining function forming operations—generic functions—with other functions as parameters to derive still other functions.

"Programs as data" deals with dynamically defined functions and self–modifying programs. Dynamically definable functions is a topic closely related to self-generating code, a technique used in LISP and other *interpreted* languages in which a function or program segment is developed at run-time. Employing this technique, data structures can be constructed and directly executed.

Ada does not directly offer the capability of producing "self-generating" code. In fact, this is possible if and only if the language involved is the "native" language of the underlying computational system (either as a virtual or physical machine). Dynamically definable functions might be possible with an Ada machine that *directly executes* Ada code (either virtually or physically).

Logic programming

Logic programming requires at least an elementary form for defining facts and rules (declarative programs). The main program component is information about the application, not procedural instructions. Algorithms are not completely under the control of the programmer. Instead an underlying mechanism known as an inference engine controls the algorithms. Programmers must master this underlying process in order to specify a correct set of assertions. These control mechanisms are inherently procedural and can be written entirely in Ada,[19] in which case traditional declarative programs (e.g., PROLOG Programs) may be considered as pure data.

Incremental and interactive compilation

A key tool in modern programming environments is an incremental compiler, which operates (usually interactively) as the source program is changed by recompiling only what is necessary. The simplest approach to incremental compilation is to determine the minimal separately-compilable unit. In System-oriented languages such as Ada which have comprehensive automatic configuration management facilities, a simple change can easily cause several compilation units to be compiled. Syntax-directed editors and the maintenance of an online intermediate program representation (e.g., DIANA[20] for Ada) makes incremental compilation more feasible for complex languages like Ada.[21]

Rapid prototyping

Rapid prototyping is a methodology that can be applied in any programming environment. For example, logic programming considers programs as executable statements of the requirements analysis. As such, logic programming can assist in the early stages of the software life cycle, unifying executable systems analysis with databases containing rules as well as explicitly stored data, and using the same formalism for both programs and specifications. The executable analysis becomes some sort of system prototype, which could be automatically converted into Ada programs. Furthermore, "interface programs" (written in Ada) can be used to handle necessary typing, subprogram calls, and error handling.[22]

Can Ada Coexist with Other AI Languages?

The Ada language definition makes provision for the possibility of inserting "foreign" code in an Ada program in the form of a pragma. However, multi-lingual, multi-paradigm programming environments in which traditional software engineering languages like Ada can directly interact with non-traditional AI languages are difficult to define for several reasons.[23]

AI languages are interpreted languages, thus there is no common (low-level) language which can be used by a linker to produce running programs made up of Ada and LISP/PROLOG code. Furthermore, a direct interface from Ada to other languages is difficult, because Ada's run-time kernel depends heavily on its data types and exception handling mechanism. Finally, pragmas are recommendations; it is up to the implementer whether to provide them.

The Ada programming environment facilitates coexistence with other AI languages. Tools can be provided for automatically converting sentences written in a "functional notation" to Ada (generic) instantiations. In such a case, we are not using a programming language; we are using a program generator: a computer-aided program generator from ("executable") specifications. Furthermore, the run-time system provides the virtual machine needed, since it can provide LISP/PROLOG-like interpretative capabilities.

AN ADDITIONAL ADA FEATURE: TASKING

Unrestricted self-modifying functions are mathematically undecideable and therefore should be avoided. Ada provides a different view of programs as data, in the form of task objects, which opens up new possibilities for "controlled" generative programs. In Ada, a (potentially concurrent) process is realized as a (constant) task object which is a data object consisting of: (1) a particular sequence of statements, (2) local data, and (3) entries for interprocess communication. As are other data objects in Ada, a task object belongs to a type: a task type. This type is a limited private type which can be used anywhere a limited private type object can be used. For example, it can be used:

- (chiefly) as an actual generic parameter
- as a subprogram actual parameter
- as a private package

However, even though we know their structure, we cannot manipulate task types as literal values. This restriction prevents the dynamic generation of completely new tasks.

Task types can be used to define task templates which, when combined with access types, can be conveniently used for dynamically creating (activating) as many tasks as needed at run-time. This is a very powerful technique leading to convenient designs of inference schemas corresponding to PROLOG clauses.[24] Ada tasks also provide an executable model of the system, something quite useful for simulation and rapid prototyping purposes.

CONCLUSIONS

The successful support that Ada gives to AI applications creates new software systems with a higher degree of portability and reliability, increasing the chances for creating reusable software and for alleviating maintenance problems.

Both traditional and non-traditional requirements of AI applications development can be satisfied by the Ada programming system at three levels: (1) the language level, (2) the programming environment level, and (3) the standard libraries level. The language support level provides basic linguistic features and programming building blocks. The environment level incorporates special AI tools. The set of standard libraries provides interoperability among the tools for supporting specific AI applications.

Large portions of AI code are procedural by nature. Other AI-intensive code can be tackled by using functional and declarative notations, automatic conversion tools, and Ada runtime kernel (RTK) support. The factors involved are Ada language features and methods, APSE tools, and RTK (CAIS dependent).

Many practical results have already been reported, some of which are:

- Several efforts have produced systems for generating Ada packages from natural language specifications as well as PROLOG prototypes.
- Several inference engines for expert systems have been implemented in Ada.
- LISP programs have been automatically rewritten in Ada. Further, it has been shown that run-time performance is much better in Ada than in current interpreted functional languages!
- Semantic networks have been implemented in Ada, producing more flexible and enhanced networks.

REFERENCES

1. Naedel, D. "Ada and Artificial Intelligence." *SIGAda Conference Proceedings,* Minneapolis, Minnesota, July 1985.
2. Lieblein, E. "The Department of Defense Software Initiative: a Status Report." *Communications of the ACM,* 29 (1986) 10, pp. 734–744.
3. Backus, J. "Can programming be liberated from the von Neumann style?: A Functional Style and Its Algebra of Programs." *Communications of the ACM,* 21 (1978) 8, pp. 613–641.
4. Martin, E.W. "The Context of STARS." *IEEE Computer,* November 1983, pp. 14–17.
5. Barnes, B. "An Introduction to The Software Productivity Consortium." SPC Internal Presentation, September, 1986, Fairfax, Virginia.
6. "Steelman." *Requirements for High Order Computer Programming Languages,* U.S. Department of Defense, June 1978.
7. "Stoneman." *Requirements for the Ada Programming Support Environments,* U.S. Department of Defense, February 1980.
8. *Requirements and Design Criteria for the Common APSE Interface Set (CAIS).* KIT/KITIA, U.S. Department of Defense, September 1985.
9. Wolfe. "Artificial Intelligence and the CAIS." *SIGAda Conference Proceedings,* Minneapolis, Minnesota, July 1985.
10. Kowalski, R. "AI and Software Engineering." *Datamation,* November 1, 1984, pp. 92–102.
11. *Rome Air Development Center Report on Knowledge-Based Software Assistant.* Kestrel Institute, California, 1983.
12. Steels, Y.L. "AI and Programming Languages." *Information Processing 86.* H.-J. Kugler (ed.), Amsterdam: North-Holland, 1986.
13. Ramamoorthy, C.V., S. Shekhar, and V. Garg. "Software Development Support for AI Programs." *IEEE Computer,* January 1987, pp. 30–40.
14. Huet, G. "In defense of programming language design." In Luc Steels and J.A. Campbell (eds.), *Progress in Artificial Intelligence,* New York: John Wiley, 1985, pp. 219–241.
15. Reeker, L.H. and K. Wauchope. "Pattern-Directed Processing in Ada." *Proceedings of the 2nd IEEE International Conference on Ada Applications and Environments,* Miami, Florida, 1986.
16. Adkins, M. "Flexible Data and Control Structures in Ada." *Proceedings of the 2nd Annual Conference on AI and Ada,* George Mason University, Fairfax, Virginia, November 1986, pp. 9.1–9.17.
17. Rine, D. "A Brief Comparison of Ada and Object-oriented Design Elements for AI." *Proceedings of the 2nd Annual Conference on AI and Ada,* George Mason University, Fairfax, Virginia, November 1986, pp. 10.1–10.10.
18. Messon, R.N. "Function-level Programming in Ada." *IEEE Computer,* March 1984, pp. 128–132.
19. LaVallee, D.B. "An Ada Inference Engine for Expert Systems." *Proceedings of the 1st International Conference on Ada Programming Language Applications for the NASA Space Station,* Houston, Texas, June 1986.
20. Goos, G. and W.A. Wulf. *DIANA Reference Manual.* Report of Institut fuer Informatik II Univeritaet Karlsruhe and Computer Science Department, Carnegie-Mellon University, March 1981.
21. Reiss, S.P. "An Approach to Incremental Compilation." *ACM SIGPLAN Notices,* 19 (1984) 6, pp. 144–156.
22. Rueher, M., M. Chantegreil, and L. Jullien. "Using PROLOG prototypes for Ada Programs Design." *Proceedings of the Annual Conference on AI and Ada,* George Mason University, Fairfax, Virginia, November 1986, pp. 6.1–6.8.
23. Wallace, D.R. "An Evaluation of Ada for AI Applications." *Proceedings of the 1st International Conference on Ada Programming Language Applications for the NASA Space Station,* Houston, Texas, June 1986.
24. Lander, L., D. Linder, and A. Ramer. "The Use of Ada in Expert Systems." *Proceeedings of the 2nd Annual Conference on AI and Ada,* George Mason University, Fairfax, Virginia, November 1986, pp. 7.1–7.12.

Artificial intelligence and security: An overview

by ALAN C. SCHULTZ
The Navy Center for Applied Research in Artificial Intelligence
Washington, District of Columbia

ABSTRACT

The junction of AI and computer security is an area of increasing concern, due to the imminent application of AI to fielded systems. Two new areas of research need are identified: artificial intelligence techniques in the development of secure systems and in analyzing the security characteristics of software; and verification of the security of artificial intelligence. Current and proposed research in these areas by the Department of Defense will be discussed.

INTRODUCTION

While the areas of artificial intelligence and computer security have been explored for many years, the intersection contains many interesting, useful, and, in some cases, dangerous implications. The intersection can be viewed from two directions. First, how can artificial intelligence techniques be used in the design and analysis of secure systems? Second, what can be said about the security characteristics of artificial intelligence software, particularly expert systems?

Artificial intelligence techniques are being relied on more in various security related tasks. Although some work has been done in both directions, the intersection still has many under-explored or unexplored areas in need of further research. This paper will briefly identify some areas under research, and areas in need of exploration.

USING AI TECHNIQUES IN COMPUTER SECURITY DESIGN AND ANALYSIS

While many software engineering tools and methodologies have been devised to help in creating reliable and easy to maintain software, secure software and systems require a greater degree of assurance about their behavior. One area that has received much attention is in formal verification of software. The necessity of formal verification is mandated by the National Computer Security Center (NCSC), which requires that for a computer system to achieve a top rating of A1, a formal top-level proof must be done for the system.[1] Artificial intelligence techniques have been introduced in the form of automated theorem provers.

Given a program and a set of formal specifications, an automatic theorem prover can be used to verify that the program satisfies the specifications. One example of a verification system that uses a theorem prover is Gypsy.[2] Although other verification systems are in use, Gypsy has been used with much success, particularly by NCSC.

Looking towards the future, it has been said that the ultimate goal of artificial intelligence applied to software engineering is automatic programming, and we might expect to have a system that automatically generates secure software when a user specifies the requirements.

While the above methods are useful in the development stage of software, experience has shown that they cannot be applied to existing software. Large bodies of software exist that need to be used in secure environments. Therefore, testing and analysis techniques are used to determine the security characteristics of the software. In this area, very little work has been done using artificial intelligence techniques.

As far back as 1974, the RISOS (Research in Secure Operating Systems) project at Lawrence Livermore Laboratory had developed a set of tools to analyze operating systems for security flaws.[3] The tools used powerful pattern-matching techniques to search the code for sequences of operations that might characterize security flaws. The tools analyzed various assembly languages, and are not currently in use; although at the time good results were obtained. The tools should be updated to analyze high-level languages.

One area that could be quite productive is the use of an expert system to analyze software and recommend testing strategies—a task well suited for an expert system. In this respect, the expert system would act as an assistant to a security analyst.

A related issue is the study of a system in operation to discover security violations. In this area, several groups have made advances using artificial intelligence techniques for intrusion detection and for on-line analysis of the system.

Discovery is the name of TRW's expert system that is used to detect anomalies in subscribers' usage of a database. The system searches for frequently occurring patterns in data and compares these patterns to daily activity to detect variations from normal behavior.[4] Sytek, under contract for the Department of the Navy, is investigating the use of pattern matching for the automated analysis of audit trails to assist security officers in detecting security violations.[5] Still others are using pattern matching and audit trails for intrusion detection.[6,7]

SECURITY OF EXPERT SYSTEMS

The other side of the artificial intelligence and computer security coin is an area of much concern. Specifically, what can be said about the security characteristics of artificial intelligence programs, in particular, expert systems. Now that expert systems are starting to be routinely created and used, computer security officers must now concern themselves with the security analysis of these systems.

Although in the early days of expert systems, they were hailed as being easy to maintain and understand, most would now agree that expert systems are actually hard to understand and maintain. The existing methodologies for software design and maintenance are not readily applied to expert systems, and this is one area that needs considerable research.

At least one research group is currently investigating design methodologies for rule-based systems.[8] More work needs to be done in the verification of expert systems in order to assure their behavior prior to installation in a security environment.

Other areas of artificial intelligence research will have even greater difficulties with computer security. What of systems that learn? There must be some assurance that these systems maintain their security characteristics. No research to date has addressed this problem, since machine learning is still in its infancy. However, the problem should be addressed now, and should not wait until systems have been implemented and installed.

CONCLUSION

Artificial intelligence techniques are starting to be applied to the analysis of secure computer systems, and, hopefully, their use will improve the utility of security analysis and verification. On the other side of the coin, more research is needed to address the security implications of artificial intelligence systems. Design, verification, and analysis techniques are needed for expert systems and systems with learning mechanisms, and these techniques should be developed now, not after the systems are fielded.

ACKNOWLEDGEMENTS

I would like to thank Randall Shumaker and Carl Landwehr for their time and insight and David Rine for the opportunity to express myself.

REFERENCES

1. "Trusted Computer System Evaluation Criteria." CSC-STD-001-83, Department of Defense, August, 1983.
2. Good, D.I. "Mechanical Proofs About Computer Programs." *Philos. Transactions of the Royal Society of London,* 312 (1984) 1522, pp. 389–409.
3. "Handbook for Analyzing the Security of Operating Systems." RISOS Project. DOD S5-2068, November, 1976.
4. Tener, William. "Discovery: An Expert System in the Commercial Data Security Environment." *Information Security: The Challenge,* IFIP, Reprints of the Fourth IFIP Security on Information Systems, 1986, pp. 283–291.
5. Halme, L. and J. Van Horne. "Automated Analysis of Computer System Audit Trails for Security Purposes." *Ninth Annual National Computer Security Conference Proceedings,* NCSC, Washington, D.C., September, 1986, pp. 71–74.
6. Denning, Dorothy and Peter G. Neumann, "Requirements and Model for IDES—A Real-Time Intrusion-Detection Expert System." Menlo Park, California: SRI International, August, 1985.
7. Kuhn, J. "Research Toward Intrusion Detection Through Automated Abstraction of Audit Data." *Ninth Annual National Computer Security Conference Proceedings,* NCSC, Washington, D.C.: September, 1986.
8. Jacob, Robert J.K. and Judith N. Froscher, "Software Engineering for Rule-Based Systems." *Proceedings of the Fall Joint Computer Conference,* IEEE Computer Society Press, November 1986, pp. 185–189.

A methodology for rule-base integrity in expert systems

by GEORGE STEFANEK
Illinois Institute of Technology
Chicago, Illinois
and
SHI-KUO CHANG
University of Pittsburgh
Pittsburgh, Pennsylvania

ABSTRACT

The incremental addition of rules over time in a rule-based system warrants the need for a system to ensure rule-base integrity. A methodology is proposed in this paper that will check the addition of new rules against the existing rule-base for conflict, redundancy, subsumption, knowledge-related limits, resource conflict, knowledge conflict, and message conflict. A relational database is used to store the rules, and relational database techniques are used to analyze the database. A directed graph is used to represent relationships between knowledge, resources, messages, and database attributes. Thus, both the relational database and the directed graph serve as unifying methodologies in the design of the system. Also, a trace mechanism is provided to show the type of conflict and the rules involved.

INTRODUCTION

This paper presents a methodology to be used along with expert system shells to check rule-based systems for rule-base integrity. The Rule Integrity Sub-System, called RISS, uses a relational DBMS to store rules making up the rule-base and to analyze them for consistency and conflict using relational database techniques. A directed graph also is used to represent interrelationships between knowledge. Together, the relational database and directed graph form the unifying approach in storing, representing, and analyzing the rule-base.

As new rules are collected from various experts and added into a rule-based system, the rule-base becomes more complex and the probability of rule-base inconsistency increases. The proposed rule-base integrity subsystem increases the integrity of the rule-base by checking for: rule conflict, redundancy, subsumption, knowledge related limits, resource conflict, knowledge conflict, and message conflict (see Figure 1). Rule conflict, redundancy, and subsumption have been discussed by Suwa,[1] but are formalized and expanded in this paper. Knowledge-related limits, resource consistency, knowledge consistency, and message consistency are introduced and formalized here. Also, a trace mechanism is included in the system to report the type of conflict that occurs, display the rules involved in conflict, and provide other useful information. Finally, a secretarial rule-base of 60 rules is used as an example rule-base for analysis.[2,3]

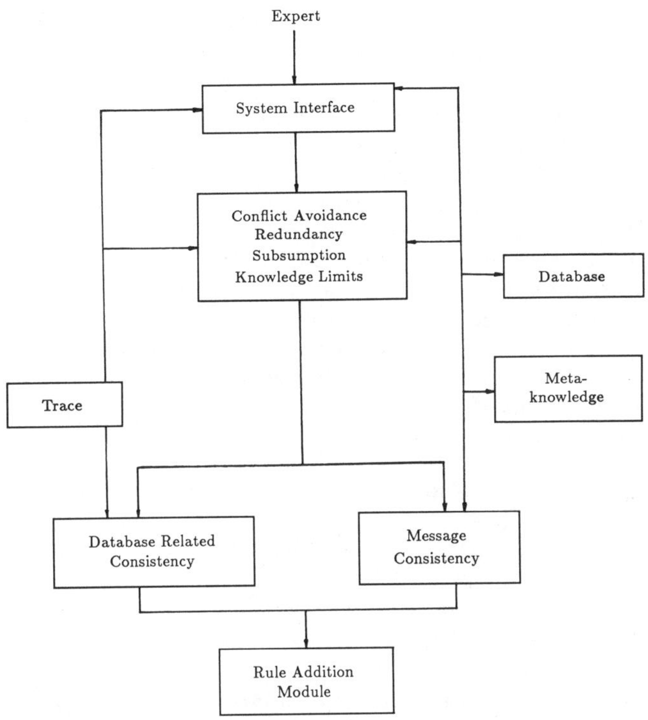

Figure 1—System diagram

KNOWLEDGE REPRESENTATION

Data organization and knowledge representation are key points in the design of RISS. These strategies form the basis for the type of analysis performed throughout the entire system.

Much of the problem solving is accomplished using meta-knowledge. Meta-knowledge[4] is knowledge about knowledge; in our case it is knowledge about various aspects of the system, rule-base, and other domain specific information. This procedural knowledge is specified in RISS as meta-rules, templates, and knowledge tables. All these forms of meta-knowledge are stored in various forms of knowledge tables.

Meta-rules are meta-knowledge in the form of "if-then rules." They are used in manipulating the internal knowledge or specifying knowledge about strategies. For example, meta-rules are used to activate groups of rules in the inference process:

r_{011}

If: category .eq. phone_call
Then: search rules 1 thru 12

Knowledge tables in the form of database relations hold mappings, function templates, and some dynamic information. Templates are in the form of list structures[4] (object, attribute, value) where object is the name of some function such as "notify," attribute is the first function parameter, and value is the second function parameter, usually indicating the type of action to be taken by the function. These templates offer a lot of flexibility because they can differ from function to function and primarily are used to check function specifications within rules.

Graph Theoretic Approach

The simple directed graph is the unifying representation for all rule and database paradigms. Related-resource models, related-knowledge models, and message models all use the directed graph approach to represent interrelated information. Formally, a digraph G consists of a set of vertices $V = \{v_1, v_2, \ldots\}$, a set of edges $E = \{e_1, e_2, \ldots\}$ and a mapping ψ that maps every edge onto some ordered pair of vertices (v_i, v_j).[5] A vertex is represented by a circle and an edge by a line segment between v_i and v_j with an arrow directed from v_i

to v_j, or v_j to v_i, or both. The digraph has no self-loops, but can have parallel edges between some nodes. This approach toward representing knowledge and its interrelationships gives a common methodology for the representation and the analysis of knowledge. Directed graphs are a mathematically formalized approach for interrelating information, and they can easily be expanded to other knowledge representations as needed. The digraph structures are stored as knowledge tables in a relational database.

Relational Database Approach

A relational database[6] is used for storing all data, rules, and meta-knowledge. It provides a cohesive way of manipulating all data. Standards can be enforced, data can be shared, redundancy reduced, and integrity increased. Relational database techniques such as restriction, projection, and division are used to manipulate and extract desired data and check for rule-base inconsistencies. That is, since all existing and new rules are stored in a relational database, all matching and checking is done within the context of the relational database.

Initially, new rules and other design information are accepted by the expert system front-end which outputs the gathered information in its own format. RISS uses an interface module to reformat the rules into a standard format understood by all its modules. The rules will be placed in temporary condition and action relations. The New_Conditions relation contains the attributes: NewRuleNo., Antecedent, Owner, Date, and Comment.

To analyze the rules for conflict, redundancy and subsumption against the existing rule-base, the rules in the New_Conditions and New_Actions relations are parsed and put into separate temporary relations that are used only during analysis. For example, in the New_Conditions and New_Actions relations the antecedent and consequent attributes hold all the conditions and actions of a rule. The conditions and actions must be broken up so that there is one condition or action per tuple in a relation. These relations are called Parsed_New_Conditions and Parsed_New_Actions. Parsed_New_Conditions contains the attributes: SeqNo., NewRuleNo., Antecedent, and Consequent.

The existing rule-base and meta-rule base are also stored in relational database form. The existing rules are stored in the Conditions and Actions relations and other rule information such as ownership and date of entry are stored in Conditions_Data and Actions_Data relations.

The Actions_Data relation contains one additional attribute called rule dependency which points to other rules, if any, that depend on the existing rule. This is necessary during deletion. Any rules associated with an existing rule in inferring a conclusion may also have to be removed given that the rule was the sole support.[7] A rule supports other rules that are used before it in an inference process. If a rule is supported by more than one rule, then all of them must be erased before it is erased.

Meta-rules that specify system-related knowledge are stored in relations having identical attributes as the relations for the existing rule-base: Mr_Conditions, Mr_Conditions_Data, Mr_Actions and Mr_Actions_Data. Other meta-knowledge is stored in database relations including knowledge tables for locks and knowledge-related limits and decision tables.

SYSTEM TRACE CAPABILITIES

RISS has a trace and error handling capability. The trace mechanism keeps track of the current module in which analysis is taking place, the type of problem encountered, the existing rules involved, a display of those rules, the new rules involved, and the new rules that have passed so far. If an error is recoverable, the trace will prompt the user to decide whether to continue or to stop. An example of a trace is found in Figure 2. The following sections present the formalized methodologies used in enhancing rule-base integrity.

RULE CONSISTENCY

When knowledge is represented as production rules and new rules are added incrementally, inconsistencies[1] may appear as:

1. *Conflict:* this may appear in two forms.
   a. *Action conflict:* two or more rules fire because they have the same conditions, but there is conflict in the action portion of the rules (that is the results are different).
   b. *CF conflict:* if certainty factors[8, 9] are used, the conditions and actions may be the same, but the associated certainty factors differ.

SYSTEM TRACE

MODULE: Consistency module

TYPE OF PROBLEM: Action Conflict

EXISTING RULE(S) INVOLVED: 036

r_{036}

If:	**category .eq. filing and** **filing.type .eq. letter**
Then:	**file(letter,filing.company) and** **notify(sender, stat7)**

NEW RULE INVOLVED: 002

r_{new}

If:	**category .eq. filing and** **filing.type .eq. letter**
Then:	**file(letter, filing.product) and** **notify(sender, stat7)**

NEW RULES PASSED SO FAR: 001

HARDCOPY? $< Y/N >$

Figure 2—Example of output from RISS trace

2. *Redundancy:* two or more rules fire because they have identical conditions and actions.
3. *Subsumption:* two or more rules have the same conditions and actions, but some of the rules have more conditions that make such rules more restrictive. Also, two or more rules have identical conditions, but some of the rules have more action clauses than other rules.

The following sections describe each area of rule conflict in detail, starting with the presentation of the problem and followed by examples.

Conflict Avoidance

Rule conflict may occur as either action conflict or CF conflict. Action conflict occurs when a rule that is being added has identical conditions with an existing rule, but the actions differ. The actions may differ completely in task execution or can merely have more action clauses in one rule vs. another.

A rule r_i is defined as the ordered pair (C_i, A_i). The set of all conditions in rule r_i is denoted by C_i and the set of all actions in rule r_i is denoted by A_i. Given two rules r_i and r_j from the set of rules in the rule-base *R,* conflict occurs when $C_i = C_j$, $A_i \neq A_j$, and A_i is not a proper subset of A_j, $A_i \not\subset A_j$. For instance, there is an existing rule in the example secretarial rule-base r_{035} which specifies that a letter should be filed according to the company to which it is addressed, and that the sender should be notified that the filing has been accomplished.

r_{035}
If: category .eq. filing and
filing.type .eq. letter
Then: file(letter, filing.company) and
notify(sender, stat7)

Suppose the domain expert wishes to add another rule into the rule-base which has the form:

r_{new}
If: category .eq. filing and
filing.type .eq. letter
Then: file(letter, filing.product) and
notify(sender,stat7)

These two rules differ in that the new rule's actions designate the letter to be filed with documents describing the product to which it pertains, as opposed to the existing rule which specifies the letter should be filed by company. This is a simple case of rule conflict: the conditions are the same, but the actons differ. The system will flag this problem and report it through the trace module shown in Figure 2. The trace will halt further analysis of additional new rules as soon as a conflict is found. From the trace, the expert adding rules will have enough information to know how to proceed. For a new rule to be added successfully, the existing rule will have to be removed first or the new rule and any related new rules may have to be modified.

The second form of conflict is CF conflict, which occurs when all conditions and actions are the same but the certainty factors (CF) associated with the conclusions differ. Given a rule r_i consisting of the ordered pair $(C_i, [A_i, CF_i])$, the set of all conditions in a rule r_i is denoted by C_i, and the set of actions having a certainty factor of CF_i is denoted by A_i. Given two rules r_i and r_j, CF conflict occurs when rule r_j has a different certainty factor from an existing rule r_i in the rule-base *R*. That is, $C_i = C_j$, $A_i = A_j$ and $CF_i \neq CF_j$. For instance, given an existing copy machine rule R_{052} and a new rule R_{new}:

r_{052}
If: copy machine is on and
copy button is pressed with no response and
no warning light is on
Then: there is strongly suggestive evidence (.9)
that the machine is broken

r_{new}
If: copy machine is on and
copy button is pressed with no response and
no warning light is on
Then: there is strongly suggestive evidence (.8)
that the copy machine is broken

Both rules are the same except that the certainty factor in the existing rule is .9 and the certainty factor for the new rule is .8. Once the certainty factor parameter of the Copy_Machine function is compared and found different, the trace will report the error and the program will terminate. The system will check whether $C_i = C_j$, $A_i = A_j$, and $CF_i \neq CF_j$ and if it is true, the system will generate a trace reporting this type of conflict and end analysis of the rule-base. After receiving the trace, the user will have to decide whether to delete the existing rule.

Redundancy

Rule redundancy[1] exists if two or more rules have identical conditions and actions. Given two rules r_i and r_j, redundancy exists when $C_i = C_j$ and $A_i = A_j$, thus $r_i = r_j$. If the conditions and actions are identical, but the order of either conditions or actions differs, then the redundancy check will still flag the rules as identical and go through the trace. To change the order of the conditions or actions in a rule which is redundant with a new rule, the existing rule must be deleted from the rule-base and the new rule added afterward. For example, the following two rules will be treated as being redundant:

r_{020}
If: category .eq. In_person
In_person.name .eq. employee
In_person.meeting .eq. 1
In_person.travel .eq. 1
free(In_person.time) .eq. t
Then: schedule(In_person.time, In_person.name)
travel(In_person.name, In_person.time,
In_person.dest)

r_{new}

If: category .eq. In_person
In_person.name .eq. employee
In_person.meeting .eq. 1
In_person.travel .eq. 1
free(In_person.time) .eq. t

Then: travel(IN_person.name, In_person.time, In_person.dest)
schedule(In_person.time, In_person.name)

The new rule's actions make travel reservations before checking a person's schedule. The order of the clauses will not be considered during the check for redundancy. Other techniques not discussed here would have to be used to check for the order of clauses. Even though redundancy may not necessarily affect the correctness or consistency of the rule-base, it will unnecessarily increase the overhead in storage and analysis of the rule-base.

Subsumption

Rule inconsistency can also occur in the form of subsumption. That is, a new rule can subsume an existing rule if it has a superset of conditions or actions of an existing rule. Subsumption has been discussed by Suwa[1] and is expanded and formalized in this section. Subsumption can occur in two forms:

1) a *superset instance*
2) a *subset instance*

The superset instance occurs when a new rule has a superset of the conditions of an existing rule. The new rule will have more conditions, be more restrictive, and include all the conditions of an existing rule as a subset of its conditions. If r_i is a new rule and r_j is an existing rule, then the superset instance occurs when, $C_j \subset C_i$ and $A_j = A_i$. Another possibility is if the new rule has a superset of the actions in an existing rule, $C_j = C_i$ and $A_j \subset A_i$. Finally, both conditions and actions in a new rule may be supersets of an existing rule, $C_j \subset C_i$ and $A_j \subset A_i$. In the event that any of these superset instances occur, the new rule will supersede the existing rule. As an example, given an existing copy machine rule r_{054} and a new rule r_{new}:

r_{054}

If: copy machine warning lights are checked and toner light is on

Then: open machine
fill with toner

r_{new}

If: copy machine warning lights are checked and toner light is on

Then: open machine and
fill with toner and
turn machine on

The new rule's actions are a superset of the existing rule's actions; therefore, the new rule will supersede the existing rule. This is an example of subsumption superset instance.

When certainty factors are involved, this check of logical consistency will flag the problem as if certainty factors didn't play a role. If the conditions or actions are a subset of an existing rule but have a different certainty factor, the trace will indicate it and the existing rule will not be superseded. It must first be deleted in order for the certainty factor to change. In the superset instance, the new rule will supersede the existing rule with the new certainty factor replacing the old.

The subset instance occurs when a new rule has a subset of the conditions in an existing rule. If r_i is a new rule and r_j is an existing rule, then a subset instance occurs when $C_i \subset C_j$ and $A_i = A_j$. Also, the situation exists when a new rule has a subset of the actions in an existing rule, $A_i \subset A_j$ and $C_i = C_j$. Finally, both conditions and actions in a new rule can have subsets of an existing rule's conditions and actions, $C_i \subset C_j$ and $A_i \subset C_j$. If any of these subset instances occur, then the new rule will not be added to the rule-base.

Knowledge-related Limits

Many higher level variables and resources may be used in a rule-base. These should be kept track of so that they are not depleted and so certain artificially set limits are not exceeded. Also, the knowledge related limits should be dynamically adjusted to accommodate changes in the rule-base. For example, suppose the following rule exists in the rule-base:

r_{056}

If: category .eq. stationery and
number of envelopes .lt. 10

Then: order a new box of envelopes

A new rule to be added is:

r_{new}

If: category .eq. stationery and
number of envelopes .lt. 8

Then: order a new box of envelopes

It can be seen initially that these are two different rules with the same conclusion. Upon closer inspection, the second condition in each rule is related. That is, the existing rule already includes the limit set by the new rule. Since the number 8 is less than 10, the new rule's limit falls under the existing rule's larger limit. However, it may be that the new rule is intentional and that the limit should be lowered from 10 to 8. In this case the system should flag the problem, report it in the trace, and the user should delete the existing rule before adding the new one. Knowledge tables hold constraint information of the form $\{a_i, r_i, \phi\}$ where a_i is an attribute such as the number of envelopes, r_i is a relational operator such as "lt" or "eq," and ϕ is the constraint or limit. Each time an attribute is encountered, it is compared against the knowledge limits table to check if it falls within some limit already prescribed. If a rule has identical conditions to an existing rule except for the constraining condition, then the knowledge limits table is searched for the attribute with the constraining condition. If it is found, the constraint is compared and reported in the trace. If it is not found, the rule is passed to the next test and the constraint flagged for update into the knowledge table.

RESOURCE CONSISTENCY

A rule-based system may make use of a database. If a database is to be updated by functions invoked by a rule which fires, then one of the considerations that should be addressed is the possibility of resource conflict. A resource is defined as a quantity of objects or allocation of time. Typically, a resource is an item quantity (e.g., the number of nuts or bolts) or a time related attribute (e.g., for scheduling or reserving dates). Resource conflict will occur when a rule fires and: (1) requires access to a resource which was recently updated, (2) rules in an inference path have access to the same database attribute, (3) rules update or access an attribute which is related to other attributes, or (4) individual rules are incomplete and therefore may contribute to a resource conflict.

To maintain resource consistency by avoiding the problem of resource conflict, the following strategies are used:

1. *lock table:* used to lock a resource on either a time dependent basis or by user ID
2. *multi-rule resource conflict model:* used to check that the same resource isn't accessed during an inference process
3. *related resource model:* used to show the relationships between various related resources.

Lock Table

A resource such as reserving a room or scheduling an appointment should be checked against being updated shortly after it has been set. A rule may fire which invokes a function that allocates a resource. Subsequent access to this resource by other rules or other functions within a rule should be restricted on a time- or ID-dependent basis. The restriction on a resource will be in the form of a lock, which will be specified in a lock table. The lock table is a knowledge table in the form of a database relation and consists of the following attributes:

1. *DB relation:* specifies the database relation containing the resource to be locked.
2. *DB attribute:* specifies the attribute in the relation representing the resource to be locked.
3. *RB function:* specifies the function in a rule that requires access to the resource.
4. *Tuple Num.:* the number of the tuple in the relation holding the resource to be locked.
5. *Lock type:* specifies the type of lock to be put on the resource. The lock type may be either time dependent or ID dependent. The time dependent lock is set on an attribute for a length of time t. The time length is set ahead of time by updating the lock table. The ID dependent lock is used to lock a resource by user ID. Only the original updater can unlock the resource. Both of these types of locks are set ahead of time in the lock table.
6. *Time:* specifies the length of time t that a resource attribute may be locked.
7. *ID:* specifies the ID of the user who updated the resource last.

The lock types are preset in the lock table and may be changed anytime. To avoid resource conflict when a rule fires, the lock table is checked by keying off the DB relation and DB attribute, which is the resource, and by checking the lock type. If the lock type is time, the time field is then checked to see if the resource can be accessed. If the lock type is ID, then the ID attribute is checked against the current updating user. Most of the problems of resource conflict can be handled by either the knowledge tables or appropriate database relations (e.g., include attributes such as "appointee," "visitor" to identify the person for which the appointment is made).

Multi-rule Resource Conflict Model

The multi-rule resource conflict model is used to check rules in an inference path for access to a single resource. A resource should not be updated more than once in a single inference since the second update will cancel out the first and make it meaningless. Therefore, a set of rules involved in an inference should be checked for functions which update the same database attribute.

To check for this potential problem, a model in the form of a directed graph G_{mrm} is constructed. All conclusions in a rule represented as functions which update the database are assigned as vertices $V_{mrm} = \{v_{mrm_1}, v_{mrm_2}, \ldots\}$ in the graph G_{mrm}. The direction of the arc e_i from a vertex v_i to a vertex v_j indicates that vertex v_i, representing a database updating function, precedes vertex v_j which represents another database function. The graph G_{mrm} contains all database updating functions of rules involved in an inference path. The functions are linked by directed arcs in the sequence they fire during an inference. If a vertex v_i has more than one arc $a_i, a_j, \ldots$ pointing to it, then there are duplicate functions or conclusions in the inference path. If this function updates a database, then it can cause resource conflict.

Related-resource Model

Resource conflict can also occur if resources that are related to one another are not updated simultaneously. That is, a resource such as a nut is related to a resource such as a bolt. For every nut there should be a bolt, or every time a trip is scheduled for a period of time, all appointments during that period should be rescheduled. These relationships or associations between resources in the database are represented by a related resource model.

The related-resource model is in the form of a directed graph G_{rr} where the vertices $V = \{v_{rr_1}, v_{rr_2}, \ldots\}$ correspond to a resource attribute and each arc from the set $E = \{e_{rr_1}, e_{rr_2}, \ldots\}$ connects two related attributes v_i and v_j. The associations between resources are predefined as world knowledge. Any new associations should be updated manually in this model. The functions in the actions portion of a new rule r_i are checked against a knowledge table holding all functions which update a database. If the new rule's function matches and therefore updates a database, then the functions' parameters are checked for the attribute being updated and this attribute is matched against the graph G_{rr}. If the resource attribute v_i is associated with another resource v_j, then the resource v_j is checked further for any other associations and so on. Last, the list of all associated resource attributes, which are found by searching the graph G_{rr}, are compared with functions updating the database. The actions portion of a rule must contain functions which update all these related resource attributes in the list.

KNOWLEDGE CONSISTENCY

An extension of resource conflict in a database domain is knowledge conflict. Knowledge is defined as an item of information or as an object of information. Knowledge conflict can occur when related pieces of knowledge are not updated simultaneously.

Some attributes in a database such as a company, its phone numbers, street address and city address may be related to one another. If a company changes its location, not only does the street address have to be changed, but probably the zip code and possibly city, state, and other attributes have to be changed as well. These are related pieces of knowledge. Also, a semantic network consists of related pieces of knowledge that may have to be updated simultaneously when a change is made.

A related-knowledge model in the form of a digraph G_{rkm} is set up to represent related pieces of knowledge. Each vertex v_i in the graph represents either an object in the form of a fact or a database attribute. Related pieces of knowledge are connected by arcs. Each time a piece of knowledge is referenced, it is checked against the graph G_{rkm} to see if other pieces of knowledge should be updated simultaneously.

MESSAGE CONSISTENCY

Some rule actions may include messages that are sent if a rule fires. If multiple rules are in an inference path, then many messages may be sent. Following is a list of some of the potential problems that may be encountered when many rules fire:

1. Identical or redundant messages may be sent by several actions invoked within a single rule.
2. Conflicting messages may be sent from more than one rule in a single inference.
3. Identical or redundant messages may be sent from more than one rule in a single inference.
4. Conflicting messages may be sent by actions invoked within a single rule.

All these message problems make up a category of conflict called message conflict. Message models are proposed as a method of increasing message consistency by checking for message conflict.

Intra-rule Message Conflict

Rules may contain a number of actions that may fire resulting in more than one message being sent from a single rule. For instance, two messages which will be sent when rule r_{001} fires:

r_{001}
If: category .eq. phone_call
phone_call.speak .eq. "boss"
phone_call.name .ne. null
location(boss) eq. "out"
Then: notify(sender,stat1)
inquire(phone_number)
generateform(type.memo,memo.info)
mailbox(memo,receiver,stat14,sender)

First, the sender is notifieed with a message *stat*1 that the person he wishes to talk to is out, *notify*(*sender,stat*1). Then the sender is notified that the intended receiver of his phone call has been notified by a mail message, *mailbox*(*memo, receiver,stat*14,*sender*).

Intra-rule message conflict is defined as conflict between messages sent from a single rule. Message conflict is defined as separate messages appearing together and having conflicting or contradictory information. A message model is used to designate what is conflicting or contradictory between messages. The message model consists of a set of vertices $V_{mm} = \{v_{mm1}, v_{mm2}, \ldots\}$, a set of arcs $E_{mm} = \{e_{mm1}, e_{mm2}, \ldots\}$ where each vertex v_i corresponds to a message m_i and each arc e_i has a flag F designating a positive or negative association $[e_i, F_i]$. A negative association, $F = -1$, from vertex v_i to v_j indicates that message m_i should not be associated with message m_j. A positive flag, $F = +1$, indicates that the association is valid. That is, both messages m_i and m_j can appear together. All messages in the graph are linked to all other messages and each link is assigned an association flag.

Intra-rule message conflict is resolved by using the message model to check whether messages in the action portion of the rule conflict or are redundant. The action functions in the rule to be analyzed are compared to a knowledge table containing templates matching the correct message to a particular function (see Table I).

The message associated with a particular action function is then matched against the message model. If additional functions in the rule send messages, they also are compared to the message model. If these messages are connected by arcs, the flag F associated with the arc e_i connecting the two messages m_i and m_j is checked to verify the validity of the association of the two messages, m_i and m_j. If the flag equals -1, then the

TABLE I—Sample knowledge table

Context	Function	Attributes	Message (M)
mail	mailbox	?x,rec,M,send	stat14
file	notify	sender,M	stat7

grouping of these messages in a single rule is not allowed, and RISS reports the problem through the trace. If the messages are the same, then this problem is also reported through the trace. Otherwise, the messages may be grouped together and RISS continues on without interruption.

Inter-rule Message Conflict

Rules may fire one after another in an inference path before coming to a conclusion. As the actions are invoked, messages may be sent that are conflicting or redundant. To avoid this problem, new rules are checked to see if they are standalone or if they are involved in an inference path. This is done by checking a rule dependency model for all rules involved in an inference. The details of this model will not be discussed here. Once all the rules in an inference path are found, the action clauses of these rules are searched for functions containing messages. Those functions are compared to the knowledge table containing templates which match the correct message to the function in the action portion of the rule. All messages involved are gathered and each message is matched to the message model to see if any messages in that inference path should not be grouped together. If any messages should not be grouped together as indicated by the association flag, then this problem is reported through the trace module.

Database Message Conflict

In a database environment, access or update of certain attributes in various relations may be monitored. Specific accesses or updates trigger messages that are sent by the monitor on the database relation. The monitor kernel may be rule-based in the form of alerter rules, which designate actions that should be taken upon any access or update of database attributes. Therefore, the techniques described in the last two sections would apply.

CONCLUDING COMMENTS

Developing and formalizing a methodology that tries to increase rule-base integrity is helpful during the ongoing addition of rules into an expanding rule-base. This paper introduces some techniques for achieving rule-base integrity and opens up some new possibilities and questions. Future work will include the development of rule models,[10] rule-set models, and knowledge belief maintenance models. Rule models will be used to check rules for completeness (e.g., whether certain conditions or actions are missing for a rule). Rule-set models will attempt to check for missing rules, and belief maintenance models will attempt to check new rules against an internal view of the world (belief) as based on existing rules and previous world knowledge. This will include the ability of a system to learn about itself in all modules including the ability to learn about the world through the addition of new rules to the rule-base and thereby expand its knowledge dynamically. Currently, world-view knowledge is predefined and added manually. Also, a friendly administrative interface should be developed to make changes to domain specific knowledge, templates, etc. Additional modules could be added to handle specifics about backward chaining and other inference mechanisms as well as analysis of other knowledge structures and the inferences that are made from them.

Although this paper focuses on rule-base integrity, the concepts presented can apply to other knowledge representations. These methodologies could easily be extended or tailored to encompass other knowledge representations. These additional extensions based on the original concepts could make this a more general knowledge integrity methodology that would be more applicable to systems which make use of several representations in their design.

RISS is implemented on a VAX 11/780 running VMS, and uses the ORACLE database to store rules, and ORACLE's SQL language to handle database analysis. C programs call embedded SQL procedures to handle rule-base analysis.

REFERENCES

1. Suwa, M., A.C. Scott, and E.H. Shortliffe. "Completeness and Consistency in a Rule-based System." *Rule-based Expert Systems,* Reading, Massachusetts: Addison-Wesley, 1984, pp. 159–170.
2. Chang, S.K., H.L. Chen, L. Leung, L.S. Liang, and G. Stefanek. "An Intelligent Message Management System." ISL Report, Department of Electrical and Computer Engineering, Illinois Institute of Technology, October 1985.
3. Stefanek, G. and C. Lin. "Alerter Rules for a Secretarial Expert System and Formal Definition using OPM." ISL Report, Dept. of Electrical and Computer Engineering, Illinois Institute of Technology, May 1985.
4. Davis, R. and B.G. Buchanan. "Meta-level Knowledge." *Rule-based Expert Systems,* Reading, Massachusetts: Addison-Wesley, 1984, pp. 507–530.
5. Deo, N. *Graph Theory with Applications to Engineering and Computer Science.* Englewood Cliffs, New Jersey: Prentice-Hall, 1974.
6. Codd, E.F. "A Relational Model of Data for Large Shared Data Bank." *Communications of the ACM* 13 (1970) 6.
7. Charniak, E. and D. McDermott. *Introduction to Artificial Intelligence.* Reading, Massachuetts: Addison-Wesley, 1985, pp. 411–415.
8. Adams, J.B. "A Probability Model of Medical Reasoning and the MYCIN Model." *Mathematical Biosciences* 32 (1976), pp. 177–186.
9. Shortliffe, E. H. and B. Buchanan. "A Model of Inexact Reasoning in Medicine." *Rule-based Expert Systems,* Reading, Massachusetts: Addison-Wesley, 1984, pp. 233–262.
10. Davis, R. "Interactive Transfer of Expertise." *Rule-based Expert Systems,* Reading, Massachusetts: Addison-Wesley, 1984, pp. 171–208.

A parallel inference model for logic programming

by JIE-YONG JUANG and DANIEL CHENG
Northwestern University
Evanston, Illinois

ABSTRACT

In this paper, we describe a parallel inference model for logic programming on general-purpose multicomputers. In the model, input clauses are partitioned into subsets, and resolution is conducted on each subset concurrently. The partitions are dynamically adjusted via clause migration as inference proceeds. This allows each processor to work on virtually the whole clause set while a shorter resolution cycle is achieved. In the context of AND/OR tree space search, the parallel model explores another dimension of parallelism in addition to AND/OR parallelism. It implicitly forces multiple processors to jointly search the same path that leads to a refutation. Problem-solving heuristics can be incorporated in the parallel model systematically to determine clause partitions and guide inference. With a distance measure derived from problem-solving heuristics, a partition that has the best combination of clause subsets and a small rate of clause migration can be obtained using existing clustering algorithms. Clause migration decisions can also be made based on the distance measure. Last, we point out that all the mechanisms of the parallel model can be efficiently supported by a connection graph. The graph also simplifies the implementation of the subsumption strategy.

INTRODUCTION

Logic inference[1–3] is a method of acquiring new knowledge from a set of known facts represented as clauses, and resolution is the most commonly used technique for logic inference. Logic programming languages such as Prolog[4] have been successfully used in solving complex problems, especially in developing expert systems.[5]

In resolution, a theorem, that is, new knowledge, is formulated as a goal statement, and the known facts are treated as a set of consistent axioms. Then, a proof procedure is applied to show that the denial of the goal statement is false, a refutation exists. The procedure involves repeated cycles of matching, unification and resolution of two clauses. The matching process identifies a pair of clauses such that the positive form of a literal appears in one clause and the negative form in the other. These two literals are unifiable if their variables can be unified by substitution during the unification process. After the two literals are unified, a new clause called the resolvent is generated by canceling them and combing the remaining literals. The two clauses involved are called *the resolvable pair* in this paper. The proof procedure terminates when an *empty clause* is generated.

The resolution procedure is slow when it runs on today's computers.[6] Many efforts have been made to speed up logic inference,[7] and parallel processing has been identified as one of the most promising approaches. Previous work in this area can be classified into five categories according to the level of parallelism they explore:[7] (1) subrule level, (2) rule level, (3) search level, (4) language level, and (5) system level. At the subrule level (or the architecture level), emphasis has been placed on the exploitation of concurrency during unification because unification is the most often invoked module in logic inference. Pipeline architectures[8] and construction of a dedicated unification hardware[9,10] fall in this category. For the rule level, efforts have concentrated on parallel matching of clause pairs that have unifiable literals.[6,11–13] Search-level parallelism mainly deals with the selection of clauses, from the whole clause set, to resolve, and is gaining attention in the field of logic programming.[14–17] Sharing resources is the main subject in system-level parallelism. To facilitate the automatic exploitation of parallelism in logic inference, many parallel logic programming languages have been proposed.[18,19] Their implementations are in progress.

However, the revelation of the low degree of parallelism in typical logic programs and the difficulty of sharing variables make extensive parallelism difficult to achieve. In this paper, we propose a parallel model of logic inference in which the clause set of a problem domain is decomposed into several distinct partitions. Logic inference on each partition is conducted at a different processor in a multiprocessor system simultaneously. Intermediate derivations in each partition are shared between partitions via clause migration. A formal method of partitioning the clause set is proposed, that includes sharing intermediate derivations via clause migration.

A PARALLEL INFERENCE MODEL FOR LOGIC PROGRAMMING

Our objective is to design a parallel logic inference scheme that will run on general-purpose multicomputers including multiprocessors and local area networks.[20] Since no specialized hardware is assumed for such a scheme, the parallelism will be explored primarily at the search level. Major problems confronting existing schemes are investigated below to motivate our design.

Problems in Existing Parallel Inference Schemes

According to recent studies, parallelism at the subrule level and the rule level is limited.[6,12,21] There was speculation, on the other hand, that search-level parallelism could offer a significant opportunity for a large degree of concurrency. Concurrency is a consequence of non-determinism in logic inference. That is, the order of resolution affects only the efficiency, not the correctness of the inference. Therefore, many clauses can be resolved simultaneously. Nevertheless, the non-determinism also has an adverse effect on logic inference. In each resolution cycle, the two clauses to be resolved can be selected out of C(n,2) possible combinations. If the selection is unrestricted, the resolution cycle can be very long when the clause set is large. To tackle this problem, two restrictions are imposed: (1) only Horn clauses[1] are allowed in the clause set, and (2) either a top-down or a bottom-up proof procedure is used. The resulting inference procedure can be viewed as a search process in an AND/OR tree space.[2] Each alternative branch in the AND/OR tree offers a possibility for parallelism since it represents a subtree that can be searched independently. The resulting inference procedure retains a high degree of parallelism, even though a strict sequence is imposed when it searches along a path. Nevertheless, due to sharing variables between AND branches and the small number of OR branches found in most existing programs,[11,15,21] concurrency in AND/OR tree search is also limited in practice.

A procedure with a high degree of parallelism is able to exploit the potential of a multiprocessor since many processors will be kept busy for most of the time. For a conventional deterministic task, such as numerical analysis, better processor utilization implies greater speedup. Unfortunately, logic inference is non-deterministic. Keeping processors busy does not guarantee a speedup. In other words, many processors may not be doing useful work even though they may be busy all the time. To prevent a processor from doing unproductive work, schemes that use the dominance relation to eliminate unnecessary clauses were shown to be very effective.[16,17] *Clause subsumption* is a notable example.[22] Unfortunately, it is difficult to implement in an AND/OR tree search procedure.

Problem-solving heuristics provide another important approach to improve the efficiency of logic inference. It may be used to guide the selection of resolvable clauses. However, in its current form, it is hard to incorporate problem-solving heuristics in an AND/OR tree search procedure.[16]

Partitioning Clause Set for Parallelism

Since a matching process selects resolvable pairs from the whole clause set, resolution on a small clause set is usually much faster than on a large one. Another fact that can be observed is that a successful inference does not always involve all the clauses. These two observations suggest that inference can be conducted on all the possible subsets of clauses concurrently; each is carried out by a different processor. The inference terminates as soon as a processor finds a proof. If the processor that found the proof happens to work on a small subset, the inference time can be very short. Although such an approach toward parallel logic inference looks very promising at the first glance, it is impractical. For a set of n clauses, there are 2^n subsets. It is impossible to exhaust all the subsets even for a medium-sized clause set. However, this approach can be made practical by the following modification. Initially, clauses are partitioned into as many subsets as the number of processors available. In this way, we can run the procedure on a system with an arbitrary number of processors, and all the processors can be kept busy all the time. Nevertheless, a subset so obtained usually does not contain sufficient clauses for a successful inference. To cope with the problem, clauses are transferred from one subset to another as inference proceeds. The migration of clauses adjusts the partition dynamically so that a refutation can be found in a subset. Thus, clause migration is essentially a robust clause partitioning scheme. To clarify this concept of parallel logic inference, the basic steps involved are outlined in the following procedure:

```
Procedure: Parallel-Logic-Inference
Begin
  Partition the input clause set into subsets;
  Load each subset into a processor;
  All the processors run the following loop concurrently:
    Loop until success or there are no more resolvable
    pairs
      Run a local inference cycle;
      If the resolvent is an empty clause, then set success
      flag;
      Invoke clause migration if necessary;
      Split into two subsets and request for another pro-
        cessor if local subset becomes too large;
    end Loop;
  end.
```

Due to clause migration, a processor in the above procedure conducts inference on virtually the whole clause set, though it is in fact working only on a small subset of clauses. Thus, the parallel inference procedure can be viewed as a form of virtual inference.

In the context of an AND/OR tree search space, the parallel model allows three forms of parallelism. In addition to AND parallelism and OR parallelism, processors may also jointly work on the same search path via sharing intermediate inference results. This parallelism is implicitly achieved by clause migration, which does not exist in the top-down or bottom-up proof procedure.

The resolution procedure is non-deterministic, and the partitioning approach creates no shared variables. Hence, no synchronization between processors is necessary. All the processors can run concurrently in the above procedure. Furthermore, resolution and clause migration from one processor to another can also be carried out asynchronously.

Issues in the Parallel Inference Procedure

The proposed parallel inference model consists of three basic components: the initial partition, clause migration, and local inference. Each involves several unsettled issues.

The initial partition is the basis of the whole inference procedure. A proper partition will reduce the rate of clause migration and improve the inference speed. Thus, clauses have to be grouped in such a way that local inference is most productive and the clause migration rate is minimal. The main issues that have to be investigated in determining the initial clause partition are the proper size of a clause subset and how related clauses are grouped together. Factors related to the target machine, such as processor speed and interprocessor communication delay, should be taken into consideration. However, problem-solving heuristics are more important since logic inference is extremely problem-dependent.

Clause migration dynamically changes the partition of the clause set. Each processor has to determine which clause should migrate, when and where. Making such decisions involves not only static information but also information about the dynamic status of the inference. Thus, besides problem-solving heuristics, an efficient data structure for maintaining status information is important to making decisions about clause migration.

Local inference is the component that does the actual work of resolution. Like a conventional inference procedure, it repeats a resolution cycle that consists of matching a pair of clauses, unifying the matched literals, and resolving the pair. Issues that have to be investigated include how to reduce inference cycle time and how to identify the most promising pair. Inference cycle time may be reduced by keeping the local clause subset small and organizing it into an efficient data structure. The *subsumption* strategy can also help to reduce the inference cycle since it can eliminate unnecessary clauses, but it requires an efficient data structure because much searching is involved. Determining which pair to resolve, on the other hand, relies on problem solving heuristics. Ranking resolvable pairs requires an effective way to capture knowledge about the problem.

Incorporating problem-solving heuristics and employing efficient data structures are two keys to a successful design of the parallel logic inference procedure. Depending on the problem to be solved and available knowledge about solving it, different heuristics may be applied. This requires a parallel logic inference procedure that adapts different heuristics from problem to problem. Few existing parallel logic inference schemes provide mechanisms for this purpose. We will describe a systematic method for incorporating different problem-solving heuristics into the parallel inference procedure and a unified data structure for supporting clause migration, local inference and subsumption.

PROBLEM-SOLVING HEURISTICS

Among resolvable pairs, some will lead to a refutation, but not all. The best inference procedure, would be the one in which every resolution makes progress toward a proof. It is hard to achieve due to the nondeterministic nature of logic inference. This motivates the use of problem-solving heuristics to predict which resolvable pair is more likely to lead to a proof so that that number of inference cycles can be minimized. For example, in the set-of-support strategy,[23] a set of clauses is "supported" and one of these clauses or their descendants should be included in each resolution. Accordingly, any resolvable pair with a supported clause is considered more useful than those without supported clauses. In the unit-preference strategy,[24] clauses with fewer literals are resolved first since these clauses are more likely to generate an empty clause. The unit-preference strategy belongs to a general class of problem-solving heuristics, called *ordering strategies.*[2,22] An ordering strategy ranks clauses to determine the order in which resolutions are performed. These strategies can be adapted to the local inference part of the proposed parallel inference model, but are difficult to apply to the initial partition and clause migration parts.

Our objective is to provide a unified mechanism for incorporating problem-solving heuristics to guide local inference, conduct initial partitioning, and determine clause migration. To this end, the problem-solving heuristic is transformed into a preference measure from which the order of resolution in local inference can be obtained directly. The measure is then transformed into another measure that helps grouping clauses into appropriate subsets.

Resolution Preference

There may be several unifiable literals in a resolvable pair, and the pair can be resolved with respect to each of them. Resolution on different unifiable literals may have different effects on the efficiency of inference, though they operate on the same clause pair. A problem-solving heuristic based on clause ordering will not reflect this fact. Thus, for a more productive local inference scheme, the preference measure should lend itself to the ranking of unifiable literals instead of individual clauses.

It is easy to encode problem-solving heuristics using a preference measure. For example, if the set of support (SOS) strategy is used, links attached to clauses having support can be placed at a preference level an order of magnitude larger than others. If the kind of strategy used in the inference process defines a function value (e.g., a priority function, a weighting, or a literal number), preference measures can be assigned values in proportion to the function values.

Another important factor is the nature of the inference procedure. As Kowalski suggests,[1] resolutions which lead to the simplification of the graph should be performed before others. With this regard, two connected literals, each of which has only this link attached, can be resolved upon without generating new clauses or links. Therefore, these links should be assigned a higher preference level than others.

Distance Between Two Clauses

The order of local resolution can be derived directly from the concept of preference. The grouping of clauses, however, cannot be determined with the same measure. Instead, it requires a measure that characterizes the similarity between clauses. We will call such a measure the *distance* between two clauses in this paper. Since the clause is the smallest unit in the initial partition and clause migration, a distance measure should be provided at this level.

The next question is how to transform the problem-solving heuristics into the distance measure. It can be done independently. However, in order to provide an unified transformation mechanism, the distance measure should be correspondingly derived from the preference measure. The advantage of doing so is that users only have to deal with the problem-solving heuristics, as in the conventional inference systems. Consequently, the partition and migration processes can be transparent to users.

For two clauses that are resolvable, their distance can be determined by a function, which combines the preference levels of those unifiable literals associated with them. The function can be provided by the system as a default. It can also be overwritten by the user with one that is more appropriate for the problem to be solved.

Two clauses may not be resolvable due to the lack of unifiable literals. However, their descendants may be resolvable. The distance between these two clauses, thus, can be obtained indirectly from other resolvable pairs. Consider an example in which Clauses Cl.1 and Cl.2 are not resolvable, but both are resolvable with Clause Cl.3. In this case Cl.2 will be resolvable with the resolvent of Cl.1 and Cl.3. Let D(x,y) represent the distance between Clause x and Clause y. Then, D(Cl.1, Cl.2) can be reasonably defined as the sum of D(Cl.1, Cl.3) and D(Cl.2, Cl.3). In general, more complex functions than a summation can be used. Nevertheless, a linear function is desirable because it is convenient to manipulate.

The distance between two non-resolvable clauses is infinite if none of their descendants are resolvable. The distance measure of a resolvent inherits that of its parent clauses with some adjustments.

Initial Clause Partitioning According to Distances

After a distance measure has been defined for every pair of clauses, partitioning can be directly converted into a clustering problem as in the fields of pattern recognition and statistics where efficient algorithms are available.[25,26] Since the work of actual partitioning is passed down to a clustering algorithm, control over how partitioning is done can be based on the assignment of distance measures.

The partition obtained in this way will have clause pairs with short distances in the same subset. This ensures that closely related clauses are grouped together. The distance of a pair of clauses in different subsets is a long one. This implies that the pair will be less likely to be resolved. As a result, the clause migration rate will be minimized.

Solving different problems with the same clause set may generate different sets of distance measures because different heuristics are used. Each set of distance measures will result in a partition that is the best for its corresponding problem, we hope.

Determining Clause Migration Based on Distances

A clause should migrate from one subset to the other when it has a higher preference to be resolved at the remote site. The difference in preference is reflected in the distances between this clause and its local and remote counterparts. If the remote distance of the clause is less than its local distance, then this clause has preference to be transferred to the remote site. When a clause is not resolvable with any clause in the local subset, its local distance is infinite. Thus, apparently, it should migrate to another partition. Essentially, the criteria for clause migration are equivalent to the protocol that realizes a distributed adaptive clustering algorithm.

UNIFIED DATA STRUCTURE

The connection graph proposed by Kowalski[1] was found to be efficient for supporting the parallel logic inference.[27] In a connection graph, each literal is represented as a graph node, and nodes representing the literals of a clause are grouped together. Unification is then conducted to match every pair of literals that have the same predicate symbol and are complementary in sign. Unifiable pairs of literals are indicated by graph links, and each link is labelled by the most general unifier (MGU) of that link. The graph representation of the clause set in Figure 1(a) is shown in Figure 1(b). Such a graph is simple, yet provides a unified framework for managing resolvable pairs, facilitating subsumption, and supporting clause migration.

Managing Resolvable Pairs

In a blind clause matching, resolvable pairs of clauses are determined by searching over the whole clause set from scratch in every resolution cycle. The procedure is highly redundant since the set of resolvable pairs does not change significantly from iteration to iteration. With a connection graph, the unifiable clauses are identified beforehand and updated during the inference process. Because information about unifiable clauses is maintained, the matching process in each resolution cycle is immediately eliminated.

Facilitating Subsumption

Subsumption is effective but may incur a large overhead. It involves exclusive searching for candidates to be subsumed, and is invoked whenever a new clause is generated. With the connection graph, those candidates can be located immediately since all of them are exactly two hops away from the new clause.

Computing Distances

To compute the distance measure of two unresolvable clauses, we need to know all the indirect resolvable pairs that relate the two clauses. This is readily available in the connection graph since these pairs form a chain in the connection graph.

Supporting Clause Migration

Local and remote distances have to be collected in making clause migration decisions. Since distance is incremental with respect to the number of indirect resolvable pairs involved, only those clauses on the partition boundary are candidates to be exchanged between subsets. If the input clause set is organized into a connection graph, these clauses can be determined immediately, and potential migration paths are represented by links crossing over the partition boundary. Hence, the overhead of clause migration can be greatly reduced by a connection graph.

```
Cl. 1. -G(a,f)                          Cl. 10. K(x,y) -W(x,y)
Cl. 2. G(x,y) -F(z,y) -M(x,z)           Cl. 11. Z(x,y) -B(x,y)
Cl. 3. M(v,w) -W(v,u)                   Cl. 12. N(x,y) -J(x,y)
Cl. 4. F(u,v) -P(u,w) -Q(w,v)           Cl. 13. L(d,e)
Cl. 5. F(u,v) -Q(u,v)                   Cl. 14. S(e,f)
Cl. 6. M(u,v) -K(u,v)                   Cl. 15. B(a,b)
Cl. 7. M(u,v) -Z(u,z) -N(z,w) -K(w,v)   Cl. 16. J(b,c)
Cl. 8. P(x,y) -L(x,y)                   Cl. 17. W(c,d)
Cl. 9. Q(x,y) -S(x,y)
```

(a) The input clause set

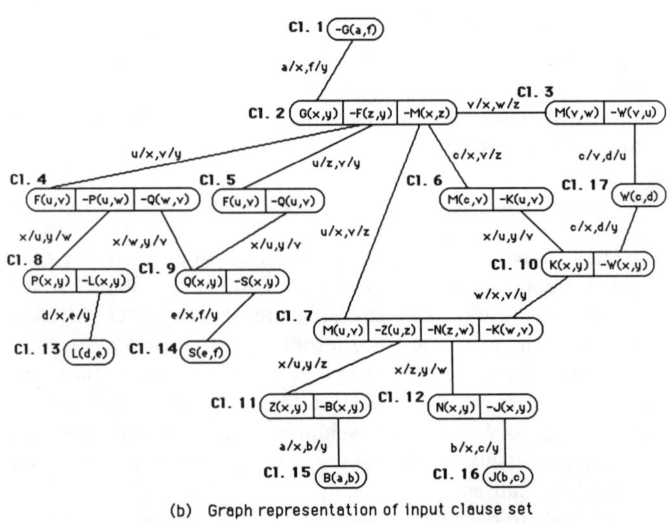

(b) Graph representation of input clause set

Figure 1—Example inference problem: (a) The input clause set, (b) Graph representation of input clause set

AN EXAMPLE

An example is described in this section to illustrate the key features of the parallel model presented in previous sections. In order to directly compare the performance of this model with that of PROLOG systems, a Horn clause set is used, as shown in Figure 1a. From the input clause set, a connection graph is first constructed as shown in Figure 1b.

Our next task, is to decompose the resulting graph through a clustering algorithm. For this example, let's define the preference measure of a pair of unifiable literals to be the sum of the literals in the two associated clauses. If there exists only one link between two clauses, the distance measure is simply set to the preference measure of their unifiable literals; otherwise, the minimum of the preference measures of the links connecting them is taken. Accordingly, the distance between Cl.1 and Cl.2 is 4, between Cl.2 and Cl.4 is 6, and so on. For clauses having no unifiable links between them, the distance measure is defined to be the shortest path between them along the unifiable links. Thus, the distance measure between Cl.1 and Cl.4 is 10(4 + 6), between Cl.1 and Cl.9 is 13(4 + 5 + 4). The complete distance measure between every pair of clauses is shown in Table I.

The clustering algorithm is then invoked to run on this distance matrix which results in three partitions of the initial graph, as shown in Figure 2, assuming three processors are available. From Figure 2, we observe that the partitions are suitably cut on unifiable links, which have the largest distance measures, as we expect. Also, notice that clauses are evenly distributed over partitions, which is a quite desirable situation. Each partition is, thereafter, loaded into one processor for execution.

The links crossing over partitions, external links, are the points where communication takes place between partitions.

TABLE I—Distance matrix of the clause set in Figure 1

Clauses	1	2	3	4	5	6	7	8	9	10	11	12	13	14	15	16	17
1	0	4	9	10	9	9	11	15	13	13	17	17	18	16	20	20	16
2	4	0	5	6	5	5	7	11	9	9	13	13	14	12	16	16	12
3	9	5	0	11	10	10	12	16	14	6	18	18	19	17	21	21	3
4	10	6	11	0	11	11	13	5	5	15	19	19	8	8	22	22	18
5	9	5	10	11	0	10	12	14	4	14	18	18	17	7	21	21	17
6	9	5	10	11	10	0	12	16	14	4	16	16	19	17	19	19	7
7	11	7	12	13	12	12	0	18	16	6	6	6	21	19	9	9	9
8	15	11	16	5	14	16	18	0	10	20	24	24	3	13	27	27	23
9	13	9	14	5	4	14	16	10	0	18	22	22	13	3	25	25	21
10	13	9	6	15	14	4	6	20	18	0	12	12	23	21	15	15	3
11	17	13	18	19	18	16	6	24	22	12	0	12	27	25	3	15	15
12	17	13	18	19	18	16	6	24	22	12	12	0	27	25	15	3	15
13	18	14	19	8	17	19	21	3	13	23	27	27	0	16	30	30	26
14	16	12	17	8	7	17	19	13	3	21	25	25	16	0	28	28	24
15	20	16	21	22	21	19	9	27	25	15	3	15	30	28	0	18	18
16	20	16	21	22	21	19	9	27	25	15	15	3	30	28	18	0	18
17	16	12	3	18	17	7	9	23	21	3	15	15	26	24	18	18	0

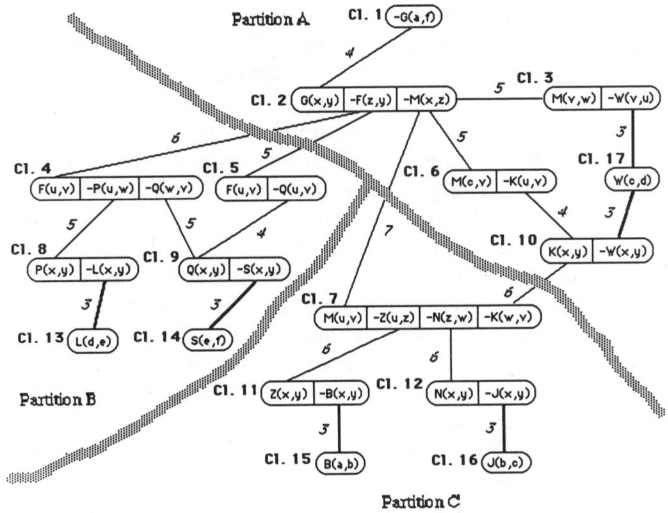

Figure 2—Distance measures and initial partition

In this case, there are two between partitions A and B, two between partitions A and C, and none between partitions B and C. A copy of the MGU of each external link is maintained in each connecting partition.

In the execution of inference on each partition, the processor picks a link of its partition, and resolves upon this link to generate a new clause, the resolvent. It selects links in ascending order of preference measures. Ties are broken randomly, but in favor of internal links.

In Figure 3, a snapshot is shown after two steps of inference have been performed in each partition through the resolution of two links, indicated by the darkened lines in Figure 2 and selected according to the strategy, assuming equal execution time for these resolutions. Except for Cl.10, whose new MGU is updated through interprocessor communication, these beginning resolutions are completely done

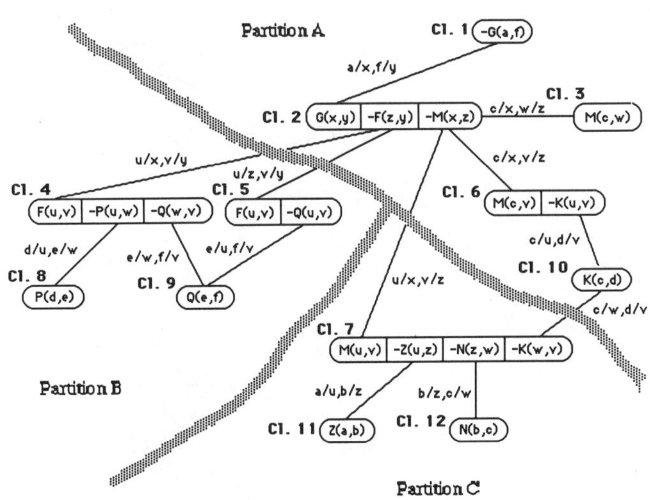

Figure 3—After 2 steps of resolutions on links indicated by the darkened lines in Figure 2
Notice that Cl.6 is to be subsumed by Cl.3

within each partition. Inside partition A, we further observe that Cl.6 ought to be subsumed by Cl.3. After the deletion of Cl.6 and its links, Cl.10 becomes isolated in partition A and is subject to migration. It migrates to partition C as its only link goes to partition C, shown in Figure 4.

During the migration of Cl.10, we assume two inference steps are also taking place in partition B and C, and one inference step in partition A. The resulting situation is shown in Figure 5. For resolution performed on clauses with external links, the new MGU is checked for compatibility, as well as, internal links. Any incompatible links are immediately deleted, as is the case, with the link between Cl.2 and Cl.3. If the external links are incompatible, they are deleted from both clauses through the communication protocol. If the new MGU is compatible with the old one, a copy of it is sent to the remote processor along the external link in order to keep the two copies consistent.

Cl.2 now becomes isolated in partition A, and is subject to migration. Since it has two links with partition B and one link with partition C, we migrate it to partition B to save the potential communication overhead. Figure 5 also shows the arrival of Cl.10 from partition A, which is thus available for resolution in partition C.

Here again, we assume that the migration of Cl.2 can be performed in approximately the same time one inference step is performed in partition B and C. Figure 6 displays the situation after these operations. Cl.7, in this case, must be migrated. Miscellaneous inference steps, thereafter, are shown in Figure 7 and Figure 8. In Figure 8, the goal statement is reached by the generation of an empty clause in partition B. Counting the migration process as one resolution step, it takes eight resolution steps to get the proof.

Presenting this example clause set to a logic inference system, a typical PROLOG, we get 28 inference steps. By carefully rearranging the order of these clauses, we can reduce it to 16 steps, and this turns out to be the best we can get from an uniprocessor inference system. Since most of the time inference problems involve a moderate number of clauses, optimal ordering of the clauses is usually not obtainable. On the other hand, the performance of the parallel model can be further improved if a more elaborated heuristic is encoded. The shorter resolution cycle in each step is another

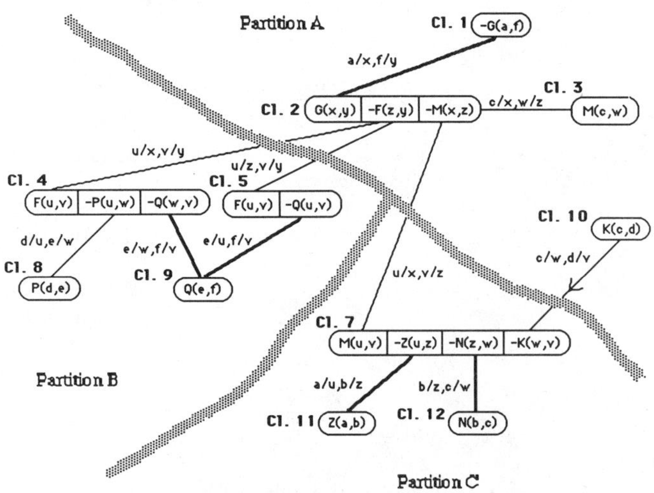

Figure 4—After the removal of the subsumed clause (Cl.6)
Cl.10 is now isolated and is subject to migration

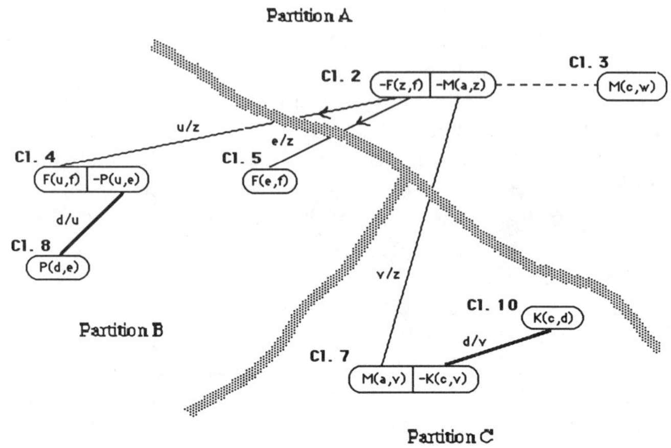

Figure 5—After the migration of Cl.10 and the resolutions indicated in Figure 4
Notice that Cl.3 is no longer unifiable with Cl.2, and is thus deleted.
Cl.2 is now isolated and is to be migrated to Partition B

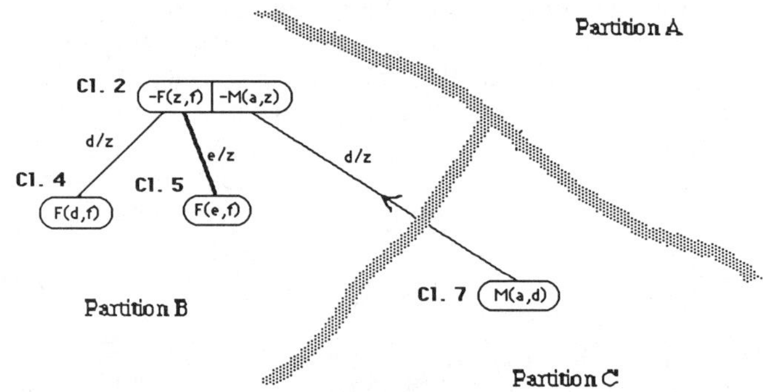

Figure 6—After the migration of Cl.2 and the resolutions indicated in Figure 5
Notice that Cl.7 is now subject to migration.

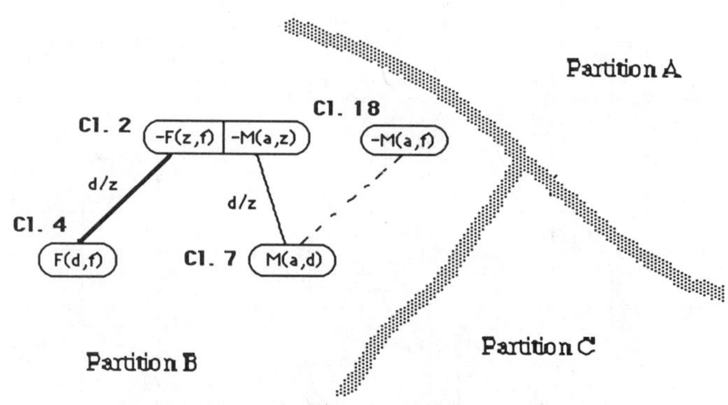

Figure 7—After the migration of Cl.7 and the generation of new resolvent (Cl.18)
However, Cl.18 is not unifiable with Cl.7 and is thus deleted.

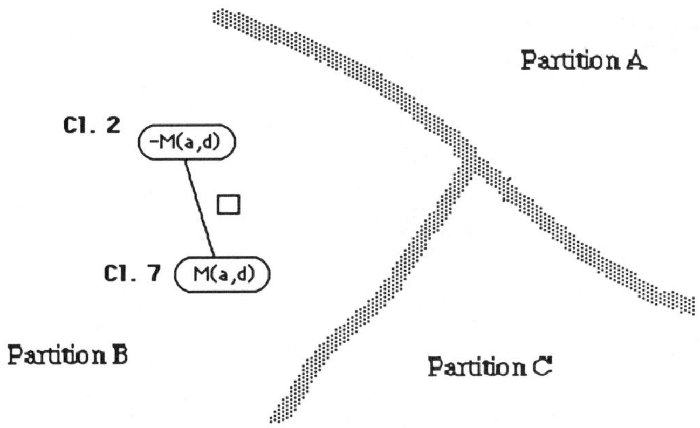

Figure 8—A proof is found in Partition B

speedup factor of the parallel model, that is implicitly illustrated in this example. Therefore, we conclude, that this parallel model will outperform uniprocessor inference systems, with the potential speedup factor in proportion to the number of partitions.

CONCLUDING REMARKS

We have described a parallel inference model for logic programming on general-purpose multicomputers. In this model, input clauses are partitioned into subsets, and resolution is conducted on each subset concurrently. All the available processors are fully utilized in this way. The partition is dynamically adjusted via clause migration as inference proceeds. This allows each processor to work on virtually the whole clause set while achieving a shorter resolution cycle. No synchronization is necessary between processors. In the context of AND/OR tree space search, the parallel model explores another dimension of parallelism in addition to the AND parallelism and OR parallelism. It implicitly allows multiple processors to jointly search the same path that leads to a refutation. Problem-solving heuristics can be incorporated in the parallel model systematically. They are encoded into a preference measure of unifiable literals to guide local inference such that the most promising clause is always resolved first. The preference measure is then translated into the distance measure between clauses. The distance measure allows closely related clauses to be grouped in the same subset using existing clustering algorithms. The partition so obtained has the best combination of clause subsets and a small rate of clause migrations. Clause migration decisions can be made based on the distance measure also. The optimal migration decision would be the one that realizes an adaptive clustering algorithm. Last, we find out that all the mechanisms of the parallel model can be efficiently supported by a connection graph. The graph also simplifies the implementation of the subsumption strategy. Therefore, we conclude that this parallel model will outperform the uniprocessor inference systems.

REFERENCES

1. Kowalski, R. *Logic for Problem Solving,* 1979.
2. Nilsson, N. J. *Principles of Artificial Intelligence,* Tioga Publishing Co., 1980.
3. Rich, E. *Artificial Intelligence,* McGraw Hill, 1983.
4. Davis, Ruth E. "Logic Programming and Prolog: A Tutorial." *IEEE Software,* (Vol. 2), 5, September, 1985, pp. 53–62.
5. Hayes-Roth, F. "The Knowledge-Based Expert System: A Tutorial." *IEEE Computer,* September, 1984, pp. 11–28.
6. Forgy, C., A. Gupta, and A. Newell. "Initial Assessment of Architecture for Production Systems." *Proc. NCAL,* 1984, pp. 116–120.
7. Douglass, R. "A Qualitative Assessment of Parallelism in Expert Systems." *IEEE Software,* May, 1985, pp. 70–81.
8. Tick, E. and D. Warren. "Towards a Pipelined PROLOG Processor." *Proc. 1984 Int'l Symp. Logic Programming,* 1984, pp. 29–41.
9. Vitter, J. S. and R. A. Simons. "New Class for Parallel Complexity: A Study of Unification and Other Complete Problem for **P**." *IEEE Tr. Computers,* May, 1986, pp. 403–418.
10. Mukhopadhyay, A. "Hardware Algorithm for Nonnumeric Computation." *IEEE Tr. Computers,* June, 1979, pp. 384–394.
11. Stolfo, S. and D. Miranker. "DADO: A Parallel Processor for Expert Systems." *Proc. 1984 Int'l Conf. Parallel Processing,* August, 1984, pp. 74–82.
12. Oflazer, K. "Partitioning in Parallel Processing of Production Systems." *Proc. 1984 Int'l Conf. Parallel Processing,* August, 1984, pp. 92–100.
13. Deering, M. "Hardware and Software Architecture for Efficient AI." *Proc. NCAI,* 1984, pp. 73–78.
14. Ciepielewski, A. and S. Haridi. "Execution of Bagof on the OR-Parallel Token Machine." *Proc. Int'l Conf. Fifth-Generation Computer Systems,* 1984, pp. 551–560.
15. Conery, J. S. and D. F. Kibler. "AND Parallelism and Nondeterminism in Logic Programs." *New Generation Computing,* (Vol. 3), 1985, pp. 43–70.
16. Li, G.-J. and B. W. Wah. "MANIP-2: A Multicomputer Architecture for Evaluating Logic Programs." *Proc. Int'l Conf. Parallel Processing,* 1985, pp. 123–130.
17. Li, G.-L. and B. W. Wah. "How good are parallel and ordered depth-first searches?" *Proc. Int'l Conf. Parallel Processing,* 1986, pp. 992–999.
18. Shapiro, E. "Concurrent Prolog: A Progress Report." *IEEE Computer,* August, 1986, pp. 44–58.
19. Clark, K. and S. Gregory. "PARLOG: Parallel Programming in Logic." *ACM Tr. Programming Language and Systems.* (Vol. 8), 1, January 1986, pp. 1–49.
20. Hwang, K. and F. A. Briggs. *Computer Architecture and Parallel Processing,* McGraw-Hill, 1984.
21. Murakami, K., T. Kakuta, and R. Onai. "Architecture and Hardware System: Parallel Inference Machine." *Proc. Int'l Conf. Fifth-Generation Computer Systems,* Tokyo, 1984, pp. 18–36.
22. Wos, L., R. Overbeek, E. Lusk, and J. Boyle. *Automatic Reasoning: Introduction and Applications,* 1984.
23. Wos, L., D. Carson, and G. Robinson. "Efficiency and completeness of the set-of-support strategy in theory proving." *Journal of ACM,* (Vol. 12), 1965, pp. 536–541.
24. Wos, L., D. Carson, and G. Robinson. "The unit preference strategy in theory proving." *Proc. Fall Joint Computer Conf.,* Thompson Book Company, 1964, pp. 615–621.
25. Hartigan, J. A. *Clustering Algorithms,* John Wiley & Sons, Inc., 1975.
26. Dube, R. and K. Jain. "Clustering Methodologies in Exploratory Data Analysis." *Advances in Computers,* (Vol. 19), Academic Press, 1980.
27. Cheng, P. Daniel. *A Parallel Theorem Prover Based on Connection Graph,* Master's Thesis, Northwestern University, Evanston, Illinois, December, 1986.

The contextual parsing of natural language

by JOHN C. WEBER and W.D. HAGAMEN
Cornell University Medical College
Point Lookout, New York

ABSTRACT

This paper describes a mechanism for parsing natural language input. The mechanism relies on context to resolve ambiguities. This ability is in turn dependent on a functional relation between the parser and the data structure which represents both the knowledge and logic of the subject matter domain. To illustrate this interdependence, the discussion is limited to a single program used to teach anatomy to medical students. However, the same parser has been used for other courses in the medical curriculum.

INTRODUCTION

The Computerized Anatomical Teaching System (CATS) is an interactive computer program used to teach gross anatomy to medical students. CATS contains no prestored questions or answers and does not rely on keyword analysis. It contains: (1) a natural language parser that interprets the meaning of a student's question or answer, (2) an abstract (numeric) representation of anatomical knowledge and logic which it uses to answer or generate questions, and (3) the ability to generate text and compose it into phrases, clauses, sentences, and paragraphs.

The anatomy each first year medical student is required to learn comprises a very large body of knowledge. Because it is a descriptive discipline, anatomy generally has been considered a memory course consisting of learning the names of things together with their functional and spatial relations. All the information that CATS contains can be displayed on approximately 15 typewritten pages. The program can use this small database to answer virtually any question that could be found in an unabridged textbook (1500 pages).

In addition to being able to use these basic relations for deducing more complex ones, CATS also has the ability to discover and articulate meaningful general principles which it offers as "reasons" for its answers to further reduce the need for memorization. It does this for 80 percent of the questions asked. The pedagogic goal of the program is to demonstrate to students the method of reasoning, and reasoning's advantage over rote memorization.

This paper is limited to a description of how the program processes input, with particular emphasis on the use of context in resolving potential ambiguities. A more comprehensive description of the program, including the mechanisms of reasoning and text generation, may be found in Hagamen and Gardy.[1] CATS is coded in APL and implemented on both 8086 (IBM PC/AT) and 68000-based microcomputers.

DATA STRUCTURE

To understand the parsing mechanism, it is necessary to know the types of information the program has about the domain in which it operates. The parsing described relies on what we shall call context. This, in turn, depends on the program's anatomical knowledge.

The program has available four types of data: (1) node descriptors, (2) relational matrices, (3) node profiles, and (4) syntactic words.

Node Descriptors

The names of anatomical structures are stored as a list of noun phrases that may be single words or groups of words. Each of these node descriptors also may contain synonyms enclosed within parentheses.

The noun phrases serve two roles. First, they are used by the utility program that automatically generates the vocabulary lists which in turn are used to determine which nodes a student is talking about. Second, they are used when the program is generating the text involved in asking or answering questions.

An example of a node descriptor is: FLEXOR DIGITI MINIMI (FIFTH FINGER LITTLE QUINTI V 5). FLEXOR DIGITI MINIMI would be used when the program is generating a question or reply. However, the program could recognize any combination of words input that uniquely identifies the structure. For example, it could recognize FLEXOR OF THE LITTLE FINGER or FLEXOR DIGITI V.

Relational Matrices

A fact such as the musculocutaneous nerve innervates the biceps is an expression of a functinal relation between two anatomical structures (nodes). Within the domain of anatomy there are more than 30 such generic types of relationships, each of which is represented by verbs or verb equivalents.

Relationship information is stored in a series of two-row numeric matrices. For the relationship of innervates (i.e., innervated by, nerve supply of), the node numbers of the structures (nerves) doing the innervating are stored in the first row of the matrix. Node numbers of the structures being innervated (e.g., muscles, viscera, and bones) are stored in the second row. The verb uniquely defines this matrix. Similar matrices exist for each different type of relationship (e.g., origin or insertion of, branches, arterial supply, venous or lymphatic drainage, spatial relations such as anterior/posterior, and distal/proximal).

Node Profile

CATS includes an integer vector that is equal in length to the number of node descriptors and which contains a number to indicate the type of tissue each node represents (e.g., 1 = artery, 2 = bone). This information is called the profile of the node. The program uses this stored information to calculate the "expected profile," which plays an important role in the parsing.

Syntactic Words

The program also includes a predefined list of approximately 128 special words or syntactic markers. Each special word has an associated decimal value (called its word type) that reflects the word's role within our rules of discourse. These tagged words include interrogative pronouns, helping verbs, anatomical "verbs," prepositions, pronouns, articles, conjunctions, and punctuation.

These syntactic words serve three main functions. First, they help in breaking a sentence into functionally useful parts or phrases. Second, the anatomical verbs direct the program to the proper numeric matrix. Third, combinations of interrogative pronouns and helping verbs define the nature of a question—whether it is asking "what is," "why," "where," or if something is true or false.

VOCABULARY LISTS, WORD TYPES, AND NODE POINTERS

After the previously defined data has been entered, a utility function scans the list of node descriptors. It takes the first occurrence of each such naturally appearing word and stores it in a vocabulary list. The utility function also records the node numbers (relative positions of the noun phrases) in which each occurrence of the word is found.

Some words in the special word list may also be found in node descriptors. This is particularly true of the anatomical verbs. The positional numbers of the nodes to which these words point is also recorded. The vocabulary lists therefore include both the special words and those that occur only as part of node descriptors.

For every word in the vocabulary there are three types of data: the word itself, its numeric word type, and the list of nodes to which each word points. All the special words have a decimal word type which, as stated, defines its syntactic role. Words found only in the node descriptor list are given a zero word type. All words found in the node descriptor list have an associated vector of node pointers. For those syntactic words that do not appear in the list of anatomical names, the pointer vector is empty.

The total vocabulary is subdivided into 27 smaller lists according to the initial character in each word. Thus we have an A-vocabulary, a B-vocabulary, and so forth. Punctuation and numbers form the twenty-seventh list. This subdivision into lists slightly reduces search time.

PARSING OVERVIEW

Parsing proceeds from left to right, one word at a time. The first character of each word determines which vocabulary must be searched. The location of a word in the vocabulary also results in retrieval of its word type and the node descriptors, if any, in which that word occurs.

The goal of the parsing is to obtain the information necessary to understand a student's question. Thus, parsing includes four features. First, it determines which nodes (anatomical structures) are being asked about. Since several of the nodes in question may occur in the same input string, individual noun phrases are isolated. Second, it identifies the nature of the relationship specified between the nodes. This involves analyzing potential verb constructions, including predicate adjectives and predicate nominatives. Third, it determines whether the domain of the verb is restricted by the presence of adverbs and prepositional phrases. Fourth, it identifies the combinations of interrogative pronouns and helping verbs which serve to define the nature of the question, and this in turn dictates the form of the answer.

A question such as: WHAT ARE THE ACTIONS OF THE LONG HEAD OF THE BICEPS ON THE FOREARM? would be parsed as follows:

WHAT ARE	1.7	1.5				
THE ACTIONS OF	3	6.2	5.7			
THE LONG HEAD *OF THE* BICEPS	3	0	0	5.7	3	0
ON THE FOREARM*?*	5.1	3	0	9		

Those words found in the syntactic word list are underlined so that a user can identify them. The numeric value (word type) assigned to each word is also shown. The first two words are interrogatives (the floor of their word types is 1), and their combination specifies this as a "what-type" question. The second row contains the relational phrase. In this example, the relational phrase is a predicate nominative. The third row is a noun phrase which indicates the anatomical entity (muscle) about which the student is asking. The fourth row is the prepositional phrase which limits the various actions asked about to those that move the forearm.

There are two types of relational words (verbals). (1) Some words define specific functions or relations. Examples include: INNERVATES, IS A BRANCH OF, and FLEXES. These words are assigned a word type with a floor of 2 (indicating that it is such a specific verbal). The relational matrix to which it points is encoded in the mantissa of its word type. (2) Other words indicate more generic relationships and have a word type with a floor of 6. Actions, for example, include such specific movements as flexion, extension, abduction, adduction, supination, pronation, internal and external rotation. The mantissa of the word type of these generic verbals points to a matrix which contains the numeric values of the specific verbals involved.

Node descriptors are separated by words that flag the beginning of a noun phrase such as determiners or, more importantly, by word types (punctuation and conjunctions) that signal the end of a previous noun phrase as in THE BICEPS and BRACHIALIS AND CORACOBRACHIALIS. Prepositions have a word type with a floor of 5. The specific type of preposition is encoded in the mantissa. In this regard, OF represents a special case. When OF separates two non-verbal noun phrases (THE LONG HEAD OF THE BICEPS), the two phrases are treated as one to define the node descriptor. Any preposition that either immediately follows a verbal (ACTIONS OF, BRANCHES INTO), or does not immediately precede an article (OF WHAT IS THE RADIAL NERVE A BRANCH?), is considered part of the verb phrase.

VERB ANALYSIS

As stated, the verbs represent the nature of the relationship. However, many of these relations are expressed as adjectivals or nominatives, rather than as verbs. At one time a word may be used to express a relationship, but at another time the same word may be used as a node descriptor. Fifty percent of the potential verbals exhibit this dual role. The program also must determine which row of the pointer matrix to search for the nodes, depending on their relation to the verb that is identified.

Identifying The Functional Verb

Potential verbs are flagged by having a word type with a floor of 2 or 6. Resolution is required when there is more than one such word in the input. The first test is whether the tagged word has any associated node pointers (can it be part of a node descriptor?). If it has no node associations, it must be a verb. If the ambiguity remains, two additional tests may be done. (1) If the word is one of the adjectivals (ANTERIOR, POSTERIOR, LATERAL, MEDIAL, INFERIOR, SUPERIOR, DEEP, SUPERFICIAL, DISTAL, PROXIMAL), it must be followed by TO or it must be the terminal word in order to be acting as a verb. (2) If it is an ambiguous nominative (BRANCH, PART), it must be preceded by a determiner (A, AN, THE), in order to be a verb. This takes advantage of the fact that these words are always preceded by an adjective when they occur in a node descriptor (CLAVICULAR BRANCH OF, SECOND PART OF). Once the active verb has been identified, the word types of the competing verbals are converted to zero, and they become available to the parser as noun phrase constituents.

Determining The Row Numbers

The verbals encountered by the program include transitive verbs, intransitive verbs, predicate nominatives, and predicate adjectives. For this reason it is not particularly useful to think in terms of subject, verb, and object. However, it should be apparent from the nature of the relational matrices that all questions are dyadic—they involve a relation between two things (or groups of things). One of these is stored in the first row of the matrix and the other in the second row. It is the program's task to determine which is which.

Some questions have the general form: WHAT IS THE ORIGIN OF THE BICEPS? or WHAT IS THE CORACOID PROCESS THE ORIGIN OF? Clearly one of the two arguments (nodes) is given in the question. The other is unknown but is tokenized by the place holding function of WHAT. This unknown represents the answer which the program must fill in. In true or false questions, both arguments are given: IS THE CORACOID PROCESS THE ORIGIN OF THE BICEPS? However, when attempting to answer this type of question, the program temporarily masks the left argument, processes the remainder as a what-type question, and then compares its answer with the masked node. In both situations the program needs to know which row contains the given node and which contains the answer.

Determining which row contains the node and which contains the answer is performed by a simple APL function. A brief introductory discussion may help in evaluating the features of the APL function. First, all verbals, except adjectivals, have an infinitive verb form. For example, ORIGINATE is the infinitive form of ORIGIN OF and INNERVATE is the verb infinitive for INNERVATED BY. The node that would be considered the subject of the verb infinitive is stored in row 1. Second, the adjectivals occur in pairs of logical opposites (e.g., ANTERIOR—POSTERIOR, MEDIAL—LATERAL). These have no verb infinitive equivalents. One half of each pair has a positive word type; its opposite is the negative of the same word type. If you think of a declarative sentence (e.g., THE AXILLARY ARTERY IS ANTERIOR TO THE POSTERIOR CORD.), the left argument (AXILLARY ARTERY) of a positive adjectival (IS ANTERIOR TO) is in row 1, and the right argument (POSTERIOR CORD) is in row 2. If the adjectival has a negative word type (IS POSTERIOR TO), the relationship is reversed. In this way the absolute value of these word types performs both roles—there are no negative values in the relational matrices.

The APL function that performs this task returns a value (1 or 2) to indicate the row number where the answer, as defined above, is located. The process involves several steps and conditional tests. (1) If the verb is followed by a noun phrase, the answer is assumed to be in row 2; otherwise it is in row 1. (2) This decision is reversed if the verb either has a negative word type (IS POSTERIOR TO) or is the nominative form of an intransitive verb (ORIGIN OF, INSERTION OF, PART OF, BRANCH OF). The reason for this depends on the transivity of the verb. In the nominative form of a transitive verb (THE MUSCULOCUTANEOUS NERVE IS THE INNERVATION OF THE BICEPS), the structure doing the innervating appears before the verb. When the verb is intransitive (THE MUSCULOCUTANEOUS NERVE IS A BRANCH OF THE MEDIAL CORD), the structure doing the branching follows the verb. (3) If the question contains a possessive, as indicated by the word types, the result is reversed again. ITS INNERVATION is equivalent to INNERVATION OF IT. (4) Passive voice, when present, causes an additional reversal. (5) A final reversal occurs if the verb is immediately followed by certain prepositions which have not already been factored in (BRANCH FROM versus BRANCH INTO). All decisions are based on the numeric (word type) form of the question which already exists.

CONTEXTUAL UNDERSTANDING

If a system justifies the term *intelligent,* it should not impose any special—even well accepted—rules of grammar or syntax on a user. The program should be as understanding and flexible as its human counterpart. Therefore, the program must be able to recognize and use the context of a dialogue. The ways in which this program uses context to help its understanding are illustrated in the following sections by specific examples.

Role of Individual Words

Given the question WHERE DOES THE EXTENSOR CARPI RADIALIS BREVIS ORIGINATE?, the program extracts a four-word noun phrase, EXTENSOR CARPI RADIALIS BREVIS. Each word (with a word type of zero) occurs as part of a number of different node descriptors. The node numbers associated with each word are shown:

EXTENSOR	41 69 70 71 72 73 74 75 76 324 325 326 327 328
CARPI	69 70 71 87 88 315
RADIALIS	33 69 70 87 234
BREVIS	2 69 75 97 197

The only node number that all four words share in common is 69 which, not surprisingly, is the EXTENSOR CARPI RADIALIS BREVIS. The first word in the sequence, no matter what it happens to be, activates (brings to mind) a number of associations. Each succeeding word, by a process of logical "anding," makes the meaning more specific. Thus, on the simplest level, the words in the noun phrase provide the context. Indeed, noun phrases have evolved as a part of language to eliminate ambiguity.

Role of The Verb–Pronoun Reference

Pronoun reference is achieved by storing the node numbers for the subject and objects (or answers) to the previous question. However, because the discussion usually involves a relation between two or more nodes, ambiguity is introduced. To which should the pronoun refer?

Q: WHAT IS THE INNERVATION OF THE BICEPS?
A: THE MUSCULOCUTANEOUS NERVE.
Q: WHAT IS ITS ACTION?
A: IT FLEXES THE SHOULDER AND ELBOW AND SUPINATES THE FOREARM.

In this example, the pronoun is interpreted to be referring to the subject of the previous question, not to the answer. However, if the second question had been WHAT ELSE DOES IT INNERVATE?, both we and the program would have coupled it to the previous answer: THE MUSCULOCUTANEOUS NERVE. This is not dependent on grammatical rules. Rather, it is based on the semantic rule that nerves, not muscles, innervate things.

In this situation the verb provides the context. Every node has an associated profile (number) that indicates the type of structure. When it searches the relational matrix representing the verb INNERVATES, it determines that all the node numbers in row 1 (representing the structure doing the innervating) have a profile of 6, which means they are nerves. We call this the "expected profile." BICEPS has a profile of 5 (muscle) and MUSCULOCUTANEOUS NERVE has a profile of 6 (nerve). For this reason, the latter node is assigned to the pronoun.

Role of the Verb-Partial Phrases

The profile and expected profiles have generic applications. In this regard consider the following question, which has nothing to do with pronoun reference: WHAT ANASTOMOSES WOULD DEVELOP FOLLOWING AN OCCLUSION BETWEEN THE SECOND AND THIRD PARTS OF THE AXILLARY? This is a very natural way to ask this question. The program extracts more information than was explicitly provided. It knows, for example, that the question refers to the AXILLARY ARTERY, as opposed to the AXILLARY NERVE or AXILLARY VEIN because it is the only interpretation that would agree with the expected profile. Similar logic indicates that SECOND refers to SECOND PART OF THE AXILLARY ARTERY rather than the SECOND RIB or SECOND DORSAL INTEROSSEOUS.

After discarding the three non-zero word types (OF THE ?), the noun phrase contains three words: THIRD PARTS AXILLARY. The APL function that takes over the selection process from this point is called GNODE. Each word in the vocabulary that has a zero word type has an associated vector of numbers indicating all the node descriptors in which that word was found. The right argument of GNODE is all of these node numbers for each of the (three) words in this phrase. For this particular phrase there are 17 such numbers. A list of the numbers, together with the complete form of each node descriptor, follows:

153	LOWER ⅔ OF ANTERIOR SURFACE OF HUMERUS (TWO THIRDS)
155	LUMBRICAL TO DIGIT 3 (FINGER THIRD)
294	THIRD PART OF AXILLARY ARTERY (3)
84	FIRST PART OF AXILLARY ARTERY (1)
251	SECOND PART OF AXILLARY ARTERY (2)
294	THIRD PART OF AXILLARY ARTERY (3)
19	AXILLA
20	AXILLARY ARTERY
21	AXILLARY GROUP OF MUSCLES
22	AXILLARY NERVE
23	AXILLARY VEIN
66	DORSAL SURFACE OF AXILLARY BORDER OF SCAPULA
84	FIRST PART OF AXILLARY ARTERY (1)
228	QUADRANGULAR SPACE OF AXILLA
251	SECOND PART OF AXILLARY ARTERY (2)
294	THIRD PART OF AXILLARY ARTERY (3)
307	TRIANGULAR SPACE OF AXILLA

Notice that the first three node descriptors contain the word THIRD; the next three include PART; and the remaining eleven all represent AXILLA-.

GNODE next eliminates all the elements of the list that do not have a node profile corresponding to ARTERY. The reason for this is that the verb in this case carries an expected profile of ARTERY—only arteries anastomose in the program's experience. The resulting shortened list follows (note that they all contain the word ARTERY, even though this was not included in the user's question):

294 THIRD PART OF AXILLARY ARTERY (3)
84 FIRST PART OF AXILLARY ARTERY (1)
251 SECOND PART OF AXILLARY ARTERY (2)
294 THIRD PART OF AXILLARY ARTERY (3)
20 AXILLARY ARTERY
84 FIRST PART OF AXILLARY ARTERY (1)
251 SECOND PART OF AXILLARY ARTERY (2)
294 THIRD PART OF AXILLARY ARTERY (3)

Notice the redundancy. Node 294 occurs three times, 84 and 251 each appear twice, and 20 is present only once. This means that node 294 is the closest match and is selected as the output of GNODE.

The program now looks at the next phrase (SECOND). The right argument for GNODE contains eight node numbers. There is no redundancy because there is only one word in the phrase.

154 LUMBRICAL TO DIGIT 2 (FINGER SECOND)
246 SECOND CERVICAL NERVE (C2)
247 SECOND DORSAL INTEROSSEOUS (2 IO)
248 SECOND FINGER (2 INDEX DIGIT)
249 SECOND METACARPAL (2)
250 SECOND PALMAR INTEROSSEOUS (2 VENTRAL IO)
251 SECOND PART OF AXILLARY ARTERY (2)
350 VENTRAL SURFACE OF SECOND METACARPAL (2 VOLAR ANTERIOR PALMAR)

Despite the fact that GNODE must determine that SECOND uniquely defines SECOND PART OF THE AXILLARY ARTERY in the context of the total question, the process actually is simpler than before. The only node number in the list that happens to have a profile number corresponding to ARTERY is 251.

Role of Complementary Phrases

As you and I read the original question, we would also realize that SECOND referred to SECOND PART OF THE AXILLARY ARTERY by an entirely different means. We would probably assume that the two phrases were parallel and that the missing parts of the partial phrase were to be found in the following one. The program also uses this logic when necessary.

Consider the question: WHAT IS THE INNERVATION OF THE SECOND AND THIRD LUMBRICALS? Processing begins with the second of the two noun phrases resulting from the parsing (THIRD LUMBRICALS). The vector of node numbers presented to GNODE is shown. Node 155 appears twice, indicating that it contains both words.

153 LOWER ⅔ OF ANTERIOR SURFACE OF HUMERUS (TWO THIRDS)
155 LUMBRICAL TO DIGIT 3 (THIRD)
294 THIRD PART OF AXILLARY ARTERY (3)
154 LUMBRICAL TO DIGIT 2 (SECOND)
155 LUMBRICAL TO DIGIT 3 (THIRD)
156 LUMBRICAL TO DIGIT 4 (FOURTH)
157 LUMBRICAL TO DIGIT 5 (FIFTH)
158 LUMBRICALS

The program next looks at SECOND. The list of competing node numbers is identical to what we showed earlier for SECOND (PART OF THE AXILLARY ARTERY). Applying the expected profile eliminates only node 246, since arteries (251), bone (249,350), and skin (248) as well as muscle (247,250,154) are all innervated by nerves. We are still left with seven nodes from which it must select one. There is no redundancy because SECOND is a single word phrase.

The program does exactly what we would do—it borrows the node pointers for the word LUMBRICALS from the previously determined node descriptor and thus uniquely identifies node 154. This is the reason it processes the phrases in reverse order. If the question had been WHAT INNERVATES THE SECOND AND FOURTH DORSAL INTEROSSEI?, it would have borrowed two words, DORSAL and INTEROSSEI to select node 247.

Adjectives Restricting The Context

Some verbals (relational words) are generic in that they each refer to several specific subtypes. Attachments include both origins and insertions. Actions refer, for example, to flexion, extension, abduction, adduction, pronation, supination, and external and internal rotation. Relations include all the logical opposites described in the VERB ANALYSIS section. Anterior–posterior and medial–lateral are two examples.

If the question is WHAT ARE THE RELATIONS OF THE WRIST?, the program will list the anterior relations and then the posterior relations because anterior relations and posterior relations are different "verbs." However, if the question is WHAT ARE THE ANTERIOR RELATIONS OF THE WRIST?, the program will list only the anterior relations. Any logical variation of this question produces the expected results. For example, WHAT ARE THE ANTERIOR AND POSTERIOR RELATIONS OF THE WRIST? produces both answers. Effectively, this restricts the meaning of the predicate nominative (ARE THE RELATIONS OF) to whatever adjectives modify RELATIONS. If there are no modifiers, all relations are listed.

Prepositional Phrases Restricting The Context

The domain of relational verbs may also be limited by prepositional phrases. Consider the following sequence:

Q: WHAT ARE THE ACTIONS OF THE BICEPS?
A: IT FLEXES THE SHOULDER AND ELBOW JOINTS AND SUPINATES THE FOREARM.
Q: WHAT ARE ITS ACTIONS ON THE FOREARM?
A: IT SUPINATES THE FOREARM.

WHAT ARE THE ACTIONS OF THE BICEPS? produces three verb-object pairings (flex–shoulder, flex–elbow, and supinate–forearm). The prepositional phrase eliminated those actions on objects not included in the prepositional phrase (ON THE FOREARM).

Contextual Interpretation of Spelling Errors

The phrase EXTENSOR ACRPI RADIALIS BREVIS contains a single typographical error—the reversal of CA in CARPI. The program never becomes aware of this mistake, because the three remaining words uniquely define the intended node. Because ACRPI is not in the vocabulary it cannot have any node pointers.

If two words are misspelled (EXTENSOR ACRPI RDIALIS BREVIS), the ambiguity in this case would be between two nodes:

69 EXTENSOR CARPI RADIALIS BREVIS (HAND SHORT)
75 EXTENSOR POLLICIS BREVIS (SHORT THUMB)

However, because the context has narowed the ambiguity to these two nodes, the misspelled words (those with no node pointers) are compared only to the words in these two node descriptors. This is done by means of the closest character match, which is essentially an APL primitive function.

DISCUSSION AND SUMMARY

In a computational sense, the parser we have described is much simpler than previous models.[2,3,4,5] It does not backtrack, look ahead, or consider parallel strategies. Despite this, it meets all our needs. The program could interpret any input we could understand—including ungrammatical but meaningful constructions.

Certainly the task is simplified by the limited subject matter domain. On the other hand, anyone who has seen a 1500 page textbook of gross anatomy could hardly call CATS a trivial application. The ability to identify nodes despite the ambiguities in all the examples included in this paper, and to do so in a fraction of a second, represents an important facility for natural language comprehension.

One explanation for the simplicity is that the parser is goal directed. It does not look for grammatical rules—any more than people do. Rather, it looks for the specific information needed to understand what is intended by a student. This includes: (1) determining the topics (nodes) a student is talking about which, in turn, involves isolating individual noun phrases; (2) looking for verbs (relations) that, if present, limit what is being asked about the topics; (3) recognizing words and phrases that may restrict the domain of the verbs; and (4) using interrogatives and helping verbs to determine the nature of the question. Minimal syntactic clues are used for these purposes.

The importance of storing the noun phrases (names of things) that define the subject matter domain rather than individual words cannot be overly emphasized. It seems intuitively apparent that people use the same technique; we think in terms of names of things and use words in various combinations to access these names. The utility of this in resolving typographical errors and other ambiguities is illustrated in this paper.

Perhaps the most important feature of the parser is the functional way in which it interfaces with the program's knowledge of anatomy (the relational matrices). The expected profile, which plays an essential role in defining the context, is dynamic; it reflects the program's own anatomical knowledge.

The two most important tools in resolving ambiguities—the pointers from vocabulary words to specific nodes and the expected profile—are calculated by the program; they are not entered by a programmer. This is labor saving and it ensures that the data is accurate and current as new information is added.

The algorithmic generation of text,[1] which is not described in this paper, also utilizes the progam's anatomical knowledge. The raw answers are columns of the relational matrices. These consist of node numbers and verb values that directly represent noun phrases and verb phrases. The program also knows the purpose of the question and takes this into account when phrasing the response. For the simplest questions, formatting the answer may involve little more than retrieving the appropriate noun phrase or verb phrase. When multiple nodes and pointers are involved, proper sentence construction requires combining nodes into logical groups (phrases) according to their profile types and adjective values and into clauses according to the associated verbs.

CATS is an example of "intelligent" CAI.[6] In addition to its ability to demonstrate the advantages of reasoning over memorization and its ability to discover and express general principles, another advantage over more conventional computer mediated tutorials[7] is that a single teacher can enter the information necessary to cover an entire discipline in a reasonable period of time. This same technique has been applied to medical diagnosis (MEDCAT),[8] and we plan to extend it to other subjects in the medical curriculum.

ACKNOWLEDGEMENTS

This work was supported in part by grants from the Anonymous Gift Fund of Cornell University Medical College, the Frances L. and Edwin L. Cummings Memorial Fund, and the Advanced Education Projects of the IBM Corporation. We would like to thank Mr. Ward Bell for writing certain auxillary processors used in the 8086 version of the programs.

REFERENCES

1. Hagamen, W.D. and M. Gardy. "The Numeric Representation of Knowledge and Logic—Two Artificial Intelligence Applications in Medical Education." *IBM Systems Journal,* 25 (1986) 2, pp. 207–235.
2. Kaplan, R.M. "A General Syntactic Processor." In R. Rustin (ed.), *Natural Language Processing.* New York: Algorithmic Press, 1971.
3. Winograd, T. *Understanding Natural Language,* New York: Academic Press, 1972.
4. Woods, W.A. "Progress in Natural Language Understanding: An Applica-

tion to Lunar Geology." AFIPS, *Proceedings of the National Computer Conference* (Vol. 42), 1973, pp. 441–450.
5. Winograd, T. *Language As A Cognitive Process,* (Vol. I). Reading, Massachusetts: Addison Wesley, 1983.
6. Barr, A. and E.A. Feigenbaum. *The Handbook of Artificial Intelligence* (Vol. 1). Los Altos: William Kaufman, 1981.
7. Hagamen, W.D., D. Linden, M. Leppo, W. Bell, and J.C. Weber. "ATS in Exposition." *Computers in Biology and Medicine,* 3 (1973) 3, pp. 205–226.
8. Hagamen, W.D., M. Gardy, G. Bell, E. Rekosh, and S. Zatz. "MEDCAT: An Interactive Computer Program for Medical Diagnosis." AFIPS, *Proceedings of the National Computer Conference* (Vol. 54), 1985, pp. 111–119.

COMPUTER DESIGN AND SUPERCOMPUTERS

JACK DONGARRA
Argonne National Laboratory
Argonne, Illinois
and
JORGE NOCEDAL and JIE-YONG JUANG
Northwestern University
Evanston, Illinois
and
EUGENE NORRIS
George Mason University
Fairfax, Virginia

Rapid advances in the development of computer architectures are revolutionizing scientific research and technological development. In the last few years, an unprecedented expansion has taken place in the boundaries of computer architectures directed towards parallel processing and high execution rates. These sessions examine the impact this expansion is having on the computer industry—specifically, the number of distinctive designs available commercially and the effects on science and technology.

The system data structure contention problem and a novel software solution for shared memory, floating control parallel systems*

by JERRY P. PLACE and ALAN A. GOERNER
University of Missouri
Kansas City, Missouri

ABSTRACT

Of the many varieties of multiprocessor architecture which have been proposed in the last five to eight years, shared memory, floating control multiprocessor systems are in many ways the most elegant. Shared memory, floating control architectures are distinguished by the structural attribute that each processor is an equal partner in the management of system resources even to the point of sharing a common copy of the operating system code and its data structures. A central feature and issue of such systems is the provision of dynamic processor load balancing. The most natural technique, however, for assuring dynamic processor load balancing by dispatching processes from a single shared queue is, we show, highly inefficient. We make the argument, validated by simulation studies, that the contention for the process dispatching queue, as they are commonly implemented, becomes so great so quickly as to severely limit the size and utility of such architectures. Examining the requirements for a solution to this problem, we derive a new, highly concurrent process dispatching queue structure with constant time average performance for all operations.

* This research was supported by grant K-5-27116 from United Telecommunications, Inc., Westwood, Kansas.

AN INTRODUCTION TO PARALLEL SYSTEMS

Parallel configurations of computing machines are being developed today across a wide range of architectures.[1,2,3] It has been recognized that parallel configurations of computing machines can provide an enormous amount of computing power for the solution of problems.

Parallel architectures may be characterized as loosely-coupled or tightly-coupled (see Figure 1). Loosely-coupled systems generally exhibit a low level of sharing. Each system has its own memory, peripherals and copy of the operating system. Tightly-coupled systems exhibit a high degree of sharing. Typically, tightly-coupled systems share memory, peripherals and the operating system.

Control in tightly-coupled systems fits into one of three categories: master/slave, separate supervisor, and floating control. The master/slave mode assigns one of the processors in the configuration as the master. The operating system kernel routines always execute on the master. The master is responsible for dispatching work to the slave processors. The separate supervisor method of control maintains a copy of the operating system kernel for each processor in the system. Other system entities such as tables and common routines must be accessible through shared memory or a shared file system. The floating control method maintains one copy of the operating system and each processor executes that one copy. Thus, each processor is responsible for satisfying its own requests for service. Floating control systems are the most difficult to design and implement. The single copy of the operating system must be reentrant and constructs to ensure determinism must be embedded in the operating system.

The basic architecture of the parallel system and the mechanism of control largely determine the granularity of the system. Granularity is a measure of the degree of cooperation possible among processors in the system. Granularity may be expressed as very coarse, coarse, medium, fine, and very fine. Very coarse granularity implies parallelism at the independent task system level. Coarse granularity implies parallelism at the program level within a task system. Medium granularity implies parallelism at the procedure level within a specific program. Fine granularity implies parallelism among instructions within a procedure, and very fine granularity implies parallelism within a single instruction. Units of work in the system can be considered as shown in Figure 2, with independent task systems at the top. Task systems are composed of programs; programs are composed of procedures; procedures are composed of instructions, and instructions can be divided into the functional actions that occur in the hardware of the system.[4]

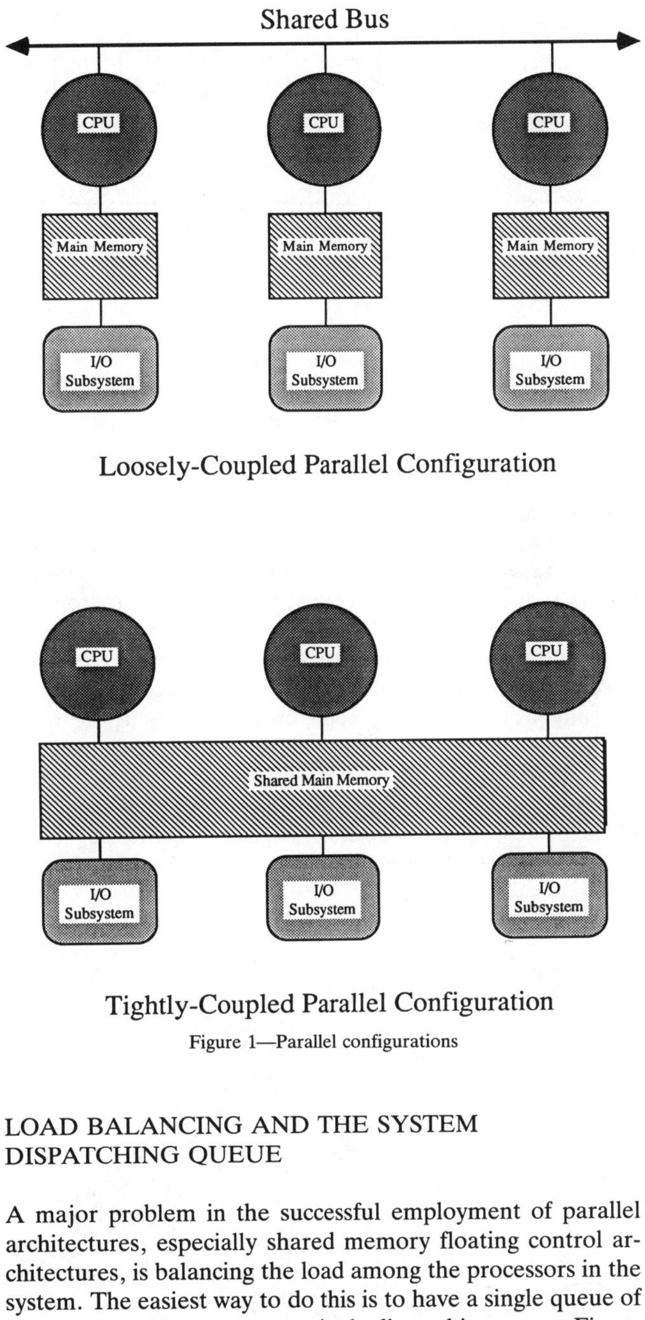

Figure 1—Parallel configurations

LOAD BALANCING AND THE SYSTEM DISPATCHING QUEUE

A major problem in the successful employment of parallel architectures, especially shared memory floating control architectures, is balancing the load among the processors in the system. The easiest way to do this is to have a single queue of processes ready to execute; a single dispatching queue. Figure 3 depicts a configuration of processors about a shared memory with a single dispatching queue. Each program in the system is divided into its component procedures. All procedures com-

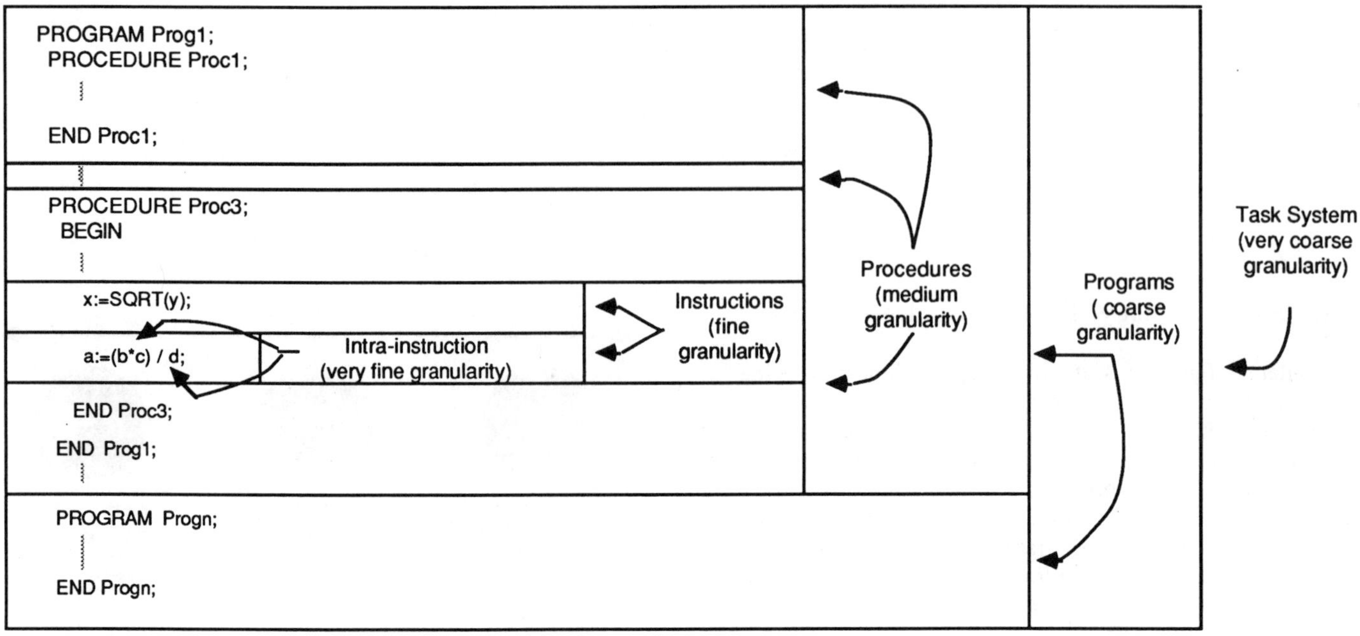

Figure 2—Granularity

peting for resources in the configuration are represented by procedure control blocks in the dispatching queue. The procedure control blocks indicate the status of the procedure, either dispatchable or not, and the dispatching priority of the procedure. The scheduling mechanism behaves like a multi-level feedback queue which allows procedures to migrate from one priority level to another, depending upon their original point of entry. Since processors share all system resources including the operating system, processors are considered equivalent, thus any procedure may execute on any processor, regardless of the procedures that are executing on other processors. Thus, it is possible that several procedures from the same program will be executing in parallel on different processors in the system. As a procedure executes, events occur that cause the status of the procedure to change, perhaps it issues an I/O request, or it consumes system resources beyond a specified limit. In order to update the procedure control block to reflect the new status of the procedure, the processor must have exclusive access to the dispatching queue to ensure determinism in the system.[4]

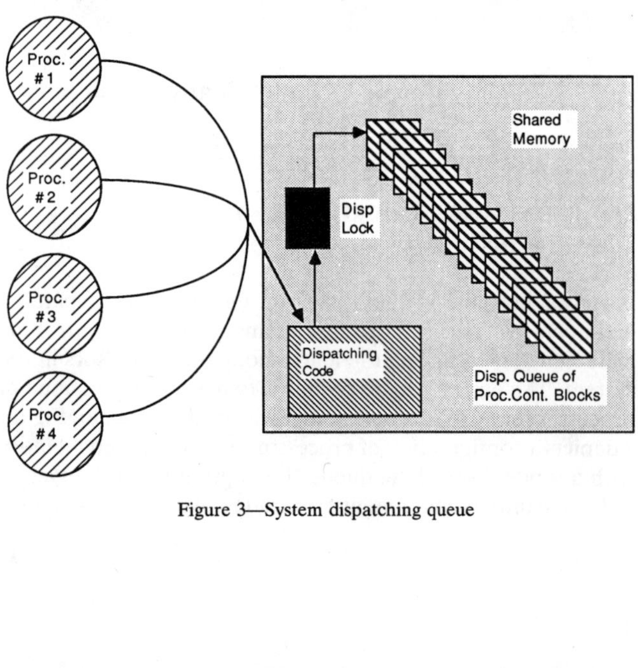

Figure 3—System dispatching queue

For example, a general purpose, moderately parallel system will support a number of concurrently active procedures; a degree of multiprogramming of several hundred is not unreasonable. The dispatching queue must support changing of priorities and setting procedure status such as EXECUTING, BLOCKED(SWAPPED-IN), BLOCKED (SWAPPED-OUT), and READY. When a procedure is first selected for execution, its control block must be marked appropriately so that it will not be selected by another processor. When the procedure is blocked for I/O or completes, the processor must again change the status in the procedure control block. Assume a single dispatching queue with several hundred procedures of varying priorities. Each processor must implement the search algorithm to find the highest priority procedure. Once the highest priority procedure is found, its status must be changed from READY to EXECUTING. Each processor must have exclusive access to the queue of procedure control blocks so that processors do not interfere with one another in the modification of the control blocks as part of the dispatching process. Processors are synchronized by requiring them to own the lock that guards the dispatching queue before they are allowed access to the queue. Thus, there must be mutually exclusive access to the dispatching queue to ensure that processor 1 does not select procedure b for execution when procedure b is in the process of getting its status changed by processor 2.

The dispatcher is enacted by each processor executing the single copy of the dispatching code that is part of the shared operating system in the shared memory. In essence, floating control means that each processor must find its own job to execute next, independently of all the other processors. A processor finds its next unit of work by searching the system dispatching queue, and at a low level of entries (under 1,000), existing implementation methods do not appear to have much impact on performance.[5] Since the dispatching queue may be used by one processor at a time, contention for its use can become a major system bottleneck.

CONTENTION IMPACT ON PROCESSOR OVERHEAD

The contention problem is graphically produced in Figure 4. Three simulation models of moderately parallel systems were created. The models evaluated degrees of parallelism from one to thirty processors. Three cases were studied, a single dispatching queue, a special dispatching processor and three equivalent dispatching queues. Each case assumed an average procedure execution time of 440 μs between context switches. The dispatching queue size was set at two hundred process control blocks and 200 ns was used as the memory access time, with a setup time of 50 μs per access. Thus, all processors required 50 μs + U(10,100) μs to update the dispatching queue and find its next procedure to execute. The simulations measured the time that processors had to wait while other processors had exclusive access to the queue (i.e., processor wait induced by contention for access to the dispatching queue).

The two alternatives to the single dispatching queue were chosen because of their practicality and because they did not materially increase the load balancing problem. The special dispatching processor searched the dispatching queue while other processors were executing user procedures. When a general purpose processor required a context switch, it was the function of the special dispatching processor to have a procedure ready for immediate switching. The dispatching function overlapped the execution of user procedures.

The three-queue case divided the dispatching queue into three separate but equal dispatching queues. If queue #1 was locked by processor b when processor a needed a context switch, processor a attempted to obtain the lock for queue #2. If that queue was locked by processor c, processor a attempted to obtain the lock of queue #3. If that queue was also locked, processor a was forced into a wait state for any one of the queues. Thus, the amount of time required to find a context-switch candidate by any processor was reduced by approximately one-third. More dispatching queues would further reduce the access time and processor contention, however, load balancing, the placement of procedures on queues, would become a significant problem.

Processor wait-time overhead for the three cases is summarized in Figure 4. The single dispatching queue presents a formidable impediment to moderate parallelism. At twenty processors, 80% of each processor's time is spent waiting for the dispatching queue lock. At a configuration greater than six processors, wait-time overhead exceeds 30% per processor in the configuration. The special dispatching processor is an improvement for configurations up to six processors. After six, however, the special dispatching processor behaves the same as a single queue. Multiple dispatching queues perform better. However, after twenty-two processors, contention for

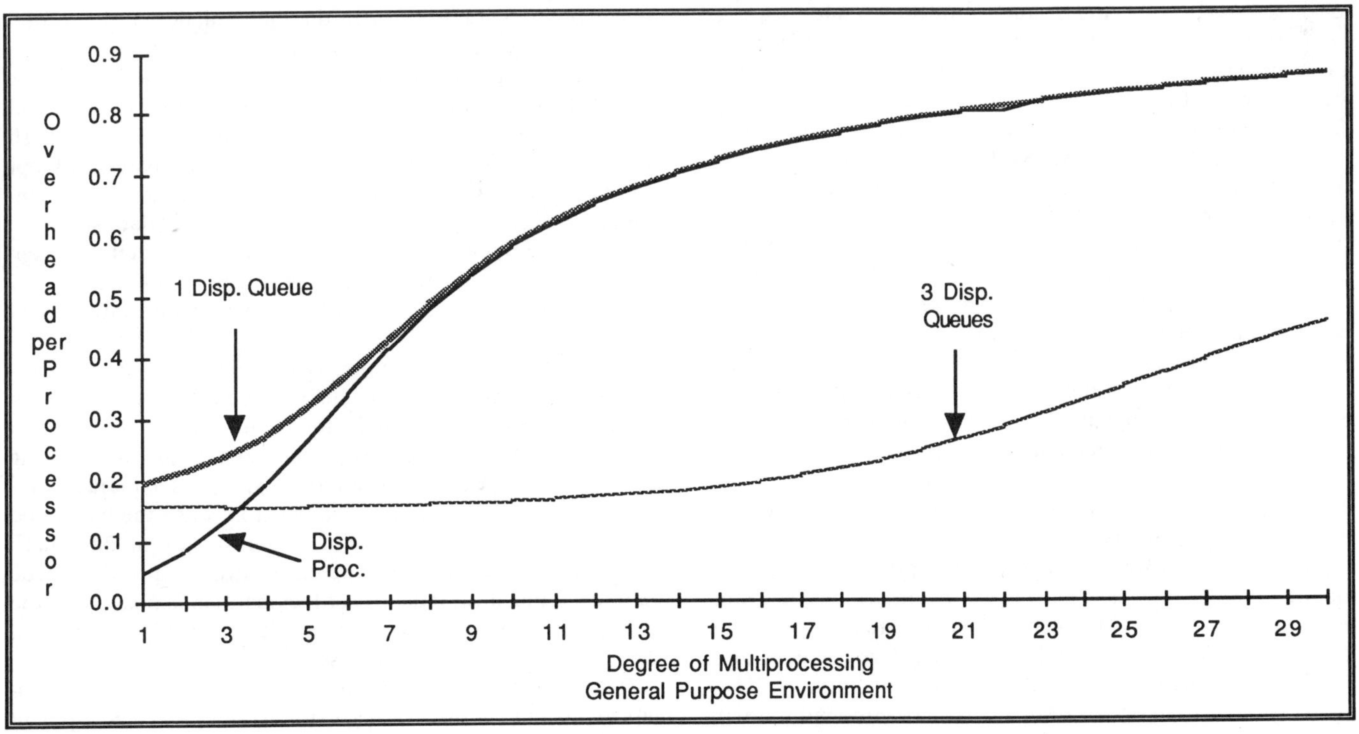

Figure 4—Data structure contention overhead

the queues again induces significant wait time on every processor in the system. More dispatching queues would improve performance, but, as the number of queues increased, load balancing among the processors would also become a significant problem. The solution to this problem is to be found in a more sophisticated data structure supporting the dispatching process rather than multiple dispatching queues.

DISPATCHER—A $\theta(1)$ SOLUTION

Our solution to the problem of contention for the process dispatching queue is embodied in a module called Dispatcher. Dispatcher is unusual in two respects; in the analysis and design methodology which gave rise to it as well as in its data structure. That is, although novel in its structure, Dispatcher is not an ad hoc solution. A specific goal of the solution phase of this investigation was that the specification and implementation of Dispatcher should, as much as possible, be derived and stated from the set of requirements drawn from the preceding analysis.

The insights of these simulation studies give rise to five such requirements, ordered from most to least important. First, a complete package of services for process dispatching must be considered, designed, and implemented, helping to ensure that one operation is not optimized at the expense of others. Second, the Dispatch operation must execute in as nearly constant time as possible. Achieving this goal means, at minimum, that processor contention will no longer be a binary function of both the number of processes and processors, and will depend only on the latter parameter; thereby reducing significantly, we conjecture, the complexity of contention. Third, for all operations, but especially for Dispatch, the Dispatcher data structure and access protocol must minimize concurrent access blocking as much as possible while ensuring database consistency. That is, within the limits of consistency, the Dispatcher data structure and protocol must: (1) reduce the likelihood of collision and, thereby, reduce blocking, and (2) reduce the duration of blocking. And finally, fourth, the Dispatcher protocol must be live (i.e., free from deadlock), and, fifth, all other operations must execute in as nearly constant time as possible.

In accord with our orientation mentioned above, the first requirement is satisfied by developing a formal specification for a process dispatching queue. The technique used is an experimental one based on the notion of an inheritance hierarchy among abstract data types.[6] In this regard, the technique is a descendant of the similar notions in object oriented programming. Although a full description of the development of the Dispatcher specification is the topic of a sequel to this paper, the derivation of Process_Dispatch_Queue, the immediate ancestor of Dispatcher in the hierarchy, exhibits most of the interesting points (see Figure 5).

The most surprising point being that process dispatching queues are not queues, nor are they priority queues. Upon examination, process dispatching queues are seen to be a hybrid data type combining features of priority queues and simple databases. For example, a Dequeue operation seldom actually removes a process from the data structure but, rather, Updates its status to "Executing." This dual heritage is represented in the "is" clause of the derivation. This clause implies that Process_Dispatch_Queue multiply inherits all the operators, exceptions, and axioms of both Priority_Queue and Database_V2.

Beyond this initial insight, the derivation also clarifies two other subtleties of this heritage. First, the bridge axioms show exactly how the priority queue function and database function of Process_Dispatch_Queue are related (i.e., that an enqueue is equivalent to a store of a process with status "Ready" and that a dequeue is not a delete but an update of the process's status to "Executing." Second, the exception conditions for Process_Dispatch_Queue are exactly the union of the exceptions for priority queues and for databases.

The end result of the derivation process is the automatic generation of a package definition for Dispatcher and a set of guidelines for the implementation of the package body. In the case of Dispatcher, the most important guideline, the one which gives the Dispatcher data structure its unique flavor (see Figure 6), can be rendered "Implement multiple inheritance as a multilinked structure." The rationale for this approach is simply the congruence of the facts that Dispatcher logically has two independent access mechanisms, the priority queue and the database, and that multilinked structures, by definition, have two orthogonal access paths. With this useful hint, the requirements on a solution point, more or less directly, to the nature of each access mechanism.

For priority queue access, Dispatcher uses a data structure similar to the process state queue of Digital Equipment Corporation's VMS operating system.[7] This structure is a variation of Henrikson's event set implementation which has recently been shown[5] to have, with splay trees, better aggregate performance than any other priority queue structure in the literature. The Dispatcher implementation, like its VMS predecessor, uses a bit vector in the maintenance of the "Top" field, thereby delivering O(1) performance for the dequeue operation Dispatch and realizing the second requirement.

The fifth requirement's goal of $\theta(1)$ performance for all other operations is guaranteed by the use of an open hash table for database access. All operations of Dispatcher except Dispatch (i.e., Create, Fetch, Block, Unblock, Terminate, Delete, ChgData, and ChgPriority) access the data structure through the open hash table. Dispatch alone enters through the priority queue mechanism, which provides access only to the subset of process control blocks with status equal "Ready."

However, the time complexity of the corresponding operations is only one reason for choosing the Henrikson and open hash table structures. Equally important is the high degree of partitioning these structures provide as a basis for satisfying the third requirement. As noted above, one technique of reducing concurrent access blocking is to reduce the likelihood of collision. The disjointness of the buckets of the open hash table and of the subqueues of the Henrikson priority queue support a much finer degree of locking than is possible in the numerous tree and list implementations which are traditional for priority queues and process dispatching queues.

The second objective of the third requirement (i.e., to minimize blocking intervals), necessitates, then, the development of a locking protocol (see Figure 7) to manage the fine grain

```
type  Process_Dispatch_Queue

    imports
        type   Proc_ID          is scalar ;   constant  Null_ID         is Proc_ID ;
        type   Proc_Data        is scalar ;   constant  Null_Data       is Proc_Data ;
        type   Proc_Priority    is scalar ;   constant  Null_Priority   is Proc_Priority ;

    is
        Priority_Queue  ( Proc_Control_Block , Proc_Priority , Null_PCB )
        and
        Database_V2  ( Proc_Control_Block , Proc_ID , Update_Field , Update_Value ,
Null_PCB ) ;

    where
        constant
            Null_PCB is             structure { Null_ID , Null_Data , Null_Priority , Terminated } ;

        types
            Proc_Status is          scalar { Ready , Executing , Blocked , Terminated } ;
            Proc_Control_Block is structure { Proc_ID , Proc_Data , Proc_Priority ,
Proc_Status } ;
            Update_Field is         scalar { Proc_Data , Proc_Priority , Proc_Status } ;
            Update_Value is         Proc_Data » Proc_Priority » Proc_Status ;

        operators
            Create_DQ is            Create_Q  and  Create_DB ;
            Enqueue has             Proc_Control_Block unfolded ;
            Store has               Proc_Control_Block unfolded , Proc_ID redundant ;
            Replace deleted ;
            ForAllItems deleted ;

        axioms
            { PDQ  : Process_Dispatching_Queue ;
                ID  : Proc_ID ;  D  : Proc_Data ;  P  : Proc_Priority ;  S : Proc_Status  }

            Enqueue ( PDQ , ID , D , P , S )  =  Store ( PDQ , ID , D , P , Ready ) ;
            Dequeue (PDQ )  =  Update ( PDQ , Front ( PDQ ).Proc_ID , Proc_Status ,
Executing ) ;

        exceptions
            No_Ready_Procs renames Queue_Empty ;
            ID_Not_Found renames Key_Not_Found ;
            ID_Already_Exists renames Key_Already_Exists ;

end  Process_Dispatch_Queue  .
```

Figure 5—Modula-2 implementation of dispatcher structure

of Dispatcher's concurrency control. This protocol has three levels of locking: bucket locks, queue locks, and node locks. Each of these locks secures a different part of the node structure. When a bucket is unlocked, all bucket links ("bNext" fields) are guaranteed to be intact and safe to traverse. Similarly, queue locks manage the integrity of the queue links "qPrev" and "qNext," and node locks manage the "id," "data," "status," and "priority" fields. The locking discipline will lock and hold a bucket only as long as necessary to traverse the bucket and lock the node. When the node is successfully seized and the bucket is released, the Dispatcher algorithms guarantee that no further changes will be made to the "bNext" fields thus allowing another processor to enter the bucket and traverse safely past the locked node as needed.

This "lock at the last moment and unlock at the first opportunity" philosophy runs counter to the prevailing theory of database concurrency control.[8] For general reasons of database consistency and deadlock prevention, the canonical approach to database concurrency control is to lock all resources at once and to release them at once. Dispatcher, as a special

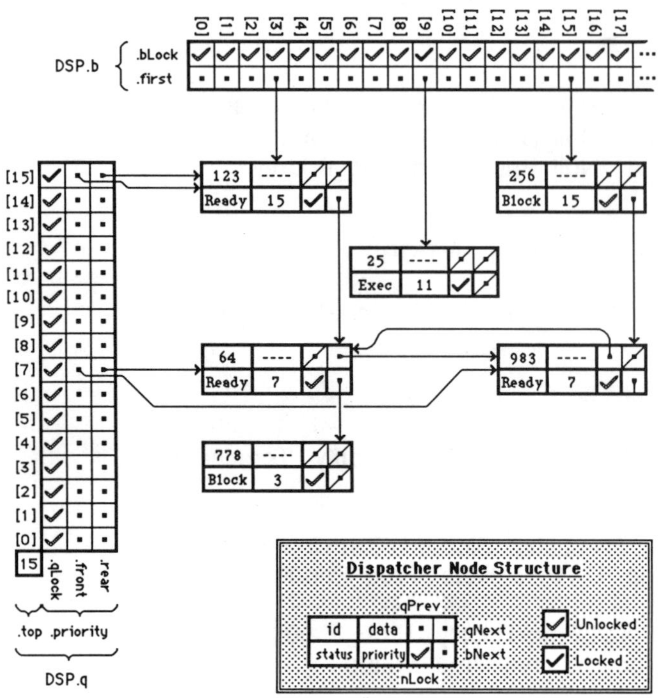

Figure 6—Dispatching data structure

purpose system data structure, satisfies a more stringent set of conditions, though, which justify the use of its looser and more efficient philosophy.

Still, the demonstration of the liveness (i.e., freedom from deadlock) of the Dispatcher protocol is a significant aspect of its development. The formal proof of liveness is developed by using the net invariant techniques of Petri net theory for colored Petri nets.[9] However, a more intuitive argument can be made based on the notion of a resource ordering.

We note that the classic deadlock situation, and the one most applicable to Dispatcher, is resource waiting. That is, deadlock occurs when processor 1 has seized resource 1, processor 2 has seized resource 2, processor 1 tries to seize resource 2, and processor 2 tries to seize resource 1. While neither processor will back off and release the resource it has, neither one can progress. This elementary, but lethal, form of deadlock arises simply because the two processors requested their resources in the opposite order. The simple resolution which Dispatcher implements, thereby satisfying the fourth requirement, is to define an ordering on resources, insist that all resources be requested according to that ordering, and to stipulate that any routine that violates this ordering will defer to the others and back off.

This observation permits us to conclude that Dispatcher is live in eight of its nine operators because they all enter via the open hash table and respect the ordering bucket→node→queue. Only Dispatch, which enters via the priority queue mechanism, violates this ordering by seizing a queue first and then attempting to seize a node. For this reason, Dispatch, and only it, implements a simple backoff subprotocol.

It is, finally, imporatnt to note that this implementation does compromise, in a small way, the second requirement's goal of O(1) performance for Dispatch. The actual complexity of Dispatch is $\theta(1)$ with the interesting caveat that its performance improves as the number of nodes in the structure increases. This latter effect arises because the probability of a back off equals the probability of a collision on the one node which is at the head of the priority queue. The probability of this collision is proportional to p/n where p is the number of processors and n is the number of nodes, a probability that decreases as n increases.

CONCLUSION

Clearly, tightly coupled, shared memory, floating control parallel processors can bring, in an elegant and incrementally extendable way, significant processing power to bear on the solution of user problems. However, we have demonstrated that neither the traditional control mechanisms and data structures nor their coarsely parallelized counterparts are effective and efficient approaches for the operating systems of this new class of computer architecture. For these new parallel processors to realize their promise in a general purpose environment, these control and data structures must be rethought and not merely translated. Failing this, we show that the contention for the essential system data structures is sufficient to fully negate the power and promise of these systems.

After a careful analysis of the requirements for a solution to the system data structure contention problem and after a thorough formal derivation of the specification for process dispatching queues, we found that there were, in fact, aspects of process dispatching queues which have gone unnoticed. These points indicated that a natural solution to the contention problem would possess three key attributes. These are: (1) a multilinked structure with orthogonal priority queue and database access mechanisms, (2) a highly differentiated structure for each access mechanism partitioning the nodes into many disjoint subsets, and (3) a fine grained, multilevel concurrency control mechanism. Dispatcher is a process dispatching queue implementation possessing these attributes and providing $\theta(1)$ performance for all operations.

REFERENCES

1. Dennis, J.B. "Data Flow Supercomputers." *IEEE Computer,* November, 1980, pp. 48–56.
2. Hwang, K. and F.A. Briggs. *Computer Architecture and Parallel Processing,* New York, NY: McGraw-Hill, 1984.
3. Hwang, K., S.P. Su, and L.M. Ni. "Vector Computer Architecture and Processing Techniques." in Yovits (ed.), *Advances in Computers,* 20, New York, NY: Academic Press, 1981, pp. 115–197.
4. Coffman, E.G. and P.J. Denning. *Operating Systems Theory,* Englewood Cliffs, NJ: Prentice-Hall, 1973.
5. Jones, D.W. "An Empirical Comparison of Priority-queue and Event Set Implementations." *CACM,* 29 (1986) 4, pp. 300–311.
6. Goerner, A.A. "Dispatcher: A Case Study in Data Type Derivation." UMKC Technical Report, March, 1986.
7. Deitel, H.M. *An Introduction to Operating Systems.* Menlo Park, CA: Addison Wesley, 1984.
8. Papadimitriou, C.H. "Serializability of Concurrent Database Updates," *Journal of the ACM,* 26 (1979) 4, pp. 631–653.
9. Jensen, K. "Coloured Petri Nets and the Invariant Method," *Theoretical Computer Science,* 14, pp. 317–336.

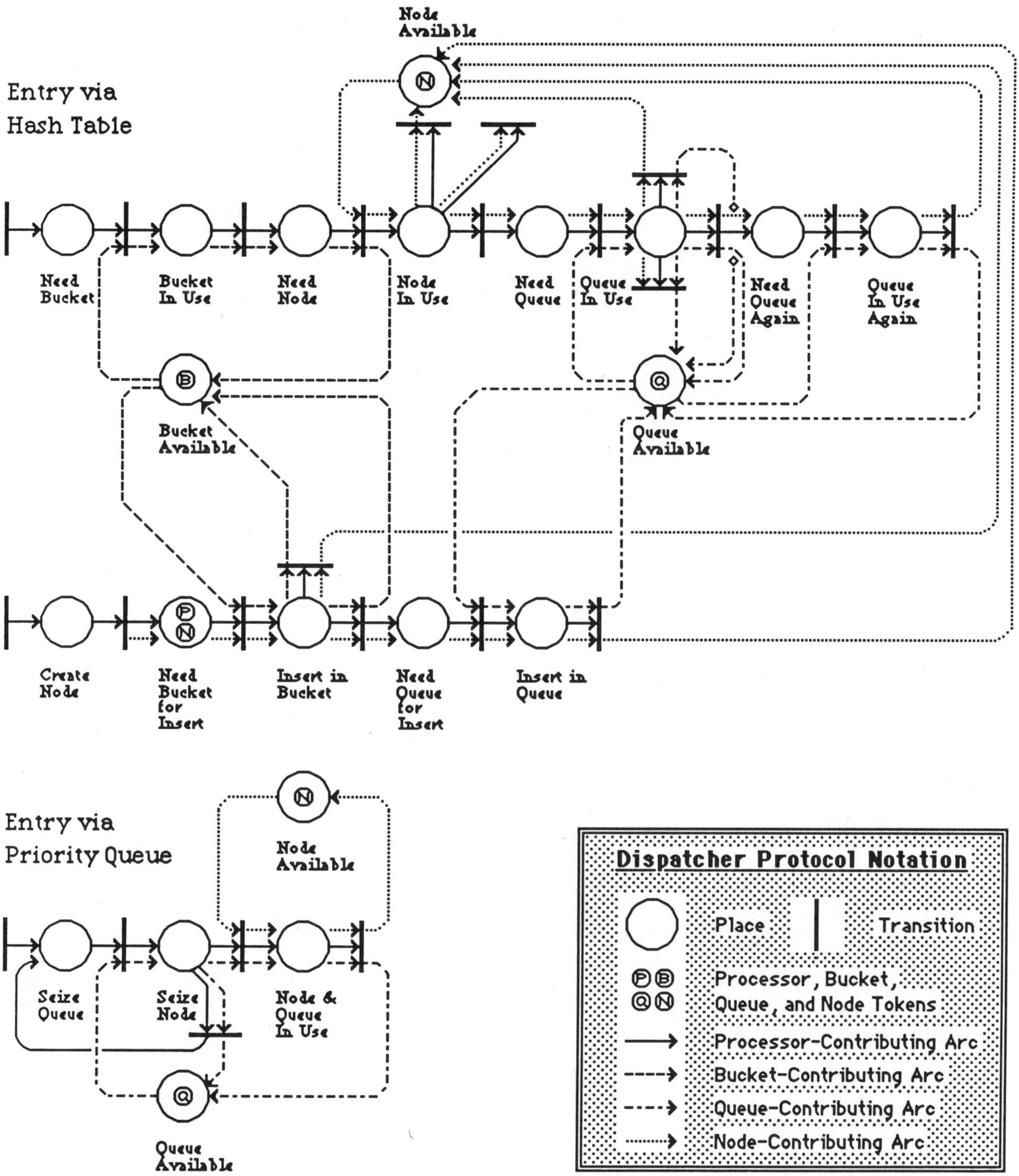

Figure 7—Dispatcher protocol

A large/fine-grain parallel dataflow model and its performance evaluation*

by BEHROOZ SHIRAZI
Southern Methodist University
Dallas, Texas
and
ALI R. HURSON
Pennsylvania State University
University Park, Pennsylvania

ABSTRACT

Data driven architecture has been widely proposed in literature as an alternative to the von-Neumann design to handle real time and fifth generation applications.[1,2] However, the network delays at the fine-grain dataflow level and handling of large arrays are some of the problems which should be addressed in these architectures. In this paper, we introduce a new model for dataflow computation which yields itself to an efficient realization of both static and dynamic dataflow architectures. Furthermore, the proposed model provides grounds for efficient handling of arrays in an SIMD fashion. Some implementation issues, the VLSI constraints, and architectural support for the model are discussed. The proposed organization achieves parallelism at the program block level (large-grain parallelism), instruction level (fine-grain parallelism), and data level (array processing). The system behavior is studied through a probabilistic simulation model and the conclusions are presented.

---

* This research was supported in part by the Department of Defense under Contract 5-25089-310

INTRODUCTION AND BACKGROUND

The recent real time applications demand a computational power of the order of 1 billion operations per second.[1,2] However, it has been proven that neither the conventional von-Neumann type computers nor the traditional concurrent systems can offer such a computational power. This computation gap is a result of factors such as: (1) the technological constraints imposed by the physical laws, (2) the sequential nature of the von-Neumann architecture, and (3) the software/hardware complexities introduced by the traditional concurrent systems. These deficiencies encourage the design and implementation of systems which are inherently parallel. The data driven computations provide the basis for such an organization. In this environment, a program is represented as an acyclic directed graph in which the nodes are operations to be performed and the arcs direct the data among the nodes. The concept of *asynchrony* embedded in the definition of a data driven architecture provides grounds for a high degree of implicit parallelism. In addition, the data driven organization eliminates the need for an updatable storage, use of identifiers, and all of their associated by-products such as global side-effects and aliasing. Such a radical departure from the sequential von-Neumann type organization has eliminated familiar concepts such as the program counter, addressing schemes, central memory, etc., with an eye towards increasing the degree of parallelism.

However, the traditional fine-grain (instruction level) data driven computation leads to the increased cost and complexity of the network, or otherwise erecting a potential bottleneck due to delays of the network for token transmission. Therefore, the large-grain data driven architectures have recently been investigated as an alternative for their fine-grain counterparts. This has led to the development of the block driven systems which explore the parallelism at the program block level.[3,4]

In addition to the network problem, the elimination of the global variables and addressing mechanisms enforces the tokens (instruction and data) to be self contained (i.e., they must carry a large volume of information in order to efficiently utilize the processing power). At the implementation phase, this violates the pin limitation constraints imposed by the current technology. Finally, the lack of updatable storage and asynchrony in the operations requires special procedures and mechanisms for handling of the data structures. The proposed data driven architectures in the literature have attempted to overcome these problems by shortening the interconnection paths and by developing new algorithms for handling the data structures and I/O operations.

A viable data driven architecture should comply with the technological constraints, offer a better performance for inherently parallel problems, reduce fine-grain communication costs, and introduce a practical and effective solution for the manipulation of the data structures. These criteria have led us to the introduction of a new model for data driven computations capable of supporting array processing. This paper discusses the proposed model, addresses the architectural support for the model, and provides a performance evaluation of the system.

THE PROPOSED MODEL

The dynamic dataflow machines allow simultaneous execution of several activations of the same block. This provides a higher potential for parallelism at the expense of more complexity. On the other hand, the static dataflow architectures provide simplicity with less parallelism. The advantages of these two classes of dataflow machines have led us to the introduction of a new model for the data driven architectures. Our goals are simplicity of the design, reduction of communication requirements, and capability to handle arrays efficiently. These goals can be achieved by distribution of the processing power among the memory cells.

In this scheme, each memory cell holds an instruction and its input operands. The system has enough processing power to perform token matching for each instruction and to carry out the operation within the cell. It is noticeable that the simple, cellular architecture will be suitable for VLSI implementation. Also, the communication requirements are reduced since the tokens only need to go through one level of networking as opposed to two or three, as in the static and dynamic models. Furthermore, the cells can be viewed as an array of processors which can be programmed in an SIMD fashion for manipulation of array structures.

Figure 1 depicts a detailed version of the proposed Processing Module (PM). The input and output ports provide communication between the PM and the outside world. The instructions of a program block are assigned to the cells, one instruction per cell. Each cell independently detects its firing condition, executes the instruction, and routes the result token to its destination cell(s) via the Sub-net. It is obvious that fine-grain data driven computation is achieved with minimal communication requirements.

A PM operates as a static data driven machine. Thus, the tokens will not carry any coloring information related to the recognition of the block activation. However, a number of these PM's can be used to efficiently emulate the dynamic data driven model through code duplication. As depicted in Figure 2, the system has a large-grain block driven organization in which program blocks can be simultaneously executed by simply duplicating the code and assigning it to a free PM.

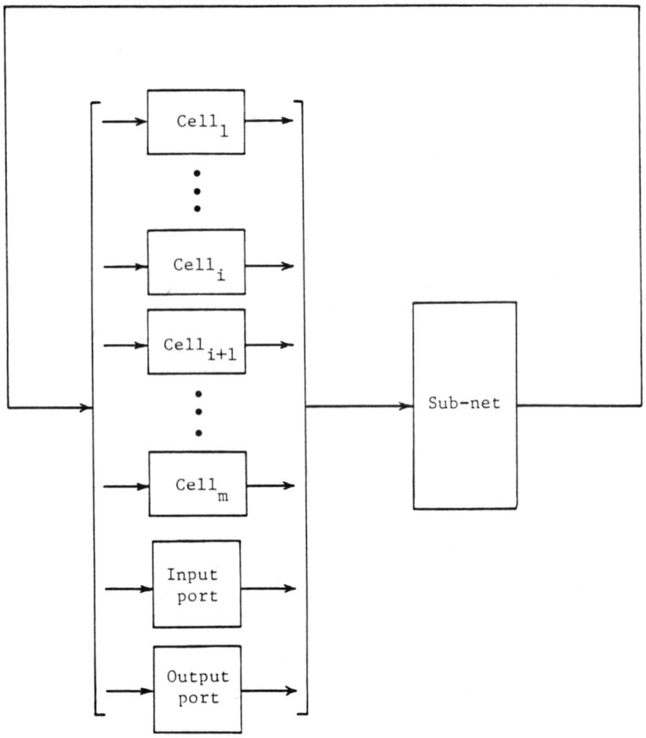

Figure 1—The organization of a processing module

The coloring information need only be kept at the program block level and individual tokens need not carry this information.

It should be mentioned that the system supports enough parallelism to tolerate network delays. For this reason and because we are concentrating on the model, not implementation, we did not specify any particular interconnection scheme for the networks used in Figures 1 and 2. Naturally, one will take advantage of the advances in interconnection technology to use the most cost efficient network during the implementation. In addition, the choice of the type of application programs to run on the system can affect the communication requirements. We assume that the application programs processed by the proposed system will be *functionl* and *block oriented* with a high degree of *locality of effect* and virtually no global variables. These characteristics imply that the independent program blocks can be executed in parallel and that the degree of communication among the instructions of a block is much higher than the inter-block communication. Therefore, we need a relatively high speed interconnection network for the sub-net (see Figure 1), while the speed requirements of the system network (see Figure 2) is not critical.

The Host Module

The *host module* holds the program blocks as they are generated by the compiler. It performs system management tasks such as: detection of the firing condition for a block, keeping track of the free processing modules, and allocation of the enabled program blocks to the processing modules. The task allocation and load balancing is performed dynamically based on the firing condition in a block driven environment. In other words, as soon as a task (function or block) is enabled (fired) for execution, it will be assigned to one of the processing modules chosen from a pool of available PM's. The firing condition consists of the availability of the input arguments for a function (block) in a functional programming environment.[10] The assumption is that the functions are strict, requiring all the inputs to be available before firing of the block.

Context switching may be used to increase the processing power utilization. Thus, if an executing function becomes inactive (e.g., due to calling another function), its current image is stored in a high speed memory in the host and the free PM can be assigned to another enabled function. The inactive block will be reactivated whenever it receives its requested item. A completely different scheme may also be employed in which an inactive block remains idle in a PM until it receives the requested data. These two schemes are compared in our simulation and the result will be discussed later.

The system management tasks are facilitated by labeling (coloring) the program blocks. A block label is a tuple (α, β), where α is the static part assigned to the block during the compilation and β is the dynamic part determined during execution. Obviously, β is used to recognize different activations of the same block during execution. For example, when a called function completes, the β part of the label of the calling function is used to determine to which activation of α the value must be returned.

The Data Structure Module

This module is used to hold the data structures and provides a smooth interface for their manipulation. The model is flexible enough to allow implementation of heaps as in,[7] I-

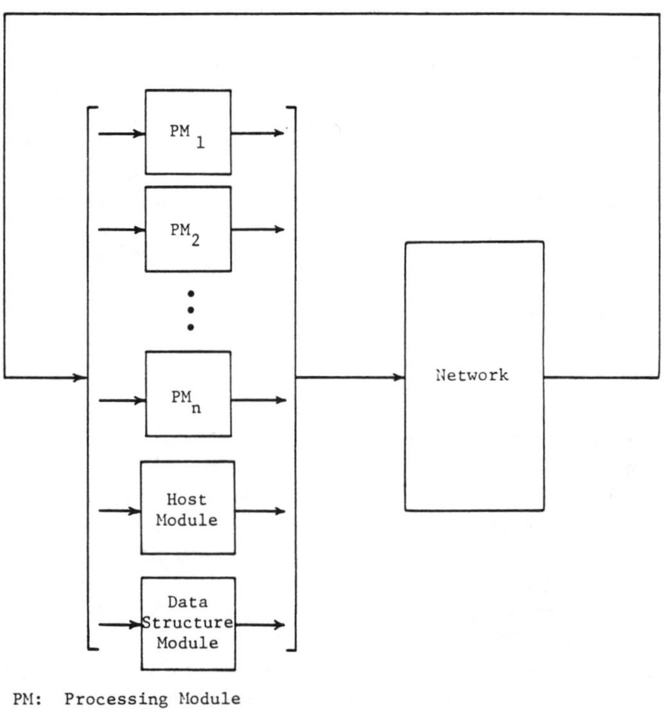

Figure 2—The overall organization of the proposed model

structures as in,[6] or array structures defined in.[11] However, one can take advantage of the functional programming style and single assignment rule to increase opportunities for parallelism. A function *consumes* its input arguments and *produces* output results. Therefore, a data structure is duplicated with a proper label (e.g., appending the dynamic label of the block to the data structure identifier) for each function to which it is passed as an input argument. However, upon the completion of the function, the input structures are deleted. The functional programming style and block driven firing conditions ensure serialization of the dependent functions which update the same data structure.

The cost of the structure duplication is justified by the reduced cost of the memory chips and the fact that the duplicated structures only exist temporarily. It should be noted that the dataflow concept has been traditionally applied to the scientific and numeric application domains in which the size of the data structures is often limited. For applications requiring the manipulation of very large data structures, the model yields itself naturally to a virtual memory organization, with the data structures stored on a secondary storage device.

Duplication of the data structures for the blocks provides opportunities for parallelism among them. However, within a block the *single assignment rule* is used to avoid the *write-after-write* problem. According to this rule, a data structure element may be assigned a value only once. The *read-before-write* problem can be avoided by using a tag bit associated to each element. If the tag is set, then the element is updated and the read can proceed. Otherwise, the read should be queued and checked for processing after each data structure update. This method was first introduced in[6] for handling of the I-structures. The tag bit can also be used for enforcing the single assignment rule during the execution.

There is a large body of scientific applications which rely heavily on manipulation of arrays.[12] Constructs such as FORALL and OVAL[13] can be used to express and exploit parallelism in SIMD type array operation. For example, FORALL defines the application of an operation to every element of an array. While, OVAL consists of application of an operation with associativity property, to the elements of an array in a binary tree fashion (e.g., OVAL.SUM (array A[1, 10])) returns the sum of the first 10 elements of array A. The proposed PM's can easily support such vector processing operations. The array of processing cells in a PM can be programmed to perform the same operation on the elements of an array. Thus as an element of an array is loaded into a PM, it can be augmented with the operation to be performed on it. This information is then used to set up the PM for the particular SIMD operation to be carried out.

The SIMD array operations are treated as function calls by a block. However, they are routed to the data structure module instead of the host module. After initiating the call, the block must wait for the result (either a value or a pointer to a data structure) to be returned from the data structure module. Upon receiving such a command, the data structure module will request access to a free PM and begins loading it with the array elements. The larger arrays have to be handled in segments. This may become expensive in OVAL operations. Let m be the number of processors and n be the size of the array. It takes $\log_2 m$ steps to apply the operations to m elements (pair-wise) and after $(n/m) \log_2 m$ steps, we will produce a temporary array of (n/m) elements. Thus, it takes $\sum_{i=1}^{k} (n/m^i) \log_2^i m$ steps to generate the final result, where $k = \log_m n$.

THE IMPLEMENTATION ISSUES AND ARCHITECTURAL SUPPORT

Due to the space limitations it is not possible to discuss, in detail, a complete implementation of the model. The interested readers are referred to.[10] However, we will briefly introduce an implementation through a presentation of the flow of operations and major characteristics of the architecture. This architecture is used in the simulation of the model which will be discussed in the next section.

The Processing Modules

It is obvious that the implementation cost of the model will become prohibitively expensive if the cells (refer to Figure 1) are complex. Therefore, we envision the cells to be simple processors called Elementary processing Units (E-unit) which can perform operations such as addition, subtraction, AND, OR, etc. The more complex operations are to be routed to coprocessors which are a collection of Functional Units (F-units). Thus, the cells of a PM are divided into E-units and F-units. The E-units are our basic cells to which the instructions and their input data are assigned. The flow of operations in an E-unit is presented in the Petri-net of Figure 3. As shown

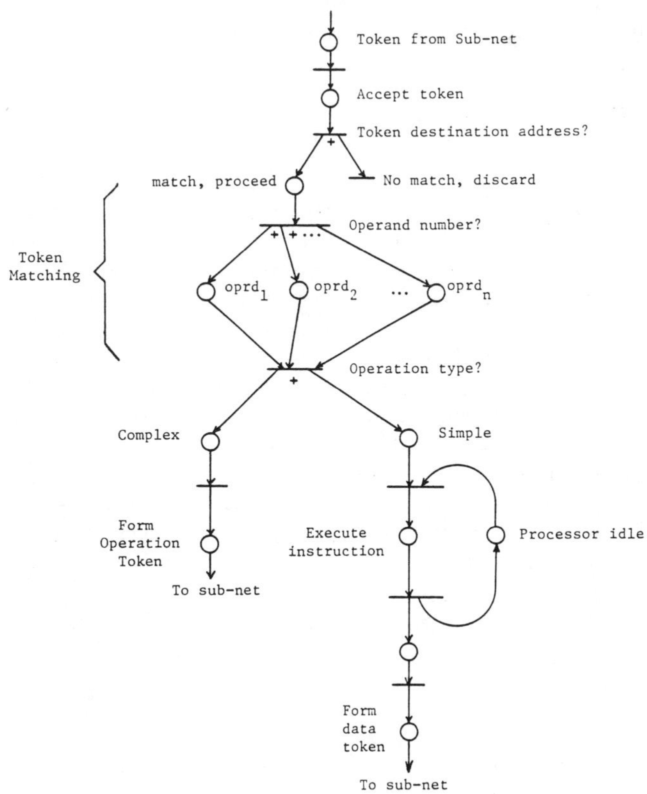

Figure 3—The flow of operations in an E-unit

in this figure, an E-unit matches the input tokens, performs simple operations, and forms operation packets for complex operations to be routed to the sub-net. An F-unit is simply a hardware implemented functional unit which performs a specific operation on the input operation token and sends the result to the corresponding E-unit (indicated by the input token) through the sub-net.

Granted the removal of the technical problems in Wafer-Scale Integration (WSI),[14,15] we suggest the processing modules be implemented on silicon wafers. WSI uses the entire wafer, instead of dicing, to condense more functionality into a single device. The intra-block communication among E- and F-units is, therefore, improved by eliminating the delays and difficulties associated to the multichip systems. However, there are some problems with WSI (heat removal, yield, etc.) which require further research and development in this area.

As previously mentioned, the sub-net can be any $n \times n$ interconnection network with a reasonable performance. We intend to investigate a variety of networks, beginning with an arbitration network. The choice of the arbitration network stems from performance and implementation issues. Dias and Jump[16] have shown that arbitration networks with buffering capability between the stages can match the performance of an equivalent crossbar network. In addition, the simple structure of these networks allows their easy implementation by WSI technology (i.e., crossovers and long parallel communication lines are avoided).

The sub-net, as an arbitration network, funnels the output tokens from the E-units and F-units in a pipeline fashion. The funneled tokens are either sent to the outside world via the output ports or distributed among the E-units and F-units through a common data bus. The PM is loaded via the input port in a bit-parallel word-serial pipeline method.

The Host and Data Structure Modules

The main function of the host module is to dynamically manage (allocate/deallocate) the program blocks during the execution using the dataflow concept as the primary task allocation principle (i.e., a function is assigned to a free processing module when it receives its input arguments). Our assumption, at this point, is that the compiler decomposes the program into blocks which best match the size of a PM. Therefore, a large logical block will be decomposed into several sequentially executable smaller physical blocks. If experimentation indicates that this scheme serializes the program extensively, we can extend the model by providing local memories for each PM. In this case, large blocks will be stored in the local memory of a PM and are processed segment by segment through some paging scheme.

The system management functions could be facilitated by a set of hardware tables which determine the status of the system during its operations. For example, the block assignment table determines the status of a block (passive, active, or inactive), while the firing condition table keeps track of the input arguments to a block and detects the firing condition for it. To improve the performance, the operations on the status tables are performed in associative fashion. This has two advantages: (1) the search of the tables are performed in parallel, and (2) we can have overlap of operation for different system operations.[10]

The host module's memory has a high-order interleaved organization in which different program blocks are assigned to different memory modules. This allows simultaneous loading/unloading of blocks among several PM's. In this particular architecture, the host and the PM's are organized in a master-slave organization with direct connections between the host and each of the PM's. This is because of the need for block transfers between the host and PM's, and due to the limited intra-block communication in a functional programming environment. However, as we will discuss later, we are considering other protocols such as a distributed host environment.

The data structure module is composed of a Data Structure Memory (DSM) and a Data Structure Processor (DSP). The DSM holds the data structures used in the data flow programs as well as the temporary data structures which are created to ensure the parallelism among different blocks. The interleaved organization of the DSM allows simultaneous access to many elements. The DSP provides smooth access to the data structures, manages the data structure memory, and initiates the execution of vector processing instructions.

The System VLSI Complexity

In order to comply with the current technology in the design of the proposed system, modularity has been explored at three levels (3-dimensional modular system). First, the architecture is composed of a few building blocks which are duplicated many times across the system (e.g., processing modules). Second, each processing module is composed of a group of basic building blocks (e.g., E-units and F-units). Third, the organization of each E-unit and F-unit is composed of a number of basic cells which are duplicated in a two dimensional space (see Hurson and Shirazi,[17] for example).

The VLSI time and space complexities of the proposed system have been evaluated through the analysis of its major components. A detailed discussion of such analysis is out of the scope of this paper, but can be found in Hurson and Shirazi.[17] Table I summarizes the geometry area and the timing delay of some of the system major components.

THE SYSTEM PERFORMANCE EVALUATION

The purpose of this performance evaluation is to study the behavior of the system and to recognize the weak points and the bottlenecks. It is not our intention to run complete programs on the simulator and compare it against the existing data driven machines; although such a study is currently underway and the results will soon be available. As such, the system simulation is based on an event-driven model which passes tokens among different resources. The token generation and routing is based on a probabilistic model reflecting the program characteristics such as the degree of parallelism in a block, execution delay of a block, number of function calls, and the type of data structure operations.

Unit	Geometry Area[1]	Timing (ηsec)[2]
E-unit	4mm×4mm	250
Sub-net	40mm×20mm[3]	150[4]
F-unit (Multiplier)[5]	10mm×10mm	97
Host Module (Associative Memory[6])	10mm×5mm	10

1. $\lambda = 2.5\ \mu m$.
2. Average inverter delay=0.3 ηsec.
3. 32-input, 4-output arbitration network, routing 64 bits in parallel.
4. Assuming no conflicts while going through the network.
5. Reference 18.
6. Reference 19.

TABLE I—The VLSI characteristics of the proposed architecture

The timing delays are based on either the VLSI timing analysis of the designed components or timing information obtained for the existing units. For example, loading of a block takes $\log_2 n\Delta t$ to fill the arbitration network pipeline plus $(n-1)\Delta t$ to go through the pipe, where n is the number of cells in a PM or the block size, whichever is less, and Δt is the delay of an arbitration switch in the sub-net.

In order to obtain realistic statistics about the execution delay of a function and its degree of parallelism, we could not rely on a probabilistic simulation model. Therefore, an emulator was written which could mimic the operations of a processing module. We were then able to write actual dataflow programs (small hand compiled functions) and run them on the emulator. The results are presented in Table II.

The system simulator would then build a complete program, running in parallel on different PM's, from these functions. The program blocks are generated by randomly selecting one of the functions and augmenting it with some global program characteristics such as function calls, data structure operations, and enabling other functions at the completion of the current function. For example, in one experiment, the number of function calls in a block is uniformly distributed between 0 and 4, while the block may enable from 0 to 3 other blocks at the end of its completion (called functions are

Program	Average degree of parallelism during execution	Program run time (μsec)	MIPS
Quadratic equation	1.01	25.0	0.44
Standard deviation	1.36	26.2	0.53
Simple data transformation	1.48	33.4	4.74
X^n, n=3	1.27	7.2	3.89
n!, n=10	1.24	23.7	4.47
$\int_0^1 x^2 dx$	1.06	21.2	3.07
$\sum_{i=1}^{n} i$, n=24	0.68	9.7	2.47

TABLE II—The processing module emulation results, running actual dataflow programs (number of E-units = 32)

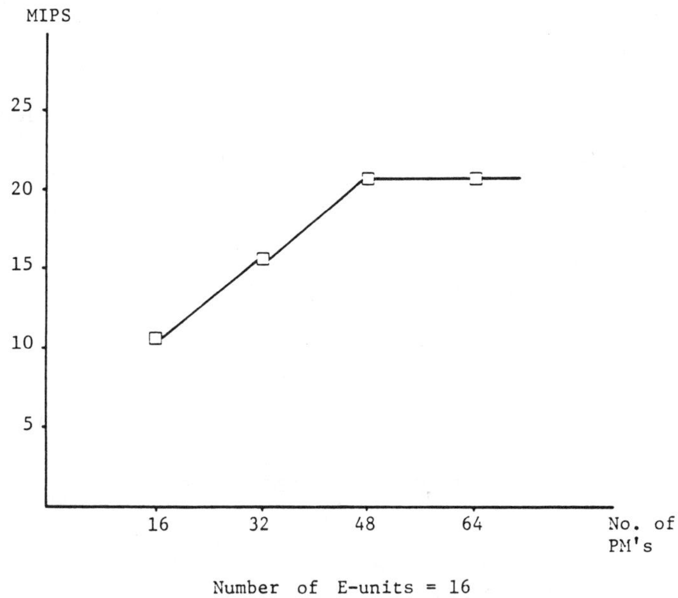

Figure 4—The MIPS performance of the proposed architecture

treated differently; they only return a value to the calling block).

Figure 4 depicts a plot of the MIPS (Millions of Instructions Per Second) performance of the system against the number of processing modules. The number of E-units in a PM is fixed at 32, while the MIPS figures presented are the average of the results collected from a number of simulations. It is noticeable that the performance saturates relatively fast and addition of the PM's does not improve the MIPS. Although not presented here, the processor utilization study also reflected a similar behavior (i.e., the PM utilization decreased as the number of PM's was increased).

Our first attempt to seek the origin of the problem was to study the loading/unloading of the blocks. The assumption was that the blocks can be loaded/unloaded in parallel from/to different modules of an interleaved memory in the host. However, instead of a bit-parallel word-serial scheme (as in the previous case), we employed a bit-serial word-parallel method. As depicted in Figure 5, this change did not improve the performance (i.e., there was no statistically significant difference). Therefore, we focused our attention toward the suspicious bottleneck, namely the host manager. In the next study, we reduced the host module overhead by a factor of 5. The results of this experiment are depicted in Figure 6. Notice that performance has improved by a factor of 2 to 5, but saturates around 64 PM due to overwhelming host overhead. As a result, we are currently studying a variation of the model in which the host tasks are distributed among a number of sub-hosts and each sub-host controls a number of PM's in a tree fashion. This model allows a better fault tolerance and scalability compared to the original model.

In the above experiments we used a context switching scheme to improve the processor utilization. In other words, an idle block is removed from a PM and reinstated whenever it receives the requested data such as function call or SIMD type array operation. If we relax the high processor utilization

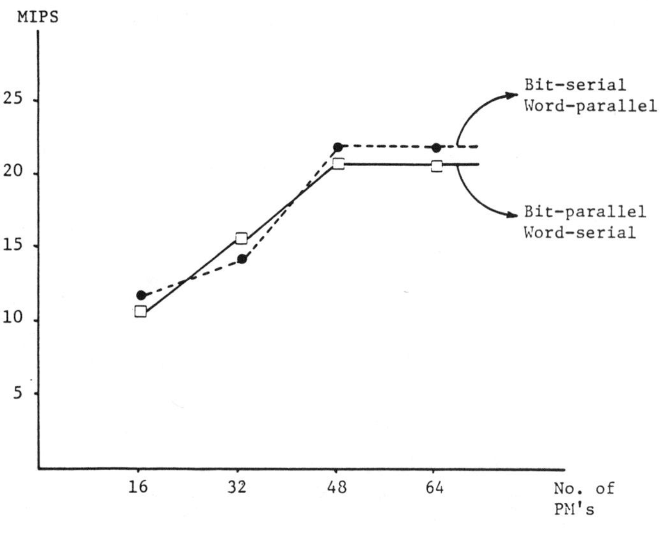

Figure 5—A comparison of the two loading/unloading schemes

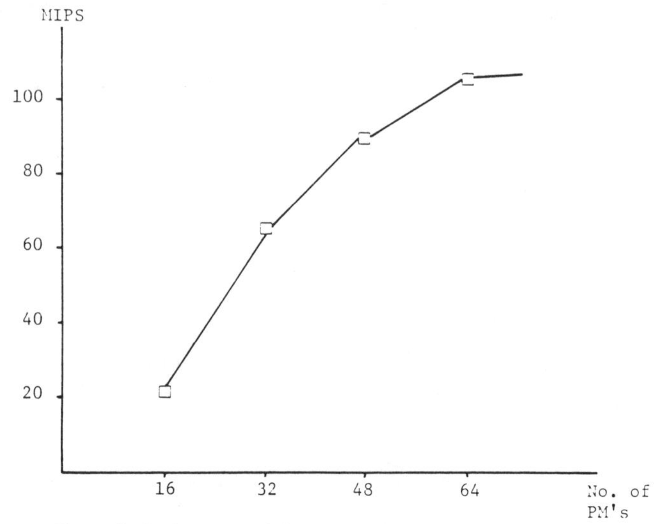

Figure 6—Performance of the system with the reduced host module overhead

requirement, an idle block may remain in a PM until its reactivation conditions are satisfied. To avoid a deadlock problem, if all the PM's are occupied, we will begin preempting the inactive blocks in a last-in-first-out basis. The major advantage of this scheme is that it reduces the number of block transfers between the host and PM's, and thus, reduces the host module overhead for setting up the blocks for transmission.

The simulator was modified to reflect the new policy "no context switching as much as possible" and the results were very encouraging. The MIPS performance was improved from 45% in case of 16 PM's to 100% in case of 64 PM's, reaching a performance of more than 200 MIPS. The processor utilization was reduced by about 40% in case of 16 PM's to about 10% in case of 64 PM's. Therefore, one can double the speed at virtually no processor utilization cost when the number of processing modules is large, more than 64.

CONCLUSION

This paper has introduced a new model for dataflow architectures based on the data driven (fine-grain parallelism) and block driven (large-grain parallelism) principles. The model is flexible enough to support both static and dynamic dataflow computation models as well as vector processing operations. It also provides opportunities for matching the underlying architecture with semantics of the functional dataflow languages. The model behavior was studied through the simulation of a system which represents an implementation of the model. The results indicated that a central host module can be the bottleneck and thus, a distributed control over the processing modules is more desirable. It was also concluded that given a large number of processors, in excess of 64, it is more advantageous to leave the inactive blocks in a processing module and only reallocate an idle module when there are no free processing modules available.

REFERENCES

1. Bernhard, R. "Computing at the Speed Limit." *IEEE Spectrum,* July, 1982, pp. 26–31.
2. Treleaven, P.C. and I.G. Lima. "Japan's Fifth-Generation Computer Systems." *Computer,* August, 1982, pp. 79–88.
3. Lecouffe, M.P. "Architecture of a Multiprocessur Using Data Flow at a Program Block Level." *Proc. of the 1981 Int'l Conf. on Parallel Processing,* August, 1981, pp. 160–161.
4. Chang, T.L. and P.D. Fisher. "A Block-Driven Data Flow Processor," *Proc. of the 1981 Int'l Conf. on Parallel Processing,* August, 1981, pp. 151–155.
5. Gurd, J.R., C.C. Kirkham, and I. Watson. "The Manchester Prototype Dataflow Computer." *Comm. of the ACM,* 28 (1985) 1, pp. 34–52.
6. Arvind, V. Kathail, and K. Pingali. "A Processing Element for a Large Multiple Processor Dataflow Machine." *1980 Int'l Conf. on Circuits and Computers,* October, 1980, pp. 601–605.
7. Dennis, J.B. "First Version of a Data Flow Procedure Language." *MAC Tech. Memorandum 61,* LCS/MIT, Cambridge, Massachusetts, May, 1975.
8. Dennis, J.B., G.R. Gao, and K.W. Todd. "Modeling the Weather with a Data Flow Supercomputer." *IEEE Trans. on Computers,* c-33 (1984) 7, pp. 592–603.
9. Cornish, M. "The TI Dataflow Architectures—The Power of Concurrency for Avionics." *Proc. 3rd Conf. Digital Avionics Systems,* 1979, pp. 19–25.
10. Shirazi, B. "WDDM—A Wafer-Scale Data Driven Multiprocessor." Ph.D. Dissertation, University of Oklahoma, July, 1985.
11. Patnáik, L.M., R. Govindarajan, and N.S. Ramadoss. "Design and Performance Evaluation of EXMAN: An EXtended MANchester Data Flow Computer." *IEEE Trans. on Computers,* c-35 (1986) 3, pp. 229–244.
12. Wetherell, C. "Desgin Considerations for Array Processing Languages." *Computer Science Group,* University of California at Davis, 1980.
13. McGraw, J.R. "The VAL Language Description and Analysis." UCRL-83251, Lawrence Livermore Laboratory, Dec., 1980.
14. McDonald, JF., E.H. Rogers, K. Rose, and A.J. Steckl. "The Trials of Wafer-Scale Integration." *IEEE Spectrum,* 21 (1984) 10, pp. 32–39.
15. Johnson, R.R. "The Significance of Wafer Scale Integration in Computer Design." *Proc. ICCD '84,* October, 1984, pp. 101–105.
16. Dias, D.M. and J.R. Jump. "Packet Switching Interconnection Networks for Modular Systems." *Computer,* 14 (1981) 12, pp. 43–53.
17. Hurson, A.R. and B. Shirazi. "A Wafer-Scale Data Driven Multiprocessor." *The 29th Int'l Symp. on Mini & Micro Computers* (MIMI '85), June, 1985, pp. 115–119.
18. Hurson, A.R. and B. Shirazi. "A Class of Systolic Multiplier Units for VLSI Technology." *Int'l Journal of Computer & Information Sciences,* 14 (1985) 5.
19. Hurson, A.R. and B. Shirazi. "The Design of a Hardware Recognizer for Utilization in Scanning Operations." *1985 ACM 13th Annual Computer Science Conf.,* March, 1985, pp. 112–119.

Rule partitioning versus task sharing in parallel processing of universal production systems

by HEE WON
SUNY at Buffalo
Amherst, New York

ABSTRACT

Most research efforts in parallel processing of production systems have focused on the rule partitioning method. This method cannot be successfully applied to the universal production systems that allow different inference mechanisms, different scopes of WM (working memory) testing, different rates of WM changes, and which do not use empirical data for partitioning.

Parallel memory configuration is essential for memory intensive applications such as production systems. Maximum parallelism cannot be achieved without sufficient memory bandwidth.

A new parallel processing method that can run the universal production systems on a parallel memory configuration is proposed, and is compared with the rule partitioning method.

INTRODUCTION

Three main issues will be addressed: how to efficiently execute parallel production systems, the importance of parallel memory for the parallel production system, and the necessity of architecture that is general enough to be applicable to universal production systems.

Most parallel production systems try to partition the set of rules by analyzing the parallel executability of the set. However, a rule can be characterized differently, depending on where it is used. A rule can be involved in more than one task. The optimal partitioning of rules changes as the task changes. Characterizing a rule according to a task is necessary in exploiting the maximum parallelism.

The main computation of the production systems is to match the condition elements to the data base.[1] It requires sifting vast amounts of information. Thus parallel memory is the key factor determining the success of parallel processing. However, most parallel production systems ignore the necessity of parallel memory. Parallel CPUs cannot be fully utilized if the information needed is not readily available because of limited memory bandwidth. Without parallel memory, the true parallel processing cannot be achieved in the production system.

In this paper, a set of heterogeneous processors are loosely coupled to form a multiprocessor system rather than a special parallel processing system such as a tree machine.[2] This configuration is more practical and less expensive because it can be easily built by connecting already existing computers rather than building a new computer system.

Another deficiency we can find in most parallel production systems is the lack of universality. Most proposed systems are based on a very narrow domain. Some proposals are only good for forward inference chaining while others specialize in backward chaining. More restrictions are imposed on its applicability by requiring empirical data to produce the optimal mapping of the rule to the parallel processor.[3]

A task sharing concept is introduced to solve the problems mentioned above. To execute the concept efficiently, a parallel memory system is advocated.

PRODUCTION SYSTEMS

Production systems consist of three basic components: a set of rules, a data base, and an interpreter for the rules.

A rule consists of a conjunction of condition elements called the left hand side (LHS) and a set of actions called the right hand side (RHS). A set of rules called productions make up the production memory (PM). Rules and productions are interchangeably used in the following discussion.

The data base contains facts and assertions. The rules act upon this data to update the state of knowledge by modifying the data base. The data base is called working memory (WM).

The interpreter may be seen as a select-execute loop in which one rule applicable to the current state of the data base is chosen and then executed. Its action results in a modified data base, and the select phase begins again. A well known OPS5 interpreter goes through the following phases in the select-execute cycle[4]:

1. MATCH: Determines which productions are satisfied in the current state of the working memory.
2. CONFLICT RESOLUTION: One of the matched productions is selected for execution based on some predefined criteria.
3. ACT: The actions specified in the RHS of the selected production are executed.

PARALLEL PRODUCTION SYSTEMS

Many parallel production systems have been proposed with the goal of accelerating the rule firing rate of each cycle.[2,3,5]

Most methods partition the rules and assign each partition to different processors. Each partition can be either a rule or set of rules that are not usually affected by the same set of working memory changes. Common characteristics of the proposed algorithms are: (1) Partitioning is made in compile time, and (2) Rule partitions are disjoint subsets. The method can be termed "Rule Partitioning" in the sense that the interdependency and the possibility of parallel execution between rules are analyzed and used as criteria of the partitioning. Thus this method tries to find the global optimum.

Another approach will be to find the local optimum. Execution of the production systems consists of tasks. The exploitation of parallelism within a task is the main idea of the task sharing algorithm. But the sequence of tasks is determined in run time. Therefore careful consideration should be given to how to make efficient run time scheduling.

ASSUMED ARCHITECTURE AND UNIVERSAL PRODUCTION SYSTEMS

The following discussion is based on a very general and realistic processing environment.

A loosely coupled heterogeneous parallel processing architecture is assumed. Each processor can store large programs and execute them independently. Each processor varies in its speed and size. Some processors might have very powerful floating point ALUs while the others can have specialized I/O units. One of the processors is used for user interface. The processors communicate through a simple bus structure.

Universal production systems are to be run on the assumed architecture. In the universal production systems, the inference mechanism can be forward or backward, or both. The condition element (LHS) of each rule requires different processing times, different resources, and different scopes of WM testing. Some condition elements might require floating point operation while others might need user's response to complete the evaluation. Global WM tests can be accommodated in the universal systems. The action (RHS) part can also have varieties of choices. The rate of change in WM can be massive or limited. The number of rules affected by a change in WM might vary to a great degree.

RULE PARTITIONING

In general, the rule partitioning method proceeds as follows:

1. Assign rules that are likely to be active at the same time to different processors.
2. Assign the WM elements corresponding to the condition elements of the allocated rules to the same processor. The WM allocation does not necessarily lead to disjoint WM partitions.
3. Repeat the following until no further rule can be fired.
   a. For each change in WM, broadcast the change to all processors.
   b. All processors where local WM has been changed conduct the match process and report results to the control processor.
   c. The control processor identifies a single rule for execution, and the action part becomes the next change in WM.

This partitioning method suffers from several significant problems in executing the universal production systems on parallel processing systems:

1. Predicting optimal partitioning is impossible in the universal production systems. For example, optimal partition for the forward chaining method is no longer optimal for the other inference methods.
2. Balancing the load amongst the processors requires predicting the processing time of each individual production in addition to the parallel executability.
3. Parallel executability might adversely effect the attention mechanism. Attention does not stay focused when a condition element shared by two rules which belong to different tasks is activated.
4. Compile time scheduling does not reflect the dynamic behavior which is necessary to make the true optimal rule partitioning.
5. Run time scheduling takes too much overhead because the entire PM and WM should be rearranged in every cycle.

TASK SHARING

Processing Grain

Different levels of processing can be defined in the production systems.

1. System level: Several independent production systems can be integrated to build one large production system.
2. Task level: Execution of a production system is made of tasks such as a series of goals or a sequence of WM changes.
3. Rule level: Each individual rule can be found under the task level.
4. Match level: Evaluating a rule involves matching condition elements to WM elements.
5. Selection level: Selecting a rule to fire requires conflict resolving task.
6. Action level: Firing a rule consists of WM-change tasks.

Parallel executability can be found within a level or across the levels. In system level, parallelism can be found if more than one production system can be concurrently activated to solve the problem of the larger production system. At the task level, sequential execution should be enforced if the next task cannot be determined before the current task is completed. One the other hand, parallel execution can be possible at the task level if more than one task can be initiated simultaneously.[6] Most efforts for parallel production systems have focused on the rule level because each rule can be evaluated independently. Very fine grain parallelism can be found within match level, selection level, or action level. Additional parallelism can be found across these levels.

How to exploit the existing parallelism depends on how the processing element is assigned to the available resources. In system level, parallel processing can be achieved by cooperatively executing individual production systems assigned to the different processors. The parallel processing method in the task level is discussed in the following section.

Task Sharing

First the difference between Rule Partitioning and Task Sharing should be made clear. In Rule Partitioning, the rules themselves are partitioned and assigned to different processors in compile time. Thus only small portions of rules are assigned to each processor. In Task Sharing, no partition is made amongst the rules. Each processor has entire PM and WM. However every processor shares the execution of the task by running different rules. The decision as to which processor executes which rule is made dynamically. This dynamic scheduling can be done without much overhead because no transference of rules across the processors is necessary. The way in which every processor can access the entire PM and WM eliminates the overhead involved in rearranging the PM and WM. The price to pay is, of course, the duplication of PM and WM in every processor.

Task Sharing Algorithm

Heterogeneous processors connected to a bus are the underlying architecture on which this algorithm is based. The main idea of this algorithm is to let each processor autonomously schedule its task. The coordination of the system is maintained by the fact that all the processors follow the same scheduling strategy, and the scheduling activity is broadcasted to all other processors if it is necessary.

Even distribution of the load to the processors should be carefully planned. For a given task, a set of rules should be assigned to the processors in an optimal way. The relationship between the ability of the processor and the computational need of the rule will determine how well a set of the rules will map onto a parallel processor. Thus the abilities of the processors and the availability of each processor should be known to the algorithm. The algorithm also should be intelligent enough to identify the computational need of each individual rule. For example, special condition elements such as user interface elements should be identified in compile time so that the information is readily available in run time. The algorithm can be described as follows.

1. Task Identification: For a given task such as establishing a goal in backward chaining or executing a match phase for each WM change in forward chaining, every processor identifies the relevant set of rules and forms a task table. The task table holds the scheduling information and the condition element matching information.
2. Initial Task Scheduling: All the processors simultaneously execute the first batch of scheduling. Each rule is characterized by its special need such as user input or floating point operation or special I/O operation. For example, a rule with floating point operation condition elements should be assigned to a processor having floating point ALU. The assignment of two rules with identical characteristics to two identical processors is determined by its rule order and the processor order which are known throughout the system. The characteristic or the rule order of the current set of rules can be identified consistently throughout the processors so that consistency of scheduling can be maintained despite its autonomous scheduling strategy. Every processor identifies its rule to execute in addition to identifying the assignment of the rest of the rules to the other processors.
3. Match: Repeat the following until all the relevant rules for the current task are matched.
   a. Every processor independently matches the rule assigned to it.
   b. Any processor having finished its match process identifies the next rule to execute, and broadcasts its results of matches (fail or success and/or its instantiated variables) with the new scheduling information.
   c. As soon as the message is received by all processors, every processor updates its task table. A possible scheduling conflict between two processors should be resolved by some arbitration method.
4. Conflict Resolution: This process can be executed independently and concurrently by every processor. The results will be the same because every processor has the same set of matched rules and the same conflict resolution strategy.
5. Act: The same action is taken autonomously and consistently throughout the system.

Further overlapping between phases of the selection-execution cycle can be achieved. When some of the processors are busy in matching the last portions of the active rules, the idle processors can proceed to the next phase so that the conflict resolution can be completed as soon as the last result of the match phase is available.

RULE PARTITIONING VS. TASK SHARING

1. Load balance: In rule partitioning, it is hard to balance the load among the processors. Balancing the load for one cycle might conflict with the balance requirement of the next cycle. Balancing the load for the forward chaining does not coincide with that of backward chaining. Moreover, evenly distributing the same number of active rules to the processors does not guarantee the load balance because execution time of each rule varies. In the worst case, the parallel processor might degrade to the serial processor when all the active rules reside in the same processor from cycle to cycle.
   In task sharing, optimal load balance is always maintained by dynamically assigning an even share of rules to the processors. A processor can process several short rules while another processor processes a long rule. A processor can grab another rule to process as soon as it has finished processing the current rule. Adaptive scheduling can be achieved by matching the need of a rule with the ability of a processor. Thus this method always guarantees optimal load balance regardless of unpredictable execution environment or execution time differences among rules.
2. Communication: In match phase, two different kinds of communications can be observed: one for testing WM, the other for reporting the matched results.
   In task sharing, no communication is necessary for testing WM because entire WM is available within the same processor. In rule partitioning, it depends on how to allocate WM. If no duplication of WM is allowed, then quite a large amount of communication is required to test the WM elements which are not available within the same processor. The situation is aggravated if global WM test is required. To eliminate communication of this kind necessitates the duplication of part or the entire WM.
   In reporting the matched result, the rule partitioning has advantage over the task sharing. Rule partitioning needs to report the results of successful matches (or the results of part of successful matches if only local maximum needs to be considered in the conflict resolution phase). In task sharing, all the results of the matches with the scheduling information need to be broadcasted to the other processors.
   Rule partitioning needs to broadcast the actions of se-

lected rule(s) after resolving the conflict while task sharing does not because every processor can resolve the conflict autonomously.

3. Universality: Three different criteria can be used to measure the universality of the algorithm: hardware, software, and application. The method should be applicable to different hardware configurations and be able to take advantage of it. It should allow dynamic software environments. It should be flexible enough to adopt new applications without difficulty. None of these important issues have been addressed in the rule partitioning methods published so far. However, the task sharing method considers all of these issues. Hardware specification can be integrated into the scheduling scheme to take advantage of it. Users can choose or change any inference mechanisms at any time without degrading the system performance. New applications can be run efficiently without extracting empirical statistics or analyzing rule dependency in advance.
4. Fault Tolerance: The task sharing method has fault tolerance which the rule partitioning method does not have. The task sharing method has achieved fault tolerance while achieving parallel processing. Each processor keeps the record of execution status relevant to the current task as well as it own copy of the scheduling mechanism, and the entire PM and WM and interpreter. This complete distribution strategy eliminates need for any hardcore element like a control processor for scheduling purposes. Any partial breakdown of the system does not effect the recovery of the overall system.
5. Hardware Requirement: Three different configurations can be envisioned in the multiprocessor system. At the low end multiple CPUs are connected to a single memory. This method might suffer from severe memory contention when that method is applied to a memory intensive application such as a production system. In the middle we can find multiple CPUs connected to shared memories via interconnection networks. This method might relieve some of the memory contention. But this solution is still far from being universal.
At the high end we can find the architecture on which task sharing is based. Each processor has its own memory which can hold the entire PM and WM. A single bus is used to connect the multiple processors. The only traffic on this bus will be the broadcasting of the matched result. All other information is readily available in each processor system including the scheduling algorithm. This method might be expensive. However, for a memory intensive application like the production systems, the importance of parallel memory outweighs that of parallel CPUs.

EXTENSION OF THE ALGORITHM

The algorithm is based on the assumption that all of the PM and WM can be stored within a processor. But only part of PM and WM can be brought into the internal memory as the volume of PM and WM grows. Every processor has its own disk where the entire PM and WM resides.

The question is: how to efficiently bring in the necessary PM and WM for a given task. It takes too much time for every processor to search the entire PM and WM residing in disk. One way of solving this problem is to partition the search area. Every processor can search for different portions of PM and WM without disk interference because every processor has its own disk under its control. After bringing in different portions of PM and WM into different processors, exchanging portions of PM and WM throughout the system is necessary for every processor to have entire PM and WM relevant to the current task. Again duplication of PM and WM in disks can help to decrease the disk search time.

A possible improvement is to decrease the communication overhead in exchanging portions of PM and WM. Partial exchange, like transferring only special rules to special processors and keeping the rest as local tasks, can decrease the communication overhead at the expense of imperfect load balancing. For example, a rule requiring user response must be assigned to the processor having a user terminal while the others can be executed in any processors.

CONCLUSION

This paper has pointed out the limitation of the rule partitioning method. The method searches for the global optimum by analyzing the parallel executability of the rules in compile time. The task sharing method has been proposed to analyze the parallelism in the context of tasks. The local optimum of a given task can be found by analyzing parallel executability in run time. This local optimum should be used to map the productions to the parallel processors in run time.

Parallel memory is essential to execute memory intensive applications such as production systems. Parallel CPUs can access the same information simultaneously because each processor has its own memory where the entire PM and WM is available. Parallel CPUs cannot be fully utilized without parallel memory. This duplication of PM and WM for every processor can decrease the overhead incurred by the run time scheduling method.

The universal system is needed in a growing area like the production systems. A special architecture based on a special algorithm will suffer from its shortcoming as the field expands. The task sharing scheme on the heterogeneous processors with parallel memory is general enough to afford the universal production systems.

REFERENCES

1. Gupta, A. and C. L. Forgy. "Measurements on Production Systems." Technical Report CMU-CS-83-167, Dept. of Computer Science, Carnegie-Mellon University.
2. Stolfo, S. and D. Miranker. "DADO: A Parallel Processor for Expert Systems." *The Proceedings of International Conference on Parallel Processing*, 1984, pp. 74–82.
3. Oflazer, K., "Partitioning in Parallel Processing of Production Systems." *The Proceedings of International Conference on Parallel Processing*, 1984, pp. 92–100.
4. Forgy, C. L. "OPS5 User's Manual." Technical Report CMU-CS-81-185, Dept. of Computer Science, Carnegie-Mellon University.
5. Tenorio, M. F. M. and D. I. Moldovan. "Mapping Production Systems into Multiprocessors." *The Proceedings of International Conference on Parallel Processing*, 1985, pp. 56–62.
6. Kumon, K., H. Masuzawa, A. Itashiki, K. Satoh, and Y. Sohma. "KABUWAKE: A New Parallel Inference Method and Its Evaluation." *The Proceedings of 1986 Spring COMPCON*, pp. 168–172.

Warp architecture: From prototype to production

by MARCO ANNARATONE, E. ARNOULD, R. COHN, T. GROSS, H. T. KUNG, M. LAM, O. MENZILCIOGLU, K. SAROCKY, J. SENKO, and Jon A. WEBB
Carnegie Mellon University
Pittsburgh, Pennsylvania

ABSTRACT

The Warp machine* is a high-performance systolic array computer with a linear array of 10 or more cells, each of which is a programmable processor capable of performing 10 million floating-point operations per second (10 MFLOPS). A 10-cell machine has a peak performance of 100 MFLOPS. Warp is integrated into a UNIX™ host system, and program development is supported by a compiler.

Two copies of a 10-cell prototype of the Warp machine became operational in 1986 and are in use at Carnegie Mellon for a wide range of applications, including low-level vision processing for robot vehicle navigation and signal processing. The success of the prototypes led to the development of a production version of the Warp machine that is implemented with printed circuit boards. At least eight copies of this machine are being built by General Electric in 1987. The first copy was delivered to Carnegie Mellon in April 1987. This paper describes the architecture of the production Warp machine and explains the changes that turned the prototype system into a mature high-performance computing engine.

* Warp is a service mark of Carnegie Mellon University.

INTRODUCTION

Warp is a high-performance systolic array computer designed to support signal and image processing.[1,2] In a typical configuration, Warp consists of a linear systolic array of 10 identical cells; each cell is a programmable processor capable of performing 10 million floating-point operations per second. The processor array is integrated in a multiprocessor host system which provides adequate data bandwidth to sustain it at full speed in the targeted applications. The host system also provides a general-purpose computing environment, specifically UNIX, for running application programs.[2]

Adequate support for programming has been a key concern for the Warp project since its conception. The Warp machine is integrated into UNIX as an attached processor and program development is supported by a custom-tailored programming environment.[3] Warp is exclusively programmed in a high-level language called W2: programs are translated into efficient microcode by an optimizing compiler.[4] Warp is implemented with conservative technology; each prototype Warp cell is built from off-the-shelf parts on a wire-warp board, and the host consists of industry-standard boards.[1] We chose to implement Warp with MSI and LSI components to reduce risk and to build the prototype quickly. A single 19″ rack hosts the Warp array with 10 cells, the host system, as well as associated power supplies and fans.

The Warp project started in 1984, and a 2-cell machine was completed in June of 1985 at Carnegie Mellon. Construction of two identical 10-cell prototype machines was contracted to two industrial partners, General Electric and Honeywell. The first prototype machine was delivered by General Electric in early 1986, and the Honeywell machine arrived at Carnegie Mellon a few months later. Both systems are used on a daily basis at Carnegie Mellon for applications that have high computation demands. The machines' first applications are low-level vision for robot vehicle navigation, signal processing, scientific computing, and research in image processing algorithms.[5]

The successful use of the prototype for several applications created the demand for additional Warp machines. Since some of the Warp machines built will be subject to environmental stress (for example, inside a moving autonomous vehicle), and since wire-wrap boards are not suited for replication due to their high production cost, we decided to implement the production Warp with printed circuit boards (PC Warp). This decision to re-implement the Warp array on printed circuit boards created the opportunity to revise and improve the architecture for the production Warp machine.

The PC Warp systems are still implemented with MSI and LSI parts, allowing us to use our experience with the prototype system as leverage. Our long-range plans call for an integrated Warp system that offers a reduction in area, power consumption, and cost by at least one order of magnitude while extending the performance into the GigaFLOPS range. We have started to develop a single-chip implementation in collaboration with our industrial partner Intel, and a VLSI Warp system is expected to be available in the early 1990s.

This paper presents the production Warp, a revision of the wire-wrapped prototype in use at Carnegie Mellon. Our goal in the architecture revision is to make it a production-quality machine thus lengthening its lifetime. Since all programs are written in a high-level language which hides the hardware details from the programmer, we do not need to maintain hardware compatibility in the evolution of the architecture. All application programs can be ported to new architectures by recompilation.

There are three primary sources for changes. First, we want to extend the application domain of the Warp machine. The primary goal of the prototype machine was to demonstrate that the architecture could be constructed and used effectively. To keep the risk low, we omitted some architecture features that are difficult to implement and are not necessary for some limited application domains. After successful construction and use of the prototype, we are now ready to expand the machine's application domain. Second, our experience in developing the compiler and application programs for the prototype system has given us insights on the strong and weak points of the architecture. With our experience in the prototype machine, we can better estimate the board area to implement different functions, tune the machine, and improve its efficiency. Last, some modifications to the implementation are made to take advantage of new and denser chips on the market.

ARCHITECTURE OVERVIEW

The Warp machine has three components: the Warp processor array (Warp array), the interface unit (IU), and the host, as depicted in Figure 1. The Warp array performs the computation-intensive routines, for example, low-level vision routines or matrix operations. The IU handles the I/O between the array and the host. It is also capable of generating data addresses and control signals for the Warp array. The host executes the parts of the application program that are not mapped onto the Warp array, and supplies the data to and receives the results from the array.

The Processor Array

The Warp array is a one-dimensional array of identical cells. Data flow through the array on two data paths (X and Y). Each cell can transfer up to 20 million words (80 Mbytes) per

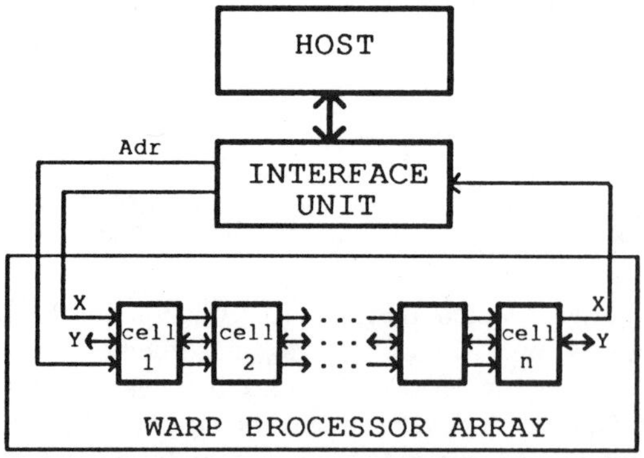

Figure 1—Warp machine overview

second to and from its neighboring cells. The direction of the Y path is statically configurable. This backward direction of the Y path is important in algorithms, such as back-solvers, the require results accumulated in the last cell be sent back to the other cells.

Each Warp cell is a 10 MFLOPS programmable processor with its own program memory and microsequencer; it executes one instruction every 200ns. The Warp cell data path for the production Warp machine is illustrated in Figure 2. Connected together through a full crossbar are a queue for each inter-cell communication path, a large local memory, a 32-bit floating-point multiplier (Mpy) and a 32-bit floating-point adder (Add). Each floating-point unit has its own register buffer. An additional small data memory backs up the limited register space of the buffers. There are three possible sources for addresses for the two data memories. Addresses can be generated on the IU and sent via the Adr path, or generated locally by an on-board address generator (AGU), or taken from the literal field of the current microinstruction.

The Host System

The Warp host, depicted in Figure 3, consists of a SUN-3 workstation*** (the master processor) running UNIX and an external host.[6] The external host consists of two cluster processors and a support processor. The support processor controls peripheral I/O devices (such as graphics boards), and handles floating-point exceptions and other interrupt signals from the Warp array. The two clusters work in parallel, each handling a uni-directional flow of data to or from the Warp processor, through the IU. The two clusters can exchange their roles in sending or receiving data for different phases of a computation, in a ping-pong fashion.

Each processor (P) is a Motorola MVME135 processor board consisting of a MC68020 microprocessor with a MC 68881 floating-point coprocessor and 1MByte memory. The processor board is connected to dual-ported memories (M). Each processor has private access to its memory via a local VSB bus, and shared access on the global VME bus to all memories. The total memory in the external host can be up to 36 Mbytes. Each cluster is connected to the IU through a

*** SUN-3 is a trademark of Sun Microsystems, Inc.

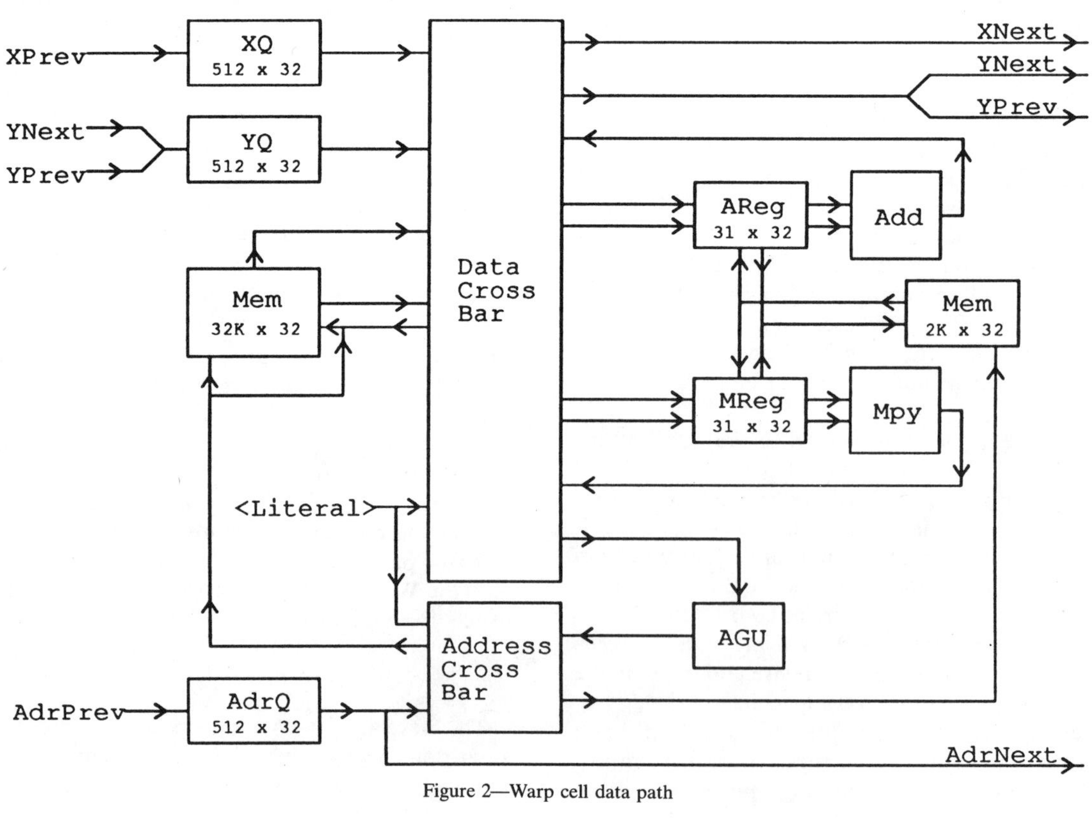

Figure 2—Warp cell data path

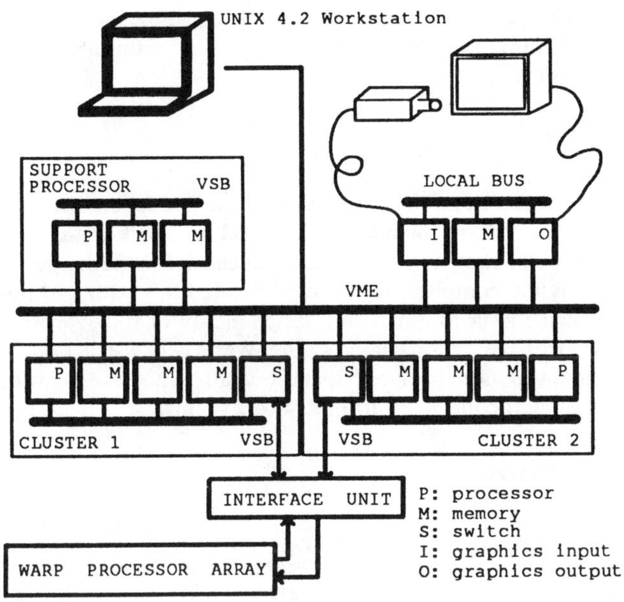

Figure 3—Warp system

switch board (S). The switch has on-board DMA devices and a VME interface. The workstation master processor workstation is connected to the external host via a VME bus coupler. All the boards except the switch and bus coupler are off-the-shelf components.

ARCHITECTURAL REVISIONS FOR THE PRODUCTION WARP

In this section we discuss the major architecture revisions in the production Warp machine: hardware flow control, local address generation, increased program and data memories, a space-saving implementation for the queues, and DMA transfers between the host and the interface unit.

Inter-cell Flow Control

As depicted in Figure 2, a queue of 512 words is placed along each communication channel. Flow control is implemented in hardware on PC Warp: when a cell tries to read from an empty queue, it is blocked until a data item arrives. Similarly, when a cell tries to write to a full queue of a neighboring cell, the writing cell is blocked until data is removed from the full queue.

The blocking of a cell is transparent to the program; the state of all the computational units on the data path freezes for the duration. Only a cell that tries to read from an empty queue or to deposit a message into a full queue is blocked. All other cells in the array continue to operate normally unless they block themselves. The data queues of a blocked cell are still able to accept input; otherwise, a cell blocked on an empty queue will never become unblocked.

The implementation of run-time flow control by hardware has two implications. First, we need two clock generators—one for the computational units whose states freeze when a cell is blocked, and one for the queues. Second, since a cell can receive data from either of its two neighbors, it can block as a result of the status of the queues in either neighbor as well as its own. This dependence on other cells adds serious timing constraints to the design since signals have to cross board boundaries.

Hardware-based flow control is not needed for all application domains, and since the implementation of the flow control hardware is complicated for a high-speed system, we elected to omit it in the wire-wrapped prototype. This decision limited our application domain to those programs whose flow control can be handled statically by the compiler.[4] However, the simplification in the design has permitted us to gain useful experience in a much shorter time.

Address Generation

As shown in Figure 2, each cell contains its own address generation unit (AGU). The AGU is a self-contained integer ALU with a set of local registers. It can compute up to two addresses per cycle (one read address and one write address). This rate is sufficient to match the memory bandwidth. The AGU is implemented by a single component, the IDT-49C402, on AMD2901 equivalent unit with 64 registers.

There are several reasons for the absence of an integer ALU in the prototype cell. First, as long as all cells execute a copy of the same program which needs only data-independent addresses, the interface unit can compute the addresses and pass them through the cells. Quite a few algorithms fall into this category.

Second, there was not enough space on the wire-warp board to include an AGU. The area cost of the AGU includes the space occupied by the address generator chip as well as a larger control store made necessary by the longer instruction word. Last, the IDT-49C402 was not available for the design of the prototype, only the AMD2901 was available and was used for the prototype interface unit. Since this component has only 16 registers, the address generation unit in the interface unit is backed up by a table that holds up to 32K pre-computed addresses. We did not have the board area to replicate this table on each cell and therefore an AGU was included only in the interface unit.

Expanded Memory

The PC Warp cell contains more program and data memory than the prototype cell. All memories in the Warp cell are implemented with static RAMs with an access time of 45ns. At the time of the redesign, higher density memory chips were available. The PC Warp cell contains 8K instruction and 32K data words, as opposed to 2K instruction and 4K data words in the prototype machine.

The large local data memory and the high inter-cell communication bandwidth are necessary to make Warp effective for numerous applications.[2] Enlarging the data memory makes it possible to use larger numbers of cells in the array just as effectively without increasing the array's I/O bandwidth requirement.[7]

The size of the instruction memory determines the size of the largest program that can run on the machine, as well as the startup time to invoke an application program. Since the W2 compiler is available, there is hardly a limit on the size of programs that can be written. Programs that exceed the 2K instruction space of the prototype already exist. A large instruction memory also allows multiple programs to reside on the cell at the same time. The application program on the host selects the programs to invoke dynamically; if the program is already present in the instruction memory, it is not necessary to download the routine each time it is called. The large instruction memory provides a fast startup time for real-time applications for which a low latency is needed.

Backup Memory for Registers

In the prototype system, the only way a data item can be retrieved from the register files is through the arithmetic units. This restriction causes problems for the compiler's code generator when spilling a register (that is, moving a value from register to memory). Since the functional units are highly pipelined, the arithmetic operation to move a register value cannot be inserted easily into the code sequence but must be considered when the instructions are scheduled. As a result, a circularity is introduced into the compilation steps: the instruction schedule cannot be determined until the register usage is known, but the register usage cannot be determined until the instruction schedule is known.

PC Warp remedies this situation with the addition of a backup memory for register overflows. This memory is connected to both register files (see Figure 2) and provides a fast way to copy a register from one file to another. This backup memory contains 2K words and is used to hold all scalars, floating-point constants, and small arrays. Addresses for this memory come from the address crossbar.

The addition of this memory also helps improve the throughput for those programs operating mainly on local data. The functional units of Warp can consume up to four words and produce two results per cycle. The local memory, however, only allows one read and one write. This data access bandwidth is improved with the addition of the backup memory.

Queues

The IDT-7202 FIFO chips, not available at the time the prototype was designed, make it possible to implement the queues compactly. In the prototype, the queues were implemented by a memory bank and a couple of pointers which together take up a lot of board space. The reduction in space allows us to implement all the other changes described. In addition, the size of the queues is increased four-fold to 512 words, a common length for a scan-line in image processing.

The size of the queues is important even with hardware flow control. Queues buffer the input for a cell and smooth the program execution. Although the average communication rate between two communicating cells must balance, a larger buffer allows the cells to receive and send data in bursts at different times.

Other Cell Changes

There are two other noteworthy changes in the cell. The prototype system included an internal feedback path: a cell could write into its own queues. Because this path was not used by the compiler, we have eliminated this path and used the board area to enrich the functionality of the Warp cell. Last, with all these changes, the Warp cell instruction becomes even more horizontal, and we had to increase the width of the microcode word from 224 to 244 bits.

Host Changes

In the prototype system, input and output between the array and the host is performed by two dedicated MC68020 processors. Data that is transferred to Warp must be read from host memory on the VME or VSB bus and written to a switch board, which is the interface between the host buses and the IU. In the PC Warp system, a DMA device was added to the switch board, increasing the peak host-array bandwidth from 4 Mbytes/s to 8–12 Mbytes/s.

Transfers between the host and the Warp array can be performed in two ways:

1. If the address pattern is not sequential, the MC68020 processor performs the transfer, and the switch board is a VSB slave.
2. If the address pattern is sequential, DMA transfer is used. In this case, the switch board becomes the bus master.

In non-sequential transfers, the transfer time depends on the complexity of the address pattern. For simple patterns, one 32-bit word is transferred in about 1 μs. The maximum transfer speed is mainly affected by the memory speed and the bus protocol. While static memory boards would allow at least a transfer every microsecond, the large storage requirement prevented us from using them.

Sequential transfers are performed by DMA, at a rate of less than 500ns per word. Sequential transfers are important in vision applications, in which digitized images are often received and sent in raster-scan order. To fully sustain the I/O requirements of the Warp array (one input data and one output data every 200ns in the worst case), the IU can unpack a 32-bit word containing four eight bit integers and generate four 32-bit floating-point values (and perform the opposite operation on the output) in 800ns. By sending bytes as packed 32 bit words, the I/O bandwidth of the external host is increased four-fold. Transferring one 32-bit word every 800ns therefore satisfies the maximum I/O requirements of the Warp array. DMA transfers easily meet this requirement (500 ns), while the nonsequential transfers miss the requirement by 20% (current time is 1μs). However, the availability of faster memory boards will allow us to meet this worst-case requirement in the near future.

Applications different from vision, specifically scientific computing, use 32-bit floating-point quantities, and packing and unpacking cannot be used. However, most of these applications seldom require the full bandwidth of the Warp array, because more operations are performed on each input data. Furthermore, input datasets are often stored into the array before processing. In this case, the latency introduced by first storing the dataset in the Warp array is small compared to the total execution time. As an example, performing a real 100×100 singular value decomposition takes about 1.3 s, whereas storing the matrix in the array takes $10{,}000 \times 1\mu s = 10$ ms. Even simpler algorithms on a problem of this size (e.g., LU decomposition, QR decomposition) always take hundreds of milliseconds since they perform several operations on each data item; reducing the I/O time does not significantly improve the overall performance.

EXTENDED PROGRAM DOMAIN

The various changes in the architecture allow us to extend the application domain of the production Warp machine. In this section, we study each of the extensions.

Data-dependent Control Flow

If the control flow of a program is data dependent, then the exact sequence of operations to be executed cannot be determined at compile-time. Structured programming constructs such as conditional statements, FOR loops with dynamic loop bounds and WHILE statements can indicate data dependent control flow. Even with homogeneous computing, in which the same program is executed by all the cells in the array, the sequences of operations actually executed by individual cells can be different. As a result, the addresses needed in each cell are different as well and must be computed on each cell. Furthermore, the accurate timing for the input and output operations of a cell is unpredictable if the execution path through the program is data dependent. This renders compile-time flow control impossible and requires runtime flow control. Since the prototype machine has neither local address generation capabilities nor dynamic flow control support, it is incapable of supporting data dependent control flow in general.

The prototype only allows one type of data dependent control flow: restricted conditional statements. No branch of a conditional statement can include any loops, and the number and type of I/O operations must be identical for both branches. The address sequences demanded by the two branches of the conditional statement can be different.

With the addition of local address generation unit and hardware flow control, the production Warp can now handle data dependent control flow. The benefits are three-fold. First, the language is now Turing-complete; we expand the domain of the language from primitive recursive functions in the prototype machine to all recursive functions. Second, the programming task is no longer complicated by the lack of WHILE statements and FOR loops with dynamic loop bounds. Previously, the user would have to predetermine the maximum number of iterations a loop may execute instead of expressing the loop with a straightforward WHILE statement. Finally, the efficiency of the machine is improved. When we had to execute the maximum number of iterations every time, we could lose a large factor in performance.

Heterogeneous Computation

The support heterogeneous computing where cells in the array execute different programs, we need the capability of efficient address generation on each cell. Different programs imply different address sequences. When heterogeneous computation is implemented on the prototype machine, addresses need to be generated slowly on the pipelined floating-point hardware in the cell. A simple integer addition requires three operations, fix-to-float conversion, floating-point addition and float-to-fix conversion, for a total of 21 clocks. The AGU included in each cell of PC Warp is as powerful as the address generator of the IU and computes an addition in half a cycle. Hence, efficient heterogeneous computation is supported.

If we can support data dependent control flow, we can also support heterogeneous computation; however, the converse is not true. The compile-time flow control algorithm does not rely on the fact that all cell programs are the same. Therefore, as long as the individual programs do not exhibit data dependent control flow, dynamic flow control is not necessary for heterogeneous computing.

Efficient Data Dependent Addressing

Some homogeneous programs need data dependent addresses which we cannot generate on the IU. The addition of a local AGU to the production Warp machine helps this class of programs as well.

Bidirectional Data Flow

General bidirectional data flow through the array is not supported by the compiler for the prototype hardware. The compilation for programs with unidirectional data flow decomposes nicely into two independent problems: cell scheduling and flow control. After the cell programs are generated, we skew the initiation of the execution of each cell with respect to the preceding cell to ensure that the input operations do not overtake the corresponding output operations. With bidirectional data flow, it may be necessary for a cell to wait for both of its neighbors at different times in the course of the execution. The analysis to determine when pauses are necessary is nontrivial; moreover, the internal hardware pipelines in the cells make efficient implementation of such pauses difficult.

Only the SIMD model of computation is supported for bidirectional data flow on the prototype machine. That is, the user must program the cells in such a way that if the programs were executed in lock step, all receives would be executed after their corresponding sends. In other words, the responsibility of flow control rests on the user.

Bidirectional data flow is difficult to implement because of the semantic gap between the programming language and the actual hardware in the prototype machine. While dynamic flow control is assumed in the language, we can only implement static flow control. In PC Warp, dynamic flow control closes this gap, making the support of bidirectional data flow straightforward.

CONCLUSIONS

The prototype Warp machine was a compromise between generality and design complexity. The program domain, although restricted, still covers a large set of important applications. The simplification in the design allowed us to construct the prototype and to demonstrate its usefulness quickly.

The development of a variety of applications for the prototype made us aware of the strengths and limitations of this machine, and led to the revisions incorporated into the production Warp system. Because we had a working compiler and a realistic set of application programs, we could evaluate each design change and assess its performance impact quite accurately. Since we had completed the implementation of the prototype, we were able to estimate the hardware cost and complexity of the revisions as well.

The production Warp machine is a major improvement over the prototype. It handles an enlarged application domain which includes programs with data dependent control flow and addressing, heterogeneous computation, and bidirectional flow. Moreover, the performance of those programs that run on the prototype Warp machine is not compromised.

ACKNOWLEDGEMENTS

The research was supported in part by Defense Advanced Research Projects Agency (DoD) monitored by the Air Force Avionics Laboratory under Contract F33615-81-K-1539 and Naval Electronics Systems Command under Contract N00039-85-C-0134, and in part by the Office of Naval Research under Contracts N00014-80-C-0236, NR 048-659, and N00014-85-K-0152, NR SDRJ-007. T. Gross is also supported by an IBM Faculty Development Award, and H. T. Kung by a Shell Distinguished Chair in Computer Science.

REFERENCES

1. Annaratone, M., E. Arnould, R. Gross, H. T. Kung, M. Lam, O. Menzilcioglu, K. Sarocky, and J. A. Webb. "Warp Architecture and Implementation." *Conference Proceedings of the 13th Annual International Symposium on Computer Architecture,* 1986, pp. 346–356.
2. Annaratone, M., F. Bitz, J. Deutch, L. Hamey, H. T. Kung, P. C. Maulik, P. Tseng, and J. A. Webb. "Applications Experience on Warp." *AFIPS Proceedings of the National Computer Conference,* (Vol. 56), 1987.
3. Bruegge, B., C. Chang, R. Cohn, T. Gross, M. Lam, P. Lieu, A. Noaman, and D. Yam. "The Warp Programming Environment." *AFIPS Proceedings of the National Computer Conference,* (Vol. 56), 1987.
4. Gross, T., M. S. Lam. "Compilation for a High-performance Systolic Array." *Proceedings of the SIGPLAN 86 Symposium on Compiler Construction.* ACM SIGPLAN, 1986, pp. 27–38.
5. Gross, R., H. T. Kung, M. S. Lam, J. A. Webb. "Warp as a Machine for Low-Level Vision." *Proceedings of 1985 IEEE International Conference on Robotics and Automation,* 1985, pp. 790–800.
6. Annaratone, M., E. Arnould, R. Cohn, T. Gross, H. T. Kung, M. Lam, O. Menzilcioglu, K. Sarocky, J. Senko, and J. Webb. "Architecture of Warp." *Proceedings, Compcon Spring 87,* IEEE Computer Society, 1987.
7. Kung, H. T. "Memory Requirements for Balanced Computer Architectures." *Journal of Complexity,* 1 (1985) 1, pp. 147–157.

The Warp programming environment

by B. BRUEGGE, C. H. CHANG, R. COHN, T. GROSS, M. LAM, P. LIEU, A. NOAMAN, and D. YAM
Carnegie-Mellon University
Pittsburgh, Pennsylvania

ABSTRACT

This paper describes the environment for developing and executing Warp* programs. The center of the program development environment is a customized shell that ties together a compiler for the Warp array, the Warp run-time system, and a debugger. The compiler translates high-level language programs to microcode for the Warp machine. It achieves a high utilization of the computation power of the processor. The run-time system supports remote execution of Warp programs across a network and makes the Warp machine available as a shareable resource. The debugger permits symbolic debugging of Warp programs. The Warp programming environment makes the Warp machine an easily programmable and accessible attached processor in a UNIX™ environment.

---

* Warp is a service mark of Carnegie Mellon University.

INTRODUCTION

In our programming environment, Warp is modeled as an attached processor accessible from an interactive, programmable, command interpreter called the Warp shell. The shell provides traditional operating system commands as well as commands to execute programs on the Warp machine. Calling a Warp program is similar to invoking a procedure: the shell calls the Warp program and passes input and output data between the application and Warp. The run-time system provides low-level support such as securing exclusive access to the machine, downloading object code, and transferring data between the host and the Warp system.

For programming the Warp, we have designed a language called W2 and implemented an optimizing compiler. The programming model, as supported by the language, allows the user to see the machine as a linear array of sequential processors and hides the low-level details from users. From a W2 program, the compiler generates microcode for the Warp array and the interface unit, as well as C programs for the I/O processors.[1]

In this paper we first describe the objectives of the Warp programming environment (WPE), and the system configuration. Then we describe the two methods for using the Warp system. The primary method is the interactive mode through the Warp shell; a library of existing Warp routines as well as user programs can be invoked interactively through shell commands. Program development is done almost exclusively with this method. The second method, used mainly for real-time systems, is the direct mode, for users who cannot afford the overhead of an interactive system. We then describe the support software in WPE: the run-time system, compiler, and debugger. We conclude with a review of the current status and a brief discussion of our experience to date.

Objectives of WPE

The primary objective of WPE is to simplify the use of the Warp machine. WPE is a uniform environment to edit, compile, debug, and execute W2 programs. Its audience includes the user who calls routines from a W2 library, the programmer who develops new algorithms for Warp, as well as the implementor who writes support software.

WPE must support efficient multiple user access because the use of the Warp hardware in a typical user session is sporadic. By allowing multiple user sessions to overlap and by serializing the use of the hardware, the Warp machine can be better utilized. WPE also provides multiple machine access; if there is more than one Warp array available, a user has the choice of connecting to any of these machines. It also provides network transparency, the user sees no difference whether he uses the Warp array remotely from his personal workstation or logs in directly to the Warp host machine.

WPE is designed to be development machine-portable. The shell, compiler, and debugger are written in Common LISP, which runs on many workstations, and the TCP/IP protocol is used in inter-machine communication. Our current release of WPE runs on SUN-3 under BSD UNIX 4.2. WPE is also designed to be target machine-portable. It has been in use for our prototype system, and it can be used with the successor Warp architectures: the production architecture implemented with printed circuit boards as well as the VLSI Warp which is currently in the design stage.

System Configuration

Figure 1 shows the configuration of WPE. Each workstation, a SUN-3, runs one or more *Warp shells.* The workstations communicate with a machine called the *Warp host.* This is another SUN-3 which is physically connected via a bus repeater to the external host and Warp array.[2] The Warp server executes on the Warp host and is the intermediator between users and the Warp array and external host.

TWO MODES OF ACCESSING WARP

There are two methods of running programs on Warp. Users may use the Warp shell which provides an interactive interface to the constituents of WPE such as the compiler, run-time system, debugger, and servers. Or, if absolute performance is necessary, users may program the machine in direct mode, without the overhead of a command interpreter.

The Warp Shell

The Warp shell binds together the components of WPE. Shell commands can be used to invoke the compiler, run a program on the array, and call debugging functions. The Warp shell is based on an extensible shell written in Common LISP.[3] The extensibility makes it possible to support different classes of users. Specifically, the Warp shell distinguishes between the novice and the experienced user. For example, the implementation language Common LISP and the components of the environment are completely hidden from a novice. This is useful for programmers interested in using the Warp shell to execute W2 programs from a library. On the other hand, the LISP implementation and all the software components comprising the Warp environment are easily available when de-

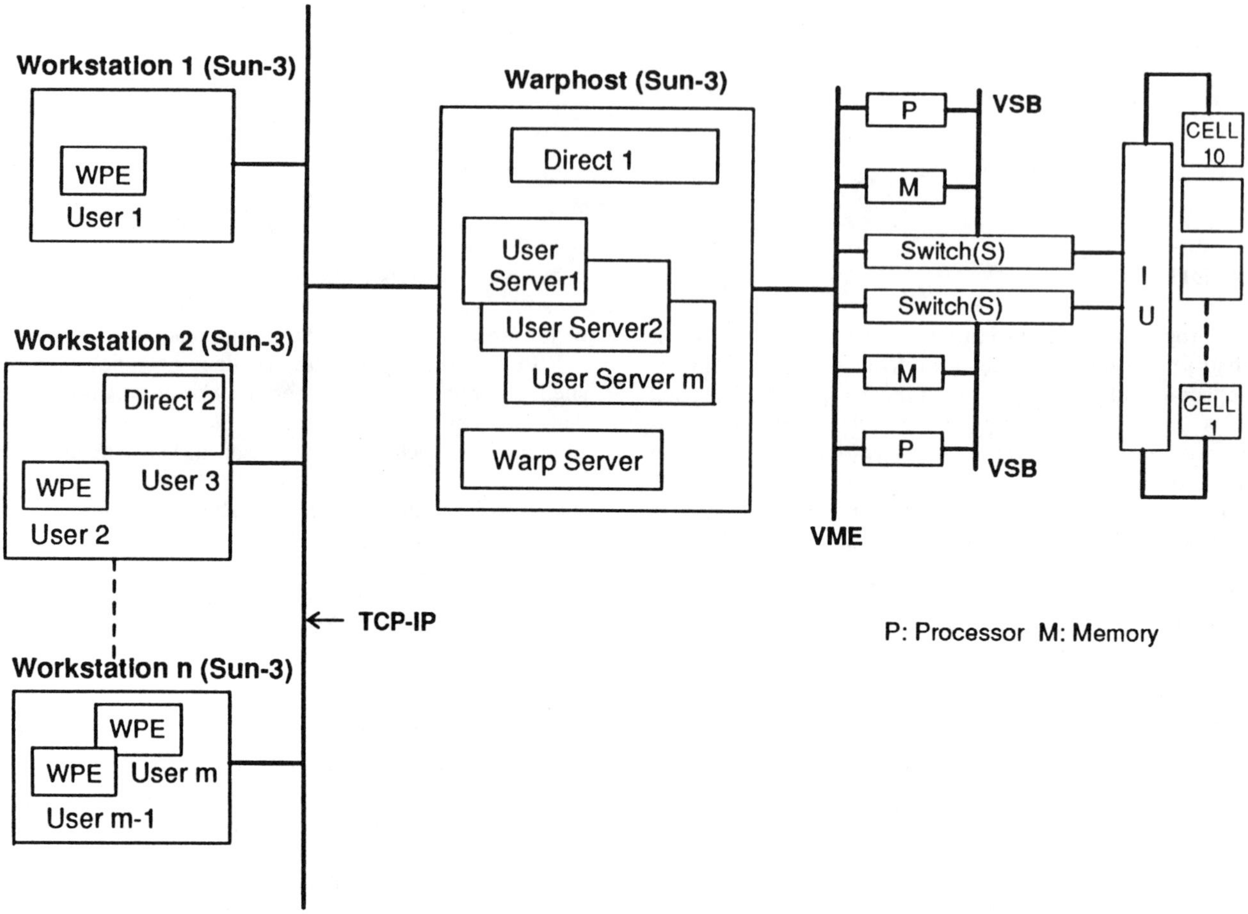

Figure 1—System configuration

sired. This means an experienced user can make use of Common LISP's powerful control structures to implement new commands.

The Warp shell allows the declaration and manipulation of variables, which can be used as inputs or outputs for Warp programs. All variables in the Warp shell are typed. The type information determines how to present a variable to a user (print as integer, floating-point number, . . .) and how to transfer it to the Warp array. The Warp shell offers predefined and user-defined types and variables. For example, an image can be defined by a user as a type "IMAGE = array [512,512] of byte" and the user can define variables of type IMAGE. User defined variables can then be passed as parameters to W2 programs.

Let us assume the user wants to invoke a W2 program "filter5by5" contained in a W2 library. This program expects an input image and transforms it into an output image. A typical sequence of Warp shell commands looks like this:

```
allocate −name IN −type IMAGE −init /img/road
allocate −name OUT −type IMAGE
filter5by5 IN OUT
```

The first command defines a Warp shell variable IN of type IMAGE and initializes it with the data contained in file "/img/road." The second command defines the variable OUT to hold the output image. The third line invokes the W2 program "filter5by5" with the actual parameters IN and OUT. When the execution is finished, the output image can be displayed or inspected in an editor buffer.

The user types commands to the Warp shell which runs inside the editor. The advantage of this structure is that such features as intra-line editing, history buffers, re-execution of previous commands and creation of script files are available automatically. The Warp shell also provides a uniform help mechanism. Each command is documented on-line and examples from the help description of a command can be fed to the command interpreter, providing easy exploration of the command language.

In addition to the Warp-specific features described in this paper, the Warp shell provides roughly the functionality of the well-known UNIX C-shell.[4] It maintains a set of environment variables such as SOURCEFILE, the name of the W2 program; HOST, the name of the Warp host in use; and BREAKPOINTS, the set of currently defined breakpoints. These environment variables can be inspected and assigned new values with Warp shell commands. By setting variables, a user can configure the environment. For example, assigning a value to HOST changes the Warp host and array on which programs are executed.

Direct Mode

The Warp shell is programmed in Common LISP and therefore garbage collection occurs regularly, making it hard to achieve predictable response times at the shell level. In addition, there is some overhead incurred in the network communication. Although this is tolerable when developing Warp programs, it may not be acceptable for real-time applications. In this case, a user calls the run-time system directly. Application programs in direct mode can be written in any language. The only requirement is that the language implementation supports the call of external C routines (the run-time system is written in C).

Direct mode is supported for both remote and local execution. Applications running remotely still use TCP/IP; application programs executed locally on the Warp host bypass the TCP/IP protocol. In Figure 1, "Direct 2" and "Direct 1" are examples of the remote and local direct mode, respectively.

The local direct mode is the mode with the lowest overhead and is the preferred mode of execution when time is critical. In this mode, the application program makes direct procedure calls to the run-time system. A program in this mode can run only on the Warp host because it is linked with the library into a single UNIX process.

SUPPORT SOFTWARE

Figure 2 shows the major software components of WPE; a compiler, a debugger, an editor, the Warp server, and the shell user interface. The different components of the environment communicate via the WPE database, which contains the W2 source files, symbol tables, and syntax trees. The shell's environment variables capture the current state of the session, for example, which Warp machine is allocated and what class of user (level of experience) is using the system. The integration of the compiler's internal tables with the shell and the debugger is important for the functionality of WPE. For example, the syntax tree produced by the W2 compiler is accessible by other components of WPE. The debugger inspects the syntax tree when a user tries to set a breakpoint. When execution on the cell reaches a breakpoint, the corresponding line is displayed in an editor buffer. Another part of the database that is used frequently is the symbol table. The Warp shell examines the symbol table when it displays the value of a variable or when it matches the actual parameters of a Warp program call with the formal parameters of the program.

The Run-time System

The WPE run-time system supports multiple user access by including two kinds of servers, the *Warp server* and the *user*

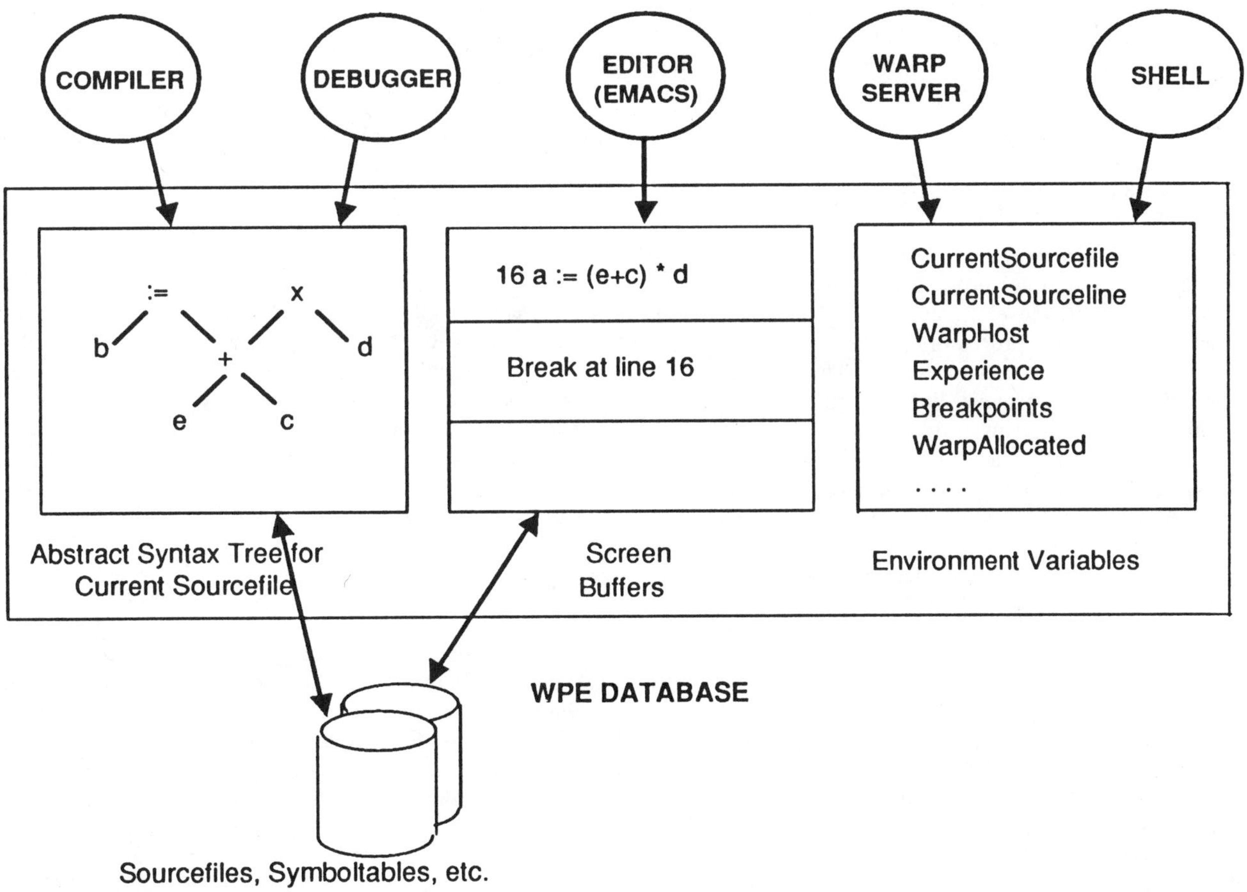

Figure 2—Software components

servers. These server processes run on the Warp host and communicate with the Warp shells on a user's workstation via remote procedure calls using the TCP-IP protocol.

For each user running either the Warp shell or in direct mode on a remote machine, there is a process called the user server which also resides in the Warp host. Variables created by a user in the Warp shell reside physically in the user server's address space on the Warp host. Variables are transferred to the user's site only when necessary. This organization reduces the performance impact of running the Warp shell remotely and accessing Warp over the network. Furthermore, because Warp shell variables are allocated in the user server, they can be initialized without possessing the Warp array. This makes it possible to perform costly file transfers (like reading an image) between the workstation and the Warp host before locking the Warp machine.

The Warp server manages the access to the Warp machine. It provides functions to lock and unlock the Warp. When the Warp server locks the machine for a particular Warp shell, the memory of its user server is copied into the memory of the external host of the Warp machine. This copy operation is done inside the Warp host and is therefore quite fast. When the Warp machine is unlocked, the memory of the external host is copied back into the memory of the corresponding user server. This scheme permits the environment to maintain user-specific state information across several locks/unlocks of the Warp machine.

The run-time system provides for sharing the Warp machine, but does not preempt a user once the Warp machine is locked. Most programs require a few seconds to run; the overhead associated with swapping processes is too high compared with the execution time.

The W2 Programming Language and Compiler

In Warp, parallelism exists at several levels. At the cell level there is a horizontal architecture with multiple pipelined functional units; at the array level there are ten cells; at the system level there are separate processors in the external host for input/output, control, and computation.[5] The potential performance of Warp is enormous, but the complexity of using the machine is proportionally overwhelming. To harness the computation power of Warp, we have designed a programming language called W2 and implemented an optimizing compiler. The W2 language provides an abstract programming model of the machine that allows users to focus on the parallelism at the array level. The compiler handles the parallelism at the system and the cell levels.

Programming model

Users view the Warp system as a linear array of identical, conventional processors that can communicate asynchronously with their left and right neighbors. Standard language constructs such as loops and conditionals are provided, as are primitives for sending and receiving data. The semantics of the communication primitives are that a cell will block if it tries to receive from an empty queue or send to a full one.

The general problem of partitioning a computation for a processor array is difficult to solve. Usually, a solid understanding of the application domain is necessary to find a good mapping of a computation onto a processor array. Therefore, the processor array configuration is exposed in the programmer's model, giving the user or higher-level tools full control over computation partitioning. Already there are application-specific tools that map sequential algorithm descriptions into parallel W2 programs.[6]

The W2 programming language

The W2 language is a simple block-structured language with assignment, conditional, and loop statements. A W2 program is a module; it defines the interface between the host and the array—the input and output to and from the array are given by the module parameters. Specified next are the cell programs, each of which describes the action of a group of one or more cells. Only one cell program is allowed for the prototype machine. When a group of cells share the same program, it does not mean they necessarily execute the same instruction at the same time. In fact, computations on different cells typically are skewed in a pipelined fashion[2] because a cell cannot start executing until it receives data from the preceding cell. Finally, a cell program may consist of several unnested functions.

Example program

Figure 3 is a simple example of a Warp program which evaluates a polynomial using an array of ten cells. The program evaluates the polynomial

$$P(z) = c_0z^9 + c_1z^8 + \cdots + c_9$$
$$= (((c_0 \times z) + c_1) \times z + \cdots + c_8) \times z + c_9$$

for a vector of 100 input data $z_0, z_1, z_2, \ldots$ By applying Horner's rule, a polynomial evaluation becomes a series of inner-product computations, each of which is computed on a cell in the array. Each cell (starting with cell 0 up to cell 9, the last cell in the system) executes a copy of the program. The first cell receives the values of the host program variables (bound to parameters c and z), and the results are sent and stored in a host variable bound to parameter "results."

The compiler

The local optimizations implemented include common subexpression elimination, constant folding, height reduction, dead code removal, and idempotent operation removal. A global flow analyzer collects detailed inter-block information for all variables of the program. For regular accessing patterns, the analysis is powerful enough to distinguish between individual array elements and different iterations of a loop so that the code generator can overlap different loop iterations. To exploit the high degree of pipelining and parallelism in the machine, the compiler has a good global scheduler. We use

```
module polynomial (z in, c in, results out)
float z[100], c[10], results[100];

cellprogram (cid : 0 : 9)
begin
    function poly
    begin
       float coeff,/* local copy of c[cid] */
        temp, xin, yin, ans;/* temporaries */
       int i;
         receive (L, X, coeff, c[0]);
         for i := 1 to 9 do begin
             receive (L, X, temp, c[i]);
             send (R, X, temp);
         end;
         send (R, X, 0.0);
         for i := 0 to 99 do begin
            receive (L, X, xin, z[i]);
            receive (L, Y, yin, 0.0);
            send (R, X, xin);
            ans := coeff + yin*xin;
            send (R, Y, ans, results[i]);
         end;
    end

    call poly;
end
```

Figure 3—Example program

two scheduling algorithms: a scheduling technique specialized for innermost loops called software pipelining, and a new unified approach to scheduling both within and across basic blocks.[7]

The Debugger

The Warp debugger provides two functions: setting source line breakpoints and symbolic inspection of variables. Because the optimizing compiler deletes redundant operations and reorders source operations, it is not always possible to set a breakpoint at a particular line in the W2 source code. A special Warp shell command permits a user to explore possible breakpoints. For a machine that executes 100 million operations per second, a simple line-oriented debugging model is not always appropriate. We must be able to qualify the breakpoint with a condition so that the program automatically resumes execution at the breakpoint if the condition is not satisfied. For example, we need to be able to stop at some particular iteration of a loop, without stopping at all the previous iterations.

For the wire-wrapped prototype, we can provide only post-mortem debugging; insufficient access to the internals of the cell makes it impossible to continue execution after resources have been inspected. This problem is alleviated in the production version of the Warp array.

CURRENT STATE

WPE is implemented in Common LISP and C, and is running under BSD UNIX 4.2 on a SUN-3 Workstation. The current release supports multiple users and multiple machine access to two copies of the 10-cell wire-wrapped prototype.[8] The core image of Common LISP is about 7 MBytes; WPE uses an additional 3 MBytes. We have found that a paging space of 25MBytes per user provides acceptable performance.

Altogether, approximately 75,000 lines of code have been written. The W2 compiler accounts for about 34,000 lines of Common LISP code, and the assemblers for 16,000 lines of C code. The shell contains 8,000 lines of LISP code; it relies on a text editor (Emacs). The debugger contains about 3,000 lines of LISP code. The run-time system is written in C and consists of 4,000 lines of code. Linkers and simulators account for the remaining lines of code.

Table I presents the performance results for some well-known programs for the prototype Warp system. The second column shows the maximum floating-point computation bandwidth that can be obtained for each program. Since there are two distinct functional units for addition and multiplication, this maximum rate is less than 100 MFLOPS if the number of additions is not equal to the number of multiplications. These numbers do not take into consideration the data dependencies in the program, but only the total number of operations. The next column presents the computation bandwidth achieved by the microcode generated by the compiler. The overhead incurred by the host is not included.

Development of the Warp programming environment started in 1984 as the architecture was defined. The major emphasis of the early work was on the programming language definition and the compiler design. Since the first prototype machine became operational in Spring 1986, increased effort has been allocated to the run-time support and the user interface. The programming environment has been continuously developed and improved, with input from our application users.

WPE provides a uniform environment for developing and running Warp routines. The massive amount of details in using the machine are abstracted out; efficient run-time support

TABLE I—Performance results

Some Benchmark Programs				
Program	MFLOPS max	MFLOPS actual	Execution (ms)	Compilation (min)
Convolution (3×3 kernel 512×512 image)	94.4	65.3	68	4.9
Matrix multiply (100×100)	99.5	74.5	25	1.7
Successive over-relaxation (225×225, 10 iterations)	88.9	45.0	180	2.6
Local average selective filter (512×512 image)	65.3	42.2	396	9.7
Mandelbrot (512×512 image, 256 iterations)	90.0	86.8	6960	5.0

is easily accessible through an interactive command interpreter. The run-time system also allows multiple user access and greatly increases the utilization of the hardware. The development of software for Warp is made easy by a highly optimizing compiler, which generates efficient microcode from a high-level language. Microprogramming has been phased out completely since the compiler became functional. In summary, the Warp programming environment has turned the Warp machine into an easily programmable and accessible attached processor in a UNIX environment.

ACKNOWLEDGEMENTS

The research was supported in part by Defense Advanced Research Projects Agency (DOD), monitored by the Air Force Avionics Laboratory under Contract F33615-81-K-1539, and Naval Electronic Systems Command under Contract N00039-85-C-0134, and in part by the Office of Naval Research under Contracts N00014-80-C-0236, NR 048-659, and N00014-85-K-0152, NR SDRJ-007. T. Gross is also supported by an IBM Faculty Development Award.

REFERENCES

1. Gross, T. and M. S. Lam. "Compilation for a High-performance Systolic Array." *Proceedings of the SIGPLAN 86 Symposium on Compiler Construction,* ACM SIGPLAN, 1986, pp. 27–38.
2. Annaratone, M., E. Arnould, T. Gross, H. T. Kung, M. Lam, O. Menzilcioglu, K. Sarocky, and J. A. Webb. "Warp Architecture and Implementation." *Conference Proceedings of the 13th Annual International Symposium on Computer Architecture,* 1986, pp. 346–356.
3. Giuse, Dario. "A Lisp Shell." Carnegie Mellon Robotics Institute Internal Report, 1985.
4. Joy, William. "An Introduction to the C Shell." in *UNIX Programmer's Manual, 7th Edition,* Computer Science Division, UCB, ed., UC Berkeley, 1981.
5. Annaratone, M., E. Arnould, R. Cohn, T. Gross, H. T. Kung, M. Lam, O. Menzilcioglu, K. Sarocky, J. Senko, and J. Webb. "Architecture of Warp." *Proceedings, Compcon Spring 87,* IEEE Computer Society, 1987, pp. 264–267.
6. Annaratone, M., F. Bitz, J. Deutch, L. Hamey, H. T. Kung, P. C. Maulik, P. Tseng, and J. A. Webb. "Applications Experience on Warp." *AFIPS, Proceedings of the National Computer Conference,* (Vol. 56), 1987.
7. Bruegge, B., C. Chang, R. Cohn, T. Gross, M. Lam, P. Lieu, A. Noaman, and D. Yam. "Programming Warp." *Proceedings, Compcon Spring 87,* IEEE Computer Society, 1987, pp. 268–271.
8. Bruegge, B. *Warp Programming Environment: User Manual,* Department of Computer Science, Carnegie-Mellon University, 1986.

Applications experience on Warp

by MARCO ANNARATONE, FRANCOIS BITZ, JEFF DEUTCH, H.T. KUNG, LEONARD HAMEY, P.C. MAULIK, P.S. TSENG, and JON A. WEBB
Carnegie Mellon University
Pittsburgh, Pennsylvania

ABSTRACT

The prototype Warp* machine at Carnegie Mellon is being used to develop new applications in magnetic resonance image processing, as a research tool in image texture analysis, and for scientific computing. In these areas, orders of magnitude speedup over conventional computers are being observed. These new applications build on our use of Warp for low level vision, which is the area for which the machine was originally designed.

Experience with the prototype Warp machine has led to rules that programmers should follow to achieve best performance in their application. These rules concern all levels of the Warp system, from input and output ordering to programming each individual Warp cell to memory use in Warp's host. The new printed circuit board version of Warp incorporates several architectural improvements, which lead to better support of a wider class of applications.

An ambitious design for implementation of Warp in custom VLSI is underway, which promises an increase of at least ten in cost-performance over the current version of Warp, together with the opportunity to build much more powerful systolic arrays delivering GigaFLOPS performance.

* Warp is a service mark of Carnegie Mellon University

INTRODUCTION

Applications experience helps the development of a special-purpose computer at many levels. It can directly influence the design of the architecture, and provide useful benchmarks to make sure the architecture performs efficiently. Applications can also help in the actual construction of the machine. For example, in the Warp project, applications programs were used first to debug the simulators, and then the prototype hardware. Once the first full-scale Warp machines were built, applications programs provided an effective acceptance test of the machines.

Since the two copies of the wire-wrapped prototype Warp machine became operational at Carnegie Mellon in 1986, there have been substantial application efforts. As we have previously discussed,[1] our first applications on the prototype Warp concerned robot navigation. The systems we have implemented on Warp include road following, obstacle avoidance using stereo vision, obstacle avoidance using a laser range-finder, and path planning using dynamic programming (DP). We have also implemented several algorithms in signal processing and scientific computing, including singular value decomposition for adaptive beamforming, fast two-dimensional image correlation using fast Fourier transform (FFT), successive over-relaxation (SOR) for the solution of elliptic partial differential equations, as well as computational geometry algorithms such as convex hull and algorithms for the shortest path through a graph.

This paper presents new applications not discussed previously; they reflect our growing effort to use Warp as a tool in realistic applications, rather than as a machine purely for research into parallelism. We are studying the use of Warp in the analysis of magnetic resonance imagery (MRI), and in research into the analysis of repetitive textures in images. We have also begun using Warp in scientific computing; algorithms in this area include partial differential equations problems and sparse matrix computation. While some of these new fields have been explored only recently, and we still do not know how effective Warp will be in realistic applications, the first results are encouraging enough to make us further pursue these areas. The performance of the prototype Warp on a range of applications will be summarized.

The success of the prototype led to the development of the production version of the Warp machine, which is implemented on printed circuit boards. The production machine is referred to as "PC Warp." Several architectural revisions were incorporated in PC Warp. These revisions are discussed, together with their impact on applications. We also briefly describe the VLSI version of the Warp machine, currently being designed by Carnegie Mellon and Intel Corporation.

MRI IMAGE PROCESSING

MRI image processing is a new application for Warp. This application is interesting for several reasons:

1. Many of the Warp programs we have already done, as part of our work on parallel vision on Warp, can be directly applied to this area without substantial modification.
2. Medical image processing requires the best and most computationally expensive algorithms be applied to images; an algorithm that can make, say, a tumor visible, can save a life.
3. Medical image processing requires fast image processing, but not real-time—something of the order of seconds or minutes per image is acceptable.[2,3] Images are acquired and examined off-line. Long processing time is not acceptable, however, because a diagnostic session occupies many resources and can be only of limited duration.

We have implemented three different algorithms for processing MRI images:

Contrast Enhancement

Typical MRI images have data values ranging over three orders of magnitude more than we can display on a standard video display device. The portions of the dynamic range the physician wants to examine must be defined, and the mapping of the image to the display device must be modified to show this range. For example, in brain imagery the physician may want to look at the dynamic range including the white-to-gray matter transition, so that the area of the image taking part in this transition is clearly identified.

Magnification

MRI images have resolutions of 1 mm or higher. Image magnification is useful to detect small-scale irregularities. Image magnification is a computationally expensive process, especially if it is done using optimal, or near-optimal, algorithms such as cubic convolution.[4] The Warp implementation of this algorithm is straightforward, and works well in the magnification of the image by a factor of eight or more both horizontally and vertically.

Edge Detection

In medical image processing, edge detection serves mainly to highlight structures that would otherwise not be visible and to precisely define the location of a structure that might be difficult to find, such as the boundary of an organ. This calls for multi-resolution edge detection, using an operator that finds, at each pixel, the edge with the best size and direction.[5] We have compared the Warp implementation of this with subroutines from a commercial FORTRAN library,[6] and observed a factor of 1100 speedup over a SUN-3 running FORTRAN code under UNIX. This remarkable speedup makes it possible to do in a reasonable time (two minutes) what would take more than a day using the FORTRAN code.

REPETITIVE TEXTURE ANALYSIS

In this research, repetitive textures are analyzed by using local point symmetry to detect the texture elements. Point symmetry is detected by an Analysis of Variance (ANOVA)[7] statistical test, which is applied to a window surrounding each pixel location.

The ANOVA method consists of partitioning the variance of the data into two portions: that which is explained by the model and that which remains unexplained. The method is applied at each pixel location to measure point symmetry. The model assumes that pixels which are located opposite each other should have similar intensities. The variance explained by the model is given by the following equation, in which I represents the window around each pixel, and W is a weighting function used to emphasize particular pixels around the central pixel, for example, by using a circular Gaussian weighting function:

$$SS_m = \sum_{ij} W_{ij}\left(\frac{I_{ij} + I_{-i-j}}{2} - \bar{I}\right)^2, \text{ where } \bar{I} = \frac{\sum_{ij} W_{ij} I_{ij}}{\sum_{ij} W_{ij}}.$$

The unexplained residual variance is given by the following equation:

$$SS_r = \sum_{ij} W_{ij}\left(I_{ij} - \frac{I_{ij} + I_{-i-j}}{2}\right)^2 = \frac{1}{4}\sum_{ij} W_{ij}(I_{ij} - I_{-i-j})^2.$$

The ratio of these two quantities is an F statistic.[7] However, the simple ratio has two faults: it is very sensitive to noise in low-contrast portions of the image, such as sky, and its values are unbounded. We therefore use the following ratio:

$$S = \frac{SS_m}{SS_r + SS_m + V}.$$

In this equation, V is a constant which is used to suppress the response to noise, and is roughly equal to the noise variance in the image multiplied by the sum of W_{ij}. The ratio S is bounded below by zero and above by one. Local peaks in an image of S values represent points of local symmetry.

In the Warp implementation of this algorithm, a pair of nested loops over the input image window compute the weighted mean surrounding each pixel. A second pair of nested loops compute SS_m and SS_r. This implementation involves 1321 floating-point multiplications and 1982 floating-point additions per pixel. For a 512 × 512 image, 346 million multiplications are required and 519 million additions. The prototype Warp processes a 512 × 512 image in 30s. The same processing would take more than an hour on a SUN-3.

SCIENTIFIC COMPUTATION

Scientific computation includes such tasks as solving systems of linear equations, determining eigenvalues and eigenvectors, and factoring matrices. Our work in this field has just started, but we have already implemented a few important algorithms, such as singular value decomposition (SVD), QR-decomposition, and LU decomposition.[8] SVD has also been used to develop a demonstration system which performs adaptive beamforming on sonar data.

Singular Value Decomposition

The SVD of an $m \times n$ matrix A is:

$$U^T A V = \Sigma$$

where Σ is an $m \times n$ nonnegative diagonal matrix, and U and V are $m \times m$ and $n \times n$ orthogonal matrices, respectively. The nonzero elements in the diagonal of Σ are the singular values of A. Here, we assume that A is an $n \times n$ square matrix; results can be generalized in a straightforward way to the case when A is rectangular.

Consider the Hestenes method[9] for computing the SVD. The method generates a sequence of J_i's such that $AJ_1 \ldots J_\sigma = U\Sigma$. Each J_i is a tridiagonal matrix obtained by a set of plane rotations that orthogonalize columns. We use a particular rotation ordering[10] that for $n = 8$ is:

(1,	2)	(3,	4)	(5,	6)	(7,	8)
2	(1,	4)	(3,	6)	(5,	8)	7
(2,	4)	(1,	6)	(3,	8)	(5,	7)
4	(2,	6)	(1,	8)	(3,	7)	5
(4,	6)	(2,	8)	(1,	7)	(3,	5)
6	(4,	8)	(2,	7)	(1,	5)	3
(6,	8)	(4,	7)	(2,	5)	(1,	3)
8	(6,	7)	(4,	5)	(2,	3)	1

where (i, j) means rotating the ith column against the jth column. Each row in this table is called a *rotation set,* and the eight rotation sets are called a *sweep.* J_i has two forms:

$$J_i = \text{diag}\{\Gamma_1, \Gamma_3, \ldots, \Gamma_{t-1}\},\ J_i = \text{diag}\{1, \Gamma_2, \ldots, \Gamma_{t-2}, 1\}$$

where $t = n/2$. The J_i on the left corresponds to odd-even column pairs (i.e., first, third . . . , rotation sets). Each Γ_i is a 2×2 matrix of rotation parameters:

$$\Gamma_i = \begin{pmatrix} \sin\theta_i & \cos\theta_i \\ \cos\theta_i & -\sin\theta_i \end{pmatrix}$$

θ_i is the rotation angle that makes $a_i^T a_{i+1}$ zero, where a_i and a_{i+1} are the rotating columns. This leads to the following rotation formulae:

$$\gamma_i = a_i^T a_{i+1},$$
$$\xi_i = \frac{\| a_{i+1} \|^2 - \| a_i \|^2}{2\gamma_i},$$
$$t_i = \text{sign}(\xi_i)/(|\xi_i| + (1 + \xi_i^2)^{1/2}),$$
$$\cos\theta_i = 1/(1 + t_i^2)^{1/2},$$
$$\sin\theta_i = t_i \cos\theta_i .$$

Two implementations on Warp are considered, storing A either row-wise[10] or column-wise. Currently, only the row-wise mapping is running on Warp, because the column-wise mapping requires right-to-left communication between the cells, "backward path," that the W2 compiler has started supporting only recently. We shall briefly examine the row-wise mapping first, and then we will discuss the column-wise mapping in more detail, since it is much faster.

In a typical 100 × 100 problem, 10 rows are stored into each Warp cell. While the array performs, in a systolic fashion, the rotation of the A matrix and the computation of $\| a_{i+1} \|^2$, $\| a_i \|^2$, and $a_i^T a_{i+1}$, called "a" terms, the $\sin\theta$ and $\cos\theta$ values are computed by one of the cluster processors. These terms leave the array from the last cell and are sent to the receiving cluster processor. This processor receives from the last cell a stream of "a" terms, and performs the above rotation.

The floating-point MC68881 coprocessor inside the cluster processor is used to compute the sines and cosines, which are then routed back to the input cluster through the VME bus. Both the use of the relatively slow coprocessor and the VME transfers introduce a significant overhead. With this implementation, a 100 × 100 SVD problem, which computes both Σ, U, and V, takes 6.5 s to run on Warp, which is 23 times faster than a Vax 11/780 with floating-point accelerator running the EISPACK[11] SVD routine. Analysis shows that more than 80 percent of the time is spent by the MC68881 computing the sine and cosine parameters, while the Warp array is heavily under-utilized.

The implementation that stores A column-wise is much more effective.[12] This works as follows. For a 100 × 100 problem ten columns are stored into each cell. The following steps are repeated until convergence:

1. All cells compute the three "a" terms for each column pair (i.e., five pairs in an odd-even rotation set).
2. All cells compute the sine and cosine parameters (i.e., five sine-cosine pairs in an odd-even rotation set).
3. All cells compute the AJ_j multiplication, (which also swaps locally within each cell the columns of A at the same time).
4. Cell 0 contains columns 0 through 9, cells 1 contains columns 10 through 19 and so on. At this point, a column swapping takes place. That is, cell 1 sends to cell 0 (i.e., right-to-left) column 10, cell 2 sends to cell 1 column 20, etcetera. This communication requires the backward path.
5. An even-odd rotation takes place. Again, all the cells in parallel compute the new "a" terms, compute the sine-cosine pairs, and perform the AJ_j multiplication. Then, a left-to-right swapping of one column takes place.

For an $n \times n$ problem, a sweep consists of n rotation sets ($n/2$ odd-even rotations and $n/2$ even-odd rotations). $\text{Log}_2 n$ sweeps are usually sufficient to ensure convergence. Therefore, the steps outlined above are executed $(n/2) \log_2 n$ times. Preliminary results show that a 100 × 100 real SVD takes 1.6 s with this mapping, a four-fold improvement over the row-wise mapping. This represents a 100-fold speedup over the Vax 11/780 with floating-point accelerator, or about 5 times slower than one CPU of a Cray X-MP (which has a peak computing power of 210 MFLOPS, vs. Warp's 100 MFLOPS). Reduction of the number of sweeps would further improve this performance.

QR and LU Decompositions

The QR decomposition of an $m \times n$ matrix A with linearly independent columns is $A = QR$, where Q is an $m \times m$ matrix with orthonormal columns, and R is an $m \times n$ upper triangular matrix.

Consider a square matrix A. Both Q and R are square. We use a two-multiplication version of the square root free Given's algorithm,[13] so that once the rotation parameters are computed two multiplications are required to update each element of each row. The computation of the rotation parameters requires eight multiplications, four divisions, and one addition. The algorithm is mapped onto the array as follows:

- Ten rows of the matrix are fed into the Warp array. The elimination with respect to the ith row is done in the ith cell, for i from 1 to 10.
- Then, the updated rows are fed back into the array through the host, and elimination is performed on the next ten rows. As each row is updated with respect to some row in a cell, it is passed to the next cell so that updating with respect to the next row can begin right away on this row while the first cell can go on updating other rows. The computation is therefore pipelined.

If we consider a 100 × 100 matrix, then at the end of the computation the first cell will contain the first, eleventh, twenty-first, . . . , ninety-first rows of Q, the second cell will contain the second, twelfth, twenty-second, . . . , ninety-second rows of Q, and so on. Each cell will also contain the corresponding rows of R.

The computation time for a 100 × 100 matrix on the prototype Warp is 264 ms. The PC Warp version will be twice as fast. This is because loop bounds must be constant on the prototype Warp, and, as a result, the program cannot avoid accessing a full rectangular matrix, even when only a triangular portion is non-zero.

A simplifed version of LU-decomposition has also been implemented. The implementation assumes a positive definite matrix, so pivoting is not needed. The mapping of this algorithm is similar to the mapping of the QR-decomposition algorithm described above. The computation time on prototype Warp is 242 ms, and the PC Warp should be twice as fast as for *QR*-decomposition.

ALGORITHM AND PROGRAM DESIGN PRINCIPLES TO MAXIMIZE PERFORMANCE

We now review a few techniques that Warp programmers use to ensure good performance of the Warp machine in their application areas. We concentrate on system-level issues, not on concurrency formulation of a computation for the Warp array, which has been covered elsewhere.[1]

Host Issues

Although the Warp array is tightly coupled with Warp's external host, and the external host is based on some of the most powerful commercially-available microprocessor boards and the highest bandwidth buses, the external host still is the weakest link in the Warp system. This is a consequence of the desire to take advantage of commercially-available, general-purpose processors, I/O boards, memory, and software. We expect that similar concerns will prevail in future Warp-like systems. Therefore, the programmer must avoid computation on the external host, whenever possible.

Input and output from host

The ratio between the maximum of the number of floating-point multiplications and additions, and the maximum of the number of inputs and outputs from the host is a crucial parameter in establishing whether the algorithm execution is bounded by the host I/O transfer speed. We call this ratio α. Our algorithms fall into two classes:

1. Pixel-based algorithms. These algorithms have α ranging as low as one, or as high as thousands (as in the algorithm to find repetitive textures). On the prototype, packing and unpacking of pixels allow α to be as low as 15 before the host becomes a bottleneck. For some simple edge detectors in vision, like the 3×3 Sobel, α is as low as 11. In this case, the host limits overall performance. DMA transfer in PC Warp can reduce this bottleneck.[14]
2. Floating-point based algorithms. That is, data are stored in the host memory as floating-point—rather than pixel—quantities. In this case, packing and unpacking cannot be used, and sequential (row-wise) transfers from the host to the Warp array are rare (which would allow us to use DMA transfer). Irregular memory access patterns, as in 1D FFT (bit reversal) and 2D FFT (corner turning) make this bottleneck worse. For these reasons, the host will be a bottleneck if $\alpha < 60$. However, many such algorithms, including many scientific computing algorithms, feature large or very large α values. For example, for an $n \times n$ SVD, $\alpha \approx 13n$, so that the host is not a bottleneck when $n \geq 5$.

Host memory requirements

The memory in the external host is quite large, from a minimum of 8 Mbytes up to 30 Mbytes, and is available to the programmer to store variables that can be used by several programs. Large data structures can be stored there, where they will not be swapped out by the operating system. This is important for consistent performance in real-time applications. The external host can also support such special devices as frame buffers and high speed disks. This gives the programmer more flexibility in moving variables from memory to other locations, but may involve some specialized hardware design; for example, a special interface card is being developed to transfer data from an Aptec bus device to the external host memory.

Host computation requirement

Sometimes computation on the host is unavoidable. Here are some examples of when the external host must be used:

1. Double-precision arithmetic. The Warp cell can perform only single-precision arithmetic. As in SVD, some floating-point operands may have to be passed out of the Warp array to the cluster processors for double-precision computation.
2. Merge results from cells. The prototype Warp cells cannot perform computations involving data-dependent loop control; sometimes such computations are not needed in the main body of an algorithm, but are needed for the combination of results from different cells. For example, in the connected components algorithm, each cell can compute the connected components of one portion of the image, but these components must be merged using a UNION-FIND algorithm[15] which a Warp cell cannot efficiently implement, because it is highly data-dependent. The component labels from the borders between cells are therefore sent to the host, where they are merged and sent back to the array.
3. Run-time decisions. Programs are executed on the Warp array under control of the external host. Therefore, when a high-level run-time decision is to be made, such as whether to execute another iteration of a loop in a relaxation algorithm, the decision must be made on the external host using data supplied by the Warp array.
4. Circular connection. The Warp array does not have a circular connection from the last cell to the first. This connection can be implemented by passing data through the interface unit, to the output cluster, and copying it from there to the input cluster, where the data can be sent in to the first cell. This technique is used in SVD, DP, and convex hull. Another way to implement this path is to use the backwards path, as in column-wise SVD. In programs that operate in phases, completely producing one output before using it in the next phase, the two clusters can exchange their roles in sending or receiving data for different phases of a computation, in a ping-pong fashion. This avoids the need to copy data

from one cluster to the other. This technique is used in SOR and could be used in DP.

Cell Issues

Intra-cell parallelism

The Warp cell is horizontally microcoded; multiple functional units can be utilized at the same time. The compiler is incapable of moving operations between different loops. Therefore, if loops using different resources are merged, the compiler can achieve better utilization.

Intra-cell pipelining

The compiler generates efficient microcode despite the Warp cell's highly pipelined floating-point adder and multiplier. This is accomplished by a sophisticated global flow analyzer and highly optimizing global scheduling techniques.[16] Since these optimizations are only applied to innermost loops, it is best to unroll all innermost loops with only a few iterations.

Use of conditional statements

The programmer must avoid the indiscriminate use of IF statements with long THEN or ELSE clauses inside short loops. Otherwise, the compiler optimizations may increase the code size enormously.

Cell memory requirements

The memory in the prototype Warp cell is quite small. This has limited the application of certain programming models, which otherwise might be quite efficient. For example, in image warping,[17] the input to output mapping is not predetermined, but is a function of the particular transformation that should be applied to the input image. Computing the mapping function is a major part of the image warping algorithm. It is not possible for the input image to be sent in the right order to produce the output image in, say, raster order, because the right input order is not known until the mapping function is evaluated by the Warp array. For this reason, the entire input image must be stored at each cell, so that the output image can be generated in raster order from the input, by accessing the input image in the order determined by the mapping function. If the cell memory is not large enough to store the entire image, multiple passes over the output image will be required. In other algorithms, such as matrix multiplication, it is possible to partition the data so that each cell has a portion of the data, and all the data are stored at the same time on the array.

PERFORMANCE SUMMARY

Table I gives the performance of the prototype Warp on a range of applications, using compiler-generated code, except for FFT, which was hand-coded. Program download (100 ms) and startup (25 ms) times are not included, but input and output of data from the external host is included. In stand-alone applications, where a small group of algorithms are used over and over, all code can be downloaded into the array before the application is started, and startup of each algorithm is not needed as long as the sequence of algorithms is fixed. In a research environment, where many new algorithms are being tested, these times may have to be counted in system performance.

PC WARP IMPROVEMENT

The re-implementation of the wire-wrapped prototype Warp machine in printed circuit board form made it possible to incorporate many improvements, some resulting from the more advanced technology now available, and others reflecting our experience with the prototype. Several changes were made;[14] here we discuss only those changes with the biggest impact on applications.

Cell Data Memory

The PC Warp cell's data memory is increased from 4K to 32K words, with a direct impact on applications. For example, the prototype cell's memory limits the largest convolution window we can presently compute for 512×512 image processing to 34×34, using the current program. With a 32K cell data memory, we will be able to compute convolution windows up to 115×115. In programs that store the entire input or output dataset, such as those that are output partitioned, like image warping, the larger memory leads to a linear speedup, until the data memory is large enough to store the complete dataset.

Cell Program Memory

The PC Warp cell's program memory is increased from 2K to 8K microwords, ensuring that we will not run out of memory for a single algorithm (certain algorithms, such as SVD, are very close to the limit). This also makes it possible to store several algorithms at once in the program memory. This is important for real-time applications which cannot afford to stop and reload the program memory.

Increased Host I/O Bandwidth

PC Warp's external host uses faster processors with on-board memories and DMA support, as well as faster memory boards. This increases host I/O bandwidth from 1–4 MB/s to 8–12 MB/s, if DMA can be used. Algorithms that do floating-point I/O, with $\alpha < 60$, will benefit from this. With DMA, α

TABLE I—Measured speedups on the wire-wrapped prototype Warp

Task (All images are 512×512.)	Time (ms)	Speedup over Vax 11/780 with floating-point accelerator	
5×5 Convolution	280	100	(*)
Quadratic image warping	400	100	(*)
Warp array generates addresses using quadratic form in 240 ms.			
Host computes output image using addresses generated by Warp.			
3×3 median filter	326		
100×100 matrix multiplication	25	200	
Road-following		200	(*)
Obstacle avoidance using ERIM, a laser range-finder	350	60	(*)
Minimum-cost path, 512×512 image, one pass	500	60	(*)
Host provides feedback.			
Detecting lines by Hough Transform	2000	387	(*)
Host merges results.			
Minimum-cost path, 350-node graph	16000	98	(*)
Convex hull, 1,000 random nodes	18	74	(*)
Solving elliptic PDE by SOR, 50,625 unknowns (10 iterations)	180	440	(*)
Warp is 2.7 times slower than CRAY-1[18].			
SVD of 100×100 matrix	1500	49	(**)
FFT on 2D image	2500	300	(*)
Warp array takes 600 ms. Remaining time is for data shuffling by host.			
Image correlation using FFT	7000	300	(*)
Data shuffling in host.			
Image compression with 8×8 discrete cosine transforms	110	500	(**)
Mandelbrot image, 256 iterations	6960	100	

(*) Further speedup by at least a factor of two with application program optimization.

(**) Further speedup by at least a factor of four with application program optimization.

can be as small as 16–25 to fully use the array. Algorithms that do byte-packed I/O can fully use the host bandwidth with DMA when $\alpha \geq 10$.

Onboard Integer ALU

Each PC Warp cell has an integer ALU, which can compute Boolean and other integer functions. This expands the range of data types that can efficiently be supported—the prototype Warp cell cannot efficiently compute bit-wise functions, making it necessary for the programmer to figure out how to do these operations using floating-point, precisely the opposite of a programmer of a machine without hardware floating-point! This makes algorithms that incorporate specialized data structures, such as graph algorithms, sparse matrix computations, histogram, and connected components more efficient.

Hardware Flow Control and Onboard Address Generation

PC Warp's most significant increase in application support comes from its hardware flow control mechanism, which, together with onboard address generation (using the integer ALU), makes the Warp cells more independent of each other.

Because the cells are independent, each cell can perform local control flow using data-dependent WHILE and FOR statements. This simplifies programming for algorithms with data-dependent control flow, such as those that must iterate a variable number of times until convergence is achieved or data is exhausted. This also gives better performance, since on the prototype machine, where control flow is data independent, worst-case estimates must be made and used for all cases.

Onboard address generation also makes support of heterogeneous programs much easier. Heterogeneous computation is known to be useful in many applications.[19] Using heterogeneous computation, it is possible to perform several operations on an image as it passes through the array. For example, an image can be filtered, histogrammed, and thresholded in a single pass through the array. This increases the number of operations that can be performed on a datum in one pass through the array, helping eliminate the host I/O bottleneck.

These mechanisms also increase the range of algorithms that can read and compute with their operands directly from the queues, reducing cell memory bandwidth. On the prototype, if a cell does too much computation before passing through operands to the next cell, the skew computed by the compiler will be too large, and the address queue on the cell may overflow. On PC Warp, this is no longer a concern.

APPLICATIONS OF VLSI WARP

Carnegie Mellon and Intel Corporation are designing an ambitious VLSI version of the Warp machine. In this machine, each Warp cell, excluding memory, will be reduced to a single chip, with at least 16 MFLOPS and 10 MIPS in the integer unit. The baseline machine will include 72 cells, for a total performance of at least 1.152 GigaFLOPS.

The implications of this machine for applications are exciting. Besides the raw power of the large array, we will also implement a more sophisticated model of inter-cell communication, which allows non-neighboring cells to communicate logically as if they were adjacent. This should help in the implementation of heterogeneous programs, which will sometimes be necessary in making effective use of such a long array. Moreover, the same chip will be used as the basis of non-linear arrays, such as two-dimensional arrays.

With the VLSI implementation, it should be possible to build much larger arrays than with the current Warp implementation. We expect that arrays of hundreds or thousands of cells will be built and used in specialized applications, leading to enormous speedups over conventional computers.

CONCLUSIONS

The ten cell prototype machines at Carnegie Mellon have proved to be useful. There are many applications which can make effective use of all ten cells. In no cases were we limited because we could not find at least ten-fold parallelism in a problem, where any parallelism was available at all. We have outlined in this paper the rules we follow to get good performance on a number of Warp algorithms.

In certain application areas (e.g., the solution of partial differential equations via successive over-relaxation) Warp's power rivals that of much more expensive supercomputers, such as the Cray-1.

Warp is particularly suited for application areas in which there is a lot of sensor information to be processed for some higher-level decisions, such as in image and signal processing. Warp's external host allows Warp to easily interface to devices for capturing such data; Warp's relatively small size and cost make it possible to put it in places where such data is used; and its power and programmability make it possible to process such data effectively.

Many of the limitations in the prototype Warp machine have been overcome in the printed circuit board version. We expect the PC Warp machines to have an even wider range of applications, especially because of their ability to support heterogeneous programs and programs with data-dependent control flow. The VLSI version of Warp will increase even more the range of algorithms supported on Warp, and give more than a factor of ten speedup for these applications.

ACKNOWLEDGEMENTS

The research was supported in part by Defense Advanced Research Projects Agency (DOD), monitored by the Air Force Avionics Laboratory under Contract F33615-81-K-1539, and Naval Electronic Systems Command under Contract N00039-85-C-0134, in part by the US Army Engineer Topographic Laboratories under Contract DACA76-85-C-0002, and in part by the Office of Naval Research under Contracts N00014-80-C-0236, NR 048-659, and N00014-85-K-0152, NR

SDRJ-007. H.T. Kung is also supported by a Shell Distinguished Chair in Computer Science.

REFERENCES

1. Annaratone, M., F. Bitz, E. Clune, H.T. Kung, P. Maulik, H. Ribas, P. Tseng, and J. Webb. "Applications and Algorithm Partitioning on Warp." *COMPCON Spring '87,* IEEE Computer Society, 1987, pp. 272–275.
2. Mansfield, P. and I.L. Pykett. "Biological and Medical Imaging by NMR." *Journal of Magnetic Resonance,* 29 (1978), pp. 355–373.
3. Matthaei, D., J. Frahm, A. Hasse, and W. Hanicke. "Regional Physiological Functions Depicted by Sequences of Rapid Magnetic Resonance Images." *The Lancet,* 2 (1985), pp. 893.
4. Vocar, J.M. and R.O. Faiss. "Image Magnification: Elementary with STARAN." Tech. report GER-16342, Goodyear Aerospace Corporation, August, 1976.
5. Rosenfeld, A. and M. Thurston. "Edge and Curve Detection for Visual Scene Analysis." *IEEE Transactions on Computing,* 20 (1971) 5, pp. 562–569.
6. Electrotechnical Laboratory. *SPIDER (Subroutine Package for Image Data Enhancement and Recognition),* Joint System Development Corp., Tokyo, Japan, 1983.
7. Rao, C.R. *Linear Statistical Inference and Its Applications,* 2nd ed., New York: John Wiley, 1973.
8. Dongarra, J.J., J.R. Bunch, C.B. Moler, and G.W. Stewart. *LINPACK Users' Guide.* Society for Industrial and Applied Mathematics, 1979.
9. Hestenes, M.R., "Inversion of Matrices by Biorthogonalization and Related Results." *J. Soc. Indust. Appl. Math.,* 6 (1958), pp. 51–90.
10. Schimmel, D.E. and F.T. Luk. "A New Systolic Array for the Singular Value Decomposition." *Proceedings of 1986 Conference on Advanced Research in VLSI,* M.I.T., April, 1986, pp. 205–217.
11. Smith, B.T. et al. *Matrix Eigensystem Routines—EISPACK Guide,* Lecture Notes in Computer Science 6, New York: Springer-Verlag, 1976.
12. Annaratone, M., E. Arnould, H.T. Kung, and O. Menzilcioglu. "Using Warp as a Supercomputer in Signal Processing." *Proceedings of ICASSP 86,* IEEE, 1986, pp. 2895–2898.
13. Hammarling, S. "A Note on Modifications to The Givens Plane Rotations." *J. Inst. Maths Applics,* 13 (1974), pp. 215–218.
14. Annaratone, M., E. Arnould, R. Cohn, T. Gross, H.T. Kung, M. Lam, O. Menzilcioglu, K. Sarocky, J. Senko, and J. Webb. "Warp Architecture: From Prototype to Production." *AFIPS Proceedings of the National Computer Conference* (Vol. 56), June 1987.
15. Aho, A., J.E. Hopcroft, and J.D. Ullman. *The Design and Analysis of Computer Algorithms,* Reading, Massachusetts: Addison-Wesley, 1975.
16. Bruegge, B., C. Chang, R. Cohn, T. Gross, M. Lam, P. Lieu, A. Noaman, and D. Yam. "Programming Warp." *COMPCON Spring '87,* IEEE Computer Society, 1987, pp. 268–271.
17. Kung, H.T. and J.A. Webb. "Mapping Image Processing Operations onto a Linear Systolic Machine." *Distributed Computing,* 1 (1986) 4, pp. 246–257.
18. Young, D. *Iterative Solution of Large Linear Systems,* New York: Academic Press, 1971.
19. Gross, T., H.T. Kung, M. Lam, and J. Webb. "Warp as a Machine for Low-level Vision." *Proceedings of 1985 IEEE International Conference on Robotics and Automation,* March 1985, pp. 790–800.

Very large database applications of the Connection Machine system

by DAVID WALTZ, CRAIG STANFILL, STEPHEN SMITH, and ROBERT THAU
Thinking Machines Corporation
Cambridge, Massachusetts

ABSTRACT

The architecture of the Connection Machine™ system is particularly appropriate for large database applications. The Connection Machine system consists of 65,536 processors, each with its own memory, coupled by a high speed communications network. In large database applications, individual data elements are stored in separate processors and are operated on simultaneously. This paper examines three types of applications of this technology. The first, which will be examined in the greatest detail, is the use of the Connection Machine System for document retrieval. The second application is parsing large free text databases and preparing them for searching. The third topic is the application of the Connection Machine to associative memory or content addressable memory tasks. This ability has been put to use in a method called "memory-based reasoning" which can produce expert system-like behavior from a database of records of earlier decisions.

INTRODUCTION

The rapid growth of on-line databases is a great challenge to information processing technology. First, databases are growing quickly in size: databases with tens of gigabytes are now quite common, and databases with hundreds of gigabytes are by no means unknown. Soon, with advances in optical disk technology, we will have to deal with databases having terrabytes or even tens of terrabytes of data.

This growth in database size creates two problems. The first is obvious: when a database doubles in size, the amount of storage it requires doubles, and the amount of compute power necessary to process it doubles. The second is perhaps less obvious: as a database grows, it becomes more and more difficult to locate and manipulate the information it contains.

For text databases, this second problem manifests itself as deteriorating search quality: as a database contains more and more information, finding the right information becomes increasingly difficult, so that the system is likely to miss desired information or to deluge the user with unwanted data. This problem can be (at least partly) overcome by the use of more sophisticated retrieval algorithms such as relevance feedback (see below). These algorithms are, however, computationally more expensive than the algorithms generally used for document retrieval today.

Databases containing numerical and symbolic data also require more intensive processing as they grow in size. In the current paradigm, a database might be abstracted to a much smaller set of statistical characteristics (e.g., "The average salary of the CEOs of Fortune 500 corporations"). However, in abstracting a database to a few statistical parameters information is inevitably lost. We believe a good solution to this problem is to search the database for precedents, a technique called "Memory Based Reasoning" (see below). In this method, decisions are made by searching a database for episodes similar to the problem facing the user, then basing conclusions on the data so located. Again, problems associated with large databases may be attacked, but the algorithms are computationally intensive.

Thus, it is desirable that computational power increase faster than the size of the database. Unfortunately, just the opposite is happening, as the performance of serial computers has reached a plateau while databases continue to get bigger and bigger. A solution to this problem is the use of a new generation of parallel computers, such as the Connection Machine™ System, which have much greater computational power than conventional (serial) machines. The remainder of this paper will consider some specific applications of this new machine to problems associated with large databases.

DOCUMENT RETRIEVAL

Document retrieval has traditionally been implemented as Boolean search on an inverted file. The main difficulties of Boolean search are that: 1) users require considerable training in the use of a query language, and 2) users generally alternate between being overwhelmed by too many documents if one uses a too general search pattern, or too few documents if one is more restrictive.[1]

We have built an easy-to-use document retrieval system that allows simultaneous searches of very large databases by a large number of users.[2] The system mixes AI ideas with methods from information science. Its basis is a weighted associative memory algorithm. In contrast to a Boolean search system, a naive user can be trained to use our system in a few minutes. The system operates very rapidly, and has high precision and recall.

Using the algorithm described here, a single Connection Machine system allows a 6 GByte free text database to be searched and browsed rapidly and conveniently by over 2000 simultaneous users. Other algorithms (not yet implemented) that are dependent on a high speed multiple disk mass storage unit will allow much larger databases to be searched.

Relevance Feedback

From the user's point of view, the search process on the Connection Machine document retrieval system has two distinct phases. In the first phase, the user types a list of a few keywords, for example, "Iran Contra arms deal." The retrieval system returns a list of documents, ordered according to how many of the keywords they contain, and how important each keyword is (the rarer the word, the more important). In the second phase, the user browses through these documents and finds one or more that bear on the topic of interest. As relevant documents are located, the user may command the system to search for related documents by performing a full-text to full-text comparison between the documents he has already found and every document in the database. This is done by automatically extracting the words from the text of the known relevant documents and rating the documents in the database according to how many of those words they contain.

This method, termed "relevance feedback," has been known since the 1960s to yield high quality searches, but to the best of our knowledge, it has never been used on a large database because of its extremely high computational requirements.

Implementation

Relevance feedback generates queries containing hundreds or thousands of terms, where each term consists of a word and the weight assigned to that word. Each processor in the system is assigned a 25 word segment from a single document. To execute a query, a serial front end processor broadcasts the word-weight pairs to the Connection Machine System. As this is done, each processor tests its segment for the presence of each word. When a word is found, the processor accumulates the word's weight to form a score for that document. After the complete query has been broadcast, the results are sorted in order of decreasing score, and the pointers to the 20–100 documents with the highest scores are sent to the user.

Documents are represented using a method of *surrogate coding* described by Stanfill and Kahle.[2] In this method, groups of 25 words are collected and used to set bits in a 1024 bit vector. Bits are set by applying n hash code functions to each term (n typically = 10). Thus, to represent a document with 75 terms, about 250 bits in each of three vectors of 1024 bits each would be set. Occasionally, more than one hash function may set the same bit. This is handled by superimposing the results. The vectors for each document are then stored in a contiguous group of processors.

In order to search for a document, the same hash codes that were used to construct the bit vectors are applied to each of the terms in the search pattern, one at a time, and the positions of the hash code bits are broadcast to all the processors. Each processor checks to see whether it has all 10 bits set for a given term and if so, it adds a score for that term to the total score for the document stored in its document mailbox. This algorithm is probabilistic: there is a small chance that a given term will hash into 10 locations which were set by other terms, causing the system to interpret it as a term occurring in a document when in fact it has not. The probability of this happening is dependent on the number of hash functions applied to each term, the size of the vector, and the number of terms in the overall database. The probability of a false hit can be made arbitrarily small by applying more hash functions or increasing the length of a bit vector. With the parameters we have been using, the probability of a false hit is about 1/1,000,000. Additionally, since each query in a relevance search contains an average of 75 terms, one or two false hits cannot make much of a difference in the overall relevance calculation.

Performance

The performance figures contained in this section assume that a Connection Machine system with 65,536 processors and 2 GBytes of fast memory. Furthermore, we assume the data preparation algorithms explained below have been applied, yielding an overall data compression rate of 3.3:1. Finally, we assume a user spends two minutes browsing between searches.

The bit vectors are much smaller than the memories of the individual processing elements. This allows us to use the Connection Machine's "virtual processor" mechanism to increase the amount of data stored in the system. To do this, each processor's memory is segmented, and the processors sequentially perform any computation on each memory segment. To the programmer or user, it appears that there are n times as many processors, each with $1/n$ as much memory as a real processor, each operating at $1/n$ the speed.[3,4]

The 2GBytes of memory in the Connection Machine System allows us to store surrogates built from 7 Gigabytes of raw text. Each processor will then simulate 64 virtual processors, and run at 1/64th the speed of a physical processor. Each surrogate may be tested for the presence of a word in 2 microseconds, and a score may be added in 6 microseconds. Allowing for the virtual processor ratio, this allows us to execute a single term in 512 microseconds. If we assume an average query generated by relevance feedback contains 75 terms, we may then perform a complete search in 38 milliseconds. This would allow our system to support over 2000 users.

FORMATTING A DATABASE

As the size of databases and the rate at which data is fed into a system increases, the problem of scanning raw data, indexing it, and adding it to the database becomes ever more difficult. We are attacking this problem by building a set of natural language and text processing tools running on the Connection Machine System.[5,6,7]

Formatting a database proceeds in several phases, gradually grouping the individual characters of the raw file into words, phrases, paragraphs, and documents. First, we use a regular expression-based lexical analysis system to break the input stream into tokens, such as words and punctuation marks. Second, several dictionaries are used to differentiate important from unimportant words and to group words into known phrases. Finally, we take groups of words, put them into surrogate tables, and write the results out to disk. We are also working on generalized parsing algorithms, which may be applied to identifying specialized forms of noun phrases (e.g., names of people, places, dates), as well as to full syntactic parsing. These parsing tools have yet to be integrated into the full system.

Lexical Analysis

The first step in processing raw text (e.g., a newswire transcript) is parsing it into meaningful units. This must be done on two levels. The words in the text must be found (and distinguished from, say, embedded formatting directives). Just as important, the incoming stream of raw text must be split into separate documents, with paragraph delimiters, identified headlines, and dates. All of this is done by a regular-expression based lexing phase, which runs the regular expressions by using precompiled finite state automata (FSAs).

The lexer is driven off an action list, which contains pointers to FSAs, and indications of what to do with the matches. For example, paragraph delimiters are handled by having the action list run an FSA which finds paragraph boundaries and inserts a special delimiting sequence. This regular expression is specific to the source of text: it might look for indented lines, blank lines, or embedded formatting directives.

The bulk of the work is done by two special directives. One of them marks all substrings of the input matching a regular expression as words. The other splits undelimited text into documents while extracting information such as the headline and date.

There are two algorithms for running FSAs on a Connection Machine System. The most direct is to put a copy of the FSA in each processor, and stream the text by them. Spurious matches like the "have" in "behave" are suppressed, by using the first match that ends at a given point. This is fine for FSAs that have only to match short strings (e.g., words), but it is excessively time consuming when the FSA needs to match a large amount of text (e.g., the headline of a newswire article). In these circumstances, the log-time lexing algorithm of Hillis' and Steel's "Data Parallel Algorithms"[8] is more appropriate.

Dictionaries

The text compression algorithm uses word frequency dictionaries. These dictionaries consist of words paired with a count of how many times they occurred in a corpus of known size. One dictionary entry is stored per processor.

To construct such a dictionary from a textual database requires four distinct steps: 1) load the Connection Machine with text from the given database, 2) accumulate the characters such that there is one word per processor, 3) produce dictionary entries for these new words, and 4) merge these new entries with the existing dictionary. This last step is accomplished by sorting the entries alphabetically, grouping entries with the same word, and summing the count fields for each group.

Look-up word frequencies in these dictionaries proceeds similarly to the dictionary building phase described above: 1) a "dummy" entry is created for each word to be looked up. This dummy contains a pointer back to the processor requesting the word's definition. 2) the dummies are sorted with the real dictionary entries so that dummy entries always follow the real entries for a word. 3) entries for the same word (both real and dummy) are grouped together. 4) definitions are copied from real to dummy entries within a group. 5) the definitions are sent back to the requesting processor via the dummy's backpointer.

Frequency Based Indexing

The text compression algorithm being used in the current Document Retrieval System is called "Frequency Based Indexing." This algorithm extracts content bearing terms based on the number of times they occur throughout some large database. Words with high frequencies, such as "the," "of," and "to" are dropped. Words with low frequencies, such as "parallel," "computer," and "algorithm" are retained. Proper nouns like "Iran" and "Reagan" are always retained.

For words which are neither rare enough to be dropped outright nor frequent enough to be automatically retained, we use a word-pair based method. For example, the word "special" is too common to be retained by the frequency considerations alone. However, when we build a dictionary of word-pair frequencies, we find the two word phrase "special prosecutor" is more common than the frequencies of "special" and "prosecutor" alone would suggest. Thus, the word "special" is retained, and marked as part of a phrase.

Building Surrogates

The final step in formatting a database is building the surrogate tables. First, each processor computes the ten hash codes for a single word. Next, 1024 bits are zeroed out in each processor as a partial hash table. The bits that the ten hash codes pointed to are then set. Finally, the 25 tables corresponding to a document segment are ORed together to form the final surrogate.

Parsing

At the moment, the system only discriminates between words on the basis of frequency. An improvement might be to detect specific types of multi-word phrases. A quick and effective way of doing this is to retrieve part-of-speech information from the dictionary and use an FSA to recognize phrases. Preliminary experiments using a dictionary of words likely to appear in names of corporations indicate that this approach can be used to find names of companies and such, with some success. Experiments have also been done with full text parsing.[9]

MEMORY-BASED REASONING

Memory-Based Reasoning (MBR) is a new paradigm for AI in which an associative memory using a best-match algorithm takes the place of rules. It is particularly well-suited to massively parallel computers such as the Connection Machine System. Memory-Based Reasoning places memory at the foundation of intelligence, rather than at the periphery. Memories of specific events are used directly to make decisions, rather than indirectly (as in systems which use experience to infer rules). In its purest form, memory-based reasoning uses the global nearest match computation to find the items in memory most similar to a current situation and then uses the actions associated with these items to deal with the current situation. In essence, reasoning is reduced to perception: the current situation is observed, it reminds the system of something it has seen before, and an immediate reaction is forthcoming without further analysis.

We can contrast memory-based reasoning in this extreme form with models based on heuristic search. In heuristic search, solutions are generated rather than looked up. To give a concrete example, in solving a medical reasoning problem, a memory-based reasoning system finds a patient or patients most similar to the current patient by a global nearest match operation, and uses the diagnosis, treatment, and outcome to find a diagnosis and treatment, and to predict an outcome for the current patient. A rule-based forward chaining system takes the patient's symptoms and applies rules one after another until it arrives at a diagnosis.

The advantages of memory-based reasoning are: 1) it is much easier to generate examples than to generate rules, so the knowledge acquisition for a memory-based reasoning system is much simpler; 2) memory-based reasoning systems inherently have a mechanism for judging confidence in an answer—if there is a very close match in memory to the current situation, one can be quite confident of the outcome. If the nearest match is far away, the system can note that its results are uncertain, "it can know that it doesn't know"; 3) memory-based reasoning systems can scale well to very large problems, and a single system can handle simultaneously a number of different kinds of problems.

Significantly, parallel hardware reverses the relative efficiency of memory-based reasoning and rule-based reasoning. On serial hardware, the best-match operation is very expensive because every data item must be considered in turn, while rule-triggering is relatively cheap due to the existence of algorithms (e.g., Rete networks) that allow a database of rules to be efficiently searched. On parallel hardware, the best-match algorithm takes constant time, while rule-invocation takes time proportional to the number of rules which must be chained to obtain an answer.

The remainder of this section will discuss work to date on memory-based reasoning, including experiments with pure MBR and MBR augmented with a generalization mechanism. We will then present our plans for further development of the paradigm.

Work to Date

In this section we will discuss memory-based reasoning applied to the classification problem. Given a database of objects, each object belonging to one of a set of mutually exclusive classes, we classify new objects by finding the best match in the existing database and looking at its class.

As reported in Stanfill's and Waltz' "Toward Memory-Based Reasoning,"[10] we implemented a memory-based reasoning "shell." This shell computes the nearest match to an input pattern (which may be incomplete) using a set of weighting and distance measures, the net effect of which is to find the distance from every individual example in memory to the current example to be classified.

The shell assumes a relational database-like format for examples. More formally, a database is a set of records. Each record has a fixed set of fields. The field specifying the class of a record is the goal field, and the other fields are predictor fields. Novel records which are to be classified are target records.

The computation of similarity is fairly complex. Field weights are computed by judging how tightly a particular predictor field constrains values of the goal field. The distance between two records is then computed by summing the weights for all predictor fields for which they have different values. For example, if a patient reports having a sore throat, this constrains the range of diseases he/she might be suffering from to a relatively small range (e.g., a viral infection, a strep infection, smoking). Thus, if a patient reported a sore throat, all records in the database which did not include a sore throat would receive a large distance measure. On the other hand, having a low fever places relatively few constraints on the possible maladies, so it would receive a small weight.

More recently, we have added a generalization algorithm to the memory-based reasoning shell. This algorithm searches for patterns in the database (e.g., "a high fever accompanied by a sore throat indicates a strep infection"), and remembers which records obey them. These stored patterns are then used to augment the best-match process: if a target record matches a stored pattern, the data records used to generate the pattern will have their similarity-measures boosted. The primary benefit of this generalization mechanism is to significantly reduce the system's sensitivity to noise. In all cases, it produces a significant improvement in the quality of MBR's decisions.

An Experiment

Memory-Based Reasoning was applied to the problem of pronouncing English words. The formulation of the task is deliberately similar to Sejnowski and Rosenberg's NETtalk system.[11] In this case, the database is a dictionary.[12] Each record in the database consists of a seven-letter window in a word (a letter, the three previous letters, and the next three letters); a three-phoneme window in the pronunciation (the phoneme plus the two preceding phonemes); and the stress of the letter (primary stress, secondary stress). For example, the word "file," which has pronunciation "fAL-" and stress pattern "1- -," would yield the following four records:

*	*	*	f	i	l	e	*	*	f	+
	*	f	i	l	e	*	*	f	A	1
	f	i	l	e	*	*	f	A	1	-
f	i	l	e	*	*	*	A	1	-	-

The 20,000 words in the dictionary thus yield 146,951 records.

It must be noted that perfect performance on the pronunciation task, as outlined above, is fundamentally impossible. First, many English words are borrowed from other languages, often retaining their original pronunciations. Thus, any system which pronounced "montage" correctly would almost certainly mispronounce "frontage." Second, the stress patterns of English words often depend on their part of speech. In some cases, a word will even have two acceptable pronunciations, depending on whether it is used as a noun or a verb ("to object" versus "an object").

In spite of the difficulty of the pronunciation task, Memory-Based Reasoning does quite well. Given the three preceding letters, the three succeeding letters, the two preceding phonemes, and the stress, MBR produces the correct phoneme 92% of the time. If we omit the previous two phonemes and the stress, MBR gets the correct phoneme 87% of the time. With a database of 128K records running on a 32K processor Connection Machine System, each classification is accomplished in 30 milliseconds.

Evaluation

The two MBR algorithms described above (pure MBR and MBR with generalization-learning) were evaluated according to sensitivity to database size, distraction, and noise. The results of these experiments are discussed more fully in Stanfill's "Memory-Based Reasoning Applied to English Pronunciation."[13]

Database size

Both algorithms exhibit graceful degradation as the size of the database shrinks from 128K down to 4K. The generalization algorithm is always slightly better. With 4K records (approximately 700 words), 78 percent of phonemes were correct.

Distraction

In an effort to distract the algorithms, between one and seven fields containing random values were added to each record in the database. These had no effect on either algorithm.

Noise

Two types of noise were considered. First, between 10% and 100% noise was added to the predictor fields.* Neither algorithm was significantly affected until noise exceeded 90%, at which point performance collapsed. Second, between 10% and 100% noise was added to the goal fields. For pure MBR, performance fell about linearly with added noise. For MBR with generalization, performance degraded more slowly until the noise level exceeded 60%.

Prospects for Memory-Based Reasoning

Work, so far, has concentrated on the application of pure memory-based reasoning to "flat" relational databases, with the representation fixed by the system builder. The next stages will be to relax some of these restrictions. Part of this work has already been started, with the addition of generalization to MBR. We also plan to allow MBR to modify its representations, as well as to allow for a greater flexibility in their form (e.g., allowing networks and hierarchies).

In the long run, we believe that memory-based reasoning will provide a unifying paradigm for Artificial Intelligence. Most aspects of intelligence, we believe, can be expressed as operations on or augmentations to memory. This includes perception, attention, generalization, learning, and deduction. Indeed, aspects of some of these phenomena appear as emergent behavior of the simple MBR model presented above.

* For 10% noise, 10% of the predictor-fields in the database would receive a random value.

REFERENCES

1. Blair, D. C., and M. E. Maron. "An Evaluation of Retrieval Effectiveness for a Full-Text Document-Retrieval System." *Communications of the ACM,* 28 (1985) 3, pp. 285–299.
2. Stanfill, C., and B. Kahle. "Parallel Free Text Search on the Connection Machine System." *Communications of the ACM,* 29 (1986) 12, pp. 1229–1239.
3. Thinking Machines Corporation, *Introduction to Data Level Parallelism.* Cambridge, MA, April, 1986.
4. Hillis, D. *The Connection Machine.* Cambridge, MA: MIT Press, 1985.
5. Sabot, G., "Bulk Processing of Text on a Massively Parallel Computer." *Proceedings 24th Annual Meeting of the Association for Computational Linguistics,* New York, June 10–13, 1986, pp. 128–135.
6. Waltz, D. L. "Applications of the Connection Machine." *IEEE Computer,* 20 (1987) 1, pp. 85–97.
7. Smith, S. "Extracting Content Bearing Terms in Parallel on the Connection Machine," Thinking Machines Corporation Technical Paper DR87-1, 1987.
8. Hillis, D., and G. Steel. "Data Parallel Algorithms." *Communications of the ACM,* 29 (1986) 12, pp. 1170–1183.
9. Thau, R., and S. Ferguson. "Context Free Parsing on the Connection Machine System." Thinking Machines Corporation Technical Paper NL87-1, 1987.
10. Stanfill, C., and D. L. Waltz. "Toward Memory-Based Reasoning." *Communications of the ACM,* 29 (1986) 12, pp. 1213–1228.
11. Sejnowski, T. J. and C. R. Rosenberg. "NETtalk: A Parallel Network that Learns to Read Aloud." The Johns Hopkins University Electrical Engineering and Computer Science Technical Report JHU/EECS-86.
12. *Merriam Webster's Pocket Dictionary,* 1974.
13. Stanfill, C. "Memory-Based Reasoning Applied to English Pronunciation." *Proceedings, Sixth National Conference on Artificial Intelligence (AAAI-87),* Seattle, Washington, July 13–17, 1987.

EDUCATIONAL AND HUMAN RESOURCE ISSUES

ROBERT L. ASHENHURST
The University of Chicago
Chicago, Illinois

The 1980s are witnessing an expansion in modes of computer use as personal microcomputers and departmental midsize systems are added alongside the once exclusive centralized mainframe systems. This results in a marked change in job requirements for many positions, both general and those specific to computing support. This, in turn, places heightened demands on education and training programs in academic and corporate settings and on an organization's personnel and human resource functions. These sessions focus on educational and human resource issues in this broadened context.

By its designation, the scope of this track is extensive, even if only considered in the institutional context (i.e., schools and colleges, personnel departments, and management). The rubric is extended even further, however, by including human factors considerations where the context is the capabilities and limitations of individuals.

Submitted papers are presented in two sessions, *Computer Technology and the Educational System* and *Human Factors in the Computer Systems Environment.* The papers address issues potentially of interest to all, but which are directly relevant to those who oversee educational efforts involving computing and organizational computing efforts.

The remaining sessions are panel presentations. Three panel sessions deal with topics of direct relevance to the management of computer personnel. In the featured session, *A New Occupational Taxonomy for Computer Specialists,* a job classification framework is presented, and issues of skill requirements and salary compensation are pinpointed. The *How to Pick Eagles* session deals with the interview and hiring process for computer professionals. The *New Technology and Human Resources* session deals with the general impact of the computer on the workplace. These sessions will interest personnel and project management specialists.

Two panel sessions deal with human factors in systems and software. The *Tackling Software Ergonomics* and *Usability of Corporate Information Systems* sessions cover the human engineering aspects of the user-system interface. These are designed to interest both managers of systems projects and the developers who have the direct responsibility for system project implementation.

Development of occupational taxonomies for computer specialists

by SYLVIA CHARP
Charp Associates
Upper Darby, Pennsylvania

EXECUTIVE SUMMARY

Background

Rapid progress in the field of computers and high technology during recent years has resulted in corresponding changes in computer specialties occupations. These changes have created new and unprecedented positions lacking common job titles and well established job descriptions. Although several taxonomies such as the *Dictionary of Occupational Titles* (U.S. Department of Labor), the *Standard Occupational Classification Manual* (U.S. Department of Commerce) and the *Taxonomy of Computer Science and Engineering* (AFIPS Taxonomy Committee) provide relevant information, none include sufficiently detailed classifications of computer specialists. This lack of detail has created problems for those in government, industry, and academia who are involved with occupational surveys and personnel functions. Perceiving a need to improve the quality of information on occupations within the computer field, the American Federation of Information Processing Societies (AFIPS) developed, under a grant from the National Science Foundation, an expanded taxonomy of computer specialist occupations which provides a contemporary, standardized set of easily understood and acceptable classifications.

Purpose

The following report is the result of a study conducted for the National Science Foundation (NSF) by AFIPS which produced such an occupational taxonomy for the computer specialists field. The term "occupational taxonomy" refers to a job classification list that specifies by title a series of related job functions. The main purpose of the study was to develop a new taxonomy which is easy to understand and use, functional in producing accurate data on actual jobs in the economy, flexible to allow for future modifications, more complete than existing taxonomies, and consistent in design with other taxonomies currently used by the NSF.

Scope

The new taxonomy consists of ten major occupational categories, representing a significant expansion of the computer specialties taxonomies currently available. Each of the general major categories includes a detailed list of specific computer specialties jobs and functional titles. These subcategories serve to clarify the general categories and provide the detail necessary for finer screening of personnel functions.

Procedures

To produce the type of taxonomy described above, the following tasks were performed:

—Researched existing sources of occupational information
—Developed an initial taxonomy
—Established an expanded taxonomy and survey questionnaire
—Evaluated the expanded taxonomy through survey pretest
—Distributed, collected and conducted statistical analysis of questionnaire based on expanded taxonomy

Two surveys of selected representatives from industry, academia, federal laboratories, and individual computer professionals provided the data on which the findings of the study were based. The pretest and survey samples consisted mainly of individual members of AFIPS' constituent organizations. The questionnaire, which includes questions about job responsibilities and titles, was filled out by 107 respondents. Further information on the statistics is shown in Appendix D of the final report.

Participants

As noted earlier, the study, launched in the Spring of 1985, was conducted for the National Science Foundation (NSF) by the American Federation of Information Processing Societies

(AFIPS). Principal investigators for the project were Dr. Sylvia Charp, Past President of AFIPS, and Arnold Eshoo, Program Manager, Technical Resource Statistics, Technical Personnel Development, IBM Corporation.

Responsibility for staff work, field surveys and preparation of the final report was sub-contracted to Edward Perlin Associates, management consultants with expertise in the data processing industry. A panel of computer specialists representing a broad range of business, government, academia, and laboratory research was selected to serve as an advisory board.

Methodology

The key tasks involved in conducting the study were as follows:

I. Research of Existing Sources
  A. Identified relevant taxonomies, job descriptions, and personnel surveys from government, industry, and other organizations
  B. Identified the target population, (i.e., organizations employing computer specialists), for the survey sample
  C. Presented initial research to AFIPS panel

II. Development of Initial Taxonomy
  A. Established list of primary computer specialties occupational areas with descriptive statements
  B. Developed and implemented survey sampling procedures
  C. Solicited and incorporated panel responses/reactions/additions to initial taxonomy and proposed sampling methods

III. Established Initial Expanded Taxonomy and Survey Questionnaire
  A. Established occupational sub-categories and selected characteristics/requirements to differentiate among sub-category levels
  B. Listed a representative sample of organizations employing computer specialists
  C. Requested, evaluated, and incorporated panel recommendations on survey questionnaire

IV. Taxonomy Evaluation Pretest
  A. Surveyed small sample of pretest respondents by mail and gathered responses
  B. Met with respondents and validated accuracy of responses
  C. Analyzed accuracy/reliability of responses and fine-tuned questionnaire and reporting requirements

V. Taxonomy Evaluation Survey and Analysis
  A. Mailed questionnaire to and gathered responses from appropriate representatives of the organizations selected for the sample
  B. Met with respondents and reviewed collected data
  C. Evaluated the results statistically for accuracy/reliability

Findings

The information obtained by carrying out the tasks provided the following taxonomy of the computer specialist occupational workforce:*

718 *Computer Scientist*—An individual, usually with an advanced degree, who is engaged as a theorist, researcher, designer or inventor (or any combination of these roles) in the fields of computer hardware or software. The computer scientist most often specializes in one of the following areas:
  A. Theory of Automata
  B. Computer Architecture/Networks
  C. Number/Information Theory
  D. Computer Logic
  E. Computer Languages
  F. Fundamental Algorithms
  G. Software Structures/Operating Systems
  H. Artificial Intelligence
  I. Theory of Complexity
  J. Graphics
  K. Other

719 *Computer Hardware Engineer*—A highly trained specialist, usually with an engineering degree, who applies state-of-the-art knowledge to the design, installation, adaptation or interfacing of computer or computer-related equipment.

720 *Computer Software Engineer*—A highly trained specialist, usually with a degree in either engineering or computer science, who applies state-of-the-art knowledge to the design of overall software systems, to the setting of operational specifications, quality standards and testing procedures, and to the definition of user needs.

721 *Telecommunications Specialist*—A highly trained specialist, usually with a degree in engineering, computer science and/or information theory who deals with the devices and techniques employed for transmission of signs, signals, writing, images, sounds or data of any nature by wire, radio, or other electromagnetic equipment, or in the interfacing of computer and communications equipment.

722 *Systems Programmer*—A high level programmer, usually with a college degree, who creates, maintains, and controls the use of computer systems software with the aim of optimizing operational efficiency.

723 *Systems Analyst*—A specialist, usually with a college degree, who gathers information about the operation of a given physical system, analyzes this information and then formulates a logical plan to achieve desired objectives for improving the system usually through the use of computer, or computer-related equipment and software.

*The numbering system used here directly corresponds to the numbered computer specialties categories included in the current NSF taxonomy.

724 *Programmer*—A specialist, usually with a college degree, who writes, tests, and applies the instructions that define the operations performed by a computer. Some programmers move easily form one field of activity to another, but the tendency is to concentrate in a single area with its own unique content, vocabulary and procedures, as indicated below:
A. Business/Financial
B. Scientific
C. Industrial Machines/Process Control
D. Graphics/Art/Animation
E. Other

725 *Computer Operations Specialist*
A. Data Center Director—An experienced professional, usually a member of management, who directs a computer installation.
B. Computer Operator—A person who performs manual activities required for efficient operation of a computer system, such as mounting tapes, aligning paper, maintaining activity logs and monitoring signals from the system on operational conditions.
C. Data Entry Specialist—A person who manually enters data for use by the computer by such means as keyboard punching, tape, disk or other storage media for processing by the computer.
D. Archivist/Librarian—A person who deals with the accumulation of computer center records, including operational manuals, program listings, documentation, and written sets of operational data as well as the tapes, disks, cards or other storage media in which the programs and data are preserved.
E. Other

726 *Technical Support Specialist*—A skilled professional who responds to technical inquires from users concerning problems encountered in using a computer system.

727 *Computer Trainer*—A skilled professional who instructs those who use computer systems.

728 *Other*

Conclusions

I. The taxonomy meets the research needs of the NSF by achieving the pre-study goals of being easy to understand and use, functional in producing accurate data on actual jobs in the economy, flexible to allow for future modifications, more complete than existing taxonomies, and consistent in design with other taxonomies currently used by the NSF.

These goals are reflected in the following characteristics of the final taxonomy:
A. Very few survey responses fell into the "other" category indicating that the taxonomy is complete and inclusive for the computer specialist field.
B. Panel review showed that the occupational titles are consonant with those used by computer professionals working in the field, thus permitting easy association between actual tasks and the nomenclature incorporated in the taxonomy.
C. The taxonomy spans the computer specialties in depth as well as range, facilitating detailed studies of labor market factors in a leading-edge technological area.
D. The classifications can be readily cross-referenced and aggregated to meet the requirements of public sector statistical groups.

II. The taxonomy is a summation of the computer specialties field as it is today. Continuing change in the industry will necessitate updates at appropriate intervals, perhaps every three to five years.

III. The problem of obsolescence already plagues existing government taxonomies dealing with the computer specialties field, with the notable exception being the Defense Department's MOTD and those used by other agencies for internal operations. The need to keep basic government taxonomies current is vital.

IV. Existing taxonomies miss relatively small, but significant groups of critical high-technology skills. Therefore, strong efforts should be made to combine existing taxonomies into a single listing which would address both the public and private sectors' needs. This would facilitate the process of planning for the future of the computer industry through an analysis of current personnel resources.

Recommendations

The following actions are recommended to the National Science Foundation:

1. The taxonomy should be incorporated as quickly as possible into all NSF surveys and studies.
2. Additional in-depth statistical analyses are needed to establish base line demographic profiles of the various computer specialist fields.
3. A dissemination plan should be developed as soon as possible to ensure the adoption of the taxonomy by other agencies and organizations. Use of the taxonomy by all federal agencies and the computer industry would establish a much needed element of consistency among studies and reports produced by each of the various groups.
4. The need to keep basic government taxonomies current is critical. The taxonomy should therefore be updated at appropriate intervals (perhaps every 3–5 years) to reflect continuing changes in the computer specialties field.
5. Small but significant groups of people employed in the computer specialties field are often not large enough to be identified in current taxonomies. A mechanism to ensure that federal agencies, educational institutions, and private sector organizations involved in personnel analysis are able to identify these critical skills should be created.
6. To simplify the use of this taxonomy, the development of

a document which would crossfoot with the DOT, SOC, OES, and MOTD classifications is highly recommended.

Adoption of these recommendations will ensure that accurate and informative data on the computer specialties field will be obtained by the National Science Foundation and other governmental agencies. The expanded taxonomy will broaden the scope of knowledge of the current characteristics of the computer specialties workforce and enable accurate projections to be made of future personnel and resource needs by the United States government.

How to pick eagles: Research and application of selection systems within information systems

by ROBERT A. ZAWACKI
University of Colorado
Colorado Springs, Colorado

International Data Corporation recently reported that United States information systems spending for salaries/benefits was 35.7 percent of the total MIS budget for the first quarter of 1986. My experience with MIS organizations is that this figure is nearer 40 percent in many firms. Because of the tremendous cost associated with selecting and training MIS professionals, this key function is too important to be left to the "professionals" in personnel. It *must* be controlled and driven by MIS managers with the support of personnel.

My research and the research of others indicates that MIS managers either leave this critical function to personnel, or they give it lip service and their ability to PICK EAGLES and eliminate losers is very poor. Further, once the MIS professional is in the firm, those who are marginal performers are rarely, if ever, eliminated from the firm.

Since 1978 over 300 articles have been written on the selection process. After reviewing the literature, conducting research myself, and consulting with numerous MIS organizations, some of the major reasons for poor selection are:

1. Biases are established early in the interview.
2. Interviewers tend to develop a stereotype of a good candidate and then match applicants with stereotypes.
3. Interveiwers are influenced more by unfavorable than favorable information because they are looking for reasons to not select the candidate.
4. If the interviewer has an early favorable impression of the candidate, the interviewer talks more and in a more favorable tone. If the early impression is negative, then the interviewer talks in a negative tone with the hope that the candidate self-selects out of the firm.
5. Seeing negative candidates before positive candidates results in a greater number of acceptances than reversing the order of interviewing.
6. Interviewers benefit very little from day to day interviewing. Training can help the selection process, however.
7. The ability of a candidate to answer questions, stay to the subject being discussed, and present a favorable appearance seems to be critical to obtaining an offer.
8. Interviewers opinions of a candidate are crystallized after a mean interview time of four minutes.
9. To increase predictive validity, interviews must be planned and structured. Yet, because of the crisis environment within MIS, many managers "wing it."

Given the pessimistic nature of the research findings, what can an MIS organization do to PICK EAGLES? What are the objectives of the MIS organization? What predicts effective job performance? How can an MIS department structure the interview to increase their "hits" and decrease their "errors"?

First, the CIO and the top management team must decide how many EAGLES they want. Intuition suggests that they should want all of the EAGLES that they can recruit. However, EAGLES are high achievers and require cutting-edge and challanging work or they become dissatisfied. As MIS departments move from development to more maintenance work, the top management team should consider a mix of people to match the jobs or attempt to enrich the jobs if they are to hire a high percent of EAGLES.

Ability, motivation, and the job all influence performance by a programmer. Figure 1 diagrams this relationship. Ability includes skill, education, aptitude, and experience.

Programmers can have all of the ability in the world. Without motivation, however, they will fail. Further, they can have all the ability and motivation; if the job does not challange them, or if it is not a good match-up between the person and the job, they will not produce to their ability.

My research and consulting with MIS organizations indicates that managers do a very good job of determining ability

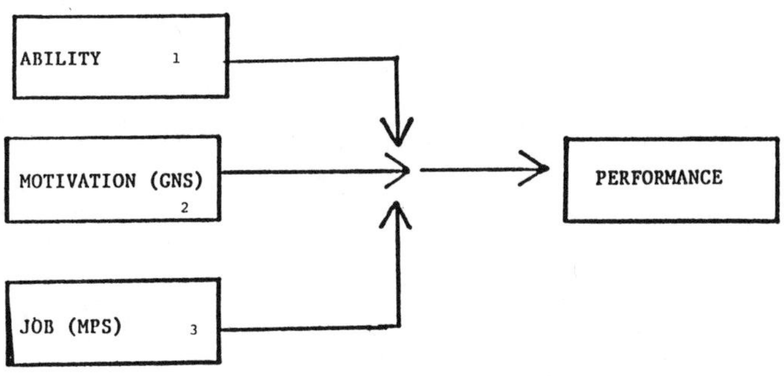

Figure 1—Determinants of employee performance

from the candidate's resume. They can review his/her education, additional courses, and previous job experience and make a good prediction. The weakness of MIS managers is in blocks 2 and 3 (see Figure 1). When we observe interviewers they tend to stay in block 1 because they are more comfortable in the technical areas. Predictive validity increased when the interviewer asks questions about the candidates motivation.

One of the major findings of my research with Dr. J. Daniel Couger (*Motivating and Managing Computer Personnel,* Wiley Interscience, 1980) is that MIS professionals have very high growth need strength (GNS). This is a measure of their motivation. Prior to the interview, the interviewer should plan four or five questions that examines candidates' need to be challenged, to continue to grow, to develop and move beyond where they are. Also, their need for education is a good indicator of high GNS.

Couger and I determined that MIS professionals believe a job is challenging if it contains: (1) skill variety, (2) task identity, (3) task significance, (4) autonomy, and (5) feedback. If a job is low or moderate in these five job dimensions, the MIS department may decide to select a person with moderate GNS. If you have a job moderate in MPS and still decide to select an EAGLE, then how the interviewers set expectations is critical. Only promise what you can deliver. Also, high GNS people in a low or moderate MPS job will soon become bored and dissatisfied. These people need a lot of feedback and encouragement, joint goal setting, and career planning. Further, you can meet some of their high GNS need by formal education while in a narrow job.

Guidelines for a Successful Match-up

1. Determine how many EAGLES you want in your MIS department.
2. Select a team of interviewers and provide training on good interviewing behavior. Include some peers on the interview panel.
3. Pre-structure the interview and plan questions that examine the candidate's GNS.
4. Conduct the interviews in a professional and timely manner. Remember the candidate is forming an impression of your firm and will talk to other people.
5. The line must own and control the interview process. Personnel specialists or psychologists are support staff to the line.
6. After the interviews, have a meeting of the selection panel and pool the evaluation of all interviewers.
7. After determining who is the best match-up with the job (MPS), make a verbal offer to the candidate as soon as possible. Also, how you notify the unsuccessful candidates can effect goodwill; they may be a source of future talent. Remember, you may only hire one person, but five or more may be talking about how your firm treated them.

Following the above guidelines can result in improved organizational effectiveness through a better match of the need of the organization with the ability and motivation of the person. PICKING EAGLES is not easy, it requires a heavy time involvement by MIS managers and peers. However, the results are well worth the effort. Either we do it right up front or we live with our mistakes. The choice is ours!

REFERENCES

1. Couger, J. Daniel and Robert A. Zawacki, *Motivating and Managing Computer Personnel,* Wiley Interscience, 1980.
2. Campbell, J. P., M. D. Dunnette, E. E. Lawler, III and K. E. Weick, Jr., *Managerial Behavior, Performance, and Effectiveness,* McGraw-Hill, 1970.
3. Zawacki, Robert A. "How To Pick Eagles," *Datamation,* September 15, 1985.

Software ergonomics research and practice: Findings and recommendations

by RICHARD P. KOFFLER
The Koffler Group
Santa Monica, California

INTRODUCTION

A major review of the software human factors engineering (ergonomics) literature conducted during 1986[1] showed that the field is growing very rapidly. Motivated by the need to make computer technology accessible to people of all ages, backgrounds and education, a growing amount of information is available to guide the development, evaluation, and use of ergonomically designed software.

This paper summarizes the results of analyzing 102 papers, magazine articles, and books. Contributions from the field of software human factors to developers, purchasers, and users of software are documented as a set of findings and recommendations. Due to the different nature of their responsibilities, there are separate sections for software developers and for purchasers and users. Table I illustrates how human factors engineering fits into the traditional software development process.

FOR SOFTWARE DEVELOPERS

Objectives, Benefits, and Costs

Conceptions of what is "ergonomic software" are becoming more concrete. The major factor is usability, which should be measured objectively and quantitatively. Developers should specify explicit and testable usability levels at the outset of design projects.

There are measureable paybacks to designing software ergonomically. Case studies show that using quantifiable criteria reveals the paybacks before product release. Software can be designed to match what people really need, rather than waiting for later versions to improve a product. Another benefit is that usability measures can improve the marketability of a product. Since many software development firms are looking for ways to satisfy users' needs, ergonomics is recommended as a means of keeping up with the competition.

The real costs of software ergonomics may be less than they initially appear. Because there is a wide choice of methods that can be used, it is possible to fit ergonomics into even a tight budget. For instance, there are ways for designers to incorporate ergonomics themselves as well as a variety of ways to use the assistance of human factors professionals.

Although there are only a few examples stated in financial terms, the evidence is sufficient to demonstrate that including ergonomics in the design process saves resources that otherwise would be needed to revise, maintain and support the software once it is out on the market. Therefore, the cost savings of ergonomics often far outweigh the initial expense.

Including Ergonomics in the Design Process

A software developer's job is quite unlike the jobs of people who use software products in offices. Therefore, it is necessary to find out about the people who will use the system and their tasks before beginning a software design project. Techniques such as task analysis, activity analysis, and controlled observations can provide this information.

The best advice an ergonomist can give to a software designer is: watch people interacting with the system, even if the design is not yet complete. A lot can be learned just from observing a few users. It must be remembered, however, that people will do things not anticipated by the designer. These behaviors are not wrong; rather, programs simply don't work the way users expect. Observations should be made with an open mind. People should be interviewed to find out why they tried to do things a certain way. Then, designs should be changed so that people are led to perform the actions that will be successful. The aim is to improve the program, not to prove it.

Sources of ergonomics guidance vary in their usefulness to designers. Although the research data base is the most current source of information, it is widely scattered and leaves many questions unanswered. For this reason, research and design methods are the most useful to designers.

A sound recommendation for software developers is to apply ergonomics methods and guidelines during the design process. This entails becoming familiar with the ergonomics perspective as represented by theoretical viewpoints. Original research papers should be referred to only to keep current on the latest developments. Also, models should be watched for of user behavior and usability that can be used instead of testing with real users.

TABLE I—Fitting human factors engineering into the software design process

The "Traditional" Software Design Process*	Possibilities for Applying Ergonomics at Each Stage
Requirements Definition	
Determine the requirements the system will meet. Establish system functions, inputs, and outputs. List constraints on system performance and economic considerations.	Establish the purpose of the system and the intended users. Determine system functionality and general level of usability. Conduct task analyses to find out how users perform these functions with similar or non-automated systems.
Specifications Development	
From the system requirements, determine the system specifications for exactly what the system must do. Specify acceptance tests the system must pass.	Determine specific user characteristics that the system must satisfy by collecting data about the user population as necessary. Perform activity analyses to find out the process of task completion. Set objective (testable) usability and learnability criteria.
Preliminary Design	
Develop models of possible solutions for satisfying the requirements and specifications. Determine advantages and disadvantages of each solution. Choose one or two promising solutions for further evaluation and investigation.	Create preliminary design ideas as potential solutions. Use ergonomics theories, models, and guidelines to evaluate each possibility. Select the most promising designs for further development. The Wizard of Oz technique begins at this stage (develop the bare-bones system).
Intermediate Design	
Develop the selected designs to demonstrate system organization and structure. Use models and analysis methods to evaluate these designs. Eliminate any design that is unsatisfactory.	Develop the proposed designs to include major organization and structure of the user-system interface. Apply theories and models to evaluate each proposal and weed out unacceptable ones. Determine if a simulation will be required before testing can be done. Create a prototype if an iterative design method is used. Begin collecting data from users if the Wizard of Oz technique is used.
Detailed Design	
Create a detailed architectural design of the proposed system. Evaluate it to determine whether it meets the system specifications and requirements. Return to previous steps if the detailed design is unacceptable. Use prototypes of sub-systems to gather further information if necessary.	Apply guidelines and standards during this stage. Refer to the research data base for information as needed. Use theories and models in making any tradeoffs required by inconsistent guidelines. Test specific aspects of the proposed design against models or in experiments with real users to determine usability effects that are unknown and likely to have large impact. Simulate system if working prototype is not available for testing. Use iterative design methods to monitor usability of different versions of the prototype as they are developed. Collect subjective assessments after users have tried the prototype or simulated system. Continue with testing and making modifications if using the Wizard of Oz technique.
Implementation	
Use the architectural design to implement the software for the system. Test each subsystem to determine that it operates properly.	Conduct usability tests as soon as an operational system is developed. Or, use the results of experiments with the simulated system to implement the real system. Or, refine the design using iterative methods so that the prototype evolves into the implemented system. Modify the design until it meets the objective usability criteria, as determined by experiments and subjective assessments.
Verification and Acceptance	
Test the entire system to verify that it meets system requirements and specifications.	Evaluate entire system (including documentation, on-line help, and system support services) after it has been completed to verify the level of usability and user acceptance. Test the system against validated models of human behavior, or use task analysis, experiments, field studies, and subjective assessments. Make any necessary changes before product release. Follow up product release with field tests to determine success of system and methods or to gather suggestions for future product designs.

* The traditional design process is adapted from Booth, Brubaker, Cain, Danielson, Hoelzeman, Langdon, Soldan, and Varanasi.[2]

Guidelines are available and can be applied directly to product design. However, an understanding of ergonomic theories is necessary to resolve tradeoffs between inconsistent guidelines and to translate general rules into design parameters.

Models are fairly new to software ergonomics. There is a movement toward models for predicting product usability, but many of these are not yet in a directly usable form. Cognitive models can help designers maintain consistency in a user-system interface.

Newcomers to software ergonomics can benefit from tested design principles that result in better software products. These principles describe the important steps in the design process. Because they have been used before, their benefits are known and the risks of experimenting with some new ergonomics techniques are reduced. These tried and true principles can even be tailored to fit into the constraints of real-world development projects.

The benefits of in-house software design guidelines should be considered. Because user-system interfaces can be standardized across many applications, in-house guidelines make the software development process faster and easier.

There are several tools and techniques that software developers can use to ensure their products are ergonomic. Some are: task and activity analyses, simulations, prototyping, iterative design, experimentation, field studies, subjective assessments, and the "Wizard of Oz" technique (described next). The decision to use any of these should be based on a project's scope and budget.

One tool that is becoming quite popular is based on a good idea that the Wizard of Oz had. The "Wizard of Oz" technique is a successful way to put an application together quickly and easily, while building usability into the program. The method combines prototyping, simulation, and iterative testing. It consists of configuring a system so all inputs to and outputs from a system can be monitored and interrupted by a hidden intermediary. The intermediary interrupts any input from a user that the program cannot handle. Outputs from the system which the user is unlikely to understand are also interrupted and rephrased before they are transmitted to the user.

FOR SOFTWARE PURCHASERS AND USERS

Ergonomic software increases productivity because it matches what users really need. Ergonomics eliminates programs that people cannot use or can use only in a limited way. Training requirements, user errors and frustrations are also reduced. To get the full benefits from computer software, usability should be included as a purchasing criterion.

Software buyers should seek out software that has been tested to meet explicit usability criteria. Ergonomic software is defined in terms that can be tested and measured. Because ergonomic software has been tested with people who represent real users, purchasers can find out how usable the software is before they buy it. It is almost a guarantee that people will be able to successfully use a tested product for its intended application.

Guidelines and standards are the most usable form of ergonomics information for software buyers and users. Models for evaluating software may also become available in the future. Currently, information contained in the research data base, ergonomics theories, and research or design methods cannot be applied directly to the selection of software.

Managers should encourage their employees to participate in software usability tests of products that are designed or purchased for in-house use. Users can give input on what they need and want before the design or purchasing decision is finalized.

To ensure consistency and enhanced usability across applications, users can collaborate with software developers to establish in-house software design guidelines based on the latest available information as well as testing within an organization. Once they have been approved, guidelines can speed turnaround time on requests for new applications. They can also reduce training requirements, since users only have to learn one standard format and set of procedures for all software programs.

Before making a request for custom software, needs and restrictions should be carefully determined. Subjective assessments of "wish lists" cannot be relied on to provide this information. More reliable data can be obtained with task and activity analyses. After the requirements are passed on to the software development staff, and effective way to keep up with the project is to periodically try the software before it is complete. Without continual feedback, reaction to the final product is likely to be, "That isn't what we wanted." By that time, software developers probably will object to changing anything on the grounds that it is too difficult or time consuming.

When considering software purchases, questions about usability should be asked. It is also important for purchasers and users to test the program themselves, rather than only watch a carefully engineered and executed demo. If intended users cannot operate the system with the salesperson or software developer standing by, they will not have much luck when they are on their own. Even after purchase, it is a good idea to give feedback to the development company on the usability of its products so future improvements can be made.

REFERENCES

1. Potosnak, K. (ed.). "Tackling Software Ergonomics, Part I: What's Available?" and "Part II: Applying the Techniques." *Office Systems Ergonomics Report,* 5 (1986) 3 and 4. Santa Monica, California: The Koffler Group.
2. Booth, T., T. Brubaker, T. Cain, R. Danielson, R. Hoelzeman, G. Langdon, D. Soldan, and M. Varanasi. "Design Education in Computer Science and Engineering." *Computer,* 19, 6, pp. 20–27.

Creating an in-house software ergonomics group: A case study

by DOREEN L. KUSHNER
Unisys
Mission Viejo, California

INTRODUCTION

They want proof. Software consumers are receiving supplier claims of "ergonomic superiority" and "ease of use" with caution. It's a buyer's market and usability has emerged as a significant competitive edge.

The field of software psychology, a branch of human factors engineering, has been a boon to the computer industry. It has expanded the market by demonstrating that, theoretically speaking, anyone can use a computer. This is not to say that a specific computer device can or should be usable by all people. In fact, the key to a successful design is to create a product targeted to a specific class of users. The design should draw upon the capabilities and compensate for the limitations of the intended users.

Establishing a successful human factors function requires careful staffing, calculated direction and appropriate tools of the trade. This paper comments on the organizational model of a human factors group and its application as an integral part of the software design process. It is the case study of creating a human factors team at Unisys.

HISTORICAL PERSPECTIVE

Human factors engineering activities at Unisys (the new company resulting from the merger of Burroughs and Sperry Corporations) have been traditionally organized and centralized at corporate levels, with a concentration on hardware-related issues. In response to market demands for more "congenial" software, though, there is a current trend toward: (1) decentralizing the function and strengthening expertise in software design, (2) assuming a "division of skills strategy for development activities, and (3) expanding the envelope of usability criteria for the mainframe software.

Prior to 1984 most human factors personnel were located at world headquarters. Their role was to participate in hardware design and to provide varied services to the development plants as requested. As a result of the more recent increased emphasis on software development, the function has since migrated away from corporate positioning. Today, 85 percent of the human factors staff is located within the separate development organizations.

In addition to decentralizing human factors to the software engineering organizations, active measures were taken to integrate their expertise with product development activity. A "division of skills" strategy was taken to maximize development efficiency. Responsibility for human-computer interface design, historically with the project programmers, shifted to the human factors specialists. This allowed the programming groups to focus attention on functionality design and implementation. It is important to note, however, that the human factors and programming staff do not work independently; rather, they work as unique members of a multidisciplinary team.

The first human factors assignment in Mission Viejo, California addressed consistency in style between and within a family of menu-driven software applications. This initial project concentrated on quality in screen layout and screen traversal techniques. Objectives of current projects also include accurate identification of user classes and renderings of user tasks.

HUMAN-COMPUTER INTERFACE DESIGN TEAM

Staffing the right people is a critical gate to any successful function. A multidisciplinary cross-section of skills in support of a human factors core is often ideal for designing human-computer interfaces.

Human Factors Technologists

When identifying the human factors talent, it is important to understand that human factors itself can be viewed as multidisciplinary. It deals with the manner in which people interact with their world. Therefore, experience in applying its principles requires an understanding of human characteristics as well as a working knowledge of the technology being studied. For the design of computer-human interfaces, formal education in human factors engineering or equivalent is basic to understanding the human side of the interface. It is also important, however, to employ designers who have specialized in computer software—the other side of the interface.

The Mission Viejo facility employs six human factors professionals, and has plans for continued growth. The current ratio of human factors-to-programming staff is 1:16. An appropriate target is estimated to be 1:8.

All six human factors personnel hold degrees in psychology and have an average of six years concentrated experience in software ergonomics. One person has a Ph.D. in cognitive psychology, two have an MS degree in industrial psychology, two are MS degree candidates in human factors, and one has a BS degree in psychology.

Multidisciplinary Support Team

The user's interface to a computer is likely to consist of a combination of: hardware control panels, monitors, keyboards or other pointing devices, reference cards, application software, on-line assistance, and user manuals. Moreover, the design of the human-computer interface is based not only on knowledge about the user and intended functionality of the computer but also on knowledge about market demands. Therefore, the development team should represent an appropriate mix of skills, and might include:

1. Human factors technologists, to design, evaluate, and specify the way in which people and a computer will interact
2. Computer scientists, to provide counsel on the relative costs and benefits of implementation alternatives and to prototype software design concepts
3. Technical writers, to prepare the prose interfaces of on-line help and printed documentation
4. Market researchers, to identify market characteristics in terms of requirements for functionality as well as characteristics of the targeted user classes
5. Hardware engineers, to provide counsel on hardware design alternatives and prototype design concepts
6. Industrial and graphics designers, to contribute expertise in aesthetics and visual communications

The proper mix is of course dependent upon the nature of the design project.

Organizationally, the Human Factors group resides, with relative autonomy, within an organization responsible for the development of system software. Lines of communication and functional relationships with other key disciplines are being established. Most design teams, consisting of talent from computer science, marketing research, user documentation, industrial design, and training lie across organizational boundaries.

ROLE OF THE HUMAN FACTORS TECHNOLOGIST

The role of the human factors technologist is to serve as the users' advocate during product development. The job begins during product conceptualization and continues until after the product is introduced to the market. During each stage of the product life cycle, broadly defined as analysis, design, and implementation, specific types of human factors activity should occur.[1]

The analysis phase is typified by functionality definition, cost/benefits projection, identification of hardware and software constraints, and scheduling. The human-computer interface design team should also define the target user by: (1) prior relevant experiences, (2) anticipated product use patterns, and (3) cognitive, physiological, and perceptual characteristics.

During the design phase, a product is designed, coded, and tested. The role of the human factors technologist is to mold the human-computer interface by applying principles of software psychology and drawing from expertise within the design team. Development of the interface evolves through an iterative process of conceptualization, simulation or prototyping, and evaluation or validation.

Lastly, the implementation stage is established when a product is distributed and installed in its final locations, the uses are trained, and the product is in operation. During implementation the best test of usability takes place, and it occurs as a function of normal product use. Human factors responsibility lies in capturing and interpreting usage data as it becomes available. Errors are then corrected, features are added, and customer-driven ideas lead to new product plans.

Projects at Unisys Human Factors

The role of the Human Factors group at Unisys has recently undergone a transition from impromptu consultation and participation just prior to the "implementation" phase, to responsibility for design across product life cycles. This shift in emphasis reflects an explicit commitment to understanding and meeting user requirements by proactively applying expertise in the human side of the interface.

The group's projects currently include human-computer interface design and evaluation for a variety of software products. The group is also developing in-house software ergonomics standards, and links are kept with the American National Standards Institute (ANSI) and the International Standards Organization (ISO). Major projects are described next.

Standard style design

Description. Design a standard presentation style for applications displayed on a family of character-mapped, monochrome displays. Prepare a specification for implementors of the User Interface Management System (UIMS). Write a style guide to accompany the UIMS as a framework of design for use by interface design teams.

Objectives. Maximize utilization of display capabilities. Meet the functional requirements of targeted applications to satisfy user needs while considering use patterns and user characteristics. Maintain consistency with associated products in such areas as keyboard functionality and pointing device behavior.

Team. Human factors specialists. Software engineers, for consultation on implementation costs.

Product design

Description. Design and specify the human-computer interface to four software products.

Objectives. Design a paradigm for functionality access so the interface predicts and reacts to a user's next move and steps aside when no prediction can be made. Involves providing a task-orientation across several user classes, accommodating users with varying levels of product expertise, and minimizing the likelihood of user error.

Team. Human factors specialists. Software engineers, for functionality definition, estimation of implementation costs, and prototype development. Marketing researchers, for competitive benchmarking and indentification of user characteristics and use patterns. Industrial designers, for keycap label design.

Development of national software ergonomics standards

Description. Participate in the Human-Computer Interaction Standards Committee of the Human Factors Society. This committee, which represents ANSI and serves ISO in an advisory capacity, is developing standards of design for the interface between computers and their users.

Objectives. The major contribution from the Unisys representative to the committee will be to create standards and guidelines for the use of color based on established human factors research and practice.

Team. Human factors specialist.

TOOLS OF THE HUMAN FACTORS TRADE

There are basic resources which, when available, substantially increase productivity, efficiency and effectiveness of the human factors function. In addition, when used to document design specifications, such resources lead to increased efficiency and timeliness of user documentation development. These resources include computer technology, printer devices, and data recording tools. The functional requirements of each are described in this section.

Computer Technology and Printer Devices

Basic to the requirements for computer technology are productivity aids, for creating design documents with textual and graphic matter, and simulation tools, for representing design concepts. The remaining requirements for computer power as well as for the print devices should be driven by intended characteristics of the targeted product. The monitor should be capable of displaying an accurate representation of the human-computer interface design concepts; the printer should produce accurate hardcopy representations; and the software simulation package should be capable of modeling the technology of the intended product.

Data Recording Devices

Design ideas should be verified by observing and analyzing some representation of use. This can be accomplished with paper-and-pencil simulations, software simulations, or live prototypes. Regardless of the technique used, it is important to have a method of capturing the data from these usability evaluation sessions for later analysis.

Several types of techniques are available for capturing evaluation data. These include audio and video recording, logging and metering, and simple note-taking by the participant or observer. The best method for recording usability data should be determined by the nature of the evaluation and by the type of information which is relevant.

HUMAN FACTORS TOOLS AT UNISYS

The functional shift of Unisys Human Factors from pre-implementation phase consultation to support across product life cycles has created new toolkit requirements. Although the current set of tools are adequate for pre-market release usability evaluations and post-release field studies, they are not useful for the remaining majority of design activities. The tools currently in use as well as near term acquisition plans are described.

Today's Computers, Printers and Data Recorders

Current tools for creating hardcopy design documentation include workstations with character-mapped displays and word processing software. These have been used in conjunction with various draft- and letter-quality printers to prepare textual matter and to capture character-driven designs. Software simulation tools are not available; therefore, paper-and-pencil and live prototyping techniques are heavily used.

Combinations of audio and video tape recording and playback equipment are used for conducting usability evaluation and validation tests. Data recording strategies can include: (1) voice only; (2) voice and computer display only; and (3) voice, computer display, and motor activity. For voice only, a mini-cassette recorder is used, synchronized voice and computer display records are captured with a video cassette recorder and motor behavior is picked up by adding one or more cameras.

Toolkit Limitations

The current set of tools is limited in three areas: (1) representing designs for use in external documentation, (2) displaying bit-mapped design concepts, and (3) simulating human-computer interactions. The workstations and printer devices work well for creating internal documents. The accuracy with which those designs can be represented, however, is not sufficient to allow direct input to customer documentation. Moreover, this technology is limited to character-driven designs. Those which are pixel-driven cannot be represented at all.

The inability to simulate presentation as well as behavior of alternative human-computer interface designs also raises issues. First, the paper-and-pencil interaction is significantly different from intended interaction. Therefore, when used as a medium for design evaluation, it is likely to have some confounding effect on evaluation results. Furthermore, inability to capture the true interaction precludes its evaluation.

The second issue has to do with using live prototypes for design evaluation. When utilizing a prototyping technique, there is often resistance to maintaining its disposability. Live prototypes are costly and therefore lead to hopeful expectations and schedule assumptions that the design will be right the first time.

Fitting the Toolkit to New Requirements

To follow the transition in human factors responsibility with an appropriate supporting toolkit, the following arrangements are planned:

1. Unisys PC/IT personal computers (IBM PC/AT compatible) with bit-mapped displays will replace the current character-mapped workstations. Software will provide capabilities for full function text formatting, advanced graphics design, and the ability to merge text and graphics. Tools for the creation of human-computer interaction simulations will also be established.
2. Laser printer devices will be added so that accurate hardcopy representations of human-computer interfaces can be created. Any design document will potentially be usable both as internal engineering specifications and as direct input to customer documentation.

In addition to increasing the functional capabilities of the Human Factors group, this new combination of tools can lead to increased product development efficiency overall. The process of customer documentation development can be initiated sooner by using product descriptions from early and accurate design specifications; documentation development can be aided by supplying high quality samples through the internal specifications; and the costs associated with evaluating interaction style design concepts can be reduced by utilizing software simulations in place of live prototypes.

SUMMARY

The most recent thrust by Unisys to tighten usability criteria was initiated by market preferences; it is reflected in product goals, and it has been carried forward by Human Factors. As a result of an enthusiastic response to the 1985 menu-driven offerings, corporate goals for new products regularly refer to ease-of-use intentions. These goals, though, are stated in general terms and require interpretation by the development groups. Human Factors has been responsible for defining measurable objectives and, according to the requirements described herein, has established a long range strategy for achieving those objectives.

Currently, a general regrouping of functional responsibilities is evolving, and changes to the product development process are being promoted and implemented. Although it is too soon to quantify the long term impact of this new approach to human-computer interface design, expectations are clear. They include:

1. Increased market opportunities from an expansion of the potential user base
2. Reduction in software development costs by more closely matching personnel expertise to development assignments, and thereby leading to fewer design iterations
3. Reduced costs associated with customer training, resulting from the design of self-evident product operation
4. Cost savings in documentation development, attributed to the use of accurate design examples from engineering specifications for user manuals

The ergonomic approach to software design offers a fresh opportunity for competitive advantages. The key to a leading edge includes unique staffing, appropriate tools, and purposeful direction.

REFERENCES

1. Anderson, N. S. and J. R. Olson. (eds). Methods for Designing Software to Fit Human Needs and Capabilities. *Proceedings of the Workshop on Software Human Factors.* Washington, D.C.: National Academy Press, 1985.

Software ergonomics guidelines and standards

by JOHN KARAT
IBM Corporation
Austin, Texas

INTRODUCTION

There are four current software ergonomics projects conducted by organizations chartered to develop national and international standards. Two projects are in the United States, one by the American National Standards Institute (ANSI) and the other by the Human Factors Society. The third is in Germany sponsored by the Deutsches Institut fur Normung (DIN), and the fourth is by a subcommittee of the International Standards Organization (ISO).

Of the four, only the DIN committee has issued a draft standard (DIN 66 234 part 8). The draft, however, has drawn intense criticism because its specifications are not easily measurable. It is not always possible to determine when a user-system interface is in compliance.

The ISO and ANSI committees are still in their formative stages. The activities of the Human-Computer Interaction (HCI) Standards Committee organized by the Human Factors Society are described in this article.

BACKGROUND

The HCI Standards Committee is working to provide a framework for the development of software quidelines and standards for human-computer interactions in a manner consistent with the professional standards of the human factors profession. It is the intention of the committee to play an active role in the development of guidelines and standards and to review and consult on the work of other standards groups.

The committee was formed in February 1985 as a task force operating under the Technical Standards Committee of the Human Factors Society. Its initial charter was to advise the Society concerning the status of existing efforts to standardize the human-computer interface and to report on the feasibility of acting as a producer of user-system interface standards.

The task force met three times in 1985. Organizations involved in developing human-computer interaction standards were identified and studied. It was decided that it was important for the Society to take an active rather than a passive role in this area. While members of the task force were skeptical about their ability to produce useful standards in a short period, there was a feeling that the skills of the Society members should provide the necessary foundation for a serious standards effort.

The task force concluded that the greatest impact would be achieved through an initial effort to develop a framework or reference model, and then to gradually add details for various areas of human-computer interaction.

CURRENT ACTIVITIES

In late 1985 the task force became a technical standards subcommittee of the Human Factors Society. During 1986 the committee created operating procedures, elected officers, established formal connections with ANSI and the ISO, produced a reference model (draft proposal) for standards activities, and began work on content areas covered in the proposal.

As stated in the committee's reference model, its objective is to create a set of software ergonomics guidelines and standards which have the following characteristics:

1. They must have a foundation on scientific evidence, empirical data, and have been generally recognized and accepted by people knowledgeable in the area.
2. They must state the criteria for when and how they will be applied relative to the type of task, type of user, the kind of technology and the environment.
3. They must be written so that they can be consistently interpreted in a clear and unambiguous way.
4. They must provide usable guidance to interface designers and provide information that can be directly applied in tradeoff decisions during the design process.
5. They must be practical and capable of being implemented within generally available technology and cost constraints.
6. They must be useful and exist only if they serve end users by offering a solution to a known problem.

   In addition to these attributes common to both guidelines and standards, standards must comply with the following:
7. They must indicate a pass-fail specification so compliance can be judged. Testing criteria must be stated.
8. They must provide some quantified, measurable benefit for users.

The areas which have been identified by the committee for the creation of standards and guidelines are:

Input devices and techniques
Output devices and techniques
Dialog techniques
User guidance (e.g., help and error handling)
Evaluation and testing

The committee's current reference model and short statements of various work efforts were published[1] for public review in the *Bulletin* of the Human Factors Society Computer Systems Technical Group. An earlier draft of the proposal was presented in May 1986 to the ISO subcommittee dealing with software ergonomics (ISO Technical Committee 159, Subcommittee 4, Working Group 5: Software Ergonomics and Man-Machine Dialogue).

TIMETABLE AND MEMBERSHIP

The committee meets four times per year for two days at a time. Two of the meetings are scheduled to overlap with major conferences (The CHI conference in the Spring and the Human Factors Society Annual Meeting in the Fall). The two other meetings are scheduled approximately midway between the conferences.

Currently the committee consists of thirteen members. Most are from industry, but they do not serve as company representatives. They act as members of the human factors profession.

REFERENCE

1. Draft Proposal of the Human Factors Society Human-Computer Interaction Committee, *Bulletin,* 13, 4. Published by the Computer Systems Technical Group of the Human Factors Society. (Available from Andy Cohill, 112 Lucas Drive, Blacksburg, VA 24060.)

Bridging the computer-user gap

by BETTY SHERWOOD
Sherwood Consulting
Chicago, Illinois

ABSTRACT

This paper deals with that portion of the computer-user interface comprising user manuals, training materials, and screen design. Several general principles are developed from learning theory including matching and schema, taxon and locale learning, and controlling the learning curve.

This paper develops more specific rules for applying these general principles to the interface. These rules cover manual design for the benefit of users, the role of typography in improving the design of any written materials, and the use of schema and matching to improve the computer screen/manual interface.

Further, the paper discusses rules particular to manuals concerning addressing different audience segments through sectioning, focusing on information, structuring the manual for each of two types of systems, and using sentence structure, graphics, and typography to improve the reference aspects of the manual. Finally, the principles of screen design which aid user acceptance, improve comprehension, and increase the rate of learning are set forth.

INTRODUCTION

The subject of user-computer interface is much too large to cover in a single paper. I focus on the user manual, training and learning materials, and screen design.

Personal computers have been a major force in improving these areas. Today, developers of hardware and software from mainframe to micro are beginning to understand that these issues can sell a product and make computerization acceptable for human consumption. The upstart world of personal computers has also attracted people with expertise from other disciplines which are important in application development such as training, learning theory, human/machine ergonomics, graphics design, and writing. Although such changes may have been addressed before, the personal computer has accelerated the process.

GENERAL PRINCIPLES

Several principles from the discipline of learning theory are vital to understanding and improving the computer-user interface.

The Human Mind

Both the computer and the brain suck up information in much the same way, but they process it differently. The computer has a very large volatile memory; the human mind has a very small one. The computer, subject to programmed rules, will store everything from volatile memory into permanent storage; the human mind is extremely picky and individualistic, and this is where the computer-user interface problem is centered.

Human volatile memory (short term memory or working memory) will hold about five of what experts call chunks for anywhere from ¼ second to one hour[1]—with practice. A chunk can be words, syllables, letter groupings, phrases, or ideas.[2] Something in those chunks must connect with something already in long term memory in order for the chunks to make enough sense for the mind to process them further. Even then only one or two pieces may ever reach permanent storage in long term memory. The more the new material relates to information already stored, the faster learning occurs.[3] To test this, try learning a foreign language without understanding either what the words mean or how to pronounce them. On the other hand, try learning BASIC after you already are proficient in COBOL, FORTRAN, and a database language; the learning time is significantly shorter than it is for a computer language novice. This process is called matching.

In addition, if the mind is given a schema for organizing these chunks in short term memory before the chunks are taken in, then these chunks can be processed even faster.[4] It's like throwing objects at someone from behind a curtain. If a person knows what kinds of objects to expect, then he can catch more objects at a faster rate than can someone who has to learn by experience what to expect. The principles of matching and schema should lead developers to use language, screen design, and system design principles that will be familiar in some way to the intended audience (matching) and to tell them first how it is organized (schema).

The most accurate model of communication I have found is shown in Figure 1. This model explains how close relatives sometimes communicate very effectively in obscure phrases. It also says that no matter how hard you try, your knwoledge base is going to bias both your communication and your comprehension of someone else's communication.

Two kinds of learning, taxon and locale, also apply. Taxon (rote) is easily lost unless it is practiced or used frequently, and it is usually taught by simple verbal repetition, much as dogs are taught tricks. Locale, on the other hand, is not lost as easily. It is understood learning and usually involves both verbal and visual stimulation in teaching. To promote total comprehension, the training impression must be as vivid as possible and may use as many kinds of sensory inputs and media as can be combined without creating confusion.[1]

Combining the model and the two learning methods, we can draw two principles: involve the user and utilize pictures, words, word pictures, demonstrations, user-centered exercises (utilizing user's own data), and any other types of media available in teaching the user about the system. Dale's "Cone of Experience" lists 12 categories of ways which are roughly age related to stimulate learning. They include direct experience, simulation, and demonstration in the lowest age categories and visual and verbal symbols at the top (comparable to a sophisticated adult learning method). Pictures of all kinds are somewhere in the middle. These categories can also relate to the subject being communicated and to prior experience of the audience with that subject and with learning itself.[6]

Therefore, the combination of media that developers choose to present their applications and machines depend heavily on the intended audience. In addition, effective learning may be stimulated by categories lower on the scale, so that user-centered exercises and illustrations may be the most effective way to teach the system (successful with the highest percentage of the audience). But a visual and verbal analysis

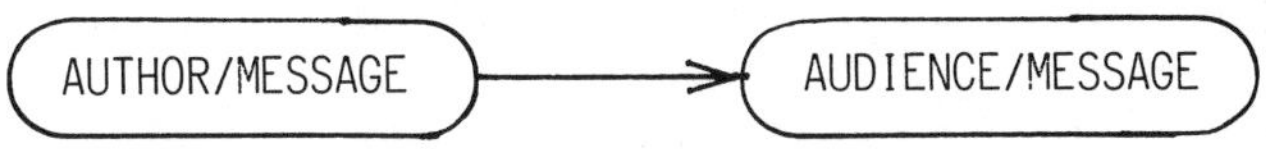

Figure 1—A communication model[5]

of how the system works may be the most efficient (promoting locale learning and using fewer resources to create and absorb training). A hint: always provide a system diagram for tree structure menu systems. This is one of the hardest concepts for users to ferret out from the system itself; it essentially requires them to infer a three-dimensional structure from the various one-dimensional pieces—almost impossible.

The Learning Curve

The learning curve (see Figure 2) is very important in designing the user-computer interface. I am interested most in the tail because with it you can get more result for your efforts, and affect the rest of the curve.

This tail, depending what is to be learned, can be very long (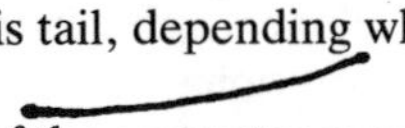) or very short (). The task of the computer-user interface is to make it short. A short tail can also affect the slope of the rest of the curve thus helping to achieve the entire learning process in less time by generating enthusiasm in users (something that has been shown to be a vital prerequisite for learning). The tail is most affected by the user manual's introductory or overview section which should give an overall understanding of the system: the easier it is for users to understand (that is, they should be provided with a schema and a basis for matching), the faster the learners will escape the tail. The tail is also strongly affected by the training materials and the approach to training. The slope will be most affected by the success with which users can find the section of the manual (or help text) they need to solve a particular problem and by the isolation of the answer from the general textual explanation of the problem (i.e., the reference aspects of the manual or help text). The slope is also affected by the screen design—the easier it is for users to relate screens to prior menus and other portions of the system, the faster (steeper) the actual learning process will be.

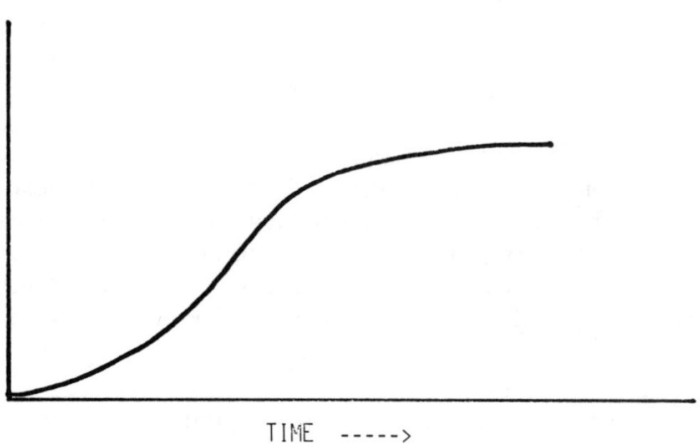

Figure 2—The learning curve

MANUALS AND SCREENS

Building on the general principles of learning theory as they apply to computer applications, this section provides specific design principles for the manual and the screen.

Patterns

Patterns are vital for reference materials and screen design. Visual images (patterns) can remain fixed in the eyes for several seconds; this physical ability can help users. When users look for something in the manual, they will probably have to deal with the instructions (once they find them) in two or more passes. The eyes will move from the book to the screen and back again to the book. If the writer/designer has used typeface, color, white space, and illustrations so that the page forms a visual pattern, there will be enough of the pattern remaining so that the eye will automatically return at least very close to where it left off.

In addition, by using exactly the same wording in the manual as is contained on the screen and as close as possible to the same typeface, the relationship between written material and screen wording is established much faster.

Typography

Boldface, underlines, color, uppercase, reverse video, italics, and type size, whether in written materials or in screen design, must be used—not abused. They serve to:

1. Call attention to warnings (bold and uppercase)
2. Set off sections of the text with headings and titles (underlining, uppercase, bold)
3. Emphasize (sparingly) text (underlining and italics)
4. Convey shorthand conventions for user input, screen output, and keytops (bold, uppercase, underlining, and italics)
5. Segregate ideas, illustrations, instructions, and reminders (boxes)

These typography graphics act as cues to memory and can improve recall as well as alert readers. They are also, of course, a part of the overall page pattern. If these aids are overused or used inconsistently (a particular problem in screen design), they will probably cause noise and hinder rather than help comprehension.[7]

Typography is therefore not purely cosmetic. But in addition to aiding learning as described, it also aids learning by generating enthusiasm, trust in the system (if the manual is professional looking, then the system is good), and the desire to learn—one of the more important components.

Overall Comprehension

Drawing on the principles of matching and increasing the slope of the learning curve, the best way to approach training materials is to plan the materials and explain the system top down; approach the training bottom up. Give users the framework of the system and the framework of the training approach. Then each step, beginning with the system base, will have an increasing amount of prior knowledge in permanent memory to match. Signal (by schema) all new material with topic sentences, headings, pointers, objectives, and summary statements.[8] You can also display pictures of the system at each step in the training to relate the new material to the entire system—kind of a "you are here" map. This can be particularly effective with the tree structure menu type of system.

MANUALS

Mainframe developers took their approach to manuals from mythology: instead of 1001 tales, you get 1001 manuals. If the single application is to be used only by users, there should never be more than one user reference manual and one training manual. If data processing personnel are going to do some technical manipulations before the users use it, then a technical (programming, installation, system adaptation) manual and a users' manual should be available.

Simple installation (except when users accidentally erase diskettes) will only be done once. Therefore, it is logical to segregate the instructions from the main body of the manual. For simple installation procedures, use a short installation booklet or card. An overview giving the installation schema should be included. If the training manual is in the same binder as the reference manual, it should be designed so it can be removed after it has been used, because it, too, will be used only once by each user. If the user has to refer to the training manual for information that isn't in the reference manual, then both manuals are badly done. Always adapt the training materials from the reference materials.

1. The purpose of a user reference manual is to provide all the information users need about a system if they are to understand it and to use it in any way it could possibly be used. The material must be organized for quick look-up, easy comprehension, and easy access. The focus must be on the information the user relies on from the system.
2. There are only two kinds of systems to use for manual organization: command-driven (word processing, database systems) and screen-driven (general ledger, order entry). This greatly simplifies developing the user manual structure.
3. The purpose of a training manual (and other training materials) is to teach the user the basic aspects of the system. Focus should be on the 20 percent of the system that is used 80 percent of the time. Also, more than one medium should be used. Simulation programs should never be relied upon to accomplish training; users must be involved and engaged as much as possible.

Audience and Communication

Some writers of user manuals seem to have a problem with the audience, particularly when a system is to be used by users with different levels of knowledge (either differentiated groups or groups with graduated degrees of expertise). For example, accounting systems are used by accounting clerks for data input and by accounting managers for analysis of reports. In some businesses, however, the clerk and the manager may be the same person. Complete business systems (such as those used by doctors, lawyers, restaurants, and other verticals) are often used by different groups of employees (e.g., accounting personnel, managerial personnel, and "expert" personnel). Don't make two manuals: handle these different readers' needs by sectioning one manual properly. Clerks and managers (even if they're the same person) aren't going to use the same screen in two different ways. Why would you explain managerial decision making when you are talking about what data is entered in a particular input screen? You talk about managerial decision making in sections on system structure and system output.

A successful reference book integrates the structure and output of the system, and segregates the instructions on how to make it go. You talk to all groups about the structure; you speak to each group separately through the segregated instructions covering the separate sections (input, reports) of the system focusing on the purpose of that section.

If the same section is to be used by two different types of readers, such as DP people and users, then write to the group with most expertise and, using typeface graphics instead of sections to segregate the information, include explanations of any technical aspects for nontechnical people. See Figure 3 for an example. Readers who understand subroutines are alerted by a boldface and indented explanatory section to skip over that part of the material. Readers who don't understand subroutines have the explanation available in the place where it's needed. Boxes, asterisks—whatever typefaces and graphics available—can be used to segregate detailed explanations.

Never write down to anyone. First, you might confuse income levels for education (such as writing down to secretaries rather than to executives), and second, most of the so-called scientific methods previously used to write down have been proven useless or even harmful. These include vocabulary levels by school grades, and the infamous fog index.

You can use the specialized vocabulary of the reader wherever appropriate, but leave out the computerese if you can possibly find an appropriate English language substitute. "Enter" is perfectly acceptable, because that's what they are doing; "file" is valid and it's an important concept to understand; VSAM, bytes, RAM, open/close a file, spool, and report image are some terms I would try to avoid.

Terminal keys are a particular problem. "Learning to Use a Word Processor"[9] contains a very amusing story about key-

```
The CALL command allows you to call a subroutine.

     Explanation: A subroutine is a....  It is
     most often used.......
```

Figure 3—Example of a manual explanation segregating instructions for different levels of user expertise.

top labeling. This happened in an experiment using only the training manual for training (wrong approach and obviously a bad manual as well as terrible keytop labeling). The novice word processing operator, wanting to remove a blank line that she had inserted in error between two text lines, used the "Required Return" key; this key was obviously the only one that might possibly have done the job since it seemed to be designed to require the bottom line to return to where it belonged. Had she first been given the basic computer file matching explanation—that there really are no such things as blanks in a computer; things that appear to be blanks are really caused by odd characters which the various keys insert into the file—she might have found her way to one of the delete or remove keys. Always remember this story when you review written materials for clarity, and remember that your readers are not programmers.

Do not write in the third person. Users are reading this. They don't like to be referred to in the third person as though they were invisible. Do not use passive voice and never, ever start a sentence with "It has" or "It is." Users don't like miracles. They want to control the system. Write the manual and training materials from this perspective.[10]

Words, Sentences, Paragraphs, and Sections

Write simply—to everyone. Eye movement tests show that longer words and unfamiliar words take longer to process in short term memory. As the number of complete thoughts in a sentence (complexity of sentence) increases, so does the time to comprehend the sentence.[11] However, the system overview section or general sections explaining concepts are designed for complete reading—not scanning. Therefore if words, sentences, and paragraphs are too simple, the reader may become bored and miss most of the material.[7] For these expository sections, vary sentence lengths.

Other problems to watch for:

1. Be rigorous in checking spelling. Misspelled words can, if the context is not absolutely clear, increase fixation duration and interfere with learning.[12]
2. Long distances between pronouns and referent nouns can also slow comprehension and perhaps even defeat it entirely.[12]
3. The index should be comprehensive. If a user looks for a word in the index and doesn't find it referenced, whether it is system specific, task specific, or just plain English, then the index has failed.

Graphics and Typography

Again in the manual, diagrams and pictures should be used where appropriate to explain the system. Each illustration should be physically as close as possible to the text which relates to it. Repeat the chapter headings and subheadings exactly for the table of contents and take great care in choosing these words. The table of contents should give readers a word picture of the structure of the system as well as giving them the schema of the manual.

You can use call-outs in addition to summaries and key words as an aid to users in skimming and learning. Short explanations can be in footnotes, but in general, regard footnotes as a last resort. Too many writing amateurs will hide vital information in footnotes not realizing that it is vital.[10]

To organize and present material succinctly, use numbered lists if things must be done in a specific sequence or have a hierarchy of importance; use bullets if listed items are of equal importance. Use rules, arrows, tabular format, examples set off from the text graphically, symbols, screen printouts—whatever you need to use in order to provide typographical and graphic clues to aid learning.[13] Don't get cute with symbolism—you are talking to adults after all. Remember the layout must be consistent throughout the manual.[14] It is meant to be scanned, and inconsistency can cause any gain in learning speed to be lost to processing dissonance.

Some obvious things which should be mentioned: readability of typefaces* (e.g., choose a typeface which distinguishes the number one, the letter el, and capital letter I) and readability of copies (use carbon ribbon for direct printing or photocopying and a good printwheel).

Balanced pages (typography and illustrations) are much less disconcerting for people, and asymmetrical balancing is preferred over symmetrical.[15] There are many rules for optimal typeface/reader comprehension. For example, wider columns require larger typefaces (10–12 words per line is optimal), and 9–12 point typeface (see Figure 4) is easiest to read.[15] The goal is to reduce that learning curve and improve the user/computer interface.

In designing the manual, remember that form follows function;[15] the manual design should come from the system design as perceived from the system/user interface. The user may use menu item 4 first, followed by item 2, then 1, and then 3; but the interface is 1, 2, 3, 4. Don't try to put the manual in the same order as the user will use it. Don't try to organize the manual to reflect the way the user will use the system. *Design the system* as the user would use it, and *then* take the manual from the system. Another problem with trying to design the manual to the user rather than to the interface is that different users will use the system differently. A manual designed for one user may completely confuse another.

This illustrates the difference in serif and sans serif typefaces. It is a 10 point typeface. 9 point is slightly smaller; 12 point is slightly larger.

This illustrates the difference in serif and sans serif typefaces. It is a 10 point typeface. 9 point is slightly smaller; 12 point is slightly larger.

Figure 4—Typeface examples. 10 point serif is on the top; 10 point sans serif on the bottom.

* In 1975, serif typeface was read 7 to 10 words faster per minute,[14] but now that sans serif is more widely used, there may be no difference.

SCREEN DESIGN

The computer screen was designed to suit technology rather than human needs. White print on black background is the hardest for humans to read.[15] Text in all uppercase letters takes more time to process and, to the average person, it signifies alarm. Yet many screen designers continue to use all uppercase, not only on input screens, but in screen instructions and in help text.

Color Problems

When given a choice between screens with text in white and one other color or text in white only, most users chose the white only as being easier to use. My opinion, based on color text studies, is that it was the choice of color and how it was used rather than the presence of color itself. People have different color preferences and needs. Yet most designers who develop for color screens continue to set the colors for the user rather than letting the user set them. Color can also be overused, causing confusion about what is important.[16]

Specialized Screen Typography

The worst mistake that developers make is with help text. A report by the American Institutes for Research says that it is 20% to 30% harder for users to read text on the screen than in a manual, yet developers insist on turing help text into a full-fledged dissertation. Keep it brief—reminders only.

Use windows rather than screen replacement. Since the brain can carry only a few chunks in short term memory, the act of reading text on a replacement screen replaces the chunks and creates a kind of "now why did I come into this room and what was I going to do with this thing in my hand?" feeling in the user. Use windows for help text and training instructions (either with or without borders and background color changes), and, if necessary, make the windows movable so that the user can comfortably examine both the problem and the solution together.

Many years of experimentation and study have gone into the effective design of today's newspapers so that readers can scan the entire page in seconds without missing a subject covered. These design principles can also apply to the computer screen. Use all the textual graphics available for designing screens, but don't make clutter from comprehension aids. Use reverse video, large letters, high intensity, and underline just as you would on paper, but remember the computer screen has more limitations than paper.

1. The computer screen is, first, unnatural. People aren't acclimated to text that is wider than it is long, so leave wide margins on text screens to make it appear longer.[16]
2. Flashing letters are irritating,[17] so use them only when you want to irritate—such as for a system crash warning.
3. All the typeface graphics call attention and pull the eye with varying intensity, so make certain you use the graphics to pull it in the general direction upper left to lower right.[17] Don't make users jump around on the screen to get the information.
4. When replacing part of the screen, leave it blank long enough for users to realize that it has been replaced.[17] This is particularly important with novice users, as they tend to think that computers eat their input.
5. Don't use animation on the same screen with text because it detracts from the text, and the text detracts from the animation.[17]
6. Some users prefer vertical input screens; some don't mind horizontal. However, line things up so users don't have to search for the cursor. (It's much easier to find the cursor on vertical screens.)

LAST WORDS

A user's interest in a system centers on information—fast, logical, understandable, efficient processing of the user's information. Users aren't directly interested in efficient hash routines or wonderful file structures. They are interested in how these things affect their information. This is the user-computer interface. Make certain users can track their information from input to output—easily and completely—including every change the programs make to the information.

REFERENCES

1. Hand, J.D. "Brain Functions During Learning: Implications for Text Design." in D.H. Jonassen (ed.), *The Technology of Text: Principles for Structuring, Designing, and Displaying Text.* Englewood Cliffs, New Jersey: Educational Technology Publications, 1982.
2. Bereiter, C. and M. Scardamalia. "Information Processing Demand of Text Composition." in H. Mandl, N. Stein, and T. Trabasso (eds.), *Learning and Comprehension of Text.* Hillsdale, New Jersey: Lawrence Erlbaum Associates, 1984.
3. Ellis, H.C. and R.R. Hunt. *Fundamentals of Human Memory and Cognition.* Dubuque, Iowa: Wm. C. Brown Company, 1983.
4. Otto, W. and S. White (eds.). *Reading Expository Material.* New York: Academic Press, 1982.
5. Sless, D. *Learning and Visual Communication.* New York: John Wiley, 1981.
6. Gagne, R.M. and L.J. Briggs. *Principles of Instructional Design.* New York: Holt, Rinehart & Winston, 1974.
7. de Beaugrande, R. "Learning to Read versus Reading to Learn: A Discourse Processing Approach." in H. Mandl, N. Stein, and T. Trabasso (eds.), *Learning and Comprehension of Text.* Hillsdale, New Jersey: Lawrence Erlbaum Associates, 1984.
8. Pace, A.J. "Analyzing and Describing the Structure of Text." in D.H. Jonassen (ed.), *The Technology of Text: Principles for Structuring, Designing, and Displaying Text.* Englewood Cliffs, New Jersey: Educational Technology Publications, 1982.
9. Carroll, J.M. and R.L. Mack. "Learning to Use a Word Processor: By Doing, by Thinking, and by Knowing." in J.C. Thomas and M.L. Schneider, *Human Factors in Computer Systems.* Norwood, New Jersey: Ablex Publishing, 1984.
10. Schneiderman, B. *Software Psychology Human Factors in Computer and Information Systems.* Cambridge, Massachusetts: Winthrop Publishers, 1980.
11. Graesser, A.C. and J.R. Rika. "An Application of Multiple Regression Techniques to Sentence Reading Times." in D.E. Kieras and M.A. Just (eds.), *New Methods in Reading Comprehension Research.* Hillsdale, New Jersey: Lawrence Erlbaum Associates, 1984.
12. Rayner, K. and P.J. Carroll. "Eye Movements and Reading Comprehension." in D.E. Kieras and M.A. Just (eds.), *New Methods in Reading Comprehension Research.* Hillsdale, New Jersey: Lawrence Erlbaum Associates, 1984.

13. Waller, R. "Text as Diagram: Using Typography to Improve Access and Understanding." in D.H. Jonassen (ed.), *The Technology of Text: Principles for Structuring, Designing, and Displaying Text.* Englewood Cliffs, New Jersey: Educational Technology Publications, 1982.
14. Hurtley, J. "Designing Instructional Text." in D.H. Jonassen (ed.), *The Technology of Text: Principles for Structuring, Designing, and Displaying Text.* Englewood Cliffs, New Jersey: Educational Technology Publications, 1982.
15. Moen, D.R. *Newspaper Layout and Design.* Ames, IA: The Iowa State University Press, 1984.
16. Christie, B. *Face to File Communication: A Psychological Approach to Information Systems.* New York: John Wiley, 1981.
17. Merrill, P.F. "Displaying Text on Microcomputers." in D.H. Jonassen (ed.), *The Technology of Text: Principles for Structuring, Designing, and Displaying Text.* Englewood Cliffs, New Jersey: Educational Technology Publications, 1982.

Prospects for improved user productivity: A visual perspective

by ROBERT ROTHBARD
Private Practice, Optometry
Santa Ana, California

ABSTRACT

Computer-related vision problems and complaints are common. Ergonomic improvements reduce such complaints by one third. All remaining problems are attributable to the visual limitations of the individual operator. These problems include poor ability to perform sustained near vision work, inadequate ocular-motor control, poor or inefficient control of focusing, aiming and teaming of the two eyes, inefficient processing of visual information, and other productivity-reducing effects of visually-induced stress. Optometric solutions are presented in this paper.

INTRODUCTION

A significant finding of the Panel on Impact of Video Viewing on Vision of Workers of the National Academy of Science was that "The symptoms of ocular discomfort and difficulty with vision reported by some workers who use VDTs appear to be similar to symptoms reported by people performing other near-visual tasks."[1]

Computer-related vision changes and problems, as well as complaints about visual discomfort are common, yet poorly understood. Computer users, their managers, unions, and other groups lobbying for new laws regulating VDTs are functioning without adequate information.

Yet a rich body of clinical and research literature on vision does exist and explains the source of vision problems and changes in vision that afflict at least half of all computer users. More important, the literature presents and explains a variety of regimens that can halt or prevent those problems.

The purpose of this paper is to provide an overview of the literature and its clinical implications and to relate that information to the prospects for improving user productivity.

NEARPOINT VISION TASKS: A RECENT PROBLEM

Beginning about sixty years ago, optometrists noticed that traditional treatment of common visual problems (nearsightedness or myopia in particular) seemed to increase both the rate of progression and the total amount of myopia. At that time, the number of people developing myopia, astigmatism, and other vision conditions was increasing rapidly.

Clinicians noted that the time of onset was beginning to change from juvenile years to the late teens and into the twenties. The data were inconsistent with genetic origin theories. Clinicians saw that vision deterioration is usually associated with periods during which the individual performed near vision tasks for prolonged periods. Other critical factors included: a confined visual target (the page of a book or a VDT screen) and high attentional demand (the material *must* be understood).

Skeffington, a leading vision theorist who integrated scientific and clinical data, noted that sharp eyesight was just one of many factors in vision. He suggested a more comprehensive model thirty years before modern brain studies confirmed his ideas.[2]

Skeffington proposed that vision is an understanding or perception which emerges from a process which involves focusing, fine ocular motor control (eye aiming and teaming), combining the images of both eyes, comparing visual input with memories of prior experience, and integration of input from all the other senses.[3]

Nearly all people are born with the mechanism for clear distance eyesight, but the precision and efficiency (speed of operation) of vision is determined largely by the level of fine ocular-motor control (visual skill) developed during early visual experiences. Skills for teaming the two eyes (binocular vision) begins to develop beginning at about four months of age.[4]

Behavioral optometrists and others have demonstrated that the nature and quality of early visual experience determines the way each individual adapts to cope with near vision tasks. Virtually no effort (oculomotor control) is required to keep the images of the two eyes aligned on distant objects. Near vision, on the other hand, requires a complex and precise interaction of focusing, aiming and alignment before visual information can be taken in.

A demonstration of the difference in visual skill and effort required for distance versus near vision work is appropriate here. To do this experiment, hold both arms straight out in front of you, then point both index fingers upward. Next, without moving your head, quickly glance back and forth from one finger to the other. Notice the effort and sensations associated with this eye movement.

Complete the experiment by bringing both hands toward you, with forefingers still pointed upward. The distance should be about 8 to 10 inches. Without moving your head, glance again from finger to finger. Note the added effort required this time, and notice any sensations of pulling or straining near the eyes.

Although the sensations are exaggerated, this demonstration provides personal experience of the effort involved in the fine motor control required to focus, aim, and align the eyes.

This is the process that occurs five times per second for a person reading at about 300 words per minute. It is a skill which is learned by trial and error from infancy to about age six.

Why is distance vision so natural? Throughout man's evolution, distance vision was a key to survival—hunting, evasion of danger, and most other visually-guided tasks were distance vision tasks. Although short periods of near visual effort were also part of living, highly developed distance vision gave the individual a considerable survival advantage.

Within the last 100 years, however, the conditions of life have changed drastically. The industrial, post-industrial, and now the information, ages require that workers do an ever increasing amount of near vision work. The impact of this shift has been profound. The percentage of the population with myopia, for example, has increased from about 12 to 14 percent at the beginning of the century to an estimated 36 percent in the 1980s.[5]

This was most clearly revealed by Young and Baldwin's study of Eskimos at Point Barrow, Alaska. Among the generations raised before compulsory education imposed near vision (reading) tasks, only a few individuals were nearsighted. Among the generations required to read, nearly 60 percent were myopic.[6]

Myopia is seen as one of several adaptive responses by an individual to the low but persistent levels of stress which is produced by near vision work.

As viewed here, stress is not a psychological feeling. It is a measurable physiological process; a flood of adrenal system chemicals to prepare the body for fight or flight. These changes are linked to increased absenteeism rates of VDT users.[7] Studies repeatedly show that prolonged, low levels of stress trigger many physical and behavioral changes (adaptations) as the individual attempts to cope with the source of stress:[8]

> Sperry states that investigation of the neurological and cytological structure of the brain reveals nothing but a mechanism for control of the musculature. Muscles only take orders. If there is a physiological drive . . . [i.e., pressure from a supervisor to complete the computer task, or a drive to achieve within the VDT user] . . . and if that drive cannot be satisfied by movement, the person will either a) cease the activity to escape (avoid discomfort induced by) the task, b) lower the achievement and understanding (reduce the performance and accuracy), c) distort the structure itself (any temporary or permanent changes in vision), or d) . . . some combination of these three alternatives.[9]

RESOLVING OR PREVENTING COMPUTER-RELATED VISION PROBLEMS

A recent study by the Data Entry Managers Association (DEMA) found that about 73 percent of VDT operators had vision-related complaints. This was up from 69 percent the year before. The lowest level of complaints we have found is in a Bell Laboratories study comparing VDT workers with operators doing the same task, but with paper materials. Bell researchers found that about 52 percent of VDT users had vision-related complaints compared to about 41 percent for the control group working with paper.

These data suggest that although environmental factors play a role in vision changes and complaints, even the installation of extensive ergonomic improvements will not resolve what are in reality the visual limitations of individual operators.

Behavioral optometrists use two major tools to deal with visual limitations and problems: lenses and visual performance enhancement training (visual training, or VT).

VISUAL TRAINING TO DEVELOP VISUAL SKILLS

As with any learned process, performance can be improved. Visual training, frequently mislabeled "eye exercise," is a programmed series of activities that provides visual feedback to the person in training about how well he or she is focusing and aiming.

Training helps the person overcome one of the most subtle but significant effects of visual stress, called "lag" by eye doctors. In simple terms, it means that a person is focusing at one distance, but aiming the eyes at another. This disagreement means the person must (1) see either an unsharp single image, (2) suppress the images of one eye to avoid seeing double, or (3) attempt to match focusing with aiming by increasing effort—which increases the visual stress, which in turn increases the lag.

Each of these responses diverts attention from understanding what is being read to struggling to overcome the deficient visual skill, thus reducing user performance speed and accuracy. Visual stress increases and a vicious cycle ensues.

Visual training disrupts the habitual ocular-motor (focusing and aiming) patterns of individuals with poor visual skills. The activities of training provide feedback which enables the person to develop more accurate and precise motor control patterns and to reduce the effort required. Reduced effort diminishes the visual stress reaction.[10] In terms of behavior, the individual is able to perform visual work more quickly and accurately. This produces an increase in on-the-job performance.

Symptomatic relief of headaches; eyestrain; intermittent blurred eyesight; and certain neck, back, and shoulder discomforts usually begins within the first few weeks of training.

Unfortunately only 3,000 optometrists and a few hundred ophthalmologists perform VT. If all VDT users with deficient vision skills sought help, there would not be enough skilled training specialists to provide it. In-plant group training may be one way to resolve this dilemma. Alternatively, a "train the trainer" program supervised by a behavioral optometrist but with visual training conducted by company staff may be viable.

LENSES, A TOOL FOR THE JOB

There are two major approaches to prescribing lenses. "Correct the refractive error" (CRE) is the most common. It assumes that the findings of an examination (refraction) show the amount of lens power needed to return the patient to maximum distance acuity (sharpness). Emmetropia, the norm, is commonly written as 20/20 eyesight. Although some CRE-oriented doctors also test for eye teaming and sharpness of near vision, the theory behind CRE does not provide for the effects of stress.

CRE often ignores nearpoint vision needs. In myopia, for example, CRE lenses clear distance but may also recreate the visual conditions which were present when myopia began. A Southern California College of Optometry study compared 100 records in both a CRE and a behavioral practice. Over a ten year span, CRE records showed an average myopic increase of nearly 3.50 diopters. Behavioral records showed less than 1.00 diopter of increase.

The behavioral model focuses on how a person's visual system responds to nearpoint tasks. Distance compensation lenses may be prescribed, but lenses for near vision tasks are always offered, sometimes as bifocals. VDT users often receive a separate (single vision) pair of spectacles specifically for computer work.

Behavioral nearpoint lenses prescriptions are based on a complex, precise formula which takes into account the way the individual responds to visual stress (case type). Individuals with poor visual skills are extremely sensitive to small differences in lens power and will often reject (find it impossible to wear) lenses just .25 to .50 diopter stronger than the most helpful lens.

Considerable research has been done over the years on the stress-relieving qualities of nearpoint lenses,[11] including studies which show that behaviorally prescribed lenses produce positive improvements in posture and work performance.[12]

Behaviorally prescribed nearpoint lenses often closely match the dioptric measure of an individual's lag. This suggests that the lens works by helping with the task of bringing the point of focus and convergence into agreement. This eliminates the lag, which seems to be a primary source of visually-induced stress.

CONCLUSION

The National Academy of Science study of VDT-related problems suggests that although the computer itself does not cause vision problems, workers with previously-existing vision problems are likely to experience difficulties. In the United States, about 54 percent of all people wear lenses to compensate for vision problems. Another 10 to 12 percent of people would benefit from, but do not wear, lenses. Thus, at least two-thirds of people have previously-existing vision problems.

One response to visual stress is to avoid visual work. But as more and more jobs become computer-centered, avoidance may not be possible. These people are unlikely to stay on the job for long and may be a source of rapid employee turnover.

For those employees already experiencing any of a variety of computer-related vision problems, behavioral optometry offers some practical solutions.

REFERENCES

1. "Video Displays, Work, and Vision," National Academy of Science, 1983, p. 2.
2. Wiesel, Thorsten N. *The Post Natal Development of The Visual Cortex and the Influence of Environment,* Harvard Medical School, Department of Neurobiology, (Nobel Prize for Medicine, 1981) Nobel Foundation, Copyright, 1982.
3. Flax, Nathan. "Functional Case Analysis: An Interpretation of the Skeffington Model." *American Journal of Optometry and Physiological Optics,* 62, 6, pp. 365–368.
4. McDermott, Jeanne. "Researchers Find There Is More to Vision Than Meets the Eye," *Smithsonian,* April, 1985, pp. 96–107.
5. Figure obtained from the Optometric Extension Program Foundation, Santa Ana, California, 1985.
6. Young, Francis, W.R. Baldwin, and R.A. Box. "Refractive Errors Within Eskimo Families," *American Journal of Optometry,* 46 (1969) 1, pp. 676–685.
7. Frank, Arthur L. *Effects on Health Following Occupational Exposure to Video Display Terminals.* Environmental Sciences Laboratory, Department of Community Medicine, Mount Sinai School of Medicine, New York, 1983.
8. Selye, Hans. *Stress Without Distress,* New American Library, Signet Books, 1975.
9. Hendrickson, Homer H. *The Vision Development Process,* Optometric Extension Foundation, 1969, pp. 8.
10. Birnbaum, Martin H. "Symposium on Nearpoint Visual Stress." *American Journal of Optometry and Physiological Optics,* 62, 6, pp. 361–364.
11. *Bibliography of Stress-relieving Lens and Visual Training Research,* OEP Foundation, Santa Ana, California, 1985.
12. Greenspan, Steven B. *A Study of Near Point Lenses: Effects on Body Posture and Performance.* Illinois College of Optometry and Illinois Institute of Technology Department of Psychology, Chicago, 1975.

Software project stress versus quality and productivity

by SARAH L. SULLIVAN and HOWARD HILL
Illinois Institute of Technology
Chicago, Illinois

ABSTRACT

Managing software project stress is the key to improving software quality and productivity. Software development is a complex intellectual process involving precise communication of abstract concepts across multiple discipline boundaries. Optimum stress maximizes communication effectiveness and the ability to deal with complexity.

INTRODUCTION

Software development is a complex intellectual process involving precise communication of abstract concepts across multiple discipline boundaries. Stress produces symptoms[1,2,3,4,5] which interfere with this process.

Stress symptoms fall into several categories. Two of these categories, cognitive and behavioral, reduce quality and productivity potential by reducing the ability to handle complexity and by reducing communication effectiveness.

Cognitive stress symptoms include decreased concentration, decreased creativity, indecisiveness, intolerance for ambiguity, mental confusion, memory problems, poor judgement, and tunnel vision. These symptoms reduce the ability of the stressed person to formulate and communicate abstract concepts, thus impairing intellectual function.

Behavioral stress symptoms reduce the ability of the stressed person to communicate because these symptoms interfere with the processes of listening, speaking, reading, and writing. These symptoms include anger, anxiety, increased anti-social acts, increased grievances, overreacting to external stimuli, reduced interpersonal skill, reduced teamwork ability, and strained interpersonal relationships.

This paper describes the effect of stress on software project complexity and communication and it shows the relationship between stress and performance. It also identifies job sources of stress on software projects and proposes suggestions for managing this stress.

STRESS AND COMPLEXITY

High levels of complexity abound on software projects. Software engineering has focused on the development of structuring techniques to master this complexity.[6] These techniques apply to various phases of development and classes of problems; they produce layers of system architecture in multiple levels of detail; they represent oblique levels of abstraction and frames of reference; and they reflect differing development styles, cultures, and philosophies. These techniques help to decompose complexity in an orderly fashion so that humans can handle the complexity without errors. But stress reduces the ability to use these structuring techniques effectively. Thus, software project stress counters the effect of software engineering advances.

STRESS AND COMMUNICATION

Communication is the vehicle for conveying quality and productivity objectives. It is also the vehicle for conveying and verifying the abstractions developed through structuring techniques. Certain techniques aid the communication process by requiring formal structured documents.

Communication problems[7,8,9,10] are often encountered in the work environment. These problems arise when communicating abstract concepts, complex interrelationships and interdependencies, and when communicating across discipline boundaries. Problems also arise from cultural differences, defensiveness, distractions, interruptions, jargon, poor listening skills, power and status, and sociological filters. These problems interfere with the sender's encoding and sending of the intended message and with the receiver's decoding and perception of the message received.

Stress intensifies existing communication problems and adds new ones. Bolton and Bolton[1] describe this reduction of adaptive behavior in interpersonal interactions as:

> ... the predictable, unconscious shift of behavior to more extreme, rigid, and nonnegotiable forms in response to a high level of stress. Backup behavior is usually counterproductive for the person using it and very hard on his relationships.... It undermines motivation; raises other people's stress thereby undercutting their productivity; and may ultimately generate more stress for the person exhibiting the backup behavior.

STRESS AND PERFORMANCE

The relationship between stress and performance is an inverted U-shaped curve[3,4] with peak performance occurring at the optimum stress point.

The optimum stress point is evidenced by optimum stress indicators.[1,3,4,11] When a person's stress level is at the optimum stress point these indicators are present. Optimum stress indicators include accurate judgement, composure during crisis, high energy, high morale, high motivation, improved memory and recall, interpersonal competence, mental alertness, optimistic outlook, sharp perception, thorough analysis of problems, and the ability to work long hours without tiring. Thus, people working at their optimum stress point can perform at their highest potential for quality and productivity.

As the level of stress moves away from the optimum stress point, cognitive and behavioral symptoms of stress increase. The severity of stress symptoms intensifies under prolonged exposure to stress. This cumulative stress comes from modern living[2] and life changes[12] as well as from the job.[3]

JOB SOURCES OF SOFTWARE PROJECT STRESS

Job sources of stress[3,13,14] include ambiguity, change, conflict, mismatch between person and job, responsibility, uncertainty, unhealthy interpersonal relationships, and work overload. Organizations unwittingly create stress. This reduces the quality and productivity of the work performed by the organization.

Something that is stressful for one individual may not be stressful for others. Each individual has a unique cultural and educational background along with a unique collection of personal interests, biases, values, skills and aptitudes. Some personalities are more stress prone. Personality factors include: achievement needs, recognition needs, growth needs and social needs.

Couger and Zawacki[15] found that computer professionals have high growth needs and Hackman[16] found that people with high growth needs perform best in jobs that have a high motivating potential. Job design affects motivating potential as a function of the core job dimensions as follows:

$$\textit{Motivating Potential} = \left[\frac{\textit{Skill Variety} + \textit{Task Identity} + \textit{Task Significance}}{3}\right] \times \textit{Job Autonomy} \times \textit{Feedback}$$

A mismatch between growth need strength and motivating potential creates unnecessary stress.

Couger and Zawacki[15] also found that computer professionals have the lowest social needs among professionals. This is consistent with job demands that require long periods of intense concentration to cope with complexity. Buie[17] found that the computer profession attracts a disporportional number of introverts. Stressed by being in the company of others, the introvert prefers to work on his/her own.[3] Thus, the computer professional's preference to avoid lengthy large group meetings and to have an individual private office with walls and a door is really a preference for an environment conducive to peak performance. One-on-one and small group meetings (one hour or less) in a quiet room free of distractions, facilitates the precise communication of complex, abstract concepts without taxing the computer professional's low social needs.

Software projects are particularly sensitive to change because change taxes the low social needs of computer professionals by demanding increased social interaction. The change process increases ambiguity about current job assignments while increasing uncertainty about the future. Frequent drastic change leads to turnover. Turnover increases time pressures and work overload. The temporarily reduced work force spends precious time recruiting and training new team members as the project re-enters the teambuilding process of forming, storming, norming, and performing.[18] A high rate of task reassignments and turnover increases the percent of time the project spends in the forming, storming and norming phases. These phases require more social interaction than the performing phase.

Just about any change generates more work and more stress. Change is inevitable. But, continual rapid uncontrolled change produces prolonged stress and intense stress symptoms.

MANAGING SOFTWARE PROJECT STRESS

Managing software project stress improves project performance by bringing the stress level of all project members to within an acceptable tolerance of their optimal stress point. Managing project stress is a three step process of tailoring and implementing stress reduction changes while minimizing change stress. The first step is to recognize stress through observation of symptoms. The next step is to identify the stress source(s). And the third step is to minimize the stress producing potential of stress sources through training, job design, project management, and change management. This is an ongoing iterative process.

Training reduces stress by developing needed skills. Participative workshops with structured group exercises that develop interpersonal skills while activating knowledge are superior to the traditional classroom lecture approach.

Job design reduces stress by engineering the job to fit the worker. On every project there is more than one way to distribute the work among team members. The distribution of work affects the complexity of the intra-project interfaces (both technical and interpersonal).[19] Here software engineering structuring techniques can be applied to define discrete work modules with minimal interfaces and high visibility to produce jobs with high motivating potential. The job design can be further tailored by matching the skills, social needs, and growth needs of individuals to role(s) and responsibilities.

The responsibility of the project management role is to keep a project on track by producing schedules and establishing budgets, by acquiring and allocating resources, by monitoring progress, and by implementing corrective action. Whether the corrective action relieves stress or creates more stress depends on the process of assessing and implementing change.

Change management[16,20,21] facilitates the change process of unfreezing, changing, and refreezing. People tend to resist change. The following change management techniques help to overcome this resistance:

1. Plan for change.
2. Prepare ahead of time for unexpected problems.
3. Confront difficult problems early.
4. Be flexible. Someone else's approach may be more effective.
5. Encourage participation. Change implementation will be smoother when people buy in ahead of time.
6. Stop the rumor mill by keeping people informed. Partial information is better than no information.
7. Avoid surprises.
8. Propose the change as an experiment.
9. Let others recognize the need for change.
10. Let others have control of their time by letting them develop their own change timetable.

Managing software project stress maximizes quality and productivity by managing stress sources to minimize the presence of cognitive and behavioral stress symptoms.

SUMMARY

Since complexity and communication are fundamental components of software projects, and since stress reduces both the ability to deal with complexity and the ability to communicate effectively, it follows that stress reduces the quality and productivity potential on software projects. Managing software project stress is therefore a key to improving quality and productivity.

Management techniques that allow software professionals to achieve and maintain optimum stress produce peak performers. This enhances the ability to simplify complexity into elegant solutions that are less costly to develop and easier to debug. It also enhances communication effectiveness, which promotes good rapport with clients, reduces tension, improves job satisfaction, reduces errors, and facilitates solving the right problem.

Managing stress on software projects enables people to work smarter.

REFERENCES

1. Bolton, Robert and Dorothy Grover Bolton. *Social Style/Management Style*. New York: AMACOM, 1984.
2. Charlesworth, Edward A. and Ronald G. Nathan. *Stress Management*. New York: Atheneum, 1984.
3. Forbes. Rosalind. *Corporate Stress*. New York: Doubleday, 1979.
4. Ivancevich, John M. and Michael T. Matteson. "Stress and Performance." in Richard M. Steers and Lyman W. Porter (eds.), *Motivation & Work Behavior* (3rd ed.). McGraw-Hill, 1980.
5. Schuler, Randall S. "Definition and Conceptualization of Stress in Organizations." in Henry L. Tosi and W. Clay Hamner (eds.), *Organization Behavior and Management* (4th ed.). Columbus, Ohio: Grid Publishing, 1985.
6. Martin, James and Carma McClure. *Structured Techniques for Computing*. New Jersey: Prentice-Hall, 1985.
7. Allen, T. Harrell. "How Good a Listener are You?" *The Toastmaster,* 42 (1976) 10, pp. 5–8.
8. D'Aprix, Roger. *Communicating for Productivity*. New York: Harper & Row, 1982.
9. Foltz, Roy G. *Management by Communication*. Philadelphia: Chilton, 1973.
10. Wells, Theodora. *Keeping Your Cool Under Fire: Communicating Non-Defensively*. McGraw-Hill, 1980.
11. Garfield, Charles. *Peak Performers*. New York: William Morrow, 1986.
12. Holmes, Thomas H. and Richard H. Rahe. "The Social Readjustment Rating Scale." *Journal of Psychosomatic Research,* 11 (1967), pp. 213–218.
13. Ivancevich, John M., H. Albert Napier, and James C. Wetherbe. "An Empirical Study of Occupational Stress, Attitudes and Health Among Information Systems Personnel." *Information and Management,* 9 (1985), pp. 77–85.
14. Saleh, Shoukry D. and K. Desai. "Occupational Stressors for Engineers." *IEEE Transactions on Engineering Management,* EM-33 (1986) 1, pp. 6–11.
15. Couger, J. Daniel and Robert A. Zawacki. *Motivating and Managing Computer Personnel*. New York: John Wiley, 1980.
16. Hackman, J. Richard. "Work Design." in Richard M. Steers and Lyman W. Porter (eds.), *Motivation & Work Behavior* (3rd ed.), New York: McGraw-Hill, 1980.
17. Buie, Elizabeth A. "Jungian Psychological Type and Programmer Team Building." *Proceedings of the IEEE Computer Societies 9th International Computer Software & Applications Conference,* (Vol. 9), 1985, pp. 249–252.
18. Licker, Paul S. *The Art of Managing Software Development People*. New York: John Wiley, 1985.
19. Weinberg, Gerald M. *The Psychology of Computer Programming*. Van Nostrand Reinhold, 1971.
20. Huse, Edgar F. "Organization Development Interventions." in Henry L. Tosi and W. Clay Hamner (eds.), *Organizational Behavior and Management* (4th ed.). Columbus, Ohio: Grid Publishing, 1985.
21. Schermerhorn, John R. *Management for Productivity*. New York: John Wiley, 1984.

Computer education in the United States of America: State policy on training, instruction, and control

by GARY D. BROOKS and BRENT EDWARD WHOLEBEN
University of Texas
El Paso, Texas
and
SANDRA BOSWELL
El Paso Public Schools
El Paso, Texas

ABSTRACT

In April 1985, a study was initiated to identify, define, and interpret national trends related to state-based priorities for computer education instruction at the elementary and secondary levels of American public education. Information was solicited from state departments of education, state senate education committees, and state legislative or general assembly committees on education policy. The four general issues under study were concerned with existing or pending state legislation or education policy related to: computer literacy and computer science curriculum for K-12 public schools, state certification requirements for teachers who use computers in the classroom, regulations concerned with the training by state teacher education institutions of computer science or literacy teachers, and rules or standards related to ethical considerations for the use of computers in education. A six-month follow-up was completed in December 1985. A critique of the formal materials received from the states formulates a current national policy perspective related to curriculum, certification, training, higher education involvement, and ethical standards for the deployment of computers in American public education.

INTRODUCTION

During April 1985, all state departments of education, state senate education committees, and state legislative or general assembly committees on education policy were contacted for information on four issues relevant to the use of computers in public and private elementary and secondary education. These four issues were concerned with existing or pending state legislation or education policy related to: (1) computer literacy curriculum for K–12 public schools, and similar curriculum guidelines or related information for higher education; (2) state certification requirements for computer literacy teachers, or general classroom teachers who use computers in their classes; (3) regulations concerning the training by state teacher education institutions, of computer science teachers; and (4) rules or general guidelines related to the ethics associated with the use of computers as an instructional medium in the classroom.

Respondents typically replied with (1) a detailed discussion of their state's attitude and progress regarding each of the four areas, and (2) documentation in the form of policy manuals, curriculum guides, and copies of attempted, pending, and enacted legislation germane to the foci of this study. A six-month follow-up study was completed in December 1985 to update the material collected earlier.

GENERAL METHODOLOGY

Each chief state school officer and the individual chairpersons of the various state senate and house education committees were contacted directly, and invited to participate in the study. The interpretive findings of this study are representative of contributed state-level responses from all states, with the exception of Alabama (AL), Delaware (DE), and South Dakota (SD), which either declined participation or provided unusable responses for inclusion in the study. Two earlier interim reports, one to the American Association of Colleges of Teacher Education in February 1986, and the other to the Association for Educational Data Systems in April 1986, did not contain information from New Mexico. A special inquiry resulted in additional information, which has been included in this final report.

Five areas of information aggregation were given priority in the analysis: (1) curricular content and focus related to computer literacy and computer science instruction, (2) state certification of computer-discipline teachers, (3) state guidelines related to policy or regulations which address the computer literacy needs for the preservice and inservice training of teachers, (4) recognized involvement or participation of teacher education institutions in the preparation of both computer literate as well as certificated computer literacy and computer science teachers, and (5) state recognized standards or guidelines related to the ethics of instructional computing.

All supporting documentation was reviewed for specific components related to the study. Structured data collection and aggregation instruments were designed specifically for this study. For each item of research interest, at least two individuals reviewed the materials independently in order to maintain inter-rater reliability.

The investigators in this study have made every effort to sustain optimal levels of validity and reliability given the normal constraints of the literacy analysis methods employed in this research. All findings, interpretations, and conclusions can be documented from the formal materials and respondent comments received from each state entity. Individual requests for specific clarification, preferably in writing, are welcomed by the principal investigators.

ANALYSIS AND RESULTS

The results of this national policy perspective on computer literacy and computer science instructional guidelines across the United States are presented in two parts. First, an analysis of each state's policy concerning each of the major foci of this study is summarized: curriculum, teacher certification, teacher training, teacher education institutional involvement, and ethical standards. Second, a detailed analysis of each state's curriculum for computer literacy instruction, where applicable and available, is summarized by instructional emphasis and state preference.

State Policy on Curriculum

A total of 27 states have developed or enacted state-level guidelines for use by local school districts. Due to decentralized authority over the curriculum in many states, most of these guidelines are offered simply as recommendations, or "model programs," for district consideration. The status of state-level guidelines for curriculum relevant to computer literacy and computer science instruction is displayed in Table I.

The supporting documentation received indicates that at least 12 states (AK, CT, HI, ID, NE, NC, ND, RI, UT, VT, VA, and WA) have enacted or are in the process of developing computer literacy/science curriculum guidelines for both elementary and secondary schools, namely, K–12 orientation. Eight states prefer a limited secondary (grades 9–12) curriculum emphasis, while four states prefer a primary or elementary school orientation (either K–8 or 7–8). Specific curricular guidelines (i.e., specified curricular objectives with demonstrable individual performance requirements) exist for 20

TABLE I—Status of state-level guidelines for curriculum relevant to computer literacy and/or computer science instruction

Alabama				Montana			
Alaska	E		1–12	Nebraska		I	K–12
Arizona				Nevada	E		K–8
Arkansas	E		3–10	New Hampshire	E		9–12
California		I	9–12	New Jersey			
Colorado				New Mexico		I	
Connecticut	E		K–12	New York	E		7–8
Delaware				North Carolina	E		K–12
Florida	E		3–11	North Dakota	E		K–12
Georgia	E		9–12	Ohio			
Hawaii	E		K–12	Oklahoma			
Idaho		I	K–12	Oregon			
Illinois				Pennsylvania			
Indiana				Rhode Island	E		K–12
Iowa				South Carolina	E		9–12
Kansas		I	K–8	South Dakota			
Kentucky	E		9–12	Tennessee	E		7–8
Louisiana	E		9–12	Texas	E		7–8
Maine		I	9–12	Utah	E		K–12
Maryland		I	9–12	Vermont	E		K–12
Massachusetts				Virginia	E		K–12
Michigan	E		9–12	Washington		I	K–12
Minnesota	E		K–12	West Virginia	E		
Mississippi				Wisconsin	E		9–12
Missouri				Wyoming			

"E" = Exists or Pending
"I" = Attempted or Introduced
K–12 = Kindergarten through 12th Grade, Inclusive

states (AK, AR, CN, FL, HI, KY, LA, NV, NH, NY, NC, ND, RI, SC, TN, TX, UT, VT, VA, and WI). The remaining 7 states have only very general statements of goals, or alternatively, are still in the delineation stages of curriculum development.

State Policy on Certification

Eighteen states responded with information regarding current or upcoming state certification considerations for computer literacy and computer science teachers. For these states, the main between-state differences centered around whether certification was perceived as mandatory, and whether formal training in computer science was considered necessary. The status of state-level guidelines regarding teacher certification for computer literacy and computer science instructional licensure is displayed in Table II.

From supporting documentation received from these states, 6 states (KS, KY, NC, OK, UT, and WI) have designated formal instruction as mandatory, although 2 other states (AK and IA) are considering a similar strategy. TX was the only state to indicate it required a test to receive certification. This practice was suspended after the Spring of 1986, but is currently being reinstituted as part of the overall teacher competency examination (ExCET) system. The remaining 9 states which have considered state certification demonstrate a preference to rely upon local school district discretion for determining certification standards, if any, for teaching computer science or literacy.

State Policy on Teacher Training

Twenty-eight states responded with information regarding current policy or future preferences for training teachers in the areas of computer literacy and science. For these states, the main differences centered around the orientation for inservice versus preservice instruction, and whether such instruction should be mandatory for any or all computer teachers and users. The status of state-level guidelines related to teacher training provisions for computer literacy and computer science instructional methods is displayed in Table III.

From supporting documentation received from these states, a total of 13 states prefer an inservice orientation, while 12 states prefer a preservice form of teaching training. HA and UT use both preservice and inservice programs. Not less than 17 states (AK, CT, HI, ID, IL, IN, CA, MN, MT, NE, NY, NC, TX, UT, VA, WI, and WY) demonstrate a preference for both elementary and secondary training opportunities. CT, HI, KS, KY, LA, ND, and OK require preservice training (usually a major or a minor) in computer science or a related field. The other fields include math, science, or business, and the requirement applies chiefly to secondary teachers. Furthermore, a total of 7 states (KS, MI, MO, MS, MT, UT, and WY) demonstrate an interest in mandatory training, though not always including the full K–12 grade level range. LA, MO, TX, UT, and WA require, or are planning to require, computer training as part of the general teacher certification at the preservice level.

State Policy on Teacher Education Involvement

The extent of involvement on the part of institutions of higher education is naturally confounded by the existence or nonexistence of certification standards and preservice training requirements. However, 21 states supplied documentation, which offers some understanding of this issue. The status of state-level guidelines for involving teacher education institutions or programs in the development of computer education curriculum and policy is displayed in Table IV.

Not less than 12 states (AK, IN, KS, LA, ME, MI, MT, NC, TX, WA, WI, and XY) have policies related to formal university-level involvement in computer literacy training, while the remaining 9 states are "formally" studying similar strategies. Of the 12 states, not less than 9 (AK, KS, CA, ME, WI, MT, WA, WI, and WY) have policies designating such involvement as mandatory. Involvement may vary from supplying the necessary training to acting as a formal planning representative during the development of training guidelines.

State Policy on Ethics

Fourteen states have formal policy, guidelines, recommendations, or "structured planning activities" directed at the

TABLE II—Status of state-level guidelines regarding teacher certification for computer literacy and computer science instructional licensure

Alabama								Montana					
Alaska					S	K–12		Nebraska					
Arizona								Nevada					
Arkansas								New Hampshire					
California								New Jersey					
Colorado								New Mexico					
Connecticut		D			S	K–6	7–12	New York					
Delaware								North Carolina	M				K–12
Florida								North Dakota		E			9–12
Georgia								Ohio					
Hawaii			E			K–12		Oklahoma	M	E			*
Idaho								Oregon					
Illinois								Pennsylvania					
Indiana								Rhode Island					
Iowa	M			P		9–12		South Carolina					
Kansas	M					9–12/1987		South Dakota					
Kentucky	M					9–12		Tennessee					
Louisiana	M					9–12		Texas			T		K–12
Maine								Utah	M				K–12
Maryland								Vermont		E			9–12
Massachusetts								Virginia				P-S	9–12
Michigan								Washington					
Minnesota				P		10–12		West Virginia					
Mississippi					S			Wisconsin	M				7–12
Missouri					S			Wyoming					

"M" = mandatory instruction
"S" = under study
"T" = test required
"*" = tentative conclusion
"D" = discretionary
"P" = proposed
"E" = experience substitute
K–12 = Kindergarten through Grade 12, Inclusive

definition of operating procedures for ethical computing activities. Of these 14 states, at least 4 are still studying the need for "policy" level guidelines. The status of state-level guidelines related to policy governing the ethical deployment of educational computing and computer equipment is displayed in Table V.

Not less than 7 states (KS, ME, NC, OH, SC, WA, and WV) have limited their interest in ethics to copyright issues. On the other hand, CA and MN have policies that also relate to the ethical responsibilities in software evaluation prior to instructional deployment. NY was the only state with a formal concern with privacy violations, although the policy guidelines resident in WI include elements of privacy in their "human values" criteria. The state of OK was particularly concerned with equity issues, especially related to the concept of equal educational opportunity. Nonetheless, WI has the most comprehensive statement on ethics. In this state, copyright, equity, human values (including privacy), and a legitimate accountability for monitoring individual student performance and progress during computer assisted instructional activities were all viewed as major components of computer ethics.

Computer Literacy Curriculum

A total of 29 states supplied interpretable documentation, which delineated state requirements or recommendations related to curriculum for computer literacy instruction at the elementary and secondary school levels. In summary, of those states who participated in the study, 19 states did not have statewide programs or guidelines; therefore, their results are not included in the curriculum synthesis of this study. NE and RI reported they had specific curriculum but did not share those documents with the investigators. Two states, IA and WA, reported they will be publishing guidelines within the next two years.

The curriculum documentation supplied by the states was analyzed for (1) specificity of instructional objectives and (2) grade level of required or recommended offering and mastery. Four generic areas of computer education goals were discernible from the curriculum, and are referred to in this study as: computer operations, computers in society, programming and problems, and computer applications. Furthermore, a total of 24 instructional objectives were synthesized

TABLE III—Status of state-level guidelines for teacher training provisions in computer literacy and computer science instructional methods

Alabama								Montana		P		M			K–12
Alaska			I				K–12	Nebraska			I		S		K–12
Arizona								Nevada							
Arkansas			I				3–8	New Hampshire							
California								New Jersey							
Colorado								New Mexico							
Connecticut					S	R	K–12	New York			I				K–12
Delaware								North Carolina		P	I				K–12
Florida								North Dakota		P				R	9–12
Georgia								Ohio							
Hawaii		P	I			R	K–12	Oklahoma		P				R	9–12
Idaho			I				K–12	Oregon							
Illinois			I				K–12	Pennsylvania							
Indiana			I				K–12	Rhode Island							
Iowa					S		9–12	South Carolina							
Kansas		P		M		R	9–12	South Dakota							
Kentucky		P				R	9–12	Tennessee			I				7–8
Louisiana	C	P			S	R	K–12	Texas	C	P	I				K–12
Maine								Utah	C	P	I	M			K–12
Maryland								Vermont							
Massachusetts								Virginia					S		K–12
Michigan		P		M			7–12	Washington	C	P					K–12
Minnesota			I				K–12	West Virginia							
Mississippi				M	S		9–12	Wisconsin					S		K–12
Missouri	C	P		M			K–12	Wyoming		P		M			K–12

"P" = preservice
"M" = mandatory
"R" = related fields
K–12 = Kindergarten through Grades 12, Inclusive
"I" = inservice
"S" = under study
"C" = part of teacher certification

from these materials, and the placement of each objective was identified across the K–12 grade continuum. The information displayed in Table VI summarizes this analysis.

The grade levels noted on the charts may be subject to a number of different interpretations. Some states' responses included the grade levels in which the subject matter was introduced. Other responses listed the level at which mastery was expected. Most states mentioned only the grades in which the materials were covered. "NG" is used in the tables to indicate that no grade level was specified. Hyphens appearing before numbers in the charts, indicate the level at which subject matter should be mastered. A hyphen following a number indicates when the materials were introduced.

Computer operations

Keyboard skills refer to the use and understanding of the functions of the keys on the keyboard. Vocabulary and terminology pertain to words and terms associated with computers and their use, including the parts of and functions of computers. Operation of the computer deals with the knowledge of all procedures and basic functions of the computer as well as the proper care of the equipment. These procedures and functions include turning the computer on and off, loading software, initializing diskettes, saving data, and copying. Use of peripherals primarily encompasses the use of printers, modems, monitors, and disk drives. Other peripherals were rarely mentioned. Use of software includes familiarity with various types of software such as CAI, simulations, and CAD. There is some overlapping with operating the computer in this topic, since the ability to run software is a necessary element in both categories. The ability to select appropriate software and to react to error messages as well as the proper use of documentation are considered under this topic.

Computers in society

History and development of computers cover the major steps and people involved in the development of computers. Daily uses of computers refer to the effects of and utilization of computers on daily life. Business uses include discussions and studies of general uses of computers in businesses. Career opportunities, careers, pertain to the study of various fields of business in which computer skills are useful in gaining em-

TABLE IV—Status of state-level guidelines for teacher education involvement in the development of computer education curriculum and policy

Alabama						Montana	U		M		
Alaska	U			M		Nebraska	U			S	
Arizona						Nevada					
Arkansas			I	M	S	New Hampshire					
California						New Jersey					
Colorado						New Mexico					
Connecticut						New York				S	
Delaware						North Carolina	U	G			
Florida						North Dakota					
Georgia						Ohio					
Hawaii						Oklahoma					
Idaho						Oregon					
Illinois						Pennsylvania					
Indiana			I			Rhode Island					
Iowa	U	G			S	South Carolina					
Kansas	U	G		M/1987		South Dakota					
Kentucky						Tennessee					
Louisiana				M		Texas	U	G			
Maine		G		M		Utah					
Maryland					S	Vermont					
Massachusetts					S	Virginia				S	
Michigan	U	G		M		Washington	U		M		
Minnesota						West Virginia					
Mississippi	U	G		M	S	Wisconsin	U		M		*
Missouri						Wyoming	U		M		

"U" = preservice, undergraduate
"I" = inservice
"M" = mandatory
"G" = preservice, graduate
"S" = under study
"*" = "tentative conclusions"

ployment or achieving advancement. Ethical issues, ethics, deals with such factors as computer crime, software protection, copyright laws, issues of privacy, and misuse of computer information. Future uses relate the many possible uses of computers in years to come. Advantages and disadvantages of computers include the cost of computers, the accuracy of information gained from computer records, duplication of information, speed of access and use, general capabilities and limitations of computers, lack of software for specific uses, and employment caused by computers.

Programming skills and problem solving

Writing programs includes use of languages to construct programs, working with sub-routines, debugging programs, and writing documentation. Learning programming languages primarily refers to the use and understanding of LOGO, BASIC, and Pascal. COBOL, FORTRAN, APL, PLI, RPG, assembly and machine languages were also mentioned in some materials. Understanding the logic of programming, programming logic, deals with developing and using algorithms and flowcharts. Problem solving has to do with the use of computers to solve specific problems. This topic includes the use of problem solving software and designing programs to solve problems.

Computer applications

Word processing, spreadsheet, and data base each refer to teaching these types of software and to students' use and understanding of their special features. Telecommunications deals with the uses of networking systems. Graphics pertains to the creation and use of graphics software and graphics programming. Robotics covers the development and study of the uses of robotics. Sound includes the uses of voice synthesizers and the production of music on computers. Artificial intelligence relates to studies and discussions of its development and possible uses.

NOTE

An annotated resource bibliography of state-source documentation, which serves as the research basis for this study, is available for session attendees. Copies may be obtained from Brent Edward Wholeben, University of Texas at El Paso, El Paso, TX 79968-0567.

TABLE V—Status of state-level guidelines related to policy governing the ethical deployment of education computing and/or computer equipment

Alabama				Montana							
Alaska				Nebraska							
Arizona				Nevada							
Arkansas				New Hampshire							
California	C	E		New Jersey						S	
Colorado				New Mexico							
Connecticut				New York		P				S	
Delaware				North Carolina	C						
Florida				North Dakota							
Georgia				Ohio	C						*
Hawaii				Oklahoma			Q			S	
Idaho				Oregon							
Illinois				Pennsylvania							
Indiana				Rhode Island							
Iowa			S	South Carolina	C						
Kansas	C			South Dakota							
Kentucky				Tennessee							
Louisiana				Texas							
Maine	C			Utah							
Maryland				Vermont							
Massachusetts				Virginia							
Michigan				Washington	C						
Minnesota	C	E		West Virginia	C						
Mississippi				Wisconsin	C		Q	V	M		
Missouri				Wyoming							

"C" = copyright
"P" = privacy
"V" = human value
"S" = under study
"E" = courseware evaluation
"Q" = equity
"M" = student progress monitoring
"*" = tentative conclusions

TABLE VI—Summary of curriculum for computer literacy instruction, delineated by curriculum objective and grade-level of offering and mastery

	AK	AR	CA	CT	FL	GA	HI	ID	KS	KY	LA	ME	MD	MI	MN	NV	NH	NM	NY	NC	ND	SC	TN	TX	UT	VT	VA	WV	WI
COMPUTER OPERATIONS																													
Keyboard	1–8	9–10	9–10	1–4	–5	9–12	3	K–5	K–8			9–12				K–8	9–12	NG	4–6		5–6	9–12	7–8		K–6			NG	9–12
Terminology	1–8	9–10	9–12	K–12	–8		3–8	K–5	K–8	11–12	9–12		NG	9–12	K–12	K–3	9–12	NG	4–6	K–5	K–9	9–12	7–8	7–9	K–6		NG	NG	9–12
Operation	1–8	9–10	9–12	1–12	–3	9–12		K–5	K–8	11–12	9–12	9–12	NG	9–12	K–12	K–3	9–12	NG	K–3	K–5	9–12	9–12	7–8	7–9	K–6	K–8	NG	NG	9–12
Peripherals	1–8	9–10			–5		8–12	K–5	K–8	11–12	9–12	9–12	NG	9–12	K–12	3–8	9–12		10–12		K–9		7–8		K–6				9–12
Software	1–8				–8		3–12	6–12	K–8		9–12	9–12	NG	9–12	K–12	K–3	9–12	NG	K–3	K–5	9–12	9–12	7–8	7–9	K–6	K–8	NG		9–12
COMPUTERS IN SOCIETY																													
History	7–8	9–10	9–12	3		9–12		K–5	K–8	10–12	9–12	9–12	NG	9–12	K–12	8	9–12	NG		K–5	9–12	9–12	7–8	7–9	7–8	2–8	NG		9–12
Daily Uses	4–8		9–12	1–12	5–8		8–12	K–5								K–3	9–12	NG		K–5	9–12	9–12	7–8	7–9		2–8	NG		9–12
Business Uses	4–8	9–10	9–12		5–8		3–12	6–9	K–8	10–12	9–12	9–12	NG	9–12	K–12	K–3	9–12	NG	4–6	K–9	9–12	9–12	7–8	7–9	7–8	2–8	NG		9–12
Careers	7–8	9–10	9–12			9–12	3–12	6–9	K–8	10–12	9–12		NG	9–12		8		NG	4–12			9–12	7–8		9–12				
Ethics	7–8	9–10	9–12	8–12	5–8	9–12		6–9	K–8		9–12	9–12	NG	9–12	K–12	8	9–12	NG	7–9	8	K–9	9–12		7–9	9–12	9–12	NG		9–12
Future		9–10	9–12	1–12	9–11				K–8				NG	9–12	K–12			NG				9–12	7–8		7–8	2–8	NG		
Advantages	4–8			1–12	8–11		–12	K–9			9–12		NG	9–12	K–12	K–8	9–12		7–9	K–5		9–12	7–8	7–9			NG		
PROGRAMMING AND PROBLEMS																													
Writing Programs	1–12	9–10	9–12	K–12	–11			6–9	K–8	9–12	9–12	9–12	NG	9–12	K–12		9–12	NG	7–12	K–5	9–12	9–12	7–8	7–9	K–6	2–8			9–12
Programming Languages	1–12	9–10	9–12	K–12			8–12	K–12								8,K–3			7–12	K–5	9–12			K–9		K–12	9–12		9–12
Programming Logic	7–12	9–10	7–12				8–12	6–12	K–8	12				9–12	K–12		9–12		7–12	10–12	9–12	9–12	7–8	7–9	K–6		NG		9–12
Problem Solving	4–12	9–10	9–12		5–8		8–12	K–12	K–8	10–12	9–12		NG	9–12	K–12		9–12	NG	7–12	6–9	9–12		7–8	7–9	K–6		NG		
COMPUTER APPLICATIONS																													
Word Processing	7–12	9–10	9–12	5–8		9–12	6–12	6–9	K–8		9–12	9–12		9–12	K–12	8	9–12	NG	10–12	8–12	11–12		7–8	7–9	7–8	K–8	NG	NG	9–12
Spreadsheet	7–12	9–10	9–12			9–12	6–12	6–9			9–12	9–12			K–12	8	9–12	NG	10–12	8–12	11–12		7–8	7–9	7–8	4–8	NG	NG	9–12
Data Base	7–12		9–12	6,8,12		9–12	6–12	6–9	K–8		9–12	9–12		9–12	K–12	8	9–12	NG	10–12	8–12	11–12			7–9	7–8	5–8	NG	NG	9–12
Telecommunications	7–12	9–10	9–12	8–					K–8		9–12	9–12			K–12	8	9–12		10–12	8–12	11–12			7–9	7–8	5–8	NG	NG	9–12
Graphics	7–8	9–10	9–12					6–9	K–8		9–12	9–12			K–12				10–12		9–12		7–8			7–8	NG		9–12
Robotics	7–12	9–10		7–12					K–8					9–12	K–12														9–12
Sound	7–12	9–10							K–8						K–12						9–12					9–12	NG		9–12
Artificial Intelligence				8–										9–12									7–9		7–8				

The computer and thinking skills: Rationale for a revitalized curriculum

by MICHAEL NEUMAN
Capital University
Columbus, Ohio

ABSTRACT

Recent reports lament the devaluation of the baccalaureate degree; too often students fail to acquire the thinking skills needed after graduation. Fortunately, the computer, besides offering utilities that increase productivity, can deliver computer-aided instruction (CAI) that helps develop thinking skills by simulating the mental processes of academic experts.

Liberal arts faculty sometimes dismiss CAI because they consider its algorithms too narrow and rigid to serve as problem-solving devices. However, such algorithms should not be viewed as capturing the essence of thinking skills, but as offering simplified problem-solving approaches that students can grasp—approaches that must be supplemented and even superseded by the professor in the classroom.

Despite objections, three recent trends are likely to hasten the advent of courseware that models and develops thinking skills: improved integration of courseware into coursework, increased attention to the ways students learn and experts think, and the introduction of sophisticated authoring systems.

INTRODUCTION

Recent reports by a number of prestigious educational task forces have brought to the attention of the American public a concern professors have recognized for some time: the decline and devaluation of the undergraduate degree. The Study Group on the Condition of Excellence in American Higher Education, the Carnegie Forum's Task Force on Teaching as a Profession, and the Association of American Colleges' Project on Redefining the Meaning and Purpose of Baccalaureate Degrees have all addressed the problem and judged it a cause for national alarm. Among the various manifestations of the decline, the one most frequently cited is this: too often students receive their college degrees without acquiring the thinking skills needed to direct their continuing education or to advance in their chosen professions.

To cure our academic ills and restore vitality to the education of our undergraduates, the commissions on undergraduate education have prescribed a coherent curriculum that subordinates the mere communication of information to the development of a wide range of thinking skills. According to the Carnegie Forum, the "core should develop the essential skills of comprehension, computation, writing, speaking, and clear thinking."[1] Among the skills deemed most important by the Association of American Colleges are logical inquiry and critical analysis, the processes of literacy (writing, reading, speaking, and listening), manipulating numerical data, understanding the scientific method, and shaping values through choices. Such a curriculum, according to the Association, would constitute "the intellectual, aesthetic, and philosophic experiences that should enter into the lives of men and women engaged in baccalaureate education."[2]

If we accept this agenda for reform, then we must enlist all the educational resources at our disposal. If the undergraduate curriculum must be reformed, not merely repaired, then educators should not overlook the advantages of the computer.

COMPUTERS AND THINKING SKILLS: A MODEST PROPOSAL

Besides the use of computer utilities to increase productivity, the computer has another, more controversial use in education. Although the notion seems incongruous to some and anathema to others, the computer can be used to guide students, step by step, through the difficult, iterative thinking processes that characterize mastery of college-level disciplines.

As an example, consider how a student could be taught critical reading, one of the thinking skills most essential for a revitalized postsecondary curriculum. According to the report of the Association of American Colleges,[2] our students

> need to be taught how to read actively, arguing along the way with every word and assertion; and how to read aesthetically and critically, seeking the word, the expression, the exact form of phrase or direction that catches the reader just when the reader wants to escape . . . (p. 18)

With the proper lesson, the computer can instruct the student how to read "actively"—either "aesthetically" or "critically" as the student's discipline demands. Making explicit the steps of the mental processes that an educated individual follows when reading the primary works of a discipline, the lesson would present a central text—a poem in a literature course, a theorem in mathematics, a syllogism in philosophy, an argument in debate—and then guide the student through a careful reading. Slowly, sequentially, the lesson would highlight and explain key points, pause to explore the implications of a phrase, and consider the rationale for analysis; in other words, the computer would simulate the process of careful reading the student needs to master. Furthermore, the computer would engage the student's attention by its interactivity; testing the student's comprehension through judicious questions and providing direction through appropriate responses and citations for further study.

Although we often consider speed to be the essence of the computer's power, in this instance the power would lie in the computer's potential for slow motion—its ability to advance more measuredly, more circumspectly than the student is inclined, to probe the significance of the text and to explain the steps of the process with sufficient depth and care.

To a seasoned professor, such a lesson might seem stultifying in its slow pace and elementary level. The professor might be eager to advance to topics of great pith and moment, such as the significance of *Hamlet*; meanwhile the student, just beginning an initiation into the academic discipline, needs to master more elementary skills, such as how to read a Shakespearean play. The professor—upholding high standards, forgetting an apprenticeship from long ago, or simply bored with the basics—may demand the fruits of thinking skills without helping develop and refine the student's ability to think. The computer, which lacks the capacity for boredom and impatience, can exercise the student at a level well below that comfortable for the professor.

Because we learn best by doing, the computer's interactive engagement of the student makes it a better device than a textbook for teaching such skills. A text may offer the advantages of lower cost and greater accessibility, but its content (for example, on how to read critically) is likely to be read at least as perfunctorily as young students tend to read their other assignments. Also, the book's interactivity is less compelling: it can pose questions, but it cannot withhold answers, judge responses, and provide direction related to students' responses. By contrast, the computer-based lesson not only describes the process of critical reading, but promotes it. By compelling students to employ the techniques of critical reading, the lesson enhances the possibility that those techniques will be learned. Furthermore, the lesson can impose a regimen of discipline and responsiveness that the student may lack. In the hours after class—the two-thirds of the learning time during which the professor is absent—many students would profit from the imposition of more discipline, rigor, and guidance than solitary study provides.

The principle being proposed here is not, of course, that the computer should replace the professor or the book, but simply that the computer should perform the tasks that it can do most profitably and efficiently. In this capacity, the computer would function not as the professor's replacement or rival but as a kind of teaching fellow, directing the basic but essential learning processes that are relegated to the machine.

OBJECTIONS TO THE USE OF COMPUTERS IN THE LIBERAL ARTS

The computer can help to revitalize the liberal arts only to the extent that the professoriate welcomes its technology. Although faculty in increasing numbers are making use of the computer, the reservations of many colleagues—especially in the liberal arts—are still strong and need to be addressed.

Recent studies show that faculty have in fact "discovered" the computer. According to a survey conducted in November 1985 by the American Council of Learned Societies, 45% of all faculty respondents either owned a computer or had access to one for their exclusive use; in 1980, by contrast, the figure was 2%.[3] This increasing use foreshadows broader educational application, according to a study prepared by the Corporation for Public Broadcasting: *Faculty Perspectives on the Role of Information Technology in Academic Instruction* reports that professors view the instructional potential of the computer favorably to the extent that they have used the technology. With respect to specific applications, 83% of the respondents stated that the computer could help develop such generic thinking skills as problem-solving, analysis, and writing; 80% stated that the computer could encourage students to be more active learners; and 79% stated that the computer could help students learn important concepts or skills that are difficult to master.[4]

Nevertheless, among faculty who do not use the computer—especially in the disciplines of the liberal arts—there is still a widespread conviction that the computer is inimical to their enterprise. "Nothing that is human," said Terence, "is alien to me;" by a strange corollary, some professors believe that nothing cybernetic is congenial.

Mind Control

For some, the notion of a computer as guide to the thinking process is threatening, conjuring up visions of Orwellian mind control. These faculty fear that if students look to the computer as a mentor, as a guide to thinking, and a source for answers, the students' own thinking processes will come to resemble the mechanism of the computer: lock-step, single-minded, relentless. Such professors fear, as did Karl Marx, "the intellectual desolation, artificially produced by converting immature human beings into mere machines."

Easy Answers

Other proponents of the liberal arts, less alarmed that the computer will dehumanize the user, nevertheless fear that students may become satisfied with the clear-cut formulas and authoritative answers of the computer and thus fail to look beyond the terminal screen for answers. These professors fear a technological perversion of Occam's Razor—the philosophical principle that, given two competing interpretations of a phenomenon, the observer should choose the simpler. They are concerned, in other words, that students who use the computer will be content with the simplified, accessible, predetermined patterns it provides and stop their quest for richer, more complex answers and solutions.

Abrogation of Thinking

Underlying both of these views is the concern that an unthinking reliance upon the computer could lead an individual to abrogate his or her mental powers. But both views overestimate the likelihood that the computer can thus undermine one of the most cherished goals of the liberal arts. Critics of computers in education frequently lack experience in using computer-based lessons and misunderstand how a computer works. Ironically, they exaggerate the power and attraction of the computer, and they underestimate the inevitable and salutary resistance that characterizes the response of most users to computer-based lessons.

However credulous the students and however circumspect the developers, postsecondary users of computer-based lessons are likely to discover that some of their choices and responses have not been anticipated. Their inevitable reaction of frustration, even to an otherwise effective program, will prevent them from becoming mesmerized and indoctrinated. In other words, the user's experience of the computer both engages and alienates. Ideally, of course, it does the former more consistently than the latter. But even the alienation can be useful in signalling the existence of alternative responses and approaches. This tendency of the computer simultaneously to engage and detach is a characteristic often overlooked by the most adamant of inexperienced critics.

Limitations of Algorithms

There are, however, other proponents of the liberal arts—not only familiar with the computer, but knowledgeable about its programming—who object to the computer on the basis of a more deeply rooted educational and philosophical principle. The opposition of these faculty colleagues is directed not to the computer as an instrument, but to the algorithm as a problem-solving device. Their views call for a more thorough examination.

An algorithm is a rule or process for solving a certain type of problem, as in basic arithmetic when we use an algorithm to find the lowest common denominator of a series of fractions. But, the use of algorithms outside the realm of mathematics and the natural sciences troubles many humanists. Can there be an algorithm for writing an expository essay? For reading critically in an academic discipline? The computer scientist, accustomed to solving a wide range of problems by means of algorithms, may answer these questions with a qualified "yes." The humanist, however, is likely to answer the same questions with a resounding "no."

Algorithms and Ambiguities

For humanists, an algorithm is of questionable worth in their disciplines because the mitigating circumstances surrounding any important human activity render rigid formulas nugatory. Humanists have studied the human condition—across the continents and throughout the ages—and they have developed a respect for the complexities and ambiguities of life. Morality, values, the deepest truths that individuals need to stabilize their psyches and enrich their experiences all are inimical to generalization. In fact, the humanities engender a tolerance for ambiguity, a wariness of simplistic formulas, final solutions, incontrovertible truths.

And so, to these critics, the computer is unwelcome as a teaching fellow, not so much because it is a technological instrument but because it proposes to solve problems in a heretical manner with tidy formulas, with algorithms. They know the computer must run its programs and solve its problems by following a single path, however rapidly and relentlessly; it does not take kindly to serendipity. By contrast, the human brain, which follows a mysterious multi-path route in solving problems, can use intuition as well as logic;[5] its wonderful vagaries cannot be simulated by machine.

Algorithms as Simplifications

In one respect, these opponents of computers are correct: algorithms in the liberal arts are oversimplifications. And, if our primary concern in the teaching of thinking skills is only the delineation of the richness and complexity of these skills, we would have to forsake algorithms and therefore computer-based instruction. Algorithms would utterly fail to capture the mystery of the thinking processes, the wonders of inspiration, what Wordsworth calls "a leading from above, a something given." However, our initial concern in the teaching of thinking skills is not to analyze and account for these skills, it is to impart them to undisciplined, maturing minds. For this purpose, the oversimplification of algorithms is not only conducive to learning, it is necessary. Later, of course, after students have developed the rudiments of thinking skills, the professor will have to supplement the algorithms and present the rest of the story.

Algorithms and the Teaching of Writing

The successful use of algorithms to devlop thinking skills is perhaps best exemplified by recent strategies in the teaching of writing. In fact, this discipline can be considered a paradigm because the process of composition is taught at so many educational levels, is undeniably a complex thinking skill, is squarely within the domain of the liberal arts, and is congenial to the use of computer-assisted instruction.

When adolescents begin to learn composition, most of them have trouble organizing their ideas. Consequently, their writing teachers have sometimes taught organization by means of the algorithm of the five-paragraph theme. According to the formula, the first paragraph introduces the subject and presents the thesis, and the fifth paragraph restates the thesis and concludes the essay; within this frame, the body of the paper presents three separate illustrations of the thesis in one paragraph apiece. This elementary organizational strategy calls for thinking skills, and the majority of students are not likely to learn to organize their essays without rigid adherence to the formula. The prudent teacher therefore will not overemphasize the fact that the five-paragraph theme is useful only for papers that call for illustration as a pattern of organization and for topics that can be developed in three examples. In other words, the limited abilities and pressing needs of the students warrant the teaching of a simplified organizational formula, an algorithm.

Eventually though, the teacher of writing in college must present techniques better suited to the developing thinking skills and broader needs of the students. The old algorithm must be superseded and a new one employed. Widely taught now is a pattern derived from the study of professional writers that is tailored to the needs of students. This much heralded writing process consists of the four separate stages of: (1) prewriting (i.e., considering audience and purpose), (2) incubating ideas, (3) composing drafts, and (4) revising the essay. Naturally, presenting this new algorithm requires dismantling the old one, and college freshmen are sometimes disillusioned to discover they can no longer rely on the handy framework of the five-paragraph theme.

Is the new algorithm of the writing process universally applicable? No. A sportswriter with a midnight deadline has scant time for incubating ideas; an executive responding to a memo may have few options for selecting a format. But, for the students in English 101 and for the writing they will be called upon to do, the algorithm of the writing process is valid, in being rooted in the actual composing process of professionals, and is educationally sound, in imposing useful and relevant guidelines suitable to the developing student. For these reasons, the prudent professor will not overstate the fact that this process can sometimes be set aside when the author's purpose or audience warrants.

To summarize the point of this lengthy example, we can concede that a central thinking process cannot be reduced to a formula; at the same time, we can maintain that at various stages of a student's education, algorithms can be useful in developing simplified and productive patterns of thinking. Such algorithms must be based upon the thinking processes of trained, mature minds; and these algorithms will have to be expanded or exploded later by the professor, even at the cost of some disorientation or disillusionment to the student.

Algorithms as Models of Thinking

Once we grant the educational value of algorithms in the liberal arts, we can begin to develop algorithms that model the problem-solving processes of various disciplines and then use those algorithms as the basis of computer-based lessons. Already available are excellent computer-based lessons in prewriting that engage students in Socratic dialogues about the salient features of the papers they are about to write (for example, the purpose, audience, length, thesis, supporting points, and likely audience response). By extension, the process of critical reading and the other thinking skills necessary for a revitalized curriculum in the liberal arts can also be distilled into useful algorithms that are rooted in the practice of experts and suited to the needs and abilities of college students.

With the computer as the students' teaching fellow, the role of the professor in the liberal arts will be to focus on the more complex, more important processes that the computer cannot address: to stay mindful of the limitations of algorithms, the complexities of life, and the value of a tolerance for ambiguity. Anticipating the students' restlessness over the computer-based lessons, the professor can use class time wisely by exploring answers that the computer did not anticipate. Thus, the professorial role is not merely to supplement or complement the computer-based lesson on thinking skills; it is also to elevate the lesson to a higher conceptual plane.

Teacher as Director

How the professor remains in control of the educational process of teaching thinking skills can be explained by a metaphor from the world of the theatre. The director of a play confronts the rich ambiguities of a dramatic text, extracts a coherent pattern of meaning, and imposes upon the theatrical production his or her conception of the work: the range of characterizations, the patterns of blocking, the tone of dramatic moments. Then the performers, having assimilated the unified and coherent conception of the show, draw upon their own talents and creativity to make natural, to fulfill, even at times to adjust the director's original conception. And they do so at the behest of the director.

In much the same way, the professor may confront the rich complexity of a thinking skill, devise patterns or algorithms to make the skill comprehensible to the students, and impose these patterns rigorously and authoritatively with the help of the computer. The student, having assimilated the thinking process imposed by the computer, must then be encouraged to discover the limitations of the imposed process and adjust the learned algorithm to deal with unique features of the problem-solving situation. Only through the combination of steps will the professor impart to the students what the Association of American Colleges calls "some sense of the wonders, complexities, ambiguities, and uncertainties that accompany the experience of learning and growing."[2]

PROSPECTS FOR COURSEWARE ON THINKING SKILLS

Even if the professoriate was of one mind in welcoming the computer as a friend of the liberal arts, using the computer in developing thinking skills would, at present, remain *in potentia*. Nevertheless, three recent trends give promise that the potential can be realized in the foreseeable future.

Improved Commercial Software

One reason for optimism is the improvement in commercial software and in teachers' skills in using the programs effectively. Educators are now successfully using sophisticated commercial programs at various academic levels and in various disciplines by subordinating the programs to the larger goals of the courses. A promising development at the elementary level is the Higher Order Thinking Skills project, which is currently in its third year and funded by the Department of Education at several sites across the country. Participating students use several commercially available instructional games that call for the same thinking skill (e.g., estimation); then they link the strategies discovered in the computer lab to concepts presented in their regular classrooms (e.g., estimation in arithmetic); finally, the students reinforce their synthesis of skills by programming questions and answers into a computer lesson with the format of a quiz show. According to Stanley Pogrow, the project director, students in the experimental group improved in thinking ability to a greater extent than did the control groups.[6]

Methods of Learning and Teaching

A second development hastening the use of the computer to teach thinking skills is also more pedagogical than technical: the heightened awareness of the way students learn and professors employ the unique thinking skills of their disciplines. In its report on the college curriculum, the Association of American Colleges[2] finds a basis for improvement in our imparting of such skills:

> A new area of research, still in its infancy, has been evolving during the last decade . . . It is directed toward understanding how students learn (or fail to learn) specific subject matter, and what difficulties they have with various modes of abstract logical reasoning, what preconceptions or misconceptions impede their mastery of concepts or principles in the given subject, what instructional approaches and devices are effective in helping learners overcome the obstacles which are encountered, what exercises and feed-back accelerate the development of various desirable skills, and how best to make use of the new instructional technology. (p. 16)

The report emphasizes the fact that the new research is not limited to the field of psychology but extends to "research indigenous to specific subject areas—research having results that can be readily understood and directly applied by teachers of the subject."[2] These investigations of the ways students learn, together with explorations of instructional approaches, may ensure that the capabilities of the computer receive careful attention.

In conjunction with the studies of how students learn is a new engagement by subject-matter experts in analysis of their disciplines. Liberal arts faculty are making explicit the steps of what they do when they employ the unique thinking skills of their various fields. Such scrutiny promises to issue in courses that emphasize the processes of analytical thought and therefore leave the students with more than notebooks of test-worthy details.

Authoring Systems

The third reason to anticipate the use of the computer for teaching thinking skills is a technological one: the development of sophisticated authoring systems. Until recently, the creation of exemplary computer-based lessons required the content expert to collaborate with a programmer and an instructional designer because the faculty member seldom possessed enough of the three skills to work successfully alone. Invariably though, the faculty member ranked lowest in the triumvirate. In the early years of courseware development, the programmer generally prevailed because he or she was most knowledgeable about the computer's capabilities. More recently, the instructional designer has generally been accorded the final word in the shaping of the lesson.[7]

Now however, authoring systems based upon principles of instructional design and offering "programmerless programming" have lessened the need for involvement by designers and programmers. So to the extent that the professor understands the disciplinary thinking process and to the extent that the lesson will be based upon an algorithm of that process, the professor can direct the form of a computer-based lesson in an authoritative way.

In summary, three developments—improvements in the quality and implementation of commercial courseware, increased understanding of how students learn and how faculty teach disciplinary thinking skills, and the advent of sophisticated systems for authoring—all suggest that in the near future professors can make the computer a teaching fellow to help students acquire the thinking skills of their disciplines. However, if this potential is to be realized, the professoriate of the liberal arts will have to keep abreast of technological developments and the pedagogical opportunities they provide. If faculty fail to take responsibility for innovative educational applications of the computer or if commercial developers do not rely upon educators for insights into the central thinking processes, then courseware to develop thinking skills is not likely to emerge, and an important educational potential of the computer will fail to materialize.

REFERENCES

1. "A Nation Prepared: Teachers for the 21st Century." *The Chronicle of Higher Education,* May, 1986, p. 50.
2. Association of American Colleges' Project on Redefining the Meaning and Purpose of Baccalaureate Degrees. "Integrity in the College Curriculum." *The Chronicle of Higher Education,* February, 1985, pp. 18–21.
3. Morton, H.C., and A.J. Price. "The ACLS Survey of Scholars: Views on Publications, Computers, and Libraries." *Scholarly Communication,* Summer 1986, 5, pp. 1–16.
4. Lewis, R.J. *Faculty Perceptions on the Role of Technologies in Academic Instruction.* Corporation for Public Broadcasting, 1985, pp. 12–13, 17.
5. Hawkins, G. *Stonehenge Decoded.* Garden City, New York: Doubleday, 1965, p. 101.
6. Pogrow, S. "Helping Students to Become Thinkers." *Electronic Learning,* April, 1985, pp. 26–29, 79.
7. Lent, R. "Courseware Development: The Role of the Subject Matter Expert." *National Forum,* 66 (1986) 3, pp. 15–17.

Developing integrated applications and installation schedules for comprehensive information management systems in education

by BRENT EDWARD WHOLEBEN
University of Texas
El Paso, Texas

ABSTRACT

Plans for the design and development of information management systems in education must be accompanied by technical implementation and evaluation aides. Important among these aides are integrated applications and installation schedules which outline (a) the overall mission of the system based upon a global needs assessment; (b) the elements of administrative and instructional computing applications that will have priority within this initial system design; (c) the anticipated acquisition, allocation, and distribution of hardware and software resources over a designated period of time; (d) strategies for assuring optimal economical centralization of resources with effective decentralization and coordination of function; (e) training requirements for all levels of intended users, and (f) a comprehensive summary of all implementation efforts appropriate for both formative and summative evaluation needs. It is imperative that these schedules denote priorities between administrative and instructional applications, demonstrating the relationship between these elements of the educational computing domain.

INTRODUCTION

The primary mission of administrative computing is to perform those service functions which directly or indirectly facilitate the instructional requirements for the individual classroom. Such service functions will range from the accounting requirements associated with the faculty payroll to inventory procedures necessary for maintaining the adequate availability of instructional equipment and materials. Any use of the computer which is not involved directly in the teaching of the individual student can be viewed as administrative in nature.

The primary mission of instructional computing is to perform those service functions that directly support the instructional requirements associated with student learning in the individual classroom. Such teaching functions might range from the introduction and demonstration to the student of various instructional objectives to the actual computerized teaching of these curricular components. Any use of the computer which is involved directly in the teaching of the individual student can be viewed as instructional in nature.

The installation of integrated administrative and instructional computing systems in the comprehensive school district requires detailed schedules that match indices of planning, preparation, and evaluation across the several years of implementation. Schedules are graphic charts which identify elemental or time requirements for implementing an integrated information management system, and which are designed for each of (a) applications integration, (b) hardware acquisition and distribution, (c) centralized control, (d) user training, and (e) overall project summary.

INTRODUCTION TO INTEGRATED EDUCATIONAL COMPUTING

The design and development of a highly functional data processing system for comprehensive administrative and instructional computing needs in a rapidly growing school district must take many issues and concerns into consideration.[1] Decisions must not be limited simply to what physical equipment (i.e., hardware), materials (e.g., software), and supplies (e.g., paper, diskette, and tapes) will be purchased. Concerns regarding which administrative and instructional applications will have priority; how such applications will be conceptualized, designed, implemented, and evaluated; and certainly, who will have primary responsibility for assuring the systematic and strategic satisfaction of district goals related to these computer-based applications, must also be addressed during these early planning and developmental efforts.

Tactical and Strategic Priorities

Tactically, the comprehensive school district must address many current problems related to computer-based applications that demand immediate resolution. These areas of immediate need include applications in the general areas of policy administration, personnel management, financial accounting, budgetary control, and instructional supervision.

Strategically, the district must assure that any selection and acquisition of equipment and materials in the immediate future must allow for continued support of district priorities in the years ahead. Such concerns are not limited to equipment alone, but include the projected life of applications software in its support of the district's data processing priorities.

Growth Potential and Applications Compatibility

A common problem with any large-scale, systematic deployment of data processing resources lies in the initial selection of hardware equipment and software materials that will support both current and future computing needs yet remain affordable to the district within budgetary constraints. In addition, initially purchased equipment must have the ability to expand compatibly in consort with district needs. Simply stated, initial computing resources should be large enough to surpass current needs, continue to support district needs for a period of five to seven years, and allow the district to add directly to the equipment when necessary so newer priorities can be addressed without any stoppage to current data processing activities.

The ability to "grow into" immediate purchases over a period of time, rather than limiting initial acquisitions to the satisfaction of then current needs, cannot be sufficiently stressed. Any changes a computing system's hardware, software, or even, applications-use components can have serious consequences for the remaining two components. Therefore, any hardware system acquired must enable expansion in accord with the district's growth pattern and, concomitantly, support enhanced software application needs demanded by future, more complex district requirements.

Integral Communications and Comprehensive Applications

The computer is an information machine, promoting the ability to integrate the communication requirements of all school district entities (e.g., administrative offices, school campuses, and warehouses) into what is often referred to as a "closed system;" that is, one allowing all necessary information to be available to all authorized decision-makers at any time and instantaneously upon demand. While such applications as word processing, electronic mail, database management, and calendaring (e.g., via electronic bulletin boards) may be the most obvious, and simplistic, of such an integral communications environment, the entire concept surrounding the "management information system" context of information processing—the provision of valid and reliable information in a timely manner for effective and efficient decisionmaking—is the ultimate strategic mission for electronic data processing and therefore is a priority goal for its use in support of school district activities.

The generalized notion of a management information system includes those comprehensive text processing, database management, and communication issues that are required for both administrative and instructional computing requirements. Computer-assisted instruction notwithstanding, equal priority must be extended towards instructional management concerns in addition to the typical priorities for an administrative computing system that supports personnel accounting, financial planning, or inventory control demands.

Standardization of Equipment and Materials

Standardization of equipment within the district-wide computing environment is a paramount priority during initial planning. The obvious advantages lie in such areas as training, cost, and communication abilities. Any changes to a standardized system of hardware also are significantly easier and more affordable than would be anticipated in a system where different "makes" and "models" of computers must be matched. These same advantages apply to the determination of standardized software packages to support application needs.

In the educational setting, however, it is typical to find that no single software package or vendor source will satisfy all application priorities for an entire school district. Therefore, several different software units, often from different sources, must be acquired to meet perceived administrative and instructional management needs. Since different software packages may only execute on certain machines, extreme caution must be exercised in determining which software will meet district priorities while remaining compatible within a single, machine-based computing environment. It is seldom advisable to employ machines from different vendors. However, equipment from different vendors may become necessary, particularly if a required software package is selected that is compatible with only one vendor's hardware.

Centralization of Management and Control

The data processing environment, including administrative as well as instructional computing applications, is a complex service setting that requires direct managerial supervision and control. All aspects of the supervision and control of data processing applications within the school district should be vested in one administrative office and assigned to a single individual for accountability purposes. In addition, the supervision and control of the data processing environment should be the primary, if not sole, responsibility of this office.

Centralized management and control of district data processing activities allow for the careful coordination and scheduling of information management requirements across all district entities, from central office administrating to classroom teacher needs. A single source is then responsible for the continued strategic planning and tactical evaluation requirements, which must be ongoing if the computing system is to remain viable and responsive to current and future district priorities and individual campus-based needs.

Decentralization of Function

Although the responsibility for adequate and appropriate planning and evaluation activities should be centralized in a single district-level officer, the actual deployment of computing functions should be decentralized to the lowest level possible. Therefore, computing services which support the responsibilities of campus level administrators, such as attendance accounting, should be accessible directly from their offices by means of remote terminal access. Other computing services that support the distinct instructional responsibilities of classroom teachers, such as student performance accounting via the essential elements, should be accessible directly from their classrooms by means of optical mark scanning units. To the extent fiscally and physically possible, the originators of data and the users of information derived from the analyses of these data should be afforded direct access to computing services and resources. Decentralized functional access not only provides a more effective and effecient use of available computing services, it also promotes a more highly participative use of available information for performing equally effective and timely decision-making related to instructional supervision, fiscal management, and policy control.

Application decentralization is desirable from the standpoint of equipment cost, associated materials support, and contingent personnel requirements. For example, certain types of software applications which would be used primarily at the high school level (e.g., student scheduling for departmentalized curricula) could be accessible directly on the high school campus, eliminating any need for intervention by individuals at the district office level. Other processing needs, such as attendance accounting, would be processed centrally at the district level but decentralized functionally on each of the various campuses.

System Integrity and Functional Backup

Throughout all district-based data processing activities, whether administrative or instructional, extreme care must be afforded to system and database security. This security is concerned with restricting access to only authorized users via specific, individual, and distinct access privileges and with assuring that any loss of system operation does not affect deleteriously the various ongoing functions of the district. System integrity need not be compromised with the requirements of a functionally decentralized system. However, formal policy concerning authorized access and specific training for these authorized users will assure the appropriate use of the information management system at all levels.

System integrity also requires the uninterrupted availability of necessary software and hardware resources for meeting prescribed needs. Therefore, provision must also be made for machine and source program backup. In the event of a system failure at one location, another station will provide immediate alternate service until the failed system has returned to scheduled operation.

Independence from Extra-District Support

Finally, the design and development of any integrated district computing system for administration and instruction must parallel the desire of the school district to become independent from outside computing resources and services. Concomitant with such service independence is the new potential for the district system to promote certain cooperative services for various extra-district entities on a periodic basis. Such services can provide a source of net revenue to the district for further system expansion and enhancement.

APPLICATIONS INTEGRATION

Functional software is defined as computer-executable instructions, written in a source code which a particular computer hardware unit will understand and which directly satisfies the data processing requirements of an organization, as identified in an *a priori* needs assessment. These data processing requirements usually include both administrative and instructional computing strategies for a school district that seeks integrated computing opportunities. The functional basis of software, namely, the remediation of those specific organizational needs via software-controlled data processing, must include the strategic and decentralized allocation of software resources to those levels of an organization which have demonstrated data processing needs.

The identified administrative and instructional computing needs of the comprehensive school district have been initially identified as comprising a total of 41 different areas of specific data processing applications. Furthermore, these particular application requirements may be generally categorized into three areas: (1) generic data processing functions, (2) generic management functions, and (3) generic instuctional functions.

A 1986 study[2] posited a list of "top 20" applications based upon the responses of district and campus level educational administrators to a system of structured interviews and questionnaires. Table I contains the "top 20" application needs expressed by those educational officers and which form the basis for the remainder of this discussion.

Table I—Top ranking 20 of 41 possible computing applications

	Top 20	Top 10	Rank
Student Attendance Accounting	84	63	3.8
Personnel Records and Payroll	68	58	4.3
Inventory Management	63	53	5.0
Student Records and Academic History	98	53	5.1
Word and Special Effects Processing	74	42	4.1
Student Progress and Grade Reporting	79	42	4.7
General Data File Management	84	42	5.1
T.E.A. Annual Performance Report	68	42	5.7
Report Formulation	63	42	6.4
Standardized Testing Assessment	68	37	4.7
Departmentalized Student Registration	74	37	6.0
Student Food Service Assignment	47	37	6.6
Student Bus Transportation Assignments	84	37	7.0
Essential Curriculum Elements Accounting	53	32	6.5
Library Functions	53	32	6.5
Finance and Accounting	53	26	1.2
Accreditation Monitoring	58	26	5.6
Computer-Assisted Enrichment, Gifted and Honors	42	26	7.8
Computer-Assisted Instruction, Grades K–6	37	21	4.5
Requisition and Distribution	53	21	5.0

Top 20: percent of frequency occurrence when 20 of 41 applications selected
Top 10: percent of frequency occurrence when 10 of 20 (viz. Top 20) selected
Rank: median of ranks assigned to Top 10 where low rank is high priority

CENTRALIZED CONTROL

Centralized versus decentralized data processing applications and the extent of shared data base utilization are based upon the particular role or function of the sub-organizational unit in question. While totally centralized data processing may lead to economies in hardware and software costs, the alternative of decentralized processing for specific applications may be more economical in work accomplished over time expended.

The role of administrative computing applications is the direct control and support of all activities which impinge upon the instructional mission on the various school campuses. This role thereby includes all activities that are not directly instructional (teaching and/or student learning). All activities identified as "instructional management" in nature, for example, student attendance accounting or student grade reporting, will be defined as elements of administrative computing for the educational organization. Alternatively, the role of instructional computing lies in direct instructional intervention within the student learning process. Typically, this intervention will be connected to one or more of the stages associated with computer-assisted instruction (CAI) or computer-managed instruction (CMI). With most instructional computing existing on microcomputers—utilizing the minicomputer networking system for related support of the instructional mission—the standardization of hardware resources becomes of paramount importance.

The standardization of instructional software resources is also a primary consideration for instructional system design and development. Such standardization is required due to the common elements of the instructional curriculum as well as the technical requirements associated with hardware and software system compatibility. Those instructional computing activities necessary for classroom instruction will be decentralized to the individual campus. Those activities best labeled as instructional support services will be physically resident on different networked stations, depending upon the actual needs of the designated primary user. Table II displays the level of centralization and shared access for both administrative and instructional applications addressed by the top 20 priorities.

HARDWARE ACQUISITION AND DISTRIBUTION

Identification, evaluation, and selection of hardware for an integrated district-wide data processing plan for both administrative and instructional computing must always be preceded by (a) a clear demonstration and understanding of perceived computing needs,[3] and (b) an equally clear demonstration of available software and courseware that will satisfactorily support these needs.[4] The hardware chosen must support, to the highest degree possible, the various software and courseware packages that will provide a systematic resolution to these *a priori* identified needs.

Administrative computing processes include, but are not limited to, the ability to perform data processing functions relative to: (1) financial accounting and budgetary control, (2) tax collection and reporting, (3) staff and student personnel recordkeeping, (4) payroll, (5) student performance monitoring and progress reporting, (6) physical plant maintenance and control, (7) real property inventory and equipment/materials accounting, (8) student attendance accounting, (9) student and course scheduling for departmentalized curricula, and (10) transportation routing and scheduling. In addition, administrative computing also includes such generic functions as word processing, data base generation with query-based access capabilities, full document transfer, electronic mail, calendaring, and decision simulation modeling.

Instructional computing is concerned primarily with the direct function of teaching and student learning in the classroom or similarly related environment. Therefore, instructional data processing activities are usually categorized as computer-assisted instruction (CAI) and computer-managed instruction (CMI). Computer-assisted instruction is concerned with the teaching of various curricular objectives within a computerized environment, and computer-managed instruction is associated primarily with the necessary monitoring and guidance functions that control such computer-assisted teaching efforts. However, computer-managed instruction need not be identified with computer-based, instructional management activities (e.g., performance monitoring via essential curriculum elements, or student grades reporting), although this obvious overlap of administrative data processing with the instructional domain of computing can appear confusing. In a sense, computer-managed instruction represents those data processing functions that assure that individual students will receive self-paced, personalized instruction within a computer-assisted environment based upon their individual need.

The optimal administrative data processing system might exist as a multi-node, minicomputer-based networking system, linking multiple minicomputer stations individually resident on each of the various administrative, instructional, and support service sites throughout the district. This configura-

Table II—Centralized and shared access to applications by station

	EDC CTR	INSTR CAMPU			CEN LIB	WAREHOU
	All	Sec	Elm	Pri	All	All
Student Attendance Accounting	C	S	S	S	—(B)	—
Personnel Records and Payroll	C	S	S	S	S(B)	S
Inventory Management	C	S	S	S	S(B)	S
Student Records/Acad History	C	S	S	S	S(B)	S
Word/Special Effects Process	D	D	D	D	D	D
Student Progress/Grade Report	C	S	S	S	—(B)	—
General Data File Management	D	D	D	D	D	D
T.E.A. Annual Perform Report	C	—	—	—	—(B)	—
Report Formulation	D	D	D	D	D	D
Standardized Testing Assessment	C	S	S	S	—(B)	—
Departmental Student Registr	S	S	S	C	—(B)	—
Student Food Service Assignment	C	S	S	S	—(B)	—
Student Bus Transport Assignment	C	S	S	S	—(B)	—
Essential Curric Elements Acct	C	S	S	S	—(B)	—
Library Functions	S(B)	S	S	S	C	S
Finance and Accounting	C	S	S	S	S(B)	S
Accreditation Monitoring	C	—	—	—	—(B)	—
Comp-Assist Enrich, Gift/Hrs	—	D	D	D	—	—
Comp-Assist Instr, Grades K–6	—	D	D	D	—	—
Requisition and Distribution	C	S	S	S	S(B)	S

C: centralized application; B: backup application; D: decentralized application; S: shared access.

tion will provide multi-user/multi-tasking capabilities which nevertheless remain transparent to the individual user. This type of configuration will promote maximum power while economizing on the comprehensive availability of software advantages to any demanding user. On the other hand, decentralization is often the best approach for instructional computing systems, including campus-centralized learning resource centers that incorporate multi-function instructional computing laboratories.

Concomitant hardware support installation can be scheduled graphically via the chart shown in Table III, which suggests an example of multiple-year scheduling for hardware installations for both academic and instructional computing applications. Such schedules not only display intended budgetary requirements over time but also demonstrate the long-range acquisition strategies of the school district.

USER TRAINING

Following the primary importance associated with (1) clearly identifying and understanding the comprehensive data manipulation needs of the school district, (2) objectively evaluating and selecting appropriate software based applications that will adequately and appropriately address these needs, and (3) efficiently installing and testing such hardware equipment as will effectively and economically operationalize these software based applications, there remains the necessity of promoting a comprehensive and diversified training regimen for all potential users of the data processing system. Such a training program must involve the direct users, namely, the individuals who will physically deploy the computing system, as well as the indirect users, namely, the individuals who will come into contact with the system only through the results of its applications.

The myriad problems connected with inadequate or inappropriate training can relegate even a superior hardware and software system to one of inferior status. Typically, the inadequately trained direct user never understands the full range of capability within the computing system. These individuals are likely to remain concerned only with particular applications identified during their initial training, and, furthermore, seldom seek or even recognize such modifications that might enhance the deployment of the system in their specific area of interest. When new direct users encounter the system, further, usually the first direct users provide initial training of later users, thereby coupling inappropriate training with an inadequate background. Indirect users have little if any understanding relevant to the capabilities of the system, and therefore indirect users remain content to accept inadequate or inappropriate applications without questioning possible capabilities.

Tactically, application training regimen for administrative versus instructional computing users is moderately distinct. For administrative computing users, the goals of training are associated with the deployment of data processing activities to support the instructional environment of the classroom. For instructional computing users, the goals of training are concerned with actual instruction within the classroom setting. Based upon these differences, the training paradigm for administrative and instructional users must be somewhat different and, moreover, lies in the context of the applications that

Table III—Multiple-year scheduling for hardware support installation

		1986			1987			1988			1989		
	Qtn	Sp	Su	Fa	Sp	Su	Fa	Sp	Su	Fa	Sp	Su	Fa
Education Center													
High-End Minicomputer	1		1										
Remote Terminal Workstation	30–35		25			10							
High-Speed Band Printer	1		1										
Medium-Speed Band Printer	1		1										
Letter-Quality Printer	1		1										
High-Capacity Removable Pack	3		2			1							
Optical Mark Sensing Device	1		1										
Optical Character Sensing Dev	1		1										
High-Speed, Reel Tape Drive	1		1										
Telecommunications, Rotary	10–12		6			5							
Elementary campuses													
Low-End Minicomputer	1		1						1*				
Remote Terminal Workstation	12–16		10			6			10*			6*	
Medium-Speed Band Printer	1		1						1*				
Letter-Quality Printer	1					1						1*	
High-Capacity Removable Pack	1		1						1*				
Optical Mark Sensing Device	1		1						1*				

*: staggered acquisition over time

guide the user of the computing system within the daily functioning of the district.

At the same time, however, administrative users in one particular area must have a clear understanding of other administrative applications, though these users may not routinely come into contact with these "remote" uses. Similarly, administrative users should have some rudimentary understanding of the deployment of instructional computing processes. Such cross-applications training objectives can be even more critical for the instructional computing user, since administrative computing processes maintain as a primary mission the support of instructional activities within the purview of the district. Table IV denotes the level of training suggested by application and station in terms of primary user, backup operator, and indirect user.

SUMMARY

The focus of the administrative computing mission is to support those peripheral activities that facilitate the primary mission of the school district, namely, student learning on the instructional campus. Various entities within the district support student instruction in different and diverse ways; nevertheless, each such organizational part exists only for the purpose of student learning. Therefore, each member of these sub-organizations must understand the total picture of administrative computing—how it functions to support education and how each individual's role impinges upon another person's functioning within the organization.

Unlike instructional computing, administrative practices exist at every level of the educational organization, from central district office to the classroom. Communicating relevant information for effective and efficient decision-making rapidly and in a timely manner is the process goal of administrative computing. Content goals are associated with types of information retrieved, which might include bus transportation routes and schedules, trial balances for various program accounts, individual student attendance histories, or the food stuffs requisition list from the food services staff.

The focus of the instructional computing mission is the direct facilitation of classroom-based activities that fulfill the primary mission of the school district, namely, student learning on the instructional campus. As with administrative computing, because various entities within the district support student instruction in different and diverse ways, each sub-organization must understand the total picture of instructional computing—how it operates in the direct teaching of the student and how individual roles impinge upon others.

Unlike administrative computing, instructional practices exist only at the decentralized level of the individual classroom or laboratory. Highly personalized communication of relevant learning paradigms, required for effective and efficient student learning based upon individual needs and differences, is the process goal of instructional computing. Content goals are associated with the types of information retrieved, which might include learning requirements of mathematics, language arts, physical science, health and physical education, foreign language, or the vocational trades.

TABLE IV—Level of training in applications by station

	EDC		INSTR CAMPU			CEN LIB		WAREHOU	
	Adm	Sec	Adm	Sec	Ins	Adm	Sec	Adm	Sec
Student Attendance Accounting	S	S	S	S	S	C	A	A	A
Personnel Records and Payroll	S	S	S	C	A	S	C	S	C
Inventory Management	S	S	S	S	A	S	S	S	S
Student Records/Acad History	S	S	S	S	C	C	C	A	A
Word/Special Effects Process	S	S	S	S	S	S	S	S	S
Student Progress/Grade Report	S	S	S	S	S	C	A	A	A
General Data File Management	S	S	S	S	S	S	S	S	S
T.E.A. Annual Perform Report	S	S	S	S	C	S	S	C	C
Report Formulatin	S	S	S	S	A	S	S	S	S
Standardized Testing Assessment	S	C	S	C	C	A	A	A	A
Departmental Student Registr	S	S	S	S	S	C	A	A	A
Student Food Service Assignment	S	S	S	S	A	A	A	S	S
Student Bus Transport Assignment	S	S	S	S	A	A	A	S	S
Essential Curric Elements Acct	S	S	S	S	S	C	A	A	A
Library Functions	S	C	S	C	S	S	S	A	A
Finance and Accounting	S	S	A	C	A	A	C	A	C
Accreditation Monitoring	S	S	S	S	C	S	S	C	C
Comp-Assist Enrich, Gift/Hnrs	S	A	S	A	S	S	C	A	A
Comp-Assist Instr, Grades K–6	S	A	S	A	S	S	A	A	A
Requisition and Distribution	S	S	S	S	A	S	S	S	S

S: skill level (primary user); A: awareness level (non-user); C: cross training (backup user).

TABLE V—Multiple-year scheduling for applications installation

	1986			1987			1988	
	Sp	Su	Fa	Sp	Su	Fa	Sp	Su
Student Attendance Accounting	P	DT	I	I	V			
Personnel Records and Payroll	P	DT	I	I	V			
Inventory Management	P	DT	I	I	V			
Student Records/Academic History	P	DT	I	I	V			
Word/Special Effects Process	P	DT	I	I	V			
Student Progress/Grade Reporting	P	DT	I	I	V			
General Data File Management	P	DT	I	I	V			
T.E.A. Annual Performance Report	P	DT	I	I	V			
Report Formulation		P	P	DT	I	I	V	
Standardized Testing Assessment	P	DT	I	I	V			
Departmentalized Student Registr	P	DT	I	I	V			
Student Food Service Assignment		P	P	DT	I	I	V	
Student Bus Transport Assignments		P	P	DT	I	I	V	
Essential Curric Elements Accounting				P	DT	I	I	V
Library Functions				P	DT	I	I	V
Finance and Accouting		P	P	DT	I	I	V	
Accreditation Monitoring		P	P	DT	I	I	V	
Computer-Assist Enrich, Gift/Hnrs				P	DT	I	I	V
Computer-Assist Instr, Grades K–6	P	P	DT	DT	DT	I	I	V
Requisition and Distribution		P	P	DT	I	I	V	

P: planning and scheduling; I: induction and evaluation; D: deployment and training; V: validation and incorporation; T: testing and piloting.

Summarizing across the total information management system development project, Table V displays a suggested schedule for the "top 20" desired applications incorporating elements form initial planning to final validation. This three-dimensional framework also provides a firm basis for both formative and summative control over the installation of all applications.

REFERENCES

1. Wholeben, B.E. "Strategic Planning for the Design and Development of Management Information Systems in Education." *AFIPS, Proceedings of the National Computer Conference,* (Vol. 55), 1986, pp. 185–192.
2. Wholeben, B.E. "Five Year Integrated Computing System Development Plan: Phase I (Needs Assessment and Priority Strategies)." Socorro Independent School District, El Paso, Texas, January, 1986.
3. Wholeben, B.E. "Designing Computerized Management Information Systems (MIS) for Offices of Field Experience and Student Teaching." Paper presented at the Annual Meeting of the American Association of Colleges of Teacher Education, Denver, February 28, 1985.
4. Wholeben, B.E. "Evaluating Existing Administrative Computing Systems for Future Management Information System Development Priorities." *Proceedings of the Annual Conference of the Association or Education Data Systems,* 1986, pp. 251–254.

Usability of corporate information systems

by JON MEADS
Jon Meads & Associates
Portland, Oregon

The ACM Special Interest Group on Computer-Human Interaction (SIGCHI) has organized this panel session. The focus is on designing and developing Corporate Information Systems for use by managers and analysts who are not likely to be computer professionals and who are not likely to have submitted themselves to the processing required to become "computer literate."

Usability of Corporate Information Systems has several aspects including access, functionality, interfacing, organization, presentation, and communication. The panelists have been asked to comment on and discuss the requirements for usability of Corporate Information Systems and the problems—physical, technological, and cognitive—that will hinder these systems from reaching their full utility as Corporate Information Systems mature and become more usable and available to a wider cross-section of users. There follows a brief discussion of some of the areas the panelists will be addressing.

INTRODUCTION

Webster's New Collegiate Dictionary defines "usability" as that which is convenient and practical to use. The interactive utilization of CPU power, in and of itself, whether in a massive mainframe distributed through networks or in a personal computer dedicated to individual use, does not make a system usable. There is more to making a system usable than simply collecting, organizing, manipulating, and analyzing data interactively. It is necessary to understand how people think about and use information. It is necessary to understand how human thought processes work and how to integrate those processes smoothly into a system so that a true cognitive symbiosis may be achieved. The ACM SIGCHI, through its newsletters, workshops, tutorials, and conferences, provides a medium for discussion and investigation in these areas and for presentation of significant results. SIGCHI presents this panel session as a forum for the presentation and discussion of those concepts pertinent to the usability of Corporate Information Systems.

Corporate Information Systems are an integral part of a corporation's management structure. They are designed to provide a service and be used by managers and analysts throughout the corporation. For the most part, these managers and analysts are living, breathing human beings with needs and requirements of their own. While it may be possible to build systems for people, it is difficult to build people for systems. Therefore, the systems we build must be designed for the people who will be using them. This is particularly true for Corporate Information Systems. Usability demands that the average manager and analyst find both the system itself and the applications to be convenient and practical to use for obtaining the service and results they require.

The issues involved span just about every aspect of a Corporate Information System. For the purposes of this paper, we have organized some of those issues into the standard components of input, functionality, and output/presentation.

INPUT

A goal of user interface development is to allow the user to specify input in a manner that fits the user's frame of reference. Current systems tend to require the translation of information as perceived and understood by the user into data items properly and precisely organized in a form suitable for the software system. Doing so not only introduces another item of work but also provides additional opportunities for error. The translation may not be appropriate or a data entry error may not be evident because of its cognitive distance from the information it represents. Reducing the cognitive distance between information as known by the user and the data tokens as input to the system requires that we know how people think about information. Although understanding the conceptual models that users employ in structuring information is of great importance, it is necessary that we understand the very basic processes of how the human brain organizes, stores, retrieves, and interrelates information, and the processes used to express and communicate information.

One of the fundamental intellectual processes of the human mind is the ability to abstract and categorize. Support for abstraction and categorization would be a major benefit for users of large data base systems. What tools can we provide the user to assist in expressing abstraction? There is no doubt that the actual interaction between a CPU and the stored data needs to be quite discrete (at least with today's technology). But can we properly map the user's abstract specification into the system's internal discrete instructions? It appears that intelligent front ends based on expert systems and neural networks may provide some solutions for this problem.

Establishing a compatible means for expressing input to a system is no trivial matter either. People do not communicate by command strings, menus, and forms alone. In fact, these methods of expression could be considered as downright unnatural. These techniques have their benefits and, in some cases, they may prove to be the most effective input method. However, improperly used, they add a burden to the user. If conscious thought, however slight, is required to convert information into a required data form, then we should search for a better method of inputting. Direct manipulation interfaces and speech input are offered as productive alternatives. Are they always better? When is it appropriate to use them and when are commands or forms more appropriate? What unexpected difficulties can we expect to encounter with these technologies? These are issues we must explore and understand more fully.

It seems at times that speech input is the Holy Grail of user interface technology. But are we being mislead by not fully understanding the problems. Consider the strong differences between communication with today's computer systems and another knowledgeable person. Are there significant factors which will make speech input inappropriate for most interaction? It is interesting to think about the differences between giving a stranger directions to a place across town and explaining a new idea to a colleague. The level of feedback and the mutual frame of reference are critical factors affecting communication, perception, and understanding. However, the technological advances in knowledge systems, pattern recognition, and hardware may result in a significant breakthrough, allowing the computer to function as a knowledgeable partner. Until such breakthroughs are achieved, we can learn how to build better user interfaces with current tools and capability by understanding the additional support and capability required for such advanced technology to be truly usable.

FUNCTIONALITY

At first glance, direct manipulation as provided by systems such as the Macintosh appears to be a very natural means of specifying desired actions and operations. However, a number of experienced computer users feel that such interfaces are relatively limited and do not provide access to the power and complexity available through command interfaces. Are direct manipulation interfaces really kid stuff? Or are they means for extending access to functionality without requiring lengthy training and in-depth system expertise? What are their drawbacks and benefits?

While some users may exult in being system gurus, making a system usable implies the elimination of arcane expertise. It is not only necessary that the average user understands how to invoke and apply a given function, but it is also necessary that doing so is convenient and practical. The conflicts between system requirements for simplicity in use and power in application are not easily resolved. Where are the bottom-lines where trade-offs have to be made and where is there need for additional innovation in user interface design?

Expert and goal-directed systems may also play a significant role in providing access to functionality by assisting the user in determining what techniques are applicable and how they should be applied. This leaves open the conjecture that the user may someday be able to simply specify the goals and let the system do all the work in getting there.

OUTPUT/PRESENTATION

Calculation and analysis does not result in new information—just new data. Before it can become information, the data must be understood by the user, placed into context, and related to other relevant knowledge. The first act in making this happen is perception. Computer graphics provides an excellent means of presenting certain types of data so that it is easily understood. But not all data lends itself to graphical interpretation. Also, quite a bit of information is transient, that is, meaningful only in the current temporal context. Making a system usable requires that the information required by the user is not only available but that access to it is either immediate or obvious and convenient. However, most software designers are not familiar with the art of presentation. Understanding the perceptual processes can make presentation more of a science and less of an art.

More critical for usability are the issues of feedback and control. With the increased power provided by personal computers, researchers are no longer measuring response times to determine if a system is usable but are looking at the semantic level of feedback provided to the user. Increasing the level of semantic feedback can reduce the cognitive distance between presented data and understood information. Such techniques, which are critical to direct manipulation interfaces, increase usability by eliminating interpretive steps and providing support for WYSIWYG (What You See Is What You Get) interfaces. But they may also require substantial changes in the design and support of information systems.

OTHER CONSIDERATIONS

Other considerations which are critical to the usability of a Corporate Information System are related to organizational and social issues. A system implies organization. How can organizations be structured to support and utilize information systems better?

Motivation and desire to use a system are also important concerns. With the autonomy provided by personal computers and the insidious nature of the individual, subversion of policy to avoid unpleasant activities can destroy the cohesiveness of an integrated Corporate Information System. The success of a system may require regular access and use by a significant portion of users so that information may be adequately shared. If access to or use of a system is sufficiently difficult, however, users will find other alternatives for managing information regardless of corporate policy. As such, usability as perceived by the individual may be critical for the success of a fully integrated Corporate Information System.

HARDWARE DIRECTIONS

JACK DONGARRA
Argonne National Laboratory
Argonne, Illinois
and
JORGE NOCEDAL
Northwestern University
Evanston, Illinois
and
EUGENE NORRIS
George Mason University
Fairfax, Virginia

The five sessions that constitute the Hardware Directions track provide an opportunity to gauge some of the shapes of computing hardware. Some of these shapes of the future are currently under active development; some are still in laboratories, where they are a gleam in an inventor's eye. All help to define the shape of the future.

As information density and throughput requirements continue to escalate, data path bandwidths must expand. The very large information content of beams of light represents an attractive possibility for the use of data paths of large information capacity that can be closely spaced in three-dimensional space. The incorporation of these ideas in hardware constitutes a major theme of this track. One session, *Current Developments in Optical Computing,* presents two papers from academic research laboratories and one from industry. The "Optical Pattern Recognition" paper discusses the application of optical computing techniques in the area of pattern recognition. "Optoelectronic Programmable Logic Arrays" outlines the successes in wedding optical computing techniques with an exciting parallel architectural concept. The third paper in this session discusses an implementation of ideas behind such neural computing concepts as architectures adaptive to a variety of fields including optical computing. This session will appeal to many technically oriented persons, especially those with interests in computer architecture or neural ideas.

Data storage using optical techniques is the basis of another session, *Optical Storage Survey: Market/Technology/Product.* The catchword is OD^3, optical digital data disks. Representatives of the OD^3 industry present and discuss the status of key issues in the optical storage market. Eleven man-years and two million dollars of effort have been expended to date in this area to develop industry standards. Presenters from four of the leading OD^3 companies discuss the status of standards and related problems, and the state of the hardware art is addressed from a number of exciting viewpoints. This session should be of interest to a large number of persons, and readers need no technical expertise.

The third session having an optical theme is database-oriented. The *CD-ROM and CD-Interactive* session is a panel discussion on the topic of CD-ROM, a standardized file format for very large microcomputer-based distributed databases. CD-ROM and a subset, CD-Interactive, databases are being marketed to businesses, libraries, and other specialized users needing up to a 500-megabyte database capability.

Another direction of interest is special-purpose computing. Interesting descriptions and progress reports on a representative and very diverse sample of special-purpose computer architectures are the subject of the *Special Architectures and their Applications* session. Technically minded persons will find presentations on such state-of-the-future systems ideas as advanced multiprocessor parallel machines, a pyramid of massively parallel processor planes, hardware for logic machines, and an application of Petri-net ideas for distributed decision making.

Lest all the progress delineated in the four sessions described above induce a certain euphoria, Gene Amdahl presents some sobering thoughts on performance limitations in inter-processor communication that have given pause to some parallel computer architects. In this featured session, Dr. Amdahl discusses these limitations in respect to one well-known architecture, the Hypercube and other pauses for thought are indicated by the relatively small performance advantage to date offered by gallium arsenide technology.

Optical pattern recognition

by GEORGE EICHMANN
The City College of The City University of New York
New York, New York

ABSTRACT

This paper surveys some recent trends in optical pattern recognition. In particular, five new optical pattern recognition techniques; the Wigner distribution, the Hough Transform, the auto- and hetero-associative memory, the symbolic substitution, and the syntactic pattern recognition-based techniques will be described. Some optical and computer-generated results will be presented.

SUMMARY

Pattern classification and recognition is a vision oriented task generic to many diverse system applications. Inasmuch as images are usually optical in nature, it is reasonable to ask that such images or patterns be processed via an optical system. Early optical pattern recognition systems evolved from coherent optical Fourier transform system concepts. Here, the idea of an optically-encoded matched filter, a filter that optimizes the signal-to-noise ratio, is used to detect and classify different visual patterns. The high degree of sensitivity to topological, in-class and intra-class variations between elements of matched filter systems, however, has recently lead to a re-evaluation of such systems. In this survey talk, some recent work on optical pattern recognizers will be described. In particular, five new optical pattern recognizer systems will be highlighted.

These new systems are based on the concepts of the Wigner distribution (WD), the Hough Transform (HT), the auto- and hetero-associative memory, the symbolic substitution and, finally, syntactic pattern recognition ideas.

The WD has been used both as a signal processing and system analysis tool to describe non-stationary signals and systems. The WD of images can also be defined. Both the one-dimensional (1D) and the two-dimensional (2D) WD can be generated optically.[1] If the 1D signal is a characteristics function of a given pattern, a function that represents a topologically invariant description of the contour, the singular values of the WD matrix are also topologically invariant descriptors of the pattern.[2,3,4] Examples of such descriptors will be presented.

The HT has been shown to be a good straightline detector. There are many patterns that can be encoded, using the Freeman chain-code, in a set of straightline segments. Recently, a number of optical HT implementations were also described.[5] Using the optical HT as a preprocessor, new topologically-invariant pattern descriptors may be formed. Examples of such coding to both visual scenes and textures[6,7,8,9,10] will be presented.

Auto- and hetero-associative memory concepts have recently been added to the repertoire of the optical image processing. Using these concepts, and using a variety of optical systems, incomplete and/or noisy images were reconstructed. By an appropriate image or pattern data encoding, and using either auto- or hetero-associative recall, different but given pattern features may be stored and recalled.[11,12,13,14,15] Application of this technique to boundary descriptors and to the superresolution of images will be detailed.

Recently, a new pattern detection technique, the so-called method of symbolic substitution, has been introduced. In this technique, a large and complex pattern is searched, in parallel, for both the location and number of times it occurs, of a given small sub-pattern. The search procedure uses a number of primitive operations that is sequentially applied upon the large pattern. These operations are unit spatial shifts, superposition, and logic, such as AND and NOR, operations. By applying these operations in a given sequence, parallel optical pattern recognizers may be constructed. Recently, it was shown that for pattern recognition only spatial shifts and a multiple-input AND element are sufficient. Examples of this approach[16,17,18] to both pattern recognition and arithmetic operation as well as some optical ultrafast implementation examples will be presented.

There are many pattern recognition problems where the pattern's structural information is important. For these problems, a syntactic pattern recognition is the proper approach. In the syntactic approach the pattern is described as a grammar or language. For each pattern, a new grammar is assigned. The syntactic pattern recognizer, also called parser, assigns an unknown pattern to a given grammar. A grammar contains, in addition to some primitive symbols, rules of how to form the pattern. By optically encoding both the symbols and the rules, via either an associative memory or symbolic substitution concepts, optical syntactic pattern recognizers can be constructed.[19,20] The application of this technique to both noise-free and noisy pattern recognition will be also discussed.

This work is supported in part by a grant from the U.S. Air Force Office of Scientific Research.

REFERENCES

1. G. Eichmann and B.Z. Dong. "Two-dimensional Optical Filtering of 1-D Signals." *Appl. Opt.*, 21 (1982), pp. 3152–3156.
2. N.M. Marinovic and G. Eichmann. "An Expansion of Wigner Distribution and its Application." *Proc. ICASSP-85*, (1985) pp. 1021–1024.
3. N.M. Marinovic and G. Eichmann. "Scale-invariant Wigner Distribution and Ambiguity Functions." *Proc. SPIE*, Vol. 519 (1984), pp. 18–24.
4. N.M. Marinovic and G. Eichmann. "Feature Extraction and Pattern Classification in Space-spatial Frequency Domain." *Proc. SPIE*, Vol. 579, *Proceeding of the 4th Intelligent Robot and Vision*, September 1985.
5. G. Eichmann and B.Z. Dong. "Coherent Optical Production of the Hough Transform." *Applied Optics*, 22 (1983), pp. 830–834.
6. G. Eichmann, M. Jankowski, and B.Z. Dong. "Optical Extraction of Pattern Shape Descriptors." *Proc SPIE*, Vol. 380, (1983) pp. 432–438.
7. T. Kasparis, N.M. Marinovic, and G. Eichmann. "Knowledge-based Image Segmentation." 1986 SPIE Conference on Robotics and Machine Vision, Cambridge, Mass., *Proc. SPIE*, Vol. 726–38, 1986.
8. G. Eichmann and T. Kasparis. "Texture Classification Using the Hough Transform." *Proc. SPIE*, Vol. 638 (1986), pp. 46–54.
9. G. Eichmann and Y. Li. "Real-time Optical Line Detection." submitted for publication, 1987.
10. Y. Li and G. Eichmann. "A Hough Transform-based Circle Detection Using an Array of Multimode Optical Fibers." to appear in *Optics Communication*, 1987.
11. I. Kadar, E. Liebman, and G. Eichmann. "Non-Baysian Optical Image Feature Extraction." *Proc. SPIE*, Vol. 752–18 (1987).
12. G. Eichmann and M. Jankowski. "Shape Description Using an Associative Memory Processor." *Proc. SPIE*, Vol. 638 (1986) pp. 76–82.
13. G. Eichmann and H.J. Caulfield. "Optical Learning (Inference) Machines." *Applied Optics*, 24 (1985), pp. 2051–54.
14. Y. Li and G. Eichmann. "Conditional Symbolic Modified Signed-digit Arithmetic Using Optical Content-addressable Memory Logic Elements." submitted for publication, 1987.
15. G. Eichmann and M. Stojancic. "Superresolving Image and Signal Restoration Using a Linear Associative Memory Filter." to appear May 15, 1987 *Applied Optics*.
16. G. Eichmann, Y. Li, and R.R. Alfano, "Parallel Optical Logic Using Optical Phase Conjugation." *Applied Optics*, 26 (1987) 1.
17. Y. Li, G. Eichmann, R. Dorsinville, and R.R. Alfano. "An AND-element Based Optical Symbolic Pattern Recognizer." submitted for publication, 1987.
18. Y. Li, G. Eichmann, and R.R., Alfano. "Optical Computing Using Polarization Encoded Shadow Casting." *Applied Optics*, 25 (1986), pp. 2636–2638.
19. G. Eichmann and S. Basu. "Parallel Optical Syntactic Pattern Recognizer." to appear in the May 15, 1987, *Applied Optics*.
20. S. Basu and G. Eichmann. "Error Correcting Optical Syntactic Pattern Recognizers." *Proc. SPIE*, Vol. 752-13 (1987).

Neurocomputer applications

by ROBERT HECHT-NIELSEN
Hecht-Nielsen Neurocomputer Corporation
San Diego, California

ABSTRACT

Neurocomputing is a new engineering discipline concerned with the design, implementation, and application of neural networks. Neural networks are non-algorithmic computing structures with the topology of a directed graph that can carry out information processing by means of their state response to continuous or initial input. The nodes in neural networks are called processing elements, and the directed links (information channels) are called interconnects. Neural networks have been shown to be capable of carrying out information processing operations in the areas of sensor processing (pattern preprocessing, pattern recognition), knowledge processing (knowledge representation, autonomous extraction of knowledge from data, reasoning with imprecise and contradictory knowledge), and control (smooth, fast robot arm and leg control, robot "hand-eye coordination"). Although neural networks cannot be cost effectively implemented using computers, it has now been shown that specialized processors called *neurocomputers* can be built that will allow neural network techniques to be affordably applied in a number of areas, including industrial, commercial, and consumer products. This paper presents an overview of some of the anticipated applications of this new technology.

INTRODUCTION

A neural network is a dynamical system with the topology of a directed graph that can carry out information processing by means of its state response to continuous or initial input. The nodes in neural networks are called processing elements, and the directed links (information channels) are called interconnects. Figure 1 illustrates a typical neural network. Each processing element's input to output relationship is described by a set of difference or differential equations. Therefore, the complete network can be viewed as a large system of coupled difference or differential equations.

Neurocomputers are information processing machines that are specifically designed to implement such systems of equations. By taking full advantage of the structure of these equations neurocomputers can implement neural networks one to three orders of magnitude more efficiently than general purpose computers in terms of size, weight, power, and cost.[1] Neurocomputers function as coprocessors to standard von Neumann computers, thus allowing the strengths of both to be freely combined. Neural networks to be implemented on a neurocomputer are expressed in a standard machine-independent neural network description language (such as HNC's AXON™ language). Such descriptions are termed *netware*—the neurocomputing equivalent of software. Netware to be implemented is loaded into the neurocomputer from a floppy disk or from a data file on the host computer and can then be called from host software when desired. The neural network is called like any other software procedure, except that the processing takes place on the neurocomputer coprocessor. Standard netware packages that implement a variety of important neural networks are now under development. It is anticipated that most users of neurocomputers will find such prepackaged, tested, and standardized netware adequate for most of their needs.

To give a feel for the types of information processing operations neural networks can carry out, two specific theoretical results are presented. The first is a reinterpretation of Kolmogorov's 1957 continuous function representation theorem.[2,3]

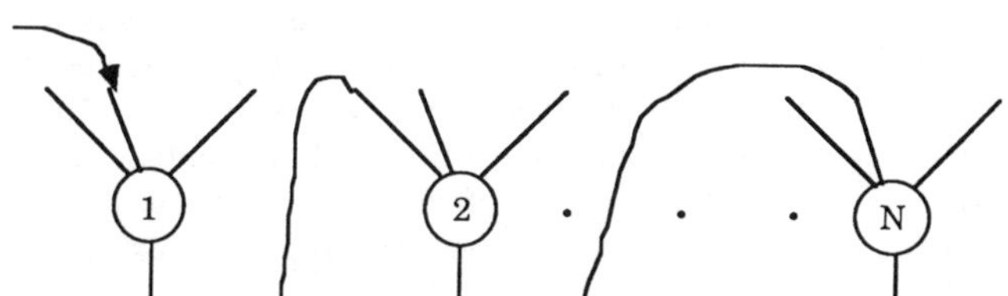

Figure 1—Typical neural network

Kolmogorov's Mapping Neural Network Existence Theorem

Given any continuous function Φ: $E^m \rightarrow R^n$, $\Phi(x) = y$, where E is the closed unit interval [0,1] (and therefore E^m is the m-dimensional unit cube), Φ can be implemented exactly by a three-layer neural network having m processing elements in the first (x-input) layer, $(2m + 1)$ processing elements in the middle layer, and n processing elements in the top (y-output) layer.

Kolmogorov's theorem guarantees that any continuous mapping or function can be implemented by a small neural network. However, it does not give us a convenient means for constructing such a network. That is the subject of the next result.

Counterpropagation Network Construction Theorem

Given a set of examples $\{(x_1, y_1), (x_2, y_2), \ldots, (x_L, y_L)\}$ of the action of a continuous function Φ: $S^m \rightarrow S^n$, where S^m and S^n are the unit spheres in m- and n-dimensional euclidean space, respectively, and where $\Phi(x_i) = y_i$ for all $i = 1, 2, \ldots, L$, a five-layer neural network with $(2m + 2n + L)$ processing elements can be constructed that implements a function Ψ, such that $\Psi(x_i) = y_i$ for all $i = 1, 2, \ldots, L$, and such that if x_j is closer to $x \in S^m$ than all other $x_i (i \neq j)$, then $y = \Psi(x)$ will be close to y_j. Further, if Φ^{-1} exists then the network also automatically implements a mapping Ψ^{-1} that has the above properties with x and y interchanged. Finally, for any $N > 0$ a five-layer neural network having $(2m + 2n + N)$ processing elements can be constructed such that the relationship $\Psi(x_i) = y_i$ (and $\Psi^{-1}(y_i) = x_i$, if Φ^{-1} exists) is approximately satisfied for all i, with the error being minimized in a certain least mean square sense. The proof of this theorem utilizes the outstar and competitive network theorems of Grossberg[4,5] and the self-organizing map theorems of Kohonen.[6]

Thus, in the case of mapping implementation, neural network theory now provides the means for developing mathematical mappings, transformations, and functions based upon examples. In many ways, this can be viewed as an advanced statistical technique in which it becomes possible to embody known constraints into the design of the network and to then allow the network to self-organize the desired mathematical operation in response to examples presented to it serially. With such networks there is no requirement to store the data used to condition the network. It can be collected, used, and discarded. As with biological systems, the ability to incorporate new data incrementally as it becomes available (rather than having to batch it up) is a major advantage over typical computer techniques. This allows neural networks to deal effectively with data sets (such as thousands of hours of imagery, 10,000 hours of sonar data, etc.) that are too large to be processed as batch data in any existing or contemplated computer.

Besides their ability to self-organize on the basis of huge data sets, neural networks have other advantages over traditional approaches. For example, neural network architectures can carry out $O(1)$-time parallel nearest neighbor searches in which the search time is independent of the number of items (patterns, knowledge, etc.) stored. They can also carry out parallel associative memory operations and hypothesis testing operations.[1,8]

Neural networks are perhaps best thought of as providing at least some of the "missing capabilities" that computer science has been unable to deliver in forty years of trying. Specifically, operations such as continuous speech recognition, image pattern recognition, sonar and radar signal exploitation, inexact knowledge processing, and autonomous learning of control algorithms, may now become possible by using neural networks. What is clear is that standard algorithmic computation and neural networks complement each other with very little overlap. Neural networks are useless for accounting. Algorithms are useless for understanding continuous speech. With the development of a simple interface between computers and neurocomputers we can now begin to use both technologies together. A number of combined software/netware packages are currently being developed for specific applications. Such combinations have been termed *cyberware.*

Neurocomputer technology has now developed to the point where neural networks that are large enough to solve many real-world problems can be affordably (in terms of size, weight, power, and cost) implemented in real time. Optical computing technology seems well matched to the needs of neurocomputing. As optical computing components are added to neurocomputers over the next decade we can expect an ever widening circle of applications to be encompassed. It may well turn out that von Neumann computing will not be able to exploit these advanced processing innovations nearly as well (because of software development and software parallelization limitations), thus making neurocomputing the primary growth element in future computing. In the following sections some potential applications of neural networks are postulated.

SENSOR PROCESSING APPLICATIONS

Sensor processing involves two primary problem sets: pattern preprocessing transformations and pattern recognition. Preprocessing transformations take patterns in one form and convert them to patterns in a more desirable or usable form. Examples include: image compression/expansion, image edge or boundary extraction, image contrast enhancement, image or signal basis function (Fourier, Fourier-Mellin, Gabor) expansion, and pattern noise suppression. Pattern recognition is the operation of mapping a pattern to its class number. This may be a fixed static mapping, or it may involve more complex operations such as hypothesis testing based on previously received patterns and stored example patterns. Neural networks can carry out a wide variety of pattern preprocessing transformations and pattern recognition operations and can deal with both spatial patterns (fixed images, fixed power spectra) and spatiotemporal patterns (dynamic video, continuous speech, sonar, radar doppler audio). Specific examples of sensor processing neural networks and some applications that they suggest are now discussed.

The Grossberg/Mingolla Vision Processing Network[9] and the Fukushima Neocognitron[10] have demonstrated that template-driven image segmentation and shift/scale/rotation invariant image pattern recognition are possible with neural networks. While all of this work has been at the small problem level and the individual pieces have not yet been put together, the techniques used appear to be directly extensible and combinable to solve full-scale image pattern recognition problems. Assuming that this is correct, the following applications would then appear to be feasible:

1. Automated object acquisition and classification for imagery. Partially obscured objects with context clues can be located.
2. Real-time image analysis for robotics. Operations such as automated paint removal, washing, assembly, could be supported.

Spectral Pattern Recognition Networks such as that of the author[8] have demonstrated the ability to classify time-series patterns by comparing their time-varying power spectra with stored examples. This spatiotemporal pattern classification approach has been theoretically shown to offer high (near-Bayesian) classification performance, near-optimal noise tolerance, and to be extensible to real-world sized problems. This approach appears to be of value for continuous speech recognition.

In summary, neural networks hold significant promise of solving a number of long-standing high-value problems in pattern recognition.

KNOWLEDGE PROCESSING APPLICATIONS

By virtue of their ability to autonomously acquire knowledge from data, to incrementally incorporate new data into their mapping functions and to carry out logical hypothesis testing, neural networks are well suited for certain types of knowledge processing. In general, if a problem involves highly quantified and/or highly deterministic knowledge, processing is best accomplished using more traditional software and artificial intelligence techniques. Neural networks seem best suited for situations where the knowledge primarily concerns causality and usuality, and where contradictions and errors may exist in the data.

Three significant neural network knowledge processing paradigms have so far been developed. These are now mentioned, along with potential applications.

First, the Anderson[11] knowledge processing neural network

works by coding knowledge in long attribute vectors. This system is very robust and can deal effectively with contradictions and missing information. In the face of contradictions it makes decisions based upon the "weight of evidence" (i.e., the response that has the largest number of supporting examples is chosen). In the case of missing information, the system guesses based upon known associations between the available attributes. One disadvantage of this system is that it requires a "hard" knowledge base. In other words, the data used to configure the system needs to be exact and not fuzzy. Anderson has demonstrated that medical knowledge can be extracted directly from medical patient records by encoding each case as a vector with multiple attributes in each of the areas of symptoms, diagnosis, treatment, and counterindications to treatment. The Anderson system would appear to be useful for the extraction of implicit knowledge from data bases. This may be of value to MIS departments wishing to exploit available data bases more fully.

Second, the Kosko Fuzzy Cognitive Map[12] is a graph-like structure, implemented in the form of a neural network, that can store causal relationships between objects known as *variable concepts*. The fuzzy cognitive map can deal with imprecise, contradictory, and erroneous data. This network would seem to be well suited for problems involving the development of a model of a complex system or organization based upon knowledge of individual interactions. For example, a functional model of an opposing sports team or corporate senior management team—to allow analysis of strategies to use against them.

Third, the Carpenter/Grossberg Adaptive Resonance Network[13] is able to carry out hypothesis testing and logical inferencing operations. It can use existing knowledge to judge the "reasonableness" of a given hypothesis. It can also find the most applicable existing knowledge by testing associated knowledge items for consistency with the given item. Because the associated items are retrieved by means of a parallel search, this process is usually completed in from 1 to 3 steps. Examples of how this capability might be applied include:

1. Context-sensitive pattern recognition systems for time-series data might be built using the ability to test each local-in-time classification as a hypothesis against the context information provided by earlier data. This might be of particular value for speech classification, automated reading, image scene analysis, etc.
2. Preliminary hypotheses regarding plans for robot activity might be tested against a behavioral rule bank to determine consistency. This might provide a mechanism for implementing a highly simplified version of Asimov's "Three Laws of Robotics."[14]

In summary, neural networks may be able to deliver valuable real-time knowledge processing capabilities that traditional knowledge based systems apparently cannot deliver. The capabilities that have been demonstrated using neural networks (albeit only at the small problem level so far) have the correct "feel," in that they are intrinsically adaptive to real-world data and are able to deal with fuzzyness, uncertainty, contradiction, and error.

CONTROL APPLICATIONS

The application of neural networks to control goes back to at least 1962. In that year Bernard Widrow of Stanford demonstrated a network that could successfully learn the control algorithm for balancing a broomstick. Since then, several other control problems have been solved by neural network techniques. A notable example is the speech synthesis system built by Terrence Sejnowski of Johns Hopkins that controls a sound generator by means of text block inputs. This network has yielded performance equal to or greater than the best commercial speech synthesis systems. Two promising control network approaches and some postulated applications are now presented.

First, the Grossberg/Kuperstein Oculomotor Control Neural Network[15] has been demonstrated to be able to carry out feedback control of an imaging sensor in the face of actuator and image plane nonlinearities. The network is capable of saccadic motions that boresight the image sensor on a designated object in one motion. Further, it can generate scan patterns for sequences of prioritized objects. A potential application of this technology is camera control in robotic systems. This could allow robots to carry out more accurate pattern recognition by boresighting objects of interest (selected by a simple neural network that views the whole image).

Second, the Rumelhart/Williams Backpropagation Network[7] has demonstrated the capability to approximate arbitrary spatial mappings by means of self-organization in response to examples of that mapping (as in the Counterpropagation Network Construction Theorem stated above). This is the network used by Sejnowski to build his speech synthesis system. It has been shown to be useful for a wide variety of applications in sensor processing, knowledge processing, and control. A possible application of this network is advanced fighter aircraft control. The network might be used to learn control laws directly from pilot inputs in a simulator. The network would "sit on top of" the usual stability augmentation and control safety systems and would be responsible for determining stick "feel" and response in various flight regimes (wing/tailpipe configurations, g-loading, thrust setting, speedbrake setting). The network could make improvements to minimize the mean square of some chosen quantity or quantities (such as average stick deflection, average deflection rate when deflected, etc.) in each flight regime. It is interesting to note that these ideas have already been tried out in flight in simplified form (using a slightly different type of network). In 1969 an F-100 supersonic jet fighter was flown using a neural network control system.[16] This test was successful, but since neural networks are nonalgorithmic and simply learn directly from data, the engineers of the day could not readily accept this approach. Given the versatile digital control systems of today, with their ability to automatically revert to simpler subsystems in the event of the failure of a higher-level system, neural network techniques may find more acceptance in flight control this time around.

In summary, neural networks may add a number of new adaptive control capabilities to the control engineer's repertoire.

SUMMARY

Neurocomputing is a technology whose time has arrived. It now seems likely that it can solve many of the problems in sensor processing that other approaches have been struggling with for over 30 years. Similarly, in knowledge processing neural networks promise to provide the means to deal effectively with the difficulties of real-world knowledge with its inexactitudes, contradictions, and errors. Finally, in the control arena, a number of new techniques that will allow better control tolerances to be achieved using less expensive components appear possible. Compensation for wear and partial damage may also be possible.

REFERENCES

1. Hecht-Nielsen, Robert. "Performance limits of optical, electro-optical, and electronic neurocomputers." *SPIE Proc.,* (Vol. 634), 1987.
2. Kolmogorov, A.N. "On the representation of continuous functions of many variables by superposition of continuous functions of one variable and addition." *Dokl. Akad. Nauk SSSR,* (Vol. 114), 1957, *AMS Translation,* pp. 55–59.
3. Lorentz, G.G. "The 13th problem of Hilbert." *Proc. Symposia in Pure Mathematics,* (Vol. 28), American Mathematical Society, 1976, pp. 419–443.
4. Grossberg, Stephen. *Studies of Mind and Brain,* Reidel, 1982.
5. Hecht-Nielsen, Robert. "Book Review of Grossberg's *Studies of Mind and Brain.*" *J. Math Psych.,* 27 (1983) 3, pp. 335–340.
6. Kohonen, Teuvo. *Self-Organization and Associative Memory.* Springer-Verlag, 1984.
7. Rumelhart, David E., and McClelland, James L. (Eds.). *Parallel Distributed Processing: Explorations in the Microstructure of Cognition,* (Vols. 1 and 2), MIT Press, 1986.
8. Hecht-Nielsen, Robert. "Nearest matched filter classification of spatiotemporal patterns." to appear in *Applied Optics,* May, 1987.
9. Grossberg, Stephen and Ennio Mingolla. "Neural dynamics of surface perception: Boundary webs, illuminants, and shape-from-shading." *Computer Vision, Graphics, and Image Processing,* in press, 1987.
10. Fukushima, K., and S. Miyake. "Neocognitron: A pattern recognition system tolerant of deformations and shifts in position." *Pattern Recognition,* 15 (1984) 6, pp. 455–469.
11. Anderson, James A., Richard M. Golden, and G.L. Murphy. "Concepts in distributed systems." *SPIE Proc.,* (Vol. 634), 1987.
12. Kosko, Bart. "Fuzzy cognitive maps." *Internat. J. Man-Machine Studies,* (Vol. 24), 1986, pp. 65–75.
13. Carpenter, Gail A. and Stephen Grossberg. "Adaptive Resonance." *SPIE Proc.,* (Vol. 634), 1986.
14. Asimov, Isaac. *The Naked Sun,* Doubleday, 1956.
15. Grossberg, Stephen and Michael Kuperstein. *Neural Dynamics of Adaptive Sensory-Motor Control,* North-Holland, 1986.
16. Roger Barron. "Avionics Flight Control Systems for Aerospace Research and Development." *Paris, France Bionics Symposium Proceedings* held September 1968, Brussels, 1969.
17. Denker, John S. (Ed.). *Neural Networks for Computing, Snowbird Utah 1986, AIP Conference Proceedings 151,* American Inst. Physics, 1986.

Optical programmable logic arrays

by RAYMOND ARRATHOON
Wayne State University
Detroit, Michigan

ABSTRACT

A review is presented in this paper of recent developments in the area of optical logic. Special emphasis is placed on optical programmable logic arrays and the development of a rudimentary optoelectronic central processing unit.

SUMMARY

In considering the granularity of multiprocessor systems, there is a linear progression in interconnection complexity from conventional von Neumann architectures to massively parallel systems such as neural networks. A content addressable memory may also be regarded as a parallel architecture. When an input is applied to such a system, the entire memory is searched simultaneously. As the degree of parallelism and the number of interconnections increases, the peculiar advantages of optical systems become apparent. One example of these interconnection capabilities in content addressable memories is provided by the recently developed optical programmable logic arrays or OPLAs.[1]

The OPLA was fabricated for use in conjunction with a rudimentary optoelectronic central processing unit capable of executing ten million two-bit instructions per second.[2] Within the OPLA hundreds of hair-thin optical fibers were connected in a specific crossbar pattern that provided the appropriate optical interconnects for the specified instruction set. Fault tolerance was designed into the unit by overlaying three redundant sets of optical connections. The system exhibited extraordinarily large fan-in and fan-out capabilities in comparison with conventional gates, moreover, fiberoptic devices in this class are potentially capable of running at considerably higher clock rates than conventional PLAs. The fan-in and fan-out advantages of the system suggest that massive content addressable memories can be built that will significantly exceed the capabilities of PLAs based on electronic logic.

Before considering the architectural implications of these devices, the issue of reconfigurability must also be addressed. The inclusion of a spatial light modulator in the system could convert the OPLA into a reconfigurable optical PLA or ROPLA. Such a device would be functionally equivalent to a dynamically programmable electrical PLA, however, the reconfiguration speed, fan-in and fan-out capabilities of the optical system would take the ROPLA into realms of content addressable memories previously inaccessible to systems based solely on electronic logic. What are the implications? At the very least, the system would be capable of implementing complex logic operations in a single clock cycle. In addition, the reconfigurable nature of such a device would permit the mapping of certain algorithms into combinational logic. This would result in substantial improvements in processing time since the algorithm would now be executed in a massively parallel mode. The advent of massive content addressable memories also permits the inclusion of adaptive algorithms as a variety of control variables could be embedded in the memory itself. These features suggest that optical programmable logic arrays are likely to prove significant in a variety of architectural considerations.

REFERENCES

1. Arrathoon R. "Historical Perspectives: Optical Crossbars and Optical Computing." invited paper, Soc. Photo-Opt. Inst. Eng. *752,* Paper 01, 1987.
2. Arrathoon R. and S. Kozaitis. "Design and Performance of a Programmable 10 MIP Optical Central Processing Unit." Soc. Photo-Opt. Inst. Eng. *752,* Paper 06, 1987.

Structure and operation of the HERMES multiprocessor kernel

by N.G. BOURBAKIS and D.K. FOTAKIS
George Mason University
Fairfax, Virginia

ABSTRACT

In this paper, we present the internal structural design and operation of the HERMES multiprocessor Kernel. HERMES is a heterogeneous, realtime, multiprocessor vision machine based on a two-dimensional array structure of ($N^2/4^r$) microprocessor-nodes. $N \times N$ is the size of the picture and r is a resolution parameter. The HERMES kernel consists of four Z-adjacent processors in the whole HERMES array configuration. The internal design of the Kernel processors and the efficient way of their intercommunication are also discussed.

INTRODUCTION

The performance of the multiprocessor vision system architectures is based on the efficient internal design of their processors and the flexible connectivity of their kernels. It is well known that there is a great variety of multiprocessor vision architectures.[1,2,3,4,5] However, the internal structural design of their processors and the processors connectivity seem to be similar for many of those multiprocessor architectures.[1,2,4] In particular, many of the homogeneous multiprocessor architectures are based on a simple processor internal structural design such as adder or ALU, which processes on one bit operands at a time.[1,2] The communication among these processors in the homogeneous structures is based strongly on the neighboring connectivity.

On the other hand, many of the heterogeneous multiprocessor architectures use a CPU as a processor.[3,4] The connectivity among the processors of those architectures has many common features with the homogeneous ones, such as neighboring. Moreover, it presents some features appearing in the local area computer network configurations.[6,7]

The goal of this paper is to deal with the internal structural design of the HERMES multiprocessor kernel and the connectivity of the processors included in the kernel. Note that, the HERMES multiprocessor kernel consists of four Z-adjacent processors, where the upper left of them in the array is their master-processor and the other three are the slave-processors.

This paper is organized into four sections. The second section discusses the Kernel internal structure and operation of two communication schemes (common-bus, parallel-buses). The third section compares these two communication schemes in a number of factors such as hardware complexity, and the last section summarizes the overall presentation.

KERNEL STRUCTURAL DESIGN AND OPERATION

HERMES Vision Machine

A brief introduction of the HERMES vision machine will assist the reader to understand the overall structure and operation of the kernel configuration. HERMES is a hierarchical, heterogeneous, real-time multiprocessor vision architecture, that has been designed and, its local and global operation has also been simulated by using Petri-net formal models.[4,8,9,10] The horizontal organization of the HERMES machine is illustrated in Figure 1. HERMES consists of $(N^2/4^r)$ microprocessor-nodes in a two-dimensional array structure, where r is a resolution parameter.

The HERMES vision machine receives image data in parallel from the environment by using a two-dimensional photo-array of $N \times N$ cells and processes them in a parallel-hierarchical (top-down and bottom-up) manner. Orders go down and abstracted picture information goes up along the HERMES hierarchy. In particular, the microprocessor-nodes process the available picture information in parallel, at the first level ($L0$) of the HERMES hierarchy. At each of the following levels of the hierarchical processing a designated node ("the upper left" in each quartet of four Z-adjacent nodes) accumulates, correlates, synthesizes, and attempts to recognize the available picture information, feeding the results upwards, as shown in Figure 2. The designated full-master node of the HERMES architecture receives various commands from its users. It then makes decisions based on both its decision making algorithms and the built in "experience." If necessary, it also sends orders down to its successors in the hierarchy, thus determining the processing tasks that they have to execute.

Kernel Intercommunication Schemes

In this section, the structural design of the HERMES kernel will be described. Two variations on the initial HERMES[9]

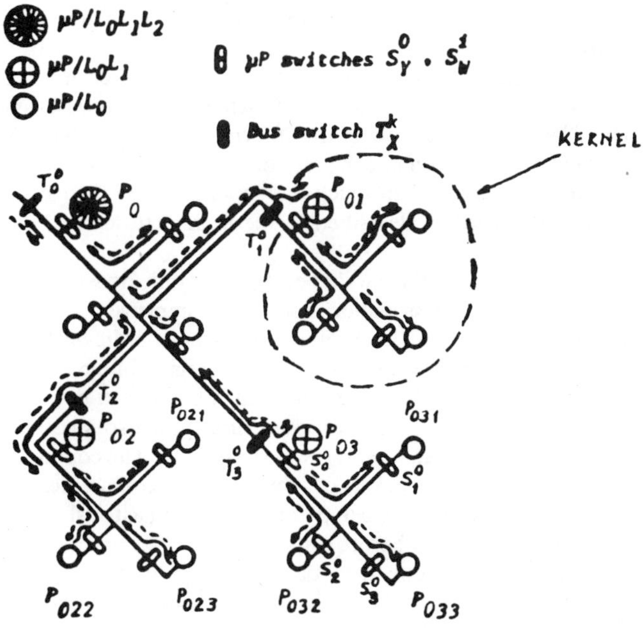

Figure 1—Busing and switching organization of the HERMES architecture of 16 nodes. The dashed arrows indicate "orders" that go down and the solid arrows indicate "abstracted" information which goes up along the HERMES hierarchy.

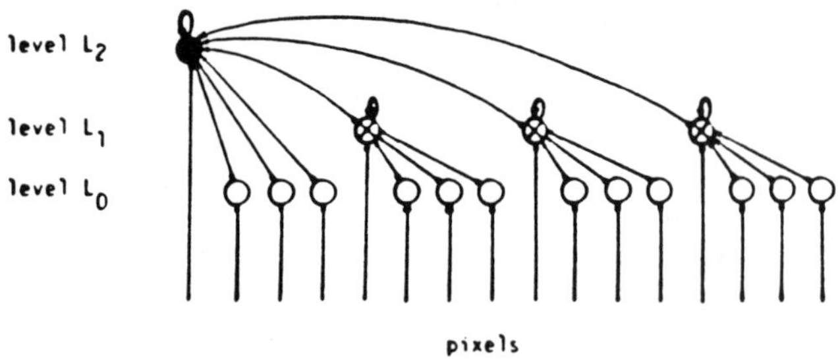

Figure 2—Pseudo-ternary tree operation of the HERMES architecture

design of the busses, interconnecting the processors of the kernel, will be presented:

1. Common bus configuration
2. Parallel bus configuration

The selection between these two different implementations is dependent on some factors such as: total processing speed of the HERMES machine,[7,8,9,10] total cost of the full design of the HERMES system, "real estate" considerations for a future VLSI realization, and architectural schemes of the "off-the-shelf" components (i.e., microprocessors) that are going to be used for the implementation of the HERMES system. In the following, the description of the two policies is given, while their comparison is presented in a third section.

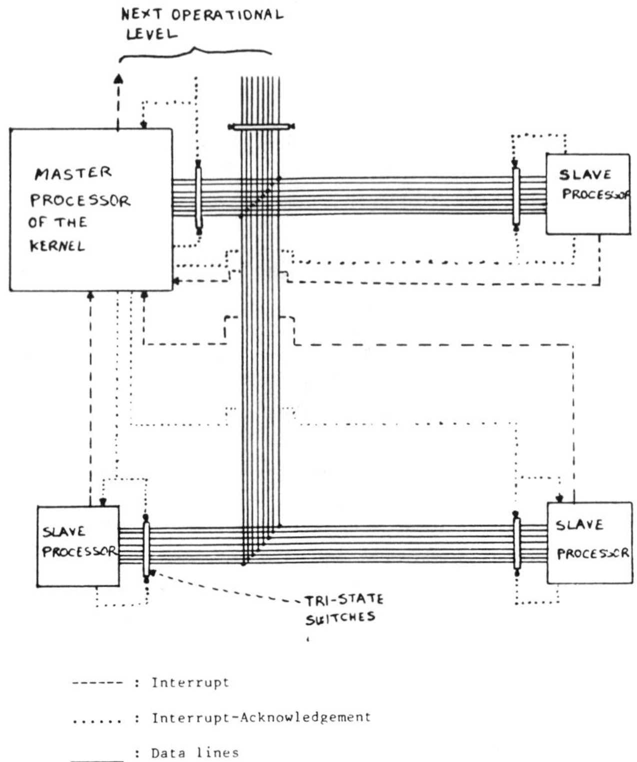

Figure 3—Common bus configuration

Common bus structure

The basic idea of this scheme (see Figure 3) is the 8-line data bus which is coming out of each processor. In addition, these buses are connected together and to the main bus of the HERMES system.[9]

The selective transmission/reception of the master of a kernel is occurred using the individual switches of the processors. The direction of the flow of the information on the data bus is selected by the enable signals of the tri-state individuals switches. The manner in which the "opening" and the closing of switches work, is described in the architectural design of HERMES.[9]

The data-bus is 8-lines wide because, not only does it represent one byte of information but, it also improves the communication procedure between the processors in the best case of the HERMES operation (i.e., when a region of a picture is of one gray level only). The data that are going to be transmitted or received in each processor (four processors per kernel) are latched on an 8-bit register (IN-OUT). The communication packages are packets of 8 bits. Once a communication session is initialized between two processors (master-slave), it has to be terminated before another session occurs.

Note that the 8-line data bus carries pure data without including control bits. Thus, the opening and the closing of a communication session is supervised by two control lines, namely: "one-way interrupt" line from a slave to the master and a "one-way acknowledgement-interrupt" line in the opposite direction. When the master wants to transmit to the slaves, there is the capability to transmit in parallel to all of the processors by opening the individual switches and at the same time interrupting them through the interrupt-acknowledgement line. This interrupt has the highest priority in the internal structure of the processors. As to what the structure of the overall HERMES architecture concerns, the same information is sent to each processor at the same time. However, there is the possibility for the master not to send information to a number of processors so that they remain idle. When a slave-processor wants to transmit information to the master, it enables its interrupt line and lets it be enabled until the last packet of information is sent to the master. In addition, the processor does not send the first packet until the master enables the interrupt-acknowledgement line. After the first packet is sent, the rest of the packets are transmitted in a synchronous manner.

On the other hand, the master has a service policy for the interrupts. The first interrupt that reaches the master is going to be serviced, and there is a fixed priority on the processors (i.e., Z-manner) in the case of the simultaneous existence of two or three interrupts. It is important to note, that any interrupt from a processor, higher in priority than the master, is of the highest priority among the three processors. The individual switch of the master is controlled by itself and by its master in a wider operational kernel (processor of higher priority). It goes without saying that the kernel structure described is compatible with the global structure of the HERMES machine.[9]

Parallel bus structure

The basic idea of this scheme (see Figure 4) is the existence of separate data buses connecting each slave to the master processor in the kernel. There is also a separate data bus for the communication of the master and the processor of the higher hierarchy. Moreover, there is no need of individual switches for each processor (including the master), since the master is capable of transmitting or receiving in a parallel manner.

The initialization and the termination of the transmission of the packets, from the standpoint of master, is set up by the interrupt and interrupt-acknowledgement lines, as discussed in the previous section. The only difference is the lack of a priority scheme in the master since transmission/reception to/from the slaves is done in a parallel manner. In addition, the transmission of packets is done in a synchronous manner for each slave separately. It goes without saying that there is a data IN-OUT register in each edge of each bus (8 bits) to latch or buffer the communication packets. Note that the slight difference of organization of the buses from the original HERMES machine design[9] does not contradict the compatibility of this structure with the HERMES design.

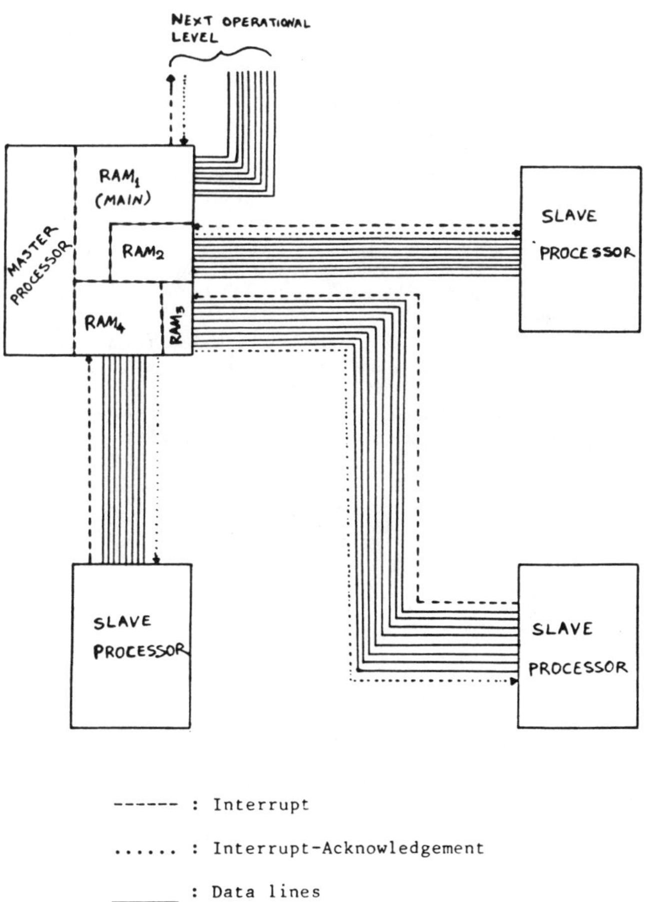

Figure 4—Parallel bus configuration

Slave-Processor Design of the Kernel

The architectural scheme of each of the three processors of the kernel is depicted in Figure 5. As was mentioned in "HERMES—A Heterogeneous Multi-processor Machine Vision System,"[9] the horizontally microprogrammed approach was utilized. In this section the basic components and the organizational role of the slave-processors will be presented:

1. Four registers of 8-bit size will accept the pixels from the photoarray in the form of 8 bits.
2. A two to four decoder will select one of the above registers.
3. A fast PROM memory will keep the micro-routines of the microprocessor operation.
4. A microprogram sequencer will always provide the control memory with the address of the next memory word to be forwarded to the control register and the address of the next instruction located in the PROM to be executed. In addition, it will accept the interrupt-acknowledgement signal and will activate the appropriate service routine. It will also arrange the communication sessions with the master.
5. The control memory (look-up-table) will contain the control words required for the execution of the micro-instructions written in PROM.
6. A control register will keep track of the control words coming out of control memory. Each bit represents a control signal connected to a part or parts of the processor, as well as, the interrupt line and the control lines required for the passing of pixel values from the photoarray to the pixel registers.
7. An 8-bit data register, MDR, will keep one of the operands to ALU.

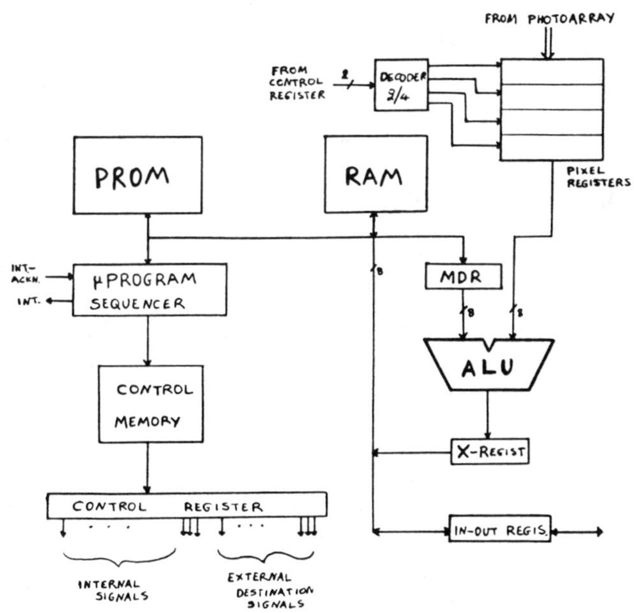

Figure 5—Block diagram of the slave processor of the kernel

8. An 8-bit IN-OUT register will keep the byte of information that is going to be transmitted or received.
9. The X-register will keep the result of an ALU operation.
10. The ALU will operate on 8-bit operands and is supposed to be a simple and fast hardware component since it is going to perform only a few basic operations (such as add, subtract, compare, change-bit, and, or, xor, and move).

Some fast off-the-shelf logic components are going to be used to implement the above design. The microprogrammed design was preferred in order to have the flexibility to change the basic operation algorithm (stored in PROM) of the processor, according to the final selection of the off-the-shelf microprocessor type used to implement the master of the kernel.

COMPARISON BETWEEN THE KERNEL COMMUNICATION SCHEMES

In this section a comparison between the structural design of the two communication schemes for the HERMES multiprocessor kernel is realized. This comparison is based on a number of factors such as number of data communication lines per kernel-processor, number of control lines per kernel-processor, number of switches, kernel processing speed, total number of components in the kernel area, and type of operational mode.

Table I provides these comparative items giving a global idea about the kernel communication schemes.

Choosing one of the two schemes discussed in this paper requires consideration of several trade-offs, as shown in Table I.

CONCLUSIONS

The structural design of the HERMES multiprocessor kernel and its operation of the interprocessor communication have been presented. Two communications schemes were described as well as the internal architectural design of the kernel slave processors was discussed. Both the communication schemes of the kernel processors include advantages and disadvantages as to what hardware complexity and processing speed of the kernel concerns. The implementation of the HERMES vision machine, using the above two communication schemes, is in progress at George Mason University at the department of Electrical and Computer Engineering.

TABLE I

Comparison items	Common Bus	Parallel Bus
# of data lines per kernel processor	a) master 8 b) slave 8	a) 32 b) 8
# of control lines per kernel processor	a) 12 b) 3	a) 8 b) 2
# of switches per kernel processor	a) 1 b) 1	a) — b) —
kernel processing speed	fair	fast
total # of components in the kernel area	4 μPs 32 data lines 21 control lines 4 switches	4 μPs 56 data lines 14 control lines —
type of operational mode	priority	full parallel

REFERENCES

1. Duff, M. "Computing Structures for Image Processing," New York: Academic Press, 1983.
2. Danielson, E.P. and S. Levialdi. "Computers architectures for pictorial information systems." Computer, November, 1981, pp. 53–67.
3. Tanimoto, S. and A. Klinger. "Structured Computer Vision," New York: Academic Press, 1980.
4. Bourbakis, N.G. "Design of a real-time supercomputing vision system architecture," *Proc. of IEEE Conf. on ICS-87,* San Francisco, California, May, 1987.
5. Fotakis, D. and N. Bourbakis. "A Simulation of a 4-bit Processing Element for Array processors using Petri-nets," GMU-ECE-TR-1986, submitted to Inter. Conf.
6. Bourbakis, N. "Data flow Simulation in Quadtree kernels," GMU-TR-1986, submitted to Inter. Conf.
7. Bourbakis, N.G. and C. Vaitsos. "A multi-microprocessor tree network configuration used on robot vision systems," *Digital Techniques,* ed. S. Tzafestas, pp. 483–490.
8. Bourbakis, N. and P. Ligomenides. "A Real Time, Hierarchical Multimicroprocessor Vision System," *Proc. of IEEE Conf. on CVPR-86,* Miami, Florida, June 22–26, 1986.
9. Bourbakis, N. and D. Fotakis. "HERMES—A Heterogeneous Multiprocessor Machine Vision System," submitted to IEEE Trans. on PAMI, 1986.
10. Bourbakis, N., D. Fotakis and D. Tabak. "On Data Flow Based Functional Model for the HERMES Multiprocessor Vision System," accepted to be published in the *Proc. of IEEE Conf. on ICS-87,* San Francisco, California, May, 1987.

Object recognition on the GAM Pyramid

by DAVID H. SCHAEFER and MAN B. CHU
George Mason University
Fairfax, Virginia

ABSTRACT

The GAM Pyramid contains 341 processing elements which are arranged in a pyramid structure that consists of five levels. A processing element can directly communicate with one "parent" on the level above its own level, with four "children" on the level below, and with four "siblings" on its own level. This structure can rapidly extract information about an image on the base of the pyramid such as the number of holes, number of end-points, number of vertices, and other parameters. This information is then used to identify an object of any size, in any orientation, and without regard to whether objects such as pliers or scissors are open or closed. Recognition of specific objects from an object vocabulary of ten has been accomplished.

INTRODUCTION

A program to investigate non-traditional computer architectures suitable for "recognizing" objects in visually sensed inputs has resulted in the fabrication of a five-level, general purpose pyramid of processing elements, augmented by a pyramid of adders. This structure, the "GAM Pyramid,"[1,2,3,4] is being used to examine pyramid algorithms suitable for identifying binary images such as triangles, cups, scissors, and pliers. The algorithms being developed will perform identification independent of orientation or whether objects, such as scissors or pliers, are open or closed.

THE GAM PYRAMID

The GAM Pyramid is a five-level pyramid machine which contains 341 processing elements. The "G" in "GAM" stands for "George Mason University," the "A" stands for "Adder," as a supplementary pyramid of full adders counts the number of "ones" on the level above the base of the Pyramid, and "M" stands for the "MPP" the Massively Parallel Processor whose custom processing elements chips are utilized.[5]

Each processing element in the pyramid can directly communicate with nine other processors (except for those located on the surface of the pyramid, where not all neighboring processors exist). A processing element is connected to a "parent" located on the level above its own level, four "children" located on the level below, and four "siblings," the northern, southern, eastern, and western neighbors, on its own level. These bidirectional connections between processing elements and the adder pyramid provide a fast and easy way of obtaining global information about the image on the base.

Each processing element is connected to 8K bits of external memory. SUMOR circuitry on each level provides the OR's of all the data busses on that level. These five SUMOR signals along with the seven-bit output of the adder pyramid provide feedback to the control computer. A camera and its associated interface produce an image, which provides input to the 16×16 pixel base of the Pyramid. The pyramid of adders provides a method for rapid counting of object pixels. For instance, in order to obtain the sum of the image pixels on the base, using the internal adder in the processing element, 178 cycles are required. With the adder pyramid, only eight cycles are required for the same operation. Pixel counting is a prime requirement for the image identification tasks to be described.

The GAM Pyramid is a modified SIMD (Single Instruction, Multiple Data) system. Every instruction can be performed by all of the processing elements. The control computer, however, generates "level enables" allowing selected levels to receive commands while other levels remain quiescent.

The motivation in building the pyramid was to provide hardware capable of rapidly identifying visual inputs. The GAM identifies input images, generally in the form of paper cutouts that are sensed by the camera. Inputs can also be provided by a cursor. Test images being examined can be one of the ten objects in the object vocabulary. Classes of objects identified are: scissors, pliers, cups, wrenches, forks, knives, L-squares, T-squares, triangles, and triangles with holes. The scissors and pliers are actual objects, not cutouts, and can assume any degree of closure. The input image is identified as one of the listed objects if its features agree with the very generalized description of that object.

The object recognition algorithms are divided into two parts. The first part extracts features of the input image. Then, based on the information extracted, the image is identified as one of the listed objects, or possibly an unknown object. Object descriptions, stored in the control computer, are of a very general nature, and apply to the object irrespective of orientation or other variables of the image.

IMAGE PARAMETERS EXTRACTION

One of the features of the input image that can be easily obtained is the number of holes in the viewed object. Since the input image is assumed to contain only one object, the Euler Characteristic Number can indicate the number of holes in the object. The Euler number (C) indicates the number of connected regions minus the number of holes in those regions. It is defined as:

$$C = V - E + F$$

where V is the number of pixels, E is the number of any pair of horizontal or vertical adjacent pixels or, in the absence of the horizontal and vertical pairs, any diagonally connected pair of pixels, and F is any two by two pixels square. If the number of connected regions (or objects) is equal to one, then the number of holes will be equal to one minus C. The equation to obtain C can be simplified to:

$$C = \begin{matrix} 1 & 0 \\ 0 & 0 \end{matrix} - \begin{matrix} X & 1 \\ 1 & 0 \end{matrix}$$

where "X" is "don't care." On the right hand side of the equation are two image patterns. The number of occurrences of each of these patterns is counted utilizing the adder pyramid. The difference in the number of occurrences of the patterns is then computed by the control computer. It requires about 50 clock cycles to obtain C by using the above equation and the adder pyramid.

The "center" of an object with one hole can be compared with the "center" of the hole. The "center" is defined as the center of the smallest rectangle enclosing the object or the hole.

Another measurable feature of the image is the number of "fingers" or small protrusions of an object. For instance, a fork has four "fingers," a monkey wrench two. To obtain the "fingers," every pixel on the base is ANDed with all of its eight neighbors. This operation leaves only those object pixels surrounded by eight object pixels, (i.e., the body of the object). This image of the body is then expanded twice, complemented, and ANDed with the original image, isolating the fingers from the rest of the object. The fingers are now each separate objects and can be counted by the Euler counting routine.

The number of extreme points is another feature associated with an image. A triangle, for example, has three extreme points, a rectangle four. An extreme point is found if any of the following patterns and their 90 degree rotations are present.

```
0 0 0       000       0 0 0 0
0 1 0  or   110  or   0 1 1 0
XXX         110       XXXX
```

If two or more extreme points are touching each other, the lower right pixel will be selected and the other will be dropped. Those points remaining will then be counted.

Narrow objects can be identified by counting the number of "end points." A "T," for instance, has three end points, an "L" only two. Before the discussion of the end point algorithm, the concept of "tail point" must be presented. A tail point is defined as one of the following patterns, their mirror image, and their 90 degree rotations:

```
00 0       000X
01 0  or   010X
0AA        0110
```

If both A's of the first pattern are "one," the second pattern is used. The tail points of the image on level 4 (the base) is obtained and stored. Then each set of children is moved up to level 3 and tail points calculated on level 3 for each of these four images. The tail point of the image obtained by ANDing the four children is also obtained on level 3. Out of those five tail point sets on level 3, if three of them are touching each other at a certain area, that area will be defined as an end point. Those areas are then moved down to the base and ANDed with the original image. Since by definition a tail point on the base also must be an end point, the two image planes are merged together by ORing. Also, in order to reduce the size of the end point, whenever an end point is covering a tail point, only the tail point will be taken to be the end point.

Long straight lines at right angles indicate the presence of an L or T-like object. A portion of a vertical line, for instance, is defined as any pixel that has both a north and south neighbor. Pixels with such neighbors are then ORed up to the level above and the same procedure applied again. This is repeated until no pixel can move up further. The further up the pyramid such a propagation can take place, the longer the line. The presence of long horizontal and diagonal lines are obtained in a similar fashion.

RECOGNITION PROCEDURE

The recognition procedure that is under investigation involves the collection of all the features, and then using all the collected evidence to determine which object in the vocabulary is being sensed. If an unknown object contains no holes, has three end points, no fingers, and two long lines at right angles to each other, then, with a high probability, the object is a T-square. The evidence, however, can be contradictory due to the imprecision of the feature extracting algorithms. Therefore a "most probable" identification is made.

The existence of holes makes identification easier. A pair of scissors is the only object in the object vocabulary that contains two holes. Several of the objects contain only one hole, but can be differentiated by comparing the center of the hole and the center of the object.

CONCLUSION

The features used in identification do not depend on the size or orientation of the input image. Sensed objects can vary in size, and have any orientation or degree of closure. It is felt that the image parameters being utilized are suitable for very large classes of image inputs. More complicated objects will consist of a collection of elementary objects. Further experimentation is being undertaken.

REFERENCES

1. Schaefer, D. H. and G. C. Wilcox. "The MPP Pyramid Computer." *Proceedings of the 1985 IEEE International Conference on System, Man and Cybernetics,* Tucson, Arizona: November, 1985, pp. 671–675.
2. Schaefer, D. H., G. C. Wilcox, and V. J. Harris. "A Pyramid of MPP Processing Elements—Experiences and Plans." *Proceedings of the 18th Annual Hawaii International Conference on System Science,* Honolulu, Hawaii: January, 1985, pp. 178–184.
3. Schaefer, D. H. and P. Ho. "Counting on the GAM Pyramid," in Levialdi and Cantoni (Eds.): *Pyramids Systems for Computer Vision,* Berlin: Springer-Verlag, 1986, pp. 125–131.
4. Schaefer, D. H., P. Ho, J. Boyd, and C. Vallejos. "The GAM Pyramid," in L. Uhr (Ed.): *Parallel Hierarchical Pyramid-Based Computer Vision,* New York: Academic Press, (in press).
5. Burkley, J. T. "MPP VLSI Multiprocessor Integrated Circuit Design," in J. Potter (Ed.): *The Massively Parallel Processor,* MIT press, 1985, pp. 205–215.

Multilayered petri-nets for distributed decision making*

by A.Z. GHALWASH, P.A. LIGOMENIDES, and R.W. NEWCOMB
University of Maryland
College Park, Maryland

ABSTRACT

Decision making networks, employed for the control of complex cybernetic systems,[6,7,8,9,10] operate on the "Command, Status, and Message Layers" of concurrent decision making activity. Decision making "nodes" function as multitasking operators on all three layers, by executing command decomposition, status reporting, and message exchanging tasks for the concurrent implementation of various control policies. Aspects of real-time concurrency in hierarchical command decomposition over the command layer of the dm-net are, more particularly, analyzed in this paper, using concepts and tools of Petri-net theory.[2,3,4,5,11,12,14]

* This work was partially supported by National Science Foundation Grant Number IST 84-08063.

INTRODUCTION

The control of systems that are significantly more complex than any single decision maker can deal with alone, has motivated investigations of distributed decision making organizations.[13, 15] The employment of multiple decision makers, coordinated in their local decision making efforts to regulate complex systems, underlines the approaches followed in these investigations.

In a more general sense, distributed decision making is used in the design of real-time management and control organizations for the regulation of "cybernetic" systems, such as various large scale business, military, and complex engineering systems. Cybernetic systems are characterized by strongly nonlinear interactions, and by regulatory processes designed to counter the homeostatic tendencies of the controlled system and the incoherent (noisy) or regulated forces from the environment, so as to derive the system away from certain intigenous behavioral trajectories and toward preferred "gainful" ones,[6, 7, 8] as illustrated in Figure 1.

Hierarchical decision making organizations for the control of complex cybernetic systems have been used by military, government, and business establishments for centuries. However, the concept of real-time, computer-based, hierarchical control of complex systems is a recent development.[4, 5, 6, 7, 13, 15] The adaptive implementation of strategies and policies along a command decomposition hierarchy, in the face of continuous environmental and system perturbations, involves the concurrent and coordinated functioning of many, level-organized, decision making modules. Command decomposition along the behavior generating hierarchy is guided by the incitement of the "best" monotonic attainment of local goals, derived from the goals and constraints contained in the input command statements, and from the options of alternative actions available.

In top-down hierarchical decision making networks (denoted "dm-nets"), high level commands are decomposed both spatially and temporally into related temporal sequences and patterns of subcommands, unfolding from top-down. This makes command decomposition a highly dynamic, behavior generating, activity. Decisions at one level of the hierarchy directly affect the decision making environment at other levels, both lower and higher, by exerting influence on the states, conditions, and alternatives available to other decision makers.

Because of the highly concurrent and dynamic character of hierarchical dm-nets, the use of concepts and tools of Petri-net theory[4, 5, 11, 12, 14] offer special advantages for performance-analysis and system-specifications. In this paper we will show the use of Petri-net concepts for the analysis of hierarchical multilayered dm-nets, in which decision making modules are allowed to operate concurrently on various policies and on the various layers of the coordinated decision making activity. In the second section we review concepts of dm nodes and nets, and in the third section we derive the equations for concurrent processing of commands along the command decomposition hierarchy, using Petri-net symbolism. We conclude with comments in the last section.

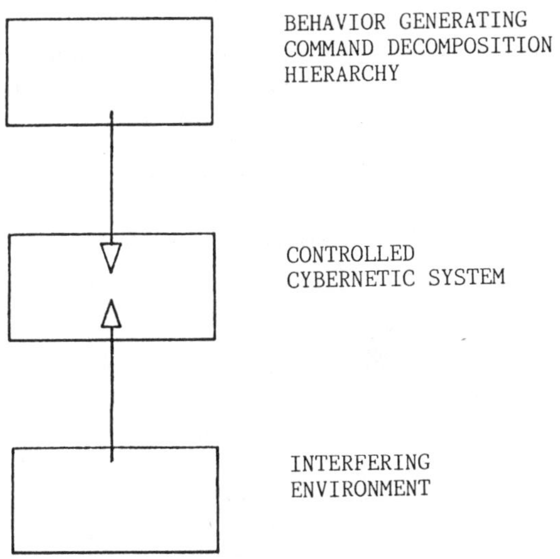

Figure 1—Designed, homeostatic, and incoherent forces on a controlled cybernetic system

DM NODES AND NETS

Decision making networks with emerging collective goal-seeking capabilities operate like highly asynchronous, real-time, cellular automata. The decision making nodes (denoted "dm-nodes") receive, process, and distribute commands, status reports, and messages from/to other dm-nodes of the network in a highly asynchronous, real-time fashion. As such, a dm-node operates concurrently on three "layers" of activity, namely the command decomposition, the status reporting, and the message exchanging layers, as illustrated in Figure 2.[2] In this paper we will limit our discussion to the role of the dm-node within the command decomposition hierarchy. As illustrated in Figure 3, the dm-node, $P_{uv}(m, n)$ (i.e., the vth node at the uth level), has m input connections and n output connections. Input commands, δ^i, are received over the m input channels in a totally asynchronous manner, and, after some processing delay, output subcommands, δ^o, are transmitted to lower level dm-nodes in the hierarchy. In output transmissions, subcommands are distributed in accordance

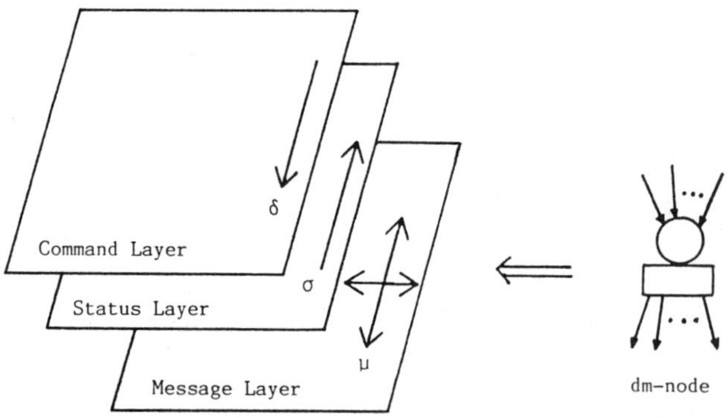

Figure 2—Layered concurrent operation of dm-nodes and nets

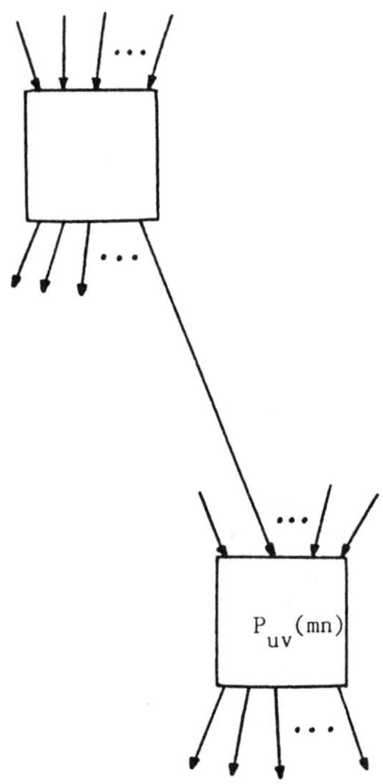

Figure 3—dm-node: $P_{uv}(m, n)$-model

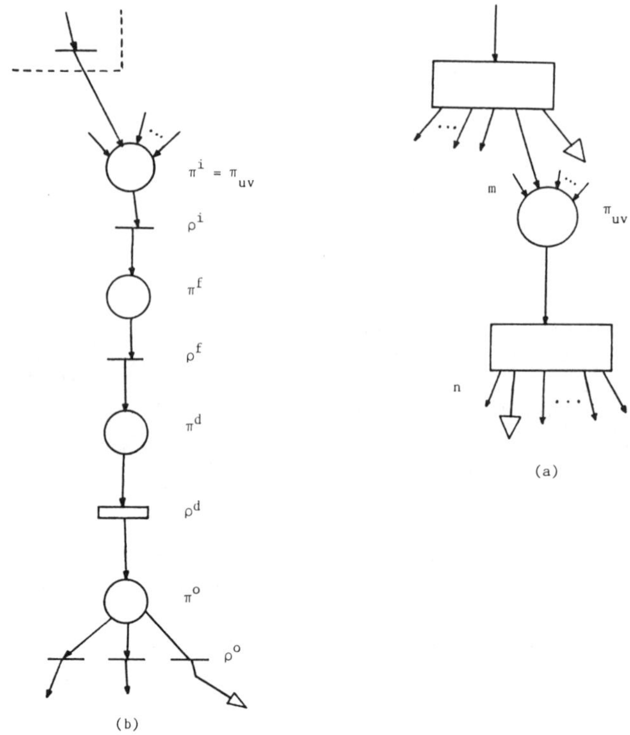

Figure 4—dm-node: (a) π_{uv}/ρ_{uv} model; (b) more detailed model.

with the spatio-temporal distribution programs, which are part of the output plan of the decision maker, functioning like microprograms of subcommand distribution.

Borrowing concepts and symbolism from Petri-net theory, we may represent the dm-node as the combination of an interface place, π_{uv}, and of a decision making transition, ρ_{uv}, where the ordered subscripts uv denote the "level, individual"-number designation of these components, as shown in Figure 4(a). In accordance with the symbolism of "binary" (also called "safe") Petri-nets,[1,2,3,4,5,11,12] places within the dm-nodes designate the presence of commands by a single "set-token." Each dm-transition has only one incident arc (place connection), and it is enabled to "fire" if a set-token is present in the incident place. Firing of a transition is also enabled by the satisfaction of a local condition.

On a more detailed level of description, the transition π_{uv} may be broken down to an input transition ρ^i, a command-fusion place and transition combination, $\pi^f\rho^f$, the actual command decomposition place and transition combination, $\pi^d\rho^d$, (further detailed in A.Z. Ghalwash's Ph.D. dissertation[2]), and an output place, π^o, connected to the output transitions, ρ^o, that distribute the output subcommands, δ^o, as it is illustrated in Figure 4(b).

Each dm-node functions within its own characteristic "decision making worlds" (denoted "dm/w"), each specified by a corresponding "domain of objectives" of the decision making activity, and each composed of domain-related attributes, objects, and events of the decision maker's concern. In response to different input command statements, specifying temporal goals and constraints, the decision maker of the dm-node (ρ^d) determines the corresponding "decision making subworlds" (denoted "dm/sw"), on which the current decision making attention is focused.[8,9,10]

The dm-nodes may operate concurrently on various temporal tasks (within corresponding dm/sw's), specified in the different, concurrently received, input command statements. Decision making tasks deal with the analysis, implementation, and monitoring of different policies specified over the various domains of objectives of the decision maker's concern, as, for example, a manager in a business organization may deal concurrently with various tasks as part of implementation of different policies of production, marketing or finance.

There are various characteristic time-delays in the operation of a dm-node. In order to analyze and determine various temporal aspects in the operation of a dm-net, processing and propagation delays must be defined and determined. Most critical of such delays are those that must be determined in real-time and are dependent on conditions and data measured only dynamically.[2]

For purposes of demonstration, we derive now the average delay in a dm-node under the following simplifying assumptions: The decision maker, ρ^d, deals with a finite set of objects in his dm/w, each object, Q_i, taking only a finite number of discrete values, q_{ij}. Input command statements contain conditions (IF part) of the type "Q_i is q_{ij}," which are found to be satisfied in the dm/w with a probability (distribution) P_{ij}. We let P_i be the probability that the next input command, δ^i, will address the object Q_i, and $P_{j/i}$ be the probability that the value q_{ij} will be addressed given that Q_i is addressed. Also we let that $P_{i\&j}$ be the probability that both Q_i and q_{ij} are addressed in δ^i.

The average time between two successive input commands is T_0, while the time required to check an IF-condition about object Q_i is T_c^i, and the actual execution time for a command when the IF-condition is satisfied is T_e.

Then,

$$P_{i\&j} = P_{j/i} \cdot P_i$$

and the average firing time delay in the ρ^d-transition is easily derived to be,

$$T_{\text{avg}} = \sum_{i=1}^{n} T_a^i$$

$$T_a^i = P_i \cdot T_c^i + \sum_{j=1}^{m_i} P_{i\&j}\left[\left(\frac{1}{P_{ij}} - 1\right)T_0 + T_e\right]$$

where m_i is the number of the discrete values of Q_i, and n is the number of objects in the dm/w. Note that the total delay in the dm-node ρ_{uv} may be determined if the delays in the other transitions of the node (see Figure 4(b)) are estimated and added to the delay in ρ^d. This derivation of T_{avg} demonstrates that temporal aspects in the command decomposition hierarchy may be computed under various statistical assumptions, or by estimations of delays from data collected in real-time.

Within a hierarchical command decomposition organization, each dm-node is appropriately connected and is designated to operate within specified dm/w's, in accordance to the various assigned domains of objectives. As new policies are generated by global commands issued at higher levels of the command decomposition hierarchy, each defining its own global goals and constraints, related decision making activity is generated and ripples-down the fired dm-nodes of the hierarchy. We classify the commands reaching and leaving each multitasking dm-node by color-coding the different policies generated by the global commands. Different color-codes are used to identify the related decision making activity, which evolves over the three concurrent layers of command decomposition, of status reporting, and of message exchanging. We distinguish three types of global commands which regulate the generation, the maintenance, and the cancellation of the active color-coded policies over the dm-net, namely: "new policy-generating," "policy-modifying," and "policy-cancelling" types of global commands.[2]

In the following section we derive functional relationships about the operation of command decomposition hierarchy, using Petri-net concepts.

RELATIONSHIPS AND EXAMPLES OF PETRI-NET ANALYSIS

A hierarchical organization of N decision makers (dm-nodes) consists of transitions and interface places, as illustrated in Figure 5. The decision making transition ρ_{uv} is connected to other such transitions through interface places that hold set-tokens according to their markings. The transitions will "fire" (i.e., will perform decision making activity) if their incident place holds a token *and* a corresponding firing condition is satisfied. The places are represented by circles, the tokens by dots in the places, and the transitions by bars. Each level of the hierarchical organization contains interface places with single outputs incident to corresponding transitions at the same level. Incident upon each place are connections from transitions at higher levels and from sources external from the hierarchy. "External" inputs incident on the place π_{uv} are denoted as x_{uv}.

At the firing time λ, tokens are moved through the fired transitions from the corresponding incident interface places into the places on which the transition is incident, in accordance with an "activity vector" associated with each fired transition. Notice that, in general, the activity vector may be time

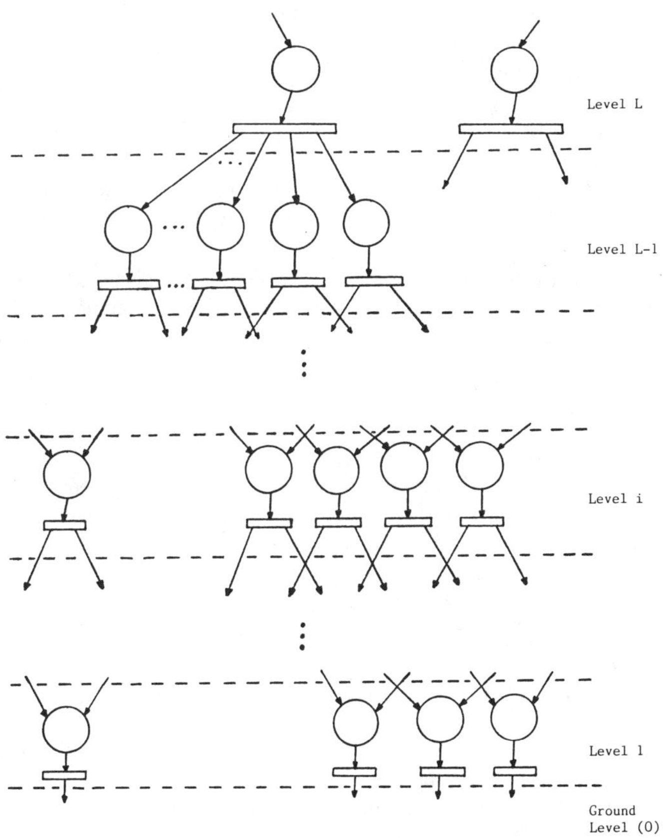

Figure 5—Command decomposition hierarchy

variable. The activity vector helps us to compute the next marking (i.e., the marking at firing time $\lambda + 1$).

If we assume that only one external incident arc x_{uv} may be accepted at most per interface place π_{uv}, and that only one external output (to an actuator) y_{uv} may be transmitted by a transition ρ_{uv}, then each dm-net is characterized by an N-bit external incidence input vector $X = [\ldots, x_{uv}, \ldots]$ and by a N-bit external output vector $Y = [\ldots, y_{uv}, \ldots]$.

Petri-net Description of Operations

For purposes of analysis we consider the hierarchical organization shown in Figure 5. For a Petri-net representation of N places and N transitions, we use the P-vector (N-bit binary) of markings at time λ, $M_0(\lambda)$ and the T-vector (N-bit binary) of firings at time λ, $F(\lambda)$. An entry equal to 1 in the firing vector F denotes that the corresponding transition will fire at time λ. In addition, the P-vector $X(\lambda)$ denotes the external inputs at λ to the interface places of the hierarchy, and the T-vector $Y(\lambda)$ denotes the outputs to external actuators at λ. An N-diagonal matrix is defined to designate whether the corresponding transitions are "ready" (i.e., conditioned) for firing. An entry equal to 1 in the Condition (diagonal) matrix, $S(\lambda)$ denotes that the corresponding transition is conditioned for firing at λ. The N-bit activity vector associated with the transition ρ_{uv} is denoted with $C_{uv}(\lambda)$.

Equations of Operations

A marking of the dm-net at time λ, $M(\lambda)$, designates the distribution of tokens over the interface places at λ. In order to take the input $X(\lambda)$ into account we use the dotted equality[1] to obtain the total binary marking vector at λ, as follows:

$$M(\lambda) \doteq M_0(\lambda) + X(\lambda)$$

For the dot equality we use normal integer arithmetic and we replace any resulting positive number with 1 and all other results by 0.

Since a transition is enabled to fire by both a token in its incident place *and* a satisfied condition, we may calculate the firing vector at $\lambda + 1$ as follows:

$$F(\lambda + 1) = S(\lambda) \cdot M(\lambda)$$

When a ρ_{uv}-transition fires, a token moves from the place incident on ρ_{uv} into those places on which the transition is incident and are designated in the associated activity vector at λ. We use again the dotted equality to compute the marking at time $\lambda + 1$.

$$M(\lambda + 1) \doteq M(\lambda) - F(\lambda + 1) + K(\lambda + 1)$$

where

$$K(\lambda + 1) \doteq \sum_{\rho_{uv} \in \phi} C_{uv}(\lambda)$$

where ϕ is the set of "firable" transitions (enabled by token and condition) at time λ.

We may calculate the Output (external actuation) vector at time $\lambda + 1$, $Y(\lambda + 1)$ as follows:

$$Y(\lambda + 1) = D \cdot F(\lambda + 1)$$

where D is a diagonal matrix, $D = \text{diag}(y_{uv}/\rho_{uv})$ and $y_{uv}/\rho_{uv} = 1$ if ρ_{uv} is connected to an external actuator (denoted with triangular arrows in Figures 4–6). Using the above derived relations we may compute the ripple-effects from an initial marking to the outputs to the external actuators.

If we assume that all transitions cause the same average delay T_{avg}, then the levels will fire synchronously and the total ripple delay from the time of global command input, λ_{input}, to the time of (say, ground level) actuation, λ_{out}, is given by

$$T_{ripple} = (\lambda_{out} - \lambda_{input}) \cdot T_{avg}$$

If the assumption of uniform delay, T_{avg}, is lifted, asynchronous firing will result, which will alter the timings over the various firing paths. An N-diagonal delay matrix, $V = \text{diag}(T_{uv}/\rho_{uv})$, will have to be defined, or determined in real time. Particularly interesting will be the formulation of a solution for the ripple-time, if the delays T_{uv} are time variable and situation (command)-dependent.[2]

Illustrative Example

Let us consider the dm-net shown in Figure 6, where

$$\Pi = [\pi_{31}/\pi_{21}\,\pi_{22}\,\pi_{23}/\pi_{11}\,\pi_{12}\,\pi_{13}\,\pi_{14}]^T$$
$$\tau = [\rho_{31}/\rho_{21}\,\rho_{22}\,\rho_{23}/\rho_{11}\,\rho_{12}\,\rho_{13}\,\rho_{14}]^T$$

We will assume that

$$M_0(0) = [0/000/0000]^T$$
$$X(0) = [1/000/0000]^T$$
$$S(\lambda) = \text{diag}(1/111/1111) \text{ for all } \lambda.$$
$$D(\lambda) = \text{diag}(0/000/1111) \text{ for all } \lambda.$$

and the activity vectors as

$$C_{31}(\lambda) = [0/111/0100]^T$$
$$C_{21}(\lambda) = [0/000/0100]^T$$
$$C_{22}(\lambda) = [0/000/0010]^T$$
$$C_{23}(\lambda) = [0/000/0011]^T \text{ for all } \lambda.$$

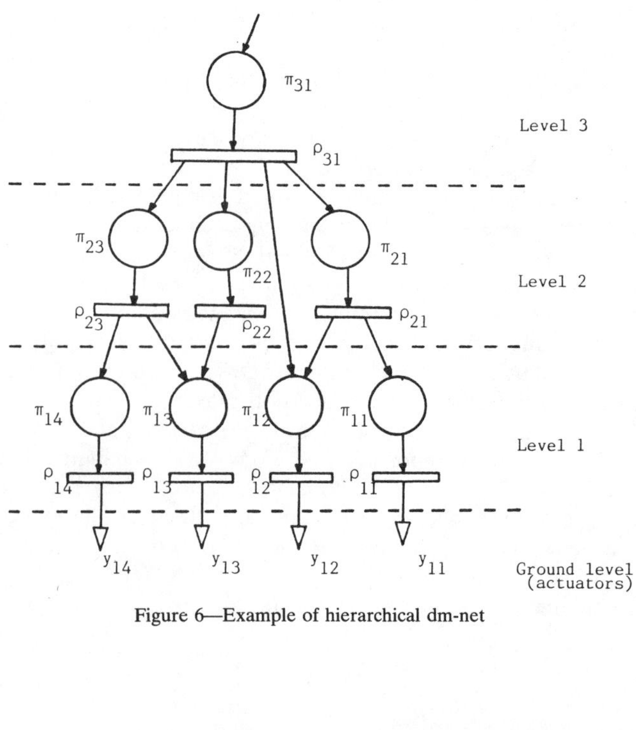

Figure 6—Example of hierarchical dm-net

At λ_{input} there is only one input to the place π_{31}, and at λ_{out} the hierarchy affects the controlled system only through the transitions $\rho_{11}, \rho_{12}, \rho_{13} \cdot \rho_{14}$. If the Condition matrix enables all transitions to fire, then

$$M(0) \doteq M_0(0) + X(0) \doteq [1/000/0000]^T$$

$$F(1) = S(0) \cdot M(0) = \begin{bmatrix} 1 &&&&&&& \\ & 1 &&&&&& \\ && 1 &&&&& \\ &&& 1 &&&& \\ &&&& 1 &&& \\ &&&&& 1 && \\ &&&&&& 1 & \\ &&&&&&& 1 \end{bmatrix} \cdot \begin{bmatrix} 1 \\ 0 \\ 0 \\ 0 \\ 0 \\ 0 \\ 0 \\ 0 \end{bmatrix} = [1/000/0000]^T$$

At the next firing time, only ρ_{31} will fire.

$$K(1) \doteq C_{31}(0) = [0/111/0100]^T$$

$$M_0(1) \doteq M(0) - F(1) + K(1)$$

$$\doteq \begin{bmatrix} 1 \\ 0 \\ 0 \\ 0 \\ 0 \\ 0 \\ 0 \\ 0 \end{bmatrix} - \begin{bmatrix} 1 \\ 0 \\ 0 \\ 0 \\ 0 \\ 0 \\ 0 \\ 0 \end{bmatrix} + \begin{bmatrix} 0 \\ 1 \\ 1 \\ 1 \\ 0 \\ 1 \\ 0 \\ 0 \end{bmatrix} \doteq [0/111/0100]^T$$

We have

$Y(1) = D \cdot F(1) = [0/000/0000]^T$, no effect on external actuators.

$M(1) \doteq M_0(1) + X(1) \doteq [0/111/0100]^T$, assuming no external input at $\lambda = 1$

$$F(2) = S(1) \cdot M(1) = [0/111/0100]^T$$

$$K(2) \doteq C_{21} + C_{22} + C_{23} \doteq [0/000/0121]^T \doteq [0/000/0111]^T$$

$$M_0(2) \doteq M(1) - F(2) + K(2) \doteq [0/000/0111]^T$$

The $M_0(2)$ marking shows that at $\lambda = 2$ there are tokens at $\pi_{12}, \pi_{13}, \pi_{14}$. Also,

$Y(2) = D \cdot F(2) = [0/000/0100]^T$, (i.e., there is an output y_{13}).

Assuming again that $X(2) = 0$, we have

$$M(2) \doteq M_0(2) + X(2) \doteq [0/000/0111]^T$$

$$F(3) = S(2) \cdot M(2) = [0/000/0111]^T$$

$$K(3) \doteq [0/000/0000]^T$$

$$M_0(3) \doteq M(2) - F(3) + K(3) \doteq [0/000/0000]^T$$

$Y(3) = D \cdot F(3) = [0/000/0111]^T$ (i.e., there are outputs at y_{13}, y_{12}, y_{11} to the corresponding external actuators).

We see that the sole initial marking at π_{31} has generated an external output at $\lambda = 2$, (y_{13}), and again at $\lambda = 3$, (y_{13}, y_{12}, y_{11}). Since the hierarchy received no further external inputs, there were no more actuations (no more tokens left in the M_0-marking).

Having assumed uniform delay in the dm-nodes, the external actuations were delayed by $2T_{avg}$ and $3T_{avg}$ respectively.

CONCLUSIONS

This paper has presented some aspects of applying Petri-net symbology and concepts to the analysis of layered dm-nets, and more particularly to policy implementation over command decomposition hierarchies. The work is currently being extended[2] on all three concurrent layers of dm-nets. Problems of reachability, timing, reconfigurability, and stability are especially being investigated, and results will be reported soon.

REFERENCES

1. Alayan, H. and R.W. Newcomb. "Binary Petri-Net Relationships," submitted for publication, 1987.
2. Ghalwash, A.Z. *Petri-Net Modeling of Decision Making Organizations,* PhD Dissertation (in preparation), EE Dept. University of Maryland, 1987.
3. Ghalwash, A.Z., P.A. Ligomenides, and R.W. Newcomb. "Modes and Job Performance Evaluation of Robot Petri-Nets." EE Dept., University of Maryland, Technical Report. (Submitted for conference publication.)
4. Ho, G.S. and C.V. Ramamorthy. "Performance Evaluation of Asynch. Concur. Systems Using Petri-Nets." *IEEE Trans. Soft. Eng.,* SE-6 (1980) 5, pp. 440–449.
5. Johnsonbaugh, R. and T. Murata. "Petri-Nets and Marked Graphs. Math. Models of Concur. Computation." *The Amer. Math. Monthly,* 89 (1977) 8, pp. 552–566.
6. Ligomenides, P.A. "An Engineering Cybernetic Model for Policy Analysis and Implementation." *Int'l J. of PAIS,* 6 (1982) 3, pp. 273–284.
7. Ligomenides, P.A. "Command Decomposition as a Decision Making Problem." in S.K. Chang (ed), *Management and Office Information Systems,* Plenum, 1983.
8. Ligomenides, P.A. "Dynamic Models for Information Quality Enhancement." *Proc. IEEE Workshop on Lang. for Autom.,* Chicago: November 7–9, 1983.
9. Ligomenides, P.A. "Specific. of an Experiential Data Base for Decision Making." *Proc. IEEE Conf. Trends and Applic.* Bethesda, MD, NBS, May 22–24, 1984.
10. Ligomenides, P.A. "The Experiential Knowledge Base as a Cognitive Prosthesis." in S.K. Chang, T. Ichikawa, P.A. Ligomenides (eds), *Visual Languages,* Plenum Press, 1986.
11. Murata, T. "Modeling and Analysis of Concur. Syst." in C.R. Vick and C.V. Ramamoorthy (eds), *Handbook of Software Engineering,* Van Nostrand Reinhold, 1984.
12. Peterson, J.L. "Petri-Nets." *Computer Surveys,* 9 (1977) 3, pp. 223–252.
13. Sandell, N.R., Jr., P. Varaiya, M. Athans, and M. Safonov. "Survey of Decentr. Control Meth. for Large Scale Sys." *IEEE Trans. Aut. Contr.,* AC-23 (1978) 2.
14. Sifakis, J. "Use of Petri-Nets for Perf. Evaluation." in H. Beilner and E. Gelembe (eds), *Measuring, Modeling and Evaluation of Comp. Systems,* North Holland, 1977.
15. Tenney, R.R. and N.R. Sandell, Jr. "Structures for Distributed Decision Making." *IEEE Trans. SMC,* SMC-11 (1981) 8, pp. 517–527.

Logic machines: A survey

by G.Z. QADAH
Northwestern University
Evanston, Illinois
and
M. NUSSBAUM
Institut fur Integrierte Systeme
ETH-Zurich/Switzerland

ABSTRACT

Logic(-based) programming languages are today the center of very many research efforts. One of these languages, PROLOG (PROgramming in LOGic), is used to program expert systems, natural language processors, computer aided design systems and compilers. A parallel variant of PROLOG is suggested as the language of the Japanese Fifth Generation computer project. Parallel to these efforts, a class of computer architectures that is suitable for supporting logic programming is emerging. Such a class is referred to as logic machines. In this paper, we propose a new taxonomy for the architectural space of logic machines. Based on such taxonomy, some of the proposed logic machine architectures are presented and compared.

INTRODUCTION

Logic Programming[1,2,3] (or programming using logic formulas) is today the center of very many research efforts around the world. Two important features of logic make logic programming attractive, namely, the fact that logic is declarative[2] and that it rests on a very powerful mathematical formalism. A language being declarative implies that the programmer needs only to specify what computations need to be performed rather than how they should be performed (the sequence of steps needed to carry them out). The language processor then decides, independent of the programmer, how such computations are to be performed. Declarative languages have many advantages, namely, higher programmer productivity and possibly high execution speed since novel hardware architectures can be used to support their execution.

The fact that logic rests on a very powerful mathematical base implies that many formal languages based on logic can be easily developed. In fact, in the last several years we have observed a good increase in the number of logic-based languages available to the programming community. In addition to PROLOG and its sequential and parallel variants,[4,5,6] concurrent logic-based languages such as PARLOG[7] and Concurrent PROLOG[8] have been developed. PROLOG and other logic languages have been used to construct expert systems, natural language processors, computer aided design systems,[9] compilers,[10] and event-driven simulators.[11] A parallel variant of PROLOG, the Fifth Generation Kernel Language (FGKL),[4] is suggested as the language of the Fifth Generation computer project.[12]

The traditional implementation of logic programming systems as complex software systems running on general-purpose von Neumann computers, has resulted in slow and inefficient systems. One major reason for this is the fact that, in such implementation, the underlying hardware is general-purpose and sequential and not tuned properly to the requirements of such systems. The recent advances in VLSI technology, the dramatic drop in hardware prices, and the fact that logic programming systems lend themselves well to novel hardware architectures has inspired a new implementation. In such implementations, the general-purpose von Neumann computer is replaced with a dedicated machine tailored for non-numeric processing and, in most cases, utilizing parallel processing to support the logic programming systems. The aggregate of software and hardware components dedicated to the support of logic programming is referred to as a logic machine. Logic machines claim to improve the performance of logic processing through hardware specialization, increased parallelism, and increased processing power.

Recently, many architectures for the logic machine have been proposed. In this paper, we propose a new taxonomy for the architectural space of logic machines. Based on such taxonomy some of the proposed logic machines are presented and compared. The following section overviews the computational model as well as the inherent parallelism of logic programming. Next, a definition and a classification scheme (taxonomy) for logic machines is presented. An overview of some of the proposed logic machine architectures follows, and finally, we offer some general comments and concluding remarks.

THE COMPUTATIONAL MODEL OF LOGIC PROGRAMMING

Logic programming is a mathematical formalism based on horn clause logic suitable for expressing certain classes of problems requiring deductive reasoning.[1,2,3] In the following, we present the elements of the computational model that underlie such programming environments as well as the various types of parallelism that exist in such a model.

Elements of the Computational Model

Conceptually, the computational model of logic programming consists of three elements, namely, a set of horn clauses, a set of goals (queries) and an inference (deduction) process. These elements are presented next.

The Horn Clauses

From a syntactical point of view and using the notations defined within the context of the logic-based language PROLOG,[13] a (horn) clause has the general form

$$S_0 :- S_1, S_2, \ldots, S_n \qquad (1)$$

where S_i $(i = 0, 1, \ldots, n)$ is a positive literal, ":–" is the implication operator, and "," is the logical AND operator. S_0 is the head literal (conclusion/goal) of the clause, while S_i $(i = 1, 2, \ldots, n)$ denotes the body literals (subgoals) of the clause. The literal in a clause is an expression of the general form

$$p(t_1, t_2, \ldots, t_m) \qquad (2)$$

where p is a predicate (relation) or functional symbol and t_i $(i = 1, 2, \ldots, m)$ is a term. A term is either a constant (whose symbol starts with a lower case character), a variable (whose symbol starts with an upper case character), or an expression of the same form as (2) except that p can only be a functional symbol. The variables in horn clauses are typeless. That is, they may assume different types throughout the process of manipulating the clauses within which these variables are defined.

From a semantic point of view, a literal may have only one of the two logical values, true and false, and the horn clause of (1), therefore, is interpreted as:

"S_0 is true if S_1 is true AND S_2 is true . . . AND S_n is true."

However, when a clause contains zero body literals, it is interpreted as "S_0:–true." That is, "S_0 is (always) true." Such a clause is called the unit clause, assertion or tautology.

Horn clauses can express both simple and complex knowledge about objects in the real world. The unit clause expresses a simple (atomic) fact about an object. For example, the unit clause,

like(arthur,john):– (3)

expresses the fact that "arthur likes john." Such a clause is called the ground unit clause. Replacing "john" of clause (3) by a variable X, the new clause, the non-ground unit clause, expresses the fact that "arthur likes X irrespective of the value that X might have." That is, "arthur likes everyone and everything."

The more complex facts about objects are expressed using clauses of the general form presented in (1). For example, the clause

uncle(bob,ruth):–sister(ann,bob),mother(ann,ruth) (4)

expresses the fact that "bob is the uncle of ruth" if "ann is the sister of bob" AND "ann is the mother of ruth." These types of facts are implicit in the sense that the body of the clause must be tested and proved to be true in order to conclude that the head literal is true. A more interesting case arises when the constants inside the literals of clause (4) are replaced by variables, as follows:

uncle(X,Y):–sister(Z,X), mother(Z,Y).

Such a clause then expresses a general "rule" that applies to members of general classes. In the above case, the rule partially defines the "uncleship" relation between human beings (a class of objects) in terms of the simpler relations, "brothership" and "fathership," defined on the same class.

Figure 1 shows a set of horn clauses. Any literal in such a set is of the form r-symb(X,Y) and can be read as "X is r-symb of Y." Most examples and illustrations in the rest of this paper will be based on this set.

The Goal(/query)

The goal is a logical statement whose truth value needs to be determined with respect to a set of horn clauses. The statement is true if it is a logical consequence of such set, otherwise, it is false. A goal has the following general format:

$:\!-S_1, S_2, \ldots, S_n$

```
C1:  brother (fred, larry) :-
C2:  brother (joe, fred) :-
C3:  brother (carl, larry) :-

C4:  sister (eva, sam) :-
C5:  sister (ann, bob) :-

C6:  father (paul, ted) :-

C7:  mother (ann, ruth) :-
C8:  mother (eva, ted) :-

C9:  uncle ( X, Y ) :- brother(Z,X), father(Z,Y)
C10: uncle ( X, Y ) :- sister(Z,X), mother(Z,Y)
```

Figure 1—A sample set of horn clauses

That is, it is a horn clause with zero head literal and one or more body literals. When a goal contains no variables (a ground goal), its answer is simply true (if a proof can be found), or false (otherwise). For example, invoking the set of clauses of Figure 1 with the following goal,

:–uncle(bob,ruth)

yields the answer "true," since "bob is uncle of ruth" is a logical consequence of the clauses C_5, C_7, and C_{10} of Figure 1. A more general situation occurs when the goal contains one or more variables, as in the following:

:–uncle(X, ruth) (5)

In such a case, the answer to the goal is a set of patterns of values to the variables in the goal under which such goal is true, if any, otherwise the answer is false. Actually, the requirement of returning patterns of values to the variables in the goal (if any variable exists) rather than returning only true or false is one of the major differences between the computational models of theorem proving and logic programming.[14] When the goal statement contains variables, it is more appropriate for the goal to be called a query since such a statement can be viewed as a specification of the set of value patterns under which the statement is true. The value patterns for the variables in a query are called solutions. Invoking the set of clauses of Figure 1 with the query of (5), yields the answer "true" and the solution X = bob.

The Inference Process

The inference (deduction) process takes a goal and a set of horn clauses and tries to prove (infer) that such a goal is true with respect to such set. Such a proof involves the establishment of the fact that the input clause (query) is consistent with (or a logical consequence of) the set of horn clauses. One of the most common inference methods that is suitable for horn clause logic is the one based on the resolution principle.[15]

At the heart of this method is the resolution (reduction) step. Such a step can be decomposed into two steps, unification and substitution. Unification is the process of making two literals identical by replacing their free variables with a common set of binding values, called the unifier. The process may succeed or fail; however, if it succeeds, then it generates the unifier. For example, the two literals, "brother(fred,larry)" and "brother(*Z*, larry)" are unifiable under the binding set {*Z*/fred} to yield the common literal "brother(fred,larry)." The two literals "brother(*Z*, larry)" and "brother (*X*, *Y*)" are also unifiable under the set of bindings {*X*/*Z*, *Y*/larry}. On the other hand, the two literals "brother(*Z*, larry)" and "brother(*X*, joe)" are not unifiable because there exists no set of bindings for the free variables of the two literals which make them identical (the second term in each of the literals has a different constant value). For the same reason, the two literals "brother(fred,larry)" and "father(fred,larry)" are not unifiable (the predicate symbol is not the same in both literals). An important feature of the unification process is that it permits a bidirectional binding of a variable from one literal to a constant, a variable, and even to a general term of the other participating literal. It is also important to notice that having the same predicate symbols and an equal number of terms is a necessary (but not sufficient) condition for two literals to unify. A general algorithm for the unification process can be found in Sterling and Shapiro.[16]

The unification of a literal from a goal with a general clause is performed by unifying the goal literal with the head literal of the clause and generating the binding set. For example, unifying "uncle(*X*, ruth)" from the goal ":–uncle(*X*, ruth)" with

uncle(*X*, *Y*):–brother(*Z*, *X*), father(*Z*, *Y*) (6)

will succeed and generate the binding set {*X*/*X*, *Y*/ruth}.

The substitution step is to replace the literal in a goal with the body literals of a clause that has unified with it; then each variable in the new expression is replaced with its value from the binding set (unifier). The expression resulting from the substitution step is a new goal and is called the "resolvent." If no body literal exists (the clause is a unit clause), then, the substitution step replaces the literal of the goal with the logical value "true" (the interpretation of the empty body of a unit clause) and replaces the free variables with their values from the unifier. "Anding" the terms in the goal yields the resolvent. In the previous example, "uncle(*X*, ruth)" has unified with clause (6) to yield the binding set {*X*/*X*, *Y*/ruth}. The substitution step replaces "uncle(*X*, ruth)" with "brother(*Z*, *X*), father(*Z*, *Y*)," and substitute for *X* by *X* and for *Y* by "ruth" to yield the resolvent

":–brother(*Z*, *X*), father(*Z*, ruth)." (7)

Unifying "brother(*Z*, *X*)" of (7) with the unit clause "brother(fred,larry):–" yields the unifier {*Z*/fred, *X*/larry}. The substitution step replaces "brother(*Z*, *X*)" with the body literals of the unit clause (the logical value "true") to yield the clause ":–'true', father(fred,ruth)" which in turn yields the resolvent ":–father(fred,ruth)." In the same way, "father(*X*, ted)" of the goal ":–father(*X*, ted)" unifies with the clause "father(paul,ted):–." The substitution step results in a resolvent of the form ":–'true'." Such a resolvent is called the empty (or null) resolvent (a clause with no head or body literals) and is given the symbol "[]."

The resolution process can be best described through the algorithm shown in Figure 2. The proof of a goal *G*, using such a process, starts by selecting one of the goal's literals *g* (step 1) and finds a clause *c* from the set of clauses that unifies with *g* and the corresponding unifier θ (steps 2 and 3). Applying, then, the substitution step to the goal *G* and the clause *c* using the unifier θ results in a resolvent *R* (step 4). Each time a new resolvent is derived (or in other words, a goal is reduced), the former steps are repeated, with the new resolvent as its input goal, until eventually one of the two states is reached, namely, the new resolvent is an empty or a non-resolvable one. (A resolvent is non-resolvable if it cannot unify with any clause in the set of logic clauses.) Reaching an empty clause indicates that the goal *G* is indeed derivable from the set of clauses (subject to whatever bindings are made to the variables in the

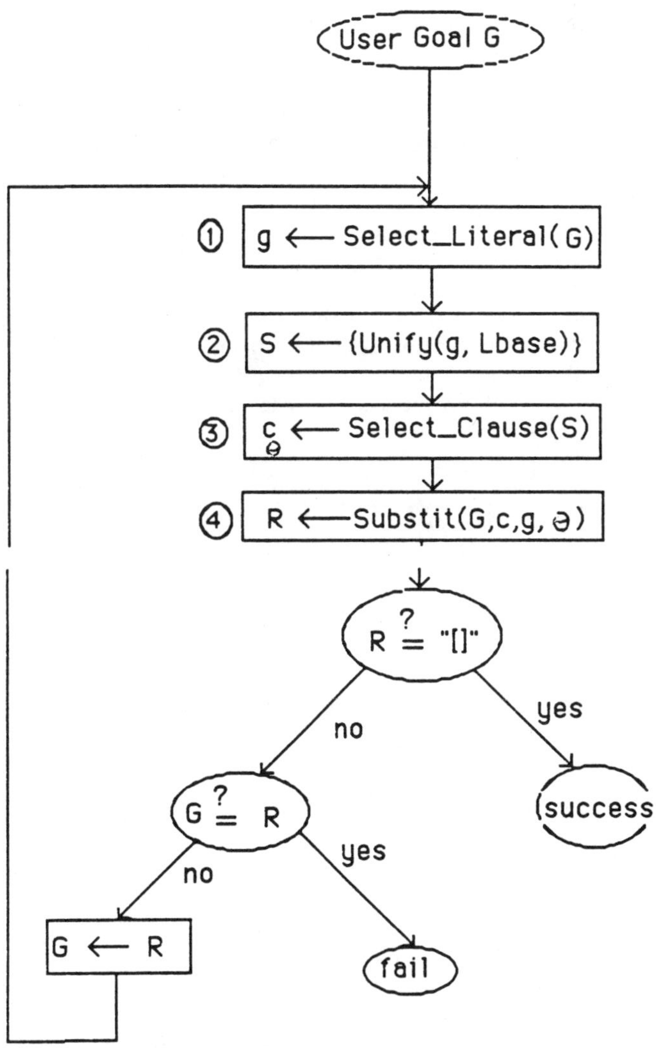

Figure 2—A non-deterministic resolution algorithm

goal statement). The sequence of resolution steps that terminates with "[]" is called a "success" proof sequence and the set of bindings that has been made to the variables of the goal throughout such sequence represents a solution to the input goal (query). On the other hand, reaching a non-resolvable clause indicates the failure of the sequence to prove the goal G. The sequence that terminates with such a clause is called a "failure" proof sequence. If neither the empty nor the non-resolvable clause is reached, the inference algorithm loops forever, producing an infinite proof sequence. Figure 3 shows a sequence of resolution steps generated by the inference process in response to the goal ":–uncle(X, ruth)," using the algorithm of Figure 2. Such proof sequence starts by unifying "uncle(X, ruth)," with C_{10} of Figure 1 to yield the resolvent ":–sister(Z,X), mother(Z, ruth)," then unifying "mother(Z, ruth)" with C_7 to yield the resolvent ":–sister(ann,X)" and finally unifying "sister(ann,X)" with C_5 to yield the empty resolvent. That is, the statement "uncle(X, ruth)" when "X = bob" is indeed a logical consequence of the set of clauses presented in Figure 1.

The set of all proof sequences (success, failure, and infinite) for a goal with respect to a set of clauses forms a space, the search space. Such a space can be represented as a tree, the search tree.[17,18] Figure 4 shows such a tree for the goal ":–uncle(X, ruth)." The root of the tree is the goal to be proved, while the rest of the nodes represent resolvents. A leaf node (if it exists) represents an empty resolvent of a non-resolvable resolvent. The arc between a node and one of its children corresponds to a resolution step and is labeled by the set of bindings generated during such step. The nodes at the ith level of the tree represent the set of all resolvents that can be obtained from the goal in i resolution steps. The path from the root of the tree to a leaf represents the sequence of resolution steps that leads to that leaf together with the sets of bindings generated throughout such sequence. A tree may contain sequences that terminate with success (1→2→3 for example), with no success (1→4 for example) or sequences

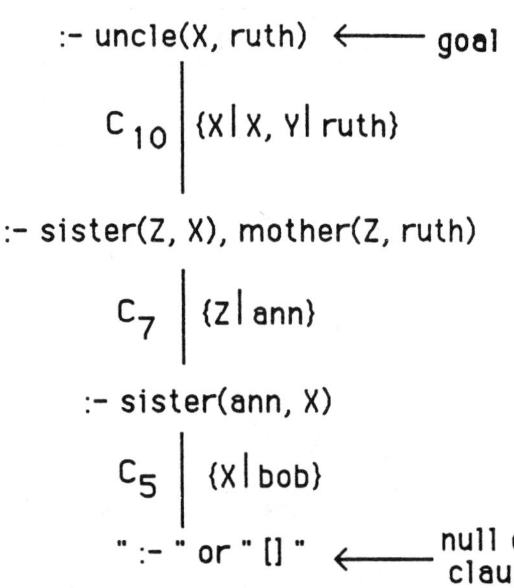

Figure 3—A possible proof sequence

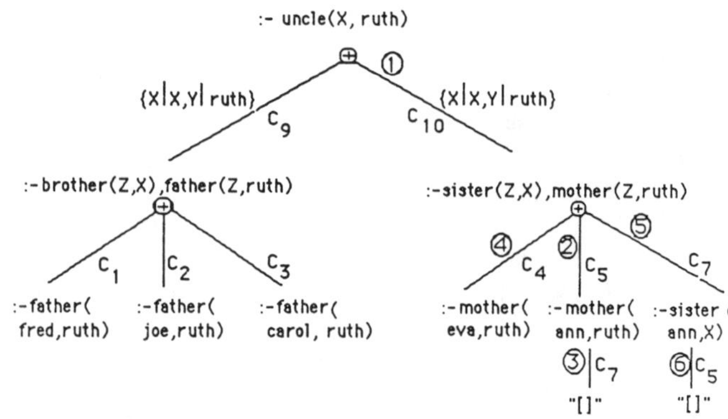

Figure 4—The search tree for the goal ":–uncle(X, ruth)"

that never terminate (not present in Figure 4). An important feature of the search tree is that it is an "OR" tree.[19] That is, to prove that any non-leaf node (resolvent or goal), in the tree is true, it is sufficient to prove that any of its children nodes ($child_1$ "OR" $child_2$ "OR" . . .) is true.

The resolution process is non-deterministic since at any step of the proof, the selection of a literal from those of a resolvent (step 1 of Figure 2) as well as the selection of a clause out of the set of ones unifiable with g (step 3) to participate in a resolution step, is performed in a non-deterministic fashion. That is, the resolution process makes, at these steps, the correct choice of a literal and a clause that leads to a solution. Therefore, the non-deterministic resolution process can be viewed as a process that finds (through making, somehow, the correct choices at the non-deterministic points) the successful proof sequences from all of the other ones in the search tree. The resolution process is semantically very powerful, since it guarantees finding all possible sequences leading to empty clauses (solutions) even in the presence of infinite sequences. Such power is not without a price. A non-deterministic process cannot be implemented (however, it can be simulated or approximated).[16] In addition, both space and time complexities of such processes are exponential in terms of number of levels in the search tree and, therefore, invoking even a small set of clauses with a goal can be very involved computationally. Practical logic-based systems try to implement deterministic algorithms that are equivalent in semantical power to (or even weaker than)* that of the presented algorithm but have improved space and/or time requirements. These systems simulate or approximate the non-determinism in the resolution process using procedures that search the different paths of the search tree (or a more efficient representation of the search space) for solutions. Such systems are presented next.

Parallelism in Logic Programming

The resolution process of logic programming contains many activities with ample embedded parallelism.[20] Step two of the algorithm presented in Figure 2 finds a set of qualified clauses

* PROLOG, for example, implements an inference algorithm that, under certain conditions, fails to generate solutions in the presence of infinite sequences.

S, each of which can unify with the literal of the current goal. Instead of selecting one of these qualified clauses to reduce the goal (producing a new resolvent), a procedure simulating the inference process can proceed to reduce the goal with two or more of the qualified clauses in parallel. Such simultaneous activities are referred to as *or* parallelism. Using such parallelism, for example, results in the simultaneous reduction of the goal ":–uncle(*X*, ruth)" using the two rules, "uncle(*X*, *Y*):–brother(*Z*,*X*),father(*Z*, *Y*)" and "uncle(*X*, *Y*):–sister (*Z*,*X*),mother(*Z*, *Y*)," of Figure 1. The *or* parallelism, when used, permits the inference process to find different solutions for the same goal (query), in parallel. The *or* parallelism is simple to exploit since *or* parallel activities, once initialized, do not interact with each other. One problem with the *or* parallelism is that when it is utilized recursively at each goal in the search tree, the generated parallel activities grow exponentially with respect to the number of levels in the search tree. The exponentially-generated activities are beyond the capability of any practical parallel processing system, and therefore, some methods have to be developed to restrict such parallelism.

A second type of parallelism is the so called *and* parallelism. Such parallelism corresponds to the simultaneous solution of two or more literals (subgoals) in a given goal (resolvent). Using such parallelism, for example, a solution for each of the subgoals ":–brother(*Z*,*X*)" and ":–father(*Z*, ruth)," of the goal is found in parallel. That is, the two search trees which correspond to the former subgoals are constructed and searched simultaneously to find a solution for each of the subgoals. When the literals in a goal have no shared (common) variables, then the solution for the goal is simply the concatenation of the individual solutions obtained for each of the literals in the goal. However, when shared variables between the literals exist (variable *Z* is shared between the two literals of the goal ":–brother(*Z*,*X*), father(*Z*, ruth)"), special care must be taken. A solution for the goal is not obtained by simply concatenating the individual solutions but by obtaining from them a solution in which the bindings for the shared variables are the same. To illustrate this point, consider obtaining the solution {*Z*/ted, *X*/bob} for the subgoal ":–brother(*Z*,*X*)," and the solution {*Z*/paul} for the subgoal ":–father(*Z*, ruth)." A solution for the conjunction of the two subgoals does not exist, because the two solutions bind different values for the shared variable *Z*. On the other hand, the solution {*Z*/ted} for the subgoal ":–father(*Z*, ruth)" together with the previous solution for the other subgoal produces a solution for the goal because the shared variable *Z* has the same value in both of the individual solutions. The problem of shared variables complicates, to a large extent, the utilization of *and* parallelism by a parallel processing system.

A third type of parallelism is the so called *search* parallelism. This parallelism corresponds to the simultaneous search of the set of clauses for those that can unify with a given literal (SIMD *search* parallelism and can be used to initialize *or* parallel activities) or the simultaneous search for clauses that can unify with different literals (MIMD search-parallelism and can be used by the *or* parallel or *and* parallel activities). *Search* parallelism is very important for parallel logic systems—especially those that contain very large logic bases.

A fourth type of parallelism is the so called *unification* parallelism. This parallelism corresponds to the parallel activities within the unification algorithm. In general, the amount of this type of parallelism is very small since the unification operation tends to have a rather sequential nature.[21] However, the *unification* parallelism can be of some advantage when both of the literals that participate in the unification operation contain many terms, each of which has a relatively complicated structure.

LOGIC MACHINES: GENERAL ARCHITECTURE AND A TAXONOMY

The entity "logic machine" can be defined as an aggregate of software and hardware components designed to simulate or approximate the computational model of logic programming. By the word "simulate" we refer to those systems that attain the full semantical power of logic programming (that is, for a query and a set of clauses, these systems generate all the solutions that can be generated by the non-deterministic inference process). By the word "approximate" we refer to those systems that implement a model of computation close to that of logic programming, but have less semantical power than logic programming (that is, they may not generate all possible solutions). In the following, an abstract (general) architecture and a taxonomy for logic machines proposed so far are presented.

General Architecture

From an architectural point of view, a logic machine, Figure 5 is organized into two major components, namely, the logic programming system and the underlying hardware system. In addition to the (user) queries (goals), the workload of such a computer system includes operations to manage, update, and maintain the knowledge stored in such a system. The logic programming system contains components for implementing or approximating the computational model of logic programming. These components, as shown in Figure 5, are the logic base (program) and the inference procedure.

The Logic Base

In general, the logic base (program) consists of a set of logical statements which express certain facts about a collection of real world objects and the relationships that exist between these objects.[1] These statements are taken from a language, a logic programming language, which serves as a tool for the user (programmer) to specify a logic program. Basically, these statements are horn clauses extended to include some extra information which helps the inference procedure (see the following section) to perform a more efficient search of the search space and/or to provide some explicit information about the sequence in which the literals in the body of a clause or the set of clauses in the logic program are to be processed by the inference procedure. For example, in the logic programming language PROLOG[13] the CUT operator "!" helps PROLOG's inference procedure to trim the space

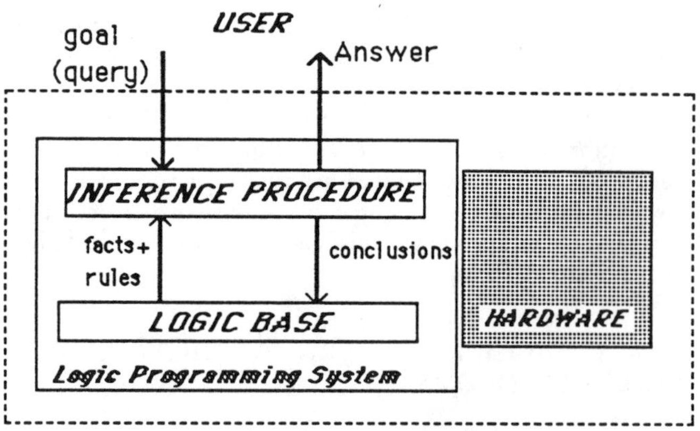

Figure 5—A general architecture for logic computers

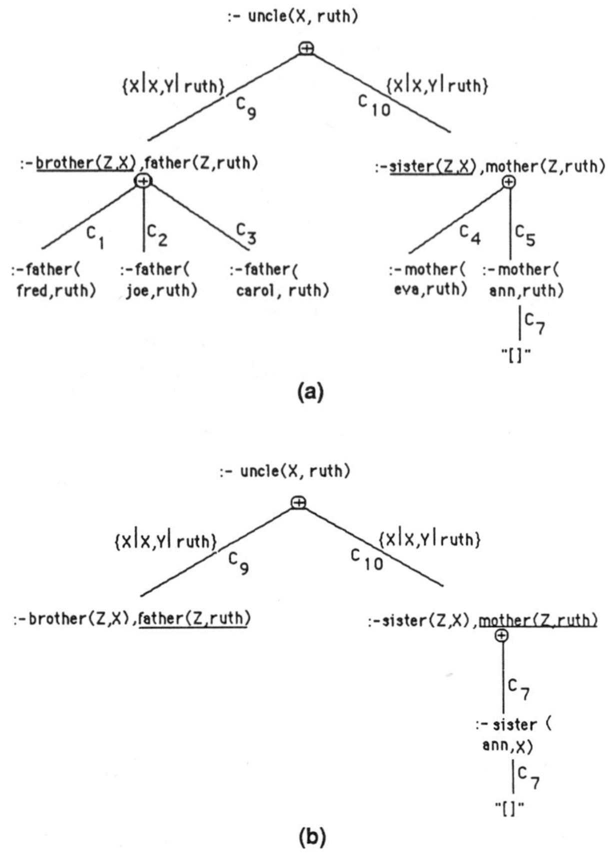

Figure 6—Two possible proof trees for ":–uncle(X, ruth)"

that is being searched for solutions for a given query. In PARLOG,[7] a parallel logic programming language, the literals in a clause are separated by either the operator "&" or the operator ",". The former indicates to the inference procedure that the literals within the body of a clause separated by such operator are to be executed sequentially, whereas the literals separated by the operator "," are to be executed in parallel. In a similar fashion, the horn clauses in PARLOG are separated by the operator "." or ";". Two clauses separated by "." are to be processed serially, whereas those separated by ";" are to be processed in parallel.

The Inference Procedure

The inference procedure simulates or approximates the resolution process of logic programming. For a given query, this procedure searches a more efficient representation of the search space than that of the search tree. One source of inefficiency in the resolution tree is the fact that it contains proof sequences which generate the same solutions (redundant proof sequences) for the same query and logic base. For example, in Figure 4, the two sequences $1 \rightarrow 2 \rightarrow 3$ and $1 \rightarrow 5 \rightarrow 6$ lead to the same solution for the query ":–uncle(X, ruth)," namely, "X = bob." An efficient inference procedure needs to generate (search) only one of these sequences but not both. The tree which has no redundant proof sequences is called the proof tree (another OR-tree). Such a tree is obtained by expanding only one literal from each resolvent at each level of the search tree (rather than by expanding all of the literals to generate all possible resolvents). Depending on which literal from each resolvent is expanded, a number of different proof trees can be obtained. These trees are equivalent[16] (that is, if a solution for the query can be obtained from one of these trees, then, the same solution can be obtained from every other tree) but have a different total number of proof sequences. A smart inference engine can take advantage of such arbitrary choice to generate and search the proof tree which has the minimum number of proof sequences. Figure 6 presents two possible proof trees for the goal ":–uncle(x, ruth)." These trees are generated by reducing the underlined literals in Figure 6 first. It is easy to see that searching both trees will generate the same solutions, however, searching the tree of Figure 6(b) will take much less time than searching the tree of Figure 6(a).

Still another source of inefficiency in the OR-tree representation of the search space is the high number of branches coming out from a node in such a tree (this factor is important for the efficient implementation of both sequential and parallel inference schemes.[22,23] To illustrate this point, consider the node (resolvent) ":–brother(Z,X),father(Z,Y)" and assume that only facts can unify with each of these literals and the number of these facts are n and m, respectively. The number of branches which come out from such a node equals $0(n \times m)$. To overcome such a high factor, a new, more efficient representation for the search space has been introduced, the AND/OR tree.[19] The basic principle underlying such representation is the replacement of each non-leaf node in the OR tree, such as the one shown in Figure 7, by two levels of nodes. The first level has only one AND node and the second level has as many OR nodes as the number of literals in the resolvent. The AND node is labeled by the (conjunctive) resolvent itself. The name AND is given to a such node because in order to prove that such a node is true, we have to prove that all of its children nodes (child1 and child2 and . . .) are true. Each OR node represents a resolvent of one literal (unit resolvent or subgoal) and needs to have only one of its children nodes to be true in order for itself to be true. A node in such representation has only $0(n + m)$ branches, a substantial reduction over that of the OR-tree representation. Figure

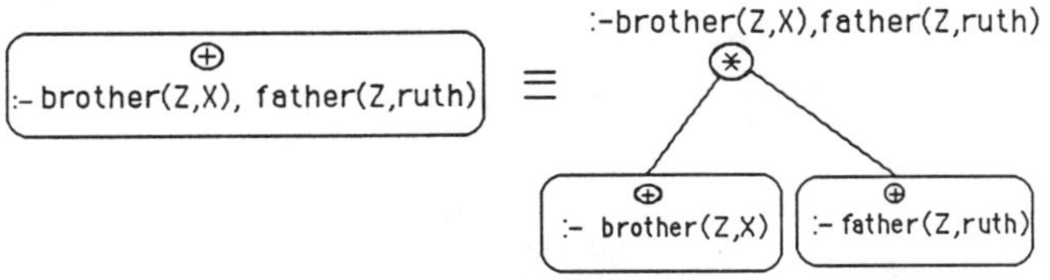

Figure 7—The transformation from the OR node to the AND/OR nodes representation

8 shows the AND/OR tree for the goal ":–uncle(X, ruth)" with respect to the logic base of Figure 1.

The AND/OR tree representation is not without problems. The search for solutions in such a tree is much more complicated than that of the OR-tree representation, since a solution in this representation has the form of a subtree rather than a sequence of branches from the root to a null leaf node.[24] For example, the subtree 1→4→5→4→2→3 of Figure 8 represents the solution for the query ":–uncle(X, ruth)." To search the OR-tree for solutions one needs to go only top down, but to search the AND/OR tree for solutions one needs to go first top-down until the leaf nodes are reached, then the search continues bottom-up.[24] Despite the complex search problem, most of the inference procedures in logic programming systems use the AND/OR tree representation of the search space because of its low branching property.

Many logic machines have been proposed so far. These machines can be viewed as points in an architectural space, the logic machine space. This space, Figure 9, is defined by two attributes which characterize the abstract architecture of Figure 5, namely, the search strategy and the hardware organization. The attribute *search strategy* specifies partially or completely the method by which the inference procedure in a logic machine performs the search of the AND/OR or the OR tree, respectively, for finding solutions. On the other hand, the attribute *hardware organization* specifies the way the hardware of the logic machine is organized to support the search of the tree. Three possible methods exist for searching a tree, namely, depth-first (DF), breadth-first (BR), and dynamic (DYN). In the depth-first method and starting from the root of the tree, the most recently generated children of an *or* node (*or* goal) get searched (reduced) first. In the breadth-first search, the children of an *or* node get reduced in the

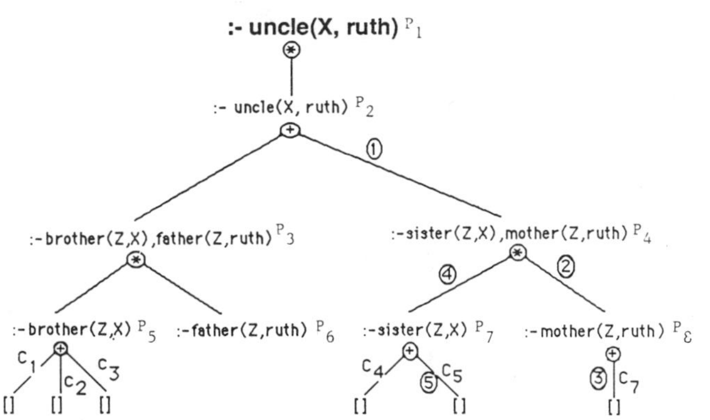

Figure 8—The AND/OR tree for ":–uncle(X, ruth)"

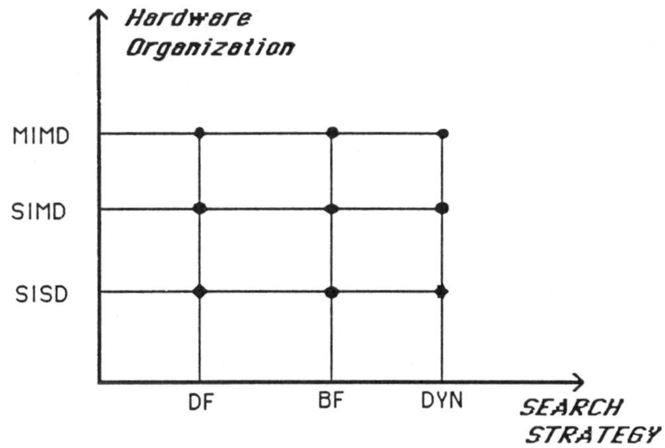

Figure 9—The architectural space of logic computers

order in which they are generated. In the dynamic search, the children of an *or* node are reduced in an order determined by some criteria. Such criteria can be preprogrammed in the inference procedure or specified by the user through the statements of the logic base (program). For the OR-tree representation of the search space, the previous methods fully specify the search strategy of the inference procedure since such tree contains nodes of only the or type. However, this is not the case for the AND/OR tree and in order to completely specify the search strategy of such a tree, one must specify the method by which the children of an and-node (subgoals) get reduced. We have omitted here such specification to keep our classification scheme as general as possible. However, such specification will be delayed until we present some of the proposed logic machines.

The hardware of a logic machine can be organized in three different ways, namely, as a single instruction stream-single data stream (SISD), single instruction stream-multiple data stream (SIMD), or multiple instruction stream-multiple data stream (MIMD) machine.[25] A logic machine in the SISD class is simply a classical von Neumann processor programmed to perform the serial search of the tree. Because of its serial nature, such a processor can be active at only one node of the tree at any point in time. The processor can be a classical processor with general-purpose instruction set or a special purpose processor that is tuned for efficiently implementing the serial search of the tree. Such tuning varies from simply extending the processor instruction set to include some more suitable instructions for the symbolic processing environment, all the way up to designing such a processor around a radically different instruction set which is more appropriate for supporting the logic processing environment. In addition, such a processor may include specialized hardware that takes advantage of the small amount of parallelism which exists in the processing of a node in the tree, such as unification parallelism, pipelined instruction, execution, and unification coprocessing.

A logic machine in the SIMD class is organized as an array of simple processors, each with its own local memory. These processors are controlled and managed by a single master processor. At any point in time, all the array processors are performing the same task on the different data elements stored in the processors' local memories. The master processor can have a general or special instruction set. An SIMD machine is a good search engine since the search operation can be performed in parallel on all the data elements in the array processors. Storing the logic base in the local memories of the array processors permits the efficient and parallel implementation of many search-based operations such as the unification operation. The SIMD class of logic machines is not popular since it can take advantage of only one type of logic programming parallelism, namely, the search parallelism (especially when processing very large logic bases). Such organization cannot take advantage of the other types of parallelism that exist in logic programming.

A logic machine in the MIMD class is organized as a set of independent processors intercommunicating over an interconnection network. The processors can be general-purpose or special-purpose ones and different types of interconnection networks[26] may be used. An important characteristic of this class of machines is the ability to perform one or more tasks in parallel. Actually, through the special design of the processor itself and through the interconnection of many of these processors together, such a machine can use not only the micro-parallelism but also the macro-parallelism imbedded in logic programs to speed up its evaluation. One important aspect of an MIMD machine is the scheme by which the machine's parallel activities are controlled and synchronized. Two broad classes of schemes have been developed, each is based on one of the basic concepts; control-flow and data-flow.[27,28] The former scheme is the parallelized version of the traditional control scheme adopted for the classical von Neumann processor. A computation in such a scheme is controlled directly by the programmer through the programming language. On the other hand, a computation in a data-flow based scheme is performed only when all of the computation's input data is available, thus permitting as much parallel activity as possible. The advantages and disadvantages of both of these approaches can be found in Arvind and Iannucci,[29] and in Gajski, Padua, Kuck, and Kuhn.[30] Both of these control schemes have been used by designers to develop MIMD logic machines.

Figure 10 presents some of the proposed logic computers classified according to the above scheme. Guided by such a classification scheme, an overview of a sample of the architectures will be presented next.

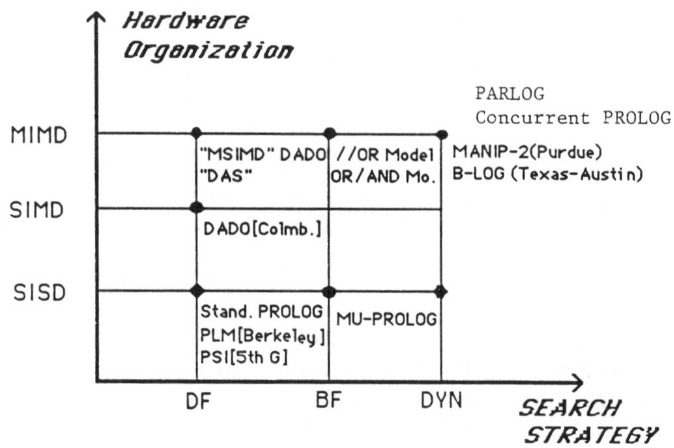

Figure 10—Some of the proposed logic computers

OVERVIEW OF SOME LOGIC MACHINES

The Depth-First-SISD Logic Machines

The logic machines in this class search the AND/OR tree representation of the search space using a single processor and the depth-first strategy to search the children of both the *or* nodes and *and* nodes of such representation. In processing the children (subgoals) of an *and* node using such a strategy, one can use one of two techniques: one-solution-at-a-time and all-solutions-at-a-time. Using the first technique, as shown in Figure 11, a solution is first obtained for $subgoal_1$. The solution is then used to instantiate the variables that are common to both the first and the rest of the node's subgoals. The processing of $subgoal_1$ is frozen and the processing of the second subgoal for finding a solution is activated. This process is repeated for all the subgoals of the *and* node. A solution to the *and* node is obtained if a solution is obtained for every subgoal in that node. Obtaining a new solution for any subgoal of the *and* node, $subgoal_i$ for example, is carried out using a technique called backtracking. Using such a technique, the $subgoal_i$ is first tried for a new solution using the old instantiations. If this fails, then the activation backtracks to the previous subgoal to obtain a new solution for that subgoal. Such a solution is then used to instantiate the variables in $subgoal_i$ and a new solution is tried. Such backtracking may propagate recursively to one or more of the subgoals previous to $subgoal_i$.

Processing an *and* node depth-first using the all-solution-at-a-time technique is performed, as shown ing Figure 11, through first obtaining all the solutions for $subgoal_1$. This set is then used to instantiate the variables that are common to the first and the rest of the node's subgoals. $Subgoal_1$ is then eliminated and the control is transferred to $subgoal_2$ to find all of its solutions. Such a process continues until all the subgoals of the *and* node have been processed. The set of solutions which has satisfied all the subgoals is then the solution set for the corresponding *and* node. It is important to note that using

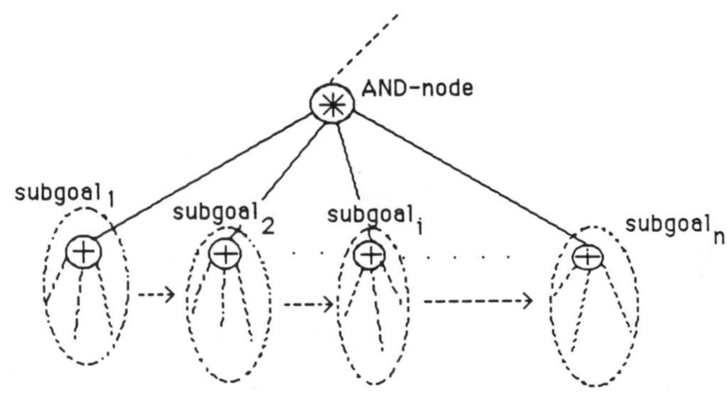

Figure 11—An AND node in and AND/OR tree

the all-solutions-at-a-time approach, the backtracking is no longer needed for processing the subgoals of an *and* node.

The search of the AND/OR tree representation using the depth-first strategy at both the *and* and *or* node levels and the use of the backtracking mechanism form the kernel of the inference procedure of PROLOG,[13] today's most known logic programming language (system). Such search strategies have permitted an elegant stack-based implementation for such inference mechanisms with excellent memory management schemes.[22] This implementation may take one of two forms: interpretation based or compilation based. In the former, the inference procedure is implemented as an interpreter program (written in some high-level language) and runs on a single general-purpose processor (the host). Such a program interprets the user query using the logic base to produce solutions. On the other hand, the compilation-based system includes a compiler which compiles the user query and the logic base to produce an object program which runs on the general-purpose processor.[31] The early implementations of PROLOG followed one of these methods. Although the compiler-based implementation is much faster than that of the interpreter-based implementation, nevertheless, both of these implementations resulted in slow PROLOG systems. To improve performance, several recent implementations which augment or replace the general-purpose processor with more suitable hardware have been proposed. PSI[32,33] and PEK[34] are special purpose PROLOG processors which implement the PROLOG Interpreter as a microprogram. In Robinson,[35] and Woo,[36,37] the general-purpose processor is augmented with a special-purpose hardware unification unit. Since the unification is a frequent operation when executing PROLOG programs, speeding up the execution of such operations results in a faster overall system.

PLM[38,39] and HPM[40] are true special-purpose PROLOG processors. These processors have been built to execute an instruction set, proposed by Warren,[41] specially designed to support PROLOG, its depth-first search strategy, and its backtracking mechanism. The instruction set is at a higher level than ordinary general-purpose instruction sets and includes instructions which directly perform the unification, memory management, and so forth. The execution of a query on such a processor is carried out by first compiling the query together with the logic base into statements using Warren's instruction set. Then the resulting program is executed by the specially designed processor. To further improve the execution speed of PROLOG programs, Tick and Warren[42] have proposed a pipelined PROLOG processor. Such a processor is essentially the same as PLM or HPM except that it is designed to pipeline the execution of Warren instructions.

The Breadth-First-MIMD Logic Machines

The logic machines in this class unfold and search the *or* nodes of the OR or the AND/OR tree representation of the query's search space using the breadth-first strategy. As a new level of *or* nodes is unfolded, one or more processes are assigned to search such nodes, thus creating a set of parallel processes which cooperate to produce solutions. Such an assembly of processes is assigned to the different processors of a multiprocessor machine for execution. The parallel OR and parallel AND/OR machines[43,44] are good representatives of this class and will be presented next.

The parallel OR machine[43,45] searches the OR-tree representation for solutions. The process assigned to an *or* node (the root node in Figure 6(a), for example) generates all of its children nodes by performing a resolution step on one of the node's literals and assigns a process to each one of the newly generated nodes (resolvents). The children processes inherit the binding environment from the parent process; thereafter the parent process is eliminated and each of the children processes repeats the parent's action. Such activities continue until a leaf node is reached by a process; thereafter, a new process for the leaf node is not generated, but rather a solution is reported to the system if the leaf node is of the null type. The assembly of processes execute on a multiprocessor system. Such execution is controlled through an elaborate token-based scheme.[45]

The parallel AND/OR machine[44,20] searches the AND/OR-tree representation for solutions. A process, the and-process, assigned to supervise the execution of an *and* node (the root node in Figure 8, for example), generates one or-process for each one of its children nodes (or, in other words, for each of the literals in the body of the corresponding resolvents). An *or* node (process), in turn, generates an and-process to supervise the execution of each of its children *and* nodes (conjunctive resolvents). For example, the or-process P_2 associated with the node ":–uncle(X, ruth)" in Figure 8, generates two and-processes P_3 and P_4 to supervise the execution of each of the resolvents ":–brother(Z,X), father(Z, ruth)" and ":–sister(Z,X), mother(Z, ruth)," respectively. As a solution is obtained for the variables in the literal of an or-process (the literal "sister(Z,X)" of Figure 8, for example), a "success" message and the obtained solution are reported to the parent and-process P_4. The P_4, then, invokes the or-process associated with its second child P_8, passes to it the variable bindings and requests a solution to the remaining free variables of the associated literal. P_7 is then blocked. When an and-process receives success messages from all of its children, it passes on a similar message to its parent together with the obtained bindings for the free variables. The and-process is then blocked. Such activities continue until the and-process of the root receives a "success" message from all of the or-processes associated with its children nodes. The bindings to the free variables in the query form a solution for the query.

The parallel AND/OR scheme is designed to run on a loosely coupled multiprocessor (no shared memory is required) in which processors (processes) exchange information via message passing. Many improvements to this basic scheme have been proposed. In Furukawa, Nitta, and Matsumoto,[46] the parallel AND/OR scheme is modified such that when a process reports a "success" message and a solution to its parent process, it is ordered to continue finding a second solution. The process is then blocked only when the second solution is found and the parent node is still processing the first one (limited form of pipelining).

In the parallel AND/OR scheme reported in Lindstorm and Pnangaden,[47] a process never gets blocked, but rather it continues supplying its parent process with solutions until it runs out of them; thereafter such a process is eliminated. Such a scheme includes many more parallel activities than the AND/OR model of Conery and approaches the amount of parallelism encountered in the parallel OR model of Ciepielewski.[43]

DeGroot[48] suggests the partitioning of the set of literals in the body of a resolvent (the children of an *and* node) into subsets such that no literals with shared variables can exist in two different subsets. The independent subsets are then processed in parallel. The new scheme is stack-based which eliminates the need to generate the large number of processes encountered in Conery's scheme.[20] It also eliminates the need to pass information around via messages; a large reduction in the overhead encountered when processing a query.

The Dynamic-MIMD Logic Machines

The logic machines in this class unfold and search the nodes in the tree representation of the query search space for a single solution in an order determined by some criteria. Such criteria can be specified by the user through the statements of the logic base (program) as in the concurrent logic-based languages, Concurrent PROLOG[8] and PARLOG[7] or preprogrammed in the inference procedure as in Li and Wah[23] and Lipovski and Hermenegildo.[49] In the latter case, a heuristic function[19] guides the search of the inference procedure for a solution.

Concurrent PROLOG[8] and PARLOG[7] bear a close resemblance to each other. They are both designed to execute on parallel machines. These logic systems use an extended version of horn clauses—the guarded horn clauses. Such a clause has the following format:

$$S0{:}{-}C1,C2,\ldots \mid S1,S2\ldots$$

where $S0$ and "$S1,S2,\ldots$" are the same as in an ordinary horn clause. "|" is the guard operator and "$C1,C2\ldots$" is a conjunction of literals which form what is called the guard condition. Procedurally, the above clause states that $S0$ can be replaced with "$S1,S2\ldots$" only after the guard condition "$C1,C2\ldots$" evaluates to "true." Or, in other words, control is passed from $S0$ to the conjunction of literals to the right of the guard (the body of an ordinary horn clause) only after the conjunction of literals to the left of the guard evaluates to "true." The literals in the guard condition are not allowed to instantiate any variables as they execute.

The Concurrent PROLOG and PARLOG search the AND/OR tree representation. As a new level of *and* nodes in the tree is unfolded (refer to Figure 8), each node is assigned a process, an and-process, to supervise the execution of the body of the corresponding guarded clause. Every and-process, in parallel, evaluates the guard condition associated with the corresponding *and* node. The first process to evaluate its guard to "true" is allowed to unfold the tree further (that is, the control is transferred from $S0$ to "$S1,S2,\ldots$"), while all of the other competing processes are cancelled. An and-process evaluates a guard condition by assigning one or-process to supervise the execution of each of the literals in such a guard condition. In Concurrent PROLOG,[8] the or-processes evaluating the different literals of a guard execute in parallel. In PARLOG,[7] the programmer can specify the sequence (serial or parallel) in which the or-processes evaluate a given guard. The programmer can also specify the sequence in which the different *and* nodes of the same level execute. PARLOG has been implemented on a reduction-based multiprocessor system called ALICE.[50] Recently, a new machine consisting of a set of processors, each specially designed to execute PARLOG, is being investigated. A processor in such a machine is built to support a newly proposed instruction set[51,52] especially designed to support the process-based search strategy of PARLOG. A multiprocessor called the Bagel[53] has been proposed to execute Concurrent PROLOG. The Bagel is a set of transputers[54] interconnected through a modified mesh network called the torus.[55,56]

The search strategy adopted by Concurrent PROLOG and PARLOG replaces the notation of nondeterminism (taking the right choice) of the resolution process with indeterminism (taking an arbitrary choice). That is, to find a solution for a query only one path in the tree is tried. If the path leads to a solution, then the query succeeds and this solution is returned to the user; otherwise, the query fails without trying to search the other paths in the tree. Because of adopting such a search strategy, both Concurrent PROLOG and PARLOG are semantically weaker than logic programming. That is, even if a solution exists for a query, there is no guarantee that these systems will be able to produce such solution. Finding such a solution depends largely on the way the various generated processes are scheduled for execution.

MANIP-2,[23] a multicomputer system consisting of a set of computers interconnected through a global broadcast bus and a selection and redistribution network, has been proposed to process logic programs in parallel. It implements a parallel heuristic search of the AND/OR or the OR/AND tree representation of the logic program for finding a single solution. Such a search is guided by a heuristic function that uses the ratio of the success probability of a literal (*or* node) to the estimated overhead of evaluating such literal.

COMMENTS AND CONCLUDING REMARKS

In this paper we have presented a taxonomy for a class of computer architectures called logic machines that use special-purpose hardware and/or parallel processing to speed up the processing of logic. Guided by such a taxonomy, some of the proposed logic machines have been overviewed. Some general comments concerning the proposed logic machines are presented below.

The taxonomy presented in the section on parallelism groups the logic machines, proposed so far, according to the strategy of search carried out by the corresponding machine; the machines fall into three classes, namely, the depth-first, breadth-first, and dynamic. From a semantic point of view, machines that use breadth-first search implement the computational model of logic programming faithfully. However, those machines that use the depth-first search implement a model of computation weaker than that of logic programming. Unless special care is taken, when infinite branches are present in the search tree of a logic program, these machines cannot produce some or all of the solutions that can be generated by the non-deterministic resolution processes. Depending on the heuristics adopted by the logic machine in the dynamic class, such a machine may implement faithfully the model of logic programming, as in MANIP-2,[23] or much weaker computational models as those implemented by PARLOG[7] and Concurrent PROLOG.[8]

Machines in the breadth-first class have exponential storage and execution time complexities with respect to the number of levels in the search tree of logic programs. Such complexities remain exponential even when a polynomial number of processors are used in the execution of logic programs.[57] The exponential storage requirement is a severe drawback of machines in the breadth-first class, especially when the search tree is deep. Some mechanisms must be designed to limit the maximum width of the tree during execution as in Epilog[58] logic system. Machines in the depth-first class require exponential time complexity and linear storage. This is a great plus to this type of machine. Machines in the dynamic class require variable time and storage complexities depending on the heuristic function being used in association with the particular machine.

From the parallelism point of view, the breadth-first machines can take advantage of all the parallelism embedded in the computational model of logic programming. However, only "and," "search," and "unification" parallelism can be used by the logic machines in the depth-first class. The amount of parallelism available to a machine in the dynamic class varies depending on the type of heuristic function being used.

REFERENCES

1. Genersereth, M.R. and M.L. Ginsberg. "Logic Programming." *ACM Communications,* 28 (1985) 9, pp. 933–941.
2. Kowalski, R., "Logic Programming." *IFIP Proceedings,* 1983, pp. 133–145.
3. Kowalski, R., *Logic for Problem Solving.* North Holland, New York, 1979.
4. Chikayama, T. et al. "A Draft Proposal of Fifth Generation Kernel Language," Technical memo of ICOT, TM-007, 1982.
5. Clark, K.L., and F.G. McCabe. *Micro-PROLOG: Programming in Logic.* Prentice-Hall, Englewood Cliffs, NJ, 1984.
6. Clark, K.L., F.G. McCabe, and S. Gregory. "IC-PROLOG Language Features." In K.L. Clark and S.A. Tarnlund (eds.), *Logic Programming.* Academic Press, London, 1982, pp. 253–266.
7. Clark, K. and S. Gregory. "PARLOG: Parallel Programming in Logic." *ACM Transaction on Programming Languages and Systems,* 8 (January 1986) 1, pp. 1–49.
8. Shapiro, E. "A Subset of Concurrent Prolog and Its Interpreter," ICOT Technical Report TR-003, 1983.
9. Suzuki, N. "Concurrent Prolog as an Efficient VLSI Design Language." *IEEE Computer,* February, 1985, pp. 33–40.
10. Citrin, W., P. Van Roy, and A. Despain. "A Prolog Compiler." *Proceedings of HICSS-19,* 1986.
11. Broda, K. and S. Gregory. "PARLOG for Discrete Event Simulation." *Proceedings of the 2nd International Logic Programming Conference,* 1984, pp. 301–312.
12. Moto-oka, T. "Overview to the Fifth Generation Computer System Project." *Proceedings of 10th International Symposium on Computer Architecture,* 1983.
13. Clocksin, W.F. and C.S. Mellish. *Programming in Prolog.* Springer-Verlag, 1984.
14. Lloyd, J.W. "Foundation of Logic Programming," Technical report 82/7, Department of Computer Science, University of Melbourne, 1982.
15. Robinson, J.A. "A Machine-Oriented Logic Based on the Resolution Principle." *Journal of the ACM,* 12(1985)1, pp. 23–41.
16. Sterling, L. and E. Shapiro. *The Art of Prolog.* The MIT Press, 1986.
17. Apt, K.R. and M.H. van Emden. "Contributing to the Theory of Logic Programming." *Journal of the ACM,* 29 (1982), pp. 841–862.
18. Clark, K.L. *Predicate Logic as a Computational Formalism.* Springer-Verlag, 1984.
19. Nilsson, N.J. *Principles of Artificial Intelligence.* Tioga, Palo Alto, CA, 1980.
20. Conery, J. and D. Kibler. "Parallel Interpretation of Logic Programming." *Proceedings of the ACM Conference on Functional Programming Languages and Computer Architecture, 1981,* pp. 163–170.
21. Dwork, C., P. Kanellakis, and J. Mitchell. "On the Sequential Nature of Unification." *J. Logic Programming,* 1984, pp. 35–50.
22. van Emden, M.H. "An interpreting algorithm for Prolog programs." *Proceedings of the First International Logic Programming Conference,* 1982.
23. Li, G. and B.W. Wah. "MANIP-2: A Multicomputer Architecture for Evaluating Logic Programs." *Proceedings of the International Conference on Parallel Processing,* 1985, pp. 123–130.
24. Nilsson, N.J. *Problem-Solving Methods in Artificial Intelligence.* McGraw-Hill, 1971.
25. Flynn, M. J., Some Computer Organization and their Effectiveness." *IEEE Transaction on Computers,* Vol. C-23, No. 2, pp. 121–132.
26. Siegel, H.J. *Interconnection Networks for Large-Scale Parallel Processing.* Lexington Books, 1985.
27. Treleaven, P.C. "The New Generation of Computer Architecture." *Proceedings of the 10th Annual International Symposium on Computer Architecture,* 1983, pp. 402–409.
28. Treleaven, P.C. et al. "Data-driven and Demand-driven Computer Architecture." *ACM Computing Surveys,* 14 (March 1982) 1, pp. 93–143.
29. Arvind and Iannucci. "A Critique of Multiprocessing von Neumann Style." *Proceedings of the 10th Annual International Symposium on Computer Architecture.* 1983, pp. 426–436.
30. Gajski, D.D., D.A. Padua, D.J. Kuck, and R.H. Kuhn. "A Second Opinion on Data Flow Machines and Languages." *IEEE Trans. on Computers,* February, 1982, pp. 58–69.
31. Warren, D.H.D. "Implementing PROLOG-Compiling Predicate Logic Programs." Department of Artificial Intelligence, University of Edinburgh, Technical Reports #39–40, May 1977.
32. Yokota, M. et al. "A Microprogrammed Interpreter for the Personal Sequential Inference Machine." *Proceedings of the International Conference on Fifth Generation Computer Systems,* 1984, pp. 410–418.
33. Yokota, M. et al. "The Design and Implementation of a Personal Sequential Inference Machine-PSI." *New Generation Computing,* Vol. 1, No. 2, 1983.
34. Tamara, K. et al. "Sequential Prolog Machine PEK." *Proceedings of the International Conference on the Fifth Generation Computer Systems,* 1984, pp. 542–550.
35. Robinson, P., "The SUM: An AI Coprocessor." *Byte,* June 1985, pp. 169–180.
36. Woo, N.S. "A Hardware Unification Unit: Design and Analysis." *12th Annual International Symposium on Computer Architecture,* 1985, pp. 198–205.
37. Woo, N.S. "The Architecture of the Hardware Unification Unit and an Implementation." *The 18th Annual Workshop on Microprogramming,* December 1985.
38. Dobry, T.P., A.M. Despain, and Y.N. Patt. "Performance Studies of a Prolog Machines Architecture." *The 12th Annual International Symposium of Computer Architecture,* 1985, pp. 180–190.
39. Dobry, T.P., Y.N. Patt, and A.M. Despain. "Design Decisions Influencing the Microarchitecture for a Prolog Machine." *Proceedings of the 17th Annual Workshop on Microprogramming,* Octobber 1984, pp. 217–231.
40. Nakazaki, A., et al. "Design of a High Speed Prolog Machine (HPM)." *The 12th Annual International Symposium on Computer Architecture,* 1985, pp. 191–197.
41. Warren, D.H. "An Abstract Prolog Instruction Set." Technical Note 209, SIR International, Menlo Park, CA, 1983.
42. Tick, E. and D. Warren. "Towards a Pipelined Prolog Processor."

Proceedings of Internatinal Symposium on Logic Programming, 1984, pp. 29–40.

43. Ciepielewski, A. and S. Haridi. "A Formal Model for or Parallel Execution of Logic Programs." *Proceedings of IFIP83,* pp. 299–306.
44. Conery, J. "The AND/OR Process Model for Parallel Interpretation of Logic Programs," Technical Report #204, University of California, Irvine, 1983.
45. Ciepielewski, A. and S. Haridi. "Execution of Bagof on the or-parallel Token Machine." *Proceedings of the International Conference on Fifth-Generation Computer Systems,* 1984, pp. 551–560.
46. Furukawa, K., K. Nitta, and Y. Matsumoto. "Prolog Interpreter Based on Concurrent Programming." *Proceedings of the First International Logic Programming Conference,* 1982, pp. 38–44.
47. Lindstorm, G. and P. Pnangaden. "Stream-Based Execution of Logic Programs." *International Symposium on Logic Programming,* 1984, pp. 168–176.
48. DeGroot, D. "Restricted AND Parallelism." *Proceedings of the International Conference on Fifth-Generation Computer Systems,* 1984, pp. 471–478.
49. Lipovski, G.J. and M.V. Hermenegildo. "B-log: A Branch and Bound Methodology for the Parallel Execution of Logic Programs." *Proceedings of the International Conference on Parallel Processing,* 1985, pp. 560–567.
50. Darlington, J. and M.J. Reeve. "ALICE: A Multiprocessor Reduction Machine." *Proceedings of the ACM Conference on Functional Programming Languages and Computer Architecture,* October 1981, pp. 65–75.
51. Gregory, S., "Implementing PARLOG on the Abstract PROLOG Machine," Research Report DOC 84/23, Department of Computing, Imperial College, London, 1984.
52. McCabe, F.G. "Abstract Prolog Machine: A Specification," Research Report Doc 83/12, Department of Computing, Imperial College, London, 1984.
53. Shapiro, E. "Lecture Notes on the Bagel: A Systolic Concurrent Prolog Machine," ICOT, Technical Report TM-0031, 1983.
54. INMOS Limited. "IMS-T424 Transputer Advance Information," INMOS, 1983.
55. Martin, A.J. "The Torus: An Exercise in Constructing a Processing Surface." *Proceedings of the Conference on Very Large Scale Integration: Architecture, Design and Fabrication,* 1979, pp. 52–57.
56. Sequin, C.H. "Doubly Twisted Torus Networks for VLSI Processor Arrays." *Proceedings of the Eighth International Conference on Computer Architecture,* IEEE, 1981, pp. 471–480.
57. Wah, B.W., G. Li, and C.F. Yu. "Multiprocessing of Combinatorial Search Problems." *IEEE Computer,* June, 1985.
58. Wise, M.J. "A Parallel Prolog: The Construction of a Data-Driven Model." *Symposium on Lisp and Functional Programming,* pp. 56–66.

CD-ROM: The Microsoft perspective

by CARL STORK
Microsoft Corporation
Redmond, Washington

Compact Disc Read Only Memory (CD-ROM) is the ideal medium for distribution of information. CD-ROM features high capacity (550 megabytes), low cost, convenience, durability, and a worldwide standard. Eight different companies manufacture CD-ROM drives.

So far, CD-ROM has been used mainly in vertical applications areas such as medicine, science, finance, and libraries. CD-ROM has provided clear benefits for these applications through reduced cost, improved accessibility of information, and easier updating.

Microsoft Corporation recently announced a general purpose CD-ROM product, Microsoft Bookshelf. Microsoft Bookshelf contains a library of ten of the most useful reference works for anyone writing or editing with a PC. The innovative product includes a dictionary, thesaurus, and a ZIP code directory, as well as, The World Almanac and Book of Facts, the University of Chicago Manual of Style, Bartlett's Familiar Quotations, and more. Microsoft Bookshelf helps the PC user write more accurately, more precisely, and more creatively by making these reference works available from within a word processor at the touch of a keystroke.

Amdek Corporation, best known for its line of PC monitors, has recently announced a CD-ROM drive, the Laserdrive-1, to be sold through retail computer dealers. Amdek will include a copy of Microsoft Bookshelf with its drive.

These developments are enabling the use of CD-ROM in a general purpose PC environment. As a larger base of CD-ROM drives is established, software developers and publishers will be able to enhance their offerings by making them available on CD-ROM without having to justify the purchase of a drive for just one application. Publication of common, low cost information will be a primary use of CD-ROM as will publication of specialized information. The benefits of CD-ROM will enhance existing applications by facilitating production of better tutorials and help systems which include audio, an increased number of examples, style sheets, templates, and product drivers, and by incorporating advances in artificial intelligence research to make possible entirely new classes of applications, such as Microsoft Bookshelf.

Microsoft has also developed MS-DOS CD-ROM Extensions which allow standard IBM PCs and compatibles to read files from CD-ROM discs in a transparent fashion. The Extensions, which are included with many CD-ROM drives, provide the CD-ROM disc interface to allow most existing programs to read CD-ROM files without modification. The MS-DOS CD-ROM Extensions read discs in the "High Sierra" format which has been adopted by most CD-ROM developers.

With CD-ROM moving from very specialized vertical applications to more general purpose uses, the CD-ROM industry is now looking at adding multi-media capabilities to CD-ROM. The concept of interactive compact disc (ICD) marries a CD-ROM player to a computer capable of displaying image-quality graphics, and playing audio. ICD will be an important concept in bringing CD-ROM (and computers!) to the broadest possible base of users, and also in delivering the benefits of CD-ROM to consumers in the home. RCA has recently announced a new technology called DVI (Digital Video Interactive) which could play an important role in ICD systems. Philips has proposed an ICD system called CD-I. There is still a lot of work to be done before ICD systems are introduced to the market.

Hardware and operating system perspectives on CD-ROM

by MARK T. EDMEAD
MTE Associates, Inc.
Del Mar, California

INTRODUCTION

This paper discusses the particular steps that take place in the integration of a CD-ROM player to a computer. The computer can treat the CD-ROM player like any other external data storage device, however, a CD-ROM has a low data transfer rate as well as a low access time. The minimum data transfer rate for a CD-ROM player to a host computer is 176Kb/sec as compared with 625Kb/sec for a hard disk. Access time to the information is around one second compared to 0.15 second for the hard disk. To improve performance special software or hardware is needed.

One way to compensate for the slow data transfer rate is to use a Small Computer Systems Interface (SCSI). Most of the SCSI configurations are single-initiator, single-target-systems, with the CPU being the initiator and the CD-ROM player the target. The SCSI bus allows quick transfers of information and commands to I/O devices via a standard command protocol. This protocol sends command-description messages to target processors that process the commands. To improve the operation, the CD-ROM drive needs to provide an interim storage space for the data between the disc and the CPU. A single-ported cache buffer can provide this capability. RAM buffers are placed in the SCSI controller to allow faster data collection. Using DMA the transfer rate between devices is increased. The current CD-I standard calls for 2 DMA channels in the microprocessor. This eliminates disc to CPU transfer time by loading the process directly into DMA.

A LOOK AT DIRECT MEMORY ACCESS (DMA)

The function of the DMA controller is to transfer a series of operands (data) between the system memory and a peripheral device. Operands can be in the form of bytes, words or long words (32 bit). With cycle stealing, the data is transferred in a single cycle. In a burst mode, the transfer is up to 64 kbytes per burst.

When the DMA controller receives a valid request for data transfer from a peripheral device, it arbitrates for and obtains ownership of the system bus. By asserting its Bus Request line (BR), it indicates that it desires to be the bus master. The processor is at a lower priority level than external devices. After completing the last cycle it had started, the processor will give control to the controller. Then, it puts the bus up for arbitration through its own Bus Grant output (BG). When a device enables the BG input, it becomes the bus master.

The controller will then wait until the Address Strobe (AS), Data Transfer Acknowledge (DTACK), and the Bus Grant Acknowledge (BGACK) signals become inactive before assuming command of the bus again. Next, the controller activates its BG line and proceeds to transfer data. At the completion of this phase, it gives back ownership of the bus by de-activating its BGACK output.

SMALL COMPUTER SYSTEM INTERFACE (SCSI)

SCSI adds flexibility and performance to many design concepts. The SCSI bus supports a maximum of 8 units. This limitation can be overcome by the use of a LAN. In addition, each SCSI device can support seven additional logical units, plus one master. Because SCSI serves as its own "traffic cop," the user's only concern is the management of the data at the host adapter.

Most SCSI devices are in the 12-Mhz range. This is about 1.5 megabytes per second. This range can be increased to about 32 MHz at distances of 50 feet. The rate then would be around 4 Mb/sec. SCSI also provides a rich set of commands and defined bus structures. The SCSI standard calls for eight command-description byte (CDB) groups. Groups 0, 1, and 5 are reserved for general purpose instructions, groups 2, 3, and 4 are reserved by the National Bureau of Standards, and groups 6 and 7 are vendor specific.

A computer equipped with a SCSI bus requires a few commands to retrieve the information from the CD-ROM player. The computer has a key to the desired record and the logical block starting address of the file. The host adapter acquires control of the bus and it sends a Search Data Equal command to the player. This provides the logical address for the file.

The player automatically moves the laser beam that reads the information from the compact disc. This is done through the SCSI based disc controller that locates the proper physical address on the disc. The CD-ROM player then signals the end of search to the source by sending a status byte with the Condition Met bit set. This is then followed by a Linked Command Complete message. The host adapter sends the disc controller a Read command which contains the number of blocks to be read and a logical block offset address. The controller then transfers the data to the host adapter. If the search for the key fails, the Condition Met bit is cleared in the status byte which is sent to the host adapter. This is followed by a Command Complete message, and the Read command waiting in the host adapter is purged and not set to the target.

The development of SCSI drivers can be very complicated. The user must have a good understanding of the device and its operating system. Problems are compounded by the makers of SCSI busses. They are insisting on system and device-specific device drivers.

In order to understand what the player is actually reading, it is important to learn the data structure format of a CD-ROM sector. One sector contains 2352 bytes. The first 12K bytes are used for synchronization purposes. The next 4 bytes contain header information. The first 3 bytes of the header are reserved for sector addressing and the 4th byte denotes the mode. The next 2K bytes are user data, then 4 bytes for error detection code, 8 bytes of space, 172 bytes of P-parity and 104 Q-parity error correction code.

The mode byte describes the nature of the user data. Mode 1 is used in applications which require maximum data integrity. Mode 2 is used for applications where the integrity is not an important issue (home or consumer applications). Mode 2 provides 288 bytes of additional user data.

After accounting for the synchronization header, and error detection and correction bytes, one disc contains 270K blocks of user data at 2048 bytes per sector yielding about 540 mbytes of usable data space. With the use of a sophisticated data search routine, the user can search the disc for a particular pattern or patterns. Each section can be encoded with an address bit which is then linked to a search pattern algorithm and the beginning of the disc. This algorithm would be placed in RAM for maximum execution speed. If the pattern is found, the program supplies the address byte sector information so the laser beam can move to the exact location. If the pattern is not found, the program notes this and exits. This reduces the wasted search time normally taken to search on hard or floppy disks.

BASIC COMPONENTS OF A CD-ROM SYSTEM

As in any computer system integration procedure, it is important to keep in mind the various components used. Design procedures require a study of the long and short term goals of the proposed system. In designing a computer system, there are six basic elements to be considered. These elements apply to CD-ROM system integration as well.

Capture

Where is the data coming from? In what form is it stored? These are important questions to answer, since without data, the system is useless. Recent developments in laser technology enable input data to be received from a number of sources. Optical Character Readers (OCR) can digitize a page and allow editing on the screen. Other digitizers allow pictures and diagrams to be digitized. These are frequently useful for CD-ROM applications.

Manipulation

Once the data are available, editing may be necessary. Recent advancements in desktop publishing software provide extensive cut-and-paste capabilities. A wide variety of editors can be used to modify textual information.

Storage

In order to maximize access time, careful thought must be given to the data storage techniques. During this process, the information is identified by name, size, and location. An indexing scheme is used to "tag" the information. There is no set procedure for this process since it is dependent on the application and retrieval software.

Of concern also is the "disc geographical layout." This refers to the physical layout of the data on the disc. Geographical location greatly affects the speed with which an application can access and display the data. Storage methods include contiguous or sequential files, mapped files (as on a hard disk), and interleaved files (files broken into 2K blocks and stored in spiral fashion). Interleaving is practical for reducing access time between related files. For instance, a file containing a database can be interleaved with a file containing its indices.

The data then needs to be compressed. This is accomplished by eliminating empty space and repetitive areas. Several data compression schemes are available for both text and video. One of the techniques is "Entropy Reduction." This method reduces data by replacing repetitive items with a short code.

Retrieval

This element is the software that determines the location of the desired information on the CD. Specialized retrieval software is necessary for particular applications. Because of the large amounts of data that can be stored on CD and the current limitations of transfer rates, careful design of the retrievel software is essential.

For most CD-ROM applications, the retrieval software will behave similarly to a database management system. The program requires a stand-alone indexing scheme to remember where each piece of information is stored.

Transmission

Some applications may call for users to access information from on-line databases. Several companies are setting up such systems. Again, careful thought must be given to the type of data to be transmitted, the transmission rate, and primarily to the type of error detection and correction techniques to be established.

Display

Depending on the application, this software can be complex or relatively simple. Display software represents a large variable in CD-ROM system design. Resolution, aspect ratios, and pixel configurations all play important roles in the selection and installation of a display system.

All of these elements play an important role in the integration of any computer system. They apply equally to CD-ROM. The design process must be laid out properly and appropriately from application to application.

Real-time operating system design for CD-ROM using OS-9

by PETER GALLANIS
MicroTRENDS, Inc.
Schaumburg, Illinois

The implementation of a multi-media compact disc product (CD ROM) requires some means of supporting and coordinating multiple tasks, where each task performs a specialized function, related in some way to others. For example, consider a multi-media version of a "how to" book. In addition to the usual text requirements, you have the considerations of sound, graphics, and possibly video. A more specific example would be a segment on automobile tuneups. This could include a video image of where the adjustment would be made, the sound of the engine as the adjustment is made, and a graphic display of a piece of test equipment.

These multi-media applications achieve their level of integration by defining specialized tasks to perform each function, like an audio processor for speech and sound, as well as a graphics task for producing graphics. This requires some level of multi-tasking, which may need to be hardware-interrupt driven.

OS-9/68000 is a small and fast multi-tasking operating system for the 68000 family of processors. The kernel, which is 13K in size, provides the functionality of a UNIX (tm) operating system, with a flexible I/O and file system. Tasks are, by design, re-entrant which make them excellent candidates for "ROMing," in fact all of the operating system and applications can be contained in ROM.

OS-9/68000 provides multi-tasking on a priority and event basis along with priority aging to ensure that a process will eventually get some CPU time. Time-slicing occurs when processes of the same priority are awaiting execution, and this occurs on each clock tick (typically 100 times a second). As an interrupt occurs, the first task in a prioritized list gets control, and can pass the interrupt on to others in that queue. By combining the re-entrancy of the processes and TRAP interrupt handling, generic run-time libraries can be accessed system-wide. In fact, the console I/O routines and mathematical routines are implemented in just such a way.

Multi-tasking also carries with it a requirement for coordination of these tasks. OS-9/68000 provides numerous methods of synchronization in addition to normal hardware-interrupt processing. One such facility is the event mechanism, that is an extension of a semaphore technique. Events are defined at runtime (and later referencable by ASCII name from any task) with a constant that is added to a counter every time a task "POSTS" the event. A task waiting for the named event can specify the range of counter values to be considered.

Another form of synchronization available is inter-task communication. Signals are used as a method of forwarding a "signal number" to a task that has defined an interception routine. In addition, named "pipes" can be used to send actual data to tasks waiting at the receiving end of the pipe.

An additional feature worth mentioning is the operating system's ability to define named data areas that may be shared among many tasks. This allows tasks to access global data in a standardized yet flexible manner.

The OS-9/68000 I/O system provides for device as well as data structure independence. An I/O device is defined at three levels. The highest level is the file manager which coordinates all access to all devices of that file category (character sequential, random block, random sequential). The next level is the device driver which is responsible for performing I/O to devices with similar characteristics much as a disk controller controls multiple disk spindles. The lowest level is a device descriptor that is really a table that ties together the file manager and device driver responsible for I/O to the specific device. OS-9/68000 treats each of these as normal processes (albeit supervisor state processes), which means that they can be loaded at any time as well as ROMable.

Another feature that demonstrates the flexibility of OS-9 is that the file system format is defined by the file manager. A native file structure is distributed with disk versions of the O/S which provides for a hierarchical structure with the USER and GROUP concept for files and directories. A completely foreign file structure can be defined by implementing another file manager, such as one supporting the High Sierra Specification structure for CD ROMs. Multiple file managers can co-exist within the O/S, and OS-9/68000 keeps track (via the device descriptor) of which file manager to use.

SUMMARY

Multi-tasking is a requirement for multi-media compact discs. OS-9/68000 provides a sophisticated multi-tasking environment, usually found only in higher-level computer systems. The synchronization and inter-task communication facilities provide an excellent structured environment for the development and execution of applications. Its small-size ROM requirement make it an ideal choice for a custom or turnkey CD operating system such as that utilized in Kiosk implementations, as well as for general 68000-family computer systems.

INFORMATION TECHNOLOGY MANAGEMENT

MARTIN L. BARIFF
Illinois Institute of Technology
Chicago, Illinois
and
RICHARD BARNIER
Digital Equipment Corporation
Rolling Meadows, Illinois
and
DAVID FOSTER
LaSalle National Bank
Chicago, Illinois

Everyone knows that the global business environment is changing at an accelerating rate. Is MIS merely reacting or working to manage the process? The Information Technology Management track brings together MIS leaders who are changing their organizations and industries. MIS can take charge and direct the organization towards high-value, leading edge technology; track participants show how.

Two of the sessions deal with change itself. *MIS in a Changing World: Living with Mergers, Deregulation, and Global Competition* describes the collision of competitive forces in the automobile and transportation industries. Among the critical trends: globalization, deregulation, and technology. Even Japan is nervously reassessing the direction of many of its industries. Deregulation is spreading to many nations that once seemed hopelessly bureaucratic. MIS is one of many elements of a successful effort to establish competitive advantage in this new global market. In some companies, the burden of building systems that provide competitive advantage falls on the CIO. In the session *The Chief Information Officer as Enterprise Change Agent,* panel members share their experiences with this relatively new and highly challenging role.

The most common theme for sessions in this track is the growing synergy between information systems strategy and the highest levels of corporate strategy. The *Using Information Technology as a Competitive Weapon* session states the issue bluntly. This session covers a range of technology and methodologies in use, while *Integrating Corporate and Information Systems Strategies* presents enterprise-wide information management as a specific approach to the complex problem of integrating the corporate information systems architecture. Since the MIS department no longer has a monopoly on systems technology, let alone the total knowledge base of the organization, another session addresses the question *Have You Discovered the Markets for Your Information Services?* Today's information systems executive sells products as both intrapreneur and entrepreneur.

In the featured session, Amy Wohl offers her views of what technology has to offer in *Management Decisions and Technology Trends.* In her words "1987 is not the Year of Anything in Particular" but technologies are delivering more power to the user in an increasingly integrated environment.

Other issues for the MIS manager remain to be dealt with. Management looks at MIS as an investment, in competition with new production facilities, stock buy-backs, and a myriad of other potential uses for scarce cash. The *Justifying and Evaluating Information Technology*

Investments session offers techniques to do just that. Old and new delivery vehicles for information are considered in two sessions: *Transforming the Data Center into a Corporate Utility* shows how to revitalize the computer center; *How to Manage End User Computing* discusses future directions for the information center.

Executive Information Systems: Putting Top Management On-Line deals with a high-visibility relationship that is changing as new on-line EIS systems replace the traditional chartbook. A different angle on MIS management challenges is given in *MIS Vendor Challenges and Opportunities: the CIO Perspective.* As the CIO's role is evolving into a strategic management function, a dramatic change in the relationship with systems vendors is needed.

The MIS manager stands at the intersection between technology that changes daily and a management structure that is also struggling with accelerating change. Managing information technology is a tough proposition. But aphorisms, buzz-words, and trendy theories are of little help in the day to day job. These sessions offer some concrete experience from the troops, as successful change agents summarize their efforts to wear manager and technologist hats at the same time.

The future will bring even bigger changes in technology, but the crucial challenge comes from the management side of the equation. Increasingly, the IS function is regarded and run as a business. To succeed in this environment the information technology executive must be first and foremost an effective manager.

Integrating corporate and information systems strategies

by RICHARD F. MITCHELL
Illinois Bell
Chicago, Illinois

The challenge for Information Systems and its user organizations is to accelerate toward an information leadership position, giving substance to a new corporate image and providing a sustainable edge to newly competitive marketing forces.

Strategic business advantage is attained by anticipating circumstances and being prepared to take advantage of opportunities. Opportunities are transient; they crop up as the business environment changes, opening during windows of time that close as other environmental events occur.

Enterprise-wide Information Management (EwIM) is planning, organization, implementation, and control of information resources to meet current and future strategic goals. EwIM is a set of concepts and tools that enable a manager to determine, for his/her enterprise, what can and should be done with information technology. EwIM results in the alignment of information technology with the enterprise plans and the alteration of the enterprise goals through the use of information technology.

Information resources must be blended into competitive business strategies, beginning with market understanding and then focusing on strengthening sales and distribution channels and customer ties. New information structures must reduce data redundancy while both intersystem and corporate internal communications are improved. Further integration with other business processes allows improved business operations control and increased productivity, while the use of information technology adds value to product and service offerings in the eyes of the customer.

The fully integrated system is the product of a corporate management committed to using data processing strategically. It provides aggregated data for decision making and effective resource control. Through improved operational efficiency and the use of artificial intelligence technology, it also offers force reduction opportunities.

An information architecture is the structure of an organization's computing technology. Similar in nature to telephone network and building architectures; it is the systematic organization of the basic components of information. These components are data, applications, communications, work stations, software, and hardware.

Data

A logical data structure, organized by subject matter (e.g., customers, products) is the most critical component of the information architecture. Data must be separated from applications and managed as a corporately shared resource to position the architecture for optimum flexibility and support the correlation of corporate and external data. Ideally, the user will access information based on needs and authorization without even being aware which system contains the data.

Applications

Applications collect, restructure, create, and distribute information for business use. When freed of the traditional data storage and management role by the newly defined data architecture, applications will become more stable and readily encompass entire processes. New applications can provide customer, channel and supplier interactive capabilities, effectively stimulating revenue and controlling operational costs.

Communications

The connection of computer environments should appear as a transparent information delivery network to the user, supporting integrated voice, data, text, image, and graphics capabilities.

Work Stations

The user's window for information access, work stations should support the capabilities of the information architecture, encourage paperless communication of information, and provide responsive delivery of information.

Software

Software is the programmer's and end user's tool kit to manipulate and analyze data and information. Advances in software technology will bring artificial intelligence potentials to reality in the work place, automating technical activities such as programming, engineering, and capacity planning. Ideally, consistent software capabilities in all information environments will provide understandable information in answer to questions posed in common business language.

Hardware

The underlying component supporting the rest of the architecture, hardware planning, and selection must allow for flexible, non-disruptive introduction of new technology and meet the increasing processing demands of the business at optimum cost.

Effective architecture development requires close coordination with the planning function of the business to ensure that implementation occurs in a timely fashion.

Management decisions and technology trends

by AMY D. WOHL
Wohl Associates
Bala Cynwyd, PA

1987 is not the year of anything in particular and yet it is a year in which much change will occur in our industry. It is also a year—like most years recently—in which managers of information systems will need to make important decisions that will have a long range effect on the success or failure of their organizations. Decision in times of change and imminent change is tough and scary, and yet unavoidable. Perfect information (a crystal-clear crystal ball) is as scarce as ever and there are no guarantees that decisions, however carefully considered, will appear solid in next morning's brighter light.

Today, there is much more pressure on Information Systems and their managers. We need to provide information of better quality, more quickly, to larger numbers of users, at lower costs. Also, at the very same time, we need to provide information via a strategy which will make profit-oriented organizations more competitive, both within the U.S. marketplace and, perhaps more importantly, in international markets. If we work in the government or non-profit sector of our economy we need to learn how to make more and more from less and less.

And we need to perform this already tough assignment in an environment in which vendor's product lines and strategies are shifting, and our end user customers are continuously redefining and upgrading their information needs.

But we are not without tools to meet these demands—or without hope that success is possible.

THE DECISION MAKING PROCESS

Making decisions about what information systems equipment to buy, when to buy it, and how to use it has changed considerably in the last few years. With the advent of the personal computer, end users and their managers now play much more of a role than before. Sometimes, they select who will get what—and when, picking from products and services preselected by their MIS department or by a committee of technologists and users. In other companies, they may make these selections entirely on their own, providing they fall within budgetary guidelines and authorities. Some companies require elaborate studies and precise systems design; others proceed on an ad hoc basis, adding technology where users or their managers identify a need and a solution, and often building the system in place as needs evolve and grow.

THE UPWARD EXPANSION OF USER CONTROL

Initially, user involvement in the selction process—and user-driven systems management—was focused on the personal computer, on small, inexpensive, individually used workstations. However, as systems grew and (importantly) as users became more sophisticated in identifying needs and aggressively seeking solutions, the user began to extend his control upward, toward the multi-user system.

This desire to control a larger and more complex information systems world was substantially aided by various technology trends.

Minicomputer systems came in smaller and smaller physical packages at lower and lower prices. This meant that even relatively small groups of users could afford the cost of connecting themselves together and sharing information and systems resources.

At the same time, the skills needed to manage minicomputer systems, especially small ones, started to shrink. Vendors eager to sell more systems and to extend their marketing into the end-user arena (particularly because this market was deemed less controlled by IBM, with its traditionally close relationships with the management of large MIS users) offered various "user friendly" tools and interfaces to make the job of systems management more and more structured and predefined. Anyone who could read the screen of the computer could perform most administrative and maintenance tasks for such systems. Frequently that anybody was a departmental clerical or secretarial employee; a considerable cost savings to the organization.

The local area network (LAN) market began to solidify. A few major vendors substantially controlled the market and offered stable, well defined, and increasingly feature-rich products. IBM entered the market, offering long-term commitment ot the LAN concept and enhanced credibility. LAN software began to appear which, together with LAN's and servers (themselves often low-cost PCs) offered an inexpensive, appealingly simple environment. Also, such LAN environments, particularly if purchased a piece at a time, incrementally to the original purchase of personal computer workstations, fell well within departmental budgetary guidelines.

This meant LANs often arrived in end-user departments (particularly in those in remote locations) without notice to the MIS department at all. In fact, MIS departments often found out about these installations when they offered plans for company-wide guidelines or implementations and found—to their chagrin—that they already had a de facto standard in place.

Other technology trends have also altered the decision making process. Many organizations are combining their telecommunications departments (both telephony and data communications) into their MIS function. Office automation, end-user computing and microcomputer support and management are also candidates for integration with the MIS function. This offers MIS an opportunity to provide more integrated planning and more integrated systems design and support. It also offers the opportunity to consider some of the new combined function hardware which it was difficult for companies with separate computer and communications functions, for instance, to contemplate, analyze or implement.

1987 TECHNOLOGY ACTIVITIES

What are the technologically centered trends we are likely to encounter in 1987? And how will they affect the Information Systems management process. A few likely technology areas to watch include:

The Legitimization of Apple and the Macintosh

Apple's Macintosh products, especially its newest family member, the Mac II, are robust, powerful personal workstations. Also, there are now more than 2,000 software programs, including personal productivity tools for almost every imaginable area of business endeavor. Too, the consistent interface, powerful performance, and image orientation of the Macintosh has attracted some of the best software; IBM PCs must often wait until later for the products which appear first, more cheaply, and with more features on the Macintosh (e.g., Aldus' Page Maker and Microsoft's Word products, to name a few popular packages with first Macintosh and only later comparable IBM PC versions).

With Macintosh II, announced in March, Apple entered a new phase. This Macintosh is open to product enhancement via additional hardware and, perhaps more importantly to corporate America, it openly embraces IBM's 80286 architecture. Users do not need to choose the simplicity of Macintosh operation instead of the software compatibility of the IBM environment. They can choose both at once.

Market reaction to this product is likely to be aided and abetted by IBM's activities this spring and the market chaos that may ensue.

The Acceptance of a Next Generation IBM PC/Compatible/Clone Standard

IBM has kept the market waiting, holding its breath, for a very long time—too long. Exasperated competitors like Compaq finally gave in and announced their own versions of -386 Personal Computers (using Intel's 80386 chip).

Some believe that IBM will announce a different kind of product incompatible, less compatible or compatible only in some strange new way with the previous IBM standard. (Actually, IBM is likely to announce more than one system, with some enhanced -286 machines in the pot for Spring, 1987 and probably one or more -386 models.) This new system from IBM seems very likely. But the market reaction to this event is much less predictable.

Customers could choose to abandon the current IBM PC standard, agree with IBM's greater wisdom, and follow IBM down whatever paths it chooses. But customers could also choose to stay in a comfortable, well-defined space, richly furnished with innumerable hardware accessories and software packages. If developers' lag cycles for new software remain long, and/or if developers continue their love affair with the Macintosh, and/or if the end users decide the industry standard has *already* been determined and cannot be redefined by a single vendor, even IBM, Compaq, and the standard continuers could triumph and IBM could stumble.

Apple could be a more than modest beneficiary in this scenario. If Apple is carrying the standard and combines the two most popular software environments, it could become a preferred product in environments (like big corporations) where it was previously overlooked, ruled an outlaw, or scorned.

LANs Replace Minicomputers as the Basis for Departmental Systems

The day of the departmental processor (read minicomputer) may be drawing to a close. Minicomputers may be too big, too expensive, and too support-intensive to be appealing to the end users who often select department computing power.

Minicomputers, will not, of course, disappear. They will continue in ever-smaller, microcomputer-based versions. They will be attached to larger LANs as servers or sources of additional or specialized computing power. They will serve to interconnect and add function to multiple LAN environments.

More and more robust LANs with more robust operating systems and substantially more multi-user software will increasingly be the selection of choice, based on ease of use and price.

Image-oriented Applications Will Change Our Workstation, Our LAN, and Our Storage Hardware Requirements

Graphics, rich word processing desktop publishing, and icon interfaces are changing our standards for workstations. Such applications require more robust workstations, with substantially larger memories and faster processors. Also, image-oriented applications and their software need substantially more storage: a single bit-mapped 8.5 x 11″ page can contain 1,000,000 bits of information. This means it's easy to fill entire hard disk drives with only a hundred or so large images. Color (still uncommon in these applications, except for low resolution business graphics and higher resolution engineering graphics) multiples the memory, processing, and storage problems by three (and doubling resolution quadruples all the hardware requirements).

Optical storage is sure to be an element in solving this problem. In both CD-ROM and WORM (writable) Optical Disk forms, optical storage is now solidly in the market, with commercial products multiplying rapidly. These products need to be built directly into larger systems, rather than being offered as specialized, separate components. Also, the necessary software for automatically indexing and quickly retrieving information on optical disk needs to be nurtured, in order to manage such vast amounts of images and other data. CD-ROM, which seems to be the medium for the reference library of the future may actually be a consumer product some day—but it seems destined to be a business product first. CD-ROM pricing for monthly services can easily compete with less information rich paper products and can be substantially cheaper for large, elaborate annual or semi-annual publications.

LANs will also need to accommodate this flow of enhanced information. We suspect that many of the early LAN designs will be too narrow and slow to carry the fast-moving, rainbow-colored information of this brave new world. Broadband LANs may see a comeback (after their retreat into academe) and enhancements to baseband technology will be critical to support these applications with reasonable performance.

The Division of the Software Market

1986 was the year when the software market started to divide; this trend will continue strongly into 1987 and beyond. This is simply a recognition of a natural end to the usefulness of emphasizing backward compatibility of new software to old hardware and the new hardware becomes more and more robust. The compromise required for this backward capability is simply too expensive.

Instead, there will be a division between software which truly exploits -286 machines and older software designed to run successfully on less powerful computers. Desktop publishing is one of the applications which will mark this line, with many desktop publishing packages simply too complex and feature rich (to say nothing of their image requirements) to fit on smaller, less powerful systems. There will be a similar division in 1988 when the first -386 software hits the market. The 68000 market is likely to have similar divisions, with software which exploits 68020 machines just too hungry to fit on older models.

The Upward and Downward Expansion of Software

A strange but necessary game is beginning to play itself out in the software market. A number of microcomputer software developers are trying to create viable multi-user versions of their products for use on LAN servers and minicomputers. At the same time, mainframe and minicomputer software developers are attempting to create microcomputer versions of their products.

This game has gone on for a long time, but previous success stories have been few. Lack of success has largely been caused by developers' assumptions that their new target market is simply a larger (or smaller) version of their current market. Actually, multi-user software environments require an entirely different, much more complex view of the world. And smaller environments aren't just smaller—they typically have users who demand much friendlier products. Failure, coupled with the rewards of success, however elusive, have fueled a new look at cross-system software and some successes seem likely to appear in 1987.

THE ISSUE OF COMPETITIVENESS

If information systems—and their managers—are to play a major role in the life and success of the organization, they need to contribute to the competitiveness of the firm. Thorough examinations of individual businesses nearly always uncover a number of areas in which better information systems (or better use of the ones already in place) can significantly improve the health of the organization. Likely areas for inspection might include:

1. The timeliness of information, particularly if faster delivery of data or analyzed data has a financial value to your organization (such as improving time to market, speeding up collection cycles).
2. The accuracy of information, especially where greater accuracy permits better decision making. This might be particularly true in consumer goods, for instance, where changes in market share of less than one percentage point can be critical.
3. Other uses for information. Information created for, or as a by-product of, one business can create other businesses. For instance, information about large groups of customers and their behavior might be valuable to other firms in their market research activities. Or an analysis of the demographics of your customers might lead you to provide other goods and services (some might be information-based) to them.
4. The integration of information. Single facts by themselves, particularly on separate, incompatible computer systems, don't tell you much. Combined in meaningful ways, these facts can give you new insights into your organization and how it should be managed. New products which cross system boundaries, and aggregate and analyze information on behalf of managers with limited computer expertise can greatly increase the information available for decision making.
5. Alerting. Computers can become agents, tracking multiple events in ways too large or too complex for the human brain to readily handle. They can be programmed to look for specific events or combination of events and to alert their human managers to act—or even, in some circumstances, act on their behalf. (A chocolate company might ask that its purchasing system automatically buy additional cocoa beans whenever the world price exceeded a certain value and bad weather was threatened in cocoa-bearing areas, for instance.)

This is an example, on a very small scale, of a so-called expert system, a computer program that embodies the knowledge of one or more experts about a particular narrow specialty. Expert systems are now coming into their own, and we expect them to blossom all over the largest companies–and some small, insightful ones—during 1987.

Change in the computer industry will not be well behaved in 1987. It will be rapid, unruly, and sometimes unpredictable. Some vendors—especially those who are flexible and fleet of foot—will do well in this era; others will find their stately style ill-served by a rapidly changing environment. User fortunes will rise and fall on the firm's ability to recognize appropriate technology and appropriate technology partners, and to reject technology that is premature or irrelevant.

Companies that move quickly to adopt relevant technology, and to adapt it to their own ends, will do best of all.

End-user computing: A grand concept running "amuck"

by J. DANIEL COUGER
University of Colorado
Colorado Springs, Colorado

ABSTRACT

A survey of 17 large firms, all with long-term computing experience and representative of major U.S. industry categories, revealed serious problems in 11 of the firms. The other firms were realizing significant benefits (i.e., ROI on the order of 2:1 to 6:1). The six successful firms used a pattern that other companies can emulate: (1) proactive rather than reactive approaches to implementing end-user computing, (2) conducting cost/benefit analyses for each potential computer application, (3) providing soft, rather than hard, controls for acquisition and use of PCs and related software. This paper explains the details of the approaches used by the successful firms.

INTRODUCTION

End-user computing has, potentially, the greatest impact of any development in the computer field. Some aspects of its growth, such as personal computing, are exponential and could easily continue that pattern through 1990. However, its cost is far greater than anticipated—much more than it should be. Worse yet, the obvious benefits realized in the past three years are threatened because of below-the-surface problems expanding and boiling like a volcano near eruption.

To identify the causes of these problems, 17 companies were selected to study, all had long-term computing experience and were representative of major U.S. industry categories. Eleven experienced significant problems in implementing end-user computing. Seven were overspending budget by a factor no less than three, and as much as ten. The situation may be even worse in four other companies because they had not prepared budgets for end-user computing!

On the other hand, six firms were realizing ROI on the order of 2 : 1 to 6 : 1. They were realizing benefits of the magnitude of millions of dollars annually.

In the 11 problematic firms, there was proliferation of micros and microsoftware and installation by inexperienced people, the users. The principal problems was lack of adequate planning for end-user computing. Had they standardized on micro hardware and software, training could have been more consistent, the learning curve simplified, and downtime reduced. Yet, the highest cost factor of all could not be easily ascertained. Without standardization, the hidden cost of errors resulting from the proliferation of hardware/software may exceed the measured excess cost.

The problems of end-user computing are not insurmountable, as shown by six of the survey companies. Analysis of their successful approaches to implementing end-user computing reveals a generic approach which will enable other organizations to leapfrog one of the three stages of end-user computing growth. The result is improvement in both efficiency and effectiveness.

In 1983, 1,850,000 PCs were shipped. By year end of 1987 the total base of installed PCs is estimated to exceed 20 million.[1] If the pattern of the 11 less successful companies in the survey is prevalent throughout the U.S., the result of installing 20 million micros could be chaotic. But risks can be greatly lowered through following the guidelines of the six successful firms, and most companies can then expect to realize the potential of end-user computing.

The number of individuals directly using computers has more than doubled in the past three years in those organizations which have implemented the EUC approach. Figure 1 shows the exponential growth of use of terminals and PCs. The data are derived from five surveys listed in the bibliography. On the other hand, the hoped-for level of managerial use has not been realized. The large user group is the professional, nonmanagerial staff, as shown in Figure 1. Managers are delegating to staff the tasks of developing models and are using the systems primarily for information retrieval. To change this pattern, more functions need to be provided in an integrated manner with more user-friendly access.

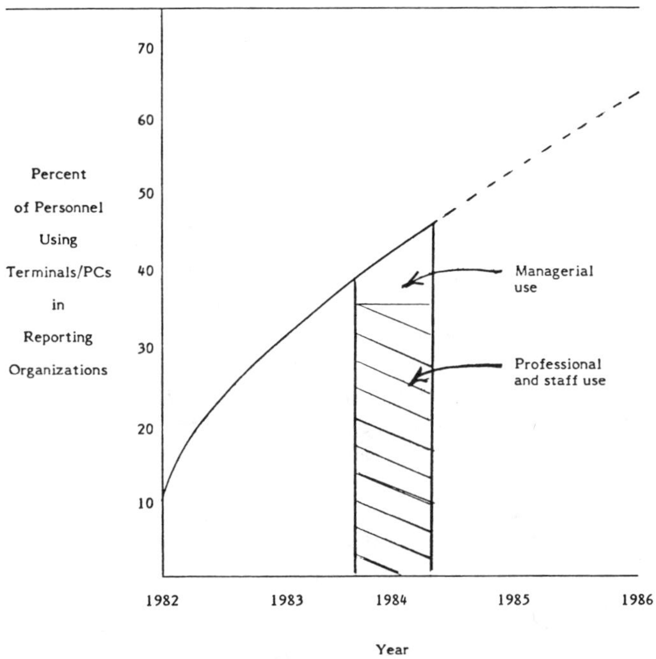

Figure 1—Growth in terminal/PC use by type of user

Those guidelines are summarized here and expanded through the remainder of this paper: 1) proactive rather than reactive approach to implementing end-user computing, 2) conducting cost/benefit analyses for each potential computer application, 3) providing soft rather than hard controls for acquisition and use of PCs and related software.

PROFILE OF THE SURVEY FIRMS

The study began with a review of five previous surveys, listed in the bibliography, on various aspects of end-user computing. Next, 17 U.S. firms were selected for in-depth analysis. Net annual income ranged from $100 million to $500 million. Total number of employees ranged from 3,000 to 45,000. All companies had experience with mainframe computers for 15, or more, years. Success in end-user computing had no correlation with size. The geographic distribution of the firms is shown in Table I.

TABLE I—Industry representation and geographic distribution of 17 firms included in the survey

Industry	Location: East	Central	West	Total No. of Firms
Insurance	1		1	2
Banking	1	1		2
Manufacturing	1	1	1	3
Pharmaceutical		1	1	2
Extraction/ Processing		1	1	2
Public Utility	1	1		2
Transportation	1		1	2
Retailing	1	1		2

EVOLUTION OF END-USER COMPUTING

The trend toward end-user computing has evolved from three distinct and parallel paths. As shown in Figure 2, all three paths provided end-user computing, but to a limited degree. Only with the convergence of the three paths is the potential of end-user computing realized, that is, integrated end-user computing.

The earliest path, interactive terminal access, primarily provided users with information retrieval capability. They could directly interact with a computer, but only in a very limited way. Only the forerunners to user-oriented languages were available and were not widely used. Technical support came from the IS personnel assigned to develop the user's transaction processing systems (e.g., order processing or inventory control) rather than from a special cadre of personnel assigned exclusively to deal with the user's personal computing needs.

The second path, information centers, was the first attempt to pull together the services needed for an individual to operate relatively independently. The early ICs were physical locations where users could go for training, technical assistant, retrieval-only access to live data bases such as the customer database, and manipulative access (ability to change contents) to copies of data bases. Today the IC is not confined to one physical location but is an IS organization entity to provide these services to users wherever they reside. Though a significant improvement over the previous delivery system, ICs did not provide many of the user-friendly benefits of personal computing.

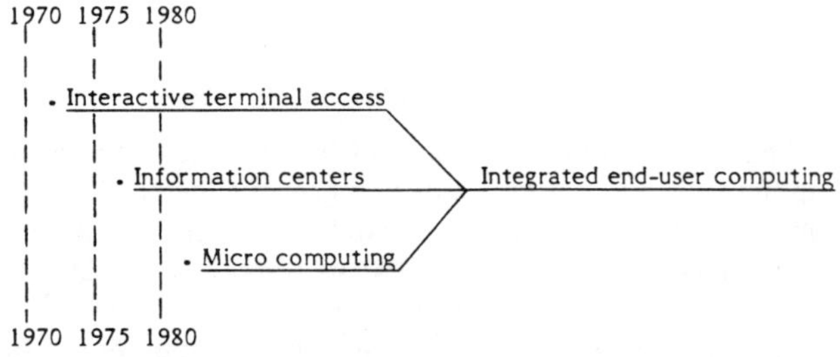

Figure 2—Evolution of end-user computing

The third path, micro computing, is the only one of the three that emerged primarily outside of the direction of the IS organization. The low cost of both PCs and PC software enabled user organizations to acquire these systems outside the purchase controls of IS. The user-friendliness of these systems enabled users to operate relatively independently of IS technical assistance. But, independence was also a disadvantage. PC users rarely had access to IS data bases. Also, most PCs were acquired without communication capability.

The convergent path, integrated end-user computing, not only provides the best of each of these earlier delivery services, but also enhances all three. PCs compatible with mainframe computers can access data bases and utilize sophisticated mainframe tools, as well as operate in standalone mode to avail themselves of the rich variety of PC software. This stage of end-user computing evolution also includes delivery of electronic mail capability with the same PC. With this concept, office and computing activities are fully integrated. Also included in this stage of evolution, is access to external as well as internal data bases.

Table II shows the functions available to users in each of the three stages of evolution of end-user computing.

ADVANTAGES OF END-USER COMPUTING

The rapid growth is itself the best indicator of the benefits of end-user computing. It is obviously meeting the needs of a large body of managers and staff. The advantages of end-user computing are as follows:

1. Simplified tools for individuals to build their own applications and models

Table II—Levels of sophistication in end-user computing in three stages of evolution

Stages	I Interactive terminal access	II Information centers and personal computing	III Integrated end-user computing
Functions Available	• Information retrieval from select internal files	• Standalone PCs and software	• Full communication capability with mainframe and other PCS
		• Widespread access to internal data bases through mainframe terminals only	• Access to external data bases • Electronic mail through same PC
	• Simplistic modeling	• Intermediate level modeling	• Sophisticated modeling

2. Improved access to data bases:
   a. For information retrieval
   b. For data as input to models
3. Increased productivity of users:
   a. Able to eliminate time required to translate their requirement to IS professionals for development of systems by IS department
   b. Able to reduce implementation time by prototyping their own systems
   c. Able to build applications tailored to their individual needs

The principal advantage needs to be viewed from the macro perspective of the effect on management in general rather than the micro perspective of individual users. The end-user computing approach has brought a result long-awaited by the computer industry—computer literacy. We are on the threshold of widespread use of the computer throughout the company.

The number of individuals directly using computers has more than doubled in the past three years in those organizations which have implemented the end-user computing. Data derived from five surveys[1,2,3,4,5] indicate an exponential growth of use of terminals and PCs.

On the other hand, the hoped-for level of managerial use has not been realized. The large user group is the professional, non-managerial staff. Managers are delegating to staff the tasks of developing models and are using the systems primarily for information retrieval. To change this pattern, more functions need to be provided in an integrated manner with more user-friendly access.

LACK OF FORMAL COST JUSTIFICATION

According to the surveys, few companies have formally analyzed the cost/effectiveness of end-user computing. Where the justification process for traditional IS applications is formalized, the one for end-user computing is rarely formalized. While each of the surveys cited benefits, few had been quantified. Why?

Surprisingly, the approach to end-user computing has followed the pattern of initiating computing in industry 25 years ago. In many companies, end-user computing began with a missionary thrust. The prevalent view was that converts could not be gained without providing the service free to users, that is, without chargeback to their budgets. Several organizations that have had end-user computing in some form for over 10 years have not emerged from the missionary stage.

Because of the burgeoning costs of end-user computing, companies are being forced to change the "free-goods" policy and to move into Stage II of the traditional IS development pattern, where chargeback occurs. In companies with a chargeback policy, the costs of computing are distributed to users according to the amount of services used. Stage III, where cost/effectiveness analysis occurs, will be realized when companies move to integrated end-user computing. Because of access to all computing facilities, data bases and software, a higher level of benefits and quantification is facilitated. A user can more easily assess the total effect on his/her job.

EXACERBATING PROBLEMS OF END-USER COMPUTING

Problems are not diminishing with the widespread growth of end-user computing. To the contrary, the problems are expanding.

1. Surface issues are:
   a. Excessive equipment cost
   b. Inefficient users
   c. Inefficient applications
   d. Friction between end-user computing technical staff and rest of IS department
2. Below-surface issues are:
   a. Proliferation of data bases
   b. Proliferation of software products and PC machine types
   c. Problems of interface between tools
   d. Developing systems difficult to maintain

With inexperienced users, computing costs soar. Much of the learning is trial and error. Even with experience, personnel without the training of an IS professional will be relatively inefficient system developers. In addition, the 4th generation languages are huge resource-burners; that is, associated computer costs are often higher than running applications developed with procedural languages. Computer costs to support end-user computing have grossly exceeded projections. For example, in four of the six progressive organizations where the in-depth analysis occurred, the three-year plan called for end-user computing usage approximating an extra shift of mainframe time; instead an entire mainframe computer was required.

Still in the missionary stage, many companies have yet to install a chargeback system. Without a chargeback system, users have less incentive to be efficient.

Although the typical end-user computing support group reports to the IS organization, there have been some disruptive results. System personnel responsible for the large transaction processing applications have complained that their user contact has been diminished by the technical personnel assigned to end-user computing. It appears that the change is not caused by the end-user computing personnel overtly usurping that privilege, but that users developing their own systems via end-user computing naturally spend more time with the person most familiar with end-user computing facilities.

The data proliferation problem is perhaps the most insidious and costly. Data base security procedures prevent users access to the on-line data bases, except in retrieval-only mode so they cannot alter the data. Users who want to manipulate data to perform analyses must be provided copies of a data base. The resultant problem is inconsistency of reports when persons are using data bases not as up-to-date as the reports produced by the transaction processing applications. The solution that has been used is to give everyone current data. In this mode a "shadow" data base copy is provided daily from the corporate mainframes. While the currency problem is resolved, a significant increase in data base cost occurs.

With PCs from a diversity of vendors with different versions of software, the cost to maintain software and hardware is higher than necessary. However, at present no single vendor meets all the needs of a customer. The different systems also complicate communication between PCs and with mainframes. In addition, some companies make available to users several 4th generation languages, causing interface problems. For interface, users must learn several sets of commands.

Some users expand their application until it becomes so large and complicated that they want to transfer its maintenance to the IS department. Because it was not developed under IS department standards, it is difficult to maintain.

IMPERATIVE TO FORMALIZE END-USER COMPUTING PLANNING

It is not surprising that the variety of approaches to implementing end-user computing has resulted in a hodgepodge of hardware and software. The essence of end-user computing is service. Although I know of only one company which explicitly uses the slogan "the customer is always right," that approach is the implicit objective of many end-user computing facilities. The goal is to undergrid improvement in user effectiveness.

The emphasis on effectiveness of computer use, rather than efficiency, can hardly be faulted. However, it is not necessary to sacrifice one to attain the other. Satisfactory results are possible. Examples in the PC area are: (1) limiting selection to compatible PCs, (2) standardizing on an operating system (e.g., a multiuser system with communication capability between PCs and to the mainframes), (3) standardizing on application packages (e.g., a single integrated spreadsheet package and a single word processor). Examples of standardizing on 4th generation tools are: (1) one language with comprehensive information retrieval capability and (2) one language with strong modeling capability.

Although the move to cost/effectiveness analysis should occur as soon as possible, a chargeback system is a satisfactory interim policy. Users who must pay for their use will prize efficiency as well as effectiveness.

Improved user training programs will produce higher levels of efficiency in computer use. For example, there are many tricks and shortcuts in spreadsheet development that can be conveyed in formal training sessions. The same is true for use of a 4th generation language.

Through improved attention to planning, the potential benefits of end-user computing are substantial, as shown by the results of the six successful firms, where R.O.I. ranged from 2 : 1 to 6 : 1.

IMPLEMENTING SOFT CONTROLS

Progressive IS organizations have found that formal planning can be introduced to achieve integrated end-user computing without resorting to increased control measures. Many of the benefits of end-user computing have been the result of the freedom to experiment with other than traditional ways to develop systems. Prototyping is an example. It has worked so well in end-user computing that the IS function is adopting it for developing certain types of transaction processing systems. In prototyping, a simple model is computerized and tested. Despite its simplicity, the model is producing useful results. It is then enhanced and retested. Each cycle of refinement produces improved results.

Tight or "hard" controls may stifle creativity of users. A better approach is "soft" controls. Examples of soft controls being adopted by the progressive IS organizations are:

1. Providing PC maintenance for a select set of PCs, encouraging users to acquire only those PC types. Providing centralized purchasing to attain quantity discounts for both PCs and software while also limiting the number of PC types and ensuring compatibility.
2. Providing training only on a select set of software and 4th generation tools, motivating users to confine their activities to that set alone.
3. Providing file sharing software, so a data set developed or acquired by one user is also available to others.
4. Serving as the central agency for obtaining new releases of software then implementing them for all interested users, thereby reducing the possibility for incompatibility/inconsistency from multiple releases existing throughout the organizations.
5. Providing training in application development methodology to enable users to better manage their own development projects and to adhere to standards in development to facilitate maintenance of applications.
6. Organizing an electronic mail (EM) system and implementing it for anyone with communication-compatible PCs as opposed to providing EM only to persons with computer terminals.

Lack of a hard controls approach will not prevent companies from moving to integrated end-user computing. On the contrary, the soft controls are a more practical approach because they permit individual creativity within an environment of cooperative, mutual objectives.

PROVIDING EFFECTIVE TECHNICAL SUPPORT

Another factor in common among the progressive firms is effective technical support. However, the key ingredient is not the availability of technical know-how; it is motivating those persons to help end-users. Some firms with adequate technical expertise are not meeting objectives in integrated end-user computing because of their approach to use of that expertise.

A major barrier is the attitude of most technical personnel toward spending the major portion of their working hours assisting users. Their terms for this activity are frequently derisive, such as "handholding" and "nursemaiding."

It is not easy to find technical personnel who find such work challenging. They would rather be back in the IS department solving complicated hardware/software issues.

These findings are not confined to the end-user study; they are also supported by other research in the behavior of computer professionals. A data base of more than 8,000 computer personnel reveals that most of these personnel have low need for social interaction and high need for challenging work.[6]

This situation need not be a deterrent. Only a small portion of the IS department personnel is required to provide the technical support for end-user computing. Those few persons at the high end of the continuum of need for social interaction will not be turned-off by the heavy interaction required to support end-user computing. The progressive firms were successful in providing effective end-user technical support because they were able to select these few personnel out of the total IS workforce.

But the selection process alone was not sufficient to ensure success. The end-user support departments of the progressive firms had one other common characteristic. The head of that support function had an ability to convince technical personnel with strong need for challenging work that end-user computing provided some unique and substantive challenges. They emphasized two things. First, the work is state-of-the-art in terms of new technical advances. Second, the impact of the work on the company is substantial because it is managerially-oriented.

In short, these successful managers of end-user computing take great care in selecting employees with the characteristics appropriate for this activity and in identifying for these employees the importance and challenge of the work.

TABLE III—Stage III: end-user computing personal workstation functions

- Standalone computing
- Access to mainframe computing power
- Remote data access (downloading and uploading)
- Sort, search, and manipulation of data
- Memo and reporting writing
- Business graphics
- Electronic mail and filing
- Document sharing

SUMMARY

Integrated end-user computing is not a utopian concept. It is a natural progression from the convergence of the three prior paths of (1) interactive terminal access, (2) information centers, and (3) micro computing. With integration, users can utilize the computing power of mainframe computers in the company as well as those external to the company which use the same communication protocols. Access to internal and external data bases is also possible. Users can also communicate with other users for electronic mail, data, and model sharing. They can also use PC software in standalone mode. With enhanced training and 4th generation tools, they can build their own tailor-made systems.

The imminent threat to end-user computing of high cost and inefficient use of resources can be avoided through more precise planning for the move to integrated end-user computing. Both effective and efficient use of computing resources is possible.

The planning process can be facilitated by analyzing the experience of progressive organizations and avoiding some of the inevitable mistakes that the frontrunners incur by being innovators. Through this approach, it may be possible to leapfrog a part, or perhaps an entire stage, in the typical three-stage process of evolution of end-user computing, producing a personal workstation with a variety of capabilities. (Table III lists end-user computing workstation functions.)

REFERENCES

1. "Effective Use of Personal Computers in Large Organizations." International Data Corporation, Framingham, MA, November, 1983.
2. "A Study of the Corporate Use of Personal Computers." Center for Information Systems Research, M.I.T., Cambridge, MA, December, 1983.
3. "Impacts of Office Automation." The Diebold Group, Inc., New York, NY, May, 1984.
4. "Microcomputer Usage Trends in "FORTUNE" Corporations." Newton-Evans Research Co., Inc., Ellicott City, MD, 1984.
5. "The Information Center Survey." Crwth Computer Coursewares, Santa Monica, CA, 1984.
6. Couger, Daniel J. and Robert A. Zawacki, *Motivating and Managing Computer Personnel,* New York: John Wiley and Sons, Inc., 1980.

The project unit costing method: Constructing a financial justification for the knowledge-based system

by MICHAEL L. MORGAN and GAIL D. WOLF
Magnavox Electronic Systems Company
Fort Wayne, Indiana

ABSTRACT

Although knowledge-based and expert systems are becoming increasingly popular, they are usually constructed incrementally and by ad hoc methods, rather than by conventional software engineering methodologies. The development of such systems often more closely resembles R&D than systems engineering, and the result is often not completely specified until the program is implemented. This makes it difficult to estimate costs and difficult to justify those costs in terms of an uncertain benefit. This paper presents one method of cost justification, which allows a direct comparison and tradeoff of costs and benefits.

INTRODUCTION

The recent media attention on artificial intelligence (AI) often leaves the impression that AI is now a mature discipline, capable of being used in a wide variety of applications and organizations. In fact, AI is still a very new field. It is difficult to find commercially viable examples of programs which equal the complexity of even a modestly-sized conventional application. In part, this is due to the fact that well-trained AI programmers and knowledge engineers are scarce, and that many of the tools are expensive. Another factor is that the exact performance of the program, and consequently its benefits, are difficult to define or quantify until the program has been written. The combination of initial high costs and uncertain benefits has made it difficult to justify AI systems using traditional cost-accounting methods, yet the corporate climate usually dictates that these methods are the only ones which are acceptable.

As part of its ongoing modernization program, Magnavox Electronic Systems Company has prepared detailed cost and technical proposals for 84 projects. Over half of these require advanced information technology methods, including knowledge-based systems, expert systems, and natural language interfaces to databases. Since Magnavox is a defense contractor, and the modernization program is performed under Government supervision, the cost justifications for projects such as these must conform to conventional cost accounting standards, while showing tangible, auditable results. To achieve these goals, Magnavox developed the Project Unit Costing Method. This method offers the following advantages when compared to the ad hoc methods currently in use:

1. Direct comparison between projects, to decide where to place the investment dollar.
2. Costs and benefits are explicit and tangible, allowing tradeoffs to be computed to maximize profit.
3. The method is standardized and readily transferable, so projects may be compared which were prepared by different user groups or subcontractors.

Although this method was developed to evaluate candidate projects for in-house use, it has additional applications in the marketing of AI systems and in steering R&D investments.

The following sections address three areas of AI cost justification:

1. The nature of AI costs, including initial costs, design and development costs, and delivery costs
2. The nature of AI benefits, and
3. The Project Unit Costing Method, which integrates costs and benefits

AI COSTS

Projects based on advanced information technology such as AI differ from their conventional counterparts in five principal ways.

1. AI projects have a higher initial investment. AI projects are frequently prototyped and developed by highly-trained knowledge engineers, working in concert with some of the company's scarcest experts. Usually, these knowledge engineers must be hired in at great cost, either as employees or as subcontractors. For less complex applications, in-house people may be trained, but training incurs the cost of time and labor. Furthermore, AI work is often done on dedicated workstations, which have a much higher cost per station than the conventional programming terminal. While simpler applications may be built in the conventional environment, there is much to be said for the high-productivity tools available on dedicated workstations.

These higher initial costs make it more important to do a thorough benefits analysis before beginning an AI project. They may also contribute to management's hesitation to fund large-scale AI development work.

2. AI design and development tends to become a goal in itself. Conventional projects are normally developed by existing software development groups, such as a Data Processing department. Their cost estimates include only the labor required to build, test, and install the given application. AI projects, on the other hand, are often costed as part of establishing an AI department. If the first few projects must bear the burden of the high initial costs mentioned above, they are not economically justifiable. Therefore, management makes an AI commitment. The company decides to support AI even if immediate benefits are not forthcoming. Unfortunately, this turns into a self-fulfilling prophecy. AI specialists are hired with no immediate expectations of demonstrating profitability and, often, with no immediate projects. These individuals may be from an academic or research environment, and have had little training in identifying or building high-payback projects. They therefore spend many months becoming familiar with their tools and developing small prototypes, but develop little or nothing that can be used in the organization to offset their costs. After some time, management becomes disenchanted with AI, and starves the AI organization of resources until it withers and dies.

3. AI costs are frequently underestimated. This is not unlike the problems which surrounded software development in general during the early years of business computing. For example, each new expert system requires a designer to choose a knowledge representation and a control method. It is usually impossible to determine if the choice is the correct one until the knowledge engineer and the human expert have

jointly developed a prototype. Frequently the poor choice does not become apparant until the system is almost complete, since some problems are functions of the size of the knowledge base. If the initial choice of control strategy or knowledge representation must be abandoned, much of the work must be redone. In addition, many of the commercial development tools, known as expert system shells, offer only one means of knowledge representation (usually production rules) and one to two control strategies (usually forward and backward chaining, with blind, depth-first search). Frequently, the designer makes an initial choice of representation and control, and buys a tool, only to be forced by the nature of the application to another methodology and another tool. Experience is of some help here, but even veteran knowledge engineers speak of the "pancake principle;" build the first one to be thrown away.

The most common defense against these redundant costs is rapid prototyping, the development of an initial version of the finished system within a few weeks. This offers the advantages of keeping the expert's interest, and of allowing the knowledge engineer to get a feel for the domain and the problem very quickly. It also allows management to see progress quickly. Another defense against wasting money on tools, is to choose the most general tool available. Unfortunately, these tools are usually the most expensive, and often require more sophistication and more work on the part of the knowledge engineer than a more tightly focused, but more powerful, tool. Furthermore, many of the most general tools do not lend themselves well for transitioning into the delivery environment.

4. AI programs are never completed. Unlike conventional programs, which are usually tightly specified, many AI application have such broad specifications that no one can agree whether they are done. There are always cases on which the human expert can outperform the machine. As those cases are discovered, there is a temptation to add "just one more" rule to improve the system. This often upsets some other, previously satisfactory, part of the system, so a bit more fine-tuning is required. This process continues until money or patience runs out.

5. Finally, the problems of transitioning an AI system into the user's environment are not well understood. Many AI systems have been built to run on specialized hardware and in a special support environment. The transition onto machines which are more accessible to the user has not been thought through, so users are forced to come to the developers to use their application. While this may have some serendipitous value in keeping developers attuned to users needs, it is not a suitable solution to the delivery problem in most domains. As an alternative, several of the manufacturers of AI workstations and tools are now offering "delivery machines" and run-time environments. These are suitable for a large class of problems. For still other problems, however, the system must end up on the machines that users have on their desktops. This may include personal computers, or access to departmental minicomputers or company mainframes. The impact of recoding the application into a conventional programming language, or the cost of a run-time copy of an expert system shell, have often been left out of the original estimate.

AI BENEFITS

AI benefits are frequently thought to be intangible. Frequently, the first expert systems are built by a company to "keep up with the technology." Due to the fatal loop described above, the initial experience with AI often does nothing to dispel the notion that AI's benefits are not readily quantifiable.

AI-based systems are frequently used to augment functions whose costs are presently captured as part of indirect and overhead expenses. For many manufacturers, direct labor represents less than 10% of total cost incurred, yet detailed accounting of the labor dollar is kept only for direct labor. This means that costs for the white-collar and non-touch functions which are reduced by AI are not visible to the accounting system. Where the costs are not visible, the reduction of those costs is not seen to be a benefit.

THE PROJECT UNIT COSTING METHOD

Based on the above observations, any method of estimating the costs and benefits of AI-based systems must have the following characteristics:

1. The in-house AI group must be run on a business basis. That is, they must generate discernable products with demonstrable benefit. While the company may serve as the investment banker, they have a right to reap a reasonable return on investment. In the case of an independent business, these returns flow from tangible benefits called sales. In any in-house business, an equally tangible measure of benefits must be found.
2. The system must be specified in terms of cost reduction. Any new (To-Be) system will grow out of existing (As-is) procedures and costs. By using the new system, those costs may be reduced. If they are not, then the quality, reliability, or timeliness of the output is increased. These non-cost benefits contribute profitability by increased market share, or by allowing the company to penetrate new markets. They can usually be translated into cost reduction terms by comparing the To-be costs with the costs of achieving a similar increase in profitability by As-is methods. This approach allows designers and management to make tradeoffs between cash flow, capital investments, and the ultimately reduced costs. This also elevates the financial side of development from a "trust-me" basis to one in which benefits are clearly visible on the bottom line.

Methods for evaluating investments based on cost reduction are well-known in the production environment, where the cost reduction is applied directly against the cost of goods sold on a per-unit basis. In that environment these methods are known as Unit Cost methods. Magnavox's adaptation is to apply these methods to the indirect and white-collar functions which do not directly contribute to product costs. The Magnavox method is described below.

Cost Analysis

The cost analysis must capture all aspects of current (As-is) costs. These may include: (1) labor, (2) burden, (3) subcontracts, (4) material, (5) capital, (6) travel, and (7) expenses (e.g. software, furniture, office supplies).

Benefit Analysis

Savings and avoidances

For cost/benefit analysis purposes, savings and avoidances are discriminated. Savings are a reduction in cost as a result of the implementation of the project, given that the business volume remains constant. Avoidances are attributable to an increase in business volume. Cost reduction from savings and avoidances come from two sources. First, there are those cost elements, such as material costs, which are directly reduced. The dollar savings of these cost elements may be captured directly. Second, there is a reduction in current or anticipated headcount attributed to the project. These are ultimately translated into dollars using the labor grades and categories, and the average cost of labor in those grades and categories for each year of the analysis.

Project unit descriptions

To define the scope and benefits of the projects, it is necessary to define a unit of the project output. Units can be defined for both touch and non-touch (i.e. process-oriented and non-process-oriented) projects. A unit must be related to the function of the project. Examples of project units include:

1. A printed wiring board
2. A work order
3. A purchase order
4. A bid

Examples of unacceptable unit definitions include:

1. Any time-related unit, such as a man-month (units must be functionally oriented)
2. A decision

As-is versus To-be cost per unit

The As-is cost per unit is defined as the dollar amount required to generate one project unit using current methods. The To-be cost per unit is similarly defined as the cost to generate one project unit, if the project were implemented and on-line today. Several options for estimating the To-be cost per unit are available: a percent reduction from the As-is can be taken, or the actual dollar amounts using the proposed techniques can be estimated.

Project volumes

Typically, there are costs which are volume dependent, such as material and recurring labor, and costs which are volume independent such as set-up costs. By reducing the As-is and To-be costs to a per project unit basis, it is possible to determine savings and avoidances based upon different business volumes. For example, a projected business volume of 200 units would have twice as much volume-dependent savings as a projected business volume of 100 units.

Cost philosophies and assumptions

It is essential to capture the philosophies used in determining cost and benefit baselines as well as any assumptions made. For example, if it was assumed that the company would continue to grow at an annual rate of 3%, it should be stated in this section. If analyses are being prepared by several different user groups, it is useful to publish a standard set of assumptions to be used throughout the company.

Definition of terms

Δ cost per project unit = As-is cost per project unit − To-be cost per project unit.
Δ labor cost per project unit = As-is labor cost per project unit − To-be labor cost per project unit.
Savings = Δ cost per project unit × current volume.
Avoidances = Δ cost per project unit × (future volume − current volume).
Headcount savings = (Δ labor cost per project unit × current volume) ÷ time element, where time element relates to units for labor, such as manhours or manmonths.
Headcount avoidances = (Δ labor cost per project unit × (future volume − current volume)) ÷ time element, where time element is as defined for headcount savings.

Project Unit Costing Forms

Following the conceptual design of a project, a detailed cost/benefit analysis is performed to justify detailed design and implementation. The sections of this analysis are described below.

Cost summary sheet

The "Cost Summary Sheet" is intended to summarize all of the essential cost elements for easy analysis by accounting, management, and auditors. These elements include As-is and To-be costs, Δ-costs, savings, avoidances, and capital retired or salvaged. The numbers for the summary sheet are aggregated from the following cost/benefit analyses:

Design-phase cost summary sheet and implementation-phase cost summary sheet

Costs for both design and implementation are estimated using conventional budgeting procedures, bearing in mind the cautions about costing described earlier.

Expense account analyses form

This standard Magnavox form is used to estimate expenses, by account code, for each quarter of a given year. Each user group, when performing their annual budgeting function, includes costs related to each project under their responsibility. These budgets are prepared to capture project costs for a five-year period beginning with the detailed design phase. The project should stand alone with respect to funding. If the project is approved, the monies associated with that project will be included in the budget. If the project is not approved, all of the monies associated with that project will not be approved in the budget.

Budget manning chart, travel and transportation analyses

These standard Magnavox forms provide backup to explain the labor and travel expenses budgeted in the Expense Account Analyses Form.

Projected volume/units of output by product

By product and by year, for the five years beginning with detailed design, the products are listed which will be affected by the project. Where "nameless" products are used, such as in the out years, this must be documented in the Cost Philosophies and Assumptions section. The Cost Philosophies and Assumptions section should also contain the rationale which links product volume with project unit volume. For example, if the number of purchase orders is a function of product complexity, and if each product today averages 200 purchase orders, and product complexity is increasing, it may be appropriate to multiply volume by 250 to estimate the number of purchase orders required per product in the out years.

As-is cost per unit calculation

This sheet captures the current cost of producing a unit of project output. Where costs are volume dependent, the calculations should be based on the most likely volumes. The backup documentation shows calculations based on other volumes. Again, the reasoning that led to the choice of a "most likely" volume should be documented in the Cost Philosophies and Assumptions section.

To-be cost per unit calculation

The To-be, or anticipated, cost, of producing a single unit of project output after project implementation are captured using the same philosophies as were used to generate As-is costs. Volumes must be the same in both the As-is and the To-be calculations.

Capital project request form

This standard Magnavox form captures depreciation and investment opportunities of interest to the accounting community.

Headcount savings

Savings are defined as the reductions which result from the project, given that the current volume of business remains unchanged. This is the place to capture the number of positions which would be eliminated if the project were implemented, and if the business volume did not increase. In order to convert this headcount to dollars, savings here are identified by labor grade and category.

Headcount avoidances

Avoidances are defined as those costs which would be incurred, due to growth in business volume, if the project was not implemented. Like savings, this list, of positions which will not need to be created, is broken out by labor grade and category.

Dollar savings

Using current and projected wage rates, the headcount savings are converted to dollar savings. Additional savings, such as material and equipment, are also captured here.

Dollar avoidances

This form is identical to the one above, except that headcount avoidances and anticipated cost reductions are captured.

Capital retired or salvaged and back-up documentation

Any capital equipment which will be retired or salvaged because of the implementation of this project is listed here. If the schedule for replacement is dependent upon the projected volumes of business, the volume assumptions must be documented in the Cost Philosophies and Assumptions section. Backup documentation shows the physical location of the equipment, associated product lines which use the equipment, and other possible applications of the equipment.

Output

The output of this analysis is a set of project costs and product cost reductions, broken out by product, by year, and by volume. In addition, the initial costs are distinguished from delivery costs, and any capital equipment retired or salvaged is shown. This set of figures is suitable for use as input to conventional cost-accounting methods such as payback, rate-of-return, or discounted cash flow models. Following that analysis, projects may be chosen which offer the highest profitability for the lowest risk. While the problems of specifying and costing AI-based systems will not disappear in the short term, this method allows the user and management to see tangible net benefits, even if bugetary estimates are exceeded.

Implementation

The Project Unit Costing Method has been implemented as a series of Microsoft® Multiplan® spreadsheets on the Apple® Macintosh.™ This allowed all computations, including links between forms, to be performed automatically. A worksheet was submitted to user groups which walked them through the process of choosing a project unit and estimating costs and savings. The results of this worksheet were entered in the Multiplan model, allowing all projections and savings to be computed automatically. Furthermore, the project model was linked to a discounted cash-flow model, giving a single figure-of-merit for each project. Once the data was collected and entered, the complete cost/benefit analysis of all 84 projects was completed in less than a week.

SUMMARY

AI-based systems are difficult to cost-justify, given that they are implemented incrementally, and their benefits are often not specified before implementation. By identifying tangible cost reduction targets as benefits, the Project Unit Costing Method makes it possible to select projects with the most attractive cost/benefit ratios. This encourages system designers to consider, before design begins, those aspects of the project which offer the greatest savings. This can be used to form a general specification which keeps design focused on those aspects, and which brings the design "tuning" cycle to halt when the most important cost-reducing features have been implemented. This also allows the design team and management to decide, if cost overruns occur, whether those overruns are justifiable with respect to the benefits expected.

ACKNOWLEDGEMENTS

This work was performed as part of Magnavox Electronic Systems Company's Industrial Modernization Incentives Program (IMIP), part of its internally funded Modernization Program. Magnavox's IMIP is performed under a business agreement with the U.S. Department of Defense, and is supervised by Air Force Systems Command/Electronic Systems Division.

Assessing IS organizational performance: Problems and suggestions

by CONNIE E. WELLS
Georgia State University
Atlanta, Georgia

Assessing the information systems (IS) function within organizations has been identified as one of the most critical issues of information systems management. Although this issue has been rated as one of the top 10 critical issues to IS managers for many years, it also appears that assessing IS performance is rated even higher in importance by non-IS managers than by the IS managers. Assessment of the IS organization is important for IS planning, and for identifying and solving IS problems. Despite the importance of the subject to both executive management and IS professionals, not much progress has been made toward understanding how to assess the contribution of the IS function to the enterprise. A true financial or economic (e.g., return on investment) IS evaluation is an illusive concept. Surrogate measures must be used. A thorough IS assessment needs to consider many factors and viewpoints, such as: attitudes of the various "stakeholders," IS planning and priority setting, system development practice and project control, the applications portfolio, operations efficiency, the IS measurement and control system, and IS organizational characteristics. We have developed a sizable list of these factors and measures within factors taken from IS literature and other sources.

Recent research indicates that the perceived performance of an IS organization on particular measures is related to whether or not IS performance on those measures are published in IS performance reports. Therefore, it is important that the measures that are used to assess IS performance accurately address the most important IS performance goals/issues. Currently, there seems to be little agreement as to which measures are appropriate to use to address the IS performance goals. In our first survey, conducted a year ago, IS managers were asked to recommend five measures to use to assess the performance of the IS organization. Approximately 170 different measures were suggested by the 94 respondents. Only 10 of these measures were suggested by at least 10 percent of the respondents. Over 70 percent of the measures were suggested by only one or two IS managers. Thus, we have many measures to choose from, but little agreement as to which measures to use.

There is, however, generally a high level of agreement between the highest IS managers (CIOs) and their counterparts in the other functional areas of the enterprise as to which performance goals/issues are most important for the IS organization. Our research indicates that the most important IS performance goals include: 1) the accuracy and reliability of data/information, 2) security of critical information resources, 3) backup and recovery planning, 4) user involvement in IS planning and systems development, and 5) IS leadership's understanding of the business. Current research is being performed to discover which of the recommended measures are most appropriate to use to address the most important goals for IS performance.

Executive information systems: Definitions and guidelines

by ALLAN PALLER
AUI Data Graphics/Computer Associates, International
Arlington, Virginia

ABSTRACT

This paper attempts to define a class of computer application, called Executive Information Systems (EIS), which has become a popular target of MIS departments in large organizations. By the end of 1987, fully 50% of the 100 largest organizations in the United States, and 33% of the largest 1,000, will have implemented information systems for use by their executives. A few of these systems will have substantially improved the productivity and profitability of their organizations, but the majority will have had little impact.

Part of the explanation for the differences between success and failure can be found in the definitions different organizations use for EIS and part can be found in the approaches they take to implementing EIS. The objective of this paper is to increase the chances of success by offering a firm definition and suggestions for effective implementation of EIS.

INTRODUCTION

An Executive Information System is a computer-based system that provides up-to-date answers to key questions raised by managers without burying the manager in unneeded data. EIS systems are action-oriented systems, because the answers lead to action by the managers.

A modern airplane cockpit is an effective model for an EIS. Key indicators are monitored constantly. When an indicator, such as elevation, moves outside an acceptable range, a warning sounds. The pilot can take immediate action to correct the problem. Hundreds of indicators are monitored, yet most of them become visible to the pilot only when a problem is apparent. A smaller number, such as speed, attitude, elevation, and course are constantly visible, because they show just how well the flight is going. These essential indicators are the ones that the pilot must watch constantly in order to "stay on course."

An EIS system has a similar hierarchy. Each executive must watch a small number of key indicators to be certain that his or her segment of the enterprise is "on course." In addition, there are hundreds, or even thousands, of additional indicators that are important, but that need to become visible only when their values go outside an acceptable range.

FINDING THE RIGHT BALANCE

An EIS system becomes more a burden than an asset when it provides too much information or, rather, when it buries the key indicators under the weight of hundreds of other pieces of potentially interesting information. On the other hand, systems that are thin on content are no more than toys. Answers to one question often lead to additional questions. An EIS must provide answers to that second level question, as well.

The problem facing designers is how to find the right balance. Too much data makes an EIS hard to use; too little makes it a toy. Yet executives do not maintain constant focus. The information they want to monitor changes as business problems ebb and flow.

A strategy that has proven effective in finding that correct balance is to include the detail, but hide it. In this strategy, you maintain data on every indicator of interest to the manager, but show only the critical success factors and other indicators that have exceeded acceptable ranges.

ON-LINE OR ON PAPER?

On-line data display does *not* appear to be an essential ingredient of successful executive information systems. On-line display may be useful when it hides unnecessary data. It also may offer a provocative "state of the art" management tool that may draw executives into testing the system. However, the excitement of on-line display should not blind EIS developers to the real needs of executives. Many executives travel a great deal and need data when they are out of the office. Others want to show information to people who are not served by the EIS. Still others want more comparative detail than can be shown on a CRT screen.

Paper-based executive information systems offer the dual advantages of portability and precision. Paper can be taken out of the office more easily than can a display. A page of charts can show ten to one-hundred times as much comparative information as a screen on a computer display. Further, a well designed page of charts can emphasize the critical indicators while also showing comparisons of dozens of lower-level indicators.

WHAT TO SHOW IS THE MOST IMPORTANT QUESTION

Whether paper or PCs are used to display the information is a far less important question than the choice of what information to display.

An EIS reaches into the heart of an organization. What indicators the executives monitor is closely watched by managers and workers throughout an organization. The most powerful impact of successful EIS systems has been the motivation it has created within an organization. Thus, picking the right indicators is the most important step toward making the system useful.

How can you find the right indicators? Two popular methods do not work well:

1. Asking the senior executives what questions they would ask when they got back from a three week vacation. Although this leads to a few good indicators, it generally misses important ones, because the senior executive's attention is focused on a limited subset of business problems.
2. Interviewing all senior managers to ask what data they think is most important. This has the benefit of getting managers involved in the process, but leads to too many indicators, with no way to limit them.

Some organizations have found a better way. Many large organizations have developed strategic and tactical plans for one, two, or five years. In these plans, the organization has laid out its objectives and how it plans to reach them. Whether it is "on course" can be measured by comparing its performance against the objectives laid out in those plans. The right indicators can be derived from a careful analysis of the plans by a team consisting of a business analyst who understands the organization and an EIS consultant who has analyzed enough EIS implementations to be able to recommend good display formats and effective hierarchies of indicators.

DATA INDEPENDENCE KEEPS YOUR OPTIONS OPEN

Information for an EIS will come from several different sources:

1. corporate data bases maintained in DB-2 or other DBMS systems
2. departmental data bases maintained in FOCUS, RAMIS, IFPS, or other planning and reporting systems
3. application programs such as MRP or financial management
4. personal data stored on minis or micros, and
5. external data bases such as Dow-Jones News Service.

In the rush to get a system operating, many EIS planners develop direct links from each of the data sources to the displays. They generate graphs or reports using programs appropriate to each data source and then combine the displays in a library for instant viewing. The benefits of this approach are quickly forgotten when the user begins to ask for changes.

Requests arise to compare data from multiple sources or to use one chart design with data from another source. Every request will create a substantial development task unless a strategy of data and graphics independence is followed.

Data independence means that data to be used in the EIS are transferred from their original source into a single holding place. FOCUS, LOTUS, or any other reporting system will all serve well. The value of data independence is created by storing all appropriate data in a common format. When a user requests comparisons or new formats, applying the display to the data becomes a simple task.

Similarly, graphics independence means using a graphics system that can chart data from any data source so that a chart design can be used regardless of the source of data to be charted.

VISIBILITY IN THE EXECUTIVE SUITE

Executive information systems offer a short-cut to information systems executives who want to participate in general management. The person who puts together the right data displays becomes an aide to the manager who uses those displays and thereby becomes eligible for management opportunities that arise. However, this visibility works two ways. If a system for executives is seen as a toy or as "too hard to use," then the visibility of its builder becomes a liability. Sticking close to the definitions and suggestions in this paper can help make certain that building an EIS system gives you the right kind of visibility.

MICROCOMPUTERS

SANDRA REED
Northern Illinois University
DeKalb, Illinois
and
HAL BERGHEL
University of Arkansas
Fayetteville, Arkansas

The Microcomputers track covers several business applications and core areas of microcomputer technology. The sessions are intended to meet the needs of novice and experienced users. Presenters provide the latest information on such major microcomputer topics as chip architecture, operating systems, and integrated software. Given the significant penetration of the business market by microcomputers, few managers and decision makers can afford to ignore these recent developments.

Micros in the workplace—the 1990s

by BRUCE GJERTSEN and CECIL PRETTY
Technology Guidance Associates
Libertyville, Illinois

INTRODUCTION

To find a setting where mainframe computers are used which has not felt the impact of the development and use of mini and microcomputers is rare if not impossible. And while the growing array of developments in the microcomputer field can generate much excitement and enthusiasm for personal computer "buffs," serious probelms can confront the data processing professional who attempts to actively implement strategies to accommodate mainframe-minicomputer-microcomputer links. This presentation will provide an overview and explanation of the events, concepts, and issues related to microcomputer applications which may provide some guidance in making the correct decisions related to the implementation and integration of these technologies.

THE FIRST TEN YEARS

In the mid-1970's, as the microprocessor on a chip became a reality, a handful of individuals dreamed of offering computers as kits. Few persons could ever have predicted the potential of such a range of relatively inexpensive microchip-based products as we understand them today. Some of the significant events to be briefly reviewed in the timeline are:

1. The development of early microprocessor chips: the 8080, the Z80, and the 6502
2. The heyday of single-tasking software
3. The Silicon Valley phenomenon
4. The emergence of significant concepts of computer design and implementation
5. The impact of the shake-out of the computer industry in the early '80s.

WHAT ARE THE CURRENT ISSUES?

As the pressure builds within organizations to attempt the forging of productive links among the various levels of mainframe, minicomputer, and microcomputer applications, a wide range of reactions and approaches result. In many cases, the outcomes mirror the tensions commonly found when cultures clash: there is much suspicion between and among advocacy and non-advocacy groups, and resistance to change becomes a major impediment to objective discussion and concrete action. More specifically, some of the user-related issues are:

Misrepresentation of Software and Hardware

The results of a recent poll are typical of those which provide fuel for the arguments of those who resent the intrusion of desktop computers and continue to resist their use in the work place. The poll of 526 businesses indicated that, in 70 percent of the cases, the software did not work as evisioned. It was claimed by many respondents that appropriate software was either unavailable or hard to find. Many charged that advertisers and vendors misrepresented the software in order to close a sale.

As for hardware: horror stories related to incompatibilities, inadequate warranties and service policies, and poor and negligent installations are countless.

Inappropriate Policies, Planning, and Training Strategies

The initial involvement with stand-alone microcomputer systems with simple applications of word processing, spreadsheets, data bases, and other tools often appears to bring quick gains in productivity. The effect may be deceptive and often leads to the possession of a shallow perspective on productive implementations of the technology. This detracts from serious long-range planning, appropriate policy making, and the establishment of effective training programs. Compared to the effort required to bring about the truly productive implementation of a constantly evolving access to resources and electronic tool-set, the initial commitment to spend money to purchase the technology is usually trivial.

The Data Base Dilemma

Data base management systems (DBMSes) have long been a major part of the mainframe and minicomputer landscape. First came the simple hierarchial models, then made more accessible by networking capabilities. But concurrent with the introduction of the IBM-PC, a marketing strategy regarded as unthinkable by some mainframe-using traditionalists, came—with IBM's DB2—the introduction of relational data bases. And then, in the opinion of many MIS managers, far too little time had elapsed before the introduction of distributed data base management systems (DDBMSes). The on-going debate is punctuated with concerns for user-access, data integrity and security, management policies, and implementation strategies.

The data base dilemma is further complicated, for some users and managers, by the continuing proliferation of on-line data bases, resources which contrast with the increasingly available laser-read optical storage media (now with 3 standards of CD-ROM) with the potential for a combination of text, audio, graphics, and animation. Any significant impact of artificial intelligence applications has yet to be measured but rumors of new developments, along with some ridiculous claims, abound.

All this, with the greatest advantages of fibreoptics and satellite transmission yet to come! One thing seems certain: the concept of information as a utility has been well-accepted.

The Push for Connectivity and Expandability

Microcomputers have gained their popularity because of low initial cost, portability, and ease of use. But many users soon find that standalone PCs are inadequate for the kind and number of tasks at hand. The dissatisfaction is often fueled by an awareness of the power of file and data sharing, and electronic communication.

With the appetite for the access to more data and increased computing power whetted, many users seek, but find impossible, the use of mainframes and minicomputers: lease or purchase, set-up, management and maintenance costs, are too expensive.

For those who turn to local area networks (LANs), questions of security and access arise. Many find the complexity of networking, especially when troubleshooting, overwhelming. And when a multitude of vendors supply a diversity of components, the excuses offered for non-performance of the network can take the form of endless loops.

So multiuser microcomputers, typically with up to 10 users on a small system, become an alternative. With a multiprocessing supermicro, a standard configuration usually includes a "birdcage" for expansion boards, a hard drive, a tape backup, all supervised by a special processor. A strong advantage in acquiring such a system is the confidence in the integrity of the design as a complete operational system.

Many of the PC enhancements—new chipsets, expansion boards and cards will permit the upgrading of existing models. Such add-on and add-in devices allow PC users to preserve the value of their investment of money and time. The brisk sales of laptop computers and the shift to $3^1/_2$ inch drives seems to indicate that the next generation of PCs will, in spite of being packed with more features, have a smaller "footprint."

SIGNS OF A MATURING INDUSTRY

On the developer/vendor side of the story, much effort is being expended to create products, operating-environments, and vendor/client relationships considerably more professional, reliable, flexible, and cost-effective than those characteristic of the pre-1985 era. The following are current efforts representative of a new level of maturity and commitment in today's computing industry:

The Concern for Compatibility

Considerable activity is currently being devoted to defining more-or-less precise specifications for hardware and software standards across the mainframe-mini-micro range. Some examples:

On the global level

Map (Manufacturing Automation Protocol) is a result of a 1980 General Motors task force recommendation to standardize communications specifications for factory floor operations. Such an action was prompted by GM's need, as an end-user to improve communication among various pieces of factory equipment such as programmable controllers and robots. GM's principal goal was to bring about a standardization of communication protocols among different vendors of equipment thus creating new levels of computer-integrated manufacturing. The original push has now evolved into the establishment of a world-wide user's group comprised of several hundred users and vendors.

TOP (Technical and Office Protocol), from Boeing Computer Services, offers a parallel and compatible set of standards applicable within office environments. Again, there is world-wide interest with participation in a users group by more than 100 companies with major data-processing departments. The goal of the group is to establish and maintain standard protocols related to office automation and resource sharing.

MAP and TOP conform to subsets of specifications contained within OSI (open systems interconnection) standards, a seven layer structure of protocols being defined by the International Standards Organization (ISO). It appears that this comprehensive set of protocols will gain high levels of acceptance thus leading to a guarantee of compatibility for manufacturing and office automation tasks throughout the world.

At the individual corporation level

In the late 1970's, Digital Equipment Corporation (DEC) made the decision (starting at that time) to build a new line of computers that could readily be linked together. The acceptance of the resulting VAX computer architecture has added to DEC's popularity in science and engineering fields and brought—during the mid-80's sales slump—new customers in other fields, including Europe, formerly served by IBM installations. IBM, with its proliferation of aging computer architectures, has been slow to follow DEC's example.

At the operating system level

Since the entry of IBM into the microcomputer market in 1981 with Micro-Soft's MS-DOS at the heart of its IBM-PC, microcomputers have largely been called "personal computers" and MS-DOS has become the *de facto* industry standard for 16-bit computers.

UNIX, an operating system originally developed for minicomputers by Bell Laboratories, has been rewritten for use with microcomputers. To this date, Unix cannot be regarded as a major commercial operation system. But considerable effort is being made to provide software which bridges the two operating systems—MS-DOS and Unix. Some experts insist that Unix will become the standard operating system for the 32-bit machines.

Towards Friendlier User Interfaces

In response to criticisms that training costs are too high, operating commands are too cryptic, operating systems are too difficult for the would-be average user to interpret, and, as a result, the transfer of skills from one software application or operating system to another is limited, a considerable amount of effort is being directed toward improving the human interface. The following are some of the devices and features that are now available, at relatively lost cost, for use with many makes of microcomputers:

1. The mouse pointing device for cursor positioning
2. Icons as pictographic representations of important objects and commands
3. Multiple windows that simultaneously display different programs
4. High-resolution graphics with the use of sound and color as a means of motivating the user and providing for clarity of presentation
5. Applications permitting touch screen input, voice recognition and optical character recognition.

HUMAN RESOURCES—THE REAL CHALLENGE

To this point, we have been primarly concerned with technical considerations. But the anwers to increased productivity through correct implementation policies and strategies will only come with a parallel consideration of issues related to "people problems".

Not much experience in a computer-intensive environment is required to bring out the realization that the most challenging problems may not be with the technology itself, but with attempting to change the ways people attempt to use it. Effective computer applications usually require changes in the "pre-computer" approaches to accomplishing specific objectives or tasks. A period of experimentation with the objective application of the technology must be matched by a period of "play" by the individual members of the human resource group who must overcome their anxiety in finding the best approach to making the application work.

A second level of increasing concern is based on some critical issues that have arisen as the implementation of computer technology in the workplace approaches the scale of a mass movement in society. Here is a cross-section:

The Design of Physical Plant Structures

The planning, designing, and construction of "intelligent" buildings and environments to accommodate computer-based technologies will increasingly demand a knowledge of ergonomics, information, communication, security, climate control, and energy systems monitored and controlled by advanced computer systems already in existence. Worldwide, there is a shortage of personnel, from architects to managers, capable of providing services and performing the necessary tasks.

The Location of Computer-intensive Businesses

The shift of the nation's economy to a service and knowledge base is a major factor in the rapid growth of urban villages—the locating of office space and related amenities in suburban communities. Computerized functions—especially those based upon the telecommunication of data and information—are essential to the operation of such services and yet do not require physical proximity to traditional city cores. Issues related to such rapid demographic change include shortages of qualified clerical, light-assembly, and service personnel, the lack of locally-available appropriate high-density housing, day-care, and transportation services for low-paid workers.

The Redefinition of Social Institutions and Professions

The impact of computerization is touching virtually every profession and occupation in society. Some of the more obvious changes:

Health care

A revolution in healthcare and delivery methods is strongly affecting hospital operation and the deployment of medical personnel. Due to competition for the provision of services there is an increasing need to contain costs while meeting the health-care related needs of a greying population. Fully integrated health-care information networks are under development which eventually will link the patient's home with doctors' offices, clinical personnel, hospitals, and sources of medical information and education.

Education

In the face of increasing enrollments and demands for higher educational and professional standards, the education field is confronted with shortages of teachers. An increase in the number of applications of computer-based and computer-assisted instructional delivery systems and a greater use of teacher productivity applications is taking place.

Libraries

The use of on-line data bases and optical storage media, microcomputer-based methods of cataloging, and patron access to information sources is changing the service and research missions of many libraries.

FINDING PATHWAYS THROUGH THE MAZE

The futurists and trend spotters continue to present arguments and provide evidence that the 1990's will be a time of rapid change and mounting uncertainty in the workplace. What are some key elements in learning to effectively implement and integrate microcomputers within these workplaces of the 1990s? Some vital strategies include:

1. Improving the flow of information throughout an organization. The main operational goals should emphasize achieving an acceptable level of productivity, strong communication within the work group, and the sharing of appropriate information throughout the organization. Effective computer implementation can elevate individual and group productivity, but only if appropriate attention is paid to establishing the most appropriate "people" links between and among each level of operations.
2. Representative participants from every level of operations and personnel clusters should be involved in assessing needs, determining objectives, and establishing procedures and policies. A considerable effort also needs to be made to implement effective assessment and evaluation standards and procedures.
3. The actual short and long-range goals of the computer-using organization must be determined and logically charted out as part of an organizational infrastructure. In most cases, these goals remain relatively constant. In the volatile world of information technology the physical configurations appropriate to achieving those goals often do not. With goals clearly defined, the comparison of ways to achieve them with computer-based technology is much easier.
4. Special attention must be paid to the strengths and weaknesses of individuals within work groups or personnel clusters. Each personnel cluster will have a unique mix of technical, application, and problem-solving skills. Attempting to mandate uniform operational strategies for each group may rob an organization of some of its richest resources: individual and group creativity, team spirit, and constructive competitiveness.
5. The available technologies to be applied to the achievement of specific objectives may also indicate the need to create new work clusters. Adopting the "islands of automation" approach may provide the best building blocks or "springboards" for eventually creating a totally integrated operation. There are some tough decisions to be made here in regard to predictability of performance vs. flexibility of performance.

CONCLUSION

The easy availability of microcomputers has brought the most important technological advance since Gutenberg's printing press to almost anyone who wishes to use it. Because of the rapidity and vast scope of development of hardware and software, the resulting potential for productive applications is enormous. The challenges of the 1990's will be to harness this potential for the benefit of organizations while effectively addressing high levels of anxiety and insecurity for personnel because of rapid change in the workplace, and society in general. To be successful will require establishing working environments that place a premium on human capital by encouraging the growth of individual responsibility and productivity and, in embracing computer technology appropriately, provide a sense of individual and group fulfilment and empowerment.

Basic networking implementation for the small computer environment

by P. TOBIN MAGINNIS
University of Mississippi
University, Mississippi
and
DONALD F. MILLER
Digital Equipment Corporation
Atlanta, Georgia

ABSTRACT

Development of a simple networking protocol which employs existing terminal line hardware and operating system services has created a separate networking category we refer to as basic networking. Basic networking provides the small computer user, especially those in a diverse computing environment such as offices, schools, and research institutes, with what appears to be a reasonable tradeoff between network implementation complexity and network services.

INTRODUCTION

Networking systems can be employed in one of four basic ways: 1) As truly distributed operating systems[1] such as the Cambridge Distributed Computing System,[2] 2) as networking operating systems such as the National Bureau of Standards Experimental Networking Operating System,[3] 3) as general networking systems such as DEC's Digital Network Architecture,[4] or IBM's Systems Network Architecture,[5,6] or 4) as basic networking systems where networking programs, like any other application program, execute without operating system modification and employ existing terminal lines.

OSI COMPARISONS

The international standards organization has developed an open systems interconnection (OSI) model for general networking schemes. The OSI model consists of seven hierarchical functional layers which provide a solution framework for many networking problems. Tanenbaum[7] provides a detailed discussion of the OSI model and contrasts it with three general networks: ARPANet, SNA and DNA.

A functional comparison shows that the OSI physical and data link layers are equivalent to the use of existing terminal line interfaces and the use of error checking. Since error free blocks are mapped directly into files, basic networking makes no distinction between a frame, packet, or message. There is no sense of the OSI network or transport layers since connections are point-to-point, or through a neighboring computer, and use existing operating system services. Thus, networking and transport layer services such as routing, congestion control, buffer deadlock prevention, addressing, connection establishment, multiplexing, and delayed packet synchronization are not issues in basic networking. At the OSI presentation layer, basic networking maps operating system specific character codes and file formats into a networking format and back into another operating system format. Other presentation layer functions such as data encryption and data compression are basic networking possibilities.

THRIFTNET IMPLEMENTATION

On the University of Mississippi campus a number of small independent computer systems exist for a variety of research and administrative purposes. These systems typically do not have adequate mass storage, data analysis programs, or specialized peripherals such as plotters and line printers. As a result, there was a need for a data transfer mechanism between these small systems and larger systems which had the desired services.[8,9,10]

A typical Thriftnet session has two basic phases: a virtual terminal phase and the file transfer phase. Initially a virtual terminal link is established between the two communicating computers during which time all characters typed on the user's terminal are uninterpreted by the local system and sent directly to the remote computer. Thus, the user's terminal appears as any terminal directly connected to the remote computer system. The file transfer phase is initiated when the user runs either the RECEIV or TRNSMT program on the remote computer system.

Figure 1 shows 11 operating systems for which Thriftnet programs are currently available. Each system may have up to four separate programs: THRIFT, RECEIV, TRNSMT and PASSON. The "T" in Figure 1 indicates that a version of THRIFT exists for the top row of operating systems. The controlling program, THRIFT, initiates a virtual terminal with any operating system. The column of operating systems on the left hand side of Figure 1 each have a version of the RECEIV or TRNSMT programs which allow file transfer with the "row" operating systems. The "E" in Figure 1 indicates that file transfer may be initiated from either operating system and in either direction.

When a timesharing operating system initiates a transfer to a single user operating system one of two configurations is assumed. One is that the single user console terminal has been directly connected to the timesharing system's output terminal port. This configuration has been helpful in laboratories where a number of single user systems collect data. Any timesharing user can use Thriftnet to control the single user machine or initiate data transfer between the timesharing system and any of the remote systems.

	CP/M™-80	MS-DOS™	OS/8™	RSTS/E™	RSX-11M™	RT-11™	TRSDOS™	UNIX™
CP/M™-80	E	E	T	E	E	E	T	E
CMS™	T	T	T	T	T	T	T	T
RSTS/E™	E	E	T	E	E	E	T	E
RSX-11M™	E	E	T	E	E	E	T	E
RT-11™	E	E	T	E	E	E	T	E
TOPS-10™	E	T	E	E	E	E	T	E
UNIX™	E	T	E	E	E	E	T	E
VMS™	T	T	T	T	T	T	T	T

Figure 1—Thriftnet File Transfer Possibilities

A second configuration assumes that the THRIFT program is executing on the controlling system. The RECEIV or TRNSMT programs are then executed on the single user system which continues the file transfer protocol over each machine's extra serial port. This second configuration is mainly used when transferring files between two microcomputers which do not have a serial connection for the console terminal.

When two timesharing systems are directly connected and either may initiate file transfer, then an additional signal (ring or carrier detect) may be employed to determine when the terminal line will be used as a login or output port. Since this strategy requires modems, we generally interconnect multiple terminal lines between local timesharing systems. Thus, there may be as many users as there are wires transferring files in either direction.

Figure 2 shows an overview of intercomputer connections and program relationships. The primary program, THRIFT, is run on the user's local computer A and indicated as "THRIFT A." The local system may be either a timesharing or a single user system but, most often, is a stand alone single user computer. The minimal configuration for a local computer system is a user terminal and an extra terminal port which is then connected to a remote computer terminal port. Remote computers may be either single user or timesharing but, most often, are timesharing systems. Two additional programs, RECEIV and TRNSMT, present on remote computer systems, negotiate the file transfer to or from local computer A and remote computer B. Executing THRIFT on remote computer B invokes "THRIFT B" in Figure 2, which is detected by the first THRIFT program. The second THRIFT program connects remote computer B to a third nonadjacent system, remote computer C in Figure 2. A virtual terminal connection then exists between local computer A and remote computer C, however, when RECEIV or TRNSMT programs are run on remote computer C, file transfer occurs between B and C. The number of successive THRIFT programs which may be executed is only limited by the number of physical connections between computer systems. Users terminate a virtual terminal session by typing an escape character, CAN (control x), for each THRIFT program run.

A fourth program, PASSON, allows two computers that are not directly connected to one another to communicate by linking through a third computer system. Thus, executing PASSON on remote computer B still allows the virtual terminal session between A and C, and when RECEIV or TRNSMT are executed, file transfer will also occur between A and C. An infrequently occurring sequence of characters is used to abort the PASSON program, three repetitions of DLE (control p) and EOT (control d). Note that binary data can assume any bit pattern, and that character stuffing would not decrease the possibility of a premature escape from PASSON since a binary file has the ability to contain any "special" data link escape character.

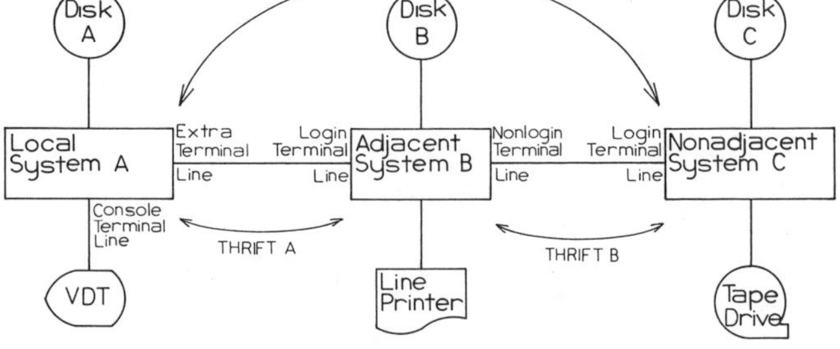

Figure 2—Thriftnet interconnections

Many times a Baud mismatch exists between the users terminal and the two communicating computers. When terminal Baud is greater than the intercomputer Baud, it gives the appearance of slower terminal speed; however, when the user's terminal has a relatively slow speed, characters can be lost when Thriftnet buffers are exceeded. Thriftnet uses a circular buffer algorithm with a small buffer to show Baud mismatches and to permit rapid escapes from lengthy typeouts. This is not a problem during file transfer since each frame is buffered and acknowledged before the next frame is sent.

Whenever possible, Thriftnet programs have been written to be logical device oriented as opposed to physical device or file device oriented. Therefore, in Figure 2, Thriftnet allows the more convenient path of transferring a file from remote computer C's tape drive directly to remote computer B's line printer instead of from tape to disk, disk to disk, and disk to printer. If remote computer B employs a spooling daemon, then THRIFT submits the file to the spooler.

THRIFTNET USER INTERFACE

As shown in Figure 3, a Thriftnet user executes the THRIFT program on the local computer system (line 1) and is placed in relay mode (line 3) during which the user's terminal appears to be directly connected to the remote computer system. While in this virtual terminal mode, the user can execute any program on the remote system. Thus, in lines 4 through 6, the user executes the login program on the remote system to gain access to the system's resources. In line 7 the user issues the command to execute the RECEIV program on the remote system. The RECEIV program will oversee the transfer of a file from the user's local system to the remote system and will cause the user's THRIFT program to initiate its complementary transmitting subsection. The transmitting subsection of THRIFT announces itself in line 8, and subsequently, prompts the user first for the name of the file to be transmitted from the local system (lines 9 and 10), and secondly for the name the user wants assigned to that file on the remote system (lines 11 and 12). If only the Carriage Return (CR) was typed, then the local system file name would have been sent to the remote system. Files are transferred by default in ASCII and arranged in an operating system compatible format. Four other possible switches are: "−b" indicating that the file should be stored as a bitstream and not interpreted; "−l" indicating that the user wishes to be auto-logoffed both systems if they are multiuser systems; "−c" indicating that both programs should recycle after file transfer for another file specification; and "−r" indicating that the file should be removed after transfer.

```
1) R THRIFT<cr>
2) ThriftNet - Version 3
3) Relay Mode
4) <cr>
5) login incorrect
6) name: harry<cr>
7) % receiv<cr>
8) Entering RT-11 TRANSMIT mode.
9) Enter local RT-11 file specs "DEV:FILNAM.EXT"
10) myfile.lst<cr>
11) Enter remote UNIX target file specs.
12) myfile<cr>
13) <lf>
14) +++++B++++L++++++++++++++++
15) File transmitted
16) Relay Mode
17) % print myfile<cr>
18) % ^d
19) login: ^x
20) Returning to RT-11
21)
```

Figure 3—Thriftnet user dialog

File transfer begins with the THRIFT program typing a plus for each successfully transferred frame, (line 14). In line 15, successful file transmission is indicated. When errors occur during the transfer, an L or B is typed to indicate a longitudinal redundancy character error or byte count error. Five consecutive errors would have caused the termination of the transfer and the issuance of an appropriate message to the user. Completion of the file transfer session is indicated by the message, "relay mode" in line 16. The user can then continue using the remote system via the virtual terminal mechanism and must remember to logoff the remote system when finished. Return to the local system is accomplished by the user typing CAN (control x). Other available user options are discussed below.

THRIFTNET FILE TRANSFER PROTOCOL

Figure 4 shows a schematic depicting the Thriftnet file transfer protocol. The left half of the diagram shows responses to and from a local THRIFT program while the right half shows the corresponding actions of a remote TRNSMT program during the transfer of a file from a remote to local system. Running the RECEIV program on the remote system would result in essentially the same protocol except that data frames would be sent in the opposite direction. Either program establishes what could be considered a virtual circuit without routing tables.

Initially, when the THRIFT program is executed on a local computer system, virtual terminal service or "relay mode" is activated. All keystrokes are relayed to the remote computer operating system or the currently running application program. Responses from the remote system are then displayed on the local computer terminal. Six special characters are not usually relayed to the remote computer. First, SOH (control a) allows the user of a multitasking operating system to return to the background leaving the remote connection intact. Second, ENQ (control e) enables local echoing of user typed characters allowing interaction with half duplex systems. Third, DLE (control p) terminates the PASSON program on the remote system by initiating three repetitions of DLE-EOT. Fourth, SYN (control v) initiates a bootstrap program which reads a file and transmits sequential characters from the file and waits for their echo. Fifth, ETB (control w) initiates a "capture mode" which saves all transmitted and received characters in a specified file. Sixth, CAN (control x) terminates the virtual terminal session and returns the user to the local operating system. Finally, Thriftnet includes an escape mechanism by which even these characters may be passed to the remote system.

Ultimately, the user executes the TRNSMT program on the remote system. TRNSMT responds with nine seven bit unsigned integers (tokens). The first token, acknowledge (ACK), signals the local THRIFT program that a special Thriftnet program has been run on the remote system. The second token is the program's version number and indicates the possibility of an incompatible earlier protocol. The third token, tarflgs, contains five target flags which indicate if the target node can or cannot perform timing, if the master should wait for the echo of each character transmitted, if the target node requires character stuffing, if the master node should honor XON/XOFF characters, and if the target node will collect file transfer statistics. The fourth token, slus, indicates the serial line unit bit size and is most often eight bits. Parallel line units are planned for the future and the seven bit integer would allow character lengths up to 128 bits. The fifth token, lins, is the maximum operating system buffer size. Thriftnet currently employs 128 or 64 byte data blocks which may grow up to 256 or 128 bytes if each data byte requires

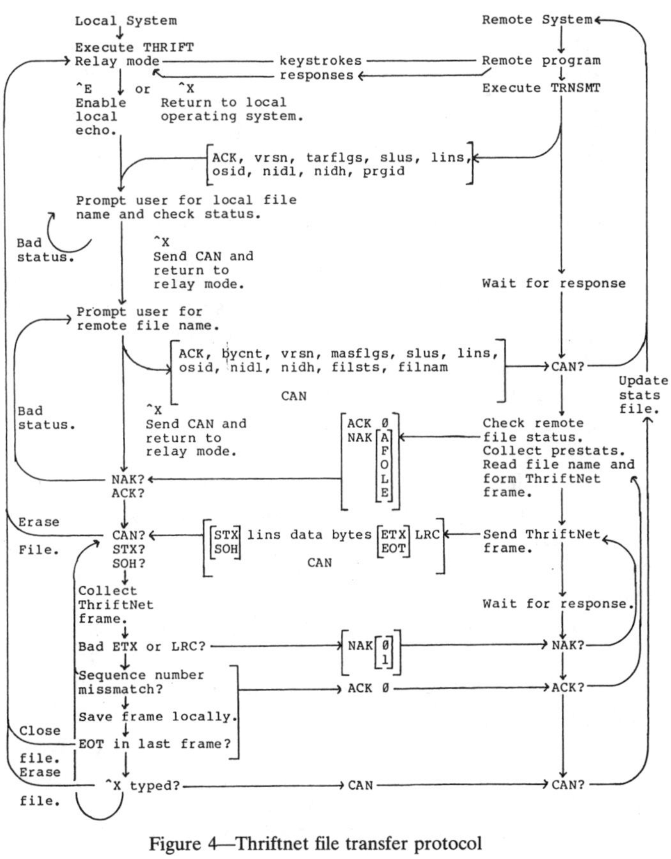

Figure 4—Thriftnet file transfer protocol

stuffing. The sixth token, osid, is the operating system type identification, while nidl and nidh represent the low and high order node identification. The ninth token, prgid, represents one of four possible codes corresponding to the various Thriftnet programs: RECEIV, TRNSMT, PASSON and THRIFT.

Upon receipt of the nine tokens from the remote TRNSMT program, the local THRIFT program prompts the user for the local system file name. After determining that the specified file can be created without overwriting an existing file, the local THRIFT program prompts the user for the target file specification. If a CAN (control x) is entered while the local THRIFT program is prompting for either file name, a CAN is transmitted to the remote system causing it to return to its operating system, while the user is returned to relay mode.

The file specification for the remote system is packaged along with ten other tokens. The first token, ACK, indicates a Thriftnet response. If the remote TRNSMT or RECEIV programs do not detect an ACK as the first response character, it is assumed the program was executed directly from a terminal and not through the THRIFT master. The remote program then exits to the remote operating system. This prevents naive or curious users from locking their terminals when directly executing the protocol programs. The second token, bycnt, indicates the length of the response packet. The third token, vrsn, indicates the master's version number. The fourth token, masflags, currently contains only one flag indicating that the master THRIFT program was run from a third remote system and that PASSON is the local program. The next four tokens, slus, lins, osid, nidl and nidh provide the same function as described earlier. The ninth token, filsts, contains four flags. The first flag indicates a binary mode transfer where incoming characters are not interpreted, but simply treated as a bitstream. The second flag indicates if the user selected the auto-logoff option. A third flag indicates that after file transfer, the remote node program should recycle for new file specifications. A a fourth flag indicates that the remote system file is to be deleted upon successful completion of file transfer.

Receipt of the file specification frame initiates the file access. If the file was successfully accessed, an acknowledge message is sent to the local THRIFT program. If the file could not be accessed, negative acknowledgement, followed by an error code indicating the type of access problem, is sent. Possible error conditions are: 1) file specification syntax error (NAKF), 2) nonexistent device error (NAKE), 3) improper access privileges (NAKL), and 4) nonexistent file (NAKO). Receipt of a negative acknowledgement code from the remote system, results in THRIFT reprompting for a new remote file name. Again, typing CAN (control x) returns the user to relay mode.

A correct file specification causes the remote system to form and transmit a Thriftnet frame which consists of a start of text (STX) or start of header (SOH) character, 128 or 64 data bytes, an end of text (ETX) or end of transmission (EOT) character, and a longitudinal redundancy character (LRC). The LRC is formed from the exclusive ORing of the preceding 66 to 260 characters. A character count of 260 occurs when all 128 data bytes and the two control characters require character stuffing. If the LRC requires stuffing, then maximum frame size would equal 262 characters. The local THRIFT program has been waiting for one of three possible characters. If the character was STX or SOH, a Thriftnet frame is collected. If the character was a CAN, the incomplete file is deleted on the local system and THRIFT returns to a relay mode. Subsequent to receipt of a Thriftnet frame, the local THRIFT program verifies the location of the ETX or EOT character, and, if present, then compares the locally calculated LRC with the received LRC. If the two LRCs match, an acknowledge message is sent to the remote TRNSMT program which initiates the transmission of the next Thriftnet frame. If the ETX or EOT character was not seen when expected, or if the local and remote LRCs did not match, a negative acknowledge (NAK) message is sent to the remote TRNSMT program which initiates retransmission of the Thriftnet frame up to four additional times before file transmission is aborted.

When the remote system reaches the end of the file being transmitted, nulls are used to fill the remainder of the last Thriftnet frame. If the pre-LRC character of the last frame was EOT, the file just received is closed, and the THRIFT program returns to relay mode. Upon acknowledgement of the last Thriftnet frame the remote TRNSMT program returns to the remote operating system. If a CAN (control x) is typed by the local system user, the THRIFT master sends a CAN to the remote system, the incomplete file is erased, and THRIFT returns to relay mode.

THRIFTNET USAGE DATA

Basic networking schemes such as Thriftnet test the ability of an operating system to deal with high terminal data rates. If three or more users of a multitasking operating system are using the virtual terminal facilities, little effect is seen when keystrokes are echoed between systems; however, other timesharing users notice a longer system response interval when several users transfer files simultaneously to/from an operating system at a relatively high terminal line Baud. Experience with a PDP-11/34 based UNIX system with two DZ-11 eight-channel terminal multiplexors has shown that operating system bandwidth appears to be approximately 7,200 characters per second, when character input and output are equal. Assuming no input, the system seems to be capable of producing 28,800 characters per second of output. These results suggest that as the number of simultaneous networking users increase above three, or as terminal speeds approach 9,600 Baud, a more general networking scheme employing a processor hierarchy should replace the basic networking scheme.

Upon completion of most Thriftnet file transfers, statistical information is logged on the target operating system. Each entry contains the date and time, the user's name, node identification numbers for master and target systems, the target system terminal line number and its Baud, the number of byte count errors, the number of longitudinal redundancy character errors, the number of successfully transferred blocks, total file transfer duration, and data bytes transferred per second.

Over a two year period, more than 350 users transferred 16,474 files to or from 10 target systems. The three highest were on the University of Mississippi campus and included a DEC-1077 TOPS system with 41.6% of the transfers, a PDP-11/34 UNIX system with 35.3% of the transfers, and an IBM-4341 CMS system with 10.9% transfers. Thirty-nine master systems, employing 10 different operating systems, initiated transfers. The most frequent file transfer initiation was from an RT-11 system with 29% transfers, next was the UNIX system with 26.4% file transfers, the third most frequent was an off-campus RT-11 system with 21.8% transfers. Target operating systems received 45.8% of the files and transmitted 54.2%. Of all transfers, 42.5% were at 1,200 Baud, 31% at 300 Baud, 17.9% at 4,800 Baud, while the remaining 8.6% ranged between 110 and 9,600 Baud. ASCII mode was employed in 93.5% of all transfers and binary mode for the remainder. Auto-logoff was selected in 5.4% of the file transfers, while 7.2% were cancelled by the user once file transfer was underway. File transfer time was highly skewed, the most frequent duration was 7 seconds, the median time was 44.76 seconds, while the average was 4.4 minutes.

Byte count errors occurred in 4.5% of file transfers and LRC errors were observed in 2.7% of all file transfers. File transfer was stopped when five cumulative byte count or LRC errors occurred within a Thriftnet block, however, 0.4% of file transfers succeeded with "random" byte count errors, and 0.2% transfers succeeded with random LRC errors. Thus, once a byte count or LRC error occurs, there appears to be 92% to 93% chance that at least four more will quickly occur. Excluding user cancelled transfers, 95.6% of all file transfers attempted succeeded. Finally, it was noted that approximately sixty percent of all transfers used 50% or less of the terminal line bandwidth. Per character interrupt processing, in combination with operating system overhead, was probably the primary reason for relatively poor line usage. This possibility was supported by an informal investigation of a serial DECnet connection which revealed similar terminal line bandwidth usage.

CONCLUSION

In conclusion, basic networking disadvantages seem to be: 1) that the network implementer and user must have an understanding of data communications fundamentals, 2) that the user must also be aware of point-to-point computer connections and each operating system command set, and 3) that basic networking offers relatively slow file transfer (between 300 and 9,600 Baud). On the other hand, a basic networking strategy such as Thriftnet seems to offer critical networking services for little, or no, cost. These services assist in the interconnection of small computers that otherwise could not employ networking. The resource sharing allowed by basic networking seems to enhance the utility of a small computer system. And basic networking may act as a gateway to more sophisticated network architectures.

REFERENCES

1. Lampson, B. W., M. Paul and H. J. Siegert (eds.) *Distributed Systems Architecture and Implementation: An Advanced Course.* New York: Springer-Verlag, 1981.
2. Needham, R. M. and A. J. Herbert *The Cambridge Distributed Computing System.* Reading, Massachusetts: Addison-Wesley, 1982.
3. Kimbleton, S. R., Wood, H. M. and Fitzgerald, M. L. "Network Operating Systems—An Implementation Approach." *AFIPS, Proceedings of the National Computer Conference,* (Vol. 47), 1978, pp. 773–782.
4. Wecker, S. "DNA: The Digital Network Architecture." *IEEE Transactions on Communications,* COM-28 (1980) 4, pp. 510–526.
5. Atkins, J. D. "Path Control: The Transport Network of SNA." *IEEE Transactions on Communications,* COM-28 (1980) 4, pp. 527–538.
6. Hoberecht, V. L. "SNA Function Management." *IEEE Transactions on Communications,* COM-28 (1980) 4, pp. 594–603.
7. Tanenbaum, A. S. *Computer Networks.* Englewood Cliffs, New Jersey: Prentice-Hall, 1981.
8. Ferguson, P. A., D. F. Miller and P. T. Maginnis "Thriftnet: An Economical Software Package for Interprocessor Communications." *Behavior Research Methods and Instrumentation,* 13 (1981) 2, pp. 251–254.
9. Maginnis, P. T. "Thriftnet: A Simple Networking Strategy." *20th Annual Southeast Regional ACM Conference Proceedings,* 1982, pp. 5–8.
10. Miller, D. F. "Thriftnet: A Reliable Networking Strategy." *20th Annual Southeast Regional ACM Conference Proceedings,* 1982, pp. 9–13.

Microcomputer word processing software: A functional perspective

by HAL BERGHEL
University of Arkansas
Fayetteville, Arkansas

ABSTRACT

We propose a taxonomy of features of word processing software which can be used to summarize their functional characteristics. This taxonomy is then applied to existing products in order to derive estimates of variation between products, and to extract meaningful trends.

INTRODUCTION

One of the most important objectives of a data processing manager is the selection of software which is appropriate for his/her objectives. Appropriateness, of course, is a complex objective. The manager must be sensitive to the cost-effectiveness of the product, its performance and ease of use, compatibility with products already in use, conversion time, error handling characteristics, quality of documentation, reliability, and so forth. But first and foremost, the manager must be able to determine whether the functionality of the software is adequate with respect to present and future data processing objectives. In plain terms: if the software fails to provide the range of features required by the application, its utility may be marginal.

In this paper, we propose an analysis of microcomputer word processing software which we have found useful in evaluating current products. So that no confusion results, it is useful to contrast an "analysis" with a "rating." Analyses, in our view, separate the components of the software and examine their properties and interrelationships. Ratings, on the other hand, assign values to products which purport to measure their quality. While ratings can be useful, they do have some drawbacks.

First, their value is proportional to the degree of rigor and thoroughness of the underlying methodology, which is usually not described in detail. Second, in order for any overall rating or ranking to be meaningful, the 'rater' and the user must agree with respect to the weighting schemes used (e.g., that feature 1 is as important as feature 2). Third, due to the volatility of the software industry, the useful life of the rating is very short. These first two weaknesses imply an uncertainty regarding the confidence level to assign to the report. The third weakness implies that most ratings will be obsolete before they are read.

In our opinion, the easiest way to avoid these difficulties is to provide the decision maker with the tools for analysis, rather than the results. The classification scheme presented here falls far short of perfection. However, we have found it to be a satisfactory framework for evaluation of word processing systems.

While the statistical results below focus upon microcomputer word processing systems, the analysis itself applies to word processing systems in general. We have chosen to apply the analysis to microcomputers because of their prominence in the office automation market. A brief glance through such trade publications as *Data Sources*[1] and *datapro*[2] will reveal the number of microcomputer word processing packages sold far exceeds the number of dedicated systems in use.

WORD PROCESSING ANALYSES

Our analysis works with a classification scheme for word processors which determines functionality by analyzing the command structure of the product. Since this taxonomy is the key to the analysis, some general remarks are in order.

We use the term "word processing software" to refer to a class of application programs which allows the user to create, display, edit, and store documents with a computer. No distinction is made between hardware environments, whether dedicated, stand-alone, microcomputer, or mainframe.

Word processing software, in our view, consists of five functionally distinct components: a text editor, a document manager, print, and display controllers, and a formatter. Each of these is interrelated and may be directly accessed by the user (see Figure 1). While we shall keep these components distinct in our discussion, we recognize that they may not be independent in a particular product. For example, it is not uncommon for modern products to merge the formatter and the text editor.

Each of these individual components relates to a particular class of activity involving an electronic document. By means of the document manager, the user creates, deletes, and stores such documents. Through the display and print controllers, the user exercises control over the media of presentation of the document. With the formatter, the user alters the form or appearance of the document. The text editor, however, is the kernel of the word processing software. Only the text editor supports the change of content of the document.

In our model, there is an input device (keyboard) and three peripherals (printer, display, and secondary storage). Input information falls into two categories: command information and text. Textual information is entered through the text editor, alone, whereas command information may be accepted by each subsystem. We seek to discover the functionality of a word processing system by means of a taxonomy of the commands supported. We argue that this is both a reasonable and concise description of the domain. It is a relatively objective, user-oriented, and inexpensive alternative to more complex analyses.

LEVELS OF ANALYSIS

There is no orthodoxy when it comes to the analysis of functionality of word processors. Even analyses which purport to describe word processors from the user's point of view differ significantly in terms of scope and detail. In fact, the level sometimes varies within the analysis. For example, Riddle[3] deals with such details as buffering techniques, command line

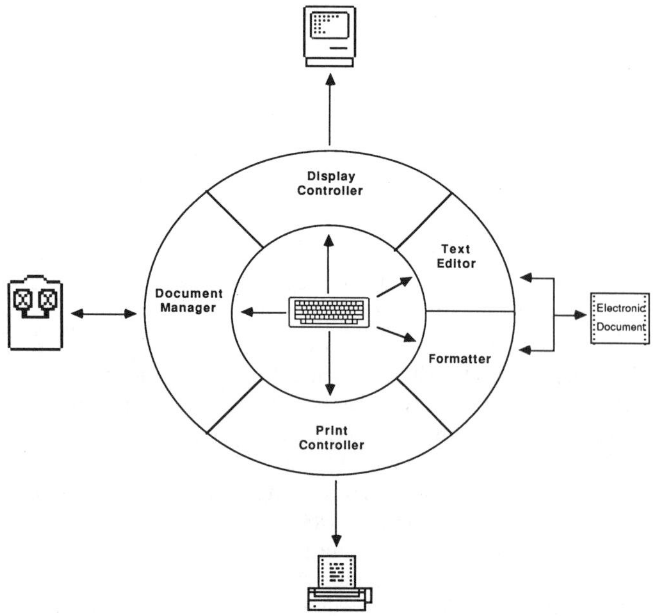

Figure 1—Five functional components of word processor

structure, and how tabs are handled but subsumes all variations of "locate" operations into one feature, and ignores the display control altogether. In this case, the analysis ranges from what Meyrowitz and van Dam[4,5] call the structural, or architectural, level to a description at the level of complex task.

Greater consistency is achieved by Roberts and Moran.[6,7,8] In this case, the analysis is usually at the level of a core editing task which is to be taken as the cross-product of a basic text editing operation (e.g., insertion and deletion) applied to basic text entities (e.g., characters, words, and sentences). This sort of analysis explicates the functionality of a product in terms of the range of core tasks supported. We have three objections to the use of core editing tasks. First, we know of no consensus regarding the appropriateness of certain core tasks to word processing applications as a whole. Failing consensus, the relevance of the core tasks to a particular work-setting must be demonstrated before the reliability of the measure may be determined. Second, all word processors, or a Turing machine, for that matter, support the same range of core tasks in one sense: it is simply a matter of how much work is involved. Thus, the issue of functionality must be further explained in terms of effort. This entails empirical study of a fast-moving and volatile market. Third, core task analyses ignore the manner of implementation of the task: generally, factors which have nothing to do with effort, but may be nonetheless, of considerable interest to the user.

For example, previewing a document with a continuous-formatting word processor is quite different than with preview-mode editors. Text editors which store control information as printable characters, as opposed to control characters not only behave differently but also generate electronic documents with distinctive properties. Similarly, insertion by split-screen might appeal to a different audience than insertion in a move-aside fashion. The point here is that the design philosophy behind a word processor is likely to affect its overall utility in ways which may not directly translate into effort. We believe that for these three reasons, at least for a first pass over the current products, the user would prefer a simpler, and less formidable, analysis than one based upon tasks.

Our study, then, attempts to extract the measure of functionality of a word processor from its command structure, including the manner of implementation of the basic operations involved, where important. We will list a feature as supported if and only if there is a specific command sequence which invokes it, or if it is a consequence of some other such sequence (e.g., automatic reformatting after deletion). In many ways, it is similar in approach to the analyses and ratings found in the popular and trade books,[9,10,11] with the exception that our taxonomy is generally of greater detail and reflects an attempt to hierarchically order the features.

PROBLEMS OF ANALYSIS

All taxonomies reflect the preferences and objectives of the taxonomist. In order to avoid inundation by detail, we have reduced the range of commands and implementation characteristics to one which we feel is both manageable and appropriate for acquisition strategies. Our selection of features is not immune to criticisms of arbitrariness. The only justification we can offer is that we have found it to be more useful than the known alternatives. Since the taxonomy serves as a filter to separate the products which match applications requirements from those which don't, the validation of the method is ultimately going to be the approbation of the user.

We specifically arranged the taxonomy to agree with what we feel are typical perceptions of features. This strategy has several implications:

1. The same underlying operation may appear as two or more separate features. This occurs when two or more commands are functionally identical, although not perceived as such. For example, some semantically simple commands (e.g., grammatically oriented operations like word and sentence deletion) are only approximated in software as special cases of other types of operations (delete-to-target). Since the user perceives the distinction between these two types of commands, the features are individuated.
2. Complex operations may be treated as simple features. To illustrate, block movement may actually be a two-stage process involving movement to and from a save buffer. In such situations, we try to orient the taxonomy toward the task rather than the method of implementation. In this case, it is our feeling that the user is more interested in adding, deleting, and permuting blocks than read/write operations on buffers.
3. A single feature may appear more than once in the taxonomy. This arises whenever a single feature affects several components of the word processor. Typographical enhancements are a paradigm case. A word processor may support boldfacing and underlining as

formatting features yet not support them on the display. Since it makes sense to speak of typographical enhancements in both contexts, they are included twice.

While complete objectivity in classification would be desirable, the complexity of current products does not allow this luxury. Our classification reflects our attitudes. Other investigators would arrive at different conclusions.

TAXONOMY OF FEATURES

The taxonomy used in this analysis appears in Appendix A. There are 168 features which break down as follows: 34 for screen control, 18 for document management, 60 for text editor, 34 for formatter and 17 for print control. In addition, there are 7 features of a more general nature (e.g., price, whether the word processor is a member of an integrated package, etc.).

Due to space considerations, we are not able to describe the features here. We only mention that we have attempted to standardize the nomenclature so that the name of the feature is descriptive of its function, without resorting to jargon. As an example, we prefer "restore text" to the often used surrogates "yankback," "undelete," and "undo," and "contextual navigation" to "find," "locate," and "search."

In addition, we provide descriptive phrases for as yet unnamed implementation characteristics. For example, "unrestricted cursor movement" refers to the ability of a word processor to move the cursor in any direction, regardless of the layout of the document. This is to be distinguished from the common restriction whereby the cursor is restricted to text boundaries as displayed. Similarly, "derivative naming convention" refers to the fact that the word processor's document manager adopts the file naming convention of the host operating system. If we have been successful, the meanings of most features are recoverable from context. Some of the concepts and terminology are covered in standard reference works.[12, 13]

As we mentioned above, the taxonomy itself is the tool of the analysis. It would be used in the following way. First, the typical applications are identified. Second, the decision maker extracts from these applications prioritized sets of desirable features. Then, products are selected according to the degree to which they possess these features. For example, a boilerplating operation may find a full range of block operations indispensable, while typographical enhancements are of minimal interest. In contrast, a medical office may not need much of a formatter but a strong editor, and so forth.

While it is not possible, or even worthwhile, to present the details of the feature analysis with respect to current products, we would be remiss if we failed to provide some understanding of the current state-of-the-art. We do this in two ways. First, we compare typical microcomputer products to their dedicated counterparts. Second, we provide descriptive statistics which summarize the features of common microcomputer software. The data used are taken from 22 microcomputer word processing products marketed within the past few years. We have intentionally included the older CP/M products so that meaningful time trends can be determined. As far as practicable, we sought to include the better selling products according to *Data Sources*.[1] Products are limited to CP/M and MS-DOS, for they represent the dominant operating systems for business applications over the past decade.

MICROCOMPUTER VERSUS DEDICATED SOFTWARE

In order to place the results that follow in perspective, we conducted a comparative analysis between microcomputer-based and dedicated products. The three dedicated systems which we used (Wang WP Plus, Decmate II, and Apple's Lisa Write) were selected because of easy access and our belief that they are typical examples.

There is no doubt that, in principle, greater power can be obtained from dedicated systems than general purpose microcomputers. Dedicated systems may take advantage of all of the hardware/software integration possible, for the details of the environment are known in advance. However, we found that the three dedicated packages which we studied failed to realize this potential.

While the dedicated systems were, on average, superior in terms of both display control and document management due to the fact that the software is designed with both a specific display and operating system in mind, their advantage eroded when it came to text editing, formatting, and print control. In fact, when one considers the percentage of features supported by the two groups of software (see Table I), the microcomputer-oriented products surpassed the dedicated products overall. The mean percentages of both groups are depicted graphically in Figure 2.

It is interesting to note that the dedicated systems fell behind the microcomputer word processors with respect to what one might refer to as the more innovative features. We have in mind such things as geometrical operations (e.g., column swap), bidirectional deletion of contextual unit (e.g., sentence deletion), searches for targets consisting of non-printable characters, complex searches (e.g., searches for multiple strings), concurrent editing of multiple documents, and so forth.

Similarly, many of the more advanced formatting features (e.g., kerning, widow/orphan adjust, footnote tie-in) and print control features (e.g., chaining, merging, queuing) were frequently unsupported. In general, the dedicated software

TABLE I—Percentage of features supported by product type and functional component

MICROCOMPUTER SYSTEMS				DEDICATED SYSTEMS		
LOW	MEAN	HIGH		LOW	MEAN	HIGH
8.8	39.3	58.5	DISPLAY	47.0	52.9	55.9
22.2	44.5	72.2	DOC MAN	27.8	64.8	88.9
39.0	53.9	67.8	EDITOR	39.0	43.5	45.8
34.2	63.1	77.1	FORMATTER	45.7	54.3	65.7
43.7	66.2	81.2	PRINT CTL	31.3	43.8	68.8

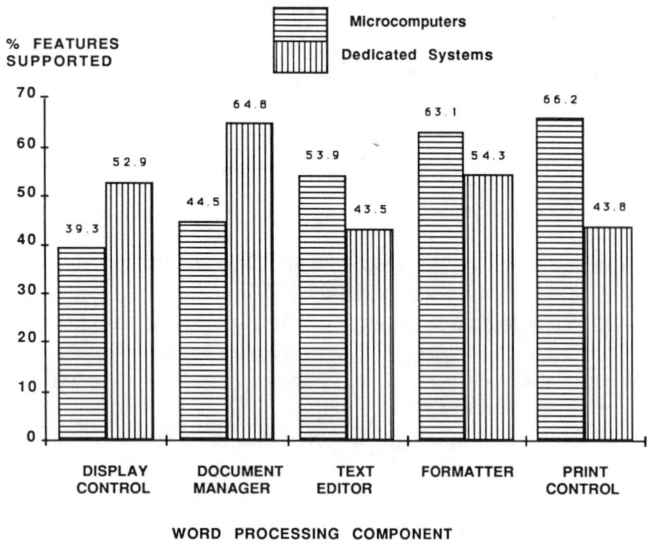

Figure 2—Mean percentage of features supported: microcomputer vs. dedicated systems

showed clear superiority only when compared to the oldest of microcomputer-based products.

One possible explanation is that the dedicated systems are not subject to the same competitive pressures as the microcomputer software. As a result, the manufacturer may be less likely to continuously revise the product. Another contributing factor might be that manufacturers of the dedicated products rely upon the advantages of convenience, power, and speed of their system, rather than the functionality of the software. Or perhaps, the prohibitive start-up costs and limited audience discourage innovators from trying to penetrate this market. In any case, we think that this comparison indicates that the results to follow may well extend beyond microcomputer software to word processing software, generally.

DATA ANALYSIS

The 22 products studied are listed atop Appendix A. For this particular sample, 16 of the 168 variables were eliminated due to lack of variance. These variables are marked {~V} in the Appendix. Of the remaining 152 variables, 135 were dichotomous, 6 were integer and 11 were nominal (categorical). The

TABLE II—Descriptive statistics for six composite variables

VARIABLE	MEAN	STD DEV	SKEW	RANGE
Display Controller	11.864	3.357	-.751	17
Document Manager	5.455	2.857	.409	9
Text Editor	26.455	3.789	.507	14
Formatter	16.364	4.635	-.694	17
Print Controller	9.727	2.142	-.505	8
TOTAL	69.864	9.593	.020	40

TABLE III—Mean composite scores as percentages of features

VARIABLE	MEAN	STANDARD DEV.
Display Controller	42.371%	11.989%
Document Manager	34.094%	17.856%
Text Editor	48.100%	6.889%
Formatter	52.787%	14.952%
Print Controller	60.794%	13.388%
TOTAL	47.852%	6.571%

integer and nominal variables are marked {I} and {N}. Of the 17 integer and nominal variables, all but two (date and price) were dichotomized for the analysis. According to Nie, et al.[14] dichotomies can be treated as interval-level measures. Four subordinate variables, marked {~v}, had less than 22 values because the values were dependent upon superordinate variables.

Of the 152 variables used in this analysis, 147 represented features of the five functional components of a word processor described above, and 5 were general descriptors. The dichotomous values were '0' and '1', indicating absence and presence of features in a particular product, respectively. The percentage of products which have a particular feature appear within parentheses alongside the feature entry in the Appendix. In addition, we have added 6 composite variables, one for each of the five functional components and a total, which summarize the data for each product. The descriptive statistics for the composite variables, in terms of both raw scores and percentages of possible features, appear in Tables II and III.

Pearson correlations among the 6 composite variables are given in Table IV. Since the directions of these correlations were not predicted, two-tailed tests of significance were

TABLE IV—Pearson correlations among composite variables

	DC	DM	TE	F	PC	TOT
Display Controller		.21	.50*	.25	.04	.73*
Document Manager			-.20	.36	.11	.49*
Text Editor				.11	-.25	.50*
Formatter					.05	.73*
Print Controller						.20
Total						

* = p < .05

TABLE V—Pearson correlations among general variables

	OS	CP	IP	D	P
Operating System		.39*	.13	.44*	.02
Copy Protection			.33	.14	-.17
Integrated Package				-.14	.17
Date					-.57*
Price					

* = p < .05

used. Pearson correlations for the general variables appear in Table V. Since the directions of three correlations (operating systems and copy protection, operating systems and date, and date and price) were predicted, one-tailed tests were used. In addition, correlations between the general variables and the composite variables were determined (see Table VI) for two-tailed tests. The correlation matrix for all 22 products appears in Table VII. For this analysis, the remaining two integer variables (date and price) were dichotomized for equal weighting. Since there is a question of whether standard significance tests have any obvious meaning when cases are correlated across variables,[15] the probability values are not reported.

A cluster analysis was performed for the 22 products in order to determine similarities in functional capabilities. The clustering method used was the hierarchical, agglomerative, average-linkage between groups method provided by SPSSX, Release 2.0. We sought to avoid the extremes of single linkage clustering and complete linkage clustering. Squared Euclidean distance was employed as the proximity measure. The five general variables were not included in the clustering. Missing values for the dichotomous variables were encoded as 0.5, so that they would not be excluded by the SPSSX procedure. The dendrogram for this analysis appears as Figure 3.

TABLE VI—Pearson correlations between general and composite variables

	DISP.	DOC. MAN.	ED.	FORM.	PRT.	TOTAL
OS	.25	.17	.002	.006	.02	.15
CP	.06	-.03	-.15	.12	.06	.02
IP	-.08	-.10	-.23	.08	-.20	-.16
DATE	.17	.17	-.32	-.27	.44*	-.05
PRICE	.09	-.12	.17	.53*	-.27	.26

* = P < .05

TABLE VII—Correlations among 22 products

1	2	3	4	5	6	7	8	9	10	11	12	13	14	15	16	17	18	19	20	21	22	
	.65	.24	.02	.14	.08	-.01	.26	-.03	.11	.30	.32	.07	.20	.13	.02	.21	.21	.21	.08	.12	.17	1
		.24	.12	.14	.21	.05	.33	.00	.17	.37	.40	.14	.14	.09	.06	.32	.35	.24	.07	.17	.19	2
			.14	.09	.32	.10	.28	.10	.18	.40	.40	.30	.27	.03	.08	.18	.40	.24	.24	.25	.17	3
				.14	.32	.34	.27	.41	.32	.07	.34	.33	.27	.35	.41	.25	.28	.35	.23	.29	.35	4
					.31	.18	.29	.17	.11	.23	.12	.23	.13	.21	.18	.09	.31	.20	.14	.28	.18	5
						.24	.46	.24	.38	.25	.46	.32	.34	.30	.35	.30	.68	.38	.35	.46	.44	6
							.12	.42	.25	.06	.16	.24	.22	.55	.56	.21	.24	.24	.21	.27	.25	7
								.30	.20	.21	.30	.27	.22	.23	.28	.33	.44	.17	.15	.22	.16	8
									.27	.00	.11	.22	.17	.43	.55	.21	.28	.26	.08	.24	.24	9
										.15	.41	.37	.19	.21	.28	.38	.42	.22	.32	.35	.53	10
											.33	.18	.20	.05	.07	.16	.31	.19	.37	.28	.26	11
												.29	.28	.27	.21	.46	.49	.24	.29	.27	.36	12
													.20	.25	.25	.19	.23	.18	.41	.33	.30	13
														.29	.22	.38	.46	.51	.30	.36	.24	14
															.78	.30	.27	.38	.15	.38	.30	15
																.21	.21	.24	.14	.38	.29	16
																	.38	.32	.21	.25	.37	17
																		.40	.32	.38	.39	18
																			.21	.36	.37	19
																				.36	.39	20
																					.47	21
																						22

DISCUSSION

Several observations can be made from the descriptive statistics in Tables II and III. First, The document manager is clearly the weakest part of these packages. This can be confirmed by reference to the Appendix. Only 18.2% of the products tested supported a document naming convention which was independent of the host operating system. In a CP/M and MS-DOS environment, this means that all file names must conform to the 8 character name/3 character extension format. Further, less than one third of the products allowed the user to identify the document by author, owner, and dates of creation and revision. Perhaps the most striking weakness, however, is the fact the less than one fourth of the products had document managers which were consistent with the file management facilities of the host operating systems. In most cases, this was a result of MS-DOS products failing to support the tree-structured domain supported in versions 2.X and above. This means that it is not possible to define multiple directories according to type of document within the word processor.

At the other extreme is the print controller. Its overall strength might suggest that software houses are investing a

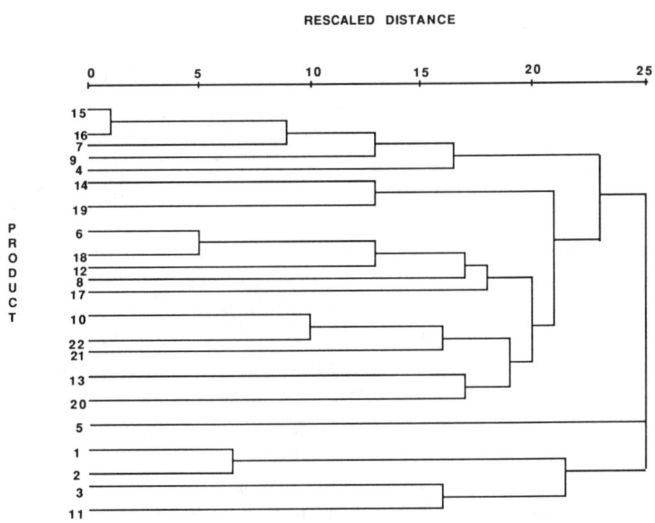

Figure 3—Cluster dendrogram

great deal of time and effort in this direction. In fact, when one looks at the correlations in Table IV, one sees that print control is significantly and strongly correlated with date. Apparently, print control is perceived to be an important component, worthy of continued attention.

Another observation is that the standard deviation in percentage of features of the "total" composite variable is less than the standard deviations for each individual composite variable (see Table III). It would appear that weaknesses in one component are generally compensated for by other components. Perhaps, as an overall design philosophy, software houses are trying to appeal to specific audiences by focusing on their particular needs. Another possibility is that they continue to refine those components with which they have the most experience. A third possibility is that software houses include features in a somewhat random fashion. This last possibility is not inconsistent with the Pearson correlations between the composite variables (Table IV). Generally, only the total composite variable is strongly and significantly correlated with the individual composite variables, which is understandable since the latter make up the former. The lack of correlation between the individual composite variables indicates that the five functional components of word processors are largely independent of one another: strength in one area says nothing of another. The exception to this rule is that the quality of screen display tends to correlate with the quality of the text editor.

Table V was created to determine the accuracy of our intuitions. It should be no surprise to anyone that copy protection is primarily associated with MS-DOS products, that the newer products tend to be designed for MS-DOS, and that the price of products is decreasing over time. We suspect that if this study had been conducted a few years ago, we would have found a positive, statistically significant correlation between date and copy protection, as well. However, this practice has recently fallen into disrespect.

The correlation of the five general variables with the composite variables (see Table VI) is strongly suggestive of some overall patterns. First, as we mentioned above, print controllers seem to be getting stronger over time. Further, price seems to be a good indication of the quality of the formatter, though little else. If one looks to the Pearson correlations between price and the individual features (not shown), one finds that it is positively correlated with only automatic hyphenation (.48, $p < .05$), the presence of screen labelling of function keys (.5, $p < .05$), whether page numbering can be included in headers and footers (.49, $p < .05$), and the capability of double striking (.49, $p < .05$). Specifically, price is not shown to correlate well with such advanced features as multiple windowing and integrated graphics. What this tells us is that price is not a measure of the overall quality of the product. Similarly, the lack of positive correlation between copy protection and the composite variables suggests that it is unlikely that there is any relation between the quality of a product and copy protection. In terms of our sample, copy protection seems to have had the unintended effect of discouraging piracy of the poorer products.

In addition, our experience indicates that the negative correlations between most of the composite variables and the general feature, membership in an integrated package, seem reasonable. Again, we predict that if a large enough sample is taken, these negative correlations can be shown to be statistically significant. We suspect that the integration comes at the expense of the quality of the subcomponents.

Table VII and Figure 3 are useful in identifying relationships between products. For example, there are three pairs of word processors which bear the same name: Perfect Writer, Benchmark and Easywriter. In one case, Perfect Writer, the CP/M and MS-DOS versions are seen to be functionally similar. Slightly less similar, though related by philosophy, are the Benchmarks. However, the Easywriters are essentially two different products. In addition, one gets the feeling the Freestyle and Select, and Newword and Wordstar have some common ancestry. This information may be of use to decision makers who would like to examine products with similar orientations.

CONCLUSIONS

In this paper, we have presented a taxonomy of features of word processing features which we have found to be useful in determining the functionality of word processing software and the relevance of software to particular applications. In addition, we have provided summary statistics for 22 existing products, when compared in terms of the taxonomy. It is our intention to provide the reader with a means of identifying distinctive and distinguishing features, as well as provide some method of assessing the microcomputer word processing software market as a whole. We hope that this information is useful in aiding decision makers who are interested in acquiring new software.

While space constraints dictate that we omit a general discussion of the correlations between features, we would like to conclude with some preliminary observations. First, the correlations indicate that innovation in word processor design is likely to be a random event. To illustrate, there is no correlation among our 22 products between multiple windowing, unrestricted text entry, complex searches, concurrent editing, and integrated graphics—features we believe are indicative of sophistication. Further, one gets the feeling that most current products suffer from a serious lack of forethought. For example, multiple windowing negatively correlates with the quality of status line information concerning the position of the cursor in the various documents in a statistically significant way. This means that for most products that support multiple windowing, the user is left in the dark concerning the location of the window. Another example is the lack of correlation between contextual deletion (delete sentence and paragraph) and delete-to-target. Since the latter is the lower-level technique used to implement the former, its absence at the command level is strange, indeed. A third case involves the frequent failure of unrestricted text entry to accompany unrestricted cursor movement. The consequence of this is that while the user may directly navigate the cursor to any position on the screen, he may not be able to do any editing once it is there. Hopefully, with further study we may better understand these design philosophies.

ACKNOWLEDGEMENT

We would like to thank D. Lavelle for assistance with the statistical portions of this paper.

REFERENCES

1. *Data Sources,* New York: Ziff-Davis Publishing Co.
2. *datapro directory of MICROCOMPUTER SOFTWARE,* Delran, NJ: McGraw-Hill.
3. Riddle, E. "Comparative Study of Various Text Editors and Formatting Systems." Air Force DataServices Center Report #AD-A-29 050, 1976.
4. Meyrowitz, N. and A. van Dam. "Interactive Editing Systems." *Computing Surveys,* 14 (1982) 3, pp. 321–415.
5. van Dam, A. and N. Meyrowitz. "Text Editing Systems." A. Ralston and E. Reilly, Jr. *Encyclopedia of Computer Science and Engineering* (2nd ed.). New York: van Nostrand Reinhold, 1983.
6. Roberts, T. "Evaluation of Computer Text Editors." PhD Dissertation, Stanford University, November, 1979
7. Roberts, T., and T. Moran. "Evaluation of Text Editors." *Proceedings of the Conference on Human Factors in Computer Systems,* March 1982, pp. 136–141.
8. Roberts, T., and T. Moran. "The Evaluation of Text Editors: Methodology and Empirical Results." *Communications of the ACM,* 26 (1983) 4, pp. 265–283.
9. Smith, B. and D. Austin. *Word Processing: A Guide for Small Business,* Brattleboro: Lewis Publishing, 1983.
10. Naiman, A. *Word Processing Buyers Guide.* New York: McGraw-Hill, 1983.
11. Donahue, B. *How to Buy an Office Computer or Word Processor.* Englewood Cliffs: Prentice-Hall, 1983.
12. Flores, I. *Word Processing Handbook.* New York: van Nostrand, 1983.
13. Sampath, G. *An Introduction to Text Processing.* Jeffersontown: River Valley, 1985.
14. Nie, N., C. Hull, J. Steinbrenner and D. Bent. *Statistical Package for the Social Sciences* (2nd ed.). New York: McGraw-Hill, 1975.
15. Aldenderfer, M. and R. Blashfield. *Cluster Analysis.* Beverly Hills: Sage Publications, 1984.

APPENDIX A: TAXONOMY OF WORD PROCESSING FEATURES

Products Tested:

Product (1) Benchmark (CP/M), v. 3.0m
Product (2) Benchmark (DOS), v. exec III
Product (3) DisplayWrite 2 (DOS), v. 1.10
Product (4) Easywriter I (DOS), v. 1.40
Product (5) Easywriter II (DOS), v. 2.0
Product (6) Freestyle (DOS), v. 1.0
Product (7) Final Word (DOS), v. 1.17
Product (8) Leading Edge (DOS), v. 1.20
Product (9) Memoplan (CP/M), v. 1.2
Product (10) Newword (CP/M), v. 1.29
Product (11) Office Writer (DOS), v. 3.0
Product (12) Palantir (CP/M), v. 1.2
Product (13) pfs:Write (DOS), v. b
Product (14) Peachtext (CP/M), v. 2.01
Product (15) Perfect Writer (CP/M), v. 1.20
Product (16) Perfect Writer (DOS), v. 2.0
Product (17) Spellbinder (DOS), v. 5.30
Product (18) Select (CP/M), v. 3.00c
Product (19) Superwriter (CP/M), v. 1.02
Product (20) Visiword (DOS), v. 1.20
Product (21) Volkswriter (DOS), v. 2.10
Product (22) Wordstar (CP/M), v. 3.32

Taxonomy:

0. GENERAL INFORMATION
    —Version
    —Operating System
    —Copy Protected
    —Member of Integrated Package
    —Date of Release {**I**}
    —Price {**I**}

I. DISPLAY
  A. Screen Imaging
    1. Layout
      —centering (100%) {−**V**}
      —justification (68.2)
      —line spacing (40.9)
      —pagination (77.3)
      —hyphenation (45.5)
    2. Typography
      —boldface (22.7)
      —sub/superscripts (0.0) {−**V**}
      —strikeouts (4.5)
      —underlining (45.5)
      —overprints (0.0) {−**V**}
      —alternate fonts (0.0) {−**V**}
      —alternate pitch (0.0) {−**V**}
      —proportional spacing (9.1)
    3. Control Suppression (50.0)
  B. Highlighting
      —block (63.6)
      —character (59.1)
  C. Column Ruler Display (77.3)
      —on/off (18.2)
      —multiple rulers (40.9)
  D. Status Line Display
    1. Document ID
        —drive id (59.1)
        —document name (77.3)
    2. Cursor Location
      —page number (59.1)
      —line number (77.3)
      —column number (63.6)
    3. Editor Mode Toggles (90.9)
    4. Systems Information
      —document size (4.5)
      —remaining space on disk (13.6)
      —remaining space in RAM (18.2)
      —time/date (9.1) {**N**}
      —screen labelled function keys (22.7)
  E. Multiple Windowing (31.8)
      —number of windows (mean = 2) {−**V**}
      —number of documents (mean = 4.5) {**I**} {−**v**}
      —variable size (18.2) {−**v**}

II. DOCUMENT MANAGEMENT
  A. Document Naming Convention
    —derivative/independent (18.2% = independent)
    —maximum character length (mean = 12) {**I**}
    —'wild card' reference (40.9)
  B. Backup
    —manual/auto (63.6% = manual) {**N**}
    —override (95.5) {**−v**}
  C. Directory
    —document size (50.0) {**N**}
    —description (18.2)
    —author (22.7)
    —creator (22.7)
    —date created (31.8)
    —last revision (31.8)
    —total worktime (0.0) {**−V**}
    —archive reference (0.0) {**−V**}
  D. Constraints and Security
    —document size (77.3)
    —access consistent with OS (22.7)
    —edit-protect (9.1)
    —exit protection (31.8) {**N**}
    —disk overflow protection (77.3) {**N**}

III. TEXT EDITOR
  A. ADD TEXT (Insert)
    1. Move Aside (95.5)
      —word wrap/cascading wraparound (27.3% + cascading)
    2. Split Screen (45.5)
    3. Unrestricted Text Entry (27.3)
  B. DELETE TEXT (Delete)
    1. Units
      a. Contextual
        —character (95.5)
        —word (63.6)
        —sentence (27.3)
        —paragraph (27.3)
      b. Geometrical
        —columns (27.3)
        —lines (72.7)
      c. Boundary
        —delete to end (45.5)
        —delete to target (22.7)
        —delegate marked block (95.5)
    2. Miscellaneous
      —bidirectional deletion (27.3)
      —deletion w/prompt (59.1)
      —restore (68.2)
      —variable save space (9.1)
      —auto-reformat (63.6)
  C. NAVIGATION (Move/Find)
    1. Geometrical
      a. Relative location
        —Directional
          —unrestricted cursor movement (50.0)
          —screen advance (95.5)
          —scrolling
            —vertical/horizontal (54.5/18.2) {**N**}
            —hard/soft (0.0 = soft) {**−V**}
            —variable speed (18.2) {**−v**}
        —Grammatical
          —word (68.2)
          —sentence (27.3)
          —paragraph (22.7)
      b. Absolute location
        —top of document (77.3)
        —bottom of document (77.3)
        —page by number (36.4)
        —marker (31.8)
    2. Contextual (Locate/Find/Search)
      a. restrictions on target
        —length (mean = 58) {**I**}
        —control characters allowed (81.8)
        —ambiguous character strings (27.3)
      b. restrictions on search
        —auto-repeat (95.5)
        —complex search (4.5)
      c. search parameters
        —complete words (45.5)
        —reverse search (54.5)
        —global search (22.7)
        —ignore case (63.6)
  C. SUBSTITUTE TEXT (SEARCH & REPLACE)
    a. restrictions on target
      —length (mean = 58) {**I**}
      —control characters allowed (77.3)
    b. restrictions on search
      —auto-repeat (100) {**−V**}
      —complex search (4.5)
    c. search parameters
      —complete words (45.5)
      —reverse search (36.4)
      —global search (31.8)
      —ignore case (63.6)
  E. PERMUTE TEXT (Block Move/Copy)
    1. Contextual Permutation (95.5)
    2. Geometrical Permutation (31.8)
      —column swap (9.1)
    3. Options
      —block move (100) {**−V**}
      —block copy (95.5)
      —block delete (100) {**−V**}
      —block file (77.3)
  F. MISCELLANEOUS
    1. Menu Type (90.9 = pass through, remaining = pop up)
      —variable help level (pass through only) (36.4)
      —menu delay (pass through only) (18.2)
      —menu bypass (pass through only) (36.4)
    2. Concurrent Editing (31.8)
    3. Integrated Graphics (9.1)

IV. FORMATTING
  A. CONTINUOUS/PREVIEW MODE (72.7 = continuous)

B. LAYOUT
1. Line Centering (100) {−**V**}
2. Variable Line Spacing (32) {**N**}
3. Proportional Spacing (72.7)
4. Kerning (9.1)
5. Justification (95.5)
—fixed/variable spacing (31.8 = variable) {**N**}
—interword (100) {−**V**}
—intraword (13.6)
6. Hyphenation (63.6)
—concurrent (50.0)
—automatic (27.3)
7. Decimal Alignment (54.5)
8. Pagination
—pagination/repagination (95.5)
—page numbering (100) {−**V**}
—with initialization ≠ 1 (81.8)
—widow/orphan adjust (63.6) {**N**}
—header/trailer insert (95.5)
—page-number merge (86.4)
—footnote tie-in (31.8)

C. TYPOGRAPHY
1. Character Enhancements
—boldface (95.5)
—complementary overprinting
—double-strike (45.5)
—underlining (100) {−**V**}
—destructive overprinting
—strikeout (59.1)
—typeover (13.6)
2. Miscellaneous
—sub/super scripts (90.0)
—multiple fonts (45.5)
—multiple character sets (36.4)
—print pause (90.9)
—print phantom character (31.8)
—multiple pitches (77.3)
—ribbon color change (22.7)
—user-definable commands (22.7) {**N**}
—typethrough (4.5)

V. PRINT CONTROL
—multiple copies (90.9)
—selective output (95.5)
—multiple pages (22.7)
—first/last page (86.5) {**N**}
—draft quality only (45.5)
—dual column printing (13.6)
—printer select (72.7)
—paper change pause (100) {−**V**}
—form feeds (90.9)
—disk file output (59.1)
—chaining (45.5)
—merging (45.5)
—queuing (36.4)
—print from edit (40.9)
—print while editing (50.0)
—print-time commands
—print stop (90.9)
—print pause/resume (86.4)

Towards the integration of integrated software within organizations

by JAMES A. CARTER, JR.
University of Saskatchewan
Saskatoon, SK, Canada

ABSTRACT

The widespread use of microcomputers is linked both to their low cost and to the promise of their being a major productivity tool for various levels of workers throughout an organization. This promise was largely supported by the introduction of a new generation of integrated software packages. These software packages typically stress their general purpose nature and their ease of use by the average office worker. The packages promise to do a variety of tasks, for a variety of individuals and to be able to combine the results produced by individuals for the good of the overall organization. The integration of these packages within an organization is assumed, but seldom planned for or achieved. This paper analyzes the promises, the types, and the uses of integrated software. It then identifies the problems with and proposes future directions towards better realizing of the promises of integration within organizations.

THE PROMISES OF INTEGRATED SOFTWARE

The range of potential users of computers in an organization is as broad as the range of the individuals in an organization. These users may range from senior management to technical workers to clerical workers and even unskilled laborers.[1] This range of individual responsibilities and skills poses a major problem in designing systems that must meet the needs of a number of individuals in an organization. The design is further complicated by the various levels of computing experience that end users in today's society may possess. This variation in experience results from the difference in the amounts and the kinds of use each individual makes of computers both within and outside the organization.

By providing an "all-in-one" solution made up of a few general purpose applications that can be used to perform a variety of fundamental business tasks, integrated software packages promise to meet the majority of needs of this diverse user body. The typical applications provided by an integrated application package include: word processing, electronic spreadsheet, business graphics, data base, and communications. Managers can use these applications for planning, while technical and clerical workers can use them for producing various types of products on a day to day basis. Integrated packages promise that their ease of use will allow each type of worker to use these applications at whatever level of sophistication best suited to them. All workers can exchange information between applications and, ideally, with the help of the communications application, between individuals in the organization. This use of communications from within integrated packages promises to integrate the levels and functions of personnel in an organization based on common sharing of data.

THE TYPES OF INTEGRATED SOFTWARE PRODUCTS

The new generation of integrated software packages is only a new generation in terms of the promises it makes and not in terms of the technology. This new generation is actually composed of three different technical approaches[2]: program environments, families of integrated programs, and all-in-one packages. Further analysis will show that these approaches are not new ones but only refinements of existing technologies.

Software integration can be analyzed into a number of integrating features. These features have been grouped into six levels of integration[3] based on the structure of the tasks performed by and for the user. Tasks performed by a user are based on FUNCTIONS of DATA that are obtained via an INTERFACE to PROGRAMS or TASKS within a unifying program. These capitalized words identify five types of possible integration of user tasks above the level of total NON-INTEGRATION.

With NON-INTEGRATION, each application is developed as a totally distinct program. Although the program may grow in complexity, the lack of integration, in its original design, limits its extent of use. Without integration of some form, the user must re-enter data into programs to fulfill other application needs. Further, similar functions may behave very differently between the various programs used.

DATA INTEGRATED programs are separate programs which share common data files or use some type of data base management system. Information generated by one program can be used by another in some manner. USER INTERFACE INTEGRATION makes separate programs, with separate data, interact with the user in the same way. The result of combining both DATA INTEGRATION and USER INTERFACE INTEGRATION is PROGRAM INTEGRATION. The barriers of accessing only one application at a time and of requiring the user to interface between programs with the computer's operating system are overcome with TASK INTEGRATION. TASK INTEGRATED systems include the various applications as tasks within a single multi-purpose program. FUNCTION INTEGRATION is a proposed level of integration beyond TASK INTEGRATION in which a user could define any number of applications as virtual tasks within a single system of shared functions.

Program Environments

Program environments, such as IBM's Top View and Microsoft's Windows, provide basic frameworks for potential integration of other application programs. As such, they are more like extensions to operating systems rather than actual end user applications in their own right.

Program environments provide primarily data level integration. They do this by providing translation services between various sources of data and various applications wishing to input that data. They allow blocks of data from one application to be used as input to other applications. In some instances, they may also provide the capabilities of reading various types of formatted data files as input into an application that would not otherwise be able to read the data.

Although program environments can provide a common user interface for their super operating system like functions, the primary interfaces between the user and the applications are those provided by the application programs running under the environment. These differences in application programs leave the area of user interface integration largely a matter of chance rather than design. To be able to utilize fully the features of a program environment, an application program must be "well behaved" by following standards, which most currently successful applications have found necessary to circumvent in order to provide adequate performance for the end user.

Families of Integratable Programs

Families of integratable programs have been around for over a decade, primarily in the area of accounting applications. The main contribution of the new families of integrated applications, such as Innovative Software Inc.'s Smart System, is their integration of general purpose applications. By utilizing separate programs for each major application, families of integrated programs tend to concentrate on the quality of the individual applications before the quality of the integration, although they may provide high qualities of both.

Families of integratable programs provide primarily program level integration. They tend to maximize both data and user interface integration while keeping individual applications separate from one another. Thus, where windowing is allowed, the multiple windows are only multiple views of data from within a single application and do not provide the user multiple applications.

All-in-one Packages

All-in-one packages, such as Ashton-Tate's Framework and Lotus' Symphony, provide the greatest emphasis on integration. All-in-one packages utilize task level integration to provide the user a number of general purpose applications. Data can be readily moved between applications or shared by them. The user interface design and functions are highly consistent throughout all applications. Multiple applications can be accessed simultaneously through separate windows which can be linked together, where necessary. To facilitate the high level of interaction and of data processing possible with all-in-one packages, they often allow the user a high level command language for defining and storing particular combinations of functions, applications, and data.

Although their aim is to provide a multi-purpose tool, all-in-one packages usually appear to be extensions of one focal application that is more highly developed than the others. This can be accomplished by adding other complementary applications to a well developed central application, such as a word processor or a spreadsheet. This focus is evidenced in the user metaphor or conceptual model of the particular all-in-one package. Thus Framework's frames appears to be more word oriented while Symphony's cells appears more number oriented.

It has been suggested that while an all-in-one package may meet most of the needs of one kind of worker, it may not meet the needs of all kinds of workers. New releases of these packages have emphasized both the continued advancement of their focal application and the strengthening of the other applications, thus expanding their potential markets.

THE USES OF INTEGRATED SOFTWARE IN ORGANIZATIONS

The introduction of personal computers and integrated software packages into organizations has often been done by individuals rather than by the organization's planners. These individuals are often rebels or at least individualists. People dissatisfied with the quality, the quantity, or the responsiveness of corporate information processing activities, often rebel against the data processing/information systems department by obtaining a personal computer to do their own information processing. Since personal computers often can be justified as low cost word processors, they can be obtained readily under misleading or false pretenses. Similarly, individualists can often prove their need for specialized systems that don't fit into [illegible]rger organizational plan for immediate systems deve[illegible]. Once a personal computer is obtained, an integrated software package may logically follow. Since most instances of obtaining personal computers and software originate with individuals, a wide variety of systems and software packages may result.

Many organizations, faced with large numbers of personal computers, are attempting to consolidate the use of these computers to meet various objectives including: standardization of operations, synergy of benefits, and the ability to save money via bulk purchasing. This requires a bottom-up organization of individuals rather than the top-down centralized design and deployment of systems that is typically used by the data processing department. Consolidation, when it does take place, generally takes the form of standardizing the hardware and software being used. The actual uses of the systems seldom are expanded beyond those initiated by the individual users. An increasing number of organizations are starting to develop consolidated plans for the purchase and use of personal computers so as to avoid future costly difficulties as the number of personal computers in the organization grows.

The traditional uses of computers, the personal nature of the relationship of individuals to personal computers, and the available software all tend to limit the use of personal computers to processing formal, structured, verbal information in largely written form. Other forms of information, such as graphical and vocalized, are largely limited by current technology, although rapid advances are being made in these areas.[4] Informal information is generally excluded from these systems due to difficulties in handling, evaluating, and utilizing it within a highly structured system. The assumption that, "If information can't be formalized that it isn't important" is often mistakenly made in order to support the value of computerization. This trend promotes individualism within organizations and limits the role of other individuals to that of reacting to the information obtained rather than of helping to produce it initially. This, in turn, may change traditional relationships within an organization.

THE PROBLEMS WITH CURRENT INTEGRATED SOFTWARE USE

By the end of 1985, various software reviewers started to ask what happened to the promises of integrated software packages. Sales of packages had leveled off, as if the market were saturated, long before everyone had converted to integrated software. Recent new product announcements have been generally only enhancements to existing products rather than dramatic improvements such as experienced in the previous few years. The promise, therefore, appears unfulfilled.

To analyze the causes of this disillusionment and to evaluate whether or not they are well founded, it is necessary to analyze how the products have, or have not, lived up to the needs of the organizations which were to be their beneficiaries. If integrated packages have failed to be all things to all people, is it the fault of the applications, the technology, the people, the organizations, or all of the above? Recent studies have suggested the answer is all of these.[2,5] In addition to recognizing the problems, it should be considered if improvements can be made to better meet the needs of organizations and to better fulfill the promise.

Applications

The benefits of the integration of applications may be offset by a variety of limitations they impose upon their adopters. The more integrated the product, the more limitations that must be accepted in order to use it. These limitations include the number and types of applications, the state of the art of the applications, and the extent of integration of the applications. They may both restrict the flexibility of the user and increase the complexity of learning and using the package. Unfortunately in some cases they cause the work involved in using the integration to be more than is involved in not using it.[5]

The set of applications integrated in all-in-one packages or families of integrated programs has remained relatively limited and fixed (generally: word processing, electronic spreadsheet, business graphics, data base, and communications). While these applications may be very powerful tools, their general purpose design (that makes them powerful) also requires the user to have a sophisticated understanding of how to apply them to specific problems. While a data base or a spreadsheet can be used to plan a schedule and then business graphics can be used to illustrate it, a scheduling application would do this for the user in a much simpler manner. Thus, in order to set up a schedule within an integrated package where no scheduling application exists, the user must become a developer as well as a user.

A variety of solutions exist to the problem of having only general purpose applications provided as the basics in an integrated system. There has developed a widespread availability of books of "spreadsheet templates" which are basically programs for the user to type into a general purpose program to produce a specific purpose application. Unfortunately, the results of using different "templates" to produce specific applications also usually results in the loss of integration between these applications. In these circumstances, using a lower level of integration, such as a program environment to integrate separate special purpose programs, may provide just as good an integration with less trouble for the user. A compromise solution is to provide a program environment within an all-in-one package, such as Framework's DOS Window, and a set of guidelines to the user as to when it is better to use a specialty package rather than trying to develop your own.

Developers of integrated packages have the dual demands of designing for integration as well as the various applications contained in them. Often, the state of the art of individual applications has progressed beyond that of comparable applications in integrated packages, leaving the integrated packages needing to catch up. Thus, the adopting of an integrated package may be seen to tie the user to capabilities that may always be trailing the leaders.

In word processing, the state of the art has grown to include spelling checking, mail merging, outlining, variable styles and sizes of print fonts, and primitive graphics. Only outlining was available first from an integrated package (Framework). Many of these other features are only starting to appear in new releases of integrated packages. Specialized decision support systems and knowledge based expert systems are being marketed to meet needs, first met by spreadsheets and data bases, in easier and more powerful manners. Distributed systems and local area networks are superseding the style of occasional communication supported by most integrated packages, providing an additional dimension of data integration. Fourth generation languages are gaining in popularity over traditional command languages for the ease they provide users in developing specific applications.

Along with each of the advances in the state of the art, there comes a period of exploring the advantages and disadvantages of the advances. Thus, working at the state of the art is most advantageous for those users who are either very sophisticated or very much in need of the new features which it provides. For the majority of users, working with slightly older, but proven and tested, versions of applications may provide the optimal level of fulfilling their needs while minimizing their trauma. Thus, the lack of state of the art applications may not be a major problem for most users. A compromise solution again would be a feature similar to a DOS Window, to be used only where absolutely necessary.

The amount of integration between each application in all-in-one integrated packages, although greater than in other cases, has remained relatively low.[3] For example, few word processors can comfortably incorporate graphics with text without considerable effort because of the traditional differences in the display handling of word processing and graphics applications. Use of alternative sources of applications, such as with program environments or DOS windows, often causes even greater concerns in integration. Decisions regarding this problem can only be made based on the need for integration and the current state of the art.

Technology

The state-of-the-art of the technology also has limited the promise of integrated packages. Hardware capacity, software complexity and the costs associated with both have forced developers to make tradeoffs between the level of integration and the quality of applications within their packages. Conflicting conceptual models and user metaphors, designed to help the user, have added to the reluctance of users to adopt integrated packages.

Many desirable integrating features require sophisticated hardware capabilities only recently introduced to personal computers. High processor speed and large main memory are required to support high resolution bit mapped graphics and the concurrency of multiple functions, applications, or users. Local area networks with external communication capability are necessary to support integration in the form of distributed systems.

Further developments in software technology will also be necessary to achieve the full promise of integrated applications. The development of functionally integrated systems can provide a technology which overcomes many of the current limitations and also allows for easy addition of other applications to an integrated package.[6] The development of knowledge bases will allow customization of systems to individual user's levels of expertise and need while maintaining compatibility and consistency between users where necessary.

Cost acts as a limiting factor both in what is available and in what the user is willing to pay. Hardware advances are continually providing better computing power for the money that users are willing to spend. Costs, however, will remain a limitation in the area of software. Typical individual users will only pay the equivalent price of two individual packages for an integrated package, since in most cases they will only make an equivalent amount of use. To be successful, developers must include much more than the equivalent of two individual packages. Thus, developers must rely on much higher volume sales to make up for their greater development costs. Recent sales trends have not justified this expectation. The similarly greater amount of effort in developing updates to integrated packages is reflected in the relatively high prices charged for upgrades to some of the popular integrated packages. Further complicating the cost situation is the expectation of organizations to be able to buy site licenses or to get volume discounts for software while the developers wish to sell only individual copies at fixed unit prices. Unless the economics of software costs can be worked out to the mutual satisfaction of users and developers, advances in integrated packages may be few and far between.

The complexities of design and marketing of integrated packages have led to the introduction of a number of conceptual models and user metaphors to explain them. Systems may be called electronic desktops, outlines, slideshows and many more names. Individual applications may reside in windows, frames, libraries, spreadsheets, and many more structures. Each of these models or metaphors is designed to show how universal and easy to use the system is to at least a target group of users. Each shows certain biases or viewpoints of the developers and certain stereotypes of the intended users. Unfortunately, familiar as all of these concepts are to most users, they may be perceived differently both qualitatively and attitudinally. Either individually or in a small consistent group, they do a good job in helping explain the purpose and workings of an integrated package. The confusion comes from the users being exposed to conflicting terms and concepts from a variety of sources besides the particular package being used. Further confusion results in the importance placed on these analogies in explaining the system to all users, even though not all users are likely to be so intuitive as to think in terms of metaphors.

People and Organizations

Difficulties with people and organizations realizing the promise may be attributed largely to the concept of the personal computer. In many cases, personal computers are thought of only as a tool for an individual to use to accomplish an individual task. Neither the power of the tool nor the value of the information, which is really a major corporate asset, is understood. Since it is individuals who are using personal computers singularly, many organizations provide little or no support to them, leaving everything to the individual's initiative and discretion. Strong efforts at providing organizational support, such as organizational information centers and new methods of managing semi-independent workers, are necessary to transform isolated individual users of integrated software packages into an integrated team of information workers.

The traditional departmental and functional specialization and segregation of workers in organizations tends to separate people who need to share information, and thus, to inhibit the full integration of organizational data. Both functional areas and individual workers often may choose whether or not to use a computer and, if so, how to use it. This discretionary use of computers by knowledge workers can lead to the lack of a critical mass of users and organizational information without which organizational level integration is incomplete and undervalued.[5] An awareness of the information structure within an organization should be shared amongst all members in order to encourage the integration of specialized work into useful information.

The co-ordination and integration of personal computers into organizations requires more than just individual initiatives. Although individual initiative is often the instigator, once the number of users and uses grows, some centralized organization is required to ensure that this growth is productive and efficient. One potential structure for providing such an organization is the concept of an information center.

Information centers are often an outgrowth of an organization's data processing department trying to provide quality user support for non-traditional data processing activities. They encourage and assist the end user to learn about data processing methodologies and to develop small or one time applications for themselves. Information centers, therefore, have a similar purpose to that of most personal computers in allowing the development and use of applications that would not otherwise have been undertaken by the data processing department.

Information centers typically provide a pool of specialists, centrally located, that support large numbers of users in different departments. This support may include: educating users in the various aspects of data processing; providing on-site resolution of problems; providing access to reference materials; providing access to hardware and software for evaluation and development purposes; providing assistance in developing small or one time applications; providing assistance in selecting and purchasing hardware and software for end user use; and providing and controlling access to corporate networks and data bases.

The information center approach is desirable since it uses "a carrot rather than a stick." It still leaves the user in control of applications and expenditures, while encouraging the user to standardize and integrate in order to obtain the various benefits of information center services. The types of hardware and software that the information center supports and which it may even make available at very attractive prices become the de facto standards for the organization. Users not following these standards do so on their own and at potentially much higher costs.

It must be recognized that integrated packages can only do some things for some people. Since typical users are limited in the number of applications they will use and since some individual packages are more powerful than their counterparts in typical integrated packages, some users will choose to use one or two specialized packages rather than one integrated package. Various users within an organization, therefore, may make individual cases for specific packages for their own use. While such a choice may be in the interests of the individual, it often overlooks the value of standardization and synergy within an organization. To overcome this difficulty, integrated packages need to not only improve the quality of their individual applications, but also to allow for the easy addition of other applications within the main integrated package.

As the use of personal computers grows, even within an integrated manner, so also grows the potential independence of the worker in the methods chosen to achieve the work. This affects both sides of the worker-manager relationship. More and more tasks can be performed directly by the worker on the computer without going through any intermediary management approval or supervision. With advances in communications technology, it will even be possible for many workers to perform their work on a personal computer at home, many miles from the manager. This increasing autonomy of workers gives rise to a number of potential problems involving the co-ordination of tasks to ensure that their results integrate appropriately without having missing parts or wasteful redundancies. It changes the emphasis of management from assigning work to be done in a certain way and supervising the work to assigning work, where the results must interface in a certain way, and synthesizing the results. This change parallels changes in software technology by concentrating on what needs to be done rather than on how it is to be done. Until managers become more involved in goal setting, arbitrating, and evaluating, and less involved with managing, the human link in integrating computing within an organization will remain weak and the integration of applications will not evolve beyond the level at which it exists in the software being used by a number of individuals in the organization.

THE FUTURE

To date, most integrated packages appear to be built around meeting the perceived needs of one or more applications rather than around meeting the actual needs of the user. Software developers have improved the level of program integration along with the current state of hardware technology, while largely ignoring the user needs for task and function integration. Advances have concentrated on increasing the data and functions in applications, and providing a more sophisticated user interface to these applications. The set of and the structure of individual applications has remained relatively fixed, and only now is starting to slowly expand.

To change the focus to the needs of individual users, a new approach to the basis of software integration is necessary, such as that of function integration. The state-of-the-art, however, has not yet reached function level integration. To do so will require both a new understanding of the user and a new state of technology to implement this understanding. To change the focus further to the needs of individual users within an organizational context requires both advances in computing and advances in the organization of the workplace. These organizational changes in the workplace are not just due to the adoption of integrated software, but have been developed and discussed in other settings. Where such methods of organization exist already, higher levels of integration may also exist.

RECOMMENDATIONS

The following are a set of recommendations for organizations wishing to achieve the promise of integrated software:

1. The decision to adopt and standardize integrated software should be made at the organizational level. Once such a decision is made, it should be communicated to all individuals in the organization in such a manner as to show them why it was a good decision and to encourage them to comply with it.
2. All-in-one packages provide the highest current level of integration and the greatest potential for achieving the promise of integration. The adoption of an all-in-one package as the basis for integration within an organization should only be made, however, if it is supported by a suitable cost/benefit analysis that proves this generalization.
3. The need for additional application programs beyond those contained in an integrated package should be recognized and allowed for in any attempt to standardize on an integrated package. The use of such additional packages, however, should be limited to those cases where the benefits to the organization are greater than the costs of deviating from the standard integrated package.
4. Where possible, additional application programs should be accessible and should be accessed from within the standard integrated package.
5. The information structure within an organization should be analyzed and then shared amongst all members of the organization in order to encourage the integration of specialized work into useful information.
6. Consideration needs to be given to how the results of integrated software packages can be integrated both with each other and with the needs of the organization.
7. Where conceptual models and user metaphors of integrated systems are used, they must be pertinent to the people in the organization who will use them if they are going to be a benefit.
8. There is a need for information center support for individual users of integrated software in an organization in

order to educate the users and to assist them in achieving the fullness of the benefits of the software.

9. There is a need for a goal oriented and integrating management approach to the user of integrated software in an organization if the fullness of the promise of integration is to be realized for the organization.
10. Since the state of the art of integrated software is evolving due to advances in technology and understanding, organizations should be prepared to change in order to achieve new benefits as they become available, rather than expecting to adopt a single package that will solve all problems both now and in the future.

REFERENCES

1. Carter, J. A. "User-Oriented Structured Design of Data Processing Applications." In H. W. Hendrick and O. Brown Jr. (eds.), *Human Factors in Organizational Design and Management,* Amsterdam: Elsevier Publishers B.V., 1984.
2. Carter, J. A., "Integrated Software: The Promise, the Product, and the Problems." In O. Brown Jr. and H. W. Hendrick (eds.), *Human Factors in Organizational Design and Management II,* Amsterdam: Elsevier Publishers B.V., 1986.
3. Carter, J. A., and J. B. Tubman. "Integrated Software: Past, Present, and Future." to appear in *Future Computing Systems.*
4. Chang, E. "Participant Systems: Group Human-Computer Interaction." *Proceedings of the IEEE International Conference on Systems, Man and Cybernetics,* 1986, pp. 1337–1342.
5. Nielsen, J., R. Makc, K. Bordendorff, and N. Grischkowsky. "Integrated Software Usage in the Professional Work Environment: Evidence from Questionnaires and Interviews." *Human Factors in Computing Systems: CHI '86 Conference Proceedings,* 1986, pp. 162–167.
6. Carter, J. A. "An Integrated Model for Defining the Role of User Interface and Other Management Systems." *Proceedings of the 1986 IEEE International Conference on Systems, Man and Cybernetics,* 1986, pp. 32–37.

MC68030: The second generation 32-bit microprocessor

by MICHAEL RUHLAND
Motorola Microprocessor Products Division
Austin, Texas

ABSTRACT

The MC68030 is a virtual memory microprocessor based on an MC68020 core with additional enhanced performance features. Increased internal parallelism is provided by multiple internal data buses and address buses, and a versatile bus controller that supports synchronous burst cycle accesses in order to maximize performance with paged mode, nibble mode, and static column DRAM technology, or even external SRAM caches. A 256-byte on-chip instruction cache in addition to a 256-byte on-chip data cache improves data flow to the execution unit and further boosts performance regardless of the actual external memory configuration. On-chip paged memory management reduces the minimum physical bus cycle time to two clocks, and provides zero translation time to any bus cycle. The paged memory management structure can be enabled/disabled by software for applications not requiring the memory management feature. The rich instruction set and addressing modes of the MC68020 have been maintained allowing a clear migration path for M68000 systems.

INTRODUCTION

The MC68030 incorporates the capabilities of the MC68020 microprocessor, a data cache, an instruction cache, an improved bus controller, and an integrated memory management structure defined by the MC68851 Paged Memory Management Unit on one VLSI device. It maintains the 32-bit registers available with the entire M68000 family as well as the 32-bit address and data paths, rich instruction set, versatile addressing modes, and flexible coprocessor interface provided with the MC68020. In addition, the internal operations are designed to operate in parallel, allowing multiple instructions to be executed concurrently. It also allows instruction execution to proceed in parallel with accesses to the internal caches, the on-chip memory management unit, and the bus controller.

The MC68030 fully supports the non-multiplexed asynchronous bus of the MC68020 as well as a dynamic bus sizing mechanism that allows the processor to transfer operands to or from external devices while automatically determining device port size on a cycle-by-cycle basis. In addition to the asynchronous bus, the MC68030 also supports a fast and flexible synchronous bus. Using its synchronous bus capabilities, the MC68030 is capable of fetching up to four long words of data in a burst mode compatible with DRAM chips that have burst capability or SRAM. Burst mode can reduce, by up to 70%, the time necessary to fetch the four long words from physical memory. The four long words are used to prefill the on-chip instruction and data caches so that the hit ratio of the caches improves and the average access time is minimized.

The block diagram shown in Figure 1 depicts the major sections of the MC68030 and illustrates the autonomous nature of these blocks. The bus controller consists of the address and data pads, the multiplexors required to support dynamic bus sizing, and a macro bus controller which schedules the bus

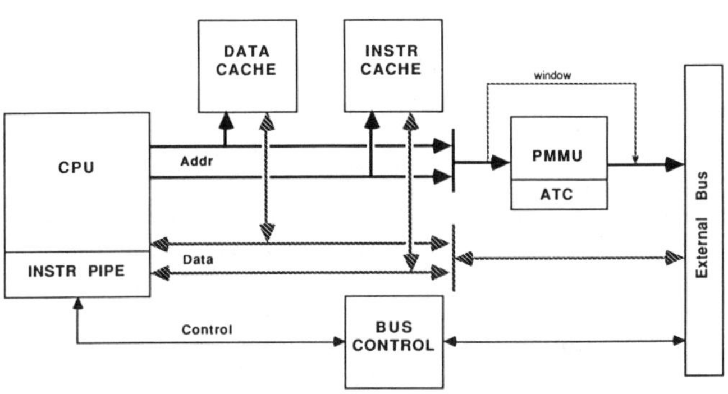

Figure 1—MC68030 block diagram

cycles on the basis of priority. The CPU contains the execution unit and all related control logic.

The instruction and data cache blocks operate independently from the rest of the machine, storing information read by the bus controller. Each cache resides on its own address and data buses, allowing simultaneous access to both. Both the caches are organized as 64 long word entries (256 bytes) with a block size of four long words. The data caches uses a write-through policy.

Finally, the memory management unit controls the mapping of addresses for page sizes ranging from 256 bytes to 32K bytes. Mapping information stored in descriptors resides in translation tables in memory that are automatically searched by the MC68030 on demand. Recently used descriptors are maintained in a 22-entry fully associative cache called the Address Translation Cache (ATC) allowing address translation and other MC68030 functions to occur simultaneously. Additionally, the MC68030 contains two transparent translation registers that can be used to define a one-to-one mapping for two segments ranging in size from 16M bytes to 4G bytes each.

PROGRAMMING MODEL

As shown in the programming model (see Figure 2) the MC68030 has sixteen 32-bit general purpose registers, a 32-bit program counter, two 32-bit supervisor stack pointers, a 16-bit status register, a 32-bit vector base register, two 3-bit alternate function code registers, two 32-bit cache handling (address and control) registers, two 64-bit root pointer registers used by the MMU, a 32-bit translation control register, two 32-bit transparent translation registers, and a 16-bit MMU status register. Registers D0–D7 are used as data registers for bit and bit field (1 to 32 bit), byte (8 bit), word (16 bit), long word (32 bit), and quad word (64 bit) operations. Registers A0–A6 and the user, interrupt, and master stack pointers are address registers that may be used as software stack pointers or base address registers. In addition, the address registers may be used for word and long word operations. All of the 16 (D0–D7, A0–A7) registers may be used as index registers. The status register contains the interrupt priority mask as well as the condition codes. Additional control bits indicate that the processor is in a trace mode, supervisor/user state, and master/interrupt state.

The vector base register is used to determine the run-time location of the exception vector table in memory, hence it supports multiple vector tables so each process or task can properly manage exceptions independently of each other.

The M68000 Family processors distinguish address spaces as supervisor/user, program/data, and CPU space. These five

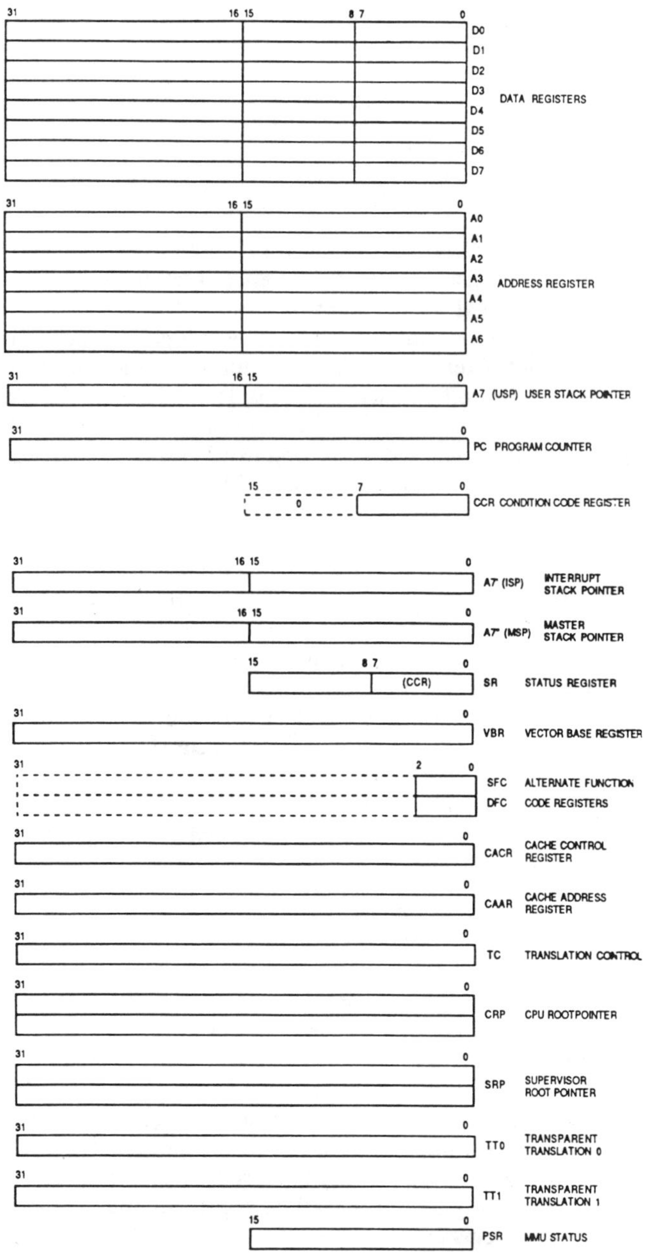

Figure 2—MC68030 programming model

combinations are specified by the function code pins, FC0/FC1/FC2, during bus cycles, indicating the particular address space. Using the function codes, the memory subsystem (hardware) can distinguish between supervisor mode accesses and user accesses as well as program accesses, data accesses, and CPU space accesses. Additionally, the system software can configure the on-chip MMU so that supervisor/user privilege checking is performed by the address translation mechanism and the look-up of translation descriptors can be differentiated on the basis of function code. To support the full privileges of the supervisor, the alternate function code registers allow the supervisor to specify the function code for an access by preloading the SFC/DFC registers appropriately.

The cache registers (control-CACR, address-CAAR) allow supervisor software manipulation of the on-chip instruction and data caches. Control and status accesses to the caches are provided by the cache control register (CACR), while the cache address register (CAAR) specifies the address for those cache control functions that require an address.

All of the MMU registers (CRP, SRP, TC, TT0, TT1, and PSR) are accessible by the supervisor only. The CPU root pointer contains a descriptor for the first pointer to be used in the translation table search for page descriptors pertaining to the current task. If the SRE (Supervisor Root pointer Enable) bit of the translation control register is set, the supervisor root pointer is used as a pointer to the translation tables for all supervisor accesses. If the SRE bit is clear, this register is unused and the CPU root pointer is used for both supervisor and user translations. The translation control register configures the table look-up mechanism to be used for all table searches as well as the page size and any initial shift of logical address required by the operating system. In addition, this register has an enable bit that enables the MMU. The transparent translation registers can be used to define two transparent windows for transferring large blocks of data with untranslated addresses. Finally, the MMU status register (PSR) contains status information related to a specific address translation and the results generated by the PTEST instruction. This information can be useful in locating the cause of an MMU fault.

The MC68030 is upward source- and object-level code compatible with the M68000 Family because it supports all of the instructions that previous family members offer. Included in this set are the bit field operations, binary coded decimal support, bounds checking, additional trap conditions, and additional multi-processing support (CAS and CAS2 instructions) offered by the MC68020. Each instruction, with few exceptions, operates on bytes, words, and long words, and most instructions can use any of the 18 addressing modes. The new instructions supported by the MC68030 are a subset of the instructions introduced by the MC68851 paged memory management unit. The MMU instructions supported by the MC68030 are the PMOVE, PTEST, PLOAD, PFLUSH, and PFLUSHA instructions and they are completely compatible with the corresponding instructions on the MC68851 PMMU. Whereas the MC68851 required the coprocessor interface to execute its instructions, the MC68030 MMU instructions execute just like all other CPU instructions. All of the MMU instructions are privileged (can be executed by the supervisor only).

INSTRUCTION AND DATA CACHES

Studies have shown that typical programs spend most of their execution time in a few main routines or tight loops. This phenomenon is known as locality of reference, and has an impact on the performance of the program. The MC68010 takes limited advantage of this phenomenon with the loop mode of operation that can be used with the DBcc instruction. The MC68020 takes much more advantage of locality with its 256 byte on-chip instruction cache. The MC68030 takes further advantage of cache technology to provide the system with two on-chip caches, one for instructions and one for data.

MC68030 Cache Goals

Similar to the MC68020, there were two primary goals for the MC68030 microprocessor caches. The first design goal was to reduce the processor external bus activity beyond what was accomplished with the MC68020. The second design goal was to increase effective CPU throughput as larger memory sizes or slower memories increased average access time. By placing a high speed cache between the processor and the rest of the memory system, the effective memory access time becomes:

$$t_{acc} = h^*t_{cache} + (1 - h)^*t_{ext}$$

where t_{acc} is the effective system access time, t_{cache} is the cache access time, t_{ext} is the access time of the rest of the system, and h is the hit ratio or the percentage of time that the data is found in the cache. Thus, for a given system design, two MC68030 on-chip caches provide an even more substantial CPU performance increase over that obtainable with the MC68020 with its instruction cache. Alternately, slower and less expensive memories can be used for the same processor performance.

The throughput increase in the MC68030 is gained in three ways. First, the MC68030 caches are accessed in less time than is required for external accesses, providing improvement in the access time for items residing in the cache. Secondly, the burst filling of the caches allows instruction and data words to be found in the on-chip caches the first time they are accessed by the micromachine, with the time required to bring those items into the cache minimized. This has the capability of lowering the average access time for items found in the caches even further.

Thirdly, and perhaps most importantly, the autonomous nature of the caches allows instruction stream fetches, data fetches, and a third external access to all occur simultaneously with instruction execution. For example, if the MC68030 requires both an instruction stream access and an external peripheral access, and the instruction is resident in the on-chip cache, the peripheral access will proceed unimpeded rather than being queued behind the instruction fetch. Additionally, if a data operand was also required, and it was resident in the data cache, it could also be accessed without hindering either the instruction access from its cache or the peripheral access external to the chip. The parallelism designed into the MC68030 also allows multiple instructions to execute concurrently so that several internal instructions (those that do not require any external accesses) could execute while the processor is performing an external access for a previous instruction. The end result is that an MC68030 operating out of on-chip cache offers much better than "no wait state" performance regardless of the external memory system.

Instruction Cache

The instruction cache resident on the MC68030 is a 256-byte direct mapped cache organized as 16 blocks consisting of four long words per block. Each long word is independently accessible yielding 64 possible entries, with A1 selecting the correct word during an access. Thus each block has a tag field made up of the upper 24 address bits, the FC2 (supervisor/user) value, four valid bits (one for each long word entry), and the four long word entries (see Figure 3). The instruction cache is automatically filled by the MC68030 whenever a cache miss occurs and using the burst transfer capability, up to four long words can be filled in one burst. Neither the instruction or data caches can be manipulated directly by the programmer except by the use of the CACR register which provides cache clearing and cache entry clearing facilities. (The caches can also be independently enabled/disabled through the use of this register.) Finally, the system hardware can disable the on-chip caches at any time by the assertion of the CDIS signal.

Data Cache

The organization of the data cache is similar to that of the instruction cache as shown in Figure 4. However, the tag is composed of the upper 24 address bits, the four valid bits, and all three function code bits, explicitly specifying the address space associated with each block. The data cache employs a write-through policy with no write allocation for data writes. In other words, if a cache hit occurs on a write cycle, both the data cache and the external device are updated with the new data. If a write cycle generates a miss in the data cache, only the external device is updated and no data cache entry is replaced or allocated for that address.

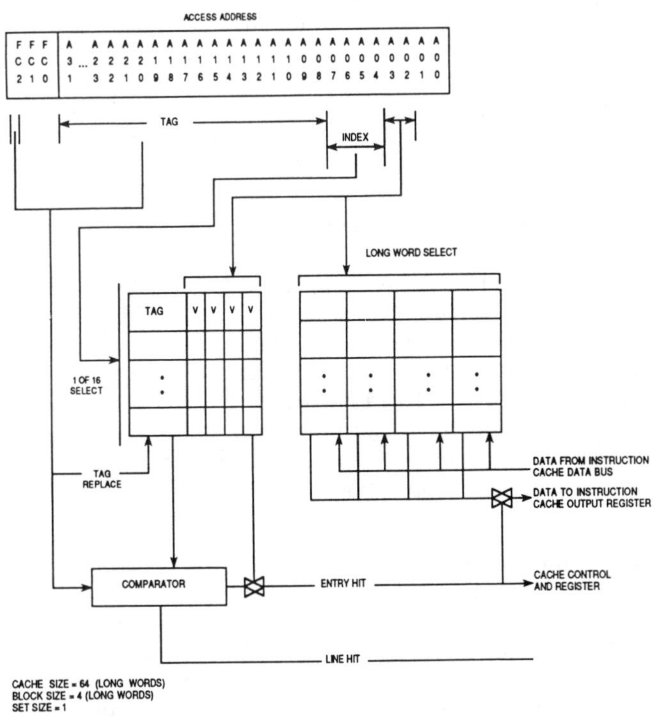

Figure 3—MC68030 on-chip instruction cache organization

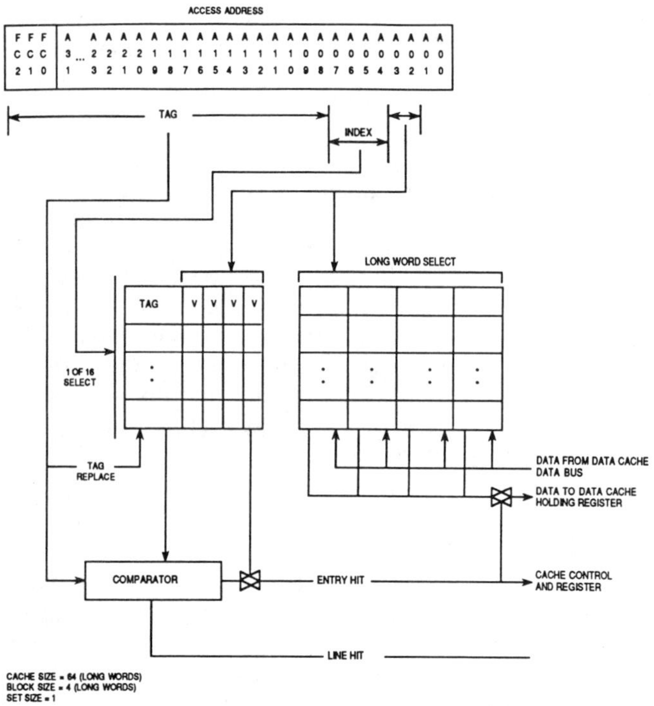

Figure 4—MC68030 on-chip data cache organization

OPERAND TRANSFER MECHANISMS

The MC68030 offers three different mechanisms by which data can be transferred into and out of the chip.

(1) Asynchronous bus cycles, compatible with the asynchronous bus on the MC68020, can transfer data in a minimum of three clock cycles and the amount of data transferred on each cycle is determined by the dynamic bus sizing mechanism on a cycle by cycle basis with the DSACKx signals.

(2) Synchronous bus cycles are terminated with the STERM (Synchronous Termination) signal and always transfer 32-bits of data in a minimum of two clock cycles, increasing the bus bandwidth available for other bus masters, therefore increasing possible performance.

(3) Burst mode transfers can be used to fill blocks of the instruction and data caches when the MC68030 asserts CBREQ (Cache Burst Request). After completing the first cycle with STERM, subsequent cycles may accept data on every clock where STERM is asserted until the burst is completed. Use of this mode can further increase the available bus bandwidth in systems that use DRAMs with page, nibble, or static column mode operation or SRAM configurations.

Asynchronous Transfers

Though the MC68030 has a full 32-bit data bus, it offers the ability to automatically and dynamically downsize its bus to 8 or 16 bits if peripheral devices are unable to accommodate the entire 32 bits. This feature allows the programmer the ability to write code that is not bus-width specific. For example, long word (32 bit) accesses to peripherals may be used in the code, yet the MC68030 will transfer only the amount of data that the peripheral can manage at one time. This feature allows the peripheral to define its port size as 8, 16, or 32 bits wide and the MC68030 will dynamically size the data transfer accordingly, using multiple bus cycles when necessary. Hence, programmers are not required to program for each device port size or know the specific port size before coding; hardware designers have flexibility to choose implementations independent of software prejudices. The MC68030, like the MC68020, offers a complete dynamic bus sizing mechanism which allows 8 or 16 bit ports or memory to be used without wasting any address space.

The dynamic bus sizing is invoked with the use of the DSACKx pins and occurs on a cycle by cycle basis. For example, if the processor is executing an instruction that requires the reading of a long word operand, it will attempt to read 32 bits during the first bus cycle to a long word address boundary. If the port responds that it is 32 bits wide, the MC68030 latches all 32 bits of data and continues. If the port responds that it is 16 bits wide, the MC68030 latches the 16 valid bits of data and runs another cycle to obtain the other 16 bits of data. An 8 bit port is handled similarly but with four bus read cycles. Each port is fixed in assignment to particular sections of the data bus. However, the MC68030 has no restrictions concerning the alignment of operands in memory; long word operands need not be aligned to long word address boundaries. When misaligned data requires multiple bus cycles, the MC68030 automatically runs the minimum number of bus cycles. Instructions must still be aligned to word boundaries.

The timing of asynchronous bus cycles is also determined by the assertion of the DSACKx signals on a cycle-by-cycle basis. If the DSACKx signals are valid 1.5 clocks after the beginning of the bus cycle (with the appropriate setup time), the cycle terminates in its minimum amount of time corresponding to three clock cycles total. The cycle can be lengthened by delaying DSACKx (effectively inserting wait states in one clock increments) until the device being accessed is able to terminate the cycle. This flexibility gives the processor the ability to communicate with devices of varying speeds while operating at the fastest rate possible for each device.

Use of the asynchronous transfer mechanism allows external errors to abort cycle upon the assertion of BERR (Bus Error), or individual bus cycles to be retried with the simultaneous assertion of BEFF and HALT, after the DSACKx signals have been asserted.

Synchronous Transfers

Synchronous bus cycles are terminated with the assertion of the STERM signal which automatically indicates that the bus transfer is for a 32 bit port. This input is not synchronized internally, thereby allowing two clock cycle bus accesses to be performed, if the signal is valid, one clock after the beginning of the bus cycle with the appropriate setup time. However, the bus cycle may be lengthened by delaying STERM (inserting wait states in one clock increments) until the device being accessed is able to terminate the cycle as in the case of asynchronous transfers. Additionally, these cycles may be aborted upon the assertion of BERR, or they may be retried with the simultaneous assertion of BERR and HALT, after the assertion of STERM. For systems operating at high clock frequencies STERM is easier to use than DSACK, because while DSACKx is asserted to the processor 1.5 clocks before the end of a bus cycle, STERM is asserted only one clock before the end of bus cycle (non-burst). This extra half clock allows control logic to be that much slower (or the clock frequency to be that much faster).

Burst Read Cycles

The MC68030 provides support for burst filling of its on-chip instruction and data caches, adding to the overall system performance. The on-chip caches are organized with a block size of four long words, so that there is only one tag for the four long words in a block. Since locality of reference is present to some degree in most programs, filling of all four entries when a single entry misses can be advantageous, especially if the time spent filling the additional entries is minimal. When the caches are burst-filled, data can be latched by the processor in as little as one clock for each 32 bits.

Burst read cycles can be performed when the MC68030 requests them with the assertion of CBREQ and only when the first cycle is a synchronous cycle as described above. If the CBACK (Cache Burst Acknowledge) input is valid at the appropriate time in the synchronous bus cycle, the processor will keep the original AS, DS, R/W, address, function code and size outputs asserted and will latch 32 bits from the data bus at the end of each subsequent clock cycle that has STERM asserted. This procedure continues until the burst is complete (the entire block has been transferred), BERR is asserted in lieu of STERM, or the CBACK input is negated. Figure 5 shows the minimum MC68030 burst cycle. To support slower memory systems, any number of wait states can be inserted before a unique long word of data is latched by negating STERM with the proper setup time. When compared to an MC68020/MC68851 system, the MC68030's burst mode provides a 220% (3.2x) improvement in the data transfer rate, assuming a four clock physical bus cycle (one long word of data, four bytes) for the 020/851 pair and a five clock burst cycle (four long words, 16 bytes) on the MC68030. This five

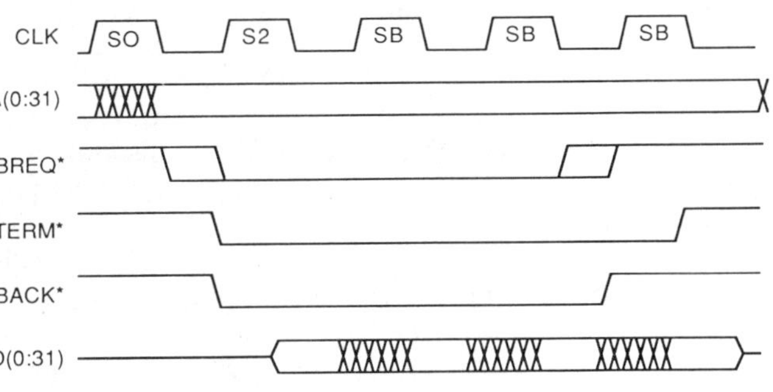

Figure 5—MC68030 synchronous burst cycle

clock burst cycle provides an effective transfer rate of one 32-bit long word every 1.25 clocks. Hence, performance of the MC68030 is better than "no wait states." In addition, the MC68030 loads this data into its on-chip caches where it if is needed again no external cycle may be required at all, improving further the better than "no wait state" performance.

Implementing an external memory system with burst capability presents several architectural options. DRAMs with page, nibble, or static column modes can be easily matched to the MC68030's burst cycle. For higher performance systems, SRAM banks can be configured in 32, 64, or 128 bit widths. For banks that are 32 bits wide an external modulo-2 counter is required to provide the addresses of the three long words not directly addressed by the MC68030's address lines. If the memory width is 128-bits, no additional addressing is necessary, but a counter will serve as a multiplexor control to gate the proper 32-bit long word onto the data bus during the burst. The 64 bit wide memory is a compromise between the two previous configurations, in that some additional addressing and multiplexor logic is required.

EXCEPTIONS

Exceptions can be generated by either internal or external causes. The externally generated exceptions are the interrupts, the bus error, and reset requests. The interrupts are requests from peripheral devices for processor action while the bus error and reset pins are used for access control and processor restart. The internally generated exceptions come from instructions, address errors, tracing, or breakpoints. The TRAP, TRAPcc, TRAPV, cpTRAPcc, CHK, CHK2, and DIV instructions can all generate exceptions as part of their instruction execution. Tracing behaves like a very high priority, internally generated interrupt whenever it is processed. The other internally generated exceptions are caused by illegal instructions, instruction fetches from odd addresses, and privilege violations. Finally, the MMU can generate exceptions when it detects an invalid translation in the Address Translation Cache (ATC) and an access to the corresponding address is attempted, or when it is unable to locate a valid translation for an address in the translation tables.

Bus exceptions are an important class of the possible M68000 exceptions. Included in this group are the bus error and retry operations, which are absent from many architectures outside the M68000 Family. Bus error exceptions for example, could be used to immediately indicate a parity error on data in the current cycle. This permits faster error detection and recovery, and prevents the processor from executing on bad data.

The retry mechanism can be used with external caches to repeat a particular bus cycle. With caches having high hit rates, this technique allows cache control logic to be slower than might be expected because hits are always assumed and signaled as such to the microprocessor by STERM or DSACK. If a miss does occur, a retry can be signaled within half a clock after STERM or one clock after DSACK. Thus with a 20 MHz MC68030, cache control logic must only be 5 ns faster than the cache data memory.

MC68030 ON-CHIP MEMORY MANAGEMENT UNIT

The full addressing range of the MC68030 is 4 gigabytes (4,294,967,296 bytes). However, most MC68030 systems implement a smaller physical memory. Nonetheless, by using virtual memory techniques, the system can be made to appear to have a full 4 gigabytes of physical memory available to each user program. In a similar fashion, a virtual system provides user programs access to other devices that are not physically present in the system such as tape drives, disk drives, printers, or terminals. The memory management unit (MMU) on the MC68030 provides the capability to easily support a virtual system and virtual memory. In addition, it provides protection of supervisor areas from accesses by user programs and also provides write protection on a page basis. All this capability is provided along with maximum performance as address translations occur in parallel with other processor activities.

Demand Paged Implementation

A typical system with a large addressing range such as one with the MC68030 provides a limited amount of high-speed physical memory that can be accessed directly by the processor while maintaining an image of a much larger "virtual" memory on secondary storage devices such as large capacity disk drives. When the processor attempts to access a location in the virtual memory map that is not resident in physical memory, the access to that location is temporarily suspended while the necessary data is fetched from secondary storage and placed in physical memory; the suspended access is then either restarted or continued.

A paged system is one in which the physical memory is subdivided into equal sized blocks called page frames and the logical (untranslated) address space of a task is divided into pages which have the same size as the page frames. The operating system controls the allocation of pages to page frames so that when data is needed from the secondary storage device, it is brought in on a page basis. The memory management scheme employed by the MC68030 is called a "demand" implementation because a process does not need to specify in advance what areas of its logical address space it requires. An access to a logical address is interpreted by the system as a request for the corresponding page.

The memory management unit on the MC68030 employs the same address translation mechanism introduced by the MC68851 Paged Memory Management Unit with possible page sizes ranging from 256 bytes to 32K bytes.

Translation Mechanism

Logical-to-physical address translation is the most frequently executed operation of the MC68030 MMU, so this task has been optimized and can function autonomously. The MMU initiates address translation by searching for a descriptor with the address translation information (a page descriptor) in the on-chip ATC. The ATC is a very fast fully-associative cache memory that stores recently used page descriptors. If the descriptor does not reside in the ATC then the MMU requests external bus cycles of the bus controller to search the translation tables in physical memory. After being located, the page descriptor is loaded into the ATC and the address is correctly translated for the access, provided no exception conditions are encountered.

The status of the page in question is easily maintained in the translation tables. When a page must be brought in from a secondary storage device, the table entry can signal that this descriptor is invalid so that the table search results in an invalid descriptor being loaded into the ATC. In this way, the access to the page is aborted and the processor initiates bus error exception processing for this address. The operating system can then control the allocation of a new page in physical memory and can load the page all within the bus error handling routine.

Address Translation Cache

An integral part of the translation function described above is the cache memory that stores recently used logical-to-physical address translation information, or page descriptors. This cache consists of 22 entries and is fully-associative. The ATC compares the logical address and function code of the incoming access against its entries. If one of the entries matches, there is a hit and the ATC sends the physical address to the bus controller, which then starts the external bus cycle (provided there was no hit in the instruction or data caches for the access).

The ATC is composed of three major components: the content-addressable memory (CAM) containing the logical address and function code information to be compared against incoming logical addresses, the physical address store that contains the physical address associated with a particular CAM entry, and the control section containing the entry replacement circuitry that implements the replacement algorithm (a variation of the least-recently-used algorithm).

Translation Tables

The translation tables supported by the MC68030 have a tree structure, minimizing the amount of memory necessary to set up the tables for most programs, since only a portion of the complete tree needs to exist at any one time. The root of a translation table tree is pointed to by one of two root pointer registers that are part of the MC68030 programmer's model; the CPU and supervisor. Table entries at the higher levels of the tree (pointer tables) contain pointers to other tables. Entries at the leaf level (page tables) contain page descriptors. The mechanism for performing table searches uses portions of the logical address as indices for each level of the lookup. All addresses contained in the translation table entries are physical addresses.

Figure 6 illustrates the structure of the MC68030 translation tables. Several determinants of the detailed table structure are software selectable. The first level of lookup in the table normally uses the function codes as an index but this may be suppressed if desired. In addition, up to 15 of the logical address lines can be ignored for the purposes of the table

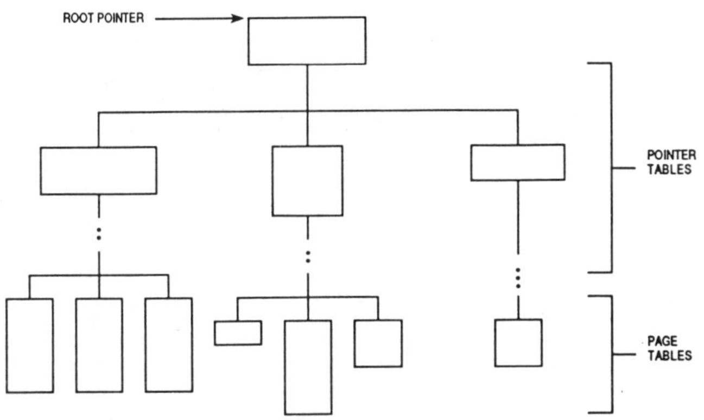

Figure 6—MMU translation table tree structure

searching. The number of levels in the table indexed by the logical address can be set from one to four, and up to 15 logical address bits can be used as an index at each level. A major advantage to using this tree structure for the translation tables is the ability to deallocate large portions of the logical address space with a single entry at the higher levels of the tree. Additionally, portions of the tree itself may reside on a secondary storage device or may not exist at all until they are required by the system.

The entries in the translation tables contain status information pertaining to the pointers for the next level of lookup or the pages themselves. These bits can be used to designate certain pages or blocks of pages as supervisor-only, write-protected, or non-cacheable. If a page is marked as non-cacheable, accesses within the page will not be cached by the MC68030 instruction or data caches and the CIOUT (cache inhibit out) signal is asserted for those accesses. In addition, the MMU automatically maintains history information for the pointers and pages in the descriptors via the Used (U) and Modified (M) bits. CIOUT is particularly useful in systems accessing shared memory or I/O devices. CIOUT directly informs any external cache that current data should not be cached. Historically, some microprocessor architects recommended dedicating an address line to indicate non-cacheable areas, but the CIOUT signal provides more flexibility without affecting the processor's addressing range.

Transparent Translation

Two transparent translation registers have been provided on the MC68030 MMU to allow portions of the logical address space to be transparently mapped and accessed without corresponding entries resident in the ATC. Each register can be used to define a range of logical addresses from 16M bytes to 4G bytes with a base address and a mask. All addresses within these ranges will not be mapped and protection is provided only on a basis of read/write and function code. These registers provide windows into memory that will never suffer from page faults regardless of previous memory activity. For example in a real time graphics application, this means that line drawing will be continuous and not jerk or step from delays caused by page faults and table searches. Many other applications will also benefit from the TT registers.

COPROCESSOR INTERFACE

The coprocessor interface is a mechanism for extending the instruction set of the M68000 family. The interface provided on the MC68030 is the same as that on the MC68020. Examples of these extensions are the addition of specialized data operands for the existing data types or, for the case of floating point, the inclusion of new data types and operations for them as implemented by the MC68881 and MC68882 floating-point coprocessors.

The communication protocol between the main processor and the coprocessor necessary to execute a coprocessor instruction is based on a group of coprocessor interface registers (CIRs) which have been defined for the M68000 family and are implemented on the coprocessor. The MC68030 hardware uses standard read and write cycles to access the registers. Thus the coprocessor interface doesn't require any special bus hardware: the bus interface implemented by a coprocessor for its interface register set must only satisfy the MC68030 address, data, and control signal timing to guarantee proper communication with the CPU. The MC68030 implements the communication protocol with all coprocessors in hardware (and microcode) and handles all operations automatically so the programmer is only concerned with the instructions and data types provided by the coprocessor as extensions to the MC68030 instruction set and data types. Up to seven coprocessors are supported in a single MC68030 system with a system-unique coprocessor identifier encoded in the coprocessor instruction. When accessing a coprocessor, the MC68030 executes standard bus cycles in CPU address space, as encoded by the function codes, and places the coprocessor identifier on the address bus to be used by chip-select logic to select the particular coprocessor.

SUMMARY

The MC68030 provides increased system performance and reduced system costs through enhanced features not found on any other commercial microprocessors. Increased performance is derived from the MC68030's on-chip caches, the on-chip memory management unit, multiple internal address and data buses, and a versatile bus controller. Reduced system cost is achieved by bringing all these features on-chip and through the improved bus controller's interface to external memory. The MC68030 does indeed represent the second generation in 32-bit microprocessors.

ACKNOWLEDGEMENTS

The author wishes to thank Clara Serrano of Motorola's M68000 Applications Group for her assistance in the preparation of this paper.

Transaction processing systems on future workstations: A feasibility study

by JACOB SLONIM, JOHN HENSHAW and AVI SCHONBACH
Geac Computers International
Ontario, Canada
and
MICHAEL BAUER
The University of Western Ontario
Ontario, Canada

ABSTRACT

An account of a benchmark test to evaluate the performance of a relational database management system, INGRES, in the context of a library circulation system. The results suggest that, within a couple of years, relational database systems running on microcomputers within distributed environments will be performance- and cost-effective in supporting transaction processing systems.

INTRODUCTION

Organizations such as banks, airlines, and libraries rely heavily on transaction processing systems in their day-to-day operations. These systems provide rapid on-line access to information for the use of both customers and employees. The emergence of powerful microcomputers and reliable communication has created an opportunity to develop distributed systems in which data locality reflects the locality of users.

The term "workstation" is used to represent a comprehensive set of tools tailored to a specific type of user—in Geac's case, a librarian's workstation. The functions of these tools are independent of the machine size. The purpose of this research is to define a minimum standard configuration for hardware and system software to cost-effectively support the workstation toolset.

We at Geac are currently involved in a project which calls for the development of a commercial transaction processing (TP) system in a distributed environment for use in libraries. Our goal is a TP system capable of operating in a large distributed environment composed of microcomputers, minis, and mainframes. This system, moreover, is to be based on existing, off-the-shelf hardware and software. These goals have led us to consider several relational database systems as a basis for the TP system, and to consider UNIX as the base operating system.

Historically, commercial transaction processing systems have relied on specialized databases, such as Tandem's ENCOMPASS/TMF[1] or Geac's GeacOS,[2] or on traditional hierarchical and network databases such as IBM's IMS/TPF.[3] These systems are commercially available, and a great deal is known about their behavior and performance. In contrast, little is known about the use of relational database systems in TP environments.

Although relational database management systems offer a number of advantages in distributed transaction processing (discussed in detail below), a common argument against their use has to do with performance. Two widely held opinions can be summarized as follows:[4]

> Relational systems are all very fine for ad hoc query, but they will never achieve the performance needed for production systems or transaction processing systems . . .
>
> Relational systems require a breakthrough in hardware technology (e.g., hardware associative memory) before they will be able to achieve acceptable performance.

In contrast, the opinion of the authors and many other researchers is that:

> there is no intrinsic reason why a relational database system should have worse performance than traditional database systems.

The next two sections discuss UNIX and the advantages of relational database systems. Thereafter follows a description of our benchmark of a commercial relational database management system in a transaction application.

WHY THE UNIX OPERATING SYSTEM?

As we have noted, one of the original aims of the project was to rely as much as possible on existing commercial hardware and software, and to take advantage of new technology as it appears on the market. This aim, coupled with requirements to support distributed systems with powerful microcomputers and reduce the cost of developing new software, led us to adopt AT&T UNIX as a logical choice for our operating system.

In practice, the development of applications to operate on multiple operating systems is a long, expensive process, and one which often results in software of poor quality. Servicing user needs across hardware from various vendors and of various sizes becomes much easier when a single operating system is used. A single operating system greatly simplifies the incorporation of industry standards in networking, database management and other software tools.

Why UNIX rather than some other operating system? We have chosen UNIX because its design stresses backward compatibility with previous versions of itself, and thereby protects the investments of Geac and its customers. This feature allows the Geac family of computers to communicate with a growing installed base of UNIX applications within the industry. The flexibility of this operating system allows Geac to add enhancements to our existing system without compromising the hardware or software investment of our customers. Since UNIX is offered by an increasing number of vendors and used at an increasing number of universities, the rate of product innovation will continue to grow rapidly.

All UNIX operating systems are not alike, but efforts are under way to find unity in this diversity. One approach is that adopted by AT&T, which has issued the Full System V Interface Definition, Issue 2, as well as a validation suite.[5] The IEEE's approach is more comprehensive: the P1003 Standard Committee is working on a single UNIX operating system standard for worldwide use.[6]

UNIX is by no means without its difficulties. For example, UNIX's i-node structure poses performance problems in the handling of large databases, and a single file cannot span multiple spindles. There is also a general concern about known bugs and built-in overheads.

WHY A RELATIONAL DATABASE MANAGEMENT SYSTEM?

A database management system is a large, complex collection of software routines positioned between the user's application program and the data to be processed. The DBMS controls access to and manipulation of the data on behalf of the application programs. Data models, which organize data logically according to genuine relationships in the data files, have been developed out of either graph or set theory.[7] The three primary models in use today are the hierarchical, network, and relational.

All three have advantages and drawbacks. The network and hierarchical models have reached commercial maturity, while the relational model has received a great deal of commercial attention in recent years. Unlike the traditional models, which have been used in the computer industry for years, the relational model has evolved along with the microcomputer. From 1983 through 1985, the number of commercially available relational database systems increased from 40 to more than 100. It is clear now, with products like DB II/III and ORACLE on microcomputers, and with companies like IBM announcing DB2 (System R) and Cullinet announcing IDM/R, that many vendors feel that relational databases represent a viable commercial technology.

The relational database model traces its roots to theories developed in relational mathematics.[8] The artificial set constructs, intrinsic to the hierarchical and network schemes, are not relevant to the relational model. Instead, data relationships are reduced to simple components and represented directly through views of data relationships. The database itself is homogeneous, and this homogeneity makes it possible to define any number of data relationships or logical views of data, and to process it by performing logical operations on attributes.

The relational model is a way of looking at data—a prescription for the representation and manipulation of data. This prescription has three components:

1. *structure,* that is, tables (rows and columns of data)
2. *integrity,* that is, a means of ensuring, for example, that every relation (table) has a unique key to identify table entries or rows, and
3. *manipulation,* consisting of operators for processing tables; these operators are straightforward: the *select* operator picks out rows; the *project* operator picks out columns; the *join* operator combines two tables.

These characteristics of the relational model provide real advantages in a distributed transaction processing environment. The relational model generally shields the application designer from the complexity of storage structures, data definitions and the design of access paths. The labor costs associated with database implementation and maintenance are thereby lowered.

Today, relatively high performance is offered in database management systems founded on the traditional (hierarchical and network) models. Nevertheless, the traditional models do have their drawbacks. The most notable is that they require a high level of effort on the part of the application designer; invariably the application designer must specify complex storage structures, data access paths, and data definitions. The network model is also inflexible, in that access paths that are not predefined when the database is loaded cannot be introduced without major restructuring of the database.

One criticism of relational systems is that they are primarily aimed at supporting query requirements, and consequently are not well suited for full-scale production and/or transaction processing. It is true that no existing commercial relational product can perform as well as, for example, IMS Fast Path. The reason for that could well be that IMS Fast Path runs on very large machines, like the Sierra 400. There are, however, no inherent theoretical or practical reasons why relational systems cannot ultimately match the top performance of traditional database systems.[9]

An advantage of the relational model is that it prevents the application developer from seeing explicit connections or links between tables (that is, physical pointers), and thereby avoiding traversal between tuples on the basis of such links. It also precludes user-visible indices on attributes, and removes the physical storage structures from the concern of users. The relational tables are a logical abstraction of what is physically stored.

The tables in a relational DBMS are a normalized structure. In systems like IMS and IDMS the physical structure is biased toward certain applications and machine architectures by the inclusion of built-in access paths. Consequently, for those particular applications, the network and hierarchical models can be very powerful. The relational model, on the other hand, permits the dynamic creation of access paths through the use of the manipulative operators. Since the application is no longer limited to predetermined access paths, data independence of the system is enhanced.

In relational systems, in contrast to traditional database management systems, the theory preceded any implementation. If a relational implementation conforms to this theory, its behavior in any given situation is completely predictable.

Under traditional database management systems, some actions may result in unpredictable events. For example, one application might delete a record which is linked to other records, with the result that none of these records are accessible to other applications.

A standard query language is an important issue because it renders database definitions and application programs portable among implementations conforming to the standard. Both ISO and ANSI have established committees to develop standard query languages, for both the network and relational models. The ANSI X3H2 committee is at the draft proposal stage for the network model.[10] The same committee has already reached agreement on a standard for the relational model based upon SQL.[11] ISO has also approved this standard.[12]

The standard for the relational query language applies to implementations in an environment that may include application programming languages, end-user query languages, report generator systems, data dictionary systems, program library systems, and distributed communications systems, as well as various tools for database design, data administration, and performance optimization.

The SQL language was developed in 1974 at IBM.[13] The

technology explored and developed in System R[14] was subsequently exploited by IBM in both SQL/DS[15] and DB2.[16] Recently, ORACLE and Fujitsu have announced an SQL product. Last year, INGRES[17] introduced their version of SQL in conjunction with supporting QUEL. QUEL was originally developed in 1974 by M. Stonebraker and others at the University of California at Berkeley as part of the INGRES system. Of the 100 or so relational products on the market, at least 30 have an SQL flavor.[18]

In distributed database systems, one important requirement is that communication traffic be minimized. Relational database systems have a number of characteristics which make them an excellent choice in distributed systems. First, the set handling capabilities within the relational data manipulation language lead to a more effective use of communication lines; the system receives one request for each set of tuples required, rather than one per tuple. Under the network model application programs operate entirely in a one record-at-a-time mode.

Second, the relational model makes it straightforward to partition tables either vertically (columns) or horizontally (rows); these partitioned tables can then be easily distributed across the network. The standard relational operators, join and union, can be used to reassemble the partitioned tables. Both these areas present considerable difficulties for systems based on traditional models.

Third, relational operators are high-level, and for that reason they can be optimized in ways essential for distributed access plan (System R*[19]).

Fourthly, the relational model provides data independence for applications. An application program is data independent if it does not require modification when the database is restructured or reorganized. Program data independence is provided by hiding from the application program the physical placement and organization of data in the database. This is particularly important for location transparency within distributed databases. In traditional systems the application must use predefined physical pointers to access the data.

An important implication for application development is that relational systems simplify prototyping. Using a relational database management system it is easy (2–3 weeks) to design and create a database, build some application (e.g., a library circulation system), and then run a prototype featuring actual screens and reports.

THE QUESTION OF PERFORMANCE

We have outlined a number of reasons why relational databases and UNIX are good tools for building distributed systems and applications. These tools will allow us to take advantage of future developments in hardware technology because of their independence from any particular hardware.

Developments in large-scale, very large-scale integration (LSI/VLSI) and integrated circuit (IC) chip technology have led to package miniaturization, minimal interconnections, economy of scale, and increased functions on an IC chip. As a result, more powerful microcomputers are continually appearing. Microcomputers are now available which provide large main memories (e.g., up to 16MB on a MicroVax II), support large mass storage devices (e.g., 420 MB drives on a MicroVax II), and provide hardware support for memory management (e.g., the INTEL 80386 and Motorola 68030). Enhanced communication capabilities, such as Ethernet, are already readily available. As hardware technology becomes more sophisticated, more software functions can be embedded within the hardware (e.g., memory management and communication protocols). This provides an opportunity to increase overall system performance, and in particular, transaction processing performance.

However, these advantages and trends do not in themselves guarantee that one can build commercially viable transaction processing systems. There remains the unresolved question of performance. To address this concern, we decided to benchmark a commercial relational database management system under UNIX in a transaction processing environment.

THE LIBRARY CIRCULATION BENCHMARK

Market requirements for our project dictate a performance of one transaction per second per $25,000. In today's market, this corresponds to the cost of a microcomputer with the performance of a Vax 8650. The purpose of our benchmark was to determine whether commercial relational database products would be capable of this level of performance on microcomputers likely to emerge within the next two years. INGRES release 4.02 was the relational database management system tested. INGRES is now marketed by Relational Technology Inc. and runs on a variety of computers. Since we were interested in the performance of "standard" commercial database systems, no tailoring of the INGRES software was made with respect to the requirements of the benchmark, in which, by the way, Relational Technology Inc. played no role.

The benchmark chosen was a library circulation system. On the basis of marketing requirements for a typical library system, a performance requirement of 5 transactions per second had been established. This is comparable to the Debit-Credit transaction benchmark[20] in terms of the number of reads and writes per transaction. The relationship to other transaction systems is illustrated in Table I. The Debit-Credit system is used as a basis for the comparison of transaction processing systems. Table I lists several different systems, presents their requirements in transactions per second, and gives a weight based upon the Debit-Credit system.

TABLE I—Transaction weights

Application	Transaction Rate/Sec.	Weight
lottery	400.0 tps/cpu	0.01 D-C
800-number	50.0 tps/cpu	0.10 D-C
video text	20.0 tps/cpu	0.20 D-C
credit authorization	10.0 tps/cpu	0.40 D-C
debit-credit	4.0 tps/cpu	1.00 D-C
"real" debit credit	2.0 tps/cpu	2.00 D-C
electronic mail	0.2 tps/cpu	20.00 D-C
phone store	0.1 tps/cpu	40.00 D-C

Environment

The benchmark was run on a VAX 8650 (8 MIPS), configured with 16 megabytes of memory, and using 120 megabytes of a 420 megabyte disk spindle. The host operating system was Ultrix 1.2 (BSD4.2). This configuration reflects our prediction of the performance of microcomputers available within a very few years. Benchmark runs were executed when there were no other active users.

An INGRES page is 2K bytes, representing four Ultrix virtual memory pages. During the course of the benchmark INGRES process cache size varied from 9 to 250 INGRES pages (18K to 500K bytes).

Ultrix imposed a number of limitations on the benchmark. In our configuration the available Ultrix lock table resources and virtual memory are exhausted when ten concurrent processes using the maximum page allocation per process are running. When this happens, INGRES cannot proceed and shuts down gracefully; INGRES processes that have sufficient resources continue to execute. Lock table size and available virtual memory size are system parameters; a system reconfiguration is necessary to set different values. Another constraint on the benchmark imposed by Ultrix is that a maximum of 24 processes are permitted for each login session; this is also an operating system parameter. Since each INGRES invocation requires a "front end" and a "back end" process, a maximum of twelve process-pairs could be run at once. In practice, this number is actually a bit lower because of the Ultrix process required to maintain a user session.

Methodology

The benchmark library circulation system involves three types of transaction: charge a book, discharge a book, and put a hold on a book. A skeleton of the current Geac library circulation system was used in the design of the benchmark. This skeleton was implemented on facilities provided by INGRES.

The benchmark data was taken from a medium size public library in British Columbia, Canada. This data was chosen because it is used internally at Geac for quality assurance testing of the current circulation system. The original database consisted of 56,000 library patron records and 222,000 library item records. Because of restrictions on space, the database size was reduced to 20,000 patron records and 120,000 library item records. A smaller database of 1000 patron records and 2100 library item records was used for prototyping and validation.

Five tables were used in the benchmark database: patron, item, statistics, library events and requests. These are summarized in Table II. As noted, three types of transactions were used within the circulation system. A Charge transaction is illustrated in Figure 1; input-output operations for the different transaction types are summarized in Table III.

Results

A summary of the benchmark results appears in Table IV. Each table entry represents one run of the benchmark, which consisted of running the same 2000 transactions to completion. The columns indicate the cache sizes available to and used by each INGRES process, the number of INGRES processes executing concurrently, the total CPU time, the elapsed time, the number of direct I/O requests (i.e., to the operating system to access the disk), cache request—the number of times the cache is accessed to read a data page, cache

TABLE II—Summary of table design parameters

Table	Primary Key	Size (bytes)	Number of Attributes
patron	patron barcode	451	28
item	item barcode	123	19
statistics	type	25	6
events	item barcode	94	13
requests	patron barcode	75	8

Get patron tuple via patron barcode.
Get item tuple via item barcode.
If item is reserved for another patron, reject charge.
Review patron's outstanding holds. If conflict, reject charge.
Update patron tuple.
Update item tuple.
Append statistics tuple.
Append event tuple.

Figure 1—Sample transaction: Charge

TABLE III—Input/output operations for transaction types

Transaction	Retrieve	Replace	Delete	Append
Charge	2–3	2	0	2
Discharge	6	2–3	1–2	1
Hold	2–3	1–2	0	2

TABLE IV—Benchmark results

Cache Avail	Cache Used	Number Process	Total CPU (sec)	Elapsed time (sec)	I/Os	Cache request	Cache read	Cache write	TPS
9	8	1	201.4	788	18265	26007	21693	6276	2.4
9	8	2	209.9	754	18657	26103	21746	6266	2.5
9	8	3	215.9	515	17847	26097	21807	6208	3.6
9	8	4	216.7	518	18376	26242	21920	6222	3.6
23	23	1	194.9	700	16499	26017	13905	6281	2.7
23	23	2	215.6	560	17355	26070	17661	6235	3.3
23	22	3	211.9	511	17750	26197	18814	6259	3.7
23	22	4	219.6	485	17484	26201	19166	6217	3.8
125	124	1	196.9	607	16778	26007	10436	6276	3.0
125	124	2	210.7	489	15820	26066	14412	6247	3.8
125	124	3	203.9	470	16420	26221	15829	6276	4.0
125	124	4	216.1	441	16445	26298	16355	6242	4.2
250	249	1	191.2	565	14562	26007	8035	6276	3.3
250	249	2	214.8	476	15424	26095	12777	6255	3.9
250	204	3	209.1	427	15495	26100	14688	6210	4.3
250	175	4	224.2	452	16286	26354	16024	6277	4.1

read—the number of times the cache must read a page from the disk, cache write—the number of times the cache writes a page to disk, and the number of transactions per second. The number of transactions per second is the number of transactions divided by the elapsed time. The following observations can be made regarding these results:

1. The best performance achieved was 4.3 transactions per second. The worst result observed was 2.4 TPS.
2. The number of direct I/Os is of primary importance. Performance decreases with an increase in the number of direct I/Os.
3. As the size of the INGRES process cache increases, the number of direct I/Os and the number of cache reads decreases.
4. The numbers of cache requests and the number of cache writes remain relatively constant, independent of INGRES process cache size.
5. The ratio of cache reads to direct I/Os is significant. An increase in the ratio decreases elapsed time. This is, however, of secondary importance to the number of direct I/Os. An increase in the number of concurrent processes causes an increase in this ratio.
6. When the number of direct I/Os is constant and the number of concurrent processes is increased, performance improves.
7. There is a strong correlation between the number of concurrent INGRES processes and the use of the available cache per process. Too many concurrent processes, however, create overhead as a result of competition for access to the data. Best performance is achieved at the point where the addition of another concurrent process causes a less than maximum use of available cache.

Experiments varying the item and patron table structures were performed on the small database with a cache size of 23 pages per INGRES process. These two tables are modified by every transaction. Table V presents these results. The ISAM access method provided the best results for our data. The hashing based storage structure failed to provide reasonable performance, since the keys in the tables were unsuitable for the INGRES hashing algorithm. The B-tree access method, used by the current Geac circulation system, is available with INGRES 5.0. This access method could offer an additional improvement in performance.

TABLE V—Benchmarks with varying file structures

Item	Patron	procs	IO reqs	reqs	cache read	write	TPS
hash	hash	1	71783	145888	144174	5203	0.4
hash	hash	2	76134	151522	144123	5204	0.4
ISAM	hash	1	29736	76033	70307	4197	0.9
ISAM	hash	2	35122	82937	71144	4198	0.8
ISAM	ISAM	1	10002	13543	7133	4034	2.8
ISAM	ISAM	2	10471	13576	7732	4036	2.9

SUMMARY AND CONCLUSIONS

Relational database management systems are a viable option in commercial transaction processing. The combination of a relational database management system and the UNIX operating system offers savings in development cost, portability among vendors and computer architectures, and the ability to take advantage of future technological innovations. UNIX is a solid platform for distributed database management systems.

UNIX and relational database management systems were first implemented, and first achieved commercial success, on small computers. They are now becoming commonly available on large and very large computer systems.

The benchmark experiment demonstrated to our satisfaction that a relational database management system can provide sufficient performance to meet market demands. In order to achieve commercial success in our market area, we must reduce the cost of a TPS. This reduction can be achieved only when the performance of the VAX 8650 is made available on a small computer like the MicroVax II. Both computers use the 32-bit word size required to run a large database management system efficiently. The benchmark results indicate that the critical performance factors are the disk access time and the size of main memory. The minimum main memory size of the Vax 8650 is already available on the MicroVax II.

We limited the benchmark to a single disk spindle, in order to match as closely as possible the hardware configuration of existing microcomputers.

Since direct I/O is the most critical factor in the performance of the system, in situations in which more than one disk is available, the tables could be stored in such a way as to allow parallel disk I/O. In our system, for example, patron and item tables would then reside on different disks.

Having started with the hypothesis that the relational model is capable of sufficient performance, we have reached the conclusion that by using one of several commercially available relational database management systems we can build a commercially successful library transaction processing system.

REFERENCES

1. Nauman, John, "ENCOMPASS: Evaluation of a Distributed Database/Transaction System." *Database Engineering Newsletter,* 5 (1982) 4, pp. 37–41.
2. Information on the Geac operating system is available from *Geac Computers International,* 350 Steelcase Road West, Markham, Ontario, Canada, L3R-1B3.
3. IBM Corporation. *Information Management System/Transaction Processing Information Manual,* IBM Form no. GH20-1260.
4. Date, C.J. *Relational Database—Selected Writings,* Reading, Massachusetts: Addison-Wesley, 1986, p. 66.
5. AT&T System V Interface Definition, Spring, 1985, Issue 2.
6. IEEE Computer Society. "IEEE P1003, Working Group on Portable Operating System for Computer Environment," IEEE, 1987.
7. Rustin, R., ed. "Data Models: Structure Set vs. Relational," *Proc. ACM SIGMOD Workshop on Data Description, Access and Control,* (vol. 11), May, 1974.
8. Codd, E.F., "A Relational Model of Data for Large Shared Data Banks," *Communications of the ACM,* 13 (1970) 6.
9. Date, C.J., and Codd, E.F. "The Relational and Network Approaches: Comparison of the Application Programming Interface," *Proc. 1974 ACM*

SIGMOD Workshop on Data Description, Access and Control, (vol. 11), May, 1974.
10. X3H2 (American National Standards Database Committee) *Draft Proposed Network Database Language,* Document X3H2-84-1, January, 1984.
11. X3H2 (American National Standards Database Committee) *Draft Proposed Relational Database Language,* Document X3H2-84-2, January, 1984.
12. ISO TC97/SC21/WG3 N147 and ANSI X3H2-86-27, "Database Language Extended SQL," October, 1986.
13. Codd, E.F. "A Database Sublanguage Founded on the Relational Calculus," *Proc. 1971, ACM SIGFIDET Workshop on Data Description, Access and Control,* November, 1971.
14. Blasgen, M.W., et. al. "System R: An Architectural Overview," *IBM System Journal,* 20 (1981) 1.
15. IBM Corporation. *SQL/Data System General Information,* IBM Form no. GH24-5012.
16. IBM Corporation. *IBM Database 2 General Information,* IBM Form no. GC26-4082.
17. Information on INGRES is available from *Relational Technology Inc.,* Alameda, California.
18. Date, C.J. "Interview Part 1," *Data Base Newsletter,* II (1983) 5.
Date, C.J. "Interview Part 2," *Data Base Newsletter,* II (1983) 6.
19. Mohan, C., B. Lindsay, and R. Obermurk. "Transaction Management in the R* Distributed Database Management System," *IBM Research Report RJ 5037,* IBM Research Laboratory, San Jose, California, February, 1986.
20. Dewitt, D.J. "Benchmarking Database Systems: A Systematic Approach," *Proc. 9th International Conference on Very Large Databases,* Florence, Italy, November, 1983.

SURF: A semantic update and retrieval facility

by FRED MARYANSKI and DARRELL STOCK
University of Connecticut
Storrs, Connecticut

ABSTRACT

The definition and design of a query language based on a semantic data model and targeted for personal workstations with color graphics is presented. The language, SURF, contains a browsing facility which permits the user to learn the structure of the database schema by exploring diagrams used in the database design phase. By using the browser, the user can create forms upon which the database operations are expressed. SURF queries are formulated by traversing diagrams and filling forms thus minimizing the keyboard input required of the user. Color is also utilized in the composition of complex Boolean expressions. The integration of a graphical interface with a semantic data model is intended to simplify database access for the nonprogramming workstation user.

INTRODUCTION

Motivation and Problem Solution Overview

The nature of interfaces to database systems is fundamentally dependent upon the functionality of the computing system and the conceptual model offered by the database package. Many of the current generation of database query languages provided keyboard directed interfaces to a tabular relational model. The shortcoming of conceptual models such as the relational model is that they present a limited set of descriptive options to the end user. The user is forced to map a mental image of the problem space into a collection of flat tables. Recently, a number of researchers have embarked on studies of a new generation of semantically rich conceptual data models which would permit the description of data in a manner closer to the user's perception. This class of data models is generally known as semantic data models.[1,2]

Concurrent with the evolution of semantic data models is the growth of personal workstations from purely ASCII character oriented devices to systems offering a variety of pointing devices, powerful graphical capabilities, and bit map color displays. It seems clear that the next generation of database query facilities must exploit the functionality of modern personal workstations and semantic data models to provide the end user with a rich, yet simple, interface to databases.[3,4,5]

The above observations have led to the definition and implementation of the SURF query facility.[6] SURF is based upon the semantic data model defined by Peckham[7] as part of the Data Model Compiler project at the University of Connecticut.[8] In order for a personal workstation to support SURF, it must provide bit map graphics with color and a mouse. The initial implementation of SURF utilized a Unix workstation which offers extensive graphical facilities beyond those required by the query facility. The software for the DMC project of which SURF is a component is presently being moved to a less powerful, Unix-based, personal workstation. While SURF is implemented in C under Unix, the choice of both the language and the operating system are independent of the basic principles of the query facility.

Design Objectives

The design of SURF was driven by the following parameters in order to produce a conceptually pleasing database access facility.

1. The ability to tailor the conceptual data model to the mind set of the end user:
   SURF is designed upon a semantic data model so that the end user may interact with the database using the concepts of his/her own discipline.
2. The provision of a graphical interface for query formulation:
   Positional information and screen context are exploited in order to simplify the task of the end user.
3. The ability to determine the structure of the database in a straightforward manner:
   A browsing facility supports the user's need to examine high and low-level details of the schema.
4. Automation of the details of integrity and consistency maintenance:
   Semantic integrity constraints are enforced to avoid inadvertent creation of inconsistent results.

QUERY LANGUAGE CLASSIFICATION

In the classification scheme of Lochovsky and Tsichritzis,[9] query languages are categorized as keyword, by-example, natural language, graphic, or multimedia. SURF combines features of by-example and graphic languages and is most closely related to QBE/OBE[10] and LID.[11]

THE SEMANTIC DATA MODEL

The data model employed by SURF is an extended entity-relationship model with a subtype/supertype inheritance structure for entities which are defined in terms of their properties, operations, and constraints.[7] A graphical application design tool, DBDT,[12] assists the designer in the specification of the entities, relationships, operations, and constraints of a given application domain. SURF's role is to map queries expressed using a combination of tables and DBDT diagrams into transactions against the semantic database.

Relationships

In general, semantic data models[2] can be distinguished by their built-in relationships. The data model employed by SURF[7] directly supports four types of relationships: IS-A, reference, nest, and association. The IS-A relationship is utilized to express generalization/specialization among entity types. The form of IS-A employed here is a template-oriented inheritance mechanism which is very strict in terms of inheritance of properties but does provide for overriding defaults and refining constraints at the subtypes.

The latter three fundamental relationship types are the basis for all user-defined relationships. They have the functionality shown below. The work of El-Masri and Wiederhold[13] strongly influenced the definition of these relationship types.

1. Reference—a mapping from one entity to another. A reference is realized as an attribute of the referencing entity.
   EXAMPLE—a STUDENT entity references a PROFESSOR entity through the attribute ADVISOR which is of type PROFESSOR.
2. Nest—a mapping from one entity, the Nest Owner, to a set of entities, the Nest Members. A nest is a set-valued attribute of the owner.
   EXAMPLE—a STUDENT entity contains a nest of the COURSE entities as its COURSE_REQUEST attribute.
3. Association—a many-to-many mapping between two or more entity types. Associations are represented as independent components of the model with their own properties, operations, and constraints.
   EXAMPLE—TAKE is an association between the STUDENT and COURSE entities that has GRADE as an attribute.

Semantic Integrity

Rules are included to preserve the semantic integrity and consistency of the database. Integrity constraints must be evaluated each time an operation is executed. This involves determining which (if any) relationships an entity participates in and then evaluating the appropriate rules for those relationships over the specified operation. The following constraints are automatically enforced by SURF.

1. If an object is to be inserted as a nest member, that member must exist as an entity object.
2. An object instance cannot be deleted if it is being used as a nest member.
3. The deletion of a nest owner instance implies the deletion of all nest objects owned by it.

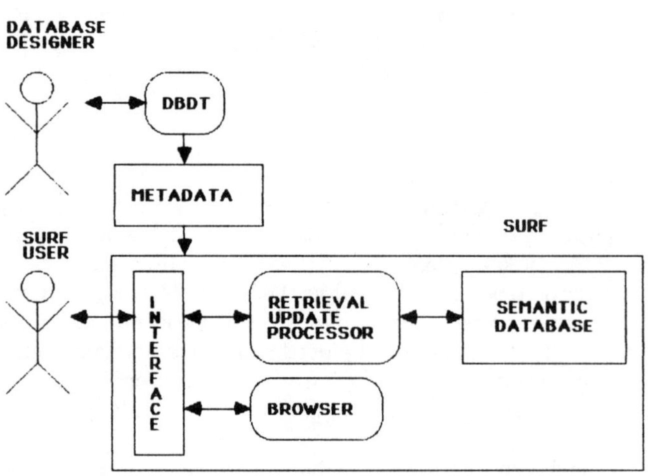

Figure 1—Organization of semantic database system

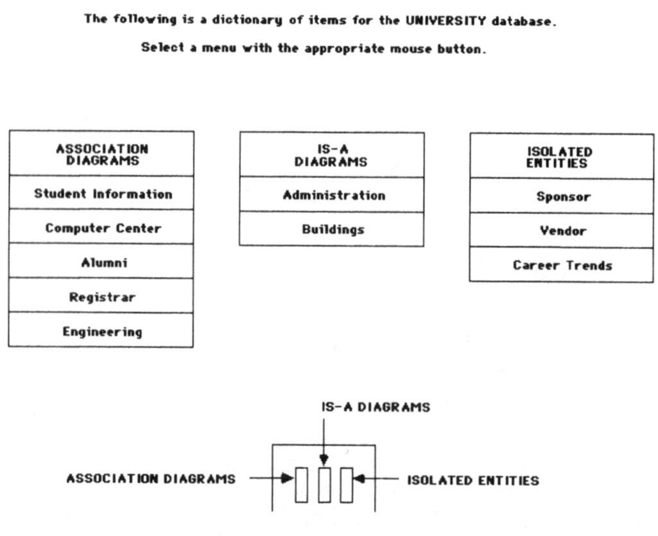

Figure 2—Diagram menus

4. If an object instance is to be inserted as a reference that reference instance must exist as an entity object.
5. An object instance cannot be deleted if it is being used as a reference.
6. The deletion of a referencing instance implies the deletion of all reference objects owned by it.
7. An object instance cannot be deleted if it is being used as an association participant.
8. All association participant instances must exist as entity objects before an association instance can be inserted.
9. Insertion of a subtype instance implies the insertion of one instance of each related supertype.
10. Deletion of a supertype instance implies the deletion of the corresponding subtype instances related to the supertype instance.

THE SURF QUERY FACILITY

A high-level view of the overall semantic database system is illustrated in Figure 1. A database designer (database administrator) applies the DBDT tool to specify the structure of the semantic database. SURF is driven by the metadata generated by DBDT. The major elements of SURF are:

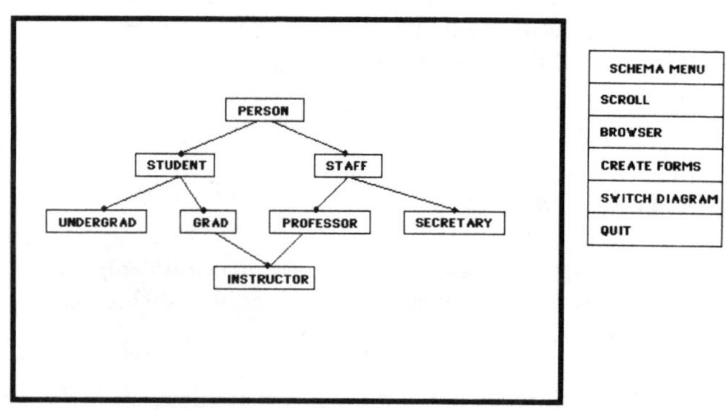

Figure 3—IS-A diagram

1. A browser program which permits database structure analysis
2. A retrieval/update processor which supplies the resources to interact with the semantic database and the SURF user

Browsing a Semantic Database

When the design phase is complete, the nonprogramming user can activate the Browser which provides a visual representation of the database structure. A SURF browsing session consists of selection, navigation, and tailoring.

Selection

In the SURF environment, a semantic database consists of a collection of diagrams. When a session is initiated, the user is presented with lists of the diagrams of the database as in Figure 2. Note that isolated entities are those which have not been included in any diagrams. The mouse icon at the bottom of the screen provides the user with a reminder of the actions associated with each button. Figure 3 illustrates the contents of the screen following the selection of an IS-A diagram.

Navigation

The navigation facility permits the user to examine the detail of database objects while retaining an overall perspective of the schema. When the user selects an object, a window describing one level of detail appears. Successive levels can be obtained by selecting complex attributes of the selected entities as in Figure 4. In the navigation facility, the system indicates the relationship among entities and attributes by lining up the top portion of a window with the entity from which it is generated. Shading is employed to indicate the most recently activated object.

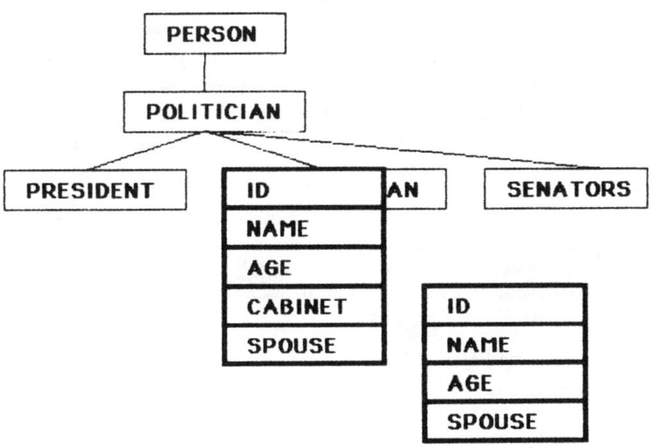

Figure 4—Navigation

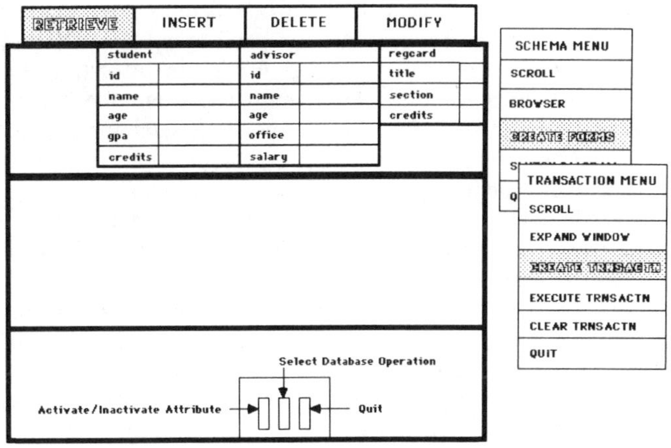

Figure 5—Transaction formulation environment

Tailoring

Tailoring involves selecting the attributes of the entities to appear on the query forms. If no tailoring is performed, all attributes of the selected entities will be available at query formulation time. Tailoring is mouse-selectable and is visualized by changing the color (highlighting) of database objects and attributes from gray to orange.

The Retrieval/Update Processor

Forms are used to represent the entities and relationships of the semantic data model. Query transactions are expressed by form filling and mouse maneuvering. Figure 5 presents an example of the screen immediately after browsing and before transaction formulation. The steps in the specification of a query are:

1. Select the operation (RETRIEVE, INSERT, DELETE, MODIFY)
2. Specify the selection criteria (or fill in data on insertion) on the forms
3. Select the attributes for output (default is output all)

Figure 6 expresses the query "Retrieve the names of all students with GPA greater than 3.8." The output of a SURF retrieval appears in tabular form, listing values for mouse-selected attributes.

One of the more difficult problems facing developers of query languages is the expression of disjunctive and conjunc-

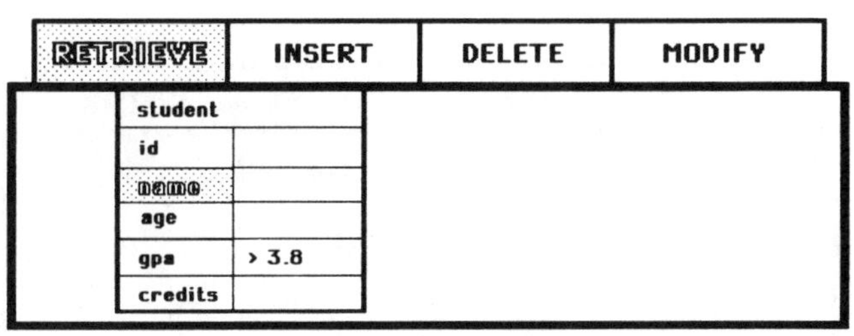

Figure 6—SURF retrieval

tive queries. The typical end user who has not been schooled in Boolean or Aristotlean logic may tend to use "AND" and "OR" interchangeably in the verbal expression of queries. SURF attempts to solve this dilemma through the use of colors. Using the function keys, terms of the selection expression can be entered in any of four colors. A boolean AND is undertaken on entries appearing in the same color. A boolean OR is undertaken on entries appearing in different colors. The use of colors provides the user with a straightforward visual representation of complex queries.

Insertions involve filling in attribute values on the forms identified in the browsing process. Key attributes require values while non-key attributes will receive a null value if the user does not elect to supply information at that time. Null values may be later assigned values by using the Modify operation. Figure 7 illustrates the insertion of the ID, NAME, AGE, and ADVISOR for the student James. Null values will be stored in the GPA and CREDITS attributes.

SURF deletions are expressed by placing selection criteria next to the appropriate attributes. The same rules as for retrievals are followed. For example, Figure 8 presents the query which deletes all students whose advisor is Brown. The highlighting of the STUDENT entity indicated that students are to be deleted.

A modification operation entails first identifying the objects to be altered and then specifying the replacement values for the appropriate attributes. Attributes to receive new values are identified by selecting the attribute name which results in the name being shaded. If an attribute is to be used for both identification and value replacement, then entries are made on multiple lines within the field for that attribute. SURF permits multiple lines per attribute for the expression of this and more advanced operations.[6] The rule for interpreting modification operations is that the value on the last line of a shaded attribute is used as the replacement value. This feature is illustrated in Figure 9 in which all students with grade point averages greater than 4.0 and with less than 60 credits, have their grade point average set to 4.0.

A design goal for SURF was to provide straightforward expression for the most common operations. As demonstrated above, the context provided by the diagrams and forms permits the statement of queries expected of the typical end user in a rather simple fashion. For a discussion of the handling of more complex operations, see the work by Stock.[6]

The Experienced SURF User

One of the more serious problems facing the designer of database query facility is that of user maturity. Features de-

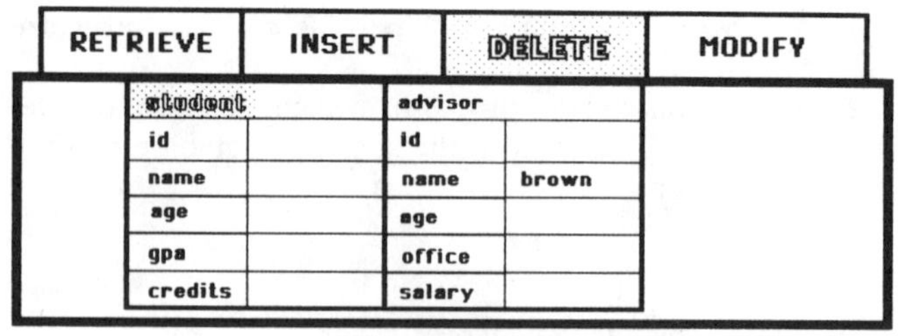

Figure 8—SURF deletion

signed to guide the first time user through a query session can become annoying to the person who has worked with the language for six months. SURF addresses this issue in two ways:

1. Macros—The experienced user who has repetitive tasks to perform may define a sequence of screens as a macro and call this operation when required.
2. Defaults—The user who is familiar with the structure and contents of the database can shortcut the browsing process by merely selecting the entities from a diagram and then moving to the transaction menu without selecting specific attributes. As a default, the system will generate a form containing all the attributes of the entity. At worst, the user will obtain a superset of the attributes required as the response to the query. However, it is a simple matter for an individual familiar with the data to visually select the attributes of interest from the screen.

CONCLUSION

Summary

SURF is a database query facility for the new generation of personal workstations and semantic data models. By exploiting current workstation and database technology it offers end users straightforward access to data which is represented in a clear conceptual model. The semantic richness of the data model allows the representation of information in a manner that is close to that of the end user's perception of the environment. Thus, the end user is not forced to learn the terminology and internal organization of the database system. Through the use of diagrams, forms, color, and a pointing device, a context is established for each operation. Therefore, the user enters simple selection expressions and data values in order to specify database operations. The end user does not use the keyboard to input keywords or any other form of descriptive text.

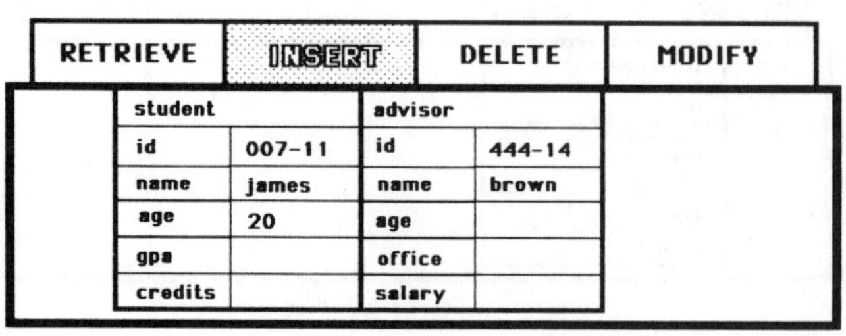

Figure 7—SURF insertion

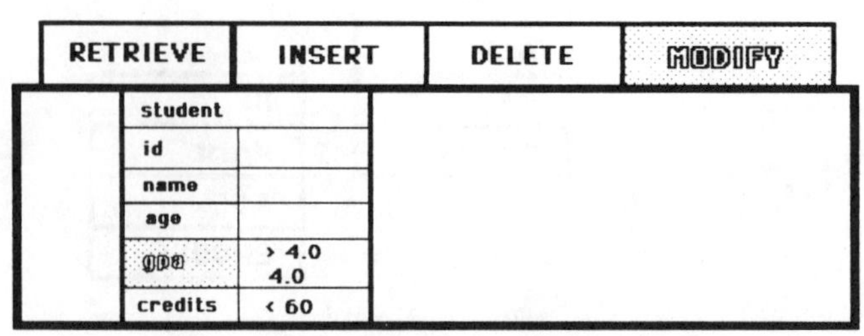

Figure 9—SURF modification

Status and Future Plans

The initial implementation of SURF has been completed recently.[6] Plans are to exercise and enhance SURF as the Data Model Compiler project continues to investigate the production of semantically rich database management systems. All components of the overall system are being moved to a smaller, Unix-based personal workstation.

As personal workstations continue to grow in functionality and the quality of their interfaces increases, database query facilities will take advantage of these features to offer the end user more options for the expression of database operations. With similar advancements in the data modeling area, the possibility of productive database manipulation by the true casual user could be realized.

ACKNOWLEDGEMENT

The research was supported in part by a grant from the National Science Foundation, ECS-8401487.

REFERENCES

1. Brodie, M., J. Mylopoulous, and J. Schmidt (eds.). *On Conceptual Modeling,* Springer Verlag, 1984.
2. Peckham, J. and F. Maryanski. "Semantic Data Models." TR CS-86-15, Computer Science and Engineering Dept., University of Connecticut, November, 1986.
3. Herot, C. "Graphical User Interfaces." in Y. Vassilou (ed.), *Human Factors and Interactive Computer Systems,* Ablex Publishers, 1984, pp. 83–103.
4. Larson, J.A. "A Visual Approach to Browsing in a Database Environment." *Computer,* 8 (1986) 6, pp. 62–71.
5. McDonald, N. "A Multi Media Approach to the User Interface." in Y. Vassilou (ed.), *Human Factors and Interactive Computer Systems,* Ablex Publishers, 1984, pp. 105–116.
6. Stock, D. "SURF: A Graphical Language for Semantic Database Interaction." M.S. Thesis, Computer Science and Engineering Dept., University of Connecticut, December, 1986.
7. Peckham, J. "A Formal Model for the Design of Semantic Databases." M.S. Thesis, Electrical Engineering Computer Science Dept., University of Connecticut, June, 1985.
8. Maryanski, F., J. Bedell, S. Hoelscher, S. Hong, L. McDonald, J. Peckham, and D. Stock. "The Data Model Compiler: A Tool for Generating Object-Oriented Database Systems." *International Workshop on Object-Oriented Database Systems,* September, 1986, pp. 73–84.
9. Lochovsky, F.H. and D.C. Tsichritzis. "On Evaluating Interactive Query Languages." *Information Sciences,* 29 (1983), pp. 93–113.
10. Zloof, M.M. "QBE/OBE: A Language for Office and Business Automation." *Computer,* 14 (1981) 5, pp. 13–22.
11. Fogg, D. "Lessons from a 'Living in a Database' Graphical Query Interface." *ACM SIGMOD Conference,* June 1984, pp. 100–106.
12. Maryanski, F. and S. Hong. "A Tool for Generating Semantic Database Applications." *IEEE COMPSAC,* October, 1984, pp. 368–375.
13. El-Masri, R. and G. Wiederhold. "Properties of Relationships and their Representation." *AFIPS, Proceedings of the National Computer Conference,* (Vol. 49), 1980, pp. 319–326.

Text database systems

by F.J. SMITH
The Queen's University of Belfast
Belfast, Northern Ireland

ABSTRACT

A text database system, often called an information retrieval system, is designed to process a text model of the data, viewed as an ordered sequence of documents, paragraphs, sentences, words (i.e., as a list structure). Although relations are *sets* of tuples, and therefore unordered, the relational model can still be used successfully for text, but surprisingly it is shown that at the physical level the two apparently different approaches are likely to be identical. However, since the human view of text is much closer to a list than to a relation, the text model is more appropriate for document handling. In addition, when tuples include a large amount of free text (as in the "soft" sciences), and when queries involve text processing more often than the eight operations of relational algebra, then also the text model is more appropriate.

INTRODUCTION

Data in the form of free text, produced on word processors, are rapidly growing in quantity and importance, and within a few years will probably outweigh the type of conventional computer data which are stored in relational, hierarchical or network databases. Text can also be stored in these conventional databases, but it is generally more straightforward and efficient to store text using database structures specifically designed for text. These text database systems have often been called information retrieval systems,[1] and perhaps for this reason, in spite of their obvious importance and wide use in industry, commerce, and information services, they are often still not mentioned in books on database systems.

A text database is a system for the storage, manipulation and retrieval of data stored in the form of free text, that is, stored as an ordered sequence (i.e., as a list) of alphabetic, numeric and control characters which normally can be printed directly onto paper. Any text prepared on a word processor can therefore be considered as the basic data of a text database, and generally word processors are now the means of data input and editing.

A text database will also have a facility for retrieving information from the data (hence the name Information Retrieval System); this is usually achieved by finding documents or parts of documents which match a search on a combination of words (equivalent to the operations of selection and projection in a relational database). For example, the search:

> "Find all Documents containing Word Processor and Database"

should find this paper amongst others.

However, there is one fundamental difference between a text database and a relational database. A relational database is able to answer directly a limited number of queries put to it about the entities and attributes described by the database, but in a text database a human must read the retrieved documents, and possibly use a great deal of inferred knowledge about the entities mentioned in the documents, before obtaining the answer to some query. So the query

> Which database can I use with my wordprocessor?

cannot be answered directly by a text database although it can find this paper, which provides one possible answer to the query. A long term aim is to design a text database system which can answer such a question, but we are many years away from this.

At best, for now, we can use some linguistic features such as synonyms, lemmas, or homographs to add to the "intelligence" of a search. We have built such a system in Belfast, called QUILL, running on a VAX.[2] It has an inverted file structure, based on an index to all of the words of the text. Although such an inverted file structure is most common in text databases, there are other possibilities (e.g., serial searching with special fast processors[3] or clustering[1]), but these need not concern us in this paper.

Just as we define a "relational model" based on a relational structure, so we can define a "text model" based on a free text structure. The "text model" can be defined as a data model of an enterprise or of part of the real world, where the data of the model takes the form of free text. Thus a report by a management consultant on a company, including text and tables, is a text model for the company, a model more appropriate for a Director's meeting than a relational model on their mainframe.

Text does not have to be stored in a text database. In the next section, we first discuss how text can be stored in a relational database and alternatively how a relation can be stored in a text database, after noting that neither model is entirely appropriate in many real examples, particularly in science and engineering. We then show that these two apparently different ways of storing text are almost identical in their implementations, so that the two are, in fact, similar.

STORING TEXT IN A RELATION

In the literature, a number of authors have discussed the storage of text within the relational model.[4,5,6] At first sight, this seems difficult because of the fundamental difference between the basic structure of free text and a relation. Text is essentially an ordered sequence of the basic units of data, words, and delimiters such as punctuation marks, spaces, and linefeeds (i.e., it is a list structure).[4] The order is obviously vital and it is rare that any two words or sequence of words, even in the largest text, can be exchanged without affecting the meaning or information content of the whole.

On the other hand, a relation is a *set* of tuples defined over a *set* of attributes. So, by the definition of a set, the basic units, tuples and attributes, are not ordered, quite different from text. It would therefore not be surprising if it was very difficult to use a relational data model, completely unordered, to store text data, completely ordered.

However, each item of a list has associated with it an implied number, giving the position of the item in the list. For example, the implied number for the 2nd item is the number 2. If we form a tuple of the implied number and the corresponding item we can turn the list into a relation. So, noting that text is a sequence of characters we could number each character and produce a valid relational model for the text, based on the relation:

CHAR(character#, character) (1)

However, it would be more realistic, noting that text is made up of a sequence of documents, made up of sentences, made up of words, to create a relation[6]

WORD-SENT-DOC
(doc#, sentence#, word#, word) (2)

in which each word is stored in one tuple and the ordering is recorded using the doc#, sentence# and word#. Both of these relations are obviously wasteful of storage space, particularly when the text is large. Alternatively, less space is wasted by storing a whole sentence, with a variable length, as a component of each tuple of a relation:

SENT-DOC (doc#, sent#, sentence) (3)

The "sentence" component is now a piece of free text, and this relation has the advantage that a sentence is arguably the basic semantic unit of text.

However, the relations CHAR, WORD-SENT-DOC, and SENT-DOC are unusual because none of the attributes contains any semantic information, as we normally expect in a relation. For example, consider the relation for the city where each employee of a company lives. It might be:

HOME (Employee#, Employee-surname, City)

then for Mr. Denver living in Denver we would need the tuple

1372, Denver, Denver.

Note that the semantic information of each component "Denver" is incomplete without adding the semantic information in the attribute.

But in the above 3 relations the last attributes, "character," "word" and "sentence" are really types rather than attributes and add no semantic information to the components. The entities to which they refer are linguistic entities (e.g., a "word") not the entities described by the text model, given by the meaning of the words: they are at a different level of abstraction. They do not model the real world, but rather the language describing the real world.

REPRESENTATION OF A RELATION IN THE TEXT MODEL

It is always possible to store the data in a relation in the form of free text. For example, consider the simple relation in Table I on Atomic Masses.

In the unlikely event of a free text structure being used for the information in Table I, it could be stored as in Table II. Table II has exactly the same information content as the relation in Table I and the software to perform the operations of selection and projection, for example,

"Find the atomic mass of Lithium"

can be performed just about as easily with a relational structure as with the free text structure. However, a join with another relation, such as the relation,

Atomic-Resistivity (Atomic Symbol, Resistivity)

to answer a query such as

"Find atoms with highest resistivity and with atomic mass <16"

is more difficult to perform with the text structure (although not inordinately so if the syntax of the text is restricted to structure and forms similar to those above) and, of course, the text takes substantially more storage space. Therefore, although it poses an interesting academic project for a student, no one would seriously consider the storage of the data in the relation in Table I in a text structure. Similarly, I contend that no one should seriously consider the storage of the content of this paper in a relational database rather than in a text database.

However, often when we want to store data in a computer system, as we will show, the situation is not as clearcut as it is in the above two examples. These grey areas are apparently more common in science and engineering than in business or commerce, because much scientific data are not exact, particularly but not only in the "soft" sciences. In business, how-

TABLE I—Atomic mass relation

Typical example of a simple relation where the components of each tuple belong to a well defined domain (e.g., the atomic numbers are all integers between 1 and 104).

Name of Atom	Atomic Symbol	Atomic Number	Atomic weight
Hydrogen	H	1	1.008
Helium	He	2	4.003
Beryllium	Be	4	9.015
Oxygen	O	8	16.000

TABLE II—Atomic mass information as free text

The atom Hydrogen, with atomic symbol H, has an atomic mass of 1.008 atomic units. The atom Helium, symbol He, has atomic mass 4.003 units. The atom Beryllium, symbol Be, has atomic mass 9.015 units and the atom with symbol O, Oxygen, has atomic mass 16.000 units.

ever, data are usually precise. A bank balance and account number have precise values and can therefore be represented perfectly in a relation in which the attributes are:

Account# Balance

and all of the information on balances corresponding to account numbers can be suitably represented in a relation:

Account-Balance (Account#, Balance)

But this is not always so. Take, for example, the attribute "telephone number." We could easily define a precise domain for such an attribute, and with a little more difficulty, allow telephone numbers in foreign countries. But consider the following example. If you were to call me and ask for my telephone number, so that you could contact me at any time, this is the information I would give you:

Telephone number
"Office: in the morning, 232-245133 Ext. 3229,
in the afternoon, 232-661111 Ext. 3234.
Home: weekdays, 232-703235
but I spend most of the Summer, Christmas and Easter vacations and many weekends at an address which has the number, 396-86684."

So, to communicate all of this information to the end user of a database, this whole text would have to be made the component corresponding to the attribute "telephone number" and the processing of this component would now involve "intelligent" text processing, not available in databases outside University research systems.

In spite of the above example, this kind of qualification or enlargement of data items is probably not often necessary in commercial databases. It is more common in science and engineering. An examination of any handbook of engineering data or source of scientific data will normally show the data displayed in tables, which appear to be exactly in the form suitable for a relational database. But on closer examination, almost invariably there are qualifications added to many data items in each table. This is true even in the physical sciences where data is known most precisely. For example, consider the data in Table III (obtained by the author by selecting one physics book,[9] opening it at random, and turning a few pages). An example of engineering data is shown in Table III where one component of the last tuple has extra information added. In both these cases, however, the relational model is still certainly the appropriate model, with some modification to allow for the comments, for errors, for alternative values (as in Table IV) and for ranges (e.g., "<0.27" in Table IV).

However, in the "soft" sciences it becomes less clear and in an example such as the ornithological record in Table V, so many of the components are expressed in the form of free text and, therefore, so many queries will involve text processing rather than the eight operations of relational algebra[8] that a text model and a text database seem more appropriate. The same is true of the Bibliographic record in Table VI.

TABLE III—Ferrous alloy properties

Example of engineering data on Ferrous Alloys with 7 attributes. This shows that, just as in Science, tuples in Engineering often need extended fields to record additional information, as in Tuple 5.

Alloy	Condition	Sigma %	Test Temp.	Creep %	Time hr	Stress ksi
3105	2000°F. ½ hr AC	0	1200	10	24	1
3105	2000°F. ½ hr AC	0	1200	100	22	1
3105	2000°F. ½ hr AC	0	1200	1000	20	1
3105	2000°F. ½ hr AC	0	1800	10	5.3	1
3105	2000°F. ½ hr AC, after a delay of 200 hrs at 1600°F	2.5	1600	10	10	1

TABLE IV—Molecular quadrupole moments obtained from microwave collision diameters

The following table illustrates that even in the Physical Sciences some components, such as those in the last column, need extended fields containing free text, to represent all of the information available. Note that two columns are used to represent the uncertainty in the diameter, *d*.

Molecule	$d \times 10^8$ (cm) Kinetic Theory	$d \times 10^8$ (cm) from NH_3 3, 3 Line Broadening	q_{rot} (cm^2) $\times 10^{16}$
N_2	4.09	5.54	0.31[a]
O_2	4.02	3.86	<0.11[b], 0.04[c]
NO	3.90	5.64	0.29
CO	3.96	5.97	0.33
CO_2	4.46	7.59	0.64
COS		7.56	0.60
CS_2		7.72	0.64
N_2O	4.35	7.32	0.91[a]
HCN		10.0	1.60
ClCN		11.9	2.39
C_2H_2		8.79	1.10
C_2H_4	4.79	6.67	0.48
C_2H_6	4.86	5.64	<0.27
H_2			0.261[d]

[a] Average of experimental values is used here to calculate q_{rot}.
[b] The value $d=4.18\times10^{-8}$ cm, which is considered to be most reliable, is used to obtain the upper limit for q_{rot}.
[c] R.S. Anderson, W.V. Smith, and W. Gordy, Phys. Rev., 82, 264 (1951), obtained this value from measurements of the line widths of the fine structure of the microwave spectrum of oxygen. The accuracy of this number is still questionable.
[d] The value q for H_2 is the value relative to the internuclear axis rather than the value for rotating molecules.

COMPARISON OF TEXT AND RELATIONAL DATABASE IMPLEMENTATIONS

In the text model, the text is represented by a continuous list of characters, including control characters which give the text its structure (i.e., pages, sentences, paragraphs, sections,

TABLE V

Example of a record in an Ornithological Database where almost every field needs free text to represent the information content. Such records are more suitably stored in a text database than using a relational database.

SPECIES:	Great Blue Heron (Ardea herodias)
HABITAT:	Common on fresh and salt water.
RANGE:	Summer and Winter in South U.S. and in Summer in North U.S., Quebec and Nova Scotia.
LENGTH:	38″.
WING SPAN:	70″.
DESCRIPTION:	Head is largely white, underparts dark and speckled, beak rich brown, back slate blue and brown. Flies with neck folded.
ALARM CALL:	Series of 4 hoarse squawks.
FOOD:	Fish, frogs.

TABLE VI—CODATA referral database record

Example of a record in the CODATA Referral Database on Sources in Science and Technology which is being stored in a Text Database. There would be no advantage in using a relational model for such records.

TITLE:	Solar Informations Centrum e.V.(SIC), Solar Information Centre, Riedlstrasse 3,D-8000 Munchen 22 (Germany FR).
SERIAL:	(e) de 001.
COUNTRY:	Germany FR.
MAIN CATEGORY:	Renewable Energy Resources.
TELEPHONE:	(089) 22-57-55.
INSTITUTION TYPE:	Information centre.
DIRECTOR:	Hegenbart, R.
COVERAGE:	Provision of information on solar energy and energy conservation: energy consulting, public information, setting up data bases.
KEYWORDS:	climatology; energy conservation; energy economics; solar energy.
OUTPUT:	Publication of printed compilations; Magnetic tapes containing data.
SERVICES:	Provision of specific data upon request; Referral to institutions or published data sources.
AVAILABILITY:	Open to all users; Fees charged.
LANGUAGE:	German; English.

chapters, documents). However, to find any part of a large text quickly (e.g., a sentence or paragraph), it is necessary, in the inverted file structure, to provide an address for each unit of the text. The physical address of the start of the unit on the disk can be used; but to facilitate edits and changes in the physical storage of the text, as in any other database, a logical address is used at the conceptual level. This might consist of "word#" measured from the beginning of the text or, as in our QUILL system, Doc#, sentence#, word#.

There needs also to be a mapping from the logical addresses to the physical addresses. This is performed using a table, which has columns such as—

doc#, sentence#, address of start of sentence (4)

But this is almost the same as the SENT-DOC relation mentioned in (3).

SENT-DOC(doc#, sent#, sentence) (5)

But the similarity is even closer if the implementation of the relational database is examined. To obtain rapid access to any tuple (i.e., to any sentence) it would be necessary to produce an index on the key doc#, sent#. This would take the form of a table with columns:

doc#, sent#, address of start of tuple (6)

which is almost identical to the table (4) used in the text database structure. In addition, the doc#, sent# values are clearly redundant if stored in the relation as well as in the index table. So for an efficient implementation they would be removed from the stored relation and the stored relation would become a set of variable length sentences, exactly as in our QUILL text database system. Also the index table in the text database, (4), becomes identical to the index table for the relation, (6). The implementations would thus be identical.

When additional software is added to the relational database to carry out the text processing functions of the text database, the responses of the two systems would be the same. The only advantage to the text database would be that, unencumbered by the eight operations of relational algebra, it would be smaller but then it would also be more limited in application.

More important is the human interface advantage, that a text model for text is much closer to a human view of text than a relational model.

REFERENCES

1. G. Salton and M.J. McGill. "Introduction to Modern Information Retrieval," New York: McGraw-Hill, 1983.
2. K. Devine and F.J. Smith. "Direct file organization for lemmatized text retrieval," *Information Retrieval,* 3 (1984), pp. 25–32.
3. L.A Hollaar. "Text retrieval computers," *IEEE Computer* 12 (1979) 3, pp. 40–50.
4. I.A. Macleod. "The relational model as a basis for document retrieval system design," *The Computer Journal,* 24 (1981) 4, pp. 312–315.
5. I.A. Macleod and R.G. Crawford. "Document retrieval as a database application," *Information Technology: Research and Development* (Vol 2), 1983, pp. 43–60.
6. M. Stonebraker, Heidi Stettner, Nadene Lynn, J. Kalash and A. Guttman. "Document processing in a relational database system," *ACM Transactions on Office Information Systems,* 1 (1983) 2, pp. 143–158.
7. A.J.H.M. Peels, N.J.M. Janssen and W. Nawijn. "Document architecture and processing," *AMC Transactions on Office Information Systems,* 3 (1985) 4, pp. 347–369.
8. E.F. Codd. "Extending the database relational model to capture more meaning," *ACM Transactions on Database Systems* 4 (1979) 4, pp. 397–434.
9. J.O. Hirschfelder, C.F. Curtis, and R.B. Bird. "Molecular Theory of Gases and Liquids," New York: John Wiley & Sons, 1966, p. 1028.

NETWORKING AND CONNECTIVITY

ROBERT VONDEROHE
The University of Chicago
Chicago, Illinois
and
RICHARD BARNIER
Digital Equipment Corporation
Rolling Meadows, Illinois
and
EVELYN MARSH
Sears
Chicago, Illinois

Harnessing the power of information and making it available to a growing audience of information users is the focus of the Networking and Connectivity track at NCC '87.

In the beginning, there were large computers; punched cards initiated work. Soon these were replaced by terminals through which jobs could be submitted. It wasn't long before these devices could do interactive tasks. The demand for remote computing power was met by connecting terminals to the mainframe via telephone lines. And thus were two giant technologies brought together. From this marriage has sprung a myriad of new innovations to tie them together more effectively as well as enable them to exist independently of each other.

As computers have become smaller and processing has become a desktop affair, connecting systems together within a building or campus using wide-area telephone facilities made less sense. Hence the demand for local area networks. What is a LAN? What commercial products are on the market, and how are they different? How can LANs connect with each other and with the mainframe? Finally, what has been the response to this new technology? Has it been embraced or is there some skepticism concerning its business value? The Networking and Connectivity track addresses these issues in five sessions on LANs.

Wide-area communication has expanded as new technologies have developed. Traditional cable connections are being replaced by high speed, reliable fiber optic cable as well as non-cable solutions such as satellite and microwave. Telephone switches are becoming digitized, and frontiers are being conquered in providing the capability to transmit voice and data on the same media. Major PBX vendors discuss their products in one session and WAN technologies is the topic of another session. How networks should be managed is the subject of yet another session. Clearly, the trend is toward reduction of unnecessary and costly connections where possible and standardization of interfaces. On a large scale, this is what ISDN is all about. The ISDN session covers the ISDN specification and its implementation to date. Speakers are drawn from the vendor community as well as business and academia.

Mobile data communications

by HOWARD J. GUNN
Gandalf Technologies, Inc.
Wheeling, Illinois

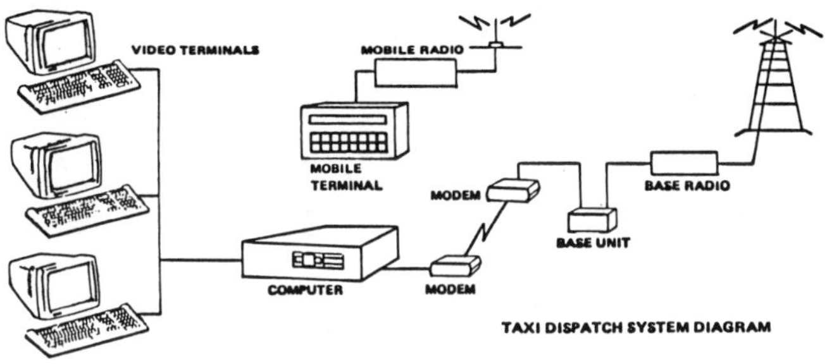

Figure 1—The communication system for Gandalf's taxi dispatch system

Gandalf is currently involved in the design and manufacturing of wide-area mobile data communications systems. We have currently targeted the computer dispatching market. By wide-area, we typically think of communication within a metropolitan range. However, wide-area mobile data communications could be expanded to include state and nation-wide interconnection through the deployment of the same kinds of techniques.

Gandalf provides mobile data communication *systems* as opposed to just equipment in that we provide application software for the end user along with the minicomputers, video display terminals, tape and hard disk storage, and a variety of printers.

This equipment is typically located in the dispatch office. The communications subsystem includes the mobile and base radio equipment, and a base signaling unit at the base radio site. The computer subsystem may also require modem links between the computer and the base signaling unit. The mobile data terminals are connected to the mobile radios in the vehicle. Mobile computer data terminals are now being used by businesses and large fleet operators in an effort to increase productivity but also to help keep costs down and aid management in running a fleet.

In Anaheim, California, for example, Yellow Cab Co. has installed the nation's first fully computerized taxi dispatch system. The system relies on our computers for dispatching taxi cabs on call. Voice communications are virtually eliminated. Those tuning in Yellow Cab's channels in Anaheim will hear computer whines and tones on the air—hardly interesting for most scanner listeners. It may also help stop other outlaw taxis from stealing fares.

Our system in Anaheim is being used in 85 taxis. Mobile data terminals are installed in the cabs and the cab company's dispatch center is equipped with computer hardware and software for dispatching and fleet management. Those who call for a cab in Anaheim don't have to wait as long as before the system was installed because the computerized system speeds up the dispatching process, which traditionally depends on the individual skill of the dispatcher on duty. At this time, they are handling nearly 30 percent more volume with the same fleet of cars and drivers.

The system also can automatically dispatch standard fares, calls for a particular time, regular runs, and priority calls. Further, the system can verify street names and numbers. The system typically includes call-taker terminals, the dispatch computer system, the communications subsystem, maintenance test equipment, and the mobile data terminals. Each communications subsystem channel can service more than 400 taxis.

In the future, we intend to continue use of radio frequency (RF) transport technologies for specific terminal to computer interconnections. We have researched the employment of RF technologies in actual LAN-type office configurations as well as wide-area monitoring via satellite systems. In the wide-area applications, data devices, modems, and radio transceivers in a vehicle would be polled periodically to determine distance related factors. Such information could be used to estimate when a truck shipment would arrive at the dock and aid in the scheduling of loads.

Overall we see continued growth in the RF delivery of data over distances. This growth will be driven by the economics of the transport medium plus the applications software that can provide efficiency and productivity in the monitoring and control of vehicles.

ISDN for MIS applications

by J.A. NEWELL and L.D. LANDY
AT&T Information Systems
Lincroft, New Jersey

ABSTRACT

This paper illustrates how existing and imminent ISDN technology can be usefully applied to the business environment. First, the ISDN interfaces and available ISDN network building blocks are reviewed. This includes the Basic and Primary Rate interfaces, telephones, work stations, personal computers, distribution media, premises switching machines, LANs, host computers, transmission facilities, and network switches. Next, useful applications with specific configurations of these building blocks are described. These applications are partitioned according to those which can be implemented within a single business customer premises and those which take advantage of the wide area networking capabilities of ISDN.

INTRODUCTION

Several major trends are apparent today which accompany the growing need to integrate the technologies of processing and communications. These trends include the increasing use of personal computers in communications networks, the use of Local Area Networks (LAN's) for local data distribution in office and factory environments, and the growing importance of distributed processing. Perhaps the most fascinating trend of all is the growing interest in the Integrated Services Digital Network (ISDN), that is the only technology on the immediate horizon which promises to bind the various communications and processing technologies into a coherent whole. Nowhere is the interest greater than in the business community that has accrued enormous commercial benefit from both communications and processing technologies while, at the same time, has suffered substantially from the incompatibilities among the various business systems and networks.

Since the definition of the first ISDN standards by the CCITT in 1984, much has happened within semiconductor, telecommunications, and processing vendor communities to bring ISDN to the threshold of deployment. The reader is referred to References 1 through 7 on ISDN for a better understanding of the ISDN interfaces and how they may be applied. For the purposes of this paper, it is sufficient to review the most important characteristics of ISDN:

1. All digital connectivity from one ISDN endpoint to the other.
2. The definition of the basic user information channel at 64 kbps (B channel) which supports voice, data, and other digital information types.
3. The definition of a common channel signaling path (D channel) between all endpoints and switching nodes of an ISDN.
4. The definition of a protocol (LAPD) and messaging structure (Q.931) for the common channel which allows intelligent endpoints and switching nodes to communicate with a common language to achieve high functionality in a multivendor environment.
5. The definition of the 2B + D structure for the Basic Rate Interface (BRI) which supports integrated voice/data and high functionality to intelligent endpoints.
6. The definition of the 23B + D and 30B + D structure for the high-bandwidth Primary Rate Interface (PRI) at 1.544 and 2.048 Mbps.
7. The applicability of the BRI ranging from simple digital telephones to sophisticated integrated voice/data personal computers with advanced communications capabilities.
8. The definition of the 4-wire S-interface for the BRI which supports 2B + D full-duplex transmission between a switch and end user terminal to distances of up to 1 kilometer. Detailed physical and electrical characteristics of the S-interface are included in this definition.
9. The definition of the 2-wire U-interface for the BRI. Although the physical and electrical characteristics of the U-interface have not yet been standardized, this interface is intended to provide full duplex 2B + D transmission like the S-interface, but over 2 wires at much longer distances (e.g., 6–8 kilometers).
10. The applicability of the PRI to high-bandwidth host computer access as well as presently-available digital carrier systems for high-bandwidth interpremises networking.
11. The applicability of ISDN interfaces to a variety of communications technologies such as circuit switching, packet switching, synchronous wide area data networks, and transparent digital carrier systems at 1.544 and 2.048 Mbps.
12. The pragmatic use of existing technology for ISDN, including twisted pair data distribution, stored program controlled circuit and packet switching, digital telephony at 64 kbps, and existing digital carrier systems. Moreover, VLSI devices which support the cost effective implementation of ISDN are becoming available.

Based on these characteristics, the remainder of the paper focuses on the equipment types to which the ISDN interfaces apply, followed by the local and wide area business applications which can be achieved in the next several years.

ISDN BUILDING BLOCKS

To position us to discuss ISDN applications, it is first necessary to discuss the components or building blocks from which ISDN networks can be established. One of the more remarkable achievements of ISDN is the wide array of product types to which the ISDN interfaces apply.

End User Equipment

In this section, we will briefly discuss those equipment types which can support ISDN interfaces and, at the same time, interface directly with end users.

Simple telephone

At the lowest end of the functional scale, a simple telephone can be supported with the ISDN Basic Rate Interface.

Using the BRI 2B + D structure, 64 kbps voice can be carried over a B-channel, and control information like addressing (dialing), and telephone status (on-hook/off-hook) carried over the 16 kbps D channel. The other BRI B channel remains unused. Using the BRI, such an instrument can be located up to 1 kilometer from a supporting switch using the ISDN S-interface for PBX applications or at 5–10 kilometer distances using the U-interface for central office applications. Powering of the telephone from the switch over the BRI can also be accommodated. Available VLSI which supports the BRI will allow the cost of a basic digital telephone to approach that which has already been achieved for the standard analog tip/ring set.

High function telephone

Simply by taking advantage of more functionality in the D-channel, a telephone which performs many more useful functions than simple dialing can be constructed. For example, a multi-line telephone which provides functions like transfer, hold, and conference with simple button pushes can and is being built for ISDN. Repertory dialing functions in which the most complicated dialing procedures are accomplished with a single button push will be commonplace in ISDN. Even more interesting, telephones with displays are achievable to identify a caller by name before the called party answers. With displays in ISDN, it becomes easy to keep track of the status of each line in a multiline station.

Integrated voice/data station

For this station, we extend the concepts introduced above to incorporate a high speed data terminal using the other 64 kbps B channel in the BRI. Now we have a high speed terminal in addition to a high function telephone, all combined in a single instrument and communicating over a single interface. The display messages described for the high function telephone can now use the data terminal display, allowing cost effective utilization at the station for both data and high function voice.

Intelligent voice/data station

Think of this as a personal computer (PC) with local processing capabilities and, at the same time, having an integrated telephone, all communicating over the BRI. For this type of workstation, the functional possibilities are enormous. Some of the applications of this workstation will be described later.

Time share computer

Using the 2B&D structure of the BRI, a small minicomputer can support two remote users through an associated switch. If the switch contains a packet capability as well, many more remote terminals or PCs can be supported (e.g., 16 terminals/B-channel). Again the reader is reminded that this occurs over two twisted wire pairs up to 1 kilometer from the switch.

Host computer

Using the 23B + D and 30B + D structure of the Primary Data Interface (PRI), many more terminals can be supported; 23 or 30 for an associated circuit switch and hundreds for a packet switch. Host computers using this interface are already available using AT&T's openly-licensed Digital Multiplexed Interface (DMI). DMI was defined in 1984 to conform to the PRI and, when its evolution is completed in 1987, is the ISDN PRI for host computer applications.

Combination workstations

Customized workstations beyond those mentioned here can also be created using both the BRI and PRI. For example, the BRI will also support intelligent Voice/Data Stations described above with a full array of peripherals like printers, plotters, and facsimile devices. The BRI also has a D-channel multiplexing scheme and a local bus arrangement (called the passive bus) to give all such devices independent communication access over the BRI. The PRI may be used for end user workstations as well. For example, the available bandwidth within the PRI allows excellent performance for high resolution graphics, video, and large file transfers.

Terminal adapters

Not to neglect existing data devices and to demonstrate the power of ISDN for system integration, ISDN provides for a wide array of terminal adapters. Simply stated, terminal adapters are digital modems; they allow the connection of existing devices like RS-232 terminals or personal computers to the ISDN BRI. Even coaxial interfaces like those found on 3270-type terminals and cluster controllers can be adapted to the BRI, thereby allowing much greater flexibility in the use of such devices in ISDN than was ever possible in the older hardwired environment.

Local Premises Distribution

To establish ISDN networks, the business customer premises distribution media and local switching vehicles are as important as the end-user stations.

Physical media

The advantages of twisted pair wiring for local data distribution are well understood. Originally used for analog tip/ring telephone distribution, twisted pair wiring has become a ubiquitous resource in most existing business premises. Equally important, straightforward wiring schemes for twisted pair have evolved over the years which allow convenient rearrangement and change from centralized cross-connect points. In short, twisted pair wiring allows cost-effective and convenient signal distribution within a business premises, primarily because of its long evolution in standard telephony applications.

Perhaps one of the least glamorous but most important aspects of ISDN is its utilization of unshielded telephone twisted pair wiring. Specifically, both the BRI and PRI are defined to work over normal twisted pair, which has reliably demonstrated since the early 1960s the ability to support digital signal distribution well beyond the Mbps range. To complement twisted pair, modern wiring systems like AT&T's Premises Distribution System (PDS) also incorporate fiber-based distribution media which will support high bandwidth data distribution into the 100 Mbps range and beyond. Finally, fiber cross-connect technology has matured to the point where rearrangement and change techniques for fiber distribution now rival twisted pair for convenience and cost effectiveness.

The pragmatic use of existing twisted pair by ISDN combined with the migration path to fiber provides the business user with cost-effective flexibility and a growth path well into the next century for signal distribution. Also, the technology of terminal adapters has matured to the point at which we can confidently state that most existing data distribution interfaces like RS-232, V.35, and 3270-coaxial cable can be adapted to the B-channels to take advantage of the power and convenience of ISDN twisted pair and fiber distribution.

Digital PBXs

Historically, Private Branch Exchanges (PBXs) have provided the functions of connection of local telephones to each other and concentration of the local phones to a much smaller number of trunks which, in turn, access wide area public or private voice networks. Modern PBXs, such as AT&T's System 75 and system 85, will play a pivotal role in ISDN evolution. Right now, System 75 and 85 use a totally digital technology and can bring two 64 kbps B-channels directly to the end user equipment along with a common signaling channel. A wide array of high function telephones, integrated and intelligent voice/data stations, and terminal adapters (data modules) for existing data equipment are already available on these PBX products. DMI, targeted to become the PRI in 1987, is also available providing high bandwidth access to local host computers. The advantage that ISDN will bring to this digital PBX environment is not necessarily the high functionality, high bandwidth, and convenient signal distribution described earlier, since these already exist. The main value of ISDN here will be the coordination, compatibility, and evolution of this functionality into multivendor networks.

Local packet switches

Packet switching products, such as AT&T's Information Systems Network (ISN), are now providing convenient, organized, and cost effective premises switching of data in much the same way PBXs have historically done for voice. Packet switches are also starting to appear in central offices. For example, several Bell Operating Companies are offering central office-based data switching using AT&T's Datakit packet switching system. A powerful feature of packet switches is their ability to statistically multiplex local end user data channels together on high-bandwidth facilities for efficient wide area interpremises transmission. It is important to note that ISDN interfaces are compatible with and will be supported by data packet switches. For example, ISN is committed to support the PRI using DMI. This allows the intimate coupling of PBX circuit and data packet switches on the business customer premises, combining the advantages of PBX circuit switching and network access with the cost effectiveness of packet switching of data. Viewing the PBX now as the ISDN Wide Area Network gateway, the packet switch may be used to statistically multiplex local data for efficient ISDN packet transmission on wide area networks using the PBX as an access gateway. This combined PBX/packet switch approach is an important step in the total integration of circuit and packet switching for ISDN networks.

Local Area Networks (LANs)

Numerous local data networks have emerged lately which fall under the category of "connectionless LANs." These networks provide communications by means of protocols implemented on plug-in boards of end user processing equipment and typically do not require a centralized switching device like a PBX or data packet switch to provide the communication paths. Such networks have names like Ethernet, Token/Ring, MAP, and STARLAN. Communication standards for such networks have been defined within the IEEE 802 committee. While not directly compatible with ISDN, it is becoming increasingly clear that these networks must be integrated with ISDN for the following functions:

1. *Bridging*. ISDN-compatible system like PBXs, packet switches, and wide area networks must provide interconnection services for such LANs. Specifically, they need to bridge a multiplicity of isolated LANs and make them appear as an integrated network. AT&T's ISN packet switch already provides such a bridging capability for IEEE 802.3 LANs including both coaxial cable-based (Ethernet) and twisted pair-based (STARLAN) varieties.
2. *Gateways*. It is necessary that processors attached to these LANs be able to communicate with ISDN-attached processors which use BRI and PRI interfaces, and protocols such as X.25, SNA, and LAPD. Therefore, ISDN gateways must be available which allow connection of individual LAN-attached processors with processors directly associated with ISDN networks.
3. *Integrated Voice/Data*. None of the LAN connection schemes provide for voice transport, although many LAN-attached PC users will want integrated voice capabilities with their PCs. Therefore, control gateways must be supported in LAN environments which allow D-channel control messages to be conveyed to individual LAN endpoints along with some form of associated voice.

With these capabilities, the ISDN-compatible LAN, individually or integrated with an associated PBX, can extend the

LAN environment to national and global networks using the universal connectivity of ISDN.

Wide Area Networks

Wide Area Networks (WANs) are defined as communication networks capable of transporting information between a number of endpoints which are separated by large distances. The public telephone network is the most widely known example of a WAN. The concept of ISDN has, at its very core, the notion of universal connection of all endpoints by means of a high function, high bandwidth, digital international network. The basic building blocks of WAN's are longhaul carrier systems and switching nodes within the network so information can reliably find its way from one endpoint to any other by proper routing through the various carrier systems.

Interface definitions based on existing WAN technology and products are the most pragmatic aspects of ISDN. No technological breakthroughs are required to implement an ISDN WAN. Virtually all of the required networking products are already available from AT&T as well as many other companies.

Carrier systems

Digital carrier systems based on the 64 kbps digital B channel already exist in many forms and are deployed all over the world. They range from systems using twisted pair (like AT&T's popular T1 carrier system at 1.544 Mbps) to systems using higher bandwidths on more specialized media. These media include coaxial cable, microwave radio, fiber guide systems, and space transmission via satellites. The speeds of these systems now extend into the hundreds of megabits. For example, the AT&T DS4 rate of 274 Mbps supports over 4,000 B-channels over a single link. The growing popularity of fiber for such carrier systems, both for buried land routes and underseas applications, promises a virtually unbounded deployment of digital bandwidth which is secure, ecologically sound, and with minimal roundtrip delays for critical data applications.

Switching systems

Virtually all new switching systems being deployed for wide area applications within a telephone company or for international applications use 64 kbps B-channel switching. AT&T's 5ESS switch for central office applications and 4ESS for toll office applications are excellent examples of modern ISDN switches. ISDN functionality for WAN's is complemented by a set of CCITT recommendations for a high function control messaging structure between switching nodes called Common Channel Signaling System 7 (CCS7). CCS7 is the equivalent of the ISDN D channel between the switching nodes in the wide area exchange network. As an important feature, CCS7 supports the transport of Q.931 messages from one end user to another through the ISDN.

To further strengthen the data transport capabilities of ISDN, access to wide area packet switched networks will soon be available by means of the ISDN B channel using both the BRI and PRI into the network. Typically, the packet switching protocol used in these networks is X.25. Such data packet switching will come in two basic forms:

1. Integrated with voice over the same interface. This form of packet switching will be accomplished by an integrated packet capability within the switch itself. Such capabilities are being provided by the 5ESS switch from AT&T.
2. Data only. This form of packet switching builds on the data packet WANs available today, especially for X.25 protocols. These networks are presently available for both public and private applications; ISDN utilization of these networks simply means providing access to these networks by means of ISDN B-channels over both the BRI and PRI. AT&T's Accunet Packet Service is an example of a widely available public packet WAN which will support ISDN interfaces.

Overall ISDN Networks

Given the wide array of ISDN building blocks for both the business premises and wide area networks, hopefully the reader can now envision the ISDN end-to-end network depicted in Figure 1.

Basically, the network is formed by the union of the ISDN interpremises network (both intra- and inter-LATA) and the customer premises equipment described earlier. End user equipment, like telephones and intelligent voice/data stations, can be attached directly to the network by ISDN central offices or by means of a customer premises ISDN switch. In addition to its classical concentration function to the wide area network as described for the PBX, the ISDN switch has two other major functions:

1. The connection and, where necessary, the protocol conversions necessary to establish communications among the various endpoints or to the interpremises network through the common BRI and PRI B-channel links.
2. The unified management and control of the various end points and the inter-premises network by means of the ISDN D-channel.

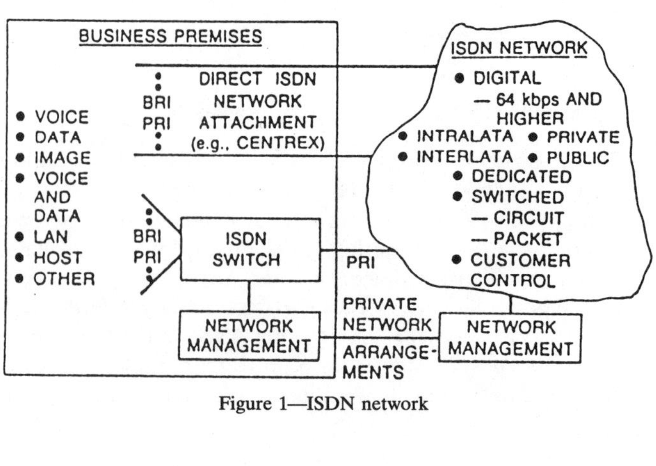

Figure 1—ISDN network

The importance of these functions within the overall ISDN should become apparent as we discuss the various business applications which ISDN makes possible.

ISDN APPLICATIONS

Now that we have discussed the framework of ISDN and the available building blocks for ISDN implementation, we can examine the wealth of business applications which ISDN permits in the international multivendor environment. We begin with those applications which apply locally, within a single business premises.

Local Applications

Integrated voice and data

Opportunities for integration of voice and data generally fall into two major categories. The first is physical integration, usually driven by the economics of sharing, flexibility for growth, and ease of management. In the ISDN local environment, these advantages are provided via a common distribution media and a single plug on the wall. For the typical end user the BRI will support simultaneous voice and data, while PRI will provide multi-channel access to more powerful shared resources.

The second area of voice and data integration involves the sharing and interaction of capabilities between the two information types. In general, integrated voice and data applications attempt to draw on the strengths of one information type to enhance the other.

Starting with primarily voice applications, there has been a trend in recent years to apply data communications technology to increase the information exchange between the user and the phone system. One set of applications is built around the use of alphanumeric displays driven by D channel information (high function telephone). Time, date, call duration, and dialed digit displays can be generated locally within the instrument, but system information is required for incoming caller identification and call coverage information (e.g., whose phone is being covered and why the call went to coverage). With an internal directory database, the system can provide names in addition to extension numbers. The combination of message storage in the system and workstation displays is particularly helpful as a means to automate short standard messages. For example, a standard "please return my call" message can be handled by the end users themselves, not requiring the involvement of attendants and secretaries.

Additional capabilities can be added with the integrated voice/data station. These include all of the features of a display phone, enhanced by the ability to simultaneously display information about multiple calls. It also allows function keys and indicators to be mapped into screen displays. These displays may be a straightforward representation of the buttons on a telephone, or they could use dynamic forms, prompting, help functions, or graphics to lead the user through complex interactions. It becomes possible to support large local directories and speed calling lists. These can include complex call setup procedures as well as logon and applications access scripts (e.g., electronic mail retrieval) for data calls, all available with a single user input. The full array of data capture capabilities including keyboard, mouse, touchscreen, and, ultimately, voice recognition is available to build a flexible, convenient communications interface for both voice and data calls.

In the area of voice capabilities used to enhance traditional data services, most applications build on the widespread availability of phone service. In the area of messaging, voice-synthesized retrieval of text messages allows for universal access. Voice mail systems are an alternative supporting both entry and retrieval from any phone. Whatever the medium, the use of a simple message waiting lamp on a subscriber's phone assures that the subscriber will know when messages arrive without having to remain logged on to a mail system or access multiple systems to check for messages. The key pad can be used as a simple, ubiquitous data entry device. Together with voice synthesized responses, Touch-Tone® entry can be used for a variety of database inquiry applications such as directory, stock quotes, and product price and availability as well as simple transactions for purchases and reservations.

Resource sharing

ISDN provides convenient high speed connectivity for isolated pockets of data functionality. The ISDN switch can be used as a local area network or to bridge local area networks. A common application is to provide access for multiple terminals for sharing a departmental minicomputer which provides local processing, file space, printing, and communications access for mail as well as network and host gateways. The ISDN switch provides call setup features such as keyboard dialing, speed calling, or hotline for direct off-hook access. Economic advantages are realized by sharing of resources as well as contention for processor ports. The ISDN switch also provides wide area connectivity through its network interfaces and can interface to non-ISDN analog facilities using modem pooling (another shared resource). With additional terminal-based intelligence, the process of accessing common resources can be made more convenient with the local directories and scripts described earlier. When these capabilities are used to facilitate access, logon, and data retrieval, it becomes important to provide options for security screening at the terminal which is facilitated by the D-channel.

In configurations where the ISDN switch is used to interconnect PCs, there is still a need for shared file servers, printers, and gateways. With some or all of the applications processing done locally on the PCs, communication functions can be handled by the local software as appropriate. This concept applies to connectionless LANs, ISDN switches and, where appropriate, both. The user gets the appearance of full-time connections even though the PC software may be establishing and disconnecting circuit or packet channels as required. Messaging and file transfer may be done through a shared server or by direct PC-to-PC connection. In either case, a major benefit is the speed. A file that would take a half hour to transfer over a 1200 baud modem can be handled in less than 40 seconds using the full B channel bandwidth available within the BRI interface.

In summary, the ISDN switch can provide an effective local area network environment. Coupled with connectionless LAN techniques, ISDN switches allow an optimum blend of local high speed data capabilities with wide area access for direct host attachment, gateways, and bridges.

Integrated host and switch functions

Connection of a processor to the ISDN switch may be by means of the BRI or the PRI, depending on the number of channels required. In either case, the user advantages associated with high speed access and enhanced signaling are supported. The host also has the ability to use the signaling channel to the switch to establish calls or activate features. In the past, such capabilities would normally have required an automatic calling unit. Since incoming caller identity is passed from the switch on demand, it is possible to enhance the normal logon/password security without resorting to a call-back procedure. In environments where ease of communications is valued as much as security, the identity passed from the switch may be used in lieu of a logon or password. In this example, security of access is largely dependent on the security of switch administration and local terminal access.

In addition to general capabilities which apply to any terminal to host access, there are a number of applications which provide a shared resource for integrated voice and data services. In recent years, adjunct processors have been used to provide increasingly sophisticated management and support capabilities for switches. These include administration of switch system data bases like directories, cost allocation reports, traffic analysis, maintenance capabilities, and various data base services such as inventory, and trouble ticket and service order tracking. User access to the adjunct processor may be done locally or remotely via the standard ISDN interfaces. Equally important, access between the support processors and the switch common control may be accomplished over the common signaling D-channel.

Large directories, resident in an adjunct processor, also provide an opportunity for integrated applications. These directories may contain organizational information, as well as related equipment inventory or other customer definable information. A common directory can provide the basis for messaging services, telecommunications cost accounting, and other applications. When accessed by an attendant or end user, it can be searched for various field matches or near matches for call set-up purposes. When the appropriate entry is found, the call can be established via D channel messages from the host to the switch.

A variety of messaging services can be supported from the adjunct processor. A pool of agents can provide personalized phone coverage based on per call data passed over the signaling link from the switch. In this case, when a call goes unanswered, the switch routes it to the next available agent. The identity of the calling and called party as well as the reason for forwarding the call (busy, not answered, or a "please handle this call for me" feature activated by the user) is passed to the processor via the D channel. The processor can then retrieve any associated data about the called party (e.g., a previously left message) and display the information for the agent. The agent can key in any received messages to be stored in an electronic mailbox. As with any regular electronic mail service or voice mail service, the signaling link to the processor is used to tell the switch to light the message waiting lamp. In all of these applications, the adjunct processor has the opportunity to provide consistency and commonality in terms of human interface, mailbox integration, and message preparation and retrieval. System integration is enhanced in the ISDN environment by use of switch-provided information when the service is accessed, and by the ability to light the message waiting lamp on the phone or terminal.

Customized local applications

One of the most exciting aspects of ISDN is the opportunity it provides for custom applications. If ISDN control functions are made accessible through a command interface to the standard programming environment on a host, PC, or switch common control, it is possible to create a wide range of new applications.

As an end user, you may wish to customize the way your phone calls are handled. By looking at the incoming caller identification, linking into a personal directory, and using standard transfer or alerting features, it is possible to specify special ringing for calls from some people, forwarding to a secretary or coverage agent for others, and a recorded announcement with a promise to call back for a third group. There's no need to worry about callers who are reluctant to leave recorded messages since the PC has already logged the time, date, and identity of all callers. If an important call is expected after working hours it can be transferred to your home phone, based on the calling party's identity without having to give out your home number. If you prefer, your PC can call you at home with a voice synthesized message (perhaps using a shared resource) leaving you the option to return the call.

Another area of end user applications can be built around data retrieval keyed to the calling party identity. If you are the manager of a large organization, you may wish to file reminders of expected work items or upcoming deadlines for each of your employees. Whenever they call, your PC can display specific information relating to that employee so you don't forget to bring up an important topic. In dealing with clients and customers, this could be an important tool to display status of past or expected orders, scheduled deliveries, or even personal reminders such as names of spouse and children, birthdays, or hobbies.

Similar applications exist for a host providing a shared service for a number of corporate users. A database in the host can be searched for customer accounts requiring special attention. For mass calling applications based on directory data, a call could be placed and transferred to the calling agent only if answered. The agent would have relevant information about the account (e.g., the criteria for placing the call in the first place) displayed on their terminal so that they could handle the call. Normal Automatic Call Distribution (ACD) applications often involve a pool of agents handling calls with the support of host-based data retrieval and entry. By using the incoming call identification, a link could be made into the relevant database to speed up the transaction and reduce errors. For airline reservations, for example, the host can search for any reservations under the customer's name and display them to the answering agent. The database could be searched for past repeated flights. The agent response could resemble "Thank you for calling Mr. Jones. Are you going to Chicago again? Do you want the same flights and hotel?" If there is no existing reservations or recent data, an entry can be started with the customer's name and telephone number, as well as any other information deemed relevant by the airline. Such information could be displayed along with outgoing schedules from the customer's home town to assist the agent.

Wide Area Applications

As a short, but extremely important, introduction to wide area ISDN applications, the reader should note that the capabilities described in the previous section can be extended to wide area networks. As a simple model, envision a nationwide array of ISDN locations with some of the local capabilities just described. By joining these locations with ISDN networking, you can immediately conclude that the functionality described earlier can be extended to this nationwide network. The reasons are straightforward:

1. End user B-channel voice or data information is simply conveyed by the carriers to the proper location, either by direct links betweeen locations or through tandem nodes in the network depending on the network configuration.
2. The D-channels carry a hierarchy of control information in a uniform messaging format which:

   a. Provides routing information for the B-channels so they always find their proper destination. The ISDN addressing structure provides for a global network of this type.
   b. Provides end user control information which allows the higher order functionality of enhanced ISDN services. For example, calling party identification messages; hold, transfer, conference messages, textual end user messages, host security queries, etc. will all be conveyed to the proper location over the D-channel and properly dispatched by the common control at the switching equipment at the destination location.
   c. Provides communications path for network information and control directly to the end user. For example, a centralized directory data base within the network can be accessed and distributed to end users on demand by means of the D-channel.
   d. Provides a communications path between each node of the network spanning all possible end-to-end routes which can be used to provide overall network management controls and maintenance. The power of this approach is the fact that faults can be quickly isolated down to specific links, paths and/or nodes. Moreover, the network can then be reconfigured dynamically by an overall network management intelligence until the fault is repaired.

These capabilities apply to both public ISDN intra- and inter-LATA networks, and ISDN private networks.

We will now discuss specific ISDN applications for wide area configurations:

SNA networking

Many of the existing wide area data networks use SNA and are composed of private analog links using modems for data transport at rates of 4.8 or 9.6 kbps which terminate on cluster controllers at terminal locations and Front-End Processor (FEP's) at host locations. It is important to note that entire SNA networks can be brought into the ISDN environment today using the existing terminal, cluster controller, FEP and host equipment while, at the same time, accruing an enormous increase in end user flexibility and convenience.

1. 3270-type Terminal Switching. SNA is a communication architecture which extends between the cluster controller and FEP. ISDN concepts allow the extension of this architecture to the end user 3270 terminals. In this case, terminal adapters are provided which translate the 3270 coaxial signal to a standard 64 kbps B-channel using the ISDN LAPD protocol. Through this conversion, the world of ISDN is now opened to the terminal, including twisted pair distribution and switching to a variety of cluster controllers for applications on demand. As an added benefit of ISDN, a 3270 terminal, once relieved of the hardwired coax restriction, can then be made to function as an asynchronous terminal in the non-SNA multivendor asynchronous environment. This functionality is made possible through a simple terminal adapter option.
2. 19.2 kbps Transmission. The availability of PRI B channels for end-to-end links in ISDN allows the standard usage of 19.2 kbps for all SNA links between cluster controller and FEP. Again, this is accomplished through terminal adapters which condition the SNA synchronous signals for B-channel transmission. Looking to the future, 64 kbps direct B-channel transmission between the cluster controller and FEP will become commonplace as this equipment migrates to support ISDN BRI and PRI interfaces. An important step has already been taken by the NCR-Comten Corporation with their announced support of DMI on their FEP equipment.
3. Remote Channel Attachment. The power of ISDN is vividly brought out by this application with a capability undreamed of in previous environments. By transporting the B-channel 3270 signals directly to a remote location by an ISDN carrier system, the local cluster controller can be totally eliminated. By terminating the 3270 signal on a remote channel-attached controller, the local 3270 terminal performs from the remote location as if it is locally channel attached. Through the techniques of ISDN, channel-attached performance, previously reserved for those lucky enough to be co-located with the

host, can now be extended to 3270 terminals any place in the country. Equally important, intelligent voice/data workstations and PC's can be made to function as locally or remotely channel attached 3270's in the ISDN environment.

All of the functionality described above is available from AT&T today. Again, the main advantage of ISDN is bringing this functionality into the multivendor marketplace.

Dynamic bandwidth allocation

An historic stumbling block in achieving truly high function wide area networks has been the cost of long distance high bandwidth facilities. Dedicated T1 routes at 1.544 Mbps are starting to be used with T1-multiplexers (Tmux's) between two endpoints to gain efficiencies in the use of the digital T-carrier bandwidth. The more advanced of these Tmux's allow the integration of voice, synchronous data, and asynchronous data for very efficient utilization of the carrier facilities. However, dedicated T1 routes at 1.544 Mbps are sometimes hard to justify when they must be paid for 24 hours a day, 7 days a week. ISDN is changing all that and, as a result, will drastically reduce the cost profile of high bandwidth digital services.

The Software-Defined Network, available from AT&T today, allows the customer access to very flexible digital private networks. With ISDN, all endpoints of an SDN may be accessed by means of the PRI. Within the SDN, individual B-channels can be routed to any endpoint according to the time of day. This allows the user to concentrate bandwidth where it is needed, when it is needed, for either voice or data or both. A specific B-channel route can be accessed for either voice or data by the end-point switching equipment or Tmux. This allows the first order of customer flexibility. With SDN, the route can be changed as a function of time-of-day. With these combined capabilities, the user can now devote a large portion of his network to voice during normal business hours. In the evening or on weekends, the network can be devoted to data and the bandwidth concentrated between data centers, allowing bulk file transfers for centralized maintenance, updates, and restoral. Again, the powerful D-channel allows this unprecedented flexibility.

Going one step further, AT&T and other carriers will be offering switched ISDN services in 1987 with access through the PRI. Switching is accomplished on the individual B-channels. End-to-end control information can be passed through the same D-channel which is used to establish the initial connection. With switched ISDN services, the customer gains enormous flexibility. Stated simply, high function ISDN wide area networks for either voice or data can be established, changed, or torn down within seconds on customer demand. The customer will be billed for switched connections only when they are established. Using this service, the concept of Virtual Private Networks is useful. The customer can simply construct the network he needs, for only as long as he needs it and pay accordingly.

For data applications, the above services of SDN and Switched ISDN can be integrated with packet data services, again through the PRI. The customer will have the option of accessing AT&T packet data networks using X-25 on a reconfigurable or switched basis. Since Accunet Packet Service is priced to be distance independent, substantial savings for ISDN data transport can be obtained, especially for long distances.

Customized wide area applications

The true value of ISDN will ultimately be demonstrated by customized wide area business applications. They will represent a breakthrough in business opportunity; not because of a technological breakthrough of communications or processing, but because of the integrated application of existing technology on a worldwide basis.

Envision the customized local applications of section 3.1.4 extended on a world-wide basis. For example, consider an international airline reservation service extended in multiple dimensions by ISDN. National data bases for the airline can be linked by worldwide B-channel connectivity. International reservations can be handled with all of the benefits of the local ISDN capabilities described earlier. The customer data base can simply be forwarded to the customers destination, for as long as he or she is there, and returned updated, with perhaps new reservations should the customer book them in the foreign country. Even language difficulties can be surmounted with ISDN. Translation of computer-based text for simple transactions will become commonplace as the market develops. ISDN allows and encourages more people-oriented solutions as well. Within a global ISDN, the following scenarios are likely:

1. A caller in the United States to a German airline at 6:00 am will be routed via international 800 service to a reservation service in Germany. Why? It will be more cost effective to route the call to the home office which will be more centralized and operating during standard business hours. Customer records are in the United States? No problem. By customization of the international 800 service, the customer records can arrive in Germany as the phone is ringing. Language difficulties are not likely. With ISDN, the network will know the originating country of the call and route the call to an English-speaking agent.
2. An Oriental caller who speaks no English calls an American airline. No communication takes place; neither the caller nor the agent understands the other. However, the agent immediately refers the caller to the single agent who is an Oriental language specialist. ISDN can find that agent instantly by means of the customized network directory, thereby retaining the caller. Although the special agent understands oriental languages, the agent is most comfortable in Japanese and is not fluent in the uncommon Chinese dialect used by the caller. Rudimentary communication does take place. The caller is instructed to be patient and that help is on the way. The call is then referred to a language specialist whose services are available to a number of reservation systems. Such a person is rare, trained in the gamut of oriental

languages and given access to a number of corporate reservation services and order entry systems by ISDN.

Real communication now takes place. The caller is a first time traveler from China to the United States. The caller became hopelessly lost and stranded because of communication difficulties. The language specialist now has facts and, through ISDN, the caller data base from a Chinese airline. By now, the reader can envision the recovery scenario.

CONCLUSION

ISDN offers the ability to extend existing applications and develop new ones based on an open standard that can provide services locally, nationally, and globally. ISDN does nothing fundamental to alter the traditional tradeoffs between network and premises-based capabilities. Even so, the technological advances which accompany ISDN encourage the use of distributed premises-based processing in combination with network intelligence. The unprecedented integration of processing and communications made possible with ISDN on a global basis promises a steady stream of new and creative business services well into the next century.

REFERENCES

1. *CCITT Study Group XVIII I Series Recommendations,* October 1984.
2. Roca, R.T. "ISDN Architecture." *AT&T Technical Journal,* 65 (1986) 1, pp. 4–17.
3. Aldermeshian, H. "ISDN Standards Evolution." *AT&T Technical Journal,* 65 (1986), 1, pp. 19–25.
4. Higdon, M., J.T. Page, and P. Stuntebeck. "AT&T Communications ISDN Architecture." *AT&T Technical Journal,* 65 (1986) 1, pp. 27–33.
5. Neigh, J.L. and L.A. Spindel. "ISDN Evolution in Information Systems Architecture." AT&T Technical Journal, 65 (1986) 1, pp. 45–55.
6. Newell, J.A. "ISDN Networks for Business Applications." *Proceedings of ISCAS, 1985,* IEEE, June 1985, pp. 711–714.
7. Morgan, K.B., P.K. Verma, H. Ibrahim, and P. Taylor. "Multivendor Network Realization Through ISDN." *Proceedings of the 8th International Conference on Computer Communications,* September 1986.

APPENDIX—ISDN INTERFACE DEFINITIONS

Bearer Channel. The ISDN channel which conveys customer information from one endpoint to another is called a bearer channel. Examples of bearer channels include a channel conveying data information from a terminal to a host computer or a channel conveying digitized voice from one telephone to another. The basic ISDN bearer channel rate is 64 kbps which can support either data or voice. The 64 kbps bearer channel is referred to as a "B" channel. Additional bearer channel rates have been defined by the CCITT as multiples of 64 kbps. These are:

HO 384 kbps (6×64 kbps)
H1 1536 kbps (24×64 kbps)
or
1920 kbps (30×64 kbps)

Signaling Channel. The ISDN channel which conveys control information from one system to the other within an ISDN network is called the signaling channel. An example of a signaling channel is a channel which conveys information from a host computer or data terminal to a switching machine which indicates the host or data terminal is ready to transmit data information. Another example of a signaling channel is a channel which conveys dialing information from a telephone to a switching machine at the initiation of a call. A signaling channel in ISDN is referred to as a "D" channel, independent of the speed of that channel. Note that, in ISDN, the signaling and control functions take place over a channel which is logically separated from the bearer channels. This provides a powerful vehicle for providing enhancements for intersystem control and maintenance without interfering with end user information (data or voice).

The capabilities for enhanced control and maintenance of ISDN systems is greatly facilitated by the provision of message-oriented signaling (MOS) defined for the D channel. The CCITT has defined a general message format for a variety of control and maintenance message types in the Q.931 recommendation. Moreover, a robust HDLC-based protocol to convey these messages between systems is defined in the Q.921 recommendation. This protocol provides flow control, error correction, and multiple simultaneous message types. Note that the efficiency of this protocol is paramount since it is intended to be cost effectively implemented in terminal equipment, including digital telephones.

Basic Rate Interface (BRI). The basic rate interface for ISDN is defined to support integrated voice and data at a customer endpoint as well as to provide economical network access. The channel structure of the basic rate interface is "2B + D" which, according to the channel definitions above, allows access to two 64 kbps bearer channels as well as a signaling channel. 64 kbps voice can be supported on one of the B channels; 64 kbps data on the other. Moreover the 16 kbps D channel can be used to multiplex low speed packet data and control information with the signaling. Using the Q.931 message structure, the D channel can be used for addressing (dialing) information for voice and data connections as well as enhanced communications features. An example of such an enhanced feature which can be supported using the D channel is "Calling Party Identification." With this feature, the user of an integrated voice/data terminal sees the name of the calling party displayed as the telephone is ringing, thereby allowing much greater user flexibility in the disposition of the call.

The CCITT has already recommended a physical interface for the basic rate called the "S" interface with the following attributes:

1. Full duplex transmission over 2 twisted-wire pairs.
2. Two optional pairs for the explicit purpose of powering the work station.
3. 192 kbps transmission rate:
   —Two 64 kbps B channels
   —One 16 kbps D channel
   —48 kbps for framing and control
4. One kilometer transmission distance using "Alternate Mark Inversion" (AMI) coding common in the digital telephony plant.

A basic rate interface for 1 twisted-wire pair called the "U" interface is presently being defined. This interface is very important in bringing ISDN to the public switched telephone marketplace.

The basic interface also supports a "Passive Bus" at the endpoint which allows the interconnection of up to 8 data terminals or peripherals using connectionless LAN techniques and D-channel contention resolution for access of these 8 devices to a single basic rate interface. Through the contention resolution process and the higher layers of the signaling protocol, each of the 8 devices can gain exclusive access to a B channel.

Primary Rate Interface (PRI). The primary rate interface has the major advantage of compatibility of digital network carrier systems presently deployed in North America, Japan and Europe. Again, the physical primary rate access is over 2 twisted wire pairs using Alternate Mark Inversion for full duplex transmission. However, the speed and channel capacity at the primary rate interface is much greater than the basic rate.

For 1.544 Mbps transmission used in North America and Japan, the primary rate interfaces supports a 23B + D structure in which the D channel is 64 kbps. Also, ISDN supports the H0 and H1 (384 and 1536 kbps) channels for the primary rate interface in this environment. For 2.084 Mbps transmission used in Europe, the primary rate interface supports a 30B + D structure in which the D channel again is 64 kbps. In this environment the H0 and H1 channels (384 and 1920 kbps) are also supported.

It is important to note that the primary rate interface has three important advantages in the business environment:

1. The primary rate interface can be used as a very high speed multiplexed interface between colocated systems using the convenient medium of simple twisted wire pairs.
2. The primary rate interface can also be used as a high speed multiplexed access point from business premises to public or private digital networks.
3. The primary rate interface can be used to create public switched networks in which the basic switched channel is the 64 kbps B channel carrying end-user information.

ISDN MIS applications

by DANIEL G. DeBUSSCHERE
EDS
Oakland, California

One of the most significant values of ISDN is the ability to provide network intelligence to the data processing world via the out of band "D" signalling channel. One of the most significant network data elements is the telephone number of the terminal that originated the call. This number is called the Subscriber Identification (SID). There are a variety of MIS applications that can be developed that would key off the SID such as a customer record look-up to support the service of an incoming call. This may even be integrated with the Automatic Call Distribution (ACD) in order to properly assign the call to a specific agent. These applications are normally classified as telemarketing applications. A generic ISDN MIS architecture is presented that will describe an integrated ISDN network to a premise based call distribution capability and access to a large remotely located host processor(s) containing

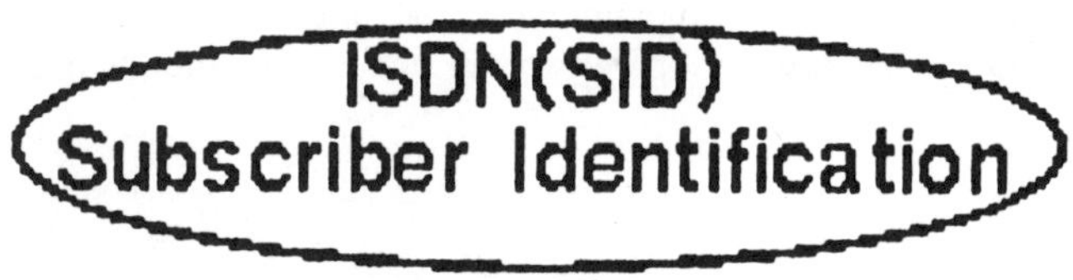

Figure 1—The architecture starts with the ISDN network and the availability of the Subscriber Identification (SID) to the end user

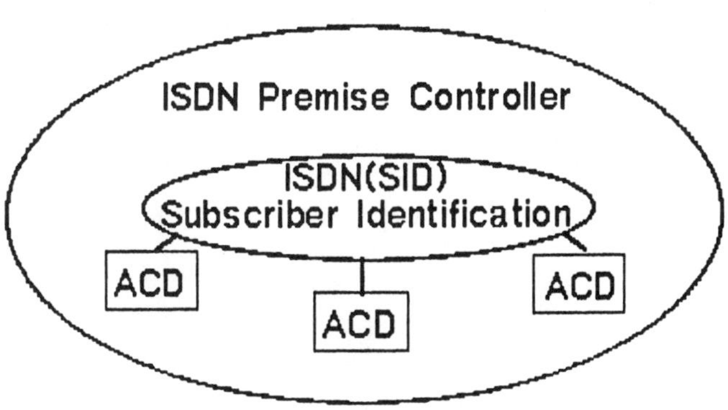

Figure 2—The next element of consideration is the termination of the ISDN primary rate interface by the ISDN premise controller. Large scale telemarketing applications, require that the incoming calls are distributed to a pool of available agents according to various algorithms. This Automatic Call Distribution (ACD) function will be, generally, a functional part of the ISDN Premise Controller

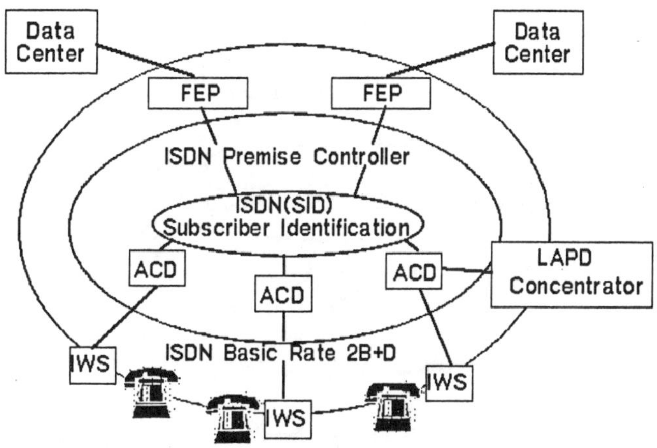

Figure 3—The call is transported utilizing the ISDN Basic Rate (2B + D) to intelligent work stations (IWS) utilizing one of the "B" channels and providing the SID on the "D" signalling channel. The other "B" channel is utilized to maintain an open session with a data base on a large remote host that is connected via the ISDN network.

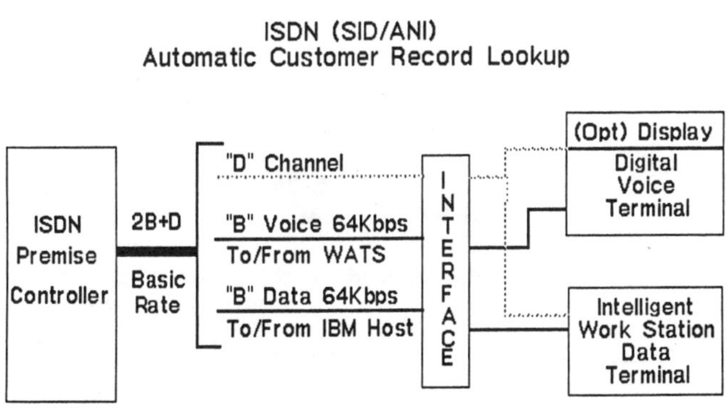

Figure 4—The SID is reformatted by the intelligent work station and an inquiry is immediately sent to the host. The voice terminal receives the call and optionally displays the SID on a small screen. Depending on the performance of the host, the completed customer record is displayed on the screen of the IWS. ISDN will provide 64Kbps data rate on the "B" channel and thus is able to provide sub-second response time if required. Generically, the intelligence of the network is passed over to the host application at the IWS location.

a large data base of customer information. Thereafter, schematics containing pre-ISDN elements are described that provide limited but functionally equivalent capability in anticipation of full deployment of ISDN.

Figure 5—Some of these capabilities may be available prior to the full deployment of ISDN. For example, AT&T may soon provide an Advanced 800 WATS service providing SID/ANI as an additional tariffed service.

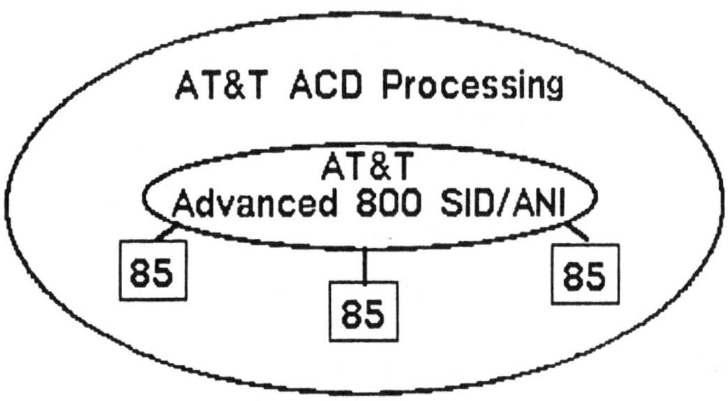

Figure 6—Large scale premise PBX's such as the AT&T System/85 can provide primary rate interface to the network and provide sophisticated ACD processing.

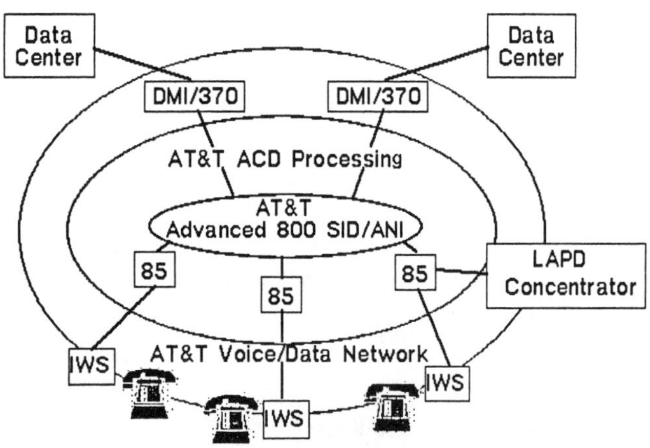

Figure 7—The AT&T PBX can distribute the call via a DCP (2B + D) interface to an IWS. Further, it is possible to maintain concurrent host sessions via a primary rate interface to the host utilizing the EDS DMI/370 interface device without the requirement for multiplexing T1 to a traditional front end processor (FEP).

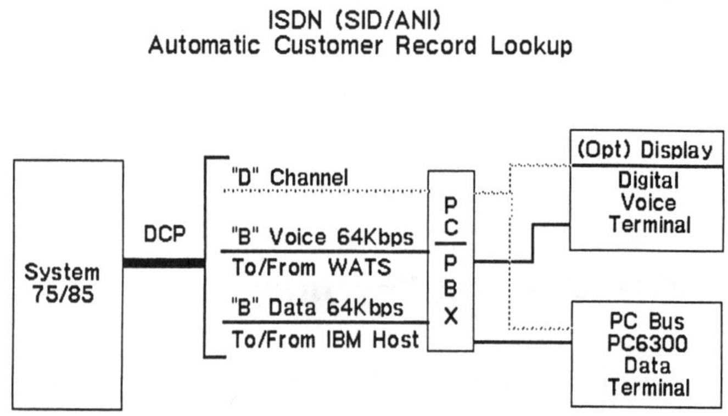

Figure 8—An AT&T product called the PC/PBX card will terminate the DCP (2B + D Like) protocol with the Voice channel terminating on one "B" channel and maintaining an open session with the host on the other "B" channel.

ISDN (SID/ANI)
Automatic Customer Record Lookup

- SID/ANI supplied to PC Program
- PC Program has open session with Host application (CICS)
- PC uses SID/ANI to retrieve customer record from Host and display to Agent
- Digital Voice Terminal operates normally and independently of PC-Host session
- Depending on speed of Host retrieval, customer record should appear just after caller presents identification in response to agent request

In Summary, ISDN MIS applications are just around the corner. Implementation planning can begin today with implementation inplace tomorrow well in advance of the 1990's.

ISDN—A new high performance platform for distributed computer systems

by R. F. HOFFMANN
The SORON Company
Sunnyvale, California

INTRODUCTION

ISDN provides distributed computer system designers new opportunities for improvement in the performance, flexibility, and cost of complex distributed applications.

This presentation will provide an overview of ISDN constructs and performance capabilities that open up these opportunities. A hypothetical real-time, distributed financial management system is described, providing as a paradigm to illuminate use and benefits of these new features.

Some of the ISDN features in this presentation are based on ISDN network attributes that are not presently available. The purpose here is to graphically illustrate distributed application possibilities from both presently defined and anticipated new service offerings expected from ISDN.

NEW DISTRIBUTED SYSTEM OPPORTUNITIES

When viewed from the perspective of higher layer networking software, and the distributed applications that this software supports, these new ISDN features represent an improved transport network "platform" for the designer. Benefits from these improved transport network capabilities, that will result from ISDNs, can be passed up through the higher layer software to aid implementation of more sophisticated and responsive distributed applications.

These improvements can be identified as benefits of:

1. more flexible and responsive system designs
2. higher performance (Error rate, throughput, delay)
3. improved network management and control
4. reduced network management artifacts imposed on information bandwidths
5. lower total system cost

The focus of the presentation is on a dynamic, interactive, distributed application. It illustrates that new and anticipated ISDN capabilities can support distributed applications with a more flexible, reliable, and responsive set of services.

A DISTRIBUTED FINANCIAL MANAGEMENT APPLICATION

A multi-node network model is assumed. Distributed throughout these nodes are mainframes, minicomputers, databases, PBXs, LANs, workstations, and personal computers. Voice is also integrated into the same system.

What will be illustrated is how a distributed application, overlaid on these disjoint heterogeneous resources, can be efficiently implemented through new ISDN services and features, and achieve a higher performance, more flexible, economical implementation than through present-day networking methodologies.

This hypothetical distributed financial application provides its users with real-time, dynamically updated graphics-based presentations. These presentations aid complex, real-time, financial decisions. Information from geographically distributed databases is required. These databases are updated in real-time from "sensors" that continuously acquire various financial and event data. Also, the databases are updated periodically from batch runs by the company's mainframes, and aperiodically from manual workstation inputs that result from user-initiated actions. Automatically generated system requests, triggered by adaptively determined conditions from sensor, processor and database sources, result in additional information transfer between the system databases.

The notion behind this real-time financial management system is that many decisions for transactions of financial instruments rely on multiple data sources. These data are changing constantly. Further, some of these decisions rely on human input from one or several "experts," but it is indeterminate when this will occur, which particular experts will be "asked" for input, and what queries must be made of these experts. AI-based applications software adaptively establishes these queries, based on real-time data from the multiple remote data and event information sources of the system. Finally, manual input of certain data is also required aperiodically from financial professionals. The interfaces that provide the end users the input/output they need to make these real-time financial transaction decisions are high-performance graphics workstations and personal computers.

The scenario then, is a setting of several locations, physically separated across distances ranging from the next desk, to next room, to near-by buildings, to locations separated over wide geographical distances. The system is highly adaptive, and both transaction- and stream-oriented in its connection requirements. *A priori* determination of connection attributes (e.g., throughput) cannot be made. Therefore, bandwidths and type of channel are selected adaptively, on a call-by-call basis, as determined by the application state at the time of connection. This has the benefit of closely tailoring the transmission resources of each individual physical and logical call to what is actually needed, greatly reducing networking costs.

DYNAMIC SELECTION OR TRANSPORT RESOURCES

The system described will provide a wide spectrum of voice and data link capabilities between these different locations, will dynamically select the type and quantity of bandwidth needed, and will adaptively change distributed network management algorithms and resources as a function of system traffic loads and network faults.

Multiple logical channels, of dynamically adaptable bandwidths, are available from each PC, workstation, minicomputer, database, PBX, and LAN. A given session will involve multiple logical connections, established to different end-points from the origination end-point. This assumes a workstation that provides multitasking capabilities. These logical channels will be established and disconnected independently from each other and will select varying bandwidths on a call-by-call basis. The attributes of each connection are selected based on the type of transaction, and its performance needs, that must be supported by the specific applications process it is interconnecting.

USER-TO-USER INFORMATION

Database, and other processing element queries, can result in unnecessary commitment of resources due to unavailable processes, for example, or data that has not been updated since the last query. Accordingly, this hypothetical distributed system makes extensive use of a new feature of ISDNs: The User-to-User Information (UUI) field in the call establishment and disconnection primitives.

This construct allows a process to conduct a quick, low overhead status query or control input to the remote process without proceeding with the resource commitments of a complete connection. It is felt that in a large distributed system, this mechanism alone can provide for substantial reductions in unnecessary resource commitments.

Also, information received back from the remote end in this UUI field, during transmission of call establishment primitives, could help determine the exact level of connection and processing resources that should be committed to the association.

IMPROVED NETWORK MANAGEMENT RESOURCES

ISDN offers a high-performance signaling channel separate from the information bandwidth. This signaling channel is available at all end points and nodes interconnected with ISDN services. The presentation will illustrate some advanced network management uses of this new signaling capability.

The original purpose of the new signaling channel, as defined by telephone administrations, was for the establishment, addressing, control, and disconnection of voice and data calls. By expanding on the definition of "control" to include management of an end users network, overlaid across the ISDN facilities, improvements in performance and efficiency of customer networks are possible.

For example, a customer's private packet network, implemented on top of the public ISDNs, could use the D-channel's UUI facilities for short, low-cost status and control updates between packet nodes. This could be used, for instance, to dynamically update flow control and congestion algorithms, and buffer resources, based on knowledge of network loads and faults.

The notion is that network signaling systems are separate resources to those used for information transmission and switching. This offers benefits in areas of functionality, reliability, and efficiency. Network management communications to the end user's system could make effective use of this resource.

SECURITY SUPPORT

Use of the D-channel facilities for passing encryption keys, separate from the information channel, can provide a much more robust security strategy. These keys could be passed around the network dynamically, making a network security compromise extremely difficult. The presentation will discuss some applications in this area.

Northern Telecom PBX LANSTAR data services

by ROBERT KELSCH
Northern Telecom
Richardson, Texas

The design and architecture of the Meridian SL-1 were specifically developed to accommodate the rapidly expanding requirements for data and voice communications. LANSTAR is the umbrella name that describes the local area networking capability of the Meridian SL-1. LANSTAR designates an entire family of data connectivity products and services. A single system can serve both voice and data communications needs by integrating the functions of a LAN and a PBX.

The most obvious benefit of using a single system for voice and data communications is the inherent efficiency of managing resources as part of one system. Cabling, transmission lines, host computer ports, terminals, personal computers, and peripherals can be administered better within a single network and a single cabling arrangement. LANSTAR also provides access to Meridian SL-1's own information services, with new capabilities such as integrated voice and text messaging.

All connections to the Meridian SL-1 are made with standard twisted pair telephone wire, already required for voice communications. By using the Meridian SL-1 for integrated voice and data connectivity, duplicate wiring is avoided. Port contention allows many users to share scarce computer ports on an as needed basis. Concentration allows multiple data devices to share a common communication line, such as a T-1 line or a modern link to a packet-switched network. Domain switching allows the connection of a single data terminal to different host computers without rewiring or manual switching.

For IBM personal computers, there is the personal computer interface card that fits inside the PC, and for the Macintosh, an inexpensive cable provides connectivity with no extra hardware. IBM personal computers may also be networked with LANSTAR-PC, which provides 2.56 megabit per second distribution to each desktop and access to a 40 megabit per second local area network. LANSTAR-PC is supported by an interface card and Microsoft Network software.

Each of these products provides a simple, economical connection to the Meridian SL-1: the standard RJ-11 jack.

Beyond ISO: The extended network

by JOSEPH B. RICKERT
Sytek, Inc.
Mountain View, California

ABSTRACT

Large organizations are faced with the problem of connecting equipment that not only represents a number of manufacturers, but a variety of disparate media, protocols, and interfaces as well. While these technologies are coexistent, their interconnectivity and communicability is desired in order to optimize use of these important corporate resources. In the short-run, one may run the transport layer throughout the entire network; however, this requires conversion of each network to the same transport layer protocol. In the long-run, ISO is projected to provide near-universal connectivity. However, ISO is not without its drawbacks. A more effective solution may be the development of the extended network, a means to join networks of different protocol families.

THE CAUSE

The local area network (LAN) industry, which is barely seven years old, grew up very quickly in a technology-rich environment where vendors were caught up in an exhilarating rush to satisfy a basic market need. Every large organization had millions of dollars of computing equipment, host machines, peripheral devices, and terminals capable of processing much more information than could be effectively acquired or distributed.

Because the environment was technology-rich, and because LAN vendors were not governed by any existing standards, several different incompatible solutions to the problem of interconnecting computer equipment developed in parallel. Ethernets, slotted rings, and many other approaches to sharing a common data communications structure in a logical and cost effective manner emerged from the laboratories and garages almost overnight. Almost all of those technological approaches worked. Many of them fit the price/performance profile to achieve some success, and nearly all were realized in mutually incompatible implementations: different media, different protocols, different interfaces.

Because the need was real, these different technologies proliferated at breakneck speed. At first, LAN companies enjoyed a nearly competition-free environment. In a large customer company, a product that filled a need was likely to be purchased without a thought as to what else was occurring in the organization. The result of all this explosive growth has been a large installed base of several different LAN technologies, with many of these technologies coexisting in different departments within the same large organization.

THE FUNDAMENTAL PROBLEM

The fundamental problem confronting those who must integrate LAN technologies within their organizations is the interconnection of multiple subnetworks, which are based in different types of physical media and which are designed around incompatible protocol architectures. Since multiple LANs are already in place, within most large organizations, the new challenge is to increase the effectiveness of corporate communications by integrating these LANs into a single, manageable whole. Moreover, integration implies more than physical connectivity. Since each LAN is presumably effective in providing a particular application, the need for inter-LAN communication is really being driven by the need for interapplication communication. Hence, the fundamental problem of inter-LAN communications hinges on the ability of higher layer network protocols to provide general services across subnetwork boundaries.

THE SHORT TERM SOLUTION

A viable solution to the problem of providing physical interconnectivity among several different LANs within an organization is to attach each LAN to a common backbone network through a standard interface. Each LAN, no matter how geographically pervasive it may be, then becomes a logical subnetwork communicating through the backbone. With today's technology, an ideal candidate for the backbone interface is the IEEE 802.3 interface. It is a common international standard that performs with adequate throughput and is available from several manufacturers.

However, the task of providing application-level connectivity among the devices residing on the various subnetworks attached to the backbone is not trival. The problem is the lack of standards in application software, as well as an absence of standardization in the high-level protocol services that support these network applications.

The short term solution to this problem is to run the same transport layer protocol throughout the entire network: all of the subnetworks as well as the backbone. The advantage of this approach is that every user is guaranteed access to any application running anywhere on any subnetwork. Its major shortcoming is that it is necessary to convert every subnetwork to the selected transport layer protocol or deny that subnetwork any meaningful connectivity. Since this was the original problem to be solved, it is a major shortcoming indeed. Nevertheless, for the present, this is the best that can be done. The situation may be somewhat mitigated by selecting a common protocol, such as TCP/IP, that has been around long enough to have implementations running on a variety of host machines and network interface units.

ISO: SCENARIO FOR THE FUTURE

But what about ISO? The dismal picture painted above appears to ignore the promised scenario of global connectivity in the all-ISO world that everyone knows is coming. The all-ISO world may indeed provide global connectivity for some very large LANs, perhaps even for some large LANs connected to other large LANs through a wide area network (WAN). However, it is unlikely that this will prove to be the universal solution to the inter-LAN connectivity problem for at least three reasons:

1. A considerable amount of money and effort has gone into constructing the present installed base of local area networks. It is likely that these networks will continue to operate for some time—well into the 1990s.
2. The promise of an all-ISO world based on a single,

homogeneous protocol suite is unlikely to ever completely materialize. The MAP community, the first group actually attempting to implement ISO protocols in a LAN environment, has already run into some trouble. Because the most robust ISO transport protocol—TP4—cannot perform quickly enough to be useful in the real-time factory cell environment, a subset of this protocol is being specified for factory cells. If such performance considerations cause transport protocols to propagate as prolifically as the ISO/IEEE 802 link layer protocols, the promised scenario will not have a chance.

3. It is unlikely that any set of standard protocols that are complete enough to be working their way through the standard organizations at the present time will be rich enough to accommodate the technical innovations that are on the drawing boards. It is not clear, for instance, that the present set of ISO protocols that are under consideration will be able to effectively handle the integrated voice/imaging applications that are on the horizon.

THE EXTENDED NETWORK

Beyond waiting for ISO, what can be done to solve the multi-subnet, multiprotocol problem? One possible answer is a kind of "protocol glue" that is capable of binding incompatible layered protocol architectures.

In concept, this glue would provide a number of capabilities that extend local services across the backbone. For example, one capability would allow a host computer on a network of one type to participate in the activity of a remote network of another type. Another capability would allow full or partial interoperation of similar, but not identical, applications operating on networks of different types.

The principal goal of the Extended Network (EN) would be to allow a customer to conserve and extend the useful life of existing network investments. With EN, the customer would control when and how fast he migrates to uniform network strategy.

EXTENDED NETWORK CONCEPTS

Underlying the EN solution are certain concepts of how networks of different types may be beneficially joined. The extended network does not attempt to perform protocol transaction or concatenation below the application layer (see Extended Network protocols).

EXTENSION OF NETWORK SERVICES

EN recognizes that the service offered by a layer to its clients is separate from the protocols used to mechanize that service. One of EN capabilities is based on the concept that the interface through which the service is provided may be stretched across one or more intervening networks (or backbones).

The service extension concept can allow a remote host to be a full participant on a remote network with no loss of functionality.

The service extension mechanisms must, however, be built into the host. This can be a problem where it is not possible to separate the client application from its underlying communications subsystem.

The service extension concept would be, for example, a useful means of enabling a Unix™ host speaking TCP on an Ethernet™ to use ISO FTAM services found on a distant MAP/TOP network.

GATEWAYS AT THE APPLICATION LEVEL

Another concept used within EN is that of application level gateways. Such gateways translate between the services offered by similar applications which exist on different types of networks. Of course, the applications must be sufficiently similar so that translation between the two is possible.

An application level gateway enables a remote application to appear to be local to the client's own network. The client interacts with the gateway and the gateway, in turn, interacts with the remote application over the remote network.

Application level gateways avoid the need for any change to the client or server.

FULL GATEWAYS

Full gateways provide the entire translation within a single device. Full gateways can be relatively efficient and can often perform a very good translation. However, a full gateway, specially designed for its role, is required for every pairing of application types. In addition, a full gateway may exist only at a point where the two networks join; there may be no intermediate backbone.

One instance where a full gateway could be used is between ×.400 on a MAP/TOP network and IBM's PROFS on an RSCS network.

HALF-GATEWAYS AT APPLICATION LEVEL

In contrast to full gateways, a half-gateway is a gateway in which the translation occurs in two steps. First, the services of a specific application are converted to a common representation. Second, the common representation is converted back to a specific form. The common representation may be transmitted over a backbone.

The half-gateway approach makes the problem of providing full connectivity to each new subnetwork a manageable engineering effort. With full gateways, it is necessary to develop one full gateway for each subnetwork that must be connected. Using the half-gateway approach, it is only necessary to develop one half-gateway for full N by N connectivity.

Half-gateways are particularly useful where there are many different, but basically very similar, applications on different network types. Terminal access protocols are one instance of applications of this nature. Half-gateways could be used in join Telnet (from TCP/IP), Sytek's V2, ISO VTP, and ×.25/×.3/×.28/×.29 PADs.

COMBINED METHODS

For utilities' sake, the service extension and gateway concepts of EN might be combined. One combination is the application forwarder.

An application forwarder is a cross between a full application gateway and a protocol service extension. From the perspective of a client, the forwarder is a full gateway. This means that the client operates with no change. However, the forwarder uses the protocol extension facilities of the EN to logically place itself on the remote network. This allows the functionality and efficiency of a full gateway to be used even when one or more intermediate networks or backbones intervene between the client and the true server.

EXTENDED NETWORK PROTOCOLS

To be effective, EN must be more than a collection of concepts. Among the specific protocols that EN might contain would be the following:

1. A concatenation protocol would provide reliable connection-oriented and reliable datagram services spanning a collection of networks and backbones. This protocol would provide the foundation upon which the service extension protocol would be constructed.
2. A service extension protocol might be developed to provide an umbrella for each of the specific protocol services being extended. For example, a specific variation of the service extension protocol might be developed to extended NetBIOS services to a remote client while another variation would be developed to do the same for ISO ×.125 session services.
3. A common terminal protocol might be developed to provide a standard method for the transport of terminal traffic between the halves of terminal half-gateways. Each half-gateway would map between the local terminal protocol and TP. These mappings would be defined for various local terminal protocols, such as Telnet (from the TCP/IP family) and Sytek's V2 protocols.

CONCLUSION

As has often been declared for LAN technology, the development of new solutions is an evolution, revolution. Since the short and long-term solutions offered by conversion to a single protocol (transport layer) or set of protocols (OSI) have their own inherent drawbacks, it is likely that the only truly effective solution will be the development of a suite of applications-level protocols to glue together the different protocol architectures that are available today and will persist into the future.

IBM's LU6.2: Implications for the future of corporate distributed processing

by BONNIE M. WEISS
Systems Strategies, Inc.
New York, New York

ABSTRACT

Logical Unit 6.2, along with the related Physical Unit 2.1, are enhancements to IBM's Systems Network Architecture (SNA) that promise to revolutionize data communications in distributed processing environments. IBM is positioning LU6.2 as a converged solution for corporate distributed processing, and is gradually incorporating LU6.2 support into virtually all of its major products. This paper examines the phenomenon of LU6.2 and some of its likely effects on office information system communications and configurations. In light of the de facto standard nature of SNA and the fact that most IBM competitors have announced or pledged LU6.2 support, LU6.2 is viewed as not only an IBM communications architecture, but as the basis for integrated multi-vendor networks.

INTRODUCTION

Until recently, corporate communications networks have relied upon a mainframe-based central control structure to manage all data distribution functions throughout the network. However, the tremendous influx in recent years of departmental minicomputers and desktop microcomputers into office information systems has created a distributed processing environment, often consisting of widely disparate systems.

Since it involves communication between multiple processors, distributed processing is intimately related to connectivity; the ability to connect systems to each other to satisfy application processing requirements. Ease of connectivity is therefore the paramount concern of communications management when configuring a distributed processing environment. Related concerns include the ability to obtain maximum functionality, ease of use, and ease of expandibility and reconfiguration.

In the ideal distributed processing environment, the effort involved in achieving connectivity should be limited to the design and implementation of the applications to perform the required functions. The underlying communications architecture should be automatically compatible for interconnection purposes.

One approach to achieving this connectivity goal has been taken by IBM Corporation through enhancements to its proprietary communications architecture, Systems Network Architecture (SNA). These enhancements are provided by the strategic Logical Unit (LU) type known as LU6.2. The marketing term given to LU6.2 by IBM is Advanced Program-to-Program Communications (APPC).

BACKGROUND: OVERVIEW OF SYSTEMS NETWORK ARCHITECTURE

As all readers may not be familiar with SNA, it is pertinent at this point to provide a brief overview in order to give the proper historical perspective, as well as to elucidate the concepts needed for a basic understanding of LU6.2 before describing its features, benefits and implications.

SNA: Theory and Structure

IBM's master plan

SNA is IBM's master plan for communications among its products. It defines the structure, formats, rules, and controls for transmitting data through networks, and for managing and operating the networks. SNA was originally conceived in 1974 to provide resource-shared communications functions between mainframe computers and peripherals. Resource sharing was designed to reduce the cost of dedicated devices, transmission lines, and other equipment, by allowing different program applications to use the same facilities at different times. SNA continues to be a single strategic architecture that is constantly evolving to accommodate new technology and market demands.

De facto standard

IBM and IBM plug-compatible systems currently account for over 90 percent of the U.S. mainframe computer market, as well as large and growing shares of most other information processing markets. It is estimated that between 70 and 80 percent of major U.S. corporations implement SNA; this base is growing. SNA is currently regarded as a de facto standard for data communications in the United States. This situation is unlikely to change in the near future.

Seven-layer definition

SNA is structured as a seven-layer architecture. The layers and their functions are depicted in Figure 1. A layered architecture divides the communications process functionally; each layer performs specific functions to pass a message between two end points in the network. A message passes through all the layers from the top down in the sending device or node and then back up the layers in the reverse order on the receiving end. In certain cases a message may pass through some of the lower layers in both directions, each time it encounters an intermediate node.

The layered nature of SNA allows a great deal of flexibility and has facilitated SNA's evolution over the years as technology advances. For instance, it is possible to alter the communications process at one layer without affecting the others, as long as the way information is passed to and from the altered layer and its adjacent layers remains intact.

This flexibility has allowed IBM to slowly advance standardizations from the bottom layers upward. Upon its introduction, SNA immediately standardized the level just above Physical (Data Link) with its SDLC (Synchronous Data Link Control) protocol. LU6.2 is now standardizing the upper layers.

Relevant SNA Concepts

Network addressable units

In an SNA implementation, special program code segments called Network Addressable Units (NAUs) are used to repre-

SNA LAYERS	FUNCTIONS PERFORMED AT EACH LAYER
NETWORK USER (APPLICATION)	
TRANSACTION SERVICES	APPLICATIONS SUCH AS DIA/DCA, DDM, AND SNADS
PRESENTATION SERVICES	PROVIDES INTERFACE TO SNA AND USER APPLICATIONS; FORMATS DATA; TURN CONTROL
DATA FLOW CONTROL	CORRELATES RESPONSES TO REQUESTS; GROUPS RELATED MESSAGES
TRANSMISSION CONTROL	END-TO-END FLOW CONTROL AND ENCRYPTION, IF NEEDED
PATH CONTROL	PACKET ROUTING FROM SOURCE TO DESTINATION; GLOBAL CONGESTION CONTROL
DATA LINK CONTROL	RELIABLE TRANSFER OF DATA BETWEEN ADJACENT NODES
PHYSICAL	PHYSICAL AND ELECTRICAL INTERFACE

Figure 1—SNA's seven layers and the functions performed at each

sent programs and devices to a network, and provide services to those programs and devices. Two types of NAU, the Physical Unit (PU) and the Logical Unit (LU), are important in a discussion of LU6.2.

Physical units

Physical Units represent devices or nodes to a network; each participating device in a network has one PU. In programmable devices, the PU is usually implemented in software; it resides in microcode or firmware in less intelligent devices. PUs provide network and resource control services for the LUs residing in their nodes.

There are four specific PU types currently defined within SNA. Each is defined by the services it provides its associated LUs. Under the initial SNA definition each PU type corresponded to a specific type of device. All the PUs and the devices they correspond to will not be reviewed here. It is sufficient to note the PU Type 2, usually written as PU2.0, represents a terminal cluster controller such as the 3274 or 3174, or a batch terminal such as the 3770, and that PU1.0 represents an individual display terminal or teleprinter. Intelligent devices such as PCs are typically linked to an SNA network through PU1.0 or PU2.0; this necessitates emulation of a 3270-type device and limits their efficiency.

Logical units

Logical Units represent end users to the network. An end user may be either an operator at a device or an application program. Multiple LUs may reside in one node; quantity depends on the type and function of the Physical Unit. LUs provide the interface through which end users gain access to network resources and manage information transmission between end users.

LU-LU sessions

LUs allow end users to communicate by establishing sessions. A session is a logical, two-way connection between two NAUs over a specific link for a specific period of time. Several types of sessions occur within SNA. This discussion is limited to LU-LU sessions.

There are currently seven LU-LU session types, and seven corresponding LU types, defined within SNA. LU and LU-LU session types are defined by the nature of the services they provide to their programs. Until recently, the definition of an LU type was also intimately related to where (i.e., in which type of device) it resided.

Two LUs may communicate with one another via an LU-LU session only if they are of the same type. This point is important to note here, as is the definition of LU Type 6 (LU6.0), a session between two application programs.

OVERVIEW OF LU6.2

LU6.2 is the strategic LU type designed by IBM as the basis for a converged solution for corporate distributed processing. LU6.2 and the related Physical Unit Type 2.1 (PU2.1) are designed to standardize all the SNA levels of a system below the application (user) level, thereby providing complete compatibility for inter-connection purposes at those levels.

A derivative of LU6.0, LU6.2 differs from the former and all other prior LU types in that it is conceived as a single, product-independent LU type. It provides a direct program-to-program interface between application programs residing on different processors. It therefore provides a base for implementing communications across a broad range of product types.

LU6.2 is supported by several PU types. Among them is the new type known as PU2.1. As LU6.2 is a derivative of LU6.0, PU2.1 is an extension of PU2.0. PU2.1 is designed to support the enhanced capabilities of LU6.2. It possesses superior capabilities over PU2.0, which give it extended connectivity ability. There are two aspects to this extended connectivity.

First, PU2.1 can connect a node to other network nodes in two ways. It can link to a mainframe in a hierarchical manner. Also, most significantly, it can connect to another PU2.1 node in a peer-to-peer relationship. The significance of this is that remote intelligent nodes, or peripheral nodes, can use PU2.1 to connect to one another directly, without mainframe intervention.

Second, PU2.1 allows multiple links, as well as parallel

session support, an improvement in resource sharing and efficiency.

MAJOR LU6.2 FEATURES

The salient features of the LU6.2 architecture and their major benefits are:

Conversations

LU6.2 provides a significant improvement in resource sharing through the use of conversations. Two transaction programs communicate via a conversation, using a session between their associated Type 6.2 LUs to exchange data. Conversations use time-sliced session segments to share the communications link, creating a very efficient use of the session resource (see Figure 2).

LU6.2 provides for two types of conversations: basic and mapped. Basic conversations are implemented on all LU6.2 products, providing a basic universal interface for communications among them.

Mapped conversations are optional; they are intended for use by products that provide an interface for user-written application programs to communicate with one another. Mapped conversations provide a simpler interface for such programs than basic conversations.

The Protocol Boundary

LU6.2 provides a standardized interface to the SNA network for use by application programs, called the Protocol Boundary. The Protocol Boundary is rigidly defined and specified by the LU6.2 verbs. The LU6.2 verbs constitute a generic Application Program Interface (API) that facilitates a programmer's task when designing distributed transactions involving different product types. This API also provides a common specification for hardware designers who want to implement LU6.2 on their products. Through use of this approach, LU6.2's product-independent nature is supported.

Parallel Sessions

LU6.2 provides parallel session capability to allow many pairs of transaction programs in a distributed processing system to connect simultaneously. Parallel sessions allow multiple sessions to exist concurrently between LUs, facilitating more efficient use of network resources and increasing system throughput.

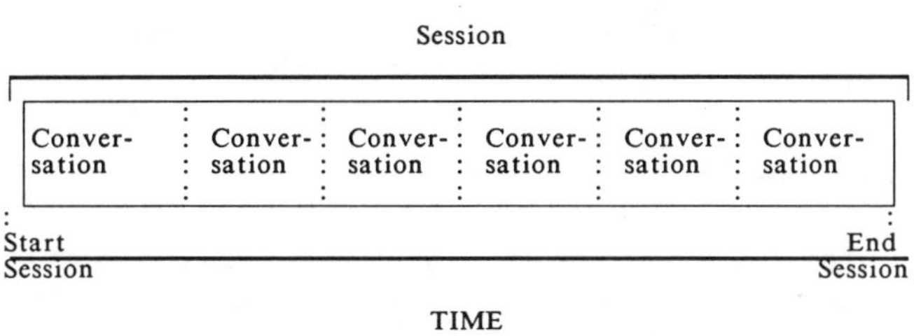

Figure 2—Conversations use an LU-LU session in a serial fashion over time (each conversation maps to an SNA bracket). In this way, logical connections can be established without the overhead of creating a new session for each connection.

Primary LU Capability

In order for application programs to communicate without mainframe intervention, both ends of the session must be capable of initiation. In SNA this responsibility lies with the primary LU; every LU6.2 implementation can assume either the primary or secondary role in any given session. This supports the peer-to-peer nature of LU6.2 communications.

Commitment Control

Commitment control involves the ability to synchronize transactions across a network (i.e., to insure that changes are committed to all appropriate resources). In LU6.2 terminology, this capability is called syncpoint. Syncpoint is the highest level of resource synchronization defined by LU6.2; it also provides error-protection recovery services, or rollback support.

ARCHITECTED APPLICATIONS

LU6.2 is the keystone in IBM's long-term office systems communication strategy. It has built-in support for a series of architected applications to be implemented at the transaction services level. These currently include Document Interchange Architecture (DIA), Document Content Architecture (DCA), SNA Distribution Services (SNADS) and Distributed Data Management (DDM). New developments from IBM in this area can also be expected.

Document Interchange Architecture/Document Content Architecture

DIA and DCA have been developed to overcome the differing commands among diverse operating systems. DIA allows the interchange of documents and other information across a network. Transmitted documents can be in final or revisable form, and can be directed to multiple destinations. DIA also provides access to the processing and distribution services of the Distributed Office Support System (DISOSS).

DCA defines uniform formatting of documents to be interchanged in an office environment, providing document compatibility across the products that support DCA. Formatting controls are included in DCA, including such functions as pagination, highlighting, heading, and centering. As with DIA, documents can be either in draft or final form.

Distributed Office Support System

DISOSS is an application subset residing in the host that stores, retrieves, and distributes documents created by IBM products that support LU6.2. Examples of these include the 5520 Administrative System, Scanmaster 1, and Displaywriter. DISOSS allows remote users to access host services, such as the host library.

SNA Distribution Services

SNADS is an architecture for asynchronous distribution of information between users. SNADS provides delayed delivery services, allowing information to be forwarded through the network as paths between intermediate nodes become available. This eliminates the need for a complete end-to-end session between the origin and the destination of a transmission.

Distributed Data Management

DDM is the most recently announced architected LU6.2 application. It provides data connectivity for record-oriented files residing on systems that support it. With DDM, System/36 and System/38 users can access such files remotely. The files may reside on a remote System/36 or System/38, or in CICS/VS on the host. Some examples of DDM functions include copying a remote file onto a local file, accessing a remote keyed file as if it were local to read, write, update, or delete records, and reading a remote sequential file.

Low-Entry Networking

Before proceeding to a discussion of the implications of LU6.2, it is highly pertinent at this point to mention a most significant extension to PU2.1, formally unveiled by IBM in mid-June 1986, amidst a flurry of announcements. This extension, given the marketing term Low-Entry Networking (LEN), exploits LU6.2 by enhancing PU2.1's capabilities. Under its original definition, PU2.1 allows an intelligent peripheral node to connect directly to an adjacent intelligent node, without mainframe intervention. The limitation is that the peer-to-peer connectivity does not extend beyond the adjacent link stations.

LEN extends PU2.1's capabilities to allow PU2.1 nodes to handle intermediate routing of sessions not intended for themselves. LEN allows the configuration of LU6.2 networks consisting of interconnected systems of widely differing sizes in an arbitrary topology. True peer-to-peer networking is now possible. LEN also provides for dynamic routing within the network, as well as dynamic reconfiguration.

LU6.2: USER'S PERSPECTIVE

True Distributed Processing

LU6.2 promises many benefits to users, both in the short and long term. It will rid intelligent workstations of their current SNA identity crisis; they will no longer need to impersonate 3270 terminals to communicate on the network. Therefore, users can begin to realize the full processing power of their ubiquitous PCs. LU6.2 will allow microcomputers to conduct work sessions in real-time with the host, as well as with all other network systems, while retaining full stand-alone processing capabilities. When the session involves a link between two intelligent devices other than the mainframe, no host intervention is required. The result will be a net gain in overall system efficiency: improved throughput, more usable computing power, no dormant excess processing power, and more effective handling of peaks. In short, true distributed processing.

Programmability

The definition of the SNA upper layers and the standard program-to-program interface provided by the LU6.2 verbs will result in the "decoupling" of programs and devices. Program-to-program communications become independent of the environments (i.e., operating system, programming language, hardware type) of the individual programs. For example, a "C" language program running on a UNIX-based system can communicate with a COBOL program on an IBM MVS machine. The language, operating system, and physical location of the program are all transparent to the programmer and user. The verbs and syntax specified by LU6.2 will provide a universal "language" for user-written programs. It will be much easier for users to configure and maintain large networks and to write distributed application programs for those networks.

Expandibility

LU6.2 will offer the same lasting use of distributed transaction processing programs that IBM's 360 operating system environment provided for batch processing programs. A capital investment in software, therefore, will be protected longer, and the cost of software maintenance support reduced.

LU6.2 will provide increased flexibility in distributing work across networks. Applications can be written for single or multi-machine environments, and value-added utility programs can be generated for many configurations. This will make expandable solutions easier to come by, and less costly.

Lower Design Costs

LU6.2 will eventually formalize the rules for creating new distributed systems. This will make everyone's life simpler, as every system designer will not have to try to "reinvent the wheel." This will lead to a decrease in cost for designing highly specialized systems, as less expertise will be required.

Configurability

The proliferation of PU2.1 nodes will greatly reduce the amount of host communications software required in LU6.2 network implementations. This is because many previously centralized control functions will be offloaded to the remote intelligent nodes, thus relieving the mainframe of some of the responsibility for communications control.

For example, in a traditional hierarchical network, centralized network control programs operating under ACF/NCP (Advanced Communication Function/Network Control Program) keep tabs on the actual physical location of every LU on the network. Therefore, if a user moves his terminal, an NCP regeneration is necessary. In an LU6.2 implementation such as a token-ring LAN, the NCP sees the virtual Logical Units but is transparent to their physical placement on the LAN. In such configuration, users will be able to move PC's as easily as one moves modular-plug telephones today. Eventually such LANs will have extremely powerful distributed processing capabilities. Figure 3 depicts just a few of the concurrent sessions which any PC on such a LAN may one day pick and choose from. Bridges between major data bases such as Cullinet's IDMS/DB and IBM's IMS/DB are possible within the same node in this context. The possibilities are many orders of magnitude more than was previously feasible (see Figure 3).

CURRENT STATUS AND LIMITATIONS

The LU6.2 future holds a great deal of promise. However, at the present time, LU6.2 is a technology in its infancy. Much development and implementation will be necessary before LU6.2 networks become a working reality in user sites. There is, however, much evidence that IBM is devoting a fair-sized chunk of its massive resources to get LU6.2 into the marketplace.

Hardware Support

As of this writing, IBM has announced LU6.2 support for CICS/VS, the System/36 and System/38, the System/88, Series 1, the 8100, and the IBM PC family, and has issued a statement of direction indicating future LU6.2 support for the

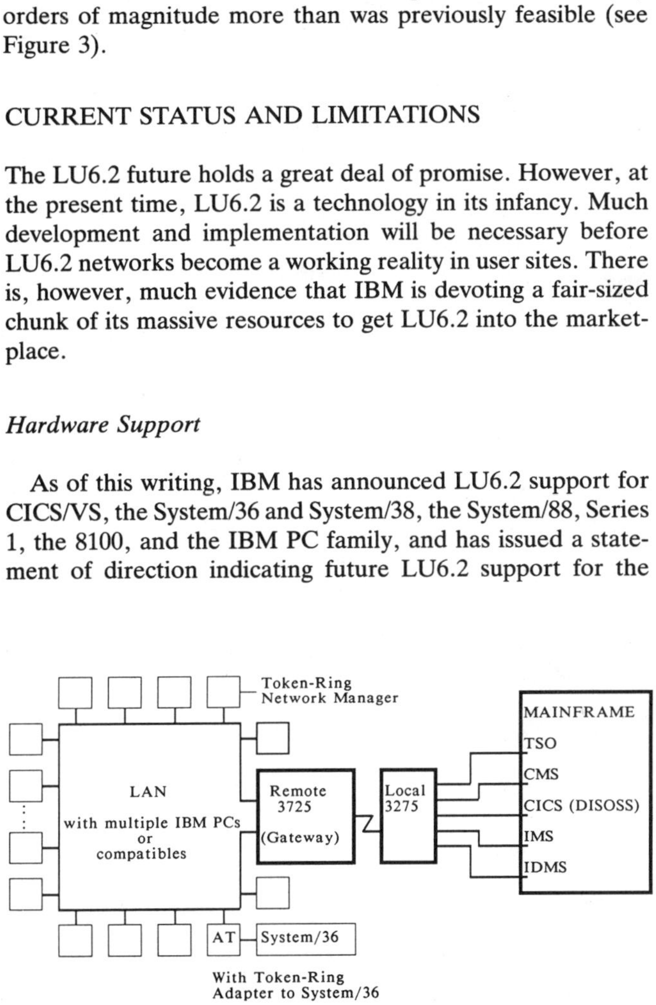

TSO = Time-Sharing Option
CMS = Conversational Monitor System
CICS = Customer Information and Control System
DISOSS = Distributed Office Support System
IMS = Information Management System
IDMS = Integrated Data Management System (Cullinet Inc.)

Figure 3—The remote 3725 controller acts as a gateway server to allow sessions between microcomputers on the LAN and programs running on the mainframe. Without an NCP regeneration, incremental physical units can be added to the LAN, as well as additional LANs via PC AT gateways.

4700. IBM has also announced support for the 5520, Scanmaster 1, and Displaywriter under its DISOSS architecture.

In mid-April, IBM announced a direct link for the token-ring network to the System/370 through the 3725 communications controller, a token-ring-to-System/36 connection via a PC/AT gateway, and a token-ring-to-token-ring bridge. IBM also announced software for the Series/I that implements links to DISOSS, System/36 and System/38 for its PCs, providing document distribution and library services.

In mid-June, IBM announced the 3174 family of cluster controllers that directly links the token-ring network to IBM mainframes. The new controllers, which replace the 3274 models, provide attachment of 3270 system displays, printers, and workstations to IBM host processors via a local channel, remote link, IBM token-ring LAN gateway and IBM token-ring LAN. At the same time, IBM also announced a physical token-ring connection for the RT, and remote PC access to the token-ring and PC Network through NetBIOS.

The announcements state a range of availability dates stretching from the present out to mid-1987. Given the apparent level of activity, more announcements can be presumed to be imminent, and may even occur between the final edit of this paper and its publication.

Software Support

Quite aside from the issue of support in hardware, there is the matter of LU6.2 applications software. IBM has published the LU6.2 specifications, and is relying heavily on third-party vendors to fill the applications software gap. Third-party development is already underway, but there is a long way to go. 3270 applications software—literally millions of lines of mainframe source code—will have to be largely rewritten to take advantage of a distributed processing environment.

Some of the 3270 applications will likely never be upgraded, because the cost in time, risk, and dollars is unwarranted. The fact that IBM has made new 3270 emulation products announcements concurrent with LU6.2 announcements is evidence of its recognition that the hierarchical environment will exist for quite some time into the future. The first LU6.2 implementations will most likely be side-by-side with 3270 technology.

Network Management

Finally, there are the issues of network management and diagnostics. As corporate processing moves away from a central control structure, these matters become increasingly complex. IBM has taken some steps toward solving these problems with recent announcements, particularly that of LEN, but it still has quite a long way to go.

LU6.2 AS AN INTERNETWORKING STRATEGY

As it provides an environment-independent, program-to-program communications technology, LU6.2 is well-suited as the basis of an internetworking strategy. The LU6.2 specifications are public, and most of IBM's competitors have already announced that they will support LU6.2. Third-party communications software vendors already have portable LU6.2 software packages on the market.

With a portable software package, the SNA and LU6.2 programming is pre-packaged in machine- and operating system-independent modules that need only to be compiled and linked. Implementation in hardware consists of a portation. The design of such packages simplifies porting to diverse operating environments.

The availability of such pre-packaged LU6.2 capability greatly reduces the development cost and time-to-market of LU6.2 products for the hardware vendor. This means that even smaller and special-purpose hardware vendors will be able to offer LU6.2 products within a fairly short period. Integrated LU6.2 networks composed of a wide variety of equipment from many different vendors is a very real scenario of the not-too-distant future.

BIBLIOGRAPHY

1. IBM Distributed Data Management Architecture: General Information (GC21-95270-0).
2. IBM Distributed Office Support System/370 Version 3 Release 3: Interchange Architecture Reference (SC30-376-4).
3. An Introduction to Advanced Program-to-Program Communication (APPC) (GG24-1584-0).
4. Systems Network Architecture: Concepts and Products (GC30-3072-2).
5. Document Interchange Architecture: Technical Reference (SC23-0781-0).
6. Systems Network Architecture Format and Protocol Reference Manual: Distribution Services (SC30-3098-2).
7. Document Content Architecture: Final-Form-Text Reference (SC23-0757-1).
8. cSNA/LU6.2 Advanced Program-to-Program Interface User Manual, Preliminary Release 4.0.
9. Networks and Architectures: IBM Systems Network Architecture (SNA), Datapro Research Corp., 1984.
10. A. E. Baratz, V. P. Gray, P. E. Green, Jr., U. M. Jaffe and D. P. Pozefsky, "SNA Networks of Small Systems." *IEEE Journal on Selected Areas In Communications,* SAC-3 (1985) 3.

Evolution of a hierarchical ring bus network

by MARK G. LARSEN
Emerson Electronic Company
St. Louis, Missouri

ABSTRACT

In this paper we discuss the evolution of a hierarchical ring bus network for use in military digital signal processing systems. Current signal processing techniques are unable to meet future requirements for speed, expandability, flexibility, and fault tolerance. After determining an MIMD architecture is required, several interconnect schemes are reviewed and evaluated. Selection of a ring bus is supported and enhancements are suggested that enable the architecture to meet required system metrics. The result is a hierarchical, segmented, multi-ring network that is ideal for use in advanced digital signal processing systems.

INTRODUCTION

Increased digital signal processor requirements for military systems have led to the realization that current programmable signal processors and pipelined processor techniques are not capable of meeting future system needs. Increased demands for system expandability, flexibility, and fault tolerance have also led to the decision to evaluate a new approach for future digital signal processing systems. The variety of processing algorithms required in applications, as well as the need for multisensor capability, have indicated that a Multiple Instruction Multiple Data (MIMD) architecture is called for.

A wide variety of interconnect schemes are available for an MIMD processing environment which includes linear, regular, crossbar, ring, and star networks. An evaluation was performed to determine which approach best answered the list of requirements for future processing applications. This paper summarizes the selection process implemented and supports the decision to use a hierarchical segmented ring bus as the target network architecture for high performance digital signal processors.

CURRENT DEFICIENCIES

Table I shows a list of near and far term requirements for digital signal processing applications. Along with requirements for increased processor performance, there is an ever increasing demand for processor flexibility, expandability, and fault tolerance. Current techniques for signal processor implementation include Single Instruction Multiple Data (SIMD) processors and pipelined arrays of high performance processors. These techniques, while being capable of meeting some near term processing power requirements, are not able to comply with long term performance, configurability, and reliability requirements.

It became clear very early on in the investigation that an MIMD architecture was required. An MIMD organization allows for concurrent execution of multiple algorithms on different sets of data that allows for processing in multiple sensor systems and for reconfiguration of a processor for multiple tasks. Spare processing power can be built in for fault tolerance, or processors capable of performing multiple tasks can be used to provide graceful degradation. The key concern of implementing an MIMD signal processing system is the selection of an interconnection scheme.

Table I—Advanced signal processing requirements

PROCESSING	REQUIRED PROCESSING POWER		
FUNCTION	CURRENT	1 - 5 YEARS	5 - 10 YEARS
RADAR PROCESSING	50 - 100 MOPS	100 - 500 MOPS	500 - 1000 MOPS
IMAGE PROCESSING	100 MOPS	800 - 1000 MOPS	1000 - 10000 MOPS
AUTO TRACKING	1 - 2 MIPS	5 - 10 MIPS	10 - 15 MIPS
FIRE CONTROL	1 - 5 MIPS	5 - 10 MIPS	10 MIPS
ATE	1 MIP	1 - 5 MIPS	10 - 15 MIPS

OBJECTIVES

The goal of the processor architecture investigation was to define a state-of-the-art busing network that will not be outgrown by future signal processing requirements. Investigation of several MIMD architectures, including linear, regular, crossbar, ring, and star networks, was undertaken to determine the most viable solution.

Whichever organization was selected must allow for: (1) massive parallelism, for required performance improvements, (2) flexibility to allow the control scheme to route data to an available processor when the primary choice is occupied, (3) ease of expandability for minimal redesign effort when increasing capability, and (4) fault tolerance for increased system reliability.

NETWORK METRICS

Each of the five network configurations was evaluated and graded in four categories: expandability, capacity, flexibility, and fault tolerance.[1] Grading of each category consisted of three possible values, high, medium and low.

Expandability is a measure of the ability to match a processor organization to a processing requirement. Each new application of the signal processing architecture should not involve a complete redesign effort in either hardware or communication software. A system should be able to be expanded incrementally with only a linear increase in interface hardware. Also, addition of processing elements to a network should not require a change in the system communication software. If a network configuration met these requirements, it received a high grade for expandability.

Capacity is a measure of the networks ability to increase communication bandwidth as more processors are added. If an organization did not exhibit this feature, a communication bottleneck would form as each of the processors attempted to communicate with each other. A network organization which naturally gave a communication bandwidth increase as processors were added was assigned a high grade for capacity.

Flexibility of a network is indicated by the ability to adapt to changes in the data or processor communication flow. Data should be capable of being dynamically routed to an available processor if the primary candidate is occupied. This process should require minimal overhead in rerouting the data flow. Maximum flexibility received a high score.

Fault tolerance involves the ability of a network to detect system failures and dynamically compensate for them. This would involve rerouting information around failed processors or communication links. The ability to dynamically compensate for faults and to do so with a minimal amount of overhead received a high grade.

One other concern in the selection of a processor organization dealt with whether the network configuration utilized a centralized or distributed control scheme.[2] A centralized controller requires less hardware to implement, but its use can limit communication bandwidth as all nodes are arbitrated sequentially by the controller. Another disadvantage of a centralized control scheme is low reliability. If the controller fails, the entire system may cease to function. This problem could be relieved by adding the overhead of a backup controller and redundant control links to the processors.

A distributed controller requires hardware consisting of a control mechanism for each node in the network. It also requires that a portion of the data direction scheme be resident in each control element. Distributed control is much more fault tolerant and allows maximum communication bandwidth between the processors in the network.

Therefore, the ideal network architecture would utilize a distributed control scheme, and have high grades for expandability, capacity, flexibility, and fault tolerance.

NETWORK EVALUATION

Illustrations of network interconnect topologies are shown in Figure 1. A review of each of the organizations with respect to the four grading catagories follows.[3] Table II summarizes the grading results of each network architecture.

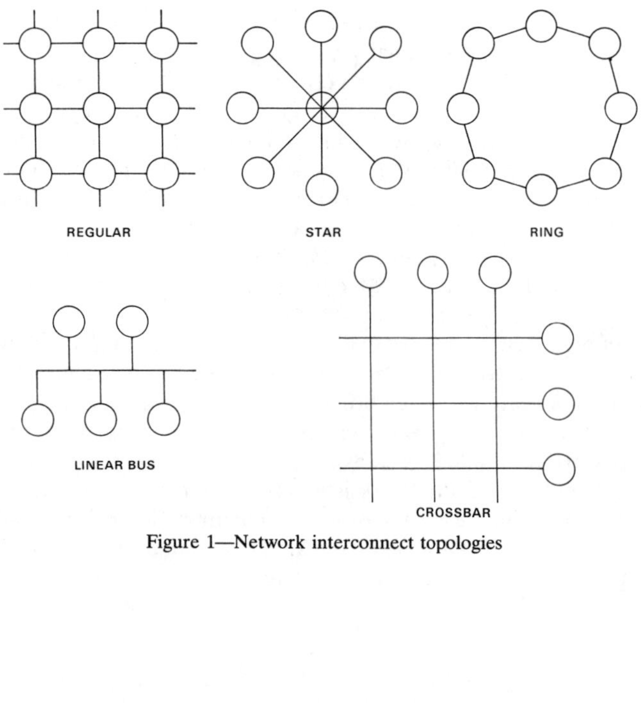

Figure 1—Network interconnect topologies

Table II—Network topology evaluation summary

NETWORK	CONTROL	EXPANDABILITY	CAPACITY	FLEXIBILITY	FAULT TOL	GRADE
REGULAR	DISTRIBUTED	MEDIUM	HIGH	MEDIUM	HIGH	3
STAR	CENTRAL	HIGH	LOW	LOW	MEDIUM	1.5
RING	CENTRAL	MEDIUM	HIGH	MEDIUM	LOW	2
	DISTRIBUTED	HIGH	HIGH	HIGH	LOW	3
LINEAR	CENTRAL	HIGH	LOW	LOW	LOW	1
	DISTRIBUTED	MEDIUM	LOW	HIGH	LOW	1.5
CROSSBAR	CENTRAL	LOW	HIGH	MEDIUM	HIGH	2.5
	DISTRIBUTED	LOW	HIGH	MEDIUM	HIGH	2.5
IDEAL	DISTRIBUTED	HIGH	HIGH	HIGH	HIGH	4

Regular Networks

Regular networks typically consist of an array of identical processors connected so that each processor performs direct communication with its adjacent neighbors. Examples of regular networks include systolic arrays, cubes, and hypercubes. Control is usually distributed throughout the network allowing the system to adapt to changing conditions. Expansion is performed by adding processors to the perimeter of the connected array. As processors are added the communication bandwidth also increases due to the fact that there is an increase in the number of communication channels. Faults are handled by routing around the failed processor or communication link.

Grading for regular arrays went as follows. Expandability was assigned a medium grade due to the fact that it is difficult to add one or two processors at a time. Also, the distributed control program for regular arrays usually needs to be recompiled for a reconfiguration. Capacity received a high score due to the increase in communication bandwidth as processors are added. Flexibility was graded only at medium because algorithms that are sequential in nature are not easily mapped onto regular arrays. Fault tolerance was rated high since a small increase in hardware can allow routing around failed processors or communication links.

Star Networks

Star networks, by nature, are centrally controlled architectures with any number of peripheral slave processors. The central control, or communication point, limits the amount of communication between nodes as the controller has a limited bandwidth. Expanding a star network is simple, but, increases the load on the controller and reduces the communication capability. The star network is not a likely candidate for systems where frequent interprocessor communication is required.

A star network is limited to central control, but, had a high score for ease of expandability. Capacity was inherently low due to the central controller having a fixed upper bound on communication bandwidth. Flexibility was low due to the fact that slave processors could not easily share a processing task due to low interface communication bandwidth. Fault tolerance was given a medium score. Redundant processors could be added to the network, however, the central controller is a single point failure. Implementation of a spare controller would require a significantly large amount of hardware for bypassing the communication bundles entering the main controller.

Ring Networks

Ring buses are used in many distributed systems including various proposed IEEE 802 standards. Usually a token passing scheme is used to allow a processor to add data or messages to the ring whenever it receives a token. With sufficient control, each segment of the ring may be allowed to transfer information simultaneously, which increases the system communication bandwidth. With a segmented ring network, system bandwidth is increased as processors are added. Use of a centralized controller reduces expandability and flexibility due to the limitation of a single controller scheduling all processor transfers. A distributed controller allows each processor to assume the transfer responsibilities. Ring buses are not inherently fault tolerant due to their architecture which includes a critical failure point, namely, the communication channel.

The ring network received a high score for capacity and a low score for fault tolerance. Expandability and flexibility depended on whether the controller was centralized or distributed. Centralized controllers required reconfiguration and became overutilized as the system was expanded. The expandability and flexibility metrics of a centralized control ring network were assigned medium grades. A distributed control ring network received high grades for expandability and flexibility.

Linear Networks

Linear networks are commonly used in microprocessor systems. All devices share a common bus and either a centralized or distributed control scheme is used to arbitrate access to the bus. As nodes are added to the linear bus, the maximum network bandwidth does not increase and more communication must take place using the same hardware. Since there is only one bus for communication, linear buses have poor fault tolerance.

The linear bus was assigned low scores for both capacity and fault tolerance. A centralized controller had a high expandability grade, but a low flexibility score. With a distributed control scheme, increased expandability requires modifications to each communication element and then receives a medium grade. Since each node is capable of implementing retry requests, distributed linear networks were rated high for flexibility. Linear buses end up being a very poor choice for an advanced signal processing system.

Crossbar Networks

Crossbar networks allow the most direct and highest bandwidth connection between processors. They are, however, very hardware intensive and the addition of processors requires a geometric increase in interconnect circuitry. Flexibility is limited by the rate at which the entire matrix can be reconfigured. Also, as long as redundant controllers exist, crossbars have a very high fault tolerance.

Fault tolerance and capacity received high marks while expandability received a low grade. Limitations to the crossbar reconfiguration rate only allowed a medium grade for flexibility.

EVALUATION RESULTS

In Table II each network was graded and compared with the ideal desired system requirements. With a low grade scored at 0, medium at 0.5 and high at 1, the grades for each network configuration were summed. Distributed regular and distributed ring networks scored the highest with three points out of four possible.

The distributed regular network showed weakness in the area of expandability and flexibility. These limitations are not easily overcome because they arise from the matrix organization of the architecture. Expansion by small incremental amounts is not easily accomplished and flexibility is somewhat limited to algorithms with specific characteristics. Much research is ongoing to resolve problems associated with regular arrays, but current application to a wide variety of signal processing applications does not seem feasible.

The distributed ring network only scored low in one category, fault tolerance. This is due to the fact that if a portion of the ring fails, processors cannot communicate past the break. This can be overcome by the addition of a redundant ring with an increase in interface hardware. Although the interface hardware must be doubled to add a spare ring, the addition can be more than justified through increased fault tolerance and increased bandwidth when the system is fully functional. The ring bus is therefore a prime candidate for the proposed digital signal processing architecture.

RING BUS ENHANCEMENTS

Segmentation of the Ring

Some basic enhancements to the basic ring network allow an even greater improvement in all of the evaluation categories. To begin with, the interconnect should be implemented as a segmented ring. This allows for each ring section between processors to execute a transfer simultaneously and allows for a linear increase in system bandwidth as nodes are added to the network.

Dual Ring Configuration

Although system messages and data can share a single ring, a redundant ring, intended primarily for improving fault tolerance, can be used for message traffic while the primary bus is used for data transfers. Since messages are typically small and far between compared with the data transferred, dedicating a ring to message communication greatly reduces the latency in preparing for data transfers. The message ring could also be used for transmission of small, time critical data, such as time tag updates or system reconfiguration information.

Variable Sized Packets

Typically, the token passing scheme used in ring networks limits transmission of data and messages to fixed length packets. In a dual ring system where messages are sent on one ring and data on the second, data packets can be made large and message packets small. This allows for more efficient transfers on both rings. The data packet header overhead is reduced because fewer packets are required to send larger data sets. Since messages are small, there are fewer empty elements to these packets.

A method to reduce overhead all together is to remove the token and have the processors use a busy/ready handshake scheme to transfer packets between each other. This way, variabled sized packets can be sent with overhead kept to a minimum. The only limitation is the maximum packet size allowed which is a system hardware constraint. This method allows the small data packets and all message packets to use only the size of packet they require. Large data transfers can always use the maximum packet size allowed by the system.

Hierarchical Rings

For more efficient utilization of processors in a multi-sensor system, those required for a given sensor processing task can be grouped in a single ring. With the use of a gateway node, results computed by the sensor ring can be passed to a data fusion processing ring. This nesting of rings can continue until the system requirements are reached. A simple example of nested rings is shown in Figure 2.

To reduce the possibility of a single point failure at the gateway node, a spare gateway path can be added. With the sensor processors grouped in a common ring, new sensors may be added or reconfigured by adding or deleting sensor rings from the fusion or integration rings.

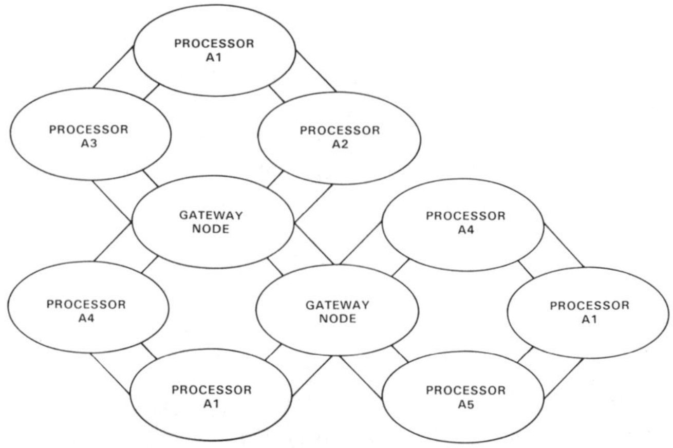

Figure 2—Hierarchical ring network example

CONCLUSION

After evaluating all five MIMD processor configurations, it was decided that the ring network was the most likely candidate for advanced digital signal processing applications. The few limitations that were involved in implementing a ring bus have simple solutions if modifications to the basic ring configuration are added. These modifications include; ring segmentation; dual, redundant rings; separate message and data rings; variable sized packets; tokenless rings; and hierarchical nesting of rings.

The result is a very powerful, dynamic signal processor which is capable of meeting and exceeding near and long term processing requirements and will not be outgrown as requirements change. This ring network scheme allows for high performance, ease of expandability, flexibility, and high fault tolerance, that are all requirements for the system of the future.

REFERENCES

1. DeMuth, G., A. Dennis, and L. Gilbert. "Signal Processor Architectures." *14th Southeastern Symposium on System Theory,* April, 1982, pp. 197–201.
2. Ezzat, A.K., and R. Agrawal. "Making Oneself Known in a Distributed World." *Proceedings of the 1985 International Conference on Parallel Processing,* August, 1985, pp. 139–146.
3. Feng, T. "A Survey of Interconnection Networks." *Computer,* December, 1981, pp. 12–27.

Token-ring local area network management

by BARBARA J. DON CARLOS
IBM Corporation
Research Triangle Park, North Carolina

ABSTRACT

This paper describes an architecture for managing a token-ring local area network, possibly consisting of several token rings joined by MAC-layer bridges in a network containing several communication subsystems. A four-tier network management hierarchy, consisting of stations, management servers, a token-ring LAN manager, and a communications network manager is presented. Stations participate in the management of the LAN by monitoring themselves and their neighboring stations. Management servers collect configuration and error reports from stations on a single ring segment. The LAN manager can coordinate the activities of the different management servers on its local ring and on rings other than its own, but within one local area network. If the token-ring local area network is part of a larger communications network, possibly a wide-area network, another tier, the communications network manager, is required to provide network-wide management capabilities. An example network configuration is presented in this paper and various scenarios involving the management of that network are described.

INTRODUCTION

The management of token-ring local area networks (LANs) involves informing management entities of errors and configuration changes in the network, honoring requests for status, and changing the state of stations attached to the token ring. Information is collected and distributed from centralized entities to allow for a single point of control from which a human operator could monitor and manage the network. A hierarchical management architecture is defined to manage stations and connections in this distributed environment. This hierarchy consists of: token-ring LAN stations, token-ring management servers, a token-ring LAN manager, and, where the token-ring LAN is part of a larger network, a communications network manager. Figure 1 summarizes the management hierarchy for the token ring.

The token-ring LAN architecture, a specification of the physical layer and the lower half of the data-link control layer (called the medium access control sublayer) provides sophisticated network management functions. This architecture is defined in the IEEE 802.5 Standard.[1]

The token-ring medium-access-control protocol provides management messages to change the configuration of stations attached to the ring, change the state of those stations, and report errors from those stations. These management activities are directed and coordinated by management servers. Three management servers are defined, each performing a different management activity for stations attached to a single token ring. In a local area network consisting of many token rings connected by bridges, each type of management server can be located on each ring to insure that all aspects of each ring in the LAN are managed. Control and coordination of the activities of the management servers is provided by a token-ring LAN manager. A token-ring LAN manager's responsibility extends across the token rings monitored by the management servers under its control.

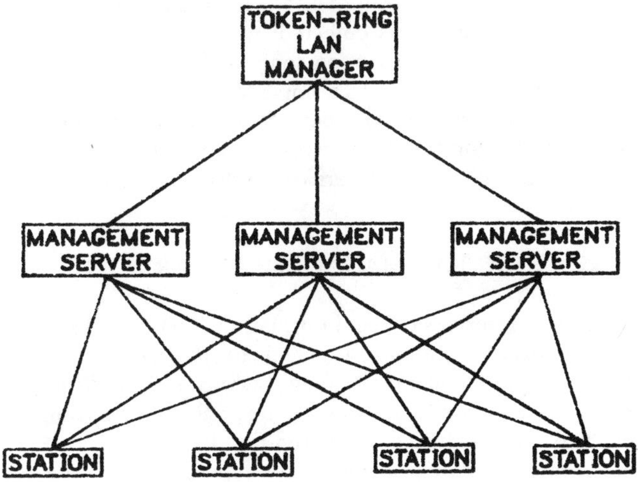

Figure 1—Token-ring management hierarchy

If the token-ring network exists as a part of a larger communications network, possibly including other types of communication subsystems, management of the token ring is included as part of the communications management hierarchy for the parent communications network. Management funcions specific to the token ring can be provided by the token-ring LAN manager, while configuration and fault information critical to the connectivity within the entire network can be reported to a higher management entity called the communications network manager. The concept of a hierarchical management architecture is very useful when several communication subsystems are to be managed from a central location. That is, each subsystem is managed to the extent possible by its subsystem manager; information about configuration and unresolved errors is forwarded to a centralized management facility. The centralized management facility could provide further fault diagnosis, maintain configuration information, and supply information about the health of the network to an operator.

TOKEN-RING LAN ARCHITECTURE OVERVIEW

A token-ring LAN consists of stations connected sequentially by a series of point-to-point physical links to form a ring. Each station is provided fair access to the shared transmission media through the use of a special bit pattern, called a *token*. Only one token is present on the ring at any time and it is passed from station to station around the ring. When a station with data to transmit receives (captures) the token, it sends the data it is holding in a *frame*. The frame consists of a header, the data, and a trailer. The header of the frame contains control information, including the destination address for the information. All other stations on the ring (not using the token) listen to the traffic on the ring while repeating all frames to their downstream neighbors. When a station recognizes its address in the destination address field of a frame header, it copies the frame from the ring. The station also repeats the frame, which propagates around the ring. The sending station removes its frame from the ring. When it finishes transmitting the frame and receives the header of the frame it sent (from around the ring), the sending station transmits a new token on the ring for use by the first downstream station with data to transmit. In this way, each station obtains fair, deterministic access to the transmission media of the ring.

Attaching to the Ring

When a station attaches to the token ring, it registers addressing information and identifies the product it attaches to the token ring to a management server called the ring parameter server (described below). The ring parameter server, if present, responds by sending a frame containing the values for operational parameters in use by stations attached to the ring. If the ring parameter server is not attached to the ring, the attaching station uses the default values for its operational parameters.

Active Monitor Function

One station attached to each ring, called the active monitor, monitors the token on the ring. Any station attached to the token ring can provide the active monitor functions, though only one does so at a time. The token-monitoring functions of the active monitor are necessary to insure that a usable token is always present on the ring. If the active monitor does not recognize a token on the ring for a specified (relatively short) period of time, it purges the ring. During the purge process, all of the stations attached to the ring are reset. The other stations attached to the ring serve as standby monitors that watch the activities of the active monitor and take over in case of failure. Active monitor errors are reported to a management server called the ring error monitor (described below). When a station becomes the active monitor (at initialization time or after a monitor error has occurred), it registers with a management server called the configuration report server (described below).

The active monitor also initiates a periodic poll, called the neighbor-notification process, in which stations identify themselves to their (downstream) neighboring station. The neighbor-notification process enables stations to isolate faults by reporting errors between them and their nearest active upstream neighbor on the ring. It also serves to notify stations that an active monitor is present on the ring. During the neighbor-notification process, the active monitor transmits a special identification frame that identifies itself to its downstream neighbor. The downstream neighbor then identifies itself to its downstream neighbor. This process continues around the ring until it reaches the active monitor again. Then, after a predetermined time, the active monitor initiates the process again. If a station detects a new upstream neighbor during the neighbor-notification process, it reports the new station address to the configuration report server (described below). Note that the upstream station could have changed because a new station attached to the ring or because the old upstream station left the ring.

Error Detection and Reporting

Two types of errors are detected by token-ring stations: hard errors and soft errors. Hard errors are faults that preclude the operation of a token ring within the normal token-ring LAN protocols. Hard errors detected by token-ring stations include a broken ring and a continually transmitting station. If a station detects a hard error, it broadcasts a special frame, called a "Beacon" frame. The Beacon frame contains the address of the nearest active upstream neighbor of the frame transmitter. All stations attached to the ring receive the Beacon frame; its destination address is defined to be the all-station group address. Upon receiving the Beacon frame, the station identified as the sender's nearest active upstream neighbor removes itself from the ring and executes a test to determine whether it and its attachment to the ring (lobe) are functioning properly. If an error is detected, the station remains out of the ring, thereby bypassing the fault. Otherwise, it reattaches to the ring.

After a predetermined amount of time, the Beacon frame transmitter removes itself from the ring and performs the same test that its upstream neighbor did. Again, if this station determines that it or its lobe is not operating correctly, it remains out of the ring and the error will have been bypassed. In this manner, many hard errors can be detected and automatically bypassed without interaction from users of stations attached to the token-ring. However, if the hard error is still present after both stations have had an opportunity to test themselves and their lobes, the token-ring LAN manager is notified and manual intervention is necessary to recover the token ring operation.

Soft errors are faults that temporarily degrade the token-ring performance; they are tolerated by the use of error-recovery procedures. Soft errors detected by token-ring stations include: cyclic redundancy check (CRC) errors in received and repeated frames, and station-congestion errors (a station recognized a frame as being addressed to it, but could not copy it due to insufficient resources). Soft errors are divided into two categories: isolating and non-isolating errors. Isolating errors isolate the location of a fault to a pair of adjacent stations and the transmission medium connecting those stations. Isolating errors detected by stations attached to the token-ring include: an error in a message detected by an error in the CRC appended to that message, a bit in the message that does not represent a zero or a one (see the IEEE 802.5 Standard[1] for description of the differential Manchester encoding used on the token ring), and an early detection of signal loss on the transmission media.

Non-isolating errors cannot isolate the fault on a token ring. The non-isolating errors detected by token-ring stations include: lost frames, stations too congested to receive a frame, and two stations attached to a single token ring with the same address. Token-ring stations periodically report the counts of isolating and non-isolating errors they detect to a management server called the ring error monitor (described below).

TOKEN-RING LAN MANAGEMENT SERVERS

Management servers collect information from, and distribute information to, stations attached to a token ring. Responsibilities of the management servers may also include analyzing reports from stations on the ring and forwarding the results of that analysis to the token-ring LAN manager. Each management server's responsibility extends only to the stations attached to its ring. The management servers defined for the token-ring LAN are: the ring error monitor (REM), the configuration report server (CRS), and the ring parameter server (RPS).

Ring Error Monitor

The ring error monitor (REM), collects, analyzes, and may log soft-error reports received from stations attached to its ring. All soft-error reports sent by stations are sent to a well-known functional address reserved for REM. Therefore, if multiple REMs are present on a ring, they all can receive soft-error reports generated by stations attached to that ring.

The function of REM is to determine when a non-random or excessive soft-error condition is present on the ring on which it resides and, if possible, isolate the most probable source of the errors to a *fault domain,* consisting of two adjacent active stations attached to the ring and the physical medium between them. REM detects excessive soft errors by analyzing soft-error reports sent by stations attached to its ring as they arrive and determining whether soft errors are occurring at a rate that degrades the performance of the token ring. When REM detects such a condition, it may notify the LAN manager, indicating the source of the error.

REM maintains a table of weighted error counts for each station attached to its ring from which it has recently received a soft-error report. The weighted error count accumulated for a station is used as an indication of the likelihood that the station is causing excessive errors on the ring. When a soft-error report is received, the information contained in the isolating error counters is used to accumulate the weighted error count for the sending station and its nearest active upstream neighbor.

When the accumulated error count for a station exceeds a threshold, REM may notify the LAN manager that excessive soft errors have been detected on its ring. REM can provide the addresses of the stations in the fault domain in which it has detected the errors in the notification, thus providing information to allow a human operator to reconfigure the token ring to bypass noisy sections of the ring.

Since even random errors may cause the accumulated weighted error count for a station to exceed the threshold eventually, a fixed value is periodically subtracted from the weighted error count for each station for which REM is maintaining a count. As a result of this periodic decrementing of the weighted error counts, only the stations continuously accumulating weighted error counts at a rate faster than the decrement rate will have error counts that grow with time.

Configuration Report Server

The configuration report server (CRS) collects reports of changes in the order of stations attached to the ring and notifications from a new active monitor on the ring. CRS may also receive commands from the LAN manager to query the stations attached to its ring for certain information, including addressing information, state information, and information about their attached software or hardware, or set the values for operational parameters in stations attached to its ring. The LAN manager can instruct CRS to force a station to remove itself from the ring if, for example, the station were part of a fault domain in which excessive soft errors had been detected (by REM). The information collected and distributed by the configuration report server could be used to maintain a configuration database for the token-ring LAN.

Ring Parameter Server

The ring parameter server (RPS) is responsible for initializing and maintaining a consistent set of values for operational parameters in use by ring stations attached to its ring. When a station attaches to a ring, it requests the current set of values for the operational parameters being used by stations attached to that ring. The station's request is sent to the well-known functional address reserved for RPS.

The request for initialization by an attaching station also contains some registration information pertaining to that station and the product it attaches to the ring. The RPS could forward this information to the LAN manager to notify it that a new station has attached to the ring and to report its characteristics.

TOKEN-RING LAN MANAGER

A token-ring LAN manager can provide centralized control for all of the management servers in a token-ring LAN. The management servers may be attached to different rings, connected by MAC-layer bridges (see "MAC Layer Interconnection of IEEE of 802 Local Area Networks"[2]). Therefore, a centralized LAN manager could provide management function, such as monitoring and controlling stations and physical media for different rings in a multi-ring LAN, from a single point.

The token-ring LAN manager coordinates the activities of the management servers in a local area network. It could obtain information about the state of management servers and set the values for operational parameters used by those servers. Examples of operational parameters for which values could be set include counter and counter thresholds maintained in the management servers. Also, for trouble shooting purposes, configuration information and version level information could be made available by management servers. The token-ring LAN manager could also receive unsolicited reports from management servers indicating state changes and errors. For example, when a management server's counter meets its threshold value or the management server detects a configuration change, the token-ring LAN manager would be notified.

In this hierarchical management architecture, servers essentially act as surrogates for the token-ring LAN manager on rings other than the one to which the token-ring LAN manager is attached. When the token-ring LAN manager needs to retrieve the status of a station on a remote ring, for example, it would instruct a configuration report server on that ring to obtain the status from the station. The station would then respond to the configuration report server, which returns the requested information to the token-ring LAN manager.

Therefore, this architecture provides a framework for information to be exchanged between stations and management servers, and between management servers and a token-ring LAN manager.

COMMUNICATIONS NETWORK MANAGER

The communications network manager receives reports of anomalies in communications subsystems from the communication subsystem managers. The token-ring LAN manager is the communication subsystem manager that is responsible for the token-ring LAN. The token-ring LAN manager notifies the communications network manager about error conditions resulting in a loss of availability of LAN resources to end users. These conditions include: excessive soft errors on a token ring, hard errors that are not automatically bypassed, and the automatic removal of stations to bypass a LAN error. Also, the token-ring LAN manager may report conditions that hinder its ability to detect errors on the token ring to which it is attached. For example, if the token-ring LAN manager detects an error in its attachment to the token-ring, it notifies the communications network manager. A single operator, using the communications network manager, can monitor all of the communications subsystems in the network, thus reducing the cost and increasing the reliability and availability of the entire communications network.

AN EXAMPLE

The following example illustrates the use of this hierarchical management framework for the token-ring. The configuration on which these example interactions are based is shown below in Figure 2. The figure shows a local area network consisting of three token rings, connected by bridges (depicted by straight lines between the rings), another separate communication subsystem, and a host containing a communications network manager. Stations attached to the token rings are shown as boxes and management servers residing in stations attached to the ring are lableled inside the boxes. Each ring has stations and the management servers described above attached to it, though only a few stations are shown on each ring. The arrow shown inside ring B indicates the direction of the token and message flows for this example. The token-ring LAN manager for the bridged LAN is shown attached to ring C. The communications network manager has links with both the token-ring LAN manager and the other communication subsystem manager.

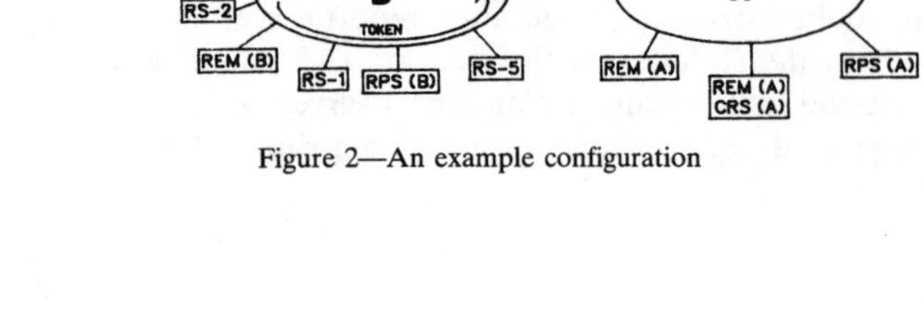

Figure 2—An example configuration

If a soft error occurs on ring B and is detected by ring station 3, then that station logs the error and will periodically send a soft-error report to the ring error monitor for ring B, REM (B). The isolating error counts in the soft error report are manipulated and added to the weighted error counts for ring stations 3 and 4, since the error may have occurred at either station or on the transmission medium between them. The non-isolating error counts in the soft error report are accumulated in a count of non-isolating errors on ring B.

If soft error reports containing isolating error indications are received at a high enough frequency from station 3, then the isolating soft error count will exceed a predetermined threshold value in the ring error monitor. REM (B) could notify the token-ring LAN manager that excessive soft errors are occurring within fault domain of ring stations 3 and 4 and the connecting medium. Similarly, if REM (B)'s counter for non-isolating errors exceeds a threshold, then the token-ring LAN manager would be notified that a non-isolating error threshold has been exceeded.

If the source of the error can be isolated, the token-ring LAN manager could take action to bypass or correct the fault. This action might involve re-configuring the ring on which the fault was detected. In the scenario above, the token-ring LAN manager could instruct CRS (B) to remove ring station 1 from the token ring in order to bypass the fault. Otherwise, the token-ring LAN manager could notify the communications network manager that excessive soft errors are occurring on ring B.

The sequence of interactions involving the ring parameter server and the configuration report server are similar. For example, when a ring station attaches to ring B, it requests the values for parameters currently in use by the other stations attached to ring B. RPS (B) responds with the appropriate values. RPS (B), since it then has knowledge of a configuration change on ring B, could notify the token-ring LAN manager of the change. The registration information contained in the original request for parameters could also be forwarded to the token-ring LAN manager.

If ring station 4 in Figure 2 removes itself from ring B, a configuration change is detected by its nearest active downstream neighbor: ring station 3. Ring station 3 reports this change to the configuration report server on ring B, CRS (B) and CRS (B) could forward the information to the token-ring LAN manager, which, in turn, may update a configuration database or display the information.

The token-ring LAN manager may request information about a ring station on ring B, say ring station 1, by instructing CRS (B) to query that ring station. On receipt of such a request, CRS (B) would obtain the information about the ring station and send it to the token-ring LAN manager. Similarly, the token-ring LAN manager could set the values for operational parameters in the ring station such as the ring number for ring B, by instructing CRS (B) to do so.

If the station attaching the token-ring LAN manager to ring

C detects signal loss, it may report this condition to the communications network manager. The communications network manager could then notify an operator that it cannot manage the token-ring LAN until the fault is corrected. NOTE: If a problem exists in the token-ring LAN manager's station or attachment to the ring, it may not affect the other stations in the network, because of the automatic bypass and recovery procedures built into the token-ring protocol.

All of the servers in the multi-ring network report to the token-ring LAN manager on ring C. It is important to also note that servers on a ring may co-reside within a single station on that ring. This is shown on Ring A, where one node houses both the ring error monitor and configuration report server functions. Also, multiple instances of a management server can be attached to a single ring. This case is also shown on ring A, where two ring error monitors are present.

CONCLUSION

To efficiently manage a token-ring network, management functions are distributed throughout the token-ring local area network (in each station). Stations participate in the management of the token-ring by monitoring the health of the ring and reporting error conditions to management servers attached to their ring. These distributed management functions are coordinated by management servers, which analyze the reports from stations and may forward the results of this analysis to the token-ring LAN manager. The token-ring LAN manager provides a centralized point of control for management functions in a token ring local area network, and may report to a communications network manager which has responsibility for the management of the entire communications network.

REFERENCES

1. IEEE Computer Society. *Token Ring Access Method and Physical Layer Specifications,* ANSI/IEEE Standard 802.5—1985 (ISO/DIS 8802/5). New York: IEEE, 1985.
2. Bernsten, J. A., J. R. Davin, D. A. Pitt, and N. G. Sullivan. "MAC Layer Interconnection of IEEE 802 Local Area Networks." *Computer Networks,* 10(1985)5.

The sub-LAN solution to office connectivity needs

by CORNELIUS PETERSON
Digital Products
Watertown, Massachusetts

ABSTRACT

Theoretically, broadband/baseband and token ring LANs will perform all the functions of an A/B switch and the sub-LAN, as well as database and software sharing. In practice, however, LANs are subject to a number of constraints. Printer sharing is not a simple task with a LAN, that often requires several operations to accomplish the task. The number of printers that can be supported is limited to two or three, which is a significant limitation in an active office environment with a great deal of printing. Heavy printing also severely limits the LAN's overall performance.

Digital Products has found that the sub-LAN will meet all the distributed printing needs of most PC users in work clusters who consider adopting a local area network, and more than those found in an A/B switch. This new market entry is based on the same technology as the data switch—a Z80 microprocessor and asynchronous RS232 communication. The sub-LAN also offers substantial improvements in software and features.

INTRODUCTION

Local-area networks have been on the market for several years, but they haven't achieved broad success as the answer to office connectivity needs. These needs have grown rapidly, in parallel with the power and acceptance of the personal computer.

There is a great deal of pent-up demand in PC work clusters for connectivity solutions. Full LANs are perceived as being complex, costly, and not focused on the most important user needs in these clusters—peripheral sharing (specifically, laser printing) and file transfer. Instead, LANs have focused on file sharing (serving) and common software applications. While such applications will probably become more widespread, most larger users already have a host computer to perform common database applications. Peripheral/printer sharing and file transfer have become the major immediate connectivity needs in large organization departmental PC clusters.

Users are becoming aware that a single type of LAN cannot satisfy all their requirements. They are developing strategies for multiple-level LAN standards based on a range of price/performance options. A typical multi-level strategy includes a full LAN, such as a token ring or Ethernet, plus several low-cost or sub-LAN offerings. Some departments need only to share a printer; others need simple networking but not the complexity or commitment required for a full LAN.

The sub-LAN offers the ideal solution in these cases, and it can be used as a server later in a larger full-LAN program.

These simpler, less expensive solutions are based on asynchronous communication, which is the dominant networking medium today. More important, Digital Products' customer surveys show that asynchronous communication will remain dominant for the next five years in most PC, printer, terminal, and modem environments.

Asynchronous communication satisfies most of the foreseeable needs of these PC clusters, including applications that are just beginning to penetrate the office, such as departmental desktop publishing. Desktop publishing calls for a PC, a good laser printer, effective software, and a reliable printer-sharing device.

The sub-LAN focuses on today's connectivity needs—printer/peripheral sharing and file transfer. It can be used later as a server in a full-LAN. Digital Products' experience is that the sub-LAN can provide 90 percent of today's connectivity requirements in PC clusters at 20 percent of the cost of a full LAN. In organizations where this scenario applies, the sub-LAN deserves consideration as an integral part of the organization's networking standards. Having sub-LAN and full-LAN products available enables a PC support organization to provide a full spectrum of price/performance alternatives for satisfying user requirements.

OFFICE NEEDS: PERIPHERAL SHARING AND FILE TRANSFER

Today's users of personal computers in office work clusters have a more pressing need to share expensive peripherals and establish data connectivity than they do for the capabilities of a full LAN. That fact is borne out repeatedly in the feedback Digital Products gets from its customers, and in results of independent studies. More than 10 million PCs are working in U.S. businesses today, along with 175,000 minicomputers and 30,000 mainframes. Some 30 percent of the PCs are used in clusters with just one PC plus peripherals, while 65 percent are in office clusters of two to 10 PCs. Approximately 5 percent of the PCs are found in clusters of more than 10.

The 65 percent of the PC users in the clusters of two to 10 represent a large potential market for some form of networking or office connectivity. This group to date has done little to interconnect computer resources—other than to use simple A/B switches—because LAN costs and complexity are substantially out of line with user's needs. Surveys of Digital Products customers and prospective customers show that users in these local clusters have three common needs: to share a few peripherals (lasers, plotters, modems); to perform simple file transfers among PCs, and to communicate with a minicomputer or mainframe; to provide gateways to future LAN developments such as 3-Com, Ethernet, or token ring.

While full LANs are focusing on high speeds and common databases, certain primary needs for most users, such as printer and peripheral sharing, are being given secondary treatment.

Organizations are looking for a solution based on existing hardware and cabling that supports their local computing, typically within a 400-foot radius. The sub-LAN has evolved in response to these needs.

WHAT IS THE SUB-LAN?

The sub-LAN consists of the NetCommander hardware—an intelligent asynchronous data exchange—EasyLAN™ and BLAST™ communication software, and a floppy-based automatic installation program for hassle-free installation and operation. EasyLAN™ uses DOS-like commands to enable printer and disk drive sharing between MS-DOS/PC-DOS PCs, while allowing them to perform applications concurrently, such as word processing and spreadsheets. BLAST™ allows the sub-LAN to get beyond the PC work cluster to communicate with every major minicomputer and mainframe with guaranteed error-free file-transfer compatibility.

Digital Products recommends a multi-level LAN strategy to ensure that both today's and future needs are met. Digital Products believes that the simple network solution technology embodied in its sub-LAN products provides the benefits that users need today and integrates well with future LAN directions. Standardizing on a Digital Products PrintDirector or NetCommander sub-LAN will meet immediate demands. Using that sub-LAN as a server to a token ring or other large LAN later will meet future needs while maintaining the functionality provided by the existing sub-LAN. No single solution meets everybody's needs, but an off-the-shelf solution such as the sub-LAN enables users to focus on the most important needs today—distributed printing and file transfer—without compromising long-term technological evolution within an organization.

LAN FUNCTIONALITIES AND NEEDS

Table I presents the LAN functions that PC users have identified as capabilities needed to improve office connectivity, and the priorities they assign to each of those needs. Almost all (80 percent) PC users want to improve their ability to share printers and other peripheral devices, and especially to share expensive laser printers. The cost per workstation of a $3,000 laser printer is substantially reduced when the printer is shared by several PCs, and the productivity of the group can be enhanced at the same time. Sharing the laser printer allows the cluster to graduate from slower dot-matrix printers. Print jobs are assigned to a high-speed buffer, freeing the PC for other work instead of having its user wait for the print job to be completed. High-speed buffering can cut PC printing time by as much as one hour per day, boosting work cluster productivity.

As application software becomes more powerful, a typical PC is called upon to run a wide variety of programs, such as spreadsheets, word processing, electronic mail and more. Various hard-copy outputs are required, including different kinds of printers and plotters. A single user cannot access multiple printers without some kind of networking or distributed-printing device.

FILE TRANSFER: EASE OF USE VS. SPEED

Table I shows that the second most important LAN function in the PC work cluster is file transfer and disk sharing—the ability to upload/download spreadsheets and word-processing files to each other, to minicomputers and mainframes, and to be able to access common disk drives on a server basis. The biggest challenge in selecting a LAN is finding a solution based on ease of use by the average user, and not speed of transfer, which seems to be the current focus of LAN development.

File transfer is the key function to fulfill the potential for PC-based distributed processing that will significantly impact office white collar labor costs and diminish management response and decision-making time. Until user-friendly file transfers are routine, operating in the background while PC users run foreground applications, local-area networking will not deliver its full promise to clustered PC users. While printer sharing is an immediate need of some 80 percent of those users, they say that file transfer and disk sharing will be major future requirements. The sub-LAN offers a user-friendly method of performing file transfer, and provides more gateways and interfaces to other LANs and CPUs than other products currently on the market. The sub-LAN's gateways and interfaces include convenient growth paths for future integration into a token ring or Ethernet LAN.

FILE SERVERS: NOW PROVIDED BY HOSTS

There are far fewer PC users who need full database file sharing and common software sharing today than there are who need to establish more basic forms of connectivity. In most large organizations, mainframes and minicomputers already provide integrated database functions: These are not immediate networking needs, but printer/peripheral sharing and file transfer are. Most corporate databases are already accessible through the PC.

BENEFITS SOUGHT THROUGH LAN FUNCTIONALITY

Today's PC users cite three principal benefits they want to realize from a LAN: reduced peripheral costs, increased data connectivity and increased user productivity (see Table II). Substantial cost reduction is possible in PC work clusters if expensive peripheral devices can be easily shared. This includes laser printers, other high-performance printers that will reach the market in the next year, plotters, hard disks,

TABLE I—LAN functions sought by office work clusters (2–10 PCs)

	Top Priority Today
1. Printer/peripheral sharing (especially laser printers)	80%
2. File transfer—disk sharing	15%
3. Database and software sharing	5%

TABLE II—Major LAN benefits sought by local work cluster users

1. Reduced cost of peripherals:
   a. Printers/terminals
   b. Plotters
   c. Modems
   d. Protocol converters
   e. Disk drives
2. Increased data connectivity:
   a. File transfer
   b. Host/mini access
   c. Local database sharing
3. Increased user productivity:
   a. Less wait for print time
   b. Direct access to wide variety of printers (including lasers)
   c. Less hassle time using PCs, printers and networks

modems, and other input-output devices. Studies show, for example, that modems are in use only about 10% of the time. A modem can be incorporated into the work cluster network and driven on a distributed basis, as a printer is. The same is true for protocol converters. Users often buy expensive built-in boards to perform IBM 3270 protocol conversion. If conversion functions are required only a small percentage of the time, a stand-alone protocol converter used on a distributed basis is highly cost effective.

Increased data connectivity is a major management goal in distributed processing. Each PC today is much like an island in the CPU sea; users are essentially "stranded" on their islands. Networks connecting these islands connect local users in an organization with each other, allow access to a mini or host computer, and eventually provide local database sharing.

Studies show that the data connectivity needs of these PC users primarily require file transfer plus host and minicomputer access. They must be able to make these connections simply and affordably, without learning new computer languages or requiring a Ph.D. in computer science. Data connectivity is the leverage pin that must be provided before the substantial organization change and reduction in decision-making time promised by distributed processing can be realized. Data connectivity will be the vehicle for management to substantially improve information transfer between organization levels, increasing the ability of an organization to respond to change.

Improving the productivity of PC users goes hand-in-hand with effective achievement of the first two LAN benefits—reduced peripheral cost and increased data connectivity. The most effective LAN products will substantially reduce CPU and peripheral access time and the "hassle factor" involved for PC users to use a simple network.

ALTERNATIVE LOCAL NETWORKING APPROACHES

Four basic approaches to local networking are presented in Table III in order of increasing cost and complexity.

Switches

Low-cost A/B mechanical and simple data switches have been available for many years, but there are practical limits to the number of users and functions they can support in a work cluster. They become impractical and ineffective for more than three users, especially at high switching rates. Most medium-to-heavy office workloads run into these limitations. A/B and code-activated data switches are acceptable solutions in clusters of two or three PCs with a low work load, but they are not a viable choice for users who need to share active peripherals to perform file transfer. Data switches are ideally suited for computer-controlled environments or very sophisticated users—two to five users—seeking access to peripherals. They do not offer buffering and are not easily operated by unsophisticated users.

TABLE III—Local networking technical alternatives

	Typical Cost/Port
1. Switches	$ 100
2. Sub-LAN	200
3. Broadband/baseband LAN	1,000
4. Multi-user minicomputer	1,500 (includes CPU cost)

The Sub-LAN

Digital Products has found that the sub-LAN, the second alternative in Table III will meet more than 90 percent of the needs of most PC users in work clusters who are considering adopting a local-area network. This new market entry is based on the same technology as the data switch—a microprocessor and asynchronous RS232 communication. The sub-LAN also offers substantial hardware buffering, and compared to data switches, substantial improvements in software and features, enabling it to support all required LAN functions. (See Figure 1 for typical applications and a comparison of LAN architecture differences.)

The typical sub-LAN offers 4-, 8-, 16- and 30-port models, which support essentially all local work cluster needs by connecting through the serial PC communication port instead of requiring complex plug-in boards. The sub-LAN also includes PC-based software to perform automatic installation, and to provide user selection menus for performing device and network function selection. The sub-LAN can also support modem sharing, simple file transfer, and micro-to-mainframe communications. The sub-LAN's asynchronous communication technology is today's dominant technology in most PC, printer, terminal and modem environments. Furthermore, Digital Products' customer surveys indicate that asynchronous communication will remain dominant for the next five years because of its low cost, ease of use and ability to support all practical levels of office connectivity.

The sub-LAN operates reliably at 9.6K to 19.2K bits per second at each port concurrently. The sub-LAN does not, however, support database sharing, which requires substantially higher speeds, more sophisticated PC-based software, and special hardware for performing file and record locking.

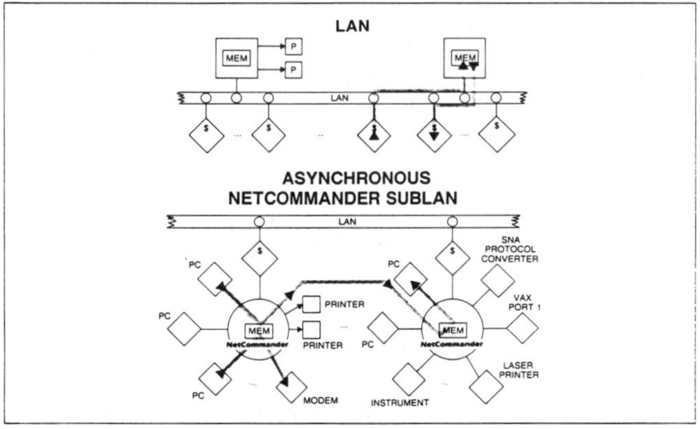

Figure 1—NetCommander sub-LAN approach versus broadband/baseband LAN approach

But users who can succeed with file-transfer speeds of 9.6K to 19.2K bps will find the sub-LAN equal or superior to a broadband/baseband LAN in all other respects. A major benefit of the sub-LAN is its ability to be operated as a server to a larger LAN. Sub-LAN flexibility allows users to meet today's distributed printing and data connectivity needs and easily interface into a broadband/baseband or token ring LAN later.

Another major benefit of the sub-LAN is that its asynchronous character means that gateway software packages, such as BLAST, can be used to enable the sub-LAN to directly interface to all popular minicomputers and mainframes as well as to other PC environments, such as UNIX and CP/M for compatible, error-free file transfer.

Broadband/Baseband LANs

Theoretically, broadband/baseband LANs will perform all the functions that are possible with A/B switches, data switches, and the sub-LAN, and will also support database and software sharing. In practice, however, LANs are subject to a number of constraints. Printer sharing, for example, isn't a simple task with a LAN, which often requires several operations to accomplish. The number of printers that can be supported is limited to two or three, which is a significant limitation in medium to heavy workload environments. Heavy printing also severely limits the LAN's overall performance. Since LANs do not easily support modem operation, their ability is severely limited. Aside from the foregoing, the major obstacles to more widespread use of these large LANs are cost, complexity, vulnerability to failure, and long installation and training time.

Multiuser Minicomputers

Given good software, multi-user minicomputers can perform all the functions that are possible with A/B switches, data switches, the sub-LAN, and broadband/baseband LANs. Minicomputers also overcome many of the technical disadvantages of broadband/baseband LANs, such as their inability to handle multi-user, multi-tasking common database applications. Minicomputers, however, carry a minimum price of about $20,000 and aren't an economical approach in PC clusters of fewer than eight to 10 users. The PC/sub-LAN combination can compete favorably with a multi-user minicomputer for up to 10 users. With more than 10 users, a multi-user minicomputer is the appropriate approach, both economically and operationally, although not all popular PC software is available for minis.

CRITERIA FOR NETWORK SELECTION

There are several important criteria which should be met when selecting the LAN that best meets organizational needs. An effective network solution should be both easy to install and simple to use. User-supplied installation aids, such as the Auto-Install program provided with the sub-LAN, should eliminate installation headaches and the need for expensive add-on boards and cabling. Fail-safe network operation should be adequately supported by a local vendor or in-house MIS management. Most important, day-to-day user operations should be performed and controlled by simple user language through DOS menus or application software.

Operationally, a network should provide excellent printer/peripheral sharing, adequate data connectivity, and a distributed buffer memory to provide transaction buffering for timely CPU and peripheral access. Printer or peripheral sharing should not be a multiple-step process and should not affect the overall performance of the net.

Finally, a network should provide multiple gateways and interfaces to other LANs, minis and host machines. Growth should be an important consideration in LAN selection. The important network investment should provide growth paths that accommodate LAN expansion or interfaces to larger LANs as they evolve—an important consideration when evaluating a "throw-away" solution such as an A/B or data switch, which has no growth potential, and a sub-LAN, which provides more gateways and interfaces than any other connectivity product on the market today.

ANTICIPATING TOMORROW'S TECHNOLOGY

That final criterion—the need for multiple gateways—is especially important so that an organization's choice to meet today's networking needs doesn't freeze it out of tomorrow's technologies. This concern has been raised because of the fast pace of technology. New products are obsolete almost as soon as they're introduced, making it difficult for an organization to plan ahead.

Digital Products recommends that an organization adopt a multi-level LAN strategy when considering immediate and long-term networking needs (see Table IV). Provide users with a solution to meet their immediate needs—printer sharing and simple file transfer—while leaving open growth paths by providing interfaces to larger, more long-term solutions. A Digital Products PrintDirector or NetCommander sub-LAN is a cost effective way to provide immediate connectivity. For users who can justify full LAN implementation later, sub-LAN capabilities can be maintained in a server role, working with the chosen large LAN standard.

TABLE IV—How to have the best of all networks: Set multi-level standards

Need	Standard
• Printer sharing only Typical work cluster (50 percent+)	• Sub-LAN PrintDirector Best printer sharing $200/Port Install in 1–2 hours without manual
• Printer sharing plus file transfer Disk sharing Cannot justify large LAN (30 percent)	• Sub-LAN NetCommander Best printer sharing Good file transfer Easily installed and operated Meets immediate needs Can be server in larger LAN
• Common database File serving Software sharing (20 percent)	• Full LAN Token ring Ethernet

Connecting terminals to multiple LANs*

by BRONSON HOKUF, PAUL D. AMER, and DANIEL GRIM
University of Delaware
Newark, Delaware

ABSTRACT

With computing facilities often distributed over sites that are both physically and administratively separate, many organizations find themselves with several unconnected Local Area Networks (LANs). Eventually it becomes desirable to enhance communication capabilities between these LANs so that users can access all hosts on all LANs. This paper describes a terminal gateway, a system that provides users having terminal access to hosts on one LAN with an ability to access all hosts on another LAN. Such a gateway solution is appropriate when: (1) separate terminal connections to each LAN are prohibitively expensive and (2) commercially available bridges or gateways are unsuitable for use. A functional specification of the terminal gateway, the communication protocol it uses, and a specification of performance metrics maintained by the gateway are described.

* This research was supported in part by the Office of Naval Research Department of Defense Contract Number 83-K-0320

INTRODUCTION

Local area networks (LANs) are clearly recognized as an economical means of connecting computing resources. With computing facilities often distributed over sites that are both physically and administratively separate, many organizations find themselves with several unconnected LANs. Eventually it becomes desirable to enhance communication capabilities between these LANs so that users can access all hosts on all LANs. Typical solutions to this problem include: combining the LANs into one LAN by using repeaters, attaching a bridge or gateway between pairs of networks, or providing separate terminal connections to hosts on the different networks. A terminal's physical connections may be extended by installing additional private lines, leasing lines, multiplexing many terminal lines over leased, or private lines, or by providing some sort of internetwork connection to allow host access using existing terminal lines.

Two LANs exist at the University of Delaware, one connecting computing center machines, ACSnet, for instructional purposes, and one connecting machines in a joint EE and CIS Department laboratory, EE/CISnet, for research purposes. Terminal connections to the ACSnet are provided via leased serial lines to a port selector. (A port selector is an intelligent switching device which establishes a virtual connection between a user's terminal line and the host computer for which they have requested a connection.) (See Figure 1.) Terminal connections to the EE/CISnet are provided by university owned lines to a terminal switch on the EE/CIS Ethernet.[1] Users that needed a connection to both networks had two lines to their terminal and a locally developed switchbox which allowed them to switch between the two lines. With the recent tripling of costs for leased lines, an alternative connection to the ACS hosts supported by the port selector process was needed to eliminate the leased lines while still providing satisfactory access to hosts on both networks. Several solutions were considered; the one selected and discussed in this paper was the development of a terminal gateway.

A terminal gateway permits users connected to the EE/CISnet terminal switch to connect to the ACSnet's port selector. The terminal switch provides users with a menu of the hosts on the EE/CIS network; one host is selected, and from then on, the user appears to be communicating directly with that host. For connections to the ACSnet, the user selects an option labeled ACS which provides a connection to the ACS port selector. The port selector then allows the user to attach to any of the ACSnet hosts; after making that connection, the user appears to be communicating directly with the ACS host just as if they had a direct serial line to the port selector.

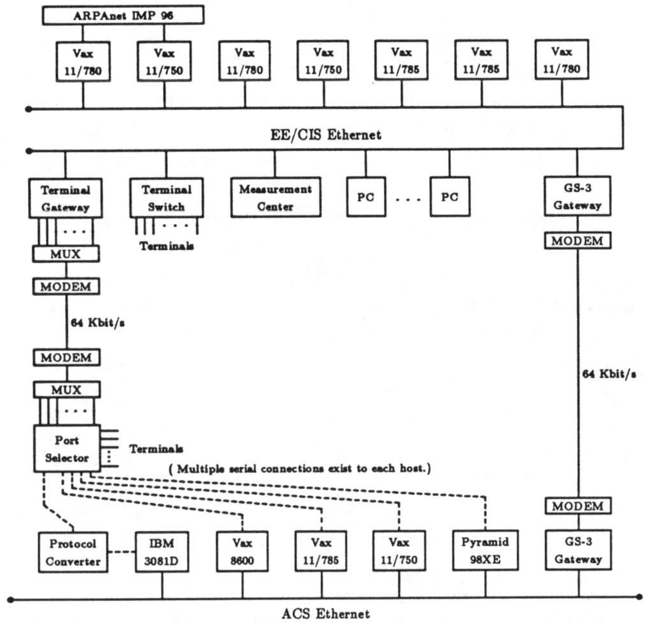

Figure 1—University of Delaware computing environment

A terminal gateway is not a general solution to internetworking multiple LANs such as one may obtain with bridges for homogeneous LANS[2,3] or general gateways for heterogeneous LANs.[4] A terminal gateway provides more economical terminal connections to other LANs for users already connected to one LAN. More general interLAN problems such as file transfer and distributed computing (e.g., load sharing) require higher level protocols for host-to-host communication and are outside the scope of this solution.

The solution presented, as it was implemented at the University of Delaware, should be applicable to other sites that seek to provide terminal connections to hosts on a distant LAN when they already have connections to an existing LAN and physically joining the LANs into one is not feasible. The computing environment serviced is discussed in the Background and Overview of the Problem section, along with the motivation for considering a terminal gateway solution. The section on the terminal gateway presents the hardware configuration, and reviews the operation and performance of the terminal gateway. This includes the gateway's functional specification, communication protocol and self-monitoring capability. Finally, the last section, concludes that a terminal gateway is a technically feasible and economically attractive solution to providing terminal access to multiple LANs.

BACKGROUND AND OVERVIEW OF THE PROBLEM

University of Delaware Computing Environment

Local networking efforts at the University of Delaware are typical of a campus with growing communication capabilities. Together, the Electrical Engineering (EE) and Computer and Information Sciences (CIS) Departments maintain a joint computing laboratory for research purposes consisting of several Vaxes and other machines linked together by an Ethernet (EE/CISnet). (See Figure 1.) In addition, the University's Academic Computing Service maintains a similar Ethernet (ACSnet) interconnecting Vaxes, a Pyramid 98XE, and an IBM 3081D for general instructional computing and non-EE/CIS faculty research.[5,6]

The main hardware on the EE/CISnet are seven Vax-11s, four running 4.2 BSD UNIX, and three running VMS. Two Vaxes are connected to the ARPAnet via IMP** 96 providing a major ARPAnet connection point in the northeast corridor. Two Bridge Communication GS-3 half-gateways directly connect the EE/CISnet to the ACSnet over a 64 Kbit/s leased line. This provides a functional LAN-LAN interconnection for file transfer (e.g., *ftp*) and remote login (e.g., *telnet* or *rlogin*). User connections to the Vax systems are accomplished by a PDP-11/45 acting as an intelligent terminal switch. Derived from software originally developed at Cornell University,[7] the switch physically connects up to 112 terminals and provides multiple, simultaneous virtual terminal connections to one or more hosts for each terminal. The gateway that is the subject of this paper resides on the EE/CISnet and allows terminals attached to the EE/CISnet terminal switch to access the port selector of the ACSnet.

Motivation for a Terminal Gateway

The desire to implement a gateway for terminal traffic came as a direct result of the divestiture of AT&T and the resulting increases in communication costs. The CIS Department maintains approximately 31 leased public telephone network lines for terminal connections to the ACSnet. The cost of these connections has multiplied dramatically over a short period of time. The Department had to find a way to reduce, if not eliminate, the prohibitive leased line costs while still providing access to all hosts on both LANs. In addition, having users deal with two physical lines to their terminal was undesirable for at least the following reasons. First, switching between the two networks, by means of a locally developed switchbox, usually meant reconfiguring the terminal for a different baud rate. Second, they could not maintain the first connection and simultaneously set up a connection to the other network. Third, the extra hardware involved meant extra maintenance costs.

** IMPs (Interface Message Processors) are now called PSNs (Packet Switching Nodes).

Alternative solutions

Several alternatives, other than the terminal gateway (TGW) that was chosen, were discussed and considered. One option was to combine the existing Ethernets into a single Ethernet connecting the two sites. This option was complicated by the legalities of not owning a right-of-way for such a connection. In general, even if a right-of-way exists, one may not be able to extend the LAN due to exceeding the maximum end-to-end length restriction. In Delaware's case, products existed, such as optical repeaters, DEC's LAN Bridge 100,[8] that appeared able to provide the desired service.*** As an added but not uncommon complication, the two LAN's are managed by separate organizations and any solution could not require major LAN changes. Repeaters were eliminated because we could not expect the ACSnet to support the software from the Terminal Switch. In addition, because EE/CISnet is an experimental network, it was undesirable to risk corrupting the ACSnet with experimental traffic; this was a real problem since repeaters forward all traffic between nets.

A related solution was to use the existing Bridge Communication half-gateways**** not only for periodic host-to-host *ftps* or *telnet* connections, but for all terminal connections to the ACSnet. The gateways are intelligent enough to isolate the traffic on the two networks, but one still would need either to: (1) port the terminal switch (TS) software to the ACSnet hosts or (2) run a *telnet* (or *rlogin*) connection for every active user. The problem of porting the TS host software is complicated by the independent management of the two networks and the fact that one of the ACS hosts, the IBM 3081D, do not support UNIX; the TS host software makes extensive use of UNIX facilities.

The problem, of using *telnet* connections over the gateways for all active ACSnet users, is this user level process consumes additional host resources at both source and destination, wasting a significant number of CPU cycles on the hosts which could be used for research purposes. *Telnet* connections require more resources from the remote host than equivalent serial line connections do. Additionally, *telnet* requires a local host to support both a TS connection and a *telnet* connection since the terminal must attach to the local host using the TS and the local host communicates with the remote host using the *telnet* protocol, neither of these are required of a host for a simple serial connection as in the TGW solution. Also, *telnet* style connections do not always provide the same level of service that a serial line might be expected to provide, for example, normal telnet connections do not support full screen terminal service on the IBM machines. The IBM machine

*** Repeaters are devices used to interconnect cable segments within a single local area network. These devices operate at the physical layer and perform no filtering on the frames received; every received frame is forwarded. A bridge has added functionality and interconnects two distinct LANs. Bridges operate at the datalink layer and are relatively simple, but intelligent, filtering devices whose function is to store-and-forward frames between two local area networks that use the same protocols.[3,9,11]

**** A gateway is a more complex device, which operates at the network layer and is designed for interconnecting heterogeneous networks. It has the ability to accommodate differences between the two networks being connected, for example: different addressing schemes, packet sizes, network speeds, as well as other differences.[4]

normally interfaces with terminals through a 7171 Protocol Converter (see Figure 1), which enables many terminals to emulate an IBM 3270 terminal. When the connection to the IBM occurs through the network interface this protocol conversion function is not available. The emulation provided by the protocol converter must be provided by from some other source, imposing an additional burden on one of the participating hosts. Additionally, using *telnet* would compete with mail and *ftp* for the resources of the GS-3 half-gateways, potentially degrading their performance. While *telnet* and *rlogin* are certainly usable on a small scale, they were eliminated as an option due to the expected large overhead they would incur and the unsatisfactory performance for connections to the IBM host.

Another option was to place a local MUX in the areas where terminals are concentrated, run private lines from the terminals to the MUX, and connect the MUX to the remote site via fewer high-bandwidth leased lines. This solution would reduce communication costs, however it required extensive rewiring, complicated by the wide and varying distribution of the terminals requiring service.

Other options included setting up a satellite link, a microwave link or installing a wide area network interconnecting all university sites. However, these solutions appeared too expensive and their realization too far in the future to be considered as viable candidates for solving the present problem.

The option decided upon was to build a terminal gateway from the EE/CISnet to the ACSnet. A TGW makes use of the existing private connections to attach terminals to the EE/CIS terminal switch and to use a 32 channel statistical MUX operating over a 64 Kbit/s leased line for the link to the ACSnet port selector. By making use of existing, privately owned terminal lines to the EE/CISnet and providing a mechanism for each terminal to connect to the ACS Port Selector via these lines, the leased line costs could be eliminated and a serial connection to an ACS host could be provided. Some experience had been gained in this type of application through the construction of the TS. The TS handles multiple, serial connections directed onto the Ethernet and the TGW would handle multiple, serial connections going off the Ethernet (see Figure 1).

The TGW solution seemed to hold the most promise for a fairly rapid solution with a minimal outlay of additional funds and labor. The hardware was available within existing department resources and no rewiring was necessary. It also provided the additional benefit of giving users a uniform connection interface to all computer systems.

Cost/benefit analysis

The cost of communications for the CIS Department goes much beyond the costs listed in this section; only the portions relevant to this discussion are listed. One can see from Table I that there has nearly been a tripling in the monthly cost of leased phone lines in the past 3 years. In contrast to the cost of leased phone lines, the TGW presents a more stable and affordable approach to providing the same services. Because the distribution of the available lines would be dynamic,

TABLE I—Cost of communications—current approach

Year	Monthly Line Cost	# of Lines†	Total Cost/yr
1983	$24	27	$7,776
1984	$28	29	$9,744
1985	$66	31	$24,552
1986*	$69	33	$27,324
1987*	$73	35	$30,660
1988*	$76	37	$33,744
1989*	$80	39	$37,440
1990*	$84	41	$41,328
		Total (1986–1990):	$170,496

* Costs projected @5% annual increases.
† Projected to increase two lines per year.

a smaller total number of connections are able to service a larger user group. The TGW solution could be implemented without a major outlay of funds and could be expected to produce substantial savings over the course of the next five years (see Table II). The cost of the TGW was arrived at by computing the replacement cost of the hardware involved in the building of the TGW. (See the hardware description later in the paper.) It also included the cost of the MUXes and modems which were purchased for the project. It did not include the cost of software development, which was funded through academic research, and did not include any amount for maintenance or replacement of the hardware. Maintenance is normally handled by the lab staff and spare hardware is available.

One can see from Table II that the difference in cost between the two approachesis significant. The rise in communication costs was significant enough to motivate a variety of cost containment procedures in the university's communication services. The TGW is but one of the attempts to contain such costs.

Problems Associated with a TGW

The TGW solution is not without problems; one need only look at the data path to see the potential for communication bottlenecks (see Figure 2). The TGW must provide a reliable, real-time interface for the user. While the level of service provided cannot be expected to be the same as when each user

TABLE II—Comparison of methods (1986–1990)

Method	5 Year (1986–1990) Total*
Multiple leased lines	$170,496
Terminal gateway†	$22,278
Projected savings	$148,218

† Includes cost of leased lines and replacement costs of hardware. Replacement costs from: Midwest Systems, Inc. Burnsville, MN 55337
* (@5% annual increases)

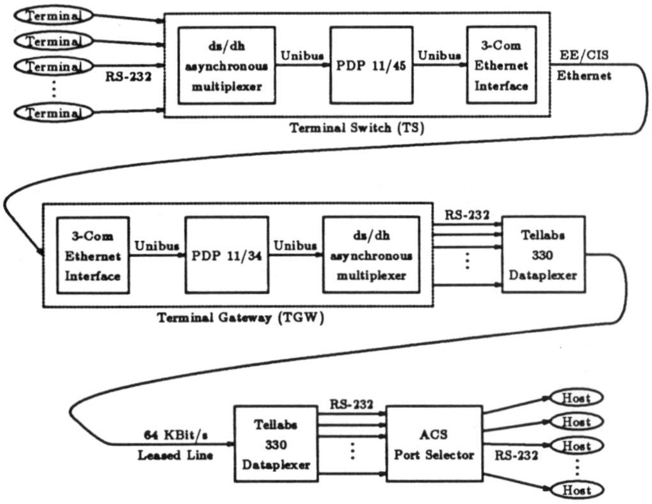

Figure 2—Data path for a remote connection through the TGW

has a dedicated 9600 baud line, the interactive nature of the traffic requires that a rapid response to user requests be given, for example, character echoes must appear to be nearly instantaneous. The TGW adds another TS-like device (which introduces delay) into the data path, plus it multiplexes 32 connections over a 64 Kbit/s link instead of a 10 Mbit/s link. Because of this, the TGW performance is expected to be poorer than the service provided by a dedicated line. However, because communication through the TGW is limited to user generated, interactive traffic, the performance is expected to be satisfactory.

Another problem is the limited number of channels available; if a thiry-third person attempts to use the link, that person is unable to do so. In contrast, when users own physical connections to the port selector, they are guaranteed a connection whenever the port selector has one to give to them.

THE TERMINAL GATEWAY

How the TGW fits into the International Standards Organization's (ISO) Reference Model of Open Systems Interconnection (OSI) is now discussed. Then the design requirements of the TGW are presented followed by a description of the operation of the TGW and its associated hardware.

One possible approach to providing gateway services is to use a standard protocol for all internetwork traffic regardless of the type of networks being connected. This is the approach taken by the ARPAnet Internet Protocol (IP) which defines the format of internet packets and the rules for performing internet protocol functions based on the information in the internet packet headers. IP provides a datagram service and fits between the network (routing) and transport (end-to-end delivery) layers of the ISO-OSI reference model. In addition to IP, ARPAnet gateways use a gateway-to-gateway protocol to exchange routing information.[10]

A second, special purpose, approach is to build a gateway that is essentially a protocol converter. The technique is to receive a packet, strip the control information from the packet, and retransmit the data using the protocol of the destination network. The principal disadvantage of this approach is that a different gateway must be built for each different pair of networks interconnected.[11] The loss of generality in this approach tends to make the implementation easier because all of the assumptions are known beforehand. This type of gateway may potentially operate faster (or as fast as, but with less sophisticated hardware) than the more general type of gateway due to the less sophisticated nature of its duties.

The terminal gateway, discussed herein, aligns most closely with the second approach. However, it is important to recall that the TGW is not a LAN–LAN gateway. The TGW does not establish a connection to a remote network, rather it establishes a connection to a port selector which, in turn, establishes a connection to a host on the remote network. It may be helpful to consider the TGW as two distinct parts (although in reality there is only one). The first part resides on the EE/CISnet and, from the point of view of the terminal switch, looks like a gateway to the ACSnet. The TS addresses packets destined for terminal connections on ACSnet to the TGW and receives packets back from the TGW just as if the TGW were the ACS host, the TS treats the TGW the same way it treats a host on its own LAN. The second part of the TGW is attached to a 32 channel, asynchronous, statistical multiplexer. This MUX is attached to an identical MUX at ACS (which is attached to the ACS port selector) over a 64Kbit/s leased line (see Figure 2). From this side, the TGW appears to behave much like a Packet Assembler/Disassembler, or PAD, taking the TS packets, disassembling them and sending each piece of data to the appropriate MUX line. The data received from the individual MUX lines is assembled into a packet and sent to the TS over the EE/CIS network. The TGW provides flow control and buffering between the two different transmission media. It does not provide for any acknowledgement or retransmission of packets received.

This last characteristic leaves a possibility of failure. There is no guarantee that a data path is reliable unless there is some sort of end-to-end internetworking protocol with extended functions,[12] usually implemented in the transport layer (e.g., the ARPAnet Transport Control Protocol—TCP).[13] Because of the low bit error rate of the Ethernet,[14] it was chosen to implement the TS-TGW communication protocol as a connection-oriented, sequenced, unreliable protocol. The reliability of the MUX link from the TGW to the ACS port selector is a different matter and is handled by a reliable MUX-to-MUX protocol.

In summary, the TGW functions in a manner analogous to a special purpose gateway which only serves the EE/CIS terminal switch. It makes use of the Ethernet as a backbone, providing virtual circuit connections***** to users attaching terminals to host computers resident on the remote network.

***** Virtual circuit connection implies that the connection behaves as if it were a single dedicated copper circuit, when it is actually implemented in software.

TABLE III—Messages processed by the console

Symbol	Name	Description
?,h	HELP	Displays a list of legal console options.
V	VERBOSE	Displays a list of options with explanations.
S	SHUTDOWN	Sends a shutdown warning to all attached lines.
A	ALL	Display all stats kept by the TGW.
L	LINE	Display status for all MUX connections.
I	IN-USE	Display line number and idle time for lines in use.
M	MUX-STATS	Display character counts for each line.
E	EN-STATS	Display stats for the Ethernet packets
H	DH-STATS	Display stats for the DH-11 boards.
Z	DZ-STATS	Display stats for the DZ-11 boards.

Requirements—What the TGW Will Do

The following requirements were established for the initial design of the TGW and they describe the functionality that the TGW provides:

1. The TGW will establish a connection with the ACS port selector upon request from a terminal attached to the TS.
2. The TGW will not introduce *unreasonable* delay into the system response time (i.e., the delay for echoing a character must remain non-noticeable).
3. The TGW will provide an option to logout idle connections if no characters are transmitted during some fixed period of time.
4. The TGW will accept messages from a console and act upon those messages. Options supported are listed in Table III.
5. The TGW will print certain events on the console device. Those events are: reception of a bad Ethernet packet, with the reason for the packet being bad; disconnection of a physical line to the MUX; refusal of a request for a connection due to no available line; and automatic logout of a line along with the line number that was affected.
6. The TGW will adapt to the failure of a TS, correctly terminating any affected connections.
7. The TGW will dynamically detect and flag MUX lines that are not connected or that become disconnected.
8. The TGW will (optionally) keep statistics on itself; these statistics are listed in Table IV.

Restrictions—What the TGW Will Not Do

There were certain functions the TGW was not to provide. The following restrictions were accepted as part of the TGW specification:

TABLE IV—Counts maintained by the TGW

1) Characters received and transmitted on each DZ line.
2) Characters received and transmitted on each DH line.
3) Characters received and transmitted on each MUX line.
4) Connections refused.
5) Lines automatically logged out.
6) Ethernet packets of length 1–10 data bytes received and transmitted.
7) Ethernet packets received grouped by multiples of 10 bytes.
8) Ethernet packets transmitted grouped by multiples of 100 bytes.
9) Ethernet packets received and transmitted.

1. The TGW will not introduce any error detection or correction as part of the communication with the TS. No reliability will be added to the Ethernet.
2. The TGW will not be designed to handle applications (e.g., *telnet* or *ftp*) other than terminal connections between the two networks.
3. The TGW will not support connections from devices other than a TS.

TS-TGW Communication Protocol

The TS and TGW exchange information between themselves using a non-standard network layer protocol on top of Ethernet's link layer service (see Figures 3 and 4). It is the purpose of this section to describe the packet format used and the function of each of its parts.

At the data link layer the packets follow the standard Ethernet packet definition. The only feature unique to this application is the value chosen for the Link Service Access Point (LSAP)—the TS uses a value of two in this field. While this value has a specific meaning in this context, it may have other meanings outside the EE/CISnet environment.

All user data and control information exchanged between the TS and the TGW at the network layer have two components. The first part is the line number and the second part is the data destined for that line. If the high bit of the first byte containing the line number is set, this flags a control message for that line and the second byte is then interpreted as a control code for that line. Control messages include setting up and terminating connections, end-to-end flow control, status messages, autologout requests and TS-TGW Ethernet flow

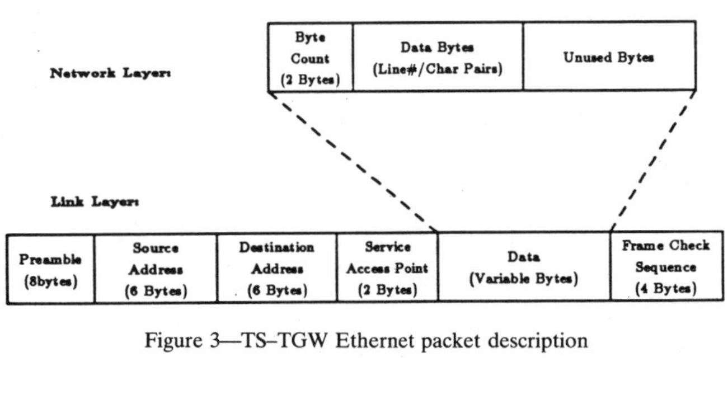

Figure 3—TS–TGW Ethernet packet description

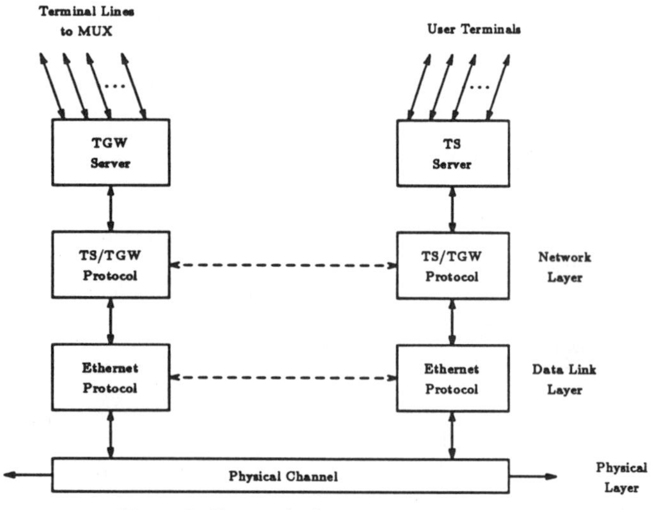

Figure 4—Communication structure for TS–TGW

control. Within a given packet, control and data pairs for the same or different lines may be multiplexed. Packets are disassembled two bytes at a time using the line number to direct each character to the correct destination. Between the TS and the TGW a lock-step flow control is observed. This prevents the TGW from ever overrunning the TS.

TGW Operation

The operation of the TGW can be best understood by first referring to Figure 2. When a user types a character at a terminal, that character is sent over serial lines to the EE/CIS terminal switch; the TS packetizes the character and sends it to the TGW. When the TGW receives the packet it disassembles the packet and forwards the character over the appropriate serial line to the MUX which sends the character to the remote MUX where it is then received by the ACS port selector and forwarded to the appropriate host. The character echo follows the same path, only in reverse order.

Figure 5 illustrates the internal operation of the TGW. The TGW buffers all data, both incoming and outgoing. When a message is received from the Ethernet, the message is stored in a buffer and the TGW begins to extract line number/character pairs from that buffer. Those pairs that represent normal data are queued to the appropriate serial output buffer based on the line number present in the pair. For the data representing control messages, the effect can be in either of two directins: if the control message is requesting that a connection be established, then a message is forwarded back to the requester by queuing an appropriate message to the current Ethernet output buffer; if the control message is requesting flow control for a particular serial line, then that request is queued to the appropriate serial line buffer.

When a character is received over one of the serial lines, an interrupt signal is generated and as soon as the TGW processor is available the character is processed. Initially, the character is placed on an input queue associated with the particular serial line. The character handler removes the characters from that queue, prepends a line number, then appends the line number/character pair to the current outgoing Ethernet buffer.

Much of the software is interrupt driven; the device handlers all react to incoming data in this manner. The main program is an infinite loop that periodically polls devices and handles the flow of data in both directions. Packets are sent from the TGW over the Ethernet either as a result of filling with data or as a result of the current polling interval expiring. Because the PDP does not have a hardware clock built in, one was implemented in software based on interrupts supplied by a DL11-W board installed in the PDP. This clock is used to control device polling and to schedule events that are time based, such as the timing of events required to disconnect a line from the Port Selector. The clock also schedules the sending of statistics on a periodic basis when that option is configured into the software.

Hardware Configuration

The terminal gateway software executes on a dedicated DEC PDP-11/34 minicomputer. The code development was done on a VAX 11/780, cross-compiled for the PDP and downloaded via the Ethernet. The PDP is configured with 128K of main memory, a 3Com 3C300 Unibus Ethernet Controller,[15] 1—DZ-11A Asynchronous 8-line Multiplexer, 2—DH-11A Asynchronous 16-line Multiplexers, and a DL-11W Serial Line Unit/Real-time Clock Option.[16]

Communication with the remote network is through a pair of Tellabs 330C Dataplexers, a statistical multiplexer with 32 asynchronous channels.[13] The Dataplexers communicate over public leased copper circuits using a pair of Amdahl 982 synchronous data sets which communicate at 64 Kbit/s. The port selector, with which the multiplexer interfaces at the ACSnet, is a Develcon Dataswitch (Model 9006/2000). As presently configured, the Dataswitch supports approximately 1440 channels or 720 user connections to ASCnet hosts.

The terminal switch software executes on a dedicated PDP-11/45 minicomputer, configured with 192K of memory, a 3Com 3C300 Unibus Ethernet Controller, 7—DH-11A

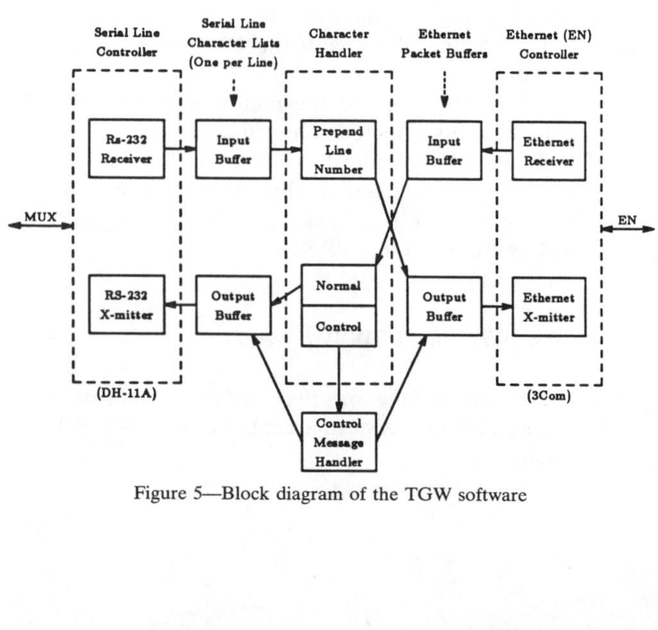

Figure 5—Block diagram of the TGW software

Asynchronous 16-line Multiplexers or their equivalent, and a DL-11W Serial Line Unit/Real-time Clock Option. The TS provides for 112 terminal connections to the EE/CIS network (both hard wired and dial-in) and is the principal connect point to the EE/CISnet systems for all EE/CIS faculty and graduate student terminals.

TGW PERFORMANCE METRICS

The TGW has been designed with an option to maintain certain statistics on itself. This was done to monitor the TGW's performance over time and to supplement statistics already gathered by an existing network measurement center.[1] A sample of the counts kept by the TGW is summarized in Table IV. Certain special events are also counted: the number of connections refused by the TGW and the number of connections automatically logged out, provided that option has been selected within the TGW software. These counts accumulate for a period of one minute and are then reset to zero. Before they are reset the TGW sends a statistics packet to one of the Vax hosts via the Ethernet where the packet is stored for later processing. A daemon process running on the Vax captures each packet and appends it to an individual file. A separate file is created for each hour during which statistics are kept.

From these counts a program running on the Vax can derive a variety of performance metrics. These metrics can be based on different intervals of time depending on how the data on file are interpreted and accumulated. Several possible metrics are listed below along with an example of how each metric is computed.

Channel utilization of the 64 Kbit/s link: This metric is a percentage based on the maximum capacity of the channel being measured.

$$\frac{(Total\ Char\ Sent)/min}{(Max.\ Possible\ Char\ Sent)/min} \times 100 = \%\ Utilization \quad (1)$$

A histogram of the average channel utilization for each minute of the day over some period of time provides a compact way to characterize the level of use of the gateway.

Mean number of lines in use: This metric is an absolute quantity and must be measured over a period of time.

$Line_i$ = number of lines active during the ith minute
N = number of minutes processed

$$Mean = \frac{\sum_{i=1}^{N} Line_i}{N} \quad (2)$$

Comparing a histogram of the mean number of lines in use during each minute of the day with the channel utilization histogram suggested above would estimate the relation between number of users and the 64 Kbit/s channel utilization. Presenting this metric as a histogram showing the mean number of lines in use for each hour of the day, as summarized over several weeks of observation, would provide an indication of typical patterns of use of the TGW resource. Such a histogram would be computed in the same manner as is suggested for the mean number of connections refused, which is presented below.

Correlate the mean number of users to the internet channel utilization: One might expect to find a linear correlation between these two metrics. At some point, however, as the number of users increases, the internet channel utilization must level out (because it will be approaching 100%). If the channel utilization turns out too high when the number of users is significantly less than the maximum, this would be an indication that the service provided is probably less than satisfactory and that steps should be taken to increase the channel bandwidth. One step might be to assign 16 lines to each of two 64 Kbit/s links instead of 32 lines to one link.

Mean transmission (or reception) rate for a connection: This rate must be expressed as a unit quantity per unit time (e.g., characters per second).

$Char_i$ = number of chars transmitted in the ith minute
N = number of minutes processed

$$Char/sec = \frac{\sum_{i=1}^{N} Char_i}{60 \cdot N} \quad (3)$$

This rate can be compared to the possible data rate for a line (9600 baud) and if this comparison is done, it can be expressed as a line utilization rate (%). This metric provides a compact way to characterize the typical load that a single user presents to the system.

Mean packet arrival rate: Since the number of Ethernet packets received, or sent, is counted each minute, it is possible to compute the mean number of packets arriving per minute and to approximate the mean number of packets arriving per second. For example, to compute the number of packets per second over N minutes of observation the following formula should be used:

$Packets_i$ = number of packets arriving in the ith minute
N = number of minutes processed

$$Packets/sec = \frac{\sum_{i=1}^{N} Packets_i}{60 \cdot N} \quad (4)$$

It should be understood that this metric does not reflect an accurate measure of packet interarrival time. This metric does offer one measure of the amount of Ethernet bandwidth consumed by the TGW-TS traffic.

Mean number of connections refused: This metric would be interesting to view as a histogram showing the mean for each hour of the day as summarized over several weeks of observation.

$$Mean\,(hr_i) = \frac{\sum_{j=1}^{Numdays} \sum_{k=1}^{60} \#\ \text{refused in}\ min_k\ \text{of}\ hr_i}{Numdays} \quad (5)$$

A display of the total number of connections refused each hour of the day over an extended period compared with the next metric would provide a means of estimating whether the TGW resource is being consumed by idle connections or by users actively working. This metric also gives some indication of user satisfaction with the TGW. If a large numbr of connections are refused on a regular basis, then the service provided has to be expanded or the period of time before idle users are logged out needs to be shortened.

Mean number of users automatically logged out per hour:

$Mean(hr_i)$

$$= \frac{\sum_{j=1}^{Numdays} \sum_{k=1}^{60} \#\ \text{automatic logouts in}\ min_k\ \text{of}\ hr_i}{Numdays} \quad (6)$$

As with the previous measure, it would be interesting to have a histogram summarizing this metric for each hour of the day. This metric may provide some indication of the manner in which people use their terminals. Large numbers of autologouts would indicate a sporadic, intermittent kind of use.

Overhead on the Ethernet: Because each data packet sent and received over the Ethernet is a fixed size and is also categorized according to the number of data bytes, it is possible to make a rough approximation of the amount of Ethernet bandwidth wasted due to partially filled data packets. The measure is an approximation because the granularity of the data byte count kept as a statistic is only accurate to the nearest hundred bytes. For an individual packet the amount of overhead in bytes is given by:

Overhead = Packet Size − *Fixed Overhead* − Data Bytes Sent

where

Fixed Overhead = Preamble + Source Address + Destination Address + SAP + FCS = 26 bytes (See Figure 3 for sizes.)

The *Fixed Overhead* is subtracted because it should not be counted as part of the wasted bandwidth. It is required that every packet have these components, therefore they are just as important as the data. For a given hour the estimated mean overhead would be computed as:

B_i = Number of data bytes sent in the ith minute
P_i = Number of packets sent in the ith minute

Mean Overhead

$$= \sum_{i=1}^{60} \frac{(P_i \cdot (\text{Packet Size} - 26)) - B_i}{P_i}\ \text{bytes/packet} \quad (7)$$

Analysis of the overhead could be useful in determining an optimal size for the packets used by the TGW. If the overhead is large and the mean number of users is near the maximum, then the packet size should be able to be reduced.

CONCLUSIONS/SUMMARY

Due to the increasing costs of leased communications facilities there was a need to consider an alternative means of providing terminal communications to geographically separate LANs. This search for alternatives led to the proposal that a TGW be built. The cost of communications affected by the TGW has been analyzed and the benefits of using the TGW have been demonstrated. The terminal gateway provides several advantages over other possible communication schemes: per line costs are significantly reduced, a standard user interface is provided, inactive terminals may be automatically disconnected, malfunctioning lines may be isolated without disrupting other users, and more users can be serviced than with an equivalent number of dedicated lines.

The TGW provides a path between the two networks that off-loads a host or dedicated general purpose gateway on each network from the tasks associated with providing an interactive communications channel; thus the TGW allows a general purpose gateway to handle its other tasks of file transfer and message forwarding more efficiently. The TGW presents some disadvantages over dedicated lines: individual line performance is degraded in the face of heavy use, failure of the 64 Kbit/s link or its associated hardware is catastrophic for all gateway users (although users may still attach to the remote hosts using *rlogin* or *telnet* from the EE/CISnet hosts), and the cost to add lines beyond the capacity of the MUX is a large, one-time expenditure.

The TGW has been described in terms of the ISO-OSI reference model and has been characterized as a special purpose gateway. The design and operation of the TGW software and hardware necessary to make the system functional have been described. The special nature of the traffic handled by the TGW made it possible to remove some of the functionality normally found in a general purpose gateway. Tasks like routing, address verification, fragmentation, and reassembly are not required. Because of this the TGW can more efficiently handle the data transfer assigned to it, allowing satisfactory real-time performance to be achieved. The requirements and restrictions placed upon the TGW have been presented.

Several performance metrics are available for measuring the performance of the TGW. A mechanism for gathering the counts necessary for computing these metrics has been implemented. It is possible to obtain significant statistical results from the data maintained by the TGW; such an analysis could yield a characterization of the gateway usage and a picture of the requirements of the clients served by the TGW.

The TGW has become a functional part of the computer communications facility of the EE/CIS computer lab and has been found to be a cost effective alternative to leasing communications services. As the University expands its networking capacity, other alternatives will become available for interconnecting existing LANs. However, the TGW will continue to serve a useful role in providing users on a local LAN with a uniform mechanism for terminal connections to hosts on a remote LAN. Until such time as the TS networking software is ported to the other types of machines available on the ACSnet (e.g., the IBM 3081), a general purpose gateway will not be sufficient for allowing the TS to communicate with those hosts. Because the TGW provides a transparent, asynchronous, serial communication channel (RS-232) for the terminal attached to it, the TGW does not depend on any proprietary protocols. Therefore, the TGW can provide connections to any device that supports RS-232 connections. In our case, this is the ACSnet Port Selector.

The TS provides a cost-effective way to allow users to make multiple virtual connections to machines on a LAN to which the TS is attached, and the TGW extends the TS's capacity by allowing connections to devices on another local network to occur in a manner that makes it appear as if the device were just another node on the local network. This connection is accomplished using leased communication facilities and represents both a technically feasible and economical solution which could be implemented by other users with similar requirements.

REFERENCES

1. Amer, Paul, Ram Kumar, Ruey-bin Kao, Jeffrey Phillips, Lillian Cassel. "Local Area Broadcast Network Network Measurement: Traffic Characterization." Department of Computer and Information Sciences, University of Delaware, January, 1986. Proceedings: CompCon Spring, 1987, San Francisco, IEEE Computer Society Press, 1987, pp. 64–70.
2. Berntsen, Janet A., James R. Davin, Daniel A. Pitt, and Neil G. Sullivan. "MAC Layer Interconnection of IEEE 802 Local Area Networks." *Computer Networks and ISDN Systems: The International Journal of Computer and Telecommunications Networking,* 10 (1985) 5, pp. 259–273.
3. Hawe, Bill and George Varghese. "Extended Local Area Network Management Principles." IEEE 802 LAN Standards Committee Meeting, October, 1984.
4. Stallings, William. "Beyond Local Networks." *Datamation,* August, 1983, pp. 167–176.
5. Grim, Daniel J. "Description of the EE/CIS Computer Laboratory." Inter-Departmental Memorandum, University of Delaware, December, 1984.
6. University of Delaware. "From the Director." *Computer News,* 13 (1986) 8.
7. Cotton, Charles J. and N. Michael Minnich. "A Local Area Network Based Computing Laboratory at the University of Delaware: Development and Impact on Campus Area Computing." *Proceedings: CompCon Fall 83,* Washington, D.C.: IEEE Computer Society Press, 1983.
8. Digital Equipment Corporation. "Digital's LAN Bridge 100 Extends Network and Improves Network Performance." Edu, no. 40, pp. 38–39, Winter, 1986.
9. Hawe, Bill, Allen Kirby, and Bob Stewart. "Transparent Interconnection of Local Area Networks with Bridge." *Journal of Telecommunication Networks,* 3(1984)2, Summer.
10. Postel, Jonathan, Carl Sunshine, and Dan Cohen. "The ARPA Internet Protocol." *Internet Protocol Implementation Guide.* SRI International, Menlo Park, California, Network Information Center, 1982.
11. *Tutorial: Local Network Technology.* Stallings, William (ed.), IEEE Computer Society Press, 1985.
12. Wainwright, Paul F. "Internetworking and Addressing for Local Networks." *IEEE Project 802 Local Network Standards, Draft C,* 1982, pp. D1–D14.
13. Tanenbaum, Andrew S. *Computer Networks,* Englewood Cliffs, New Jersey: Prentice-Hall, 1981.
14. "The Ethernet, A Local Area Network: Data Link Layer and Physical Layer Specifications, Version 2.0." Stamford, Connecticut, Xerox Corporation.
15. *Unibus Ethernet Controller Reference Manual,* Mountain View, California, 3Com Corporation, 1982.
16. Tellabs, Inc. *Tellabs Technical Manual: 330 Dataplexer,* Lisle, Illinois: Tellabs, Inc., 1982.

SECURITY, PRIVACY AND LAW

GEORGE B. TRUBOW
John Marshall Law School
Chicago, Illinois
and
JOSEPH E. COLLINS
Data Processing Management Association
Park Ridge, Illinois

The growth of technology has increased at a rapid rate in recent years. Undoubtedly, advancements in technology will continue to increase and change society as the United States moves into the Information Age. As with other areas, high technology has shed its effects on society before policymakers could come to grips with its societal implications.

Is the Nation able to move into the Information Age and retain its beliefs in the principles of the U.S. Constitution? The opening session focuses on the increasing capability to disseminate information rapidly and efficiently and its impact on an individual's right to privacy. The intent and accomplishments of the Privacy Act of 1974 along with current developments in the area of information privacy are assessed, and the argument that information privacy is eroding as a result of new technologies is addressed.

Is the Nation able to protect its citizens and businesses from new types of crimes derived from advancements in technology? Another area where the law has not kept up with the technology is in the Nation's criminal codes. Three sessions in the Security, Privacy and Law track will address computer crime legislation, law enforcement and prosecution, and corporate security measures.

The U.S. Congress recently adopted the Computer Fraud and Abuse Act of 1986. Most states have passed computer crime legislation. However, the laws vary in their ability to effectively prosecute those involved in computer crime. Federal and state laws regarding computer crime are reviewed to identify what constitutes a computer crime.

Security measures adopted by corporations have proved to be the best way to defend against computer crime. Security specialists explain how an organization can address the task of developing or assessing a program to protect computers and information systems.

If a breach of security or a computer crime is suspected, what procedures should be implemented to investigate the matter and make a case? How should the matter be disposed of? Law enforcement agencies have only recently addressed the need for specialists in tracking down computer criminals. Experts in computer crime investigations describe the investigating team that should be assembled, the relationship between governmental and private police work, the rights of suspects, the identification of evidence, and prosecution policies.

Software transactions and contracting for services has raised questions not easily identifiable in current law. One session focuses on the relationship between vendors and users—their respective needs and obligations to each other. The session will explore the legal and practical aspects of contracting for computer goods or services. Discussion covers protection and use of software, liability for delivery or systems failures, financing and payment, and tax implications.

Is the Nation capable of maintaining its leadership position in the world economy? Can the workforce be prepared for new job requirements as the Nation moves from a manufacturing-oriented economy to a service-oriented economy? Two sessions in the track address the overall issues revolving around high technology and public policy.

One session discusses options for the development and implementation of a national information policy. Questions raised involve the relationship among Federal, state and local governments in policy development; appropriate government mechanisms for policy oversight; and the extent to which the private sector should be free from information regulation.

The final session explores the role, if any, of Federal and state governments in encouraging the economic development of computer technology and research. The international implications of market share and protection, technology transfer, intellectual property protection, investment tax benefits, and antitrust implications are also discussed.

The Information Age and the growth of technology affect every segment of society. The Security, Privacy and Law track provides a better idea of the issues and concerns that impact all of us.

Development and management of a national information policy

by JOHN CLEMENT
American Federation of Information Processing Systems
Reston, Virginia

Policymakers in the information field have been hollering for concerted action for years. "We need an information policy!"—you could quote leaders in bunches on that one, from the executive and legislative branches, or from university and corporate settings. In truth, everyone would admit that we *have* an information policy or, more accurately, many information policies. What we don't appear to have is agreement on a single set of guiding principles, or even on a common pragmatic approach. This is not more than one might expect from our polyfacetic system, in dealing with an area with such rapid technological change.

Not having a consensus on policy, a preliminary step is to set up some process for arriving at a consensus.

The Information Age Commission bill—sponsored by Senators Sam Nunn (D-GA) and Frank Lautenberg (R-NJ)—was introduced in early 1985. It is not a new bill, nor is the Commission it creates a new idea. The idea of a national discussion of the changes wrought in our society stems from a call for a "Temporary National Information Committee"; akin to the Depression-era Temporary National Economic Committee. Its authors began expressing their concern in the late 1960's.

How broadly should the mandate of such a Commission range? Prior proposals for a government information function have, I believe, gone in three policy directions:

1. Aimed, alone or predominantly, at international issues.
2. Aimed at one or more narrow policy areas, such as dissemination of scientific and technical information.
3. Spanning the entire range of information policy issues.

The prospect of a very broad mandate raises fears of massive government regulation among some stakeholders; and yet the interrelatedness of information policy issues makes delimiting the mandate of such a group a difficult and perhaps self-defeating task.

And what should such a Commission do? Conduct or contract research, commission papers, conduct hearings and produce hearing transcripts, issue reports? And, if so, to whom should these materials be directed? The bills that just died in Congress leave many of these issues open. Rather than debate these questions here, I will just stipulate that there are a number of groups that already conduct competent information policy research, and that the usual run of reports will generate the same enthusiasm and political action that the reports of other recent Commissions have—little or none.

If we need a Commission on the Information Age—and I'll add my voice to the chorus and say we do indeed—it should do something different than the usual such group.

What we need is to create a process by which we can reach a consensus. We don't have to get to a consensus in order to derive benefits from working at it; the process itself clarifies viewpoints, acquaints people with the insights of others, and gets the uninvolved interested. All of these are important things to have happen.

Everyone who has ever wanted to kick their bank's automatic teller machine, everyone who has their paycheck directly deposited or their house payments directly withdrawn from their bank account, everyone who spends hours at work or at home or in a college in front of a CRT screen and a keyboard—everyone who pays taxes, in fact, since their information can be used in computer-based matches for research, for determination of benefits, for evidence of fraud—is affected by new technology. All of these people are participating in a revolution, and they probably don't know it. They might have something to say about it if they were made aware.

We need to create a consensus-reaching process. A Commission could do that, if it viewed its mandate as promoting dialogue—as synthesis, summary, and communication. A Commission should not necessarily do research, but might identify issues and opportunities. A Commission could hold hearings and entertain viewpoints from scientists, corporate heads, technicians, and the public at large. A Commission, finally, could report in different ways and at different technical levels to policymakers, to professionals, to the corporate world, and to the public at large.

Corporate computer crime and abuse policy statement

by RICHARD CASHION
Tennessee Technological University
Cookeville, Tennessee

SURVEY

In the Spring of 1986 the Data Processing Management Association (DPMA) conducted a survey of its members and a random selection of corporate CEO's to determine the general attitude toward a Corporate Computer Crime and Abuse Policy Statement. DPMA conducted this survey as a starting point in developing a model policy statement.

181 surveys were returned. Of those responding only 27 percent of the organizations have a published policy statement; 10 percent were working on one. At the same time, only 5 percent of the responses indicated that a policy statement was not needed.

WHY HAVE A POLICY STATEMENT?

DPMA feels that it is important for each organization to have a published Computer Crime and Abuse Policy Statement. Without a published statement, certain computer crimes will go unpunished even when the culprit is caught. Most computer crime legislation uses the term "unauthorized" in every area to describe the criminal act. The organization must take steps to ensure that everyone in the organization is aware of his/her authorization and responsibilities in respect to computerized information and the computer itself. If it does not, the only legal remedy that the organization may have is to fire the individual involved.

WHO SHOULD DEVELOP THE POLICY STATEMENT?

It is clear that the policy statement should be endorsed by top management. However, it may not be as clear that top management must be involved in its development with guidance from the MIS, legal, and security staff. Top management must realize the full impact of the change in our resource base.

America is moving from an industrially-based to an information-based society. Information has become a valuable resource in the same way that people, building, equipment, and money are considered valuable resources. It is becoming increasingly clear that the success of any institution is more and more dependent on its ability to create, store, retrieve, transfer, and protect vast amounts of information.

WHAT SHOULD BE IN THE POLICY STATEMENT?

The goal of the policy is to make a short concise statement about the organization's views of computer crime and abuse. The statement should not spell out the detail procedures. There should be several levels of detail in the overall policies and procedures for computer crime and abuse.

Some large organizations start with a "policy statement" of one or two pages. Then the policy statement is broken down into "standards." The standards expand on the policy and provide more detail for the development of the "minimum requirements statement." The minimum requirements statement defines the minimum general procedures that must be followed to conform to the policy. The next level is the actual "procedure manuals." This many levels are needed in a very large multi-division organization. In most organizations only two levels are needed.

The one or two page policy statement is the focal point of the entire operation and must lay a foundation for the procedures.

Access control—the key to information security in a remote user system

by BRUCE E. SPIRO
Advanced Information Management Inc.
Woodbridge, Virginia

We are moving to remote user systems with alarming speed and often with little thought for security. Market forces and operational necessity are the driving factors that make this movement necessary. We cannot obstruct this movement with overzealous protestations. On the other hand, we must not overlook the essential need for security in this expanding environment. The proper people must have relatively easy and convenient access to the data and processing support to which they are authorized—and only to that which is authorized.

Effective access control is not a simple matter of installing IDs and passwords, and trusting that things will work out. We start with a security analysis of the communications network to determine where there are weak points and what controls can be applied that decrease the likelihood that an unauthorized individual can use the communication capability of the system.

We then proceed inward, looking at each level of the system to determine what protection is required and what controls are available. When a series of processors are coupled together, each will have different requirements based on the criticality and sensitivity of the data and programs contained. Each will have different protective capabilities based on the specific operating system and security features installed. The objective is to ensure separation and control of datasets and programs so that there is no opportunity to crossover from an authorized process to one that is not authorized.

The integrity of the operating system is critical. What is possible may not be what is there. A close review by qualified people is essential. Often techniques to bypass security features are installed to make work a bit easier for test and development effort. Sometimes these bypasses remain in a production system and create openings that destroy the protective barriers that have been built.

Finally, the entire security process must be reviewed to ensure that it is consistent across the board. All too often we see technically accurate and well thoughtout security systems that in reality provide no protection at all because there is no administrative procedures to manage passwords or something else as seemingly innocuous.

Effective security is the combination of network control, system integrity, identification, protection, and procedures brought together in a consistent access control package. Weakness in any area may mean that you have no security at all.

SYSTEMS SOFTWARE AND LANGUAGES

CARL K. CHANG
University of Illinois at Chicago
Chicago, Illinois
and
CONRAD WEISERT
Information Disciplines
Chicago, Illinois
and
SANDRA TAYLOR
Britton Lee, Inc.
Los Gatos, California

Systems software and languages encompass the tools used to build, maintain, and operate application systems. While many of these tools are implemented in software, others are based on concepts and techniques (i.e., methodology). Recent explosive growth in the number and variety of vigorously acclaimed software and methodology components is generating uncertainty and controversy over their value to a user organization, their impact on development organizations, and their relationship to one another.

Among the specific topics in this area are:

Computer languages, including specification languages, very-high level languages, database query languages, and distributed languages.

Methodologies and tools for design and coding, including structured programming, libraries of reusable code, in-house standards, design reviews, workbench facilities, and design methods for distributed software systems.

Data management tools, including data modeling, design, and analysis methods, entity-relationship approaches, relational technology, data dictionary and directory systems, information retrieval systems, and techniques of data administration.

Tools for systems analysis, including structured analysis concepts, structured documentation software, prototyping, generalized transaction processors, and methods for choosing packaged application software.

Project management tools, including standardized life cycles, project planning techniques, project control techniques, project management software, productivity measurement methods, software maintenance strategies and tools, and quality assurance programs.

Operational tools, including operating systems, storage management methods, sorting and searching techniques, resource scheduling algorithms, resource accounting methods, system performance measurement facilities, and teleprocessing monitors.

Support structures, including methodology development, training, methodology integration, and revised role and skill definitions.

Software workbenches: The new software development environment

by CARMA L. McCLURE
Extended Intelligence, Inc.
Chicago, Illinois

ABSTRACT

Software workbenches provide computerized assistance for the development, maintenance, and management of software systems. They differ from earlier programming environments in their breadth of coverage of the software life cycle. They are general-purpose software development environments with powerful tools for specification, design, implementation, testing, and documentation. A complete software workbench must have these characteristics:

1. A graphics interface for drawing structured diagrams
2. A central information repository for storing and managing all software system information
3. A highly integrated toolset sharing a common user interface
4. Tools to assist every phase of the life cycle
5. Prototyping tools
6. Automatic code generation from design specifications
7. Support of structured methodologies

INTRODUCTION

As new advances in hardware and software technologies have occurred, the software development environment has changed from a standalone mode in the 1950s and early 1960s to a batch mode in the late 1960s and early 1970s, and then to a timesharing mode in the late 1970s and early 1980s.[1] In the late 1980s, a new mode based on personal workstations is becoming the preferred environment for developing software. Workstations have potentially far reaching implications for changing and improving software development. The introduction of powerful workstation tools and accompanying engineering-like structured methodologies transforms and automates the software development process.

A workstation is a complete environment including hardware and software. Its function is to provide computerized assistance for the production, maintenance, and project management of software systems. It is a personal machine dedicated to providing the maximum possible support for the individual software developer.

An extensive set of intelligent, integrated software tools called the *workbench* makes up the "soft part" of the workstation environment. Workbenches are tailorable to each developer's preferences and to specialized tasks such as project management, design, and maintenance; and replace traditional tools that are bound to batch processing and third generation languages of the 1960s and 1970s.

Workbenches differ from early programming environments such as UNIX and Interlisp in their breadth of coverage of the software life cycle. UNIX is a timeshared operating system in which a uniform file format is the primary means of integrating a rich array of programming tools.[2] UNIX is a general-purpose programming environment in that it does not support a particular programming language or software development methodology. Interlisp, on the other hand, is a programming environment that supports only the programming language LISP. This gives Interlisp the advantage of tailoring and optimizing its tools for a single programming language.[3] All Interlisp tools are written in LISP and provide tightly integrated operating systems, utility functions, editors, and debuggers.

Whereas such programming environments as UNIX and Interlisp have concentrated on tools for the coding and implementation phases, software workbenches provide powerful tools for specification, design, implementation, testing, and documentation. Workbenches are general-purpose software development environments attempting to support the full range of the software job as well as its management.

To meet its objectives of enhancing productivity and simplifying the process of software development, the software development workbench cannot simply consist of a collection of even the best tools of the 1970s and 1980s. These tools were not designed to be used in a dedicated, personal computing environment allowing customization for individual workstation owners. They were not designed to use powerful graphics capabilities to enhance the human interface. They were not designed to be used in cooperation with one another, linking together all aspects of the development process. They were not designed to capture information about an ongoing development process and evolution of a software product. Further, they were not designed as intelligent tools capable of performing many development tasks on their own.

For these reasons, a workbench providing a complete software development environment must have at least the following characteristics:

- Graphics capability
- Central information repository
- Tightly integrated tool set
- Full life cycle coverage
- Prototyping support
- Automatic code generation
- Development methodology support

GRAPHICS

When viewing a software development workstation, one is first impressed by the graphics. The ease with which objects can be made to appear, disappear, and move around the graphics screen with a mere click of a mouse button is amazing. More important, however, the better the graphics, the more productive the user interface can be.

Most people prefer pictures over words because the human mind is pictorially oriented. Narrative text is one-dimensional, but pictures are multi-dimensional, borrowing such properties as size, shape, and color from the physical world. Because the language of pictures is richer than the language of text, more information can be represented in pictures than in text, and people can grasp their meanings more quickly.[4]

Graphical representations (or diagrams) have always played an important role in software development. Diagrams are used to define program specifications and to represent program designs. They provide the blueprint for implementing a design into code, and are an important form of software documentation.

Diagrams are really the language of software modeling because they offer a concise, unambiguous way of describing software. They are so fundamental to software analysis and design that different structured methodologies can be characterized in terms of the diagramming techniques they use to model a software system.

Diagramming techniques have evolved along with programming methodologies. In the 1950s and 1960s, flowcharts were used to plan out detailed and complicated program logic. Flowcharts fell out of favor because they can give neither a high-level nor a structured view of a program. In the 1970s, structured techniques became widespread, and structured diagramming techniques such as data flow diagrams and structure charts were introduced along with them.

Although many different structured diagramming techniques are in use, an essential trio of diagramming types is needed for representing a software system:[5]

1. *Data flow diagram*—a friendly and familiar diagram used during analysis to define the problem components and to sketch a first, rough cut of program components and the data that pass among them (see Figure 1).
2. *Data model diagram*—a diagram used during the data modeling processing to represent the data items and the logical associations among them.
3. *Tree structure diagram*—a hierarchical diagram created during program design to define the overall architecture of a program by showing the program modules and their relationship to one another.

Minimally, a software development workbench should provide the capability of automatically drawing and updating each of the three types of diagrams. Other types of diagrams such as decision trees, finite state diagrams, and data navigation diagrams also are useful for modeling software systems.

Beyond Automatic Drafting

Although important in increasing productivity, a graphics capability must go beyond automatic drawing functions.

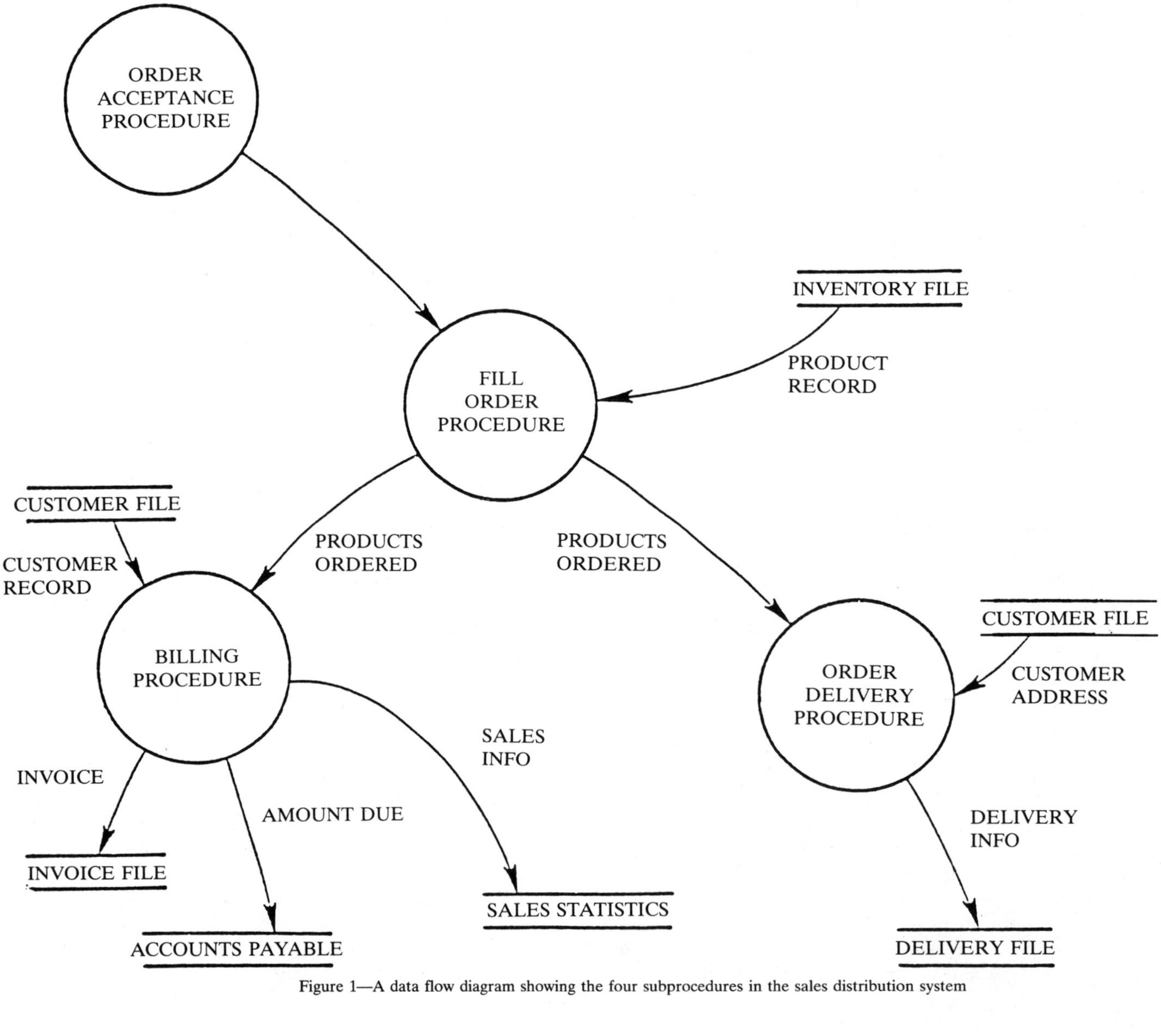

Figure 1—A data flow diagram showing the four subprocedures in the sales distribution system

There must be an underlying logical meaning associated with the graphics. This is important for several reasons.

First, when there is a meaning associated with the graphics, the correctness and completeness of the diagrams can be checked more thoroughly. Some examples are included in the Error Checking section. Second, when the meaning of the graphics symbols is captured, the same information can be represented in different but equivalent forms. For example, a data flow diagram can be automatically converted into a tree structure diagram (e.g., a structure chart) after the root is identified. Or, a tree structure diagram can be automatically converted to an action diagram.[6] In both cases, it is the same information; only the form in which the information is represented has been changed. Thus, a workbench can accommodate the preferences of different developers and can conform to the diagramming standards of different organizations. Third, when the meaning of the symbols is stored, information necessary for automatically generating code from the diagram is captured.

Also, the logical meaning of the diagram must be stored when a diagram is drawn. Most workbench tools store the diagram or its logical meaning in some sort of dictionary or other kind of repository. This is essential to providing the capability of quickly changing and redrawing a diagram as well as automatically changing all of the affected associated diagrams. We know from past experience that this is a tedious, almost impossible task when done manually. The storage capability of a workbench is discussed further in the Central Information Repository section.

Finally, error checking of the diagrams must be automatically performed.

ERROR CHECKING

Error checking is one of the most important capabilities of workbenches. There are four basic types of error checking for diagrams.

The first type of checking is for syntax and type errors. As an example, consider the data flow diagram in Figure 1. One syntax rule for a data flow diagram is that each process bubble must have at least one data flow entering it and at least one data flow leaving it. Notice that ORDER ACCEPTANCE PROCEDURE is incorrect because there is no data flow arrow entering it.

The second type of checking is completeness and consistency checking for a diagram. Again consider the data flow diagram in Figure 1. In a completed data flow diagram, all the data flow arrows between processes are labeled with the data that is passed between the processes. Notice that in Figure 1 the data flow arrow between ORDER ACCEPTANCE PROCEDURE and FILL ORDER PROCEDURE is not labeled. A completeness check should identify this kind of missing information.

The first two types of error checking are concerned with errors in one diagram. Checking one diagram is the simplest type of error checking and the minimum expected from a software development workbench. The third type of error checking is concerned with not just one diagram but with a family of diagrams. One example of a family of diagrams is a set of leveled or layered data flow diagrams in which successive levels describe processes in increasing detail. Figure 1 identifies the ORDER ACCEPTANCE PROCEDURE and Figure 2 shows in detail what happens inside the ORDER ACCEPTANCE PROCEDURE. Consistency checking across a family of diagrams checks whether information is consistent from level to level.

Notice that the data flow diagrams in Figures 1 and 2 are not consistent because they do not show the same number of data flows going into and out of the ORDER ACCEPTANCE PROCEDURE.

The fourth type of error checking is concerned with tree structure diagrams in which functions or procedures are decomposed into more detailed subfunctions as one proceeds "down" the tree. Some structured methodologies provide guidelines for decomposing functions. For example, no function should be decomposed into itself. Workbenches should incorporate these types of refinement rules into their error checking.

CENTRAL INFORMATION REPOSITORY

Although not as visually impressive as the graphics capabilities, the central information repository is the heart of a workbench. It is the basis for integration, standardization, documentation, code generation, and reusability. No other workbench characteristic is more important.

A central information repository is a mechanism for storing and organizing all components of a software system including data structures, architectural design, process logic, screen definitions, report layouts, system diagrams, source code, test data cases, project management forms, schedules, and user documentation. A key to high productivity is getting information to developers when it is needed and in a form that is directly usable.

In some workbenches, a dictionary serves as the central information repository. However, a mere dictionary mechanism is inadequate because it does not provide information management. In other workbenches a more sophisticated mechanism called an *encyclopedia* is the central information repository. An encyclopedia is more than a dictionary because it coordinates and analyzes information as well as stores it. An encyclopedia is more than a database and an accompanying management system because it is a knowledge base containing facts and rules about checking the completeness and consistency of the data stored.[7] Whereas a database and a dictionary are passive tools in which control lies with a user, the encyclopedia is an intelligent tool that can provide multiple views of information and can choose which information is to be shared. It performs a more active role in control to maintain data consistency and integrity.

INTEGRATION

Specification languages, diagramming tools, prototyping tools, dictionaries, database management systems, compilers, various types of generators, and so on are the high productiv-

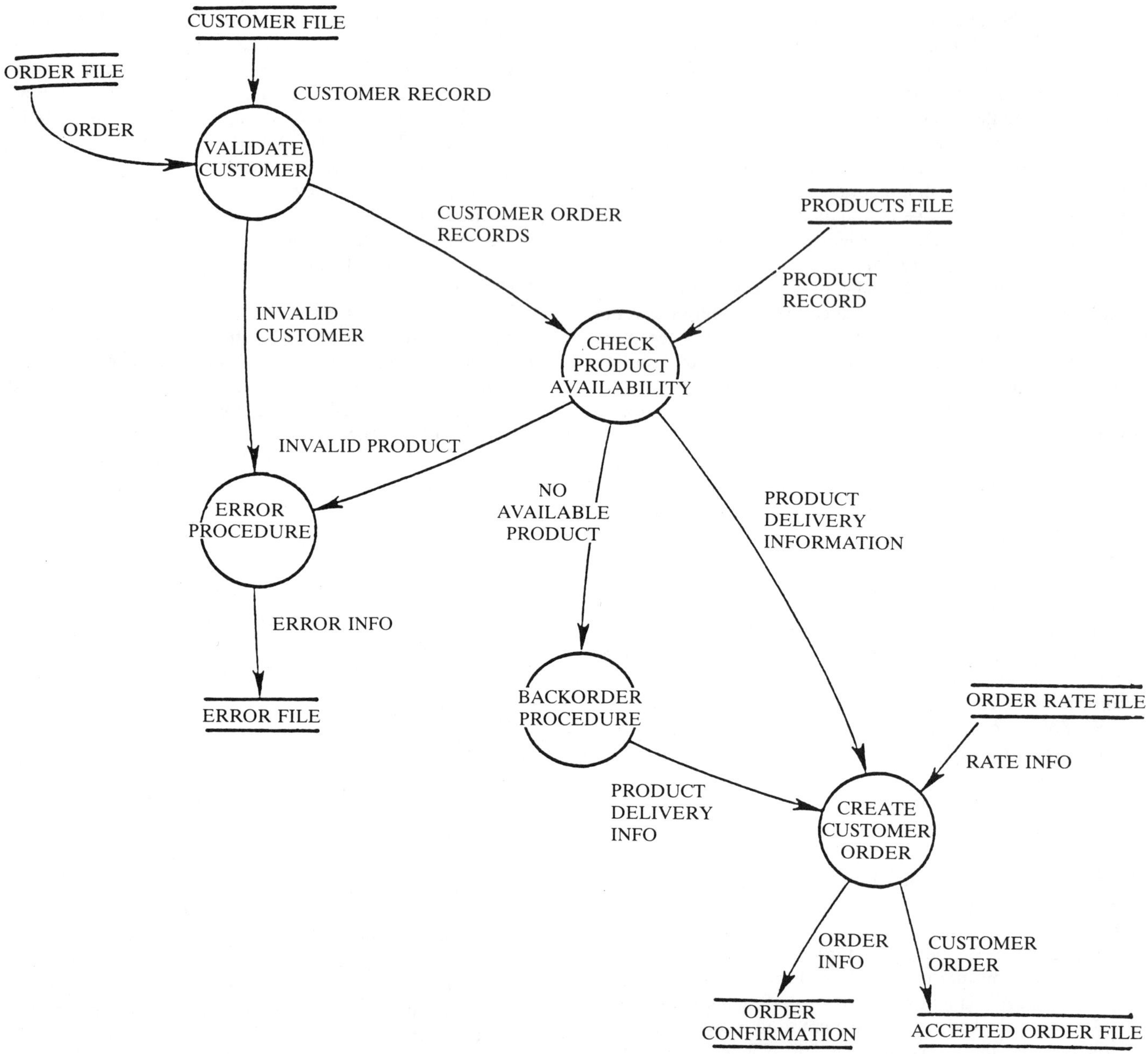

Figure 2—A data flow diagram for the order acceptance procedure

ity tools of the early 1980s. However, a major obstacle to their ease of use is their tendency to be standalone tools capable of supporting only part of the software process. Usually they do not have standard interfaces to one another; and they are highly dependent upon a particular computer, operating system, and programming language. As a result, software developers must learn to use a different set of tools for each environment in which they work. Even within a single environment, developers cannot apply their knowledge of one tool to another because each tool has its own command format, specialized file structure, and range of available options.

In spite of their power, many potentially powerful tools have failed to substantially improve software productivity and quality because they do not provide integrated, continuous support to software developers in day-to-day work.[8]

Tools integration lies at the very foundation of the software development workbench concept. It is the key to making powerful software tools practical to use. Workbench tools should interact with each other in a consistent, intuitive way and should conform to a set of well-understood standards. They should appear to a user to be cooperating with each other and aware enough of each other not to duplicate functions or messages.

There are five levels of integration. The first level, common user interface, is the minimum expected in a software development workbench. It reduces the learning curve associated with the workbench since experience acquired using one part of the workbench can then be applied to learning other parts. A common user interface is the bridge connecting various workbench tools. When third party tools are added, individual tool differences are covered under the umbrella of a common menu system.

The second level of integration, transferability of data between tools, is another kind of bridge connecting workbench tools. When necessary, conversion routines and file transfer routines are supplied to automatically convert data into an appropriate input format for a particular tool or software package. In a smoothly running workbench, it is easy for a user to pass data from tool to tool. It is expected that the output of each tool will become the input to another.[9]

The first two levels of integration are concerned with integrating across tools—a way of linking tools together for ease of use and ease of learning. The third level of integration is concerned with linking the phases of the software life cycle—integrating across the process of developing and maintaining software systems. In this case, the bridge between the various life cycle phases is one common representation of the system (but which allows multiple user perspectives or views), stored in a central information repository and shared among project teammates. This level of integration unites teammates, users, and management and reduces communication problems by providing one easily updated source for all information about a system.

The last two levels of integration are concerned with integrating across hardware environments—linking mainframe and micro levels, and in some cases a "middle" minicomputer level as well. The objective is to be able to perform development activities in whichever environment is most expedient. This is possible only if text, code, data, and graphics can be transferred easily between software packages and between hardware environments. In addition, some workbenches offer integration across functions—graphics, word processing, data processing, and office automation—by providing all these functions at the workstation level.

LEVEL CYCLE COVERAGE

Workbenches for general-purpose software development environments provide tools for automating the entire software life cycle with a concentration on the early life cycle phases. This front-end emphasis, or "front-end loading," of the life cycle comes from recognizing analysis and design as the most critical life cycle phases.

Specification errors can be very expensive if they are not detected and corrected in the early phases. Correcting a specification error during the maintenance phase may be 100 times more expensive than if it is corrected during the analysis phase.[10] The completeness and correctness of the system specification affect the success of the entire software development effort. Poorly understood system requirements cause software failures. The specification is the basis for project schedules and assignments, test plans, user documentation, and program design.

Design errors often dominate software projects because of their number and the cost to correct them, especially when they are not detected early. In large projects, design errors often exceed coding errors.[11]

More care given to design means lower-cost and more reliable systems. A system design is the blueprint for system implementation. If the blueprint does not exist or is incorrect, the system produced is probably poorly organized, poorly documented, and a nightmare to maintain.

PROTOTYPING

Prototyping tools play an important part in automating the early software life cycle phases. They are used to determine system requirements and answer questions about the behavior of the emerging system.

Screen generators, report generators, and menu builders are used mainly to prototype the user interface as a quick, friendly way of clarifying user requirements. The prototype provides users with a concrete model of how the system will look from the users' perspective. This is an effective method for identifying and correcting misunderstandings about user expectations for the system.

Fourth generation languages can be used to develop a more complete model of a system. In such cases, the prototype includes the major functions of the system but does not check for exceptions or invalid input data and does not worry about execution performance. The purpose is to give a user experience with the system by using a fairly complete model. Sometimes the model is found to be adequate enough to serve as the actual system.

Executable specification languages are the most sophisticated prototyping tools. They change system development into an iterative process whereby the system is specified and the specifications are executed to determine if the system is complete and correct. Then, based on the experience of this prototype version, the specifications are refined and re-executed. The iterative process continues until the system is able to perform in a manner that meets all user requirements.

DEVELOPMENT METHODOLOGY SUPPORT

The software development workbench concept supports structured techniques by providing tools to automate the techniques. There are two levels to automation:

1. Automate documentation preparation
2. Automate the steps of a structured methodology.

Automating documentation preparation means providing graphics support for drawing structured diagrams such as data flow diagrams, entity relationship diagrams, state transition diagrams, and action diagrams. It also means automating the production of textual specifications such as mini-specs and pseudocode. The textual specifications are used to provide more detailed information about program procedures and data structures referenced in higher-level structured diagrams.

Since different structured techniques use different diagrams to model a software system, the types of structured techniques supported by a particular workbench will be determined by the types of structured diagrams and the notation conventions that it offers. For example, the Yourdon Structured Design Methodology uses a structure chart derived from a data flow diagram to represent a program design; the Jackson Design Methodology uses tree structured diagrams; and the Warnier-Orr Design Methodology uses Warnier-Orr diagrams. One approach for standardizing program documentation is to restrict the diagrams and the notation conventions offered in the workbench.

The second level of methodology support, automating the process steps, means the workbench guides a user in correct use of a structured methodology. This requires that at least some level of understanding of the methodology is embedded in the tools. This could be as simple as embedded help panels that describe each step in the methodology or checklists that include the input required by and the output produced by each step. It also might include a checking mechanism to ensure that each output deliverable required by the methodology is present, correct, and complete before a user is allowed to go to the next step. In this case, a user is not simply guided through the methodology; rather, the user is forced to perform the steps in a standardized order and way. The purpose is to standardize and systematize the process of developing software.

There are two schools of thought on whether a development methodology should be embedded into the workbench. The argument for separating the methodology from the tools is that such separateness gives users flexibility in choosing the methodology or the part of a methodology that is appropriate for developing a particular system. The argument for embedding the methodology into the workbench tools is that it introduces control over the development process.

KEY WORKBENCH CONCEPTS

In summary, software development workstations differ from other powerful high-productivity tools because workstations:

1. Provide a highly interactive, responsive, and dedicated environment in which to develop software
2. Automate many software development tasks
3. Provide a pictorial view of software by means of powerful graphics
4. Enable rapid prototyping for creating models of the system to help discover and clarify user requirements
5. Collect the information necessary for automatic code generation from system analysis and design
6. Perform automatic checking to get the errors out early

These concepts enable workstations to dramatically change and improve programmer productivity.

REFERENCES

1. Gutz, S., Wasserman, A., and Spier, M. "Personal Development Systems for the Professional Programmer." *Computer,* 14 (1981) 4, pp. 45–53.
2. Kernighan, B. and Mashey, J. "The UNIX Programming Environment." *Computer,* 14 (1981) 4, pp. 12–24.
3. Teitelman, W. and Masinter, L. "The Interlisp Programming Environment." *Computer,* 14 (1981) 4, pp. 25–34.
4. Raeder, G. "A Survey of Current Graphical Programming Techniques." *Computer,* 18 (1985) 8, pp. 11–25.
5. Martin, James and McClure, Carma. *Diagramming Techniques for Analysts and Programmers.* Prentice-Hall, 1985, pp. 1–22.
6. Martin, James and McClure, Carma. *Action Diagrams.* Prentice-Hall, 1985.
7. Martin, James. "Information Engineering." *Savant Technical Report,* Savant Institute, England, 1986.
8. Osterweil, L. "Software Environment Research: Directions for the Next Five Years." *Computer,* 14 (1981) 4, pp. 35–44.
9. Osterweil, L. "Software Environment Research: Directions for the Next Five Years." *Computer,* 14 (1981) 4, pp. 35–44.
10. Haase, V. and Koch, G. "Developing the Connection Between User and Code." *Computer,* 15 (1982) 5, pp. 10–11.
11. Boehm, B., McClearn, R., and Unfrig, D. "Some Experiences with Automated Aids to the Design of Large-Scale Reliable Software." *IEEE Transactions on Software Engineering,* 1 (1975) 1, pp. 125–133.

It's not the technical problems . . .

by DONALD M. McNAMARA
General Electric
Bridgeport, Connecticut

ABSTRACT

The important issues concerning operating environments are not technical issues. They are managerial, business, marketing, integration, and application issues that are shaped primarily by the changes in how we develop and implement software systems. Fortunately, hardware, software, and communications technology will keep advancing to meet these development needs. The big problem is for vendors to package and deliver the operating environment technology in a way that business, academia, and government, can use it. The other problem is for those of us who are users to exploit it to the fullest.

INTRODUCTION

My perspective at General Electric (GE) is that of a Software Development Program Manager. My job is to understand and direct trends in the use of software developent methods, tools, and management approaches throughout GE. As a member of the Corporate Information Technology Staff and as a Software Engineer, I help GE's (very) independent businesses exploit the best computer hardware, software, and communications to develop GE's products and support systems.

With over 15,000 software developers at GE, even a five percent improvement in productivity means millions of dollars on the bottom line. For that reason, my perspective is also that of a businessperson. I see dramatically increasing demands for software and systems in every part of GE, as well as in many other United States businesses. Yet, neither GE nor most other United States businesses are going to be able to increase the number of software developers in proportion to the increase in demands. Developers of software systems simply must start using new approaches that increase productivity by orders of magnitude. Fortunately, new software tools, more disciplined methodologies, and new management approaches that can make dramatic improvements in productivity, are available and are being adopted.

So, what do these software development trends have to do with operating environments? The answer is: everything! The approaches we use to develop and implement software are changing so fast (thank goodness) that they are the major forces in shaping new needs for operating environments. In addition, these forces are too strong for anyone to change.

Fortunately, hardware, software, and communications technology will keep advancing to meet these development needs. If there's a market, technology can meet its requirements. In most cases, the technology already exists. I am not worried about it. Where it needs to advance, it will advance quickly. The big problem is for vendors to package and deliver the operating environment technology in a way that business, academia, and government, can use it. The other problem is for those of us who are users to exploit it to the fullest.

My position is that the really important issues concerning operating environments are not technical issues. They are managerial, business, marketing, integration, and application issues that are shaped primarily by the changes in how we develop and implement software systems. The key issue is that both vendors and users need to focus on the forces of change in software development in order to understand how to deliver and use operating environment technology.

The forces of change are rapid expansion of end user computing, development using individual PC workstations, and information resource development for distributed processing.

Rapid Expansion of End User Computing

End user computing, that is systems development and implementation by non-professional system developers, is the information systems success story of the 1980's. In many of GE's businesses and in other United States businesses, end users far outnumber professional system developers. End users use non-procedural Fourth Generation Languages to develop and implement rudimentary systems. Many end users use personal computers while others work solely on mainframes. A growing percentage work on both.

GE now has 26 information centers. They are staffed by three to ten information systems professionals especially assigned to support and promote end user computing. As end users become more experienced, they expand their horizons and frequently install local area networks so they can share data and programs. They quickly outgrow stand-alone applications and want ready access to corporate databases and external databases.

Most of these end users do not know the meaning of the words "boot," "crash," "operating system," or "data flow diagram." They do not want to design systems. They want to start implementing systems immediately and to easily change them later. Since they are the people who originate the system requirements, they do not need "treacability" between requirements, design, and code. They do not want to have to refer to user manuals. They want easy access to corporate data bases and outside databases that are administered by others. They definitely do not want the system to crash and do not know what to do if one does. They want complete fault tolerance. They want a seamless development, implementation, and operation environment in which the operation system is invisible and development can be accomplished using only screens, menus, screen pointers, and other non-procedural interfaces.

Development Using Individual PC Workstations

The hottest topic among software developers in GE these days concerns software development on Personal Computers (PCs). Managers want to use PCs to develop systems that will run on the mainframe. They want to offload as much mainframe development work as possible to take advantage of the significantly lower costs on the PC. They want to use the PC to develop systems for multiple types of mainframe computers. Developers of PC applications want to be able to have the functionality of mainframe tools available on PCs at PC software prices.

A big disadvantage of systems development on PCs is the difficulty of defining and accessing common data from multiple PCs. In addition, integration test and systems test of mainframe applications is almost impossible in most PC operating environments.

Developers want PC operating environments that provide all the comforts of a centralized mainframe at PC prices. Obviously developers want operating environments where linked PCs have common and concurrent access to databases under development. They want mainframe development tools that work on PCs to develop applications that can run on different target mainframes. They want operating environments that enable systems integration and test on the PCs as well as easy transfer to mainframes. They want to be able to change database structures in a transparent mode without effecting the applications in any way.

Information Resource Development for Distributed Processing

The third force of change is the realization by many organizations that data and information need to be developed and managed as a distinct and integrated resource separate from the processing systems that support and use them. Organizations encounter their Information Resource Management (IRM) problems as smaller subproblems such as data base integration needs or availability of distributed data for relational access by end users. They quickly realize, though, that they need solutions that encompass the entire enterprise. Often, the data and information is controlled by distributed organizations using a mix of incompatible communication and processing facilities.

IRM developers want enterprise-wide active data dictionaries and data repositories that can be used by developers operating in a distributed environment. They want an operating environment that handles the communication and control, making the data appear as if it resides locally. They want to be able to change the physical characteristics of the data without impacting the applications. In short, they want to be able to develop and manage information resources in a way that is transparent to developers and users.

SUMMARY

The operating environment characteristics that I have said we need are: invisibility, fault tolerance, non-procedural fourth generation interfaces, seamless interfaces between development and operation facilities, global information resource development and management, PC development for mainframes execution, application portability, and data independence.

All of these technological capabilities exist today in one system or another. The three forces of change are demanding that they be integrated under one operating environment for each major computer and software system vendor. As soon as vendors understand this and see the market potential, they will provide the capabilities. We as users must understand how to exploit the new capabilities. Since the technology already exists, it is almost certain that the major operating environments of the late 1980's will include them.

Evolution of operating environments for new communication service control

by SHUZO MORITA
Fujitsu Laboratories Ltd.
Kawasaki, Japan

Traditionally, software in the communication field, especially switching software, has followed a specific path different from that in the information processing field. Individual processings in switching software are simple, but in multiplicity, "real-timeness," and reliability, it has unparalleled features. Communication software itself, which manages a huge amount of communication resources spread over a global scale and assigns them on a real-time basis according to enormous amounts of service orders, constructs a large operating system.

However, telecommunication systems are now going to change significantly. With the advance of the information society, there is a large demand for new communication services using various communication media such as text, image, and video as well as voice. To respond to these demands, much effort has been devoted to evolving communication networks to digital and broad-band networks, and new communication networks such as Integrated Service Digital Network (ISDN) have just begun to be introduced. In the 1990s, multimedia information "pipelines" will be economically available for the general public as well as business users. On the other hand, even if these broad and efficient information pipelines are provided, they are only a treasure left unused if there are no mechanisms for efficiently controlling information streams in the pipeline. In parallel with the advance of physical capabilities of the network, the advance of operating environments for network and service control is necessary. The expectations for the advance of operating environments in communication systems are:

1. Enhancement of user programmability of communication services—the drastic allowance of users participation in service customization. Conventionally, communication services have been one-sidedly and uniformly provided by service providers such as common carriers and system vendors. However, considering diversification and personalization of future communication services, it is impossible to avoid feeling some limitation in the conventional mechanism of service provision. This is the time for us to introduce the idea of user programmability into the communication world by which users themselves can customize services to meet their own requirements.
2. Provision of communication services with much freedom, independence of time, place, and media—the basic subject of communication service control. Much effort has been devoted to achieving the subject so that everybody can freely communicate whenever, wherever, and using every media they want. However, a systematic approach is necessary now when new communication networks such as ISDN have just begun to be constructed. The concept of virtual network control which is realized in AT&T advanced 800 service, for example, points the way we should follow. Service control on virtual networks, which are independent of physical networks consisting of terminals, transmission lines, and so forth, makes it possible to realize communication services with much freedom without physical constraints.

To provide these new services, the operating environments of communication systems must be evolved. The basic point is to depart from the closed world of telecommunications to be in harmony with the information processing world. Communication software should not only be system software but provide higher level operating environments for supporting advanced communication services. To realize user programmable services, it is necessary to provide various utilities by which end users as well as some few specialists, who have been developing communication software as an operating system, can easily define their own services. Furthermore, in virtual network control, operating environments for complex processing using large amount of data are necessary. These basic features are similar to those of information processing, and commonality of various resources including man-power for the development of application packages will become more and more important. Thus, commonality with the operating environments of information processing resources is the basic direction of the evolution of the operating environments of communication software, but it should be done strictly considering specific features of communication software: ultra multiplicity, "real-timeness," and high reliability. RTR (Real Time Reliable) operating system of AT&T and HSOS (Hybrid Structured Operating System) of FUJITSU, which integrate UNIX and real-time operating systems, are examples of new operating environments meeting the above requirements. The operating system offering multi-environments for the control from real-time/ultra-multiprocessing to complex data processing will be the main stream of operating environments for future communication service control.

An overview of the Pick Operating System

by RICHARD PICK
Pick Systems
Irvine, California

INTRODUCTION

Information management is the heart of the Pick Operating System. This easily used, multi-user operating system with virtual memory has an English-like retrieval language in which a data base manager, an extremely efficient programming language, and system utilities are all integral. Because of this structure and capabilities, Pick is actually more than a traditional operating system, it is an integrated decision support system. In addition to its use as a management decision tool, the Pick system has proved to be exceptionally efficient for applications development. As a result, the Pick approach has won converts from both professional and non-professional data processing ranks for nearly two decades. This software architecture remains technically very different from other operating systems with data storage and accessing concepts that are truly unique.

THE PICK ARCHITECTURE: A SOFTWARE MACHINE

The term *architecture* applies to software written free from hardware constraints in a virtual assembly language, or pseudo code. In mainframe and mini-computer implementations, the Pick architecture is interfaced to hardware at the micro-instruction level and much execution is at the firmware micro-instruction level. With microprocessor-based machines, the system is in software. This micro-instruction layer includes terminal I/O operations and a virtual memory manager that treats core memory as a scratchpad and addresses the entire disc. With assembly language executing in this high-level software, the Pick system provides a remarkable degree of transportability which contributes to its reputation for being machine, or hardware, independent. Some of the major system components incorporated in the Pick system's architectural construct are:

- An advanced VIRTUAL MEMORY MANAGER
- A versatile SYSTEM MONITOR
- A unique FILE STRUCTURE
- An efficient DICTIONARY SYSTEM
- A sophisticated DATA BASE MANAGER
- An easily used INQUIRY LANGUAGE, (ACCESS*)
- An exceptionally powerful high-level PROGRAMMING language, (Pick/BASIC)
- An efficient STORED PROCEDURE LANGUAGE INTERPRETER, (PROC)
- A TEXT-PROCESSING PROGRAM with expanded capabilities, (EDITOR)
- A flexible, productivity-enhancing TERMINAL CONTROL LANGUAGE, (TCL)

In the Pick Operating System, all these major system components and several additional system utilities are integral parts. This is not the case with most traditional operating systems in which many of these features are technically add-ons. Although this may be transparent to the user, such add-on constructs are inefficient.

VIRTUAL MEMORY MANAGER

Embedded in the quick of the system, the virtual memory manager allows data and programs to move in and out of main memory as needed, dynamically. Disc is addressed as if it were an extension of main memory. It allows the active processes to use only the portion of a program, or data, needed at any particular instant. With the Pick system, users need not concern themselves with the memory requirements of programs, files, or reports. In effect, main memory is as large as the available disc space.

SYSTEM MONITOR

The Pick system is a video display, or CRT, terminal-oriented multi-user system designed for interactive use to facilitate decision making from a shared data base. The system monitor provides the vital interrupt-driven multi-user scheduling required. It ensures system users inter-active access to data resources and it allows simultaneous performance of such processes as program compilation, system utility functions, multiple application program construction, and data base back-up without conflict.

FILE STRUCTURE

The Pick file structure is unquestionably unique. It features data strings of variable length in a structure that is considered mathematically "three dimensional." Although this concept may be difficult to grasp at first, the system is much easier to use than traditional structures, and a Pick system user can easily process data in a very real world environment.

THE DICTIONARY SYSTEM

For speed and ease-of-use, the Pick software incorporates a hierarchy of special files called "dictionaries." They are "road maps" for retrieving data from the various files using the inquiry language, ACCESS. They provide the mnemonic names for the various attributes (fields), describe their contents, and reveal how information is to be displayed when printed.

FILE DICTIONARIES

The Pick dictionaries contain file and attribute definition statements that describe the structure of the data files with which they are associated. They describe, on an attribute-by-attribute basis, the type of data within each, the conversion specifications, relationships between attributes, and similar information. The file dictionary's definitions assist substantially in the information retrieval process and are used with the English-like ACCESS inquiry language processor.

DATA BASE MANAGEMENT AND THE ACCESS LANGUAGE

The business orientation of the Pick system is most evident in the interactive inquiry processor and the high-level inquiry language, ACCESS, associated with it. A data base has been described as an accessible collection of separate information values and Pick, a data base management system, was designed to manage varied operational data, or information, in a coherent way using one set of standards. The Pick Operating System was created specifically to manage information practically. It was purposely written in a pseudo code with logic free from the constraints of hardware and traditional programming approaches. Classified as a relational system by many, it actually includes desirable features from all three traditional structures and is, in fact, something entirely new—ideally suited to data base management. A special purpose inquiry language, ACCESS, provides a programming tool to enter the data base and generate reports with exceptional speed. In the hands of non-programmers it can be used to easily generate simple inquiries from a visual display terminal on an ad hoc basis, and programmers and trained personnel can use it to generate extremely complex reports, with relative ease.

PICK/BASIC

Pick/BASIC is a high-level, general purpose programming tool. When combined with the non-procedural ACCESS inquiry language and the flexible Pick data structure, it enables programmers to bring new applications on-line in a remarkably short time. A new language, Pick/BASIC, is specifically tailored for data base management in a multi-user environment. BASIC was chosen because of universal appeal. It is an easy-to-use, flexible programming language adaptable to quickly solving specific business application needs.

PROC

A handy procedure language called PROC is provided to create a time-saving list of commands to ensure the proper execution of sequential processes. It permits the storage and execution of a lengthy series of commands or operations and the ability to customize data base input, inquiry, retrieval, and report generation.

EDITOR

The Pick Operating System's editor is used to examine and alter any attribute, item, or file.

TERMINAL CONTROL LANGUAGE (TCL)

The Pick Operating System is terminal oriented. Although hard-copy reports are generated, it is a multi-user interactive system activated through various video display terminals. As such, the Terminal Control Language, or TCL, plays a major role. With TCL, an unlimited number of user-defined procedures, and more than 200 system utilities, menus, and procedures can be initiated. TCL serves as a command processor where action is initiated and passed to other system modules.

As new faster and smaller computers appear on the scene almost monthly, the need for a machine-independent operating system becomes more and more necessary. The Pick system fulfills that requirement and will continue to do so in the coming decades.

Concurrent phasing: When time means money

by RICHARD G. LEFKON
Citibank, N.A., and New York University
New York, New York

INTRODUCTION

Those responsible for improving the efficiency of software generation and maintenance, sometimes overlook an obvious but nonetheless critical fact: If there were no users, there would be considerably fewer programmers to manage.

One problem with large-scale programming efforts is that by the time the system is finished, the business it serves may have evolved into something distinctly different. Users will not stand by quietly without good cause if their key systems are frozen for a lengthy period to accommodate the programming department.

EXTRA COSTS MEAN SAVINGS[1]

When time means money, time frame acceleration can make a large-scale project more costly, but the extra expense may be more than justified by a much larger return on the investment. Bringing a new system live significantly earlier means that the resulting benefits in savings, profit increment or marketplace leadership are cumulatively in effect for that much longer. Business users pay attention to this return on investment.

Even from the programming department's standpoint, there are benefits:

Employee salaries and consultant costs will be billed at today's rates rather than increase steadily over time; the new system can use state-of-the-art software rather than, for instance, a database package that has aged several additional years upon system delivery; the necessary freezing of present procedures will be shorter and cause correspondingly less disruption to the conduct of business.

INTRODUCTION TO CONCURRENT PHASING

Concurrent phasing is a two-dimensional project management approach that integrates the management practices of task subdivision, subtask ganging, functionally distinct development teams, early completion of the common database, and extensive prototyping. This approach facilitates coordinated delivery of subsystems to the user as integral wholes. It makes testing, fixes, and user sign-off much less awkward.

The chief benefit of concurrent phasing is that it smooths and reduces the staff load required to complete a software development project in a greatly accelerated time frame. The final software products delivered are not necessarily any better than those produced with other approaches, and completing a project in 1½ years with this strategy will cost significantly more than permitting the same project to take five years to go live. But when time means money in its effect on the business, this more expensive project management strategy may be just the right one.

HOW TO IMPLEMENT CONCURRENT PHASING

Concurrent phasing is definitely not the place for laissez-faire managers. Because many tasks usually done in sequence will now be performed concurrently, the project management team must take an active role, meeting at least weekly to discuss problems and alternative solutions.

Senior management may be unfamiliar with concurrent phasing and at first may have difficulty conceptualizing this management-intensive method. It is imperative that this accelerated approach be presold to those with systems influence in either the data processing or end-user departments and explained carefully as new individuals enter the management chain. Because it runs counter to the traditional linear schedule, concurrent phasing should periodically be discussed with those to whom it has already been explained. A loud "This method will never work!" can decelerate progress if left unanswered often enough.

A simple memorandum format can be used to express the worth of the management processes involved here. Such a memo, circulated in one's own department and subsequently discussed with key users, can offer the following recommendations:

1. A prerequisite starting point is a complete set of known data items.
2. The first internal product delivered should be a comprehensive database—thinly populated but logically complete.
3. Before the conclusion of formal specifications, coders should construct a skeleton of the full system for tuning and hands-on feasibility studies.

4. Major subsystems should be planned, designed, and coded and tested with phased starting points. This will leave intact the three respective teams throughout the project, guarantee team-to-team handoffs, and minimize misuse of staff such as coders interviewing users, CICS learners designing transmissions, or user contacts writing code.
5. The management and staff of each team should work together to report progress based on the smallest components of each task and to gang labor on critical-path items.
6. To facilitate phasing, a list of cumulative features for subsystems should be enclosed.

LIMITATIONS

Except for subtasking, the synthesis of techniques discussed here will not produce the projected acceleration with projects of less than four to six work-years. Not only do projects of shorter duration have insufficient resources to facilitate ganging; but also the complexity of the task is probably not great enough to reap a net time gain from prototyping.

Software development projects managed by concurrent phasing still need the application of other accepted good programming management practices. Coding standards must be introduced and enforced,[2] and quality testing must be thoroughly and consistently applied.[3] Moreover, non-programming considerations affecting users[4] cannot safely be ignored either.

Even within this approach, common sense should be applied. Coders should be discouraged from breaking up a program in circumstances where the time for component linkage coding and testing is comparable to the time to be gained by coding in parallel (ganging). And, too, subordinates must understand that the deadlines are real and that 80 percent completion is not good enough.

Finally, if a new software technology is used, veteran practitioners of only the old technology should be kept off the project design team. Otherwise, their knowledge of the business, seniority, and self-confidence may converge so strongly that they lead the real software experts to come up with the wrong system architecture.

REFERENCES

1. Lefkon, R. G. "Speeding Software Delivery." *Computerworld* 20(May 12, 1986)19, pp. 97–108.
2. Lefkon, R. G. "Large-Scale Telecommunications and Data Base Standards." *Data Management,* 25(May, 1987)5, pp. 18–24.
3. Lefkon, R. G. "Maintenance manager: How to be a drill sergeant and a good guy, too." *Computerworld,* 21(February 9, 1987)5, pp. 61–75.
4. Lefkon, R. G. "Quantitative Evaluation of Networks." *Selecting a Local Area Network,* American Management Association, 1986, pp. 106–118.

TABLE I—Five subsystems with phasing and balance loading

Responsible Individual or Group:	Period I:	Period II:	Period III:	Period IV:	Period V:	Period VI:	Period VII:	Period VIII:	Period IX:
Business Analyst:	A functionals	B functionals	C functionals	D functionals	E functionals	train operators and clerical staff			
Systems Analyst:	Design database	A specifications	B specifications	C specifications	D specifications	E specifications	perform maintenance and small upgrades		
Programmer/ Analyst:	Create a Model System	Create the Database	A coding unit testing	B coding unit testing	C coding unit testing	D coding unit testing	E coding unit testing	Perform maintenance	
Quality Control:	Procedures	Document	Ensure Database	A integration testing	B integration testing	C integration testing	D integration testing	E integration testing	Maintenance testing
User:	A functionals	B functionals	C functionals	D, E functionals	A acceptance testing	B acceptance testing	C acceptance testing	D acceptance testing	E acceptance testing

Software engineering in the large

by JOHN C. CHIANG
Hayes Microcomputer Products, Inc.
Norcross, Georgia

Software engineering practices typically develop, first, from coding activities and then move to more global applications of tools and engineering practices that affect the entire development cycle. There is a growing recognition that successful software engineering depends upon factors beyond practices that apply to a single project. These factors encompass multiple projects, longer time frames, and affect many groups in the organization. Borrowing from DeRemer and Kron's "Programming in the Large,"[1,2] we will refer to these broader factors as "Software Engineering in the Large". The five examples below illustrate topics from this broader view software engineering.

Software Development Environments Extend Over Time

A series of related projects may be developed by an organization over an extended period of time. Projects in the series might be elements in a family of products. The stability of the development environment across time and projects becomes an important factor in development productivity. UNIX, with its tool box approach, provides an opportunity to stabilize the development environment.[3] Gandalf[4] is another example of a set of similar development environments that offer stability over projects.

The Culture of Communication

Desire alone does not fulfill the long recognized need for communication in software development. There should be a central system to archive documents, to make knowledge available to more personnel, and to serve as a future reference source. Individual project books or libraries tied to single projects do not support the larger family of projects over extended time periods.

Early Prototypes

One solution to rapidly changing project requirements and technology is to develop early prototypes that solidify requirements and build up technical know-how before implementation begins. The key to successful prototypes is to resist the temptation to patch the original prototype into a finished product.[2]

Life Cycle Model in Software

The traditional life cycle model[5] partitions the software life cycle into rigid steps, such as specification, design, and implementation. This model, also referred to as "The Waterfall Model," does not properly reflect the dynamic nature of software development. The newly formed "Spiral Model,"[6] recognizing the dynamic nature of software development, emphasizes risk analysis and discipline in planning. It is believed that this model will be widely accepted, and a host of supporting tools and practices will emerge from it.

Physical Environment and Organization

The concept of a "software factory,"[7,8] addresses office arrangements, computing environments, project team structure, and supporting organizations. The result of applying this approach can be finely tuned software development machine.

REFERENCES

1. DeRemer F. and H. Kron, "Programming-in-the-Large versus Programming-in-the-Small." *IEEE Trans. Software Eng.*, (Vol. SE-2) June, 1976, pp. 80–86.
2. Ramamoorthy, C. V., V. Garg, and A. Prakash, "Programming in the Large." *IEEE Trans. Software Eng.*, (Vol. SE-12), July, 1986, pp. 769–783.
3. Kenighan B.W. and J.R. Mashey, "The Unix programming environment." *Computer* (Vol 14), April, 1981, pp. 25–34.
4. Habermann A.N. and D. Notkin, "Gandalf: Software Development Environments." *IEEE Trans. Software Eng.*, (Vol. SE-12), December, 1986, pp. 1117–1127.
5. Royce, W. W. "Managing the development of large software systems: concepts and techniques." *Proc. WESCON,* August, 1970.
6. Boehm, B. M. "A spiral model of software development and enhancement." *Proce. IEEE Second Process Workshop,* 1986.
7. Nakamura K. "Approach to a Software Factory in the Telecommunications Field." *Proc. COMPSAC85,* October, 1985.
8. Matsumoto Y. et al, "SWB System: A Software Factory." *Software Engineering Environments,* North-Holland Publishing Company, 1981, pp. 305–318.

Design methods for distributed software systems*

by CARL K. CHANG, MIKIO AOYAMA,** AND TSANG MING JIANG
University of Illinois at Chicago
Chicago, Illinois

ABSTRACT

As modern software systems tend to be more and more distributed, the design for such systems becomes very complicated. Design validation for distributed software systems is particularly difficult. Not only must a suitable design representation first be obtained, but automatic analysis tools have to be developed to validate essential design decisions and their impact on the resulting software. In other words, a formal specification method based on a chosen representation at the design level of distributed software systems is highly desirable.

This paper first reviews various design methods for distributed software systems. A new approach to design specification based on the well known *Petri* nets model is then presented. Methods for design validation of distributed software systems are also discussed.

*This work is currently supported by Fujitsu America, Inc. under contract number 052-80136
**Aoyama is with Fujitsu Limited in JAPAN and currently visiting University of Illinois at Chicago.

INTRODUCTION

During the design phase, a computer system is normally specified as a model. Based on its model specification, a system can be gradually implemented. If the specification is formal, meaning that automatic analyses can be performed to a satisfactory extent, certain design errors can be detected and corrected at the design stage and later implementation errors can be avoided. Greater software economy can thus be achieved.[1]

Specification of a computer system can be effectively used as a communication vehicle among all parties involved in the same development project, including both technical and nontechnical personnel. Therefore, the system model should provide a precise and complete description of the modeled system so that desirable analyses can be carried out earlier and easier. Moreover, the model should be flexible enough to facilitate different views at different levels by all parties developing the same system.[2,3,4]

Distributed software systems, as opposed to conventional sequential software systems, become more and more popular. With the advent of fast advancing microprocessor technology as well as widely spread use of powerful workstations, software architects in various applications tend to adopt distributed computing architecture to implement highly effective and efficient software as solutions to a wide spectrum of real-world problems. In parallel to the adoption of distributed architecture, the design of a system to realize such an architecture becomes highly sophisticated.[5]

A variety of design methods have been proposed for real-world applications exhibiting distributed properties. The selection criteria used to determine design methods for the underlying models depend on the nature of the world, the design support environment tailored to the chosen model, and the analysis tools available in a particular environment.

This paper reviews two major classes of design methods. First, a number of representations based on the graph model are reviewed. Second, the one-dimensional specification language oriented design methods are surveyed. Pros and cons of different specification languages are discussed to address the suitability of applying them to distributed software design. The paper then proceeds to discuss design methodologies for distributed software systems from different perspectives pertaining to a number of distinguishable development paradigms. Design approaches of a specific application, namely, the switching software, are scrutinized to examine and determine the generality and usefulness of these methods.

A new design approach is then presented as a token of the new generation of design methods for distributed software systems. The approach integrates two forms of design representation: the graphical form and the language form. Advantages and applicability of this approach are then evaluated.

Finally, this paper addresses the design validation issue. In fact, design validation is very distinct, difficult, and important for distributed software systems. We point out future research directions in our conclusion.

DESIGN METHODS FOR DISTRIBUTED SOFTWARE SYSTEMS

Since the behavior of distributed software systems is very complicated, a desirable design method must be able to capture such behavior completely and translate it faithfully into a specification. For that purpose, a number of methods have been proposed. In general, they can be classified into two major groups: graph based and language based.

Graphical Approach

A number of graphical modeling methods have been developed.[6] However, with the rapid advance of software technology, the architecture, requirements, and style of these graphical models have changed. Note that one of the original design representations is flow charts. The concept of structured programming introduces a number of standard structures into the topology of graphs. Meanwhile, hierarchical decomposition also has been playing a very important role in design modeling. Examples are SADT,[7] HIPO,[8] R_Net of SREM,[9] and various other graphical models. Another driving force sprang from real-time software such as process control systems, switching systems, and communication protocols. Such systems require high performance and high reliability, hence precise descriptions of execution timing and process behavior are essential to modeling such systems. The State Transition Machine (STM) has been used widely for modeling real-time systems, especially switching systems.[10,11] As a definite trend with the advancement of high-performance, systems are now evolving into (fully) distributed control. The introduction of distributed architecture requires significantly enhanced modeling capability due to the following reasons:

1. Complex behaviors such as concurrency, non-determinancy and asynchronism.
2. Needs of analytical capability, especially for real-time systems.

As we mentioned before, to model distributed software systems graphically, a number of modeling methods have been proposed. They can be classified into two groups: control-flow model and data-flow model. Control-flow models include Petri Nets (PN) and some extended PN models.[12,13,14] The Data Flow Diagram (DFD)[15] is an example of the data-flow model. Since the original proposition by Petri in 1962, Petri nets have been the focus of many researchers because of not only their strong modeling capability, but also their various analytical capabilities based on graph theory. Important characteristics of Petri nets are summarized below:

1. Representation of concurrent execution of multiple processes.
2. Representation of non-determinant and asynchronous executions.
3. Modularity, that is, capability of various ways of decomposition and composition of multiple graphs.
4. Various analytical capabilities of model structuredness and dynamics.

However, Petri nets are a difficult tool to use to model systems involving timing requirements, data flow information, and stochastic information. Based on the generalized Petri nets, a number of extensions have been proposed as well as its subclasses.[13] The relationship among these models has been investigated. However, to describe the behavior of distributed software systems comprehensively, it is necessary to represent both control flow and data flow. Yau and Caglayan proposed Modified Petri Nets (MPN)[16] which integrated Petri nets and a data flow representation. MPN supports hierarchical decomposition as well as reuse of software components. Since PN is an asynchronous network model, it does not provide a timing concept. Recall that Ramchandami introduced Timed Petri Net (TPN).[17] TPN is further extended as Stochastic Petri Net (SPN) and both models are applied to performance evaluation of distributed systems. We extended the MPN model by using a timer mechanism and defining more concrete data flow information. Our new model is referred to as Extended Modified Petri Net (EMPN) hereafter. A recent survey revealed some formalization effort on graphical models as visual languages.[18,19] Moreover, the widely spread uses of graphical workstations make it easy to display graphical models and enhance the software development environments a great deal.

Language Approach

A good specification language should meet the following requirements.[20]

1. What the system intends to do should be unambiguously described.
2. The specification written in that language should be complete for implementation.
3. Implementation errors should be precisely pinpointed based on the specification.

Because distributed software systems are more complicated than sequential ones, a specification language for distributed software systems, in addition to these basic requirements, should have features to accommodate the complexity of such systems. These features include formal development, easy human comprehension, and levels of abstraction.

Formal development refers to a set of well defined design processes to obtain the specification from informal and unstructured information. The Ina Jo specification language is an example as the formal specification language for the Formal Development Method (FDM).[21] A specification language must be sufficiently precise so that a sequence of specification statements can be checked for consistency, nonredundancy, and completeness. This characteristic is normally in conflict with easy human comprehension. In fact, the diagrammatic representation is one way to improve human comprehension. As an example, in SREM, a graph representation (R_Net) is incorporated into the specifications to alleviate the problem.[9]

In addition to these two features, to provide formal development facilities (usually through implementation refinements or function refinements), a distributed software system specification language must support levels of abstraction. For example, Event-Base Specification language (EBS) considers the conceptual models of distributed software systems from different levels of abstraction.[22]

Design Methodologies

Much work has been done on actually designing software systems. However, the design methodology of real-time distributed software is not well developed so far.[23,24] Designing such systems requires integrating more sophisticated techniques and procedures into the conventional methodology. Key issues to be considered in a well integrated design methodology include:

1. For real-time software,
   —rigorous timing design
   —performance design
   —quality design
2. For distributed software,
   —partitioning
   —allocation
   —communication design
3. For software productivity,
   —affirmity with modeling and testing methods
   —affirmity with software support and automation

Due to space limitation, the authors concentrate on the design methodology for telecommunications software systems, such as switching software and communication protocols, which widely adopt the real-time distributed architecture.[25,26]

STM and its various extensions have been applied to the design of telecommunications software due to the fact that many telecommunications systems are actually finite state machines.[10] However, significant enhancements to the current STM based design techniques are necessary because STM provides very limited design capabilities for such systems.[27,28]

1. STM models force sequential thinking; concurrent computations are not expressed naturally.
2. Certain computations, such as those involving a queue or stack of arbitrary length, cannot be completely specified.

3. The performance cannot be evaluated directly.
4. The hierarchical structure or stepwise refinement are not supported naturally. Our model which will be discussed in the next section intends to provide some remedy to the limited specification power of most current design techniques especially for telecommunications software.

A NEW APPROACH

A basic model for distributed software systems is shown in Figure 1. An application world is normally divided into two sub-domains, namely, environment domain and system domain. The environment consists of many ports. Ports are abstract data types which are the sources of triggering stimuli to a system and the sinks of responses from the system. Port can be global or local. Each kind of port can be further divided into two different types. Active ports can generate signals on their own demand, while passive ports never generate signals unless on the system's demand. A system is composed of views that are executed in the course of functional components. As far as the interface is concerned, there are two levels of communications among views and components. At the view level, different views use the procedure calls to communicate. At the component level, components in different views use the message passing mechanism through ports for communication.

The design methodology based on this basic model is shown in Figure 2, in which each transition between successive steps is detailed as follows:

STEP 1 TO STEP 2: Each user's need is defined as a generic service.

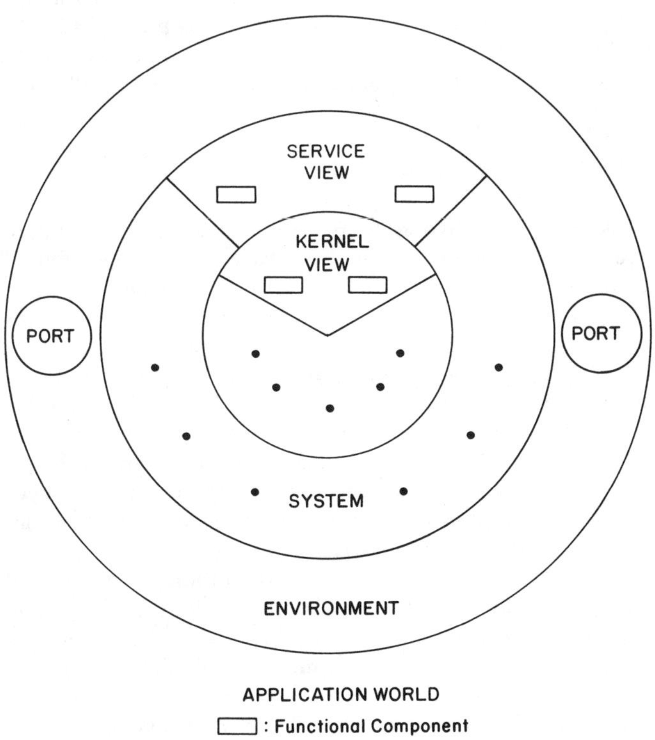

Figure 1—Basic model for distributed software systems

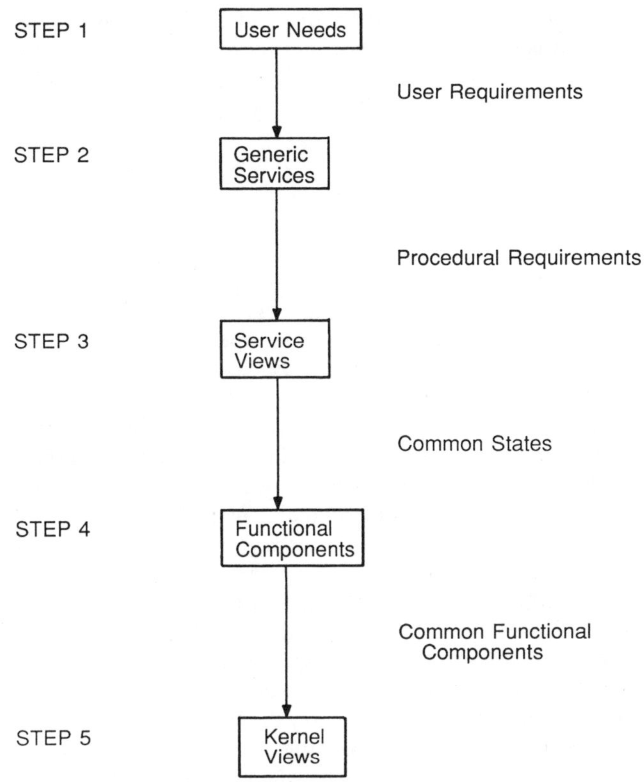

Figure 2—Design methodology

STEP 2 TO STEP 3: Based on procedural requirements, find common procedures among all generic services. We define these common procedures collectively as a service view. The criteria that we may use in defining service views are:

1. number of processes
2. process size
3. hardware architecture
4. etc.

STEP 3 TO STEP 4: A functional component is the maximal set of functions under the same state which includes system markings and an environment for each service view.

STEP 4 TO STEP 5: Among all service views, find those common functional components, and define them as the kernel view.

The basic model can be represented by an EMPN which includes the data information (signals), timing requirements (timer ports), and the hierarchic structure (views). The EMPN can be described by a logic oriented language to be discussed in the next section.

EMPN DESCRIPTION LANGUAGE: EMPNDL

Based on the EMPN, the EMPNDL is developed not only to extend the model but to provide certain analysis capabilities without a graphic editor. EMPNDL is the description language of the EMPN model with the basic system model in mind. For example, the structure of a component that is responsible for message receiving and send back acknowledgement is shown as follows:

Precondition: the component is enabled and receives message and *check(message) = valid*
Postcondition: the component sends acknowledgement and enables *next_components*

In our model, a system interfaces with its environment by exchanging signals with the environment. For example, in a telephone switch, lifting the handset is a caller's signal to the system of the intention to dial a number. In response, the system sends a dial tone to the handset as a signal to the caller that dialing can now proceed.

Just identifying signals exchanged between the system and its environment is insufficient in describing the interface completely. For example, a telephone switching system involves two parties in its environment, namely, the caller and the callee. The two parties can be represented as two ports through which signals enter or leave a system.

By examining the nature of signals, two distinct signal types can be derived: impulse signals and level signals. An impulse signal is an infinitely short event, such as off-hook in the telephone switching system. An impulse signal can not only trigger system action but also carry data with it. For example, when the caller dials a number, the signal given to the switch is associated with a value, which is the number just dialed. On the other hand, a level signal represents a continuously monitored condition, such as the dial tone in the switching system, which lasts from the moment the caller goes off hook until the first digit of the number is dialed. A level signal may have several continuous conditions. As a real-world example, the colors of a traffic light signal have three levels: red, yellow, and green.[29]

A signal can trigger a transition in the system. At some moment in time, the system is in a certain stable state, waiting for input. When the system receives a signal applicable to its current state, it performs a set of actions such as updating internal resources and sending messages to the environment. It then settles into another (not necessarily different) stable state, waiting for the next input.

Sometimes system's behavior depends on whether an expected input signal from the environment arrives in a finite period of time. Consider the following requirement:

If the caller does not dial a number within 30 seconds, the switch shall send a howler tone to the caller.

To express this kind of time-dependent system behavior, the model provides the timer mechanism. A timer is a port which interprets signals as operations and responds properly. A timer can be an alarm clock, with a fixed timing interval. It start running when it is explicitly started by the system. When the timer's interval expires, the timer issues an alarm. An alarm has the same effect as an impulse signal in triggering a transition in the system. For example, to impose the above timing constraint upon a telephone switch, we can have a timer port called digit-receiving-timer. The system starts the digit-receiving-timer with 30 seconds when an off-hook signal from a caller is detected. If the caller dials a number promptly enough, the system will cancel the digit-receiving-timer. Otherwise, the digit-receiving-timer raises an alarm and triggers the system to send a howler tone to the caller.

In certain situations, system's behavior may depend on the history of previous signals. Consider the following behavior of a telephone switch:

If the dialed number is inoperative, the user should receive a recorded message; if the dialed number is busy, the user should receive a busy tone.

The status of a dialed number is not part of the behavior of the telephone switching system to be specified. But, the telephone switch's reaction to the status is and must be modeled.

To handle this kind of hidden information, our model provides a decision construct. A decision is associated with a finite set of results. For example, the decision to be made for checking on the status of the dialed number may have three results: inoperative, busy, available. Depending on the result of a decision, a certain transition in the system may be triggered.

Our model provides the view mechanism to allow for the expression of the relationships among structural modules of a complex system. Systems in our model are specified mainly in terms of views. Each view is a subsystem that deals with a subset of the whole system's signals. For example, a telephone switching system can have views of plain old telephone service (POTS), call forwarding service (CFS), automatic callback service (ACS). It is often the case that a specification is written by a team, rather than by a single author. The view mechanism lends itself very well to this situation, because views are independent components and can be elaborated separately. However, the combined views present a complete picture of the whole system. In spirit, views resemble modules in programming methodology and subschema in database theory.

DESIGN VALIDATION

Distributed software systems are more difficult to analyze then conventional centralized software systems. Distributed systems are inherently concurrent, asynchronous and nondeterministic.[30] As an example, distributed switching systems can be verified by generating all reachable states and checking whether any of them is a nonprogressive state, such as deadlock, overflow, and unspecified receipt. This technique is referred to as state exploration. A major problem with state exploration is that it requires large execution time and storage. The problem is caused by the assumption that one needs to consider all possible progressive speeds for all parties contained in the distributed systems.

An efficient variation of state exploration for distributed switching systems has been studied.[31–33] Briefly, in that study, the task of generating all reachable states is divided into N independent subtasks. In each subtask, only the states reachable by forcing maximal progress for one party are generated. Since the N subtasks are completely independent and, in most instances, the time and storage requirements for each subtask are fewer than those for the original task, the proposed method can save time and/or storage over conventional state exploration methods. Moreover, the method is also suitable for parallel processing.

CONCLUSIONS

This paper reviews several software design techniques with most of the discussion centering around distributed software systems which are inherently nondeterministic, hard to design, and very difficult to analyze.

A new model, EMPN, is presented for modeling distributed software systems. EMPN integrates representations of both control and data flow, and is extended primarily for real-time distributed software systems. The associated logic oriented language, EMPNDL, is also proposed for formal specification. For further research, there are three directions to be investigated.

First, there are many analysis tools available for PN models. However, due to the complexity of distributed software systems, the maximal progress technique should be utilized to reduce the complexity of analyzing the entire system.

Second, since the EMPNDL is a logic oriented language, it is natural to use AI reasoning techniques to find inconsistency, incompleteness, and redundancy at the specification level. As a tradition, these flaws are normally detected by a state transition matrix which expresses the relationships between the stimuli and responses based upon compiler techniques. An evaluation is necessary to compare these two techniques.

Finally, a testbed based on our new technique should be implemented to perform dynamic testing. Dynamic errors can thus be detected in this phase.

REFERENCES

1. Liskov, B. H. and V. Berzins. "An Appraisal of Program Specifications." *Software Specification Techniques,* edited by P. Wegner, Cambridge: MIT Press, 1979, pp. 276–301.
2. Riddle, W. E., Wileden, J. C., Sayler, J. H., Segal, A. R. and Stavely, A. M. "Behavior Modeling During Software Design. *IEEE Transactions on Software Engineering,* SE-4 (1978) 3, pp. 283–292.
3. Yau, S. S., C. C. Yang, and S. M. Shatz. "An Approach to Distributed Communicating System Software Design." *IEEE Transactions on Software Engineering,* SE-7 (1981) 4, pp. 427–436.
4. Kleinrock, L. "Distributed Systems." *Communications of the ACM,* 28 (1985) 11, pp. 1200–1213.
5. Watson, R. W. "Distributed System Architecture Model." in B. W. Lampson, M. Paul, and H. J. Siegert (eds.) *Distributed Systems: Architecture and Implementation,* New York: Springer-Verlag, 1981, pp. 10–43.
6. Alford, M. W., J. P. Ansart, G. Hommel, L. Lamport, B. Liskov, G. P. Mullery, and F. B. Schneider. *Distributed Systems: Methods and Tools for Specification,* New York: Springer-Verlag, 1985.
7. Ross, D. "Structured Analysis(SA): A Language for Communicating Ideas." *IEEE Transactions on Software Engineering,* SE-3 (1977) 1, pp. 16–34.
8. Stay, J. F. "HIPO and Integrated Program Design." *IBM Systems Journal,* 15 (1976) 2, pp. 143–154.
9. Alford, M. W. "A Requirements Engineering Methodology for Real-Time Processing Requirements." *IEEE Transactions on Software Engineering,* SE-3 (1977) 1, pp. 66–79.
10. Kawashima H., K. Futami, and S. Kano. "Functional Specification of Call Processing by State Transition Diagram." *IEEE Transactions on Communication Technology,* COM-19(1971)5, pp. 581–587.
11. CCITT, Z101–104: *Functional Specification and Description Language,* Geneva: CCITT, 1980.
12. Agerwala T. "Putting Petri Nets to Work." *IEEE Computer,* (1979) 12, pp. 85–94.
13. Peterson, J. L. *Petri Net Theory and the Modeling of Systems,* Englewood Cliffs: Prentice-Hall, 1981.
14. Murata T. "Modeling and Analysis of Concurrent Systems. in C. R. Vick and C. V. Ramamoorthy (eds.), *Handbook of Software Engineering,* New York: Van Nostrand Reinhold, 1983, pp. 39–63.
15. Chambers, F. B., D. A. Duce, and G. P. Jones (eds.). *Distributed Computing,* Orlando: Academic Press, 1984.
16. Yau, S. S. and M. U. Caglayan. "Distributed Software System Design Representation Using Modified Petri Nets." *IEEE Transactions on Software Engineering,* SE-9 (1986) 6, pp. 733–745.
17. Ramchandani, C. "Analysis of Asynchronous Concurrent Systems by Petri Nets." *Ph.D. dissertation, Department of Electrical Engineering,* Cambridge: Massachusetts Institute of Technology, July, 1973. Also *Technical Report 120, Project MAC.* Cambridge: Massachusetts Institute of Technology, February, 1974.
18. Raeder G. "A Survey of Current Graphical Programming Techniques." *IEEE Computer* 18 (1985) 8, pp. 11–25.
19. Chang, S. K., "Visual Languages: A Tutorial and Survey," *IEEE Software* 4 (1987) 1, pp. 29–39.
20. Levene, A. A. and G. P. Mullery. "An Investigation of Requirement Specification Languages: Theory and Practice." *IEEE Computer,* May, 1982, pp. 50–59.
21. Berry, D. M. "Towards a Formal Basis for the Formal Development Method and the Ina Jo Specification Language." *IEEE Transactions on Software Engineering,* SE-13 (1987) 2, pp. 184–201.
22. Chen, B. and R. T. Yeh. "Formal Specification and Verification of Distributed Systems." *IEEE Transactions on Software Engineering,* SE-9 (1983) 6, pp. 710–722.
23. Yau, S. S. and J. J.-P. Tsai. "A survey of Software Design Techniques." *IEEE Transactions on Software Engineering,* SE-12 (1986) 6, pp. 713–721.
24. Filman, R E. and D. P. Friedman. *Coordinated Computing: Tools and Techniques for Distributed Software,* New York: McGraw-Hill, 1984.
25. Anderson, L. G., J. R. Gibbons, Y. W. Han, and E. C. Lee. "5ESS Switching System Software Architecture." *Proceedings of the International Computer Symposium 1984,* December 12–14, 1985, Taipei, pp. 517–523.
26. Ogawa T., S. Kamioka, Y. Ogawa, and T. Koyano. "A New Generation PBX for Integrated Office Services." to appear in *Proceedings of the International Switching Symposium 1987,* March 15–20, 1987, Phoenix.
27. Chandrasekharan, M., B. Dasarathy,and Z. Kishimoto. "Requirements-Based Testing of Real-Time Systems: Modeling for Testability." *IEEE Transactions on Computer,* April, 1985, pp. 71–80.
28. Boute, R. T. "Towards System Specification Languages." *Proceedings of the 4th International Conference on Software Engineering for Telecommunication Switching Systems,* July 20–24, 1981, Warwick, pp. 31–37.
29. Wang, Y. "A Distributed Specification Model and its Prototyping." *Proceedings of COMPSAC 1986,* October 8–10, 1986, Chicago, pp. 130–137.
30. Eckhouse, R. H. and J. A. Stankovic, "Issues in Distributed Processing—An Overview of Two Workshops," *IEEE Computer,* 11 (1978) 1, pp. 22–26.
31. Chang, C. K. and T. M. Jiang. "A Design Method for Recoverable Distributed Communicating Systems." *Proceedings of COMPSAC 1986,* October 8–10, 1986, Chicago, pp. 427–431.
32. West, C. H. "General Technique for Communications Protocol Validation," *IBM Journal of Research and Developments,* 22 (1978) 4, pp. 394–404.
33. Yu, Y. T. and M. G. Gouda, "Protocol Validation by Maximal Progress State Exploration." *IEEE Transactions on Communications,* COM-32 (1984) 1, pp. 94–97.

An analysis of the roll-back and blocking operations of three concurrency control mechanisms

by VIJAY KUMAR
University of Missouri at Kansas City
Kansas City, Missouri

ABSTRACT

Transactions in database systems are run concurrently to achieve optimal resource utilization. Concurrent execution of transactions is managed by concurrency control mechanisms for maintaining the database consistency. These mechanisms use activities like transaction roll-backs and transaction blockings for serializing the concurrent execution, and they have significant effect on the performance of database systems; however, their relationship with throughput, workload, and other aspects of the system is unclear. Further it is not clear how the read : write ratio affects the performance. This paper attempts to show the effect of roll-back, blocking, and read : write ratio on the performance of database systems under several different types of workloads. We have used detailed and realistic simulation models to conduct our investigation; and, unlike other performance studies, we have avoided simplifying assumptions as far as possible to include most of the attributes of real database systems. In this study we show that neither a roll-back nor a blocking scheme is consistently better for all types of workloads; they are rather workload sensitive. We also show that it is not the write-only transactions but the read-only transactions that need special treatment for efficient processing. We report that transaction wait-time does not have significant effect on the throughput and the effect of read : write ratio is very short lived. We have introduced a new term *Domain of Efficiency* (DoE) to explain the behavior of these mechanisms.

INTRODUCTION

Recent performance studies of concurrency control mechanisms (CCMs)[1,2,3] have shown that mechanisms based on two-phase strategy outperform others. However, CCMs based on two-phase locking suffer with the problem of deadlock.[3,4,5,6] A deadlock may involve several transactions and must be detected and resolved. A large number of algorithms are available for deadlock detection[7,8,9,10,11,12,13,14] and for deadlock prevention.[15,16,17,18] Resolution of deadlocks is usually done either by rolling-back or by blocking concurrent transactions. It is not clear which method is suitable for what kind of environment or how these activities (rolling-back and blocking) affect the system behavior. In this paper, we study in detail the effect of transaction blockings and transaction roll-backs on the performance of database systems. Although a great deal of work has been done in this area, we feel that performance models used in these works do not incorporate some important attributes of a real database system. We try to bridge this gap with our detailed study.

We begin our study by constructing detailed simulation models which incorporate most of the attributes of a real database system such as transaction failure and database recovery, deadlock detection and its resolution. We define the common terms used here, describe the CCMs studied in this paper, and provide their comparative study. Next we review previous work done in this area as well as our approach. Next we explain model parameters and the construction of transactions used in our work. We describe simulation models, and the statistical approach taken for data collection and their validation. Finally, we discuss the simulation results and conclude our findings.

TERMS

In this section we define the common terms used in this paper.

Entity: We consider a database as a set of entities of fixed size. An entity is a lockable unit.

Read: A transaction reads an entity. The contents of the entity is not changed. It is an atomic action.

Write: A transaction after reading an entity modifies its contents. It is an atomic action in the sense that the read and modify operations are not separable.

Conflict: Operations of any two transactions $T1$ and $T2$ accessing an entity conflicts if one of the following conditions is satisfied:

1. $T1$ is performing a read (write) operation and $T2$ wants to perform a write (read) operation. This is read-write (RW) or write-read (WR) conflict.
2. $T1$ is performing a write operation and $T2$ wants to perform a write operation. This is a write-write (WW) conflict.

Blocking: The execution of a transaction is suspended (blocked) temporarily upon encountering a conflict.

Restart: A blocked transaction is rescheduled for execution. The point of restart of a blocked transaction depends upon the CCM.

Roll-Back: A process in which all the write actions of a transaction are undone. There are two situations under which a transaction is rolled-back:

1. a blocked transaction is rolled-back.
2. an aborted transaction.

Commit: A transaction is said to be committed if and only if it has unlocked all its locked entities.

Degree of Concurrency (DoC): Total number of active transactions in the system at any instant. For two-phase locking, an active transaction is a transaction with at least one of its lock requests granted, and which is in a state ready to be scheduled for execution. (The term degree of multiprogramming has also been used in literatures for DoC.)

Degree of Cycle: Total number of transactions involved in a deadlock.

TRANSACTION PROCESSING AND CONCURRENCY CONTROL MECHANISMS

We describe here in detail the mechanisms of the CCMs we have studied. We analyze their behavior to define the domain of our investigation and we use this domain to perform the simulation experiment. The entire processing of transactions can be divided into the following three phases:

Locking Phase—The scheduled transactions lock the required entities. Locks can be applied into two different modes: the *share* mode (read lock) and the *exclusive* mode (write lock).

Execution Phase—The transaction processes the locked entities.

Release Phase—The transaction unlocks the locked entities.

Execution of these phases by concurrent transactions depends on the CCM used. Next we explain, in terms of these three phases, how concurrent transactions are processed by the three concurrency control mechanisms we investigated in this work.

Incremental Locking and Simultaneous Release

In this mechanism the first two phases (i.e., locking and execution) are interleaved and the end of the execution phase initiates the release phase. Entities are locked only when demanded by the execution phase. Consequently, only those entities are locked which are actually processed by the transaction, although the transaction might have referenced many more entities in its code.

A conflict is resolved by blocking the transaction which is trying to lock the entity. A blocked transaction retains all the locks it obtained before getting blocked; it is unblocked and resumes its execution when the entity it required becomes free. We also refer to this activity as transaction *restart*. Resolving conflicts by blocking a transaction may create deadlocks which must be resolved by rolling-back a transaction. A rolled-back transaction may be rerun or may be removed from the system. At the end of the execution phase all the entities locked by the transaction are released in one atomic action (simultaneously). In this report we refer to this mechanism as D1 protocol.

Wait-Die (WD) and Wound-Wait (WW) Mechanisms

Rosencrantz and others[19] have discussed Wait-Die and Wound-Wait mechanisms which can be described as follows:

Let T_1 and T_2 be two transactions and (T_1 *-ts*) and (T_2 *-ts*) their associated timestamps. Suppose that T_1 makes a lock request (requester) for an entity *E* currently locked by T_2 (holder), thus generating a conflict over *E*.

Such conflict is resolved by these techniques as follows:

a. The Wait-Die System (WE Protocol)
If (T_1 *-ts*) < (T_2 *-ts*) then wait else die. If the requester's timestamp is smaller, then it waits for the holder—otherwise, the requester dies (roll-backs).
b. The Wound-Wait System (WW Protocol)
If (T_1 *-ts*) < (T_2 *-ts*) then wound else wait. If the requester's timestamp is smaller, then wound the holder—otherwise, wait for the holder (T_1 wounds T_2) to release the entity.

Comparison of Protocols

In this section we hypothesize the expected behavior of the three mechanisms and later we verify the hypotheses. As mentioned earlier, the strict two-phase (D1) locking resolves conflicts by blocking transactions. Blocking transactions does two things: increases transaction *wait-time* (amount of time transaction remains blocked) and creates the possibility of deadlocks. A blocked transaction reduces the availability of entities for other transactions; the higher the number of blockings the lower the availability of entities. Reduction in the availability of entities would in turn increase transaction blockings which might increase the probability of deadlock occurrence. This increase, however, remains very low and becomes significant only at very high transaction arrival rates.[20] An increase in deadlock increases transaction roll-backs. Thus we see that these activities are interdependent and a change in one affects in some way all the other activities.

It seems that if transaction wait-time is reduced, some improvements in system performance may be achieved. One of the ways this can be done is by rolling-back transactions instead of blocking them. This approach is taken in WD and WW, which assume that blocking a transaction is likely to create a deadlock and hence they roll-back the transaction when a conflict arises. On one hand this policy increases the availability of entities and minimizes transaction wait-time, but on the other hand it consumes, comparatively, more CPU and IO resources and also rolls-back transactions which may never cause a deadlock. We refer to this type of roll-back as *redundant roll-backs*.

It has been shown[20] that even at very high arrival rates the degree of cycle (number of transactions in a cycle) remains low. In this situation it would seem that redundant roll-backs are expensive and might get worse for larger transactions. Another important factor which should be considered is the size of roll-back (number of entities to be restored in a roll-back). If the average roll-back size is small, then the process would not be expensive. Blocking a transaction which is holding one entity for some length of time is certainly more expensive than rolling it back. The latter is even less expensive if the entity happens to be in the main memory.

Intuitively it seems that if the average transaction size is large then the average roll-back size may be large and may become expensive. We aim to verify if there is any relationship between the average transaction size and the size of roll-back. We aim to compute the Domain of Efficiency (DoE) of these mechanisms. We define the DoE of a CCM as the set of ranges of those parameter values inside which there exists a linear relationship among these parameters. For example, we might discover that in a CCM up to an average transaction size of *N,* the average roll-back size increases linearly. When the average transaction size becomes larger than *N,* this relationship may become unpredictable. The relationship among other parameters may be observed in a similar way to define the DoE of a CCM. We aim to establish the set of parameters and their acceptable ranges.

In D1 a roll-back is not instantaneous. It can take place only when the deadlock is detected and resolved. There are several criteria for selecting a transaction to be rolled-back to resolve a deadlock;[21] we have selected the youngest transaction for this purpose. A blocked transaction resumes its execution when other transactions are rolled-back or committed. Since these operations are not instantaneous in D1, transaction wait-time will keep on increasing. In contrast, in WD and WW a roll-back may be instantaneous, and blocked transactions do not wait longer than they do in D1. In WW the number of blocking is much higher and these blocked (waiting) transactions may get wounded. In WD mechanism, a blocked transaction never dies: either a transaction's waiting-time is increased or, in the case of its death, its recovery time is increased but never both. We aim to verify these points in this work.

REVIEW OF PREVIOUS WORK

The database literature is full of performance reports. Each report emphasizes certain aspects of some mechanisms. In Kiessling and Landherr[22] the effect of roll-backs and transaction blockings have been looked into in a limited way. They do not take into account the effect of deadlocks on throughput and they assume that the entire database is divided into 100 granules, which is not very realistic. Also, a performance comparison of timestamping and strict two-phase locking has been done.[23] They report that when average transaction size is small (4–8 entities), resolving conflicts by rolling-back is better than blocking transactions and for larger transactions rolling-back becomes too expensive. The report contains few details about the effect of varying transaction arrival rates and different types of workloads. Tay, Suri, and Goodman[24,25] report that in all the situations, the no-waiting case performs better than the waiting case. Their studies show that transaction blockings have a significant detrimental effect on the system throughput and concludes that locking with no waiting seems to be a practical approach, if the cost of transaction restarts is brought down to a minimum. They do not say how this can be achieved. Ries and Stonebraker[26] reported that the optimistic method (conflicts are resolved by rolling-back transactions) always performed better. A possible reason for this result could be that they assumed the roll-back cost to be negligible. Further, a detailed study of deadlock has been done[29] in which the authors have basically looked at the effect of transaction blocking and restarts on system performance and tried to find a deadlock treatment technique which is consistently better. They report that there is no such deadlock treatment strategy that performs consistently better and the performance of a strategy very much depends on the type of workload. They found that in a situation in which resources are fairly heavily utilized, continuous deadlock detection is preferable, but in Kumar[20] it is reported that even at high transaction arrival rates deadlock occurrence is very low and a continuous deadlock detection does have some effect on the performance.

Our Approach

Our model has its origin in the model of Ries,[28] however, we have avoided simplifying assumptions as far as possible to simulate a real system as precisely as possible. In almost all the work we have reviewed, no one has included transaction failure and they have assumed that the IO and CPU requirements of transactions depend on their size. Also, in some reports they have simulated deadlocks, transaction blockings, and restarts simply by introducing estimated delays. Most of these works have used only one type of workload to drive their simulators except one[3] in which three different types of workloads have been simulated.

It can be argued convincingly that these simplifying assumptions do affect the simulation, and the results so obtained may fail to explain the behavior of CCMs correctly. In our investigation we have included most of the attributes of a real system to study the behavior of these CCMs precisely. For this reason we feel that a direct comparison of our work with others would not be very meaningful.

We have studied the performance of D1, WD and WW under strictly identical environments. We selected D1 protocol to avoid cascade roll-backs and the same locking policy (incremental locking) as D1 was used in WD and WW mechanisms for a meaningful comparison of transaction roll-back and blocking. We have coded the deadlock detection and resolution, database recovery, transaction blocking, and transaction roll-back algorithms as they would exist in a real database system. In this respect our system, to a large extent, represents a real database system. On this basis we claim that our results may be more reliable and informative than the results obtained in other reports.

The assumptions we have made to build our models follow:

1. There is one IO processor and one CPU.
2. Transaction IO requirements are partially and transaction CPU requirements are totally independent of their size. This means that the probability that a large transaction would use more IO than a small transaction is high, and two same size transactions may not use the same amount of IO.
3. The CPU resource is shared between locking and processing activities.
4. Recovery operation is required in the case of transaction failure and in deadlock resolution, and has been given the highest priority (i.e., a transaction to be rolled-back goes to the top of processing queues and is processed in the next event) #34.
5. Our models are open-ended, i.e., a set of transactions does not cycle in the system for repeated execution. Also a rolled-back transaction is not rescheduled. We used open-ended models to study the worst case behavior of the CCMs we tested.
6. Transaction failure is unpredictable. A transaction can be aborted by the user, it can fail due to disk fault or due to some other system problems. In [32] it is reported that transactions failures are not frequent and the failure percentage lies usually between 2–3%, so we assumed that 2% of transactions would fail in a simulation run.
7. Lock table always resides in the main memory.

MODEL PARAMETERS

The system parameters for our models are:

1. IO processing time (time taken by IO processor to transfer an entity from the disk)
2. CPU processing time (time taken by the CPU to process an entity)
3. CPU locking time (time taken by the CPU to lock an entity)
4. CPU recovery time (time taken by the CPU to restore the last consistent state of an entity)

5. Node check time (time taken by the CPU to check one node in a wait-for graph)
6. Deadlock detection cost (time taken by the CPU to detect a deadlock)
7. Cycle detection frequency (defines after how many transaction blockings the deadlock detection is performed)

Input Parameter

To generate the three different transaction size mixes we have used the approach taken in Ries and Stonebraker:[28]

1. All transactions are roughly the same size. This transaction mix is generated by uniform distribution.
2. About 35–40 percent of transactions are large and the rest are small (accessing about 25–30 percent of average transaction size). This transaction mix is generated by exponential distribution.
3. About 95–97 percent of transactions are very small (accessing about 3–4 percent of the average transaction size) and the rest are very large (accessing maximum number of entities). This transaction mix is generated by hyper-exponential distribution (it should be noted that the exponential distribution is a special case of hyper-exponential distribution).

We have assumed that most of the real transaction processing environment would fall into the defined domain. We do not claim that these transaction mixes completely represent the real transaction processing environment; however, they have some flavor of such an environment.

Workload Parameters

1. *Total number of transactions to be processed.*
2. *Database size.*
3. *Read : Write ratio.* We define the read : write ratio of a transaction as the ratio of the number of read actions and the number of write actions. Under this scenario, if a transaction size is 30 and its read : write ratio is 20 : 10, then the transaction will perform 20 reads and 10 writes. The selection of entities for read and write operations are done randomly under a uniform distribution. Thus any entity out of 30 entities is equally likely to be selected for a read or write operation. To study the effect of this ratio, we start our simulator with read-only transactions (read : write ratio is $m : 0$, where m is transaction size and it also indicates the number of read operations in a transaction). We collect all the statistics for this run. The same set of transactions are then run, each with n number of write locks, such that the read : write ratio is $m - n : n$, where $n = 1, 2, 3, \ldots, m$, and statistics are collected for all the runs. When $m = n$ then all transactions of the set become write-only transactions.
4. *Percentage of transaction failure.* We have modeled this kind of failure by parameterizing the failure percentage. A required failure percentage can be supplied and the system randomly selects so many transactions (victims) which will fail during execution. The failure points of these victims are selected randomly and represented in terms of sub-transactions which would be processed successfully before the transaction fails. For example, if the total number of sub-transactions in a transaction is 10, then the failure point may be any number between 1 and 10. In this case the transaction will fail after processing so many sub-transactions and will then be scheduled for roll-back (recovery).

Output Parameters

1. *Average number of transaction restarts.* Transaction restart means the resumption of the execution of blocked transactions. A blocking point may be anywhere in the transaction (i.e., a transaction may get blocked at its first lock request or it may get blocked after occupying some locks).
2. *Degree of cycle.*
3. *Throughput.*
4. *Average response time.*
5. *Average Recovery Time.*
6. *Degree of Concurrency (DoC).*
7. *Average number of deadlocks.*
8. *Average transaction roll-back size.*
9. *Average transaction wait-time.*
10. *Average wait-time of wounded/dead transactions.*

CONSTRUCTION AND SCHEDULING OF TRANSACTIONS

A transaction for our simulation is viewed as an ordered set of several sub-transactions, each of which holds a certain number of entities as shown below:

$$T(m) = \{t_1(e_1), t_2(e_2), \ldots, t_n(e_n)\}$$

where

T = parent transaction, m = total number of entities required by T,

$t_1, t_2, \ldots, t_n$ = sub-transactions. e_n = number of entities required by t_n, and

$$m = \sum_{i}^{n} e_i$$

During the locking and execution phases of T, t_1 locks e_1 entities and processes them, then t_2 locks e_2 entities and processes them, and so on. When t_n has successfully locked and processed e_n entities, m entities are released in one atomic action.

SIMULATION MODELS AND EXECUTION OF TRANSACTIONS

The simulation models are shown in Figures 1 and 2. The dotted lines represent the use of CPU and IO resources by the related activities. The *flow of transaction* (execution) through it is as follows:

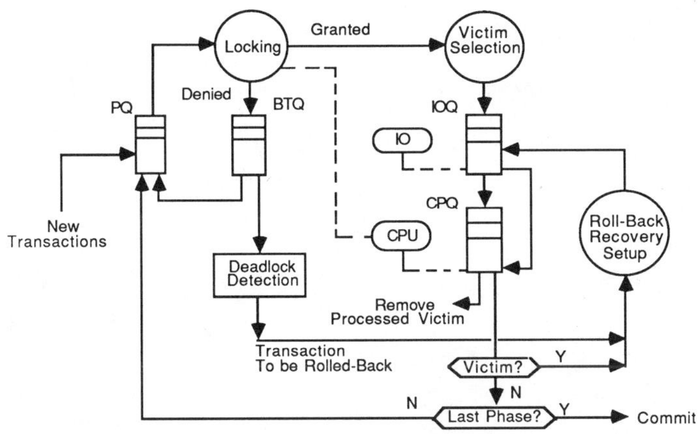

Figure 1—Simulation model of D1 protocol

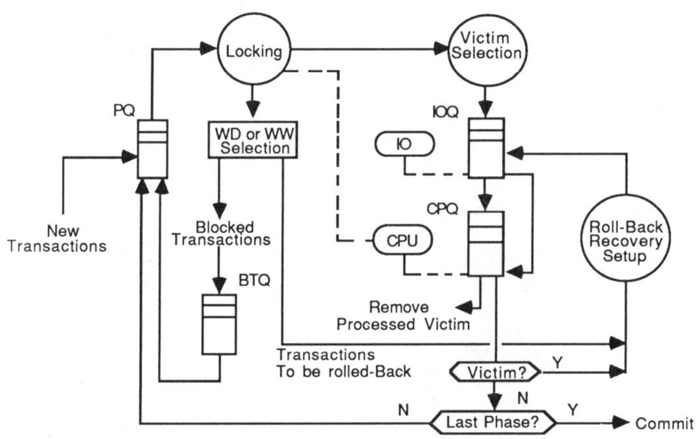

Figure 2—Simulation model of WD and WW protocols

1. A transaction arrives (poisson arrival) and joins the pending queue (PQ).
2. A transaction is picked up from the top of PQ, the total number of entities required by this transaction is calculated, and its sub-transactions are created by a random process. Another process randomly distributes the total entities of this transaction among its sub-transactions. A FIFO is used in processing the PQ.
3. The first/next sub-transaction of the parent transaction requests the required locks one at a time.
4. If any of the locks of that sub-transaction is denied, then, depending upon the CCM being simulated, a proper action (roll-back or blocking) is taken to resolve the conflict. A blocked transaction goes to blocked transaction queue (BTQ). In the case of D1, a deadlock detection is initiated after every conflict or after a prespecified number (can be specified via a parameter) of transactions are blocked. If a deadlock is found, then the cycle is broken by rolling-back a transaction from the cycle. Several transaction selection criteria can be specified by a parameter; we selected the youngest transaction for this purpose. As mentioned earlier, a roll-back process is given the highest priority, so such a transaction is put at the top of IOQ and is processed before all those transactions which joined IOQ before it.
5. After a successful locking phase, a transaction goes through a random victim selection process. The parameters of this selection process are set so that it achieves a 2% transaction failure. A transaction goes through this process only once.
6. IO request of a sub-transaction is processed.
7. CPU request of a sub-transaction is processed.
8. If more sub-transactions of a parent transaction are left to be processed, then the parent transaction is moved to the bottom of PQ.
9. At the end of processing all the sub-transactions, the parent transaction is committed and all BTQ transaction are moved to PQ and resume their normal processing.

Simulation Parameters Values

All three simulators have been tested with the following parameter settings. One simulation time unit may be interpreted as one millisecond.

Transaction arrival rate range:	0.5–20 transactions/second.
Read : write ratio range:	$m - n : n$ ($n = 0, 1, 2, \ldots, m$).
Victim selection parameter:	set to give 2% transaction failure.
Database size:	3000 entities.

(We selected this value after running our simulator with several different values. In the case of very large database size (9000–20000) and with uniform entity access probability the number of conflicts was too low to observe any difference in the performance of these CCMs. They gave nearly similar performance results.)

CPU processing time: 2.50 time unit/entity.
CPU locking time: 1.05 time unit/entity.
CPU recovery time: 3.55 time unit/entity.
Deadlock detection cost: 1.05 time unit.
IO processing time: 25.15 time unit/entity.
Cycle detection frequency: set to perform after 1, 10 and 15 conflicts.

The parameter values were chosen so as to be able to simulate from lightly loaded system (one or less active transaction in the system) to heavily loaded system (more than 25 active transactions in the system). Using the rule of thumb proposed in Tay, Goodman and Suri[27] we expect our system to start *thrashing* at heavy workloads, which in our case is likely to occur when DoC is between 25 and 30.

The Statistical Approach

We describe in this section the statistical approach we took to discriminate between throughput differences owing simply to statistical variations and those actually owing to algorithm performance characteristics.

Several simulation analysis techniques are available (a survey of these techniques may be found in[31,32,33]). We selected the method of batch means from the options of batch means, regenerative method and the independent replications. In our test runs we found that following initial set-up, an *idle state,* where all transactions input sources (terminals) are in their *stagger delay* does not occur with sufficient frequency to allow the use of regenerative method. The batch means has the advantage over independent replication that initial transients do not bias each of the throughput observations.[32] From the implementation view point, the batch means method is simpler than the method of replication since in the latter the simulator has a garbage collect and reinitialize simulation and the data structures between the observation periods.

Under the selected method (batch means) a simulation run is divided into a set of batches. Each batch is a fixed simulation time-units long and each such batch provides one throughput observation. All individual throughput observations are averaged to estimate the overall throughput. Standard techniques with the assumption that the throughput observations from the batches are independent and indentically distributed[32] are used to compute the confidence intervals. In our simulation run we used the following values of batch-num and batch-time:

Batch_num = 20; Batch_time = 50000; Total simulation time units = 20 × 50000

RESULTS AND DISCUSSION

We present the results of only two types of transaction size distributions: uniform and hyper-exponential. The results of exponential distribution follow a similar pattern as the uniform distribution except they have higher values of output parameters. We have taken the liberty of mentioning the results of exponential distribution without providing graphs for them.

Arrival Rate Versus Deaths, Restarts and Wounds

The graphs in Figures 3 and 4 show the relationship between average transaction arrival rate and number of deaths (WD), number of transactions wounded (WW) and the number of transaction restarts (D1). Figure 5 shows the relationship between the arrival rate and transaction restarts for all the three mechanisms.

The number of restarts in D1 increases comparatively rapidly with arrival rate. In the hyper-exponential distribution (Figure 4) the increase is even sharper. At lower arrival rates the number of restarts in all the CCMs is nearly the same and it widens after an arrival rate of 12 transactions per second on the average. A comparison of D1 and WW mechanisms indicates that in WW only the younger transactions are blocked to resolve conflict, since the younger requesters never cause deadlocks to occur. At higher arrival rates D1 suffers with deadlock occurrences which increase the transaction blockings and WW with wounded transactions which reduce the number of such blockings. The situation in WD is just the opposite; all younger transactions are rolled-back to resolve conflicts and consequently the number of restarts remains quite low even at higher arrival rates. A low number of restarts is bound to increase the number of roll-backs (deaths) and that is shown to happen (Figures 3, 4, and 5). The number of restarts is the highest in D1 and the lowest in WD, and the number of roll-backs is the highest in WD.

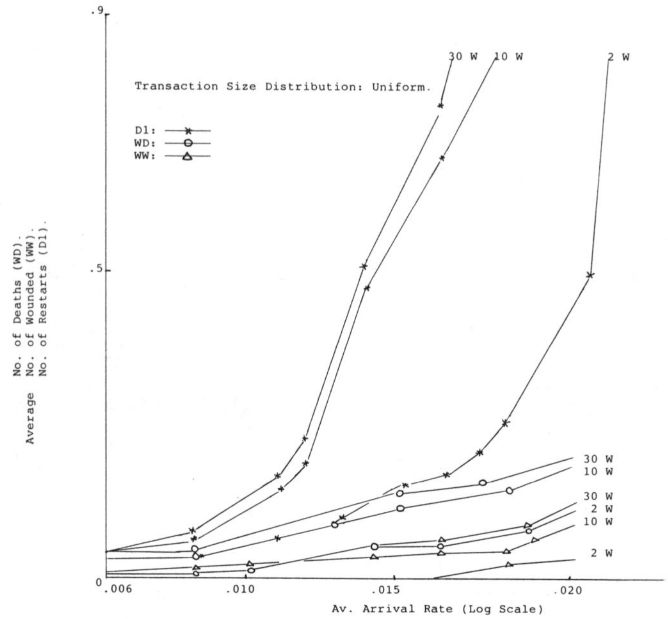

Figure 3

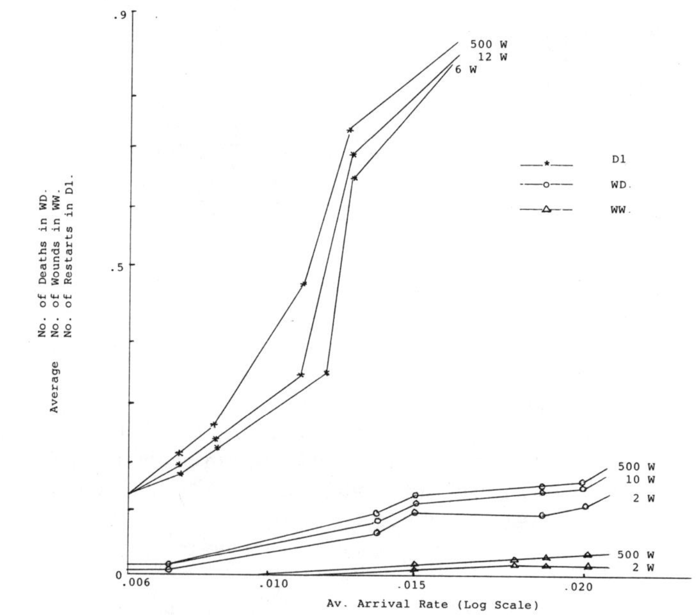

Figure 4

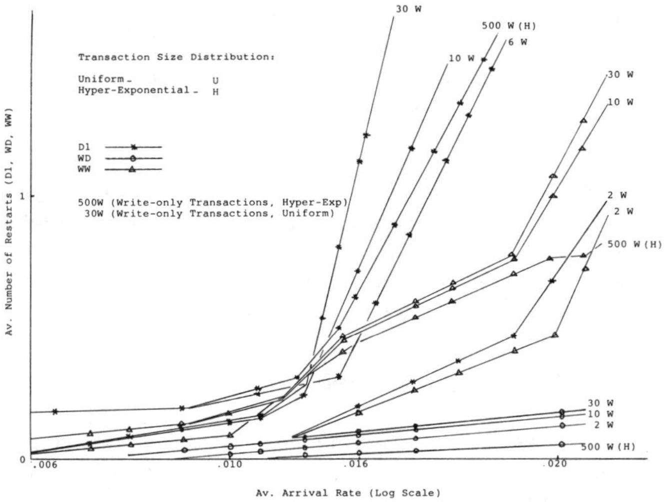

Figure 5

Transaction Wait-Time and Restarts

To evaluate the effect of restarts we look at the average time a transaction has to wait (transaction wait-time) for the required entity to become available. As stated earlier, one of the aims of CCMs is to minimize the wait-time. Figure 6 shows the relationship between average transaction wait-time and arrival rate. At very low arrival rates there is no significant difference in this parameter value for these CCMs. The difference between D1 and the other two mechanisms widens after the arrival rate of 11 transactions per second on the average. One noticeable result in Figure 6 is the wait-time for read-only transactions under these CCMs. Under WD and WW, transactions with 0 or 2 write locks wait longer than transactions with higher values of write locks.

Read-only transactions experience wait only in IO and CPU queues. Every transaction after lock requests joins IO queue and waits there for its turn. How long a transaction would wait in IO queue depends totally on the efficiency of IO processor. In D1, as the number of write locks increases so does the number restarts, and a transaction may experience wait at three places: in blocked queue, in IO queue, and in CPU queue. The situation is different in WD and WW mechanisms. As the number of write locks increases, so does the number of conflicts. The increase in the number of conflicts increases transaction deaths or the number of wounded transactions where some transactions would never reach IO queue, and these do not block the IO activity of other transactions. To verify this unexpected result we measured the average waiting-time experienced only by successfully completed transactions and found a further reduction in the waiting-time. We also looked at the waiting-time experienced by wounded and dead transactions (see Figure 7). As expected, on the average a wounded transaction experiences much higher waiting-time than a dead transaction, simply because a blocked transaction in WW is likely to get wounded. This implies that for lower values of the read : write ratio (higher number of write locks in a transaction) WD and WW mechanisms minimize transaction waiting-time, but transaction waiting-time increases as the value of this ratio increases (higher number of read locks).

Figure 7 shows the relationship between the arrival rate and average transaction wait-time of only wounded/dead transactions. The wait-time is higher in WW than it is in WD, which is expected since in WW a higher number of transactions are blocked than in WD (see Figure 4). A higher number of restarts in WD keeps the transaction wait-time to a minimum.

Since transaction restarts increase wait-time, and transaction roll-backs reduce this time, we next look at the average transaction roll-back size. Intuitively, if this size is large then transaction roll-backs would gradually become expensive as the average transaction size increases.

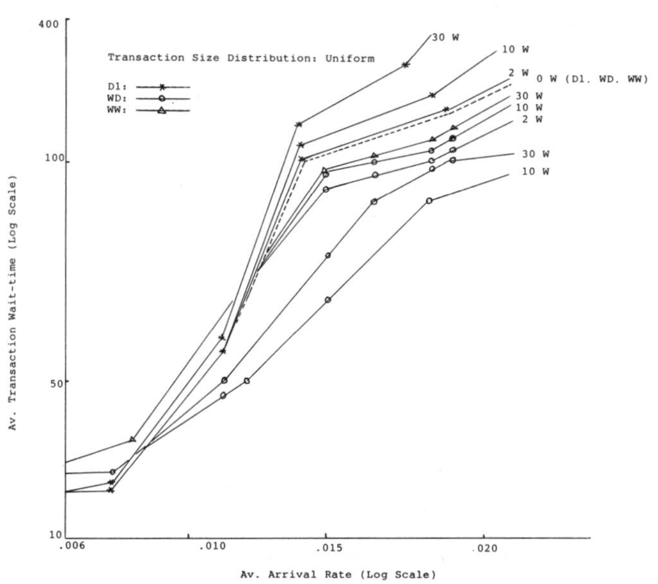

Figure 6

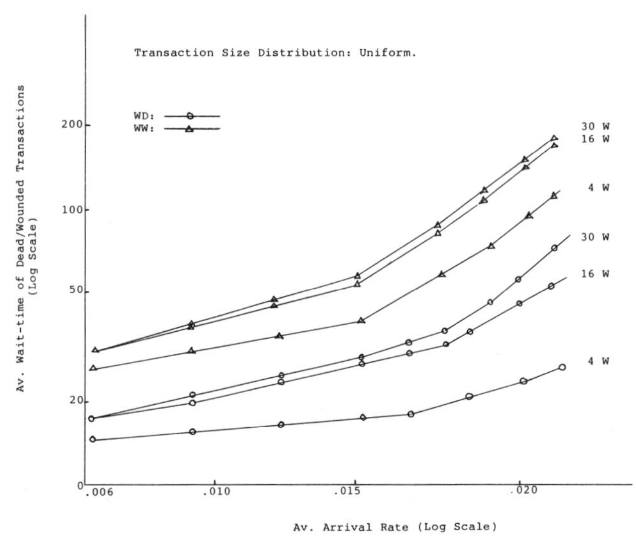

Figure 7

Arrival Rate and Roll-Back Size

As mentioned earlier, average roll-back size is the number of entities required to be restored to get the last consistent state of the database. Figures 8 and 9 show the relationship between the arrival rate and average roll-back size. In WD and WW the average roll-back size decreases with arrival rate. At higher arrival rates, on the average, fewer number of entities are restored because at lower arrival rates a transaction manages to lock more number of entities before it conflicts with other transactions. The probability of conflict increases with the arrival rate, consequently, transactions begin to conflict with other transactions sooner and the average roll-back size begins to shrink.

In the hyper-exponential distribution (Figure 9), the region of higher roll-back size for the WW mechanism begins from the arrival rate of 10 transactions per second on the average. This size begins to decline slowly after the arrival rate of 18 tansactions per second on the average. The situation is slightly different in the WD mechanism, where the average roll-back size shows a slight increase after the arrival rate of 17 transactions per second. It seems that under WD between the arrival rate of 10 through 17 transactions, almost all very large transactions go through successfully, keeping the roll-back size to a minimum. After this arrival rate, however, large transactions get rolled-back and the roll-back size increases.

In WW, it seems that most of these large transactions face roll-back between the arrival rate of 10 through 18 transactions per second on the average. This is possible since in WW a blocked transaction can also be rolled-back at any time.

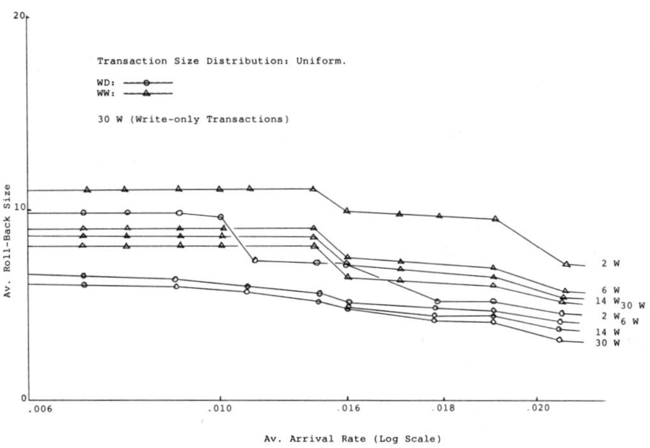

Figure 8

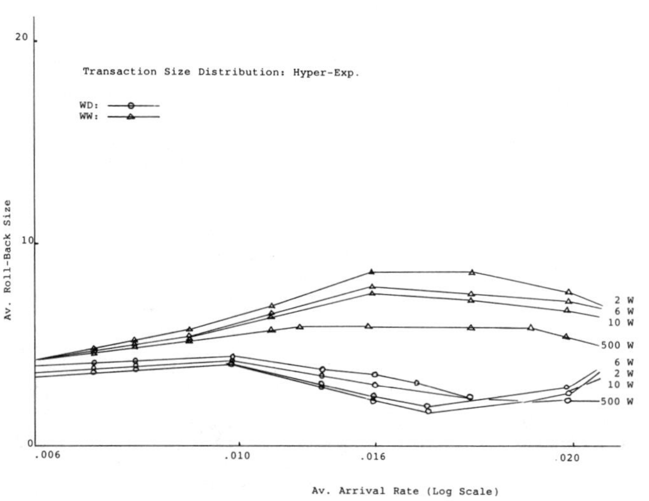

Figure 9

Deadlocks and Degree of Cycle

Deadlocks do not reduce the DoE drastically. Table I lists the number of deadlocks at various transaction arrival rates for different read : write ratios. We observe that the number of deadlocks is affected more by the type of workload than by the arrival rate. In hyper-exponential distribution, the frequency of deadlock occurrence is higher, and they also occur at lower arrival rates.

The problem of deadlock would have stronger effect, if the degree of cycle is large. We observe in Figure 10 that the degree of cycle at all arrival rates remains low. In fact in our investigation, in uniform distribution, it never exceeded three transactions. At an arrival rate of 20 transactions per second with write-only transactions we observed 8 deadlocks when about 500 to 600 transactions are run. The average degree of cycle never exceeded 2 transactions. This is low when we consider the transaction processing environment. However, its effect on throughput is noticeable. The picture is somewhat

TABLE I

Average Arrival Rate	Transaction Size Distribution Uniform (No. of Write Locks)								Transaction Size Distribution Hyper-Exponential (No. of Write Locks)			
	2W	6W	10W	14W	18W	22W	26W	30W	2W	6W	10W	500W
.006										2	2	3
.007										2	3	4
.008										2	3	4
.009									1	2	3	4
.010									1	2	3	5
.011									1	2	3	5
.012									1	2	3	4
.013									1	2	3	4
.014			2	2	2	2	2	2	2	2	2	5
.015			2	2	2	2	2	2	2	1	2	4
.016			1	1	3	3	3	3	2	2	3	5
.017		1	2	2	2	2	2	2	2	2	4	8
.018		1	2	2	2	2	2	2	2	3	4	8
.019		1	2	3	4	4	4	7	2	3	7	10
.020		2	4	5	5	5	5	8	2	5	7	13
.021	2	1	4	5	5	6	7	10	3	6	10	15
.022	1	1	4	6	6	7	8	10	6	10	12	18

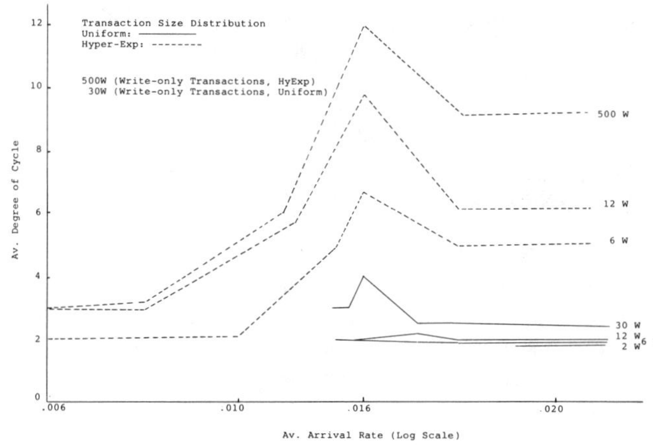

Figure 10

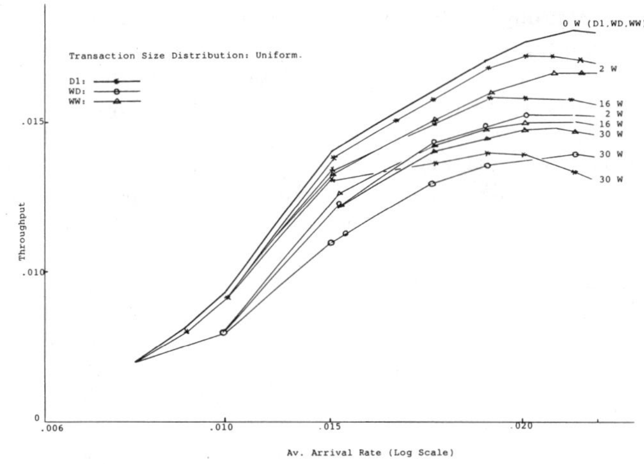

Figure 11

different in hyper-exponential distribution. The degree of cycle here shows sudden increase between the arrival rates of 10 to 16 transactions per second. We believe these peaks are caused mainly by the very large transactions. It seems that within this range of arrival rates, large transactions acquire a large number of entities, raising the probability of conflict among transactions. At higher rates outside this range, a higher number of very small transactions manage to acquire their locks without conflicting with large transactions.

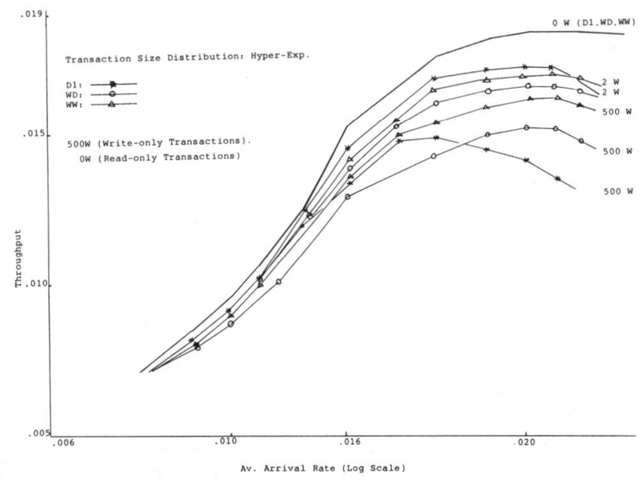

Figure 12

Read : Write Ratio

One common observation is that the behavior of read-only transactions is more noticeable than transactions with some write locks. When the number of write locks varies from 10 onward, the behavior of transactions does not change significantly. Our results show that write-only transactions and read-only transactions show distinct behavior, and transactions with all intermediate values of this ratio exhibit nearly the same behavior. We do not think the read : write ratio plays a significant role in shaping the performance of a CCM.

Arrival Rate, System Throughput, and Boundary of Efficiency

Figures 11 and 12 show the relationship between the system throughput and the arrival rate for uniform and hyper-exponential distributions respectively. At higher arrival rates, the throughput of D1 compared to WD and WW declines rapidly. As noted earlier, D1's performance suffers with high transaction wait-time due to transaction blockings. At lower arrival rates, the probability of deadlock occurrence is nil (see Table I) and the number of restarts is high (see Figure 5). As the arrival rate increases, the throughput begins to decline because of the higher restarts and deadlocks. Eventually, after the arrival rate of 20 transactions per second on the average (Figure 11), its throughput becomes the lowest. In the case of hyper-exponential distribution, the decline begins to take place after 18 transactions per second on the average. A glance at Figure 12 shows that at that rate the average number of deadlocks and the degree of cycle are higher than they are in the uniform distribution (Figure 11). To see the effect of larger size transactions, we repeated the same experiment with exponential size distribution of transactions. We found that as the transaction size increases the throughput declines more rapidly due to the increased number of restarts and deadlocks. However, at lower transaction arrival rates (lower than 20 transactions per second on the average (Figure 11), and 18 transactions per second (Figure 12), D1 performs better than WW and WD. It seems then that the domain of efficiency (DoE) of D1 is narrow compared to WW and WD, and D1 should be used for smaller size transactions under certain arrival rates.

The throughput of WD is between WW and D1. The main factor affecting the throughput of WD is the higher number of deaths (Figures 3 and 4). Although the average roll-back size remains low (Figures 8 and 9) its effect predominates from 15 to 16 transactions per second onward. It is interesting to note that a large reduction in transaction wait-time (Figure 6) does not seem as effective as we expected. It should also be noted that the effect of deaths begins to show as early as an arrival rate of 10 transactions per second on the average. The throughput of WW is the highest in the two transaction size distributions. The strategy of WW can be said to be a compromise between excessive transaction roll-backs and transaction wait-time. Similar results have been reported.[29] The average number of wounds is smaller than the number of deaths in WD, but the transaction wait-time is higher due to higher transaction blocking. A combination of these two seems to be more effective in enlarging the domain of efficiency of WW.

To test the consistency of DoEs of D1, WD, and WW, we tested these mechanisms under extreme cases, that is, large transaction sizes (100 entities on the average) and very high transaction arrival rates (100 transactions per second). In these cases we discovered that WW is comparatively more sensitive to these variations than the other two. In particular, the rate of decline of throughput was much sharper in WW compared to D1 and WD. The reason seems to be the slow increase in the average roll-back size and the frequency of deadlock occurrence.

The last point we would like to mention is that the degree of concurrency (level of multiprogramming) does not have any direct relationship with the DoE. The larger the degree of concurrency does not necessarily mean wider DoE, because after a certain value of degree of concurrency the system starts *thrashing* and the throughput begins to decline rapidly.

CONCLUSIONS

We have investigated the effect of transaction roll-backs and transaction restarts on the performance of the system. Our aim was to define in some clear terms the DoE of two-phase concurrency control mechanisms under varied transaction processing environments. We observed that the DoE is sensitive to a number of parameters. The degree of sensitivity varies among CCMs, which makes us unable to claim one CCM to be uniformly superior to others. In the case of D1, we found that the effect of deadlock is negligible up to a certain transaction arrival rate and after this rate the efficiency of D1 declines, making it inferior to WD and WW. The largest DoE is offered by WW; however, in extreme cases it appears to be more sensitive to transaction size than D1 and WD. The DoE declines more rapidly here when the average transaction size is increased. We conclude that under the worst transaction processing environment performance of WW is the worst.

The DoE of WD can be placed between D1 and WW and we found it to be the least sensitive. It does not vary significantly when other parameters such as transaction size and arrival rates are varied. However, the performance of WD is superior to D1 only at higher arrival rates.

Read-only transactions have the same performance results under all the CCMs. We notice that read-only transactions experience longest transaction wait-time in WW and WD. The situation is just the opposite in D1, where read-only transactions experience the least amount of wait.

We contradict our earlier observation that a reduction in transaction wait-time would considerably improve the performance of CCMs. A balance between the wait-time and the number of restarts seems to be more suitable for improving performance.

We notice that deadlocks are not so harmful and their detection and resolution are not so damaging to the resource utilization. In our opinion D1 should be preferred for a lightly loaded system and WD for a heavily loaded system.

REFERENCES

1. Eswaran, K.P., J.N. Gray, R.A. Lorie, and I.L. Traiger. "The Notions of Consistency and Predicate Locks in a Database System." *Comm. ACM,* 19 (1976) 11, pp. 623–633.
2. Bernstein, P.A., D.W. Shipman, and W.S. Wong. "Formal Aspect of Serializability in Database Concurrency Control." Technical Report CCA-79-14, Computer Corporation of America, February 28, 1979.
3. Coffman, E.G., M.J. Elphic, and A. Shoshani. "System Deadlocks." *ACM Computing Surveys* 3 (1971) 2, pp. 67–78.
4. Gray, J.N. "Notes on Database Operating Systems." in R. Bayer, R.M. Graham, and G. Seegmuller (eds.), Lecture Notes in Computer Science 60, *Operating Systems: An Advanced Course,* Springer-Verlag, New York, 1979.
5. Bernstein, P.A. and N. Goodman. "Concurrency Control in Distributed Database Systems." *ACM Computing Surveys,* 13 (1981) 2, pp. 185–221.
6. Bernstein, P.A. and N. Goodman. "A Sophisticate's Introduction to Distributed Database Concurrency Control." *Proc. 8th Int'l. Conf. on Very Large Data Bases,* September 1982, pp. 62–76.
7. King, P.A. and A.J. Collmeyer. "Database Sharing—An Efficient Method for Supporting Concurrent Processes." *AFIPS, Proceedings of the National Computer Conference (Vol. 42),* pp. 271–275.
8. Macri, P.P. "Deadlock Detection and Resolution in a CODASYL Based Data Management System." *Proc. ACM-SIGMOD 1976 Int'l Conf. on Management of Data,* June 1976, pp. 45–49.
9. Menasce, D.A. and R.R. Muntz. "Locking and Deadlock Detection in Distributed Databases." *Proc. 3rd Berkeley Workshop on Distributed Data Management and Computer Networks,* August 1978.
10. Newton, G. "Deadlock Prevention, Detection and Resolution: An Annotated Bibliography." *ACM-SIGOPS Operating Systems Review,* 13 (1979) 4, pp. 33–44.
11. Glogor, V.D. and S.H. Shattuk. "On Deadlock Detection in Distributed Systems." *IEEE Trans. Software Eng.,* SE-6 (1980) 5.
12. Beeri, C. and R. Obermarck. "A Resource Class Independent Deadlock Detection Algorithm." *Proc. 7th Int'l. Conf. on Very Large Data Bases,* September 1981.
13. Obermarck, R. "Distributed Deadlock Detection Algorithm." *ACM Trans. Database System,* 7 (1982) 2.
14. Mitchell, D. and M.J. Merritt. "Distributed Algorithm for Deadlock Detection and Resolution." *Proc. ACM-SIGACT-SIGMOD Conf. on Principles of Distributed Computing,* August 1984.
15. Lomet, D.B. "Deadlock Avoidance in Distributed Systems." *IEEE Trans. Software Eng.,* SE-6 (1980) 3.
16. Lomet, D.B. "A Practical Deadlock Avoidance Algorithm for Data Base System." *Proc. ACM-SIGMOD 1977 Int'l Conf. on Management of Data,* August 1977, pp. 122–127.
17. Korth, H.F. "Edge Locks and Deadlock Avoidance in Distributed Systems." *Proc. ACM-SIGACT-SIGPOS Symp. on Principles of Distributed Computing,* August 1982, pp. 173–182.
18. Chamberlain, R.F., R.F. Boyce, and Traiger. "A Deadlock-Free Scheme for Resource Locking in Database Environment." *Proc. IFIP 1974,* pp. 340–343.
19. Rosencrantz, D.J., et al. "System Level Concurrency Control for Distributed Database Systems." *ACM Trans. on Database Systems,* Vol. 3 (1978) 2, pp. 178–198.

20. Kumar, V. "Performance Evaluation of Concurrency Control Techniques for Database Management Systems." Ph.D. Thesis, University of Southampton, England, 1983.
21. Munz, R. and G. Krenz. "Concurrency in Database Systems—A Simulation Study." *Proc. Int'l. Conf. on MOD.,* August 1977, pp. 111–120.
22. Kiessling, W. and G. Landherr. "A Quantitative Comparison of Lock Protocols for Centralized Database." *9th Int'l. Conf. on VLDB,* Florence, Italy, October 1983, pp. 120–130.
23. Lin, W.K. and J. Nolte. "Basic Timestamp, Multiple Version Timestamp, and Two-Phase Locking." *9th Int'l. Conf. on VLDB,* Florence, Italy, October 1983, pp. 109–119.
24. Tay, Y.C., R. Suri, and N. Goodman. "A Mean Value Performance Model for Locking in Databases: No Waiting Case." Aiken Computational Laboratory, TR-16-83, Cambridge, Massachusetts, May 1983.
25. Tay, Y.C., R. Suri, and N. Goodman. "A Mean Value Performance Model for Locking in Databases: The Waiting Case." *Proc. 3rd ACM SIGACT-SIGMOD Symposium on Principles of Database Systems,* Waterloo, Canada, April 1984, pp. 311–322.
26. Kung, H.R. and J. Robinson. "On Optimistic Methods for Concurrency Control." *ACM Trans. on Database Sys.,* 6 (1981) 2, pp. 213–226.
27. Tay, Y.C., N. Goodman, and R. Suri. "Performance Evaluation of Locking in Databases: A Survey." Aiken Computational Laboratory, TR-17-84, Cambridge, Massachusetts, 1984.
28. Ries, D.R. and M. Stonebraker. "Effect of Granularity in a Database Management System." *ACM TODS,* 2 (1977) 3, pp. 233–246.
29. Agrawal, R., M.J. Carey, and L.W. McVoy. "The Performance of Alternative Strategies for Dealing with Deadlocks in Database Management Systems." UW-CS-TR #590.
30. Gray, et al. "The Recovery Manager of System R Database Manager." *ACM Computing Surveys,* 13 (1981) 2, pp. 223–242.
31. Sargent, R. "Statistical Analysis of Simulation Output Data." *Proc. of the Fourth Annual Symposium on the Simulation of Comp. Sys.,* August 1976.
32. Ferrai, D. "Computer System Performance Evaluation." Englewood Cliffs: Prentice-Hall, 1978.
33. Saur, C., and M. Chandy. "Computer System Modeling." Englewood Cliffs: Prentice-Hall, 1981.

Implementing distributed algorithms using remote procedure calls*

by HENRI E. BAL, ROBBERT VAN RENESSE, and ANDREW S. TANENBAUM
Free University
Amsterdam, The Netherlands

ABSTRACT

Remote procedure call (RPC) is a simple yet powerful primitive for communication and synchronization between distributed processes. A problem with RPC is that it tends to decrease the amount of parallelism in an application due to its synchronous nature. This paper shows how light-weight processes can be used to circumvent this problem. The combination of blocking RPC calls and light-weight processes provides both simple semantics and efficient exploitation of parallelism.

The communication primitive of the Amoeba Distributed Operating System is based on this combination. We describe how two important classes of algorithms, branch-and-bound and alpha-beta search, can be run in a parallel way using this primitive. The results of some experiments comparing these algorithms on a single processor and on Amoeba are also discussed.

* This research was sponsored in part by the Netherlands Organization for Pure Scientific Research (Z.W.O.) under project number 125-30-10

INTRODUCTION

As computing technology advances, it becomes increasingly difficult and expensive to make computers faster by only increasing the speed of the chips. Electrical signals in copper wire travel at ⅔ the speed of light, or about 20 cm/nanosecond, so very fast computers must be very small, which leads to severe heat dissipation problems among other things. The obvious solution is to harness together a large number of moderately fast computers to achieve the same computing power as one very fast computer, but at a fraction of the cost.

Many ways of organizing multiple processors into distributed systems have been proposed. At one end of the spectrum are the *loosely-coupled systems* consisting of a number of independent computers, each with its own operating system and users, exchanging files and mail over a public data network. At the other end of the spectrum are *tightly-coupled systems* with multiple processors on the same bus and sharing a common memory. In between are systems consisting of minicomputers or microcomputers communicating over a fast local network and all running a single, system-wide operating system. We have used a system in the latter category as a testbed for the implementation of some distributed algorithms.

In this paper we briefly describe this system, called Amoeba, and its communication primitive, which is essentially a remote procedure call (RPC). The main intent of the paper is to describe how some fairly complex distributed algorithms can be implemented on such a system using RPC. Measurements on the performances of these algorithms are presented in the last section.

THE AMOEBA SYSTEM

The Amoeba Distributed Operating System[1,2,3,4,5] consists of a collection of (possibly different) processors, each with its own local memory, which communicate over a local network. Currently, we mainly use Motorola 68010 processors connected by a 10 Mbps token ring (Pronet), although Amoeba also runs on the VAX, NS16032, PDP-11, and IBM-PC. Amoeba is based on the client-server model.[6] The system is composed of four basic components. First, each user has a personal workstation, to be used for editing on a bit-map graphics terminal and other activities that require dedicated computing power for interactive work. Second, there is a pool of processors that can be dynamically allocated to users as needed. For example, a user who wants to run a 5-pass compiler might be allocated 5 pool processors for the duration of the compilation to allow the passes to run largely in parallel. Third, there are specialized servers including: file servers, directory servers, process servers, and bank servers (for accounting). Fourth, there are gateways that connect the system to similar systems elsewhere.

The Amoeba communication primitive is based on remote procedure call (RPC).[7,8] RPC is a mechanism for communication across a network. It resembles a normal procedure call. Amoeba uses a simple form of RPC: the client sends a request to any server that is willing to offer a certain service and some server sends a response back. RPC has the advantage of simple semantics, similar to the procedure calls with which every programmer is familiar. Because it is a higher level construct than asynchronous message passing it is potentially easier to use.

One problem with RPC is that the caller (client) is blocked during the call, so a separate mechanism is needed to obtain parallelism. In Amoeba, a process (or *cluster*) consists of one or more light-weight processes called *tasks*. Tasks share a common address space and run in parallel. While a task is blocked in an RPC other tasks in its cluster may run if they have work to do. The combination of blocking RPC calls and light-weight processes provides both simple semantics and efficient exploitation of parallelism. In the following sections we describe how they can be used together to implement parallel algorithms for branch-and-bound and alpha-beta search.

PARALLEL BRANCH-AND-BOUND USING RPC

The branch-and-bound method is a technique for solving a large class of combinatorial optimization problems. It has been applied to integer programming, machine scheduling problems, the Traveling Salesman Problem, and many others.[9] We have chosen to implement the Traveling Salesman Problem (TSP), in which it is desired to find the shortest route for a salesman to visit each of the n cities in his territory exactly once.

Abstractly, the branch-and-bound method uses a *tree* to structure the space of possible solutions. A *branching rule* tells how the tree is built. For the TSP, a node of the tree represents a partial tour. Each node has a branch for every city that is not on this partial tour. Figure 1 shows a tree for a 4-city problem. Note that a leaf represents a full tour (a solution). For example, the leftmost branch represents the tour London–Amsterdam–Paris–Washington.

A *bounding rule* avoids searching the whole tree. For TSP, the bounding rule is simple. If the length of a partial tour exceeds the length of any already known solution, the partial tour will never lead to a solution better than what is already known.

Parallelism in a branch-and-bound algorithm is obtained by searching parts of the tree in parallel. If enough processors are

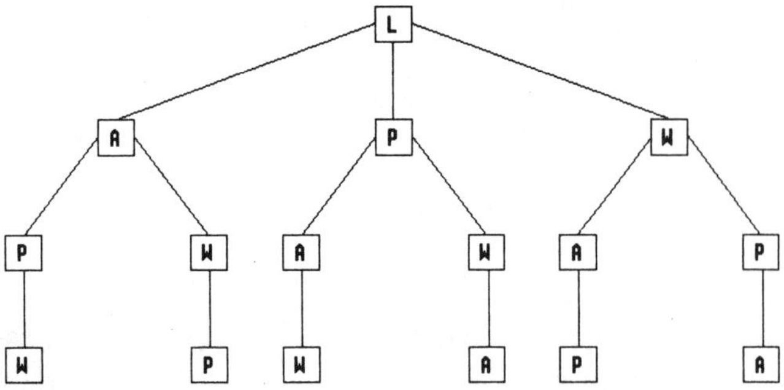

Figure 1—Tree for a 4-city Traveling Salesman Problem for London, Amsterdam, Paris, and Washington.

available, a new processor could be allocated to every node of the tree. Every processor would select the best partial path from its children and report the result back to its parent. If there are N cities, this approach would require $O(N!)$ processors. More realistically, the work has to be divided among the available processors. In our model, each processor starts at the node given to it and generates the complete partial tree reachable from that node down to *depth* levels. Each time the processor generates a node at level *depth* it hands out this node to a subcontractor for further evaluation. These evaluations and the generation of the partial tree occur in parallel. Figure 2 shows how the tree of Figure 1 can be searched using a 2-level processor hierarchy (i.e., a subcontractor has no subcontractors itself).

In Figure 2, the processor that traverses the top part of the tree (the root processor) searches one level. It splits off three subtrees, each of depth two, which are traversed in parallel by the subcontractors. This algorithm is shown in Figure 3. The algorithm sets the global variable "minimum" to the length of the shortest path. This variable is initialized with a very high value.

A processor only blocks if it tries to hand out a subtree while there are no free subcontractors. Each subcontractor executes the same traversal process, with a different initial node and probably with a different initial depth. In general, a subcontractor may split up the work over even more processors, so a subcontractor may also play the role of a root processor.

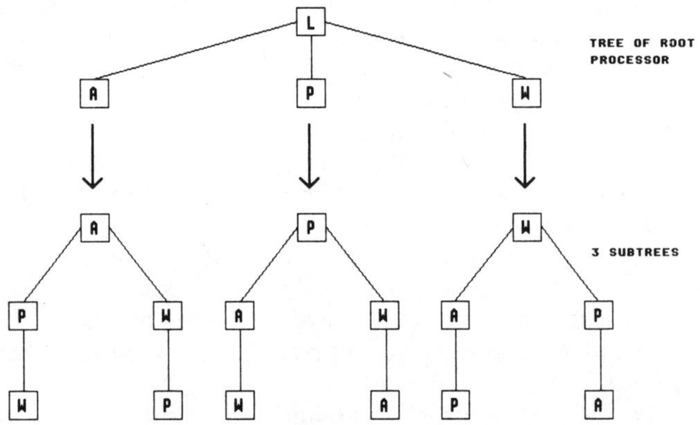

Figure 2—Example of a distributed tree search

The Traveling Salesman Problem has been implemented under Amoeba using the algorithm described above. A processor playing the role of a subcontractor can be viewed as an Amoeba *server*. The service it offers is the evaluation of a TSP subtree. Each server repeatedly waits for some work, performs the work, and returns the result. A processor playing the role of a root processor is a *client*.

The "handing out of work" is implemented using RPCs. As stated before, a problem with RPC is the fact that the caller (client) is blocked during the call. Therefore, the client cluster is split into several tasks (see Figure 4). A cluster C_p running on processor p contains one *manager* task M_p that performs the tree traversal. If the cluster has N subcontractors, it also contains N *agent* tasks $A_{p,1} \cdots A_{p,N}$. An agent $A_{p,j}$ controls the communication with subcontractor j.

After the manager task M_p receives a subtree T to evaluate, it starts the tree traversal of Figure 3. When it finds a subtree that has to be subcontracted out, it tries to find a free agent, say $A_{p,j}$. The agent $A_{p,j}$ sends the work to be done to the

```
procedure traverse(node,depth,length);
begin
   { 'node' is a node of the search tree. It contains
     a list of the cities on the current partial tour.
     'length' is the length of the partial path so far.
     'depth' is the number of levels to be searched
     before the rest of the tree should be handed
     out to a subcontractor }
   if length < minimum then
   begin { if length >= minimum skip this node }
      if 'node' is a leaf then
         minimum := length;
      else if depth = 0 then
         hand out subtree rooted at 'node'
         to a subcontractor;
      else
         for each child c of 'node' do
            traverse(c,depth-1,length+dist(node,c));
```

Figure 3—Tree traversal algorithm

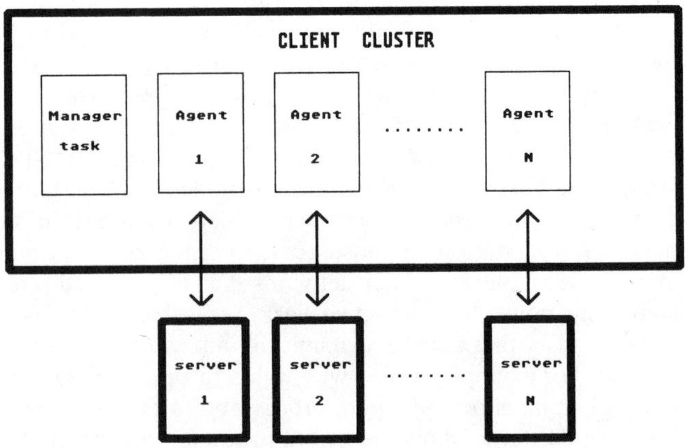

Figure 4—Process structure of the TSP program

Manager M_j of subcontractor j, using an RPC with a partial path and the current best solution as parameters. This manager M_j starts executing the process we describe here on processor j. When M_j finishes the evaluation of the subtree, it returns the result to $A_{p,j}$. This agent checks if the current best solution has to be updated, and then becomes available again for the next request from M_p. In the meantime, the manager M_p continues its tree traversal and eagerly tries to find new work to distribute. The entire client cluster only blocks if the manager tries to deal out work while all agents (and thus all subcontractors) are engaged.

This implementation fully utilizes the parallelism present in the algorithm. Furthermore, the implementation is highly flexible. It uses depth-first search, but it can easily be adapted to other strategies, such as breadth-first or best-first.

PARALLEL ALPHA-BETA SEARCH USING RPC

Alpha-beta search is an efficient method for searching game trees for two-person, zero-sum games. A node in such a game tree corresponds to a position in the game. Each node has one branch for every possible move in that position. A value associated with the node indicates how good that position is for the player who is about to move (let's assume this player is "white"). At even levels of the tree, this value is the *maximum* of the values of its children; at odd levels it is the *minimum,* as the search algorithm assumes black will choose the move that is least profitable for white. Most implementations negate the values of the odd level nodes, so the values are maximized at all levels.

The alpha-beta algorithm finds the best move in the current position, searching only part of a tree. It uses a *search window* (alpha,beta) and prunes positions whose values fall outside this window. The algorithm is shown in Figure 5.

Alpha-beta search differs significantly from branch-and-bound in the way the best solution is constructed. A branch-and-bound program (potentially) updates its solution every time a processor visits a leaf node (see Figure 3). That processor only needs to know the current best solution and the value associated with the leaf. An alpha-beta program, on the other hand, has to *combine* the values of the leaves and the interior nodes, using the structure of the tree. Some parallel alpha-beta programs realize this by having a dedicated processor for every node (up to a certain level) that collects the results of the child processors.[10] A disadvantage of this approach is that processors associated with high level interior nodes spend most of their time waiting for their children to finish.

Our solution avoids this problem by working the other way round; the child processors compute the values for their parent nodes, so there is no need for their parent processors to wait. To do this, an *explicit* tree structure is built, containing the alpha and beta bounds at each node. The search tree is no longer just a concept, it is actually built as a data structure. This tree is distributed over all processors, each processor containing that part of the tree on which it is working.

The process structure of alpha-beta is somewhat simpler than that of TSP because the shared tree can be used for synchronization within the client cluster. Hence there is no need for a manager task. The client cluster contains as many tasks as there are subcontractors (see Figure 6).

Each task essentially executes the sequential alpha-beta algorithm of Figure 5. To keep other tasks from evaluating the same positions, each task leaves a trace of what it has done already by building the tree. Each task does a depth-first search in the tree until it either finds an unvisited node or it decides that the subtree rooted at the current node should be evaluated by another processor. In the first case, it generates all children of the unvisited node and continues with the first child node. In the second case, it sends the node to a subcontractor using RPC and waits for the result.

After a subtree has been evaluated (whether local or remote) its result should be used to update the alpha and beta values of other nodes in the tree. This is illustrated in Figure 7. In Figure 7(a), the subtrees rooted at nodes 3, 4, 6, and 7

```
function AlphaBeta(node,depth,alpha,beta): integer;
begin
  if depth = 0 then
      alpha := evaluation(node)
  else
    for each child c of 'node' do
    begin
        r := -AlphaBeta(c,depth-1,-beta,-alpha)
        if r > alpha then
        begin
            alpha := r;
            if alpha >= beta then
                exit loop;   { pruning }
        end
    end
  AlphaBeta := alpha
```

Figure 5—Sequential alpha-beta algorithm

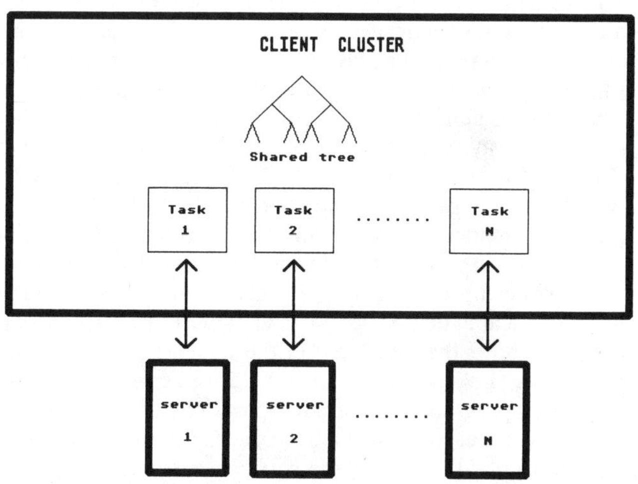

Figure 6—Process structure of the alpha-beta program

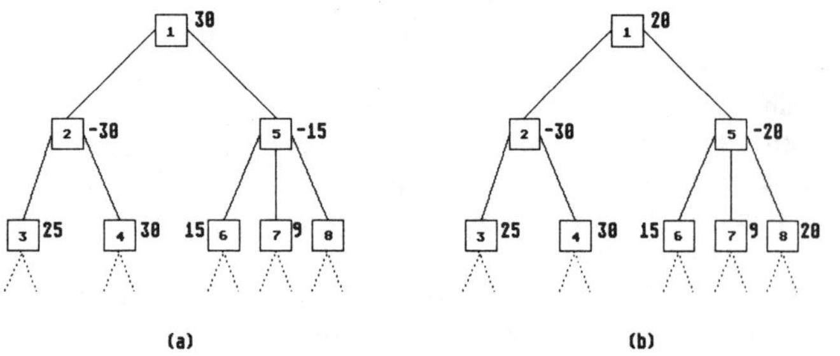

Figure 7—Example of alpha-beta search

TABLE I—Results for 11-city traveling salesman problem

version	time(secs)	speedup
sequential	637.2	
1 server	548.1	1
2 servers	309.7	1.77
3 servers	218.2	2.51
4 servers	171.7	3.19
5 servers	141.5	3.87
6 servers	124.2	4.41

TABLE II—Results for *Othello* implementation of alpha-beta search

Table 2 Results for Othello implementation of alpha-beta search

version	time(secs)	speedup	#evaluations	search overhead
sequential	266.9		2670	1
1 server	324.6	1	2670	1
2 servers	196.2	1.65	3925	1.47
3 servers	153.3	2.12	4732	1.77
4 servers	125.1	2.59	5676	2.13
5 servers	114.0	2.84	6424	2.40
6 servers	111.5	2.91	6719	2.51

have been evaluated. After the subtree rooted at node 8 has been evaluated the value of the parent of node 8 (node 5) is updated (as $20 > 15$). This is shown in Figure 7(b). Furthermore, the evaluation of the subtree rooted at 5 has now been completed. As its final value (-20) is the highest value of level 1, the value of node 1 is updated too.

After the value of a node has been improved this new value can be used as a tighter alpha bound for its children. Each child can use this new alpha value as a tighter beta bound for its own children, and so on. Thus, new values are propagated down the tree to ensure each node uses the smallest possible alpha-beta window. In principle, new bounds can even be propagated across processor boundaries. However, this would also increase the communication overhead. We have not yet experimented with this kind of propagation.

DISCUSSION

We have done some measurements on the TSP and the alpha-beta programs. The hardware used was a collection of 10 MHz 68010 CPUs connected by a 10 Mpbs token ring. For each program, we ran both a sequential (single processor) version and a parallel (multi-processor) version. For simplicity, the parallel versions use only a 2-level processor hierarchy. They use one processor for the client process and a varying number of processors for the servers.

The depths of the subtrees are important parameters of the TSP algorithm. If the client processor distributes work at a too high level, the effectiveness of pruning will be severely weakened. For example, if it traverses just one level, then the best solution in the leftmost branch of the tree cannot be used as a bound in its neighbor branch, as these branches are searched simultaneously. Increasing the depth of the root subtree will decrease this effect, at the cost of more communication between the root processor and its subcontractors. To achieve high performance, a good compromise has to be found. For an 11-city problem we found the optimal search depth of the client to be three levels. The results for an 11-city problem using this search depth are shown in Table 1. The last entry in the table shows the speedup over the 1-server version. With 7 processors (1 client and 6 servers) a 5-fold speedup over the sequential program is achieved. Note that with only one server, there is still some parallelism; the client can find the next subtree to hand out while the server is working on the previous subtree.

To measure the performance of the alpha-beta algorithm, we implemented the game *Othello,* using this algorithm. Table 2 shows the time to evaluate a position, averaged over five different positions with a fan-out (number of moves) of approximately fifteen. The depth of the search tree was four plies. As for TSP, the division of labour between the client and the servers is important. For the parallel versions the client searched three plies, the servers searched one ply.

The results show that the speedup achieved is significantly worse for alpha-beta search than for TSP. The main reason is that alpha-beta search suffers more from the decrease in pruning efficiency than TSP. The third entry in Table 2 shows the number of leaves visited by alpha-beta (i.e., the number of static evaluations). This number is a yardstick for the total amount of work done. The last entry shows the search overhead over the sequential version.

Initially, our implementations of TSP and alpha-beta search have been deliberately kept simple because we implemented them just to gain some experience with programming using RPC and light-weight processes. However, our results indicate that the primitives offered by Amoeba are sufficiently general for more advanced implementations.

REFERENCES

1. Mullender, S.J. and A.S. Tanenbaum. "A Distributed File Service Based on Optimistic Concurrency Control." *Proceedings of the 10th ACM Symposium on Operating Systems Principles,* Orcas Island, Washington, December 1985, pp. 51–62.
2. Tanenbaum, A.S. and S.J. Mullender. "An Overview of the Amoeba Distributed Operating System." *Operating Systems Review,* 15 (1981) 3, pp. 51–64.
3. Mullender, S.J. and A.S. Tanenbaum. "Protection and Resource Control in Distributed Operating Systems." *Computer Networks,* 8 (1984) 5, pp. 421–432.

4. Mullender, S.J. and A.S. Tanenbaum. "Design of a Capability-Based Distributed Operating System." *Computer Journal,* 29 (1986) 4, pp. 289–299.
5. Tanenbaum, A.S., S.J. Mullender, and R. Van Renesse. "Using Sparse Capabilities in a Distributed Operating System." *Proceedings of the 6th International Conference on Distributed Computing Systems,* Cambridge, Massachusetts, May 1986, pp. 558–563.
6. Tanenbaum, A.S. and R. Van Renesse. "Distributed Operating Systems." *Computing Surveys,* 17 (1985) 4, pp. 419–470.
7. Birrell, A.D. and B.J. Nelson. "Implementing Remote Procedure Calls." *ACM Transactions on Computer Systems,* 2 (1984) 1, pp. 39–59.
8. Nelson, B.J. "Remote Procedure Call." CMU-CS-81-119, Carnegie-Mellon University, May 1981.
9. Lawler, E.L. and D.E. Wood. "Branch-and-Bound Methods: A Survey." *Operations Research,* 14 (1966) 4, pp. 699–719.
10. Finkel, R.A. and J.P. Fishburn. "Parallelism in Alpha-Beta Search." *Artificial Intelligence,* 19 (1982), pp. 89–106.

Hardware assists for relational database systems

by PAULA HAWTHORN
Britton Lee, Inc.
Los Gatos, California

ABSTRACT

Hardware assists tackle problems that have long been associated with relational database management systems: namely, slow response time and heavy CPU consumption. This paper explores why these problems have surfaced on many relational systems and how specialized hardware systems can improve relational database performance. It will also discuss how database machines fit within an overall database system and how the database machine itself operates.

INTRODUCTION

Why do relational database management systems require hardware assists? Much has been written about slow response times and heavy CPU consumption of conventional relational DBMS. The paper discusses the motivation behind special-purpose hardware for RDBMS and the performance issues involved with this technology.

IS RELATIONAL SLOWER?

The question as to whether relational systems are slower than non-relational systems has puzzled researchers ever since the relational model was first proposed. The answer to that question, however, has much more to do with procedural vs. non-procedural than relational vs. non-relational.

In a procedural high-level interface system (such as a relational DBMS), one must depend on the computer to perform the optimizations that the programmer performs in a low-level system. For instance, although assembly language programs generally operate faster than high-level language programs, writing assembly code is extremely labor-intensive. Therefore, most applications are written in the high-level language because *people time is more expensive than computer time.* The situation with respect to database systems is the exact same as that for high-level language compilers: the high-level relational DBMS can result in less efficient use of computing resources.

While it is quite common for a user to implement an entire application using a relational DBMS in a fraction of the time that it would take using another method of managing data, it is also quite common for that user to then have problems with performance. Database machines were designed and are built to alleviate performance problems that are inherent in database systems. The performance problems existed before there were relational systems. These problems exist because the user is trying to access a large quantity of data (if there isn't a large quantity of data the user doesn't generally bother with a DBMS) and is trying to do some complicated action on the data (otherwise, a file system would serve the user just as well).

What relational systems have brought into this situation is a well-defined, highly regular, high-level interface. Such an interface is ideal for designing a computer to off-load the data management task from a general-purpose computer.

HARDWARE TO INCREASE PERFORMANCE

Research on database machines began in academic environments not long after the relational model was introduced. The University of Toronto system, RAP (1975), was the best-known of the research systems (several others are listed in the bibliography).

Figure 1 shows the database machine connected to a "host" (also called a "front-end") system that handles the interaction with the user. This separation of functionality allows the back-end database machine to be completely dedicated to the task of data management, so that the entire management of system resources is within the domain of the DBMS. The DBMS is then able to run in fully optimized mode, without affecting the user running on the general purpose system.

The user interface is located on the general-purpose system because application code is generally site-dependent. Since the code in the database machine is not modifiable by ordinary users (if it were, the consistency and security of the data would be compromised), the application code needs to be in the front-end, where it can be modified by the users.

Britton Lee's BL700 performs its database functions as a back-end machine. A block diagram is shown in Figure 2.

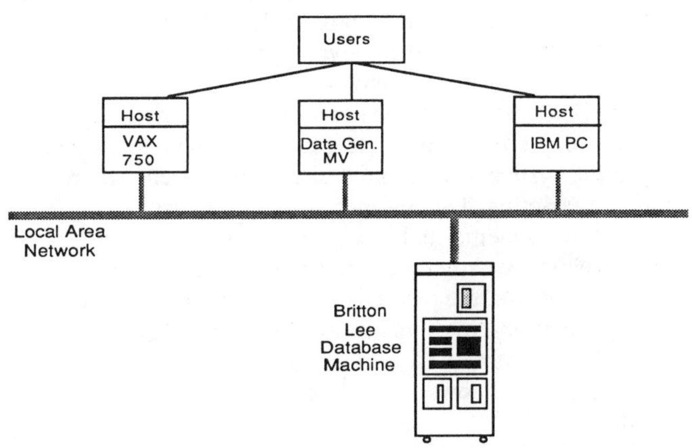

Figure 1—Illustration of the use of a database machine

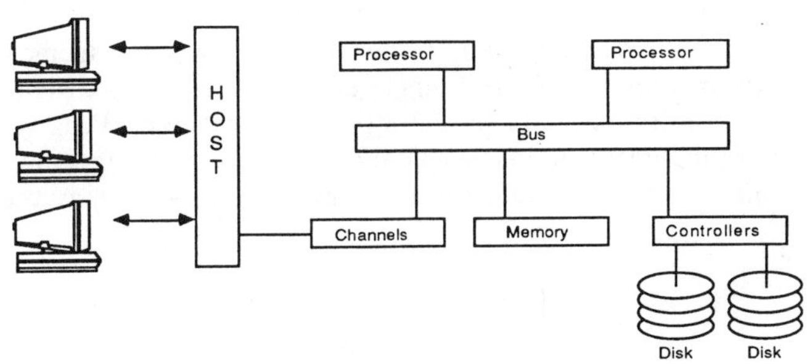

Figure 2—Block diagram of the Britton Lee system

Front-end systems—typically single-user personal computers and/or more powerful multi-user systems—can accommodate several users. The key requirement of the front-end is the ability to parse the user's database command and send it to the Britton Lee system. In Figure 2, the "host interface" program resides in the "host," or front-end box. This program translates the commands to parse trees and sends those trees to the BL700.

At this point, the BL700 handles all transaction management, recovery, security and protection issues surrounding the command, as well as executing the command itself. This split (parsing in the front-end, executing in the back-end) was first used by DeWitt on the Wisconsin database machine, DIRECT.[1]

Figure 2 shows that the data command enters the back-end system via a channel. Each channel has a dedicated processor that handles communication between the outside world and the database machine, providing the services for buffering, protocols, and so on. After a command has been received by a channel, it notifies the main processor that there is something new to do.

The BL700 has two processors dedicated to command execution: the general-purpose processor, and Britton Lee's Database Accelerator (DAC) processor.[2] The DAC is an eight MIPS reduced-instruction-set machine which executes data management instructions specifically. The DAC is called as a co-processor by the general purpose processor via subroutine calls.

The performance of the BL700 is a result of two sources: the hardware (as in the DAC) and the specialized operating system in a dedicated environment. In a dedicated machine, optimizations can be taken advantage of that would be difficult in a general-purpose environment.

The BL700 performs one function only: data management. Therefore, at every possible point the data management/operating system is cognizant of the special environment in which it is acting. For instance, the buffers are managed according to a scheme that recognizes what type of buffer it is, thus deciding whether the buffer needs to stay in memory longer. Likewise, the process manager is aware that it is a data management process manager and doesn't schedule out a process before it is finished with its buffers. And the disk allocation algorithm knows it is allocating space specifically for databases.

Much has been written about the problems that general purpose operating systems give data management systems.[3,4,5] However, the point is not that general-purpose operating systems are so bad; it is that specialized systems can be very efficient.

The BL700's operating system and the data management system were written as a single entity. There are occasional attempts to put more specialized operations in operating systems to make data management systems run more efficiently, but doing so would only make general-purpose operating systems more complex. In addition, discriminating in favor of the DBMS user could negatively affect the non-DBMS user. Therefore putting more specialized operations in general purpose operations in general-purpose operating systems will never be as effective as making a special-purpose database machine.

THE RESULTS

In G. Adams' article "VAX/DBMS Combination Requires Tuning For Maximum System Performance,"[6] it is shown that a popular software-based VAX-resident DBMS has the following characteristics:

Processor	*Amount of Memory Required*	*Number of Software DBMS Users*
725/730	3–5 Mbytes	2
750	6–10 Mbytes	6–10
μvax II	8–12 Mbytes	8–12
780	10–15 Mbytes	10–18
785	15 Mbytes or more	15–25

Adams does not state what the DBMS users are doing, and the application type would be very important to any such estimate, but the following has been observed at Britton Lee customer sites:

Processor	*Amount of Memory Required*	*Number of Britton Lee Users*
725/730	3 Mbytes	10
750	4 Mbytes	40
μvax II	4 Mbytes	40
780	12 Mbytes	70
785	12 Mbytes	90

The results are clear: specialized hardware and software result in more cost-effective use of computing resources.

REFERENCES

1. DeWitt, D.J. "DIRECT—A Multiprocessor Organization for Supporting Relational Database Systems," *IEEE Trans. Computers,* June, 1979, pp. 395–406.
2. Ubel, M. "The Intelligent Database Machine (IDM)," in Won Kim (ed.), *Query Processing in Database Systems,* Springer-Verlag, 1985.
3. Gray, J. "Notes on Database Operating Systems," in R. Bayer, R.M. Graham and G. Seegmuller (eds.), *Operating Systems: an Advanced Course,* Springer-Verlag, 1979.
4. Hawthorn, P. "Evaluation and Enhancement of the Performance of Relational Database Management Systems," ERL Memo M79-70, Univ. of California, Berkeley, 1979.
5. Stonebraker, M.R. "Operating System Support for Database Management." *Comm. of the ACM,* 24 (1981) 7, pp. 412–418.
6. Adams, G. "VAX/DBMS Combination Requires Tuning For Maximum System Performance." *Hardcopy,* November, 1986.

Deployment strategies for new software technology

by KENNETH C. LATOZA
Digital Equipment Corporation
Schaumburg, Illinois

ABSTRACT

Strategy selection for the deployment of software technology is a key part of putting software to work within organizations. Several different deployment strategies are examined in this paper—diffusion, test site, and edict. Also some of the key elements in strategy selection are reviewed. Finally, three agents of strategy implementation are discussed—technology managers, information flow, and application centers.

INTRODUCTION

The deployment of software is an integral part of the software life-cycle. In any organization, a strategy must be adopted for deploying that technology. In this paper, several different types of strategies are examined.

Generally, any type of software technology that is significantly different from those an organization currently uses should be considered as new software technology. Typical examples are: significant new languages (e.g., Ada or OPS5), new technology areas (e.g., artificial intelligence or distributed computing), new software development methodologies (e.g., higher order software, object oriented design, or rapid prototyping).

Where the software technology is going to be used will affect the deployment strategy. Although one could examine the types of strategies that would be used if the technology would be deployed to customer organizations, this paper discusses deployment of new software technology within a parent organization. Three strategies are examined, ways to determine which strategy to use are presented, and general deployment tools are described.

STRATEGIES

Of the many different strategies that can be identified, three are discussed here: diffusion, test site, and the blanket or edict strategy.

Diffusion

The diffusion strategy is used to introduce a new software technology in non-selected areas and allow the technology to permeate the organization through word of mouth. This strategy forces the technology to sell itself and asks the users of the technology to become the salespeople. The diffusion strategy allows an organization to accept the technology on its own time-scale and to make choices about local deployment. Diffusion of technology by area in large organizations can take a long time and can cause various levels of the deployment to be apparent in the organization for long periods of time.

This strategy frequently is used when a small group of individuals determines the need for some type of technology. The technology is then implemented and spread through the organization by word of mouth. As an example, the precursors to the electronic conferencing tool VAX Notes were deployed within Digital Equipment Corporation using this strategy.

Test Site

The test site strategy is used to select a test location or test group to pilot a technology. Using this method, an experiment is run to see if the new technology is truly applicable within an organization. This strategy forces technology managers to decide on a test location and to enlist a test group as active participants. Test sites can later become showcases of the technology. By enforcing formal review procedures, valuable insights can be gained into the usefulness and problem areas of given technology. The test site strategy also consumes time and sometimes the results can be inconclusive.

As an example, Digital Equipment Corporation has formalized this deployment strategy through the field test methodology. Field test sites are carefully chosen and monitored to determine the effectiveness of the new technology. All Digital products must pass through this phase.

Edict

The edict strategy involves selecting a technology and then enforcing use of that technology across an organization. With this method, either a ramped or start date implementation plan is chosen and the technology is spread through the organization. This strategy forces the technology managers to make an excellent guess on the needs of the organization for this technology and to develop a "well oiled" implementation strategy. This strategy removes the problems that result when dissimilar technologies coexist.

This strategy can also be used "negatively." For example, the retirement of a particular product and subsequent discontinuation of its support is a form of the edict strategy. Digital uses a product life cycle methodology that contains a retirement phase for a given product.

STRATEGY SELECTION

Selection of a deployment strategy depends on a number of factors, some of which are discussed here. One element in strategy selection is how well original requirements are filled by the software technology selected. Another aspect is how the software was selected; that is, was it internally developed, externally developed, or purchased. The effect on the organization and the problem to which the technology will be applied must be examined.

Technology impact information can be gathered in a number of ways. One way is to survey targeted users of the technology. When designing such a survey, it is important to ensure that useful results will be obtained and that a majority of users are questioned. Another way to gather information about how a new technology may affect a company is to form committees of technology managers and the target users. The composition of any committee should include the most vocal and most active members of the user community; however, typical members also should be included.

The goal of information gathering using these techniques is to reveal the attitudes of the users about a new technology and how they feel about the possible ways the new technology can be used to solve a problem. Frequently, users will feel that a problem does not really exist even if the problem has been identified by business or technology managers. Therefore, part of the deployment strategy will be to gain a consensus that a problem exists and is amenable to a new technology. Differing opinions about whether a problem exists typically result when a user community is large but only a small portion of the user community is included in technology selection. This problem can also occur when a change in business direction occurs and a new technology is needed to meet a business goal. For example, when companies with differing technology products merge, discrepancies in problem identification are likely to arise.

Once the receptiveness of the user population is determined a risk analysis[1] should be performed to evaluate:

- Whether the correct technology has been chosen
- Time to deploy
- Return on investment for cost of deployment

The costs of deployment must include training, support, and distribution of user and reference manuals. The size of the user community will obviously affect this cost. Another aspect to study is if the organizational structure will change (or should change) with the deployment of the technology. Further, the complexity of the technology will affect training and support issues and may also affect the cost of the technology. For example, the complexity of the technology affects the length of training time and the amount of effort needed to complete the training. Also, the new technology could increase maintenance costs and payments to vendors and require additional computer equipment.

When the risk assessment is finished, the deployment strategy (or strategies) can be selected and a deployment plan developed. This plan should include the risk analysis, the deployment timetable, and a list of resources used to deploy the plan. A presentation can be developed and toured through the organization. This presentation should include the background to the problem for which the software technology is being deployed, the background to the technology, some of the options considered, the resources available and used within the organization during deployment, and the highlights of the deployment plan.

If the diffusion strategy is used to introduce a new technology, the deployment plan can become the formal recognition that a technology is in place and is meeting the solution to some problem within an organization.

Replication of effort and use of different strategies can increase the chances of success. Often a problem exists but either no reasonable technological solution exists or equally valid multiple solutions exist. In such cases different groups can develop and deploy different technologies and time will determine which will be the most successful.

OVERALL DEPLOYMENT TOOLS

The role of a technology manager[2] is key within an organization. As an example of using technology managers, Digital has a team that consists of a staff manager and consultants. They are responsible to respond to both business management and the user community with effective choices of technology and deployment strategies for the technology. The technology management team is used for deploying different types of technology, including software technology. These players play the lead role in ensuring successful deployment of technology within the organization.

The benefits of having a technology manager are:

- Technology leadership
- Focus point for software technology issues and information
- Organization responsibility to respond to technology change issues
- Responsibility for long term technology plans

Another key deployment tool within an organization is information flow. Large amounts of current information must be moved within the organization. Adopting multiple lines of communication is necessary to service the needs of all members. Digital, for example, has several types of communication formats. Videotex databases are used for bulk delivery of current information on technologies. VAX Notes electronic conferencing is provided for both private and public discussions of technical and non-technical issues. Scheduled review meetings between users and technology managers are used to provide face to face communication.

Providing current information to the user community has many benefits. These include reduction in printed material, quick feedback on problems and questions, forums for timely discussions, and quick changes to rapidly changing information.

Finally, software needs hardware on which to execute. To provide focus points for software technology tools, technology information centers should be provided.[3] For example, Digital has introduced Application Development Centers to provide common locations where software technology can be found. These centers are linked to facilities throughout the organization through Digital's internal computer communications network.

Technology information centers are beneficial when used as:

- Test sites for software technology introduction
- Catalogue and inventory sources of available software technologies
- Known software information interchange locations.

CONCLUSION

Successful introduction of software technology requires the selection of an appropriate deployment strategy. This strategy is embodied in a deployment plan that describes the risk analysis and deployment timetable. Finally, technology managers, good communication channels, and focused hardware resources are necessary to develop and implement effective deployment strategies.

REFERENCES

1. Strassman, Paul A. *Information Payoff.* New York: The Free Press, 1985.
2. Kanter, Rosabeth Moss. "Technological Change—A Threat or An Opportunity." *The Consultant,* May/June 1985, pp. 6–11.
3. Boar, Bernard H. "The Prototyping Center." *Application Prototyping.* New York: John Wiley, 1984.

Evidence on separately organizing for software maintenance

by NED CHAPIN
InfoSci Inc.
Menlo Park, California

ABSTRACT

Software maintenance activities can be organizationally combined with or separated from software development. Proponents have argued advantages for each mode, but factual evidence on the respective results and conditions has been missing. This paper reports evidence gathered from sites organized in the two ways and contrasts their characteristics. Significant differences appear that give a better factual basis for selecting an appropriate organizational position for application software maintenance.

INTRODUCTION

Our purpose in doing and reporting this work is to clear the air on the consequences and conditions associated with two alternative organizational modes. One mode is to keep application software maintenance activities organizationally combined with software development. The other mode is to keep a clear separation organizationally between application software maintenance and development.

A survey reported in 1980,[1] revealed that only about one-sixth of organizations kept those two activities separate. No survey reported since has profiled the characteristics and results associated with each organizational mode. Publications that could reasonably be expected to have covered these matters have neglected or passed over them. For example, the *Proceedings* of the four Software Maintenance Conferences have not addressed this matter.[2,3,4,5] The *Proceedings* of the CSM-85 and of the Software Maintenance Workshop of 1983 gave this matter no explicit attention.[6,7] *Software Maintenance News* has largely passed over this matter.[8] The National Computer Conference has not addressed this matter in its *Proceedings* even though software maintenance is given some attention.[9]

Which mode to adopt and the pros and cons about each mode have received passing mention in several articles and papers. For example, Canning offers a summary of pros and cons.[10] Reynolds can be interpreted as saying that organizational separations also build walls affecting communication with users, and hence are bad.[11] On the grounds that maintenance is a specialized task, Parikh favors a separate organizational status.[12] Bronstein and Okamoto argue that a separate organizational position reduces conflicts in priorities.[13] Marks and Strowbridge advocate specializing the staff, but stop short of advocating a separate organizational status.[14]

What little has been reported on this matter has not had a strong or broad factual base. We did the study reported here because our discussions with management at computer sites detected a warm interest in evaluating the applicability of these two alternative modes. Some managers seem to seek reassurance that the mode they have chosen is a good selection given their circumstances; other managers wonder if that other pasture is indeed as green as it looks and is touted to be. Opinions abound, but reliable facts are in short supply. We therefore decided to gather facts and report the evidence found.

In the gathering and reporting process, we used a four-part definition of software application maintenance presented by Chapin since it matches the current reality of software maintenance work better than some earlier definitions.[1,15] In brief, the four parts can be termed *enhancive, corrective, adaptive,* and *consultative* maintenance. Application software maintenance itself is any servicing done to, on, or about existing application software. That servicing may result in: 1) modifying the application software (usually to extend, alter, or to correct its functionality), 2) adapting the software to perform in a changed data processing environment, or 3) consulting with (e.g., by interpreting, guiding, or training) the user personnel in securing the desired results from the use of the existing software. Packaged software in this definition is not distinguished from in-house developed software. Work related to system software is conventionally excluded by the definition of software maintenance.

DATA GATHERED

We solicited data by means of a written questionnaire from persons with managerial roles in data processing sites sprinkled all across the United States. We solicited information from sites with a data processing (DP) staff believed to number more than nine. We did a vigorous follow-up to get the questionnaires back, although some were returned only partially completed. As expected, we found the common organizational position for software maintenance is that it is combined with software development. Since our sampling process was not designed to determine the current proportion of the various organizational modes for placing software maintenance, we report neither data nor conclusions on the relative frequency of the modes.

For statistical confidence, we sought a sample of at least sixty organizations in each of the two modes, but attempted to draw a larger sample than that, anticipating some unusable returns. We attempted to secure responses from more than one person at each organization since different people in an organization often view the organization differently. After discarding clearly questionable or seriously incomplete responses, we had 232 responses spread over 130 organizations, and 684 statements of problems recognized by the respondents. The modal number of responses was one per organization and the average number of responses per organization was two.

In checking our data gathering, we found that one question on the questionnaire was interpreted variously by different responders. That question asked about the years of backlog of maintenance work. Some responders framed their responses for the full size (staffing) of the organization they represented, whereas others framed their responses in terms of years of backlog per person primarily doing maintenance work. This makes the total or overall magnitude of the gathered backlog data meaningless. Also, a few large responses pull up the averages. The medians for the backlog are 4.0 years for the separate mode of organization, and 2.5 years for the combined mode. However, we found only random differences in the varied responder interpretation with respect to the mode of organization. Hence, on a contrast basis, any comparison or difference can still be meaningful even though the absolute levels reported are not meaningful for this item.

ANALYSIS

After making validation checks, we applied ordinary statistical analysis techniques to the distributions of the data. Then we applied tests of statistical significance. Table I summarizes our analysis.

CONFIGURATION

The analysis points to distinctive configurations for the two modes of organization of application software maintenance. In the following paragraphs, we summarize the statistically significant aspects first and then some aspects showing no significant differences.

Organizations that organizationally combine software maintenance with software development display the following configuration of characteristics compared to the other mode: 1) The respondents see their organizations as smaller. 2) They believe their organizations do more enhancement and less new development. 3) They see the maintenance backlog as smaller but have a more negative attitude toward software maintenance. 4) They believe they have more management problems in maintaining software and that they have software that is generally harder to maintain, although old software is not seen as being as much of a problem.

Organizations that organizationally separate software maintenance from software development display the following configuration of characteristics compared to the other mode: 1) The respondents see their organizations as larger. 2) They believe their organizations do more new development but less enhancement. 3) They see the maintenance backlog as larger but have a more positive attitude toward software maintenance. 4) They believe that the age of the software makes software maintenance difficult. 5) They believe their software maintenance work suffers from fewer management problems.

In a number of important ways, both organizational modes are alike. The experience level of the personnel doing the software maintenance is about the same for both groups. Personnel turnover is seen about equally by both groups as a problem area, as is, to a lesser extent, a shortage of qualified staff. The groups show no significant difference in the extent to which they see documentation as a problem, and they do about equal proportions of corrective maintenance. The groups show no significant differences on such personnel-related matters as staff availability, motivation, morale, and turnover. Both groups regard maintaining good communication with users and others as a problem area and regard user relationships as about equally difficult to keep satisfactory.

TABLE I—Analysis of data gathered on software maintenance for different levels of significance by mode of organization for software maintenance

```
ATTRIBUTES

    Significant at one per cent level
        Size of organization, average staffing level
            Separate--95.1 persons; Combined--80.7 persons
        Enhancement effort, average as per cent of total
            Separate--42.5%; Combined--51.9%

    Significant at two per cent level
        None

    Significant at five per cent level
        New development effort, average as per cent of total
            Separate--37.3%; Combined--27.2%
        Backlog of maintenance work, average (see text)
            Separate--15.8 years; Combined--10.5 years

ATTITUDES

    Significant at one per cent level
        Negative attitude toward software maintenance
            Separate--18.1%; Combined--31.9%

    Significant at two per cent level
        Positive attitude toward software maintenance
            Separate--15.5%; Combined--7.8%

    Significant at five per cent level
        None

PROBLEMS RECOGNIZED as proportion mentioned in categories

    Significant at one per cent level
        Management problems in total
            Separate--6.7%; Combined--13.5%
        Old software to maintain
            Separate--11.0%; Combined--3.3%

    Significant at two per cent level
        Difficult to work with software characteristics
            Separate--2.3%; Combined--8.6%

    Significant at five per cent level
        Unstructuredness in the source code
            Separate--8.1%; Combined--15.2%
```

DISCUSSION

Statistical analysis does not tell what are the causes and what are the effects. Management personnel in organizations may be seeking some particular effect, such as "How to free some time for increasing effort on new development projects." They want to know likely causes. Also, the data presented here may be more representative and descriptive as a constellation or configuration of characteristics than are the characteristics individually.

A perception of a difference in the size of the organization is noted in the configuration. The averages are far above the median sizes of 52 persons for the separate mode and 25 persons for the combined mode. Many respondents in each group did not report the size of the entire data processing organization; rather, they reported the size of their own unit. Hence, size is rarely overstated but often reflects a esprit de corps view of personal identification—an attitude cultivated by some managements. The smaller size reported by the combined-organized group could reflect a measure of more success in such attitude cultivation. We verbally explored this possibility informally with personnel in a few organizations, and believe it contributed little to the size difference noted here. Generally, larger organizations are more likely to use a separate organizational mode for software maintenance than are smaller organizations, but the separate mode is still a minority for all sizes of organizations. This evidence is consistent with what has been reported elsewhere.[1]

The differences in the proportion of effort on enhancements and on new development are probably untrustworthy.

We found no organizations other than software houses that systematically and consistently recognized and recorded consultative maintenance as a distinct entity, even though all respondents recognized the existence of the activity in their organizations and most indicated it was an increasing drain on personnel time. To a lesser extent, and not concentrated in software houses, the same observation applies to adaptive maintenance. In the data gathered, respondents spread effort in both categories over the categories of corrective and enhancive maintenance, increasing both, with no detected differences by organizational mode.

A more serious complication is the variability used in practice in defining what effort is corrective maintenance, what is enhancive maintenance, and what is new development. Where maintenance is separately organized, these distinctions have more often been given some explicit attention than where the combined organization mode is used. Nonetheless, variation is rampant for both modes. A fairly common criterion is a set level of effort that "distinguishes" new development from maintenance. Such a criterion might be: Any application software work estimated at more than six person-months is classified as new development, irrespective of its other characteristics. Such criteria are pragmatically useful and not uncommon, since socially or politically unpopular (negative attitude) maintenance work can be made to disappear and new development appear at the stroke of a pen. For example, one could define any application software work of more than two person-months duration as new development, any work of more than one person-day (but less than two person-months) as enhancement (maintenance), and anything smaller as corrective (maintenance). It is our assessment that the differences noted above in enhancement and new development effort primarily reflect differences in definition, not differences in the amounts, character, or nature of the work being done.

If the work *is* equivalent, then the real differences in the organizational modes are the differences seen in the management area.[16] Segregating the personnel doing the maintenance work into a separate organization unit weakens the lines of communication to those (few) personnel still around who did the development work on the software. With less of that knowledge to call upon, any impenetrability in the software looms larger. Concern with documentation is not significantly different between the two modes. Recognition of these factors appears to be an effect of selecting the separate-organized mode, but does not appear to be a cause of the mode selection.

When a separate organization is put in place for any function, securing enough qualified personnel to staff it is a common management concern, along with securing other needed resources. Yet no significant differences appear between the two modes. In the absence of such a separate organization, development personnel get assigned to do the software maintenance. This provides a staff (which may be qualified) but documentation deficiencies are still the number one complaint in both modes. In this regard, it must be remembered that *no* significant differences are seen by the respondents in the turnover, motivation, morale, qualifications, and experience level of the personnel between the two organizational modes.

Attitudes are seen as significantly different too. Negative attitudes are associated with the respondents' greater frequency of mentions of management problems, and are significant for the combined-organized group. Positive attitudes are associated with the respondents' lesser frequency of mentions of management problems, and are significant for the separately-organized group. This relationship is not surprising given the respondents' management responsibilities. It also points to what appears to be an effect of selecting the separate organization mode—a more positive attitude by those managing the software maintenance. The significance of this has been noted before.[17] The specific causes of this attitude difference are not seen in the work reported here.

The differences between the two organizational modes with the greatest statistical significance are the differences in the proportion of enhancement effort (see prior qualification), in management problems, in groupings of software attributes, and in the size of the organizations (see prior qualification). One of the two main groups of significant software attributes consists of the fewer problems reported by the combined-mode respondents for old software, interactions among software, and poor implementations. The other consists of the fewer problems reported by the separate-mode respondents for source-code unstructuredness, difficult-to-work with source code, and large program and system size. From the evidence reported here, the causes and effects for these characteristics are not seen directly for most of them.

CONCLUSIONS

Given the qualifications presented in the discussion about the configuration of characteristics described here, some conclusions emerge. One is that we detected no differences in the nature or characteristics of the demand for or performance of the software maintenance work between the two organizational modes. Hence, any motivation to adopt one or the other of the modes apparently arises from other sources. A hope to reduce the burden (cost or total amount) of software maintenance work in order to get more personnel time for new development appears to be a tempting motivation, but the achievement appears to be more a matter of definition rather than of any actual change in the work getting done.

What those organizations adopting a separate organizational place for software maintenance have achieved is fewer management problems and a more positive attitude toward software maintenance by those managing it. What adopting the separate organizational mode has required is an explicit definition and recognition of what is to be encompassed as software maintenance. This sharper definition may contribute to the larger backlog recognized in the organizations that organize separately for software maintenance.

Larger organizations are more receptive to a separate organizational place for software maintenance. Maintenance management personnel in the separately-organized mode report fewer problems with maintaining poorly structured and poorly implemented source code but more problems with old programs and systems. It is not known whether a recognition of these is a predisposition to or a consequence of adopting the separate-organized mode.

In summary, management's use of a separate organizational position for application software maintenance appears to have little effect upon the maintenance work, its cost, and its quantity. It does appear to reduce management-oriented problems with getting software maintenance done and to improve attitudes. From this survey, the evidence appears to us that an old management dictum—if you want something managed better, then make the managing of it be someone's prime responsibility—also applies to managing application software maintenance.

REFERENCES

1. Lientz, Bennet P. and E. Burton Swanson. *Software Maintenance Management.* Reading, Massachusetts: Addison-Wesley, 1980.
2. *Proceedings of the First National Conference on EDP Software Maintenance.* Silver Spring, Maryland: U.S. Professional Development Institute, 1983.
3. *Proceedings of the Second National Conference on EDP Software Maintenance.* Silver Spring, Maryland: U.S. Professional Development Institute, 1984.
4. *Proceedings of the Third National Conference on EDP Software Maintenance.* Silver Spring, Maryland: U.S. Professional Development Institute, 1985.
5. *Proceedings of the Fourth National Conference on EDP Software Maintenance.* Silver Spring, Maryland: U.S. Professional Development Institute, 1986.
6. Arnold, Robert S. and Roger Martin (eds.). *Proceedings of the Conference on Software Maintenance—1985.* Long Beach, California: IEEE, 1985.
7. Arnold, Robert S. (ed.). *Proceedings of the Software Maintenance Workshop.* Long Beach, California: IEEE, 1984.
8. *Software Maintenance News.* 1984 through 1987.
9. *AFIPS, Proceedings of the National Computer Conference.* (Vols. 48 through 55), 1979 through 1986.
10. Canning, Richard G. (ed.). "Easing the Maintenance Burden." *EDP Analyzer,* 19 (1981) 8, pp. 1–6.
11. Reynolds, Carl H. "Issues in Centralization." *Datamation,* 23 (1977) 3, pp. 91–94.
12. Parikh, Girish. *There Is a Fortune to be Made in Software Maintenance.* Chicago, IL: Shetal Enterprises, 1985.
13. Bronstein, Gary M. and Robert I. Okamoto. "I'm OK, You're OK, Maintenance is OK." *Computerworld,* 15 (1981) 2, pp. In-depth 19–20.
14. Marks, William W. and William D. Strowbridge. "Dedicated Maintenance Staff Key to Smooth Operation." *Computerworld,* 19 (1985) 34, pp. SR/45.
15. Chapin, Ned. "Software Maintenance—A Different View." *AFIPS, Proceedings of the National Computer Conference* (Vol. 54), 1985, pp. 507–513.
16. Perry, William E. "A Plan of Action for Software Maintenance." *Data Management,* 23 (1985) 3, pp. 44–45.
17. Chapin, Ned. "Supervisory Attitudes Toward Software Maintenance." *AFIPS, Proceedings of the National Computer Conference* (Vol. 55), 1986. pp. 61–68.

PC proliferation: Minimizing corporate risk through planning for application maintenance

by LINDA SHAFER
Los Alamos National Laboratory
Los Alamos, New Mexico
and
JOHN CONNELL
Martin Marietta Denver Aerospace
Denver, Colorado

ABSTRACT

The rapid proliferation of personal computers, offering tremendous productivity gains for knowledge workers, often creates new application maintenance tasks. Specific concerns include security, data integrity, and access authorization. Distributed networks require security and communication systems. Distributed data entry requires file servers, network support personnel, and synchronization methods to preserve the integrity of corporate data. Much personal computing software which must be maintained is developed outside of standard-imposing environments and without benefit of formal training. A recommended method for limiting future maintenance problems is the formation of a staff possessing skills specific to problem solving in the areas mentioned and functioning as personal computing consultants for the area of the knowledge worker.

INTRODUCTION

There is better than a 100 to 1 ratio of personal computers (PCs) to mainframes in this country and more than 100,000 commercial application packages available to support those PCs. Management and knowledge workers have embraced the use of PCs and generic software, gaining degrees of freedom from data processing departments. No longer do users have to wait months or years for the delivery of a new application system—they choose from packaged software or write their own.

Knowledge workers are using PCs for the following kinds of tasks:

- *Word processing:* specifications, documentation, agendas, memos, and reports
- *Graphics:* view-graphs, diagrams, design concepts, planning charts, graphs, layouts, and artwork for documents
- *Database management:* inventory, action status, compensation analysis, task analysis, design decomposition, new application rapid prototyping, and problem tracking
- *Spreadsheet:* estimates, financial analysis, expenditure tracking, trade-off analysis, and criticality analysis
- *Outline processing:* to-do lists, presentation outlines, agendas, and document outlines
- *Project management:* task planning, cost estimating, and critical path analysis
- *Telecommunications:* mainframe access, rapid remote data transfer, and electronic mail

No doubt many other types of applications could be cited, but the list is sufficient to illustrate that a good PC offers great assistance with everyday work tasks. Increased use of computers by the average knowledge worker is the obvious result even though productivity gains are difficult to measure since PC users accomplish tasks that they would not have attempted before.

Despite well-documented advantages of using microcomputers, accelerated and unmanaged growth of networks has left a vacuum in support services. Software maintenance, presumed to be a non-issue with respect to personal computers, is still a required task.

The PC and Data Maintenance Issues

Many companies download data into applications running on PCs, realizing that micro users' direct access to corporate data saves re-keying and gives all users the same up-to-date information. Sophisticated links download only selected portions of voluminous mainframe files, a procedure that may soon become the norm. This and other uses for the PC are growing daily—their real potential has only begun to be exploited. Yet the personal computer has not been a commonplace fixture in organizational settings long enough for surrounding maintenance issues to be documented.

In a centralized computing environment, software maintenance consists of making changes to production programs—modifying, adding, and deleting lines of code. A catalyst for software maintenance is user dissatisfaction with the functionality of current systems. A system may not be functioning properly, not be functioning at all, or functioning perfectly but not solving the desired set of current information management problems. To correct such situations in actual practice, maintenance programmers perform a wide range of activities in addition to code modification.

When a production problem occurs with code that has been functioning properly, the problem may not be with the program logic. The most common cause for such problems is imperfect data. Problems may occur when someone accesses the wrong file, when inaccurate information is entered into a file, or when a file update is executed at the wrong time or not at all. There are so many opportunities for such mishaps to occur in most information systems that maintenance programmers spend a great deal of time tracking down and correcting data problems.

Relating these traditional production problems to PCs, suppose that with increases in the number of operators of computer systems there are directly proportionate increases in mishaps causing imperfect data. If all computing was done on PCs and all knowledge workers had personal computers on their desks, the resulting increase in data problems would be significant.

Such a scenario already is in the making. The number of centralized data entry operations and the proportion of MIS/dp staffers devoted full time to data entry has declined while PCs have added to the number of remote data entry sources. In addition, the "linear approach" of many jobs, in which one person must wait for another to finish before beginning a task, has changed. Rigid procedures have given way to broader job functions; few workers are strictly dedicated to data entry anymore. For example, a financial analyst may now concentrate on all aspects of one client and enter data for all aspects instead of entering the data for one narrow category of all clients. Data entry has become distributed—often with no central, controlling, responsible, organizational entity.

The PC and Software Maintenance Issues

Software departments, hesitant to take responsibility for modifications to PC software, are becoming concerned that desktop computing may be creating future maintenance problems. Undocumented and unstructured code developed for mainframes before the days of structured analysis and design causes many of today's maintenance nightmares. An analogous situation with micros may be in the formative stages today.

Personal computers are proliferating because they are extremely useful. Organizations wholeheartedly endorsing the personal computer revolution need adequate software maintenance personnel dedicated to PC application support. Such specialists, perhaps referred to as microcomputer support analysts, could reduce corporate risk by consulting with PC users as well as performing PC-specific application maintenance.

PERSONAL COMPUTING AND MAINTENANCE RISKS

Potential maintenance problems are abruptly different with PCs than with traditional centralized computing environments. Emerging technology, protocols, standards, and accepted practice are not yet well-defined for PC environments. Personal computers present a potential for adding new dimensions to the software maintenance task.

Potential Security Problems

Early distributed networks allowed users inter-departmental access to data on private minicomputers distributed among separate departments. These networks allowed users to move freely from node to node using menu choices or different log-on commands as long as they had authorized access to the desired node. Physical barriers and access controls, used as security measures during the era of centralized computing, often are not as effective when applied to distributed processing in complex PC networks. Connections to remote sites allow intruders into systems and possible insertion of malicious programs known as "trojan horses," "logic bombs," and "trap doors." Students ranging from the university level to grade school have been known to access computers using information present in electronic bulletin boards, spread by word of mouth, or appearing in underground publications.[1] Every networked system allowing telephone dial-in has three built-in security weaknesses: the telephone lines and modems, the log-on procedures, and the passwords.[2] Security software, such as encryption/decryption and log-on controls are often developed in-house and must be maintained.

In addition to security issues posed by the intrusion opportunities naturally present in PC networks, communication protocols between machines must be considered. Some networks have approximately one personal computer per user with shared peripherals and no large central mainframe in the loop. Often, the PCs on such networks are made by a variety of companies. Networks including PCs from multiple vendors frequently are practical because different micros have capabilities to match different user needs. The trend toward multiple hardware vendors can only be expected to increase.

Figure 1 illustrates a distributed network containing many makes and sizes of computers, from mainframes to micros, in which personal computers are the dominant workstation. In this environment, it can be imagined that there are some communication complexities. Many organizations in which similar configurations exist have no clearly identified team of specialists assigned to solve communication problems. In such situations, software specialists must increase their scope of knowledge to span multiple machines.

To help solve networking problems, many users understandably are turning to their central software department and requesting custom built security and communication software involving passwords, log-ons, encryption, transmission degradation, and file transfer. These custom solutions then become additions to the inventory of software applications that require maintenance effort when users' needs or vendors change.

Potential Unreliable Information Problems

Much of the PC application maintenance job consists of tracking causes of imperfect data. Most often, the origin is with the operator or user, not in software correctness. The job of controlling the flow of data in an automated and secure fashion typically falls on a software maintenance professional. Commercially developed software applications are just as vulnerable to imperfect data as custom built software, and users probably will always demand professional help in solving the resulting anomalies.

Consider a PC desktop publishing package used to produce a complex contract proposal. This package will be used to receive and integrate information from many sources. The data flow interfaces for such a system are shown in Figure 2. It can be seen that when figures and text in the proposal draft require revision the source of these elements must be isolated from within a maze of programs and entry points.

Classic maintenance problems will not disappear by moving an application from custom software running on a central computer to commercial software running on a network of personal computers. However, personal computing has added a new dimension to the problem of data integrity—the proliferation of decentralized data storage devices. Newer PC networks may have information scattered over many floppy disks on the desks of many users or on hard disk file servers at several locations. Such files may have differeent backup versions, which means that users unaccustomed to file management tasks are now expected to be responsible data librarians.

Floppy disks can be a menace where data integrity is concerned. They do not hold much data, compared to the disk drives of larger computers, so they tend to proliferate in abundance at each user location. Cataloging the data storage of a large computer is typically an automated feature of the operating system and often is augmented by application software. Floppy disks, on the other hand, are usually cataloged manually by listing the contents on a paper label affixed to the disk and storing the disks in a small desktop filing cabinet with index labels.

As data storage spreads outward to points of origin, data responsibility no longer rests with a professional file clerk in

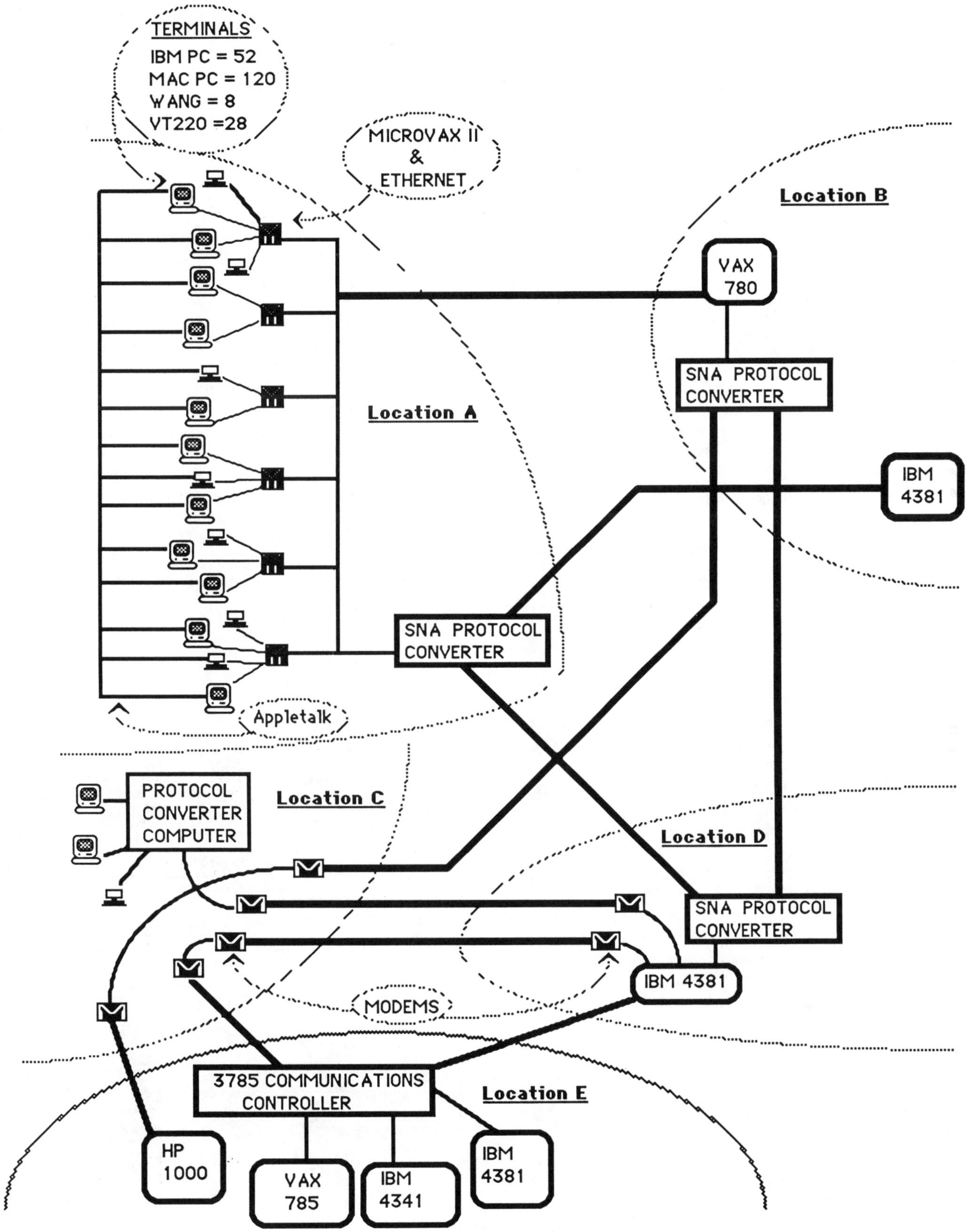

Figure 1—Complex distributed network

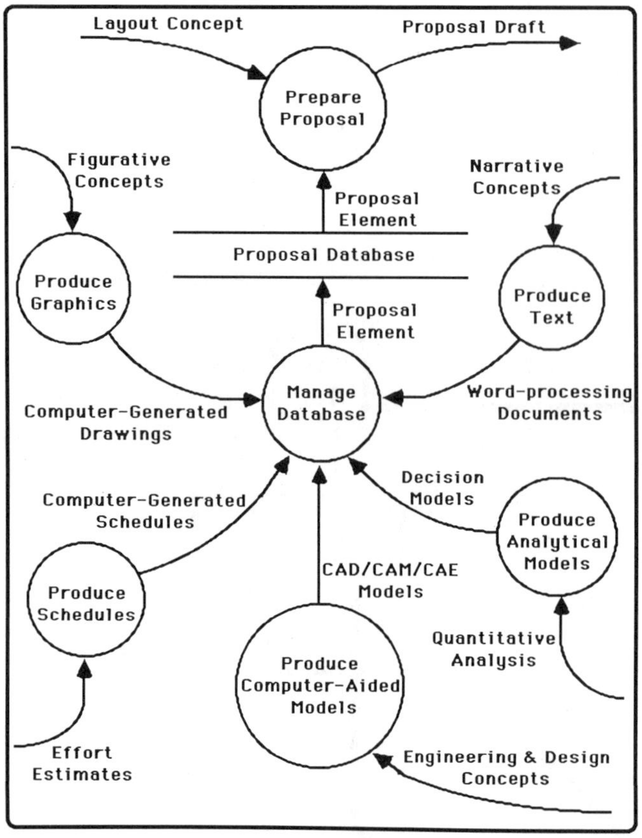

Figure 2—Desktop publishing system

servers. When mistakes occur, software maintenance professionals will be asked to provide solutions.

Potential Access Authorization Problems

Data access problems occur both when there are authorized persons *without* access to information and when there are unauthorized persons *with* access to information. When access is denied, information processing often stops because necessary data cannot be entered, updated, or used. When unauthorized access occurs, unknowledgeable persons may be entering data for which they have no official sources.

These types of application maintenance difficulties are not new to the industry, but personal computers provide new ways in which such events may occur. A primary area of consideration is the floppy disk. If a user has a need for information that only exists on a floppy locked in the desk drawer of a coworker who is on vacation, project progress may halt. In addition, floppy disks are not subject to a controlled backup system. If they become damaged, data recovery may be difficult.

Floppies are portable. They can be carried in a briefcase or even in pockets much more conveniently than magnetic tape reels or disk drives. Such portability makes floppy disks easy targets for damage, loss, or theft. Data files are usually not copy protected, so it is easy to move them from one disk to another. Thus, a potential exists for unauthorized access to data. One cannot discern from looking at printed output whether the data came from an authorized floppy or a bootleg copy.

charge of centrally located corporate data. Each PC user has a personal filing system and style, ranging from efficient to sloppy. If every diskette were clearly and meaningfully labeled and placed in a distinctive jacket in an easily accessible place, problems would be minimal. But in everyday practice there is no control over what is basically a manual filing system, and maintenance professionals are at the mercy of individual filing systems. The distribution of data on floppies should at least be considered in the context of the normal risk analysis procedure for computer security.[3]

Some file server approaches re-centralize data storage by providing a central file library on a hard disk. Other networks utilize a software-based approach, transparent to the users, whereby shareable files are not centralized but may reside at any node. These systems all provide services similar to a public library, allowing users to electronically check out files. Available files may be designated as originals or copies with read/write privileges or read-only access specified. Users may have private storage areas as well as limited access to public files. A personal computer network incorporating a file server scheme is illustrated in Figure 3.

Some file servers have software that prevents concurrent access of files. However, this does not mean that the second user to access a file cannot undo the work of the first user by overwriting good data with corrupt data. The job of a network support person becomes complex in such environments, particularly in environments of large networks with multiple file

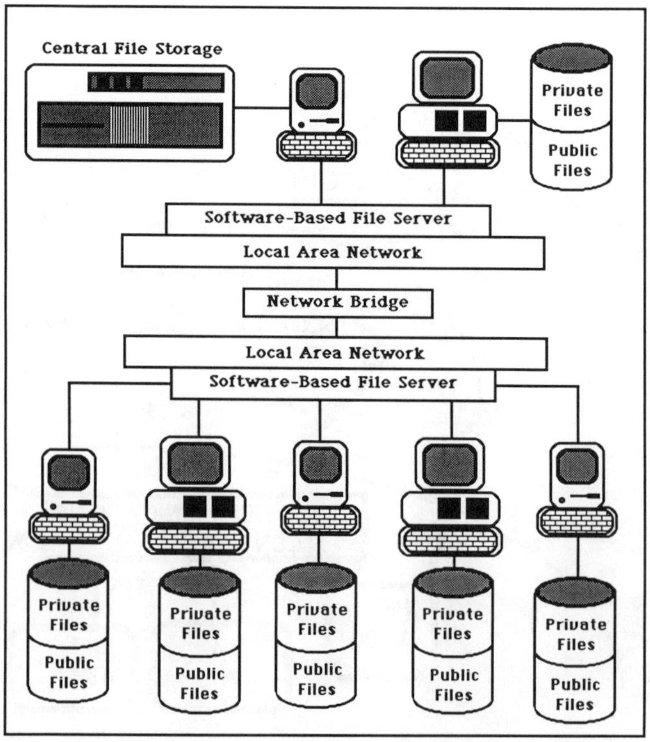

Figure 3—Software-based file server approach

Some file server schemes attempt to prevent unauthorized data access by requiring a system administrator to be responsible for user access to centralized data files. However, a system administrator can rarely be expected to know enough about every user's job to be able to make optimal decisions about which user should have access to what data. In addition, an authorized user with a personal computer still has the ability to copy an official file from the central library to a floppy disk and pass the floppy on to an unauthorized user.

Potential User-developed Application Problems

Software development practices including structured programming, structured analysis, system specification methodologies, structured design, and structured technical reviews have become accepted as standards for software engineering. These practices consist of techniques aimed at producing better products and reducing future maintenance effort. Colleges are teaching these techniques and software departments are enforcing their use.

When users develop customized software applications using personal computers, accepted software engineering standard practices may not be applied. Most users have no formal training in such practices, nor are they bound by software department development standards. Few user-built applications will be developed with ease of maintenance as a feature. Yet, user-developed PC software may sometimes become critical to an organization's operations. The developers of such applications can be promoted, fired, transferred or they might quit, retire, or die. Modifications will then become someone else's responsibility and the ease of maintenance issue will surface.

Personal computer users often develop their own software despite a rich variety of commercial applications from which to choose, simply because the opportunity to do so exists. In the days of centralized computing, end users typically were not permitted access to software development tools. With personal computers, vertical application development environments are available on users' desktops and managers do not often care to risk reduced motivation by enforcing discipline typically associated with the duller aspects of computing. Commercial software provides generic functionality to broaden a vendor's market potential. However, users often want to tailor application systems to their unique needs.

When user-written software becomes critical to business operations (e.g., because of success in providing unique solutions to unique problems) and when someone other than the original developer becomes responsible for maintenance, maintenance problems may be worse than in centralized environments. For example, user-developed programs may be written in a little-used programming language with which no one in the company is familiar, they may have been modified many times, or there may be no documentation and no comments in the programs.

SOME PARTIAL SOLUTIONS

Personal computer proliferation in the workplace will not decrease application maintenance efforts as is sometimes predicted. This should not lead to a conclusion that personal computers should be banned from the workplace or that the proliferation should be controlled. Because PCs are such tremendous productivity aids for knowledge workers, intelligent management will wholeheartedly endorse PC acquisition despite incidental problems such as those cited here. However, "security . . . cannot be delegated away; it must be closely integrated with the overall information resource management planning and control."[4]

Anticipating Maintenance Effort

New areas of application maintenance can be planned for and included in the cost of raising knowledge worker productivity. A preliminary planning step would be to identify the new skills required of the software maintenance staff in order to solve problems arising from personal computing.

Medium to large size organizations could take an "expert" approach. For example, the network shown in Figure 1 might be supported by a staff including IBM PC™ experts, Macintosh™ experts, network experts, file transfer experts, communications experts, and database experts. To qualify as an expert one would have to demonstrate unusual capabilities in an area of specialty.

In addition to tracking data anomalies that may be passed to a central processor or network file server, a microcomputer support team assumes the maintenance function of tracking software versions passed out to PC users. Bookkeeping will be involved and physical distribution considerations will emerge. For example, the support team might require that previously distributed floppy disks must be returned before new application versions will be distributed. Further, new integrated software links that move files from mainframe applications or a database management system into micro applications require communications software at both the micro and mainframe level, often involving custom programming. Custom software will have to be maintained when any of the links is modified by a new version of the commercial micro software, a change in format of the mainframe data, or in some other way.

Typically, today's maintenance programmers do not have PC problem-solving skills. There is a need for providing maintenance staff with specialized PC training. Once a cadre of specialists in microcomputer software maintenance has been trained and provided with proper equipment (PCs included), a personal computer support group can be formed. The support group could solve unique end user problems related to personal computing. Funding this new maintenance activity could be on a rechargeable basis; that is, funds would be transferred from users' departments to the support organization based on effort provided.

Limiting Maintenance Problems

Poor planning in any one of the areas of maintenance mentioned will result in data imperfections and user-developed applications that are difficult to modify. Personal computer proliferation within a problem-limiting framework could confine future maintenance problems to manageable proportions.

Network complexity can be limited. Every knowledge worker in an organization does not have a legitimate need to download the corporate general ledger to a spreadsheet on their personal computer. Further, network links to every personal computer in an organization are not needed. Typically, information sharing occurs within the confines of a small departmental or project group (i.e., five to fifty workers) because the information processed is of primary interest only to that group.

The number of workers with responsibility and authority for entering and updating official data can be strictly limited, preferably to one user for one data file. Official data files should not be kept on floppy disks except in rare instances for backup purposes. Updating a hard disk file from a floppy should not be allowed without approval of knowledgeable management.

With respect to user-developed software, end users should be required to abide by the same software engineering standards in current use by the software department if that software might become part of the corporate application library. Advanced users developing custom applications need adequate training in modern software development techniques and their applications should be subject to the same pre-implementation review procedures as those developed by software department staff.

A micro support group will ease transition into a personal computing environment. Tasks of this group could include evaluating new products, helping to select equipment, procuring equipment, setting up equipment, assisting with software maintenance, assisting with the development of new system and application software, and providing users with technical assistance and training.

Software managers must realize that application maintenance will not be eliminated by PC proliferation. Intelligent management of personal computing environments must rely on the experience and skill of software maintenance professionals to make personal computing work effectively in a corporate setting.

REFERENCES

1. Edison, Tom A. *TAP,* January, 1983.
2. "Ex-hacker Offers Supplemental Security Checklist." *Computerworld,* July 8, 1985, p. 15.
3. Fisher, Royal P. *Information Systems Security.* Englewood Cliffs, New Jersey: Prentice-Hall, 1984.
4. Schweitzer, James A. *Computer Crime and Business Information: A Practical Guide for Managers.* New York: Elsevier, 1986.

A measure of program nesting complexity

by ELDON Y. LI
California Polytechnic State University
San Luis Obispo, California

ABSTRACT

For more than a decade, metrics of software complexity has been an intriguing topic for discussion. Many metrics have been proposed. Among them, the cyclomatic complexity metric is the easiest to understand and compute. In this paper, the cyclomatic complexity metric and its extensions are reviewed. The strengths and weaknesses of the cyclomatic metric are identified. One of the major weaknesses of the cyclomatic metric as well as its extensions is that they are insensitive to the level of nesting within various constructs. To remove this shortcoming, a "nesting" complexity metric is proposed. The process of deriving this new metric is described in this paper. This new metric is proved to be superior to the cyclomatic metric in reflecting program complexity.

INTRODUCTION

Since the emergence of structured programming concepts, program complexity has received tremendous attention from researchers in software engineering. "Program complexity" may be classified into two categories: computational complexity and psychological complexity.[1] Computational complexity refers to the difficulty of deriving expected output and of verifying an algorithm's correctness, and psychological complexity refers to the characteristics of software which make it difficult to understand and work with. Both types of complexity are not easily measured or described, and are often ignored during the system planning process. "But when this complexity exceeds certain unknown limits, frustration ensues. Computer programs capsize under their own logical weight, or become so crippled that maintenance is precarious and modification is impossible."[2] Based on Mills's observation, it seems wise to apply the "divide-and-conquer" principle to program design by decomposing the entire program into modules and submodules. Each module and submodule will have much less complexity and will, in turn, be much easier for programmers and users to comprehend and maintain.

Numerous metrics have been proposed to measure program complexity. Excellent reviews of these measures are provided by Fitzsimmons and Love,[3] Mohanty,[4] and Berlinger.[5] Several empirical studies have applied some selected metrics to measure program complexity and correlate such complexity with the number of errors occurring in the measured modules. It was found that the occurrence of program errors correlates significantly with the complexity of the target program.[3,6,7,8,9,10,11,12,13,14] This finding supports the popular hypothesis that program complexity is a major factor influencing the quality of computer programming.

Among various current complexity measures, the cyclomatic metric[15] is the easiest to understand and calculate. It is also the only one that lends itself to determining a minimum test set for program testing. In this paper, we review the cyclomatic metric and its extensions. The strengths and weaknesses of cyclomatic metric is identified as well. Further, a new metric to reflect the levels of nesting is proposed.

THE CYCLOMATIC COMPLEXITY METRIC

The cyclomatic complexity metric was proposed by McCabe.[15] His metric is based on the decision structure of a program and the cyclomatic number[16] (also called the cycle rank,[17] or the nullity[18]) of the classical graph theory. The cyclomatic complexity metric, $V(G)$, as defined by McCabe, is

$$V(G) = E - N + 2P$$

where E is the number of edges (or arcs), N is the number of vertices (or nodes), and P is the number of connected components. A component is a subgraph representing an external module that either is calling or is being called by another module. For example, consider a main program M and two called subroutines A and B having a control structure shown in Figure 1.

The total graph in Figure 1 is said to have three connected components and each subgraph has only one connected component (itself). Therefore, the cyclomatic complexity numbers are:

$$V(M) = 3 - 4 + 2(1) = 1,$$
$$V(A) = 2 - 2 + 2(1) = 2,$$
$$V(B) = 4 - 4 + 2(1) = 2,$$

and

$$V(M + A + B) = 9 - 10 + 2(3) = 5.$$

It can be easily shown that $V(M + A + B) = V(M) + V(A) + V(B)$.

McCabe further demonstrates two alternate ways of finding the complexity number V. One is to count the number of both inner and outer regions on the plane control graph. Notice there should be one outer region for each subgraph. In fact, if we form a closed subgraph by drawing an imaginary arc from the exit node to the entry node for each subgraph in Figure 1, and count all the inner regions afterward, we would yield the same number. We believe that the latter approach is less confusing than the former. For example, Figure 2 shows the closed subgraphs derived from Figure 1. By counting the inner regions (I_1 through I_5), we get a $V(G)$ of 5.

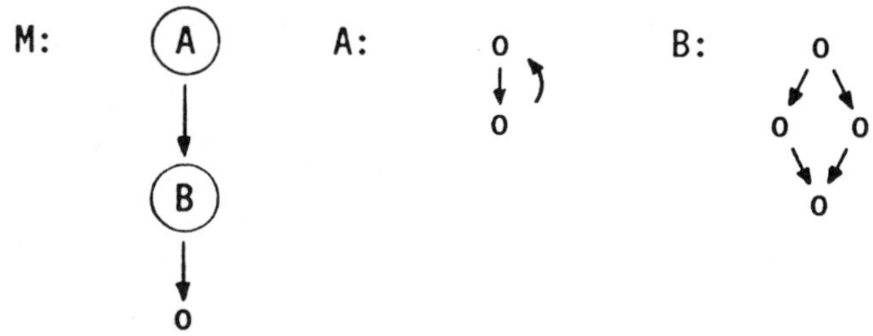

Figure 1—A graph with three connected components

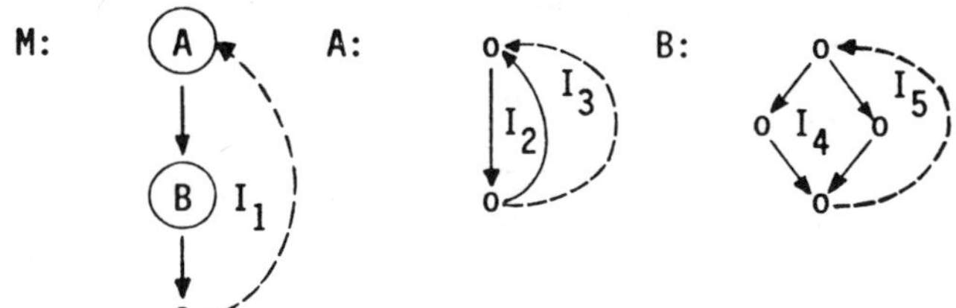

Figure 2—A graph with three closed subgraphs

The other way of calculating V is to count the number of predicate conditions in the program. Then the cyclomatic complexity is:

$$V(G) = \text{Number of predicate conditions} + 1.$$

The attractive aspect of this method is that one can find the $V(G)$ directly from the program text without arduously constructing a flow graph. For example, consider the following PL/1 program:[19]

```
M: PROCEDURE(A,B,X);
IF ((A > 1) & (B = 0)) THEN DO;
                          X = X/A;
                     END;
IF ((A = 2) | (X > 1)) THEN DO;
                          X = X + 1;
                     END;
END;
```

Notice that each "IF" statement in procedure M has two conditions in its predicate. This type of "IF" statement is called a *compound* "IF" construct. In contrast, an "IF" statement with only one condition is called a *simple* "IF" construct, hereafter. Since each condition in procedure M contributes one cyclomatic complexity count, the complexity number is thus $V(M) = 4 + 1 = 5$.

Figure 3(a) shows that the flow graph corresponds to procedure M. Notice that it reflects the compound predicate by placing an extra exit edge for the second condition on each alternation node. For the convenience of counting, we substitute a traditional decision symbol for each alternation node and create Figure 3(b). It can be seen that Figure 3(b) is more readable and understandable than Figure 3(a). Therefore, we highly recommend adopting a decision symbol in flow-graph construction because it not only helps in counting the number of predicates but it also improves substantially the readability of the flow graph.

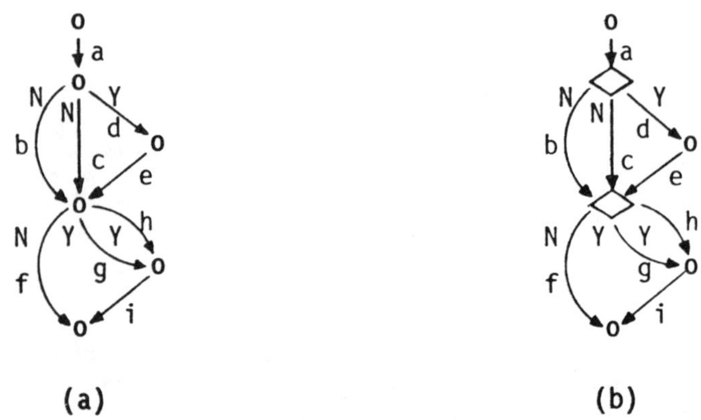

Figure 3—A control graph with compound predicates

THE ANOMALY AND THE EXTENSIONS OF THE CYCLOMATIC COMPLEXITY METRIC

One of the anomalies of cyclomatic complexity measure is that it does not accurately reflect the complexity of various "IF" structures; namely, simple "IF," compound "IF," and nested "IF." Myers[20] recommends an interval measure having one plus predicate counts as the lower bound, and one plus condition counts as the upper bound for the complexity level. Myers clearly demonstrates that this new metric can accurately reflect the complexity of various "IF" structures. However, the measure does not lend itself to quantitative analysis due to its "interval" data representation.

Hansen[21] indicates that the cyclomatic complexity metric does not reflect "expression" complexity. In other words, "a program with more operators is simply bigger . . . (and) . . . more complex" and thus [has a] higher expression complexity.[21] He proposes two measures in a pair to measure both control flow complexity and expression complexity. The former is measured by one plus predicate counts (including repetitive construct), the latter operator counts in the program. However, Hansen's metric suffers the same deficiency as Myers's; that is, it does not lend itself to quantitative analysis due to its "interval" data representation. Moreover, it is somewhat difficult to compute and can be applied only to program text.

Another major weakness of the cyclomatic complexity metric is its insensitivity to the level of nesting within various constructs. For example, three "WHILE" loops in succession result in metric values similar to those for three nested "WHILE" loops. This anomaly was brought forward by Curtis, Sheppard, Milliman, Borst, and Love,[1] but they did not offer any solution to it. Inspired by this anomaly, we examine various structures and propose a new metric to accurately reflect their complexity levels.

STRENGTHS AND WEAKNESSES OF THE CYCLOMATIC COMPLEXITY METRIC

Although the cyclomatic complexity measure has many anomalies, it has several strengths. We summarize its strengths and weaknesses in this section.

Strengths

1. It is easy to compute from the program text and the flow graph.
2. It supports a top-down development process to control module complexity in the design phase, that is, before actual coding takes place.
3. It lends itself to determining the maximum set of independent test paths.
4. It can be used to control the complexity of program modules. (McCabe recommends that an upper bound of 10 should be used as a guide to control the complexity of program modules. This recommendation is endorsed by Schneidewind and Hoffmann[13] and Walsh.[22])
5. It can be used to evaluate alternate program design to find the simplest possible program structure.

6. It serves to partition a program structure into high or low error occurrence according to its value.
7. It serves to partition a program structure into high or low error finding and removing times according to its value.
8. It can be used as a guide for allocating testing resources.

Weaknesses

1. It measures the psychological complexity, not the computational complexity.
2. It views all predicates as contributing the same amount of complexity.
3. It is insensitive to the level of nesting within various constructs.
4. It is insensitive to the frequency and the types of input and output activity.
5. It is insensitive to the size of purely sequential programs.
6. It is insensitive to the number of variables in the program.
7. It is insensitive to the intensiveness of data operations (i.e., the number of operators and operands) in the program.
8. It is insensitive to the dependency of control flows on foregoing data operations. (See, for example, the program listed on page 43 of Myers.[19])
9. It is insensitive to a situation in which one condition is "masked" or "blocked" by another within a nesting construct. (See, for example, the program listed on page 43 of Myers.[19])
10. It is insensitive to the program style and the use of "GOTO" statements.
11. It measures neither the types and levels of module interaction, nor the levels of module invocation.

DERIVATION OF THE NESTING COMPLEXITY METRIC

The purpose of our new complexity metric is to reflect the level of nesting within various constructs while keeping the computation process as easy as possible. Bearing these two objectives in mind, a new metric called "nesting complexity metric," $L(G)$, is formulated.

Consider the six structured programming control flow constructs[23] depicted in Figure 4. The "sequence" construct has a complexity V of unity while the "IF," the "WHILE," and the "UNTIL" constructs each has a V of 2, but the "CASE" construct of n branches has a V equal to $n - 1$ nested "IF" statements. That is, a "CASE" statement with two branches is equivalent to a simple "IF" statement. The relationship of the complexities of various constructs is thus:

sequence < (simple IF) = (simple WHILE)
= (simple UNTIL) = (two-branch CASE).

This relationship, along with our belief that nesting increases program complexity, are the premises of our metric to be derived subsequently.

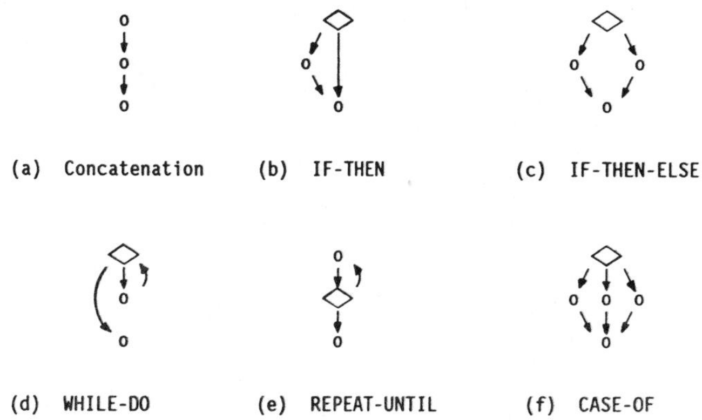

Figure 4—Structured programming control flow constructs

Now, consider the following structured programming statements:

A: IF (X = 0) THEN a
ELSE b
B: IF (X = 0) AND (Y = 0) THEN a
ELSE b
C: IF (X = 0) THEN IF (Y = 0) THEN a
ELSE b
D: IF (X = 0) AND (Y = 0) AND (Z = 0) THEN a
ELSE b
E: IF (X = 0) THEN IF (Y = 0) THEN
IF (Z = 0) THEN a
ELSE b
F: WHILE (X = 0) DO a
G: WHILE (X = 0) AND (Y = 0) DO a
H: WHILE (X = 0) DO WHILE (Y = 0) DO a
I: WHILE (X = 0) AND (Y = 0) AND (Z = 0) DO a
J: WHILE (X = 0) DO WHILE (Y = 0) DO WHILE (Z = 0) DO a
K: REPEAT a UNTIL (X = 0)
L: REPEAT a UNTIL (X = 0) AND (Y = 0)
M: REPEAT REPEAT a UNTIL (Y = 0) UNTIL (X = 0)
N: REPEAT a UNTIL (X = 0) AND (Y = 0) AND (Z = 0)
O: REPEAT REPEAT REPEAT a UNTIL (X = 0) UNTIL (Y = 0) UNTIL (Z = 0)
P: CASE X OF
0 : a
Q: CASE X OF
0 : CASE Y OF
0 : a
R: CASE X OF
0 : CASE Y OF
0 : CASE Z OF
0 : a
S: IF (X = 0) THEN a
IF (X = 1) THEN b
T: IF (X = 0) THEN a
IF (X = 1) THEN b
IF (X = 2) THEN c
U: IF (X = 0) THEN a
ELSE IF (X = 1) THEN b

```
V: IF (X = 0) THEN a
   ELSE IF (X = 1) THEN b
                   ELSE IF (X = 2) THEN c
W: CASE X OF
     0 : a
     1 : b
X: CASE X OF
     0 : a
     1 : b
     2 : c
Y: CASE X OF
     0 : a
     1 : b
     ELSE : c
Z: CASE X OF
     0 : a
     1 : b
     2 : c
     ELSE : d
```

Based on the foregoing premise, we begin ranking the complexity of the constructs one pair at a time. Finally, the following complexity ordering is derived:

$A = F = K = P,$
$B = G = L,$
$C = H = M,$
$D = I = N,$
$C = D,$
$E = J = O,$
$H = I,$
$M = N,$
$Q = C,$
$R = E,$
$S = W = Y,$
$T = X = Z,$
$U = C,$
$V = E,$

and

$A < B < D,$
$B < C,$
$D < E,$
$C < E,$
$F < G < I,$
$G < H,$
$I < J,$
$H < J,$
$K < L < N,$
$L < M,$
$N < O,$
$M < O,$
$P < Q < R,$
$S < T,$
$U < V,$
$S < U,$
$T < V,$
$W < X,$
$Y < Z,$
$P < W,$
$P < Y,$
$W < Q,$
$Y < Q,$
$X < R,$
$Z < R.$

Therefore, the final relationship is

$$\{A,F,K,P\} < \{B,G,L,S,W,Y\} < \{C,D,H,I,M,N,Q,T,U,X,Z\} < \{E,J,O,R,V\}.$$

In contrast, the relationship from McCabe's cyclomatic metric is

$$\{A,F,K,P\} < \{B,C,G,H,L,M,Q,S,U,W,Y\} < \{D,E,I,J,N,O,R,T,V,X,Z\},$$

which does not reflect the proper complexity ordering depicted above.

After comparing both relationships illustrated above, ten constructs—*C, E, H, J, M, O, Q, R, U, V,* which were ranked differently by the authors and McCabe's metric—are identified. All of these constructs are nested. We decided to increase the complexity number of any nested construct by one less the number of its nested levels. This practice consequently allows us to derive the following process of calculating the nesting complexity metric.

PROCESS OF CALCULATING THE NESTING COMPLEXITY METRIC

The final relationship derived in the last section is the premise of our proposed metric. Since the purpose of our new complexity metric is to reflect the level of nesting within various constructs while keeping the computation process simple, we have formulated the process of calculating the "nesting complexity metric," $L(G)$, from the program text as follows:

1. Count and mark all the Boolean logical operators, "AND," "OR," and "XOR," in the program and assign *one* unit of complexity to each occurrence. However, do not count "NOT."
2. Count and mark keywords "IF," "WHILE," "UNTIL," and "CASE" at the first level of nesting within each flow construct. Once again, assign each occurrence with *one* unit of complexity. Note that if a control statement has at least one branch which leads directly to the program exit, any immediately following control statement should be considered to be at the first level of a new nested construct.
3. Count and mark all the remaining "IF," "WHILE," "UNTIL," and "CASE" keywords and assign *two* units of complexity to each occurrence.
4. Count and mark all but the first and the "ELSE" conditions in each "CASE" statement, and assign each occurrence with *one* unit of complexity. Remember to ignore the first and the "ELSE" conditions, otherwise each

level of the construct will be unnecessarily inflated by two units of complexity.

5. Sum up all the complexity units derived by the previous four steps and then add one into it. The total is our new complexity measure, $L(G)$.

Alternately, we can obtain $L(G)$ from the following two-step process:

1. Find the cyclomatic complexity measure, $V(G)$, using McCabe's approach.
2. Identify the second, the third, the fourth, and subsequent levels of nesting constructs and assign each occurrence with *one* unit of complexity. Do not forget that if a control statement has at least one branch which leads directly to the program exit, any immediately following control statement should be considered to be at the first level of a new nested construct.

Notice that the new nesting metric, $L(G)$, possesses all but one of the strengths and weaknesses of the cyclomatic metric, $V(G)$. It exchanges a weakness of $V(G)$ for one of its own strengths; namely, the $L(G)$ is now sensitive to the level of nesting but no longer is able to determine the maximum number of independent test paths. Three characteristics of the $L(G)$ metric are worth mentioning. First, the $L(G)$ metric assumes that nested constructs are more complex than simple constructs, but a nested control statement having one branch directing to the end of the program does not contribute additional complexity. Second, the $L(G)$ penalizes the excessive use of nested constructs and encourages substituting the "CASE" statement for the nested "ELSE IF" construct. Third, the $L(G)$ converges to the cyclomatic complexity metric if there is no nested construct in the program text.

After applying the counting procedure to the constructs A through R of the previous section, we have four groups of complexity:

1. Complexity of 2: $\{A,F,K,P\}$,
2. Complexity of 3: $\{B,G,L\}$,
3. Complexity of 4: $\{C,D,H,I,M,N,Q\}$,

and

4. Complexity of 6: $\{E,J,O,R\}$.

The relationship established earlier is therefore preserved.

In contrast, McCabe's $V(G)$ gives the following three groups of complexity:

1. Complexity of 2: $\{A,F,K,P\}$,
2. Complexity of 3: $\{B,C,G,H,L,M,Q,S,U,W,Y\}$,

and

3. Complexity of 4: $\{D,E,I,J,N,O,R,T,V,X,Z\}$.

Those constructs that have different metric values between $L(G)$ and $V(G)$ are shown in Table I.

TABLE I—Value of $L(G)$ versus $V(G)$ under the same construct

Construct	L(G)	V(G)
C	4	3
E	6	4
H	4	3
J	6	4
M	4	3
O	6	4
Q	4	3
R	6	4
U	4	3
V	6	4

TABLE II—Comparison of the outcomes of four complexity metrics

Algorithm from Kernighan and Plauger [24]	McCabe	Myers	Hansen	L(G)
A checkers move generator: ([24], pp. 41-42)				
Original version	17	(17:17)	(15,60)*	25
Improved version	17	(10:17)	(10,46)	17
Julian to Gregorian date conversion: ([24], pp. 43-46)				
Original version	19	(17:19)	(17,85)	30
Improved version #1	10	(5:10)	(5,25)	11
Improved version #2	11**	(6:11)**	(6,25)**	13
Merge two lists: ([24], pp. 18-19)				
Original version	5	(5:5)	(8,10)***	7
Improved version	5	(3:5)	(3,16)	5
Computer dating service: ([24], pp. 21-22)				
Original version	7	(7:7)	(7,10)	8
Improved version #1	6	(3:6)	(3,12)	6
Improved version #2	3	(3:3)	(3,6)	3

* Computed GOTO construct is regarded as CASE construct in this case.

** One unit of complexity is introduced by an additional DO-WHILE construct.

*** Arithmetic IF construct is counted as twice the complexity of logical IF's in this case.

APPLICATIONS OF THE NESTING COMPLEXITY METRIC

To validate the $L(G)$ metric, four algorithms from Kernighan and Plauger[24] were measured. A comparison of the outcomes of applying four different complexity metrics is illustrated in Table II. After scrutinizing the outcomes of these metrics, four major findings are notable:

1. The difference between the two elements in Myers's metric indicates the number of logical compound operators, that is, "AND," "OR," and "XOR."
2. The first element of Hansen's and Myers's metrics are the same if the program contains no "CASE" construct.
3. The only metric that does not reflect program improvement correctly is McCabe's metric. Although program improvement might introduce more operators, the control flow complexity should definitely be reduced.
4. The difference between $L(G)$ and $V(G)$ metrics indicates the number of nested levels. When $L(G)$ equals $V(G)$, the program contains no nested construct.

CONCLUSION

We have reviewed the cyclomatic complexity metric and its extensions, and have discussed strengths and weaknesses of the metric. An extension of the cyclomatic complexity metric, the "nesting complexity metric," has been proposed herein to remove the weakness of being insensitive to the level of nesting. Although the "nesting complexity metric," $L(G)$, is no longer able to directly determine the maximum number of independent test paths, it is superior to the cyclomatic complexity metric because it is now able to reflect the level of nesting structure and to penalize the excessive use of nested constructs thus encouraging the practice of substituting the "CASE" statement for the nested "ELSE IF" construct. Therefore, the nesting metric $L(G)$ is better than the cyclomatic metric $V(G)$ in measuring program complexity. However, we highly recommend using a pair metric of $(V(G),L(G))$ because is supplies more information than the $L(G)$ alone. Besides, the $V(G)$ number is readily obtained since it is a by-product of finding the $L(G)$ value.

REFERENCES

1. Curtis, B., S.B. Sheppard, P. Milliman, M.A. Borst, and T. Love. "Measuring the Psychological Complexity of Software Maintenance Tasks With the Halstead and McCabe Metrics." *IEEE Transactions on Software Engineering,* SE-5 (1979) 2, pp. 96–104.
2. Mills, H.D. "Mathematical Foundations for Structured Programming." FSC 72-6012, Gaithersburg, MD.: IBM Federal System Division, 1972.
3. Fitzsimmons, A.B. and L.T. Love. "A Review and Evaluation of Software Science." *ACM Computing Surveys,* 10 (1978) 1, pp. 3–18.
4. Mohanty, S.N. "Models and Measurements for Quality Assessment of Software." *ACM Computing Surveys,* 11 (1979) 3, pp. 251–275.
5. Berlinger, E. "An Information Theory Based Complexity Measure." *AFIPS Proceedings of the National Computer Conference,* Vol. 49, 1980, pp. 773–779.
6. Bulut, N. and M.H. Halstead. "Impurities Found in Algorithm Implementation." Technical Report CSD-TR-111, Computer Sciences Department, Purdue University, 1974.
7. Cornell, L. and M.H. Halstead. "Predicting the Number of Bugs Expected in a Program Module." Technical Report CSD-TR-205, Computer Sciences Department, Purdue University, 1976.
8. Elshoff, J.L. "Measuring Commercial PL/1 Programs Using Halstead's Criteria." *ACM SIGPLAN Notices,* 11 (1976) 5, pp. 38–46.
9. Fitzsimmons, A.B. "Relating the Presence of Software Errors to the Theory of Software Science." Presented to the 11th Hawaii International Conference of Systems Sciences, January 1978.
10. Funami, Y. and M.H. Halstead. "A Software Physics Analysis of Akiyama's Debugging Data." Technical Report CSD-TR-144, Computer Sciences Department, Purdue University, 1975.
11. Halstead, M.H. "An Experimental Determination of the "Purity" of a Trivial Algorithm." Technical Report CSD-TR-73, Computer Sciences Department, Purdue University, 1972.
12. Love, L.T. and A.B. Bowman. "An Independent Test of the Theory of Software Physics." *ACM SIGPLAN Notices,* 11 (1976) 11, pp. 42–49.
13. Schneidewind, N.F. and H.-M. Hoffmann. "An Experiment in Software Error Data Collection and Analysis." *IEEE Transactions on Software Engineering,* SE-5 (1979) 3, pp. 276–286.
14. Sunohara, T., A. Takano, K. Uehara, and T. Ohkawa. "Program Complexity Measure for Software Development Management." *Proceedings of the Fifth Internatinal Software Engineering Conference,* San Diego, California, 1981, pp. 100–106.
15. McCabe, T.J. "A Complexity Measure." *IEEE Transactions on Software Engineering,* SE-2 (1976) 4, pp. 308–320.
16. Berge, C. *Graphs and Hypergraphs,* Amsterdam, The Netherlands: North-Holland, 1973.
17. Harary, F. *Graph Theory,* Reading, Massachusetts: Addison-Wesley, 1969.
18. Chan, S.-P. *Introductory Topological Analysis of Electrical Networks,* New York: Holt, Rinehart and Winston, 1969.
19. Myers, G.J. *The Art of Software Testing,* New York: Wiley-Interscience, 1979.
20. Myers, G.J. "An Extension to the Cyclomatic Measure of Program Complexity." *ACM SIGPLAN Notices,* 12 (1977) 10, pp. 61–64.
21. Hansen, W.J. "Measurement of Program Complexity by the Pair (Cyclomatic Number, Operator Count)." *ACM SIGPLAN Notices,* 13 (1978) 3, pp. 29–33.
22. Walsh, T.J. "A Software Reliability Study Using a Complexity Measure." *AFIPS Proceedings of the National Computer Conference,* Vol. 48, 1979, pp. 761–768.
23. Ledgard, H.F. and M. Marcotty. "A Genealogy of Control Structures." *Communications of the ACM,* 18 (1975) 11, pp. 629–639.
24. Kernighan, B.W. and P.J. Plauger. *The Elements of Programming Style,* New York: McGraw-Hill, 1974.

Towards automatic software fault location through decision-to-decision path analysis

by JAMES S. COLLOFELLO
Arizona State University
Tempe, Arizona
and
LARRY COUSINS
GTE Communications Systems
Phoenix, Arizona

ABSTRACT

Software development is a complex and error prone process. As a result of this process, much time is spent debugging software. This debugging process actually consists of two activities, fault localization and repair. For most problems, much of the debugging effort is devoted to fault localization. In this paper, current fault localization techniques are surveyed and a new technique called relational path analysis is proposed. Relational path analysis suggests that there exists information associated with stored execution paths of programs that, when analyzed heuristically, can localize faults with statistical significance. This paper presents a set of candidate heuristics for relational path analysis and the results of an experiment utilizing the heuristics. Conclusions regarding the effectiveness and usability of this technique and future research in this area are also discussed.

INTRODUCTION

Software development is a complex and error prone process. Although hardware costs during the last 30 years have consistently dropped, software costs have continued to climb.[1,2,3,4] One of the significant factors in these increased costs is the expense incurred performing software fault (error) localization and repair. As the complexity and size of software systems continues to increase dramatically, emphasis is needed on developing automated methods to help perform fault localization and repair activities.

It is important to distinguish between the terms fault localization, fault repair, and debugging. Myers defines debugging as:

> the activity that one performs after executing a successful test case [successful in the sense that it found a bug]. Describing it in more concrete terms, debugging is a two-part process; it begins with some indication of the existence of an error (e.g., the results of a successful test case), and it is the activity of (1) determining the exact nature and location of the suspected error within the program and (2) fixing or repairing the error.[5]

Thus, debugging entails both fault localization and repair. In the remainder of this paper, only the fault localization aspect of debugging is addressed.

CURRENT FAULT LOCALIZATION METHODS

Currently, many techniques and tools are used to perform fault localization. These methods can be classified either as knowledge-based or non-knowledge-based. Most of the existing fault localization approaches can be classified as non-knowledge-based. Over 100 such approaches were cited by Myers[5] in 1979. There are two common threads that most of these non-knowledge-based approaches possess. The first is that they usually provide powerful control over the program under test (e.g., symbolic execution of code). The second is that a user is required to provide all the intelligence necessary to guide and especially interpret the testing/debugging session.

Knowledge-based fault localization systems can be identified by their autonomous behavior. The systems themselves interpret the information they generate to localize faults; the information is not passed to a user for interpretation, as is the case in non-knowledge-based systems.

An example of a knowledge-based fault localization system is PROUST.[6] The goal of PROUST's designers was to create a framework sufficient to catch all possible errors in small programs. They also wanted the program to understand the nature of the bugs, state it, and suggest a form of solution. To accomplish these objectives, the system requires that the program be totally and correctly specified. The major practical limitation of this system is that it is extremely difficult to form such specifications even for small programs, and there is no way to guarantee the specifications are correct even after they have been stated.

Another interesting system that approaches debugging through the avenue of a knowledge-base is the Program Testing Assistant developed by Chapman.[7] The unique quality that Chapman's system possesses is that as programs are developed and tested, a user can request that the system automatically store the test cases for future use. When a bug arises in a feature being tested, the system in coordination with the user can request that the appropriate saved test cases be rerun automatically—either before the system has been repaired to aid in identifying the problem or after the system has been repaired to ensure its correctness. In conjunction with this capability, the Programming Testing Assistant heuristically modifies the corresponding test cases when the source code is changed. This preserves the ability of the system to continue to use, if possible, previous test cases to perform a type of automated regression testing of the code.

The major disadvantage of this system is that it only works with LISP code. Given the indistinguishability of LISP code and data, it may in fact only be practical with LISP. The major advantage is the way the system relieves users from having to manually save and execute test cases.

RELATIONAL PATH ANALYSIS

In this section a theory called relational path analysis is described that suggests that there exists information associated with the execution paths of programs which when analyzed heuristically can produce statistically significant fault locations.

The basis of this theory stems from analysis of DD-path (decision-to-decision-path) executions. A DD-path is a section of straight-line code that exists between predicates in a program. The theory suggests that a database of test cases that execute correctly can be utilized to locate DD-paths that contain faults in an incorrect program execution. To accomplish this objective, the database of test cases is supplemented to contain execution path information consisting of the DD-paths traversed for each test case. Various heuristics are then applied comparing the execution path for the incorrect program with those of correct program executions in an attempt to locate DD-paths on the incorrect program path which may be the source of the error.

In the remainder of this section, ten such heuristics based upon various strategies for program debugging are described. Each heuristic examines both the current execution path and the execution path database to identify DD-paths in the program which may contain the error. In the next section, experimental results utilzing these heuristics will be presented.

Heuristic 1

The first heuristic returns all of the DD-paths on the erroneous path that are not executed in any of the correct execution paths in the database. This heuristic is based on the theory that if a DD-path is traversed by an error-producing test case that has never been traversed before, it is likely to contain the error.

Heuristic 2

Heuristic 2 returns all the DD-paths that are elements of the erroneous execution path whose sum of all executions in the correct execution paths is less than or equal to 50. The number 50 was chosen as a possible lower bound for experimental purposes and certainly is not sacred.

The rationale for this heuristic is similar to that for heuristic 1 except that it was thought that the bound would allow flexibility in tuning the heuristic for finding different types of errors. Heuristic 2 recognizes that code paths may be executed several times correctly before some condition occurs that may create an error.

Heuristic 3

Heuristic 3 returns all the DD-paths that are elements of the erroneous execution path and whose sum of all executions, both correct and incorrect, is less than or equal to 50. Again, the number 50 is chosen for experimental reasons. Heuristic 3 is the same as 2 except that the sum of all test case executions is utilized.

The rationale for heuristic 3 is analogous to that for number 2, and is based on the idea that the fewer times a DD-path is executed, the higher the probability that it contains an error.

Heuristic 4

Heuristic 4 returns DD-paths in the erroneous execution path with the maximum ratio of times executed in the erroneous path to total number of executions in the correct execution path database. For example, if one DD-path is executed 500 times by the error producing test case and 100 times by all other test cases, and another DD-path is executed 3 times by the erroneous test case and once by all the others, the ratio values for each would be 5 and 3 respectively. Heuristic 4 would then choose the first as the likely candidate to contain the error.

The rationale for heuristic 4 suggests that DD-paths executed with a higher relative frequency in the erroneous path than in the correct paths may be more likely to contain the error than those with fewer executions.

Heuristic 5

Heuristic 5 returns the DD-path on the erroneous execution path that has been executed a minimum number of times (but non-zero) in the execution path database. Heuristic 5 is based on the theory that the DD-path that has been exercised least by the nonerror producing test cases may be the source of the error.

Heuristic 6

Heuristic 6 returns the DD-path on the erroneous execution path that has the corresponding minimum localized sum. A localized sum for a particular DD-path is defined as the sum of all the execution counts from the execution path database of three contiguous DD-paths which contain the particular DD-path in the center.

This heuristic attempts to locate a localized pocket of minimum contiguous DD-path executions with the assumption that those areas least exercised are more likely to contain the error.

Heuristic 7

This heuristic is analogous to heuristic 5 but it identifes the DD-path with the minimum number of executions by all test cases, including the erroneous path, instead of trying to locate the DD-path in the erroneous execution path with a corresponding minimum number of executions in the execution path data base.

The rationale for including the erroneous execution path in the minimum calculation is that traversals of a DD-path (even on an erroneous execution path) increase the likelihood that the DD-path does not contain the error.

Heuristic 8

This heuristic returns sets of pairs of contiguous DD-paths that have been executed in the erroneous execution path and that have never been executed as a pair in the execution path database. This heuristic is based on the theory that some types of errors are caused by the sequencing of contiguous DD-paths. If a sequence has never been tested, it may be a likely candidate for the error.

Heuristic 9

Heuristic 9 is analogous to heuristic 8 except that this heuristic examines sequences of three contiguous DD-paths instead of examining contiguous sequences of two DD-paths.

A sequence length of three was chosen to increase the accuracy of heuristic 8.

Heuristic 10

This heuristic extends the rationale utilized in heuristics 8 and 9 to examine all contiguous sequences of DD-paths that have been executed in the erroneous execution path that have never been executed as noted in the execution path data base.

RELATIONAL PATH ANALYSIS EXPERIMENT

This section describes the experimentation utilizing relational path analysis. The experimental design is presented first, followed by the actual results and their interpretation.

Experimental Design

The first step of the experiment was to develop a Pascal path analysis tool that could automatically calculate the ten heuristics currently utilized by relational path analysis for a set of sample programs. Ten small Pascal programs were chosen from Jensen and Wirth's *Pascal: User Manual and Report*[8] and Grogono's *Programming in Pascal*[9] to provide a non-biased test set. The programs selected are summarized in Appendix 1.

The next step involved creating test cases for each of the programs using a black box testing approach. The path analysis tool was then invoked for each test case preserving a record of the test case execution. The result of this step is a test suite for each program as well as the information needed for relational path analysis.

To actually determine the effectiveness of relational path analysis, errors then had to be inserted into each program. Ten different error types were chosen from Myers' book *The Art of Software Testing*[5] to seed into the programs. The error types are described in Appendix 2. To simplify testing, each program was associated with only one error type.

After assigning the error types, one error was randomly seeded into the code of each of the ten programs. Then, each program was executed with the previously generated test suite, and an analysis was performed utilizing the relational path analysis heuristics. The results of each error analysis were saved, and the seeding of errors was repeated four more times providing a total of five error analysis results per program.

There were ten null hypotheses to test during the experiment. Each null hypothesis corresponded to a heuristic and could be stated as: "The probability that the heuristic is capable of finding errors is 0." Thus, if a heuristic was capable of finding errors, this experiment would have to reject the null hypothesis at a 90% confidence level. When calculating a heuristic's error localization ability, all ten error types were utilized.

RESULTS

The results of using the ten heuristics on the ten programs are shown in Table I. Each entry in this matrix contains the fraction of time in which the heuristic corresponding to the column found the DD-path(s) that were in error in the program corresponding to the row. The mean at the bottom of each column corresponds to each heuristic's ability to identify errors across all ten programs (i.e., all ten different error types). The standard deviation (SD) and half length (HL) of a 90% confidence interval using the t statistic are also shown. Also shown is the average fraction (MDD) of DD-paths returned by each heuristic over the total number of DD-paths. This number provides an indication of the precision of a heuristic. Finally, the mean number of times each error type was found by all of the heuristics is shown in the column labeled "MEAN."

Table II contains the 90% confidence intervals for the ten heuristics tested along with the average percentage of DD-paths returned by each heuristic. The confidence intervals and the percentage of DD-paths returned provide the means of assessing the relative utility of each heuristic.

INTERPRETATION

An analysis of the confidence intervals in Table II shows the null hypotheses for all of the heuristics rejected at the 90% confidence level. Thus, all of the heuristics possess some error localization ability. Table I also illustrates that the heuristics

TABLE I—Results of heuristics

	Heuristic										
	1	2	3	4	5	6	7	8	9	10	MEAN
1	.4	1	.6	.4	.2	.2	.4	.8	.8	.8	.56
P 2	.4	1	.6	0	0	.2	0	.6	.6	.8	.42
R 3	.6	1	1	1	.2	0	.2	.6	.6	.6	.58
O 4	.8	1	1	.4	0	0	0	1	1	.8	.60
G 5	.2	1	1	.8	.4	.2	.4	.6	.6	.6	.58
R 6	.6	1	1	1	.4	0	0	.6	.6	.6	.58
A 7	.6	1	.4	1	.4	0	0	.6	.6	.6	.52
M 8	.4	.8	.8	.8	.2	.2	.2	.4	.4	.4	.46
9	.4	1	1	.8	.2	0	0	.4	.6	.8	.52
10	.2	1	.8	.6	.2	.4	.2	.2	.2	.2	.40
MEAN	.46	.98	.82	.68	.22	.12	.14	.58	.60	.62	
S.D.	.19	.06	.22	.33	.15	.14	.16	.22	.21	.20	
H.L.	.11	.03	.13	.19	.09	.08	.09	.13	.12	.11	
MDD	.15	.95	.90	.09	.09	.09	.09	.45	.48	.42	

TABLE II—Confidence intervals and percent DD-paths returned

Heuristic	C.I	Percent DD-paths
1	(.35, .57)	15%
2	(.95, 1)	95%
3	(.69, .95)	90%
4	(.49, .87)	9%
5	(.13, .31)	9%
6	(.04, .2)	9%
7	(.05, .23)	9%
8	(.45, .71)	45%
9	(.48, .72)	48%
10	(.51, .73)	42%

are not very sensitive to the ten error types (as demonstrated by the mean number of times each error type was found by all of the heuristics). These results suggest there is some basis for relational path analysis as an error localization technique.

The usability of a heuristic requires an examination of both the confidence interval and the percentage of DD-paths returned by the heuristic. Based on the results in Table II, the most usable heuristics appear to be numbers 1 and 4.

CONCLUSION AND FUTURE RESEARCH

In this paper relational path analysis is presented as a new technique for software fault localization. An experiment is also described in which the heuristics comprising relational path analysis were tested and found to localize errors with statistical significance. Although this experiment was limited to small programs and a small number of error types, the results were promising and suggest additional research should be performed. The ultimate goal of this research into relational path analysis should be to develop a powerful fault localization tool. Such a tool could apply sophisticated heuristics to help isolate errors. Although such a tool would be applicable throughout a product's life cycle, its diagnostic capabilities would be most powerful after some systematic testing has been performed. Thus, the fault localization tool would be most beneficial during the later stages of testing and during software maintenance. Considering the high cost of performing maintenance activities and the difficulty of isolating errors during this phase, this tool could be very cost effective.

Several additional research areas must be explored before an effective fault localization tool based on relational path analysis can be developed. First, the current heuristics must be examined and experimented with for additional types of errors and bigger programs. Additional heuristics may also be needed for detecting errors in large programs. Another interesting area to explore is the combination of various heuristics. Although much research remains to be done in this area, the need for automated fault localization is high and the potential benefits are significant.

REFERENCES

1. Boehm, B.W. "Software Engineering." In *Classics in Software Engineering*, E.N. Yourdon (ed.), New York: Yourdon Press, 1979, p. 326.
2. Boehm, B.W. *Software Engineering Economics*. Englewood Cliffs, New Jersey: Prentice-Hall, 1981.
3. Booch, G. *Software Engineering With Ada*. Menlo Park, California: Benjamin/Cummings, 1983.
4. Zelkowitz, M.V. "Large-scale Software Development." In *Principles of Software Engineering and Design*, Englewood Cliffs, New Jersey: Prentice-Hall, 1979, pp. 2–11.
5. Myers, G.J. *The Art of Software Testing*. New York: John Wiley, 1979.
6. Johnson, W.L. and Soloway, E. "PROUST An Automatic Debugger for Pascal Programs." *BYTE* (April 1985), pp. 179–190.
7. Chapman, D. "A Program Testing Assistant." *Communications of the ACM*, 25 (1982) 9, pp. 625–634.
8. Jensen, K. and Wirth, N. *Pascal: User Manual and Report*. New York: Springer-Verlag, 1974.
9. Grogono, P. *Programming in Pascal*. Reading, Massachusetts: Addison-Wesley, 1980.

APPENDIX 1—PASCAL TEST PROGRAMS

1. A simulation program that models passenger buses traveling between stops and shows the passenger throughput.
2. A calculator program that evaluates arithmetic expressions in infix notation.
3. A program that finds the circular radius and center of the circle that intersects three distinct points.
4. A cosine program that arithmetically finds the cosine of a number through iteration.
5. A program that produces a cross-reference for all distinct words contained in a file.
6. A square root program that arithmetically finds the square root of a number through iteration.
7. A program that finds the matrix multiplication of two matrices.
8. A program that changes an infix notation expression to postfix notation.
9. A program that converts regular numbers to Roman numerals.
10. A program that performs a shell sort on a list of numbers.

APPENDIX 2—SEEDED ERROR TYPES

1. Unset or uninitialized data values (value is zero).
2. Wrongly set data (values set randomly).
3. Logic errors; that is, misuse of "and," "or," and "not."
4. Computation errors; that is, incorrect arithmetic precedence, mixed mode problems, and integer division.
5. Incorrect procedure or function output.
6. Does not correctly handle all legal input; that is, boundary conditions not checked, no checks for valid input, and exhaustive decision are not made.
7. Off-by-one arithmetic errors (not loops).
8. Placing of program statements is incorrect; that is, placed external from or internal to the place they should be (e.g., incorrect begin/end grouping).
9. Misuse of comparators; that is, =, <, >, >=, <=, <>.
10. Incorrect looping; for example, wrong assumptions, off-by-one errors, etc.

Tool integration in lifecycle support environments

by JAYASHREE RAMANATHAN*
Universal Energy Systems
Columbus, Ohio
and
VASUDEVAN VENUGOPAL
Ohio State University
Columbus, Ohio

ABSTRACT

Two pragmatic requirements are placed on lifecycle support environments: (1) one must be able to integrate existing tools into the environment, and (2) the environment must possess an open-ended architecture. The approach must therefore consider the large number of tools that support various phases of a lifecycle. The diversity of such tools makes them hard to integrate into an environment such that they can operate in a coordinated manner and can communicate with each other.

This paper provides a possible approach to the tool integration problem in which the environment architecture and user interface issues are also taken into account. It is shown herein that such an approach leads to a very general and powerful technique of integrating tools. Apart from being able to handle evolution both in the environment and in tools, the approach allows the enforcement of policies on tool invocation and on tool operation.

* The author currently is on leave of absence from Ohio State University.

INTRODUCTION

This paper addresses the issue of integrating diverse tools into lifecycle support environments. The integration problem is examined in the context of the following architectural characteristics:

- A logical database serves as the repository for all project information.[1,2,3]
- The database is object-oriented and its conceptual model allows the representation of all objects involved in the lifecycle (for example, objects representing people such as programmers, generated objects such as source code, and derived objects such as object code) and their interrelationships (like the "owns" relationship between a programmer and a code object or a "part_of" relationship between an object describing the project and another describing a programmer involved in the project).[2]
- Tools that are integrated into this environment access existing objects (by means of views) and tool products are distributed into the database in a manner consistent with the conceptual model.
- The environment allows diverse types of existing tools to be integrated regardless of the idiosyncrasies of their operation. It also allows new tools to be added without any major modifications to the tools.
- The environment has at least a rudimentary notion of an activity and such relationships between activities as sequencing and concurrency.[3,4,5]

The first two characteristics are widely accepted among software environment builders. The next two are unique to the environment described herein; however, they are essential pragmatic requirements for a real-world environment. Given the breadth of activities that such an environment supports and the diverse tools that are involved, it would be impossible to come up with a single representation for all tools or, for that matter, to predict all the tools that would be integrated into the environment. The emphasis on existing tools does not preclude the possibility of building tools for such an environment. As for the last point, any software environment attempting to enforce policies on users must have a conception of software development as a set of related activities. Much of the policy enforcement at a macro level is done by permitting, denying, or constraining specific activities at specified times.

"Loose integration" is proposed here as an appropriate, widely applicable paradigm for tool integration in lifecycle support environments. Broadly speaking, loose integration is a view-oriented mechanism for bidirectional communication between the tool and the database through input-extraction and output-distribution views.

The distinctness of this approach stems from the fact that tool integration is treated as an issue to be examined in the larger context of modeling the software process. It does not treat tool integration as an issue of tool communication and therefore independent of the process model.[6,7] Further, it does not treat the process model as being, in some sense, a "merging" of tool views.[8] Such an approach would subsume the model aspect as one necessary for tool communication rather than as a separate issue.

Listed below are some advantages of the loose integration scheme proposed here. Many of these advantages accrue because of the unified treatment of tool integration with other environmental issues.

- *Encapsulation:* When integrating a tool, you need not be aware of the other tools in the environment.
- *Tool communication:* Communication between tools need not be set up. It happens automatically and indirectly if their input view specifications intersect (i.e., the two view specifications refer to the same object(s)).
- *Tool coordination:* Since tool invocation is an activity, the activity model can coordinate this tool's invocation with others in much the same way as it coordinates any other activities. Thus, tool coordination is merely a special case of activity coordination.
- *Enforcement of policies on tool invocation:* Policies such as automatic invocation of tools, constraints on their invocation, and so on can be implemented using the same mechanism that is used to monitor activities (the activity model) and enforce system policies (using daemons described in the next section).
- *Increased tool versatility:* Since the same tool can be associated with many views, it can be used in many ways. For example, one view specification may extract the view for compiling an entire project while another might be meant to let an individual programmer compile his or her module. Both views would be associated with the same compiler tool.

Some other advantages are better illustrated by specific examples presented in a later section.

The next section briefly digresses to a description of the object model that is used for the software process. This description is brief and is added only to facilitate an understanding of the examples that follow. Later sections describe and illustrate loose integration of tools with examples and discuss the scope and limits of its applicability. Lastly, the status of our implementation is discussed.

THE OBJECT MODEL

Information Frames (see Figure 1) are used to model all the data objects involved in the lifecycle. Information frames correspond to physical and logical entities in the software process. *Slots* of a frame describe properties of an object. Some slots link the parent frame to other frames or slots. The link type represents a particular relationship between participating frames. Slots and frames may possess *attributes* that serve as variables for recording local state and history information as well as protection and display information.

The real difference between information frames and structured objects of other object-oriented models[9] lies in the attachment of procedures to slots or frames. These procedures (called *daemons*) are triggered (as against being explicitly invoked) under a variety of environmental conditions. These conditions could be user and tool operations on slots and frames (such as Visit, Modify, Exit and so on), the occurrence of certain environment states (such as design in progress), or change in environment states (such as design completed), to name a few. The variety of triggering conditions allows daemons to help in a variety of activities such as assisting a user, maintaining data consistency in an object base and enforcing policies on users and tools. Most of the policy enforcement by daemons is of an "all or none" nature. An ongoing activity or subactivity could trigger a daemon. Successful execution of the daemon validates the activity. If the activity or subactivity violates some environment policy, an exception is raised during the execution of the daemon leading to a rollback of the errant activity. The environment is then reverted to the most recent consistent state.

A frequently used display view for frames is called a *form*. Forms consist of *panels* which correspond to the underlying slots of a frame. A user navigates through the object base by moving between text panels and down links to other frames. Any daemons related to user focus are fired as the user navigates through the database. The comamnds that a user can issue when in a panel are controlled by a menu. Forms are, however, only one of many possible unparse schemes for a frame.

CONCEPTUAL ISSUES IN TOOL INTEGRATION

The decision to integrate a tool is not a mere data conversion issue. Integrating a tool involves resolving such issues as the nature of the user-tool interface, the tool's input and output views, and the policies one wants to enforce on tool usage. Provided here is a classification of the kinds of knowledge involved in integrating a tool.

1. *Interface-oriented knowledge:*
   a. Commands involved in tool invocation. (That is, should the tool be invoked by users using menu selection, control keys, or some other scheme. Should the user's focus be inferred from the cursor position, mouse position, or by some other mechanism?)
   b. Granularity of data. (That is, on what chunk of information should the tool be applied, and how does this relate to the user focus when invoking the tool?)

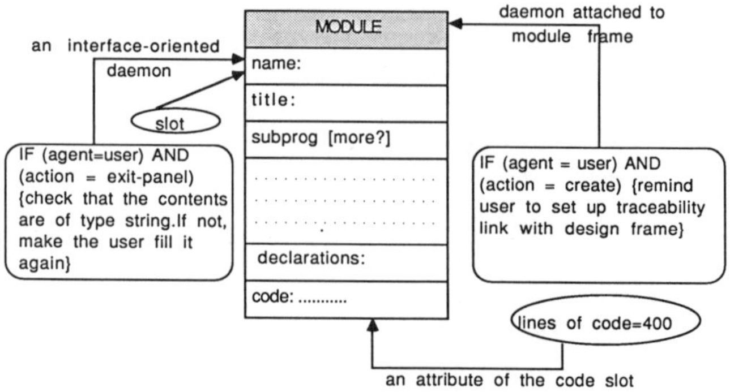

Figure 1—An information frame

   c. Granularity of control. (That is, should the command provided to users constitute one tool command or should one design user commands that are implemented as combinations of underlying tool commands? Also, how and when should users get back control and how should users be notified of and made to look at tool outputs and diagnostics?)
   d. Interface-oriented daemons. (That is, is there a need to include consistency-checking daemons beyond whatever was implemented in the object-model? For example, completeness and validity of user-supplied data can be ensured by associating daemons with data panels that monitor the data even as it is being keyed in.)

2. *Tool-oriented knowledge:*
   This comprises of knowledge needed to reconcile the tool and information-base disparity. To do this, it is necessary to specify the input-extraction and output-distribution views as well as parse-up and parse-down procedures between the tool and the information base. The view definition language must have primitives not only for specifying network traversal but also for specifying view modifications, view dependencies, and exception handling primitives to handle exceptional situations that might occur during traversal.

3. *World-oriented knowledge:*
   Concurrently with the integration of a tool, the system may need to enforce tool-related policies. For example, along with the integration of a compiler to allow compilation of modules, it may be desirable to enforce the protocol to automatically inform the project manager of a successful compilation. To do so requires knowledge about other objects in the "world-model" of the enterprise such as the manager's frame. Implementing the protocol may also require knowledge about what the manager is to be informed and how. Much of this would depend on personnel hierarchy and system policy about protection and distribution of information. Generally some world-oriented knowledge is required about the tool's role in the enterprise as well as policies and protocols relating to tool application.

EXAMPLES

1. *Tool:* Editor

Assumed tool characteristics:
- Interactive nature of the tool.
- Works on buffers.

Desired interface behaviour:
The user should be able to use the editor in a panel in much the same way as he edits a buffer.
Steps in integrating such a tool:
- Associate a buffer with each panel.
- Intercept user commands and pass them on to the editor with the buffer context.
- Redisplay the updated buffer on the affected panel.

Policies that can be implemented:
- Sense the language in which the user is coding (on any given coding panel) and put the editor in the appropriate model (e.g., C-mode in EMACS[10] if the user is coding in C). This assumes that the editor provides language sensitive assistance.
- Automatically save changes after every 10 commands.

2. *Tool:* RCS (Revision Control System)[11]

Salient tool characteristics:
- Batch tool
- Not a data transformer but a repository for textual information.

Some policies that can be implemented:
a. Maintain "revisions" of any slot that contains more than 500 lines of text.
Implementation:
- Associate a linecount attribute with any slot containing text that stores the number of lines in the slot (this could be computed every so often).
- Have a daemon associated with each such slot that fires whenever the user exits the associated panel, and if the panel is larger than 500 lines, have checks in the slot text to RCS (the slot can be uniquely identified by the frame-id/slot-heading pair).

RCS handles the versioning of slots, allowing us to implement such environment policies as:
b. Allow the owners of the participating frame to decide when they want to store a modified text as a new revision and to retrieve any particular version.
Implementation:
Tie the "check in a new version," "check out version," and "create a new version" commands to keystrokes and invoke in the context of the panel that is the user-focus.
c. In a project, only the chief programmer has rights to create new revisions. Subprogrammers are not to be aware of the underlying versioning.
Implementation:
- Have a daemon that is triggered when the chief programmer visits his frame.
- This daemon should augment the displayed menu with "create a new revision" as an invocable command.
- If the chief programmer issued this command, traverse each of the "subprogrammer" links out of this frame and check in the "source code" slots of these frames for a new revision.
- The name of the RCS file associated with the "source code" slots of the subprogrammers is stored as an attribute of the subprogrammer frame.
- Whenever any subprogrammer visits his frame, display it in the usual manner except to check the text associated with the "source code" slot and display it in the corresponding panel.

3. *Tool:* Compiler

Salient tool characteristics:
- Batch tool
- Data transformer

Mode of integration:
Given that the coding frame has the form shown in Figure 2 and that "uses" and "subprogrammer" links exist between such frames, it is desired that the chief programmer be provided with a single command to compile the entire project's code. Any error messages are to be distributed to the appropriate places.
Some comments:
Shown below are the input and output views for integrating a compiler in the manner mentioned above. The following aspects of the problem and the working of the view-interpreter are worth noting:
- There is only an implicit ordering among the subprogrammer modules. The view specification includes exception handlers that cause backtracking until the modules are incorporated into the view in the right order.
- The contribution of any frame instance depends not only on the type of the frame but also on the contents of some panels in the frame instance. Each unique selection criterion forms and "instance_view." Many such instance views *combine* to form the input view for the tool (com-

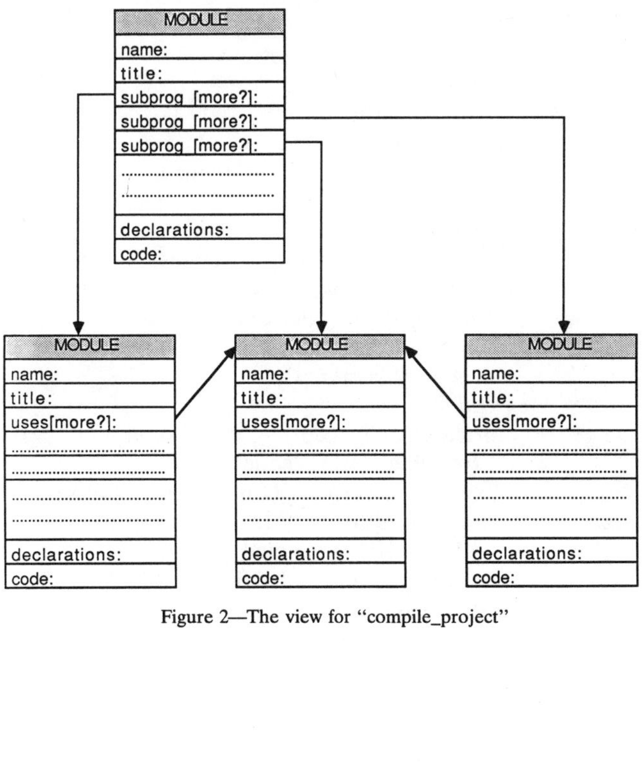

Figure 2—The view for "compile_project"

bine is a scoping mechanism such that control passes out of the combined view only if the encountered frame does not conform to any of the selection criteria described within the combined view).

- One of these instance views outlines the selection criteria for the root frame (i.e., the frame from which the traversal begins). This view also includes a "termination condition" whose fulfillment indicates that the view is complete.
- The result of navigating through the database according to an input-view description is a sequence of slots (their headings and contents). It might need to be unparsed to suit the tool.
- Frames and slots that have been visited are tagged to facilitate easy detection of view termination.

```
Compiler view:
 combines
   chief_programmer_instance_view
     begin view
       frame instance selection:
         (heading(slot) = "title") and
         (contents(slot) = "chief programmer");
       slot selection:
         (type(slot) = "LINK") and
         (heading(slot) = "subprogrammer") and
         (untraversed_link(slot))→traverse_link(slot);
         heading(slot) = "declaration"
         or (heading(slot) = "code")
         → add_to_view(slot);
       exceptions:
       forall(((heading(slot) = "declaration") or
         (heading(slot) = "code")) and
         (contents(slot) = NIL)) handled by foo;
       forall((type(slot) = "LINK") and
         (content(slot) = NIL)) handled by foo;
       terminate condition:
       forall(type(slot) = "LINK"→traversed(slot))
       end view
   subprogrammer_instance_view
     begin view
       frame instance selection:
         (heading(slot) = "Title") and
         (contents(slot) = "subprogrammer");
       slot selection:
         (type(slot) = "LINK") and
         (heading(slot) = "subprogrammer") and
         (untraversed_link(slot))→traverse_link(slot);
         (heading(slot) = "declaration") or
         (heading(slot) = "code")
         → add_to_view(slot);
       exceptions:
         forall(((heading(slot) = "declaration") or
           (heading(slot) = "code")) and
           (contents(slot) = NIL)) handled by foo;
         forall((type(slot) = "LINK") and (content
           (slot) = NIL)) handled by foo;
         forall((type(slot) = "LINK") and (heading
           (slot) = "uses")
             → is_visited(object_pointed_by(contents(slot)))
             handled by untraverse;
     end view
   end combine
     output_distribution_view for compiler
     begin dist
       associate(error_message,line_text)
         using assoc_procedure;
         insert_in_slot(find_slot_in_view(line_text,
           slot_num, location),
         error_message, location + 1);
     end dist
```

4. *Combinations of tools:*

Policies and activities requiring combinations of tools to be invoked in a coordinated manner is handled in one of two ways. In the case that the coordination is complex, it is handled in the activity model which treats each tool invocation as an activity and models the entire coordinated transaction as a petri net. Simple and hardwired interactions between tools can be implemented using daemons.

SCOPE AND LIMITATIONS

The ease of loose integration of any tool depends on the ease with which the environment can mediate and arbitrate between the tool and the user. In almost all *batch tools,* the semantics of tool commands and the nature of input required by the tool are quite well defined. Normally, user commands correspond closely to single tool operations. It is therefore straightforward to integrate batch tools into the environment. The integration is more graceful if the underlying operating system provides "virtual screen" or "pseudoterminal" (UNIX) facilities so that tool diagnostics and messages that are directed to the screen can be intercepted and the environment can decide what it wants to do with them. In an operating system devoid of these facilities, the environment cannot filter out these diagnostics but it can still restore the earlier screen status once the tool has finished executing.

Interactive tools that interact through textual data and commands are integrated by using a pseudo-terminal interface to the tool. The environment arbitrates by isolating the interactive tool from the physical screen. Each command during an interaction is treated like one invocation of a batch tool with that command. The results of the interactive command are captured by the pseudo-terminal interface and relevant parts presented to the user in the right context.

For interactive tools in which the interaction involves both textual and graphical information as well as the use of pointing devices (e.g., mouse or light pen), the very advantage of such tools causes problems in integration. The fact that a user can point at any object on the screen makes it harder for the environment to control user actions than it was in the case where the system could track or control cursor motion. The fact that simple graphical figures can represent textual information in a greatly condensed form leads to the problem that for any graphical figure, the underlying frame representation (which is essentially textual) can be very complex. Moreover, incremental changes to the graphical representation may lead to major changes in the underlying frame representation due to the difficulty in translating the graphical context of the change into an underlying frame context and because we cannot guarantee that there exists a mapping between an arbitrary set of graphical operations and underlying frame operations that ensures consistency under composition. For example, the effect of adding a link between an SADT[12] box A and another box B can be understood only in the context of other boxes in the diagram.

IMPLEMENTATION

The paradigm of loose integration has been examined and tested as part of the TRIAD project in progress at The Ohio State University and the KI shell being developed at Universal Energy Systems (see[13] for a detailed description of the environment architecture). Some examples include the integration of a C compiler and the dbx debugger as well as the integration of synthesized tools such as a tool for providing graphical views of project information. The TRIAD shell has also been used to bring up process support environments for non-software lifecycles allowing the opportunity of integrating a variety of design and simulation tools used in manufacturing an expert system as well as numerous other domain-specific tools. The language framework for describing views is under development.

CONCLUSIONS

Given the trend in software environments towards having a common database for storing project information, we examine a view-oriented approach to tool integration for permitting bidirectional communication of information between a tool and the database. We also believe that a carefully designed object-oriented architecture suitable for lifecycle support goes a long way in solving the problems that are typically encountered in integration. A common interface for database access and tool invocation as well as an active database in which user actions and changes to data are monitored as they go on eases policy enforcement and leads to significant enhancements in the ways in which an already existing tool can be used on incorporation into the environment.

REFERENCES

1. Penedo, M.H. and Stuckle, D.E. "PMDB—A Project Master Database for Software Engineering Environments." *Proceedings of the Eighth International Conference on Software Engineering,* 1985, pp. 150–157.
2. Dittrich, K.R., Gothard, W. and Lockemann, P.C. "DAMOKLES—A Database System for Software Engineering Environments." *IFIP WG2.4 International Workshop on Advanced Programming Environments,* 1986, pp. 345–364.
3. Ramamoorthy, C.V., Usuda, Y., Tsai, W.T. and Prakash, A. "Genesis: An Integrated Environment for Development and Evolution of Software." *Proceedings of COMPSAC,* 1985, pp. 472–479.
4. Ramamoorthy, C.V., Garg, V. and Aggarwal, R. "Environment Modeling and Activity Management in GENESIS." *Proceedings of SOFTFAIR-II: 2nd Conference on Software Development Tools, Techniques and Alternatives,* 1985, pp. 2–9.
5. Cheatham, T.E. "A Computer-Based Project Management Assistant." *Digest of Papers, Fall COMPCON,* 1984, pp. 156–160.
6. Kaplan, S.M., Johnson, R.E., Campbell, R.H., Kamin, S.N., Purtilo, J.M., Harandi, M.T., and Liu, J.W.S. "An Architecture for Tool Integration." *IFIP WG2.4 International Workshop on Advanced Programming Environments,* 1986, pp. 109–124.
7. Osterweil, L.J. "Toolpack—An Experimental Software Development Environment Research Project." *Proceedings of the Sixth International Conference on Software Engineering,* 1982, pp. 166–175.
8. Garlan, D. "Views for Tools in Integrated Environments." *IFIP WG2.4 International Workshop on Advanced Programming Environments,* 1986, pp. 317–340.
9. Goldberg, A. and Robson, D. *The Smalltalk-80 System: Its Implementation and Language.* Reading, Massachusetts: Addison-Wesley, 1983.
10. Stallman, R.M. "EMACS, The Extensible, Customizable, Self-Documenting Display Editor." Memo 529, Artificial Intelligence Laboratory, June 1979.
11. Tichy, W.F. "Design, Implementation, and Evaluation of a Revision Control System." *6th Conference on Software Engineering,* 1982, pp. 58–67.
12. Ross, D.T. and Schoman, K.E. "Structured Analysis for Requirements Definition." *IEEE Transactions on Software Engineering,* SE-3 (1977), pp. 6–15.
13. Ashok, V., Ramanathan, J. and Sarkar, S. "A Tightly Coupled Software Assistant." OSU Report OSU-CISRC-86TR1TRIAD, September 1986.

An interactive software maintenance environment*

by STEPHEN S. YAU, SYING-SYANG LIU, and SHEAUSONG YANG
Northwestern University
Evanston, Illinois

ABSTRACT

In this paper, an interactive software maintenance environment is presented in which software maintenance tools, such as a syntax-directed editor, a pretty-printer, control and data flow analyzers, a data flow anomaly detector, a program slicer, and logical and performance ripple effect analyzers, are integrated together for effective software maintenance. The environment is based on a unified program representation model which is constructed by a *pair syntactic-semantic tree.* The advantage of this environment is that it allows software maintenance tools to use the common information which is supported by the database manager for the environment. The communications among different software maintenance tools are high because each maintenance tool can retrieve data from the common database. An experimental system has been implemented to demonstrate this interactive software maintenance environment.

* This work was supported by the Office of Naval Research under Contract N00014-80-C-0167.

INTRODUCTION

It is well known that software maintenance has become the dominant factor of the high cost of software, and software maintenance costs are still increasing.[1] Maintenance is frequently performed on a large-scale software system because of the existence of system errors, changes of operating environment, code optimization, functional enhancement, deletion of obsolete features, and improvement of efficiency.[2] Because of lack of effective maintenance techniques, the reliability of software systems likely deteriorates as more maintenance activities are performed on the systems. Consequently, the systems soon become unmaintainable and hence unusable. An effective approach to reducing the high cost of software and increasing the useful life of many software systems is to establish a software maintenance environment that would facilitate the proper use of various techniques and tools for effective maintenance.

Traditionally, a maintenance tool included in a software maintenance environment operates on the basis that the necessary program information needed by the tool is extracted from the program. The disadvantage of this approach is that a large number of special software packages must be written to extract the necessary information from the program and organize it in various forms required by the maintenance tools. The information generated by some software maintenance tools is frequently used by other software maintenance tools. For example, the graphical program flow generator, data flow anomaly detector, and program slicer need control and data flow information which has already been generated by the control and data flow analyzers. The communications among software maintenance tools in this type of environment are usually very low because one translator is required between each ordered pair of related maintenance tools. In this case, it is better to directly extract the information from the program under maintenance than to construct a translator between each ordered pair of related maintenance tools. Since maintenance tools are usually developed continuously and independently of the software maintenance environment, the total system for software maintenance would be huge, expensive, and difficult to control and maintain.

In this paper, we present a software maintenance environment based on a unified program representation model that facilitates the integration and interface of various software maintenance tools. The advantage of this environment is that it allows the software maintenance tools to use the common information that is supported by the database manager for the environment. The communications among different software maintenance tools are high because each maintenance tool can retrieve data from the common database. An experimental system has been implemented to demonstrate this interactive software maintenance environment, and has shown that the productivity for software maintenance using this environment is improved by a significant order of magnitude.

MAINTENANCE OF LARGE-SCALE SOFTWARE SYSTEMS

Before we present our software maintenance environment, let us review the maintenance process for large-scale software, which involves several phases and can be illustrated as shown in Figure 1.[3]

The first phase determines the overall maintenance objectives. The second phase consists of analyzing a program to understand it. This phase is affected by the complexity, documentation, and self-descriptiveness of the program. The third phase consists of generating a particular modification proposal to accomplish the implementation of the maintenance objective. This phase is affected by the extensibility of the program. The fourth phase consists of accounting for the ripple effect. The primary attribute affecting ripple effect is

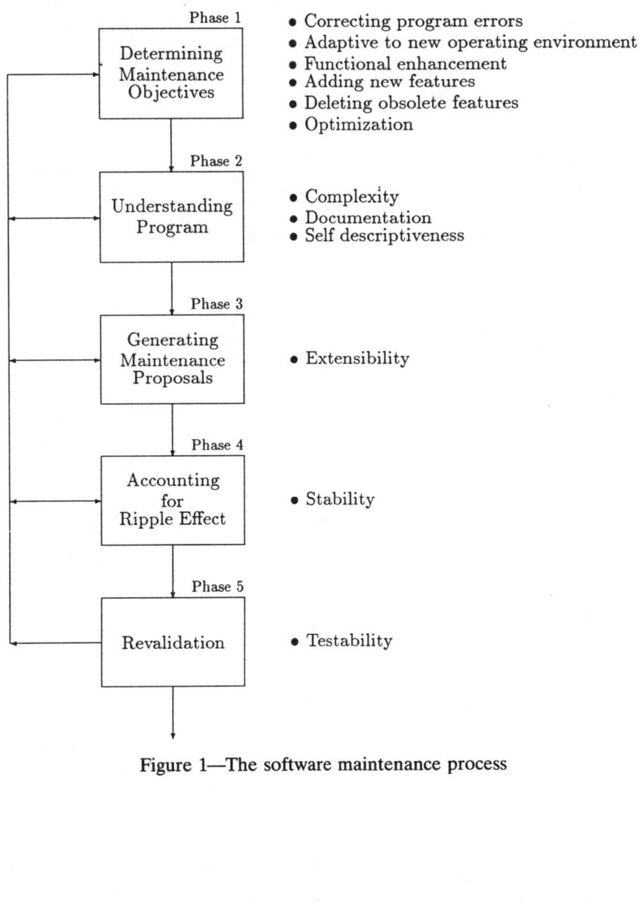

Figure 1—The software maintenance process

the stability of the program; the stability of a program is defined as the resistance to the amplification of changes in the program. The fifth phase consists of revalidating the modified program to ensure it has at least the same reliability as before. This phase is affected by the testability of the program. The whole or part of phases one through five is repeated until the modified software system passes the test.

The tools in our maintenance environment are used for software maintenance as follows: At the beginning, a graphical program flow generator[4] is invoked to generate a graphical view of the software system under maintenance so that the system hierarchical structure can easily be understood. At the same time, a pretty-printer displays the structured program source code on the terminal. After locating the program information and deciding how to achieve the maintenance objectives, the user will use a syntax-directed editor to modify the program. During modification, other software maintenance tools may be invoked by pressing a function key to analyze program flow,[5] detect data flow anomalies,[6] slice the program,[7] and accommodate ripple effect[8,9] revalidate modified program, and compute important metrics[10] whenever it is necessary.

MAJOR FEATURES OF THE ENVIRONMENT

Our interactive software maintenance environment is shown in Figure 2. The major features of the environment include a modified compiler, a syntax-directed editor, control and data

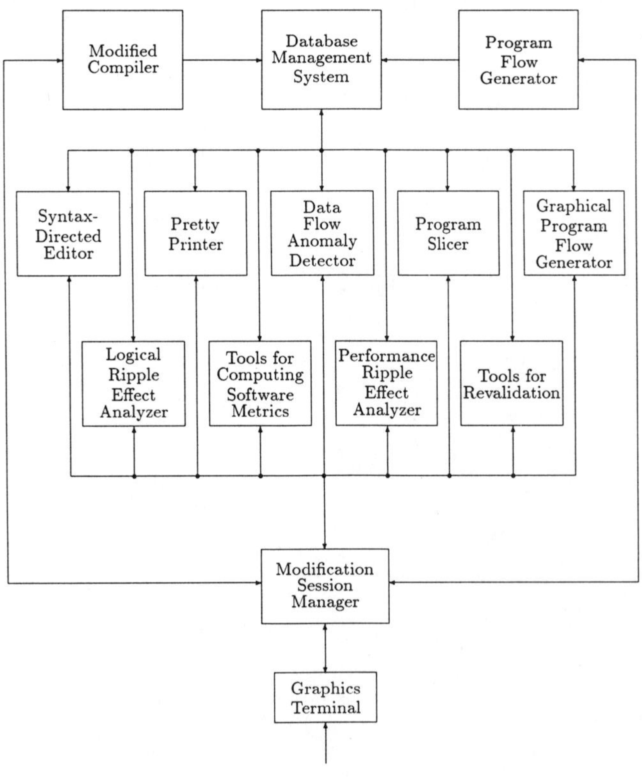

Figure 2—A software maintenance environment

flow generators, a graphical program flow generator, a data flow anomaly detector and a program slicer. In addition, a database manager is used to provide the interface between software maintenance tools and the database. All these software maintenance tools can be used interactively.

Database Manager

To support a large-scale software maintenance system, we need a database to store the whole syntactic and semantic information of the program to be maintained. The database manager provides an effective way to access the database and supports the interface for various software maintenance tools.

Modified Compiler

The purpose of the modified compiler is to translate the program source code to the internal syntactic and semantic structures and store them in the database. Various software maintenance tools can access the database through the database manager.

Modified Syntax-Directed Editor and Pretty-Printer

The pretty-printer (PP) and syntax-directed editor (SDE) offer an enviornment for creating and manipulating VAX-11 PASCAL programs. (VAX-11 PASCAL is an extension of standard ANSI PASCAL with the separate compilation capability.) The PP and SDE environment provides an easy-to-use editor that promotes step-wise refinement of PASCAL programs by simulating the program conception at a high level of abstraction. All input is type-checked for syntactic and semantic correctness and the program is automatically indented to emphasize the program structure.

The major features of SDE and PP include:

- A menu-driven facility to make SDE and PP user-friendly.
- A structured program representation facility for online modification and understanding.
- Using program templates to enforce the user to type in a well-structured and syntax-correct program.

Control and Data Flow Generators

When a program is input, control and data flow generators generate control flow and data flow information which is used by the graphical program flow generator, data flow anomaly detector, and program slicer.

Graphical Program Flow Generator

The graphical program flow generator draws the system hierarchical structures including the relation between modules, subprograms, and statements that are shown in Figure 3. With the aid of the graphical hierarchical structures, a user can take a graphical view at different levels of the program and understand its control and data flow information. Such information is helpful for understanding and modifying the program. Figure 4 shows the hierarchical view of the system-module level on a graphics terminal.

Data Flow Anomaly Detector

Data flow anomaly includes *defined-undefined, undefined-referenced,* and *defined-defined* anomalies which indicate possible program errors. The data flow anomaly detector displays data flow anomaly on the terminal whenever it is invoked.

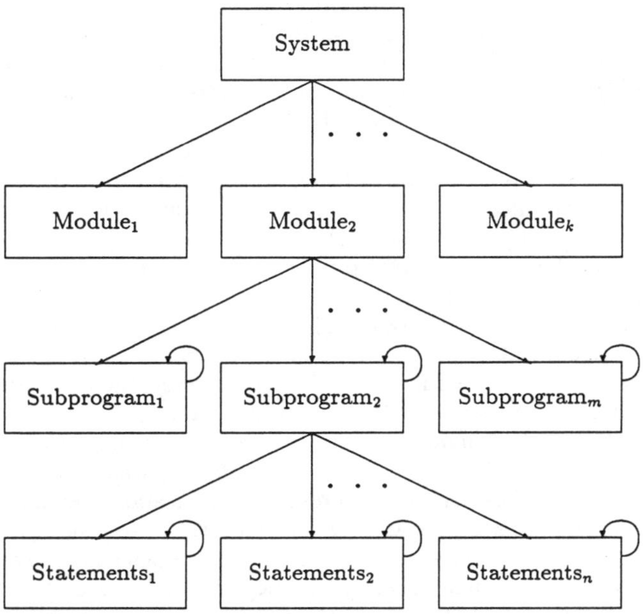

Figure 3—A hierarchical system structure

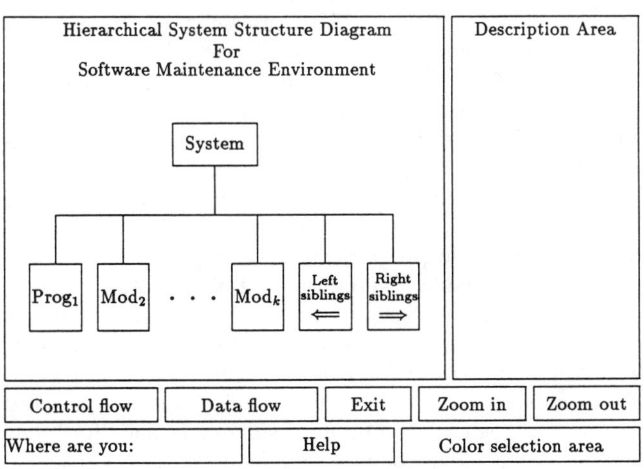

Figure 4—The hierarchical system structure diagram for the system-module level

Program Slicer

The program slicer decomposes a program into a reduced program subset with respect to some statement and variables. Since a reduced program subset is greatly smaller than an entire program, modification and debugging are easier and more efficient to perform on reduced program subsets than on a whole program.

SOFTWARE MAINTENANCE USING THE ENVIRONMENT

A user may use the commands provided by the syntax-directed editor to create a new program or modify an existing program. Cursor movement can be node-oriented, line-oriented, or page-oriented depending on the user's request. Movement is controlled by moving terminal keys, such as, [↑], [↓], [←], [→], or by specifying a line number to jump to a destinated line. To make any modification, a user first moves the cursor to a destinated program node and then types in the correct command and code.

As shown in Table I, the whole program template is displayed on the screen when a user creates a new program. To find the features of all keys, the user may press PF2 to invoke the help menu screen as shown in Table II. Starting from

TABLE I—A program template

```
program <Identifier> (<External-File-List>) ;
{ Declaration Part }
{ LABEL Declaration }
{ CONST Declaration }
{ TYPE Declaration }
{ VAR Declaration }
{ MODULE Declaration }
begin
    {Statement-List}
end. { Of program }
```

TABLE II—A key feature menu

[I] : insert template
[D] : delete a node
[R] : replace a node
[F] : go to parent node
[S] : go to first child
[P] : go to previous sibling
[N] : go to next sibling
[DELETE] : delete line feed
[RETURN] : insert line feed
[↑]: to 'up' node
[↓]: to 'down' node
[←]: to 'left' node
[→]: to 'right' node
[L] : move by line number
Press Any Key To Continue

invoke command menu	help	to first line	to last line
move section down	move section up		graphical flow generator
anomaly checking on/off			program slicer
boldface on/off	insert after/ before	syntax checking on/off	enter/ leave edit mode
		show line number	

Table I, the following steps would allow the user to key in a program similar to the program shown in Table III.

1. Move the cursor to the ⟨identifier⟩ by pressing [→]. Press [ENTER] to enter edit-mode and edit ⟨identifier⟩ to program name "Max" and then press [ENTER] to leave edit-mode. Repeat this step to edit ⟨File-Identifier⟩ to "(input, output)."
2. Press [↓] to move the cursor to "{LABEL Declaration}"-node and press [D] to delete this node. Repeat this step to delete "{CONST Declaration}"-node and "{TYPE Declaration}"-node.
3. Now, the cursor is positioned on "{VAR Declaration}"-node. This node will be replaced by a new node "*var* ⟨Identifier-list⟩:⟨Type-Specification⟩;" by pressing [R]. Entering edit-mode by pressing [ENTER], the text "a,b,c: integer" is input.
4. Repeating steps 1 to 3, the whole program will be input through the aid of screen online menu-driven features which provide all the possible selections. For example, when the cursor is positioned on "{Statement-List}"-node and [R] is pressed, then a menu, as shown in Table IV, is displayed. After selection, for example "D. If-Then-Else," this menu will disappear, and "{Statement-List}" will be replaced by an "if"-statement template.

To perform program slicing, we need to specify the software module name, the starting statement, and variables. The graphical program flow generator is used to improve program understanding and facilitate program analysis by displaying program flow information on a color graphics terminal.

TABLE III—A sample program for demonstrating SDE and PP features

```
{1} program Max (input, output);
{2} var a,b,c : integer;
{3} begin
{4}     readln(a,b);
{5}     if a>b then c := a;
{6}     else c := b;
{7}     writeln(c)
{8} end.
```

TABLE IV—A statement node insertion menu

A. Module-Call	G. For-To
B. Label	H. For-Downto
C. Assignment	I. With-Do
D. If-Then-Else	J. Case
E. Repeat-Until	K. Goto
F. While-Do	L. Compound
X. Quit	

THE UNIFIED MODEL OF THE ENVIRONMENT

In this section, the unified model for the environment is described. *Hierarchical graph model* (HGM)[9] and *Typed tree representation* (TTR)[10] are two unified program representation models for incremental modification. HGM is based on the concepts of recursive graphs and Codd relations to represent a program. The major disadvantage of HGM is that the internal program representation structure, which is in a relational form, is inconsistent with the program hierarchical structure, which is the interface between the user and the syntax-directed editor. Therefore, each movement on the program hierarchical tree needs several relational tables to reconstruct the program tree and display it on the screen. TTR is a program tree representation, but the tree also contains semantic information. The disadvantage of TTR is that the syntactic and semantic information of a program is combined together and associated with the nodes of the tree. In this case, the internal tree structure is still inconsistent with the program structure displayed on the screen. The syntax-directed editor and pretty-printer have to reformat the positions of nodes on the screen. Obviously, the implementation of software maintenance tools based on HGM or TTR will be more difficult and complicated than on a model which is consistent between the internal program representation and the external representation from the user's view.

The unified model used in our environment is a *pair syntactic-semantic tree* which consists of two parts: (1) a syntactic tree for incremental program modification and (2) a semantic tree for the storage and retrieval of semantic and flow information for various software maintenance tools. The syntactic information and semantic information are stored independently, but connected by several pointers for syntactic and semantic checking whenever it is necessary. To define a structure that is suitable for interactive modification, the program hierarchical structure should be maintained and should be consistent between system internal view for retrieval and external view for display. The syntactic and semantic structures of our system can be described as follows: A program is composed of two parts: (1) declaration parts, including "label," "constant," "type," "variable," and "procedure and function" declaration and (2) statement parts, including assignment statement, procedure statement, go-to statement, compound statement, conditional statement, repetitive statement, and with statement. Syntactic nodes are defined through the whole program, such as program header, type declaration, variable declaration, and statement in statement parts. Because the control and data flows exist in statement parts only, flow information is only defined in semantic nodes for statement parts. For each statement, variables in the "assignment" and "for" statements and expressions in various statements, such as "conditional" statements and "for" statements, are considered as semantic nodes. A syntactic or semantic node can be a simple node, such as "expression" node and "go-to" node, or a structured node, such as "com-

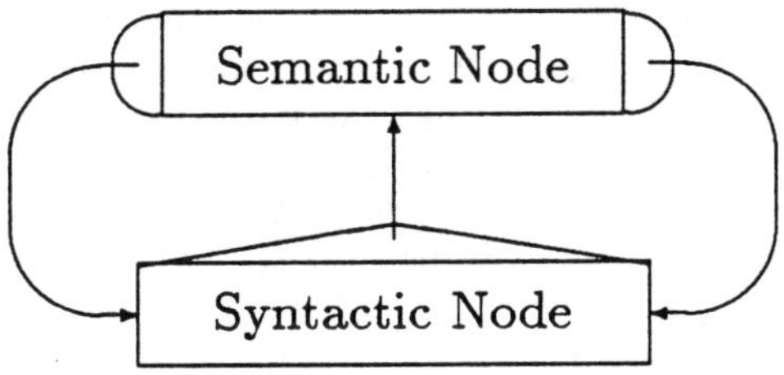

Figure 5—The relation between a syntactic node and a semantic node

pound" node, "conditional" node, "repetitive" node and "with" node.

In order to have good system performance, semantic nodes and syntactic nodes are stored independently except that some pointers indicate their relations. The relation of each pair of a semantic node and a syntactic node is illustrated in Figure 5 and can be described as follows: (1) There are two pointers from the head and from the tail of a syntactic node referring back to its semantic node. (2) There is one pointer from a semantic node point to its syntactic node. Figure 6 shows the semantic node structures, syntactic node structures, and their relationship for six common statements—"assignment," "compound," "if," "while," "repeat," and "for" statements.

The cursor is positioned on a syntactic node, which is exactly the same as the cursor on the program source code displayed on a terminal. If a user modifies a text; for example, ⟨expression⟩ in "while"-statement, then it can be done in syntactic structure by moving and editing key features. After modification, the updated information will be inherited to related semantic nodes for semantic checking and flow computation. The flow information will be associated with semantic nodes. If a user tries to add a new node, update or replace an old node, then the system will locate the semantic meaning from the semantic node, determine the necessary action, and then tell the user what to do by displaying a menu on the screen. Therefore, the syntactic and semantic information can be handled independently and be connected together whenever it is necessary.

The following example explains the data set stored in semantic nodes, which is used in graphical program flow gen-

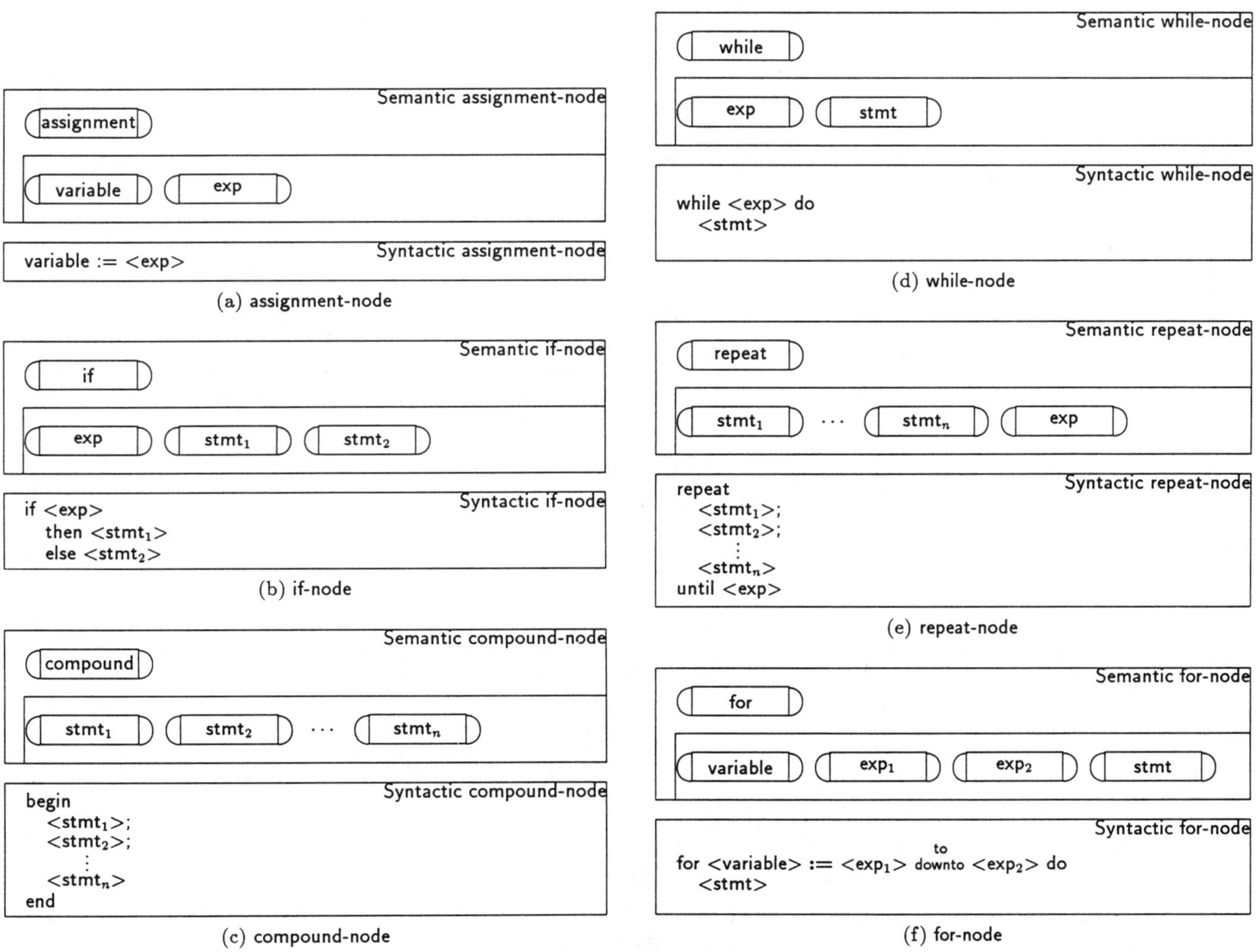

Figure 6—The structure of semantic nodes and syntactic nodes

eration, data flow anomaly detection, program slicing, and logical and ripple effect analyses. Consider a statement "if a > b then c: = a else c: = b" and assume that $D_i(n)$ and $D_o(n)$ denote the input and output data sets of node n respectively. Then, we have the following equations:

$$D_i(\boxed{\text{exp}}) = \{a, b\}$$
$$D_i(\boxed{stmt_1}) = \{a\}$$
$$D_o(\boxed{stmt_1}) = \{c\}$$
$$D_i(\boxed{stmt_2}) = \{b\}$$
$$D_o(\boxed{stmt_2}) = \{c\}$$
$$D_i(\boxed{\text{if}}) = \{a, b\}$$
$$D_o(\boxed{\text{if}}) = \{c\}$$

IMPLEMENTATION AND EXPERIMENTS

So far, we have integrated the following tools in our environment: a syntax-directed editor, a pretty-printer, control and data flow generators, a graphical program flow generator, a data flow anomaly detector, a program slicer, and part of a modified compiler. We have not yet integrated logical and performance ripple effect analyzers in the environment; however, even with only the tools already integrated, we have experienced major improvement in productivity of performing software maintenance. Comparing our experimental results, shown in Table V, for maintaining a program of about 2,000 lines with and without using the environment, we notice that the improvement is in a significant order of magnitude. Larger programs will also be experimented after we complete the modified compiler so that large programs can be automated, input, and formatted in the environment.

The current environment is being implemented in a DEC VAX/VMS 11/785 using PASCAL. The necessary space used by our model is about eight times the space required for the program source code. The number of nodes is proportional to the number of lines of the program source code. In the worst case, the space occupied by data set in semantic nodes is $O(cd)$, where c is the number of lines of the program source code, and d is the number of identifiers in the program. Since a program usually contains many subprograms and each subprogram has few identifiers, the space used by the data set is usually much less than $O(cd)$. In practice, the space used by the data set is usually close to $O(c)$. However, the data set can be calculated dynamically instead of being stored in the semantic nodes if the size of the memory space causes any implementation problem. As usual, there is a tradeoff between the amount of memory space used and the execution time.

CONCLUSION

Based on the unified model, various software maintenance tools can be integrated to form an effective software maintenance environment. The major advantage of this environment is that a user works with a two-dimensional, graphical representation of a program, instead of a linear text string representation. Specifying a program as a two-dimensional structure results in better understanding and easier modification of the program, which reduce the time and effort for software maintenance. At present, we have integrated several software maintenance tools in our environment including a

TABLE V—Some experimental results for using the software maintenance environment

	without our tools (in minutes)	with our tools
Understanding system structure	60	15
Algorithm analysis	same	same
Adding new feature (each local area)	(assume the adding process is compiling error, linking error, correct code)	
* Typing added text	same	same
* Compiling, linking, and correcting errors	10 + 10 + 3 (assume correct at 3rd time)	3
Debugging run-time error	(assume the correction process is guessing error, modifying, correct code)	
* locating error codes	same	same
* understanding statements	60 + 60 + 30 = 150	(10 + 6) * 3 = 48
* debugging error codes	same	same
* recompiling and linking	0 + 13 + 3 = 16	0 + 0 + 3 = 3

syntax-directed editor, a pretty-printer, a graphical program flow generator, control and data flow generators, a data flow anomaly detector, and a program slicer. We are integrating logical and performance ripple effect analyzers in the environment. We plan to use artificial intelligence techniques to develop a software maintenance tools synthesizer to construct software maintenance tools automatically.[13]

REFERENCES

1. Lientz, B.P. and E.B. Swanson. *Software Maintenance Management,* Reading, Massachusetts: Addison-Wesley, 1980.
2. Swanson, E.B. "The Dimensions of Maintenance," *Proceedings of the 2nd International Conference on Software Engineering,* 1976, pp. 492–497.
3. Yau, S.S. and J.S. Collofello. "Some Stability Measures for Software Maintenance." *IEEE Transactions on Software Engineering,* SE-6 (1980) 6, pp. 545–552.
4. Yau, S.S. and J.P. Tsai. "GQL: A Graphic Query Language for Software Maintenance Environment." *Proceedings of COMPSAC 83,* November 1983, pp. 218–228.
5. Hecht, M.S. *Flow Analysis of Computer Programs,* New York: Elsevier North-Holland, 1977.
6. Forman, I.R. "An Algebra for Data Flow Anomaly Detection." *Proceedings of the 7th International Conference on Software Engineering,* March 1984, pp. 278–286.
7. Weiser, M. "Program Slicing," *IEEE Transactions on Software Engineering,* SE-10 (1984) 4, pp. 352–357.
8. Yau, S.S., J.S. Collofello, and C.C. Hsieh. *Self-Metric Software—A Handbook: Part I, Logical Ripple Effect Analysis.* Final Technical Report RADC-TR-80-138, Vol II (of 3), April 1980, NTIS AD-A086-291.
9. Yau, S.S. and J.S. Collofello. *Self-Metric Software—A Handbook: Part II, Performance Ripple Effect Analysis.* Final Technical Report RADC-TR-80-139. Vol. III (of 3), April, 1980, NTIS AD-A086-292.
10. Yau, S.S. *Methodology for Software Maintenance.* Final Technical Report RADC-TR-83-262, February, 1984, NTIS AD-A143-763/1.
11. Yau, S.S. and P.C. Grabow. "A Model for Representing Programs Using Hierarchical Graphs." *IEEE Transactions on Software Engineering,* SE-7 (1981) 6, pp. 556–574.
12. Yau, S.S., C.K. Chang, and R.A. Nicholl. "An Approach to Incremental Program Modification." *Proceedings of COMPSAC 83,* November 1983, pp. 588–597.
13. Yau, S.S. and S.S. Liu. "A Knowledge-Based Software Maintenance Environment." *Proceedings of COMPSAC 86,* October 1986, pp. 72–78.

The design of distributed databases with cost optimization and integration of space constraints

by DALIA MOTZKIN and ELMO IVEY
Western Michigan University
Kalamazoo, Michigan

ABSTRACT

This paper presents methods for the logical design of distributed relational databases. The design procedure consists of fragmentation of global relations and allocation of fragments to sites. Fragments are allocated to sites in a way that optimizes local and global costs. Storage constraints are taken into consideration. The design algorithms are efficient. The algorithms have been implemented and tested. This design methodology integrates and extends previous work.

INTRODUCTION

The problem of configuring optimal data distribution over a computer network is not a trivial one. Tradeoffs between the decreased cost of communications and increased speed and parallelism when multiple copies of data are available at local sites, and the increased cost of communication due to multiple updates of copies must be considered. The availability of space should also be taken into consideration.

The data distribution problems have attracted a substantial amount of research. Significant results have been published by Ceri et al.,[1–6] Chang et al.,[7–9] Duta,[10] Irani and Khabbaz,[11,12] Lin and Liu,[13] Mazzarol et al.,[14] Navathe et al.,[15] Rakes,[16] Reddy,[17] Yu,[18] and others. Additional bibliography can be found in Yao et al.[19] and in Dowdy and Foster.[20]

Current distribution schemes typically deal with subsets of the issues above. Some address complete file allocation rather than the allocation of fragments of files. Some ignore local storage limitations and some are too complex for practical use.

The design method described here integrates and extends previous work. It especially builds on techniques developed by Ceri, Deen, Martella, Navathe, Negri, Pelagatti and Wiederhold.[1–6] However, a new approach is presented for computing the cost/benefit of allocating fragments to sites. The global cost computations are configured in a way that provides cost optimization of each site individually. These provide for a simplified, yet considerably more accurate, cost optimization. In addition, storage requirements are incorporated into the scheme.

Thus, the overall distribution scheme achieves improved performance and reduced communication cost. In addition it can meet storage constraints. An initial version of the design method described here has appeared in Motzkin.[21] The work described here provides an extension and revision of Motzkin's work.

TERMINOLOGY, NOTATIONS AND ASSUMPTIONS

We are concerned with distributed relational databases. We assume that a global relational database is fully defined, and is composed of global relations denoted by $r_1, r_2, \ldots, r_k$. See Table I for an example of global relational database. The global database is to be distributed to sites denoted by $S_1, S_2, \ldots, S_n$. See Figure 1 for an example of a network with three sites. At each site there are applications which need to use the DDBMS (distributed database management system). Each application is assumed to have a home site from where it is executed, and from where the DDBMS is used. An application j is denoted by a_j. An example of applications associated with the database and sites of Table I and Figure 1 is depicted in Table II.

TABLE I

Employee Relation				Project Relation		Plant Relation	
E#	Skill	Salary	PR#	PR#	Skill	PL#	PR#
E1	SK1	18000	PR1	PR1	SK1	PL1	PR1
E2	SK1	20000	PR1	PR2	SK1	PL1	PR2
E3	SK3	20000	PR2	PR2	SK3	PL2	PR3
E4	SK1	19000	PR2	PR3	SK2	PL3	PR4
E5	SK1	25000	PR2	PR3	SK3		
E6	SK2	22000	PR3	PR4	SK1		
E7	SK2	22000	PR3				
E8	SK3	25000	PR3				
E9	SK3	21000	PR3				
E10	SK1	20000	PR4				

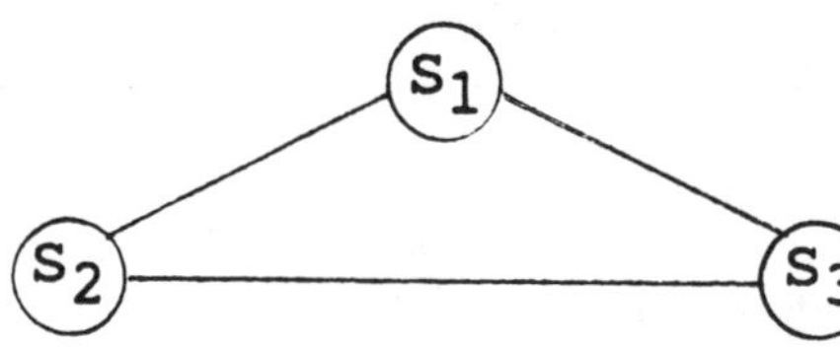

Figure 1

A portion of a global relation that is allocated to a site (or sites) is called a *fragment.* During the design phase each global relation is broken into fragments in a way such that the fragments are pairwise disjoint and that the union of all fragments of each relation is equal to the relation. We deal here only with horizontal fragmentation. Horizontal fragmentation is defined as in Ceri and Pelagatti.[6] A *horizontal fragment* consists of a subset of the records of a file or, more formally, it consists of a subset of the tuples of a relation. We are not concerned here with vertical fragmentation.

AN OVERVIEW OF THE DESIGN METHOD

The data distribution to sites is achieved in two phases. The first phase is the *fragment definition phase,* and the second phase is the *fragment allocation phase.*

During the fragment definition phase each relation is broken into horizontal fragments based on application requirements. The fragments defined during this phase meet the following conditions:

1. The fragments are pairwise disjoint.
2. The union of all fragments of a given relation is equal to the relation.
3. Given a fragment and an application, the fragment is either completely required by the application or not at all.

During this phase, cost and storage requirements are not considered. However, this fragment definition technique greatly facilitates the optimization of data distribution. It insures that allocation can be accomplished without allocating fragments to sites where some records will be useless.

During the fragment allocation phase, the fragments that were defined during the first phase are allocated to sites. During this second phase communication costs, processing costs and storage constraints along with statistics regarding the frequency and type of use of fragments by applications are utilized. The fragments are first allocated in a way that provides *optimal* (minimal), local, and global cost. This initial allocation of some of the fragments is then revised, if needed, to meet storage constraints.

FRAGMENT DEFINITION

The fragment definition algorithms are achieved in two stages. During the first stage, the segment definition stage, subsets of relations, called here *segments,* are defined using application requirements. These segments have the property that each segment is required by some application, but the segments are not necessarily pairwise disjoint. During the second stage, the fragment determination stage, disjoint fragments that meet the conditions 1–3 are generated.

TABLE II

Site #	Application #	Application Requirement
S_1	a_1	Records of employees at plant PL1
S_1	a_2	Records of employees having skills needed for projects at plant PL1
S_1	a_3	Projects at plant PL1 and required skills.
S_1	a_4	List of all plants and their projects.
S_2	a_5	Records of employees of plant PL2
S_2	a_6	Records of employees with skills needed for projects at plant PL2
S_2	a_7	Projects at plant PL2 and required skills
S_2	a_8	A list of all plants and their projects
S_3	a_9	Records of employees at plant PL3
S_3	a_{10}	Records of employees with skills needed for projects at plant PL3
S_3	a_{11}	Records of projects at plant PL3 and required skills
S_3	a_{12}	A list of all plants

Segment Definition

Let a_j be an application which requires data from the database. A segment w of relation r_i denoted as $SEG_W(r_i a_j)$ is defined as a subset of the tuples of r_i that meet the following conditions:

1. All the tuples in the segment are required by the application a_j.
2. No tuple in $r_i - SEG_w(r_i a_j)$ is required by a_j.

Informally a segment is the smallest subset of records of a given relation r_i that are required by a given application a_j. In the following sections we will often denote the segments simply as SEG_w and omit the reference to the relation and application.

The requirements of the applications* are provided as sets of relational operators.

The following algorithm is used to define the segments:

```
ALGORITHM DEFINE-SEG
 w←1
 FOR i = 1 TO number of sites DO
   FOR j = 1 TO number of applications DO
     k←relation number of the relation
        required by a_j
     SEG_w←records of R_k required by a_j
     w←w + 1
   ENDFOR
 ENDFOR
END of ALGORITHM
```

The segments defined this way are associated with an application, a site, and a relation.

To illustrate the results of the segment definition algorithm consider the global database of Table I, the network of Figure 1 and the application requirements of Table II. The resulting segments of the relation EMPLOYEE are shown in Table III.

The relational operators are used to formally describe the requirements of each application. For example, the relational operators associated with the applications that use data from the employee relation are shown in Table III.

The following symbols are used in Table III for relational operators:

σ—select
π—Project
|x|—Natural join

Fragment Determination Algorithm

Next, the second stage of the fragment definition is executed. During the second stage the disjoint fragments are defined. Disjoint fragments are achieved in the following way:

*The assumption that an application is associated with one relation is not necessarily a restriction. If an application requires data from two relations it is simply broken into two sub-applications.

TABLE III

Application #	Seg #	Relational Operators	Tuples
a_1	SEG_1	$\Pi_{E\#,\ SKILL,\ SALARY,\ PR\#}(\sigma_{PL\#=PL1}(EMPLOYEE\vert x\vert PLANT))$	E1 SK1 18000 PR1
			E2 SK1 20000 PR1
			E3 SK3 20000 PR2
			E4 SK1 19000 PR2
			E5 SK1 25000 PR2
a_2	SEG_2	$EMPLOYEE\vert x\vert(\Pi_{SKILL}\ (\sigma_{PL\#=PL1}(EMPLOYEE\vert x\vert PLANT)))$	E1 SK1 18000 PR1
			E2 SK1 20000 PR1
			E3 SK3 20000 PR2
			E4 SK1 19000 PR2
			E5 SK1 25000 PR2
			E8 SK3 25000 PR3
			E9 SK3 21000 PR3
			E10 SK1 20000 PR4
a_5	SEG_5	$\Pi_{E\#,\ SKILL,\ SALARY,\ PR\#}(\sigma_{PL\#=PL2}(EMPLOYEE\vert x\vert PLANT))$	E6 SK2 22000 PR3
			E7 SK2 22000 PR3
			E8 SK3 25000 PR3
			E9 SK3 21000 PR3
a_6	SEG_6	$EMPLOYEE\vert x\vert(\Pi_{SKILL}\ (\sigma_{PL\#=PL2}(EMPLOYEE\vert x\vert PLANT)))$	E3 SK3 20000 PR2
			E6 SK2 22000 PR3
			E7 SK2 22000 PR3
			E8 SK3 25000 PR3
			E9 SK3 21000 PR3
a_9	SEG_9	$\Pi_{E\#,\ SKILL,\ SALARY,\ PR\#}(\sigma_{PL\#=PL3}(EMPLOYEE\vert x\vert PLANT))$	E10 SK1 20000 PR4
a_{10}	SEG_{10}	$EMPLOYEE\vert x\vert(\Pi_{SKILL}\ (\sigma_{PL\#=PL3}(EMPLOYEE\vert x\vert PLANT)))$	E1 SK1 18000 PR1
			E2 SK1 20000 PR1
			E4 SK1 19000 PR2
			E5 SK1 25000 PR2
			E10 SK1 20000 PR4

Each pair of segments v, w which are not disjoint are replaced by three segments v', w' and t' where $t' = v \cap w$, $v' = v - t'$, $w' = w - t'$. If either v' or w', is empty, it is removed. The fragment definition algorithm is detailed below.

Table IV contains the fragments of the relation EMPLOYEE of Table I which were generated from the segments in Table III using the algorithm DETERMINE-FRAGMENT.

ALGORITHM DETERMINE-FRAGMENT

(* A simplified notation of segments is used here; the ith segment of a relation in context is simply denoted by SEG_i *)

FOR $k = 1$ TO number of relations DO
  $t \leftarrow$ number of segments in relation r_k
  $u \leftarrow 1$
  $w \leftarrow$ index of first segment of relation R_k
  WHILE $w < t$ DO
    $v \leftarrow w + 1$
    WHILE $v \leq t$ DO
      IF $SEG_w \cap SEG_v \neq 0$
      THEN $SEG_{t+1} \leftarrow SEG_w \cap SEG_v$
        $SEG_w \leftarrow SEG_w - SEG_{t+1}$
        $SEG_v \leftarrow SEG_v - SEG_{t+1}$
        $t \leftarrow t + 1$
      ENDIF
      $v \leftarrow v + 1$
    END WHILE (* At the end of each pass of this while loop the ith SEGMENT is disjoint from all other segments *)
    Define fragment $f_u \leftarrow SEG_w$
    $w \leftarrow$ index of next segment of relation R_k
    $u \leftarrow u + 1$
  END WHILE
  $f_u \leftarrow SEG_w$
  IF $r_k \neq \bigcup_{u=1}^{t} f_u$ THEN output error message:
    "$r_k - \bigcup_{u=1}^{t} f_u$ is not defined by any application".
  ENDIF
END FOR
Remove all empty segments
(* Note that when $SEG_i \leq SEG_j$ an empty SEGMENT will be generated *)
END OF ALGORITHM

TABLE IV

Fragment #	Used by Applications/Sites	Tuples			
$F1$	a_5S_2, a_6S_2	$E6$	$SK2$	22000	$PR3$
		$E7$	$SK2$	22000	$PR3$
$F2$	a_1S_1, a_2S_1, a_6S_2	$E3$	$SK3$	20000	$PR3$
$F3$	a_2S_1, a_5S_2, a_6S_2	$E8$	$SK3$	25000	$PR3$
		$E9$	$SK3$	21000	$PR3$
$F4$	a_1S_1, a_2S_1, $a_{10}S_3$	$E1$	$SK1$	18000	$PR1$
		$E2$	$SK1$	20000	$PR1$
		$E4$	$SK1$	19000	$PR2$
		$E5$	$SK1$	25000	$PR2$
$F5$	a_2S_1, a_9S_3, $a_{10}S_3$	$E10$	$SK1$	20000	$PR4$

FRAGMENT ALLOCATION

Cost computation

We use the following notation:

$CA(f,s_i)$ = Local cost at site s_i of allocating fragment f to site s_i

$CN(f,s_i)$ = Local cost to site s_i of *not* allocating fragment f to site s_i

$B(f,s_i)$ = benefit of allocating fragment f to site s_i

CA is computed as the sum of the following quantities:

- Cost of the space occupied by the fragment
- Cost of local retrievals
- Cost of local updates
- Cost of updates sent from other sites

CN is the sum of the following quantities:

- Cost of local retrievals from remote sites

We are assuming that the site who owns a copy of a fragment is "paying" for all updates of its copy of the fragment. Also, obviously each site is paying for all retrievals issued by local applications.

The cost of a remote retrieval issued from site s_i to site s_j is composed of the cost of communication between site s_i and site s_j, plus the cost of retrieval at site s_j.

The cost of an update issued from site s_i to site s_j is similarly composed of the cost of communication between site s_i and site s_j, plus the cost of updating at site s_j.

In the computation of communication costs, we assumed an average communication cost which is the same for all pairs of sites. This approach is suitable for distributed databases where the costs of communicating between two sites are close. This approach is applicable to local area networks, or to networks within small geographic regions and other networks where the cost of communications between pairs of sites is nearly equal.

Similarly, an average retrieval cost and an average update cost are assumed. This approach is especially appropriate when the database is distributed over a network of similar computers such as a network of VAXes or a network of microcomputers.

Using the averages provides considerable simplification to the computations, and at the same time reasonably accurate values are obtained. An extension of the cost computation into the general case is being developed. See the section "Concluding Remarks."

Now the benefit of allocating fragment f to site s_i is defined as:

$$B(f,s_i) = CN(f,s_i) - CA(f,s_i)$$

Note that if an application a_j at site s_i issues an update to fragment f, then this update is not a function of the fragment allocations, it is simply a function of the nature of the application, Thus whether fragment f is allocated to site s_i or not, the update will be issued, and each site which owns a copy of f will accrue the communication cost and its own local update cost.

Thus, we achieved a fragment allocation benefit computation which can be computed for each site independently, that is, the cost benefit of allocating a fragment to a given site is independent of what is allocated to other sites.

This approach is a major departure from previous work. A similar approach in computing benefit of access structure was introduced in Motzkin.[22,23]

Note also that the sum of all local DBMS's costs is equal to the global DDBMS cost, since all retrievals, updates and communication costs are included and are not duplicated.

Thus, maximizing the benefit of each local site will result in overall maximal benefit of the global DDBMS.

Furthermore, if it costs a site more to own a copy of a fragment than it costs if the site does not own a copy, a negative value for the benefit of allocating a fragment to a site will result.

Therefore, a maximum benefit results when allocating all fragments to sites where $B(f,s_i)$ are positive, and not allocating otherwise. However, storage constraints may affect the allocation.

The problem of guaranteeing optimal global benefit while meeting storage requirements is NP complete. In the worst case all permutations of ordering of sites must be tried. A heuristic approach is taken.

The Space Constraints

Each site s_i provides input concerning maximum available space, denoted $ASP(s_i)$. If space is not limited ∞ can be provided as an input. Space constraints are more likely to exist in DDBMS of microcomputers.

Now all the sites are checked to see if they have sufficient storage space to store all the fragments allocated to them. If a site s_i is found with insufficient storage space all the fragments of site s_i are sorted on their benefit to this site. Starting with the fragment of least benefit and continuing until there is sufficient space or all fragments have been checked, the following is done: If the fragment is allocated elsewhere, its allocation to site s_i is cancelled. If the fragment is not allocated elsewhere the sites are checked in the order of the benefit of allocation, for this fragment, and the fragment is allocated to the first site, s_j, with enough space, and then removed from s_i. At the end of this process a message is issued if space constraints were not met. See part 2 of the algorithm ALLOCATE in the section "Fragment Allocation Algorithm."

Fragment Allocation Algorithm

From the discussion of costs above, it follows that the benefit of allocating a fragment to a site can be computed for each site individually, regardless of what happens at other sites. The benefit value is obviously either positive, negative or zero, and is a function of local applications' queries and remote applications' updates.

The algorithm has two parts.

1. Allocate fragments to all sites where $B(f,s)>0$
2. Adjust to meet space requirements

The algorithm is as follows:

```
ALGORITHM ALLOCATE
(Part 1: allocate fragments to sites with positive benefit value)
  FOR m = 1 to number of fragments DO
    ALLOCATED ← FALSE
    FOR each site s_i which uses fragment f_m DO
      Compute B(f_m, s_i)
      IF B(f_m, s_i) > 0
      THEN allocate f_m to site s_i
        ALLOCATED ← TRUE
      ENDIF
    END FOR
      IF ALLOCATED = FALSE
      THEN issue an error message 'fragment f_m was not
      allocated'
      ENDIF
  END FOR
(Part 2: adjust to meet space requirements)
  FOR i = 1 TO number of sites DO
    SP(s_i) ← total space used by fragments allocated to site
    s_i
    ASP(s_i) ← available space at site s_i
    IF ASP(s_i) < SP(s_i)
    THEN sort fragments at s_i in ascending order on B(f_m, s_i)
    ENDIF
    Denote sorted fragments by f_1, f_2, . . . , f_t
    Denote the space used by fragment f_m as SP(f_m)
    m ← 1
  REPEAT
      IF f_m is allocated elsewhere
        THEN cancel allocation of f_m to s_i
          SP(s_i) ← SP(s_i) − SP(f_m)
        ELSE sort the sites in descending order on the
            benefit of allocating f_m to each site.
          j ← index of site with greatest benefit
          DONE ← FALSE
          REPEAT
            IF SP(s_j) + SP(f_m) ≤ ASP(s_j)
            THEN allocate f_m to s_j.
              SP(s_j) ← SP(S_j) + SP(f_m)
                DONE ← TRUE
            END IF
            j ← index of next site in the sorted list
            UNTIL DONE = TRUE for all sites have been
            checked
      END IF
      m ← m + 1
    UNTIL SP(s_i) ≤ ASP(s_i) or all fragments have been
    checked
    IF ASP(s_i) < SP(s_i) THEN OUTPUT message
      'insufficient storage at site S_i'
  END FOR
END of part 2
```

Assume input data for the database of Table I as shown in the Appendix. All resulting fragments are shown also in the Appendix. The benefits calculated from this input is shown in Table V. The allocation of fragments based on optimizing cost alone is shown in Table VI. After executing part 2 output as in Table VII, results.

TABLE V—Benefit of allocating fragments to sites

	S_1	S_2	S_3
F_1	−5.47	28.53	−5.47
F_2	15.16	31.16	−10.84
F_3	35.83	33.83	−8.17
F_4	6.96	−19.04	8.96
F_5	27.76	−16.24	11.76
F_6	27.83	−8.17	−8.17
F_7	−13.55	46.45	−13.55
F_8	−5.42	−5.42	38.58
F_9	3.60	−0.40	11.60

TABLE VI—Optimal fragment allocation based on benefit only

Fragment	Relation	Records	Sites
1	1	6 7	2
2	1	3	1 2
3	1	8 9	1 2
4	1	1 2 4 5	1 3
5	1	10	1 3
6	2	1 2 3	1
7	2	4 5	2
8	2	6	3
9	3	1 2 3 4	1 3

TABLE VII—Reallocation of fragment subject to space constraints

Fragment	Relation	Records	Sites
1	1	6 7	3
2	1	3	1
3	1	8 9	1
4	1	1 2 4 5	1 3
5	1	10	1 3
6	2	1 2 3	1
7	2	4 5	2
8	2	6	3
9	3	1 2 3 4	1 3

Note that the allocation of fragments 1,2 to site 2 have been cancelled. Fragment 1 was not allocated anywhere in the network, so the algorithm reallocated it to site 3. The space situation before and after adjusting to space constraints is shown in Tables VIII and IX. The corresponding costs and benefits are shown in Tables X and XI.

COMPLEXITY OF COMPUTATION

The complexity of DEFINE-SEG is $0(A \cdot N)$ Where A is the number of applications and N is the average number of records per relation.

The nested WHILE loop lines 6–19 of the DETERMINE FRAGMENT algorithm has time complexity of $0(F^2)$ where F is the average number of fragments generated for a relation. The worst case occurs when each fragment consists of a single tuple. Therefore the worst case for this nested loop is $0(N^2)$. Lines 21 through 22 have complexity $0(N)$ where N is the average number of records per relation. The outer FOR loop deliminated by lines 1–23 has 0(R) time complexity, where R is the number of global relations, DETERMINE-FRAGMENT algorithm has the time complexity $O(RF^2)$. The worst case is $0(RN^2)$ where N is the average number of tuples per relation.

Part 1 of algorithm ALLOCATE is bounded by $S \cdot N \cdot R$ where S is the number of sites while the time of executing part 2 is bounded by the time needed to sort the fragments at each site. The worst case occurs when all sites have insufficient space and none of the fragments are allocated elsewhere. In such a situation all fragments at all sites are checked for reallocation. The time complexity of this process is $0(N \cdot R \cdot S \cdot \mathrm{LOG}(N \cdot R/S) \cdot \mathrm{LOG}(S))$.

Therefore the entire set of design algorithms has time complexity that is bounded by $0(R \cdot N^2 + R \cdot N \cdot S \cdot \mathrm{LOG}(R \cdot N/S) \cdot \mathrm{LOG}(S) + A \cdot N)$.

TABLE VIII—Space situation following optimal allocation of fragments

Site	SP	Free Space	ASP
$S1$	456	44	500
$S2$	228		100
$S3$	300	200	500

TABLE IX—Space situation following allocation constrained by available space at site 2

Site	SP	Free Space	ASP
$S1$	456	44	500
$S2$	48	52	100
$S3$	372	128	500

TABLE X—Optimal costs and benefits with unconstrained allocation

Site	Cost	Benefit
1	148.86	117.14
2	118.02	139.98
3	82.60	70.90
	349.48	328.02

TABLE XI—Costs and benefits after space constrained allocation

Site	Cost	Benefit
1	148.86	117.14
2	211.55	46.45
3	88.07	65.43
	448.48	229.02

CONCLUDING REMARKS

A method for logical design of distributed relational database management systems has been developed. The scheme is an extension of previous work. It uses a new approach for calculation of cost benefit. This approach provides the computation of maximum cost benefit of each site independently. It is shown that optimal local sites benefits yield optimal global benefit for the entire distributed database. It was shown that the optimal local and global cost benefit is achieved by allocating fragments to all benefiting sites. The ability to compute the optimal costs independently for each site contributes considerably to the efficiency of the design algorithm. It eliminates the need to compare a large number of design configurations.

The algorithms can utilize parallel processing. Fragmentation of each global relation can be computed in parallel, during the definition phase. During the allocation phase, the benefits fragment assignments of each site can be done in parallel.

The model also incorporates storage constraints. When storage space is not sufficient at some site S_i, then the allocation of some of the benefiting fragments is cancelled. Reallocation is done if needed. This process guarantees that if space is available elsewhere on the network the fragments of lower benefit to s_i will be available on other sites. When reallocation is needed the sites of highest benefit values are chosen. The space adjustment algorithm is heuristic and provides reasonable but not necessarily optimal allocation.

The model uses average figures for retrieval costs, update costs and communication costs. Thus it is appropriate for a network where communication costs are nearly equal, and the computers in the network have similar processing costs. Thus the model will work well in situations such as local area networks of microcomputers, or local area network of VAXes etc. This is often the case when there are distributed databases within a company or an institution.

An extension to the general case is being developed, and will be submitted for publication at a later date. The general idea behind the extension is the clustering of similar computers, with similar communication cost between them. Fragments will be assigned to a cluster based on actual communication costs between clusters and also based on the average processing cost of computers in the cluster. Within a cluster, the method that was described here will be used. The design algorithms described here have been implemented with a PASCAL program and tested.

Additional details concerning the cost computations, the details of the algorithms, implementation, and simulation runs will be published at a later date.

ACKNOWLEDGEMENT

The authors wish to thank Dr. Kenneth Williams for very valuable comments and suggestions.

REFERENCES

1. Ceri, S., G. Martella, G. Pelagatti, S.M. Deen, and P. Hammersley. "Optimal file allocation for a distributed data base on a network of minicomputers." *Proceedings of the International Conference on Data Bases,* Aberdeen, Scotland, 1980, pp. 216–237.
2. Ceri, S., G. Martella, G. Pelagatti. "Optimal file allocation in a computer network: a solution method based on knapsack problem." *Computer Networks*, 6 (1982) 5, pp. 345–357.
3. Ceri, S., M. Negri, and G. Pelagatti. "Horizontal partitioning in database design." ACM-SIGMOD, 1982.
4. Ceri, S., and S.B. Navathe. "A methodology for the distribution design of database." *Proceedings of Comcon '83,* San Francisco, California, 1983.
5. Ceri, S., S.B. Navathe, and G. Wiederhold. "Distribution design of logical database schemas." *IEEE-TSE,* 1983.
6. Ceri, S., and G. Pelagatti. *"Distributed database principles and systems."* McGraw-Hill, 1984.
7. Chang, S.K., and W.H. Cheng. "A methodology for structured databases decomposition." *IEEE-TSE,* 1980.
8. Chang, S.K. and A.C. Liu. "A database file allocation problem." *Proceedings of COMPSAC '81. IEEE Computer Society,* 1981, pp. 18–23.
9. Chang, S.K., and A.C. Liu. "File allocation in a distributed database." *International Journal of Computer and Information Science,* II (1982) 5, pp. 325–340.
10. Duta, A. "Modeling of multiple copy updates for file allocation in distributed database." *International Journal of Computer and Information Science,* 14 (1985) 1, pp. 29–34.
11. Irani, K.B., and N.G. Khabbaz. "A model for a combined communication network design and file allocation for distributed database." *Proceedings of the First International Conference on Distributed Computer Systems,* Huntsville, AL, 1979, pp. 15–21.
12. Irani, K.B., and N.G. Khabbaz. "A combined communication network design and file allocation for distributed databases." *Proceedings of Second International Conference on Distributed Computing Systems,* Paris, France, 1981, pp. 197–210.
13. Lin, J., and M.T. Liu. "A distributed double-loop data network for very large on line distributed databases." *Proceedings of a symposium on reliability in distributed software and database systems, IEEE,* 1981, pp. 83–88.
14. Mazzarol, G., E. Tomasin, and J. Stoer. "Optimal file allocation problem and relational distributed databases." *Proceedings of the Eighth IFIP Conference on Optimization Techniques,* Wurzburg, Germany, 1977, pp. 484–494.
15. Navathe, S., S. Ceri, G. Wiederhold, and J. Dou. "Vertical partitioning algorithms for database design." *ACM Transactions on Database Systems,* 9 (1984) 4, pp. 680–710.
16. Rakes, T.R., L.S. Franz, and A. Se. "A heuristic approximation for reducing problem size in network file alloction models." *Computers and Operations Research,* 11 (1984) 4, pp. 387–395.
17. Reddy, C.N. "Distributed data base systems." *Electro-Technol,* 25 (1981) 1, pp.15–22.
18. Yu, C.T., M.K. Siu, K. Lam and F. Tai. "Adaptive clustering schemes: general framework." *Proceedings of COMPSAC '81 IEEE Computer Society,* 1981, pp. 16–20.
19. Yao, S., S.B. Navathe, J.L. Weldon, and T.L. Kunii. "Database design techniques." *Proceedings of NYU Symposium on Database Design,* 1982.
20. Dowdy, L.W., and D.V. Foster. "Comparative models of the file assignment problem." *ACM Computing Survey,* 14 (1984) 2.
21. Motzkin, D. "Horizontal fragment allocation in distributed databases with optimal integration of cost reliability and storage constraints." *Technical Report TR-01 Computer Science department Western Michigan University,* 1986.
22. Motzkin, D. "An optimal physical database model." *Proceedings of Fifth International Conference on Mathematical Modelling,* 1985.
23. Motzkin, D. "Database performance optimization." *AFIPS, Proceedings of the National Computer Conference,* (Vol. 54), 1985, pp. 555–565.

APPENDIX—STATISTICAL INPUT WITH SPACE CONSTRAINTS

NUMBER OF SITES: 3
NUMBER OF RELATIONS: 3

Relation Input

Relation	Number of Records	Bytes per Records
1	10	36
2	6	24
3	4	24

Site Input

Site	Available Space
1	500
2	100
3	500

Cost Input

Cost of Space Unit	Cost of Unit Retrieval	Cost of Update	Cost of Communication
0.001	0.30	0.70	2.00

Workload Input

Site	Application	Frequency of Retrieval	Frequency of Update	Average Retrieval Size
1	1	10	3	3
	2	20	2	5
	3	15	3	2
	4	10	4	3
2	5	15	2	4
	6	20	1	3
	7	25	5	2
	8	10	2	3
3	9	15	3	1
	10	10	4	4
	11	20	2	1
	12	15	3	3

The Fragments

Relations	Records				Fragments
EMPLOYEE	E#	Skill	Salary	PR#	
	E6	SK2	22000	PR3	F1
	E7	SK2	22000	PR3	
	E#	Skill	Salary	PR#	F2
	E3	SK3	20000	PR2	
	E#	Skill	Salary	PR#	
	E8	SK3	25000	PR3	F3
	E9	SK3	21000	PR3	
	E#	Skill	Salary	PR#	
	E1	SK1	18000	PR1	
	E2	SK1	20000	PR1	F4
	E4	SK1	19000	PR2	
	E5	SK1	25000	PR2	
	E#	Skill	Salary	PR#	F5
	E10	SK1	20000	PR4	
PROJECT	PR#	Skill			
	PR1	SK1			F6
	PR2	SK1			
	PR2	SK3			
	PR#	Skill			
	PR3	SK2			F7
	PR3	SK3			
	PR#	Skill			F8
	PR4	SK1			
PLANT	PL#	PR#			
	PL1	PR1			
	PL1	PR2			F9
	PL2	PR3			
	PL3	PR4			

How sensitive is the physical database design? Results of experimental investigation

by PRASHANT PALVIA
Memphis State University
Memphis, Tennessee

ABSTRACT

The structure and efficiency of a physical database design depends on the logical data structure, the activities to take place in the database, the computer system characteristics, and the physical characteristics of the computer system. This paper identifies specific underlying factors within the broad general categories that may potentially influence the physical database design. In an effort to conduct a detailed sensitivity analysis of the underlying factors, an experimental design is developed. Sensitivity experiments are conducted as per the experimental design, and, finally, the experimental results are reported.

INTRODUCTION

The database literature has reported several research studies on selecting an optimal physical design given a set of underlying independent factors.[1,2,3,4,5] However, reports of research and experience on the sensitivity of a physical database design to the same underlying factors are practically non-existent. Such research has significant practical value to designers, who are constantly faced with restructuring databases because of changing user and technical requirements. Such findings will help designers assess the effects of major changes in the influencing factors on physical design.

This paper reports the results of sensitivity analysis based on several controlled experiments conducted in a laboratory setting. This paper includes a discussion of the objectives for physical database design and the general categories of independent factors. One of the factors is the physical design model itself, and the abstract model used for this study is described. Also, the specific factors, the factor levels and, in some cases, methods to quantify factor values are described. The experimental design is also described. The major section of the paper presents and discusses the sensitivity results from the experiments. Finally, some conclusions are presented.

PHYSICAL DESIGN OBJECTIVES AND DESIGN DETERMINANTS

Among the objectives for designing a physical database, the over-riding criterion is to minimize the operational costs of using the database (the studies referred to earlier largely use this criterion). In this study, two operational costs are considered: the cost of storing the data and the cost of accessing the data. Access costs are estimated in this paper by the surrogate measure of the total number of pages accessed from secondary memory.

The operational costs of a physical database design are influenced by four major factors: (1) the logical data structure, (2) the activities to take place on the database, (3) the computer system characteristics, and (4) the physical design model. Each category is briefly reviewed here.

The logical data structure (LDS) is designed using a logical design model, which is provided on the basis of prior design activity. The LDS for a particular design problem contains several entities and relationships joining the entities. For example, Figure 1 is the LDS of an organization's employee database. The LDS can be directly obtained using data structure diagrams[6] or by converting from entity-relationship diagrams.[7]

The activities on the database may be either retrieval or update. This work primarily focuses on retrievals. A retrieval may require selected instances of only one entity (e.g., data about certain employees only), or may require data across several entities and their instances (e.g., data about certain departments and data about employees who work in those departments). The second type of retrieval is more complex and requires "traversing" several entities.

The physical design also depends on the computer system characteristics. In a high contention multi-user environment, each access may be considered a random access, and then the total number of pages accessed can be used as a measure of access costs. The relevant computer system characteristics are the page size, the cost per page access, the storage cost, and the direct pointer size.

Finally, such physical factors as the access paths available and the data access/navigation strategy also influence the physical database design. Foremost among physical factors is the physical design model itself. The physical design model describes the permissible alternative physical designs. Different commercial DBMSs use different physical design models for the physical representation of a database. This work uses an abstract design model, which is described next.

The Physical Design Model: Record Structuring

Whereas the LDS is represented by entities and relationships between entities, the physical design is comprised of various record types, their instances, and pointer linkages between records. Additionally, access paths (e.g., indexes) may be created to permit rapid access of records.

Record structuring should be so done so as to represent the entities as well as the relationships between entities. Record structuring strategies in a file and database environment have been proposed in the literature.[1,4,5,8,9,10,11,12] A common

Figure 1—Example of a logical data structure

theme emerges from these works; that is, two principles are used for representing a relationship between two entities. The first principle is basic: indicate a relationship between two entities by storing appropriate pointers in the entities' instances. The pointers may be in the form of linked lists or inverted lists or some combination. The second principle for indicating a relationship is the concept of clustering/aggregation, in which all instances of one entity that are related to an instance of a second entity are clustered near the second entity instance.

The two concepts yield substantially different designs. The present abstract model captures the spirit of the two concepts; more variations and details will be included in future experiments. The abstract physical design model allows for five ways of representing a relationship between two entities X and Y: X points to Y, Y points to X, they both point to each other, X aggregates (clusters) Y, and Y aggregates X. Further, the pointers may be direct or symbolic. Aggregation of Y into X in the abstract model is actualized by making the related Y instances part of the X record.

Hierarchical and CODASYL systems incorporate the concepts of pointers and aggregations. For example, aggregation is supported in IMS by permitting hierarchical segments in the same data set, and in CODASYL systems by storing MEMBER records near the OWNER using VIA SET and NEAR OWNER. Relational systems prohibit aggregation at a logical level; however, substantial efficiencies may be achieved by its use.[13,14]

The physical options start multiplying and become more complex to evaluate as the number of entities in the LDS become large. An evaluator/simulator reported in Palvia[10] is used to evaluate the storage and access costs of any given physical database design as per the specifications of the physical design model. The evaluator is used in an exhaustive-search manner to find the optimal physical design for a given problem.

In the experiments conducted, it was soon realized that one of the three pointer options could be fairly easily selected without significantly affecting the optimal physical design. For this paper, the physical design model is simplified by permitting only one pointer option of the three options described. This option will be either mandatory two-way pointers or one-way pointers selected by the designer or by the software. With only one pointer option, a physical design can be fully specified simply by indicating the aggregations. A short-form notation devised by the author to represent a physical design is to name the "aggregator" or "absorber" (also called "parent") entity of each entity. A root entity does not have a physical parent; so its parent is numbered 0. Designs for the 6-entity problem of Figure 1 expressed in short-form include:

0 0 0 0 0 0 . . . (unclustered flat-file design)
0 1 0 2 2 0 . . . (1 clusters 2; 2 clusters 4 and 5; 1, 3 and 6 are rooted)
0 0 0 0 6 0 . . . (only 6 clusters 5; except 5, all entities rooted)

With this background, the experimental factors are described in full detail.

THE EXPERIMENTAL FACTORS

Since no assumptions are made about the sensitivity of the factors, a priori, the factors considered are comprehensive in that they make the problem character vary in most ways. The experimental factors are developed along the four exogenous dimensions; namely, the logical data structure, the activities on the database, the computer system characteristics, and the implementation characteristics. It is believed that the factors discussed in this section capture the most important features, in the spirit of the 80-20 rule, in which a relatively few number of factors tend to be the most significant.

LDS Related Factors

A. Number of entities in the logical data structure

A measure of logical data structure size and complexity is the number of entities and/or relationships in the LDS. The number of entities and the number of activities in an LDS are highly correlated, so only the number of entities is considered. Since this is the most important factor representing the LDS, four levels are chosen for this factor; that is, LDS with four, six, eight, and ten entities. The ability to generate an optimal physical design (by enumeration) prevented us from considering higher sized problems.

Activities Related Factors

The number of activities and the "structure" of activities can significantly affect the optimal physical design. Four factors relating to the structure of activities have been used. The activities related factors are: (1) the number of activities on the database, (2) the number of contexts per activity, (3) the proportion of entity instances addressed, (4) the distribution of activities on the LDS, and (5) the degree of conflict between activities.

B. Number of activities on the database

Three levels have been chosen for this factor. For the six-entity problem, the three levels are three, six, and nine activities on the database.

C. Number of contexts per activity

The number of contexts for an activity refers to the number of entities the activity traverses. The average number of contexts per activity is used as an indication of this characteristic. The three levels used are 1.67, 3.17, and 4.5 average number of contexts per activity.

D. Proportion of entity instances addressed

The proportion of entity instances addressed by an activity depends on the operating environment. For example, a production/batch environment is characterized by activities addressing a large proportion of entity instances whereas an executive environment has activities addressing only a small proportion of entity instances. Three levels have been selected, one for which 100 percent of the instances are required, one for which a medium proportion of instances are required, and one for which a very small proportion of instances are required. Call these high, medium, and low proportions.

E. Distribution of activities on the LDS

The activities on the LDS may concentrate on one or a few entities of the LDS, or may be distributed uniformly over the entire LDS. Again, use three levels: high, medium, and low concentration over the LDS. This is achieved by changing the frequencies of the various activities.

F. Degree of conflict between activities

If all activities traversed in the same direction in the LDS, there would be no conflict between activities, and it would be relatively easy to obtain the optimal physical design. In fact, it may be argued that it is the conflict among the activities which makes the design problem hard. Since a measure for the degree of conflict is not readily found in the current literature, the author developed a method to measure the degree of conflict.

In this method (see Figure 2), focus on the number of activities along each relationship. Split these activities into two categories, one for each direction along the relationship. Let $F1$ be the sum of the frequencies of all activities in one direction along a given relationship, and $F2$ be the sum of frequencies of the activities along the other direction. The greater of $F1$ and $F2$ is called FH and the smaller of the two is called FL. FH and FL are computed for each relationship in the LDS. Let FHS be the sum of all FHs and FLS be the sum of all FLs. The ratio of FLS to FHS is termed the degree of conflict. Note that this ratio varies between zero and one. A higher value represents higher conflict, while a zero value represents minimum conflict. Figure 2 also illustrates the computation of the measure of conflict.

Based on this measure, sets of activities were constructed for the six-entity problem to provide high, medium, and low degrees of conflict among activities.

Computer System Related Factors

G. Access and storage

The relevant factor is the cost of access and storage. Three cases have been considered: only access costs, only storage costs, and a realistic case of both access and storage costs. Generally, the access costs alone are of primary importance.

H. Page size

Two levels have been used for this factor; a page size of 2000 and a page size of 4000 characters.

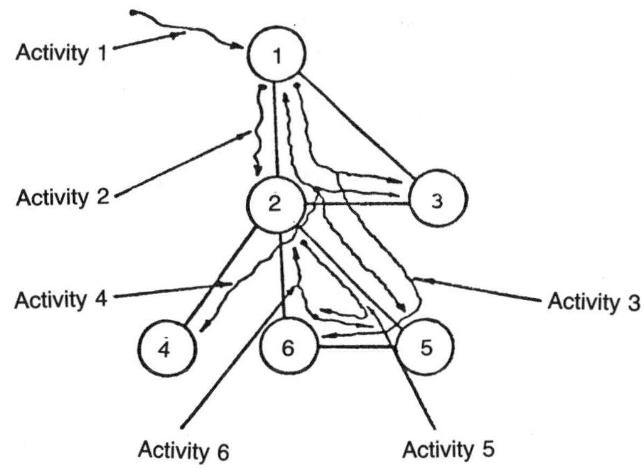

Relationship	FH	FL
1-2	2	1
1-3	0	0
2-3	2	0
2-4	1	0
2-5	3	0
2-6	1	0
5-6	2	1
Total	11	2

Conflict = 2/11 = .182

Figure 2—Measure of degree of conflict

Implementation Factors

I. Method of accessing data

The normal mode of accessing records is to bring the records into the main memory as needed while navigating through the database. Here, this method is called AM1. A second method, called AM2, was considered for which maximum batching was assumed. AM2 requires extremely large buffer sizes so that all required records from each file are brought in all at once and the files need not be re-accessed. Unless queries are simple or main memory is very large, real systems provide a certain limit on look-foward and the extent of batching. Thus, the AM2 results should be interpreted as the asymptotic case, while the AM1 results are more realistic.

J. Random versus sequential access path

Random access paths are more suitable for today's multiuser databases requiring fast on-line retrieval speeds. Sequential access paths are also evaluated for the sake of completeness and because batch-oriented systems use sequential access paths. Thus, there are two levels.

K. Symbolic versus direct pointers

These are two levels. The mixing of pointer types is not allowed.

L. Mandatory versus non-mandatory two-way pointers

In the mandatory case, only two-way pointers are considered. In the non-mandatory case, selection among the three pointer options is made based on pair-wise consideration of entities. Thus, there are two levels.

THE EXPERIMENTAL DESIGN

For the twelve experimental factors, the total exhaustive number of cases to evaluate for a full factorial design are A(4).B(3).C(3).D(3).E(3).F(3).G(2).H(2).I(2).J(2).K(2).L (2) or 62,208 cases. For the first six factors, a new problem also has to be generated, for a total of 972 cases.

Clearly, the large number of cases precludes considering the full factorial design; the number of cases has to be reduced to a realistic proportion. Since the experiments on the evaluator are deterministic (and not stochastic), statistical methods cannot be used in developing a partial factorial design. Instead, the methodology used is to intelligently select the most important cases for experimentation. This was accomplished by first defining a "reasonable case," called the base case. The base case has each of the problem factors set at a specified value. To keep the case reasonable and average, the value of each quantitative factor is set at the middle value, and the value of each qualitative factor is set largely to reflect the current practice in database design. Table I describes the parameter values of this "average and reasonable" base case. The base case has six entities, as shown in Figure 1. (It may be noted that although six entities is not a very large number, many organizational databases can be represented by that many entities).

The next step is to change each factor, one at a time, to all of their possible values without changing the other factors. Thus, the sensitivity of each factor is tested individually without regard to each factor's interaction with other factors. If a solution is extremely sensitive to different values of a factor, then another base problem is defined by altering the value of the factor to the new value. The process is then repeated for the new base problem. In fact, Table I also lists the second base case generated in this manner. The two base cases are based on the method of accessing data, i.e., AM1 and AM2. In all, there were twenty cases for each base case, or a total of forty cases.

The philosophy of this experimental design is to evaluate the effects of each factor near the base problems. The base problems are created and recreated to assure that all significantly different experimental regions are examined.

TABLE I—Experimental factors and their levels, and parameters of the base case

Factor	Levels	Base Case Value
A. Number of entities in the LDS	4	6 entities
B. Number of activities	3	6 activities
C. Number of contexts per activity	3	Medium (3.17)
D. Proportion of entity instances addressed	3	Medium
E. Distribution of activities on LDS	3	Low concentration
F. Degree of conflict between activities	3	Medium
G. Access and storage	3	Access costs
H. Page size	2	2000 characters
I. Method of accessing data	2	AM1 for base case 1 AM2 for base case 2
J. Access Path	2	Random
K. Pointer type	2	Direct
L. Mandatory vs non-mandatory two-way pointers	2	Mandatory

SENSITIVITY ANALYSIS

Sensitivity analysis refers to the extent to which the final optimum design changes because of changes in the values of the experimental factors. The cost of the final design almost invariably changes with changes in the experimental factors. However, the change in the optimum design is the sensitivity issue and not the change in the cost of the optimum design.

The assessment of the extent of change in the optimum design remains subjective and its measurement is not readily available in the literature. To quantify this change, a measure was developed to capture the relative difference between two alternate designs. The measure determines the physical parent of each entity in the two designs and counts the number of entities with different parents. Let this number be D. D is divided by the total number of entities, N to obtain the physical design difference measure (PDDM). To illustrate, consider the following two physical designs:

0 0 0 2 6 0
0 1 0 2 2 0

In these two designs, entities 2 and 5 have different physical parents; thus $D = 2$. Since $N = 6$; PDDM $= 2/6 = .33$.

The optimal designs for the forty cases, found by exhaustive enumeration, are reported in Table II. Note that cases 1 to 20 are the AM1 cases and the first case is the base case for AM1; cases 21–40 are AM2 cases and the twenty-first case is the base case for AM2. As suggested earlier, the access costs are the more important costs to consider; the optimum designs minimize the access costs unless otherwise stated. In Table II, each experimental case is described by its difference from the base case. The case description is followed by the optimal design listed in its short form, followed by the operational cost of the design and the number of total designs required to be evaluated for exhaustive enumeration. To appreciate the improvement obtained by using the abstract physical design model, the commonly used operational cost of the flat-file (expressed as all zeroes in short form) design is also listed. Finally, the ratio of optimal to flat-file costs indicates the relative inefficiency of the flat-file design.

The sensitivity analysis results for the forty experimental cases are reported in Table III. Each case is compared with the base case and the PDDM value is computed. The PDDM

TABLE II—Optimal and naive design characteristics

Case	Diff. from Base Case 1 (AM1 cases)	Optimal Design: Design	Optimal Design: Operational Cost	Optimal Design: Designs Evaluated	Flat-File Oper. cost	Ratio Optimal/ flat-file
1.	None	0 1 0 2 2 0	4717	176	18869	.25
2.	4 Entities	0 1 2 2	102	20	2944	.03
3.	8 Entities	0 1 0 2 2 0 6 0	5025	956	19164	.26
4.	10 Entities	0 1 0 2 2 0 6 0 0 4	5842	5773	46656	.13
5.	3 Activities	0 0 0 0 6 0	250	176	708	.35
6.	9 Activities	0 1 0 2 2 0	5912	176	20710	.29
7.	Lo cntx/actv	0 0 0 2 0 0	443	176	623	.71
8.	Hi cntx/actv	2 3 0 2 2 0	5332	176	21499	.25
9.	Hi proportn	0 1 0 2 2 5	9658	176	53448	.18
10.	Lo proportn	0 0 0 2 6 0	543	176	858	.63
11.	Med concentr	0 1 0 2 2 0	6429	176	19337	.33
12.	Hi concentr	0 1 0 2 2 0	6634	176	19877	.33
13.	Lo conflict	0 5 0 0 6 0	9011	176	17347	.52
14.	Hi conflict	0 1 0 2 2 0	6642	176	22072	.30
15.	Storage cost	0 1 0 2 2 0	676800	176	796800	.85
16.	Acc & Strg	0 1 0 2 2 0	87.49	176	202.87	.43
17.	4000 pg sz	2 3 0 2 2 0	3407	176	18684	.18
18.	Seq acc path	2 3 0 2 2 0	38799	176	715857	.05
19.	Symbolic ptr	2 0 0 2 2 5	6739	176	18912	.36
20.	Flexible ptr	0 1 0 2 2 0	4687	176	18843	.25
	Diff. from Base Case 2 (AM2 cases)					
21.	None	0 0 0 2 6 0	593	176	642	.92
22.	4 Entities	0 1 0 2	89	20	105	.85
23.	8 Entities	0 0 0 2 6 0 6 0	682	956	790	.86
24.	10 Entities	0 0 0 2 6 0 6 0 0 4	1025	5773	1428	.72
25.	3 Activities	0 0 0 0 6 0	222	176	249	.89
26.	9 Activities	0 0 0 2 6 0	1264	176	1362	.93
27.	Lo cntx/actv	0 0 0 2 0 0	385	176	388	.99
28.	Hi cntx/actv	0 0 0 2 6 0	1238	176	1354	.91
29.	Hi proprtn	0 0 0 0 6 0	1193	176	1265	.94
30.	Lo proprtn	0 0 0 2 6 0	410	176	469	.87
31.	Med concentr	0 0 0 2 6 0	1009	176	1050	.96
32.	Hi concentr	0 0 0 0 6 0	1486	176	1515	.98
33.	Lo conflict	0 0 0 0 0 0	1090	176	1090	1.00
34.	Hi conflict	0 0 0 0 6 0	1275	176	1278	.998
35.	Storage cost	0 1 0 2 2 0	676800	176	796800	.85
36.	Acc & Strg	0 0 0 2 6 0	98.44	176	109.51	.90
37.	4000 pg sz	0 0 0 2 6 0	345	176	369	.93
38.	Seq Acc Path	0 0 0 0 6 0	1298	176	1370	.95
39.	Symbolic ptrs	0 0 0 2 0 0	696	176	723	.96
40.	Flexible ptrs	0 0 0 2 6 0	530	176	552	.96

reflects the sensitivity of a particular case. Since there are multiple cases for each factor, the combination of the multiple cases' PDDM values projects the sensitivity of the factor. Because the base case is the "middle" case of the multiple cases, the higher PDDM of the multiple cases is used as a measure of the sensitivity of the factor (this reflects the maximum change in the physical design that can occur due to change in the factor level). Note that the sensitivity rating (and PDDM) can vary between 0 and 1; where 0 means no sensitivity and 1 means maximum sensitivity. The sensitivity ratings have been classified as "high" if the rating is greater than or equal to .50, as "medium" if the rating is between .25 and .50, and as "low" otherwise.

As suggested in the experimental design section, the most sensitive factor has been the method of accessing data (i.e., AM1 vs AM2), so much so that two separate base cases were used for the two methods. For this reason, this factor's effect is explored first.

TABLE III—Sensitivity analysis results

Factor Name	Factor values (differences from base case)	AM1 Results PDDM	AM1 Results Sensitivity Rating	AM2 Results PDDM	AM2 Results Sensitivity Rating
Number of entities in the LDS	4 Entities	*		*	
	8 Entities	0	Low	0	Low
	10 Entities	0		0	
Number of activities	3 Activities	.50	High	.17	Low
	9 Activities	0		0	
Number of contexts per activity	Lo context/actv	.33	Medium	.17	Low
	Hi cntx/actv	.33		0	
Proportion of entity instances addressed	Hi proportn	.17	Medium	.17	Low
	Lo proportn	.33		0	
Distribution of activities on the LDS	Med concentr	0	Low	0	Low
	Hi concentr	0		.17	
Degree of conflict in activities	Lo conflict	.50	High	.33	Medium
	Hi conflict	0		.17	
Access and Storage	Storage cost	max	High	max	High
	Acc & Strg	of .67		of .50	
Page size	4000 pg sz	.33	Medium	0	Low
Access path	Seq acc path	.33	Medium	.17	Low
Pointer type	Symbolic ptr	.50	High	.17	Low
Mandatory 2-way vs flexible ptrs	Flexible ptrs	0	Low	0	Low

* The four-entity LDS was structurally different from the six-entity LDS, so PDDM was not calculated.

Method of Accessing Data

The method of accessing data, AM1 versus AM2, is an extremely sensitive factor. The PDDM values between corresponding cases of AM1 and AM2 (not shown here) were as high as .67. As the number of activities and the contexts per activity begin to increase, the differences between the AM1 optimal design and AM2 optimal design begin to be substantial. With few and simple activities, the AM1 and AM2 solutions are not much different. (Table II shows that the AM1 and AM2 solutions for three activities and low contexts per activity are identical.) The AM2 designs are not much sensitive to the activities on the database, but the AM1 designs are. The AM2 argument is to access each required file only once. Thus, if the file sizes are small, there will be few accesses on the file. Therefore, it may be stated that:

Assertion: The objective of minimizing accesses in the AM2 (batching) case is strongly correlated to the objective of minimizing storage.

This is not so in the AM1 case where each file may be searched multiple times depending on the characteristics of the activities.

As observed earlier, a physical design technique commonly used by many designers is to store each entity independently in its own file with proper pointers to reflect relationships (e.g., in relational implementations). This design is called the flat-file design. Table II shows that, in the AM2 cases, the flat-file design is a very good design. Of the twenty AM2 cases, one flat-file design turned out to be optimal, and in fourteen cases, the cost difference between the optimal and the flat-file design was less than 10 percent. This observation is a direct corollary of the above assertion because the flat-file design is a good design from the standpoint of minimizing storage requirements (the only storage overhead is due to the pointers and no data redundancy is caused due to absorptions).

On the other hand, the flat-file design is not always good for the more commonly used access strategy as in the AM1 cases. In all of the twenty AM1 cases, the cost difference between the optimal and the flat-file design was more than 10 percent and in only one case was less than 20 percent. Further, it was found that some designs are extremely poor, costing far more than the flat-file design (on the order of 5 to 10 times more). The AM1 strategy in combination with activity factors becomes extremely sensitive and one has to be very careful in laying out the physical design. Again the reason is that in AM1, the first file is searched once, while subsequent files are searched many times. Since the flat-file calls for the maximum number of files possible, the total searches are also multiplied accordingly. This results in the flat-file being a poor design choice. The physical design selected has to minimize the total number of accesses, which is a combination of the number of searches of the files as well as the accesses at each search. This is a much more difficult design goal.

One final word on this factor. Although we have only discussed the two extremes AM1 and AM2, there are other data access strategies which fall between the two extremes (e.g., limited batching may be applied). The sensitivity of the factor is then diluted accordingly. As stated earlier, AM1 strategy is more commonly applied in most DBMSs, and the sensitivity of the underlying factors in AM1 is much higher; therefore, the remaining sensitivity results generally focus on the AM1 cases.

LDS Related Factors

The LDS related factors (i.e., the number of entities in the LDS) alter the total character of the problem. Thus, the optimal design changes to the extent the problem description changes. In a sense, it may be unfair to conduct sensitivity analysis if the changes in LDS alter the problem definition drastically. However, it does make sense to conduct sensitivity analysis by changing the LDS size without changing its basic structure (e.g., entities are merely dropped from or added to an existing LDS).

When such changes were made to the LDS of the base problem and minimal changes were made in the activities on the LDS, it was found that the optimal physical design was only moderately affected. When we experimented with adding entities to the LDS, only the physical storage of the added entities was affected with no or minimal effect on the entities previously stored. As in Table II, in both AM1 and AM2 cases, when entities 7 and 8 were added to the six-entity LDS, 7 was absorbed into 6, and 8 was stored independently. Entities 1 through 5 were stored unchanged.

LDS-based guidelines have been proposed for physical design.[1,6] The guidelines in Carlis[1] suggest that (a) a 1 : 1 relationship should be represented by pointers and (b) a 1 : *M* relationship should not be represented by the "*M*" entity absorbing the "1" entity. Evidence of the applicability of these guidelines is found in all AM2's batching cases, but not in all of the more realistic AM1 cases. For example, cases 8 and 9 violate these guidelines. Further, the experiments show that these guidelines remain valid when the activities on the database are very few and are relatively simple (e.g., each activity focusing on a very few number of entities). However, this is not the case in large multi-user databases, where there are many activities on the database and the activities may be fairly complex. It is therefore inferred that pure LDS based guidelines have limited applicability; they are applicable only when the activities on the database are few and relatively simple.

Activities Related Factors

The sensitivity experiments findings are again summarized in Table III. One of the important conclusions of the experimentation is that not only the number of activities, but also the "structure" of the activities, affect the choice of the optimal design. The amount of change in the activities related factors is a continuum, from very low to very high. The amount of change induced in the optimal design also varies similarly.

It might be said at the outset that the activity effects are more pronounced in the AM1 case than in the AM2 case. In the AM2 case, all of the activity factors had low sensitivity with one exception, and the optimal designs differed in, at most, one clustering. However, in the realistic AM1 cases, the findings were different. As expected, the sensitivity was high as the number of activities on the database increased. It is important that even when the number of activities on the database remains the same, the optimal design can change considerably with "structural" changes in the activities. These structural changes in the activities include the number of contexts per activity, the degree of conflict between entities, the proportion of entity instances addressed, and the distribution of activities on the LDS. The design changes caused by these factors are shown in Table II, and the factor sensitivity ratings are shown in Table III. As can be seen, all have a medium-to-high sensitivity to the optimal design, with the possible exception of the factor: distribution of activities on the LDS.

The sensitivity of the activity factors can be explained in an intuitive manner. Since the activities are the cause of accesses on the database, it is natural for them to be a critical factor. Clearly, when there are few activities on the database, the LDS characteristics dominate. As the number of activities increases, different design choices start to be more appealing. But, more important than the number of activities is the structure of activities. If each activity focused on one entity alone (i.e., one context activities), then a flat-file design in which each entity is placed in its own file will be a good design. However, as the contexts per activity increase, certain clusterings become desirable. For example, if an activity addresses entity *B* instances only via entity *A* instances, then it is best to cluster entity *B* into entity *A*. The proportion of entity instances addressed has the "volume" effect in that the differences due to absorption and non-absorption are multiplied according to the proportion of entity instances addressed. Finally, the effect of distribution of activities is to localize or spread the considerations of absorption/non-absorption over the LDS, thus generating different physical design choices. Perhaps the low sensitivity indicated due to this factor may be because the factor levels are not significantly apart or are not able to properly capture the factor meaning.

The last activity related factor of degree of conflict between activities makes the physical design problem especially complex. For example, consider two conflicting activities, one going from entity *A* to entity *B* and the other going from entity *B* to entity *A*. For the first activity, clustering *B* near *A* will be advantageous, while the reverse will be true for the second activity. The design choices become very sensitive as shown by the "high" sensitivity rating for the AM1 cases and the "medium" rating for the AM2 cases.

As stated earlier, designers have developed intuitive guidelines for physical design based on the logical data structure alone. In the author's opinion, this view offers a microscopic perspective on the design problem. For example, consider two LDS based guidelines suggested in Palvia.[10] The first guideline is that in a related entity pair, the entity with the higher outdegree should absorb the entity with the lower outdegree. This guideline works in most common cases, but does not work well when the activity is directed predominantly through the entity with the lower outdegree. Another guideline suggested is: if the length of an instance of the entity related to another entity is quite small in comparison, then the larger instance entity should absorb the smaller instance entity. This guideline also does not perform very well if the activity is predominantly from the smaller instance entity. Thus, as a result of these experiments, the author concludes that any physical database design guidelines or heuristics should be based both on the logical data structure and the activities to take place on the database.

Computer System Related Factors

Storage cost or access cost is a critical sensitivity factor in optimizing the physical design. This is apparent as these two are different dimensions. The storage cost for a given physical design depends only on the physical design itself; while the access cost depends both on the physical design and the activities on the database. For this reason, the "minimizing storage cost" objective function yields the same optimal solution irrespective of the other problem-related factors as long as the LDS contents and structure remain the same. On the other hand, the "minimizing access cost" objective function yields a different optimal solution based on the activity characteristics. In the AM1 cases, the PDDM values between "minimizing storage" designs and "minimizing accesses" designs ranged as high as .67.

Another factor, page size, had a medium level of sensitivity in the AM1 cases (and low in the AM2 cases). Page size has an effect on clusterings because it dictates the amount of data that can be brought into memory at once; thus, it affects the size of clusterings.

Physical Factors

The most important physical factor is the method of accessing data (discussed in a previous section). Of the remaining physical factors, mandatory versus non-mandatory two-way pointers has low sensitivity to the optimal design. Of course, the non-mandatory two-way pointers option costs less because it allows more flexibility in the direction of pointers. The low sensitivity can be easily explained because the mandatory two-way pointers automatically include the one-way pointers of the non-mandatory option.

The symbolic versus direct pointers factor had high sensitivity in the AM1 cases (and low sensitivity in the AM2 cases). As can be expected, direct pointers yield fewer page accesses because they can directly retrieve records, as opposed to going via an access path with symbolic pointers. Since direct pointers give direct address of the related record, the effect of clustering becomes largely irrelevant.

The random access path versus sequential access path factor had medium sensitivity in the AM1 cases (and again low in the AM2 cases). One would expect that absorptions would be less desirable in the sequential access paths because one would have to scan through much unnecessary data to get to the required data.

This completes the discussion of the sensitivity analysis results. As said earlier, Table III summarizes the experimental results of sensitivity analysis and may be used as a quick reference.

CONCLUSIONS

The relatively unexplored area of sensitivity of the physical database design is addressed in this paper, and contributing factors that may influence the physical database design have been identified. To study the effect of these experimental factors, a practical experimental design was developed. Based on this design, forty experimental cases, with different combinations of factor levels, were created. For each experiment, optimal physical database design was obtained using a simulation based software. Based on the experiments, the sensitivity of the optimal physical design due to changes in the factor values was analyzed.

The results of the sensitivity analysis have been reported here. An important conclusion is that activity related factors are as important in physical database design as are the logical data structure factors. The activity related factors include both the number of activities on the database as well as the structure of the activities. Several activity structural factors have been identified as sensitive factors.

Conducting sensitivity analysis of the physical database design is important, especially when restructuring the physical database. It is hoped that this exploratory study will trigger future studies as well as reports of current experience, which will validate and extend the findings of this paper.

REFERENCES

1. Carlis, J.V. "An Investigation into the Modeling and Design of Large Multi-User Databases." Ph.D. Thesis, University of Minnesota, 1980.
2. Gambino, T.J. and R.A. Gerritsen. "A Data Base Decision Support System." in *Proceedings of the VLDB,* Association for Computing Machinery, 1977.
3. Hoffer, J.A. and A. Kovacevic. "Optimal Performance of Inverted Files." *Operations Research,* 30 (1982) 2.
4. Katz, R.H. and E. Wong. "Resolving Conflicts in Global Storage Design Through Replication." *ACM Transactions on Database Systems,* 8 (1983) 1.
5. Schkolnick, M. "A Clustering Algorithm for Hierarchical Structures." *ACM Transactions on Database Systems,* 2 (1977) 1.
6. Bachman, C.W. "Data Structure Diagrams." *Data Base,* 1 (1969) 2.
7. Chen, P.P.S. "The Entity-Relationship Model—Towards a Unified View of Data." *ACM Transactions on Database Systems,* 1 (1976) 1.
8. Batory, D.S. and C.C. Gotlieb. "A Unifying Model of Physical Databases." *ACM Transactions on Database Systems,* 7 (1982) 4.
9. Maech, S.T. "Techniques for Structuring Database Records." *Computing Surveys,* 15 (1983) 1.
10. Palvia, P. "An Analytical Investigation into Record Structuring and Physical Database Design of Generalized Logical Data Structures." Ph.D. Thesis, University of Minnesota, 1984.
11. Severance, D.G. "Some Generalized Modeling Structures for Use in Design of File Organizations." *Information Systems,* 1 (1975) 2.
12. Yao, S.B. "An Attribute Based Model for Database Access Cost Analysis." *ACM Transactions on Database Systems,* 2 (1977) 1.
13. Chamberlin, D.D., et al. "History and Evaluation of System R." *Communications of the ACM,* October 1981.
14. Guttman, A. and M. Stonebraker. "Using a Relational DBMS for Computer Aided Design of Data." *IEEE Bulletin on Database Engineering,* June 1982.

Design of a distributed data dictionary system

by HONGJUN LU, KRISHNA MIKKILINENI, and BHAVANI THURAISINGHAM
Honeywell
Golden Valley, Minnesota

ABSTRACT

To function effectively, every organization requires a dictionary or directory as an informant of the metadata on databases, users, applications, and systems within the organization. To date, the current use of data dictionaries within the organizations is limited owing to the failure of bringing about their full capital capacity. Two important factors are responsible for this deficiency of current systems. First is the complexity and cost and second, the absence of any integration of organizational information. Our primary focus of attention is on developing interface services between the existing and the new dictionary systems which will permit the distribution of metadata across various functional domains in the organization by providing users with a mechanism to gain access from any of the dictionary systems. The work presented here provides a sound foundation upon which practical solutions to the problems encountered in the design of distributed data dictionary systems can be developed.

INTRODUCTION

To function effectively, every organization requires a dictionary or directory as an informant of the metadata on databases, users, applications and systems within the organization. It would provide a logical catalogue of general and specific questions concerning the organizational informational resources and can also be a useful managerial implement by providing a more efficient documenting, controlling, and managing system which will ultimately lead to an improvement of the overall productivity.[1,2]

Another more important role that such a dictionary will fulfill within the organization would be that of support mechanism for system life cycle methodology.[1] This would involve several functions including:

1. Verifying the internal consistency of dictionary data
2. Analyzing the impact of changes
3. Ensuring naming standards for the data elements
4. Maintaining the data management policies, procedures and statistics
5. Audit records
6. Providing access to multiple configuration of database schemas
7. Indicating the value and quantity of information

To date, the current use of data dictionaries within the organizations is limited owing to the failure of bringing about their full capital capacity. Two important factors are responsible for this deficiency of current systems. First is the complexity and cost and second, the absence of any integration of organizational information. We are of the opinion that this situation can be remedied by providing cheaper and more simple, but, nonetheless, highly functional dictionary systems as well as integratory services between new and existing systems.

Our primary focus of attention is on developing interface services between the existing and the new dictionary systems. They will permit distribution of metadata across various functional domains in the organization by providing users with a mechanism to gain access from any of the dictionary systems.

We define in this paper an architecture of a distributed dictionary system and present a design for the interfaces within the architecture. The specific objective is as follows: Develop the specification for the canonical interface which, when coupled with each dictionary system, allows integration with others within the architecture. The interface overcomes the differences in different dictionary systems and their various data representations so that the metadata may pass between them. It provides an elegant and uniform medium for transfer and also complements the functionality which may be lacking in the different domain dictionaries.

In the remaining sections, we describe the organizational dictionary system architecture and the essential features of the object based canonical interfaces in the architecture. Finally, we conclude the paper by outlining our future considerations.

ORGANIZATIONAL DICTIONARY/DIRECTORY SYSTEM ARCHITECTURE

The purpose of this section is to provide a comprehensive description of an architectural framework which integrates distributed dictionary systems. The framework is comprised of:

1. A collection of domain dictionaries meeting the specific needs of the various domains in the organization
2. A hierarchy of dictionaries providing relevant information at the different levels
3. A system of interfaces among both the distributed domains and hierarchical dictionaries

The proposed architecture of the dictionary system, as illustrated in Figure 1, consists of a Central Organizational Dictionary/Directory System (CODS), together with an unspecified number of Domain Dictionary/Directory Systems (DDS), all of which are incorporated within a hierarchical structure. The central and domain systems are interconnected through a canonical object based and distributed metadata interfaces. Together, these provide an effective system for the transfer of metadata between the various domain dictionaries and make access to them readily available.

The architecture has been flexibly designed to allow for extensions both horizontally and vertically, so that the number of domains or levels can be increased should they be demanded by the functional needs of the organizations. With reference to Figure 1, we concentrate primarily on discussing both the central and domain dictionaries and secondly on presenting an overall view of the system and its operations.

Central Organization-wide Dictionary/Directory System

Some of the major functions of the CODS within the architecture are described below.

1. Initially, it provides an extensive resource information center and permits ready access to that information which is essential. It would be possible to distribute some of the metadata among the various DDS.

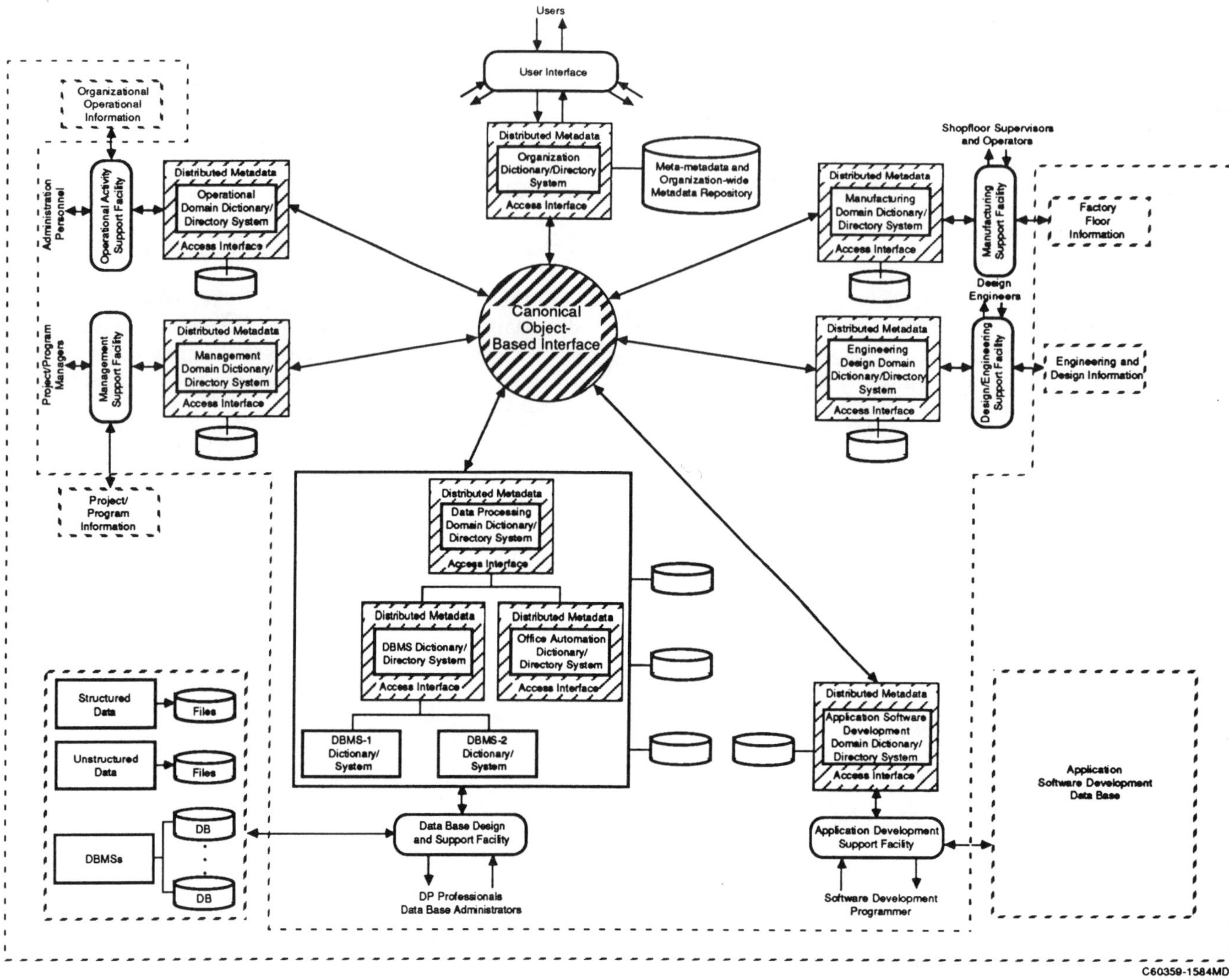

Figure 1—An organizational dictionary/directory system architecture

2. Such a system would enable a centralization of the meta information with the main control being held by the CODS.
3. Consistency and integrity of the meta information throughout the distributed domain dictionary systems would be maintained.
4. An impact analysis would be available should changes occur in any of the domains.
5. Different types of user interfaces would be provided and may include input/output facilities for non-procedural languages, menu systems, high level programming language interfaces, report generators and graphic displays.

Domain Dictionary/Directory Systems

The DDSs are specifically designed as support facilities to be advantageous to the various users in their particular domains and therefore their functionality depends largely on each particular domain. In accordance with some of the principal domains of a typical manufacturing organization, we have briefly listed below a series of their possible functions.

Data processing domain dictionary

The data processing domain dictionary manages the general requirements of the data processing department of the organization. The information within this domain, if it is to be effective, has to be well organized.

As illustrated in Figure 1, there are two separate sections to the main domain, respectively containing the office automation dictionary and the DBMS dictionary systems. The former controls the meta information pertaining to the business management while the latter combines meta information, for example, the various schemas and constraints originating from the dictionaries of many database management systems. The database design and support facility provides the opportunity for schema manipulation and metadata design and loading. It also provides tools that aid in the daily maintenance of the data resources.

Application software development domain dictionary

The application development domain dictionary is a culmination of metadata information concerning software documents and packages, reference manuals, on line help programs, library routines and user specific menus and forms. Its primary function is to be a repository for the generation, development, maintenance, and sharing of software and documentation for various applications in the organizations. It also provides a facility for the retrieval of library of software routines, documentation, and for version and configuration controls of these packages.

Engineering/design domain dictionary

Design and engineering specifications are incorporated into the engineering/design domain dictionary, together with version and configuration information on the results on design analysis and simulation experiments. Its users would include design engineers, and technicians. Its primary concern is to provide for the version control of the design documents, but it also extends to information exchange among various design groups as well as location of designs and drawings.

Manufacturing automation domain dictionary

This particular domain dictionary catalogues the information connected with the production operations on the shop floor, for example, manufacturing and assembly guidelines, quality control, and numerical control program specifications. Therefore it would benefit and be used by shopfloor managers and supervisors. The user support facility for this domain provides for the location for those guidelines, specifications, and for the verifications against the production databases as well as integrity control between the design and manufacturing documents.

Project management domain dictionary

Project management domain dictionary is used in particular by managers and project leaders for information on various projects, management and administrative policies, plans and schedules. The support facility provides for the global view of the resources, projects, plans and schedules. It also assists in the automation of daily management activities.

Operational domain dictionary

The operational domain dictionary assists in the daily concerns of an organization, and it is chiefly used by the support staff. It is an informant of the organization's operational information including available resources, equipment and future requirements. The support facility provides for the easy access of personnel, inventory, and bulletin board information. Office automation systems may use the information contained in this dictionary.

Basic Functions Provided by the Dictionary System Interfaces

As shown in Figure 1, each domain dictionary system has its own distributed metadata access interface attached. This interface can be complemented with a canonical object interface. An alternative solution is to centralize this canonical interface. The choice depends on the ease of implementation and performance considerations. The main functions of these two interfaces are as follows.

1. They provide metadata transfer between the various DDSs.
2. They provide an intermediate logical metadata model, which can represent the information in the various DDSs and can also provide the transformation between the different metadata models used in these DDSs.
3. They provide the routing capability for locating the information not available in a particular domain.

Overall flow of data among the various operations of the system is shown in Figure 2. In this figure it is assumed that the canonical interface is centralized, and some of the meta-metadata is distributed among the various distributed metadata interfaces. When a user poses a query, it is first checked whether the required information is in the local DDS. If so, the necessary translation is performed between the interface and the DDS, and the query is processed. If the information is not present in the local DDS, then the CODS is queried via the canonical interface, and the result is returned to the user.

DESIGN OF THE DISTRIBUTED DICTIONARY SYSTEM INTERFACES

We present in this section a description of the canonical and distributed metadata interfaces, as illustrated in the architecture described in the previous section. We shall first present the metadata model used in the interface and then discuss its functionality. The various domain dictionary systems may utilize different models in accordance with the specific needs. As the interfaces to the domain dictionary data are meant to provide communication between the various domain dictionary systems, the model embedded in the canonical interface should be:

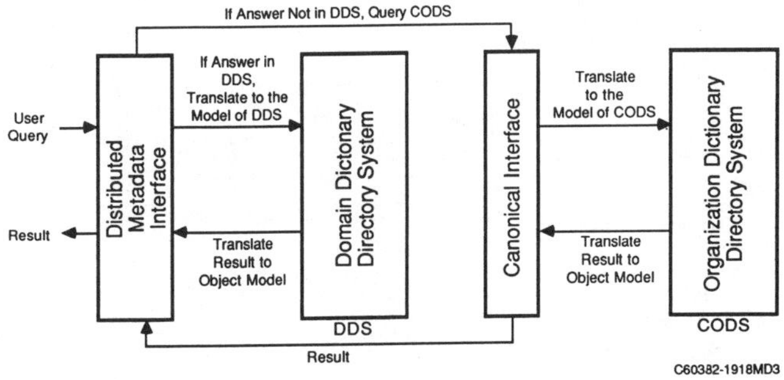

Figure 2—Operational flow in the distributed dictionary system

1. Uniform and flexible in order to allow interfaces to various domains
2. Simple so as to avoid performance penalty
3. Powerful to allow semantics of different metadata models to be imposed upon it.

The Information Resource Dictionary Systems (IRDS), as designed by the National Bureau of Standards, together with many commercial data dictionary systems, has made use of the Entity-Relationship-Attribute (ERA) model.[3] Figure 3 is representative of a meta-database schema taken from the IRDS, and therefore illustrates the ERA model. In this example, finance department, payroll system, personnel department, personnel system, etcetera, represent dictionary "entities." As depicted, the finance department is responsible for the payroll system, and the personnel department is responsible for the personnel system. The "relationship" between these entities reflect these responsibilities. Both the payroll record and the personnel record data entities contain Social Security number and employee ID as attributes. The length of the Social Security number an that of employee ID represent dictionary "attributes" for the dictionary entities of payroll record and personnel record.

Although the ERA model is simple and flexible, we believe that it is not powerful enough to store all the required metadata information such as constraints, views, and version controls. Furthermore, since the interfaces should operate with diverse dictionary systems of the present and the future, the interface should be based on a more general model than the ERA model. After examining in depth many of the existing models such as Frames[4] and the Entity-Category-Relationship model[5] we have chosen the object model for the logical design of the interfaces.[6,7] The main reasons for this choice include its simplicity, flexibility, and generality. The concept of an "object" provides a powerful modeling paradigm supporting classification, generalization, aggregation, and the inheritance properties.

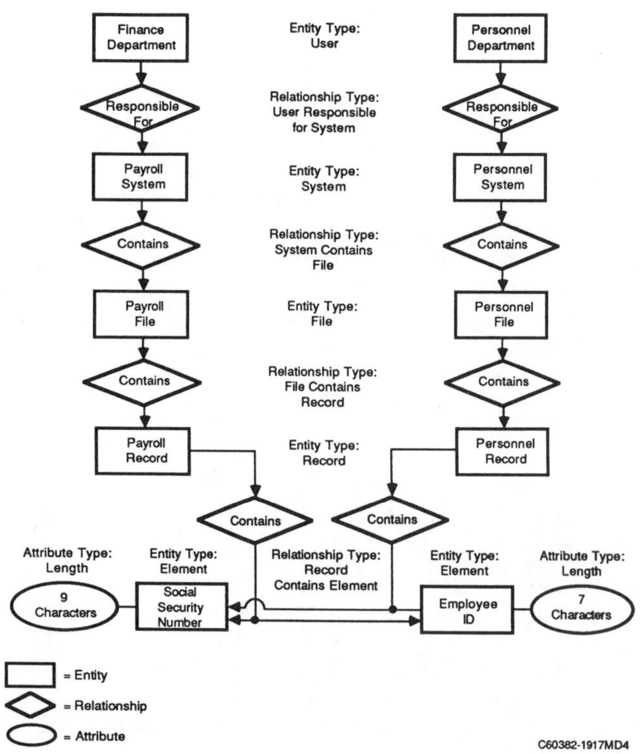

Figure 3—An example of a meta-database

The essential features of the object model, that we have found useful, are the following:

All conceptual entities are modeled as objects. The straightforward notion of an object is sufficient to represent both simple and complex entities.

Objects are abstract in the sense that the physical implementation of objects and their operations are separated from their specifications. The user need not be aware of physical representations and complex interobject operations to understand and manipulate relationships. This property makes the object model an ideal candidate to model the interfaces, which are built on top of different dictionary systems.

The notions of object class lattice, inheritance of properties, and operations along the lattice facilitate top-down development of the definition of a metadata base. At higher levels of the class lattice, general properties and operations may be introduced. They are augmented and specialized at lower levels. This inheritance mechanism is a very powerful concept, which effectively captures the notion of generalization and abstraction of metadata.

Description of the Object-based Interface Model

The object model we have used to represent the interfaces follows closely to the model of the Object Data Base System (ODBS) designed by MCC. Although some significant differences between the two models exist, the basic notions are common to both systems. Our model is different from the ODBS model mainly by eliminating the notion of instance variables present in the ODBS model mainly by eliminating the notion of instance variables present in the ODBS model and by including the concept of attributes associated with objects.

Using the object model, all entities are modeled as objects. Similar objects may be grouped together to form a class. A collection of classes may form a hierarchy. The instances of a class are objects. Properties of an object are described by its attributes. An object consists of some private memory that holds its state. The private memory is made up of the values for its attributes. The behavior of an object is determined by its operations or methods. Methods consist of code that manipulate or return the state of an object. Objects communicate with each other through messages.

Figure 4 illustrates an example of the object model which models the metadata in the FINANCE_DEPARTMENT, PERSONNEL_DEPARTMENT examples depicted in Figure 3. The classes in this object model are USER, SYSTEM, FILE, RECORD, RELATIONSHIP, CONSTRAINT and VIEW. Some of these classes form a hierarchy as shown in the

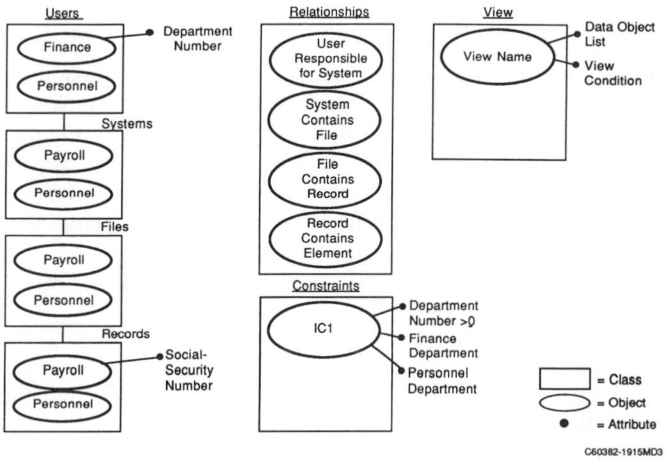

Figure 4—An example of meta-database using object model

Figure. For example, SYSTEM is a superclass of FILE and a subclass of USER. A class consists of many objects. For example, the class USER has objects FINANCE_DEPARTMENT and PERSONNEL_DEPARTMENT and the class SYSTEM has objects PAYROLL and PERSONNEL.

An object has associated attributes. The object FINANCE_DEPARTMENT may have attributes department number, manager, and the subdivisions within the department.

A subclass inherits all the properties of its superclass. The class RELATIONSHIP consists of objects which are the relationships between entities. In this particular example, RELATIONSHIP consists of objects USER_RESPONSIBLE_FOR_SYSTEM, SYSTEM_CONTAINS_FILE, FILE_CONTAINS_RECORD, and RECORD_CONTAINS_ELEMENT.

The constraints associated with metadata objects are modeled by the class CONSTRAINTS. Different classes may be used for modeling different types of constraints such as mandatory security constraints, integrity constraints and discretionary constraints.

The integrity constraint:

IC1: The Department Number in Finance and Personnel Departments have to be a positive number

is modeled as follows:

An object of the class CONSTRAINT is IC1. The attributes of IC1 are the condition in the constraint: Department Number $> = 0$, and the entities on which the constraint is applied: Finance Department and Personnel Department.

Similarly, multiple views of different data objects are modeled by the class called VIEW. An object belonging to this class is the view name. The attributes of this object are the data objects described in the view definition and the conditions used to specify the view. As briefly illustrated here, it can be seen that the constraints associated with the ERA model of metadata can be easily mapped onto our object model. Furthermore, constraints and views can be modeled fairly simply with the object model.

Functional Design of the Interfaces

In this section, we present a high level design of the canonical object interface and the distributed metadata access interface. As shown in Figure 5, the canonical object interface consists of query translator, metadata translator and the remote meta-metadata repository. The distributed metadata access interface consists of the front-end user interface and the distributed metadata access controller. We first describe each of these components and then, discuss their functions.

The query translator translates a user's query in a dialect familiar to the local domain ito a universal query language based on the object model.

The metadata translator translates the metadata from a remote domain into the form familiar to the local domain.

The remote meta-metadata repository consists of the directory information for metadata in other domains. Each domain dictionary system may contain total or partial meta-metadata information concerning the remote domains. If a user's query to the dictionary involves metadata in remote domains, then the Remote meta-metadata repository associated with the local system is examined first. If an entry is found, then the query is routed directly to the appropriate system. Otherwise, it is routed to the central organization-dictionary where all metadata information is stored.

The front-end user interface is the communication medium between the user and the local system. If the user's query can be solved by the local domain, the result is returned to the user. Otherwise, the Query translator is invoked.

The distributed metadata access controller performs the following functions. First, if a query cannot be processed locally, the controller will invoke the query translator. Second, if a remote system has issued a request for metadata retrieval from the local system, the controller will invoke metadata translator to translate the metadata retrieved. The functions needed for the operation of our system fall into two categories. Functions in the first category are used to create, delete, and modify the classes and objects. Functions in the

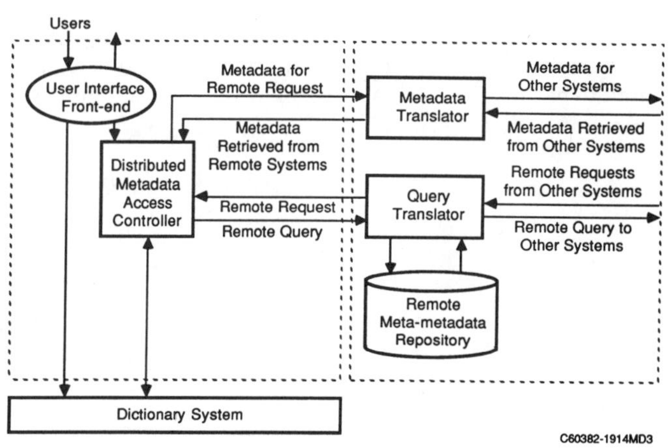

Figure 5—A functional breakdown of the combined distributed meta-data access and canonical interface

second category control the distributed metadata access. The essential functions belonging to these two categories are included in the following list.

Functions that are defined on classes are:
Define-Class(name, description)
Modify-Class(name, description)
Delete-Class(name, description)

Functions that are defined on objects are:
Insert-Object(class, object, attributes)
Modify-Object(class, object, attributes)
Delete-Object(class, object, attributes)
Insert-Attribute(class, object, attribute)
Modify-Attribute(class, object, attribute)
Delete-Attribute(class, object, attribute)
Retrieve-Object(class, object)
Retrieve-Attribute(class, object, attribute-name, qualification)

Functions that control distributed metadata access are:

local-cmd-obj(local-id, local-cmd, obj-cmd) (This function translates a local query into the object form.)
obj-cmd-local(local-id, obj-cmd, local-cmd) (This function translates a remote query based on the object form into a language familiar to the local system.)
send-request(source, destination, request) (This function is called when a request has to be sent to a remote system.)
local-data-obj(local-id, local-data, obj-data) (This function translates a local metadata into the object form.)
obj-cmd-local(local-id, obj-data, local-data) (This function translates remote metadata in object form into a language familiar to the local system.)
send-data(source, destination, data) (This function is called when metadata has to be sent to a remote system.)
receive-data(source, destination, data) (This function is called when a system has issued send-request and is waiting for metadata from the remote system.)

We are currently investigating the mappings between the functions described and the functions associated with the other models such as the ERA model and the Relational model. These mappings could be achieved fairly easily due to the fact that any entity, relation or attribute could be considered to be an object. We are also in the process of defining an implementation specification for our design.

FUTURE CONSIDERATIONS

In this work, we have proposed a distributed data dictionary system architecture that allows for integration of metadata in the organization. Since information integration technology has been widely accepted as a key ingredient to achieving manufacturing and office integration, the integration of metadata through a common architecture is the first pragmatic step towards achieving a total organizational information integration. Our immediate goal is to successfully implement our design.

The proposed work can be extended in many directions. One direction is to extend the distributed dictionary system interfaces to manage distributed data as well as metadata. Another direction might be to incorporate knowlege into the metadata and to extend the dictionary system functionality with inferencing capability. We are of the opinion that the work presented in this paper provides a sound foundation upon which practical solutions to the problems encountered in the design of distributed database management systems and dictionary systems can be developed.

ACKNOWLEDGEMENT

We thank the following people: Dr. Alan Goldfine at NBS for the helpful discussions and Dr. Amit Sheth and Mr. Amrish Kumar at Honeywell Corporate Systems Development Division for their valuable suggestions.

REFERENCES

1. Lefkovitz, H., E. Sibley, and S. Lefkovitz. *"Information Resource/Data Dictionary System."* QED Information Sciences, Inc., 1983.
2. Leong-Hong, B., and B. Plagman. *"Data Dictionary/Directory Systems,"* John Wiley & Sons, 1982.
3. *"A Technical Overview of the Information Resource Dictionary System."* U.S. Department of Commerce, National Bureau of Standards, April, 1985.
4. Fikes, R., and T. Kehler, "The Role of Frame-Based Representation in Reasoning." *Communications of the ACM,* September, 1985, pp. 904–920.
5. Elmasri, R., J. Weeldreyer, and A. Hevner. "The Category Concept: An Extension to the Entity-Relationship Model." *Data and Knowledge Engineering,* 1 (1985) 1, pp. 75–116.
6. Derrett, N., W. Kent, and P. Lyngbaek. "Some Aspects of Operations in an Object Oriented Database." *Database Engineering,* December, 1985, pp. 66–74.
7. McLeod, D., and S. Widjojo. "Object Management and Sharing in Autonomous, Distributed Data/Knowledge Bases," *Database Engineering,* December 1985, pp. 83–89.

Protecting statistical databases by combining memoryless table restrictions with randomization

by ERNST L. LEISS and DAVE J. KO
University of Houston—University Park
Houston, Texas

ABSTRACT

Statistical databases are databases that provide access to statistics about groups of people (or organizations) while protecting the confidentiality of the individuals represented in the database. Unfortunately, protecting confidentiality is difficult to achieve, since the statistics contain vestiges of the original information. Hence, users of statistical databases have a host of inference techniques at their disposal for retrieving information about identifiable persons.

This paper reports on simulations that combine simple restriction criteria such as order control, table size control, and minimum frequency control with unrestricted randomization techniques, and compares them with respect to their cost, accuracy, and security. Our simulations demonstrate that these methods provide an acceptable level of security for many applications without being overly restrictive or costly.

INTRODUCTION

Starting in the late 1970s[1] computer scientists began to look at the inference problem in on-line, general-purpose database systems that provide both statistical and nonstatistical access. Statistical databases contain sensitive information about individuals or organizations and provide access to statistics about groups of persons or organizations such as sums and averages, while protecting the confidentiality of the individuals represented in the database. In a hospital, for example, doctors may be given direct access to a database of patients' medical records, but researchers are only permitted access to statistical summaries of the records.[2,3] Census Bureaus, for example, are responsible for collecting information about all citizens and reporting this information in a way that does not jeopardize individual privacy.[5,6]

Unfortunately, the confidentiality objective is difficult to achieve, since the statistics contain vestiges of the original information. By correlating different statistics, a clever user may be able to deduce confidential information about an individual.[6,7,8,9] The problem of protecting against such indirect disclosures of sensitive data is called the inference problem.[4] The objective of inference controls is to ensure that the statistics released by the database do not lead to the disclosure of confidential data.[4]

Generally, the most efficient mechanisms for inference control have the least security or greatest information loss. Recently, the results related to inferenc controls of on-line database systems have become more positive. This paper reports on simulations that combine memory-less table restriction criteria[3,4] with unrestricted randomization techniques,[8,10,11] and compares them with respect to cost, accuracy, and security. The results are attractive in that these hybrid methods can provide an acceptable level of security for many applications without being overly restrictive or costly.

We describe a statistical database in terms of an abstract model. The model describes neither the database schema nor its implementation; rather, it describes a conceptual view of the data in the database.[12] Its simplicity allows us to focus on the disclosure problem and to compare different controls. We also discuss the simulations and results of a prototype statistical database system. Finally, some conclusions are drawn about the controls described.

STATISTICAL DATABASE MODEL AND INFERENCE CONTROL TECHNIQUES

Statistical Database Model

We assume a statistical database, stipulate that no dependencies between attributes exist and ignore the problems caused by insertions, deletions, and modifications.[8,13,14] Also, we restrict our attention to exact disclosure and consider only the queries for such additive statistics as COUNTs and SUMs, and statistics which can be easily computed from additive statistics (e.g., AVEs). These statistics computed over groups of records having m attribute values in common, corresponding to cells of m-dimensional tables in a lattice of tables.

A database can be viewed as a collection of N logical records, each describing an individual data item. The ith record ($1 \leq i \leq N$) contains values $x_{i1}, \ldots, x_{iM}$ for M attributes $A_1, \ldots, A_M$. Each attribute (or variable) A_k has $|A_k|$ possible values in its domain. Statistics are computed for subsets of records having common attribute values. A set of records is specified by a characteristic formula C called the query set of C, and we use C to denote both a formula and its query set, and ALL to denote a formula whose query set is the entire database (the universe). A query set that can be specified using the values of m distinct attributes (but no fewer) is called an m-order query set or m-set for short. An elementary m-set is an m-set specified by a formula of the form.

$$E = (A_1 = a_{i1}) \& \ldots \& (A_m = a_{i_m}),$$

where $A_1, \ldots, A_m$ are attributes and each a_i is some value in the domain of A_j. Note that all m-order query sets over $A_1, \ldots, A_m$ can be expressed as unions of the elementary sets of the attributes. In our simulation, we shall consider elementary sets only. Given $A_1, \ldots, A_m$, the total number of elementary m-sets is $S_m = \prod_{j=1}^{m} |A_j|$. These S_m sets define an m-dimensional table or m-table T_m, where each attribute A_j corresponds to one dimension of the table.

A database with M attributes has 2^M such tables, corresponding to all possible subsets of the attributes, and each table partitions the database. The set of 2^M tables $T_1, \ldots, T_{2m}$ is a subset of the set of all partitions of the database. The above subset forms a lattice of partitions under the partial ordering relation refinement. Thus, $T_i \leq T_j$ implies that T_i is a refinement of T_j and each elementary set in table T_j corresponds to a union of elementary sets in the table T_i. An example is the lattice of tables defined over four attributes A, B, C, D[4,15] We have, for instance, $ABCD \leq ABD \leq AB \leq B \leq ALL$. An elementary 2-set $(A = a)\&(B = b)$ in table AB, for example, is a union of elementary 3-sets over all possible values of attribute D in table ABD.

$$(A = a)\&(B = b) = \bigcup_{d \in D} (A = a)\&(B = b)\&(D = d)$$

Statistics derived from the values of d attributes are called d-order statistics and it is customary to speak of tables of statistics, where the cells of an m-table contain d-order statistics $f(C,D)$ for the m-sets C of the table. A statistic is sensitive if confidential data could be deduced from the statistic alone. The exact criterion for sensitivity is determined by the policies of the system. In this paper, we shall assume that a sensitive statistic is one with a query set having only one record. Let S be a set of statistics released to some users. Statistical disclosure occurs when release of S allows a user to deduce something about a restricted statistic q. Exact disclosure occurs when q is determined exactly.[2,16,17] If a disclosure occurs without supplementary knowledge, it is called resultant disclosure.[2,18] The disclosure risk, or identification risk, of a table is given by the number or the percentage of sensitive cells in the table.[15,19]

Inference Control Techniques

To control inference, information must be removed from tables with sensitive statistics. There are two broad categories of inference controls, namely, controls that place restrictions on the set of allowable queries, and controls that add noise to the released statistics.[4]

Restriction techniques can be classified according to whether they restrict at the table level or cell level, and according to whether they are a priori, audit based, or memoryless.[4] Table-level controls restrict complete m-tables of statistics in the lattice, including the statistics for all m-sets over the associated attributes. Cell-level control aims to restrict only the sensitive cells of an m-table, and just enough nonsensitive statistics over the associated attributes to prevent inference. A priori controls determine in advance a fixed set of statistics that can be released without compromising any individual's privacy. Audit-based controls keep a history of queries to determine whether release of a statistic, when correlated with previously released statistics, could lead to compromise. Memory-less controls are potentially the most efficient because they are applied at query processing time and do not require an audit trail.

By adding noise to the statistics, perturbation techniques try to permit more statistics than can be permitted with restriction techniques alone. Perturbation techniques can be classified according to whether they are record based or result based (rounding). Given a query $q(C)$, record-based techniques perturb the input to the statistical function for q. Perturbation is accomplished either by taking a sample of the records and estimating $q(C)$ from the sample or by perturbing the data used to compute $q(C)$ from the sample or by perturbing the data used to compute $q(C)$ as they are extracted from the records satisfying C. The cost and variance of both approaches are proportional to the query set size.[4] Rounding techniques perturb the result $q(C)$ after it has been correctly computed. The perturbation typically involves some form of rounding. The cost is small, and the variance is usually a constant proportional to the square of the rounding base. Because errors are confined to a known interval, rounding is more acceptable to users.

Inference controls are judged by three factors, namely cost, accuracy, and security. Cost is determined by the initial implementation requirements, including any computation, plus the overhead in query processing. Accuracy is measured by the number of nonsensitive statistics or tables of statistics that are unnecessarily restricted by the control, and by the amount of noise injected in permitted statistics. This measure does not account for the relative importance of a statistic for a particular study; however, the statistics in m-tables for small m values (i.e., those near the top of the lattice) are more correct than those further down. Security is measured by the relative number of sensitive statistics that can be inferred by circumventing the control and by the difficulty of doing so. Because higher levels of security usually imply higher levels of information loss and cost, the challenge is to find a control with the right balance for the given application and associated risks.

SIMULATIONS AND RESULTS

Simulation

We chose the maximum order,[3,4,20] the maximum table size[3,4,20] and the minimum frequency criterion,[3,20] to combine with the randomization technique[8,10,11] in our simulation. Randomization adds enough noise to the released statistics that most nonsensitive statistics can be released without endangering sensitive statistics, but not so much that the released statistics become meaningless. The amount of noise introduced in our simulation comes from an uniform random number generator with S_m/N as seed. The level of security provided by the three memoryless table restriction controls that we have chosen is determined by the control's threshold.[3,4] The strategy used to set this threshold in our simulation is to adjust the threshold for a somewhat lower level of security and use the randomization technique to control the remaining risk.[4] Each combined scheme has been investigated by a simulation with query types of AVEs for a statistical database with $S_m/N = 1.8$. We also applied the unrestricted randomization technique alone to the same database for comparison. From the simulation results of these candidates, the relative table size criterion looks most promising.

The flow chart of the main modules of this simulation program is shown in Figure 1; they are written in VAX extended PASCAL language compiled under the VAX optimizing PASCAL compiler and run on several VAX-11/730 with VMS Version 4.1. A database has been chosen with S_m/N equal to 1.8 and containing 606 records; this is appropriate for a detailed investigation.

The input is generated by a program; it consists of all possible queries of the same type and on the same m-table.

Required input is as follows:

N : Total number of records
M : Total number of attributes
$|A_1|$: Number of possible values in the domain of attribute A_i $(1 \leq i \leq M)$
⋮
$|A_M|$ (assume the range of its domain is [0, |Ai|])
d : Parameter for order restriction
k_t : Parameter for table-size restriction
k_f : Parameter for mini-freq restriction
order : Order of query set

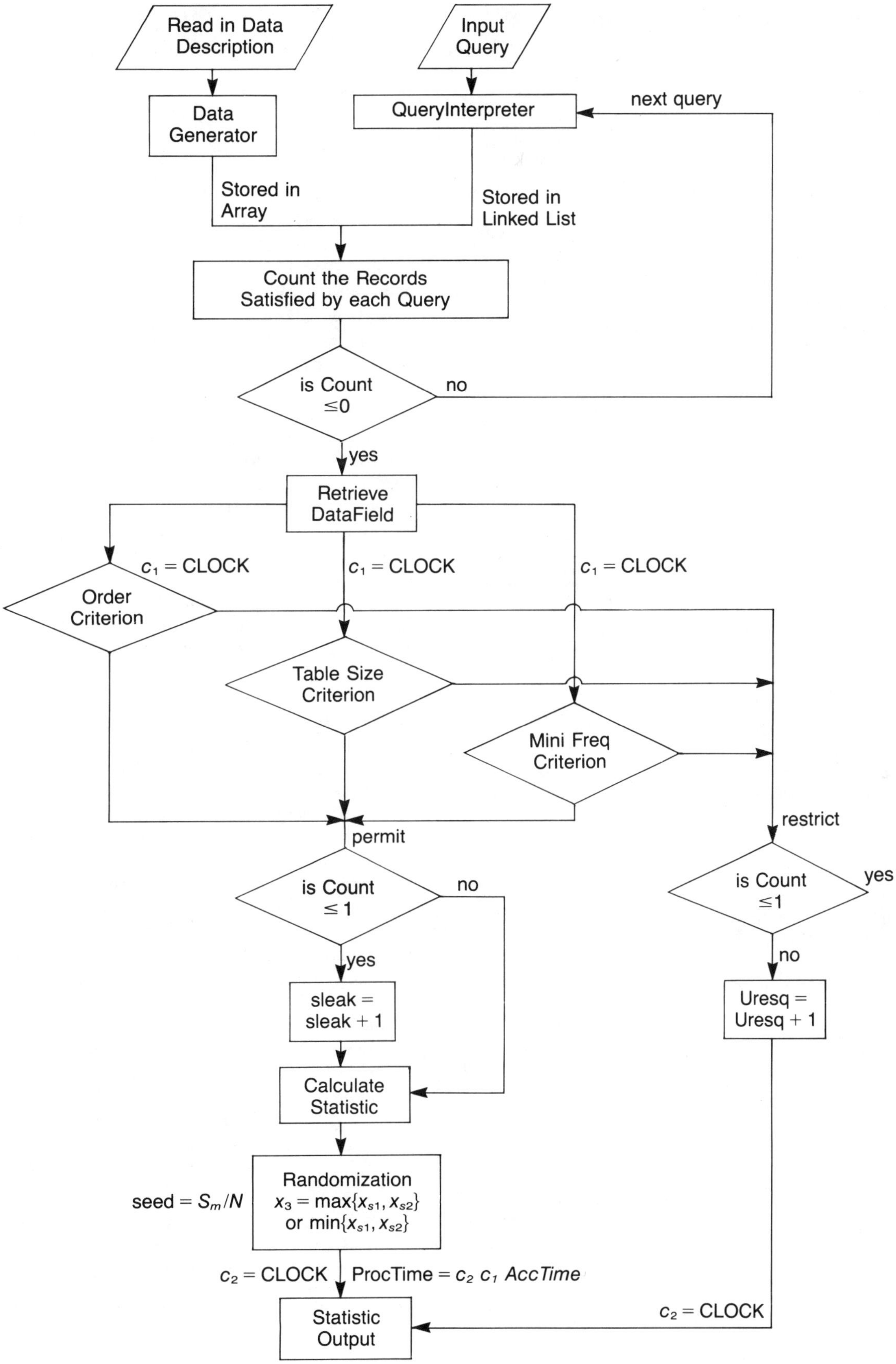

Figure 1—Flow chart of the simulation program

f(C,D) : All possible queries of type f on the *m*-table

⋮

f(C′,D′)

In our simulation procedure, cost is determined by the extra processing time for each security checking which we take to be the time of all required computations plus 1 msec seek time for each extra record retrieved for the security checking. Accuracy is measured by the number of nonsensitive statistics or tables of statistics that are unnecessarily restricted by the control method, and by the amount of noise injected in permitted statistics by randomization. This measure does not account for the relative importance of a statistic for a particular study; however, the statistics in *m*-tables for small *m* values (i.e., those near the top of the lattice) are more correct than those further down.[3] Security is measured by the relative number of sensitive statistics that can be inferred by circumventing the control. For simplicity, we restrict our attention to exact and resultant disclosure only; that is, no approximate disclosures and no supplementary knowledge are included.

Produced output is as follows:

order restriction:
  average processing time: msec
  (assume 1 msec for the accessing of each extra record)
  average % error introduced by randomization: %
  % of unnecessarily restricted queries: %
  % of permitted sensitive statistics: %
table-size restriction:
  average of extra processing time: msec
  (assume 1 msec for the accessing of each extra record)
  average % error introduced by randomization: %
  % of unnecessarily restricted queries: %
  % of permitted sensitive statistics: %
mini-freq restriction:
  average of extra processing time: msec
  (assume 1 msec for the accessing of each extra record)
  average % error introduced by randomization: %
  % of unnecessarily restricted queries: %
  % of permitted sensitive statistics: %

index	A	B	C	D	E	F	G	H	I
1	0	0	0	0	0				
2	0	2	2	2	2				
3	2	4	0	3	1				
.									
.									
.									
606	1	2	4	1	3				
.									
.									
.									
32767									

Figure 2—The 2-dimensional array structure for the simulated statistical database

j	1	2	3	4	5	6	7	8	9
Aij									

Figure 3—The 1-dimensional array structure for the domain of attributes

The simulator models our statistical database by a two dimensional array of size 9 × 32767 stored in main memory via row-major. The first index is with respect to the attributes *A* through *I* and the second index is with respect to the record number. The data structure of the statistical database that we have chosen is illustrated in Figure 2.

Since we assume that the range of the domain for each attribute is between 0 and $|A_{ij}|$, only $|A_{ij}|$ needs to be stored. The data structure for storing $|A_{ij}|$ is illustrated in Figure 3.

The simulated data items stored in memory are created by a uniform random number generator provided by the VMS run time system library. The data are generated and stored row by row. The alphabetical order of each attribute has been used as the original seed to generate the data of each row. The random number generator generates a real number *r* between 0.0 to 1.0. We multiply *r* by $|A_{ij}|$, then apply the VAX extended PASCAL function UTRUNC to give an unsigned integer between 0 and $|A_{ij}|$.

The input queries are interpreted by the procedure QueryInterpreter. For each query, the query type is put into a variable QueryType (a string of length three), the data attribute is put into an integer variable DataField, and the alphabetical order and its required value of each attribute in the characteristic formula are put into an element of a linked list. An example is shown in Figure 4.

The procedure OutputStatistics will call the procedure DataRetrieve to find each record satisfying the formula and to retrieve the value of DataField. For the 0-table *ALL*, it simply goes through all records to retrieve DataField. At the same time the procedure will count the number of records in each query set; if the count is greater than zero then the query is legitimate and it will call procedure Security to check each restriction to see whether to reject the query. If the count is less than or equal to the record number of a sensitive query set (we assume 1 here) and if the statistic has not been restricted, the counter variable sleak (for security leak) will be incremented by one. If sleak is greater than 1 and if the statistic has been restricted, the counter variable *uresq* (for unnecessarily restricted query) will be incremented by one. The VAX extended PASCAL function CLOCK returns an integer value indicating the amount of CPU time in msec used by the current process. The processing time for each security checking is obtained by calculating the difference between two process

```
+----+---+      +----+---+      +----+---+
| *1 | 3 |--->  | *2 | 2 |--->  | *3 | 5 |---+
+----+---+      +----+---+      +----+---+   |
                                             V
QueryType = 'AVE'  DataField = *4

*  Alphabetical order of the attribute
```

Figure 4—The linked list structure for store the input quere AVE ((A = 3)&(B = 5)&c = 5,D)

TABLE I—Number of queries for the 0-table and the results of unrestricted randomization

Table	#Q	ProcTime	%Err	I_m
ALL	5	8.00000	0.0832706	0

CPU times (one before and the other after the security checking procedure), then one msec seek time is added if an extra record accessed for the security checking is necessary. If the query has not been restricted then the procedure calculates the statistic and calls the procedure Randomization which uses a uniform random number generator with a seed equal to S_m/N to get the noise that needs to be added to the statistic and finds out the average error introduced by the randomization technique.

Results

We find that a control combining randomization with table restriction should be very difficult to circumvent.[15] Tables I through VI show that the S_m/N ratios range from 0.003300 to 0.014851 for the 1-tables, from 0.009901 to 0.074257 for the 2-tables, from 0.039604 to 0.297029 for the 3-tables, and from 0.198019 to 0.891089 for the 4-tables. The ratio for the 5-table is 1.78217. Using $k = 10$ with the S_m/N criterion, for example, would restrict none of the 1- and 2-tables, five out of ten 3-tables, all 4-tables, and the 5-table.

The simulation results of applying only the unrestricted randomization technique for each m-table of the statistical database that we have chosen are given in Tables I through VI. The processing time for each security checking is obtained by calculating the difference between two process CPU times (one before and the other after the security checking procedure), then one msec seek time is added for each extra record accessed for the security checking. We count the number of identifications, sets with cardinality equal to one in each m-table, for each complete input query set.[19] The identification risk of a table is given by the number of sensitive cells in the table. Table VII summarizes the simulation results for unrestricted randomization. Tables VIII through X give the simulation results for each restriction with randomization applied to the same database for each m-table.

TABLE II—Number of queries for each 1-table and the results of unrestricted randomization

Table	S_m	S_m/N	$\#Q_1$	$\#Q_2$	ProcTime	%Err	I_m
A	2	0.003300	10	5	2.00000	0.180262	0
B	9	0.014851	45	40	3.75000	1.82666	0
C	5	0.008251	25	20	4.50000	0.593532	0
D	4	0.006601	20	15	2.00000	0.430914	0
E	3	0.004951	15	10	4.00000	0.311046	0

$\#Q_1$ = number of queries tried
$\#Q_2$ = number of legitimate queries (has at least one record in the statistical database)
ProcTime = The Average query processing time of a query in msec
% Err = Average error in % introduced by randomization
I_m = Identification risk

TABLE III—Number of queries for each 2-table and the results of unrestricted randomization

Table	$\|A_1\|$	$\|A_2\|$	S_m	S_m/N	$\#Q_1$	$\#Q_2$	ProcTime	%Err	I_m
AB	2	9	18	0.029703	90	40	4.75000	2.22530	0
AC	2	5	10	0.016501	50	20	5.50000	0.864639	0
AD	2	4	8	0.013201	40	15	5.33333	3.92019	0
AE	2	3	6	0.009900	30	10	2.00000	0.361694	0
BC	9	5	45	0.074257	225	160	4.68750	5.37981	0
BD	9	4	36	0.059406	180	120	4.33333	9.38679	0
BE	9	3	27	0.044554	135	80	3.62500	11.9946	0
CD	5	4	20	0.033003	100	60	4.16667	2.51948	0
CE	5	3	15	0.024752	75	40	5.00000	1.88171	0
DE	4	3	12	0.019802	60	30	5.00000	1.27045	0

$|A_x|$ = number of values of attribute A_x
S_m = number of elementary sets = $|A_1| \times |A_2| \times \ldots$
$\#Q_1$ = number of queries tried
$\#Q_2$ = number of legitimate queries (has at least one record in the statistical database)
ProcTime = The Average query processing time of a query in msec
%Err = Average error in % introduced by randomization
I_m = Identification risk

TABLE IV—Number of queries for each 3-table and the results of unrestricted randomization

Table	$\|A_1\|$	$\|A_2\|$	$\|A_3\|$	S_m	S_m/N	#Q_1	#Q_2	ProcTime	%Err	I_m
ABC	2	9	5	90	0.148514	450	150	5.44828	5.46738	5
ABD	2	9	4	72	0.118811	360	110	5.33333	10.0003	5
ABE	2	9	3	54	0.089768	270	80	5.25000	7.14603	0
ACD	2	5	4	40	0.066006	200	60	4.8333	1.91466	0
ACE	2	5	3	30	0.049504	150	40	3.50000	3.11083	0
ADE	2	4	3	24	0.039603	120	30	4.00000	1.38749	0
BCD	9	5	4	180	0.297029	900	295	5.54717	11.1632	30
BCE	9	5	3	135	0.222772	675	320	3.44332	11.5581	20
BDE	9	4	3	108	0.178217	540	235	3.65217	11.2909	5
CDE	5	4	3	60	0.099009	300	120	4.16667	6.39226	0

$|A_x|$ = number of values of attribute A_x
S_m = number of elementary sets = $|A_1| \times |A_2| \times \ldots$
#Q_1 = number of queries tried
#Q_2 = number of legitimate queries (has at least one record in the statistical database)
ProcTime = The Average query processing time of a query in msec
%Err = Average error in % introduced by randomization
I_m = Identification risk

TABLE V—Number of queries for each 4-table and the results of unrestricted randomization

Table	$\|A_1\|$	$\|A_2\|$	$\|A_3\|$	$\|A_4\|$	S_m	S_m/N	#Q_1	#Q_2	ProcTime	%Err	I_m
ABCD	2	9	5	4	360	0.540594	1800	166	9.88123	9.51869	25
ABCE	2	9	5	3	270	0.445544	1350	265	9.76744	11.7464	50
ABDE	2	9	4	3	216	0.356435	1080	175	6.06897	7.36407	30
ACDE	2	5	4	3	120	0.198019	600	120	6.00000	6.45210	0
BCDE	9	5	4	3	540	0.891089	2700	439	14.3770	11.8939	134

TABLE VI—Number of queries for each 5-table and the results of unrestricted randomization

Table	$\|A_1\|$	$\|A_2\|$	$\|A_3\|$	$\|A_4\|$	$\|A_5\|$	S_m	S_m/N	#Q_1	#Q_2	ProcTime	%Err	I_m
ABCDE	2	9	5	4	3	1080	1.78217	5400	280	8.83986	9.24305	100

$|A_x|$ = number of values of attribute A_x
S_m = number of elementary sets = $|A_1| \times |A_2| \times \ldots$
#Q_1 = number of queries tried
#Q_2 = number of legitimate queries (has at least one record in the statistical database)
ProcTime = The Average query processing time of a query in msec
%Err = Average error in % introduced by randomization
I_m = Identification risk

TABLE VII—simulation results of applied unrestricted randomization technique only

Table	ProcTime	%Err
ALL	8.00000	0.0832706
1–	3.55555	1.06013
2–	4.45217	5.87829
3–	4.49114	9.65619
4–	8.27923	10.2809
5–	8.83986	9.24305

TABLE VIII—Simulation results of order restriction (d = 2) with randomization technique

Table	Rlt	ProcTime	%Err	uresq	sleak
ALL	All Permitted	6.00000	0.117099	0	0
1–	All Permitted	201.778	1.06014	0	0
2–	All Permitted	2728.10	5.87831	0	0
3–	All Restricted	4193.42	9.65622	0	65
4–	All Restricted	5495.56	0	926	0
5–	All Restricted	6894.45	0	180	0

uresq = # of unnecessarily restricted query
sleak = # of permitted sensitive statistics
ProcTime = Processing time in msec (no extra record accessed)
%Err = Average error in % introduced by randomization

TABLE IX—Simulation results of table-size restriction (k = 5) with randomization technique

Table	Rlt	ProcTime	%Err	uresq	sleak
ALL	All Permitted	6.00000	0.117099	0	0
1–	All Permitted	202.889	1.06014	0	0
2–	All Permitted	2728.95	5.87831	0	0
3–	8 Permitted 2 Restricted	4196.67	9.19620	565	15
4–	1 Permitted 4 Restricted	5457.89	0.664594	806	0
5–	All Restricted	6902.36	0	180	0

ProcTime = Processing time in msec (no extra record accessed)

TABLE X—Simulation results of mini-freq restriction (k = 0.015) with randomization technique

Table	Rlt	ProcTime	%Err	uresq	sleak
ALL	All Permitted	30968.0	0.117099	0	0
1–	All Permitted	6389.11	1.06014	0	0
2–	All Permitted	15697.7	5.87831	0	0
3–	All Permitted	22113.4	9.15622	0	65
4–	All Permitted	31716.7	10.2813	0	239
5–	All Restricted	39645.8	0	180	0

ProcTime = Processing time in msec (includes 1 msec for each extra record accessed)
%Err = Average error in % introduced by randomization
uresq = # of unnecessarily restricted query
sleak = # of permitted sensitive statistics

COMPARISON

This section draws some conclusions about each of the controls.

Order Control with Randomization

Table VIII shows that for the order restriction, we conclude that order is probably not useful as a standalone control, but it appears to be a very simple and useful control when combined with the randomization technique. Because higher order tables have already been restricted, no noise is introduced to higher order tables.

Relative Table-size Control with Randomization

Table IX shows that the S_m/N-criterion can control disclosure without falsely restricting too many tables. The most appropriate value for the parameter k, however, depends on the whole database. Moreover, from Table IX we see that considerable information will be lost if we restrict too many tables, such as restricting the descendents of every table having a nonzero identification risk. In our simulation of table-size control with randomization, only those tables with a high risk have been restricted, and we use randomization techniques to thwart attacks on the permitted tables. The 3-tables have a lower average relative error than with the randomization technique alone, because eight of them have already been restricted and so no noise has been introduced there. Also after order control, table-size control is the simplest of the controls to implement.

Nevertheless, we suggest that dynamic strategies, for example those in which the amount of noise introduced increases with S_m/N, could be even better in terms of minimizing information lost.

Minimum Frequency Control with Randomization

The πrmin-criterion is highly secure but overly costly and restrictive. It has the disadvantage over table-size control of requiring more CPU time and more information about the databases (i.e., their frequency distributions). Although the cost need not be prohibitive, if only 1-dimensional frequency distributions are used, another way is to compute and store these frequency distributions periodically as needed to account for the dynamics of the database.

CONCLUSION

In conclusion, our simulation results clearly indicate that the simple schemes—namely, order control and table-size control—when combined with randomizing are very attractive inference control methods, from both the point of view of security and that of associated cost.

REFERENCES

1. Hoffman, L. J. and W. F. Miller. "Getting a Personal Dossier from a Statistical Data Bank." *Datamation,* 16 (1970) 5, pp. 74–75.
2. Denning, D. E. "Restricting Queries that Might Lead to Compromise." *Proceedings of Symposium on Security and Privacy,* 1981, pp. 33–40.
3. Denning, D. E., J. Schlörer, E. Wehrle. "Memoryless Inference Controls for Statistical Databases." Computer Sciences Dept., Purdue University, West Lafayette, Indiana, 1982.
4. Denning, D. E., J. Schlörer. "Inference Controls for Statistical Databases." *IEEE Computer,* July 1983, pp. 69–82.
5. Cox, L. H. "Suppression Methodology and Statistical Disclosure Control." *Journal of the American Statistical Association,* 75 (1980) 370, pp. 377–385.
6. Denning, D. E. *Cryptography and Data Security,* Reading, Massachusetts: Addison-Wesley, 1982.
7. Dobkin, D., A. K. Jones, and R. J. Lipton, "Secure Databases: Protection Against User Inference." *ACM Trans. on Database Syst.* (1979) 1, pp. 97–106.
8. Leiss, Ernst L. *Principles of Data Security*. New York: Plenum Press, 1982
9. Reiss, S. B. "Medians and Database Security." in Demillo, R. A. et al. (eds.) *Foundations of Secure Computation,* New York: Academic Press, 1978.
10. Leiss, Ernst L. "On the Security of Randomized Database: A Simulation." Tech. Report UH-CS-81-01, Dept. of Computer Science, Univ. of Houston, Univ. Park, Houston, February 1981.
11. Leiss, Ernst L. "Protecting Statistical Databases Through Randomizing." Tech. Report UH-CS-81-07, Dept. of Computer Science, Univ. of Houston, Univ. Park, Houston, December 1981.
12. Chin, F. Y. and G. Ozsoyoglu. "Update Handling Techniques in Statistical Databases." *Proceedings of the First LBL Workshop Statistical Databases Management,* Lawrence Berkeley Laboratory, December 1981.
13. Ozsoyoglu, G. and M. Ozsoyoglu. "Update Handling Techniques in Statistical Databases." Technical Report 80-2, Dept. of Computer Science, Cleveland State University, May 1981.
14. Yu, C. T. and F. Y. Chin. "Study on the Protection of Statistical Databases." *Proceedings of ACM SIGMOD International Conference on Management of Data,* 1977.
15. Denning, D. E. "A Security Model for Statistical Databases." Computer Sciences Dept., Purdue University, West Lafayette, Indiana, 1983.
16. Friedman, A. D. and L. J. Hoffman. "Towards a Fail-Safe Approach to Secure Databases." *Proc. Symp. Security and Privacy,* April 1980, pp. 18–21.
17. Schlörer, J. "Identification and Retrieval of Personal Records from a Statistical Data Bank," *Methods Inf. Med.* 14 (1975) 1, pp. 7–13.
18. Haq, M. I. "Insuring Individual's Privacy from Statistical Data Base Users." *AFIPS, Proceedings of the National Computer Conference* (Vol. 44) 1975, pp. 941–946.
19. Schlörer, J. "Disclosure from Statistical Databases: Quantitative Aspects of Trackers." *ACM Trans. on Database Syst.* 5 (1982) 4, pp. 467–492.
20. Schlörer, J. "Confidentiality of Statistical Records: A Threat Monitoring Scheme for On Line Dialogue." *Methods Inf. Med.* 15 (1976) 1, pp. 36–42.

Some thoughts on intelligence in information retrieval

by RAVI SHANKAR SHARMA
St. Francis Xavier University
Antigonish, Nova Scotia, Canada

ABSTRACT

Information retrieval is the process of selectively disseminating relevant information stored among a variety of information objects. A useful method of storing these objects adopts the notion of clustering, where similar objects are placed into homogeneous groups with the expectation that objects within the same group are similar and likely to be relevant to the same queries. The search process during retrieval is thus expedited. Most currently used techniques in information retrieval systems are basically of a statistical nature. However, it is felt that they have reached their performance limits in terms of precision and recall, the common measures of user-satisfaction. New techniques are necessary to maintain the progress in efficient (in terms of computer resources used) and effective (in terms of user-satisfaction) retrieval. We propose a framework incorporating some artificial intelligence strategies for intelligent information retrieval. The experimental prototype of the proposed framework has yielded quite encouraging results.

AN OVERVIEW OF MODERN INFORMATION RETRIEVAL

Information retrieval is the process of selectively disseminating specific information that is stored among a great number of information items; a discipline involved with organization, structuring, retrieval, and display. While the most common use of these methods is in the referencing of bibliographic data, it can also play a vital role as an integral component of the all-encompassing management information system. In general, information retrieval applies methods that select from a given universe of information objects some information relevant to a user's query. By relevance, it is meant that the information is judged by the user to be of interest with respect to a given query. The efficiency and effectiveness of the retrieval are measured in terms of computer resources used (CPU time, memory space) and the degree of satisfaction of fulfilling a user's information needs in reasonable time. The two most commonly cited indicators of user-satisfaction are precision and recall, where precision is the proportion of the retrieved objects that are relevant and recall is the proportion of the relevant objects that are retrieved.

The environments in which information retrieval may be applied are disparate and, consequently, so are the levels of sophistication of the techniques used. Information retrieval today is not limited to library and office applications alone; scientific uses have also been found in biology, chemistry, and engineering. From the bookstack-catalog reading room systems of second century B.C. Alexandrian libraries to the emerging North American "office-of-the-future," the trend has been a progression from systems that provide mere access (storage and retrieval) to those involving calculation (computing), deduction (rule-based instructions, such as, if – then – else), and now, induction (inference).

About 10 percent to 12 percent of the typical workday of managers and executives is occupied by the filing and/or retrieval of information.[1] It is understandably higher for secretaries and library workers. Therefore, the motivation for "automatic" information retrieval is quite unequivocal. In the morass of information that surrounds "real-world" situations, there is an imperative requirement for a conscious, organized, and systematic effort to develop automated systems that will deliver the right information to the right person at the right time. In this day and age of information explosion, automatic and computerized information retrieval is necessary to combat existing and potential situations of information overload.

A simplified concept of information retrieval is shown in Figure 1. An information retrieval system is, in essence, the interface between the document collection and the user. The main elements of such a system are: a finite set of documents, a finite number of user's queries, a document and query representation scheme, a matching function, and an output criterion. The document collection may be articles, books, serials, and other published work in a library, or electronic messages, memos, reports, and organizational statements in an office, or even files and records in a distributed database. Users (library staff and patrons, office workers, management, application programmers) have specific information requirements addressed to the information retrieval system in the form of queries. The system accesses the database of documents and returns to the user the documents that it considers to be what the user wants. This is also known as the response set and is determined according to some matching function and selection criterion. The response set might not always exactly match the user's queries. It is this imprecise nature of the response set that differentiates document retrieval from the more specific data or fact retrieval which returns all and only relevant objects, thus achieving a precision *and* recall of unity.

In the more sophisticated methods of information retrieval, the user is then given the option of providing relevance-feedback. That is, the user is allowed to pass judgement on the system's retrieval, indicating which of the retrieved items are

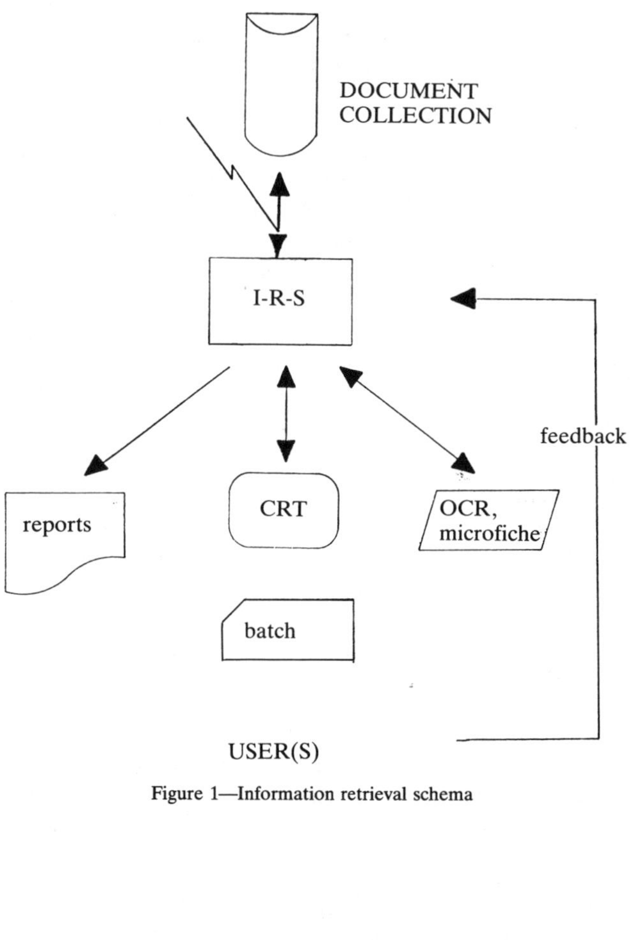

Figure 1—Information retrieval schema

also relevant. This examination of the response set involves the user's browsing through documents, extracting syntactic and semantic information from the text to deduce whether the documents meet the initial information requirements. The feedback provides the basis for correction and enhancement of future performance.

For example, if a user had the query:

What are the economic prospects in Nova Scotia for the next decade?

in mind, the information retrieval system should ideally focus on "economic prospects." "Nova Scotia" and "decade" to initiate a search on the document collection and retrieve budget statements, portfolio management reports, economic forecasts, job market statistics, (at best, on agriculture, forestry, fisheries, and oil), for the user's examination. Now, if the user strictly intended to query the prospect of seeking employment, only the job market information would be accepted (by the user) and all else would be returned as non-relevant, a form of feedback. It is this relevance-feedback feature that makes a system adaptive. The system then automatically senses the emphasis suggested via feedback and continues the search on job market information. The scheme described is known as query reformulation, which addresses the problem of automatically modifying the user-query based on feedback information obtained about the relevance of the response set. In any event, the session terminates on meeting the user's satisfaction. The tradeoff between precision and recall that the user is prepared to be satisfied with depends of course on the application. A casual library patron using an online integrated library system might be content with the first batch of citations rather than wait for more similar documents. On the other hand, a lawyer researching for a case would want all relevant citations (recall approaching unity).

A wide variety of retrieval strategies for determining the relevance (from the system's point of view) of documents relative to a query can be found in the literature.[2,3,4] Figure 2 shows a simple method for this determination. In this scheme, documents and queries are represented by terms, keywords or descriptors. These words are used to describe the content of a document. The process of extracting these words is known as indexing which usually entails tasks such as the removal of non-content words (articles, prepositions, pronouns), suffix stripping, and detection of equivalent stems. Terms are often assigned weights indicating their frequency of occurrence or their discriminating power. There is a host of statistical techniques for exploiting relevance information to weight search terms, rationalized by the fact that they allow the user to state a preference. When a user submits a query to the system, it is in the form of a string of terms (weighted or otherwise). The system then matches the query with the documents in the collection, using certain standard similarity functions, and determines an order of the documents in which the most similar document is first, then the next most similar and so on. The number of documents to be displayed can be controlled by a cutoff rank or threshold similarity value, until the user is satisfied.

This computation of similarity for ranked selection is $O(i*j)$ for i documents with j terms, if the search is sequential. To

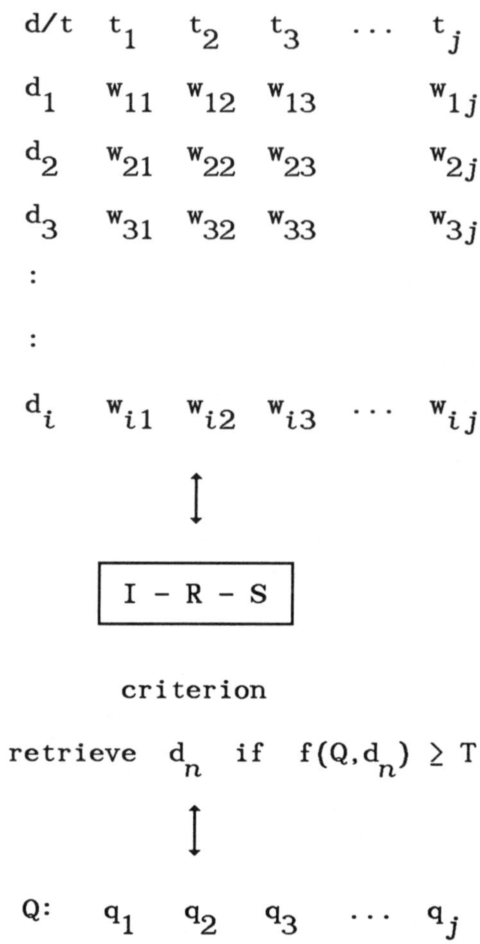

Figure 2—A simple mechanism for document selection

enhance the response time for retrieval, the notion of classification or clustering is adopted. Classification or clustering refers to the process in which similar documents (or their surrogates, such as abstracts, summaries) are placed into homogenous groups (interchangeably called classes or clusters) with the expectation that documents relevant to the same queries will be in the same clusters. It is rationalized by the cluster hypothesis which states that *"closely associated documents tend to be relevant to the same requests."*[3] Thus, searching is limited to comparing the typical document from each cluster, known as the centroid, to the query and possibly retrieving the entire cluster if its centroid is deemed close enough. In this way the search space will be greatly reduced.

Information retrieval systems can thus be seen as possessing the three levels of complexity of management information systems. The technical level includes the routine transactions such as storage and maintenance. The tactical level involves semi-structured decisions like query reformulation and output selection. The strategic level faces the long-term challenges of automatic indexing, clustering. But even these are not without certain problems. In the following section, the shortcomings of the general method of information retrieval outlined above are discussed.

LIMITATIONS OF THE TRADITIONAL APPROACH

Several commercial information retrieval systems currently exist. Among the best known are: Dialog of Lockheed Information Systems; Orbit, a product of System Development Corporation; Medlars, from the National Library of Medicine; and IBM's Stairs.[2,4] These systems, however, go no further than to implement the rudimentary techniques of information retrieval with flat or inverted file structures.

These standard treatments have many shortcomings and limitations associated with them. For one, certain fundamental problems stem from the terms themselves. Indexing is still in a primitive, unsophisticated state notwithstanding the progress made through basic research on the subject.[3] Often, important contextual and semantic considerations are ignored and it is difficult, if not impossible, to describe a hundred-page document with ten to twenty keywords. Furthermore, the assignment of weights to the terms that represent the documents is, at best, a difficult task. Terms are subjective in importance and weights based on frequency of occurrence do not consider the context and semantics. Keyword extraction on graphics-oriented documents (an important consideration given the emerging popularity of visual information systems) and text in, say, Kanji, is not yet possible.

Second, the matching functions that define similarity and therefore relevance (as seen by the system), are computationally tedious. For instance, if there are i documents using a vocabulary of j terms, then a query (similarly represented) would require $O(i*j)$ comparisons to determine the similarities for a simple algorithm reading from a sequential file. Another pitfall is that the feedback in a simple system is performed in the context of a single user query. There is only a limited amount of gain that can be made with such small amounts of feedback. As well, what the system "learns" is quickly forgotten once the current user completes the query session. Finally, the methods of classifying the documents seem to be wanting in many respects. The standard approach is based on $O(i^2)$ associative measurements between the documents, and the clusters are judged against the cluster hypothesis almost as an afterthought!

It has been felt that the traditional statistics-based methods have reached their performance limits in terms of precision and recall.[6] Despite considerable efforts in research, increases in precision and recall have been very small, and researchers have been looking elsewhere for improvement. Techniques from artificial intelligence have been suggested for incorporation into the conventional methods. This has led to the production of some systems which are of the "question-answering" type, such as MYCIN, PROSPECTOR, DENDRAL, HEARSAY, PAM, TAXMAN and MECHO. In the following section, this strategy is outlined with a survey.

INTELLIGENT INFORMATION RETRIEVAL

The study of artificial intelligence primarily embodies the motive of designing and developing more sophisticated systems. Its foundations (representation, problem solving, architecture, and knowledge) already have wide-spread applicability in the more futuristic management information systems. Information retrieval, which seems to have reached a limit on precision and recall with existing techniques, must adapt and adopt new tools and techniques that, if done by humans, would be termed intelligent.

Artificial intelligence is intuitive to, and has tremendous scope in, information retrieval applications. Much work has been done in attempting to overcome the limitations of the conventional approach with such novel, innovative methods. Knowledge representation techniques have been applied to automatic indexing (for example, semantic networks or frames in thesauri construction) to produce expert systems; natural language understanding aids in translating a simple vocabulary into predicate calculus for document representation and query reformulation, heuristic state space searches have been used in attempting to optimize retrieval selection, and learning in clustering. This is in addition to hardware features such as associative and parallel processing in the search phase of retrieval.

An intelligent system is one that is capable of acquiring knowledge so as to improve its performance. Central to this notion of intelligence is the process of learning as defined by Simon.[8] Information retrieval systems depend on the knowledge of bibliographers for indexing and clustering, logico-linguists for text understanding, and, experienced users for search strategies. What is needed is an integrated approach that will acquire knowledge in these areas in a modular form. Several packages, commonly known as question-answering systems, such as MYCIN, PROSPECTOR, DENDRAL, Q&A, HEARSAY, PAM, TAXMAN, MECHO, already do this. Quite expectedly, their design architectures are a hybrid of expert/knowledge-based systems and information retrieval/database systems. In our opinion, the four main techniques of artificial intelligence (drawn among others)[7] that have potential applications in the information retrieval environment are:

Knowledge Representation[9]

The common methods of using frames and scripts seem to be apt for indexing strategies. In a broad sense, signatures may be thought of as frames and abstracts (document surrogates) as scripts. Another promising scheme appears to be the use of semantic networks and conceptual dependencies that attempt to *understand* text. In all cases, a set of rules to extract meanings from phrases in documents to form thesauri before matching with the users' queries in a deductive fashion is clearly superior to straightforward indexing where the stems of the most frequent or discriminatory phrases are selected as representatives. A good declarative mechanism for the representation of structured knowledge from documents is an integral part of the information retrieval problem.

Heuristic Search Strategies

There is considerable agreement in the literature that one of the functions of an expert intermediary is the choice of an appropriate search strategy. Knowledgeable users select a strategy based on their experience, their knowledge of the database, and the query. This approach is relatively easy to conceptualize, but as there are several strategies available, determination of the heuristic will depend on the database and the a priori knowledge of the user. A range of problem-solving techniques[9] including divide-and-conquer, dynamic programming, greedy, breadth- or depth-first, backtracking, seem successfully applicable. But the emerging trend is in the adoption of parallel or associative processing strategies for searching indexes and/or clusters.

Logico-linguistics

Natural language research has yet to come up with a unified theory that will neatly, upon input, transform user queries in natural language sentences into symbolic logical language to be used internally for searching and deductive purposes. Although it is already possible to translate English statements into first order predicate calculus or other logical formations, from which deductive searches could proceed according to well-known methods of theorem proving,[5] it is limited to a subset of the natural language vocabulary making it yet another query language!

Learning[7]

The greatest "proven" potential in applying artificial intelligence to information retrieval seems to be with learning. The notion of learning is intuitive to the classification of documents so as to categorize what users co-access frequently. Probably because there is no dearth of experts—indexers, catalogers, casual users all have some form of contribution to make, either in keyword or document clustering or in retrieval. Several combinations of learning strategies: rote learning (without processing); learning-by-being-told (by an expert); learning-from-examples (induction); learning-from-observation (without a teacher), have been used to improve the storage and retrieval process. In the following section, one instance of the application of learning which is intuitive to the information retrieval problem is outlined.

A FRAMEWORK AND PROTOTYPE

A fundamental problem in artificial intelligence is the automation of inductive inference. Clustering can be viewed as an inductive process. Sharma[10] has proposed a learning algorithm for document storage and retrieval as an alternative to designing an expert system with decision rules. It is an adaptive algorithm[11] that, given training examples with expert decisions, can infer a classification of the document collection and also infer (-by-example) which cluster[5] a user requires. A metric from the theory of Rough Sets[12] guides the learning process.

This work is an attempt to overcome the traditional limitations. It is a novel, self-organizing procedure that provides a setting in which multi-expert-input into the information storage and retrieval is possible and does away with the usage of terms and their weights to describe documents and queries. No similarity computations are therefore required. Feedback is handled by dynamically incorporating user-input during clustering and retrieval. The work therefore advocates a classification-based retrieval-by-example scheme. The framework proposed incorporates learning as a means of attaining intelligent information retrieval. The major disadvantage of the traditional mode of feedback is that the performance element is single-step, indirect learning. There is also no attempt to reconcile inconsistencies and redundancies. All this is overcome.

In the proposed framework, the way of introducing user-input from several experts into the clustering process makes it a sophisticated learning system capable of handling both the case of many experts and the case of an imperfect expert. The method draws from Rough Set theory and an adaptive clustering strategy in order to achieve some amount of self-organization in the database. The relevance judgements of weighted queries are used as the basis for influencing the classification of documents, thus enabling user-input to direct clustering and allow the clustering sub-system to learn. An evaluation metric based on the theory of Rough Sets is used as the clustering criterion, which is enhanced in an iterative fashion.

The clustering algorithm begins with an arbitrary placement of the documents in the collection on a one-dimensional linear space and, as each query arrives, uses the relevance judgements to generate movement along the line so that "similar" documents are moved closer together and "dissimilar" ones moved further apart from each other. The precise definitions of what is meant by similar and dissimilar are also based on ideas from Rough Set theory. After a number of queries are processed, the initial positions change as the system "learns" the users' profiles. The classification, however, is re-clustered only when this movement is deemed significant as defined by a variation of a common measure for determining the similarity between classifications. The general method of clustering places boundaries on gaps so as to optimize the clustering criterion. Efficient and effective retrieval is sought by using a learning scheme known as retrieval-by-example. The prototype experimental implementation of the scheme indicates remarkable potential, producing recall and precision results of between 40 percent to 80 percent.

However, several enhancements to the prototype as it stands may be feasible. First and foremost, a heuristic strategy has been formalized to expedite the re-clustering process. In addition, associative processing[13] seems appropriate for the examination of several clusters concurrently. Rough Set theory also allows for decision rules to be generated as descriptors of the clusters. Implementing such a module will help achieve expert-system capability so that new documents added to the collection can immediately be placed. And, finally, it is pointed out that since the framework does not require the representation of documents as terms, the method is not limited to the traditional Information Retrieval environment alone. This potential for integrating (or including) database management with Information Retrieval must be exploited.

CONCLUDING REMARKS

Some artificial intelligence techniques that can overcome the shortcomings of the standard approach to information retrieval have been surveyed. It is felt strongly that although their application is not altogether new, more of such techniques are imperative if steady improvement in retrieval results are to be gained. Current literature in information retrieval shows that many researchers look beyond the standard statistical techniques and are willing to incorporate more complex artificial intelligence ideas into their work. Some groups have actual working systems (such as SMART, RESUDA, IFS) which possess some amount of intelligence. Future directions in information retrieval can no longer bypass artificial intelligence techniques.

ACKNOWLEDGEMENTS

The clustering and retrieval scheme was supervised by Vijay Raghavan, with financial support from the Faculty of Graduate Studies and Research, University of Regina, Canada. Many thanks are also due to my colleague, Ernst Schuegraf, for discussing with me the theme of the paper, and to St. Francix Xavier University for continuing to fund this project.

REFERENCES

1. Somberg, B. "Cognitive Processes in Information Storage and Retrieval." *Proceedings of the ACM Conference,* 1982, pp. 79–81.
2. Bartschi, M. "An Overview of Information Retrieval Subjects." *IEEE Computer Magazine,* 18 (1985) 5, pp. 67–84.
3. van Rijsbergen, C. J. *Information Retrieval,* (2nd ed.), London: Butterworths, 1979.
4. Blair, D. C., & M. E. Maron. "An Evaluation of Retrieval Effectiveness for a Full Text Document Retrieval System." *Communications of the ACM,* 28 (1985) 3, pp. 289–299.
5. Cooper, W. S. "Bridging the gap between AI and IR." in C. J. van Rijsbergen (ed.), *Research and Development in Information Retrieval,* Cambridge: Cambridge University Press, 1984.
6. Croft, B. "Artificial Intelligence and Information Retrieval—Performance for a price." Invited presentation at the 8th Annual International Conference on Research and Development in Information Retrieval, 1985, Montreal.
7. Cohen, R. R., & E. A. Feigenbaum. *The Handbook of Artificial Intelligence,* (Vol. 1–3), Los Altos: William Kaufmann, 1982.
8. Simon, H. "Why Should Machines Learn?" In R. R. Michalski et al. (eds.), *Machine Learning: An Artificial Intelligence Approach,* California: Tioga Publishing, 1983.
9. Rich, E. *Artificial Intelligence,* New York: McGraw Hill, 1983.
10. Sharma, R. "Adaptive Information Retrieval: A Framework and an Experimental Prototype." Computer Science Dissertation, University of Regina, July, 1986.
11. Yu, C. T., Y. T. Wang, & C. H. Chen. "Adaptive Document Clustering." Invited presentation at the 8th Annual International Conference on Research and Development in Information Retrieval, 1985, Montreal, Canada.
12. Pawlak, Z. "On Learning—A Rough Set Approach." In A. Skowron (ed.), *Lecture Notes in Computer Science (208),* Berlin: Springer-Verlag, 1986.
13. Schuegraf, E. "Indexing for Associative Processing." *Canadian Journal of Information Science,* (Vol. 5) 1980, pp. 93–101.

Beyond the command-response model for PC-based front-ends: Some design principles and their application

by DAVID E. TOLIVER
Institute for Scientific Information
Philadelphia, Pennsylvania

ABSTRACT

Personal computers are often used for front-end software that mediates retrieval of information from databanks. The native information retrieval language of databank systems usually follows a command-response model of user interaction. PC front-end software has often conformed to this model. However, this is neither necessary nor optimal, as more acceptable models for user interfaces on PCs can and should be used by front-ends. This paper states five practical principles for breaking away from the older to the newer models. Examples of the application of these principles are taken from the author's experience in developing a new software product, tentatively named CC-Mate, that assists with access to Current Contents Search, a new database from the Institute for Scientific Information.

DEFINITIONS AND SCOPE

A "databank" is a commercially accessible mainframe with a selection of databases. Users access the mainframe in order to search these databases. Databanks give access to bibliographic, full text, scientific, business, and econometric databases. Examples of databanks include Dialog, Mead, BRS, Dow Jones, and services of CompuServe.[1]

A "front-end" is any computer system placed between users and databanks with the intent of monitoring activities or assisting users with databank transactions. Some front-ends provide access to a broad range of databases and databanks while others focus on a small number of databases, often from one provider. Three places have proven to be practical for implementing front-ends: on the databank host itself (e.g., BRS AfterDark); on a shared access remote computer (e.g., EasyNet); and on distributed PCs, (e.g., the Sci-Mate Searcher).[2]

Front-ends give easier, faster or more complete search results and improve the cost-performance of information retrieval. Front-ends do some or all of the following: assist in preparing a strategy before the online session; automate logging on and off databanks; simplify use of the retrieval language; assist with syntactic details of particular databases; capture results in electronic form; and process the results after the session.

THE COMMAND-RESPONSE USER INTERFACE MODEL FOR INFORMATION RETRIEVAL

Databanks first became available when 300-baud telecommunication with TTY terminals was standard. The relatively slow rates of 300 to 2400 baud via packet-switching networks is still the standard link to databanks. On many databanks, the native retrieval language has not evolved much since it was first designed: the databank prompts the user for some command and responds to the command with results.

Most front-ends also follow this model of interaction. This is not necessary and underutilizes a PC's potential. Very little of a PC processor is needed to handle the arrival of asynchronous characters. Most front-end packages, though, use the PC processor for much of the session only to serve characters to the screen.

THE FULL-SCREEN USER INTERFACE MODEL ON PERSONAL COMPUTERS

In contrast to the slow serial command-response model, the entire video display of a PC can be refreshed almost instantly. The screen can be divided into regions through which the user can navigate with the mouse or cursor. Windows imply additional regions "hidden" behind the screens. Internal memory and external mass-storage accommodate programs, supporting data, and even complete electronic transcripts of results.

The principles below emphasize taking advantage of the full-screen user interface found in many PC application packages. They have been applied at ISI in the development of a new front-end program, CC-Mate. This program assists users of a new ISI database, Current Contents Search, available on the BRS databank.

DESIGN PRINCIPLES FOR FRONT-ENDS AND APPLICATION EXAMPLES

Principle 1: The front-end should support user activities before and after the online search session itself. CC-Search's built-in full-screen editor allows users to prepare their search profile. Data tables with details about the structure and content of the database can be recalled. The same edit commands can be used to clean up transcripts of search results, both during the session and after logging off.

Principle 2: Front-ends should provide ongoing status and options as well as innovative features made possible by full-screen access to the profile and results. Detailed status is continually on display in CC-Mate; action and information options are continually available. Terms in the results can be selected as profile queries by "pointing and clicking"; the full text of referenced items can be ordered from ISI or from the reprint author by pressing a single function key.

Principle 3: The user and database interfaces should be isolated from each other in their own modules of the computer program. These distinct interfaces are linked only in a main event loop. Code isolation simplifies maintenance and makes it easier to extend the product to support users of other databanks and databases.

Principle 4: Temporal interleaving of the user and database interface activities improves the cost-effectiveness of the front-end. As results continue to stream into buffers from the serial line, the user can examine and edit all results, summaries, status data, and options. Immediate information gives the user more control over the session, while not halting the incoming flow of results.

Principle 5: The functions carried out by the user and database interfaces need not correspond one-for-one. For example, CC-Mate merges the Select, Limit, and Print functions of BRS under a single function called Display. This gives users results from a query in a single step. Also, when the user alters a query in the profile, the sequence of commands to the databank will be redirected without changing the profile's own sequence with which the user is familiar.

REFERENCES

1. Pemberton, J. "Databank." *Online,* (9) May, 1985, p. 95.
2. Toliver, D.E. "Whither and Whether Micro-based Front-Ends." In *Proceedings of the Second Conference on Computer Interfaces and Intermediaries for Information Retrieval.* DTIC/TR-86/5, Alexandria, VA: Defense Technical Information Center, 1986, pp. 225–234.

Expert front ends in the environment of multiple information sources

by GABRIEL JAKOBSON
GTE Laboratories, Inc.
Waltham, Massachusetts

Among many different aspects of information retrieval from a single source one may separate three major tasks performed by a database intermediary (either person or system): conceptual analysis of the request and formal specification of the query; planning and control of the search process; and representation of the results. The addition of at least one more information source creates one new obligatory task: data (or document) base selection, and two optional tasks: data integration from multiple sources and unification of the data (document) display formats.

The multiple database environment poses challenging tasks to expert database front-ends. In many cases the database request may be decomposed into a set of isolated sub-requests and a particular independent database should be selected to satisfy each sub-request. The existence of alternative databases leads to the task of optimization of the selection procedure, where criteria like user model, cost, level of data abstraction, may be taken into account.

In a more complicated case, the request may be integrated (i.e., several dependent databases should be accessed simultaneously in order to satisfy the request). This case brings us to the task, which may be called database navigation. Database navigation implies that a sequence of related databases should be planned: the result from one database in this sequence is used for specification of the data selection condition for the next database. The database navigation task is performed by joining cross-database files. It includes two optimization tasks: selection of the path of the cross-database join fields and selection of the file join methods. Both analytical and heuristic rule-based methods may be used for solving these problems. The database navigation task is most naturally associated with relational and hierarchical databases. It is hard to justify the database navigation task for document retrieval systems, unless we know how to extract meaningful parts from the test, or read it by machines.

There is one important aspect of a general nature in data retrieval: the user's understanding of the subject area and now the initial request is described are not necessarily directly related to the actual data files and fields. Many different views and interpretations may be built on top of the stored data. We may consider these views as virtual databases. The end user communicates with the database intermediary using the terms of the virtual database; the task of the intermediary is to map these terms into the real databases, files and fields. This task, as well as the database selection and navigation tasks, is knowledge extensive and needs expertise.

Finally, there is a result representation task. The primitive solution is physical concatenation of records retrieved from different sources. However, in most applications the unification of the data display formats adopted by different databases is required. A more complicated solution evolves semantic data fusion with resolution of conflicting data, eliminating duplicates, and extrapolating gaps. The response returned to the user may be aggregated and contain general meta-statements about the data.

The solution of building front ends capable to perform the above mentioned tasks lies in the area of knowledge based expert systems. The examination of the behavior of human experts—database analysts or information retrieval specialists—gives us a picture of what kind of knowledge and decision making procedures are required to perform the data (document) retrieval tasks. The knowledge may be classified as follows: (1) subject area knowledge, (2) user profile, (3) knowledge about database structures (data dictionaries), (4) knowledge about inter-database relations, (5) knowledge about network communication protocols, and (6) knowledge about database query languages and DBMSs.

We will present general architectural principles and design solutions of a specific expert front end called Intelligent Database Assistant (IDA) developed at GTE Laboratories.[1] IDA is designed to retrieve data from multiple heterogeneous databases. IDA performs the tasks of automatic database selection, database navigation, formal target database query generation, and connection to different remote databases. The user may communicate with IDA, either formulating a natural language query or interacting through a menu interface. The process of converting the virtual query into the set of target database queries includes the steps of selecting the database(s), finding the optimum cross-database join fields, finding the best join algorithm, mapping from the subject area objects and relations into the database files and fields, and shaping the query according to the syntactic constraints of the target database query languages.

IDA is built in an expert fashion: it contains a generic procedural part and a compartmental knowledge base. The knowledge base has parts representing the subject area, database management, database, and communication knowledge. The experimental version of the system is implemented on XEROX 1186 Artificial Intelligence workstation, and it accesses databases residing on remote hosts. The current implementation accesses ORACLE, DB2, and FOCUS relational databases, and also ASI-STable files.

REFERENCE

1. Jakobson, G., C. Lafond, E. Nyberg and G. Piatetsky-Shapiro. "An Intelligent Database Assistant." *IEEE Expert,* 1 (1986), 2, pp. 65–79.

Thoughts about intermediary systems in information retrieval

by GERARD SALTON
Cornell University
Ithaca, New York

In information retrieval, we must deal with many hundreds of different data bases, and with several dozen search and retrieval services used to provide access to these databases. In view of the common operating requirements of all retrieval services, namely large file sizes, on-line operations conducted by end-users or search intermediaries, and system responses provided to users in real time, the normal sequential search methods cannot be used. Instead, it becomes necessary to use auxiliary indexes capable of providing access to specific subsections of the files. At the present time, all operating retrieval sevices use large (inverted) index files to obtain fast search output with acceptable retrieval effectiveness.

Even though the internal data organization and the search strategies are effectively identical, the access protocols and command structures used by the many retrieval services are very different, and generally incompatible with each other. To bridge the gap between the common internal operating characteristics and the multiple external access protocols, user accessing aids have been designed consisting of easy-to-use front-ends, expert advice systems for query formulation and submission, and gateways capable of reaching the proper retrieval service and record files. The regrettable proliferation in noncompatible retrieval services is now matched by an equally large number of noncompatible intermediary and gateway systems.

The many different retrieval systems and intermediary services can effectively be replaced by a common query formulation and query submission system based on natural language manipulations. Such a system would provide the following facilities:

1. Initial query analysis in terms of weighted attribute vectors
2. Global collection matching facilities designed to identify the relevant document collections that must be searched in a particular instance
3. Global document matching facilities designed to provide ranked output of retrieved documents in response to submitted queries
4. Displays of expanded query vocabularies consisting of thesaurus contents and relevant phrases to be used in generating improved query formulations
5. Relevance feedback facilities designed to construct improved query formulations by automatic methods.

Such a common interface system could serve as a cornerstone for a highly effective and easily usable retrieval facility.

Graphical query languages for semantic database models

by BOGDAN CZEJDO, RAMEZ ELMASRI, and MAREK RUSINKIEWICZ
University of Houston
Houston, Texas
and
DAVID W. EMBLEY
Brigham Young University
Provo, Utah

ABSTRACT

Graphical representations of database schemas such as entity-relationship diagrams are commonly used to support database design. In this paper we discuss graphical representations of semantic data models and their application to interactive query languages. Operators that are appropriate for graphical query formulation are defined for several semantic data models. We also discuss a general method for implementing graphical interfaces to database systems that can be applied to a wide range of semantic data models.

INTRODUCTION

Graphic display can frequently enhance user understanding of complex objects. Since database schemas have considerable complexity, it is not surprising that several graphic representations, such as Bachman diagrams and entity-relationship (ER) diagrams, have emerged.[1,2,3] These diagrams can conveniently represent database schemas and have been used extensively to support database design activities.

Graphic representations may also be used to support database query formulation. Rather than require a user to write a symbolic expression in a disciplined style using a formal query language, a graphical language could allow a user to formulate queries interactively, by working directly with some kind of diagram. This method of query formulation would take advantage of available graphical interfaces and pointing devices to provide a friendlier user interface to a database system and benefit both novice and experienced users. Two of the earliest query languages specifically designed for use with an interactive two-dimensional interface are QBE[4] and CUPID.[5] Graphical query interfaces are also discussed in several additional papers.[6,7,8,9,10,11,12,13]

In this paper we present a method of query formulation for various semantic data models with natural graphical representations. For each data model, our approach is to define graphical operators that allow an end-user to manipulate a diagram until it represents a desired query. In the same way that a semantic-model diagram represents the schema of the database, a modified diagram (usually much smaller) can represent the query. From the end user's point of view the data in a stored database is manipulated in a manner consistent with changes made to a graphic representation.

We also describe the semantics for these operators and discuss ways of implementing them efficiently. We assume that an underlying database system exists that can be described by a relational schema and manipulated by relational operators. The graphical operators specified by a user are transformed into relational operators for processing.

Three data models will be discussed as an example of our approach. The entity-relationship model[3] has a natural graphical representation in the form of ER-diagrams. The second example is based on the entity-category-relationship (ECR) model.[14] This model constitutes an extension of the ER model by introducing the concept of a category. The third example is based on an extended relational model.[15] In addition to relations, this model also contains connectors, which allow a natural graphical representation of a database schema.

The paper is organized as follows. First, a general approach to graphical query formulation for semantic data models is discussed. The application of our approach to interactive query formulation is illustrated for an ER model, for the ECR model, and for an extended relational model. We describe an implementation method applicable to these and other similar semantic data models and illustrate the approach by giving details for the ER model. Finally, conclusions are drawn.

GRAPHICAL QUERY FORMULATION

A graphical representation of a database using a particular semantic data model is an abstract description of the schema of the database. Views and queries can also be represented using this same abstract description, and thus, graphical query formulation can consist of manipulating a schema diagram so that it represents the query. The general approach is to discard unneeded portions of the diagram and modify the remainder of the diagram such that it defines the desired query. Diagram manipulating operators are defined to perform these actions. The final result of a query is produced when the graphically formulated query is applied to the current database instance.

A possible screen layout for a graphical interface would be to display a schema diagram together with the list of applicable operators and reserve an area on the screen for messages between the system and user. Large diagrams can be viewed using a windowing mechanism. A user manipulates a diagram by pointing to an operator and then to its operands. Depending on the operator, the user may also enter text in the message area. After each operation, a new diagram is displayed. The diagram displayed on the screen corresponds to the current view of the data and can always be interpreted as a query.

This approach to query formulation has the following advantages:

1. The query language is two dimensional. Pictorial diagrams that depict a view of the database schema are displayed and can be manipulated interactively.
2. Query formulation is flexible. A query can be formulated in many different ways since the order in which the diagram manipulating operators are invoked is often immaterial.
3. The user always has a convenient frame of reference. The current diagram reflects the current status of query formulation and is always a valid query.
4. The approach is applicable to a wide range of semantic data models.
5. An undo operator, which reverses the last operation(s), can be easily implemented by keeping a copy of the model state, corresponding to the previous step(s), on a stack.

6. Immediate feedback is provided whenever an operator is invalid in the current context. Thus, a user is assisted by being immediately informed about possible errors.
7. The intended query can be specified in several different ways corresponding to different levels of diagram reduction. The strategy to be used can be selected by the user.

We now illustrate how queries are formulated graphically for an ER model, the ECR model, and an extended relational model.

GRAPHICAL QUERY FORMULATION FOR AN ER MODEL

Figure 1(a) shows an ER diagram corresponding to a simple database for a university. Queries can be formulated by manipulating ER diagrams with the following operators.

Relationship-Set Delete (R1): This operator removes the relationship set R1 from the diagram.

Entity-Set Delete (E1): This operator removes the entity set E1 from the diagram. All relationship sets associated with E1 are also removed.

Relationship-Set Project (R1, Z): This operator restricts the attributes of the relationship set R1 to the (possibly empty) set of attributes Z. Thus, attributes of relationship sets may be removed by invoking this operator.

Entity-Set Project (E1, Z): Like relationship-set projection, this operator restricts the attributes of the entity set E1 to the (possibly empty) set of attributes Z. Entity sets with no attributes are useful for specifying indirect relationships, for example, the courses taught by a particular student's advisor.

Relationship-Set Restrict (R1, e): This operator restricts a relationship set to the subset of relationship objects that satisfy a boolean restriction expression e.

Entity-Set Restrict (E1, e): This operator restricts an entity set to the subset of entity objects that satisfies a boolean restriction expression e. This operator not only imposes a boolean restriction expression on entity set E1, it also alters the associated relationship sets to ensure that referential integrity is maintained. Thus, the operator guarantees that when an entity e1 is removed from an instance of E1 by condition e, every relationship instance involving e1 is also removed.

There are also operators for set union, set intersection, set difference, renaming attributes and entity and relationship sets, duplicating diagrams to formulate self-referencing queries, and creating new relationships among existing entities. A minimal set of operators has been identified and has been shown to have the expressive power of Codd's relational algebra.[16]

As an example of query formulation by manipulating ER diagrams, consider the following query: "Get names of all faculty members who are currently teaching the student whose Id# is '123456789'." We assume that the current ER diagram is the one shown in Figure 1(a).

This query can be specified in several phases. In the first phase, unnecessary entities and relationships are removed. This can be achieved by selecting the delete operator and pointing at ADVISES. This generates the following ER-algebraic operator:

Relationship-Set Delete(ADVISES)

In the second phase, the selection conditions are specified by choosing the restrict operator, pointing at the attribute Id# of STUDENT and entering the value '123456789'. This generates the following operator:

Entity-Set Restrict(STUDENT, Id# = '123456789')

In the third phase, unnecessary attributes of entities and relationships are deleted by selecting the operator project and pointing at STUDENT, CLASS, and Name (of FACULTY). This generates:

Entity-Set Project(STUDENT, ϕ)
Entity-Set Project(CLASS, ϕ)
Entity-Set Project(FACULTY, {Name})

At this point the schema diagram is as shown in Figure 1(b). This ER diagram specifies the query and can be interpreted as explained in the Implementation section.

EXTENSIONS FOR THE ECR MODEL

The ECR (Entity-Category-Relationship) model extends the basic ER model with the concept of category. An ECR diagram extends ER diagrams to graphically display categories. In the ECR model, there are two types of categories: subclass categories and generalization categories.

The graphical representations of categories is shown in Figure 2(a). Subclass categories are used to model a subset of entities from an entity set. In Figure 2(a), GRAD-STUDENT is a subclass category of the entity set STUDENT. STUDENT is called the defining entity set of GRAD-STUDENT. A category can have additional specific attributes that apply only to entities that are members of the category. In addition, a category can have specific relationships in which only entities that are members of the category can participate. In Figure 2(a), a specific attribute, Undergrad-School, and a specific relationship, IS-THESIS-ADVISOR, are specified for the GRAD-STUDENT category.

A subclass category specifies a restriction on the entities in the defining entity set. Hence, GRAD-STUDENT contains only the entities from STUDENT that are graduate students. The subclass category inherits all attributes and relationships of the defining entity set, since every entity of the category is also a member of the defining entity set. Hence, GRAD-STUDENT will also have all attributes of STUDENT.

For graphical query formulation, we can include additional operators to deal with subclass categories. All the operators that apply to entity sets can also apply to categories. Deleting a defining entity set E results in automatic deletion of all subclass categories of E. Deleting a subclass category, however, does not affect entities in the defining entity set. To ensure that entities in subclass categories are subsets of the

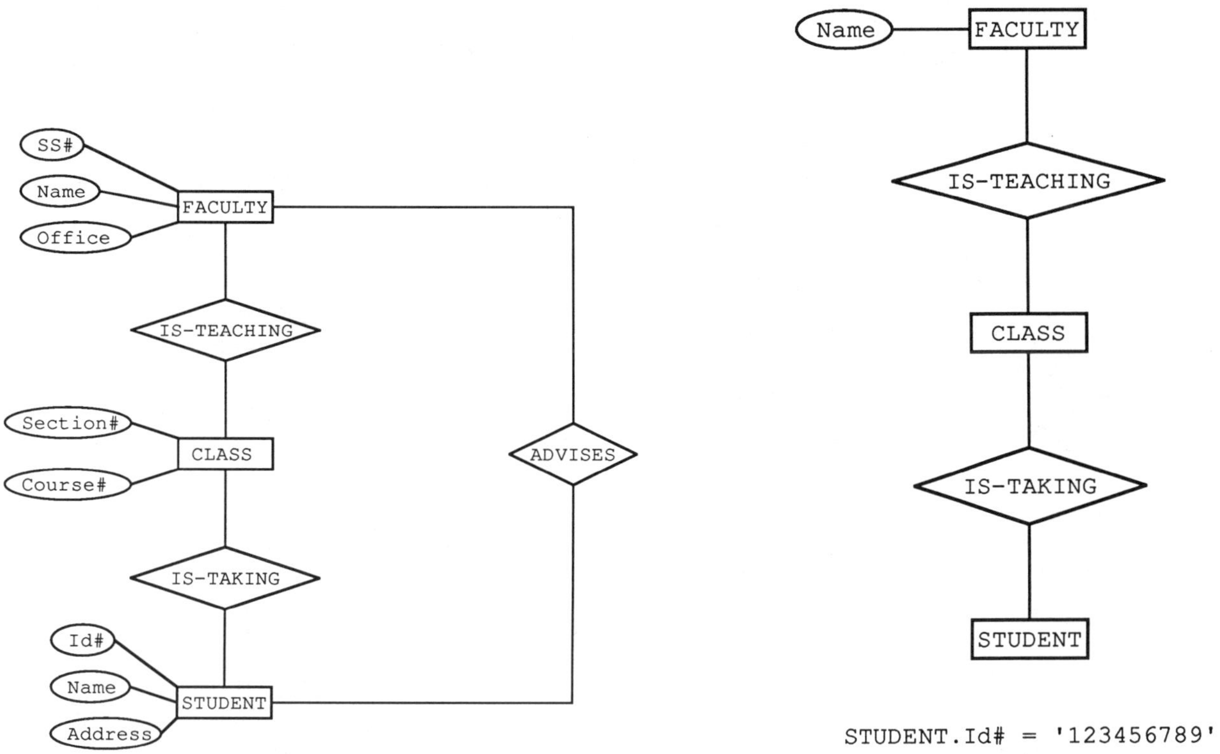

(a) A sample ER schema diagram

(b) Transformed ER schema diagram

Figure 1—Example for the ER model

entities in their defining entity set, restricting a defining entity set E results in automatic restriction of all subclass categories of E. Restricting a subclass category, however, does not affect entities in the defining entity set.

In addition, we can include an operator subclass-category-combine that restricts a defining entity set to those entities that are members of a category. Hence, this operator is similar to an entity-set restrict without an explicit condition—the condition is that entities must be members of the category.

Subclass-Category-Combine (E1, C1). The category C1 is combined with its defining entity set E1 to yield a new entity set E2 with the same name as C1. The entities in E2 are restricted to those in C1, and the attributes of E2 are the union of the attributes of E1 and C1. E2 will participate in any specific relationships in which C1 or E1 participated. To maintain referential integrity, all relationship instances in which any removed entity of E1 participated are removed. All other subclass categories of E1 are removed from the ECR diagram.

The second type of category in the ECR model is the generalization category, which represents the union of entities from two or more disjoint entity sets that participate in some relationship in the same role. Figure 2(a) shows a generalization category VEHICLE-OWNER that is (a subset of) the union of the FACULTY and STUDENT entity sets. The entities in the category VEHICLE-OWNER participate in the role of owners in the OWN relationship with the VEHICLE entity set.

All the graphical operations that apply to entity sets can also be applied to generalization categories. However, a delete operation on one of the defining entity sets E automatically implies that entities in the generalization category that are members of E are automatically deleted. For example, a Entity-Set Delete(FACULTY) also deletes all FACULTY entities from the VEHICLE-OWNER category. This is necessary to maintain the category subset constraint. Similarly a restrict operation on one of the defining entity sets E implies that if entities removed from E are also in the generalization category, they are automatically removed.

A generalization category can also be combined with one of its defining entity sets to restrict members of the category to those entities in the defining entity set. This operator is called Generalization-Category-Combine.

Generalization-Category-Combine (E1, C1): The category C1 is combined with one of its defining entity sets E1 to yield a new entity set E2. The name of E2 is the concatenation of the names of E1 and C1. The entities in E2 are restricted to those in C1 that are members of the entity set E1, and the attributes of E2 are the union of the attributes of E1 and C1. E2 will participate in any relationships in which E1 or C1 participated. To maintain referential integrity, however, all relationship instances in which any removed entity participated are removed. All defining entity sets of C1 (including E1) are removed from the ECR diagram.

The two category combine operations are used to restrict a set of entities, as well as to cause explicit attribute inheritance

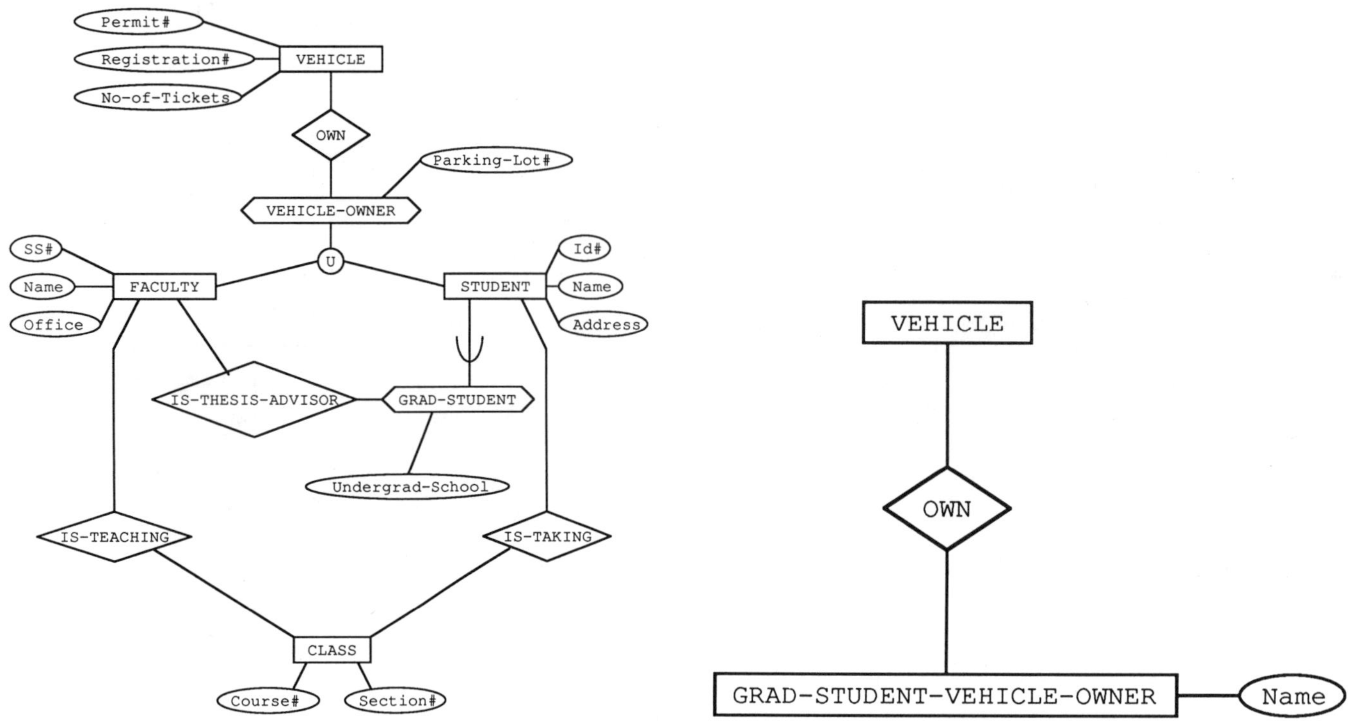

(a) A sample ECR schema diagram

(b) Transformed ECR schema diagram

Figure 2—Example for the ECR model

in the displayed ECR diagram. Hence, they are used for queries in which only some of the entities in an entity set or a generalization category are selected. For example, suppose we want to formulate the query to retrieve the names of all graduate students who have at least one parking ticket outstanding. Assume that the ECR diagram shown in Figure 2(a) represents the database schema.

In the first phase, we remove all unneeded entity sets, categories, and relationships. This is accomplished by pointing at the delete operator and then at FACULTY and CLASS, which generates the following operators:

Entity-Set Delete(FACULTY)
Entity-Set Delete(CLASS)

In the second phase, we graphically specify operators to combine GRAD-STUDENT with STUDENT and then to combine the resulting GRAD-STUDENT entity set with VEHICLE-OWNER. The operators generated are:

Subclass-Category-Combine(STUDENT, GRAD-STUDENT)
Generalization-Category-Combine(GRAD-STUDENT, VEHICLE-OWNER)

Finally, we use the graphical interface to restrict VEHICLE to those with at least one ticket outstanding, and then to project on the GRAD-STUDENT name. The operations generated are the following:

Entity-Set Restrict(VEHICLE, No-of-Tickets > 0)
Entity-Set Project(VEHICLE, ϕ)
Entity-Set Project(GRAD-STUDENT-VEHICLE-OWNER, {Name})

Figure 2(b) shows the final reduced diagram. Since this is a regular ER diagram, it can be interpreted as discussed in the Implementation section.

GRAPHICAL QUERY FORMULATION FOR AN EXTENDED RELATIONAL MODEL

Figure 3(a) shows a schema diagram for an extended relational model.[15] Each relation of the database is represented on the schema diagram by a relation descriptor consisting of the relation name and the relation attributes. We extend the relational schema diagram by adding connectors. Pairs of attributes of relation descriptors can be connected and a boolean-valued operator over the connected attributes can be specified. (The model can also include connectors that relate more than two attributes.) We formulate queries by manipulating diagrams for the extended relational model with the following operators.

Delete Connector (C1): This operator deletes connector C1 from the diagram.

Add Connector (R1, A1, R2, A2, θ): This operator creates a θ-comparison connector between attribute A1 of relation descriptor R1 and attribute A2 of relation descriptor R2. A1 and A2 must, of course, be θ-comparable attributes.

Delete Relation (R1): This operator removes relation descriptor R1 from the diagram and also removes any connectors associated with the removed relation descriptor.

Add Relation (N1, Z, T): This operator creates a constant relation named N1 whose attributes are given in the set Z and whose tuples are given in the set T, adds the relation to the stored database, and adds its relation descriptor to the model. We may use this operator along with add connector to restrict our query to particular constant values.

Delete Attributes (R1, Z): This operator removes the set of attributes Z from the descriptor of relation R1. Any connection descriptor that references a deleted attribute is also deleted.

There are also operators for combining relations using set union and set difference, explicitly reducing diagrams by joins, renaming attributes and relation descriptors, and duplicating diagrams to formulate self-referencing queries.[15]

As an example of query formulation for the relational model extended by connectors, we show how to manipulate the diagram to specify the sample query: "Get names of all faculty members who are currently teaching the student whose Id# is '123456789'." We assume that the current diagram is the one shown in Figure 3(a).

As before, the query can be specified in several phases. In the first phase, unnecessary relations and connectors are removed. For our example a user points at the delete-connector operator and then at the connector to be removed. This generates the following algebraic operator:

Delete Connector((STUDENT, Advisor, FACULTY, SS#,'='))

In the second phase, the selection conditions are specified. This can be done by pointing at a graphical select operation, pointing at the Id# attribute (of STUDENT) and entering '123456789'. This generates the following operators:

Add Relation(T1, {Id#}, {<Id#:'123456789'>})
Add Connector(STUDENT, Id#, T1, Id#,'=')

In the third phase, the attributes to be displayed are marked, resulting in the schema diagram of Figure 3(b) where marked attributes are underlined with stars. This diagram specifies the query and can be translated into executable code as explained next.

IMPLEMENTATION MODEL

The operators for the semantic data models can be implemented in several ways. If the underlying database management system supports a data manipulation language (DML) corresponding to the semantic data model (e.g., GORDAS[17] for the ER model), our operators can be directly translated into equivalent semantic DML queries. An alternative and more general solution is to map graphical operators into equivalent algebraic operations on a corresponding relational database schema. This approach will be presented below using the ER model as an example.

A mapping from an ER diagram into an equivalent relational schema can be defined as follows. For each entity set, we assume the existence of a relation scheme whose name is the name of the entity set and whose attribute set consists of the attributes of the entity set plus a surrogate key attribute.[18] For each relationship set, we assume the existence of a relation scheme whose name is the name of the relationship set and whose attribute set consists of the attributes of the relationship set plus the surrogate key attributes of the associated entity sets. For Figure 1(a), the derived relational database schema is shown below.

FACULTY(eFACULTY, SS#, Name, Office)
CLASS(eCLASS, Course#, Section#)
STUDENT(eSTUDENT, Id#, Name, Address)
IS-TEACHING(eFACULTY, eCLASS)
IS-TAKING(eCLASS, eSTUDENT)
ADVISES(eFACULTY, eSTUDENT)

The attributes prefixed with "e" are surrogate key attributes.

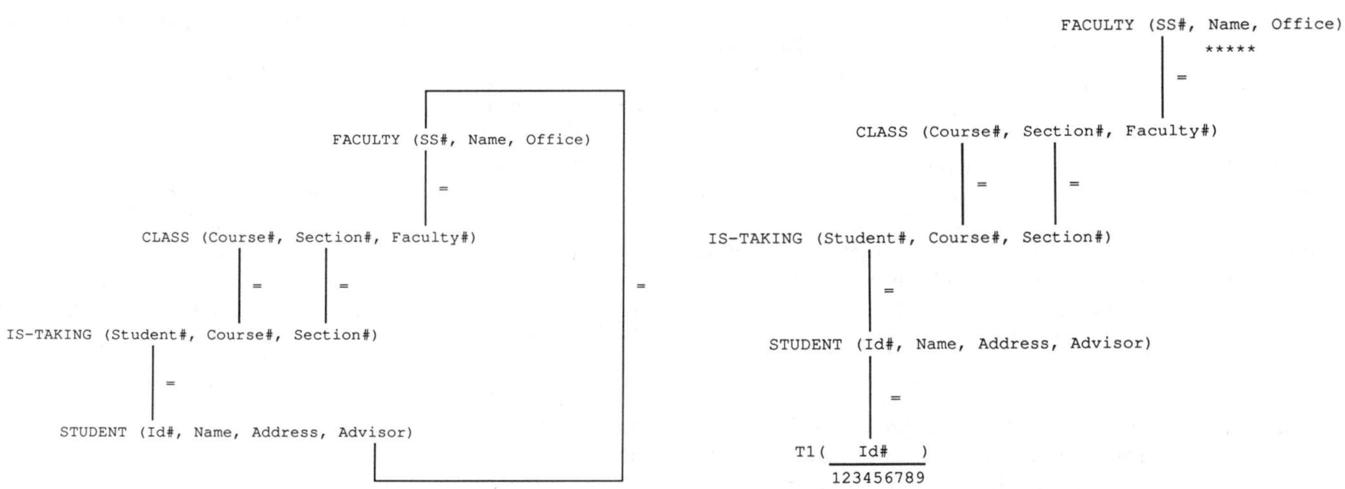

(a) A sample extended relational schema diagram

(b) Transformed extended relational schema diagram

Figure 3—Example for the extended relational model

Each graphical operator corresponds to an operation that maps a set of relation instances into another set of relation instances. The initial instance is the current database state. For our example the initial set of relations is {faculty, is-teaching, class, is-taking, student, advises}. The first operator invoked for the query in the section on graphical query formulation for an ER model was relationship-set delete (ADVISES) which corresponds to removing the relation advises from the set of relations. The second operator invoked was entity-set restrict(STUDENT, Id# = '123456789') which corresponds to replacing the relation student with

$$\sigma_{Id\#='123456789'}\text{student}$$

and, to maintain referential integrity, replacing is-taking with

$$\pi_{eSTUDENT,eCLASS}(\text{is-taking} \,|\times|\, \sigma_{Id\#='123456789'}\text{student}).$$

The last three operators invoked were entity-set project (STUDENT, ϕ), entity-set project(COURSE, ϕ), and entity-set project(FACULTY, {Name}). These operators each correspond to appropriate projections. The final set of relations is

$$\begin{array}{l}\pi_{eFACULTY,Name}\text{faculty},\\ \text{is-teaching},\\ \pi_{eCLASS}\text{class},\\ \pi_{eSTUDENT,eCLASS}(\text{is-taking} \,|\times|\, \sigma_{Id\#='123456789'}\text{student}),\\ \pi_{eSTUDENT}\sigma_{Id\#='123456789'}\text{student}.\end{array}$$

This set of relation instances is the database instance for the query in Figure 1(b). To produce a single table for this query, we join the relations in the final set of relation instances and project on the attributes of interest shown on the diagram.

Of course, actually manipulating the stored relation instances as the query is formulated, would be very inefficient. Instead, we can accumulate information about how to create the relation instances as the diagrams are manipulated, and thus obtain a relational algebra expression equivalent to the graphically specified query. For this example, the equivalent query is:

$$\begin{array}{l}\pi_{Name}(\pi_{eFACULTY,Name}\text{faculty} \,|\times|\, \text{is-teaching} \,|\times|\, \pi_{eCLASS}\text{class} \,|\times|\\ \quad \pi_{eSTUDENT,eCLASS}(\text{is—taking} \,|\times|\, \sigma_{Id\#='123456789'}\text{student}) \,|\times|\\ \quad \pi_{eSTUDENT}\sigma_{Id\#='123456789'}\text{student}\end{array}$$

In such an implementation, the application of a graphical operator causes transformation of the diagram, and corresponding relational algebra expression(s), but does not affect the underlying stored database. This means that the proposed graphical interface can be treated as a front-end to an existing relational database. As a consequence, the relational algebra expression can be optimized before execution by the relational query processor.

This approach also has the significant advantage that the formal definition of the semantics of graphical operators can be described by providing translation rules to generate relational algebra expressions. Entity-relationship diagrams can be described formally as a pair that includes a set of entity-set descriptors and a set of relationship-set descriptors. Each operator transforms a particular ER diagram into another diagram. Most operators are partial and are valid only if certain enabling conditions are satisfied.

We enhance the above model by associating a relational algebra expression with each descriptor (entity-set descriptor and relationship-set descriptor). This relational algebra expression is referred to as the X-component and defines a set of tuples associated with the given set descriptor. Thus, when an operator is specified on an entity or relationship set, a corresponding relational-algebra operator is concatenated (using applicable syntax rules) with the X-component of the set descriptor. Hence, the state of the X-component for an entity or relationship set W defines the view generation for W as displayed on the diagram.

The semantics for a basic set of operators for our ER model are formally defined.[16] Semantics for graphical operators for the ECR model, the extended relational model, and other semantic models can be defined in the similar manner.

CONCLUSION

A general approach to graphical query formulation for semantic data models has been discussed. Three data models—an ER model, the ECR model, and an extended relational model—have been used as examples. Our approach is to define graphical manipulation operators that allow queries to be specified by manipulating schema diagrams. Diagrams are transformed until they represent a desired user query. The resulting diagram (as well as all intermediate diagrams) can be interpreted in terms of the graphical representation of the data model used.

We have also explained how the operators can be defined and efficiently implemented. These graphical operators can be defined in terms of functions that operate on an abstract data model. Based on the definition of these operators, the result of formulating a query can be expressed as a relational algebra expression. Thus, it is unnecessary to manipulate the stored database while the schema diagrams are manipulated. This approach allows an efficient implementation of graphically-specified queries because the relational algebra expression can be optimized, using standard techniques, before it is executed.

Our method is general and is applicable to a wide range of semantic models. For each model, the graphical query interface provides a convenient and dynamically changing frame of reference. Immediate feedback is provided whenever an operator is invalid in the current context. Assistance in both formulating and understanding a query is provided at a higher level of abstraction, closer to the application domain of the end-user.

These graphical query interfaces can be implemented as a front-end to an existing (relational) database system. Hence, multiple interfaces can be implemented over the same underlying database system, so a user can select the interface that corresponds to his/her favorite data model.

REFERENCES

1. C. W. Bachman. "Data Structure Diagrams." *Data Base,* 1 (1969) 2, pp. 4–10.
2. C. W. Bachman. "The Programmer as a Navigator." *Communications of the ACM,* 16 (1973) 11, pp. 653–658.
3. P. P. Chen. "The Entity-relationship Model—Toward a Unified View of Data," *ACM Transactions on Database Systems,* 1 (1976) 1, pp. 9–36.
4. M. M. Zloof. "Query by Example." *AFIPS, Proceedings of the National Computer Conference,* (Vol. 44) 1975, pp. 431–438.
5. N. H. McDonald. "CUPID: A Graphics Oriented Facility for Support of Non-programmer Interactions with a Database." Memo No. ERL-M563, Ph.D. Dissertation, University of California, Berkeley, 1975.
6. Vassiliou, Y. and M. Jarke. "Query Languages—A Taxonomy." in Y. Vassiliou (ed.) *Human Factors and Interactive Computer Systems,* Norwood, New Jersey; Ablex, 1984.
7. M. E. Senko. "DIAM II with FORAL LP: Making Pointed Queries with Light Pen." *Information Processing,* Amsterdam: North-Holland, 1977.
8. Chang, N. S. and K. S. Fu. "Query-by-pictorial Example." *Proceedings of IEEE COMPSAC,* 1979.
9. D. C. Tsichritzis. "LSL: A Link and Selector Language." *Proceedings of ACM SIGMOD,* Washington, DC, 1976.
10. Zhang, Z. Q. and A. O. Mendelzon. "A Graphical Query Language for Entity-relationship Databases." in C. Davis, S. Jajodia, P. Ng & R. Yeh (eds.) *Entity-Relationship Approach to Software Engineering,* Amsterdam; North-Holland 1983.
11. Larson, J. and J. Wallick. "An Interface for Novice and Infrequent Database Management System Users." *AFIPS, Proceedings of the National Computer Conference* (Vol. 53) 1984.
12. Elmasri, R. and J. Larson. "A Graphical Query Facility for ER Databases." *Proceedings of the 4th International Conference on Entity-Relationship Approach,* Chicago, Illinois, 1985, pp. 236–245.
13. Bryce, D. and R. Hull. "SNAP: A Graphics-based Schema Manager." *Proceedings of the IEEE International Conference on Data Engineering,* Los Angeles California, 1986.
14. Elmasri, R., A. Hevner, and J. Weeldreyer. "The Category Concept: An Extension to the Entity-relationship Model." *Data & Knowledge Engineering,* 1 (1985) 1, pp. 75–116.
15. Czejdo, B., M. Rusinkiewicz, D. M. Campbell, and D. W. Embley. "A Graphical Query Language for the Relational Data Model." University of Houston Technical Report UH-CS-5, August 1985.
16. Campbell, D. M., D. W. Embley, and B. Czejdo. "A Relationally Complete Query Language for an Entity-relationship Model." *Proceedings of the 4th International Conference on Entity-Relationship Approach,* Chicago, Illinois, 1985, pp. 90–97.
17. Elmasri, R. and G. Wiederhold. "GORDAS: A Formal High-level Query Language for the Entity-relationship Model." *Proceedings of the 2nd International Conference on Entity-Relationship Approach,* Washington, DC, 1981, pp. 49–72.
18. Codd, E. F. "Extending the Database Relational Model to Capture More Meaning." *ACM Transactions on Database Systems,* 4 (1979) 4, pp. 397–434.

A network forms database management system

by SHUHSHEN PAN
Bell Communications Research
Red Bank, New Jersey

ABSTRACT

This paper describes a network forms database management system *(netfords)*. Netfords is a UNIX tool used to maintain a collection of forms which can be related in a network fashion. The basic concepts about forms are introduced. The entire database architecture is presented. A form editor has been developed to help edit the forms. A simple query capability was built into the editor to help retrieve forms. A manual page system has also been incorporated into netfords for documentation. Also discussed are the file structures of a netfords database, a library to access the database from C programs and the accommodations to traditional data models.

INTRODUCTION

Many business systems have been using forms as input sheets and output reports. There have been a number of table oriented systems commercially available; for example, QBE.[1] The major reasons for adopting forms as a user interface are that office workers are familiar with business forms in their daily work, and most office work is carried out through forms. Even though office workers may be unfamiliar with programming and query languages, they still can perform operations on predefined forms through interactive interfaces provided by the computer technology. Netfords is a network forms database management system. The relationships among forms can be as complex as a network. The difference between a table and a form can be seen in Formanger.[2] In the context of ths paper, however, we assume that a form is a more general term than a table. Each form or table can be defined in terms of *tbl* commands.[3] Henceforth, we are going to use the words *table* and *form* interchangeably.

The goal of netfords is to provide an information system based on forms and with the following features:

1. An interactive methodology for data entry, deletion, revision, and retrieval
2. A mechanism to express the relationships among forms
3. Formation of complicated forms
4. Project-related documentation
5. Accommodation of relational, hierarchical, and network models
6. Batch processing of form manipulations

Netfords mainly consists of a form editor, query mechanism, a manual page system,[4] and a C library. The form editor *(eform)* is used either to build or revise a form. The query mechanism provides a simple query capability with which to retrieve forms. The manual page system helps document application-related executable files. The C library provides a mechanism to access the database from C programs.

This paper is organized as follows: The first section provides an introduction and basic definitions. Next, an architecture for a netfords's database is presented and the form editor discussed. The operation and the implementation of netfords follows. Finally, a library for C programs is addressed, the accommodation of traditional data models is discussed, and the results and future extensions are summarized.

Definition of Forms

Associated with a form are a *form type* and a set of *form instances.*[5] A form type is a template that describes the format of the form. It consists of a set of attributes which can be further divided into heading attributes and body attributes. Heading attributes appear as the headings of a form, and body attributes define the body of a form. A form instance is a form type with complete or partially complete attribute values. The term form will be used informally to refer to a form instance. Heading attributes can be used to uniquely identify forms. Normally a form type can be defined in terms of tbl commands. A command called *mft* is provided to define a form type. Consecutive question marks (?) are used to signal the heading attributes and asterisks (*) for the body attributes. The number of question marks or asterisks indicates the length of corresponding attributes.

Figure 1(a) is the example for a form type ast1. Figure 1(b) displays a blank form instance of form type *ast1*. We can see from Figure 1 that form type ast1 has five heading attributes: feature code, side 1, side 2, signaling attributes, and transmission attributes; and six body attributes: FTC, &/OR, SIC, TFC, T&S REQD, and ARRAY#. Each field length is indicated by the number of ?s or *s. For the sake of illustration, Figure 1(b) contains ?s and *s. However, in the actual editing,

```
.in + 1.8i
.PH ""
.ce 2
Array Selection Table
Complete and Partial Array Types
.sp 2
.TS
 ssssss.
Feature Code:????????     Side 1:??????     Side 2:??????
 Signaling Attributes:?????????????????????????????
Transmission Attributes:??????????????????????????????
.T&

.TE
.TS  H
center, tab(;);
cccssss
c|r1ssss|
c|r1ssss|
c|ccssss|
c|c|csss1
|c|c|c|c|c|c|1
|c|c|c|c|c|c|1
|1|c|1|c|c|c|1.
;_;_;
;&; : FTC "&" SIC --< FS-POT  ARRAY
;OR; : FTC --< Complete ARRAY "or" SIC --< TS-POT  ARRAY
;;_;
_;;_;
FTC;;SIC;TFC;T&S;ARRAY;
;;;;REQD;#;
_;_;_;_;_;_;
.TH
******;**;*********;****;****;**;
_;_;_;_;_;_;
.TE
.in -2.0i
```

Figure 1(a)—A form type ast1 defined by tbl commands

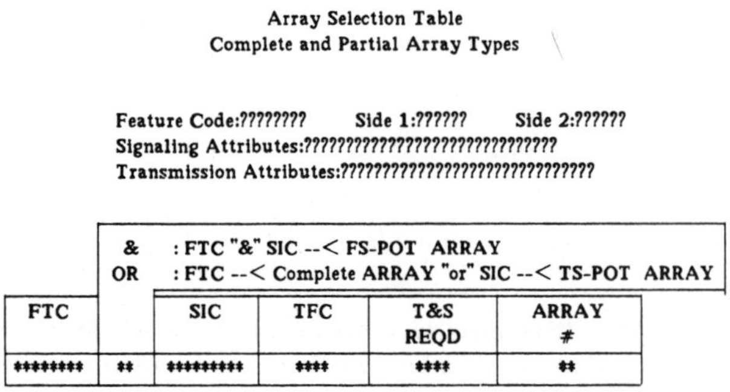
Array Selection Table
Complete and Partial Array Types

Feature Code:???????? Side 1:?????? Side 2:??????
Signaling Attributes:?????????????????????????????
Transmission Attributes:?????????????????????????????

& : FTC "&" SIC --< FS-POT ARRAY
OR : FTC --< Complete ARRAY "or" SIC --< TS-POT ARRAY

FTC		SIC	TFC	T&S REQD	ARRAY #
********	**	*********	****	****	**

Figure 1(b)—A blank form generated by the form type ast1

those ?s and *s will disappear and can be replaced by actual values.

THE ARCHITECTURE OF A NETFORDS DATABASE

A netfords database is comprised of the following subdirectories: admin, backup, bin, data, dict, doc, and temp. Figure 2 gives a simple structure for a typical netfords database where *db* is the database name. Admin is used for administrative information, for example, broadcasting message. Backup is a duplicate storage for all the forms. At the end of each interactive session of netfords, all the forms will be copied into backup. This provides an on-line backup storage capability. It will help users to retrieve the backup copies during the course of a netfords session. Bin is used to store the executable files which are specific to the database. Data is a regular store for all the forms' data. Dict is further divided into three subdirectories: data, forms, and sets. Data stores all of the files, each of which contains the allowable entries for a particular field defined in forms; forms stores all of the form type definitions; and sets stores all of the defined relationships among forms. Doc is used to keep the manual pages which document the commands stored in bin. The manual page system[4] has been incorporated into netfords to facilitate the maintenance of project-related documentation. This will be discussed later. Temp is used as a temporary working space.

FORM EDITOR

One important feature about netfords is the provision of a form editor called *eform*. The form editor provides users an easy way to edit data. This avoids the traditional database management approach which requires users to learn data manipulation languages (DML) in order to enter or revise

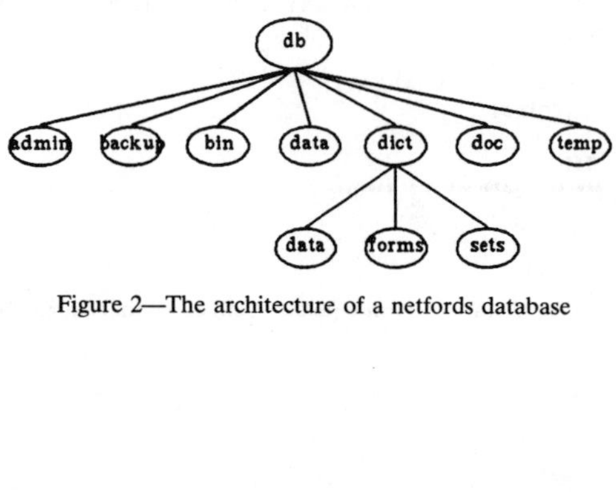

Figure 2—The architecture of a netfords database

data. Eform was built to help users edit forms from the screen on a field-to-field basis. The editor commands mainly follow the conventions of the *vi* editor. Before the invocation of eform for a form, a screen file for the form type must have been defined. By using the msc command (which stands for making screen), we can generate a screen file from a form type. A screen file provides information for eform to create and edit a form instance. A screen file's name is the form type's name concatenated with ".scr." However, a form instance's name is form type's name followed by "." and a string of characters. For example, given a form type called ast1 which is defined in Figure 1, *msc* can generate a screen file called ast1.scr. By using eform which utilizes ast1.scr, we can create a form instance called ast1.LE4ENCC. Figure 3 explains the relationships among form type, forms, screen file, and commands mft, eform, and msc. Eform can insert characters, delete characters, replace characters, open lines, and delete lines.

Command Mode Verse Editing Mode

Eform is similar to any regular editor which can have both command mode and editing mode. At the beginning of the invocation of eform, users are in the editing mode. In the editing mode, users can add, change, or delete entries in a form. However, in the command mode, users can escape to Shell, exchange forms, write into disk, or even query the database. Command mode can be entered by typing ":" which will bring the cursor down to the command line which is preceded by the character string "CMD=⟩". At the end of the execution for each command, users will be brought back to the editing mode.

Query Capability

A simple query capability has been built into eform to retrieve forms. This can be done by calling a blank form using eform, filling heading attributes' values, and typing ":query" which will access command mode and query the entire database. A set of retrieved form instances then will be displayed on the screen one after another in terms of eform, and users can edit them in the normal manner. At the time of writing, neither the AND/OR condition nor the more sophisticated query capabilities have been implemented.

OPERATION OF NETFORDS

Netfords is invoked as in the following command:

netfords[/⟨name⟩[/⟨name⟩ . . .]]⟨database⟩

where ⟨name⟩ is a directory name and ⟨database⟩ is the database name. To avoid misspelling the database names, netfords first checks if the database already exists. For a new database, netfords will ask users the following:

Create a new database *db*, errno = no? (y or n)

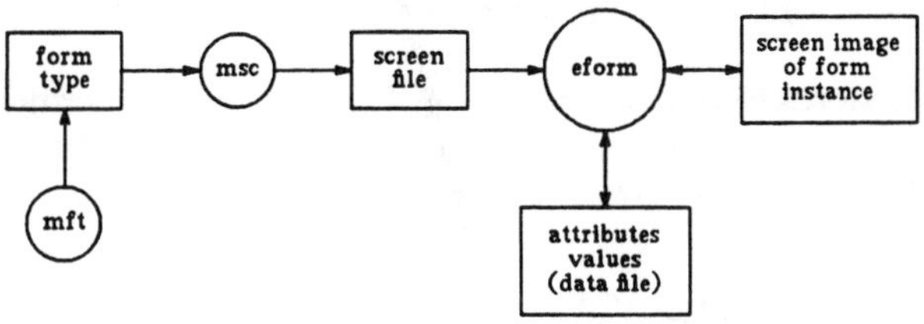

Figure 3(a)—A generic description of the form operations

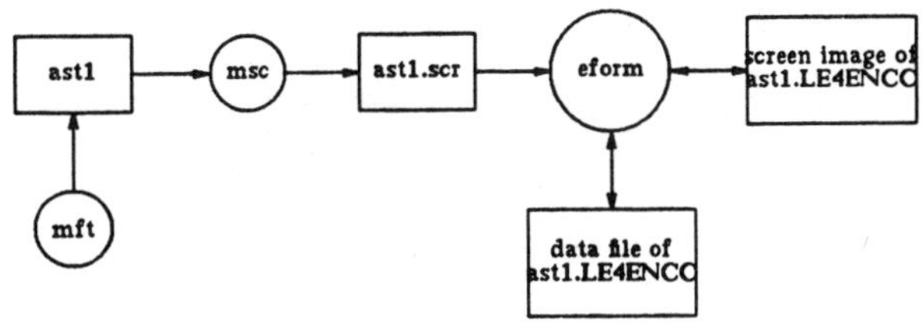

Figure 3(b)—An instance of form operations

where *db* is the database name, a "y" will enable netfords to create a new one, and errno = no is an indication about the error. Users can check the System V Programmer Reference Manual to find out the error message. After successfully getting into the specified database, users can create form types, edit forms, print forms, and even post some messages to notify other users.

Netfords Commands

In this section, we are going to discuss some of the netfords commands.

Accessing other databases

To access other databases easily without exiting from the ongoing netfords session, a command called *attach* is provided. The original database is called the Master database, whereas the attached ones will be called alien databases. Several alien databases can be attached at any given time. Users can access both the attached forms and executable files. Command *lisa* which stands for *lis*t attached database will list the Master and attached databases. To unattach a database, there is another command called *purge.* Purge will not allow the Master database to be unattached.

Making form types

Command *mft* is provided to define a form type. Actually, mft creates a subdirectory underneath a netfords database subdirectory, data, and invokes the *vi* editor to edit a form type. Mft can also be used to revise an existing form type.

Making screen files

Since eform requires a screen file to aid in editing forms for any given form type, a command called *msc* is provided. Msc takes a form type and generates a screen file whose name is obtained by concatenating the form type name with ".scr." A screen file provides information about the locations and length of different attributes. To protect against accidentally overwriting, the mode of the screen file should be changed to 666 after satisfying with the formating of the screen file. The formating can be done by using tbl commands. Familiarity with the tbl commands is necessary to efficiently create a form type.

Building relationships among forms

As suggested by the name *netfords* which stands for *net*work *for*ms *d*atabase management *s*ystem, several commands are provided to build the relationships among forms. Adopting the conventions from the DBTG report,[6] we use the word "set" to represent a one-to-many relationship from one form type to another form type. The former is called the owner and the latter the member. Notice that both owner and member can be of the same type. The available commands are described as follows:

1. *defset setname ownertype membertype:* will create a relationship definition called *setname* whose owner is of type *ownertype* and has members of type *membertype.*
2. *delset setname ownertype membertype:* will delete a relationship definition called *setname* whose owner is of type *ownertype* and has members of type *membertype.*
3. *addmen* -s*setname* -o*owner* -m*mem:* will add a member *mem* into a set *setname* owned by *owner.*
4. *delmen* -s*setname* -s*owner* -m*mem:* will delete a member *mem* from a set *setname* owned by *owner.*
5. *addset* -s*setname* -o*owner:* will add a set owner *owner* into a set defined by *setname.*
6. *rmset* -s*setname* -o*owner:* will delete a set instance defined by *setname* and owned by *owner.*

Broadcasting message

Netfords is intended to be a multi-user database system. The communication among users is provided by a command called *nbc* which stands for *n*etfords *b*roadcasting. *Nbc* is simply an editor which allows users to post information which will post on the screen at the time of login. Command *addmsgs* will store the broadcasted information into a mailbox called "mbox" which is a file in the netfords database subdirectory admin. Command *netsmsgs* will display the stored information.

Current users

Command *user* will list the current users' login id, tty, and login time.

Printing forms

In addition to viewing forms on the screen, users can print hard copies of the forms. A command called *pform* provides such a tool.

Leaving netfords

To leave netfords one can simply type *logout.* Logout will automatically trigger a command called *backup* to copy all the forms into the subdirectory "backup." This operation is behind the scene. It is suggested that, during any netfords' session, users use command backup to get a latest copies of all forms before issuing any doubtful command which may corrupt the regular database.

Intrinsic Forms

Every netfords database has one predefined form type. It is used to facilitate the communication among users. It will be interesting to add some other form types to every database.

Message form

A pre-defined form type called "_notice" is built into every netfords database. Users can use eform to edit message, and use pform to get hard copies. Command nbc provides a mechanism to post on-line message, however, form type "_notice" provides another off-line message.

Interactive Mode Versus Batch Mode

Although netfords is initially designed to be an online, screen-oriented database management system, users can also run it in a batch mode. This can be done by simply writing netfords commands to a file and using that file as input to netfords. For example,

netfords smetds40<cfile

will let netfords read commands from cfile. It should be noted that command eform is prohibited in the batch mode.

Documentation

To ease the maintenance, a manual page system has been incorporated into netfords so that users can write application-related manuals and store them in the same database. These commands are:

1. newman: write a new manual.
2. upman: update a old manual.
3. lman: list all the available manual names.
4. hman: print manual on the screen.
5. pman: print manual pages on the image printer.
6. ptxm: print a permuted index for all manual pages.

Current Applications of Netfords

Netfords has been used to work for an engineering project. It also has been used to write the converting algorithms[7] to extract data from RAMIS database in TSO.

DESIGN AND IMPLEMENTATION OF NETFORDS

The purpose of this section is two-fold: first, to disclose the program structures of netfords in order to facilitate the maintenance of the system, and second, to open the architecture of a netfords database to the sophisticated users. Netfords is implemented in the UNIX operating environment of System 5.2. It uses the curses library[8] in the design of the form editor eform. All the commands are written either in C programming language or UNIX Shell.

System Administration

Currently netfords resides in the VAX 11/780. The entire system consists of the following files or subdirectories:

- README: contains the general information about the whole directory.
- aux: contains all the predefined form types and the associated screen files.
- bin: contains the executable files to be invoked by general users.
- doc: contains the general user's guide and this paper.
- lib: contains the procedures to be called in C programs.
- src: contains all the source codes and a makefile file.
- system: contains all of the structures necessary for the procedures listed in the above lib subdirectory.

Handling of Signals

The current implementation considers three kinds of signals. They are SIGHUP (hanghup), SIGINT (interrupt) and SIGILL (illegal instruction). Only SIGHUP is caught; SIGINT and SIGILL are ignored.

Concurrent Control

To make the entire database accessible to multiple users, a locking facility is added to take care of the concurrent updating. The locking facility provides a mechanism in such a way that at any particular time, only one user can revise a file, however, more than one user can read the same file. When invoked, eform will first check if the associated lock file exists. If it does, which means the actual file is being edited, netfords will notify the login id who is editing the file, and the user must try eform again. Otherwise, a lock file will be created and the user will gain the exclusive right to revise the file. The lock file is created in the system subdirectory /tmp and has the same name as the one to be edited. Such a lock file will be removed at the end of editing. If for some reason the lock files fail to be removed, users can remove the lock files themselves.

The File Structures of a Netfords Database

The storage of a netfords database was built upon the UNIX file system. Figure 2 gives the file structure for a typical netfords database. All the user-created form instances (or data files) reside in the netfords subdirectory data. The data files are organized as follows: for each form type there is a subdirectory under data. All of the data files of the same form type are stored in the same subdirectory. Each subdirectory under data has at least two files—the form type and the screen file.

Manual pages

All of the project-related manual pages are stored in the netfords database subdirectory doc. All of the manual pages are under the control of SCCS.[9] Users can always retrieve different versions of manual pages.

System catalog

In addition to those regular data files, netfords also keep a system catalog for all the form definitions, set definitions, set instances, data definitions, and dictionary files. The purpose of this catalog is to facilitate system maintenance, auditing, and validation. C programs can also access those files. This will be discussed shortly.

Form definitions

Every time a screen file is produced by the msc command, a definition file for that form type is generated and stored in the subdirectory dict/forms. For the form type as defined in Figure 1(a), Figure 4 shows the corresponding definition file. As we can see from Figure 4, the file contains the field numbers; the types, which indicate the type of field, that is, h (heading) or b (body); the length, which indicates the field length; the datafiles, which give the file names containing the allowable data entries; and the definitions, which provide the verbal description for each field. Users can also use eform to edit such a definition file. In general, a definition file for form type xx is indicated by _form.xx which actually is the file dict/forms/xx. For example, users can type the command "*eform_form.ast1.*" to edit the definition fields for form type ast1.

Form: ast1				
field	type	length	datafile	definitions
1	h	8		feature code
2	h	6	d.side	side1 attributes
3	h	6	d.side	side2 attributes
4	h	30	d.sigattr	signaling attributes
5	h	30	d.tranattr	transmission attributes
6	b	8	d.ftc	ftc
7	b	2		and/or
8	b	9	d.sic	sic
9	b	4	d.tfc	tfc
10	b	6	d.tsreqd	t&s eqpt
11	b	2		array number

Figure 4—Form type definition

Sets Definitions		
set	owner	members
ast1toarray	ast1	ary
ast2toarray	ast2	ary

Figure 5—Set definition

Set definitions

A set definition file indicated as _setdefs is automatically produced whenever a database is created. Such a set definition file is used to store all the user defined set definitions. A set definition defines the owner type and the member type of a set. To define a set, users can either use "*eform*_setsdef" or command "*defset.*" In fact, _setsdef is the file dict/sets/definitions. It is similar to a form in that a set consists of a set definition and a collection of set instances. Each set instance has at least one owner and one or more members. Every time a set, say *S*, is defined, a subdirectory dict/sets/S is created. For each set instance associated with *S*, a file whose name is the same as the owner is created under dict/sets/S which stores all the members associated with the particular owner with respect to the set *S*. Figure 5 shows two sets or relationships defined from form type ast1 and ast2 to form type ary.

Data definitions

Included in the subdirectory dict/data is a data definition file which provides the description of all the data dictionary files which contain all the allowable entries for the fields in form types. Figure 6 shows the data definition file. Users can use "*eform*_datadef" to edit the data definition file. Actually, _datadef is dict/data/definitions.

Dictionary files

Users can store the allowable data entries for different attributes defined in form types. Those files or data dictionary files are also sitting in the same subdirectory dict/data. Those files can edit and revise by using "*eform*__data.xx" where xx is the file name which, in fact, is dict/data/xx.

Form instances

All of the form instances are further classified and stored in different subdirectories under data according to their form

file	definitions
d.entid	entry id
d.ftc	FTC(Facility Type Code)
d.lds	LDS(Location Data sheet)
d.otr	the Other field in ARRAY
d.sic	SIC(Smetds Interface codes)
d.side	side1 and side2
d.sigattr	signalling attributes
d.tranattr	transmission attributes

Figure 6—Data definition

types. In other words, each subdirectory under data represents a particular form type, and all of the form instances pertinent to the same form type are kept there. Each such subdirectory has at least two files: form definition file and the associated screen file.

A screen file is an aid to eform which contains the left margin, the field type, field number, y-positions, lengths, and the a blank form. The blank form is going to be reflected on the screen. Figure 7 shows a screen file (whose path is data/ast1/ast1.scr) of form type ast1. Although revising the screen file is not recommended, sometimes it is necessary to customize the screen file for special application. This can be achieved by using regular editors. Upon the invocation of eform, the related data dictionary files sitting in the netfords subdirectory dict/data will also be loaded into the main memory for online validation. For each newly-entered or revised entry, eform will check against the data dictionary files, and produce error messages if violations happen.

System Structures

Figure 7 gives the process structures. It consists of three phases: initialization phase, command phase and finish phase.

The initialization phase

The initialization phase (indicated by box "init") is first to identify the presented database. If the database does not exist, then a new one will be created if users so desire. For a new database, seven subdirectories will be created. After recognizing or creating a database, netfords checks if file descriptor 0 is a terminal. If it is, three windows will be created: the welcome window which will appear at the very beginning of a netfords session; the information window which is prepared for the command phase; and the finish window which will appear only at the end of a session. In the batch mode, netfords reads commands from a regular file.

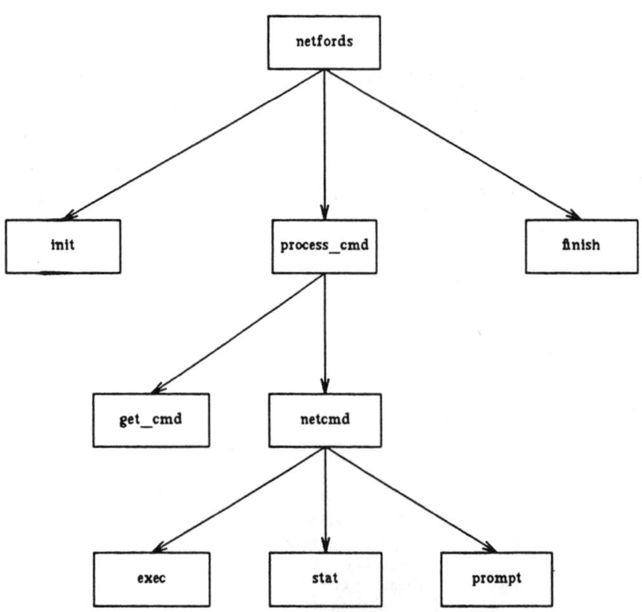

Figure 7—Process structures

The command phase

During the command phase (indicated by box "process_cmd"), netfords takes commands from users or files (indicated by box "get_cmd"), executes them and updates the information window (indicated by box "netcmd") when in the interactive mode. Netfords provides several generic commands which are embedded in the netfords system. However, users can also create project-related commands which are stored in the netfords database subdirectory bin. When the input string is received by netfords, it is first checked by netfords to see if the string is a generic command. If it is not, then netfords checks to see if it is projected-related command. If it is not a project-related command either, then it will be treated as a Shell command and passed to the Shell. Indicated in the information window are the current database name, recently edited form, current owner, member, and time. A READ ONLY sign will also appear on the window if the user does not have the write privilege. All the Shell commands have to be proceeded by "!."

The finish phase

By typing "logout," users will be brought into the finish phase (indicated by box "finish") and ready to leave a netfords session. During such a finish phase a command called *backup* will be triggered to copy all the regular files in the netfords subdirectory data into the netfords subdirectory backup. In interactive mode, a finish window also will appear on the screen showing some statistics including number of command being executed, number of files being updated, and number of newly-created files.

A LIBRARY OF C FUNCTIONS

To enable C programs to access the database, a library of C functions is also provided. User-provided C programs can be used either to print or validate the database. As we can recall, a C program has to reside in the netfords database subdirectory bin. In order to use the library, it is required to have a line

#include "path"

at the top of the program. The path is dependent on the installation. In the current version, the path is /h3/sjp/Netfords/system/netfords.h. Two commands are also provided to facilitate the compilation and loading. They are *nc* and *nload:*

- *nc* prog.c: will compile a C program *prog.c* in bin.
- *nload* prog: will load both the object code *prog.o* in bin and the library and generate the executable file called

prog which, again, will reside in the same subdirectory bin.

Data Structures

Several data structures have been defined in the "netfords.h" file. They are FORM, FORMTYPE, SET, SETDEF, SETSDEF.

The Functions

The library consists of several functions which are to be invoked from a C program to access the database. They are listed below:

```
getf(F,file)
FORM *F;
char *file;
```

Getf will get a form instance, pointed by F, of *file*.

```
getft(Ft, ftype)
FORMTYPE *Ft;
char *ftype;
```

Getft will get a form type or form definition, pointed by Ft, of type *ftype*.

```
getset(S,r)
SETDEF *S;
char *r;
```

Getset will get a set definition, pointed by S, defined by *r*.

```
getsetins(S,set,owner)
SET *S;
char *set;
char *owner;
```

Getsetins will get a set instance, pointed by S, which is defined by *set* and owned by *owner*.

```
getsetsdef(S)
SETSDEF *S;
```

Getsetdef will get all the defined set definitions pointed by S.

ACCOMMODATION OF TRADITIONAL DATA MODELS

Although netfords is intended to be a form-oriented system, it can also accommodate the traditional database models. In this section, we are going to show that netfords has the equivalent power as traditional database models. To do this, we are going to give some netfords representation for traditional database models.

Relational Model

In the relational model, data is organized into tables. Let's look at the definition:[10] Given a collection of sets $D_1, D_2, \ldots, D_n$ (not necessarily distinct), R is a relation on these sets if it is a set of ordered n-tuples $\langle d_1, d_2, \ldots, d_n \rangle$ such that d_1 belongs to D_1, d_2 belongs to $D_2, \ldots d_n$ belongs to D_n. $D_1, D_2, \ldots, D_n$ are the domains of R. The value n is the degree of R. Figure 8 shows a sample relation model from;[10] it consists of three relations, S (the SUPPLIER relation), P (the PART relation), and SP (the QUANTITY relation). Each row of the table represents one n-tuple of the relation. An attribute represents the use of a domain within a relation. For example, the PART relation is defined with five attributes (PART#, PNAME, COLOR, WEIGHT, and CITY). It is not difficult to use the tbl commands to define a relation. Moreover, users can also utilize the library functions already discussed to define the standard relational operations such as join, projection, select, and so forth.

Hierarchical Model

In this model the data is organized as a tree structure. The record type at the top of the tree is usually known as the root. In general, a root may have any number of dependents, each of these may have any number of lower-level dependents, and so on, to any number of levels. A hierarchical data model is given in Figure 9. It represents the prerequisite courses and offerings for each course. Each offering may have several

S#	SNAME	STATUS	CITY
S1	Smith	20	London
S2	Jones	10	Paris
S3	Blake	30	Paris
S4	Clark	20	London
S5	Adams	30	Athens

P#	PNAME	COLOR	WEIGHT	CITY
P1	Nut	Red	12	London
P2	Bolt	GREEN	17	Paris
P3	Screw	Blue	17	Rome
P4	Screw	Red	14	London
P5	Cam	Blue	12	Paris
P6	Cog	Red	19	London

S#	P#	QTY
S1	P1	300
S1	P2	200
S1	P3	400
S1	P4	200
S1	P5	100
S1	P6	100
S2	P1	300
S2	P2	400
S3	P2	200
S4	P2	200
S4	P4	300
S4	P5	400

Figure 8—A relational data model

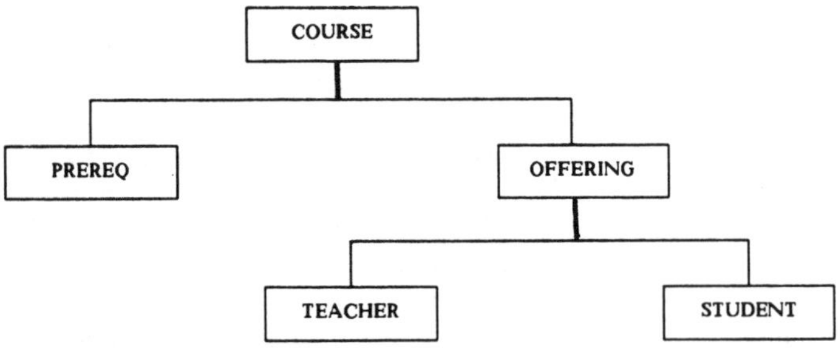

Figure 9(a)—A hierarchical schema

teachers and students associated. Assuming that we have used tbl commands to define the four record types: COURSE, OFFERING, STUDENT and TEACHER, we can use the following commands to establish the hierarchical data model:

1. defset -sprereq -oCOURSE -mCOURSE
2. defset -soffering -oCOURSE -mOFFERING
3. defset –sstudents -oOFFERING -mSTUDENT
4. defset -steacher -oOFFERING -mTEACHER

Set definition 1, prereq, defines the relationship between COURSE and pre-request COURSEs. Definition 2, offering, defines the relationship between COURSE and OFFERINGs. Definition 3, students, defines the relationship between OFFERING and STUDENTs. Definition 4, teacher, defines the relationship between OFFERING and TEACHERs.

Network Model

The network model, as in the hierarchical approach, represents data by records and links. However, a network is a more general structure than a hierarchical approach because a given record occurrence may have any number of immediate superiors as well as any number of immediate dependents. The network approach thus allows one to model a many-to-many correspondence more directly. A network model is given in Figure 10. An equipment array represented by an ARY table may consist of more than one piece of equipment, and each one may be represented by an ECT table. Similarly, a single piece of equipment can be used by more than one array. Therefore, an ECT table can have many ARY tables associated with it. We can define these two relationships as follows:

1. defset -sary_to_ect -oARY -mECT
2. defset -sect_to_ary -oECT -mARY

where ARY is the table for arrays and ECT for equipment. "Ary_to_ect" defines the relationship from an ARY to ECTs. "Ect_to_ary" defines the relationships from an ECT to the associated ARYs.

CONCLUSION

Netfords is a UNIX tool intended to maintain a collection of tables. Each table is treated as a file. Using eform, users can

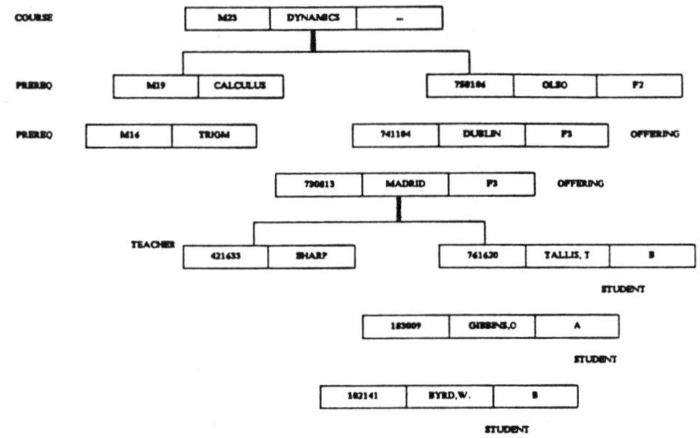

Figure 9(b)—A hierarchical model

edit forms on the screen. To enhance netfords, several extensions have been proposed:

1. *Undo command:* This will enable users to undo the previous command and restore the database. For the present, it is suggested that the *backup* command be used before issuing a command which may corrupt the database.
2. *An organized tree structure for forms:* Currently, netfords utilizes the UNIX file system. All the forms are treated as ordinary files. This approach is only good for a small database. For a large database, it is better to have a B-tree to organize all the forms. This will increase the efficiency.
3. *A more sophisticated query capability:* Currently users can only make simple queries by specifying some heading attributes. As the database grows, more complicated query capabilities which involve AND/OR conditions will be possible.

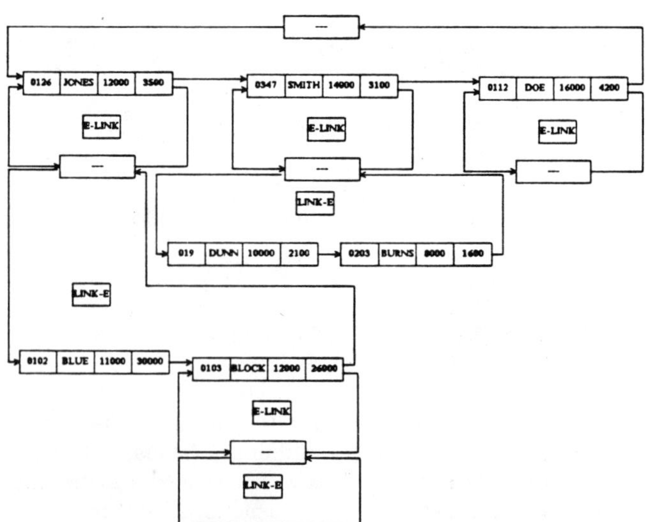

Figure 10—A network model

4. *A general screen form type:* So far a form type is only allowed to have heading and body attributes. However, adding bottom attributes to a form type will generalize the style of a form type and increase the applicability of netfords.
5. *A more powerful form editor:* The current form editor, eform, can only supply a small set of commands. In order to increase the ease of usage, more commands have to be added in the future.

ACKNOWLEDGEMENT

Many thanks to Mary Ward-Callan and Rob Fredericks. It would not have been possible to finish this project without their encouragement. Special appreciation also should be given to Charlie Salvaggione, Harvey Stowers, and Jack Hannan. They pointed out many early bugs and made judicious suggestions.

REFERENCES

1. Zloof, M.M. "Query by Example: A Data Base Language." *IBM System Journal* 16 (1977), pp. 324–343.
2. Yao, S.B., A.R. Hevner, Z. Shi, and D. Luo. "FORMANGER: An Office Forms Management System." *ACM Transactions on Office Information Systems,* 2 (1984) 3, pp. 235–262.
3. Lesk, M.E. "TBL—A Program to Format Tables." Bell Laboratories, 1976.
4. Pan, Shuhshen. "A Manual Page System." Bell Communications Research, TM-TSY-001210, 1985.
5. Tsichritzis, D. "Form Management." *Communications of the ACM,* 25 (1982) 7.
6. Data Base Task Group of CODASYL Programming Languages Committee Report, April, 1971.
7. Pan, Shuhshen. "The Software Support for SMETDS-40." Bell Communications Research, TM-TAP-006015, August 1986.
8. Arnold, Ken. "Screen Updating and Cursor Movement Optimation: A Library Package." Computer Science Division, University of California, Berkeley.
9. Bonanni, L.E. and C.A. Salemi. "Source Code Control System User's Guide." Bell Telephone Laboratories.
10. Date, C.J. "An Introduction to Database Systems." Addison Wesley, 1975.

Translation of queries to account for direct communication between different DBMSs

by MEHDI OWRANG
American University
Washington, D.C.
and
L.L. MILLER
Iowa State University
Ames, Iowa

ABSTRACT

A translation process designed to translate queries between data models is examined. In particular, this paper concentrates on translating queries between the relational and network data models. Such a translation mechanism will enable the user to have access to the database resource in a distributed database for which different database management systems coexist. The translation process is described and examples illustrating the process are given. The discussion has been limited to operating in the environment where the source and target databases have the same semantics. Hypergraphs are used as the intermediate representation format for the query during the translation process. The semantics of both the source and target databases are described in terms of hypergraphs. In addition, the hypergraph is extended to incorporate the operations of the data manipulation language in order to define a general model for query translation. The quality of the translated query is examined.

INTRODUCTION

The problem of translation is not new. Each time a new generation of computer systems evolves, data from the old database must be regenerated and the old query set must be translated. In addition, there is a need for translation when we restructure the database. Such restructuring can be motivated by

1. A change of the use environment of a database management system (DBMS).
2. A change in DBMS.
3. Modification of the design for efficiency reasons.
4. A change in database semantics.

Su and Reynolds[1] studied the problem of high-level sublanguage query conversion using the relational model[2] with SEQUEL[3] as the sublanguage, DEFINE[4] as the data description language and CONVERT[5] as the data translation language. They examined sublanguage query conversion where query modification is due to changes in the schema and subschemas. The changes they considered were

1. A large relation split into several relations.
2. Several relations combined into one.
3. Changes of the mathematical mapping between/among entities.
4. Adding or deleting entities and/or associations.

Their conversion algorithm is specific to the environment they studied and serves pedagogically when an attempt is made to extend their work into the general translation problem.

Other researchers, Katz and Wong,[6] have studied the program conversion due to the changes in application programs that are caused by converting between database systems that support a different level of procedurality in the data sublanguage. In particular, they present an algorithm for mapping from the procedural operations of CODASYL DML[7] into the nonprocedural relational calculus.[8] Their mapping algorithm is restricted to only the conversion from CODASYL DML to relational calculus and therefore does not introduce a general model for translation.

The advent of lower-cost computer systems has paved the way for decentralization of computing resources. Decentralization has enabled designers to enhance local performance by allowing the freedom of design and software choice for each local system. Such freedom provides the necessary enhancement of local computing, but complicates the task of providing access to the database resource on a system-wide basis. In particular, it either forces the user to be aware of the location and format of all of the data in the system, or the computer software/hardware must have the ability to provide access to the local databases through a single data manipulation language. Systems, such as MULTIBASE[9] provide such access but force the user to use both the data manipulation language (DML) of MULTIBASE and the local system to get the enhanced local performance.

What is needed is a model that can provide both the dynamic query translation necessary to allow the direct communication of different DBMS so the user only needs to be proficient in the DML of his/her local DBMS and the ability to provide general query translation to allow the extension of Su and Reynolds'[1] work. In recent work on database design, a number of authors[10–14] have found the hypergraph to be a useful means of modeling relational database designs. When the hypergraph is extended to incorporate the DML operations, it is helpful in defining a general model for query translation.

In the present work, the space limitation forces us to examine the topic in narrower terms. In particular, we will concentrate on translating queries where the source hypergraph attempts to model the same semantics as the target hypergraph (as in dynamic query translation). We also restrict our discussion to the relational and network data models, although similar results are available for the hierarchical model as well.[15,16]

REPRESENTATION IN HYPERGRAPH

This section examines the use of hypergraphs to model both the logical designs and the DML operations of the relational and network data models. A great deal has been written in recent years about the use of hypergraphs in representing the logical design of database schemes,[10–14] and we assume that the reader is familiar with hypergraph concepts to the level of Fagin, Mendelzon, and Ullman.[13] To be of use in translating queries, the hypergraph model has to be expanded to incorporate the operations of the DML. In the remainder of this section, the hypergraph representations for the relational and network data models are described.

Relational Data Model and Its Hypergraph Representation

Fagin, Mendelzon, and Ullman[13] use the hypergraph to model the full join dependency which defines the universal relation (UR). For example, the well known supplier-parts database is defined by the dependency set $\{\bowtie[R_1, R_2, R_3],\ S\# \rightarrow C,\ C \rightarrow S,\ S\#P\# \rightarrow Q\}$, where $R_1(S\#, P\#, Q)$, $R_2(S\#, C)$, and $R_3(C, S)$. The join dependency (jd) $\bowtie[R_1, R_2, R_3]$ can be represented by the

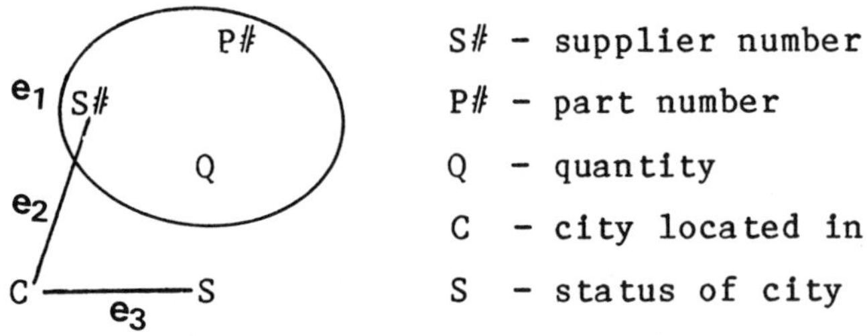

Figure 1—Hypergraph representation of the supplier parts database

hypergraph of Figure 1, where the nodes of the hypergraph are the attributes of the relation schemes and the edges are the relation schemes. Fagin, Mendelzon, and Ullman[13] have shown that the semantics of any database can always be represented by such a full join dependency and a set of functional dependencies (*fd*). Ullman[17] in his survey of universal relation assumptions denotes this as the *UR/JD* assumption.

In the following, we incorporate the DML commands of relational algebra into the model to fit the needs of the translation process. The inclusion of the three fundamental operators of relational algebra—join, project, and select—in the hypergraph model is described by the following set of actions.

Join: The natural join is introduced into the model by the creation of a new edge containing the combined attribute set of the two joined relations. The new edge is labeled as a join edge. To consider the more general question of the theta join requires an extension of the edge labeling process to describe the restrictions on theta.

Project: Projection is introduced into the hypergraph by inclusion of a new edge containing the projected attributes. The new edge is labeled as a projection edge.

Select: A selection operation on a relation creates a new relation of tuples which have been defined by the given condition. The condition involves a boolean combination of simple conditions. Simple conditions or combinations of conjunctive simple conditions can be indicated in the hypergraph by simply labeling the appropriate attribute nodes with the condition. Conditions formed by the disjunction of simple conditions requires the insertion of a new edge which is labeled as an "OR" edge and the appropriate condition.

Figure 2 illustrates the inclusion of a relational algebra query into the hypergraph model of Figure 1.

```
Query: Select e1 where S# = S1 or P# = P1 giving T0 ;
       Join T0 and e2 giving T1 ;
       Project T1 over C.
```

Resulting Hypergraph:

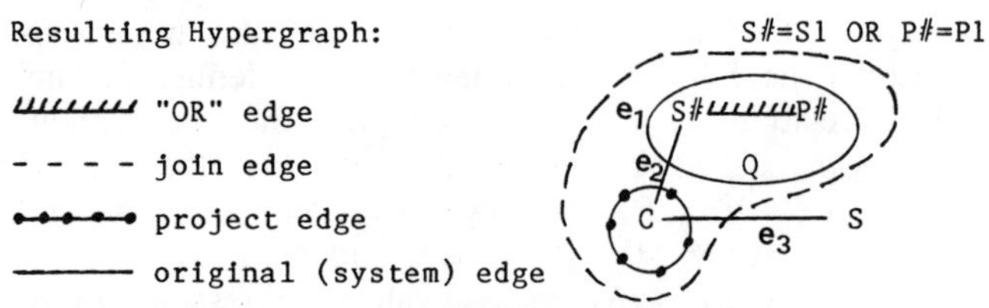

Figure 2—Example of including relational algebra in the hypergraph model

Network Data Model and Its Hypergraph Representation

The network schema consists of a set of record types $R_1, R_2, \ldots, R_n$ and a set of set types in which a set type is an association between one owner and one or more member record types.[18] Figure 4 provides the hypergraph representation of the network data model for the course offering database. Note that the fields of record types $R_i (i = 1, 2, \ldots, n)$ are the nodes in the hypergraph and the record types $R_i (i = 1, 2, \ldots, n)$ are the edges of the hypergraph. In addition, the hypergraph model is expanded to include the owner-member relationship between the edges. To do this, we use the node $L_{record\text{-}name}$ in each record to act as the identifier for the record. To indicate an owner-member relationship between the records "offering" and "student" in Figure 4, an arc is used to connect $L_{Offering}$ to $L_{Student}$.

In the remainder of this subsection the DML operation of the network language (FIND) is incorporated into the hypergraph model. As in the relational model, the selection criteria imposed on the network query contains a boolean combination of simple conditions. Conjunctive simple conditions are indicated in the hypergraph by simply labeling the appropriate nodes with the restriction on its value. Conditions formed by the disjunction of simple conditions require the insertion of a new edge which is labeled as an "OR" edge. The concept of projection (choosing data values from a record) is included in the network language by using SELECT FROM record-name:list. The concept is introduced into the hypergraph by enclosing the relevant nodes in a projection edge.

The inclusion of an OUT OF THE BLUE FIND and RELATIVE FIND in the hypergraph model is implied by two paths—the positioning path and the answering path. The positioning path contains all of the selection criteria that is required to establish a starting position in the network database. A positioning path implies an OUT OF THE BLUE FIND operation and possibly a RELATIVE FIND if there is more than one in the positioning path.

An answering path contains all of the selection criteria and projection information required to generate the result of the query. To process the answering path, three paths are examined—the common path, the selection path, and the projection path. The common path consists of the nodes (owner or member) that are common to both the selection path and projection paths. This path is used to establish the initial position for processing the selection and projection paths. The common path will always imply a RELATIVE FIND operation.

A selection path contains all of the selection criteria required to satisfy the query. It implies a RELATIVE FIND operation. The projection path consists of all the projection fields and the required selection criteria for the records that make up the projection path. It implies a special RELATIVE FIND (FIND FIRST, an operation to allow backing up to the beginning of the named record type for the current path) and a RELATIVE FIND operation. (Example 2 illustrates the inclusion of a network DML query into the hypergraph model.)

In the next section the hypergraph models are used as the basis of a translation process between the two database models.

QUERY TRANSLATION

We assume that we have two database designs. The source design attempts to retain the same semantics as the target design although they are supported by different database management systems and may be based on different data models. The data is stored in the format required by the target design, but the user views the data as though it were stored in the source design. As noted in the introduction, our motivation for examining this problem is to provide a local user in a distributed database environment with the ability to work with only one query language and to allow him/her to access the local DBMS directly.

The two designs are represented in the hypergraph format described in the previous section. To translate the query, we require three operations:

1. Map the source query into the hypergraph space of the source design.
2. Translate the resulting source query hypergraph into the hypergraph space of the target hypergraph.
3. Map the target query hypergraph to the target data manipulation language.

In the first operation we have the task of creating a source query hypergraph that has sufficient information content to provide a basis for translation. We have found four types of information to be useful. Naturally, the set of attributes that represents the result of the source query and the attributes used in search conditions are essential. In addition, we include information used in the network model to establish a position in the database. The hierarchical model operates in a similar manner.

The last type of information taken from the source query is navigational information, useful in navigating the target hypergraph. The path used in the source query is passed with the source query hypergraph. In target hypergraphs with ambiguous path selection, the source query path can be used to choose the correct path. For example, if the target database is relational and the hypergraph contains a cycle, we may have two paths connecting the relevant attributes.[14] The two paths have somewhat different semantics which can be resolved in the translation process by falling back and using the user's interpretation of the semantics from the source query path. A similar approach is taken for navigation in the network model.

The format used to pass the four types of information to the translation process is a three edge hypergraph, and the path information passed as a set. The first edge of the source query hypergraph (P) is the set of attributes used to establish position. The second edge (C) is the set of attributes used in the search conditions, and the conditions are used to label the attributes in the manner described earlier. The final edge (R) is the set of attributes which represents the result of the source query. Examples 1 and 2 provide the source query hypergraphs for the network and relational queries, respectively. Note that the position edge (P) is always empty for relational source queries.

The translation process makes use of the source query hypergraph, the source path set, and the target hypergraph to

EXAMPLE 1

Translation of a source query written for the network design of Figure 4 to the target query for the relational design of Figure 3.
Query: Get the names of all students who made a grade of A in all offerings of 1985 CS courses after 2500.

Network Source Query:

```
FIND Course Record Within SS-Course SET where
Course# = '2500'
Skip if fail
Repeat
FIND NEXT Course Record Within SS-Course SET where
dept = 'CS'
Exit if status-check
  Repeat
    FIND NEXT Offering Record Within HASOFFER SET
    where date = '1985'
    Exit if status-check
      Repeat
        FIND NEXT Student Record Within HASSTU SET
        where grade = 'A'
          Exit if status-check
          Select From Student: sname
      end
    end
end.
```

Source Query Hypergraph (Q_S):

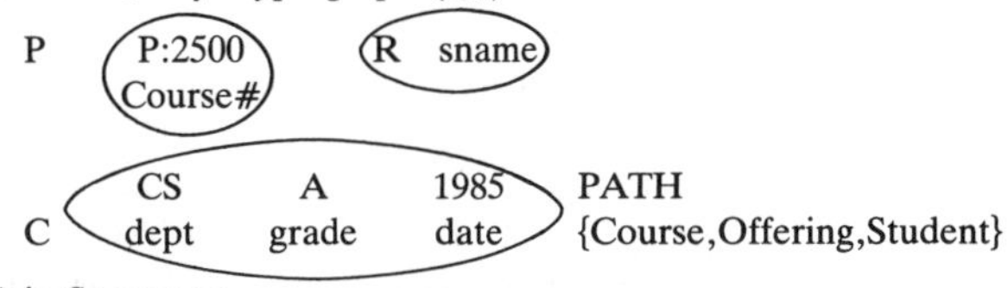

Join Sequence:
Course Offering Student

Target Query Hypergraph (Q_T):

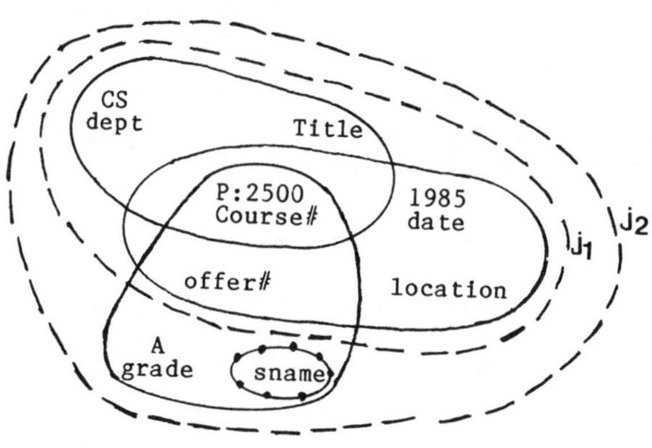

Note: The value P:2500 denotes that the label (2500) is used in the position edge (P).

Target Query:
Select Course where dept = 'CS' giving T_0
Select Offering where date = '1985' giving T_1
Join T_0 and T_1 giving T_2
Select Student where grade = 'A' giving T_3
Join T_2 and T_3 giving T_4
Find partition of T_4 where Course# $\geq$ 2500 giving T_5
Project T_5 over sname giving Result.

translate the source query into the target query hypergraph. When the source and target database designs have the same semantics (as in dynamic query processing), the source path set can be used directly to determine the path in the target hypergraph. For the case in which the target data model is relational, the source path is used to determine the join sequence required to incorporate the attributes used in the selection conditions and the projection attributes in the same relation. We assume that the join sequence produced is lossless. There are several methods that exist in the literature of ensuring the generation of a lossless join sequence, for example, γ-hypergraph,[12] hinges,[19] and maximal objects,[14] and we will assume that one of the techniques is used in the remainder of this work. The edges forming the join set are used as the initial edges of the target query hypergraph. Join edges are added to the target query hypergraph to imply the order in which the join operations will take place. As a final step the labels from the nodes in the source query hypergraph are copied over to the nodes in the target query hypergraph. Labels from the position edge of the source query hypergraph (if any) are marked as position labels before they are copied to the target query hypergraph. The concept of positioning is handled in the relational environment in one of two ways. In cases where the positioning is such that it can be implemented by simply using the condition on a selection, relational algebra operators are sufficient to answer the query. In more complex cases, we may require a sort of the resulting tuples followed by a partition of the sorted set.

Example 1 illustrates the process of translating a query from a network DML to the relational environment. The mapping of the target query hypergraph into the appropriate DML is naturally language dependent. The target query hypergraph for the relational environment uses relational algebra as its basis to allow the mapping algorithm to be basically a translation from relational algebra to the appropriate DML.

Translation from the source query hypergraph into the environment of a target database in the network format requires the creation of a target query hypergraph made up of a positioning path and an answering path. The source query path set is used by the translation process to determine the segments required in the target query hypergraph. The position edge (P) is used in conjunction with the path information to create the positioning path. The selection and projection edges of the source query hypergraph, C and R respectively, are used by the translation algorithms to create the answering path required to generate the target query in the network DML. To enhance the process of generating the target query, the answering path is processed to create the common parent path, selection path, and projection path as described before.

To simplify our discussion in this presentation we make two assumptions concerning the nature of the source query. First we assume that the translation process considers a class of queries which are tree queries (or acyclic queries)[20]—queries which do not have a cycle. We also assume that network source queries look at the data from some starting point (position) in the database and continue until the end of the database is reached. Such an assumption can be removed in the general case but requires unnecessary complexity in this discussion.

EXAMPLE 2

Example 2:

Translation of a source query written for the relational design of Figure 3 to the target query for the network design of Figure 4.

Query: Get the name of all students who made a grade of A in all offering 2 OR offered in Washington and taught by a male teacher for all CS courses.

Relational Source Query:

```
Join Course and Offering giving T1
Join Teacher and T1 giving T2
Join Student and T2 giving T3
Select T4 where dept='CS' and (offer#='2' OR location='Washington')
     and sex='male' and grade='A' giving T4
Project T4 over sname giving Result.
```

Source Query Hypergraph (Q_S):

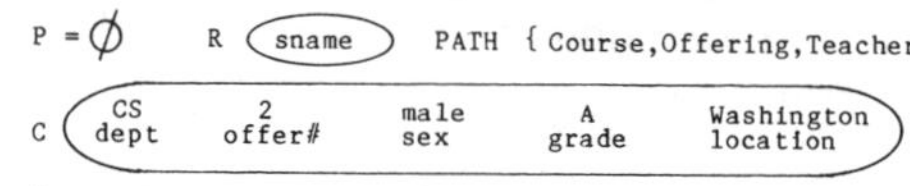

Target Query Hypergraph (Q_T):

Target Query Answering Path: Target Query Positioning Path:

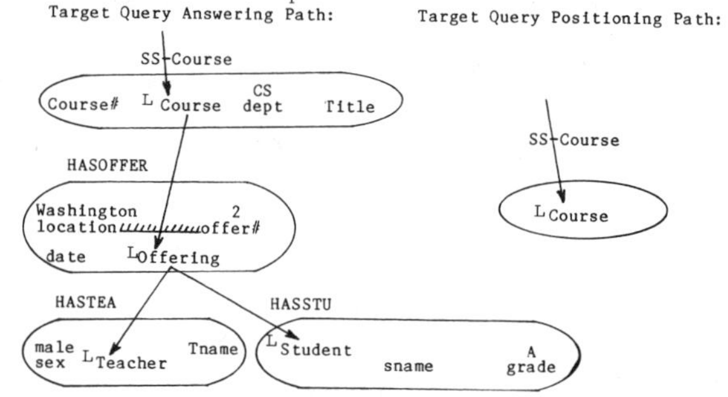

Common Path: Selection Path: Projection Path:

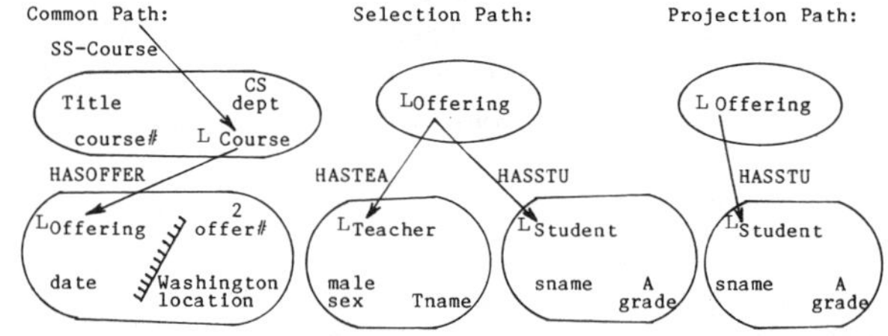

Target Query:

```
FIND Course Record Within SS-Course SET
Skip if fail
 Repeat  /* process common path */
  FIND NEXT Course Record Within SS-Course SET wher dept='CS'
  Exit if status-check
   Repeat
    FIND NEXT Offering Record Within HASOFFER SET
              where offer#='2' OR location='Washington'
    Exit if status-check
                          /* process selection path */
      FIND NEXT Teacher Record Within HASTEA SET where sex='male'
      Skip if fail
      FIND NEXT Student Record Within HASSTU SET where grade='A'
      Skip if fail
                     /* process projection path */
       FIND FIRST Student Record Within HASSTU SET
        Repeat
         FIND NEXT Student Record Within HASSTU SET where grade='A'
         Exit if status-check
         Select From Student: sname
        end
   end
 end.
```

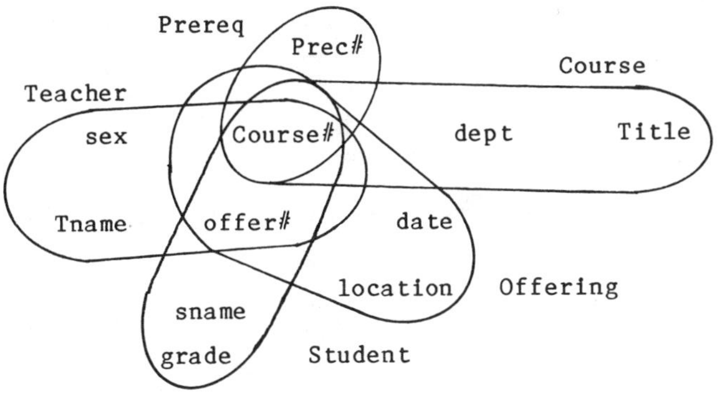

Figure 3—Hypergraph representation of relational course offering database

Example 2 illustrates the translation process, where the source query is written for the relational design of Figure 3, and the target design is the network design shown in Figure 4.

CONCLUSION

A process for translation of queries between the network and relational data models has been presented and shown to produce valid queries.[16] The translation scheme uses the hypergraph as an intermediate representation format between the two DMLs. The translation process requires three steps:

1. Map the source query into the hypergraph space of the source design.
2. Translate the resulting source query hypergraph into the hypergraph space of the target hypergraph.
3. Map the target query hypergraph to the target manipulation language.

The second step is the heart of the translation process and is model dependent, but not DML dependent. Steps one and three are language dependent, but based on the algorithms that we have developed to this point are not difficult to implement.

The work presented here represents the basic description of the translation process as it relates to the relational and network data models. Space limitations keep us from providing the algorithms used to create the structures given in Examples 1 and 2 (see Owrang[16] for details). Currently we are working on expansion of the system to handle the cyclic queries, and work has been started on implementing the translation system. Note that the discussion has been limited to operating in an environment in which the source and target databases have the same semantics. The algorithms used in this translation process can be easily expanded to handle the case in which some changes have been made in the semantics, such as is the case in the work by Su and Reynolds.[1]

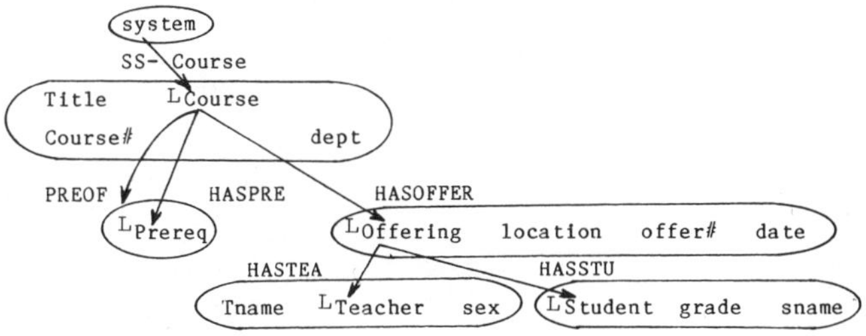

Figure 4—Hypergraph representation of network course offering database

REFERENCES

1. Su, S.Y.W. and M.J. Reynolds. "Conversion of High Level Sublanguage Queries to Account for Database Changes." *Proceedings of the 2nd International Conference on VLDB,* Brussels, September 1976, pp. 143–157.
2. Codd, E.F. "A Relational Model of Data for Large Shared Data Bank." *CACM,* 13 (1970) 6, pp. 377–387.
3. Chamberlin, D. and R. Boyce. "SEQUEL: A Structured English Query Language." *Proceedings ACM SIGMOD Workshop on Data Description, Access, and Control.* Ann Arbor, Michigan, 1974.
4. Housel, B., D. Smith, N. Shu, and V.Y. Lum. "DEFINE: A Nonprocedural Data Description Language for Defining Information Easily." *ACM Pacific Regional Conference,* San Francisco, 1975, pp. 62–70.
5. Shu, N., B. Housel, V.Y. Lum. "CONVERT: A High Level Translation Definition Language for Data Conversion." *CACM,* 18 (1975) 10, pp. 557–567.
6. Katz, R.H. and E. Wong. "Decompiling CODASYL DML into Relational Queries." *ACM TODS,* 7 (1982) 1, pp. 1–23.
7. CODASYL Cobol Committee. J. Dev., 1978.
8. Codd, E.F. "Further Normalization of the Database Relational Model." *Current Computer Science Symposia 6, Data Base Systems,* New York: Prentice-Hall, 1971.
9. Smith, J.M., P. Berstein, U. Dayal, N. Goodman, T. Landers, K. Lin, and W. Wong. "MULTIBASE: Integrating Heterogeneous Distributed Database Systems." *AFIPS, Proceedings of the National Computer Conference* (Vol. 50), 1981, pp. 487–499.
10. Beeri, C., R. Fagin, D. Maier, and M. Yannakakis. "On the Desirability of Acyclic Database Schemes." *JACM,* 30 (1983) 3, pp. 479–513.
11. Chase, K. "Join Graphs and Acyclic Database Schemes." *Very Large Database Conference,* 1980, pp. 95–100.
12. Fagin, R. "Degrees of Acyclicity for Hypergraphs and Relational Database Schemes," *JACM,* 30 (1983) 3, pp. 514–550.
13. Fagin, R., A.O. Mendelzon, J. Ullman. "A Simplified Universal Relation Assumption and Its Properties." *ACM TODS,* 7 (1982) 3, pp. 343–360.
14. Maier, D. and J. Ullman. "Maximal Object and the Semantics of Universal Relation Databases." *ACM TODS,* 8 (1983) 1, pp. 1–14.
15. Owrang O.M.M., and L.L. Miller. "Query Translation Between Data Models." *Proceedings of Sixth Annual International IEEE Phoenix Conference on Computers and Communications,* Scottsdale, Arizona, February 1987, pp. 308–314.
16. Owrang O.M.M. *Query Translation in a Heterogeneous Distributed Database Based on Hypergraph Models.* Doctoral Dissertation, University of Oklahoma, Norman, Oklahoma, May 1986.
17. Ullman, J. "The Universal Relation Strikes Back." *Proceedings ACM Symposium on Principle of Database Systems,* Los Angeles, March 1982, pp. 10–22.
18. Ullman, J., *Principles of Database Systems,* Second edition, Computer Science Press, Rockville, Maryland, 1982.
19. Gyssens, M. and J. Paredaens. "A Decomposition Methodology for Cyclic Databases." *Advances in Database Theory,* 2 (1984), pp. 85–122.
20. Bernstein, P.A. and N. Goodman. "Power of Natural Semijoin." *SIAM Journal of Computing* 10 (1981) 4, pp. 751–771.

A new approach to version management for databases

by VINIT VERMA and HUIZHU LU
Oklahoma State University
Stillwater, Oklahoma

ABSTRACT

Following an overview of version management databases, a new approach for implementing these databases by employing the use of persistence in height balanced trees is proposed. Persistence in a tree is obtained by path copying. In classical databases, version management is performed by checkpoints which require O(n) time, and O(n) space. This new methodology maintains historical data in O(lg n) space, and O(lg n) time for a binary search tree. The paper discusses how the concept of persistence is superimposed on B-trees, which are the primary storage structures utilized in present day databases. A search operation on this persistent B-tree of order 'm' is $O(\lg(k) \lg_m n(\lg .80(m-1)))$, where 'k' is the number of nodes in an index time stamp tree, 'n' is the number of nodes in the B-tree, and the B-tree is assumed to have 80% node utilization.

INTRODUCTION

Human memory essentially has a no deletion mechanism. Memory does exhibit a decay characteristic with time, but people simply do not delete. The concept of deletion was invented to reuse expensive computer storage. With the falling computer storage costs, and new storage technologies (e.g., optical disks),[1,2] this deletion policy will eventually give way to a non-deletion policy in database applications.[3] All accounting, financial, and legal databases require a non-deletion policy. This policy is usually required by law for good reasons. Once this policy comes into effect, then a version management strategy will need to be imposed on current databases.

Conventional database management systems lack the ability to store and process time dependent data.[4,5,6] Without this temporal support the burden comes on the application programmer to build some temporal information management strategy. The resulting applications are inefficient in terms of data storage and processing costs. Most decision support systems require trend analysis and historical queries which are not readily supported by DBMSs of today. Even error corrections have been implemented in DBMSs via audit trails which require space intensive checkpoints to preserve past states.[7,8,9]

The initial part of this paper describes the four types of databases which support temporal information processing. The four database types are differentiated by their ability to support these time concepts and their temporal information processing capability. Snapshot, rollback, historical, and temporal databases are the four types of databases which are discussed.[10] In the second section of this paper, the authors propose the use of persistent search trees to implement these version management databases. Persistent search trees primarily utilize path copying for maintaining historical information.[11] The concept of path copying to save historical versions can be carried over to any height balanced tree—height-balanced trees, weight-balanced trees, or B-trees for example.[12,13] The paper discusses persistence on an HB(1) tree using path copying. The persistence can be obtained without path copying and this is also shown for the same HB(1) tree. By far the most common file structure or access method utilized in databases today is VSAM (virtual storage access method). VSAM is implemented using B-trees. So if this version management can be superimposed on B-trees, we have an appropriate data structure to implement version management databases. The final section of this paper discusses how B-trees can be made persistent.

CLASSIFICATION OF DATABASES WITH TEMPORAL SUPPORT

The four types of version management databases are described below. The relational data model has been used for this discussion. In the mentioned data model the user views the data in the form of tables. The rows in the table form tuples and the columns form the attributes. Inserts, deletes, and updates occur instantaneously on these tables in a conventional system. The table below shows two attributes name and salary, and two tuples (rows).

Name	Salary
Jack	$1000
Tim	$1500

Snapshot Databases

A state, or instance, of a database is its current content, which does not necessarily reflect the current status of the enterprise. Dynamic changes in such an environment are preserved by snapshots. Insert, delete, and update operations on the payroll table occur instantaneously and no historical information is recorded. Such a database is described as a snapshot database. A snapshot database cannot support the following types of temporal queries: (1) trend analysis (statistical information on the number of employees during the past three years), (2) historical query (What was Jack's pay two months ago?). Further, snapshot databases cannot support (1) retroactive change (Tim got a raise of $100 starting last month), or (2) a proactive change (Jerry is joining the company next month) information.

These snapshot databases provide no historical retrievals or updates. The burden to preserve and maintain historical information falls on the application programmer. As the variation of data over time is not related to any application, so the DBMS, rather than the application programmer should take care of this version management.

Rollback Databases

A rollback database stores a sequence of snapshot states indexed by transaction time. Transaction time is defined as the time during which a database update is performed. An update refers to insert, delete, or update database operations. Historical queries can be supported by moving along this transaction time axis and selecting a particular snapshot state. The operation of selecting a snapshot state is termed rollback, and a database supporting it is called a rollback database.

For example, the relation in Figure 1 has three transactions. Starting from an empty relation, two tuples were added at time A, a third tuple was added at time B, and finally a tuple was deleted at time C. Modifications on a rollback database can only be made to the most recent snapshot state. As is evident from the above transaction, each transaction results in a new snapshot being appended on the transaction time axis. Since snapshot database stores only the most current state of the database, historical queries are not supported. But rollback databases can back up on the transaction time axis and support an historical query. Note, rollback databases support historical queries, not historical updates, that is, insert, delete, update. Thus a rollback database can support the following query on the payroll database: "What was Tim's salary last month?" The database will roll back on the transaction time axis and display a snapshot of the needed relation. Rollback databases record the history of database transactions. A tuple becomes effective as soon as it is entered into a rollback database. Retroactive and proactive changes cannot be recorded. If it is discovered that Tim got a raise a month earlier than the month that is stored in the database, there is no way to resolve this in a rollback database.

Historical Databases

Historical databases record a single historical state per relation. They support valid time—the time during which the relationship being modeled was valid. Since previous states of the database are discarded, historical views are not supported. Historical databases have a resemblance to snapshot databases in that error corrections are not recorded. These types of databases need extra high-level language support to be able to support the complex semantics of valid time. They support the following types of historical queries: "What was Tim's salary when Jerry joined the company?" The result of the query will be an historical relation which can be used in further historical queries. These databases support arbitrary modifications, whereas rollback databases only allow snapshots to be appended. This historical relation can show that a later transaction has changed the time when a tuple takes

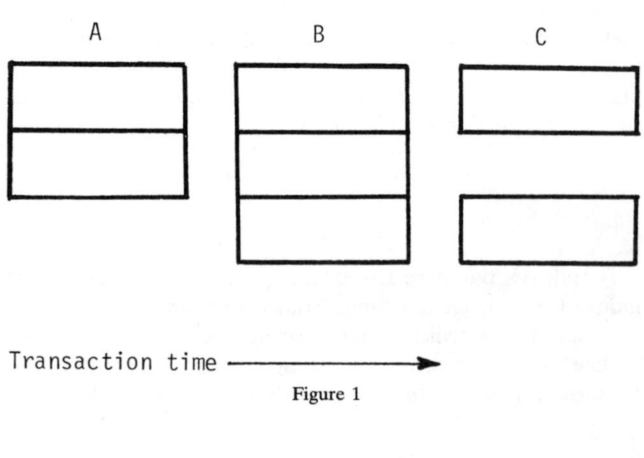

Figure 1

effect in the relation. Thus historical DBMSs can represent correct information about the past, whereas rollback databases can back up to an incorrect previous snapshot. Historical relations can be viewed as interval relations, in which a tuple is valid until the next tuple with the same key becomes effective.

Temporal Databases

The plus points of the rollback and historical databases are integrated to form temporal databases. These support both transaction time and valid time in the same relation; and both these times can be manipulated by a query. A rollback database views stored tuples, whether valid or not, as of a certain instant in time. An historical database views tuples valid at some instant as of now. Finally, a temporal database views tuples valid at some instant seen as of some other instant and thus can capture both retroactive and proactive changes.

A temporal relation is a sequence of historical states, each a complete historical relation. A rollback on a temporal relation selects a particular historical state on which an historical query is executed. A new historical state is appended to each transaction. Temporal databases are capable of answering the following kinds of queries: According to the state of the database as of December 1985, "What was Tim's salary when Jack joined the company?" Notice that the query is manipulating both the valid time as well as the transaction time.

The following analogy should prove helpful to an understanding of the temporal classification of databases. A snapshot relation can be compared to the latest payroll stub showing the current salary of the recipient. If the recipient gets a raise, the next stub shows the new salary, but the latest stub gives no information about the recipient's previous salary. The collection of all payroll stubs forms a rollback relation, a slice of which is a snapshot relation comparable to a payroll stub. No corrections are allowed on past stubs. An historical relation can be compared to a chart containing the salary history of a person until the instant of making the chart. If an error is found in the chart, or a person gets a raise, then a new chart reflecting the change is made. The current chart should always be up to date. A temporal relation is a file of all such payroll charts marked by the date when each was prepared. It is possible to refer to an old chart as it was known at some instant of time. An in-depth discussion on temporal databases has been presented in Snodgrass and Ilsoo.[10] Having built the needed background for version management databases, we now consider methods for implementing these databases.

A NEW APPROACH FOR VERSION MANAGEMENT

Path copying can be utilized to maintain previous versions of a tree after insertions and deletions.[11] Basically, the path in a tree along which an update operation is performed is replicated to maintain the previous version. These trees which maintain previous versions are termed "persistent trees." A persistent tree differs from an ordinary search tree in that following an insert/delete operation the old version of the tree is still accessible. The old version of the tree needs to be maintained after a new version has been created during an update operation. If the entire tree is copied on each update operation, then the processing time is O(n) and the space utilized in O(n). Thomas[14] addresses the concurrency problem of these multicopy databases. Severance and Lohman[15] discuss the use of differential files to maintain versions in large databases. In path copying, only those nodes are copied in which a change is made. Thus any node which contains a pointer to a node that is copied, must, itself, be copied. If every node contains pointers only to its children, this means copying one node requires copying the entire path to the node from the root of the tree. Thus, in effect, a set of search trees is created, one per update, having different roots but sharing common subtrees. The processing in a path-copying search tree is O(lg(n)) since only one path in the tree is traversed. The space utilized is also O(lg(n)) since only one path will be copied. If there exists a large number of updates then the roots of these tree versions can reside in an array, or better still, in a search tree. If a search tree is utilized to hold roots for the different tree versions, then a search time of O(lg(m)lg(n)) is obtained, where 'm' is the number of updates and 'n' is the number of nodes in the tree. This path copying works on any kind of balanced tree, for example, a height-balanced tree, or weight-balanced tree. In a balanced tree, the balance is maintained by storing certain balance information in each node and rebalancing after an insert/delete operation by performing a series of rotations along the access path. Aho, Hopcroft, and Ulmann[16] and Knuth[17] provide a good description of height-balanced trees.

The example below shows how a height-balanced(1) tree can be made persistent using path copying. The keys CD,AE,BG,QK,RR are inserted in that order into an HB(1) tree. The resulting HB(1) tree after balancing is shown in Figure 2. This is the state of the tree at time 0 in Figure 3. The numbers to the left of each node are the time stamps, and the numbers to the right reflect the balance information. At time 1, suppose SS is inserted into the tree. The tree undergoes a rotation as BG becomes critical. The balanced tree with the path BG→QK→RR copied is shown under the time 1 root. The tree version under time 2 results after TT is inserted into the tree at time 1. Appropriate rotations have been performed to balance the tree. Note the path QK→RR→SS has been copied from the time 1 tree to result in the time 2 tree. Once a node is copied or a new node is inserted, the appropriate time stamp is placed on the node. A new index tree can be made which holds the pointers to the various time stamp roots. Figure 4 addresses the previous point. If the version 1 tree needs to be accessed, the pointer with key equal to one in the index tree is taken to direct the search in the appropriate tree version. This time-index tree can be made height balanced too.

A search tree can be made persistent without node copying. The nodes are allowed to grow arbitrarily large after updates, that is, each time we need to change a pointer, a new pointer

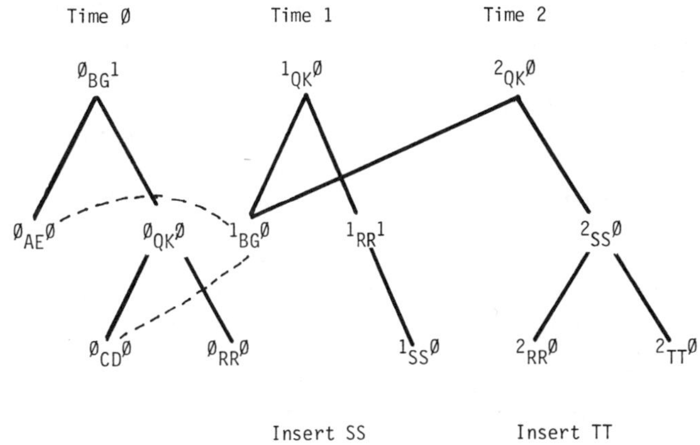

Figure 3

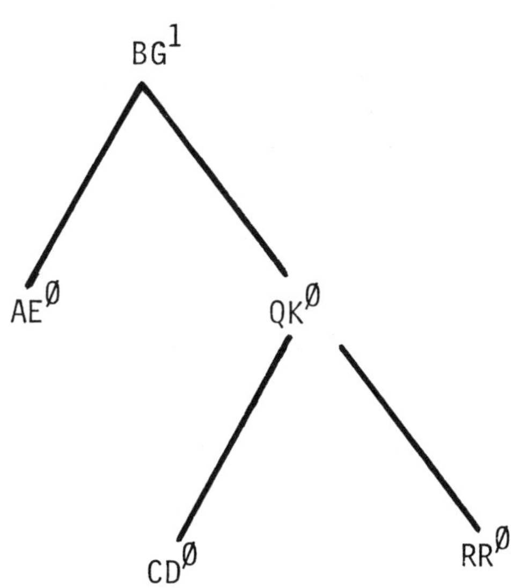

Figure 2

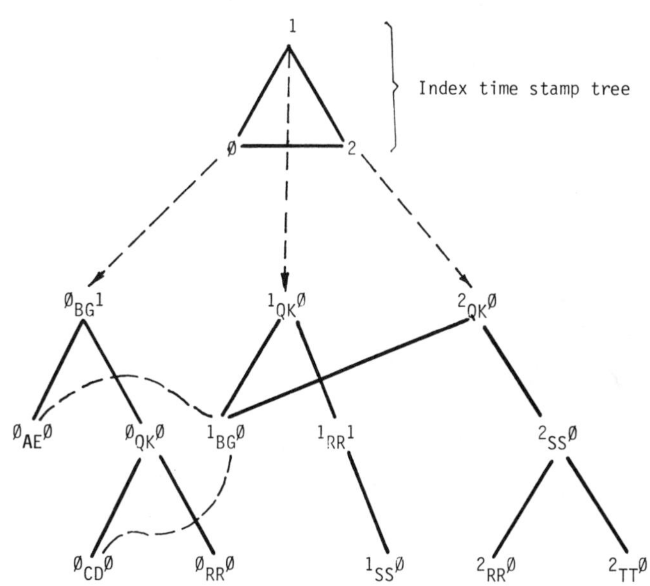

Figure 4

is stored in the node along with a time stamp indicating the time of the update. Thus the space requirement is O(1) during an insertion as only one node is inserted and no copies are made. The pointer change also requires O(1) space since only one pointer is inserted. The drawback of the method is the time spent deciding on the correct pointer in a node, as the node has an arbitrary number of left and right pointers. If a binary search on an index time stamp tree is performed, choosing the correct pointer takes O(lg(m)), and an access, insert, or delete takes O(lg(n)lg(m)), where "m" is the number of time stamps and "n" is the number of nodes in the tree.

Starting with the tree in Figure 2, a persistent HB(1) tree without node copying is obtained (see Figure 5). The tree in Figure 5 results after the insertion of SS and TT into the tree in Figure 1, at times 1 and 2 respectively. Again pointers to the different version of the tree need to be maintained in an index time stamp tree. The balance tags are overwritten each time, and the arcs reflect the time of creation. To traverse the tree at time 0, the appropriate pointer in the index tree is accessed.

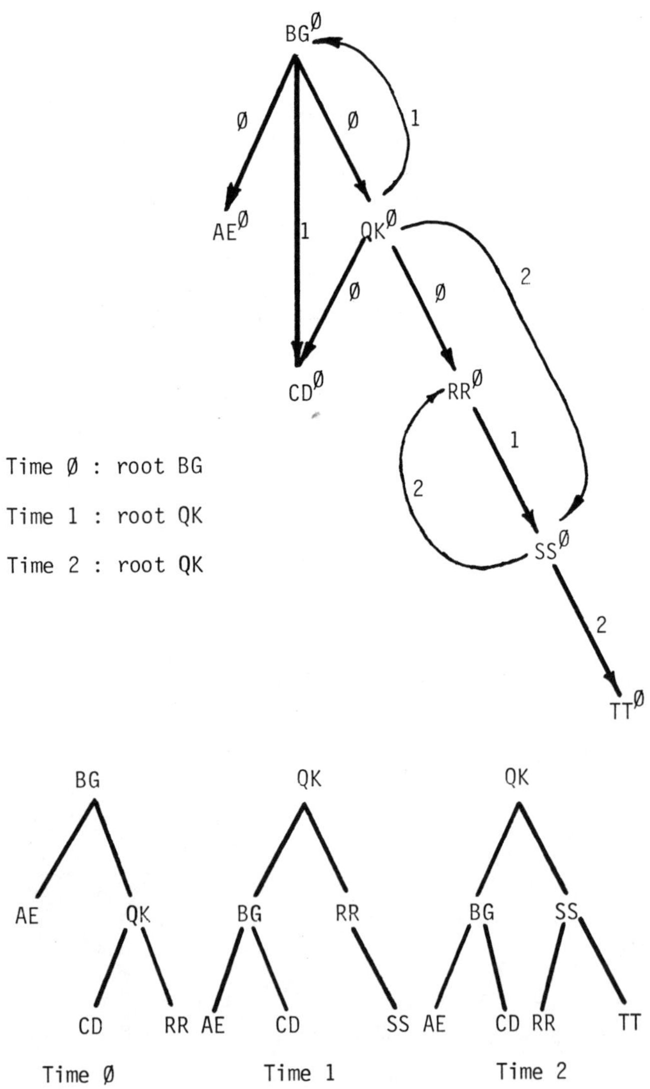

Figure 5

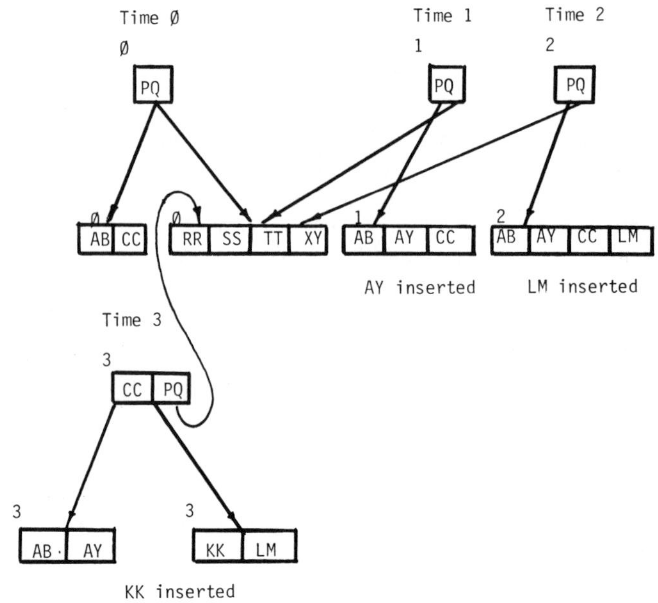

Figure 6

All 0 arcs are accessed once the correct tree version is located. To reveal the time 1 tree, the appropriate index tree pointer is taken again. Then from each node a 1 arc is taken. If a 1 arc doesn't exist, a 0 arc is taken. The same is done for the time 2 tree. As a tree version is traversed, each visited node needs to be flagged to avoid cycles during the traversals.

Path copying can be carried over to a B-tree also. Figure 6 depicts an order 5 B-tree. At time 0 the B-tree has keys AB,CC,PQ,RR,SS,TT and XY. At time 1, AY is inserted into the B-tree. Notice that the nodes in the path are copied and a new root with time stamp 1 results. At time 2, LM is inserted—again with appropriate node copying. Finally at time 3, KK is inserted resulting in a node getting overfull. The condition is resolved with a 1-2 split. The nodes along the path are again copied, and a new root results. An index time stamp tree indexes this B-tree. It takes O(lg(k)) to search the index tree for the appropriate time stamp. In a B-tree all leaves are at the same level. Therefore a search operation takes, on a average, $O(lg_m n)$ to locate the node of interest. Let us suppose that a node in the B-tree has 80% node utilization, and the number of keys in a node justify a binary search. Then the search operation gives a processing order of $lg_m n$(lg .80(m-1), where (m-1) is the maximum number of keys in a node of a B-tree of order "m," and "n" is the number of nodes in the B-tree. Thus the total search time in this version management B-tree will be lg(k)$lg_m n$(lg .80(m-1)).

B-trees are by far the most frequently utilized data structures with which to implement databases. IBM's VSAM is based on B-trees. So the path copying on a B-tree will provide version management for VSAM databases. Figure 7 depicts the proposed version management support for VSAM. The index tree, which points to different tree versions, can be maintained in primary memory. Once the tree version to be queried is located in the index tree, the appropriate page can be retrieved from the VSAM file on disk.

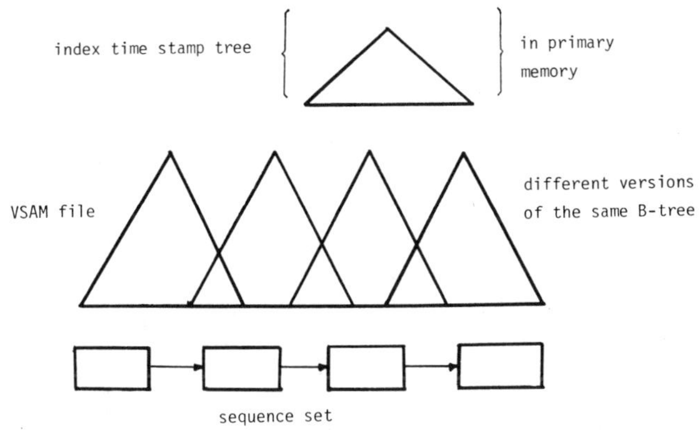

Figure 7

CONCLUSION

The paper provides an overview of version management databases. The version management systems are categorized as snapshot, rollback, historical, and temporal databases. The concept of persistence in balanced trees is utilized to create an efficient data structure with which to implement these temporal databases. The classical method of checkpointing proves extremely expensive in both memory usage and processing time. Path copying in a tree provides the needed persistence of historical data. A height-balanced(1) tree depicted the persistence characteristic. A persistent B-tree is proposed as an appropriate data structure to support version management on databases. A search operation on this persistent B-tree of order "m" is $O(\lg(k)\ \lg_m n(\lg .80(m-1)))$, where "k" is the number of nodes in an index time stamp tree, "n" is the number of nodes in the B-tree, and the B-tree is assumed to have 80% node utilization. The space utilized is $O(\lg_m n(m-1))$, as all nodes along one path of an "m" way B-tree need to be replicated.

REFERENCES

1. Rathman, P. "Dynamic Data Structures on Optical Disks." *Proceedings of the IEEE International Conference on Data Engineering,* April 1985, pp. 175–180.
2. Hoagland, A. "Information Storage Technology: A Look at the Future." *IEEE Computer,* 18(1985)7, pp. 60–67.
3. Copeland, G. "What if Mass Storage Was Free?" *IEEE Computer,* 15(1982)7, pp. 22–35.
4. Weiderhold, G. "Databases." *IEEE Computer,* 17(1985)10, pp. 211–233.
5. Date, C.J. *An Introduction to Database Systems.* Vol. I, 4th ed., Reading, Massachusetts: Addison-Wesley, 1986.
6. Weiderhold, G. *Database Design.* 2nd ed., New York: McGraw-Hill, 1983.
7. Chandy, K.M. "A Survey of Analytic Models for Rollback and Recovery Strategies in Database Systems." *IEEE Computer,* 8(1975)5, pp. 40–47.
8. Verhofstad, J.S.M. "Recovery Techniques for Database Systems." *ACM Computing Surveys,* 10(1978)2, pp. 167–195.
9. Chandy, K.M., J.C. Browne, C.W. Dissly, and W.R. Uhrig. "Analytic Model for Rollback and Recovery." *IEEE Transactions on Software Engineering,* SE-1(1975)1.
10. Snodgrass, Richard and Ilsoo Ahn. "Temporal Databases." *IEEE Computer,* 19(1986)9, pp. 35–42.
11. Sarnak, Neil and Robert E. Tarjan. "Planar Point Location Using Persistent Search Trees." *Communications of the ACM,* 29(1986)7, pp. 669–679.
12. Comer, D. "The Ubiquitous B-tree." *ACM Computing Surveys,* 11(1979)2, pp. 121–137.
13. Maier, D. and S.C. Salveter. "Hysterical B-trees." *Information Processing Letter,* 12(1981)4, pp. 199–202.
14. Thomas, R.H. "A Solution to the Concurrency Control Problem for Multiple Copy Databases." *Proceedings, CompCon,* Spring, 1978.
15. Severance, D.C. and C.M. Lohman. "Differential Files: Their Application to the Maintenance of Large Databases." *ACM Transactions on Database Systems,* 1(1976)3, pp. 256–267.
16. Aho, Alfred V., John E. Hopcroft, and Jeffrey D. Ulmann. *Data Structures and Algorithms.* Reading, Massachusetts: Addison-Wesley, 1985.
17. Knuth, D.E. *The Art of Computer Programming, Vol. I: Fundamental Algorithms.* 2nd ed., Reading, Massachusetts: Addison-Wesley, 1973.

The impact of data models on application development at Pacific Bell

by RAY STRAKA
Pacific Bell
San Ramon, California

INTRODUCTION

The evolution of data models from reflections of physical database management systems to powerful conceptual tools has had a profound impact on the way systems have been developed at Pacific Bell over the past decade. We will focus on the impact data models have had on our System for Building Systems,[1] will describe our migration from classical data models to more advanced models, and will consider the impact future classes of models may have on our capability to develop applications.

STRATEGIC BUSINESS AND SYSTEMS PLANNING

Pacific Bell came into being on January 1, 1984 with the divestiture of Pacific Telephone & Telegraph from AT&T along with the other Bell Operating companies. Pacific Bell found itself in the position of a 17 billion dollar new venture with a need to build strategic business plans reflecting its own destiny. Using an ensemble of strategic systems planning techniques, an application, data, and technology architecture were developed based on the identified future business direction. In this way those groups of entities associated with the subject areas of data most leverageable by the business were identified.

We found that 80 percent to 90 percent of our business functions, processes, and activities utilized the customer, product, and location data entities. Early implementation of these entities would have substantial leverage. The application model also indicates related entities which must be implemented early in order to support the implementation of the primary entities. In this way, a base of strategically significant data is developed upon which future applications can be built.

Strategic systems planning indicates that the systems we need do not look anything like the systems we have currently. This does not come as a great surprise as the new architecture is based on an analysis of the needs of our business; former systems tended to reflect the capabilities and interests of the information systems community. The Entity-Relationship Model[2,3] played a significant role in several of the methodologies employed in the strategic systems planning effort. It is unlikely that the complex interrelationships of the business' data could have been understood without such powerful modeling techniques. However, the use of data models has not always played such a central role in the systems development lifecycle.

SYSTEMS DEVELOPMENT HISTORY

Prior to divestiture, many of our operational systems were built by Bell Labs or AT&T. Many of these systems continue to this day and are either supported locally or through Bell Communications Research. Internally built systems tended to be in the business support arena including accounts payable, accounts receivable, general ledger, payroll, facilities tracking, and order distribution.

In the 1960s and early 1970s, formal data models played almost no part in the systems development lifecycle at Pacific Bell. Systems were developed independently around applications areas with no emphasis on data sharing among applications. These applications for the most part made no use of database technologies, or if they did it was only to use the DBMSs as if they were an access method.

In the late 1970s and early 1980s the structured revolution, which began several years previously, was "discovered" at Pacific Bell. A small number of internal systems developers embraced the process-oriented structured approach as taught by Yourdon, DeMarco, and Gane & Sarson.

One of Pacific Bell's most stable and well designed systems was built using the DeMarco approach.[4] It was originally implemented using a network data model, but was subsequently rewritten as a relational design. As the DeMarco methodology lacked support for logical database design at that time, the relational database was developed using James Martin's approach: canonical synthesis and normalization.[5] The final database consisted of 32 tables in 3NF.

Though the process-oriented methodologies were a great improvement over the previous chaos, as our applications became increasingly database and management information system oriented, the inability of the process-oriented methodologies to directly support database design became more troublesome.

As a result, we went looking for a more suitable approach when confronted with a large personnel application intended to activate our first subject database, employee. We adopted a methodology developed and marketed by Ken Orr & Associates. Known as the Data Structured Systems Development (DSSD) approach,[5] this methodology directly yields a tabular logical database design in at least 2NF and usually in 3NF. This approach uses a combination of top-down and bottom-up methods which combine aspects of both the Entity-Relationship Approach[2,3] and the Relational Approach.[7,8]

We have found this methodology to work well; however, there is a danger that the logical database design will be too biased toward the single application's view of the data. Therefore, it is important for a company entity-relationship data model to provide guidance and context while applying the DSSD methodology. This mixture of models is the approach currently being used for new application development at Pacific Bell.

In the future we hope to find even more support for our application development efforts from advanced data models and database management systems based on those models. Our research indicates that commercially feasible DBMSs based on the entity-relationship model or other models which express more of the business "semantics," such as the SDM model proposed by Hammer and McLeod,[9] will be available in the near term. We look to the vendor community to develop robust systems development methodologies which will enable large corporations such as Pacific Bell to utilize these tools to their greatest advantage.

REFERENCES

1. Straka, R. "System for Building Systems at Pacific Bell." *Data Base Newsletter;* Boston, Mass., Database Research Group, Inc., January–February, 1987; pp. 11–12.
2. Chen, P.P. "The Entity-Relationship Model: Toward a Unified View of Data." *ACM Transactions on Database Systems,* 1(March, 1976)1.
3. Chen, P.P. "The Entity-Relationship Model: A Basis for the Enterprise View of Data." *AFIPS Conference Proceedings,* Dallas, Texas, (Vol. 46) 1977.
4. DeMarco, T. *Structured Analysis and System Specification,* New York, New York. Yourdon Inc., 1978.
5. Martin, J. *Computer Data-Base Organization,* Englewood Cliffs, New Jersey. Prentice-Hall, 1977.
6. *The Design Library,* Topeka, Kansas. Ken Orr & Associates, 1981.
7. Codd, E.F. "A Relational Model of Data for Large Shared Data Banks."*Communications of the ACM,* 13(June 1970)6, pp. 377–387.
8. Codd, E.F. "Extending the Relational Database Model to Capture More Meaning." *ACM Transactions on Database Systems,* 4(Dec. 1979)4, pp. 397–434.
9. Hammer, H. & D. McLeod, "Database Description with SDM: A Semantic Database Model." *ACM Transactions on Database Systems,* 6(Sept. 1981)3, pp. 351–386.

The ER approach, relational technology and application development

by MARTIN MODELL
Merrill Lynch
New York, New York

Among the tasks facing many application development teams today are the development of a logical data model, and using that data model to choose a data base management product. In the past many applications were limited to a single DBMS, one which was either based upon the hierarchic or the network data structure model. Most firms used DBMS products which supported one or the other, but usually not both.

The availability of a number of working relational implementations either as separate software, or as relational versions of existing DBMS products, and the high degree of visibility and favorable publicity attached to the relational model itself has persuaded an increasing number of firms to acquire them. Thus, many application teams now must make a choice of two supported, but substantially different data base structural architectures.

In the past, the application data modeling process created designs which were oriented toward the available DBMS. The logical data model was often framed in the manner of the logical data structure model of the prevailing DBMS, that is either in hierarchic or network form. Because of the popularity of the relational products, and the comparative simplicity of the relational model, many designers today attempt to frame their data in tabular form.

However, just as the analysis of the application processing requirements must be objective and unbiased toward any particular processing mode, the data modeling process must be objective and data structure independent, to avoid biasing the analysis toward one or the other of the products. Those designers who develop an ER model but do not take the additional step of evaluating the model against each DBMS's natural data structure will find that they have caused themselves unnecessary problems when they force their data into an incompatible data structure model.

Each application's data has a natural structure. The use of the Entity Relationship model can graphically illustrate this natural structure and can be a strong indicator of which DBMS will be most effective. Although most analysts assume that their application's data can be stored under any DBMS with equal effectiveness, in practice the natural structure of the data will make one DBMS more effective than another.

The fully attributed ER model provides a wealth of information for the analyst to make a proper DBMS evaluation. A detailed evaluation not only of the entity structures, but also of the attributed relationships provides a sound guide to an appropriate DBMS choice. Thus a true logical data modeling step, using a structurally independent modeling technique has become indispensable to the application analysis and design process.

A retargetable vector code generator

by TOM C. REYES*
Oklahoma State University
Stillwater, Oklahoma

ABSTRACT

This paper describes the prototype implementation of a retargetable vector code generator which applies recent advances in automatic (scalar) code generation techniques to the task of generating code for a vector source language. The source language is a subset of Fortran 8X, the proposed successor to the Fortran 77 standard. The target machine is an attached vector processor. This work extends Cattell's maximal munch method to vector code generation. Variants of TCOL are used for the intermediate representation of both the source program and the target machine description table. The prototype implementation demonstrates the feasibility of template-driven vector code generation and emphasizes the importance of code optimization in a vector compiler.

---

* The author's present address is: Amoco Production Company Research Center, P.O. Box 3385, Tulsa, OK 74102

INTRODUCTION

Most vector processors are programmed using either a low-level machine-specific language or a scalar high-level language (usually Fortran 77) with a vectorizing compiler. Code written in a low-level language is inherently nonportable. Writing good efficient code in a low-level language is also a difficult and often expensive task. Pure Fortran 77 code is portable but inherently sequential, obscuring the parallelism present in the application program and requiring a vectorizing compiler to rediscover vector operations in sequential loops. In practice, most Fortran programs which are run on vector machines are not completely portable either. It is not uncommon to maintain multiple versions of Fortran programs[1] which are regularly run on different machine and compiler combinations.

The recent development of compilable vector languages such as Fortran-8X,[2] Vector-C,[3] Actus,[4] and modified APL[5] has made it possible to write scientific code using a more concise and higher level notation. The parallelism inherent in array operations can now be directly expressed in these languages obviating the need for vectorization of scalar code.

The implementation of these languages on vector machines presents some new, interesting problems. Besides generating good vector (and scalar) code, it is also important for a vector language compiler to be retargetable to other new and existing vector processors. A family of retargetable vector compilers which implements the same language on different machines and shares a common machine-independent core is more likely to enhance program portability than a collection of vectorizing compilers. Recent advances in compiler technology, particularly in the automatic code generation area, have largely focused on scalar machines and scalar languages.[6,7,8,9,10] Previous vector language implementers[3,4,5] have taken an approach to retargetable code generation similar to that used in the Pascal P-compiler, producing code for an abstract machine and then expanding this virtual code into the real code appropriate for the target machine. A major problem with this approach is the fundamental conflict between the need for a truly machine-independent abstract machine model and the need to fully exploit the power of a particular target machine.

A more promising approach, which allows the realization of the optimization goals of a vector compiler without sacrificing compiler retargetability, is pattern-matched vector code generation. This paper describes the application of a template-driven code generation technique to the task of implementing a vector language on an attached vector processor. This work extends Cattell's tree-matching algorithm[11] to vector code generation.

SOURCE LANGUAGE

Our source language is a subset of Fortran-8X, the proposed successor to the Fortran-77 standard. Fortran-8X[2] is a superset of Fortran-77 and has a rich array processing facility among its set of new features.

Fortran-8X's Array Processing Facility

Fortran-8X's array processing features are designed to allow the programmer to implement numerical algorithms in a more concise and natural notation. For example, the following Fortran-8X code may be used to compute the variance of n sample points ($n > 1$) contained in a vector x (of size n):

$$\text{variance} = \text{SUM}((x - \text{SUM}(x)/n)^{**}2)/(n-1)$$

Note how clearly this single statement indicates what is being computed without the distraction of an extraneous loop and loop index variable which in Fortran-77, and in other scalar languages, would have been required to index thru the vector x.

Fortran-8X carries even further the idea of allowing whole array operations by extending all scalar operations to apply element-wise to any conformable operands. An element-wise operation applies a scalar operation on the corresponding elements of its operands to produce the corresponding element of the result array. These element operations can be performed in any order simultaneously.

Fortran-8X allows subsets of an array, called array sections, to be used as operands. An array section is an array itself and is the result of subscripting a parent array with one or more non-scalar subscripts and zero or more scalar subscripts. An array section is the set of elements from the parent array selected by the non-scalar and scalar subscripts. One way of specifying non-scalar subscripts is by triplet notation which consists of three scalar integer expressions separated by colons, namely:

⟨array⟩ (⟨begin⟩ : ⟨end⟩ : ⟨stride⟩)

This triplet notation represents a sequence of integer subscript values starting from ⟨begin⟩ to ⟨end⟩ in increments of ⟨stride⟩.

Fortran-8X provides many other array processing features including array constructors, dynamic arrays, and masked array assignments. However, we chose not to complicate our prototyping efforts with these features.

TARGET MACHINE

Our target machine is the IBM 3838 attached vector processor.[12,13] Although the 3838 has been rendered largely obsolete by more recent vector processors, it provided us almost unlimited and very inexpensive access to a real target machine with vector instructions. A vendor-supplied interface called the Vector Processing SubSystem (VPSS)[12] provided 40 memory-to-memory vector instructions, 21 scalar arithmetic and branching instructions, and 13 housekeeping operations for programming the 3838.

COMPILER STRUCTURE

Our compiler design and choice of intermediate representation were heavily influenced by Intermetrics' compiler projects.[9,14] The Intermetrics projects were, in turn, inspired by W. Wulf's Production Quality Compiler-Compiler project[6] at Carnegie-Mellon University.

We greatly simplified our compiler design by deliberately deferring inclusion of any optimization phases until the feasibility of a retargetable vector code generator was established. Our compiler design is diagrammed in Figure 1.

No attempt was made at implementing a compiler front-end to process Fortran-8X statements. We simply hypothesize the existence of a Fortran-8X scanner, parser, and semantic analyzer. We also assume the existence of an array-to-vector transformation phase (labeled Vectorizer in the diagram) which unravels multi-dimensional array expressions and assignments into one or more nested loops, bracketing the same expressions and assignments but operating only on vector and scalar operands.

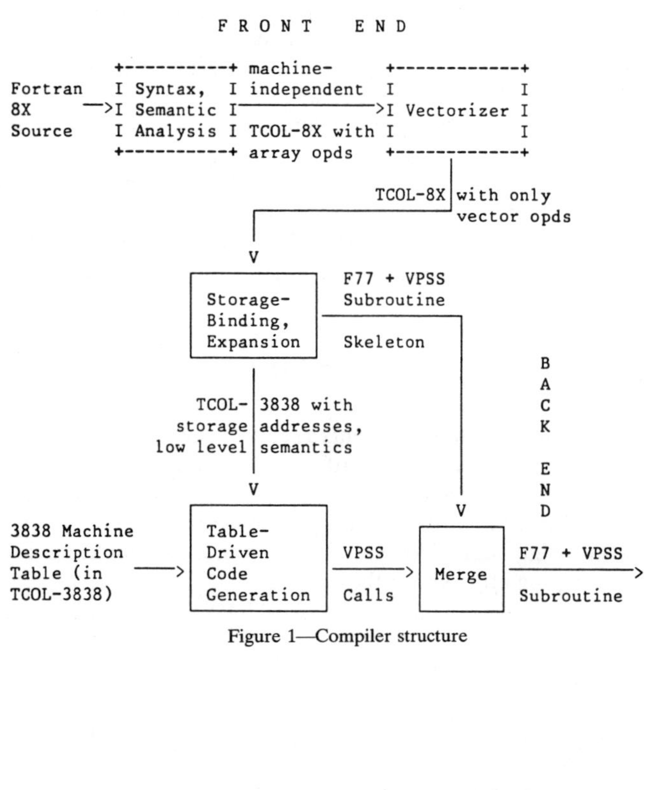

Figure 1—Compiler structure

The Compiler Back-End

The compiler back-end consists of two major phases: a storage binding/expansion phase and a table-driven code generation phase. The storage binding/expansion phase performs the following operations:

1. Takes the high-level TCOL-8X form of the source program and generates the low-level TCOL-3838 input to the code generation phase
2. Binds variables to target machine storage locations
3. Expands all implicit computations into explicit arithmetic operations (e.g., exposes all address arithmetic implied by vector subscripting)
4. Outputs a Fortran-77 subroutine skeleton

This subroutine skeleton consists of a subroutine heading, declaration statements, and Vector Processing SubSystem CALL statements to do housekeeping operations. The subroutine skeleton is given to a subsequent MERGE step which combines the skeleton with the subroutine body from the code generation phase.

The table-driven code generation phase performs the following functions:

1. Reads in the target machine instruction templates, and
2. Performs pattern matching operations on the TCOL-3838 program trees and the instruction templates to determine which instructions should be generated to implement the low level semantics of the source program

The output of the code generation phase is a sequence of properly formatted CALL statements to the Vector Processing SubSystem. These VPSS CALL statements constitute the body of a subroutine which can be compiled with a Fortran compiler and linked with the Vector Processing SubSystem to create an executable module.

INTERMEDIATE REPRESENTATION

Two intermediate languages, both variants of TCOL,[6,15] are used in our compiler design:

1. TCOL-8X is the output of a Fortran-8X compiler front-end and the input to the back-end.
2. TCOL-3838 is the intermediate representation used in the back-end.

TCOL-8X

TCOL-8X is the high-level Fortran-8X-specific and machine-independent notation used in the output of the compiler front-end. TCOL-8X closely reflects the structure and the semantics of Fortran-8X constructs. A TCOL-8X VECTOR node reflects the structure and the attributes of a Fortran-8X array reference which it represents. It references a parent ARRAY node and a sequence of SCALAR, TREE, or SECTION nodes representing the subscripts. It does not expose implicit machine-dependent address computations. Similarly, a TCOL-8X SCALAR node models the attributes of the Fortran-8X scalar variable it represents. It has no storage location attribute because storage binding is a machine-dependent operation which is deferred to the Storage-Binding/Expansion phase. Fortran-8X control constructs retain their basic structure in TCOL-8X. A Fortran DO-loop is represented in TCOL-8X as a loop-control part and a loop-body. It is not decomposed into conditional and unconditional branches which are often machine-dependent (e.g., some machines have a "do-loop" instruction).

TCOL-3838

In contrast to the machine-independence of TCOL-8X, TCOL-3838 closely reflects the data types, operations, addressing modes, and instruction formats available on our target machine.

The main motivation for the low-level nature of TCOL-3838 notation is the need to represent the low-level semantics of both program constructs and machine instructions in the same notation. The low-level semantics of program constructs are represented as TCOL-3838 program trees. The effects of executing a target machine instruction are represented as a TCOL-3838 pattern tree. This uniform representation of program trees and pattern trees allows the instruction selection problem of code generation to be recast into a pattern matching problem. If the TCOL-3838 program tree representing the low-level semantics of a particular program construct matches the TCOL-3838 pattern tree representing the effects of executing a particular 3838 machine instruction, then the corresponding target machine instruction can be emitted to implement the program construct.

The TCOL-3838 VECTOR node type closely models the target machine representation of vector operands. A TCOL-3838 VECTOR node has four attributes: a base, a count, a stride, and an operand class. The base attribute references another TCOL-3838 structure which represents the computation of the address of the first vector element. The count attribute references another TCOL-3838 structure which represents the computation of the number of elements in the vector operand. The stride attribute references another TCOL-3838 structure which represents the distance between consecutive elements of the vector operand. The operand class attribute represents the vector operand access modes of the target machine. TCOL-3838 completely exposes all operations that are implicit in the TCOL-8X notation including the arithmetic operations involved in determining the number of iterations in a general Fortran DO-loop.

To completely specify a target machine instruction for code generation purposes, the description of the effects of the instruction must be associated with a code generator action to emit the properly instantiated instruction according to a specified instruction format. TCOL-3838 is also used for describing these code generation actions.

VECTOR CODE GENERATION

The code generation phase is essentially a three-step operation:

1. A pattern matching step searches a target machine description table for instruction templates to match against the program tree. The goal of this step is to find an instruction template which matches the program tree structurally and semantically.
2. A pattern instantiation step fills in the "holes" of the instruction template with values obtained from the program tree. These "holes" in the instruction template correspond to the memory addresses, the register numbers, and the literal values of the instruction's operands.
3. An action sequence executes the code generation directives specified by the instruction template. These directives may call for:
   a. The recursive invocation of the code generator to generate code for a program subtree or to instantiate an operand of a vector instruction
   b. The writing out of a fully instantiated instruction into the output object file
   c. The creation of a statement label
   d. The return of the instantiated values of a vector operand's base, count, and stride

The code generation algorithm, as implemented in our compiler back-end, is essentially Cattell's maximal munch method.[11] Published applications of maximal munch seem to have been directed exclusively to scalar code generation.[6,11,14] We did not have to extend Cattell's maximal munch method in order to use it for vector code generation. The three-step pattern-matching/instantiation/action-sequence model is equally applicable to both scalar and vector code generation.

We did extend the TCOL intermediate representation (TCOL-3838) to reflect the vector operand addressing modes and instructions available on our target machine and to represent the four kinds of code generation directives in the action-sequence step. Correspondingly, our target machine description table has two new sections devoted to vector instruction templates and to vector operand access mode templates respectively. The code generator was also extended to interpret the new code generation directives specified by these templates.

Just like other maximal munchers,[9,11,14] our code generator knows about partial matches which can be transformed into complete matches by fetch or store decomposition. When the offending operand is a vector source operand, vector fetch decomposition obtains a vector temporary and conceptually creates a new program subtree to move the offending source operand into the required vector operand storage and recursively invokes the code generator on this new subtree. Having fixed the offending source operand(s) in a partially matching template, the code generator can then execute the template's code generation directives and fix any offending destination operand(s) by store decomposition. In a simple one-pass code generation scheme such as ours, the allocation and deallocation of vector and scalar temporaries associated with vector and scalar fetch, and store decomposition, is performed during the single code generation pass. In a multi-pass optimizing compiler, the binding of temporaries to program tree nodes is done in a separate pass.

TARGET MACHINE DESCRIPTION TABLE

We have not attempted to automate the creation of the target machine description table. Instead, we simply wrote the instruction templates by hand.

Organization of the Machine Description Table

The target machine description table is organized for efficient access by the code generator. It consists of five major sections:

1. Scalar arithmetic instruction templates
2. Vector arithmetic instruction templates
3. Vector operand class and access mode templates
4. Control construct templates
5. Conditional branching templates

Within each section, templates whose pattern trees represent similar instructions (e.g., "add" and "add-immediate") are sorted by increasing cost per number of node.

Completeness

The completeness of the machine description table is an important issue in retargetable code generators. Code generator blockage is usually a symptom of an incomplete or incorrect machine description table. Tools for writing code generators[11] find their most important use in this area of assuring completeness in the machine description table.

Due to our lack of such a tool and our rather specialized target machine, we could not completely cover all legal program constructs that can be generated by a Fortran-8X compiler front-end. We had to restrict our source programs precisely to those programs whose computations can profitably be off-loaded to our target machine.

Exotic Instructions

On our target machine, about half of the 40 algorithmic vector operations can be considered exotic instructions. Examples include fast Fourier transforms, vector square root, and vector tangent. We did not write any templates for these exotic instructions because of their limited applicability to the translation of general-purpose Fortran-8X constructs.

Despite their specialized nature, these exotic instructions can be used to implement the "high-level" operations they were designed for. Equally exotic TCOL-3838, and TCOL-8X, operators and structures can be defined to model the semantics of these fancy instructions. Adding templates using these exotic operators to our machine description table and extending our source language by predefining these fancy operations as intrinsic operations, would allow our compiler to provide the user all the native capabilities of our target machine.

AN EVALUATION OF THE COMPILER BACK-END

To establish a reference point for comparing the quality of the output code of our compiler back-end, we hand assembled and optimized some of the Livermore kernels into Vector Processing SubSystem CALLS. The output from the execution of these two versions of the test routines were compared and found to be identical, giving us some confidence that our compiler back-end is generating correct code.

A static analysis of the compiled code against the hand-crafted code yielded the results shown in Table I. Our compiler back-end generates only vector arithmetic instructions which are absolutely necessary. However, it also generates too many unnecessary scalar instructions. A large proportion of these redundant scalar instructions are loads and stores.

A closer examination of the compiled code indicates that most of the redundant loads and stores arise from the allocation and deallocation of vector, and scalar, temporaries during vector, and scalar, fetch decomposition. On-the-fly vector, and scalar, temporary management is the main culprit. Some scalar instructions are redundant because they constitute common subexpressions or invariant computations which can be eliminated or moved out of loops. Our design decision to exclude any optimization phases in our compiler back-end has come back to haunt us.

To measure the execution efficiency of the compiled code against the hand-crafted code, we timed the execution of the compiled code and the hand-crafted code on an essentially unloaded IBM 3090 with a similarly unloaded 3838 attached processor. The benchmark code is Livermore kernel 8 which is a fragment of a P.D.E. integration routine. We performed two sets of timing runs for two different size settings of the

TABLE I—Static analysis of compiled vs. hand-crafted VPSS code

	Number of VPSS Calls		
	C Compiled	H Hand-Coded	C/H Ratio
Setup	4	4	1.0
Transfers	20	13	1.5
Housekeeping	24	17	1.4
Scalar Arithmetic	281	33	8.5
Scalar Moves	397	25	15.9
Branches	4	2	2.0
Scalar Operations	682	60	11.4
Real Arithmetic	36	36	1.0
Vector Operations	36	36	1.0
Total	742	113	6.6

array operands. For each set, we isolated data transfer times from actual target machine computation times. The results are shown in Table II.

The run-time numbers are worse than those for code size because most of the redundant scalar instructions happen to be inside loops. The megaflop rates indicate that our target machine executes scalar and simple vector instructions with short operands very inefficiently compared to the exotic vector instructions (over 20 megaflops for some fast Fourier transforms).

CONCLUSION

Advantages of TCOL as an Intermediate Representation

TCOL by itself does not assume any abstract machine model. It is sufficiently extensible to accurately model all of the instructions and operand access modes available on machines with reasonable architectures. Accurately modeling the available target machine resources allows better exploitation of these resources.

With adequate support tools,[14,15] the use of TCOL as an intermediate representation can significantly speed up and facilitate the construction of compilers, especially those with optimization goals. TCOL suits the multipass nature of an optimizing compiler. Since the program is internally represented by pointers and nodes, traversing the whole program can be done very efficiently any number of times. It also facilitates the implementation of optimizing transformations by simple pointer manipulations.

TABLE II—Dynamic analysis of compiled vs. hand-crafted code

	Minimum Execution Time (in milliseconds)		
Array Size	Compiled Code	Hand-Coded	Comp/Hand
80 × 80			
Data Transfer + Computation	16935.9	1787.5	9.5
Data Transfer Only	112.6	111.0	1.0
Computation Only	16823.3	1676.5	10.0
Floating-Point Operations	219024	219024	1.0
Scalar Operations	47883	2139	22.4
Megaflops	0.0130	0.1306	
40 × 40			
Data Transfer + Computation	8260.4	846.6	9.8
Data Transfer Only	34.5	33.3	1.0
Computation Only	8225.9	813.3	10.1
Floating-Point Operations	51984	51984	1.0
Scalar Operations	23363	1059	22.1
Megaflops	0.0063	0.0639	

Disadvantages of TCOL as an Intermediate Representation

Using TCOL as an intermediate representation requires the development of tools.[9,14,15] In the absence of adequate tool support, the use of TCOL can complicate, rather than simplify, the implementation of a compiler and it may even introduce an unacceptable compilation overhead.

Tree matching is not as well understood as string matching. Tree matching is often implemented by ad-hoc methods whereas string matching can be implemented by very well understood bottom-up parsing techniques.

Retargetability

We have designed retargetability into the structure of our compiler back-end. Although a large part of our design provided for retargetability, our implementation did not. The prototyping nature of our project allowed us to make many machine-dependent shortcuts in our implementation work. Thus, about 5100 lines (43%) of the total 12000 lines of Pascal code in our compiler back-end is target machine specific. The alert reader may have noticed that the storage-binding/expansion phase is heavily machine-dependent and should have been implemented as another table-driven maximal muncher.

We believe that the amount of target-machine-dependent code in a vector compiler back-end can be dramatically reduced in a more careful implementation. The only parts of the back-end code that may be inherently machine-dependent are the routines which implement the code generation directives.

ACKNOWLEDGEMENTS

I thank Rex L. Page for giving me the opportunity to work on this project, and for reviewing an earlier draft of this paper.

REFERENCES

1. Becker, E., "A Preprocessor for Version Control." *Technical Symposium on Computing Environments and Software Tools,* Amoco Production Research Center, Tulsa, Oklahoma (1985), pp. 37–46.
2. American National Standards Institute, Inc., X3J3. *American National Standard for Information Systems Programming Language Fortran S8(X3.9-198x),* (Revision of X3.9-1978, Draft S8, Version 99.), 1986.
3. Li, K.C. and H. Schwetman, "Implementation of the Vector C Language on the Cyber 205." *Supercomputer Applications,* Plenum Publishing Corp., 1984, pp. 69–84.
4. Perrott, R., D. Crookes, P. Milligan, and W. Purdy. "A Compiler for an Array and Vector Processing Language." *IEEE Trans. on Software Engineering,* 11 (1985), 5, pp. 471–478.
5. Budd, T. "An APL Compiler for a Vector Processor." *TOPLAS,* 6 (1984), 3, pp. 297–313.
6. Leverett, B., R. Cattell, S. Hobbs, J. Newcomer, A. Reiner, B. Schatz, and W. Wulf. "An Overview of the Production-Quality Compiler-Compiler Project." *Computer,* 13 (1980), 8, pp. 38–49.
7. Glanville, R. *A Machine Independent Algorithm for Code Generation and Its Use in Retargetable Compilers.* UMI, Ann Arbor, Michigan, 1977.
8. Johnson, S. "A Portable Compiler: Theory and Practice." *Proceedings of the 5th ACM Symp. on Principles of Programming Languages.* pp. 97–104, 1978.
9. Haradhvala, S., B. Knobe, and N. Rubin. "Expert Systems for High Qual-

ity Code Generation." *IEEE 1984 Proceedings of the First Conference on AI Applications*. pp. 310–313.
10. Ganapathi, M. and C. Fischer. "Affix Grammar Driven Code Generation." *TOPLAS*. 7 (1985), 4, pp. 560–599.
11. Cattell, R. *Formalization and Automatic Derivation of Code Generators*. UMI Research Press, Ann Arbor, Michigan, 1978.
12. IBM. *OS/VS1 and OS/VS2 MVS Vector Processing Subsystem Programmer's Guide* (2nd ed.), 1978.
13. IBM. *IBM 3838 Array Processor Functional Characteristics* (3rd ed.), 1982.
14. Avakian, A., S. Haradhvala, J. Horn, and B. Knobe. "The Design of an Integrated Support Software System." *Sigplan Notices*. 17 (1982), 6, pp. 308–317.
15. Marshall, H. "The Linear Graph Package, A Compiler Building Environment." *Sigplan Notices*. 17 (1982), 6, pp. 294–300.

Incremental generation of high-quality target code

by MARY P. BIVENS and MARY LOU SOFFA
University of Pittsburgh
Pittsburgh, Pennsylvania

ABSTRACT

Although conventional compilers frequently apply optimization techniques in the generation of target code, some current *incremental* compilers do not support commonly used optimizations. This work extends the concept of incremental compilation to fine-grained, high-quality target code generation. The proposed incremental code generator changes only the affected target code and register allocations in response to a source program edit. In this paper, we first discuss some issues and analyze the actions and information needed for developing incremental code generators. From the analysis, incremental techniques for allocating registers and generating target code are developed. Both local and global register allocation are considered, using graph coloring as the allocation scheme. To evaluate the performance of the incremental system, both incremental and non-incremental systems are implemented on a VAX, and their performance is compared in terms of the quality of the target code and the savings (40% to 80%) in time for making changes incrementally rather than completely regenerating the target code.

INTRODUCTION

In the evolution of compiler technology, the production of high quality code has been an overriding concern, especially for embedded and real-time systems. Thus, numerous techniques to improve the quality of code through the application of machine independent transformations, effective register allocation schemes, and machine dependent optimizations have been developed. Major advances in these optimization techniques have increased their effectiveness in reducing the time and space requirements of target code.[1]

Recently, the growing recognition of the importance of programming environments in software development has led to an interest in incremental compilers.[2,3,4,5,6] While a traditional compiler uses the entire program as its compilation unit, an incremental compiler decreases the size of the compilation unit and recompiles only the affected parts. Fine-grained incremental systems use a source or intermediate code statement as the incremental unit and recompile only those statements directly changed by the programmer or indirectly affected when a program is edited. Thus, compilation time is reduced and response time improved, especially for small changes in large programs.

Although traditional compilers frequently apply optimizations including sophisticated register heuristics to reduce time and space requirements of target code, work in incremental compilers has mainly focused on the front end of compilation. Thus, current incremental compilers either do not support the traditional compiler techniques for machine dependent and independent optimizations, code generation and register allocation, or they limit the applicability of the techniques to the changed incremental unit. For example, the incremental programming environment of Feiler and Medina-Mora[2] regenerates target code for an entire procedure in response to a change, while Fritzson[3] regenerates code only for the source code statement that is changed. In both cases, all register allocation and optimizations are restricted to the concerned incremental unit. This restriction severely affects the quality of target code produced, especially when using a statement as the incremental unit, for the capability of allocating registers or performing optimizations across statements is prohibited. Although the quality of code improves on increasing the size of the incremental unit to a procedure, it is reported that if a procedure rather than a source code statement is recompiled in response to a change, recompilation costs are greater by a factor of ten.[3] Other restrictions sometimes placed on existing incremental compilers include the assumption that all references to a particular variable are always mapped into a single, unchanging location. Thus, these restrictions on current incremental compilers negatively affect the quality of code produced and the performance of the compiler itself.

The problem of incrementally compiling intermediate code that has been optimized through machine independent transformations was recently undertaken.[7,8,9] In addition to identifying important aspects of incremental optimizations, techniques for incrementally compiling both local and global machine independent optimizations were developed, demonstrating the feasibility of extending the concept of incremental compilation to include these types of optimizations.

Incrementally generating optimized target code complicates the incremental process in that the forms of the intermediate and target code, the code generation algorithm, and the register heuristics must all be considered. An analysis must be performed to determine the effect on the target code of changing a source code statement, and this analysis is complex for high-quality code. Introducing a change in a source statement causes both direct and indirect changes in the intermediate code and target code. If a variable in the intermediate code resides in a register in the target code, inserting and deleting uses and definitions of that variable can result in changes to register allocations as well as changes to the target code instructions that load and store values between memory and registers. A number of allocations and deallocations of registers during incremental code generation may result in register fragmentation, which could lead to less efficient code than that produced in a non-incremental environment.

This work addresses the problem of incrementally generating high quality target code by further extending fine-grained incremental compilation, using techniques that are compatible with traditional compilers.[10] To be widely applicable, this work concentrates on local and global register allocation, the machine independent phases of target code generation. The machine dependent task of instruction selection is handled by pattern matching on a set of templates. A goal of the work is that the incrementally generated code be similar in quality to that produced by non-incremental compilers.

In order to help meet the goal of high quality code, the incremental unit chosen is the three-address intermediate statement, thus supporting commonly used register heuristics and machine independent optimizations. The intermediate representation of the source program is the standard control flow graph with nodes that are basic blocks.[11] A change in the source program is represented by a set of changes to intermediate code statements. We assume the target code is 2-operand register-based assembly code that has not been peephole optimized. The available general purpose registers are assumed to be partitioned into two sets, one set for local allocation and the other for global allocation. A local register is allocated for use within a basic block; a global register is allocated for use across several basic blocks. In keeping with the goal of high quality code, the value of a variable is kept in a register until it has no more uses or until a register is needed and there are none available.

OVERVIEW

This paper describes the overall design and implementation of an incremental code generator of optimized target code. The first step in this work is to analyze how various changes to intermediate code statements affect the target code and, in particular, the register allocation. Both changes that affect statements within the basic block and those that affect the control flow graph structure are considered. One use of this analysis is to determine the information that should be gathered and maintained to permit incrementally changing instructions and register allocations. To make incremental changes, a record of register usage is necessary, so a model that represents the mapping of variables into physical registers is developed. And lastly, techniques are developed to incrementally update target code instructions, the model of register usage, and register allocations. This produces either target code or attributes the intermediate code with information about the target code that can be used to generate target code when execution is demanded.

ANALYSIS OF EFFECTS OF PROGRAM EDITS

When a source code statement is edited, the incremental compiler front end performs incremental syntactic and semantic analyses and creates a list of intermediate code statement insertions and deletions and a list of flow graph changes for the incremental code generator. To determine the effect that a change has on target code and incrementally incorporate the change, we make the distinction between a variable and the value of a variable, termed a name. A span of a name in a basic block consists of all its occurrences in the block. A name in a program can either have global extent or local extent, based on its usage. A name has local extent if all uses of the name are confined to the defining basic block; otherwise it has global extent.

Each name span in a basic block is mapped into a local or global physical register. For efficiency, if a name X with local extent gives up its register at its last use in the basic block to the result Y of an operation, then both X and Y would be mapped into the same register. A name with global extent has a name span in each block that has an occurrence of the name. This sequence of name spans forms a global span, which is the unit for global register allocation.

The mapping of names into the available local and global registers is performed using a register allocation heuristic. All names with local extent have local allocation, although the span of a local name may have to give up its register because of competition for registers. If insufficient global registers are available, a variable with global extent may have local allocation rather than global allocation, necessitating a "spill" from a register to memory. Spill code stores definitions of a spilled variable and then loads the value of the spilled variable into a register at its next use.

We examine the direct effects which include modifying the target code and register allocations for the changed statement and then consider the indirect effects which are modifications to other target code and register allocations, not marked as being changed by the edit. When a program edit causes the deletion of an intermediate code statement, the direct effect is the deletion of the corresponding target code instructions. In a system that does not keep values in registers across source code statements and does not include target code optimizations, this would be the extent of the target code changes. Similarly, the insertion of an intermediate code statement would result in the generation and insertion of the appropriate target code. In neither case would any other target code be affected. However, when the code generation scheme includes efficient use of registers and target code optimizations, intermediate code changes also cause indirect effects.

Changes That Affect One Basic Block

We first consider changes whose direct and indirect effects are local to the basic block that contains the change and thus have no effect on target code or register allocation in other blocks. Since values are kept in registers between source code statements, if a variable in a changed intermediate code statement is at the beginning or at the end of a span of uses of that variable, then the change can affect the register allocation by extending or reducing the span. These modifications can also result in creating or removing spills and in reassigning a physical register for that span of uses.

The indirect effects for locally allocated variables generally involve the target code for the intermediate code statements that correspond to the last and next occurrences in the basic block of the variables in the altered intermediate code statement. These changes consist of inserting or deleting target instructions that move variables between memory and registers.

Since the code generation scheme being considered includes the efficiency of storing only the last definition of a variable in a basic block, we must be able to mark each intermediate code statement that stores its result and update this information in response to a change. When a statement is marked for deletion and contains the last definition of a variable X in the basic block, then the previous definition of X must be marked as a store and a store instruction added to its target code. If the statement is an insertion, then the store status of the previous definition of X must be changed and the target code that stored it to memory deleted.

If a changed statement contains the first occurrence in the basic block of a variable X, then it must be determined if changes, such as the insertion or deletion of an instruction that loads a register, must be made to the target code for the next use of this variable. For example, if the statement containing X is to be deleted and X has a next use, then target code must be inserted at the next use to load X from memory to a register.

If the insertion or deletion of an intermediate code statement that contains a variable X results in a change in the local liveness (a value of X is locally live if it has a further use in the basic block) of the last occurrence of X, then target code may be changed at the statement that contains the last occurrence of X. Given the intermediate code statement $Z := X + Y$, if X is not locally live, then the result Z can be generated in the register that contains X. However, if X is live, then the value of X should be copied to a new register and the result Z computed in the new register. Thus, a change in the liveness of a variable that is a first operand can result in changes in the number of registers necessary to compute the statement, in the span of uses for the variable and possibly in the physical register allocations.

The effects of changes on the name spans and register allocation are illustrated by an example. In Figure 1, we examine the effects of increasing the length of a name span. Figure 1a represents a basic block with each circle denoting an occurrence of a variable. The spans *A, B, C,* and *D* are assigned local registers *LR*1, *LR*2, *LR*1, and *LR*2, respectively, which is an optimal register assignment for this block. However, when the span *B* is lengthened, so that *B* and *D* overlap, these spans cannot both be assigned *LR*2. If a third register *LR*3 is available, then the assignment in Figure 1(b) can be made and the register number in the target code is altered. When a third register is not available, span *B* is spilled, so that a register is freed, as in Figure 1(c), and spill code is inserted.

Changes That Affect Several Basic Blocks

In a scheme that includes global register allocation, a change to an intermediate code statement can affect the target code in a number of blocks. A change affecting a control statement can produce a change in the flow graph such as the insertion or deletion of an edge or a node, or the merging or splitting of a node. This may result in altering the extent of variables and the size of name spans, as well as reallocation of global and local registers.

Program changes can alter the span of occurrences of a name in the following ways:

1. create a new name
2. delete a name
3. change the length of the span of occurrences of a name such that
   a. the extent remains unchanged
   b. the extent changes from local to global or global to local
4. change the priority of a name for global allocation

A name with global extent and allocation is assigned a global register for the basic blocks in its global span. The effects of changing the length of a global span are similar to the local example in Figure 1. The results of changing the extent of a name from global to local are shown in Figure 2. The names *X* and *Y* are defined respectively at statements *Si* and *Sj* in block *B*1, and the only uses of these definitions outside *B*1 are in *B*2. Although both *X* and *Y* have global extent, *X* has global allocation and resides in register *GR*1, *Y* has local allocation and is assigned registers *LR*1 in *B*1 and *LR*2 in *B*2 (see Figure 2(a)). The deletion of the only use of *X* at *Sk* in *B*2 changes the extent of *X* from global to local, which frees the register *GR*1 in *B*1 and *B*2 and requires that a local register be found for *X* in *B*1. Since *X* no longer has global extent, its span is deleted from the set of global spans, which allows *Y* to be globally allocated and assigned register *GR*1. The spill code for *Y* in *B*1 and *B*2 is removed.

The changes to the name spans for block *B*1 are the deletion of a span with local allocation for *Y* and insertion of a span with local extent and allocation for *X*. The change to the name spans in *B*2 is the deletion of the span for *Y*. In both blocks, these changes may cause creation or removal of spills and changes in register allocation. The changed register assignments are shown in Figure 2(b).

From this analysis of changes to variables with local and global allocation, it is evident that a solution to the incremental code generation problem requires the gathering of pertinent information, the development of models to represent this information, and the creation of techniques to update the models in response to a change. The models and algorithms must be able to perform these functions:

1. maintain a mapping between the intermediate code and the target code instructions
2. determine name spans and whether the name has local or global extent
3. determine allocation and physical register assignment of name spans
4. detect register spills

INFORMATION STRUCTURES AND MODELS

Based on the characteristics of the system and on the analyses of the direct and indirect effects of a change in an intermediate code statement, the allocation of registers through a coloring scheme was found to be particularly suitable in an incremental setting. Coloring in this work is applied to local register allocation as well as global allocation,[12,13] although the techniques for incremental allocation of global registers using coloring are valid without local coloring. Thus, the following models

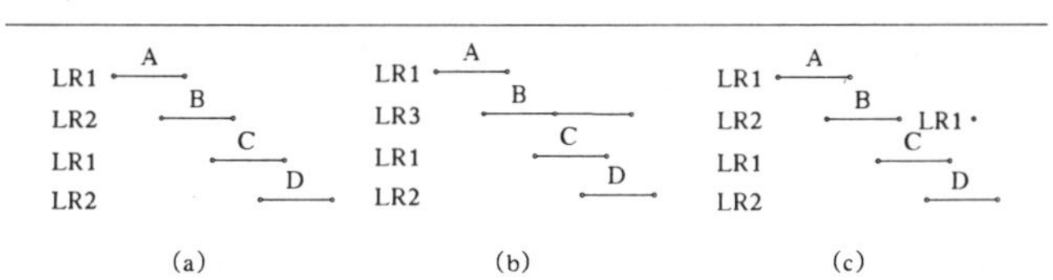

Figure 1—Name spans and register assignments

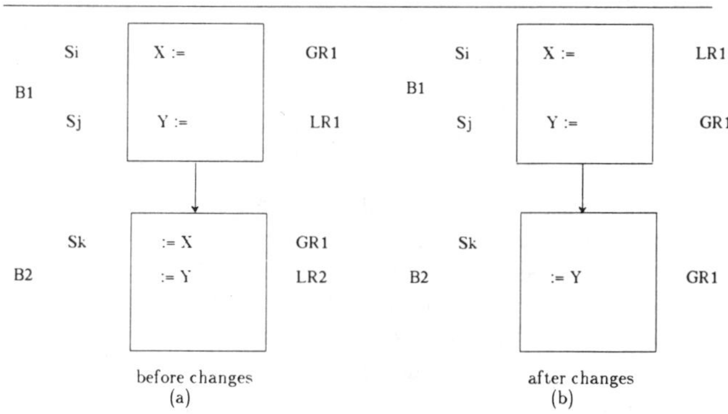

Figure 2—Effects of changing the extent of a span from global to local

and information structures are developed for use in the incremental code generator.

The information needed about the intermediate code, structured as a linear list or a directed acyclic graph, includes:

1. a mapping between the intermediate code and the target code
2. for each variable in an intermediate code statement—the last occurrence, next occurrence, local liveness and the register usage

Since register allocation can be changed by the incremental code generator, it is necessary to keep a record of register usage. For each basic block, the register usage is represented by a list of virtual register spans, each composed of one or more name spans. Each virtual register span comprises the following information:

1. the list of name spans that forms this span
2. a bit to indicate the type of extent of the span
3. a bit to indicate the class of allocation, i.e. local or global
4. the physical register assigned to the span
5. two bits to indicate the spill status of a span

The extent represents the ideal class of register for a virtual register span and the allocation is the actual class of register that is assigned to the span. A name with global extent has a global span. The global span consists of virtual register spans in each block that has an occurrence of the name. Data flow information is used to determine the extent of a name.

Spilling and physical register assignment for virtual register spans with either local or global extent are done by building interference graphs. The nodes in an interference graph are either virtual register spans or global spans, and there is an edge between two nodes if the regions of the two spans overlap. The nodes in a local interference graph are a subset of the virtual register spans in that block and contain all those with local allocation. The local interference graphs are interval graphs and, unlike general graphs, can be optimally colored in time linear in the number of edges.[14]

The global interference graph is similar, with a node representing all the virtual register spans in the global span. In general, two global spans interfere if a virtual register span of one interferes with a virtual span of the other. The global interference graph is not an interval graph, so a heuristic is used to obtain a good, but not necessarily optimal, coloring.

INITIAL CODE GENERATION

When target code is initially generated non-incrementally, intermediate code information structures, virtual register spans, global spans, and interference graphs are constructed. The virtual register spans in the basic blocks are first constructed. From the traditional data flow information, the extent of the names are determined and the global spans are constructed.

The global spans are sorted according to a priority that weights the number of occurrences of the variables in the global span by the depth of nesting of the blocks and by the number of blocks in the global span. The global interference graph, represented as an adjacency matrix, consists of nodes that are global spans and edges that represent interferences. Two global spans interfere if they have a basic block in common. If there are k global registers, then any node with fewer than k interferences can always be colored, since its neighbors will use at most $k-1$ registers. Such nodes are called unconstrained nodes; nodes with k or more interferences are constrained. The interference graph is colored by assigning registers to the constrained nodes with highest priority until all the nodes are colored or until no more nodes can be colored. Constrained nodes that are not colored are locally allocated and will compete for local registers in each basic block of their global span. Finally the unconstrained nodes are colored.

After the global spans have been allocated, the local interference graph, represented as an adjacency matrix, is built for each basic block. In the construction of the graph, if adding a node causes that number of interferences to exceed k, the number of local registers, then one of the registers must be spilled. Common heuristics for local register allocation include spilling the span least recently used, the span least recently loaded, the span with fewest remaining uses or the span with next use furthest in the future. Regardless of the heuristic used to determine which span should be spilled, spilling involves splitting a virtual register span into two virtual spans and inserting spill code in the target code. When spilling is done, the second part of the spilled virtual register span becomes a new node. Spilling ensures that the interference graph can be colored with k colors; that is, that the virtual register spans can be mapped into k physical local registers.

After a k-colorable graph is constructed, it is colored by assigning a local register to each node, in the order that each was added to the graph. The graph can be colored in $O(|E|)$ time since each edge is represented only once in the graph and each edge is only considered once. After coloring, the target code for the basic block is generated, using the physical register assignments obtained from both global and local graph coloring.

Figures 3 and 4 illustrate the data structures for a basic block in which all the variables have local register allocation. Figure 3 is the intermediate and target code for a basic block. In Figure 4, virtual register spans and the adjacency matrix

INTERMEDIATE CODE	*TARGET CODE*
1. A := B − C	MOVE B R1 MOVE C R2 MOVE R1 R3 ADD R2 R3
2. C := C + A	ADD R3 R2 MOVE R2 C
3. A := B − C	ADD R2 R1 MOVE R1 A
4. X := A + Z	MOVE Z R2 ADD R2 R1 MOVE R1 X

Figure 3—Intermediate code and target code for a basic block before changes

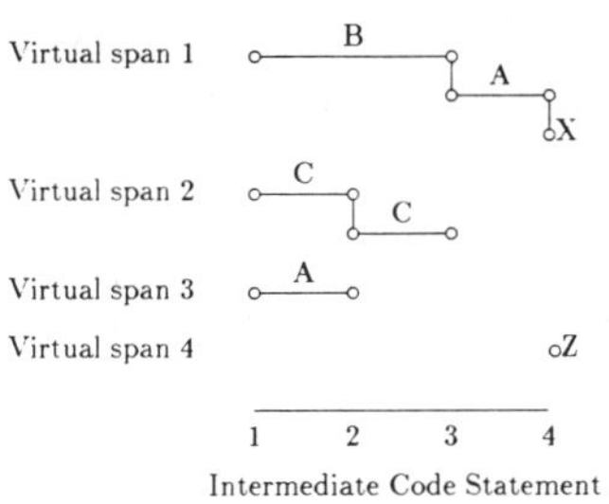

Node	1	2	3	4	Register
1					R1
2	1				R2
3	1	1			R3
4	1	0	0		R2

Figure 4—Virtual register spans, local interference graph and physical registers before changes

are shown. The matrix indicates that nodes one and two overlap, that node three interferes with nodes one and two, and that node four overlaps node one. Without spilling, this graph can be colored with three registers; the physical register assignments are indicated.

INCREMENTAL TECHNIQUES

Using the analyses and the models described above, algorithms have been developed to incrementally generate target code for a group of changes to intermediate code statements. In the incremental process, the values of the affected intermediate code attributes are changed, target code is inserted and deleted, and virtual register spans, global spans, and physical register allocations are changed. These algorithms produce code that is of similar quality to that produced in a non-incremental environment, since they detect the destruction and creation of opportunities to use registers efficiently. The algorithm for the incremental process is outlined below.

ALGORITHM: GLOBAL_PROCESS_CHANGES.

This algorithm processes a list of changes in a procedure *P*. The changes are insertions and deletions of statements in a basic block *B* and changes in the flow graph.

```
BEGIN {GLOBAL_PROCESS_CHANGES}

For each basic block B with intermediate code changes DO
BEGIN
    FOR each quad q that is marked 'delete' or 'insert' DO
      Update_Quad_Information(q);
    FOR each quad q that is changed DO
      IF (q is marked 'delete') THEN
      Update_Virtual_Reg_Delete(q)
      ELSE Update_Virtual_Reg_Insert(q);
  END;

  FOR each change C in the flow graph DO
    Process_Flow_Graph_Changes(C);

  Update_Global_Adj_Matrix;
  ReColor_Global_Adj_Matrix;

  FOR each basic block B marked as changed DO BEGIN
    Update_Local_Adj_Matrix(B);
    ReColor_Local_Adj_Matrix(B);
    Update_Target_Code(B);
  END;
END.{GLOBAL_PROCESS_CHANGES}
```

Changes to Locally Allocated Variables

The incremental process for variables with local register allocation is illustrated by inserting an intermediate code statement in the example described in Figures 3 and 4, and incrementally updating the information structure, the virtual register spans, the local adjacency matrix and the target code. We assume that three physical registers are available for local allocation.

To insert the statement $Z := B + A$ before statement 1 in Figure 3, the following is done. Since the inserted statement becomes the first statement in the basic block, none of its variables has a last occurrence. Statement 0 is marked to store its result as this is the only definition of *Z* in the block.

The next occurrence of *A* is a definition at statement 1, so *A* is not locally live and a new virtual span is created for it. The variable *B* is locally live since it has a next use at statement 1, and it will become part of the virtual span that includes *B* at statement 1. As an indirect effect, the target code for statement 1 is marked to remove the instruction that loads *B* from memory. The result *Z* has a next use at statement 4, so *Z* is locally live and will become part of the virtual span that is a use of *Z* at statement 4. The target code for statement 4 is marked to remove the instruction that loads *Z* from memory.

Figure 5 shows the updated virtual spans and the updated adjacency matrix. When span 3 is added to the matrix, it overlaps three other nodes so four physical registers are needed. Since only three registers are available, one virtual span must be spilled. Virtual spans 1 and 2 are used at the start of span 3, so only span 4 can be spilled.

Span 4 is broken into span 4A with range [0, 0] and span 4B with range [4, 4]. The adjacency matrix after spilling is also shown in Figure 5. *Z* is spilled, and statement 1 is checked to

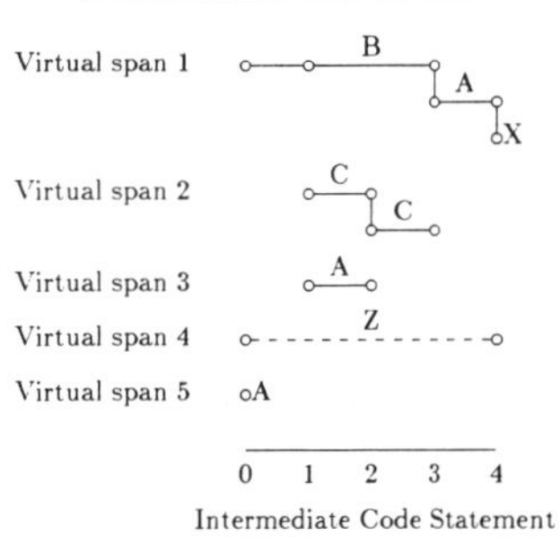

Node	1	4	5	2	3
1					
4	1				
5	1	1			
2	1	1	0		
3	1	1	0	1	

Before spills

Node	1	4A	5	2	3	4B	Register
1							R1
4A	1						R3
5	1	1					R2
2	1	0	0				R2
3	1	0	0	1			R3
4B	1	0	0	0	0		R3

After spills

Figure 5—Virtual register spans, interference graph and physical registers after changes

see if the value of Z in memory is current. Statement 4 is marked to insert an instruction to load Z from memory. The updated adjacency matrix is incrementally colored by examining the changed nodes and keeping their old colors if possible. The intermediate code, the old target code and the updated target code are shown in Figure 6.

Incremental Global Coloring

When a change involves variables with global extent, the incremental process may include creating, deleting, merging, and splitting global spans, and updating and recoloring the global adjacency matrix. Although similar to local changes, the algorithms for incorporating these changes are more complex since one change can affect several basic blocks. In addition, the global interference graph is not an interval graph, since two virtual spans may represent parallel regions in the control flow graph and cannot be ordered. To give a flavor of the technique, we briefly describe the incremental coloring algorithm.

The incremental global update algorithm processes changed nodes in order of their priority. Changes to nodes in the graph include deletion, insertion, change in the length of a span, increase in priority and decrease in priority. The deletion of a node *Ni* that has global allocation causes each of its neighbors with lower priority and local allocation to be marked for recoloring since the global register assigned to *Ni* is available to another span. The deletion will also reduce the number of interferences for each neighbor and may change some constrained nodes to unconstrained. When the priority of a node with local allocation is increased, or the priority of a node with global allocation is decreased, the node is marked for recoloring. Similar changes are made when a node is inserted and when the size of the span of a node is changed. After all changed nodes have been processed, nodes with local allocation that are now unconstrained have their allocation changed to global and are marked for recoloring.

Recoloring is done in order of decreasing priority. A constrained node *Ni,* marked for recoloring, is globally allocated if there is a color that is not used by its higher priority neighbors, or else it will be locally allocated. When a color is available for a node, the colors of its neighbors with lower priority are checked to see if the color is being used. If the color is in use by a neighbor, this neighbor is marked for recoloring. Since nodes are recolored in order of their priority and a neighbor with higher priority is never disturbed, incremental recoloring can be done in one pass.

INTERMEDIATE CODE	*OLD TARGET CODE*	*NEW TARGET CODE*
0. Z := B + A		MOVE B R1 MOVE A R3 MOVE R3 R2 ADD R3 R2 MOVE R2 Z
1. A := B + C	MOVE B R1 MOVE C R2 MOVE R1 R3 ADD R2 R3	MOVE C R2 MOVE R1 R3 ADD R2 R3
2. C := C + A	ADD R3 R2 MOVE R2 C	ADD R3 R2 MOVE R2 C
3. A := B + C	ADD R2 R1 MOVE R1 A	ADD R2 R1 MOVE R1 A
4. X := A + Z	MOVE Z R2 ADD R2 R1 MOVE R1 X	MOVE Z R2 ADD R2 R1 MOVE R1 X

Figure 6—Intermediate code and target code after changes

PERFORMANCE AND IMPLEMENTATION

To experimentally evaluate the performance of the incremental code generator, a prototype of the system has been implemented for the VAX/780 as well as a non-incremental code generator that uses the same register allocation heuristics. The performance of the incremental system is evaluated by:

1. comparing the quality of the target code that is produced by the incremental system versus that produced non-incrementally
2. measuring the savings in compilation time when a change is incorporated incrementally rather than regenerating the target code

The implementation uses the front end of an ADA compiler to generate 3-address intermediate code. A data flow analyzer then creates data and control flow information for the intermediate code, and the non-incremental target code generator creates the virtual registers, global spans and target code for the program.

The incremental code generator takes as input the structures built by the non-incremental code generator and a list of program changes and incrementally incorporates the local and global changes. Although the code produced by the two systems may not be identical, when it differs, it is only in the physical register assignments.

Experimental studies done so far indicate savings of from 40% to 80% when approximately 4% of the intermediate code is changed. Edits that involve only local changes and those that include both local and global changes were both tested. The results for both types of changes are in the same range. The variance in the results is based on the perturbation caused by the changes. If a change is local and involves a virtual register span that is at the beginning of the basic block, it is more likely to disrupt the register allocation for that basic block than is a change that occurs at the end of the block. Likewise, a change in a high-priority global span that has many interferences will disrupt its neighbors more than a change in a low-priority span that has few interferences. Work is currently underway on categorizing the changes that are well-suited for incremental target code generation.

ACKNOWLEDGMENTS

This work was partially supported by NSF under Grant DCR 811934.

REFERENCES

1. Harrison, W.H. "Position Paper on Optimizing Compilers." *Conference Record of the Eighth Annual ACM Symposium on POPL,* (1981), pp. 88–89.
2. Feiler, P.H. and R. Medina-Mora. "An Incremental Programming Environment." *5th International Conference on Software Engineering,* (1981), pp. 44–53.
3. Fritzson, P. "Preliminary Experience from the DICE System—A Distributed Incremental Compiling Environment." *Symposium on Practical Software Development Environments,* (1984), pp. 113–123.
4. Ford, R. and D. Sawamiphakdi. "A Greedy Concurrent Approach to Incremental Code Generation." *Conference Record of the Twelfth Annual ACM Symposium on POPL,* (1985), pp. 165–178.
5. Schwartz, M.D., N.M. Delisle and V.S. Begwami. "Incremental Compilation in Magpie." *Proceedings of SIGPLAN '84 Symposium on Compiler Construction,* (1984), pp. 122–131.
6. Reiss, S.P. "An Approach to Incremental Compilation." *Proceedings of SIGPLAN '84 Symposium on Compiler Construction,* (1984), pp. 144–151.
7. Pollock, L.L. and M.L. Soffa. "Incremental Compilation of Locally Optimized Code." *Conference Record of the Twelfth Annual ACM Symposium on POPL,* (1985), pp. 152–164.
8. Pollock, L.L. and M.L. Soffa. "INCROMINT—An Incremental Optimizer for Machine-Independent Transformations." *Proceedings of SOFTFAIR II—A Second Conference on Software Development Tools, Techniques, and Alternatives,* 1985.
9. Pollock, L.L. "An Approach to Incremental Compilation of Optimized Code." Ph.D. Dissertation, Department of Computer Science, University of Pittsburgh, 1986.
10. Bivens, M.P. "Incremental Generation of High-Quality Target Code." Ph.D. Dissertation, Department of Computer Science, University of Pittsburgh, 1987.
11. Aho, A.V., R. Sethi, and J.D. Ullman. *Compilers Principles, Techniques, and Tools.* Reading, MA: Addison-Wesley Publishing Company, 1986.
12. Chow, F. and J. Hennessy. "Register Allocation by Priority-based Coloring." *Proceedings of SIGPLAN '84 Symposium on Compiler Construction,* (1984), pp. 222–232.
13. Chaitin, G.J. "Register Allocation and Spilling Via Graph Coloring." *Proceedings of SIGPLAN '82 Symposium on Compiler Construction,* (1982), pp. 98–105.
14. Even, S. *Graph Algorithms.* Rockville, MD: Computer Science Press, 1979.

Ripple effect analysis based on semantic information

by JAMES S. COLLOFELLO
Arizona State University
Tempe, Arizona
and
D.A. VENNERGRUND
TRW Federal Systems Group
Fairfax, Virginia

ABSTRACT

Maintenance of large-scale software systems is a complex and expensive process. This process is often unreliable due to the ripple effect of modifications in one component of the system adversely affecting other components. Although syntactic techniques exist for tracing ripple effect, their results are often crude and require considerable interpretation by maintenance personnel. In this paper, a prototype ripple effect analysis tool based on both syntactic and semantic information will be described. This tool enables maintenance expertise to be captured in the form of semantic conditions which can then be linked to syntactic components. The ripple effect tool can then guide the maintenance personnel in tracing ripple effect as a consequence of a program modification. The functional capabilities of this tool are presented in this paper as well as an overview of the tool's architecture. Some experience with the tool as well as suggestions for future research are noted.

BACKGROUND

The development and maintenance of large software systems is a difficult and complex task, compounded by both technical and management factors including the size and complexity of the software system and the teams developing it. Today's larger systems contain thousands of software and hardware components developed by large teams with varying levels of experience. Development may take years with maintenance of many systems spanning decades. Ensuring a working system over long development and maintenance life spans is a difficult task.

A major software engineering concern is that software maintenance accounts for such a large percentage of the total cost of software systems. J. Martin, C. McClure, and B. Patkau[11,15] estimate that from 40% to 80% of a system's cost is maintenance, costs incurred after the initial release. The goal of several software engineering techniques and research methods[3,11,20] is to lower this cost.

Software maintenance, in this context, encompasses the correction of incorrect software, the adaptation of software to a new or changing environment, the perfection of software, and the addition of new software. In short, software maintenance can be defined to be any change made to an existing software system. With this definition, a model of software maintenance can be described.

The software maintenance model proposed in "Ripple Effect Analysis of Software Maintenance"[25] provides a useful basis for describing the software maintenance process. The model presents four phases followed to make a change: understand the software, propose a solution, account for ripple effect, and test the solution in the system. Each of these tasks is difficult and requires a great deal of knowledge about the system under maintenance. Unfortunately most of this knowledge is experiential, unformalized, and thus unavailable to the novice maintainer.

The software maintenance tasks are difficult to begin with; compound this with out-of-date and incomplete information, high turnover rates of experienced designers, inexperienced designers assigned to maintenance, and a cumbersome methodology, and the tasks become very costly.

Improvements to the difficult task of software maintenance can be made by providing formalization in the form of automated assistance. Tools are needed for each of the software maintenance tasks including: creating, managing, and storing maintenance information, suggesting solutions, verifying changes, and enforcing methodologies. With such tools and information, a body of knowledge useful for software maintenance can be built and maintained for future generations of maintainers.

Few such tools exist to date. Most maintenance activity is accomplished with the aid of a minimal toolset containing a text editor and a compiler. More advanced maintenance environments may contain syntax-directed editors, diagnostic compilers, change tracking data bases, design languages, online documentation relating to requirements, design and testing information, and various metric and syntax analysis tools. Such tools might include data and control flow mappers, symbol cross-references, data dictionaries, ripple effect analyzers, code auditors, and complexity analyzers. Few environments provide a coherent integration of these tools and fewer still capture and provide experiential knowledge of the system under maintenance. Semantic information is desperately needed to perform effective software maintenance.

The remainder of this paper focuses on the providing some experiential information to the novice in one task, ripple effect analysis, the process of examining system software for impacts that may result from changes. A tool which ties semantic information to syntax information based on today's systems is described.

CURRENT RIPPLE EFFECT ANALYSIS TECHNIQUES AND TOOLS

Analyzing the effects of change on software is a difficult task, complicated by program size, complexity, and information hiding. Complicating factors external to the program include: multiple representations of information, out-of-date documentation, undocumented previous changes, and difficulty in tracing code to the design and requirements. Several ripple effect analysis tools and techniques are known, and two distinct categories of these tools can be identified.

The first, syntax-based ripple effect analysis techniques, work on source code representations alone. These techniques determine the effects of changes by examining syntax information like control and data flow. The second, semantic-based ripple effect analysis techniques, work on higher-level information not derivable from the source. This semantic information reflects the intent of a program and represents knowledge of the basic assumptions which must be true for the correct operation of the system.

There are many differences between these two strategies; syntactic information is easily derived from the source code, semantic information is difficult to derive, and difficult to verify. Analysis based solely on syntactic information is worst case, and may implicate many sections of code not truly affected, whereas semantic analysis can pinpoint effects more precisely at the cost of being incomplete. Semantic information is informal and manually-derived, thus any analysis based on it is incomplete at best.

Syntax Methods

The most basic ripple effect analysis method, manual inspection, is performed with no tools except perhaps a text editor. This method is the most labor-intensive and incomplete yet it is widely practiced in industry. Automatically derived control and data flow information[8,14,24] help the manual inspection method by providing details on the possible propogation of the change. Program data bases[2,17] are useful change impact tools since they provide a consistent representation of program information which can be queried. Data dictionaries and symbol cross-references are basic program data bases. Tools like DAVE,[13] FAST[5] and ISUS[9] detect certain ripple effect errors in a data base query fashion.

Typestate[19] and Assertion statement[20] methods are also useful in detecting ripple effect at compile and run-time. Both methods detect nonsensical errors, many caused by ripple effect. The highest level of syntax analysis is embodied in logical ripple effect analysis tools[22,23,25] which are focused on determining the worst case extent of change effects. The weakness of this method is that in large systems it produces far too much information. The need to reason about change is apparent.

Semantic Methods

Semantic methods attempt to reason about the meaning of changes. Many approaches have been taken to meet this task.[1,6,7,10,12] Each recognizes the need to represent and use knowledge of the application domain as well as the programming language. Formalizing this kind of knowledge is a difficult task, as represented by the many varied approaches. Each of these approaches require the following:

1. Formal representations for requirements, design and related documentation
2. Formal representations of programming constructs
3. Methods for manipulating all representations
4. Methods for relating all representations
5. Methods for acquiring the representations

The trend in ripple effect analysis, as well as software engineering, is toward representing and using higher level concepts. The conceptual leap from assembler to high-level languages opened a new world of programming opportunities. A similar jump to another level of languages has been predicted and anticipated for years. Studies in artificial intelligence, data base technology, conceptual modeling and cognitive sciences all attempt to answer the basic questions which will open the door to higher-level language programming: How to represent knowledge, and how to reason with knowledge.

Recent success and popularity in the expert system subfield of artificial intelligence has sparked a new euphoria. The application of expert system technology is appropriate for limited domains of knowledge, problems already solvable by a set of best guesses, or heuristics. Unfortunately, most of the problems associated with reasoning about computer programs remain unsolved, or contain far too much knowledge to be represented.

In the ripple effect problem, many interesting pieces may be solved with expert system technology. The derivation of interesting, subtle or confusing dependencies can be based on knowledge of programming constructs and application intent. Such dependencies could be partially derived from source comments and design documents. Smart documentation assistants, as described in the Intelligent Program Editor[18] and the Programmer's Apprentice[16,21] are essential to the organization and derivation of such dependency information.

Change propagation libraries may also be amenable to expert system technology. Such libraries would contain a pattern-matchable description of all manner of ripple effects, both logical and performance. Thus when a certain change is made, the change propagation knowledge base can pinpoint with best guesses all effected components.

Unlikely expert system applications include the derivation of semantic impact from a syntax change. To understand the effects of a change, a semantic representation of the change must also be made. No method for inferring the meaning of a change, based on syntax alone is possible.

Other approaches to semantic representation are found in the integration of software engineering environments. Based on data base techniques, this approach can model any relationship and enforce any constraint. Thus semantic information is able to be represented and manipulated. Conceptually, then, the knowledge-based approach and integrated environment are equivalent. Clearly, in order to reason about meaning we need to represent meaning.

A PROPOSED SEMANTIC INFORMATION TOOL

Introduction

The existing software base is a significant asset, and little of it contains any semantic information. Reasoning about this software is a difficult and mostly manual task. Providing automated assistance to the maintenance of such programs is the goal of today's tools. Semantic annotations of syntactic relationships is a first step towards incorporating information useful in formalizing the meaning of syntax. Later steps will build on this information until a new development paradigm[1,7] evolves. This incremental development of support tools, that transform today's meaningless programs into tomorrow's meaningful programs, is a viable approach.

A tool which can provide the maintainer with up-to-date semantic information tied directly to source code and express the meaning of the source is necessary for the efficient and effective analysis of ripple effect. The many approaches to this need were discussed in the previous section. Yet most of the approaches cannot be applied to today's software base, because they are designed for symbolic languages and specially created programs. Examples include the formally verified programs built by the Designer/Verifier's Assistant[12] and the Programmer's Assistant.[21]

A tool that captures and presents semantic information directly related to program dependencies is now described. The tool, Semantic Information Tool (SEMIT), is targeted for the majority of today's software systems written in imperative, high-level programming languages.

Imperative programming languages achieve their primary effect by changing the state of variables with assignment statements. Since ripple effect is propogated through the path of variable assignments, a documentation of critical assignment statements will aid ripple effect analysis.

SEMIT addresses programs with these characteristics by assuming an imperative-based syntax analysis, creating a syntax and semantic data base, and directly linking the semantic information to the program syntax. The combination of semantic information and program source present a model of the program that can grow with software maintenance.

SEMIT Overview

SEMIT provides the ability to link semantic information to source code by representing the syntax in a relational format which captures data flow dependencies and any useful descriptions of the dependency in the form of semantic conditions. Semantic conditions are assumptions or assertions about data item properties or program states. Examples include, "the array is sorted," and "the input value is non-negative."

The conceptual model of SEMIT is based on the Semantic NET.[10] A network records all syntax relations. Logical relations describe key information derived from procedures and data. Figure 1 shows a simple network for a procedure FIND_TOP_SALESPERSON. Procedures and data items are represented by boxes, relations between them with arcs. Note how the relationships between the procedure and other program components are represented with relations. Modified data, used data, called procedures, and passed parameters are easily represented. These relations are strong enough to describe all possible logical ripple effect paths for inter-procedure cases.

The syntax in Figure 1 represents the fact that "the procedure PRETTY_PRINT is called by the procedure FIND_TOP_SALESPERSON with the parameter TOP_SALESPERSON which has been modified by the procedure FIND_TOP_SALESPERSON." Stated in a set of logical relations:

1. modifies (FIND_TOP_SALESPERSON, TOP_SALESPERSON)
2. calls (FIND_TOP_SALESPERSON, PRETTY_PRINT)
3. called_with_parm (PRETTY_PRINT, TOP_SALESPERSON)

A simplification of this relationship is noted by the existence of a modifies-uses chain between the modification of TOP_SALESPERSON by the procedure FIND_TOP_SALESPERSON and the usage of TOP_SALESPERSON by the called procedure PRETTY_PRINT. There exists a dependency between these two procedures, since a change in the procedure FIND_TOP_SALESPERSON in the modification of TOP_SALESPERSON may affect the correct operation of the procedure PRETTY_PRINT. This dependency may be stated with the pair of logical relations:

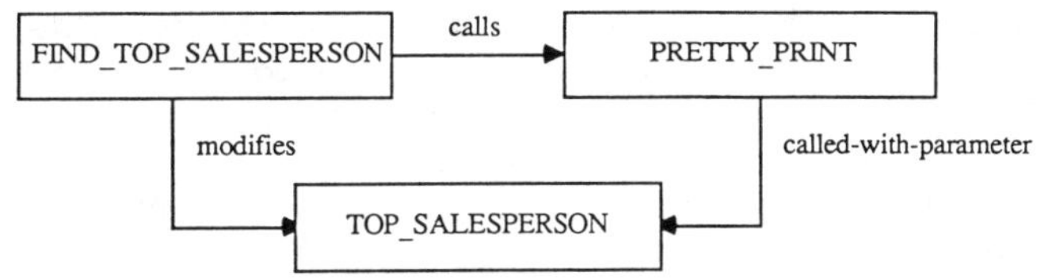

Figure 1—Semantic network

1. modifies(FIND_TOP_SALESPERSON, TOP_SALESPERSON)
2. uses(PRETTY_PRINT,TOP_SALESPERSON)

Semantic conditions can be used to describe the dependency between the modifies and uses relations. A semantic condition, for example, may describe the condition established by the procedure FIND_TOP_SALESPERSON and used by the procedure PRETTY_PRINT. Examples include: TOP_SALESPERSON must not be the TOP_SALESPERSON from the previous month, or TOP_SALESPERSON is a record containing first and last names. Only the more interesting, subtle, or confusing relations need be described. Typical semantic conditions include the assumptions on program control, whether an action has been performed or not, and constraints on data item values, especially input and output parameters.

If component *A* establishes a condition and component *B* uses that condition to execute correctly, then component *B* is said to be semantically dependent on the condition established by component *A*. Figure 2 illustrates a simple semantic condition between a procedure *A* and procedure *B*. Procedure *B* depends on procedure *A* properly sorting the array *Y*. With semantic conditions linked to syntax, the effects of a change to syntax can be traced to semantically dependent components. In this manner, knowledge of semantic dependencies effectively reduces the very large set of possible ripple effects to a much smaller set of probable ripple effects.

The construction of such a base of semantic knowledge linked to syntax information will limit ripple effect analysis to

Component	Relation	Component	Semantic Condition
procedure *A*	modifies	data-item *Y*	"Array *Y* is sorted"
procedure *B*	uses	data-item *Y*	"Assumes Array *Y* is sorted"
procedure *B*	depends-on	procedure *A*	"Array *Y* is sorted"

Figure 2—Semantic dependency

simple network transversal. When a syntax change affects modifies-uses relations, the linked semantic condition is implicated. If the maintainer determines the semantic condition is still valid, no further analysis occurs. Otherwise a display of all the components dependent on the semantic condition is presented. The semantic data base will serve as "corporate memory," a structured repository for information typically embedded and forgotten in comments and supporting documentation.

Capabilities

SEMIT provides capabilities to the software maintainer in performing the following tasks: linking semantic descriptions to syntactic dependencies, using the semantic information in ripple effect analysis, and linking semantic conditions to external documents.

Syntax and semantics linked in a semantic data base

SEMIT creates a semantic data base by deriving default syntax relations from the source code, grouping the relations into possible dependencies based on modifies-uses paths, and then prompts the maintainer to describe the dependent components with semantic conditions. This keeps semantic and syntax information in-step and consistent.

Semantic ripple effect analysis

SEMIT provides semantic ripple effect analysis by presenting the semantic information in the semantic data base to the maintainer. This allows the maintainer to determine the effects of change based on both syntax and semantic information. If a procedure which establishes a semantic condition is changed in such a manner as to affect that condition, then all other components which depend on that condition are possibly impacted. In doing so, the analysis ignores the numerous syntactic ripple effects as derived by data and control flow analysis and thus focuses the analysis to more probable paths as defined by the expert maintainer.

External documentation mapped to semantic conditions

Semantic conditions are also useful for describing dependencies to system documentation external to the source code. These dependencies provide the traceability necessary for up-to-date and consistent documentation. The addition of one-directional dependencies is an ad-hoc procedure, based on the existence and format of existing documentation. The maintainer must explicitly describe the dependency, no syntactic defaults are derivable.

Architecture

The architecture of SEMIT is composed of two basic components, the Semantic Data Base and the SEMIT system. External components include the Source Code and the Syntax Analysis module which builds the default Semantic Data Base.

Figure 3 represents the architecture of SEMIT. Note the bidirectional flow of information from the user to the Semantic Data Base via the SEMIT Control. This represents the two modes of SEMIT usage, adding information and using information.

Syntax Analysis

The Syntax Analysis program builds the initial Semantic Data Base based on program control flow and data flow. For each procedure in a program, all external data used and modified by the procedure are represented in the network. All data item and control flow relations are represented with the following relations:

1. uses (procedure_name,data_name)
2. modifies (procedure_name,data_name)
3. calls (procedure_name,procedure_name)

SEMIT Control

SEMIT Control performs three different functions. It assists the annotation of default dependencies with semantic conditions, maps syntax changes to semantic conditions, and lists the dependent components of changed semantic conditions.

Annotating default dependencies to create semantic conditions is the primary knowledge acquisition function of SEMIT. The maintainer documents the more interesting syntactic or performance dependencies internal to the source, and dependencies to external documentation. As the description is made, a consistency check is made to insure at most one establisher and at least one user of the semantic condition exists.

The Change Analysis function is an interactive tool to aid the user in the process of making a change. It maps a syntax change to existing semantic conditions if directly linked. The impacted conditions are a list of all the semantic conditions established by the procedure which may now be inconsistent. The user examines the list and filters out those that are still valid, then performs dependency analysis on the changed conditions.

The Dependency Analysis function examines the Semantic Data Base for all components reliant on the impacted semantic condition. It lists those components while prompting the maintainer for verification of correctness. SEMIT cannot reason about the consistency, and must rely on the maintainer's

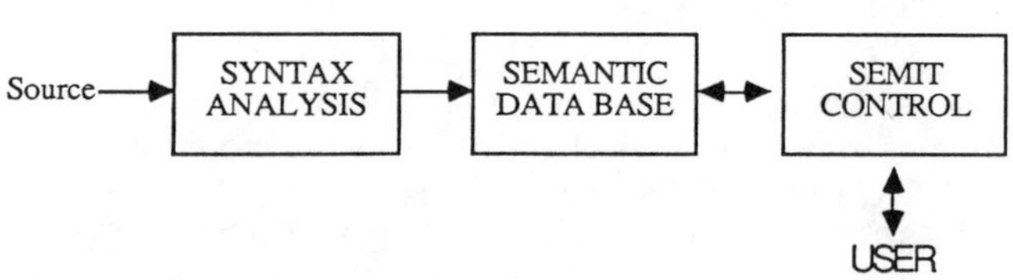

Figure 3—SEMIT architecture

skill and judgment. Dependency chains may then be followed by the maintainer if a change ripples through more than one set of dependencies.

Prototyping Experiences

SEMIT was prototyped to show the feasibility of the concept and model the user interface. A series of adjustments to the tool were identified based on the prototype. The first observation involved the nature of ripple effect error flow and the types of semantic conditions typically entered into SEMIT. Examples tended to emphasize modifies and uses pairings. Thus a simplification of all syntax relations summarized by a modifies-uses pairing seems possible. Annotation of these syntax pairs is a simple and useful solution.

Further understanding of the difficulty of performing semantic ripple effect was also discovered in the prototype by the attempt to map syntax changes to semantic conditions. The prototype only considered the simplest class of syntax changes; a modification of an existing source line. SEMIT then checked for all the semantic conditions which referred to that source line, and considered them impacted. Deleted lines, too, were merely mapped to any semantic condition which used it. All semantic conditions that were linked to source lines after the deletion were implicated.

A more interesting situation becomes apparent when the addition of source lines is considered. In the event of a maintenance operation which added syntax lines, the prototype initially assumed no impact on existing semantic conditions. In practice, the adjacent semantic conditions, the conditions linked to source before and after the added lines are often affected.

User interface issues were also identified by the prototype experience. Menus were useful in coordinating the user activities. A fully interactive interface, however, would provide more benefits. Stereotyped action patterns (schemes) which lead the user through maintenance actions should be developed. For example, a common scheme involves making a syntax change, mapping its impacts to semantic conditions, pursuing a breadth-first examination of all primary and secondary dependent components, followed by the iterative examination of all dependent components. Primary dependent components are those components directly dependent on a particular semantic condition, secondary dependent components are those components indirectly dependent on a particular semantic condition via dependency on a primary dependent component. Other schemes might enforce a particular methodology, requesting reports, creation of documentation, and communication of impacts to other maintainers.

In following semantic ripple effects, it quickly became apparent that many screens (or windows) are necessary to fully understand the current situation. A single screen was used with a small work list tracking actions taken and actions to take. This list was useful. A more appealing solution would utilize multiple windows: displaying source code, the change, semantic conditions, users of conditions, and a network of related components. Especially important is the need to use such a tool from within an editor, thus allowing maintenance and analysis in parallel. With such a wide-band of information, maintenance would be easier to relate back to the original change, rather than through a long string of dependent impacts.

Finally, feasibility was shown in the sense that semantic information can be stored and used for an approximation to semantic ripple effect analysis. The power of the information used to reason is only as useful as the information originally entered.

FUTURE RESEARCH

In the course of prototyping, many ideas toward integrating and extending SEMIT surfaced. User interface concerns and functional extensions were noted. Considering SEMIT primarily as a semantic data base representation of a program's dependency information, the following capabilities would extend SEMIT into a more useful maintenance tool.

Incorporate Schema-Driven Assistance. A Software Maintenance assistant, similar to the Designer/Verifiers Assistant[12] or the Programmer's Apprentice,[21] could lead maintainers through the basic tasks of creating and using semantic conditions in a mixed-initiative interaction. Schema-driven assistance is based on the knowledge of a stereotypical interaction. The assistant would lead and follow the maintainer based on the type of actions being performed. Such an assistant would eventually be knowledgeable of all system documentation and helpful in its presentation.[4]

Improve User Interface. A multi-window based approach is required to present the wealth of information necessary. Work on multiple tasks in the same ripple analysis needs to be supported.

Incorporate Semantic Data Base in A Relational DBMS. The prototype of SEMIT does not represent the semantic information in a relational manner. However, the semantic dependencies are relations between objects, perfectly suited for a relatonal data base representation.

Develop a Relationship Library. The prototype SEMIT creates default dependencies based on syntax analysis alone. The relations "modifies," "uses" and "calls" are system defaults. Any relation can be represented. A library of the most common and useful relations could be developed. Examples include the performance relationships described in "Ripple Effect Analysis of Software Maintenance,"[25] and relationships to related documentation external to the source. Automatic derivation of some of these relations is possible during the syntax analysis stage.

Integrate Syntax-Directed Editor. A link between an existing semantic data base and a syntax-based editor would provide intelligent editing. Any syntax change made that affected a semantic condition could be examined and processed in the background unbeknownst to the maintainer. Special considerations would be necessary when reasoning about the effects of partial changes, and the addition and deletion of source lines.

Provide Analysis Control. Finally, the analysis performed by SEMIT should be controllable by the maintainer. Extent options might include program, sub-program, or module level analysis. Summary information options would limit deep analysis, producing various summary lists of possible impacts.

REFERENCES

1. Balzer, R., T. Cheatham and C. Green. "Software technology in the 1990's: Using a new paradigm." *IEEE Computer,* November, 1983.
2. Blaylock, J. *A Syntactic Analyzer for a Maintenance Engineering Environment,* Computer Science Department, Arizona State University, 1983.
3. Boehm, B. *Software Engineering Economics,* Englewood Cliffs, N.J.: Prentice-Hall, Inc., 1981.
4. Bortman, S. *Display of Maintenance Information,* Computer Science Department, Arizona State University, 1984.
5. Browne, J. and D. Johnson. "FAST: A second generation program analysis system." *Proceedings Third International Conference on Software Engineering,* May, 1978.
6. Colofello, J. and S. Woodfield. "A proposed software maintenance environment." *Proceedings Software Maintenance Workshop,* December, 1983.
7. Green, C., D. Luckham, R. Balzer, T. Cheatham and C. Rich. "Report on a knowledge-based software assistant." Kestrel Institute, RADC-TR-83-195, August 1983.
8. Hecht, M. *Flow Analysis of Computer Programs,* New York: North-Holland, 1977.
9. Hirschberg, M., W. Frickel, W. Miller. "A semantic update system for software maintenance." *Proceedings COMPCON,* (1979).
10. Ince, D. "A program design language maintenance tool based on semantic nets." *Proceedings Software Maintenance Workshop,* December, 1983.
11. Martin, J. and C. McClure. *Software Maintenance: The Problem and Its Solutions,* London: Prentice-Hall, 1983.
12. Moriconi, M. "A designer/verifier's assistant." *IEEE Transactions on Software Engineering,* July, 1979.
13. Osterweil, L. and L. Fosdick, "DAVE—A validation error detection and documentation system for FORTRAN programs." *Software Practice and Experience,* September, 1976.
14. Oviedo, E. "Control flow, data flow and program complexity." *Proceedings IEEE COMPSAC,* 1980.
15. Patkau, B. *A Foundation for Software Maintenance,* Department of Computer Science, University of Toronto, 1983.
16. Rich, C. and H. Shrobe. "Initial report on a LISP programmer's apprentice." *IEEE Transactions on Software Engineering,* November 1978.
17. Rudmik, A. and D. Vines. "Modeling the static and dynamic properties of software engineering projects." GTE Communication Systems, Phoenix, Arizona, 1985.
18. Shapiro, D., J. Dean and B. McCune. "A knowledge base for supporting an intelligent program editor." *Proceedings IEEE International Conference on Software Engineering,* March, 1984.
19. Strom, R. and S. Yemini. "Typestate: A programming language concept for enhancing software reliability." *IEEE Transactions on Software Engineering,* January, 1986.
20. Stucki, L. "New directions in automated tools for improving software quality." *Current Trends in Programming Methodology,* London: Prentice-Hall, 1977.
21. Waters, R. "The programmer's apprentice: Knowledge-based program editing." *IEEE Transactions on Software Engineering,* January, 1982.
22. Yau, S. "Methodology for Software Maintenance." Northwestern University, RADC-TR-83-262, 1984.
23. Yau, S. and S. Chang. "Estimating logical stability in software maintenance." *Proceedings IEEE COMPSAC,* 1984.
24. Yau, S. and P. Grabow. "A model for representing the control flow and data flow of program modules." *Proceedings IEEE COMPSAC,* 1980.
25. Yau, S., J. Collofello, and T. MacGregor. "Ripple effect analysis of software maintenance." *Proceedings IEEE COMPSAC,* 1978.

Computer information system development methodologies—a comparative analysis

by DANIEL T. LEE
Pan American University
Edinburg, Texas

ABSTRACT

A computer information system is one of the main constructs through which a business firm gains a competitive edge over its competitors. Unfortunately, after four decades of effort by computer scientists and management specialists, ideal methodologies of CIS development are still lacking. The purpose of this paper is to conduct a comparative analysis of CIS development methodologies, trace their historical evolution, and develop integrated methodologies which can be used for logical system design and physical implementation. During the past four decades, CIS development methodologies concentrated on structured methods which are efficient for small systems, but they will soon be overwhelmed by complex and large systems. Only recently, fourth generation languages and automatic design techniques have begun to emerge as driving forces in CIS development. This paper tries to integrate these new technologies into a unified whole for CIS development. It will not only be used for transactional processing, but also for office automation and decision support.[1]

PREFACE

Computer information system development methodologies have evolved through several stages. The information system development life cycle (ISDLC) method is one of the most widely known methodologies.[2] According to Ahituv, the traditional ISDLC has always been a troublesome, complex, costly, and time-consuming process. This inadequacy is primarily caused by the rigidity of its development process and there is no match between its logical design and physical implementation.

In the early days of system analysis and programming, according to Martin,[3] there were few rules other than those of the programming language itself. The methods used in CIS development were often inefficient and caused many problems. The structured techniques represented a search for better methods in system analysis, design, and programming. They did improve the quality of programs and system development but were not building applications fast enough and were bogged down by maintenance problems. This led to the development of new languages, report generators, application generators, database systems, decision support tools, mini-macro computers, operating systems, data communication and networks, multifunctional work stations, automated techniques, expert systems, and integrated systems.

Under automated methodologies computers are used as design workbenches for creating, editing, expanding, and changing structured diagrams. They can also be used to automate data modeling from system specifications, extract subsets of data models for individual applications, check the design being created, and automate the generation of code. Automated designs are based on mathematical axioms so that the overall design can be mathematically verified. This is an extension of structured design; computers can rigorously check the entire design, eliminate all misuse of the constructs, and automate codes which are bug-free and can be used in applications.

Many tools are involved in the automated methodologies. These tools cannot stand alone for effective function. They have to be integrated for combined efforts. The integrated methodologies are therefore the last, but not the least, CIS development techniques with which strong CIS can be built.

This paper first discusses traditional ISDLC and follows with a discussion of various structured methodologies. Automated design methodologies, iterative design methodologies and integrated methodologies are also described.

TRADITIONAL METHODOLOGIES

The ISDLC techniques were introduced to the academic community in the 1950s and 60s. According to Awad,[4] system development revolves around a life cycle that begins with the recognition of users' needs. Following a feasibility study, the key stages are the evaluation of the present system, information gathering, cost/benefit analysis, detailed design, and implementation of the candidate system. Kanter[5] illustrates the application, development, and implementation cycle as being composed of three general phases: analysis, synthesis, and implementation. Analysis is defined as the analysis of company operation and the division of the total operation into logical and workable units for measurement and evaluation. Synthesis, the opposite of analysis, begins to combine and build the parts or elements into a whole. The implementation phase is the "proof of the pudding." The phases of analysis, synthesis, and implementation are never-ending cycles. Prince[6] divides the CIS analysis and design into five phases: (1) the planning phase, (2) the organization review and administrative study phase, (3) the conceptual system design phase, (4) the equipment selection and program design phase, and (5) the implementation phase. Unfortunately, this method almost stops at phase 3, the conceptual system design. The descriptions of the methodology are quite clear, but physical implementation is lacking.

Murray[7] views the maturation of a system as going through the stages of analysis, design, implementation, and operation. He conceives of the cycle as beginning with a feasibility study that precedes a formal systems analysis. The systems design and implementation are followed by operation of the new (or revised) system. This cycle may repeat. Ahituv[8] summarized that the traditional ISDLC typically contains four major phases such as definition phase, construction phase, implementation phase, and operation phase. Each phase in turn consists of several steps.

Ahituv finished this work in 1982. In 1984 even he admitted that, primarily because of the nature of the systems that must be built with it, this traditional ISDLC has always been a troublesome, complex, costly, and time-consuming process.

Actually there are hundreds of information systems development methodologies which follow this established pattern. The big flaw of this traditional method is that though the phases or steps relating to system analysis and design seem to be clear, there is no practical way to bridge the gaps among analysis, design, and implementation. Most of the traditional design methodologies concentrate on logical system design; it is very difficult, if not impossible, to follow up with physical implementation. Information technology personnel have been trying hard for three decades to find ways out of this inadequacy. They found out that the structured techniques represent an advancement in information development research; it clarifies the many uncertainties embodied in the traditional ISDLC and largely bridges the gaps among system analysis, design, and implementation. The detailed mechanism of the structured techniques is the topic in the following section.

STRUCTURED TECHNIQUES

Structured techniques evolved from a coding methodology (structured programming) into techniques consisting of analysis, design, test, project management, and documentation tools. According to Martin,[3] structured techniques were intended to be a step toward changing software-building methods from a manual craft to an engineering discipline. In a sense, it is more an attitude than a particular methodology.

Structured Techniques

This has evolved into a set of technologies encompassing the whole software life cycle. It consists of both technical and management issues, ranging from programming to problem solving procedures such as structured programming, structured analysis, structured design, automated techniques, and computer-aided system analysis.

Structured programming

Structured programming focuses on the program itself. It involves structured coding, top-down programming, and stepwise refinement.

Structured analysis

This is the process of defining the information requirements for operation, including system constraints and performance requirements. The functions to be performed are precisely defined, but how these functions work together is not defined. The main output of the analysis is a statement of the function specification and information requirements. This statement bridges between the system analysis and design because the requirements of the system to be built, including functional specifications and constraints, are used as input to the design process.

There are two similar versions of structured analysis: Gane and Sarson,[9] and De Marco[10] and Yourdon.[11] Both are based on structured disciplines such as top-down, bottom-up, divide-and-conquer, graphic presentation, and functional decomposition.

The structured specification is composed of data flow diagram (DFD), processing logic, data store, data dictionary, and data immediate access diagram (DIAD).

A DFD is a network representation of the process (functions or procedures) and the data used in this process. It shows what a system does, but not how it is done. It is the central modeling tool of structured analysis and is used to partition the system into a process hierarchy. DFD can be used in a top-down design and can be exploded to lower level of details.

DFD only provides an informal description of the system. The data dictionary is used to add rigor to the specification. It is a set of formal definitions of all data including data elements and data relationships.

A process specification describes what happens inside a process box in a DFD. It follows the input-process-output specification which is also used for the construction of databases. The DIAD is designed for identifying the data elements or record types (relations) needed in on-line processing or immediate access.

De Marco defines the structured analysis as a seven-step process; Gane and Sarson define a similar process, but in five steps. Both approaches are informal applications of the functional decomposition method to divide the problem into its component parts. But neither methodology offers sufficient guidelines to provide the rigor necessary for defining a precise, computable specification. Gane and Sarson's book,[9] improves upon their 1977 edition and adds more rigorous specifications.

The greatest improvement in structured analysis is a change in the system specification from a large, unreadable tome to a user-friendly graphic model. A higher-level DFD can be drawn quickly to show the general picture of the system. Perhaps the most impressive improvement in Gane and Sarson's structured system analysis is that the data stores and data dictionaries are directly related to relational database systems.

However, there is no checking mechanism in DFD. It emphasizes process components; data analysis receives only secondary attention. Structured analysis techniques should only be used for small systems and simple problems with formal data modeling. For complex systems, DFD can be used to sketch a high-level view of the system. But beyond this point, more rigorous analysis and specification methods should be used to develop a precise and computable specification. The higher-order software methodology is better for this. It is the topic in the next few sections.

Structured analysis and design

Structured analysis and design emphasize a higher-level view of the system which is then applied to the lower-level process. The concept of modulization was implemented by standardizing the structure of program modules and restricting the interfaces between modules.

System design

System design is defined as finding ways to satisfy the information requirements identified in the system analysis phase. It is the process of planning how the system will be built, by determining the procedural and data components, and planning how these components will be organized to produce the information needed. Functional specifications, information requirements, and constraints defined in the analysis phase are used as the input to the design process.

Structured Design Methodologies

Functional decomposition, top-down, and bottom-up are the main techniques used in system design, but the most widely used structured design methodologies are top-down design, Yourdon's structured design, Jackson design methodology, and Warnier-Orr design methodology.

Top-down design

The top-down design begins with the most general function and breaks it down into subfunctions which may follow with a bottom-up approach for detailed design of the subfunctions. The step-wise refinement process is the key technique. Input, function, and output should be specified for each module. Details should not be delayed until late in the design process.

Structured design methodology

The structured design methodology (SDM) defined by Steven, Myers, and Constantine,[12] and Yourdon,[13] is a composite of techniques for system design. Actually, it is a refinement of the top-down design method and consists of four steps.

First, a data flow diagram (DFD) composed of processes that operate on the data is drawn to represent the system. These processes and data link together as the basis for defining the programming components. The DFD is built from four basic components: the data flow, the process, the data store, and the terminator. The DFD shows how data flow through a logical system and a procedure for processing applications. For details on drawing the DFD, De Marco[10] and Martin[3] completely describe the techniques.

Second, a structure chart is drawn to represent the program design. It is a hierarchy of functional components. The structure chart is derived from the data flow diagram produced in the first step. There are two design strategies for guiding the transformation of a DFD into a structure chart: transform analysis and transaction analysis. Page-Jones[14] has a detailed description of the two strategies.

Third, the design is evaluated by using transform analysis and transaction analysis and is also measured by the techniques of coupling and cohesion of modules.

Fourth, the design is prepared for implementation. This is called packaging design and is the process of dividing the logical program design into physical implementation units; these units are called load units. Each load unit is brought into memory and executed as one unit by the operating system. The purpose of packaging is to make sure that the components of the physical system can be executed in an actual computer environment. The packages should be functionally related with high cohesion but loose coupling. At the end of analysis the system is packaged into jobs and job steps. A job is a sequence of job steps. A job step is composed of a main program and its subprogram. The data flow diagram is packaged at this point by establishing three boundaries: hardware boundaries, batch/on-line/real-time boundaries, and operating-cycle boundaries. Each job step is defined in terms of a structured chart which is packaged into executable programs and load units. The smallest possible load unit is one module. Yourdon's structured design[13] has a complete description of procedure and techniques.

The drawback of the structured design is that the rules guiding the transform analysis, transaction analysis, and factoring techniques are very vague. They offer no real improvement over the simple functional decomposition method of top-down design. The introduction of such new terminology as afferent streams, efferent streams, and central transforms confuses rather than enhances the top-down design process. The biggest problem of the structured design is that the design process will break down when used for the design of complex and large systems with many input, output, and transform processing streams. The combined strategy of using transaction analysis to divide the system into more manageable pieces and using transform analysis to design each piece can be difficult to apply in practice. No guidelines are offered for accomplishing the top level division. Besides, there is a lack in data design which constitutes a serious omission in the structure design methodology. The role of databases or data dictionaries in program design is not discussed. This limits the usefulness of the structured design methodology to designing small and simple programs with simple file systems. For these simple problems, the top-down design methodology is easier to use.

The Jackson design

The Jackson design methodology is also a refinement of the top-down design method and separates the implementation phase from the design phase. The main difference between the Jackson design and structured design is that the former is based on analysis of data flow. The former is data-oriented and the latter is process-oriented. The Jackson method advocates a static view of structure while the structured design focuses on a dynamic view of data flow. The Jackson method derives the program structure from data structure. It assumes that the problem has been fully specified and that the program will be implemented in a procedural language. Thus, system analysis and program implementation concerns lie outside the design process. The design process first defines the data structure and then orders the procedural logic or operations to fit the data structures. There are four steps in the design process. First, each input and output data stream is described as a hierarchical structure. Second, all the data structures are combined into one hierarchical program structure. Third, a list of executable operations required to produce the program output from the input is prepared. Then each operation on the list is allocated as a component in the program structure. Fourth, the ordered operations are written in the form of structure text, a formal version of pseudocode.

The major strength of the Jackson design methodology is that it emphasizes data structure design. It produces a hierarchical program structure from hierarchical data structures. The major weakness of the Jackson design is that it is very difficult to apply directly to real world problems. The design process assumes the existence of a complete and correct problem specification. This is rarely possible for most application situations. Another weak joint is that it is limited to simple programs. Third, it is batch-processing-oriented, which is not an effective design technique for on-line systems or database systems. In simple program applications it is an overkill; in complex situations it provides very few guidelines for managing the problems.

It is fair to say that the Jackson design methodology is more difficult to use than other structured design methodologies;

the steps are tedious to apply. It is only helpful for a certain class of problems such as serial file systems. It breaks down completely when applied to database systems. For simple problems with simple data structures, the extra effort is not worthwhile. The simpler-top-down method may be the choice.[15,16,17]

The Warnier-Orr design

The Warnier-Orr design methodology is a hybrid form of LCP and SPD. LCP stands for logical construction of programs while SPD represents structured program design. The Warnier-Orr design uses set theory from mathematics to describe program design. A set is an ordered collection of objects. It also adopts a top-down design method and functional composition to derive program design. There are six steps in its design procedure:[18,19] First, the program output is defined as a hierarchical data structure. Second, the logical database is defined. It consists of all the data needed to produce the program output. Third, event analysis is performed to define all the events that can affect the data elements in the logical database. Fourth, the physical database is developed, which is composed of the primary data items in the logical database. Fifth, the logical process that is needed to produce the desired output from the input is designed. Sixth, the physical process is designed to complete the program design.

The Warnier-Orr design methodology is similar to the Jackson design because both are data-driven and derive the program structure from the data structure. They both work with hierarchical data structure only and stress that logical design should be separate from physical design. The main difference between the two is that the Jackson design merges old input and output data structures to form a single program structure while the Warnier-Orr design derives the program structure and the input data structures from the output data structures. Therefore, in the Warnier-Orr design, the program output completely determines the data structure which, in turn, determines the program structure. It is, therefore, an output-oriented analysis in addition to being a data-driven approach.

The Warnier-Orr design methodology limits the design to a strict hierarchical model for data and processes. Network-like data structures cannot be described. The fact is that not all databases are hierarchical. It also does not address the design of database systems or the role of data dictionaries. This is a serious omission from what is claimed to be a general-purpose design methodology. Warnier claims that the control logic is not part of the logical design, and therefore provides no guidelines for control logic design.

In general, the Warnier-Orr design methodology is suitable for small problems with simple, report-oriented systems. For these problems the methodology provides an easy-to-follow design method, but for such small and simple report designs, the methodology is too tedious to follow in detail.

AUTOMATED DESIGN METHODOLOGIES

Structured techniques for system design suffer common weaknesses in that they are only fit for small systems and not fit for complex problems. The human brain is limited and has difficulty handling complex details with precision. Structured techniques often make mistakes so higher-level automation is the predominant trend. The system analyst will create his designs at a work station in a computer-aided fashion. The work station may use mini-microcomputers to help create and edit data models or diagrams. These diagrams may become a language themselves, and from this language executable code will be automatically generated.

USE.IT is a completely general specification language that can be applied to any type of system. It is mathematically based so that it completely checks the internal consistency of specifications and generates bug-free codes. USE.IT would not rate high on a scale of user friendliness, but it is clearly shown that mathematically-based rigor applied to tools can be built into user-friendly constructs for system specification. USE.IT has an automatic documentation generator for generating documentation in U.S. Department of Defense format. Design and documentation of systems are closely linked.[20,21]

Data modeling is vital for database design. The task is too tedious and error-prone to be done by hand. It should be designed and maintained with computers. For example, the canonical synthesis is very tedious to apply to large installations unless it is automated. Once computerized, it automatically produces fully normalized data models. A data model shows the functional dependencies and associations among data items. Data redundancy in different areas can be avoided.[22,23]

DDIs data designer is one of the data modeling tools.[24] The user's view and functional dependencies can be input to the data designer, which synthesizes them into a non-redundant data model, plots the result, and produces various reports for data administrators. If the input functional dependencies are correct, the output is in third normal form.

The future of computing lies with computer-aided design in which the analyst builds applications at a workstation screen and the machine generates executable code. Much computing will be decision support operations done by individuals at workstations. Personal, departmental, and central computing will be tightly interlinked. Most end users' computing will not involve programming, but will employ report generators, spreadsheet facilities, decision support tools, personal databases, and many other packages.

The data models are kept in a computerized form, and the users at work stations use computerized tools to build applications that use data. These tools are selected or designed to aid and automate system analysis and design, and application development.

ITERATIVE DESIGN METHODOLOGIES

Iterative design methodology (IDM) is an interim method between structured design methodologies and integrated system design techniques. As indicated earlier, the traditional information system development life cycle methodologies are troublesome, costly, complex, and time consuming. There are no rigorous rules which the system analyst can follow to develop computer information systems. There is almost no database arrangement with the traditional ISDLC. The development of structured design techniques in the 1970s represents an advancement in the search for better methods. Unfortunately, structured design methodologies are only fit for small systems and simple programs. For large systems and complex programs, the structured methodologies are completely overwhelmed. Also, there are no rigorous rules which can be used for guiding the system design process. The structured methods try to change the system design methodologies from an art to a science. This effort has only been partially successful. When faced with a very complex situation like decision making, rigid methods such as structured techniques are totally inappropriate to the ever-changing environment.

Practitioners and academicians alike are diligently searching for alternative methods to meet the needs of the executives because the tasks they face are basically unstructured. Both the traditional ISDLC and the structured design methodologies are inadequate for decision support system development. An alternative, iterative design methodology, is advocated by Sprague and Carson.[25] This is an interim design methodology which can be used until an effective integrated design methodology can be developed for developing decision support systems.

The iterative design method is based upon the premise that the environment of decision making is volatile. It is difficult, if not impossible, to completely identify the information requirements before system design begins. Under such circumstances, the best way is to identify an important subproblem, develop a small but usable system first, then gradually refine it, and finally expand this usable subsystem to other areas. After all the subsystems are developed, efforts will be directed toward integrating these workable subsystems into a unified whole. So far there is still no perfect solution to system integrations. Tremendous progress has been made recently in individual areas. Eventually integrated methodologies may be developed.

The iterative design methodology also adopts the divide-and-conquer tactic. It first defines the requirements of DSS, then defines what capabilities the DSS can provide. This methodology was developed by Sprague and Carson and named the ROMC approach; it will be discussed in the next section.

There are six objectives which include three types of tasks and three types of support needed in DSS:

The three types of tasks are: (1) to support all types of structures—structured, semistructured, and unstructured,[26] (2) to support all levels of management—strategic planning, management control, and operational control,[27] and (3) to support the communication between all levels of decision makers—independent, sequential, and pooled.[28]

Three types of support are needed: (1) it needs to support all phases of decision making—intelligence, design, and choice,[29] (2) it needs to support a variety of decision-making processes but not be dependent on any one type since each person's cognitive organization and style are different, (3) it should be easy to use and modify in response to changes in the user, the task, or the environment.[1,5]

Gory and Morton[26] combined Anthony's levels of management and Simon's types of decisions into a paradigm which can be used for identifying to which categories applications belong.

In a design DSS for poorly-specified environments, Sprague and Carson suggested an approach called ROMC (representation, operation, memory aids, and control mechanisms). The ROMC is intended to identify requirements in each of three capabilities of DSS: databases, analytical models, and query interface. This approach is based on a set of four user-oriented entities: R, O, M, and C. The capabilities of DSS from a user's point of view are that it provides representations to help users conceptualize and communicate the problem or decision situation; to operate, analyze, and manipulate those representations; to provide memory aids for the users in linking the representations and operations; and to control the entire system. Through this approach, the gap between the requirements and the capabilities of DSS can be reduced.

The iterative design of a specific DSS consists of an iterative addition or deletion of Rs, Os, Ms, and Cs. These combinations of R, O, M, and C are carried out by the three capabilities: databases, analytical models, and query dialogue. The ROMC approach is a framework for identifying the end user's requirements and the capabilities of DSS which will support these requirements. It is a process-independent approach. One set of representations and operations may support a variety of decision-making processes. The differences among the decision-making processes are more or less in the sequencing of operations and in the decision makers' interpretation of representation rather than in the set of representations or operations to be used in the process.

The major drawback of the iterative design methodology is that there are no rigorous rules which can be followed by the system designer. When one specific DSS is developed, it may not fit the second application and another one may have to be developed. It is, of course, costly and time consuming. With the automated design tools, the cost and time needed for system development may be reduced, but the effectiveness of this approach may still be a problem. The solution may be to have integrated rules which can be followed for system integration. The integrated design methodology is the topic of the following section.[25,30,31,32]

SYSTEM INTEGRATION METHODOLOGIES

The Present State of the Art

So far four major information system design methodologies have been discussed. There is not one among them that is completely fit for designing complex systems. Perhaps there will never be one that is perfectly fit. It may also be true that for some tasks it is more appropriate than for others. For example, structured design methodologies are more appropriate than the traditional ISDLC if it is applied to structured tasks and environments. For volatile and unstructured tasks and environments, iterative design methodologies are more useful than both the traditional ISDLC and SDM. Automated design methodologies (ADM) are in the infant stage but are progressing rapidly. If ADM can be integrated with other design methodologies and tools, a new design methodology will emerge. Actually, this new methodology has popped up and is called systems integration methodology (SIM).

The ISDM integrates many design techniques: the top-down and bottom-up are the two most important techniques in the design tool kits. The top-down design is a macro system design beginning with the general function or the root of a hierarchical tree and working down to the lower level leaves of the tree. It is usually based on information planning which lays down the information development guidelines in the system analysis phase. These guidelines are used in the system design phase as input. Under such high-point guiding principles, a bottom-up micro system design can be carried out for detailed program development.

Another important characteristic of the SIM is that information system development usually involves two groups of people. One group is business oriented, and the other is technically oriented. During the system analysis phase, the main duty of the system development team is to define the information needs. The business-oriented people are in a better position to define the information requirements of the organization. When the problem and the information requirements are defined, the technical people take over and identify the technologies which can be used to meet the requirements. This is usually carried out in the system design phase. Actually, there is no clear-cut separation of the two phases. There is some overlap between the two, and sometimes they are iterative. For more information on unified design methodology, please refer to Lee.[32]

Conceptual Models for Integration

In office automation there is another effort working toward integrated methodologies. Bracchi[34] classifies the conceptual office models into four types: data-based models, process-based models, agent-based models, and mixed models. Most of the recent office models belong to the mixed category. This is actually an integrated method for office information development. Office information systems are one of the main components in the overall information construct.

The mixed models consist of more than one type of element as the basis for system specification, and define relationships among these elements. The semantic office system (SOS) is an example of a mixed model. SOS classifies office elements into three different submodels: the static, the dynamic, and the evolution submodels. The static submodel contains the specification of data-related elements such as documents, dossiers, and agents. The dynamic submodel contains the specification of operations and activities performed in the office. The evolution submodel specifies, through two sets of rules, both the normal evolution of office work and the possible structural modifications of office tasks. Some of the rules support office activities with information for performing normal operations or for decision making; other rules may be used for triggering the automatic execution of operation. These mixed specifications and operations actually work in an integrated fashion. This new mixed technique turns many original models into mixed models. For example, the OFFICETALK-D[35] is transformed from OFFICETALK-ZERO[36] (a data based model) and information control nets[37] (a process-based model).

Integrated Models

Lyngrack and McLeod developed an integrated design methodology which can be applied to distributed environments. It does not employ any one of the traditional high-level database models. For example, SDD-1,[38] distributed INGRES,[39] R*,[40] and the system for managing structured messages[41] are more or less related to the relational data model.[42] The simple object-oriented database model (ODM) was defined, and now this model has been extended to work in distributed environments and is called distributed object-oriented database model (DODM). It concentrates on distributed information management at object-level. Both ODM and DODM provide end users with the basic primitives for object definition, manipulation, and retrieval. The DODM supports object sharing, location transparency, and access control, and allows relationships to be established among objects in the databases. The best feature of the DODM is that the location transparency can be supported without having to have a central data structure.

The DODM can be incorporated for use with multi-functional workstations. Each workstation has a unique name. Several workstations can be grouped together at a single mode in the computer network. All the workstations have the same interface for communication, but they do not have to establish the same data model. The DODM models the distributed environment as a logical network of many workstations. Each workstation contains information such as databases. The distributed workstations can be thought of as a logical network of distributed databases.

The ODM and DODM are both modeled as a collection of objects and relationships. The relationships between objects are modeled as structural objects. Each object in the database corresponds to a relation in the set of all database objects.

Implementation of ODM can be straightforward by using existing database technology. A prototype has been built by using the INGRES relational database management system[43] running UNIX operating system. The object heap is implemented as a direct access file.

DODM is a very simple database model for specification of objects and relationships in a logical network of databases. Mechanisms are provided to allow relationships to be established across database boundaries, objects are allowed to be copied and moved from database to database, and access control and object sharing among databases are accommodated.

Neither ODM nor DODM is a high-level system for inexperienced database users. Both lack semantic expressiveness, mechanisms for integrity control, and high-level operations for database integration. The contributions were made in defining a small set of fundamental concepts and constructs that can be used as building blocks for integrated systems.

Efforts are being made at the University of Southern California to design and develop a personal information system and experimental prototype called INFOBASE, which is intended to provide information management facilities to support a wide spectrum of transactional, professional, managerial, and clerical processing. Based on the above modeling concepts and facilities recently developed, integrated systems can doubtlessly be achieved. These integrated systems are capable of supporting multi-functional workstations, database processing, and personal computing. INFOBASE is not only an example of integrated systems but is also intended to provide a basis of information management in engineering applications including software engineering and CAD/VLSI design.[40,47]

System Integration Recapitulated

After four decades of effort by both computer scientists and management experts, a legitimate model that can be used for system integration is still missing. Though complete integrated models are still in short supply, there are plenty of quasi models which can be combined for unifying the various components of an integrated system. The various models and components relating to system integration have been illustrated and examined, but further efforts are needed to integrate them into a unified whole.

Before integration, the question must be asked, "What is the integration for?" The answer might be, "for transaction processing, decision making, and/or office automation." According to the definition of an integration system, it may be designed to provide any one, or all, of those functions. For transaction processing, the system design is easier; for decision making it is harder; for both transaction processing and decision making it is difficult. For transaction processing, decision making, and office automation, it is even more difficult because the current technologies are more appropriate for structured tasks, and the tasks a decision maker faces are largely unstructured.

In addition to the structure of tasks, the current trend is toward distributed processing. Theoretically, distributed processing involving concurrent control, security, and recovery is not a problem, but actually integrated systems in a distributed environment are still in an infant stage. Though system integration has a long way to go, the basic technologies required for system integration do exist. What is needed now is to try patiently using the integrated methodologies introduced in the previous sections.

So far the structured techniques, structured design methodologies, automated design methodologies, iterative design methodologies, and system integration methodologies have been discussed. Before putting them in an appropriate format, we should keep in mind the basic ingredients needed in an integrated system. In order to solve problems, task analysis is vital for identifying information requirements. These requirements are the basis for preparing a system specification which, in turn, is used for system design.

During the system design stage, the basic job is to identify the alternate ways to meet the information requirements identified in the system analysis stage. In the system design stage, data and process analysis are necessary. Data and process analysis involve data modeling, database systems, and processing logic. All the structured techniques and methodologies can be used. In addition to the above-mentioned techniques, data communication and networking, expert systems, fourth generation languages, computer-aided design techniques, and system automation methodologies should be used and integrated into the overall construct of the integrated systems.

Integrated Systems

After comparing 12 commercial systems in 1983, MacFarlane classified them into three kinds of systems: software-only, hardware/software, and time-shared.

In the software-only systems, the organizations buy the software and run it on their new or existing hardware. Though these are not total systems, they can perform professional and managerial tasks and can be tied into broader hardware and databases.[34]

The hardware/software systems are total turnkey systems. All provide local and remote area networking capabilities serving as integrated systems.

In the time-shared systems, the organization only needs to install work stations. All the software and processing power can be obtained through these work stations. This is a cost-effective method for obtaining the services of integrated systems.

There are many more disciplines and methodologies working toward integrated systems development. It is beyond the scope of this paper to go into detailed discussion of these efforts. Interested readers may refer to Lee,[33,44,45,24] Martin,[22,23,3,46] Lyngback,[47] and Bracchi.[34]

CONCLUSION

This paper has intensively investigated the various CIS development techniques: the traditional ISDLC methodology is loosely defined, and there are no rigorous rules which can be followed for effective CIS development. The various structured design methodologies are only fit for small systems and simple programs. There are also no rigorous rules for the system analysts and designers to follow for checking the consistency of the system being designed. When facing complex situations, they will be quickly overwhelmed. The automated techniques and system integration methodologies are still in their infant stage. Remarkable advancement in automated techniques has been reported recently. There is no doubt that integrated systems will be within reach in the near future. Some prototypes of integrated systems have already been built. Though they are still in the primitive stage and not for user-friendly use, it can be expected that near perfect integrated systems are imminent due to the rapid growth in technology.

REFERENCES

1. Alter, Steven L. *Decision Support Systems*. Reading, Massachusetts: Addison-Wesley, 1980.
2. Ahituv, Niv and Seev Neumann. "A Flexible Approach to Information System Development." *MIS Quarterly,* 8 (1984) 2.
3. Martin, James, and Carma McClure. *Structured Techniques for Computing,* Englewood Cliffs, New Jersey: Prentice-Hall, 1985.
4. Awad, Elias M. *Systems Analysis and Design,* 2nd ed. Richard D. Irwin, 1985.

5. Kanter, Jerome. *Management-Oriented Management Information Systems,* 2nd ed. Englewood Cliffs, New Jersey: Prentice-Hall, 1985.
6. Prince, Thomas R. *Information Systems for Management Planning and Control,* third ed., Irwin, 1975.
7. Murray, Thomas J. *Computer Based Information Systems,* Richard D. Irwin, 1985.
8. Ahituv, N. and S. Neumann. *Principles of Information Systems for Management,* William C. Brown, 1982.
9. Gane, C. and T. Sarson. *Structured Systems Analysis: Tools and Techniques,* Englewood Cliffs, New Jersey: Prentice-Hall, 1979.
10. De Marco, T. *Structured Analysis and System Specification,* New York: Yourdon, 1978.
11. Yourdon, E. "The Emergence of Structured Analysis." *Computer Decisions,* 8 (1976) 4.
12. Stevens, W., G. Myers, and L. Constantine. "Structured Design." *IBM Systems Journal,* 13 (1974) 2.
13. Yourdon, E. and L. Constantive. *Structured Design,* Englewood Cliffs, New Jersey: Prentice-Hall, 1979.
14. Page-Jones, M. *The Practical Guide to Structural System Design,* New York: Yourdon, 1980.
15. Jackson, M.A. "Constructive Methods of Program Design." In *Proceedings, First Conference of the European Conference in Informatics,* 1976.
16. Bergland, G.D. "A Guided Tour of Program Design Methodologies." *Computer,* October 1981.
17. Adrion, R., B. Branstand, and J. Cherniavsky. "Validation, Verification and Testing of Computer Software." *Computing Surveys,* 14 (1982) 2.
18. Higgins, D. *Program Design and Construction.* Englewood Cliffs, New Jersey: Prentice-Hall, 1979.
19. Orr, K. *Structured Systems Development,* New York: Yourdon, 1977.
20. Razdow, A., N. Albertson, Jr., and D. Rose. *Design Systems by Documenting Them With USEIT,* Cambridge, Massachusetts: Higher Order Software, Inc., 1979.
21. *USE.IT Reference Manual,* Cambridge, Massachusetts: Higher Order Software, Inc., 1982.
22. Martin, James. *Managing the Data Base Environment,* Englewood Cliffs, New Jersey: Prentice-Hall, 1983.
23. Martin, James. *System Design from Probably Correct Constructs,* Englewood Cliffs, New Jersey: Prentice-Hall, 1985.
24. Lee, Daniel T. "Decision Support in a Distributed Environment." AFIPS, *Proceedings of the National Computer Conference* (Vol. 53) 1984.
25. Sprague, H. Ralph and Eric D. Carson. *Building Effective Decision Support Systems,* Englewood Cliffs, New Jersey: Prentice-Hall, 1982.
26. Gory, G.A. and M.S. Scott Morton. "A Framework for Management Information Systems," *Sloan Management Review,* 13, Fall 1971.
27. Anthony, R.N. "Planning and Control Systems: A Framework for Analysis." Harvard University Graduate School of Business Administration, Studies in Management Control, Cambridge, Massachusetts, 1985.
28. Hackathorn, R. and P.G.W. Keen. "Organizational Strategies for Personal Computing in Decision Support Systems." *MIS Quarterly,* 5 (1981) 3.
29. Simon, H.A. *The New Science of Management Decisions,* New York: Harper & Row, 1960.
30. Zmud, Robert W. "Design Alternatives For Organizing Information Systems Activities." *MIS Quarterly,* 8 (1984) 2.
31. Bonczek, H., Clyd Holsapple, and Andrew Whinston. *Foundations of Decision Support Systems.* New York: Academic Press, 1981.
32. Keen, Peter and Michael Morton. *Decision Support Systems,* Reading, Massachusetts: Addison-Wesley, 1978.
33. Lee, Daniel T. "A Unified Method for Information System Development and Database Application." *International Journal on Policy and Information,* 8 (1984) 2.
34. Bracchi, G. and B. Dernici. "The Design Requirements of Office Systems." *ACM Transactions on Office Information Systems,* 2 April (1984) 2.
35. Ellis, C. and M. Bernal. "OFFICETALK-D: An Experimental Office Information System." In *Proceedings ACM SIGOA Conference on Office Systems,* Philadelphia, 1982.
36. Ellis, C. and G. Nutt. "Office Information Systems and Computer Science." *ACM Computing Surveys* 12 (1980) 1.
37. Cook, C. "Streamlining Office Procedures—An Analysis Using the Information Control Net Model." In *AFIPS, Proceedings of the National Computer Conference* (Vol. 49), 1980.
38. Rothnie, J.B., P.A. Bernstein, S. Fox, N. Goodman, M. Hammer, T.A. Landers, C. Reeve, D. Shipman, and E. Wong. "Introduction To A System for Distributed Database (SDD-1)." *ACM Transactions on Database Systems,* 5 (1980) 1.
39. Stonebraker, M. and E. Neuhold. "A Distributed Data Version of INGRES." In *Proceedings of Berkeley Workshop on Distributed Data Management Systems,* May 1977.
40. William, R., D. Daniel, L. Haass, G. Lapis, B. Lindsay, P. Ng, R. Obermarck, P. Selinger, A. Walker, P. Wilms, and R. Yost. "R*: An Overview of the Architecture." IBM Res. Rep. RJ3325, IBM Research Laboratory, San Jose, California, Feb. 1981.
41. Tsichritzis, D.C., F.A. Rabitti, S. Gibbs, O. Nierstrasz, and J. Hogg. "A System for Managing Structured Messages." *IEEE Transactions Commun.* COM-30 (1982) June.
42. Codd, E.F. "A Relational Model of Data for Large Shared Data Banks," *Communications of the ACM* 13 (1970) 6.
43. Stonebroker, M., G.D. Held, and P. Krep. "The Design and Implementation of INGRES." *ACM Transactions on Database Systems* 1 (1976) 3.
44. Lee, Daniel T. "A Unified Methodology of Combining Distributed Systems and Distributed Databases for Decision Support." *DSS-84 Transactions, 4th International Conference on Decision Support Systems,* 1984.
45. Lee, Daniel T. "Personal Computing for Decision Support." *Oxford Surveys in Information Technology Journal,* 2 (1985).
46. Martin, James and Carma McClure., *Fourth Generation Languages,* Englewood Cliffs, New Jersey: Prentice-Hall, 1985.
47. Lyngback, Peter and Dennis McLeod. "Object Management in Distributed Information Systems." *ACM Transactions on Office Information Systems,* 2 (1984) 2.

A model for monitoring software integration

by MARY LOU LANCHBURY
St. Edward's University
Austin, Texas
and
DAVID A. GUSTAFSON and AUSTIN MELTON
Kansas State University
Manhattan, Kansas

ABSTRACT

When managing software development, it is difficult to assess progress. This paper describes a general method for modeling software development; in this method, the development is considered to be a sequence of documents. The new perspective provided by this method is that much can be learned by examining the changes in successive document versions. In particular in this paper, the connections between the changes and the progress in software integration are studied. It is shown that the changes present a "picture" of development. This picture can be understood by both technical and non-technical personnel; thus, this model allows for the development of methods which software managers can use to monitor progress during software integration. The example presented is based on empirical data collected from team projects written in C.

INTRODUCTION

If one were to examine the sequence of documents written by an author in the development of a book, one would notice different types of changes being made at different stages in the book's development. In fact, after examining several sequences of documents for several books, one could probably determine with much accuracy where in a book's development an author was by examining the changes made to a particular document. The general claim of this paper is that, in writing software even more than in writing a book, much about the development can be determined by examining the changes made to successive versions. In particular, the sequence of changes made to a program during integration provides a picture that describes the integration process.

Managing software integration is a difficult task. It is made more difficult by the inability to accurately assess progress during this phase. A model of the integration phase that can be used to monitor the progress of the software integration would be very useful. It would be a first step toward a management tool to accurately assess the effectiveness of the integration phase.

This paper presents a model of successful code change patterns for the integration phase of the software development cycle. The model was empirically derived from data from successful projects; it is contrasted with failed project data to highlight those characteristics that empirically and intuitively should distinguish a successful development pattern from possibly unsuccessful development patterns. This model should enable project personnel, including non-technical personnel, to visualize the progress of the integration phase of the project. It can be used for decision making about the extension of deadlines and/or the expansion of budgets. It is understandable and provides visibility of progress in the form of patterns of changes to the data, that is, code. While using technical concepts and tools, the results of the model are non-technical enough to be understood and used by personnel who may not have a technical background. Thus, the model can be used by non-technical and technical personnel alike. Appendix A presents a checklist format of the model to aid managers in the use of the model.

OTHER APPROACHES

Most approaches to software management involve estimating the cost of a software project.[1,2,3,4,5,6,7,8,9] These approaches involve determining characteristics of the project or of the environment and then predicting the cost, time, etcetera, based on past data. Only a small amount of the literature specifically addresses the issue of general management of the software development cycle. Most models and mathematical equations presented to aid in project management only support cost estimation. Further, Thayer, Pyster and Wood[10] in investigating the major problem areas in software project management, found that procedures, techniques, strategies and aids that provide visibility of progress to the project manager are not available.

THE INTEGRATION PHASE

The model presented in this paper addresses the integration phase of the software development cycle. Integration is the systematic technique of assembling software unit modules into an overall system while testing to uncover errors associated with interfaces. Experience has shown that software integration requires a large amount of time because of errors that arise in the transfer of information between modules. There are three common approaches to software integration: top-down integration, bottom-up integration, and sandwich integration. The top-down and the bottom-up integration strategies (which are well known) are combined in the sandwich integration strategy.[11] It is predominately top-down, but bottom-up strategy techniques are also used. Sub-systems are built using the bottom-up integration strategy. Integration of the sub-system into the system in its entirety is done by using the top-down integration strategy. Thus individual modules and sub-systems are tested prior to replacement of stubs. The advantages of the top-down integration strategy are retained while some of the problems are eased.

DATA COLLECTION

The data used for this research consists of modules and programs written in the language C and implemented under UNIX. During the final days of the integration phase, "snapshots" of the modules and programs were taken. For each module and program there exists a collection of versions of the code that depicts the integration activities.

The modules and programs were developed and written by junior and senior computer science/information science students enrolled in CMPSC 341 Software Engineering Project II. This course is required in the undergraduate curriculum in the Computer Science Department at Kansas State University, Manhattan, Kansas. There were seven teams for which data is available.

ANALYSIS METHODOLOGY

Three change measures were chosen to be used in the analysis and definition of this model of progress for the integration phase. The measures are:

1. Changes by statement type
2. Changes within the software hierarchy or structure
3. Changes in complexity

CHANGES BY STATEMENT TYPE

The initial measurement analyzes the types of statements being changed. This was a logical starting point since a similar analysis of changes during the maintenance phase proceeded and suggested this research.[12] To measure the changes in various statement types, a tool was used that had been developed for analyzing changes during the maintenance phase. This tool compares two source code files for differences using the UNIX utility program "diff." A total count for occurrences of each statement type is determined, and the total number of each statement type that is changed is also determined; that is, 100 "if" statements of which 8 were changed. The percentage of change for each statement type is then calculated (total changes of a statement type divided by total number of that same statement type). These figures show which types of statements were changed most frequently during the integration phase. For a given statement type it can be stated that X% of this type of statement changed during the integration phase of the project.

HIERARCHY CHANGES

The location of changes within the software hierarchy or structure was also examined for the data sets. If a pattern in the location of the changes within the hierarchy could be found, it would be indicative of the technique of integration actually being used (the actual technique may be different from the intended integration technique). If no pattern could be found, this would reflect a serious disorganization of the integration phase and a need for corrective action.

To evaluate the location of changes within the software hierarchy, the actual software hierarchy itself had to be identified. Although hierarchy diagrams for each project existed, it was felt that a more valid hierarchy would be obtained from the source code itself—a case of what is said to be done versus what is actually done. A tool extracted the function calls from the source code, and the hierarchy diagrams for each snapshot were built by hand.

A total percentage change for each module was found. Modules showing the most significant change were identified in the hierarchy diagrams. As the changes from one change period or delta to the next were recorded, the successive hierarchy diagrams were examined for integration patterns.

A top-down integration pattern should be associated with top level modules having the higher percentages of change in the initial change period and these higher percentage positions appearing at subordinate levels as integration progressed. A downward growth of the hierarchy would be expected as more modules replaced the stubs.

A bottom-up pattern would show the lowest level modules exhibiting the higher percentages of change in the initial change periods with an upward progression in the later change periods. The hierarchy would also be expected to grow both horizontally and upwards as sub-systems were added and additional pieces were integrated.

A sandwich integration would show a pattern that at first may appear to have little order. Lower modules would exhibit higher percentages of change in the early change periods. Horizontal and upward growth would also appear in early diagrams. At some point, the entire structure would be available and the change percentages would go through a top-to-bottom progression as in the top-down integration pattern.

COMPLEXITY MEASURES

A measurement of the complexity of the programs and modules was also used to look for patterns. For this research, complexity measures were chosen for data analysis to determine patterns of change in code complexity and not to provide an understanding of a program's complexity.

McCabe's cyclomatic complexity measure[13] and Halstead's software science volume[14] were used in the data analysis; they were chosen for several reasons. Both have been around long enough for people to be familiar with them. Also, automated tools were available to calculate their values, eliminating the necessity of calculations by hand. Finally, the two complexity measures have been shown to give complementary results.[15,16]

Part of the analysis of the complexity measures dealt with inter-module versus intra-module complexity or the complexity of the whole versus the complexity of the parts. The inter-module complexity or the complexity of the integrated system was evaluated for patterns in accordance with the integration technique (top-down, bottom-up, or sandwich) identified in the hierarchical change analysis. Both top-down and bottom-up would show a significant increase in overall complexity as integration progressed. The increase in complexity during a sandwich integration would not be as significant as the increase during top-down or bottom-up integration and would level out prior to the end of the integration phase when all modules were in place.

Intra-module complexity would not be expected to fluctuate significantly throughout the integration phase. Individual modules should have been unit tested prior to the beginning of the integration phase and should be stable in complexity.

The automated metric tools were run on the programs for each delta or change period. The results for each complexity measure were examined to note any increase or decrease in the complexity of the whole program and of the individual modules. Patterns of increase or decrease in complexity were identified.

The three change measures were all evaluated for patterns (or lack of patterns) during the integration phase. These patterns were compared with a model for an idealized case which had been developed based on experience and intuition. From the patterns identified, a revised model for successful patterns during the integration phase of software development was built. Details of the idealized case and the revised model are described elsewhere.[17]

CASE STUDIES

Although a large amount of data was available and was analyzed during this research, there were two teams whose data were chosen for presentation as case studies. The first team, G3, was successful. It was able to finish its software development project on time while meeting the specifications. Its data exhibited identifiable patterns of progress during the integration phase. The second team, G5, was unsuccessful. This team did not finish their project and did not seem to be making progress towards completion. Its data exhibited a randomness which was not identifiable with anything—especially progress.

SUCCESSFUL CASE

Team G3 completed its test coverage project on time meeting its defined requirements. The project had nine individual modules. Four versions were examined representing three change periods that occurred during G3's integration period.

The statement type with the highest percentage of change during the integration phase for G3 was subroutine/system calls. Twenty-one percent of all subroutine/system calls were changed during integration. Assignment statements also exhibited a fairly significant amount of change with 18% of all assignment statements changing during integration. However, the percentage of change for assignment statements steadily decreased during the integration phase. Thirteen percent of "if" statements were also changed. All other types of statements showed less than 13% change. Percentages for overall changes in all statement types are presented in Table I. The raw data for types of statements changed are presented in Table II.

Hierarchical analysis revealed some rather surprising results in that a strict application of any of the three integration strategies was not used. Instead, all modules were put together into one system similar to the starting point of the sandwich technique. However, from then on the bottom-up integration technique was utilized. At first, the lowest level modules exhibited the highest percentages of change. This was followed by an upward movement through the hierarchy of the higher percentages of change. This technique was called G3's big-bang strategy. Table III presents the percentages of change for each delta or change period. The hierarchy itself was stable during the integration phase.

McCabe's cyclomatic complexity measure (see Table IV) remained relatively stable for both inter-module complexity measures and intra-module complexity measures throughout the integration phase. The stability of the inter-module pattern is not unreasonable given the integration technique used.

Halstead's software science measure (see Table IV) showed more change than the McCabe's complexity measure. At the intra-module level, change ranged from no change at all to a large change—in some cases doubling from one change period to the next. The inter-module figures showed an increase overall of about 40%.

UNSUCCESSFUL CASE

Team G5 did not complete its test coverage project and did not show any signs of progress towards integration. Eleven individual modules were in its project. As with team G3, four versions were examined which represented three change periods that occurred before team G5's project was abandoned.

TABLE II—Raw data for types of statements changed—Team G3

type	# changes	total occurrences
Assignment	24	127
Begin/End	14	114
Subroutine Calls	48	226
If	9	71
Else	5	45
Do	1	13
Return	0	6
While	4	33
Declarations	10	138
Include	0	6
Comments	3	46
Break	0	0
Case	0	0

TABLE I—Statement changes by change period—Team G3

STATEMENT TYPE	PERIOD 1	PERIOD 2	PERIOD 3	OVERALL
Subroutine Calls	14.7%	32.9%	16.5%	21.2%
Begin/End	11.1%	21.1%	5.0%	12.3%
Assignment	33.3%	14.3%	10.9%	18.9%
If	13.0%	20.0%	4.3%	12.7%
Else	20.0%	13.3%	6.7%	11.1%
Do	0.0%	20.0%	0.0%	7.1%
Return	0.0%	0.0%	0.0%	0.0%
While	18.2%	9.1%	9.1%	12.1%
Declarations	15.2%	2.3%	4.1%	7.2%
Include	0.0%	0.0%	0.0%	0.0%
Comments	0.0%	33.3%	0.0%	6.5%
Break	0.0%	0.0%	0.0%	0.0%
Case	0.0%	0.0%	0.0%	0.0%

TABLE III—Percent changes by module—Team G3

Procedure	Delta 1	Delta 2	Delta 3
Main	18.6%	20.0%	11.1%
Findword	89.5%	21.4%	0.0%
Beginproc	11.7%	20.0%	16.2%
Thenproc	15.8%	62.2%	41.9%
Getword	52.6%	0.0%	0.0%
Check	4.1%	9.2%	2.5%
Skip	30.8%	0.0%	0.0%
Declare	0.0%	0.0%	0.0%
Initial	5.3%	0.0%	0.0%

TABLE IV—Complexity measures—Team G3

McCabe's

Procedure Name	Period 1	Period 2	Period 3	Period 4
Beginproc	8	8	8	8
Check	11	12	12	12
Declare	1	1	1	1
Findword	3	3	3	3
Getword	2	3	3	3
Initial	2	2	2	2
Main	5	5	5	5
Skip	2	3	3	3
Thenproc	5	6	3	9
OVERALL	39	44	40	46

Halstead's

Procedure Name	Period 1	Period 2	Period 3	Period 4
Beginproc	137	159	178	160
Check	179	193	192	195
Declare	27	27	27	27
Findword	41	49	39	39
Getword	39	53	53	53
Initial	35	35	35	35
Main	36	36	55	61
Skip	11	23	23	23
Thenproc	72	93	59	117
OVERALL	577	669	661	710

Almost every type of statement was changed significantly during G5's integration phase (see Tables V and VI). Assignment statements, subroutine/system calls, declarations, breaks, and case statements all exhibited percentage changes of greater than 30%. "If" statements and "while" statements showed change percentages between 22% and 27%. All other statement types had less than a 14% change. The fact that almost 34% of all declaration statements were changed indicates some significant design deficiencies. Table V presents the percentage change for each statement type for G5's integration phase. Table VI presents the raw data for the statement type changes.

Team G5's statements exhibited a much higher precentage of change overall than did team G3. The types of statements being changed and their high percentage of change indicates significant design deficiencies and lack of progress towards project completion.

Changes in the hierarchy also exhibited no pattern. Although the hierarchy itself was stable, the integration technique, if one was used, escaped identification. Table VII presents the module change data.

TABLE V—Statement changes by change period—Team G5

STATEMENT TYPE	PERIOD 1	PERIOD 2	PERIOD 3	OVERALL
Assignment	73.3%	9.1%	32.4%	36.0%
Begin/End	0.0%	0.0%	18.1%	6.1%
Subroutine Calls	29.8%	10.6%	76.6%	39.0%
If	22.2%	11.1%	33.3%	22.2%
Else	0.0%	0.0%	40.0%	13.3%
Do	0.0%	0.0%	0.0%	0.0%
Return	0.0%	0.0%	0.0%	0.0%
While	80.0%	0.0%	0.0%	26.7%
Declarations	33.3%	21.9%	45.5%	33.7%
Include	0.0%	0.0%	0.0%	0.0%
Comment	0.0%	1.2%	8.2%	3.2%
Break	100.0%	0.0%	0.0%	33.3%
Case	100.0%	0.0%	0.0%	33.3%

TABLE VI—Raw data for types of statements changed—Team G5

statement type	# changes	total occurrencs
Assignment	66	194
Begin/End	12	250
Subroutine Calls	118	292
If	12	54
Else	4	30
Do	0	18
Return	0	0
While	8	30
Declarations	52	170
Include/Define	6	20
Comments	14	504
Break	10	30
Case	10	30

McCabe's cyclomatic complexity measure (see Table VIII) shows virtually no change at either the inter-module or intra-module levels. Although this might seem to point to progress, it probably does not. Instead, it probably indicates that the same statements are being changed over and over with no progress being made towards integration.

Halstead's software science measure (see Table VIII) appears relatively stable at the inter-module level, but this can be explained by examining the intra-module level complexity figures. Fluctuations from one change period to the next can be seen with both increases and decreases occurring. These increases and decreases appear to offset each other and give the illusion of inter-module stability.

A TOOL

By combining several shell programs utilizing UNIX utility functions and two C programs, an automated tool was developed that would extract the data necessary for a manager to take advantage of the decision structure in Appendix A. The shell programs find the percentage change for statement type and the percentage change per module. One C program calculates the Halstead's and McCabe's complexity measures for

TABLE VII—Percent changes by module—Team G5

Procedure	Delta 1	Delta 2	Delta 3
Instcode	27.3%	0.0%	18.2%
First_Pass	55.9%	0.0%	21.4%
Second_Pass	13.0%	0.0%	13.0%
Mes_Proc	12.5%	0.0%	25.0%
Umes_Proc	28.0%	0.0%	11.5%
Comment	5.0%	0.0%	25.0%
Insert	13.6%	0.0%	27.3%
Putsymbol	25.7%	0.0%	21.4%
Stack	14.8%	25.9%	32.1%
Push	25.0%	31.8%	66.7%
Pop	15.0%	9.1%	63.6%

TABLE VIII—Complexity measures—Team G5

McCabe's

Procedure Name	Period 1	Period 2	Period 3	Period 4
Comment	2	2	2	2
First_Pass	6	6	6	6
Insert	2	2	2	2
Instcode	1	1	1	1
Mes_Proc	1	1	1	1
Pop	2	2	2	1
Push	2	2	2	1
Putsymbol	1	1	1	1
Second_Pass	3	3	3	3
Stack	4	4	4	4
Umes_Proc	5	5	5	5
OVERALL	29	29	29	27

Halstead's

Procedure Name	Period 1	Period 2	Period 3	Period 4
Comment	29	24	24	30
First_Pass	57	52	52	67
Insert	39	40	40	52
Instcode	13	13	13	15
Mes_Proc	12	13	13	19
Pop	28	35	35	9
Push	28	35	39	9
Putsymbol	15	14	14	17
Second_Pass	41	37	37	40
Stack	37	40	43	35
Umes_Proc	116	124	124	133
OVERALL	415	427	434	426

programs written in C code. A second C program was written that takes its input from a shell program that gives information about calling modules and the modules called. It then produces a hierarchical representation of the program structure. From this collection of data, the changes for one delta or change period could be collected. By combining change data for several deltas, patterns or pictures for the changes occurring during the integration phase would be visible if they existed. These patterns or lack of patterns could then be related to the manager's decision structure in Appendix A for evaluation of visible program or lack of visible progress.

CONCLUSIONS

During integration, subroutine/system calls are the statement type expected to exhibit the most significant change. Further analysis may support inclusion of significant changes in assignment statements. Other statement types should exhibit relatively little or no change during integration.

Declaration statements should be representative of data structures that were thought out and defined in earlier phases. These statement types should show very little or no change during integration. Likewise, decision structure statements such as case statements, if statements, returns, breaks, and else statements should show little or no change during integration. These statement types represent the algorithmic structure of the project which should have been defined in an earlier phase.

A stable hierarchy should evolve during the integration phase. An identifiable integration technique should be found. However, which integration technique used will depend upon the situation and the project team members. Top-down integration strategy, bottom-up integration strategy, sandwich integration strategy or G3's big bang integration strategy are examples of integration techniques that may be identifiable.

The pattern of the complexity measures for the inter-module measures will be dependent upon the integration strategy. The top-down integration strategy and the bottom-up integration strategy would exhibit dramatic increases in inter-module complexity. Sandwich integration strategy would indicate a visible increase early, with a leveling off as integration progresses. G3's big bang integration strategy would exhibit inter-module stability throughout the integration phase. Intra-module complexity should remain relatively stable throughout the integration phase regardless of the integration strategy identified.

Since none of the patterns in the proposed model require extensive technical analysis to show progress during integration, the model can be used by non-technical project personnel as well as members of management and technical personnel. Patterns are easily recognizable. Recognizing the patterns outlined for this model will enhance the visibility of progress during a project's integration phase and enable non-technical and technical project personnel to make rational, data-based decisions about software projects. Appendix A presents a checklist for the model to aid managers in its use.

Future work to identify models of patterns for the other phases of the software development cycle is needed to build an overall model of patterns of progress for software development. A search for a theoretical/logical explanation for this percentage of change for assignment statements would also be valuable. Research is continuing in the analysis of change during the integration phase to lend credence to the proposed model or to refute it. Evaluation of additional change measures could also expand the proposed model.

REFERENCES

1. Bailey, John W. and Victor R. Basili "A Meta-Model for Software Development Resource Expenditures." *5th International Conference on Software Engineering,* 1981, pp. 107–116.
2. Boehm, Barry. *Software Engineering Economics,* Englewood Cliffs, New Jersey: Prentice-Hall, 1981.
3. Itakura, Minoru and Akio Takayanagi. "A Model for Estimating Program Size and Its Evaluation." *6th International Conference on Software Engineering,* 1982, pp. 104–109.
4. Putnam, Lawrence H. and Ray W. Wolverton. *Quantitative Management: Software Cost Estimating,* New York: IEEE, 1977.
5. Putnam, Lawrence H. and Ann Fitzsimmons. "Estimating Software Costs." *Datamation,* September-November, 1979.
6. Putnam, Lawrence H. *Software Cost Estimating and Life-Cycle Control,* New York: IEEE, 1980.
7. Putnam, Lawrence H. "The Real Metrics of Software Development," EASCON 80 Record, New York: IEEE, 1980, pp. 310–322.
8. Shooman, Martin L. "Tutorial On Software Cost Models," Workshop on Quantitative Software Models, New York: IEEE, pp. 1–19.
9. Warburton, R.D.H. "Managing and Predicting the Costs of Real-Time Software." *IEEE Transactions on Software Engineering,* 9 (1983) 5, pp. 562–568.
10. Thayer, Richard H., Arthur Pyster, and Roger C. Wood. "Validating Solutions to Major Problems in Software Engineering Management." *Computer,* August, 1982, pp. 65–77.
11. Fairley, Richard. *Software Engineering Concepts,* New York: McGraw-Hill, 1985.
12. Gustafson, David A., Austin Melton, and Chyuan Samuel Hsieh. "An Analysis of Software Changes During Maintenance and Enhancement." *Conference on Software Maintenance,* Washington, D.C., November, 1985.

13. McCabe, Thomas. "A Complexity Measure." *IEEE Transactions on Software Engineering,* 2 (1976) 4, pp. 308–320.
14. Halstead, Maurice. *Elements of Software Science,* New York: Elsevier, 1977.
15. Mata Toledo, Ramon. "A Factor Analysis of Software Complexity Metrics." PhD Thesis, Kansas State Univeristy, 1984.
16. Mata Toledo, Ramon and David A. Gustafson. "A Factor Analysis of Software Complexity Measures." Submitted for publication.
17. Lanchbury, Mary Lou. "A Model of Successful Patterns of Progress During the Integration of Software." Masters Thesis, Kansas State University, 1986.

APPENDIX A—MANAGER'S DECISION STRUCTURE FOR PROGRESS EVALUATON

Step One—Statement Types

Identify which statement types are being changed most frequently.
If it is *Declarations, If, While, Else, Begin/End, Case, Break*
then this indicates unsuccessful pattern for step one.
stop—predict unsuccessful
if it is *Subroutine/System Calls, Assignment*
then it indicates successful pattern for step one.
continue to step two—successful pattern
if it is *Comments, Include, Return, Do*
then it indicates no pattern established for this model.
continue to step two—no pattern

Step Two—Hierarchy Structure

Identify pattern of integration which matches one of the following:
if TOP-DOWN INTEGRATION
Higher percentages of module change at top level modules.
Downward movement of location of higher percentages.
Downward growth of hierarchy structure.
Hierarchy calls stable (if A calls B in early phase then A calls B throughout).
then proceed to step three—complexity A.
if BOTTOM-UP INTEGRATION
Higher percentages of module change at lower level modules.
Upward movement of location of higher percentages.
Upward growth of hierarchy structure.
then proceed to step three—complexity A.
if SANDWICH INTEGRATION
Higher percentages of module change at lower levels.
Upward movement of location of higher percentages.
Appearance of total hierarchy.
Higher percentages of module change at top levels.
Downward movement of location of higher percentages.
then proceed to step three—complexity B.
if BIG BANG INTEGRATION
Hierarchy structure is complete and stable.
Higher percentages of module change at lower levels.
Upward movement of location of higher percentages.
then proceed to step three—complexity C.
if NO PATTERN
Higher percentages of module change randomly distributed.
Hierarchy structure may be stable or may be fluctuating rapidly.
then no visible progress is being made—stop

Step Three—Complexity Measure Evaluation

if Complexity A and complexity matches one of the following:
Inter-module complexity growing significantly
or Intra-module complexity showing slight change but relatively stable
then predict PROGRESS
if Complexity B and complexity matches one of the following:
Inter-module complexity growing significantly then leveling off
or Intra-module complexity showing slight change but relatively stable
then predict PROGRESS
if Complexity C and complexity matches the following:
Both intra-module and inter-module complexity showing slight change but relatively stable.
then predict PROGRESS
If neither McCabe's or Halstead's exhibits a pattern
then predict NO PROGRESS

Software risk assessment

by SUSAN A. SHERER and ERIC K. CLEMONS
The Wharton School, University of Pennsylvania
Philadelphia, Pennsylvania

ABSTRACT

This paper presents a framework for software quality that is firmly grounded in the economic significance of software failure. We introduce the concepts of software exposure and software risk—the magnitude of the potential loss due to software failure, and the expected value of this loss, respectively. These, we feel, are far more meaningful measures of software quality than the more traditional expected number of residual errors or mean time between failure, which have been adapted from hardware reliability theory. Our measures can be used by management in software engineering; examples of such use include allocation of test time to modules and the determination of optimal release time for systems.

INTRODUCTION

The past decade has shown an increasing reliance by government, corporations and individuals on computer software. Evidence suggests that this reliance on software will increase even more rapidly in the future. Many functions previously performed manually are being computerized; few functions, once automated, lose computer support. The increasing computerization of society is creating more dependence on software, particularly for very critical functions such as air traffic control and nuclear power plant control. A growing number of systems are operating in real time, which decreases or eliminates the opportunity for human intervention, further contributing to our reliance on software. Corresponding to the increased dependence on computers has been the development of much more reliable hardware. This improvement in hardware has increased the significance of software as a source of failure.

As reliance on software grows, the importance of developing and ensuring high quality and, in particular, reliable software increases. This requires improved methods for evaluating and controlling quality and reliability in software development. Since software failures have different consequences, any measure of software reliability must include the measurement of the consequence of failure. A measure of software risk—the cost of failure weighted by the probability of failure—is necessary.

Software risk measurement can be used in developing and maintaining high quality software in several ways. First, it may be used to guide software testing. Generally, it is not possible to test a software system until perfection is assured. Trade-offs must be made concerning allocation of test resources: although all portions will be tested, some may be tested more intensively than others. It is reasonable to consider allocating test resources based upon software risk since consequences of failures differ among modules.

Risk measurement of software can be used to determine optimal release times for a software product. The risk of software failure can be weighed against the cost of additional test time to determine the most cost effective time to release the software.

Since the consequences of software failure can be catastrophic, it is reasonable for producers and, perhaps, users to want to have some insurance against their losses. If software risk were quantifiable, insurance could be offered on software products. Just as the insurance industry has grown to meet the demand to support risky ventures, it is reasonable to expect that it should consider encompassing the risk of software failures as this risk becomes a significant part of organizations' and individuals' operations. A means of quantifying this risk is necessary to establish insurance requirements.

This paper begins with a background of the software reliability research and an overview of testing methodologies. Neither traditional reliability measurement techniques nor traditional testing methodologies consider the fact that the implications of software failures vary. Software reliability measurement techniques have been adapted from hardware reliability, where a failure typically has a single consequence. However, since different software failures have different expected consequences, traditional reliability measurement techniques are inappropriate for measuring the true economic risk associated with failure. Traditional testing methods do not consider expected consequences of errors and thus are of only limited use in allocating available resources to the portions of the system with the greatest risk.

The paper introduces and discusses a methodology for assessing software risk that considers both the magnitude and likelihood of loss. Measurement of risk begins with an assessment of external exposure, that is, the magnitude of loss due to invalid actions. The external exposure is mapped onto the system to determine the magnitude of loss due to failures caused by faults in individual modules. Assessment of the likelihood of failure for each module is based upon characteristics of the code and the development process as well as results of test efforts.

BACKGROUND

Software Risk Versus Reliability

Software risk is defined here as the cost of failure weighted by the probability of failure. This definition differs significantly from current definitions of software reliability. The major difference is its inclusion of a measure of the cost of failure. Software reliability models have not considered the cost of failure. They have been adapted from hardware reliability assessment, which models failure as producing a single, known consequence, generally total system failure. However, the consequences of software failure are more varied. Furthermore, the causes of failure differ: hardware may fail after use as components fatigue or wear out; software may fail as new use encounters old errors. We may therefore expect different statistical properties for hardware and software failures. Thus, software risk assessment differs from hardware reliability assessment, and it is not surprising that traditional software methods, grounded in the hardware tradition, should prove less than wholly satisfactory.

There have been several definitions advanced for software reliability. The early software reliability models defined reliability in terms of the number of residual errors in a program.[1–7] Other models have adapted the traditional hardware definition of reliability, mean time to failure, in defining software reliability as mean time between software failures.[8–10] Littlewood defines reliability as a strength of our belief in the operation of the software without failure for a given time period.[11–14]

The major problem with all of these definitions lies in the assumption that all errors or failures are the same. Whereas hardware failures typically have the same consequence (i.e., the system is not operational), a software error can have a variety of consequences. There are different types of software failures. A software failure can be a system crash or a misread number. If the latter, the consequence of this misread number can vary. In an air traffic control system, if the hardware fails, we typically lose sight of all aircraft. If the software fails, we might lose sight of all aircraft, or we might unknowingly lose sight of a single aircraft, or we could transpose a digit on the aircraft identification. The consequence of these different failure modes are quite different. The point is that software errors and resulting failures have varying consequences, while hardware failures typically have a single consequence; this makes hardware models of software failure of limited usefulness.

There are other differences between software and hardware that distinguish software risk assessment from hardware reliability measurement. Hardware failures are due to degradation of components as well as design errors. The former source of failure produces statistically measurable failure patterns. Software components, however, do not degrade as a result of environmental stress or fatigue. In fact, an older program is usually more reliable. Software failures are often due to design and implementation errors that occur as a result of unanticipated or untested inputs. The correction of software errors usually alters the software; it does not just replace it as in hardware. Finally, software can be copied, retaining the reliability, whereas hardware cannot.

Software Testing

Complete testing of a software system, conclusively demonstrating the absence of any errors, is usually impossible. Therefore, the key issue in software testing has been the selection of the subset of all possible test cases that has the highest probability of detecting the most errors.[15]

Several methodologies are used for accomplishing this task. These can be classified as:

White box testing
Black box testing
Random testing

These methodologies are used in various phases of the testing process. We review the testing process to show that traditional methods have not adequately addressed the economic consequences of software failure. Since errors can produce consequences of different significance, testing ought to be concerned with the selection of test cases with the greatest expected loss.

White box, or structural testing, uses the internal structure of the program to develop test cases. Coverage criteria include statement coverage, decision coverage, condition coverage, and combinations of these.[15–19]

Black box, or functional program testing, is largely data driven. The testing process involves partitioning the input space into equivalence classes. These are sets of input states that appear to be similar, so that a test of a representative value in a class should yield results equivalent to a test of any other value in that class.[15] Boundary values of these classes in particular are usually tested.[15, 16, 19]

Random input testing chooses test cases by randomly selecting inputs from the input space, using the same probabilities of selection of input states as occur during operation.[20] In many cases, more efficient testing is accomplished if one recognizes that once an input state has been selected, it does not have to be repeated. In this case, the failure intensity* must be divided by a test compression factor, or ratio of execution time required in operation to execution time required in test phase, to obtain the corresponding failure intensity to be expected in operation.[20]

Software testing is a major component of systems development, typically accounting for as much as one half of the development effort.[21–22] The testing process generally comprises several phases:

1. Module test
2. Integration test
3. Function test
4. Systems test
5. Acceptance test

Module, integration, and function testing are typically performed by the systems development group. These phases verify the code against the design and specification. They typically consume 45% of the total development effort.[23] Systems and acceptance testing are generally performed by an independent group, which verifies the system against the user's objectives. These phases typically consume only a small part of the total systems development effort.[23]

The purpose of module testing is to compare the code to the module specification. The objective is to show how the module contradicts the specification (i.e., to find faults in the code). Typically, module testing involves a combination of white box and black box tests. The test manager is faced with many decisions such as what modules to test, what test data are necessary, and how to allocate personnel. In many cases, test resources are constrained. Commonly, test time is limited. Personnel may also be limited. Thus, the manager must decide how to allocate test effort to each module so as to locate as many errors as possible. Typically, this is done on an ad hoc basis based upon the logic in the code (white box testing) and the equivalence partitions (black box tests).

During integration testing, the parts of the code are put together and the integrated code is compared to the program structure and systems design. White box and black box testing may be used. The integration strategy chosen and the testing sequence affect the form in which module test cases are writ-

* Failure intensity has been defined as failures per unit time.[20]

ten, the types of test tools used, the cost of generating test cases and the cost of debugging errors.[15]

Function testing is the comparison of the system to the external specification, a description of the system from the user's point of view. Thus, the system is not tested against the design but against the user specifications. Function testing is typically a black box process. During this test phase, management must decide how to allocate test effort to different data categories so as to uncover as many errors as possible. Typically, time and personnel constrain testing efforts.

The function of the systems test is to compare the system or program to its requirements.[15] Its purpose is to assess the system against its original objectives, as opposed to the specifications. The objective of the systems test phase is to produce a reliable software product. During this phase, testing generally proceeds by randomly choosing inputs based upon the user objectives. Software is tested until the deadline for system release is reached or the test team feels that the software is reliable enough for release.[23] Software reliability measurement techniques have been developed to determine when desired reliability levels are reached.[20] Since they do not consider the consequence of failure, costs and benefits cannot be addressed, and desired reliability cannot adequately be defined or measured.

In all of these types of testing, prior theory never explicitly considers the fact that the errors that we are looking for vary in their consequence. This is a critical factor. Given the constraints that exist during each testing phase, we should be considering the consequence of failure when allocating test efforts. During the module test phase, management should be allocating efforts not only based upon the structure of the code and the equivalence partitions but also considering the different consequences of failure in different modules. During function testing, we ought to be allocating efforts based upon the criticality of the function. During systems test, test effort should be allocated to requirements with the greatest consequences of failure. Optimal release times considering the cost of failure can then be determined. These points are addressed in our research, which is introduced in the following section.

ASSESSMENT OF SOFTWARE RISK

Introduction

We present in this section our extensions to software quality assessment, intended to capture the economic significance of software malfunction.

We define software risk as the expected loss due to failure during a given time period. Risk is measured by the frequency or likelihood of loss (events resulting in loss per unit time) times the magnitude of loss or the level of exposure due to loss (consequences of events).**

In order to develop a measure of software risk that may be used to guide testing, we need to perform several functions. These will be briefly described here and then will be discussed in more detail later in this paper:

1. External exposure identification: What actions, external to the system, can result in losses and what are the consequences of these actions?
2. Structural exposure analysis: What system failures can result in these actions? What is the potential magnitude of loss due to failures caused by faults in each module?
3. Prior predictions of failure likelihood and risk: What is the *a priori* estimate of the likelihood of failure due to faults in each untested module? What is the resulting estimate of risk?
4. Updating priors using test results: How do we use test results to update failure assessments?

External Exposure Identification

The first step in the measurement of software risk is external exposure identification. This involves an assessment of factors operating in the environment, external to the software, that can contribute to loss. First, we must identify potential actions that can result in loss. Then, we must assess their consequences, that is, the magnitude of loss due to these actions.

Assessment of the external environment involves identification of sources of catastrophe, typically operator actions (or inactions) that can cause disaster by violating norms of behavior. For example, in an air traffic control system, the collision of two airplanes may be caused by an operator who does not take action to change headings when two planes are on a collision course. Our analysis of behavior linked to catastrophic events may reveal items that may have inadvertently been left out of the system requirements. This may yield an additional benefit from this analysis giving us another technique for validating the system design.

The magnitude of loss that may result from inappropriate actions is a function of the environment and the context in which the system operates. The potential loss if an air traffic controller operates inappropriately in situations where planes are on potential collision courses will be much larger if the controller is working during rush hour in a large airport than if he were working on an off hour in a small airport that does not handle wide-bodied aircraft. Generally, there are a large number of environmental factors that must be considered. We will begin by using expected values for the magnitude of loss.

Structural Exposure Analysis

In structural exposure analysis, we map invalid actions, identified in external exposure identification, back to system causes. We try to associate these system causes with potential faults in various modules; we can then identify the magnitude of loss due to faults in various portions of the system.

The magnitude of loss due to system failure is defined as the exposure level. The exposure level is based upon the magnitude of loss due to actions that can result from this failure. Failures are due to faults, or defects, in the system. Our

** This is analogous to the work of Henley & Kumamoto.[24]

objective is to assign an exposure level due to faults in the basic interconnected components of the system, the individual modules.

Operator, or environmental, malfunction results from invalid system output. (Note: The absence of expected output may itself also be considered invalid output.) This invalid output is a result of a failure, due to one or more faults in the system. Thus, it is necessary first to relate invalid actions to system failures. For example, failure of an operator to respond to aircraft on a collision course may be due to the system's failing to display more than one aircraft with conflicting headings.

After identification of potential system failures, we attempt to determine which modules or paths in the system may have faults that can result in these failures. In the above example, we must determine which modules process data related to the display of aircraft heading. To do this, we need to determine how the output resulting from the system malfunction is produced. Invalid output, triggering actions resulting in losses, is produced by invalid processing of data by the system.

To assign exposure levels to modules, we will assume that the fault potential of a module is a function of the type of processing taking place in each module. The functions relating to data with the potential for producing invalid outputs causing loss are identified.

The module's function at any time, and the associated exposure level, may vary with the way the system is using it; this, in turn, is related to the way the system itself is being used. For example, response to an air traffic control display produced by a module can result in different actions, based upon the purpose of the display at the time of failure. Thus, it will be necessary to evaluate the complex relationship of module functions to system functions.

In sum, the exposure level of a module is based upon the actions that can result from failures due to faults in the module. It depends upon what data is processed by the module and how that data relates to invalid output. It also depends upon how the module processes the data, itself a function of the nature of use of the module.

Prior Prediction of Failure Likelihood and Risk

The likelihood of a software failure depends upon the number of faults or errors in a program and the probability that a fault or program defect will be encountered in operation, causing a failure.

The number of faults is a function of the product as well as the development process. Most research has concentrated on studying the relationship between characteristics of the final product and the number of faults found. Many researchers have found that the size of a program, measured in terms of the number of executable source statements, has the most effect on the number of faults it contains.[20,25] Research relating measures of program complexity to the number of faults has been inconclusive.[25–27] Characteristics of the development process also affect the number of faults. This includes such factors as skill level of the development team, communication among the team members, quality of reviews, and familiarity with application and techniques. However, it is difficult to develop objective measures of these characteristics.

One means of relating the number of faults to both the product and the development process would be to gather historical information concerning the number of faults in modules developed by individual programmers. We will assume that programmer performance, measured in terms of number of errors per line of code, remains fairly stable over time after an initial learning period. This assumption may be relaxed at a later date to account for experience and learning factors. By measuring the number of errors per line of code for each programmer, we gain useful historical information concerning the development process; this information can be used to make prior assessments of the programming product.

The probability that a fault produces a failure depends upon the number of ways in which the module can be used and the frequency with which the module is used. If a module has a large number of paths and input classes, the probability of a specific fault causing a failure on any given run is much less than if a module has only a single path and a single input class. Typically, in operation, certain sections of code are used more often than others, resulting in unequal per fault hazard rates. The operational profile, or set of all possible input states with their associated probabilities of occurrence, will determine which sections of the code will be used most frequently. If the fault is located on a main branch of the code or in a portion of code well traversed, it should have a higher probability of causing a failure than if it is located in a section of code rarely traversed.

The risk for each module is equal to the probability of each type of failure times the cost of that failure. Since we do not know the probability of each type of failure, we will begin by estimating risk for each module as the product of the expected exposure level times the aggregate failure likelihood for that module. The expected exposure level will depend upon the expected use of the system during operation. Failure likelihood depends upon the number of faults and the probability that faults will produce failures.

Updating Priors Using Test Results

As testing proceeds, we gain information concerning the software risk. This may change our initial perceptions, or prior assessments, of the magnitude and location of the risk. Before testing, we assessed the exposure level based upon our prior identification of the types of failures that could occur and of their consequences. We estimated the number of faults and the likelihood of failure based upon *a priori* perceptions of the development process and characteristics of the code. Examination of failure and debugging information will yield new knowledge about the system.

The frequency and number of failures due to faults in each module may change our initial estimate of the failure likelihood for each module. One means of doing this is to assume a statistical distribution for software reliability growth. As failure data become available, statistical inference procedures may be used to update the parameters of the distribution.[8,10,11,28] In most cases, these parameters are the number of faults and the probability that a fault will cause a failure.

A second means of using failure data to update our prior estimates is based upon the observation in many systems that errors tend to cluster. As one example, this phenomenon was observed in IBM's S/370 operating systems. In one of these operating systems, 47% of the errors found by users were associated with only 4% of the modules within the system.[15] In fact, one of Myers's testing principles is that "the probability of the existence of more errors in a section of a program is proportional to the number of errors already found in that section."[15] Thus, the location of many faults in a single module may change our prior estimate of the number of faults still to be found in that module.

Test results also give us new information about programmer performance that may be used to update our estimates of failure likelihood. Test data on several modules by the same programmer indicating many more faults than initially expected in those modules would cause us to increase our expectations of faults in as yet untested modules by this programmer. We can use this information to update prior estimates of number of faults and, thus, the probability of failure in modules by this programmer.

CONCLUSIONS

We have developed a new measure of software quality, software risk. Measures of software reliability should attempt to consider the varying significance of software failures. Once we can assess the variation in software risk between different portions of a system, we can more cost effectively test our systems.

We have presented a framework for measuring software risk and using the measurement in testing. The next step is to develop the supporting mathematics representing our assumptions about the failure likelihood. This will be needed to develop prior estimates of failure likelihood as well as to update these estimates with test information. Empirical results will then be needed to support the theory.

REFERENCES

1. Jelinski, Z. and P. Moranda. "Software Reliability Research." In W. Frieberger (ed.) *Statistical Computer Performance Evaluation.* New York: Academic Press, 1972, pp. 465–484.
2. Shooman, M.L. "Probabilistic Models for Software Reliability Prediction." In W. Frieberger (ed.) *Statistical Computer Performance Evaluation.* New York: Academic Press, 1972, pp. 485–502.
3. Shooman, M.L. "Operational Testing and Software Reliability Estimating During Program Development." *IEEE 1973 Computer Software Reliability Conference,* New York, pp. 51–57.
4. Moranda, P.B. "An Error Detection Model for Application During Software Test Development." *IEEE Transactions on Reliability* R-30 (1981) 4, pp. 309–312.
5. Schneidewind, N.F. "Analysis of Error Processes in Computer Software." *Proceedings International Conference on Reliable Software,* April 1975, pp. 337–346.
6. Shooman, M.L. and A. Trivedi. "A Many State Markov Model for Computer Software Performance Parameters." *IEEE Transactions on Reliability* R-25 (1976) 2, pp. 66–68.
7. Ohba, M. "Software Reliability Analysis Models." *IBM Journal of Research Development,* 28 (1984) 4, pp. 428–443.
8. Musa, J.D. "Theory of Software Reliability and Its Application." *IEEE Transactions on Software Engineering,* SE-1 (1975) 3, pp. 312–327.
9. Musa, J.D. and K. Okumoto. "A Logarithmic Poisson Execution Time Model for Software Reliability Measurement." *Proceedings 7th International Conference on Software Engineering,* Orlando, Florida, 1984, pp. 230–238.
10. Goel, A. and K. Okumoto. "Time Dependent Error Detection Rate Model for Software Reliability and Other Performance Measures." *IEEE Transactions on Reliability* R-28 (1979) 3, pp. 206–211.
11. Littlewood, B. and J. Verrall. "A Bayesian Reliability Growth Model for Computer Software." *IEEE 1973 Computer Software Reliability Conference,* New York, pp. 70–77.
12. Littlewood, B. "MTBF Is Meaningless in Software Reliability." *IEEE Transactions on Reliability* R-24 (1975) April, p. 82.
13. Littlewood, B. "How to Measure Software Reliability and How Not To." *IEEE Transactions on Reliability* R-28 (1979) 2, pp. 103–110.
14. Littlewood, B. "Theories of Software Reliability: How Good Are They and How Can They Be Improved." *IEEE Transactions on Software Engineering* SE-6 (1980) 5, pp. 489–500.
15. Myers, G.J. *The Art of Software Testing.* New York: John Wiley, 1979.
16. Howden, W.E. "Reliability of the Path Analysis Testing Strategy." *IEEE Transactions on Software Engineering* SE-2 (1976) 3, pp. 208–215.
17. Huang, J.C. "Error Detection through Program Testing." In R.T. Yeh (ed.) *Current Trends in Programming Methodology Vol. II Program Validation.* Englewood Cliffs, New Jersey: Prentice-Hall, 1977, pp. 16–43
18. Goodenough, J.B. and S.L. Gerhart. "Toward a Theory of Testing: Data Selection Criteria." In R.T. Yeh (ed.) *Current Trends in Programming Methodology Volume II Program Validation.* Englewood Cliffs, New Jersey: Prentice-Hall, 1977, pp. 44–79.
19. Redwine, Jr., S. "An Engineering Approach to Software Test Data Design." *IEEE Transactions on Software Engineering* SE-9 (1983) 2, pp. 191–200.
20. Musa, J.D., A. Iannino, and K. Okumoto. *Software Reliability: Measurement, Prediction, Application.* Manuscript in progress, to be published by McGraw Hill, 1987.
21. Yourdon, E. and L. Constantine. *Structured Design: Fundamentals of a Discipline of Computer Program and Systems Design.* Englewood Cliffs, New Jersey: Prentice-Hall, 1979.
22. Zelkowitz, M.V. "Perspectives of Software Engineering." *ACM Computing Surveys* 10 (1978) June, pp. 197–216.
23. Kubat, P. and H.S. Koch. "Managing Test-Procedures to Achieve Reliable Software." *IEEE Transactions on Reliability* R-32 (1983) 3, pp. 299–303.
24. Henley, E. and H. Kumamoto. *Reliability Engineering and Risk Assessment.* Englewood Cliffs, New Jersey: Prentice-Hall, 1981.
25. Feuer, A.R. and E.B. Fowlkes. "Some Results from an Empirical Study of Computer Software." *Fourth International Conference on Software Engineering,* Munich, Germany, September 17–19, 1979, pp. 351–355.
26. Basili, V.R. and B.T. Perricone. "Software Errors and Complexity: An Empirical Investigation." *Communications of the ACM* 27 (1984) 1, pp. 42–52.
27. Shen, V.Y., T. Yu, S. Thiebaut, and L. Paulsen. "Identifying Error-Prone Software—An Empirical Study." *IEEE Transactions on Software Engineering* SE-11 (1985) 4, pp. 317–323.
28. Kubat, P. and H.S. Koch. "On the Estimation of the Number of Errors and Reliability of Software Systems." Working Paper Series No. 8013, Graduate School of Management, University of Rochester, New York, May 1980.

WORKPLACE APPLICATIONS

S. KRISHNA DRONAMRAJU
AT&T Information Systems
Naperville, Illinois
and
JULIE M. HURD
The University of Chicago
Chicago, Illinois
and
ROBERT K. CLARK
Boeing Computer Services
Seattle, Washington

The various environments in the modern workplace encompass not only technical and business activities but also structural issues of the department, the company, and the ever changing larger society. In this track, some timely applications and associated problems are presented in detail, and their relationships to organizational and societal concerns are shown, in addition to their taxonomy and interrelationships. A featured session examining the general environment of workplace applications is arranged to introduce the professional and nonprofessional alike to this track. Following are some glimpses into the activities of the other sessions scheduled:

A plethora of intelligent applications in the office of the future and the connected problems on the human side.

A well-orchestrated battle to decide the winner among the page description languages.

CIM, computer integrated manufacturing, which will be the panacea for the problems associated with the factory of the future and the different facets of these stages of integration.

Effective data analysis and interpretation associated with the mechanical CAE, where various techniques are introduced to handle the specific problems.

Industry's attempts to standardize the CAE systems for electrical design applications, thus aiming at improved productivity, data sharing among various diverse systems, and the current status in these efforts.

The expert systems for reliability in complex designs with stringent requirement constraints.

The rapid pace of computing in the modern financial world, covering the spectrum from applied AI to technological advances in the marketing field.

The advance of computers in medical research, pharmaceutical product management, and private practice.

ABF: A system for automating document compilation

by JAMES SPROWL, MARTHA EVENS, and MOHAMED RAGAIE SAYED OSMAN
Illinois Institute of Technology
Chicago, Illinois
and
HENRY HARR
DePaul University
Chicago, Illinois

ABSTRACT

The ABF system, named after the American Bar Foundation, its first sponsor, was designed to aid lawyers and paralegals in the compilation of legal documents. The ABF interpreter processes a skeleton document from a library of templates, and automatically generates questions about whatever client-specific information is needed to produce a client-customized document, ready to be formatted. The user can interrupt the processor at any point to change the document; the system will then reprocess the new document using answers to questions asked previously. The templates in the ABF System Library may contain conditional expressions, loops, and complicated arithmetic expressions, like those sometimes needed in tax computations. Other documents may be included by reference. The goal is to make model documents written by legal experts available to lawyers in small offices and to law students.

INTRODUCTION

ABF is an expert system designed to assist attorneys in drafting legal documents. The system starts by extracting, from a library of legal forms, a skeleton template document that has embedded within it programming constructs such as conditionals, loops, references to other documents, and variables. The variables are later replaced by client-specific information in the course of an automated interview. Alternative and repetitive passages are included, or excluded, dynamically as the interpreter encounters conditionals and loops. The system analyzes the document and if it discovers that information is missing, it first checks to see if it already has the value stored, then it checks to see whether the document designer gave it a rule to compute the value, or supplied a special question that is to be displayed to the user when the value is needed. If these measures fail, the system generates an English question asking the user for the missing data. The user can stop the interpreter at any time, edit the draft document, and reinitiate automatic processing. Since the answers to previous questions are saved, the system will never ask a question a second time. ABF was implemented in Pascal on an IBM PC in a joint venture with IBM.

The facilities that ABF offers to automate the assembly of legal documents will, we feel, make it just as useful in other applications, such as marketing, insurance, and hospital recordkeeping. We are currently using ABF in an experiment in the automatic generation of hospital discharge summaries.

HOW THE ABF SYSTEM WORKS

The ABF system library contains a number of document templates designed to help the law student learn how to frame simple documents of the kind that must be handled constantly in ordinary practice. One of those model documents is a simple will that begins:

> I, [the name of the testator], do give my entire estate to my [the testator's spouse, a husband or wife] [the name of the testator's spouse], if my [the testator's spouse, a husband or wife] survives me by at least 30 days. If my [the testator's spouse, a husband or wife] [the name of the testator's spouse] predeceases me, then I give my entire estate to my children. . . .

Suppose the problem is to draft a will for a client named John Smith with a wife named Mary Smith and three children. To start this assignment, the user types into the system:

> PROCESS Will OF John Smith

The words "PROCESS" and "OF" are typed in capitals, so that the system interpreter will recognize them as system command words

On receiving this command, the ABF processor pulls out the model will and starts to process it. When it comes to the first set of square brackets, the processor stops and looks to see if it already knows the name of the testator. Since the processor does not know the name in this instance, the system displays the following question on the screen:

> What is the name of the testator?

The user types in the answer:

> John Smith

and the system displays on the screen:

> I, John Smith, do give my entire estate to my

followed by a question about the next item of information it needs:

> What is the testator's spouse, a husband or wife?

The user answers:

> wife

The system now asks:

> What is the name of the testator's spouse?

and the user answers:

> Mary Smith

The system now displays:

> I, John Smith, do give my entire estate to my wife Mary Smith, if my wife survives me by at least 30 days. If my wife Mary Smith predeceases me, then I give my entire estate to my children.

Since the processor saves the answers to the questions it asks, it does not need to ask for the same information again. Indeed the processor is asking for just the information the user would need to elicit in a client interview in order to draw up a will manually.

The version of the document produced by the system in asking questions and filling in the answers is called the

> DRAFT Will OF John Smith

To see what the document will look like in finished form the user can issue the command

DISPLAY DRAFT Will OF John Smith

and the system will display the draft on the screen. The user can make further changes by editing this draft using the command

EDIT DRAFT Will OF John Smith

Once the document is in satisfactory shape, the user calls the formatter with the command

FINISH DRAFT Will OF John Smith

This will cause the will to be printed out in a nicely formatted fashion.

Variable Names

The strings in square brackets are variable names. Because the variable names used in the questions generated by the system need to be self-explanatory, they are often long and cumbersome. To make the task of the document designer easier and to avoid misspellings, which confuse the system, the ABF system allows short names (abbreviations) to be associated with variable names. The association is declared by including both the short name and the long name in the square brackets, separated by a colon. Short names may not contain colons. For example, the document designer decides to use the abbreviation "testname" for the name of the testator, and "spname" for the name of the spouse, and "horw" for "the testator's spouse, a husband or wife." Our model document then becomes much shorter:

> I, [testname: the name of the testator], do give my entire estate to my [horw: the testator's spouse, a husband or wife] [spname: the name of the testator's spouse], if my [horw] survives me by at least 30 days. If my [horw], [spname], predeceases me, then I give my entire estate to my children.

The system stores both short and long variable names. It also stores the answers to questions as the values associated with the variable names. The long name is always used in asking questions, however.

Various Ways to Answer Questions

Most of the time the user will type in an answer and the system will accept that answer and insert it in the correct spot in the document. But occasionally the system receives an answer it does not understand. In that case, it will explain what kind of answer is appropriate and ask the same question again. For example, if the system expects a number and gets text instead, it will explain that a number is needed and then give the user another chance to answer the question.

If the system asks a question that the user is not ready to answer, the user types a question mark. Suppose the system asks for the address of the residuary legatee and the user does not know it yet. If the user types a question mark, the system will continue to process the will, without asking that question again. When the will is printed out, it will look perfectly normal except that where the address should be there will appear instead "[the address of the residuary legatee]." This address can easily be filled in using the editor as soon as the address is known, or the document may be reprocessed.

Help is also available. F1 brings up help with the editor, and F2 brings up help with the document processor. If a question is not clear, then the user presses the F2 function key. The system will display an assistance document at this point if it has one, that is, if the document designer realized that users might get confused at this point. Shift F1 and shift F2 bring up, respectively, the editor and the system help documentation in outline form.

Alternative Passages

The last sentence in our model will is not really appropriate if the testator is childless. This is one of many situations in the law when different circumstances call for alternative passages. To make our model more sophisticated, we can rewrite the last sentence to include:

```
IF the testator HAS any children
   INSERT I give my entire estate to my children.
END IF
```

When the system arrives at the variable named "the testator HAS any children," it displays the question:

Has the testator any children?

If the user answers this with a "yes," this passage will be inserted.

In a situation like this where the name of the variable is preceded and followed by a capitalized command word, it is unnecessary to enclose it in square brackets. We could have written this section without the brackets:

```
IF the testator HAS any children
   INSERT I give my estate to my children.
END IF
```

This variable is different from those we saw earlier in another way. Most variables have many possible values, but this has only two: true or false. Such variables are called propositions. The kind of "What is . . . " questions that the system generates for other variables would sound very strange with propositions. If there is a capitalized word in the proposition, like the "HAS" in our example, it is moved to the front when the question is formed. If there is no capitalized word, the system asks the question: "Is it true that . . . ?"

At some time we may want to insert one passage in one situation, but a different one in another situation. In our sample we will need to insert one passage if there is to be a single executor and a slightly different passage if there is to be an executor and an alternate. ABF gives us a very simple way to express what we want to do here:

IF you DO wish to name only one executor,
  rather than an executor and an alternate
INSERT
  I name as my executor [exnam: the executor's name] who shall not be required to post security upon [exposs: his or her, the possessive pronoun for the executor] bond.
OTHERWISE INSERT
  I name [exnam] to be my executor, but if [expers: he or she, the personal pronoun for the executor] is unable or unwilling to serve, I name [exalt: the alternate executor's name] as executor. My executor shall not be required to post security upon his bond.
ENDIF

The ABF interpreter will ask the question:

Do you wish to name only one executor, rather than an executor and an alternate?

If the answer is "yes" the first passage will be inserted; if the answer is "no," the second passage will be inserted.

At some time we may want to insert an already existing document in the middle of another document. For example, one or the other, or both, the alternative passages in the IF statement may be an already prepared document. To incorporate such a document by reference, simply place its name, enclosed in brackets, in the other document.

IF [the testator HAS any children]
  INSERT [the gifts to minors passage]
  OTHERWISE INSERT [the unborn child passage]
END IF

Document names are thus a kind of variable name.

Rules and Replacement Questions

The user of ABF will see the system mainly as a collection of nagging questions, so it is important to cut down the number of questions wherever possible and to make the remaining questions both clear and crisp.

The document designer may notice that the value of a variable can be computed by the system once the values of other variables are known. For example, if the system knows the value of [sex: the testator IS a man], then it should be able to compute the values of [sppersрron: the personal pronoun of the testator's spouse, he or she] and [sppossрron: the possessive pronoun of the testator's spouse, his or her]. The document designer writes a special rule to tell the ABF system how to perform the computation. The first step is to enter the command:

EDIT RULE sppersрron

Then the designer enters the rule body:

IF [sex: the testator IS a man]
  LET sppersрron = ⟨she⟩
  LET sppossрron = ⟨her⟩
OTHERWISE
  LET sppersрron = ⟨he⟩
  LET sppossрron = ⟨his⟩
END IF

When the system needs the value of sppersрron or sppossрron, it will activate the rule instead of asking a question.

Sometimes a question cannot be avoided, but it can always be rephrased. The system-generated question may sound very awkward. From the variable "chnam: the names of my children" the ABF system will form the question:

What is the names of my children?

The document designer who looks at this question will doubtless decide to change it immediately by entering the command

EDIT QUESTION chnam

and then type in a substitute, perhaps:

List the names of the testator's children.

Client Data Files

As a document is processed, the system automatically writes a record of the values obtained for variables in a file. As John Smith's will is processed, the system produces a file called DATA OF John Smith. It will begin:

LET the name of the testator = ⟨John Smith⟩
LET the testator's spouse, a husband or wife
  = ⟨wife⟩
LET the name of the testator's spouse
  = ⟨Mary Smith⟩

As you can see, this file takes the form of a rule. If it is necessary to stop in the middle of an interview, the client data file will be saved. When the system starts to reprocess the draft, the rule contained in John Smith's data file will be executed first and the values will be assigned to the variables. This means that the questions asked in the previous interview will not be asked again. The processor will start from the point where the previous interview finished.

The client data file also gives the user a way to correct earlier mistakes. If the user discovers that a previous answer was wrong, it is easy to change the values by editing the client data file. This may be done in mid-interview.

Constructing Lists and Repetitive Passages

Our model will also include an optional paragraph containing a list of special gifts of property. It uses a REPEAT clause to construct this list.

REPEAT
WHEN #the testator DOES NOT wish to give another gift of property to someone EXIT
I give my [#the description of the gift] to my [#the relationship of the recipient to the testator] [#the name of the recipient]
IF #the recipient IS an individual
INSERT if living 30 days after my death
END IF.
END REPEAT

When this block is processed, the system begins by asking:

Does the testator wish to give another gift of property to someone?

If the answer is no, the proposition in the WHEN clause is true and the system exits from the REPEAT block immediately. If the answer is yes, the system starts to process the rest of the block. Let's suppose that John Smith wants to give his golf clubs to his nephew Russell Walton. Then the following interview results:

What is the description of the gift?
golf clubs
What is the relation of the recipient to the testator?
nephew
What is the name of the recipient?
Russell Walton
Is the recipient an individual?
yes

When the processor reaches the END REPEAT, it jumps back to the beginning of the repeat block and again asks:

Does the testator wish to give another gift of property to someone?

Suppose that John Smith also wants to give his coin collection to his cousin Peter Ames. This question will be answered yes and the processor will proceed as before through the REPEAT block.

What is the description of the gift?
coin collection
What is the relationship of the recipient to the testator?
cousin
What is the name of the recipient?
Peter Ames
Is the recipient an individual?
yes

Again the processor reaches the end of the REPEAT block and jumps back to the beginning. We have come to the end of Mr. Smith's gifts of property. The question generated by the WHEN clause:

Does the testator wish to give another gift of property to someone?

is now answered no and the processor exits from the REPEAT block.

The result of processing the REPEAT block is the addition of the following two sentences to the draft of John Smith's will:

I give my golf clubs to my nephew Russell Walton if living 30 days after my death. I give my coin collection to my cousin Peter Ames if living 30 days after my death.

The variables in the REPEAT block look distinctly different from those we have seen before; they are prefixed with a number sign. The function of the number sign is to indicate that we do not need one, but a number of copies of each variable in the REPEAT block. In fact, the system gives us a new copy of each variable every time it jumps back to the beginning of the block. In technical terms, a variable prefixed with a number sign is an array variable.

Why is this necessary? Consider what would happen if we had only one copy of the first variable [the testator DOES NOT wish to give another gift to someone]. Suppose we answered the question "Does the testator wish to give another gift to someone?" with a yes on our first trip through the REPEAT block. Then the second time through the block the system would look the variable up in its tables, discover that it already had a value, and start to process the rest of the block without asking the question again. It would do the same thing the third time, the fourth time, and so on. The processor would never escape from that block; it would go on asking about gifts until the user gives up in disgust and walks away.

If the number sign were omitted from another variable, the name of the recipient, for example, the system would be convinced after the first time through the block that it knew who the recipient was and would not ask that question again. All gifts would go to the same recipient.

A look at John Smith's client data file at this point would show that the processing of the REPEAT block added a lot of information:

ASSERT #1 the testator DOES wish to give another gift of property to someone
LET #1 the description of the gift = ⟨golf clubs⟩
LET #1 the relationship of the recipient to the testator = ⟨nephew⟩
LET #1 the name of the recipient = ⟨Russell Walton⟩
ASSERT #1 the recipient IS an individual
ASSERT #2 the testator DOES wish to give another gift of property to someone
LET #2 the description of the gift = ⟨coin collection⟩
LET #2 the relationship of the recipient to the testator = ⟨cousin⟩
LET #2 the name of the recipient = ⟨Peter Ames⟩
ASSERT #2 the recipient IS an individual
ASSERT #3 the testator DOES NOT wish to give another gift of property to someone

Proposed Extensions

Experience with earlier versions of ABF has already led to a number of design changes, particularly the integration of the editor with the system.[1,2] Our work during the last two years[3,4,5] has suggested a number of additions to ABF. We want to add the ability to SELECT a passage from several alternatives, or even to RANDOMLY SELECT one, to facilitate CAI applications. We would also like to add the concepts MAY, MUST, SHALL, and SHOULD to the ABF language to increase our ability to model legal reasoning. We also feel that it is time to experiment with these same techniques in other applications.

OTHER APPLICATIONS OF ABF

The ABF system will prove useful in any situation where the user needs to write a series of customized documents, as in marketing or insurance. Imagine a marketing application in which the user is the owner of a computer store called PC World. An invoice document template is used to draw up invoices automatically, as it asks the client a series of questions about the configuration being purchased. This process will establish a client data file that can then be used to produce customized follow-up letters. A very simple invoice template might look like this:

```
                                                  [date]

[customer's name]
[customer's address]
IF pc:the customer DOES want a pc
  INSERT P C [modelno] [pcprice]
OR IF at:the customer DOES want an at
  INSERT A T [modelno] [at price]
END IF
IF the customer DOES want more memory
  INSERT additional memory [addon: the additional
  memory desired / 64000 * $49]
END IF
IF hard:the customer DOES want a hard drive
  INSERT hard drive [hard price]
OR IF [double:the customer DOES want two floppies]
  INSERT double floppy [double price]
OTHERWISE
  INSERT one floppy [single price]
END IF
IF mono: the customer DOES want a monochrome monitor
  INSERT monochrome [monoprice]
OTHERWISE
  INSERT color monitor [colorprice]
END IF
```

While the invoice is being processed, a client data file will be set up for this customer and kept in the library. This will allow us to process a customized follow-up letter without asking for further data at a later date.

```
  IF [mono]
    INSERT [customer's name]
           [customer's address]
           Dear [customer's name]:

           On [date] you purchased
  IF [pc]
    INSERT a P C
  OR IF [at]
    INSERT an A T
  END IF
  with a monochrome monitor. Here at P C World we are
  running a special on color monitors at a one time price of
  [special price].
END IF
IF memsize<257
INSERT if you want to extend your memory size from your
initial [memsize] to 640K, a special added discount price of
20% will be available to purchasers of color monitors.
END IF
```

This is just a simple illustration of the possibilities.

SUMMARY

The ABF environment permits one to design arbitrarily complex interviewing and document assembly systems for use in any application where standardized text is routinely assembled into customized drafts, in accordance with predefined rules. While this technology was originally developed to serve the specialized needs of the legal profession, it appears promising for applications in insurance and marketing. We are working on automating the construction of medical discharge summaries in using ABF also.

The ABF approach makes all the constructs of structured programming available to word processing specialists in a very supportive environment.

REFERENCES

1. Sprowl, J.A. "Automating the Legal Reasoning Process: A Computer That Uses Regulations and Statutes to Draft Legal Documents." *American Bar Foundation Research Journal,* (1979), pp. 1–8.
2. Sprowl, J.A., and R.W. Staudt. "Computerizing Client Services in the Law School Teaching Clinic: An Experiment in Law Office Automation." *American Bar Foundation Research Journal,* (1981), pp. 699–751.
3. Saxon, C.S. "Computer-Aided Drafting of Legal Documents." *American Bar Foundation Research Journal,* (1982) pp. 685–754.
4. Sprowl, J.A., P. Balasubramanian, T. Chinwalla, M. Evens, and H. Klawans. "An Expert System for Drafting Legal Documents." *AFIPS Proceedings of the National Computer Conference,* (Vol. 53), 1984, pp. 667–673.
5. Sprowl, J.A., K. Applegate, M. Evens, H. Harr, and R. Rueb. "Human Interfaces in a Legal Expert System." *AFIPS Proceedings of the National Computer Conference,* (Vol. 55), 1986, pp. 135–142.

AI/expert system applications for the automated office

by JANET PALMER
Western Kentucky University
Bowling Green, Kentucky

ABSTRACT

AI/expert systems enable machines to emulate human thinking. Originally, AI technology was directed toward scientific applications, but now office applications are available for all computer configurations. AI/expert systems can enhance the quality of human thinking by decision makers in an organization and increase productivity. Organizations can develop expert systems following a customized, semi-customized, or off-the-shelf software approach. Expert systems "clone" the best thinking of company gurus and distribute that knowledge wherever and whenever required. Programs currently available for office applications include decision making, training, word processing, and retrieval systems. The problems solved by AI/expert systems can be large or small but should be of a nature to justify the time and expense involved in developing such systems. Just as the acquisition of office automation was once deemed critical to company survival, so too will be the development of expert systems, the newest competitive edge.

INTRODUCTION

Office automation is about to take a quantum leap forward because of rapid advancements in artificial intelligence (AI). AI is the field of study linking computer science and cognitive psychology. Its goal is the development of machines that emulate human thinking. These processes involve hypothesizing, reasoning, guessing, perceiving, associating, speculating, concluding, and learning. Originally, the capabilities of AI technology were directed toward scientific applications, such as medicine and geology, but now computer programs called expert systems are being generated for office applications.[1] Office automation experts agree that AI/expert systems will play an important role in the integration of office systems in the future. Truly user friendly systems are expected to be the result. These expert systems will be so transparent, users will not even be aware of their existence.[2]

EXPERT SYSTEMS

Expert systems are composed of two parts: a knowledge base and an inference engine. A knowledge base consists of a collection of facts, assertions, inferences, observations, hypotheses, rules, and procedures required to solve a particular class of problems. An inference engine is the control structure of the expert system which manipulates and applies the information stored in the knowledge base. Artificial intelligence combined with office automation produces powerful expert systems capable of the following functions: interpretation, prediction, diagnosis, instruction, control, design, planning, monitoring, debugging, and repair.[1] However, just as office automation needs to be designed carefully in order to achieve its benefits, so too must expert systems.

EXPERT SYSTEM DEVELOPMENT

Ostensibly, the chief benefit of AI applied to the automated office will be increased productivity. Ultimately, the greatest contribution of AI to the office environment will be its subtle alteration of the way people function in an office; their relationship to their colleagues, their mastery and creative use of the tools before them.[3]

Organizations desiring the benefits of expert systems have three options. The first approach is the most expensive and time consuming. This method involves the custom development of an expert system. An AI specialist called a knowledge engineer "mines" the expertise of individuals in order to create a knowledge base. Then a highly skilled programmer designs the inference engine. The second approach involves the semi-customized development of an expert system. With this approach, a commercially available package is used which contains a "shell." A shell is a development tool which frees the knowledge engineer from creating the raw code for the expert system. With the services of a programmer, such packages can be developed to build the knowledge base around the shell. The third approach involves the use of an off-the-shelf, pre-written software package which can be slightly modified to suit a particular user. Many of these commercial packages are designed to be so user friendly that even a non-programmer can enter information into their shells.

Expert system development packages are available in a price range from $50 to $50,000 and can be configured for specialized AI workstations or standardized mainframe, mini, and microcomputer systems. Some top-selling expert system development packages include The Knowledge Engineering Environment from Intellicorp, The Automated Reasoning Tool from Inference Corporation, and Micro-Expert from McGraw-Hill.[4]

Organizations develop their own expert systems in order to "clone" the expertise of their best thinkers and distribute their thinking to remote locations. Expert systems provide organizations with "distributed knowledge" to accompany the popular trend of "distributed systems." Capturing and storing for future use the wisdom of company gurus will help protect an organization from sudden loss of such expertise by death, retirement, or resignation. Not all organizations, however, will need to develop their own expert systems. Software for office applications is now being developed which incorporates AI technology.

EXPERT SYSTEM OFFICE APPLICATIONS

The market for expert system software is just beginning. An estimated three thousand such packages have been sold. However, software industry experts predict that by 1988 all new software will have AI embedded in it.[5] Programs currently available for office applications include decision making (decision support, spreadsheets, and databases), training, word processing, and retrieval systems.

Decision Making

Executives and managers in the office already use decision support systems (DSS) software to query databases as an aid in problem solving. AI technology, however, has produced a new class of software called expert support systems (ESS). Whereas DSS software is designed to handle deterministic problems, ESS software is designed to deal with probalistic problems. Deterministic problems can be codified, calculated, and solved according to well-defined rules of logic. Probalistic problems resist easy coding, are often referred to as "fuzzy," are best expressed in words, and are solved with rules-of-thumb (heuristic knowledge).[6] While deterministic problems are well suited for solving with spreadsheets or traditional data processing programs, probalistic problems are ideal candidates for expert systems. In practice, the user provides input to the expert system which then refers to its knowledge base to develop a solution to the inquiry. The answer given represents a determination of the probability of something occurring. This process is much the same as that of a human expert offering his/her "best guess" for a particular problem. An example of a best-selling computer program combining artificial intelligence with a database is Symantec's Q and A. AI technology eventually will allow users to query databases using natural language processing (conversational English). However, not all executive and managerial decision making is appropriate for use with expert systems. For example, extremely complex, single-time tasks requiring high degrees of social interaction might not be appropriate.[7]

Many decisions made in an office are on a small scale, repetitive, and solved by following standardized procedures. Such decision making generally is handled by support staff members, often secretaries and clerks. Slight deviations in such problems usually result in the staff members seeking assistance from their office supervisors. Cases of such indecision result in work interruptions and loss of office productivity. Expert systems can remedy such situations.

The expertise of office supervisors can be incorporated into a knowledge base for the benefit of inexperienced or untrained office workers. These individuals can then acquire the answers needed to complete their tasks quickly with a minimum of work disruption. Application of expert systems for this type of decision making is known by various names, such as small expert systems, knowledge systems, or intelligent job aids. Such systems provide an interactive, computerized database, which can be conveniently updated to accommodate changes in office procedures. Decision making can become more efficient and effective with such small expert systems rather than reliance on employee memorization of procedures or printed office manuals.[8] Another application of AI which will be of direct benefit to office employees is in the area of training.

Training

Lack of training among office employees is often cited as the chief reason for failure of the automated office to achieve increased productivity. Office employees often do not understand all of their equipments' features and thus are unable to use the equipment to its best advantage.[8] AI technology is now being combined with computer-assisted instruction (CAI) resulting in intelligent computer-assisted instruction (ICAI). Training experts predict that such programs will revolutionize training.[9]

What distinguishes ICAI from CAI is its greater degree of flexibility in assessing the learning difficulties of trainees. Traditional CAI presents information to trainees, permits interaction between trainees and the instructional program, provides evaluation to trainees, and tracks the progress of the trainees. When a particular instructional approach fails to produce effective learning, the ICAI program can provide more instructional options to trainees. The traditional CAI program can only assess the trainees' lack of performance according to test scores, which are the result of matching the trainees' responses against predefined, anticipated answers.

The ICAI program makes use of its inferencing capability to analyze trainees' difficulties. Also, ICAI programs can provide to trainees the reason why a particular instructional strategy was selected.[10] An example of an ICAI program is the Technology Based Training Series from HyperGraphics Corporation in Denton, Texas. This program provides users wth an authoring system to create intelligent training programs featuring graphics, animation, and eventually voice. Intelligent software can also be used advantageously for training in word processing.

Word Processing

IBM is developing an intelligent word processing software package called Critique. This program uses AI technology to assist authors of business correspondence. The program will not only correct grammatical errors but also generate original documents.[11] Another custom-designed expert system has been developed to diagnose operators' difficulties with a word processing program and/or procedures. Such diagnosis by the program aids word processing supervisors. Operators who need additional training can be identified and operators' difficulties remedied. In addition, an expert system word processing program can constantly update the users' files.[12] Retrieval systems are yet another area in which AI technology can be applied.

Retrieval Systems

Expert systems can be used to link diverse office automation tools under one interface on a multiuser system.[13] One example would be a retrieval system which integrates AI/expert system technology with databases. Such retrieval systems can provide file access to users in a multivendor computer environment including main, mini, and micro computers. These programs called network file systems allow all users to share files, even when systems are linked by more than one network. The development of a network file system frees users from worrying about different operating systems or different file structures, enabling users to access files in remote systems. What makes a network file system different from a local area network is that a network file system accesses files without copying them, thus protecting the integrity of the files resident on remote computers. An example of such a program is manufactured by Sun Microsystem.[14]

CONCLUSION

From all indications, AI/expert systems appear ready to become a dominant force in the automated office for the 1990s and beyond.[1] According to a study by Electronic Trend Publications, the expert systems market will reach $1.2 billion by 1990.[5] The total AI hardware and software market has been predicted to reach $4 billion by 1990.[3]

Although rapid advancements are being made in AI/expert systems, such systems will not imminently replace human thinking. Professor Edward A. Feigenbaum of the Computer Science Department and Knowledge Systems Laboratory at Stanford University predicted that AI general computer systems able to cover the full range of human knowledge are at least 50 to 100 years in the future.[15] At least for the time being, then, human thinking will remain more flexible and creative, while machine thinking will be aimed at solving a specific class of problems. Expert systems, however, complement human thinking and are expected to become routinely incorporated into office hardware and software.

Currently, about half of the companies in the Fortune 500 are actively pursuing the development of expert systems. Companies such as Lockheed, Digital Equipment Corporation (DEC), Boeing Computer Services, General Electric, and General Motors hope that by so doing they will gain a competitive edge. Just as the acquisition of office automation was seen as critical to company survival, so too is the development of expert systems. AI/expert systems are expected to infiltrate organizations gradually, department by department, just as PCs once did. Organizations striving to stay abreast of technological developments need to assess their organizations' needs for the development of appropriate AI/expert systems applications.[4] Perhaps as humans become more computer literate, fairness dictates that computers become more human literate.[6]

ACKNOWLEDGEMENT

The author acknowledges the assistance in the preparation of this paper from Jennifer Backer, a graduate assistant in the Department of Administrative Office Systems at Western Kentucky University.

REFERENCES

1. Canter, J. "Expert Systems." In *Proceedings of the Fourth Annual Research Conference,* Office Systems Research Association, Atlanta, 1985, pp. 371–394.
2. Fiderio, J. "Voice, Image Processing, AI Likely Additions to OA Systems." *Computerworld,* June 30, 1986, p. 38.
3. Johnson, D. "Making Computers Work 'Smarter.'" *Administrative Management,* October, 1986, pp. 28–33.
4. Newquist, III, H.P. "Expert Systems: The Promise of a Smart Machine." *Computerworld,* January 13, 1986, pp. 43–57.
5. Myers, E. "Making Micros Experts." *Datamation,* September 1, 1985, pp. 51–54.
6. Becker, H.B. "Information Management and Artificial Intelligence." In *Proceedings of the Fourth Annual Research Conference,* Office Systems Research Association, Atlanta, 1985, pp. 1–14.
7. Wohl, A. "Artificial Intelligence: Myth vs. Reality." *Computerworld,* October 7, 1985, p. 17.
8. Harmon, P. "Intelligent Job Aids: The Use of Small Expert Systems in Office Automation." In *Proceedings of the Fifth Annual Research Conference,* Office Systems Research Association, Houston, 1986, pp. 184–209.
9. Hickingbottom-Brown, B. "Increasing Your Artificial Intelligence Quotient." *Training and Development Journal,* January, 1984, p. 69.
10. Crews, P. "tbt EXPERT: A case study in integrating Expert System technology with computer-assisted instruction." *Unpublished study,* 1986. HyperGraphics Corp., Denton, Texas, pp. 1–14.
11. Harder, L. "An Artificial Intelligence Approach to Document Preparation." *AFIPS Proceedings of the National Computer Conference* (Vol. 55) 1986, p. 149.
12. Rushinek A. and S. Rushinek. "The Effects of Word Processing Software on User Satisfaction: An Empirical Study of Micro, Mini, and Mainframe Computers Using An Interactive Artificial Intelligence Expert System." *Office Systems Research Journal,* 3, Fall, 1984, pp. 1–16.
13. Wright, B. "AI and Integrated Office Systems: Intelligent Workgroup Assistants." *ComputerData,* 10, Canada: September 1985, p. 21.
14. Harmon, P., ed. "Close-up on Sun Microsystem's Network File System." *Expert Systems Strategies Newsletter,* March, 1986, pp. 10–11.
15. Nofel, P. "There's Nothing Artificial About A.I." *Modern Office Technology,* February, 1986, pp. 40–44.

WE: A writing environment for professionals

by JOHN B. SMITH, STEPHEN F. WEISS, GORDON J. FERGUSON,
JAY D. BOLTER, MARCY LANSMAN, and DAVID V. BEARD
University of North Carolina
Chapel Hill, North Carolina

ABSTRACT

We have developed a visually-oriented environment for writing and thinking, designed for professionals using workstations linked by a communications network. Users represent ideas as labelled nodes, move them into spatial clusters, link them into an associative network (directed graph), and transform the network into a tree. The content for each node can be expanded with either a text- or a graphic-editor. Editing the structure of the tree changes the structure of the corresponding document. We are also using the system to support a series of experiments to map users' cognitive strategies. Protocols are collected automatically by the system and then parsed with a cognitive grammar. The results are used to refine both the system and the cognitive model on which it is based.

INTRODUCTION

Technical and scientific professionals are writers. Regardless of title or job description, they write. Most spend 25% to 75% of their time doing something related to writing; gathering and organizing information, writing *per se,* revising, talking with others about something they have written, giving oral presentations accompanied by documents, etc. They write many different forms: letters, reports, specifications, plans of various sorts, proposals, justifications, articles, oral presentations, to name some of the more prevalent forms. These documents are important. They form the skeleton of the writer's organization. While that skeleton must be fleshed out by other activities, the collection of written documents is the core. If new tools can lead to more effective documents and can help skilled professionals work more efficiently, the payoffs will be substantial.

Current tools for writing and producing documents fall into four major groups: editors, formatters, checkers, and organizers. The first two are well-established and need no additional comment. Checkers are less universal, but still widespread. The most common are the spelling-checkers, but style-checkers are also beginning to appear. While those that use table lookup and limited pattern matching are of questionable value, checkers that will eventually include full parsers may have more impact, when they appear. The final group, the organizers, include structure editors and outline processors. The former tend to be mainframe-oriented and are often experimental or demonstration systems; Nelson's hypertext[1] and Engelbart's NLS[2] are early examples. More recently, the microcomputer outline processor has become widespread, but the jury is still out on its value.

Current tools for writing were not designed for professionals. Most were designed for technical writers concerned with layout and physical production, or for microcomputer hobbyists. What is needed are tools designed specifically for the sophisticated professionals who use workstations within distributed environments.

We are developing a comprehensive Writing Environment (WE) for this application. Parts of this work are supported by IBM, NSF, and the Army Research Institute. In describing this system, we will emphasize five key concepts:

1. The system is based on a cognitive model for written communication.
2. The system is highly visual.
3. The system was prototyped in Smalltalk and then ported to Objective C.
4. The system will be used in a series of cognitive experiments.
5. The system can be extended to other applications.

The emphasis placed on cognitive aspects in this description probably needs more explanation. WE is one instance of an increasingly important kind of software that provides users with an environment in which to think, or with functions that supplement human cognitive skills. To be successful, these intelligence augmenting systems must reflect the cognitive processes of the people using them. We suggest that a modified development cycle is needed that begins with an explicit cognitive model of the user interacting with the system to perform specific high-level tasks, includes formal testing of the model as well as the software, and ends (the first cycle) with systematic refinement of both. Therefore, our discussion of WE will include not just a description of the system but also its underlying rationale and the methods we used to develop and test it.

COGNITIVE MODEL FOR WRITTEN COMMUNICATION

WE is based on a cognitive model of written communication. The model was derived from a review and synthesis of the literature in cognitive psychology, composition theory, human/computer studies, as well as our own experience. However, it is put forth more as a question than as an assertion. We are testing the model in a series of cognitive experiments and will revise it accordingly. It stresses the structure of information, particularly the transformations writers and readers produce as they write and read documents, and views writing and reading as symmetrical processes in several important respects (see Figure 1). In this section, we describe the model, briefly, and then explain how we have used it in designing WE.

Whether readers read a document from beginning to end or jump from one place to another, when they "settle down" to read a passage they do so linearly. That is, they decode a linear sequence of words. However, they do not comprehend linearly. Rather, they comprehend by relating bits and pieces of information to one another hierarchically. They see that

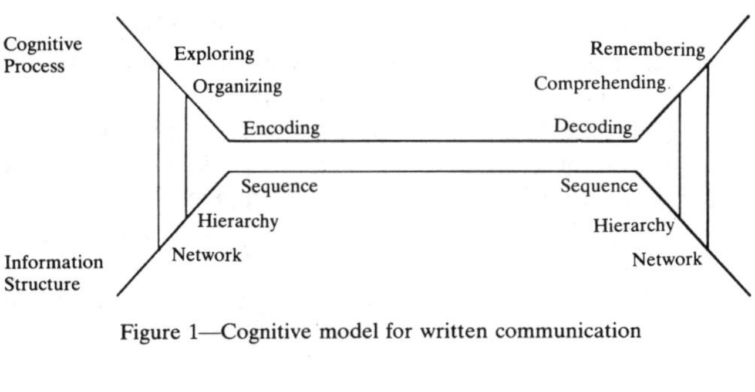

Figure 1—Cognitive model for written communication

several points do, indeed, add up to the conclusion the writer has drawn, or that a general point is supported by the evidence or examples cited. As the process continues, readers relate what they are reading to what they already know. This process is particularly active as new information is integrated into the network of associations that underlies long-term memory. Thus, readers read, comprehend, and remember what they read by transforming information in one structural form into another: from *linear sequence,* to *hierarchy,* to *network.*

The key to the reading process, however, is the hierarchical step. If a document signals its hierarchical structure through features included in it, such as a system of headings, overviews, topic sentences in paragraphs, readers use these clues to advantage. That is, they read and comprehend the document more quickly, and the structure they infer for the document will match more closely that intended by the writer.[3] If such features are omitted from the document, no headings or inconsistent headings, flat narrative, few topic sentences, to the extent readers understand what they are reading, they will construct their own hierarchy for the document. However, the hierarchy they construct may or may not resemble that intended by the writer. Consequently, organizing expository information into a hierarchical structure and then signaling that structure is a particularly effective strategy for writers to follow.

Writing involves a similar series of transformations, but in reverse order. Writers normally begin with a need to write. The content is likely to be scattered through the writer's long term memory or through various external sources, such as books, databases, or other people's heads. The "structure" of that information is likely to be a very loose associative network, derived as the information is brought to consciousness. A key step for the writer, then, is to gather information and to organize it. Most writers do so by constructing a hierarchy, in the form of an outline or a tree. Once the hierarchy has been constructed, the task of writing becomes a traversal of the hierarchy during which the writer encodes the concepts into prose, graphics, or other forms. Thus, writing involves a similar but opposite sequence of transformations: *network,* to *hierarchy,* to *linear sequence.*

Several conclusions can be drawn. First, writing involves both networks (directed graphs) and hierarchical structures but at different stages of the process. All earlier structure editors with which we are familiar have adopted one principle or the other, but not both. The hypertext family of editors, such as Nelson's hypertext system,[1] its Brown University derivatives,[4] and ZOG,[5] support directed graphs. A similar group support hierarchical structures such as Engelbart's NLS,[2] Thinktank[6] and the other outline processors, and XS-2.[7] While users can construct a hierarchy within a directed graph environment, they may find the environment more supportive when they can voluntarily relinquish some function during certain stages of the process in exchange for greater discipline. Consequently, we have constructed an environment that includes both, permitting writers to develop graphs and hierarchies separately but also to transfer conceptual structures from one mode to the other.

Another key conclusion is that writing requires a number of different cognitive skills, not just linguistic encoding skills. Writers think associatively, hierarchically on a small scale (individual inferences and deductions), hierarchically on a large scale (constructing a single large hierarchy), and analytically (as they revise). For many writers, particularly those in scientific and technical fields, these stages also include visual and spatial reasoning. This is particularly true during early exploratory thinking and during the organizational stage. Consequently, we have built our environment around the notion of an abstract space in which users can represent and manipulate concepts visually.

A third, and related, implication is that writing includes both bottom-up and top-down thinking. During early exploration, writers often think bottom-up as they trace paths of associations, gather information, and explore various relations. While an entire document can be organized hierarchically by continuing a bottom-up strategy, it cannot be "aimed" easily or reliably using this approach. To focus a document and to ensure that it achieves a clearly recognized goal, experienced writers often begin with a single large objective and derive the hierarchical structure from that point. Thus, writers also need tools that let them work top-down. The point is not that one form of thinking or the other is best; both are needed but at different stages of the process. Consequently, the environment we are developing is strongly multimodal.

While cognitive psychology has had a strong impact on human factors studies and the design of computer interfaces, it has had less impact on the underlying architecture and function of systems. In WE, the cognitive model has influenced not just the interface; it is central to the entire design and is a concept that will be evaluated experimentally. Thus, the system itself and the thoretical basis on which it is built emerge as a question: How do users write and think while working within this particular computing environment? A substantial part of our effort is directed at answering this question, as we explain below in the section on Cognitive Experiments.

Description of WE

Three aspects of WE distinguish it from other writing support systems: the visual interface, its multimodal architecture, and an underlying relational database.

Visual interface

The interface for WE is based on three major factors derived from the cognitive model:

1. Writers use a number of different cognitive skills in writing.
2. Writing involves a series of transformations in which information in one structural form is changed into another.
3. Structures can be more easily comprehended, constructed, and manipulated when they are represented visually (e.g., in a tree) than when they are represented linguistically (e.g., in an outline, as in 1.3.2.4).

Consequently, the user interface is distinctly visual and graphical, as opposed to language-oriented.

The default layout for the screen shows five tiled windows (see Figure 2). The two largest are a *graph* window and a *hierarchical* window. The first supports operations that conform to the rules of a directed graph embedded in a Euclidean space. The second obeys the rules of hierarchies. A smaller window is available for either a text or a graphic editor used to write or draw the content of the document, associated as blocks of data with individual nodes. The fourth window is used to search the relational database for other structures or nodes that might be inserted into the current document. The last window is a control panel for managing the environment. Each window is described in more detail below in relation to its corresponding mode.

Users can easily change the default configuration by resizing and moving the various windows. Thus, the entire screen can be used for the directed graph window during, say, the early brainstorming stage of writing. Or the entire screen can be used to show a tree in hierarchical mode during organization. Another option is to split the screen between a directed graph and a hierarchical window so that small hierarchical substructures can be copied from one mode to the other (see Figures 2–8).

Modes

A second key architectural feature of WE is its multimodal structure. Although the tide of opinion is currently running against such designs, separating the function of the system into separate domains is desirable for this particular application. Since writing involves several different kinds of thinking, WE supports each with functions specific to that cognitive mode. An hypothesis we will test experimentally is that users will prefer to "drop into" different modes of thinking for

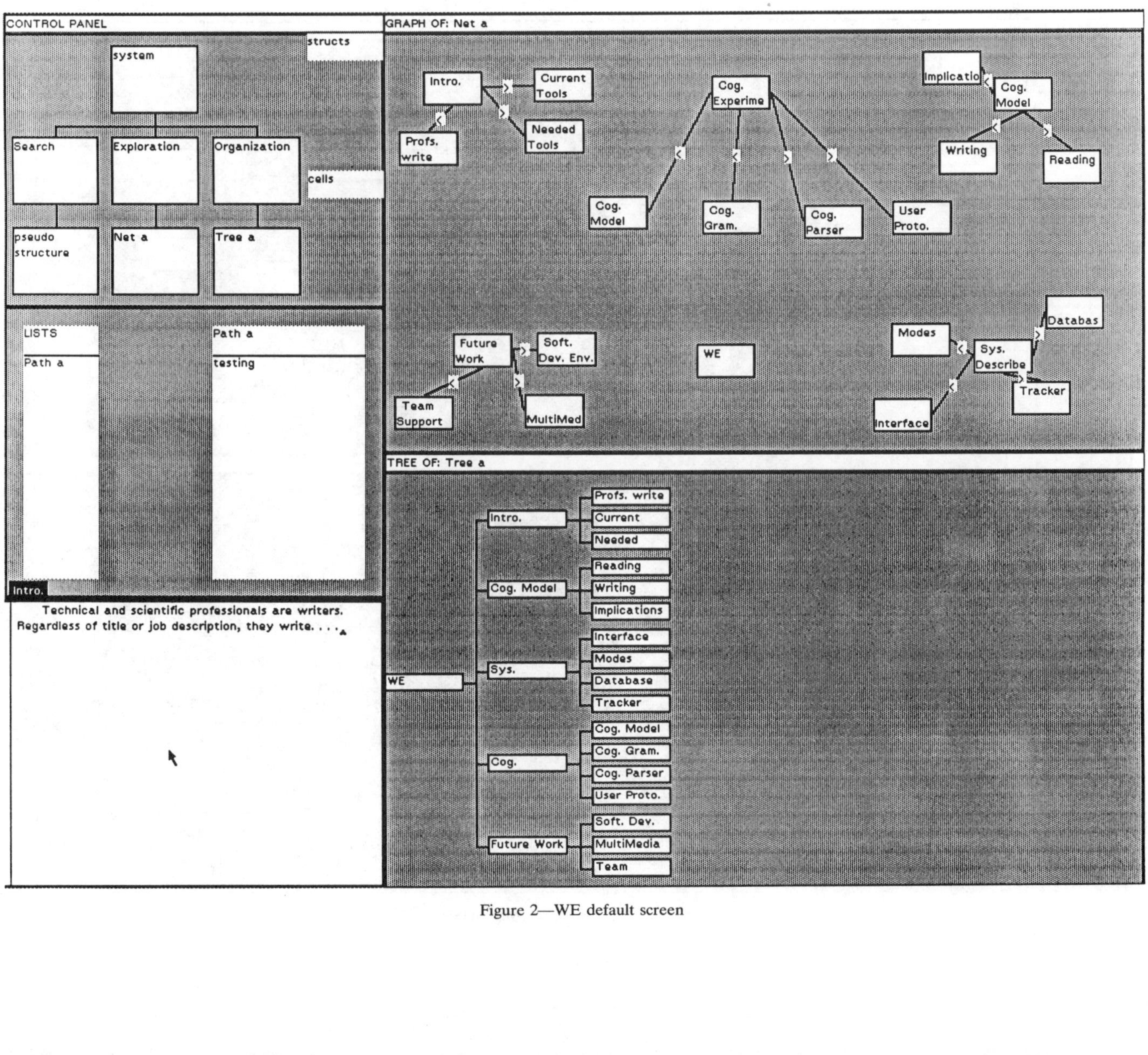

Figure 2—WE default screen

different activities, gaining flexibility in some cases, giving it up in others, in exchange for greater rigor and consistency.

We expect most writers to begin a project by working in a directed graph window. This mode is particularly well suited for bottom-up thinking. Using a mouse, users can open a window to cover the entire screen. They can then create nodes at any spot in the windows simply by pointing with the mouse, clicking for a menu, and selecting the "create node" option. (Since the last option selected on a particular menu is retained as the default, subsequent clicks produce additional nodes without further selection.) They can label each with a word or phrase, either when the node is created or later as an editing operation. Users can also move nodes into clusters of related concepts (see Figure 4) and can join pairs of nodes with directed links to denote specific associations (see Figure 5).

A second mode/window provides functions that conform to the rules for hierarchies (see Figure 6). Users begin in this window by creating a root node and labeling it, as in graph mode. They can then create child nodes under the root, indicating the major divisions of the document. The process of division can be continued until the nodes represent sections that can easily be written, usually a few paragraphs, or represented in a single graphic. A number of structure editing functions are also provided. These permit users to move nodes or branches around in the hierarchy, add and delete both leaf and interior nodes, etc. Users may also import nodes or structures from graph mode into tree mode. That is, they can go back to a directed graph window created earlier and select a node that is a root for a small hierarchical relation; when they return to the hierarchical window, they can point to the place where the branch should be placed and the system will insert the subtree into the tree at that point.

The system provides four different visual representations for hierarchies. The first is a conventional horizontal tree in which parent/sibling relations are indicated by left to right relations (see Figure 6). The second is a vertical tree that extends from top to bottom (see Figure 7). Zoom and roam functions are provided for each. In fact, since users can open

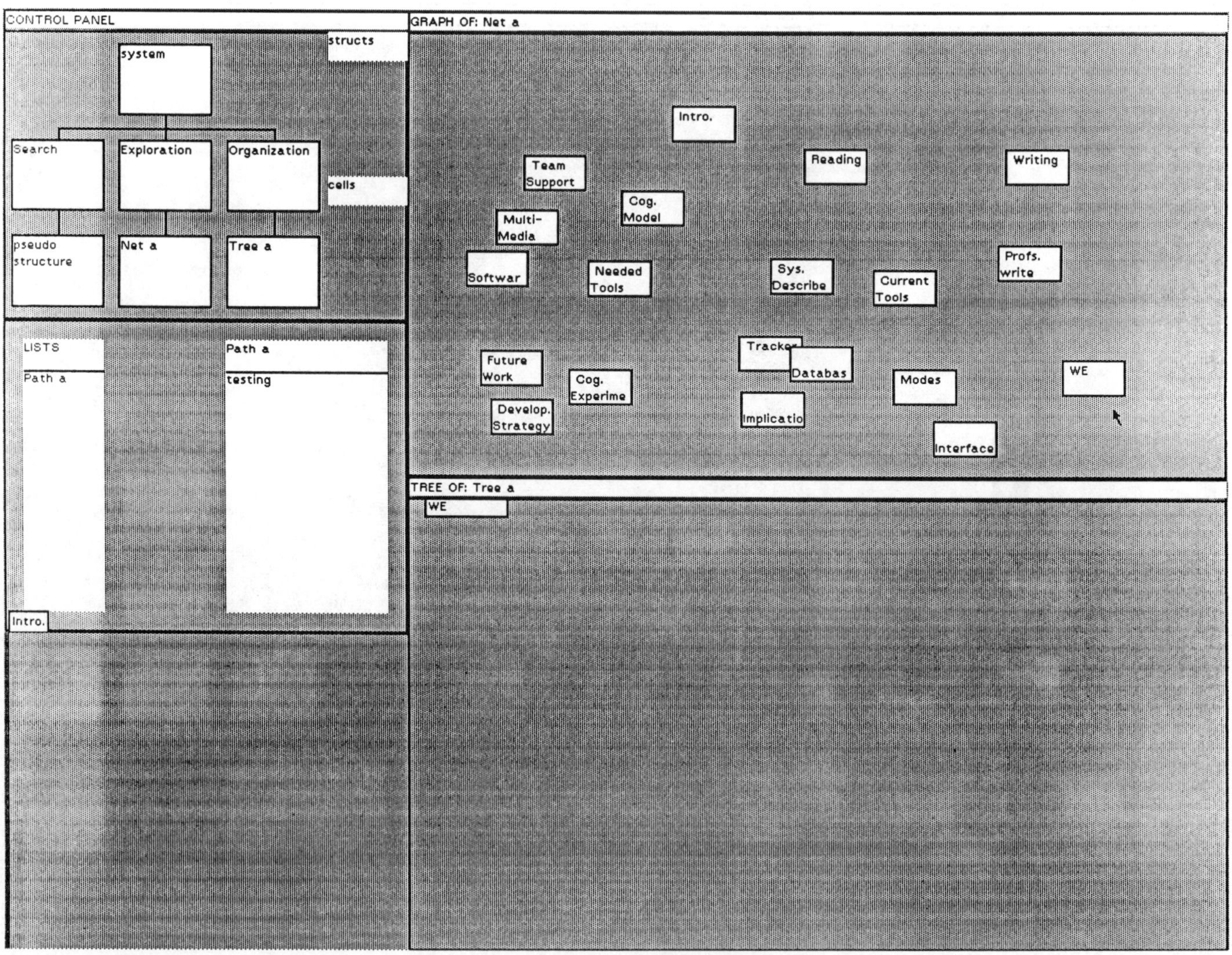

Figure 3—WE spatial graph mode

several different windows on the same structure, they can show a small schematic view of the whole tree in one, an enlarged view of a section in a second, and a still larger image of the particular branch being worked on in a third. This is particularly useful for large structures, for team development efforts, or other projects where managing technical complexity is an issue. A third view presents a Chinese box representation of the hierarchy in which child nodes are shown as small boxes inside the larger box representing the parent node (see Figure 8). Since the system shows only three levels of depth with this view, it provides a form of information hiding. The last view is a standard outline view.

At any point, in either graph or hierarchical mode, the user can open a node and insert content. This is done by invoking either a conventional text or graphic editor. Typically, users write a paragraph or several paragraphs or create a single visual image. In this mode, the function provided is that of the particular editor. When users finish with a content unit, they close the node and the content is saved in a file system. Thereafter, whenever a node is moved using any of the structure editor functions, the associated content is also moved along with it. Since a node is a typed object bound to a particular editor/display program, the kinds of data that can be associated with a node can be extended simply by extending the set of types and associated editor/display programs. We describe several planned extensions in the section on Future Work.

A fourth mode helps users search the relational database in which nodes, links, and structures are stored. We explain its purpose and function in the following section. Here, we merely call attention to its existence.

All four modes—graph, hierarchy, content, and search—are "held together" by a control panel. The control panel includes two major fields: mode tree and a pair of stacks. The mode tree represents the different modes, as first-level children, and the specific named instances of each (i.e., windows), as second-level children. It provides a variety of management functions. For example, to move a buried window to the forefront, users merely point to it in the mode tree and

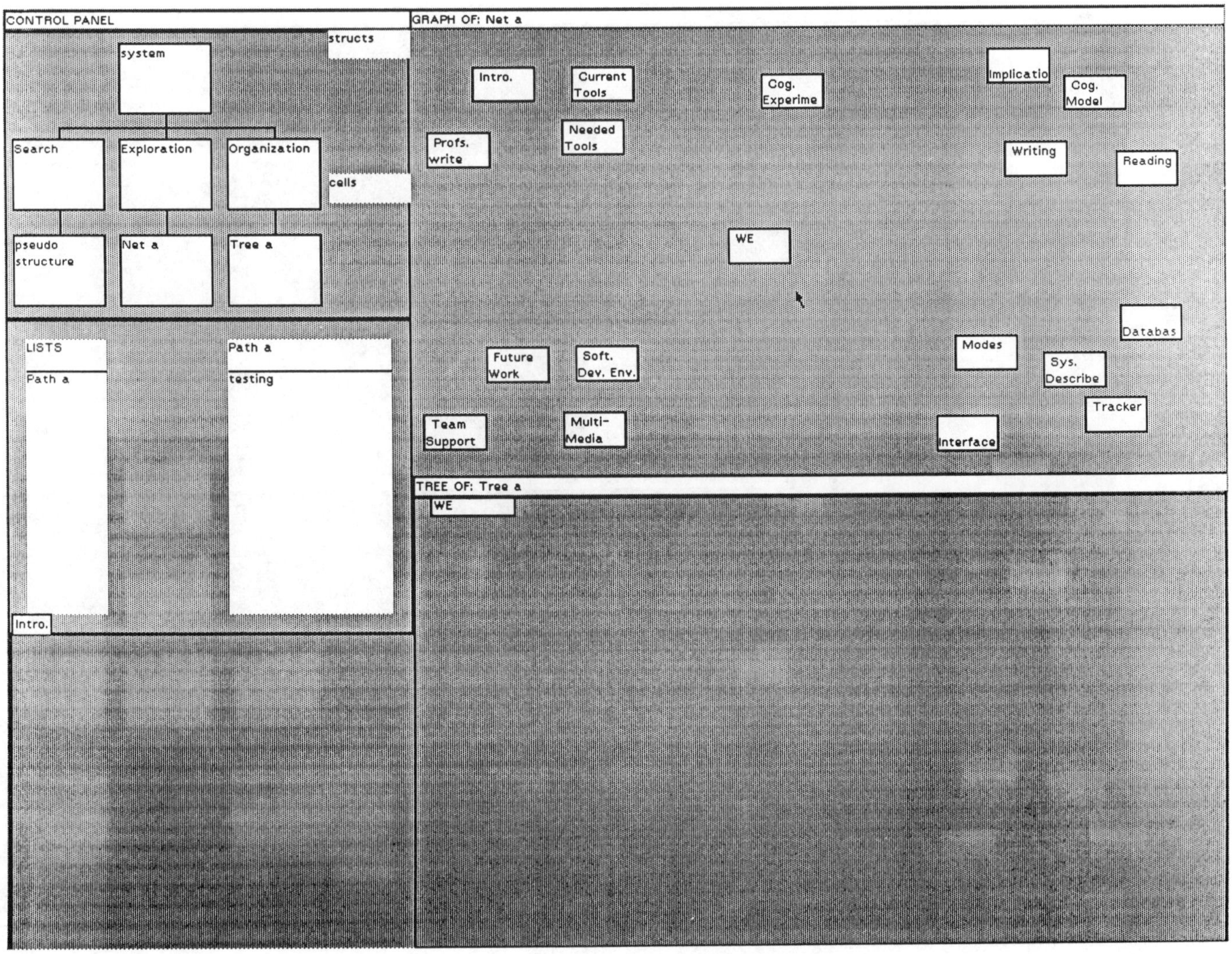

Figure 4—WE spatial graph mode, conceptual clusters

select the appropriate operation. Thus, users can quickly get an overview of the entire "screen space" they have created, including windows covered by other windows. The stacks receive the nodes and structures created by the yank operation. They permit users to make copies of several different nodes or structures while working in one mode/window and then selectively move them at their leisure into the structure being created in another.

Database

A third major innovation in WE is the use of a relational database system as the store for all structural information. The database holds three kinds of entities: structures, nodes, and links. Structures are typed, named sets of links and, by implication, associated nodes. The type indicates whether the structure is a graph, hierarchy, or path; this information is used by the system to determine the operations that can be performed on the particular structure. Each node is also viewed as a typed object. Associated with it are various attributes that identify the type of content "within" that node and, thus, bind it to an editor/display program; its spatial dimensions in graph-mode space; and both its associative and hierarchical links. Links are attributed pairs of node identifiers. The node identifiers define the directed arc; and the attributes indicate the kind of link (e.g., graph), the structure of which the link is a part, and other system information.

Users can search the database for a structure, node, or link by its identifying label or by its attributes. This is done through the search window/mode, mentioned in the preceding section. In the current system, the database is confined to a single project, but we will extend its definition to permit teams and departments to store collections of documents and other kinds of data. Thus, future users will be able to search the database for information relevant to the current project. Once a usable node or structure is found, it can be imported into the environment and included in the structure currently being

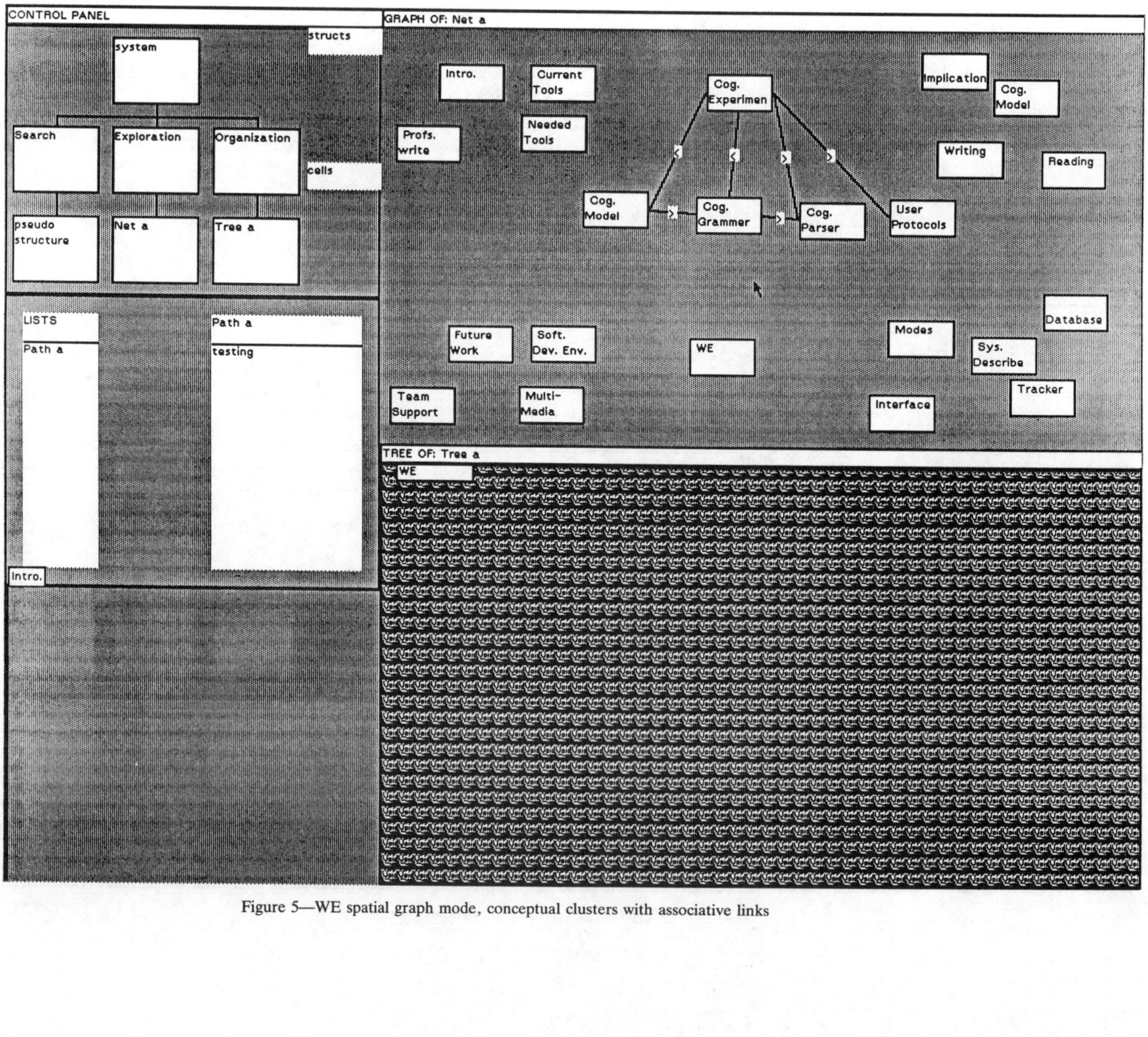

Figure 5—WE spatial graph mode, conceptual clusters with associative links

developed. A longer term goal is to merge another system we are developing, MICROARRAS,[8] an advanced full-text retrieval and analysis system, with WE to support content-based searches as well.

IMPLEMENTATION

We have followed an unusual path in implementing WE. First, we designed and implemented a prototype system in Smalltalk running on a SUN-3 workstation. Smalltalk provides an object-oriented environment that encourages information hiding and hierarchical modular design in which each level of the system is implemented in terms of the tools defined at lower levels. It also provides a complete development environment including a sophisticated system browser, extensive graphic tools, and access to the full Smalltalk source. Since Smalltalk is an interpreter, changes can be made and tested quickly and easily. The prototype system, shown in Figures 2–8, provides full functional capability and can support documents up to about fifty nodes. Using it, we were able to test our original design by actually using the system to see how various features worked in conjunction with one another. However, since Smalltalk is not suited for large, high performance applications, we planned from the beginning to port the system to other software and hardware environments.

To facilitate this move, we developed device-independent toolkits for drawing and for managing user interaction with the system. Both toolkits were designed as Smalltalk classes. In Smalltalk, they were implemented directly, using methods provided by the system. To port them to other environments, we are writing drivers that use the graphics and window management facilities provided by the target system. We have completed the porting of both toolkits to Microsoft Windows for the IBM PC/AT, and we are currently moving them to X Windows for the SUN workstation.

Finally, we are porting the entire system from Smalltalk to Objective C, a synthesis of Smalltalk and C developed and

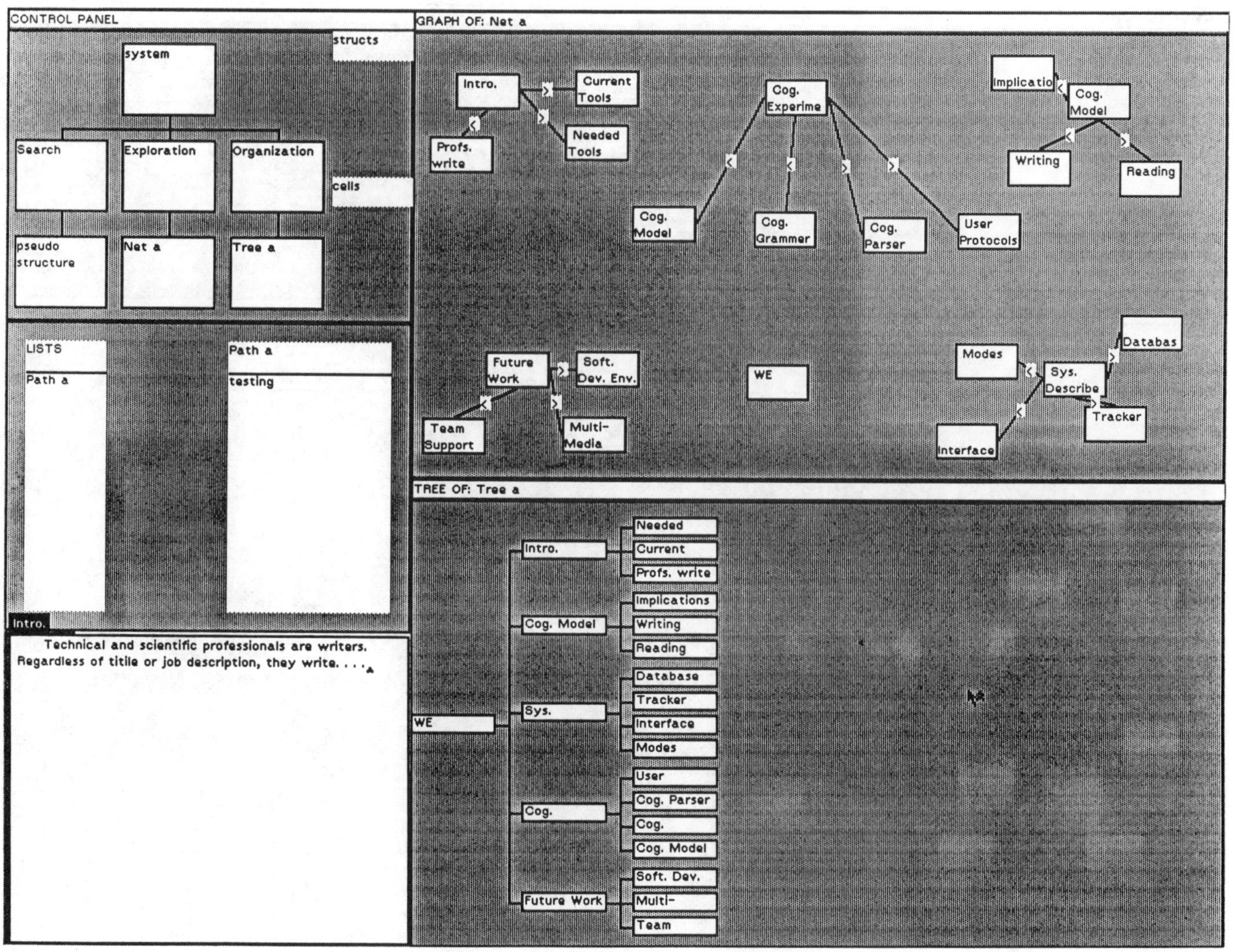

Figure 6—WE hierarchy mode horizontal tree

marketed by Productivity Products International, Inc. Objective C provides a large-grain structure of classes, methods, and inheritance characteristics nearly identical to Smalltalk. But, it also provides the small-grain capability to replace system primitives with C functions for greater speed and processing efficiency. While we can foresee the possibility of translating Smalltalk classes into Objective C automatically, for the present we must still rewrite the syntax manually. This is largely a direct, line-for-line translation that requires virtually no changes to overall system architecture.

COGNITIVE EXPERIMENTS

As we noted earlier, WE was designed in accord with a cognitive model of the writing process. We are using the system as an observational instrument in a series of formal experiments to evaluate that model as well as other cognitive hypotheses, and to test specific system features and representation schemes. In this section, we will not describe these experiments in detail, but rather the technical features of the system that support them.

A built-in tracking facility permits us to record the actions of users at a functional or operational level. Thus, we can observe the sequence of operations employed to create nodes, move them into spatial clusters, and link them into associative relations. Each operation is recorded along with the time it was performed and its associated parameters, and stored in the same relational database as the document. These data constitute a high-level concurrent protocol of the session, collected unobtrusively and in a machine-readable form ready for analysis.

Traditional approaches to concurrent protocols have employed video recordings of users interacting with a system, "thinking aloud" protocols in which users attempt to narrate the thinking processes they are using, and keystroke records. All three result in enormous volumes of data. Both video tape and thinking aloud protocols also require extensive encoding

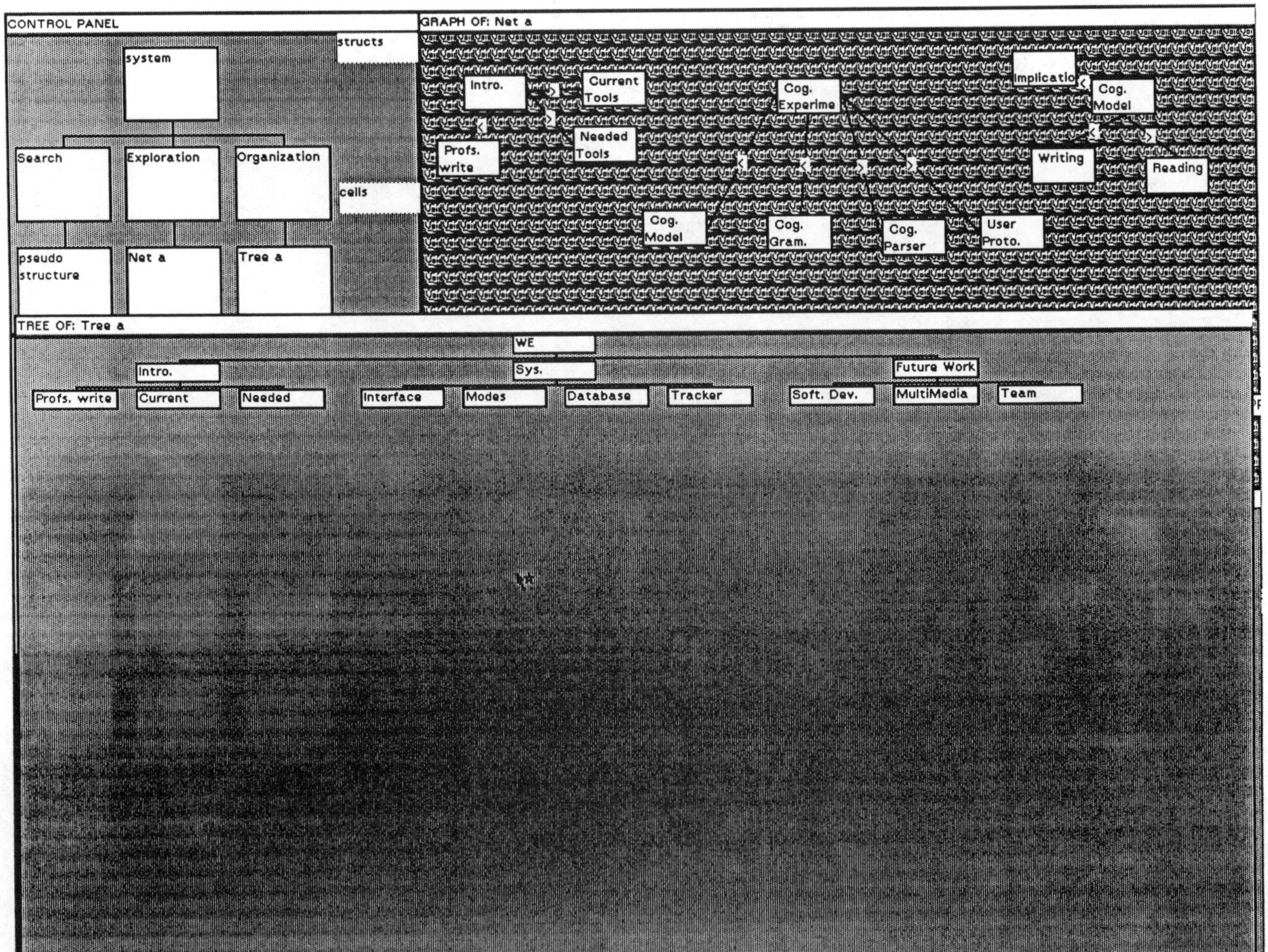

Figure 7—WE hierarchy mode vertical tree

to produce machine-readable data that can be analyzed. Thinking aloud protocols present further theoretical problems for situations where verbalization is not an integral part of the task being performed, such as tasks in which users manipulate spatial forms.[9] This is exactly the situation presented by our system. Writers, particularly during the exploratory and organizational phases of writing, often think spatially and abstractly, rather than verbally. For these reasons, we believe the relatively large-grained record produced by the tracker, representing the operational history of a session will provide more usable and reliable data for our purposes than more traditional protocols.

The cognitive model on which the system was built is expressed as a grammar. While it superficially resembles the GOMS model of Card, Moran, and Newell,[10] it goes beyond their framework. One distinction is the extension to a quasi context sensitive grammar. Context free productions are not powerful enough to handle user operations for this application. More importantly, the grammar can be used to develop a parser to analyze the protocols generated by the tracker. The trees that result from parsing the sequence of operations performed by a user during a session constitute a formal representation of that user's strategy for the session. Thus, we have a concrete way of comparing the strategies of different groups of users, such as those of experts and novices. Additional display and statistical analysis techniques will permit us to play back a user's session, graph distributions of specific operations over time, look for "cognitive rhythms," and note combinations of functions frequently used together.

On the basis of this information, we will revise the cognitive model, as appropriate, and then refine the system. Thus, we hope to set-up a development loop in which the system is designed in accord with a well-defined model of the user's interaction with the system at a cognitive level, implemented in a fast prototype environment for initial testing, ported to an actual-use configuration for more extensive experimentation, and then systematically revised in accord with empirical results.

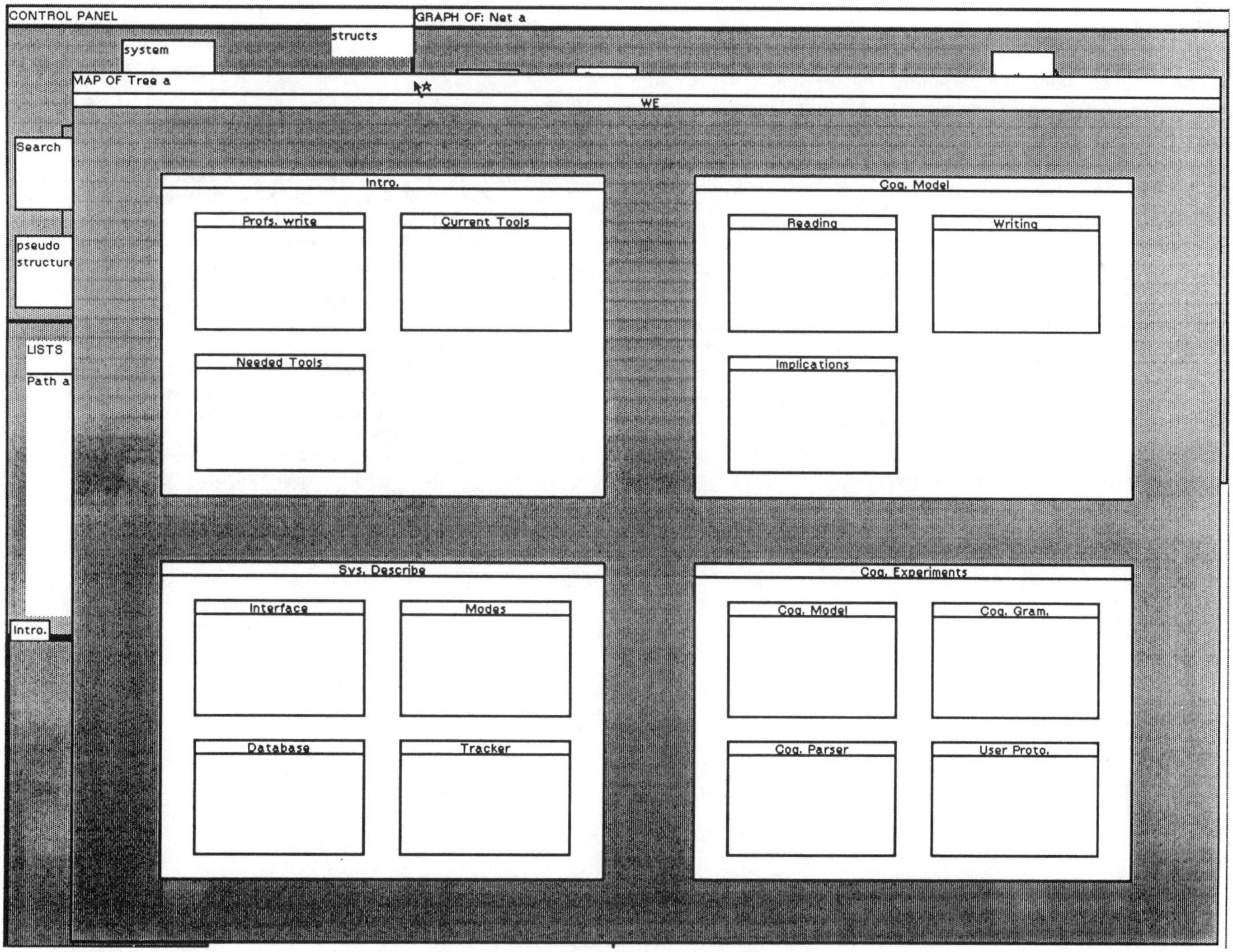

Figure 8—WE hierarchy mode vertical box

FUTURE WORK

While the system we have described is intended as an aid for professionals who write, it can be extended to other applications. Basically, the system provides a general visual interface for creating, editing, and displaying directed graphs of abstract nodes that can be associated with typed data. A number of other applications can be modeled in these terms. We plan to extend our work into three other areas.

First, we want to extend the system from a single user system to a multiple user system for distributed environments. The central database underlying the system can facilitate team development of a structure and collaborative efforts. We also want to add a simultaneous teleconferencing facility in which several team members can view the same display on their respective workstations while they work on the same underlying data structure. This will be done in an environment in which switchable voice and video can be added to permit them to discuss their work and to see one another. We will also try to extend the cognitive model to characterize the cognitive/communication acts of a team of individuals working together to construct a single, integrated conceptual structure and then test that model, analogously.

Second, we will extend the system to include other forms of data. Since a node is an abstract, typed entity, other forms of content can be included by extending the set of node types and by providing the necessary display and edit functions. The system can, thus, include sound and video sequences from conventional video disks as well as emerging cd/roms by including in the nodes the instructions necessary for the bound function to display that data.

A third application will extend the system to form a vertically integrated environment for software development. The primary extension necessary is to make the graph multi-dimensional. In this way, one two-dimensional plane can be assigned to functional specifications, a second to source code, a third to executable modules, a fourth to test results, and so on. While each level represents a large field of research, we will limit our work to a small subset of tools in each, such as Objective C and C in the source level, so that we can concentrate on issues of interaction between levels.

ACKNOWLEDGEMENTS

A number of people have contributed their ideas and their labors to this project. We wish to thank the following graduate students: John Walker, Valerie Kierulf, Greg Berg, Paulette Bush, Yin-Ping Shan, and Katie Clapp. Many of the ideas on which WE is based were refined in discussions with Catherine F. Smith. We also wish to thank Myra Reaves for her help in preparing the manuscript.

REFERENCES

1. Nelson, T.H. "Getting it out of our system." In Schecter, G. (Ed.), Information Retrieval: A Critical View, Washington, D.C.: Thompson Book, 1967.
2. Engelbart, D., and W. English. "A research center for augmenting human intellect." *Proceedings of 1968 FJCC,* 33, Part I, Montvale, N.J.: AFIPS Press, 1968, pp. 395–410.
3. Meyer, B.J.F., D.M. Brandt, and G.J. Bluth. "Use of top-level structure in text: key for reading comprehension of ninth grade students." Reading Research Quarterly, 1, 1980, pp. 72–103. Kieras, D.E. "Initial mention as a signal to thematic content in technical passages." *Memory and Cognition,* 8 (1980) 4, pp. 345–353. Williams, J.P., M.B. Taylor, and S. Ganger. "Text variations at the level of the individual sentence and the comprehension of simple expository paragraphs." Journal of Education Psychology, 73 (1981) 6, pp. 851–865.
4. Feiner, S., S. Nagy, and A. van Dam. "An experimental system for creating and reporting interactive graphical documents." *ACM Transactions on Graphics,* 1 (1982) 1, pp. 59–77.
5. Akscyn, R.M. and D.L. McKracken. "The ZOG approach to database management." Tech. Rep. #CMU-CS-84-128, Pittsburgh: The Carnegie-Mellon Computer Science Department, 1984.
6. "Thinktank." Palo Alto, CA: Living Videotext, Inc., 1984.
7. Stelovsky, J. "XS-2: The user interface of an interactive system." Ph.D. Dissertation, Zurich: Swiss Federal Institute of Technology, 1984.
8. Smith, J.B., S.F. Weiss, and G.J. Ferguson. "MICROARRAS: An Overview." Technical Report #86-017, Chapel Hill, NC: UNC Department of Computer Science, 1986.
9. Nisbett, R.E. and T.D. Wilson. "Telling more than we can know: Verbal reports on mental processes." *Psychological Review,* 84 (1987), pp. 231–259. Ericsson, K.A. and A.S. Simon. "Verbal reports as data." *Psychology Review,* 83 (1980) 3, pp. 215–251.
10. Card, S., T. Moran, and A. Newell. "The Psychology of Human-Computer Interaction." Hillsdale, NJ: Erlbaum Associates, 1983.

Managing data and design process in engineering development

by WILLIAM S. JOHNSON
Sherpa Corporation
San Jose, California

ABSTRACT

A software system model is described which provides effective management of documentation development. The system is particularly well suited for a variety of computer-aided engineering development environments. The system combines for the first time the management of the data files and the development process which creates the files.

INTRODUCTION

Writing is the principal way we have to store and organize information which we want to share with other people. We live increasingly with written documents. Our world overflows with them. They are the essence of modern civilization.

Paper has long been the most efficient medium in which to store documents, but its limits have been exceeded. Paper documents are:

1. Difficult to change
2. Hard to store in large quantities
3. Difficult to deliver quickly
4. Tedious to produce repetitive parts within
5. Not usable by automated tools

These shortcomings are easily overcome with computers. Computer stored data is more compact than paper. It can be easily edited. Repetitive parts need only be produced once, and can then be placed where needed. Single electronic copies can be updated centrally and made widely available to multiple users. And automated tools can both use and produce them.

Some shortcomings of paper documents have not been commonly overcome with computer equivalents. Paper documents:

1. Can only be filed in one order
2. Cannot be located by query on contents
3. Cannot have updates apply automatically to duplicates
4. Require manual handling to: organize, store, control access, retrieve, copy, distribute, and track status

DOCUMENTATION IN ENGINEERING

Of course, the trend to word processing for text documents hardly needs elaboration, but prime examples of the broad application of computer generated documents are also evident in engineering development. The product of development is, after all, just documentation; documentation which tells the manufacturing organization how to build a product. Outstanding examples of computerized documentation in engineering include: drafting in mechanical design, drafting in integrated circuit layout, drafting in printed circuit board layout, and schematic entry in electronic design.

These are graphics documents. The advantages of electronic documentation for graphics is particularly persuasive because graphics documents contain extraordinary amounts of data which is often repetitive and requires frequent editing. Furthermore, electronic graphics documents offer the capability of providing direct input to software development tools like simulators, place and route programs, and automatic checking software. Direct input not only avoids the extra labor of special data entry for these tools, it also guarantees correctness between the document and the input data.

Despite the advantages, organizations still have many problems with electronic documents. The advances of the last few years have focused on improved hardware and document entry and editing. On the hardware side, graphics workstations and personal computers have provided vastly better functionality at greatly improved cost. Drafting software, schematic editors, and improved word processors have complemented these tools on the software side. The result has been to transfer more and more document production to computer. The efficiency of engineering design has been improved for the individual engineer.

Now, new problems are becoming apparent. Overall efficiency of a development project does not depend solely on the productivity of an individual. For example, if a design is partitioned among several people and the results of one person's efforts become the starting point for another, the whole is more than the sum of the parts. Bottlenecks may no longer result from the throughput of an individual; they may now occur at coordination and control points of information shared by a group.

The problems now being recognized include:

1. Ensuring all development steps are completed
2. Reporting the state of completion
3. Keeping track of versions
4. Ensuring correct versions are used
5. Coordinating changes among cooperating users
6. Ensuring compatibility within document sets
7. Facilitating retrieval of documents
8. Preventing unauthorized access
9. Maintaining an audit trail

OVERVIEW OF THE DMS

Sherpa Data Management System™ (DMS) is a software model which provides management services for documentation development and control. The significance of the model is that it integrates in one system heterogeneous design tools and documentation control with total management control.

Here, documentation is meant in the broadest sense. It includes any form of data from text to graphics to machine code, manually generated to machine generated. Thus, the documentation of an engineering project includes the specifications, the mechanical drawings, the schematics, the simulation and checking results, and even the software tools.

By controlling the documentation, the DMS controls the deliverables and hence the development project. This is project management in its truest sense.

Unlike traditional project planning and scheduling software, which can only store information about the deliverables, the DMS controls the deliverables themselves. Without this link, the status of a project must be fed separately into the project planning software. Not only is this extra work but, more importantly, it cannot be guaranteed that the planning system is accurate and up to date at any point in time. DMS does not suffer from this deficiency because it automatically records key management data whenever a document is accessed.

In addition, DMS can control the actual access to data. It prevents access by unauthorized people. It automatically directs access to the appropriate version for the intended use. It even automatically adjusts access privileges depending on the completion status of a document.

In examining the DMS, we divide its functionality along two lines: data and process. The data includes the documents. DMS provides many functions for storing, cataloging, protecting and retrieving documents. The process includes the actions and methodology for developing documents. DMS provides many additional functions for managing the development process. For example, it can store and administer an organization's rules for developing and releasing deliverables.

LIBRARY ANALOGY

Table I compares various terms used with DMS to their common equivalents in a library. The files DMS stores are like the books in the library. A library stores books securely in the stacks, and DMS stores files in a secured directory. Just as the library keeps a record of information about each book on a card in the card catalog, DMS keeps a record for each file in the database.

Books are located in a library through a card catalog, removed from the stacks, and signed out. Only persons who are library members are allowed to check out books. With the DMS, a file is located through its record and copied to a user's directory. Only users with the proper privilege can obtain files. Making a copy of a file is an advantage the library cannot afford. With the DMS, the original is always safely secured; it cannot be lost. The library relies on users to return each book.

The cards in a library card catalog are organized alphabetically for easy retrieval. There are several cards for each book: one filed by title, one filed by author, and one or more filed by subject. This is convenient for users, but requires extra maintenance to coordinate the update of all the cards when a change is made. The DMS allows flexible retrieval and eliminates the duplicate update problem. Only one record is stored for each file, and it can be located by a query on any part of its contents.

Like a library, DMS does not alter the contents of the files it controls. It only catalogs them, secures them, and manages access to them.

TABLE I—Comparison of a reference library and the DMS terms

Reference Library Terms	DMS Terms
book	file
stacks	secure directory
card catalog	database
card	record
subject divider	group record
librarian	database administrator

DOCUMENT SETS

A key feature of Sherpa DMS is the ability to track and control document sets. For example, the mechanical assembly document set in Figure 1 consists of the original specification, a mechanical drawing, a parts list, a group of manufacturing tests, and the user's manual. As each document is developed it is revised several times; it is essential to keep corresponding versions of each deliverable matched.

The DMS permits defining a record to represent a set of documents (e.g., the documents for the mechanical assembly in Figure 1). Such a record is called a group record because it serves to group other records; the records referenced are called component records. The group record is, however, completely identical to any other record. In fact, it too can have a file attached. Since the records it points to might also be group records, a hierarchical set of relationships can be constructed to any nesting depth. In addition, a record can be a component of as many group records as desired. This can be useful in many ways. For example, as shown in Figure 2, a set of drawings of standard parts might all belong to a group record representing a "library" of parts. Each part record might also be referenced by a group record representing any assembly in which it is used. This would give excellent

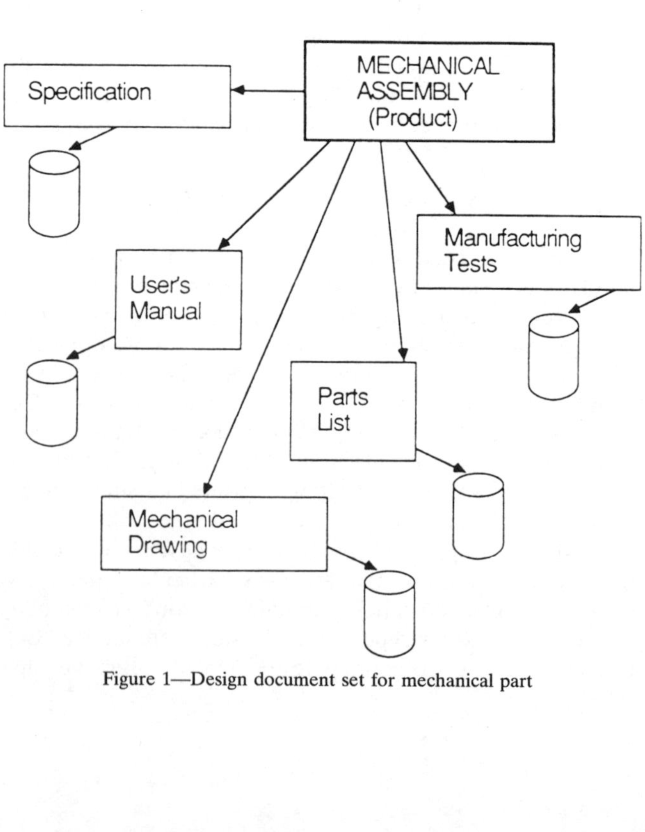

Figure 1—Design document set for mechanical part

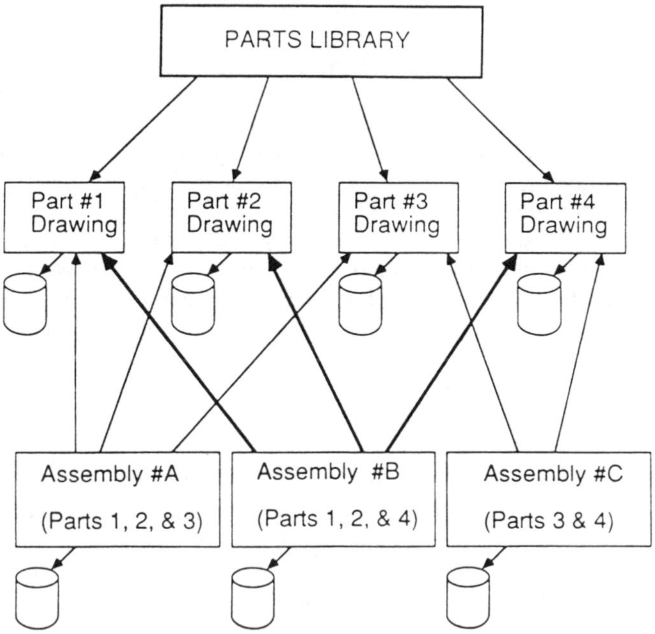

Figure 2—Components library and using assemblies

traceability of where parts are used. An equally useful application would be to track application-specific integrated circuit (ASIC) cell libraries.

This capability is indispensable for retrieval purposes. In the example, the query can be made: "What parts were used in Assembly A?" This, in fact, can become a dynamic parts listing facility which is updated automatically and therefore is always current. Moreover, the inverse query is also supported: "What assemblies use Part 2?" The ability to query by part can be particularly important when a problem is found with a part. All assemblies in jeopardy can quickly and accurately be located. In Figure 2, if a problem is found in the design of Part 3, a quick query of the DMS system would reveal that Assemblies #A and #C must be reviewed to correct the problem. There is no limit to the size of the parts library, nor to the number of higher level references to a parts library. As can be seen from the discussion, group and component records give Sherpa DMS the capability of defining deliverables more complex than a single document. In the following sections, the term *deliverable* is used in this more general sense: a single document, a group of documents, or even a group of other deliverables, each with its own arbitrary hierarchical definition.

GENEALOGY

Group references are useful beyond defining matched sets of deliverables. One use is recording the genealogy of a deliverable. For example, after a design is checked by an automated tool, a reference to the tool can be inserted in the design record, presuming that the tool is also represented by a record in the DMS. Similarly, simulation results for an electrical design might be linked to the drawing they represent as well as to the simulator and the models used.

In the Figure 3 file genealogy, the electrical schematic is verified by the simulation results. The simulation results were produced by executing the simulation program using the netlist as input. The netlist is derived from the component list contained within the electrical schematic. The DMS keeps track of these relationships as both the component and schematic files move through the design process. There is no limit to the size of a defined file genealogy.

The existence of this reference serves to verify that the check was made, and to save an audit trail determining which version of the tool was used. As another example, in software development, an object code module can reference the source code module from which it was derived, as well as the compiler that was used.

When coupled with an environmental shell which sets up such references automatically whenever a tool is run, genealogy tracking can become a very powerful audit trail mechanism capable of reproducing the entire development history of a product. All of this can be accomplished invisibly to users.

PROCESS CONTROL

The DMS provides a substantial set of functions for managing the process of developing documents. In these functions DMS departs from the concept of a library.

A process is an activity which transforms data from one form to a useful new form. The first data in a development may be a creative idea that is transformed by a process into the specification; the specification is processed to produce a drawing; the drawing is processed to check the specification and produce a list of errors, and so on. The entire development project can be modeled as a chain:

data → process → data → process → data

The key object in the DMS's tool kit for process control is the release procedure. The release procedure is similar to a standard policy in an organization; it stores the rules for

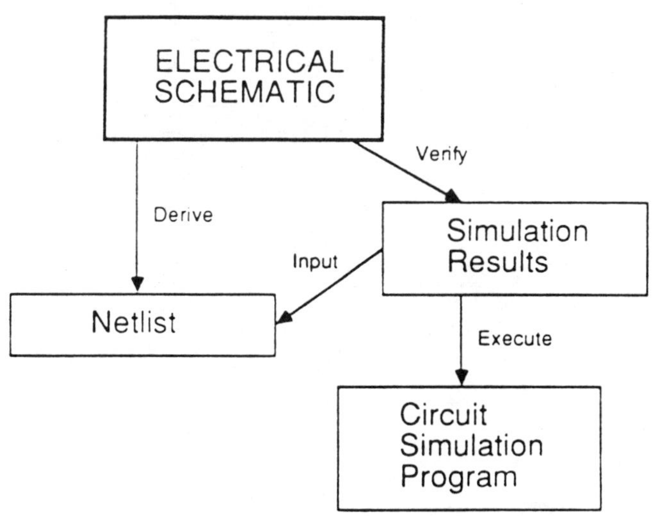

Figure 3—Design file genealogy for electrical product

completing a deliverable. The rules can describe required relationships within the database as well as external signature approvals.

Release procedures are entirely defined by users. As many release procedures as required can be defined and applied to different records. Normally, records are grouped by type with a single release procedure applying to all records of a given type. As shown in Figure 4, each release procedure defines a set of promotion levels representing different stages of completion. In this case, the release procedure is defined for the electrical schematic design process illustrated in Figure 3.

To control the passage of a deliverable from one level to the next, a set of rules, or checks, is defined for each such transition. Rules can define, for example, required component references. It might be required that an ASIC cell be checked by a certain design rule check (DRC) program before release. Using the genealogy relationships described, the release procedure might check to see that the required references are present before allowing promotion.

In addition, electronic signature approvals are supported. The checks in a release procedure for a given level might require that the "owners" of the deliverable approve their own work, or that the project manager approve it. To signify approval, the designated person need only issue a simple command from his or her computer account. DMS checks the user identification of the approver and logs the approval in the record for the deliverable.

Thus, the basic components of a release procedure are promotion levels and checks. Figure 4 illustrates a four-level release procedure for the electrical schematic of Figure 3. In this procedure, design completion checks and management approvals must be completed to allow the design to be promoted. For the design to move from Level 0 to Level 1, ALL of the following conditions must be met: The design must be approved by the design originator engineer using an electronic

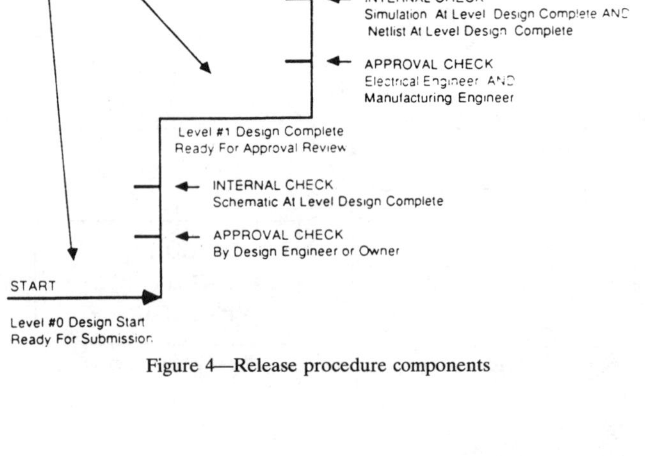

Figure 4—Release procedure components

password signoff, AND DMS must perform an internal check that the schematic does exist and is at Level 1 Design Complete. All of the levels and checks in a release procedure are user-defined and there is no limit to the number of steps or the number of approvals between levels.

Access privileges for difffering types of user classes may be defined for each level. DMS allows classes of users to be defined, and allows those privileges to change as the promotion level of a design using the release procedure changes. A typical example is to allow a design engineer full access privilege prior to design review, but to limit the engineer's privileges to read-only after the design is submitted for review.

ACCESS MANAGEMENT

At each level of a release procedure a set of access privileges for all users is defined. When a deliverable reaches a new level, access privileges are automatically adjusted to those prescribed at that level. In another example considering an ASIC cell library, access at lower levels might be confined to the developing engineers but at a higher level, for example at a level called "released," access might be opened up to the community at large for execution, but not for update.

Part of the power of release procedures is the ability to define them once and apply them over and over again to records of the same type. This implies that release procedures are defined before a project is started, before individuals have been assigned to the project. To support this notion but still allow access privileges to be defined within the release procedure, Sherpa DMS supports the notion of user classes.

A user class is a generic group of people with similar job functions. User classes are completely defined by the user organization. They would commonly be job titles within the organization like engineer, draftsperson, and project manager. Any number of user classes can be defined. Within a release procedure, access privileges are assigned to user classes.

In the release procedure introduced in Figure 4, the access privileges could be defined, for example, for the design originator or design engineer, an electronic engineer, a manufacturing engineer, and the engineering manager. The access privileges for each person can change as the promotion level of the design changes. For example, once the design originator submits a design for review, his or her access privilege changes. In "Level 0 Design Start," the design originator may list, modify, update, delete, export, and promote the design. However, once the design has been submitted and promoted to "Level 1 Design Complete," the design originator's privilege is changed to list and export only.

User classes are associated with the personnel on a design project. Sherpa DMS understands the notion of a project in essentially the same sense it is used in most development organizations. As defined by the DMS, a project is a group of people collectively working on common data. When a project is formed, individuals are assigned to user classes for that project. If a record requires approval by the project manager, DMS checks to which project the record belongs, and then requires that only the project manager of that project approve. Further, the DMS accommodates different job responsibilities on different projects. The project leader on one job may be a design reviewer on a second job, and the design originator of a third.

ALERT FACILITY

Often the completion of a deliverable requires commencement of activity by someone else. Efficient communication of completed tasks is essential to keeping a project rolling. The DMS provides a mechanism for automatic communication of messages based on activity in the database. This is called the alert facility.

An alert has a trigger and an executable. The trigger is a description combining a list of records with a list of commands. When one of the commands is executed against one of the records, the alert is triggered. To trigger an alert means to execute the command procedure associated with it. Commonly the procedure would send a mail message to a predefined distribution list, but actually it can process any legal commands. It could even cause further activity within the DMS itself.

Alerts may be tailored from almost any definable DMS event. (See Figure 5.) An alert has a trigger and an executable. The trigger is a description of what DMS event must occur in order for the alert to execute. The executable defines what the trigger will do and to whom it will be distributed. In Figure 5, the trigger event occurs when any design within the release procedure reaches Level #1 Design Complete. The alert executable triggers the electronic mail utility to send a message to the electronic and mechanical engineers and to the engineering manager. The triggered action will distribute the message: "New Design Submitted on 09/30/86 At Level #1 Design Complete. Ready For Approval Review."

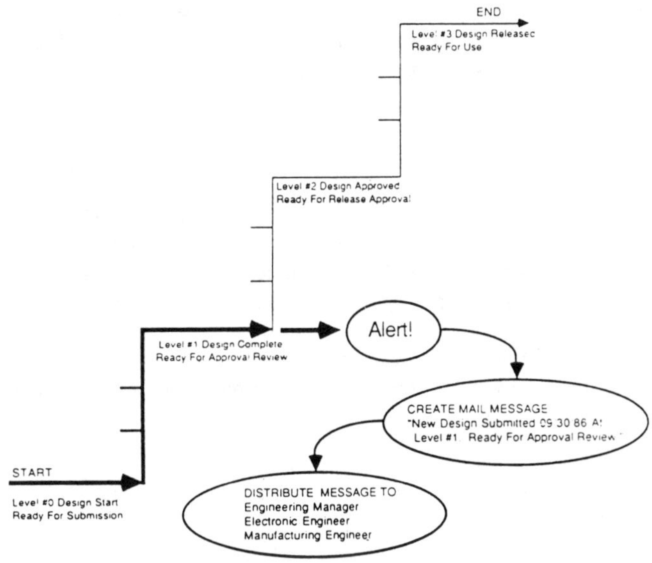

Figure 5—Alert creating electronic mail message

THE DMS SUMMARY

As summarized in Figure 6, the DMS manages the computer files containing documentation and it manages the process of development as well. Running in the DEC VAX/VMS environment, the DMS is able to create an exact model of the design engineering organization as well as its release policies and procedures.

The key element is the ability to create a release procedure that defines the design process at all management levels. Using dynamic access privileges and internal checks, the DMS makes sure that the design process follows exactly the procedure specified by the engineering organization's management and simultaneously automatically creates audit and status information about the progress of the design.

Any type of computer file may be managed by the DMS, including data files, software applications, utilities, and tools. In addition, the DMS will manage off line data in the form of archive files or specifications. It provides full security and audit trail functionality to provide total management accountability for design validity and verification. Management status reporting is provided through both formalized alert reporting and ad-hoc queries.

By creating a model of the engineering organization, the DMS provides design process control that matches exactly with the way an organization has always wanted to manage the design process.

Thus, the DMS enhances productivity of designers, engineers, and management for a number of computer-aided design applications, including VLSI, electronics, mechanical, and software. It can integrate all parts of the design process while controlling the release procedures and access privileges to all engineering data. When a project is promoted up through its various levels, the DMS ensures that those access privileges are automatically updated and the release procedures enforced. Any design file can be managed by the DMS, including schematic diagrams, parts lists, design drawings,

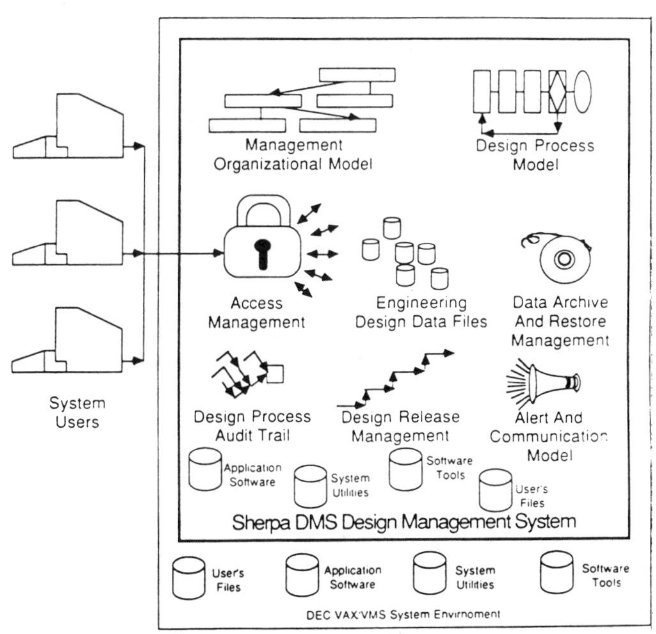

Figure 6—The DMS functional summary

manuals, specifications, as well as archived versions of any of these. The DMS keeps track of the relationship of each file to various projects so that engineers can share common data.

CONCLUSION

We have described a new software system, the DMS, for managing documentation and documentation development. It is particularly applicable to engineering development. The principal benefits to the end user organization are:

1. Shorter development cycles
2. Reduced errors and blunders in managing CAD/CAM/CAE data
3. Greater confidence in design integrity
4. Faster reaction time to new market opportunities
5. More engineering time to design, rather than just managing the data
6. More accurate status reporting to all levels of an organization
7. Improved engineering communications
8. A complete record of engineering and management actions

Presently the DMS is being applied in mechanical, electronic, and software engineering applications. Its principal strength is that it is equally applicable to many applications, and therefore can be efficiently applied to complex projects with components in several engineering disciplines.

Possible productivity improvements using PDES

by LARRY O'CONNELL
Sandia National Laboratories
Albuquerque, New Mexico

ABSTRACT

Product Data Exchange Specification (PDES) is being developed to package product model data for communication among disparate computer-aided systems. Early hopes were that data transfer would be less costly than manual reentry of the design. However, transferring a design to a different computer-aided system can also involve costly manual intervention. PDES concerns the augmented packaging of data so that the data can be "understood" by systems that receive it. PDES uses a 3-schema methodology. The two normal views for describing data are the internal storage schema and the external application view. The third schema interposes a way of organizing the information to provide a more stable reference for each of the other two views. Application data modeling is also used in the development of this conceptual schema. Important public-domain research on product-design information exchange is being conducted for PDES. Because it is the first systematic investigation of product-design information transfer, it may represent the best chance for realizing the goal of improved productivity through CAE Systems Interface Standards.

BACKGROUND

The Product Data Exchange Specification (PDES) is a project which intends to develop a better way to package product model data. The aim is to communicate meaning as well as facts among disparate computer-aided systems. It is one of the four current projects of the Initial Graphics Exchange Specification (IGES) Organization.[1] The National Bureau of Standards sponsors the organization and is currently providing the following personnel: (1) Chairman, Bradford Smith, (2) Coordinator, Gaylen R. Rinaudot, and (3) two committee chairmen. Other officers and members are from private industry, other government agencies, universities, and small partnerships. The opinions expressed in this paper, however, remain those of the author alone; they do not necessarily reflect those of Sandia National Laboratories or the IGES organization.

The IGES organization has developed an exchange format for transferring design information between disparate CAD systems. This format is the IGES Version 3.0[2] and is upwardly compatible with IGES Versions 1.0[3] and 2.0.[4] However, PDES is being developed to provide new capabilities which will not be compatible with the IGES file format. A one-way translator will be furnished and will convert IGES files to PDES files. IGES files frequently need additional human interpretation; this need will be minimized with PDES files.

Data transfer is productive whenever the time and effort expended is less than that required to manually reenter a design into the target system. However, transferring designs to a different, computer-aided system often involves some costly manual intervention. Packaging the data to enable the receiving system to "understand" it is the problem the PDES addresses. PDES, unlike most other data exchange formats, seems to be unique in the use of information modeling together with a 3-schema methodology. This methodology interposes a third way of organizing the data between the internal storage schema and the external application view(s). This provides a more stable reference for the other two views. It also reduces the trauma caused by changes to internal storage methods, or to application data formats.

The goal of PDES is to make a product-design model, created on one computer-aided tool, that is readily communicable to other computer-aided systems.

PRODUCTIVITY IMPROVEMENTS

Improvements within Islands of Automation

One of the primary benefits of Computer-aided engineering (CAE) is the increased productivity realized by the enhanced automation at each workstation. Many vendors and users appear to be working hard to enhance productivity in this way. Unfortunately, many naive users have assumed it would be easy to transfer finished designs to computer-aided manufacturing systems. However, Thomas R. Smith[5] writes: "An integrated design and manufacturing process composed of an ever-changing set of independently developed and rapidly evolving tools, configured by different organizations, places severe demands on the design of the structures and transfer mechanisms used to 'glue' the process together."

Minimization of Repackaging and Rekeying

Another way to enhance productivity would be to reduce the human involvement needed on receipt of a file from another workstation. It often happens that the file received has useful data that must be reformatted or that must be associated with a meaningful feature of the receiving system. For example, one user may have developed some utilities to extract printed wiring board outline data from Level 12. If the sender had stored that type of information in Level 34, the recipient might have to discover this was done and then adjust for it. If the meaning of the data had been attached to the data in a way that made sense to the machine, the rearrangement could be automated or eliminated. Examples of netlist reformatting are also available. Another duplication of effort is frequently encountered when information, available at the source, gets lost in the exchange process and must be rekeyed by the recipient.

The area of enhancing productivity seems amenable to standardization, and is being addressed by many groups. Among the U.S. groups working on exchange formats or design languages for Electrical or Electronic products are: ANSI Y14, IEEE, VHSIC, ATLAS, EDIF, IPC, ICAM, CAM-I, EIA, and NEMA. Others, mentioned in an unpublished paper by A. J. Gibbons,[6] include ISO TC 184, ESPRIT, ISO TC 97, DIN, AFNOR, MAP, TOP, ASTM, and IEC. The scope and methodology of only one of these groups, Working Group 1 of Subcommittee 4 of ISO TC 184, is of interest here. This group (ISO TC184/SC4/WG1) includes many members of the IGES organization working on PDES.

At present, those working with the PDES project are concentrating their efforts on communicating a complete product model; this model must contain sufficient information so it is readily interpreted by numerous receiving systems. The intended receiving systems include computer-aided systems to do generative process planning and directed inspection plus generation and verification of numerically controlled cutter paths. The methodology being used borrows from lessons learned in database design. In particular, the 3-schema approach described by the ANSI/X3/SPARC Database Task Group in 1975[7] has been adopted. Even though an exchange file is not exactly equivalent to a data-base, it is subject to some of the same pitfalls. Use of the 3-schema approach should help avoid these pitfalls. The PDES methodology[8,9] consists of 3-layer architecture, reference models and formal languages.

PDES seems unique in the breadth of applications which can be addressed and in functions which can be supported. It also seems to be among the first exchange standardization efforts to apply an information modeling methodology to develop a conceptual schema.

BREADTH OF APPLICATIONS AND FUNCTIONS

Application disciplines include mechanical, electrical, architectural, and finite-element modeling. Reference models are also being developed for support functions which include solid geometry, curves and surfaces, presentation, drafting, manufacturing, tolerances, and technical publications.

Mechanial Products

The mechanical products for which reference models are being developed are: piece parts (flat plates, turned parts, bent plates, complex surface parts, and extruded parts); permanent groupings of parts (like welded assemblies); and temporary groupings of parts (like bolted assemblies).

Electronics

The electrical/electronic products for which reference models are being developed are: integrated circuits and standard cells, hybrid microcircuits, printed wiring boards and assemblies, cables, and 3-dimensional wiring harnesses.

Architecture

The Architectural Engineering and Construction Committee has begun work on reference models for distribution systems, plant/building/sites, structures, geographic information, buildings, and power-generating plants.

Finite Element Modeling

The Finite Element Modeling Committee has begun working on reference models for local coordinate systems, geometric properties, material properties, post processing, analysis, and results.

Support Functions

No less important than the above application areas, are the reference models for support functions, such as, solid geometry, curves and surfaces, tolerances, presentation, drafting, manufacturing, and technical publications. PDES is being developed to provide support throughout the life cycle of the modeled products.

METHODOLOGY APPLIED IN PDES

Need for 3-schema Methodology

Even though a standardized exchange format for use among different computer-aided systems is not identical to a database, some similarities exist. Finding certain kinds of information in either the database or the exchange file depends not only on the information having been included, but on a format that enables retrieval of that information. For example, a database of address labels needs a separate field for ZIP codes if one ever intends to sort data by ZIP code. If the ZIP code is simply the last 5 or 10 characters in the city-state-ZIP line of the address, it will usually be impractical to ask the database to give you any information on ZIP codes.

The same assertions apply to a file of address labels you wish to send to a colleague. If the file structure does not isolate and identify ZIP codes, the recipient will be hard pressed to have his software find them quickly. Note that the receiving system might easily throw away the carefully crafted distinction if the target database was not designed to use it. Furthermore, asking for the street address of "Mike Hall" might not give the desired result if the database or the exchange file has more than one "Mike Hall."

The 3-schema methodology was developed to circumvent such difficulties in the design of databases. The three schemas[7] are: (1) the internal view of the data as seen by the system, (2) the external view of the data as seen by the application programmer, and (3) the conceptual schema (the enterprise's description of the information as modeled in the database). Tsichritzis and King[7] write: "Without the assistance of the indirection provided by the conceptual schema it becomes awkward to write applications that can survive the inevitable variations in the characteristics of the stored data."

Importance of the Conceptual Schema

The ANSI/X3/SPARC DBMS Framework Report[7] emphasizes the importance of the conceptual schema:

> "The conceptual schema contains the definitions of entities and their properties and relationships. No entities or properties may be referenced in the database unless they are defined in this schema. . . it is likely to remain more stable than either the internal or external schemas; hence, internal and external schemas are prepared and mapped against the relatively stable conceptual schema rather than against each other, in order to insulate one from the other."

Information Modeling of Applications

Information modeling is also being used in PDES to help define a small, integrated, and clearly labeled set of data packages which will efficiently provide all the data needed in each application or function. In the PDES methodology, the various external schemas are being developed by different groups at the same time. The group most knowledgeable in each application or subject area has been developing an information reference model for that particular application. Each model is equivalent to an external schema. Where necessary, the groups have been considering many application views at the same time and have been incorporating all the data needs into one model.

The Electrical Application Committee faced an unusual situation. Because the background of the people in the Committee did not cover the full range (integrated circuits, standard cells, hybrid microcircuits, printed wiring boards and assemblies, cables, and 3-dimensional wiring harnesses) of applications to be addressed, help was obtained from the Design Automation Standards Subcommittee (DASS) of the IEEE Computer Society. At this writing, the models are being developed by the Cal Poly Task Team in Pomona, California under the sponsorship of the IEEE DASS. The host for this activity is the Department of Electrical and Computer Engineering at the California Polytechnic University.

Integration at the Logical Layer

Those models judged to be ready are also now being integrated by the Logical Layer Committee. (The PDES term, "Logical Layer," corresponds to the conceptual schema used by ANSI/X3/SPARC.) As deemed necessary, this Committee will consult with designated developers of the reference models being reviewed to make sure nothing significant gets lost in the integration process.

The integration task involves minimizing the kinds of entities needed. In this context, entities are roughly equivalent to labeled data receptacles. This minimization is done while concurrently assuring that the conceptual schema has everything needed to support both the physical layer (the internal schema) and all the reference models which constitute the external schema. The resulting logical layer will be described in a formal computer-readable language known as EXPRESS. The reference models will also be described in EXPRESS and will be made available to application programmers.

The application modeling and integration of models must be done well, or redundant data may be filed and transmitted needlessly. Worse, needed data may be retrieved or received too slowly, too expensively, or not at all.

To ensure the widest possible coverage and to ease conversion from a national standard to an international standard, the work is partly being done and is being reviewed by members of the ISO TC 184/SC4/WG1. This is in addition to those workers/reviewers who reside in the United States. Our liaison reports: "The work to be accomplished under ISO TC 184/SC4 is the development of a new International Standard (IS), currently called STEP, for the exchange of digital product data between computer application systems."[10] Thus, it is our hope that PDES will not only be the principal contribution to, but that it will be identical to STEP (Standard for Exchange of Product Model Data). A resolution to that effect has been adopted by both the IGES Steering Committee and the ISO TC 184/SC4/WG1.[11] The identity of the two standards would conform with the General Agreement on Tariffs and Trade (GATT) Standards Code. According to John Rankine,[12] the code "stipulates that governments should use international standards, where they exist, in national technical rules and regulations."

CONCLUSIONS

The aim of the efforts described in this paper is the exchange of product model data with no human intervention. This may be the first time that the 3-schema methodology will have been applied to an exchange format, rather than to a database. PDES is conducting important research on information exchange as it relates to product data. The lessons learned will be made available to all who are striving for Computer Integrated Manufacturing. Moreover, because it is the first systematic investigation of product-design information transfer, it seems to offer the best hope for realization of the goal of improved productivity through CAE Systems Interface standards.

ACKNOWLEDGEMENTS

The support of Bert Gibbons and Jack Jones is gratefully acknowledged. Jack reviewed drafts and helped clarify ideas; Bert assisted the author by suggesting references and by reviewing drafts.

REFERENCES

1. Smith, B., and G. R. Rinaudot. "Welcome to Initial Graphics Exchange Specification." (Newcomer Material). National Bureau of Standards, January, 1987.
2. Smith, B., and J. Wellington. "Initial Graphics Exchange Specification (IGES), Version 3.0." NBSIR 86-3359, National Bureau of Standards, April, 1986.
3. Nagel, R. N., W. N. Braithwaite, and P. R. Kennicott. "IGES Version 1.0." NBSIR 80-1978 (R), National Bureau of Standards, January, 1980.
4. Smith, B. M., K. M. Brauner, P. R. Kennicott, M. Liewald, and J. Wellington. "Initial Graphics Exchange Specification (IGES), Version 2.0." NBSIR 82-2631 (AF), National Bureau of Standards, February, 1983.
5. Smith, T. R. "A Data Architecture for an Uncertain Design and Manufacturing Environment." In *Proceedings of the 22nd Design Automation Conference,* Los Alamitos, California: IEEE Computer Society Press, 1985.
6. Gibbons, A. J. "Information about Standards Development for Support of Information Management, Data Sharing, and Data Exchange," 1986. A private communication.
7. Tsichritzis, D., and A. King, (eds). "The ANSI/X3/SPARC DBMS Framework. Report of the Study Group on Database Management Systems." Montvale, New Jersey: AFIPS Press, 1975.
8. Brauner, K. "The Preliminary Report of the Ad Hoc Committee on the Content, Methodology, and Scheduling of IGES Version 3." July 11, 1984.
9. Brauner, K., and D. Briggs. "The Second Draft Report of the Ad Hoc Committee on the Content and Methodology of the IGES Version 3. (The Second PDES Report.)" November 12, 1984.
10. Gibbons, A. J. "Evolving from CAD/CAM/CAE/CAP/CAT to CIM: The role of Information Management and Industry Standards," 1986. An unpublished article.
11. ISO TC 184/SC4/WGI, Document Number N96. "Update to Document 0.0, STEP Project Plan. Joint Development Agreement." January 6, 1987.
12. Rankine, L. J. "Leadership and Responsibility in International Standardization." *ASTM Standardization News,* December, 1984.

A real world application of EDIF

by MICHAEL A. WATERS
Motorola SPS, Inc.
Mesa, Arizona

ABSTRACT

This paper describes the first application within Motorola of the Electronic Design Interchange Format (EDIF), which is used to exchange Macrocell Array design information. The software based on this development is in regular use to support Motorola's Macrocell Array products in the marketplace. The paper examines some of the issues involved, including both the design library and the completed design portion of the problem, illustrating the solutions that EDIF provides. An actual example from one of Motorola's Macrocell Array libraries and a small design example using those libraries are used to show how the relevant information is expressed using EDIF.

INTRODUCTION

This paper describes the first use within Motorola of the first release of the EDIF standard, version 1 0 0.[1] The application is oriented to a mainframe based Macrocell Array design system, which was in use when the project began. In each case, examples are derived from actual library or design data used in commercial designs although in some cases numeric information has been altered to protect proprietary information. Copies of the actual design databases and reference documents may be obtained by contacting Motorola's ASIC customer engineering group.*

Figure 1 shows the overall scheme used; EDIF is used as a bidirectional interface between Motorola and an external customer. In planning this interface, six distinct classes of data were identified—three types of library and three types of data—to describe the completed design. For convenience, this paper is organized along these same lines, describing first the three types of library data and then the three types of completed design data.

In many cases, cell names and other EDIF identifiers have been chosen to aid human understanding of the EDIF information. This information would not be used by a computer system other than as a unique identifier of some EDIF object. That is to say, if the library identifier "MOTOROLA_MCA2" was to be changed to some other unique character string, such as "FOO_BAR", throughout the file, then the semantics of that file are unchanged.

The examples used in this paper were drawn from Motorola Macrocell Array libraries for semicustom integrated circuit (IC) design, but the techniques presented apply equally well to any component library that EDIF can handle. This can include all types of electronic components, semicustom ICs, full-custom ICs, standard part ICs, passive components, board level parts, or complete modules.

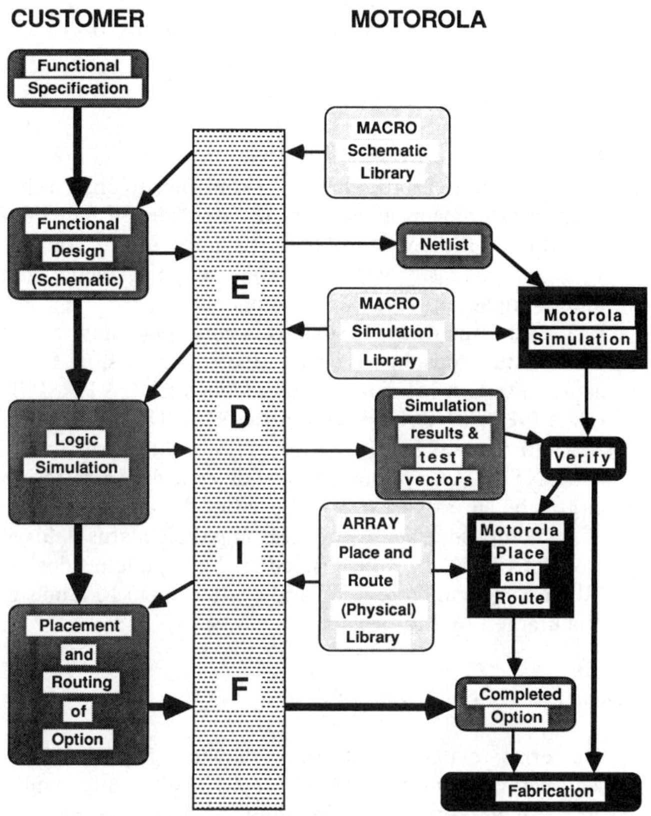

Figure 1—An overview of the EDIF based Macrocell interface

MACROCELL ARRAY COMPONENT LIBRARIES

A component library typically reflects the product offering of a particular manufacturer. It must include enough information for a designer to successfully use the part in a design and to order the correct part from the manufacturer.

For semicustom integrated circuits (ICs) such as Macrocell Arrays, this library becomes an integral part of the design and ordering process for the entire integrated circuit. Since the entire design must then be built by a single manufacturer, the library becomes the basis for the product specification as well. As a result, the accuracy and completeness of the library is a concern of both the manufacturer and the ultimate user of the CAE system. One of the earliest motivations for developing EDIF was to simplify and expedite this transfer of semicustom IC libraries from the manufacturer to the ultimate user.

One of the useful features of EDIF is the tree-structured data organization, which allows an EDIF user to quickly isolate the small portion of an EDIF file of interest for the task at hand, consisting of a LIBRARY, CELL, and VIEW organizational hierarchy. The power of this structure is that it reflects the natural divisions of design information by source and intended use.

Note that the term VIEW implies there is some relationship between different VIEWs of the same cell (although EDIF does not force this), and that the actual object being described by each VIEW is the same object with different information being expressed in different VIEWs. Any number of VIEWs of a cell may be defined; the user selects only those VIEWs of interest for the particular application being addressed.

*Motorola Semiconductor Products Inc., Application Specific Integrated Circuit Division, Customer Engineering Support, Box 20912, Phoenix, Arizona 85036

Motorola divides these libraries by EDIF VIEW as follows:

SCHEMATIC view	Schematic symbols of each macrocell.
NETLIST view	Macrocell internal interconnection of simulator primitives.
BEHAVIOR view	Basic models of simulator primitives.
SYMBOLIC view	Physical information needed to place and route a design. This view includes the appropriate base array information and data for each macrocell.

Component Library Revision Control

One of the concerns of a manufacturer that is maintaining libraries that are not under his direct control is to ensure that any design referencing these libraries uses current and valid information. If there is a problem, it is important to identify it as quickly and easily as possible so it can be corrected with minimum impact on schedules and budgets.

As a result, one of the first steps in checking a design sent for manufacture must be to check the software revision, EDIF revision, and data revision. EDIF supplies EDIFVERSION and ACCOUNTING fields within the STATUS for this purpose. Motorola uses EDIFVERSION for problem tracing and ACCOUNTING as a preliminary validity check of a design on receipt to be sure that every cell used in the design is valid. This is accomplished simply by returning these status fields as part of the EDIF file, which specifies the completed design, and then comparing a revision code within them to a master list maintained by Motorola.

Schematic Symbol Library

The terms related to schematic drawings are often used loosely within industry. To understand a schematic symbol library, it is important to understand the difference between a "schematic symbol," a "schematic drawing," and a "netlist" for our purposes:

netlist:	connectivity data ONLY (which may be extracted from a "schematic drawing")
schematic drawing:	both graphics and connectivity data; references a number of "schematic symbols"
schematic symbol:	a cell with graphics and "connect points" which may, or, may not contain, a "schematic drawing" to describe its contents

The schematic level component library consists of schematic symbols for each macrocell. These symbols can be interconnected to form a schematic drawing for the complete design. Each port of the macrocell is defined as a connect point, both as a symbol, and by using a flag for the user's CAE system. Standardized graphics are defined to display the same symbol both on a workstation and on a drawing. Several property values are supplied for each port to define such items as

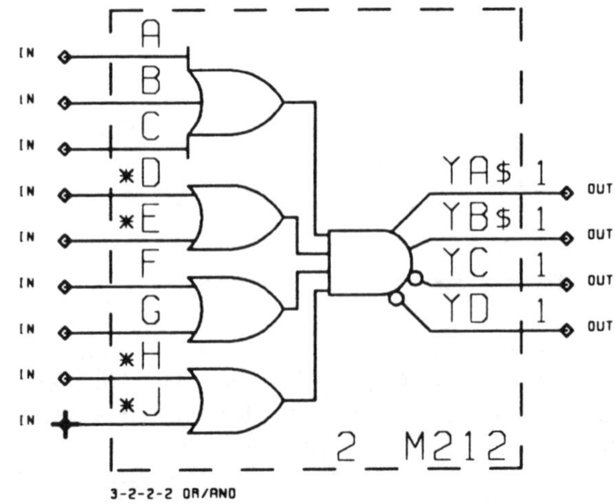

Figure 2—Schematic symbol of the M212 macrocell as displayed by a workstation

loading factors and port names. Similarly, some macrocell related properties, such as macro name and function, are supplied for each macrocell.

Figure 2 shows the schematic symbol of a typical macrocell from Motorola's bipolar macrocell library as it would appear on a workstation. Figure 3 shows a sample of the corresponding EDIF file used to transfer this cell to the workstation. This particular macrocell is a 3-2-2-2 OR/AND function taken from the design manual for the M2500ECL Macrocell Array.[2]

The information in the EDIF file is an electronic form of the data found in the design manual, but it also includes such added information as explicit designation of pin functions.

The basic structure of the file fragment starts at the CELL level, defining the CELL name, its STATUS, and the VIEW of interest. An INTERFACE section defines the external symbol to be used for the macrocell, while the internal schematic may also be defined in the CONTENTS giving as much

```
(CELL M212
 (STATUS (EDIFVERSION 1 0 0)(EDIFLEVEL 0)
  (WRITTEN (TIMESTAMP 1986 6 6 16 37 42)
   (ACCOUNTING PROGRAM "SYM2EDIF v2.00")
    (ACCOUNTING AUTHOR "Motorola ASIC Div.")))
 (VIEW SCHEMATIC MACRO_SCHEMATIC
  (INTERFACE
   (DEFINE INPUT PORT A)
   (PORTIMPLEMENTATION A (FIGUREGROUP SYMBOL_PIN
    (DOT (POINT 0 20000)))
   (DEFINE INPUT PORT B)
    (PORTIMPLEMENTATION B ...)))
   (BODY
    (FIGUREGROUP SCHEMATIC_SYMBOL (FILLPATTERN 1 1 "0")
     (PATH (POINT 5000 15000)(POINT 6750 15000))
     (PATH (POINT 5000 20000)(POINT 6750 20000))
     (PATH (POINT 5000 17500)(POINT 7500 17500))
     (SHAPE
      (ARC (POINT 6750 15750)(POINT 7500 17500)
       (POINT 6750 19250)))...)
    (USERDATA BORDER MACRO_BORDER
     (FIGUREGROUP BORDER (BORDERPATTERN 6 "001111")
      (RECTANGLE (POINT 2500 -2500)
       (POINT 25000 22500))) ...)
```

Figure 3—EDIF SCHEMATIC view of the M212 library cell

or as little data as required about the internal working of the macrocell. For this library, no CONTENTS were required: the INTERFACE provided all of the data required to use the cell in a semi-custom IC design.

Within the INTERFACE, each port of the cell is specified with the DEFINE and PORTIMPLEMENTATION constructs, which give direction, pin symbol, swapability, and display information for the port. The graphical information is an important part of the symbol and is found in one or more FIGUREGROUPs, a construct EDIF uses to identify figures with common attributes, such as layer or color. Finally, a DOT shape is used to define the actual location and shape of the port. EDIF uses similar mechanisms to specify graphical data, whenever needed.

The BODY is used to supply information about the actual graphics of the symbol as seen on a workstation, once again using FIGUREGROUPs containing a number of EDIF SHAPE constructs. This time, a FILLPATTERN specifies that the SHAPE is left "white," or unfilled. A BORDER is defined for the symbol, with a dashed line (BORDERPATTERN).

Simulation Library

The simulation library is divided into two parts, corresponding to usage within simulators. First, a library of cells containing simulator primitive data (BEHAVIOR view) provides a model of each primitive modeled by Motorola's internal simulator. Then, the main macrocell library defines the macrocell functional connections (NETLIST view), which connect the simulator primitives to make a particular macrocell.

Since EDIF V100 does not support an adequate BEHAVIOR view for this purpose, the library contains only the NETLIST view, which interconnects primitives that must be defined outside the EDIF library. This is far from ideal but has proven workable as an interim step and has allowed gate level simulation libraries to be ported with minimal effort.

Simulation example

Figure 4 shows NETLIST view of the M212 library cell shown in Figures 2 and 3. The logic primitives may be found in the LOGCAP user guide;[2] they essentially are Boolean gates with rise and fall delays for each input and output.

The CELL, VIEW, and STATUS are given as before, but the INTERFACE is used merely to DEFINE the ports seen by the user. The CONTENTS is used to describe the inner workings of the cell. First, a LOGCAP primitive is referenced by INSTANCE, with PARAMETERs specifying rise and fall time. Next, the ports of this primitive cell are connected by JOINED statements, either to external cell ports or to other ports within the cell or to instances of primitives. The QUALIFY is used to specify that the named port is the port in a particular instance, rather than the port of the cell being defined. Thus, the complete internal connectivity of the cell is modeled using commonly known primitives. This description provides a highly accurate reference for the receiver, who may

```
(cell M212
 (view netlist LOGCAP
  (STATUS (EDIFVERSION 1 0 0)(EDIFLEVEL 0) ...)
  (interface
   (define input port (multiple A B C D E F G H J))
   (define output port (multiple YA YB YC YD)))
  (contents
   (instance (qualify LOGCAP OR) netlist AA
    (parameter risetime 2 falltime 4))
     (joined AA (qualify AA output_port))
     (joined D (qualify AA input_ports_1))
     (joined E (qualify AA input_ports_2)) ...
   (instance (qualify LOGCAP AND) netlist YYY
    (parameter risetime 0 falltime 0))
     (joined YYY (qualify YYY output_port))
     (joined AA (qualify YYY input_ports_1))
     (joined AD (qualify YYY input_ports_2))
     (joined AC (qualify YYY input_ports_3))
     (joined AF (qualify YYY input_ports_4))
   (define local signal
    (multiple YYY YY AF AC AE AB AD AA)))))
```

Figure 4—LOGCAP NETLIST view of the M212 library cell (ACLOGLIB)

then decide to generate more efficient models using his own system's native primitives.

Physical Library

Structurally, the physical level library is the most complex and the most specific to a given technology. For a Macrocell Array, the library consists of three parts: the base array, the macrocells and the packages available for that array.

Defining the base array

The base array consists of the preassigned components (e.g., transistors, resistors) which are prefabricated, ready for the customizing metal layers. In a Macrocell Array, these metallization patterns come from two sources: pre-designed cells or macrocells, which perform a specific function when placed at the appropriate location; and interconnect wiring, which connects the macrocells to make the design. The places where a macrocell may be used are called sites and have complex symmetry rules associated with them.

The base array cell first defines the sites allowed for placement of the various classes of macrocells using a special section of EDIF called SOCKET definitions. This section defines such information as placement rules, symmetry of the sites, and the location of sites on the chip.

Since the underlying array is quite complex, a hierarchical definition has been used, as shown in Figure 5, with the basic sites defined as cells (e.g., INTERNAL_SITE) containing the basic SOCKET definitions. These are then instantiated into quads of four sites (e.g., INTERNAL_QUAD_SITE). These, in turn, are instantiated into the base array, with a STEP to specify the placement of each array of quad sites on the underlying array. This results in a pattern that can be flattened to show a simplistic representation of the placement sites, or maintained as a hierarchy for a sophisticated placement algo-

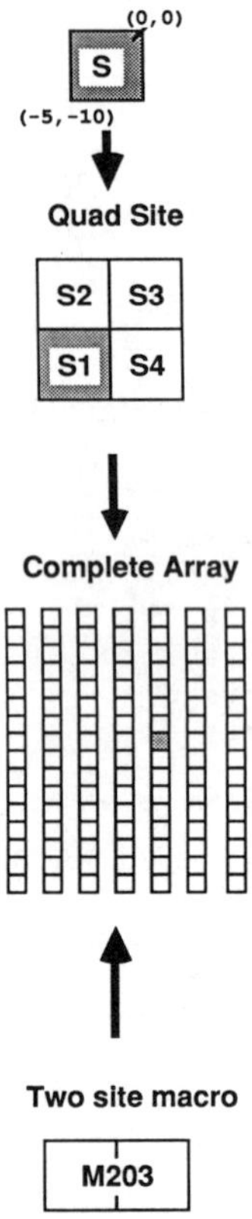


```
(Cell S (View . . .
    (ArrayRelatedInfo ArraySite
    (Socket))))

 (Instance S Physical S1)
 (Instance S Physical S2 (Transform MX))
 (Instance S Physical S3 (Transform R180))
 (Instance S Physical S4 (Transform MY))

(Instance Q Physical Sites
  (Transform (Translate
   (Step 0 7 45)
    (Step 0 16 20))))

(SocketSet
  (Instance S Physical IS1)
  (Instance S Physical IS4 (Transform MY)))
(SocketSet
  (Instance S Physical IS3 (Transform R180))
  (Instance S Physical IS2 (Transform MX)))
```

Figure 5—Definition of sites in a Macrocell Array

rithm or perform complex group interchanges according to the natural structure of the base array to better utilize the available space.

Routing barriers are defined in a similar hierarchical fashion, but using cells which contain only a BODY to define a protection frame consisting of shapes in the appropriate FIGUREGROUPs. Finally, various symbols may be defined, including text, to aid in the consistent display of the base array features on a workstation. This may include such objects as potential sites for macrocell placement, company logos, and boundaries to routing areas.

Figure 6 shows part of an EDIF file that describes the base array for the M2500ECL from the design manual. In this case, the graphical information given reflects the drawing published in the M2500ECL design manual, rather than the actual array geometries.

The individual macrocell

The macrocell library includes the placement site requirements for each macrocell, including any special restrictions (such as a macrocell which may occupy more than one site), and the orientation of the macro required to correctly occupy a site. This data uses a section of EDIF that is complementary to the SOCKET called a PLUG, and the relationships between different PLUGs and SOCKETs define the often com-

```
(CELL BIPOLAR_BASE_ARRAY
 (VIEW SYMBOLIC PHYSICAL (INTERFACE
  (DEFINE INPUT PORT (MULTIPLE P002 P003 ...
   P122 P123 P124 ))
   (DEFINE INOUT  PORT (MULTIPLE P019 ...
   P104 P105 P106 P107 ))))
 (VIEW SYMBOLIC SITE
  (INTERFACE
   (ARRAYRELATEDINFO BASEARRAY))
  (CONTENTS
   (INSTANCE CLOCK_GENERATOR_SITE SITE ID
    (TRANSFORM R0 (TRANSLATE 59 10)))
   (INSTANCE INTERNAL_QUAD_SITE SITE ID1
    (TRANSFORM R0
     (TRANSLATE (STEP 19 10 10) (STEP 17 11 10)))) ...
   (INSTANCE ARRAY_ROUTING_BARRIERS_LEVEL_1 SITE ID6
    (TRANSFORM R0
     (TRANSLATE (STEP 23 10 10) (STEP 17 11 10))))
   (INSTANCE ARRAY_ROUTING_BARRIERS_LEVEL_2 SITE ID7
    (TRANSFORM R0
     (TRANSLATE (STEP 16 10 10) (STEP 17 11 10))))
     ... )))

(CELL INTERNAL_QUAD_SITE
 (VIEW SYMBOLIC SITE
  (INTERFACE (BODY
    (FIGUREGROUP  ROUTING_LEVEL_1
     (RECTANGLE (POINT 0 0) (POINT 5 6))
  (CONTENTS
   (INSTANCE INTERNAL_SITE SITE IS1 )
   (INSTANCE INTERNAL_SITE SITE IS2 (TRANSFORM MX))
   (INSTANCE INTERNAL_SITE SITE IS3
    (TRANSFORM R180))
   (INSTANCE INTERNAL_SITE SITE IS4 (TRANSFORM MY))
(CELL INTERNAL_SITE (COMMENT "INTERNAL ARRAY SITE")
 (VIEW SYMBOLIC SITE
  (INTERFACE
   (ARRAYRELATEDINFO ARRAYSITE (SOCKET)))))
```

Figure 6—A Macrocell Array base array definition

plex rules for correctly using a given macrocell in a given site. Also defined in the cell are any macrocell related routing barriers, physical port names, port locations, and relevant data about internal port to port connections, if any. Symbols may be defined for display of the macrocell on a workstation during the placement process. These symbols are distinct from those defined for the schematic drawing, and are used only for the PHYSICAL view of the design.

Figure 7 shows the SYMBOLIC view of the M212 library cell from Figure 2. This view gives the information required to successfully place this macrocell on the base array and to route wiring to the appropriate pins. Note that the internal routing of the cell (CONTENTS) is not given since this is not needed to use the macrocell in the array.

The INTERFACE defines a BORDER for display purposes similar to the one defined for the schematic symbol. As before, the physical appearance of each port is defined in a PORTIMPLEMENTATION. But in a PHYSICAL view, this specifies a routing target for a router, in this case a DOT. Some connectivity is specified, showing that port YD and SYD are equipotential and that a router may wish to use this as a feed-through connection. Finally, the ARRAYRELATEDINFO section defines the correct placement information using SOCKETSETs to specify the required sites and the orientation of the cell if it uses the site.

```
(CELL M212
 (VIEW SYMBOLIC PHYSICAL
  (STATUS ...)
  (INTERFACE
   (BODY
    (USERDATA BORDER BORDER
     (FIGUREGROUP BODY_EXTENT
      (RECTANGLE (POINT -320 -400)(POINT 320 0)))))
   (PORTIMPLEMENTATION YD
    (FIGUREGROUP R_LEV_2 (DOT (POINT 0 -50)))) ...
   (JOINED YD SYD)
   (DEFINE INPUT PORT (MULTIPLE A F C G B E H D J))
   (DEFINE OUTPUT PORT (MULTIPLE YD SYD YA YC YB))
   (ARRAYRELATEDINFO ARRAYMACRO
    (PLUG
     (SOCKETSET (INSTANCE INT SITE IS1)
      (INSTANCE INT SITE IS2 (TRANSFORM MY))
                             (TRANSFORM MY))
     (SOCKETSET
      (INSTANCE INT SITE IS3 (TRANSFORM R180))
      (INSTANCE INT SITE IS4 (TRANSFORM MX))
                             (TRANSFORM MY)))))))
```

Figure 7—PHYSICAL (place and route) view of the M212 macrocell

THE COMPLETED DESIGN

The requirements and capability of Macrocell Array users varies widely—from a small customer that is a first time user of Macrocell Arrays to a large sophisticated customer that designs dozens of arrays a year. This disparity is reflected in the different levels of required interface to the manufacturer. The small customer needs to minimize the risk involved and will use its own equipment just to generate a schematic drawing of the part, extracting just a netlist from which the rest of the design work is done. The large customer usually has installed equipment and procedures to do most, if not all, of the design in-house, sending a netlist, test patterns, and even physical or macrocell placement and interconnect routing information.

The sections of this paper are organized to correspond to each of the types of information to be transferred by means of the EDIF description. These three information groups are:

Netlist: Connectivity information normally derived from the schematic drawing, including the macrocells used for the design and their interconnection.

Test Pattern: Simulation input and output, in terms of signals applied to, and expected from, each pin of the device.

Physical: Defines macrocell placement in the array, routing of wiring and other manufacturing related information.

Three EDIF LIBRARY level sections are required regardless of the information sent: DESIGN, EXTERNAL, and TECHNOLOGY.

The DESIGN construct specifies the "root" or topmost cell in the design hierarchy, and is used as a starting point when extracting information about a design. The VIEW NETLIST within this cell contains the netlist data, the VIEW BEHAVIOR contains the test pattern data, and the VIEW MASKLAYOUT contains the macrocell placement and interconnect routing data. In each case, VIEWNAMEs for these three VIEWTYPEs have been chosen to help a human reader to understand their usage rather than to give some semantic understanding to a CAD system.

The macrocell library used for the design is specified using the EXTERNAL construct. For example, the EDIF statement (EXTERNAL M2500ECL) specifies that the Motorola M2500ECL Macrocell Array library was used. This allows reference to the library and its contents without requiring that the complete library be sent with each design.

A TECHNOLOGY section must be present to give at least the technology identifier for a simple netlist, but may also be needed to add information such as the scale factor to be used for timing information. For example, (TECHNOLOGY MOTOROLA_MCA2) specifies that Motorola's MCA2 technology is being used and that the technology specific scaling and definitions will be found in that library. In this example, the definition case refers to the TECHNOLOGY section in the M2500ECL library previously supplied by Motorola.

Netlist Information

A 4-bit binary counter is used as a design example to illustrate the way data is expressed in EDIF. As in the library examples, only the basic information required is shown for clarity. The example is called "MOTO2500," the schematic drawing is shown in Figure 8, and a partial EDIF file of the netlist is shown in Figure 9.

Test Pattern Information

A "Test Pattern" refers to a sequential set of logic states applied to or expected from each signal named in the EDIF file during the test sequence or simulation run. The data supplied consists of a series of logic states High (H, HIGH, T, or TRUE), Low (L, LOW, F, or FALSE), Ignore (X), or high impedance (Z).

Referring to the MOTO2500 example in Figure 8, a functional test is performed using the waveforms shown in Figure 10. If inputs are driven to the states shown, then the outputs shown are to be expected. To transmit this information a new

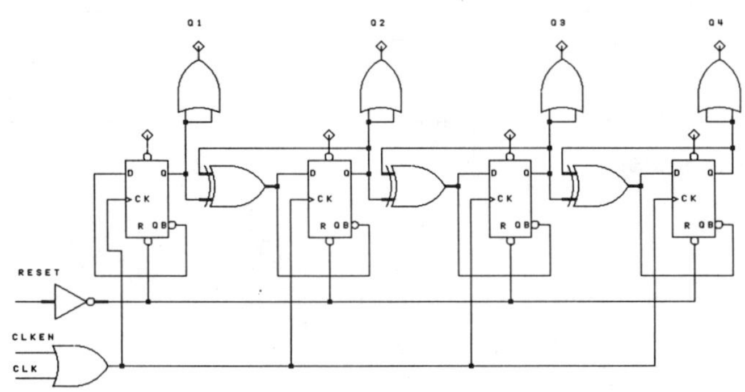

Figure 8—Schematic drawing of the MOTO2500 example

```
(EDIF MOTO2500
 (DESIGN MOTO2500 (QUALIFY EXAMPLES MOTO2500_CELL))
 (EXTERNAL M2500ECL)
 (LIBRARY EXAMPLES
  (STATUS ...)
  (TECHNOLOGY ...)
  (CELL MOTO2500_CELL
   (STATUS (EDIFlevel ... ))
   (VIEW NETLIST LOGCAP
    (INTERFACE
     (DEFINE INPUT PORT (MULTIPLE RESET CLK CLKEN))
     (DEFINE OUTPUT PORT (MULTIPLE Q1 Q2 Q3 Q4)))
    (CONTENTS
     (INSTANCE (QUALIFY M2500ECL M202) logcap RST)
     (JOINED RST (QUALIFY RST YA))
     (JOINED RESET (QUALIFY RST A))
     (INSTANCE (QUALIFY M2500ECL M291) logcap FF1)
     (JOINED RST (QUALIFY FF1 R))
     (JOINED CLOCK (QUALIFY FF1 C))
     (JOINED (QUALIFY FF1 D) (QUALIFY FF1 QB) ...))
```

Figure 9—EDIF Netlist for MOTO2500, extracted from Figure 8

view is added to the EDIF file, as shown in Figure 9, resulting in the file Figure 11. Note that a PORTMAP has been added to identify the name of each port in the two views.

Physical Structure Information

The physical implementation of this array requires that each macrocell be placed in a legal site in the correct orientation and that interconnect wiring be routed to connect the ports of the macrocells. The rules for this process were supplied in the physical library description shown in Figure 6. Referring again to the MOTO2500 example in Figure 8, yet another view is added to the EDIF file (as shown in Figure 12), and gives a complete specification of the three types of information required to correctly build this design.

CONCLUSIONS

Both the software described and EDIF V100 have proven useful for exchange of actual designs. Because of the limitations of both the first version of this software and of EDIF V100, the software described will be replaced by EDIF V200 based production software in the near future. Since these two versions of EDIF are not upward compatible, a potential user of the EDIF interfaces described here should check with Motorola to be sure of the current status of

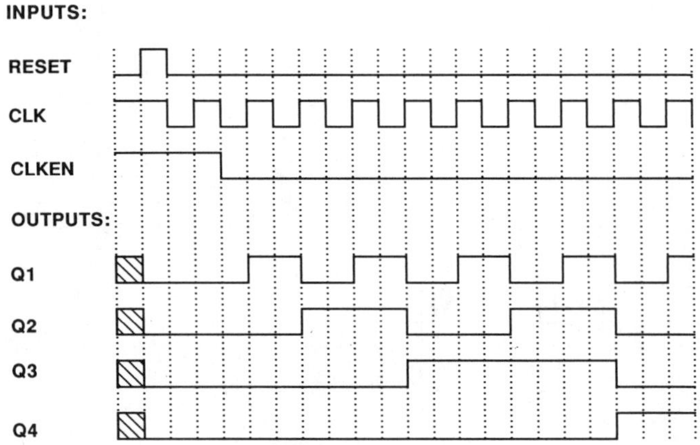

Figure 10—Functional test patterns for the MOTO2500

```
(EDIF MOTO2500
 (DESIGN ...)
 (LIBRARY EXAMPLES
  (STATUS ...)
  (TECHNOLOGY M2500ECL)
  (CELL MOTO2500_CELL
   (STATUS (EDIFlevel ... ))
   (VIEWMAP
     (PORTMAP (QUALIFY LOGCAP RESET)
              (QUALIFY LOGIC  RESET) ... ))
   (VIEW NETLIST LOGCAP ...)
   (VIEW BEHAVIOR LOGIC
    (INTERFACE
     (DEFINE INPUT PORT (MULTIPLE RESET CLK CLKEN))
     (DEFINE OUTPUT PORT (MULTIPLE Q1 Q2 Q3 Q4)))
    (CONTENTS
     (SIMULATE MOTO2500 FUNCTIONAL_TEST
      (IGNOREVALUE X)
      (APPLY 25 1
       (LOGICINPUT RESET
        (LOGICWAVEFORM L H L))
       (LOGICINPUT CLK
        (LOGICWAVEFORM H H L H L H L H L H ...))
       (LOGICINPUT CLKEN
        (LOGICWAVEFORM H H H H L))
       (LOGICOUTPUT Q1
        (LOGICWAVEFORM X L L L L H H L L H ...))
       (LOGICOUTPUT Q2
        (LOGICWAVEFORM X L L L L L L H H H ...))
       (LOGICOUTPUT Q3
        (LOGICWAVEFORM X L L L L L L L L L ...))
       (LOGICOUTPUT Q4
        (LOGICWAVEFORM X L L L L L L L L L ...)))))))))
```

Figure 11—EDIF file with test pattern information added

```
(EDIF MOTO2500
 (DESIGN ...)
 (LIBRARY EXAMPLES
  (STATUS ...)
  (TECHNOLOGY M2500ECL)
  (CELL MOTO2500_CELL
   (STATUS (EDIFlevel ... ))
   (VIEWMAP
     (PORTMAP (QUALIFY LOGCAP RESET)
              (QUALIFY LOGIC  RESET)
              (QUALIFY PHYSICAL P001) ... ))
   (VIEW NETLIST LOGCAP ...)
   (VIEW BEHAVIOR LOGIC ...)
   (VIEW NETLIST PHYSICAL
    (INTERFACE
     (DEFINE INPUT PORT (MULTIPLE P001 P003 P015))
     (DEFINE OUTPUT PORT (MULTIPLE P028 P002 P004 P009)))
    (CONTENTS
     (INSTANCE (QUALIFY M2500ECL M291) physical Site_122
      (TRANSFORM R180 (TRANSLATE 20 25)))
     (FIGUREGROUP LEVEL_1
      (SIGNALGROUP RST
       (FIGURE
        (PATH
         (POINT 21 25) ... )))))))
```

Figure 12—The EDIF file now includes physical information

Motorola's software before writing their interface software, and with the EDIF User Group for the latest information on EDIF.*

*EDIF User Group, 2222 South Dobson Road, Building 5, Mesa, Arizona 85202

REFERENCES

1. EDIF Steering Committee. *EDIF Specification, EDIF – Electronic Design Interchange Format Version 1 0 0,* EDIF User Group, 1985
2. *MCA2500ECL Macrocell Array Design Manual.* Motorola Inc., 1985, p. 38.
3. *LOGCAP Reference Manual,* Phoenix Data Systems Inc., Albany, N.Y., 1980.

CitiExpert: Artificial intelligence applied to banking

by KENAN E. SAHIN
Consultants for Management Decisions, Inc. and *Massachusetts Institute of Technology*
Cambridge, Massachusetts
and
ROBERT K. SAWYER
Consultants for Management Decisions, Inc.
Cambridge, Massachusetts

ABSTRACT

This paper describes the CitiExpert system, an artificial intelligence system developed for a commercial bank to increase the productivity and effectiveness of funds transfer telex request operations. These telexes were previously processed manually. Data entry operators would read and analyze the telex and then type information at a standard ASCII terminal interface. CitiExpert applies a combination of natural language processing techniques and rule-based expert system techniques to automatically analyze the telex and to generate a formatted equivalent. CitiExpert also provides a sophisticated intelligent user interface which aids users by applying the system's domain knowledge to the interactive session.

The paper discusses the previously existing technical and organizational environment at the client bank, and the factors and technical solutions which made CitiExpert a success. CitiExpert has been in production use since June of 1985.

INTRODUCTION

The CitiExpert system was designed and implemented to increase the productivity of funds transfer telex processing, a labor-intensive area. English text telexes are read by bank professionals, and important data in the telex is typed into a data entry console. This data must be entered according to both general banking guidelines and strict formatting rules.

Because of the bank's need to process English text input and to incorporate a significant amount of domain expertise, traditional programming techniques were inadequate. Artificial intelligence (AI) technology was identified as the appropriate solution. AI offers two groups of techniques which are used by CitiExpert: natural language processing techniques, and rule-based expert system techniques.

CitiExpert was first implemented by Consultants for Management Decisions (CMD) as a standalone prototype in the Summer of 1984. A prototype approach was selected to allow management to evaluate the potential of artificial intelligence in banking and to determine the potential success of a full production implementation. The prototype was standalone to allow the design team to concentrate on knowledge engineering. This standalone prototype was successful, and system integration became the major development issue. CitiExpert was integrated with the bank's system environment, and a production version was readied and installed in June 1985.

The development and management of the CitiExpert project provides a case study of the implementation of new technology within traditional corporate data processing environments. Several conclusions can be drawn from this experience which may benefit other applications of advanced technology in business environments.

THE EXISTING CLIENT ENVIRONMENT

The environment at the bank displayed a unique set of management and technical characteristics. Careful management and coordination of both executive desires and technical reality was a key factor in the success of the development effort.

Selection of the Application Domain

Late in 1983, the management of the bank's international transaction processing area began to realize the importance of artificial intelligence technology for their business: large-volume transaction processing of international transaction requests. These requests include funds transfer requests, requests for issuance of trade financing instruments such as letters of credit, and inquiries and investigation requests. These transaction requests arrive via several international electronic networks, such as TELEX, SWIFT, and CHIPS.

The majority of the area's traffic was formatted according to banking conventions and was processed automatically by conventional computer systems. However, a significant percentage of the processing costs were associated with the unstructured, or *free format* messages, which arrived as English text messages over the telex wire.

The use of artificial intelligence technology was an attempt to leapfrog the existing, more gradual, upgrade and improvement of transaction processing systems. The risk of new technology was balanced by the potential for a three- or four-year advance in transaction processing technology.

The initial application chosen as a test area for a prototyping effort was unstructured funds transfer telex processing. This application domain satisfied all of the accepted conditions for a successful AI project. A subset of the key conditions satisfied follows:[1,2]

1. The domain is characterized by the use of expert knowledge, judgement and experience.
2. Conventional programming solutions are inadequate.
3. There are recognized experts that solve the problem today.
4. The completed system is expected to have a significant payoff for the corporation.
5. The task requires the use of heuristics, or "rules of thumb."
6. The task is neither too easy nor too difficult.
7. The system can be phased into use gracefully.

The Technical Environment

The system for funds transfer processing at the bank is known as the Funds Transfer Network (FTN). After the success of the standalone prototype, integration with this system became the key issue.

A moving target

The FTN was built in the late 1970s using several PDP-11s and many different serial line network protocols. In 1984, as we were completing our prototype, an effort was initiated to upgrade the entire FTN to VAX Cluster architecture. This was a three-year effort, involving all of the machines and network connections.

The authors were involved with the internal system group's planning process, in an effort to integrate CitiExpert with the PDP-11 and schedule the transition to the new VAX as painlessly as possible. Corporate MIS systems are rarely static, and the need to coordinate to "hit a moving target" is even more critical with integration of a strategic technology such as artificial intelligence. Strong management desire for rapid implementation of the technology resulted in a reworking of the entire three-year development plan, to bring CitiExpert online at the earliest possible date.

Networking

The CitiExpert prototype was developed in LISP on the LISP Machine. In 1984, the LISP Machine did not provide an interface to the PDP-11. The implementation dates set by management did not allow time to develop a port to another language or machine.

A solution was provided by the availability of a UNIX processor for the LISP Machine. Citibank made available a C-language based protocol for UNIX which would communicate with one of their PDP-11 routing nodes. CMD substantially revised and enhanced the protocol to increase its robustness to a production quality.

Communication with the new VAX-based FTN, over DECnet, was pursued via several paths. First, a vendor was engaged to develop a custom DECnet for the Lambda UNIX processor. Second, a port to the Symbolics LISP machine was completed soon after Symbolics announced DECnet, in November of 1985. Third, a port to Common LISP on the VAX itself was completed early in 1986.

Careful attention to network integration issues was the primary factor affecting the project's success. Performance of the knowledge engineering components could be excellent from a technical perspective, but the system could not be cost-effective without an appropriate system integration.

The client's technical staff

A further complicating issue was the unavailability of the bank's technical staff for CitiExpert. This staff was fully utilized developing the VAX-based FTN, which was critical to the bank's operations, and they could not be spared to aid with the networking issues. Thus it became even more imperative that we provide this expertise as well as artificial intelligence knowledge. Insisting that we were "knowledge engineers" and above such work was not an option in this environment, and we suspect such is the case in most other business environments as well.

Performance requirements

Because funds transfer is a transaction processing environment with large volumes and strict time constraints, we were required to design from the beginning with speed efficiency in mind. We could not afford the luxuries of powerful, overly general formalisms for processing. This required us to pursue a custom development approach.

The initial prototype processed each telex in 70 seconds on the LISP Machine. The current microVAX II Common LISP version processes each telex in under 30 seconds. This speed improvement was necessary to make the system cost-effective.

FACTORS CONTRIBUTING TO SUCCESS

The complex management demands and the difficult combination of technical factors resulting from application of new technology to a traditional DP environment required a unique combination of solutions to bring CitiExpert to successful completion. Decisions too numerous to itemize were each responsible in some way for the success; the most critical factors are described in this section.

Support of Top Management

Key executives at Citibank were our contact point. These executives had the vision to identify the potential of combining AI technology with this application. In addition to the backing of these executives, the manager directly responsible for system development and operations became a strong proponent of the technology, and the entire management team worked together to implement the initial vision. This strong management backing was critical to the project's success for several reasons.

Knowledge acquisition was necessary from several sources. To develop an effective system, we interviewed Citibank staff in systems development and operations as well as the end-users and managers. Without the strong backing of top management, organizational dynamics might have jeopardized our access to one of these groups. In particular, had our initial contact been within the systems group itself, contacts with end-users and with higher-level management would have been difficult to establish.

Management demonstrated their commitment to the system by producing a professional quality videotape of CitiExpert. The first version of this videotape was prepared immediately after the prototype, making a strong statement early in the project about management's commitment to the technology. This videotape was used both as a marketing tool for overseas clients and as an internal tool for the dissemination of the technology.

Because of the success of CitiExpert, follow-up applications were requested which leveraged the initial effort. Several related applications are currently past the prototype stage and are being prepared for production implementations. Management's continued commitment to CitiExpert, in the form of both the videotape and the follow-up applications, indicates the success of the project.

Strong management backing also allowed us to proceed with a unique, important development relationship described in the following section.

The Client-consultant Relationship

The typical paradigm for managing consultants involves viewing them as extensions to the in-house development team. The client's existing project management structure is used, and the consulting firm provides programming talent.

This paradigm may not work when applied to advanced technology such as artificial intelligence. With such a different technology, new management techniques are often required to correspond to the difference in development styles and issues. We insisted on providing the project management expertise as well as the technical expertise. Thus we delivered a custom turnkey system, rather than simply providing various code modules and routines according to a client-specified schedule.

This arrangement at times resulted in strained relations with the systems development staff, as they were not used to relegating management control of consultant-developed projects. Once again, the strong backing of top management allowed us to proceed.

CitiExpert also benefited from the knowledge engineers' concurrent involvement with other, more traditional decision support efforts at Citibank. These concurrent efforts proved synergistic. Together the efforts increased the trust relationship between the development team and the bank. The larger number of projects resulted in more frequent access to the key managers. These more traditional projects provided CMD with a better understanding of the bank systems and staff.

Broad Expertise of Development Team

A research-oriented knowledge of artificial intelligence is far from adequate when approaching a real-world production application. We found that much more important is the breadth of experience within the project staff. In addition to abilities as knowledge engineers, the development team was required to aid in scheduling a three-year development effort; to optimize rules and formalisms, at times even in assembler; and to debug and optimize a serial network protocol for integration with the PDP-11.

Our experience was that knowledge engineers must be willing and able to immerse themselves in all aspects of a project's development, and that this versatility is more critical than the arcane knowledge associated with advanced research.

Porting the System to the VAX

Continued success of CitiExpert has been dependent on the evolution of the code to run on different computers. The LISP Machine was not feasible for the new FTN since no acceptable network protocols were available. To retain cost effectiveness and achieve network integration, it became necessary to port the application to the VAX. This was a major effort, porting from ZetaLISP to Common LISP. After the port was completed, we decreased the time performance by more than an order of magnitude.

All of these efforts were undertaken to retain the cost-effectiveness of CitiExpert. Cost-effectiveness is *the* key issue for implementations of new technology which move from the laboratory into a production enviornment. A cost justification must be demonstrable at the onset of development, and cost-effectiveness must be achieved during the course of the project, especially with a "showcase" project for new technology such as artificial intelligence.

```
 FROM: BANK OF MASSACHUSETTS, CAMBRIDGE, MA
7/13/84
CAMBRIDGE MASS   13/7/84
TO NEW YORK BANK
1/5642
VALUE 16TH JULY
DEBIT OUR ACCOUNT AND PAY USDLRS 7,406.94 TO YOURSELVES
IN NEW YORK N Y FOR
CREDIT ACCOUNT OUR TOKYO BRANCH
 BEING REIMBURSEMENT OF AMOUNT
EXPENDED ON BEHALF OF THE OFFICE OF THE PRESIDENT FOR
PERIOD 24TH MAY 1983 TO 17TH MAY 1984 BY ORDER JOHN SMITH,
VP ACCOUNTING
RESERVE
CAMBRIDGE
```

Figure 1—A typical funds transfer telex. (Bank names are fictitious.)

THE TECHNICAL SOLUTION

Technical Requirements

The knowledge domain for CitiExpert is the reading and translating of English text messages into a structured format. The messages are sent to the bank electronically via the telex network. Each funds transfer request is from 80 to 200 words long. A typical telex, with fictitious bank names, is shown in Figure 1. The subset of English used in these telexes is highly terse and abbreviated. The people typing in the telex messages are under time pressures, so abbreviations and typographical mistakes are common. Many of the telexes are entered by people for whom English is a second language. Often information which is necessary for the bank, but not required of the sender, will be omitted to reduce the sender's message entry time. For example, the name of a bank is often specified without the corresponding account number. In many telexes, information is supplied which is not needed by the bank; this information is ignored.

The domain is such that a direct mapping from individual phrases to structured values is not possible (see Figures 2 and 3). The structured values depend on the context of the entire message. Some structured values depend on several different phrases in combination. Some values may depend on a particular combination of yet other structured values. The possible combinations of situations resulting in a given value are thus very large. Application domains in which combinatorial effects become significant usually do not submit to a cost effective, traditional programming solution. These complex-

FROM **THE BANK OF ALLBANKS**
DATED 11/23/86
REF EH-2323
PLEASE DEBIT OUR **TUSCALOOSA BRANCH**
CREDIT THE BANK OF CAMBRIDGEVILLE
FOR USDOLLARS 1000,000.--
PAYMENT TO THEIR GENEVA BRANCH
THEIR REF. LOAN NO. 25563
REGARDS,
FT DEPT.

Figure 2—A telex where two phrases together (in bold) indicate the exact branch to debit. Also note that the credited bank branch is indicated in two distinct phrases.

Dollar Amounts

```
15,904:00        387.50              1000 US-DOLLAR-
60,352.72        26.643,--           ONEZERONINEONE CENTS 13
64,500.-         100,000/=
1405.03          200.000,--,
25110.00         50.000,--
1,000.00         86,875.00.
825.95           1'142'546.72
650,000.00       167.702 US DOLLARS 48 CENTS
1565.00          2.014.833 US DOLLARS 33 CENTS
1.200.000,--     1.747 DECIMAL 50
1.338,75         18.000,--
```

Value Dates

```
VALUE 840509             VALUE MAY/16/84
VALUE MAY 11,1984        VALUE 10.5.
VALUE TODAY              VALUE DATE MAY 9, 1984
VAL. MAY 8/84            VALUE TODAY, 5/9/84
VALUE 9TH MAY 1984+++    VAL. 05/10,
VALUE 9.5.84             VAL. 9.5.84
VALUE 11/5/84            VALUE 11. MAY 1984
VALUE 10/5/84            VAL 9TH PAY
VALUE 10/05/84           VALUE THIS MAY NINTH 1984
VALUE MAY 9,             VALUE MAY ELEVENTH 1984
VALUE DATE: 10.5.84      VAL. 10.05.
VALUE 10.05.84           VAL. 10TH MAY 1094
```

Figure 3—Samples of the variations in two CitiExpert domain phrase types.

ities are an indication that artificial intelligence techniques may be appropriate. These techniques are designed to manage such combinatorics by representing the basic structure of the knowledge. In addition to these domain requirements, the production environment required that each telex be processed in under sixty seconds.

System Design

The particularly abbreviated version of English found in these telexes led to the use of a *flexible parser* approach.[3] We combined elements of *case frame grammars*[4] and *semantic grammars*[5] to arrive at the final linguistic formalism. The characteristics of our formalism satisfied the domain requirements:

1. The formalism was capable of identifying single phrases and incomplete sentence fragments.
2. The formalism was able to identify useful information and ignore irrelevant information.
3. The formalism provided for the identification of abbreviations and misspellings.
4. The formalism was capable of identifying information even when incorrect grammar was used.
5. The individual parsers could be *compiled* to provide a significant decrease in processing time.

The basic formalism was designed using a variation of the Augmented Transition Network[6] to build semantic units. Each semantic unit is responsible for the identification of one key piece of information from the telex. As information is identified, it is stored within the semantic unit.

In addition to the linguistic formalism, we employed a rule-based expert system to incorporate domain knowledge. The expert system receives input from the semantic unit values (see Figure 4). The expert system was used to make decisions based on overall message content, to infer values using combinations of phrases, and to implement constraints among different structured values. This expert system was also customized to achieve production level speed performance. In the current production version, the rules have been rewritten directly in LISP code, resulting in a ten fold performance increase.

A successful technical design was achieved through two primary emphases. First, no single technique was identified as the best, or preferred technique. The design team was encouraged to blend the most appropriate elements of several formalisms, a hybrid approach, which resulted in a system highly optimized for performance in this domain. Second, speed performance was a design consideration from the onset. The formalisms were designed to provide powerful knowledge engineering capabilities, while providing for ease of optimization in the implementation phase.

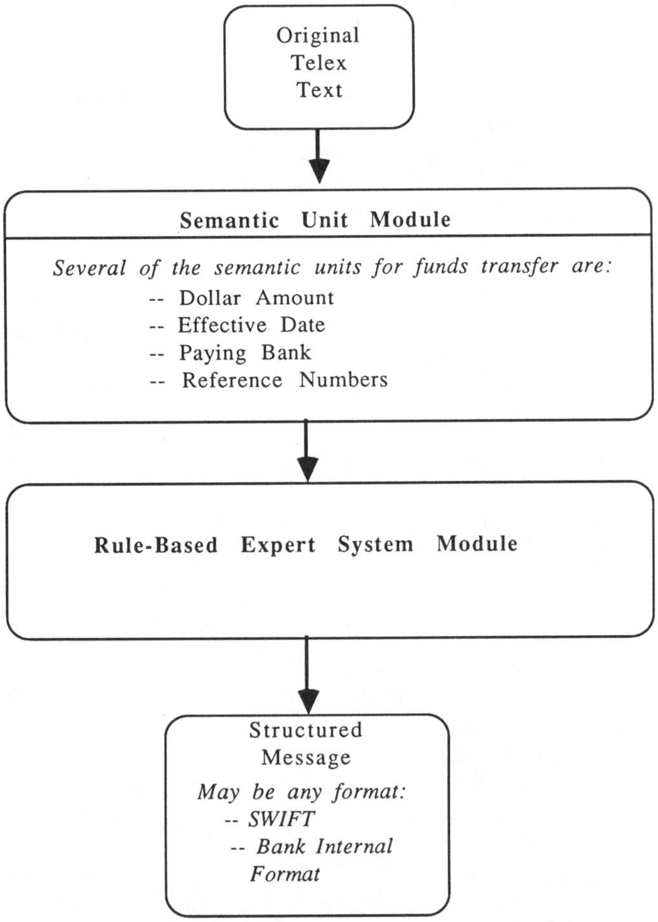

Figure 4—CitiExpert internal architecture, with a representative set of semantic units shown.

THE INTELLIGENT USER INTERFACE

CitiExpert was designed to process a telex fully, then to pass the telex and the corresponding structured information to a user edit interface. CitiExpert identifies an average of over 80% of the structured information. An operator must complete the remaining structured information, usually one or two values.

The existing FTN data entry stations could not support display of both a telex and a structured equivalent. These interfaces were designed to be used with a printed copy of the telex, and provided for structured value entry only. Designing CitiExpert to print out the telex for these operators would have reduced the cost effectiveness of the process considerably. Instead, we implemented an "intelligent assistant" interface within CitiExpert. This interface was conceptualized as a low-level assistant to a human operator which would provide much of the processing expertise, freeing the operator to perform higher level conceptual activities.[7] Similar functionality was implemented on both the LISP Machine and the VAXstation.

This interface employs mouse cursor control, multiple windows, and pop-up menus and windows to improve operator productivity. Two primary windows are displayed: one containing the original telex message, and the other containing the structured values identified automatically (see Figure 5). The mouse can be used to mark a region of text in the telex window and move that text into one of the structured values.

Incomplete or ambiguous values identified by CitiExpert are made available to the user through pop-up windows. One such window is for English-text notifications of problems encountered during processing. A second window contains suggested values which are each mouse-selectable. For example, if several branches are found in the CitiExpert bank database for the name "CREDIT SUISSE," the notification window would say "Several branches found for CREDIT SUISSE," and the suggested values menu would display each of the branches, with the corresponding city and account numbers (see Figure 6). This mechanism allows the user to benefit even when CitiExpert cannot uniquely identify a value.

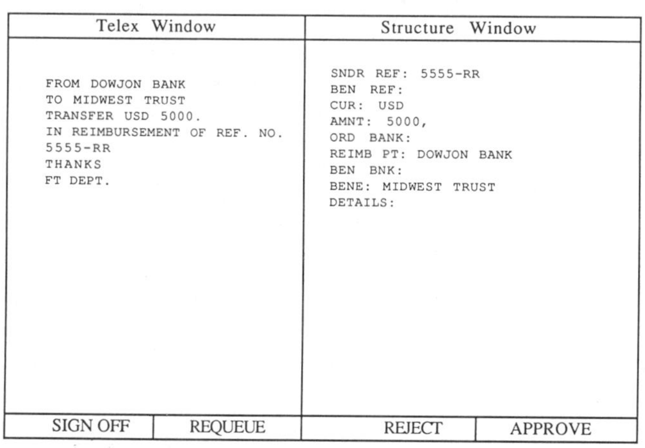

Figure 5—The CitiExpert interface. "Mouse" selection of all screen items is supported to aid the editing session.

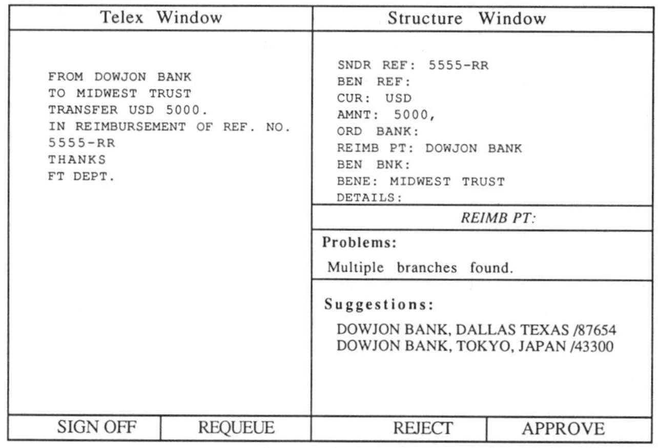

Figure 6—The CitiExpert interface, with suggestions and problems displayed for the "REIMB PT" field.

The linguistic and domain knowledge used in the automatic processing is also available to the user. For example, when a region of text is moved to a structured value using the mouse, the user can request intelligent processing for that text. The parsers and domain rules are then invoked to process the text. A correctly processed value will be entered by the interface. In addition, other values which may have been affected by this change will be flagged with a notification for the user.

The intelligent user interface is a critical component of CitiExpert. The power of this "intelligent assistant" concept, employing mouse cursor control, multiple windows, and pop-up menus, significantly increases the productivity of the users. Providing a broad interface between the user and the intelligence in the system results in maximum value for the knowledge engineering effort.

SUMMARY

The CitiExpert system provides a case study of technological innovation within a traditional data processing environment. A number of conclusions, both organizational and technical, can be drawn from this experience.

Management Conclusions

The most significant organizational lesson is that the key executives must be personally involved in the project. The organizational dynamics can become quite complex, especially when new technology is involved. Managers below the key decision-making level do not have the authority to manage these conflicts. Also, because new technology requires a new management approach, the involvement of key executives is necessary to smooth the transition to a new management style. We observed that the vision of these executives is often more important than technical expertise. Executives can often achieve success with new technology by pursuing a firm vision while not allowing themselves to be dissuaded by a lack of technical knowledge.

A second management lesson is that traditional implementation issues are magnified when a new technology is used. The languages and machines used are likely to be different from the existing DP systems. Network protocols may not exist for these machines. These issues must be considered at the onset of development, and a path, from prototype to production, must be available. This requirement may result in the selection of a less optimal machine or language for development. An alternative is the "two track" approach of using separate machines for development and delivery. The CitiExpert solution of the LISP machine development environment with the VAXstation delivery system is one example of this approach.

A third lesson is that new technology often requires new management techniques. Managing development of a new technology, such as artificial intelligence from a traditional DP orientation, can be problematic. In some cases, the ability of the project team to adapt to the new management techniques may have more effect on project success than the team's technical expertise.

A fourth lesson is the importance of a custom design orientation. In a production environment, producing cost-effective results for new technology requires this orientation.

CitiExpert also benefited from CMD's concurrent involvement with other, more traditional decision support efforts at the bank. These concurrent efforts proved to be synergistic, providing the development group with a broader understanding of the client's needs and establishing a stronger trust relationship.

Technical Conclusions

Several technical recommendations can be drawn from the CitiExpert experience. The key lesson is that theoretical dogmatism or purity hinders a production implementation. In most cases, a hybrid of several techniques and formalisms will result in the best solution. At points throughout development, new variations in the formalism may be suggested which would never arise in a research environment. These variations should be welcomed, rather than rejected as theoretically unsound.

A second lesson for artificial intelligence system designers is that partial results should be made available to the users. If this information on partial results is lost, a significant portion of the system's capabilities is being wasted. When cost-effectiveness is the key management issue, designers cannot afford to keep this information from the users.

Third, for maximum cost-effectiveness, the system's intelligence should be made available to the user through an intelligent interface. With the typical expert system consultation model, this is standard; however, in a transaction processing environment, an intelligent interface is not required. Partially processed messages can be routed through the existing systems, removing the need for a special interface; this temptation should be avoided.

A fourth lesson is the importance of speed performance. Designers should anticipate the need for speed optimization and design accordingly. Options such as assembler rewrites of speed critical code should be available on the delivery machine. Formalisms should be carefully tailored to the needs of the application, rather than generalized for a large class of applications; a generalized formalism will usually result in reduced performance.

The fifth lesson is the importance of system integration issues. The system may contain superb knowledge engineering, but will be useless without a clear implementation path. The system must blend in with the existing system environment. Initial implementation must be supported by the development team, and follow-on releases should address user comments during this period. The system is successfully completed when the development team can "cut the umbilical cord" so that users can take over the system as their own.

REFERENCES

1. Davis, R. "Expert Systems: Where Are We? and Where Do We Go From Here?", MIT AI Memo No. 665, 1982.
2. Prerau, D.S. "Selection of an Appropriate Domain for an Expert System." *AI Magazine,* 6 (1985), 2, pp. 26–30.
3. Hayes, J.H. and G.V. Mouradian. "Flexible Parsing." *American Journal of Computational Linguistics,* 7 (1981), 4, pp. 232–242.
4. Fillmore, C. "The Case for Case." In E. Bach and R. Harms (eds.) *Universals in Linguistic Theory*. New York: Holt, Rinehart, and Winston, 1968.
5. Hendrix, G.G. "The LIFER Manual: A Guide to Building Practical Natural Language Interfaces," Technical Note 138, SRI International, 1977.
6. Woods, W.A. "Transition Network Grammars for Natural Language Analysis." *Communications of the ACM,* 13 (1970), pp. 591–606.
7. Rich, C., and R.C. Waters. "Abstraction, Inspection and Debugging in Programming," MIT AI Memo No. 634, 1981.

Use of expert systems in medical research data analysis: The POSCH AI project

by JOHN M. LONG, JAMES R. SLAGLE, MICHAEL WICK, ERACH IRANI, JOHN MATTS and the POSCH GROUP*
University of Minnesota
Minneapolis, Minnesota

ABSTRACT

Artificial Intelligence (AI), especially expert systems technology, has very promising possibilities for more fully automating the analysis of medical research data. The Program on the Surgical Control of the Hyperlipidemias (POSCH), a national multi-centered clinical trial has been experimenting with using AI in its data analyses for several years. Three projects are described in this paper.

The first experiment, designed to automate the clinical judgment used to evaluate the data from serial graded electrocardiograms has been a success. Early efforts to automate one step of the evaluation of serial coronary arteriography data has also been successful, but major difficulties must be overcome to extend the work.

The initial motivation for the POSCH AI Project was to build an expert system that can search for interesting relationships among, and between, the POSCH variables. The problems encountered are different from those of other investigators who are attempting similar projects. Efforts to segment and/or collapse the problem into smaller units are explained. Issues related to the data structure and query languages have been identified. Statistical and other logically based reasoning methods, fundamental to the entire project, are discussed in conjunction with the heuristic methods used by expert systems.

* The work of J.R. Slagel, M.R. Wick, and Erach Irani is partially supported by NSF Grant DCR8512857 and by the Microelectronics and Information Sciences Center of the University of Minnesota.

INTRODUCTION

Artificial Intelligence (AI), primarily expert systems technology, is being widely explored in medicine.[1] There are several large, multi-centered clinical studies that accumulate extensive files of data on a large number of patients.[2,3,4] AI has promising possibilities for them. As an example, the Program on the Surgical Control of the Hyperlipidemias (POSCH) has been experimenting with using expert systems to automate more fully the analyses of its large database of clinical trial research data. In our first two projects, we are using expert systems to automate the element of clinical judgement required for some analyses.[5] Ultimately we hope to use AI to automate the search for interesting relationships between, and among, the variables that are collected annually on POSCH patients.

The POSCH database comes from a randomized controlled clinical trial that uses a standard patient visit protocol and records all data on standard data forms.[2] The timing and frequency of patient visits are also standard. POSCH has some missing data and a few missed visits, but the frequency is quite low. This allows us to focus our efforts on the interesting aspects of building a system to search for medical knowledge that may now be hidden in the database. In other words, the POSCH database is ideal in many ways for experimentation in the use of AI for data analysis.

POSCH AI PROJECT

The long range objectives of the POSCH AI Project are to use this new technology to:

1. Develop an automated system that will assist our staff of analysts in a comprehensive examination of all of the POSCH data.
2. Identify and test relationships that exist over time between and among the variables.
3. Identify an optimal subset of variables that can predict the outcome of the POSCH study endpoints (for example, a heart attack or atherosclerotic death).
4. Compare the AI based automated system's results with the results accomplished in a more conventional manner and thus provide an evaluation of the AI methods.

Basis For the Study

The POSCH study is a national, multi-clinic, clinical trial designed to test the lipid-atherosclerosis hypothesis in a population where all have had a heart attack. It is known that higher rates of heart attacks and atherosclerotic deaths occur in people with higher levels of cholesterol. The lipid-atherosclerosis hypotheses, yet to be fully proven, says that lowering cholesterol will also lower the rates of heart attacks and atherosclerotic deaths. In order to test this hypotheses, POSCH lowered the cholesterol in half of its patients, the intervention group, using the other half as a control group. POSCH is now collecting a large amount of data on each of the POSCH patients over a 7 to 14 year period.

POSCH's data collection, editing, storage, retrieval, and analyses problems are typical of a number of other large medical research projects.[6,7] The focus of this paper is on the uses of AI in data analyses. A variety of manual and automated methods are used by POSCH, and other large clinical trials, to analyze the medical research data. The analysis of certain complex tests, especially for changes in the patient's performance over time, requires clinical judgement. This requirement is especially difficult because it has traditionally required manual processing by human experts, usually busy and expensive medical specialists.

POSCH has an additional problem. The designers of POSCH chose to collect about 1400 data items at each annual visit, 600 of which are placed in our computerized database. Even the 600 variables stored in our database are more than our staff can examine in a comprehensive way. At the present time, the POSCH analysis staff examines in detail about 100 of the 600 variables. These so called major variables are known to be related to the lipid-atherosclerosis hypothesis, the focus of our study, and/or the partial ileal bypass surgery, the intervention modality used to lower cholesterol. We are especially concerned with the potential effects of changes in these variables on the POSCH patients, either beneficial or not beneficial. The other 500 so called minor computerized variables are collected because there is some possibility that they could be related to our study focus. They are examined in much less detail. The remaining 800 items that are not entered into the computer are useful at the time of data collection but are judged to have little long term value. They consist primarily of series of questions asked by the physician in order to determine the patient's health status in a certain area. The relevant health status is entered into the automated portion of the patient's record.

POSCH is attempting to resolve the problem of analyzing so many variables by finding supplemental and automated methods for searching for relationships between, and among, all of the computerized variables; especially the ones that cannot receive the special attention our staff has devoted to the 100 or so major variables.

There is a potential trap in such a detailed examination of the POSCH data, such as finding spurious or irrelevant relationships. Statistically significant differences that are clinically unimportant are apt to be found when one examines such a large database in so much detail. The analyses must be performed in an intelligent way. We expect to avoid such pitfalls by designing the expert system rules to do the same thing that a human would do to avoid such errors. Direct human intervention will be used as a last resort. That is to say, we accept the possibility that we may not be able to fully automate the process. Even partial success, which we have already achieved, makes this work very practical.

The project has been under development for several years and this paper presents the current status. At this stage a basic plan has been formulated, the necessary resources have been assembled, and two prototype expert systems have been developed.

The Resources

1. *The POSCH Database.* The database is an hierarchically organized database that includes about 600 computerized variables collected on 838 patients upon entry into the study (that is, the baseline data) and at annual visits for a minimum of seven, and up to 14, subsequent annual visits. At present the database is about 75% of its ultimate size and includes a total of about 200 million characters broken down into about 160 million in MEDDB, the main data storage area, and 40 million in STATFILE/LOCATOR, an on-line administrative type database that includes the status and location of all patient visits, data forms and documents.
2. *Catalog of Variables.* The catalog classifies and organizes, into clinically logical groupings, all data items collected by POSCH. We may use the classification system as a basis for simplifying and directing the discovery phases of the project.
3. *Human Resources.* The POSCH Group has the necessary statistical and medical expertise. POSCH has clinical expertise related to the lipids, electrocardiographic stress testing, coronary arteriography, surgery, and other areas. The project is a joint effort with the AI group within the Department of Computer Sciences at the University of Minnesota. They have many years of experience in AI including the design, development, and implementation of many expert systems. The Project is using an expert system development tool built by members of our AI team called AGNESS (a generalized network-based expert system shell).[8]
4. *Computer Hardware and Software.* Existing minicomputer facilities in the POSCH data center have been supplemented with an IBM PC AT workstation and with SUN AI workstations in Computer Sciences. Virtually any computer type or size is available for our use at the University, including the largest supercomputers in existence and parallel computers. We anticipate the need for one or both of these in future phases.

AN EXPERT SYSTEM FOR ANALYSES OF SERIAL GRADED ECG TESTS

Our first expert system was designed to compare the data from a pair of graded exercise electrocardiogram (ECG) tests taken several years apart in order to determine whether the patient's performance was better, unchanged, or worse over time. This system can approximate the decision reached by a cardiologist evaluating the same data. We will only briefly describe this system because it has been reported previously.[5,9]

The expert system rules for the ECG system were developed using an iterative process in which the knowledge engineer and expert met to discuss and analyze sample cases. The set of cases were carefully selected so as to present a variety of typical situations and to stimulate explanations by the clinician as to what he was doing to solve the case. The clinical expert explained the factual knowledge he used from scientific literature, often citing results of research performed by himself and others. He also used and explained the "rules of thumb" or heuristics that he found helpful. These are based on his experience, rather than on book knowledge, and their incorporation into the system is one of the unique reasons expert systems work. As these sessions progressed, the knowledge engineer formulated, modified, discarded, replaced, and expanded the rules used by the domain expert, either stated or implied. The computer version of most of the rules is of the "IF . . . THEN" type. The IF part, called the antecedent, or premise, contains the pattern or attributes that must be matched for the rules to be used. The THEN part, called the consequent, contains the action to be taken, or the assertion to be made when the antecedent is satisfied.

The resulting expert system was tested on 100 cases that were used to validate the system. Each case consisted of a pair of tests taken by a POSCH patient two years apart. The cases were selected to be representative of a variety of situations.

The cases were also evaluated individually by two different members of a panel of five expert cardiologists. Each one evaluated 40 cases. The 100 pairs were evaluated in such a way that each reader's cases were equally distributed among the other four readers for the other reading. Table I illustrates how this was done. We then compared the conclusions made by the expert system with the individual cardiologist's evaluations.

TABLE I—ECG Panel reading pattern

	P-P	P-N	N-P	N-N	Total
Reader A	16	4	4	16	40
Overlap of					
B with A	4	1	1	4	10
C with A	4	1	1	4	10
D with A	4	1	1	4	10
E with A	4	1	1	4	10

Typical pattern of overlap of each reader with the other readers for the set of 100 pairs of exercise ECG tests evaluated by them.
P = Postiive Test N = Negative Test

Since a more conventional way to automate this situation would be to use a statistical approach, we also developed a set of multiple linear regression equations as a third method of evaluation. We briefly digress here to mention that, although the equations worked, several variables used in the multiple regression equations had obscure clinical meanings, a matter of concern to POSCH clinicians.

All three methods used a seven category scale to describe their conclusions. When a given pair of tests was evaluated by either of the two cardiologists, or the expert system, or the multiple regression equations, they concluded whether or not a patient's result was better or worse from the first to the second test using the seven category scale shown below:

much worse	worse	slightly worse	no change	slightly better	better	much better

Because of the strong element of subjective clinical judgement in these evaluations, the three methods for evaluating the test data were not necessarily expected to draw the same conclusions. For this reason the evaluation methods were compared in two ways as to how well they agreed. "Exact" agreement means that the same category on the seven category scale was selected as the conclusion for both of the evaluations being compared. Agreement "within one category" means that the two evaluations selected the same or immediately adjacent categories of the seven category scale. The comparisons were made based on the percentage of agreement.

Table II summarizes the results. For "exact" agreement the expert system agreed with the cardiologists about as well as the cardiologists agreed among themselves and did better than the multiple regression equations. For agreement "within one category," the expert system performed best and the multiple regression equations' evaluations did better than the cardiologists among themselves.

After allowances for normal variation, it can be seen that even a very basic expert system can evaluate serial graded exercise ECG test data about as well as either an individual cardiologist or the multiple regression equations.

AN EXPERT SYSTEM FOR ANALYSIS OF SERIAL CORONARY ARTERIOGRAMS

The next system we are attempting to build is one to evaluate serial coronary arteriograms. The general concept is the same as for the ECG system but the medical aspects are far more complex. A brief background on the medical nature of the problem is needed in order to explain this. Narrowing of coronary vessels by lipid based deposits (stenosis) can cause decreased blood circulation to the heart muscles. In extreme cases the blood flow can be restricted enough to cause severe chest pain (angina pectoris) and can cause the death of those parts of heart muscle (myocardial infarction) whose blood supply depends on the blocked artery. Arteriography (a procedure that photographs the pattern of blood flow in the coronary arteries) yields useful information about the condition of the coronary vessels. The technique involves injecting a contrast medium sensitive to x-ray film into the heart vessels followed by a series of 35mm x-rays taken in rapid succession. A cine film strip is thus produced that shows how the blood fills the arteries of the heart. By repeating this procedure from several angles, a cardiologist can examine the films and tell which vessels have stenosis as well as the nature and extent of stenosis. Narrowing of the blood vessels by either a lipid deposit stenosis or a blood clot (thrombus) shows up on the arteriogram as dark regions within the artery.

TABLE II—Average agreement of cardiologists' readings with themselves, the equations and the expert system (ES)

	Card. vs Card.	Card. vs Eq.	Card. vs ES
Exact	42.0%	34.0%	41.7%
Within one Category	76.0%	81.5%	83.5%

Cases from the POSCH study are used to build and test the experimental system. Coronary arteriograms of participants in POSCH are taken at the time they enter the study and at 3, 5, and either 7 or 10 years later. An arteriography review panel of cardiologists and radiologists has been formed by POSCH to clinically evaluate pairs of these serial coronary angiograms taken three to ten years apart. The methods they use to evaluate these clinical data are subtle and require a considerable amount of clinical judgement. The current method of assessment is for a subpanel of two members from among the eight doctors on the arteriography review panel to take turns meeting for two days, about once a month, to review about 30 to 40 pairs of arteriograms. This is an extremely tedious task for the doctors on the panel and logistically complex. The panel members live all across the United States.

Here are some of the details of the assessment process. The subpanel review is conducted in a double-blinded fashion. The members know neither the identities of the participants nor the temporal sequence of the arteriograms. The film pairs are identified simply as Film A and Film B. Film A is evaluated and all stenoses found are recorded. Film B is then evaluated for change from Film A. In the final step of their evaluations, the subpanel carefully reviews all of their findings and provides a global assessment of change using a scale similar to the one used for the ECG system. The total process requires about 20 minutes of the subpanel's time to review one pair of films with the global assessment taking only a few minutes at the end. The findings of the subpanel are recorded on a standard form and the information is entered into the computerized database.

The coronary vessels in the arteriogram appear in a treelike branching structure wrapped around the heart myocardium (muscle). What is visible in one frame of the cine may be obscured in another. Stenoses near the branching point of arteries are especially difficult to estimate. A factor affecting visualization is the presence of collateral arteries. When the normal blood flow in one branch of the system is blocked, collateral arteries (arteries at the ends of an adjacent branch of the system) will sometimes open up and extend their perfusion field (provide a blood supply) to the affected muscle tissue. This amazing ability of the heart to adjust can complicate the task of determining stenoses. For example, if the blockage of the normal flow decreases, the collateral flow may also decrease and can disappear altogether. Another factor that must be assessed by experts is whether the blockage is caused by a thrombus or stenosis.

Assessing the change in stenoses is further complicated by the fact that vessels tend to develop stenosis more quickly after coronary bypass grafts have been placed on them. Medical procedures such as recanalizations (opening up the vessel by angioplasty) are also fairly common and complicate the evaluation.

These are examples of the many complex and interactive factors that make assessing the percentage change in stenosis difficult. For these reasons we chose to build only one part of the evaluation process in our first phase. As the first phase of this system, we chose to approximate just the global assessment process.

The initial knowledge base was built to perform this one task. Data elements from the consensus report (all previous steps) of the experts are used as the expert system's input and they form the leaf (entry) nodes of the network. The top-node represents the systems global assessment of the overall disease change. The interactions between the tree-like structure of arteries are not required at this point because the heart, as a pumping organ, is not to be evaluated. Thus, each artery can be treated independently. The change in each artery is assessed and the individual changes combined to obtain the overall change. The inference network therefore consists of a subnetwork that is evaluated 22 times; once for each of the 22 arterial segments under study by POSCH; and a top-level network that merges the information passed up by the subnetworks.

Table III gives the results obtained by the global assessment expert system when applied to 56 test cases. Terminology and comparison methods are similar to those used for the ECG system.

The POSCH quality surveillance program has shown that two different panel evaluations will agree "exactly" on a seven category scale 55% of the time and agree "within one category" (select the same or adjacent categories on the scale) 91% of the time. The expert system's assessments of the set of 56 test cases agreed "exactly" with the panel 50% of the time, and agreed "within one category" of the panel assessments in 96% of the cases. The system's performance is roughly comparable to that of the panel for the global assessments.

The current, early version of the system does not consider many of the factors used by the subpanel. For this reason, the results obtained by this system are somewhat surprising and should be reviewed with caution. Further tests are needed. It is doubtful that the final version of the expert system for evaluating serial coronary arteriograms can perform this well, because the system does not include many of the facets of subjective clinical judgment that are used by the human experts for these evaluations. For example, the current version of the expert system does not translate many of the subtle things observed on the film by the arteriographers. Furthermore, we do not know how to interpret and record many of these data. Nonetheless, our success encourages us to hope that we can build a system that can closely approximate the results of these subpanels using a single simplified reading of each film by trained technicians.

TABLE III—Average agreement rate of subpanel (SP) compared to expert system (ES)

	SP vs. SP	SP vs. ES
Exact	50%	55%
Within one Category	96%	91%

AN EXPERT SYSTEM TO AUTOMATE THE SEARCH FOR NEW MEDICAL KNOWLEDGE

The initial motivation for the POSCH AI Project was to build an expert system that can identify relationships that exists between, and among, the POSCH variables. This entails building an expert system that can automate what biostatisticians do when faced with the analysis of a large database like that in POSCH. The idea for this was inspired by the early work of Robert L. Blum in his RX discovery project, now renamed RADIX.[10,11] His effort to build an expert system to discover and confirm causal relationships in a medical record database appears to be the first attempt to use this approach in medicine. The system obtained its initial hypothesis by selectively combing through a database using a discovery module. It combed through a selected subset of 50 patient records to produce an hypothesis such as A causes B. What it actually did was to determine that A precedes B and is correlated to B. A study module then designed a comprehensive study of the most promising hypotheses as determined by the human researcher. A statistical module was then used to test the hypothesis on the entire database. Newly discovered data were added to the knowledge base and then used in future phases of the study. In the more recent work of the RADIX project, he and his co-workers have a more advanced system using more sophisticated statistical methods.[11]

TABLE IV—Comparison of POSCH study to RX project

	RX (RADIX)	POSCH
Number of Patients	Large	838
Number of Variables	Non-Standard	1400
Number of Visits	Variable (up to 50)	8 to 15
Protocol	Nonrandomized	Randomized
Time of Visits	Variable	12 Months
Data Elements	Variable	Standard
Total Size	Very Large	Very Large
Setting	Clinical	Clinical Trial

Much of the work required in the development of the original RX system had to deal with the fact that the data were nonrandomized and included many missing data elements. The frequency and timing of patient data were also variable. POSCH does not have these problems. Instead, it must deal with a much larger number of variables and other issues. Table IV summarizes the differences.

As we attempt to put substance to our efforts, we have identified several things that must be done before we can begin to build the expert system designed to search for knowledge now hidden in the POSCH database.

Unifying Concepts

Some unifying concept must be used to pull together into fewer units the diverse variables in POSCH's database. We have been examining several classification schemes to accomplish this. Logically formed clinical groupings already exist within our Catalog of Variables. We can use either a statistical clustering method or clinical knowledge or some combination of them to produce a dozen or so groups into which all POSCH variables are placed. By using a single entity as a representative of each group, we will reduce the initial complexity of the problem.

Role of Statistics and Reasoning Systems

Standard statistical methods provide the basis for examining the database and for describing and explaining the relationships that exist between and among the variables. These methods are based in probability theory. However, the key to the success of the system is its ability to imitate what a biostatistician does in the discovery phases of his work.

It may seem to be a contradiction for us to attempt to use expert systems in data analysis because most successful expert systems use heuristics. These expert defined heuristics or "rules of thumb" are usually necessary in order for the system to work at the level of an expert. The heuristics often have no conventionally based scientific foundation and rely solely on the expert's experience. They represent that "knowledge" of an expert that goes beyond book knowledge and this "knowledge" is what makes the expert an expert. He may not always realize that a part of his expertise lies in those intuitive things he relies on when selecting, using, and interpreting the "tools of his profession." It appears that heuristics will be especially important in the search and discovery phases of our system and it may not be possible to accurately place them into any conventional system of logic because we are trying to automate the creative phases of data analysis. Once the search and discovery phases are done, confirmation can be provided using the more routine statistical processes.

Database Issues

Another issue to be resolved has to do with finding the most efficient database structure to use in order to facilitate the needed logical manipulations of the data. Once identified, we must rebuild the database into that structure. This seems to mean that we should convert to some form of a relational database. We also need to obtain or build a reasonably efficient query language that will allow our searching module to run efficiently.

The computing capacity requirements of our system are apt to be enormous. We may need a supercomputer, but preliminary investigations indicates that a parallel processing architecture is suitable for the expert systems processing.

SUMMARY AND CONCLUSIONS

We have briefly described the POSCH AI Project. In this project we are attempting to automate many aspects of clinical research data analysis previously requiring manual processing; usually because clinical and statistical judgment are necessary components of the analysis. We are meeting with success in automating the evaluation of serially administered tests that require such clinical judgment in their evaluations. Our efforts to automate the search for medical knowledge in the POSCH database are now focused on preliminary problems that need to be resolved. This involves some means of simplifying the problem by use of unifying concepts, identifying the role of statistical reasoning, and of other reasoning systems, and developing an efficient database structure and query language.

ACKNOWLEDGEMENTS

The Program on the Surgical Control of the Hyperlipidemias (POSCH) is funded by NHLBI Grant HL15265.

REFERENCES

1. Waterman, D.A. *A Guide to Expert Systems.* Boston: Addison Wesley, 1986, pp. 319–328.
2. Buchwald, H., R.B. Moore, J.P. Matts, J.M. Long, R.L. Varco, G.S. Campbell, M.G. Pearce, A.E. Yellin, D.H. Blankenhorn, W.H. Holmes, R.D. Smink, H.S. Sawin, and the POSCH Group. "The Program on the Surgical Control of the Hyperlipidemias: A Status Report." *Surgery,* 92 (1982), pp. 654–662.
3. Multiple Risk Factor Research Group: Multiple Risk Factor Intervention Trial. "Risk Factor Changes and Mortality Results." *Journal of the American Medical Association,* 248 (1982), pp. 1465–1477.
4. Lipid Research Clinics Program: The Lipid Reserch Clinics Coronary Primary Prevention Trial Result. "1. Reduction in Incidence of Coronary Heart Disease," 251 (1984), pp. 351–364.
5. Long, J.M., J.R. Slagle, A.S. Leon, M.W. Wick, J.P. Matts, J.N. Karnegis, J.K. Bissett, H.S. Sawin, and J.P. Stevenson. "An Example of Expert Systems Applied to Clinical Trials: Analysis of Serial Graded Exercise ECG Test Data." *Controlled Clinical Trials,* (accepted for publication).
6. Long, J.M., J.R. Brashear, J.P. Matts, J.E. Bearman, and the POSCH Group. "The POSCH Information Management System: Experience with Alternative Approaches." *Journal of Medical Systems,* 4 (1981), pp. 355–356.
7. Long, J.M. "The POSCH Data Processing Experience: The Problem of Metadata." *Journal of Medical Systems,* 10 (1986), 173–183.
8. Slagle, J.R., M.W. Wick, M.O. Paliac. "AGNESS: A Generalized Network Based Expert System Shell." *Proceedings of the Fifth National Conference on Artificial Intelligence,* (Vol. 1), 1986.
9. Slagle, J.R., J.M. Long, M.R. Wick, J.P. Matts, A.S. Leon. "The Eta Project: A Case Study of Expert Systems for Analysis of Serial Clinical Trial Data." *Proceeedings of MEDINFO '86,* (Vol. 1), 1986, pp. 155–159.

10. Blum, R.A. "Discovery, Confirmation and Incorporation of Causal Relationships from a Large Time-Oriented Clinical Database: The RX Project." *Comput Biomed Res,* 15 (1982), pp. 164–187.
11. Walker, W.G., and R.L. Blum. "Towards Automated Discovery from Clinical Databases: The RADIX Project." *Proceedings on MEDINFO '86,* (Vol. 1) 1986, pp. 32–35.
12. Holland, P.W. "Statistics and Causal Inference." *Journal of the American Statistical Association,* 81 (1986), pp. 945–960.

PIONEER DAY

GEORGE RYCKMAN
General Motors, Retired
Grosse Pointe, Michigan

The challenge was seemingly never-ending. Six months of hand calculation could be carried out in fifteen minutes on one of these stored program machines, and the resulting time and cost advantages rapidly made these machines a scarce resource. A few of us dedicated ourselves to devising methods of using this resource more efficiently, and one result was a set of programs called an operating system. This is the story of those efforts and the theme of the 1987 NCC Pioneer Day: "Early Operating Systems."

The first session of the Pioneer Day program describes a period of time in the 1950s when the ideas for operating systems were germinating. Pre-operating system days are described when a programmer entered a room full of computer equipment, card deck in hand, and bent every effort to get the most out of a scheduled fifteen-minute time period. The experiences of the people at MIT with Whirlwind and at North American Aviation with the IBM 701 computer are related. Out of this background several organizations worked on methods of improving efficient use of both programmers and machines. In the words of George Mealy "There was no single line of development . . . [so] . . . I have chosen to examine a number of threads in the tapestry, for it is far from clear how to describe the tapestry as a whole." Some groups were working toward increased efficiency by providing libraries of programs such as assemblers, decimal to binary conversion, and debugging aids. Others concentrated on reducing computer idle time through automatic sequencing of a number of jobs in a batch. Both are part of the modern operating system.

The second session explores a number of systems that were implemented in the mid to late 1950s. An operating system developed jointly by General Motors and North American Aviation is described. Both automatic job sequencing and libraries of programs were features of this system which began operation in 1956 on an IBM 704 computer. The Bell Telephone Laboratories followed with BESYS in late 1957, also running on an IBM 704. The story of BESYS takes us through a series of versions culminating in a powerful system with file handling capabilities, buffered I/O, and many other features found in modern systems. The program continues with a paper on the FORTRAN Monitor System developed by IBM in the late 1950s. A number of organizations had installed FORTRAN on their own systems and, through SHARE, were urging IBM to provide and maintain a system for FORTRAN. The author describes the IBM interactions with SHARE and the development of IBM's first operating system (FMS). IBM's follow-on work with IBSYS and IBJOB in the 1960s is also recounted. Concurrent with the FMS effort, SHARE was also working with IBM on the development of the SHARE Operating System (SOS). The final paper in the afternoon session describes this last major effort undertaken in the 1950s. Many of the features revealed in this paper, such as job management, data management, and run-time facilities, are direct ancestors of today's IBM operating system.

The 1950s were exciting times, and the papers in the Pioneer Day sessions reflect that excitement. Young and old conferees will share in the experiences of thirty years ago, not only to learn why and how operating systems came about, but also to learn how to build better systems in the future.

Some threads in the development of early operating systems

by GEORGE H. MEALY
Scituate, Massachusetts

ABSTRACT

This paper discusses many of the important themes in design of the early operating systems and their libraries. Historically, the library preceded the development of the early batch system but many of its utility functions gradually migrated to the system proper. Important ideas concerning system structure which were further elaborated in the sixties are briefly discussed.

INTRODUCTION

The broadest definition of an operating system (OS) is *an environment for developing and running programs.* The motivation for invention of the earliest batch systems was economic: computers were a scarce resource, thus it was important to minimize idle time and make running time as productive as possible. The early designs concentrated on the process of sequencing jobs and keeping the machine running.

The Times

During the early fifties, the field was still small enough for most of us to become personally acquainted. Few meetings required parallel sessions, and attendees were more or less conversant with both hardware and software. As the decade wore on, specialization necessarily increased.

By 1960, programmers were rapidly becoming a scarce resource; a typical installation was spending roughly the same amount of money for software development as for hardware. Programming, and especially system programming, was then coming to be regarded as a professional activity. In the early fifties, by contrast, few of us viewed ourselves as being programmers first and foremost. Typically, we had taken up programming in order to get our primary job done; many of us never entirely returned to our previous discipline.

The rapid advances in hardware technology and architecture forced programmers to become more and more inventive. In 1950, we must remember, the first commercially developed computers had yet to be delivered. At Bell Telephone Laboratories Inc. (BTL), the main computing resources in 1950 were the Bell Model 5 relay calculator and the GPAC analog computer. Within the decade, BTL went from these to the IBM Card Programmed Calculator, the IBM 650, rental of time on the IBM 701, and finally the IBM 704. Each change of hardware caused an upheaval in our way of doing business. By the end of the decade, large open shops had developed. FORTRAN was in widespread use, but machine language programming had far from disappeared.

Installations were dissimilar, even within the airframe industry. North American Aviation used an operating system quite early. The RAND Corporation did not use an operating system until 1960. Only one RAND closed-shop programmer then used FORTRAN, and the open-shop programmers were forced to use JOHNNIAC rather than the IBM 704. (The theory, I was told, was that the open-shop programmers might waste precious machine time.)

Design of the early systems was profoundly influenced by the fact that main storage was miniscule by today's standards. The IBM 704, for instance, at first had only 8192 36 bit words of core storage and at most 16384 words of drum storage. Cards were the primary input medium. While tape reliability was a major concern throughout the fifties, after the introduction of magnetic core storage main storage reliability had come more or less under control.

Scope

This report cannot pretend to be a comprehensive treatment of operating systems or of their libraries. To a great extent it reflects the author's personal involvement with the field. (I do not know, for instance, whether systems were developed for UNIVAC I, the RAYDAC, or the early 1100 series machines. Again, Holt and Turanski are said to have made important early contributions to the organization of the library, but I did not know them during that period.) A dispassionate historian would attempt to write a very different paper. But, since few of the systems of the fifties were described in the literature, such an historian would have great difficulty in researching the subject. There was no single line of development, even among systems designed for the IBM binary computers, and the wheel was probably reinvented many times over. Description of even a single system is a complex task, especially since the ideas of many people are involved; I have chosen to examine a number of threads in the tapestry, for it is far from clear how to describe the tapestry as a whole.

The gradual development of the online system library is in many ways a more interesting story than that of the batch system. Many functions now classed as OS functions were first embodied as utility subroutines and programs. The early assemblers, interpreters, and compilers (classed here as utility programs) were developmed entirely outside of any OS context and in the almost complete absence of any theoretical guidance. Today, the library is an integral part of the OS—to the extent, for instance, that many programmers identify the UNIX system with its library rather than with its nucleus and shells.

During the fifties, a number of systems were developed which had no recognizable relation (we thought) to batch systems or to each other; in hindsight, I have little hesitation in calling them operating systems. Examples are the SAGE system (the first multiple-access computer?) and the BTL electronic switching systems (ESS.) There was a strong family resemblance, on the other hand, between the batch systems of the fifties and their structure was quite simple.

Most of the organizational ideas which became important in the following decade were present in rudimentary form during the fifties. This report ends by briefly tracing their roots in the fifties.

THE SHARE ORGANIZATION

SHARE, the first computer user group, was formed about the time of announcement of the IBM 704 in 1955. "SHARE" was not an acronym, but was aptly rendered as the "Society to Help Avoid Redundancy of Effort." Its founders were among the organizations then using the IBM 701 and in desperate need of additional computing power. Their most immediate problem in conversion from the 701 to the 704, which was not upward compatible, was the development of basic math routines, utility subroutines, and utility programs. Only a few then existed, such as the assembler developed by IBM (NY AP1) which was shortly abandoned by SHARE in favor of that developed by Roy Nutt of United Aircraft (UA SAP).

A crucial event was IBM's acceptance of the idea that it should reproduce and distribute at no charge routines and programs submitted to the SHARE Library. This was not unalloyed benevolence, for existence of the library became an important sales tool for IBM.

Cooperative development of operating systems started immediately, in the form of the General Motors and North American system for the 704, really a side effect of the formation of SHARE although not an official SHARE effort. (As late as 1959, barely half of the SHARE installations believed that an operating system was a good thing.) During the first three SHARE meetings in 1956, there had been discussion of possible improvements to the design of the 704. This resulted in announcement of the IBM 709 and in the formation of the 709 System Committee at SHARE IV in January, 1957. The system in question was SOS.

An important function of SHARE (and later user groups) has been informal education. This has taken place during committee meetings, formal presentations, the informal evening sessions in the SHARE Suite (which was well stocked), and in the SHARE Secretary Distribution—mailings to the member installations.

THE ONLINE LIBRARY

In 1955, the library was a set of file cabinets containing card decks. The decks were, variously, math and utility subroutines and utility programs. Typically, the programmer wanting to make a computer run submitted a card tray or one or more drawers of cards, any data tapes required, and a detailed set of operator instructions. To assemble and test a program, for instance, the card deck started with the binary form of the first pass of the assembler followed by the source deck followed by the assembler's second pass. There followed a separator (which could not be swallowed by the card reader) and test data cards. The operator was directed to load and ready the card reader, mount a scratch tape, and push the Load Cards button. At the conclusion of the assembly, he then took the object deck out of the card punch, substituted it for the separator, and let the machine continue with the test. Given a scratch tape, it was possible to write the assembled binary output to the tape and then load from it directly, punching the binary deck on the side.

The early OS used a library tape only to hold the system code and its utility programs. User programs and data were submitted much as described above. Roy Nutt found a way to obtain the benefits of an OS without requiring resident code. His system consisted of the library tape, a one card library call program which identified the library program to be loaded, and a set of installation standards for use of the system. The cardinal rule was that each program would conclude by issuing a load-card sequence to the card reader. As with any system of the era, the machine operator was required to intervene in case of disaster.

A few compilers had been developed for UNIVAC I by both Grace Hopper's group and by Holt and Turanski. IBM 704 FORTRAN, delivered in 1957, was a stand-alone compiler which did not allow separate compilation of subroutines. It was, with some difficulty (only octal dumps of the compiler were available), integrated by users into systems at Bell Telephone Labs (BESYS), General Motors (the F system), North American (the FORTRAN monitor or FMS), and very possibly elsewhere.

The concept of PUBLIC and EXTERNAL symbols was introduced in compiler modifications made by Monte Minami and Kei Shimizu of North American. This allowed the FORTRAN object decks to contain references to library routines (which had been written in assembler language), avoiding the necessity of punching them out as part of the compiler output. It became the job of the loader to combine library routines with the object program—a process called "linkage loading." FORTRAN II later allowed separate compilation of subroutines.

Since the FORTRAN relocatable object format followed the SHARE standard, UA SAP could be used to assemble routines to be loaded with compiled routines. More important was the fact that this allowed compiled programs to communicate with OS common data and routines. So, although the early versions of FORTRAN did their best (we thought) to defeat any integration into an OS, it was possible to ameliorate the effects of FORTRAN's inexperience.

LANGUAGE PROCESSORS

The earliest language processors were interpreters. The design of the IBM Card Programmed Calculator precluded any other approach: the interpreter consisted of the hardware and suitable plugboard wiring—in effect, it was microprogrammed. At that time, interpreters were often, as on the IBM 650 before development of the SOAP assembler, written in decimal machine code.

While it was generally recognized that interpreters did not make for efficient use of the machine (by a factor of roughly 100 or worse), compilation was in its infancy, and many of us believed that compilers could not, even in principle, match the efficiency of good assembled code. But, interpreters were ubiquitous during the early fifties, and many if them survived through the early sixties, having been moved from one machine to another in the meantime, principally to avoid reprogramming applications.

A quite different activity on the language front was t invention of the list processing languages IPL (Newell, Shaw, and Simon of Carnegie Tech and the RAND Corporation) and LISP (McCarthy's group at MIT). The ideas of pointer data and the pushdown stack introduced by list processing swiftly became indispensable tools in compiler and OS design.

Of the advances in assembler design, the invention of macro substitution was the most important. I do not know where and when it originated, but the idea was a component of the development of SOS, and a macro preprocessor for UA SAP was developed by Irwin Greenwald of RAND about 1957. In 1958-59, macros were developed much further by Eastwood and McIlroy at BTL and implemented in BE SAP, descended from UA SAP. Many of their ideas survive in current assemblers. (During the sixties, a number of unreconstructed machine language programmers seriously proposed discarding compilers in favor of macro-assemblers!)

The one theoretical advance of the fifties which had any immediate effect was the invention of Backus-Naur form, based on the work of the logician E. L. Post during the mid-thirties. Finite-state automata, discovered in the early fifties and based on the work of A. M. Turing, became important in the design of compilers only in the sixties. Chomsky's discovery of phrase-structured grammars about 1955 was also based on Post's ideas, but again did not influence compiler design until much later. While some of us felt intuitively that the grammar must be the guide to compilation of a syntactically correct program, the first syntax-directed compiler was not developed until about 1960 by Ned Irons.

COMMAND LANGUAGES

The idea of an OS command language developed rather slowly. The earliest systems used control cards in a fixed field format, and the processing pattern within a batch job was pretty much restricted to variations of that described earlier. Later, the assembler source format was adopted, the operation code field being used to call the assembler or compiler from the library, load a user program, specify breakpoint dumps, and the like. Despite the Byznatine semantics of the later OS/360 job control language, its syntax remained that of the assembler.

The MIT Compatible Timesharing System (CTSS) first allowed the operation field to be the filename of an arbitrary program, a development which preceded the widespread use of mass storage and thus online storage of user programs and data files. At this stage of OS evolution, the command processor became (or should have become) just another program. The way was now clear for development of command processors which used different linguistic styles but could coexist on the same OS. The Bourne and Berkeley shells for UNIX are examples.

SYMBOLIC MODIFICATION

Deplorable as it was, the practice of patching object programs was widespread. That there was a net saving in machine time is doubtful. Many programs ended up being such a welter of patches that it was difficult, if not impossible, to update the sources correctly. The original FORTRAN compiler and its runtime input-output library are cases in point: In order to embed the runtime routines into BESYS, I was forced many times to iterate the process of using Arthur Samuels's disassembler on the relocatable decks, commenting the resulting source code, and reassembling. The effort was worthwhile quite apart from what I learned while trying to understand Roy Nutt's code, for it was then easy to include new features in FORMAT statements and even to allow FORMAT statements to be read at runtime.

At the first meeting of the SHARE 709 System Committee in 1957, Chuck Baker of RAND presented a proposal which he called the "Alpha System." His idea was that the source program should be encoded into a form which allowed rapid loading but also retained the information necessary to reconstruct the source program. The loading process would collate in modifications written in the source language. If desired, an updated compressed (SQUOZE) deck and listing could be obtained. The symbol table was then to be used to aid in formatting dump output.

I can attest to the fact that the difference this made in the life of a machine (or assembler) language programmer was extraordinary. Unfortunately, this did not help the FORTRAN programmer. A version of the assembly pass of 709 FORTRAN which would produce a SQUOZE deck was coded, but never debugged. The basic problem here was that the idea of linkage loading did not come early enough to have any impact on the design of SOS. In the event, while we eventually got FORTRAN working within SOS, it was used in conjunction with the assembler written by Dave Ferguson of UCLA.

DEBUGGING TOOLS

Machine designs often incorporate features intended to assist in diagnosing machine and program bugs. The SAGE system, for instance, had an extremely elaborate diagnostic console. The Lincoln Laboratories utility control program (UCP) was designed to simulate the actions of an operator using that console and was directed by control cards; UCP was the immediate ancestor of BESYS. But, debugging through use of the machine console was very expensive and thus of limited utility. Post-mortem dumps were often uninformative, and a program trace usually unsurveyable.

The idea of the breakpoint, rather than post mortem, dump was to get a picture of the console state and selected portions of storage at points specified by the user. While one could insert code at these points to output information, two severe difficulties existed in practice: The breakpoint code was frequently buggy, and the cost of reassembly was high. In SOS, breakpoints were specified by inserting debugging macros, thus effectively eliminating these difficulties.

The notion of a breakpoint dump was not new at the time, but combining it with the idea of symbolic modification and macros was. Marty Belsky and his group at the IBM service bureau in New York City invented a different approach, described next, that was implemented on the IBM 704 in a matter of a few months.

The design of the 704 had included a feature designed to facilitate program tracing. When the trapping mode was enabled, any successful jump instruction sent control to location 1, depositing the address of the trapped instruction at location 0. A special instruction, trap transfer, would never be trapped. As far as I know, the trapping mode was never used for its intended purpose, but it could be used for obscure forms of subroutine and coroutine linkage.

In the case of NY SNAP, a table containing one four word

entry per breakpoint was built and an instruction in each entry was swapped with the instruction in the program at the breakpoint. Dumps were written in binary to a scratch tape and converted following the end of the program test. This scheme is still in use, although dump output conversion is now done on the spot.

Roy Nutt used the trapping mode for communication between FORTRAN compiled code and his runtime routines which interpreted [*sic*] FORMAT statements.

THE SIXTIES

The early batch systems considered only one job at a time, and the order of execution of the jobs was fixed once a batch started. Job scheduling could not become a system function until the advent of plentiful random access storage, nor could a system designer contemplate switching control between members of a set of partially executed jobs. The latter, given a suitable adjustment of terminology (read "job" as "unit of processing," "task," or "process") was the typical processing pattern in the real-time systems and became that of the operating systems of the sixties and later.

Apart from the presence of mass storage, this development benefited from a number of earlier hardware and programming advances. These are summarized below.

Multiple Access

SAGE, under development in the fifties, had a number of consoles of different types. The most numerous displayed radar plots and other data related to missile tracks. The console operator gave direction to his part of the enterprise by keying in data. The SAGE program was responsible for monitoring all system inputs (radar, communications lines, and consoles) by polling each class of inputs on a regular basis and yielding control to an appropriate subprogram whenever it noted a change of status. The ESS program was not unlike the SAGE program in that its overall control was based on polling inputs. Batch systems, by contrast, had only one input source (apart from switches on the operator's console) to worry about.

Hardware Interrupts, Multiprogramming, and Multiprocessing

The practice of polling elevated what should ideally have been a low level concern—noting the presence of new input data and other status changes—to a high level concern in system design. The introduction of hardware interrupt systems by STRETCH corrected this situation and, in principle at least, reduced system overhead and response time.

Input-output channels allowed input-output operations to overlap central processing unit (CPU) operation. On the output side, this was relatively easy to accommodate in OS design, even when the interrupts were not used. On the input side "anticipatory buffering," as the practice came to be called, was a more complex proposition. The design of the SOS buffering subsystem was predicated on the presence of these hardware facilities. Ironically, the official version of SOS was never run with the interrupts enabled.

The term *multiprogramming* derived from the view that a computer runs programs and an interrupt diverts its attention from one program to another. *Multiprocessing* referred to a computer configuration with multiple CPUs, whether or not they shared main storage. Both terms are more suggestive than exact and have meant different things to different people. Regarding the former term, the principal focus in designing a real-time system has been the data rather than the program; use of the term *multiprogramming* would be inappropriate, quite apart from the use by the early systems of polling rather than hardware interrupts. Regarding the latter term, CPUs have been joined within single hardware systems by other types of processors, such as array processors, numeric processors, and input-output channels; by only a slight abuse of terminology one could call STRETCH, the IBM 709, and their suite, multiprocessing systems. The GAMMA 60 was, to use Doug McIlroy's word, multi-everything.

By late 1963 it was clear that scheduling and dispatching of whatever units of processing was already an important system function. Whatever one called the unit of processing in any context, it must be accompanied by a sort of a job ticket which identified among other things the program, the data, and the type of processor to be used. Scheduling and dispatching then arranged these in queues and from time to time assigned each processor to a given unit of processing. The terms *task* (OS/360) and *process* (MULTICS) were neutral with respect to program and data. Hence my coined term *multitasking*. Multitasking was not a new invention but a revisionist view of the early system organizations.

Dynamic Relocation and Paging

Linkage loading of relocatable object programs had made it unnecessary for programs to directly reference absolute locations in storage or to be assembled at absolute origins. However, once the program was loaded, it was bound to absolute storage addresses and could not be moved. Even before the advent of timesharing, there were situations in which it was desireable to write a partially executed program out to a backing store and then read it later into a different location in main storage. Further, a buggy program had to be prevented from destroying its near or distant neighbors.

The solution to these problems embodied in the STRETCH hardware, and later built into the augmented 704 on which CTSS was first implemented, was to provide machine registers to dynamically relocate addresses in the program and to bound the range of allowable memory references, on the pain of a memory protection interrupt. A quite different and more elegant solution was provided by the British ATLAS computer's paging hardware. An additional benefit of the ATLAS design was provision of a much larger (virtual) memory than that implied by the width of the machine's memory address registers.

ACKNOWLEDGEMENTS

Bernie Galler, Doug McIlroy, Owen Mock, George Ryckman, and Kei Shimizu have jogged my memory and suggested changes of emphasis, for which I thank them.

A batch-processing operating system for the Whirlwind I computer

by CHARLES W. ADAMS
Hudson, New Hampshire

ABSTRACT

The Whirlwind I computer was developed at M.I.T. in the late 1940s and early 1950s primarily for use in real-time applications, most notably in early development of the U. S. continental air defense system. It was the fastest first-generation machine and the first to use magnetic core memory. Under sponsorship of the Office of Naval Research, time on Whirlwind was made available for general-purpose use by M.I.T. students and researchers on a program-it-yourself basis, their use coordinated and supported by the small so-called Scientific and Engineering Computation Group. During 1951 through 1955, this group developed a variety of coding techniques and aids for using Whirlwind, including a batch-processing operating system incorporating many of the logical capabilities which appear in today's systems. The hardware available, the operational philosophy, and the accomplishments of the group are briefly described.

THE WHIRLWIND I COMPUTER

The development of operating systems for the Whirlwind I computer was an evolutionary process which extended over the entire decade from its early operation in 1950 until its retirement in 1959, with the greatest effort concentrated in the early half of the decade. It also extended over Whirlwind's two distinct areas of intended application as: (1) a real-time control system, and (2) a general-purpose computational tool. I can only report on the latter application area. Before I attempt to describe some of the operational thinking and accomplishments of the 1951–1955 period, let me outline the evolving hardware context which led up to and through that time period.

History

I joined Project Whirlwind in the Servomechanisms Laboratory at the Massachusetts Institute of Technology on a part-time basis in December 1947, while I was still an undergraduate. The project had been in existence for three years under the sponsorship of the Special Devices Section of the Navy's Bureau of Aeronautics before being transferred to the new Office of Naval Research (ONR).[1] Its original purpose had been to develop an aircraft flight simulator incorporating a real-time stability and control analyzer, for which its young project leader, Jay W. Forrester, had first thought in terms of analog computation. After visiting the University of Pennsylvania in the Fall of 1945, he decided instead to build a general-purpose digital computer which would be called Whirlwind I.

Logical Design

Whirlwind's intended real-time applications required high speed and high reliability but not particularly high precision. The logical design which Robert R. Everett completed in 1947 called for a 16-binary-digit parallel machine with instructions comprising a 5-bit operation code and a single 11-bit address capable of addressing an internal storage of 2048 words. In today's terms, this would be a 4K-byte RAM, although the use of pure binary numbers made each word capable of storing a sign and about 4.5 decimal digits.

Whirlwind's instruction code, like many other first-generation machines, bore considerable similarity to von Neumann's IAS computer (which was to store 1024 40-bit words with two instructions per word). Operating in parallel at a one megahertz cycle rate with eight cycles per instruction exclusive of memory access (specified at 8 microseconds, a speed achieved with magnetic cores in 1953 though not with the original electrostatic storage tubes) and built-in multiply and divide (at about 16 and 32 microseconds), Whirlwind performed some 17,000, and after 1953, some 40,000 operations per second, by far the fastest first-generation machine.

Early Programming

I completed my graduate work in the Mathematics Department (my thesis included a Whirlwind program which was never run) and joined Project Whirlwind in February 1949 as a full-time, about-to-be programmer. Programming was a relatively untrodden field at the time since no stored-program computer had yet gone into operation anywhere in the world. (Wilkes's serial, mercury-delay-line-storage EDSAC at Cambridge University became the first on May 5, 1949.) My job was to develop programs intended to aid future scientific and engineering users in making use of a portion of the time available on Whirlwind for research projects of their own. This allocation was to continue despite the high priority of the intended real-time control applications which, over the next three years, evolved from flight analysis through air traffic control to continental air defense (and, ultimately, the SAGE system). By 1951, hardware development was under Air Force sponsorship, though ONR retained an interest in the use of Whirlwind for general-purpose computation, and Project Whirlwind had become the M.I.T. Digital Computer Laboratory.

Initially, these user aids were envisioned as pre-programmed sub-routines to handle such things as decimal-to-binary and binary-to-decimal conversions for input and output, the computation of roots, trigonometric and other mathematical functions, the solution of algebraic and differential equations, and the processing of complex variables, matrices and the like. But practical experience, hard and slowly learned, suggested that these facilities, though important, were not the crux of the problem.

Test Storage

By 1950, the central processor was in operation, but due to difficulties with the specially-designed electrostatic storage tubes which were to provide the main memory, our only hands-on experience with Whirlwind for many months involved the use of a so-called test storage comprising 32 words of what is today called programmable read-only memory or PROM, with each bit represented by a toggle switch, and five words of flip-flops (vacuum-tube circuits storing one bit each) that could be substituted for any five of the PROM registers. Each flip-flop register could be preset to a value set in front-panel toggle switches and its contents were continuously indicated on the front panel. In addition to its extensive use to test hardware and to demonstrate the early Whirlwind, this test storage served permanently as Whirlwind's "bootstrap" loader.

Early Peripheral Devices

The early input equipment was limited to, besides the quite useful toggle switches mentioned above, a slow punched-paper tape reader. Output, in addition to the indicator lights on the flip-flop and internal registers, and the audio output mentioned below, comprised a ten-character-per-second printer and, more importantly, a device unique to Whirlwind among early machines and crucial to its air defense applications—a cathode-ray-tube (CRT), the beam of which could be deflected to arbitrary x and y coordinates by output instructions. Probably the most widely seen demonstration of Whirlwind, before electrostatic storage become operational, used the CRT to display the solution to the differential equation describing a ball bouncing on a horizontal axis, repeated at successively-increased horizontal speeds until it hit a hole in the floor and fell through.

After electrostatic storage made possible more elaborately scaled and calibrated graphics, and computer-generated dot-matrix decimal and alphanumeric displays of a thousand or more characters per frame at about 200 characters per second, an automatic camera was attached to a second CRT so that graphs and, more importantly, memory dumps and other aids to program debugging, could be recorded for future reference. Another off-beat but useful output, incorporated after we noted the sound of unintentional audio crosstalk on intercom wires strung around the 2500-square-foot computer area to permit maintenance engineers to talk to operators, consisted of intercom stations connected to selected flip-flops in the accumulator, program counter or elsewhere, so an operator could hear how things were progressing and know when a bug had put the program into an endless loop. This also led inevitably to programs to make the computer play recognizable tunes.

Full-scale Storage

When reasonably reliable operation of the early 16 × 16 bit electrostatic storage tubes began late in 1950, the availability of 256 additional words of storage opened whole new vistas after months of cramming things into 32 words. Reasonably reliable operation was unfortunately preceded by some months of reasonably unreliable operation—I can still feel the pain of watching on a monitor while a small black cloud would slowly overspread the pattern of bits in a defective tube and my program would sputter and die, with an audio accompaniment not unlike the sound of an encephalogram of a patient dying on TV today. By late 1951, a second bank of tubes, each capable of storing a 32 × 32 array, expanded the memory to 1280 words, not counting test storage and the 100 or so unconsecutively numbered locations we sometimes used, that lay inside the circumference but outside the 16 × 16 square array in the first bank of tubes. Almost 3K bytes; this was heaven indeed.

By that time, work on a coincident-current magnetic core memory conceived by Forrester in the Spring of 1949 had progressed to the point at which it appeared more promising than the electrostatic tubes, both in speed and in reliability, but the electrostatic memory continued in use until it could be replaced in August and September 1953 by 2048 words of 8 microsecond-access cores in two 16-high stacks of 32 × 32 core arrays. This form of memory quickly became the standard of the computer industry and remained so for roughly the next 15 years.

Later Peripheral Devices

The 1951 to 1953 period also saw the addition of: a magnetic drum system with a 64K-byte capacity and 64K-byte-per-second transfer rate; four magnetic tape drives each with 250K-byte capacity and about 800-byte-per-second transfer rate in which the tapes were for all practical purposes not removable; a 200-character-per-second photoelectric paper tape recorder which to our great joy could stop and start between individual characters rather than requiring an inch or two of blank tape for stopping as an earlier, slower unit had; a real-time clock useful in logging; a 1200-digit-per-second character generator for the CRT; and a joystick and later a light gun for use with the CRT (facilities important for air defense applications and for demonstrations but not used in the general-purpose system). In a 1954 description of the system,[2] I described the core, drum, and tape capabilities as "a storage hierarchy of ample sizes, speeds, and versatility," something I would hardly say today.

THE GENERAL-PURPOSE OPERATING SYSTEM

As mentioned, the intent of Whirlwind's so-called Scientific and Engineering Computation (S&EC) Group which I headed under ONR sponsorship was to make the computer available to qualified users with the proviso that they do their own programming, and to provide support for training offered to graduate and undergraduate students, and (through special one and two week full-time summer session courses) to interested people from business and industry. Wearing a second hat as Assistant Professor of Digital Computation in the Electrical Engineering Department, I had the pleasure of preparing and teaching both the regular and the summer programs at M.I.T. during that period. During 1953 and 1954, Whirlwind was used by 10 staff members of the S&EC Group, by some 35 graduates and four undergraduates in connection with their theses, and by about 25 undergraduates, 40 graduates, and 100 summer students in connection with M.I.T. courses.

Batch Processing

With so many users sharing the 40 or so hours per week of Whirlwind time available to this activity, much of it scheduled in the middle of the night and on weekends, hands-off batch processing was the order of the day. Whirlwind's file storage capabilities may have been "ample" for one user at a time, but would have been grossly inadequate for online multi-task moment-by-moment time sharing developed a few years later by another group on another computer at M.I.T.

It is perhaps interesting to note that the luxury of time-shared access to supercomputers and of full-time access to powerful personal computers are enjoyed by today's users at monthly costs approximating their own salaries for a single day. In the early 1950s, the daily salary of a Whirlwind user, if indeed he had one, would not normally have covered the cost of half a minute of machine time.

Assemblers and Interpreters

Operating as it did on short fixed-point pure-binary words, Whirlwind clearly required input and output conversion routines and some way of extending the effective word length for computational purposes. It took only a little exposure to the problems of assigning absolute memory locations to variables and instructions to suggest that the task should be handled along with decimal-to-binary conversion by the computer itself, through the actual implementation of assembly programs with symbolic (we called them "floating") addresses extended over several years.

Double-precision arithmetic seemed best accomplished by an interpretive routine, a program which treated the instructions specified by a user as data to be interpreted and then executed one at a time. Given a double-precision interpreter, a floating-point capability could be included at little extra cost in machine time. Furthermore, an interpreter could greatly facilitate the debugging of a program by pre-checking for some kinds of mistakes and by storing a trail (a "trace") of the logical path followed and of intermediate results to the extent desired by the user.

There was also no great additional time required to interpret instructions written in a form unrelated to the single-address instruction logic built into Whirlwind. This led to the development of fairly powerful and more easily debugged (but still machine-like) languages such as the Summer Session and the TAC and SAC languages used in the 1953 and 1954 summer courses. An interpreter was also used to implement an Algebraic Language developed by two users of Whirlwind, J. H. Laning and N. Zierler, which was an early precursor to the FORTRAN language later implemented with a compiler.

The "Comprehensive System"

Most users, other than students in M.I.T. courses, used the so-called Comprehensive System. They wrote their own programs as machine-language instructions in assembly-language form with numerical computation to be executed by an interpreter in double-precision floating point (signed 24-bit numbers with signed 6-bit scale factors, roughly equivalent to 7-decimal-digit precision with magnitudes ranging from 10^{-10} to 10^{10}) while logical computation was executed in Whirlwind's internal format (signed integers from −32767 to 32767).

Operational Procedures

Whether written in the Comprehensive System, the Summer Session or other languages, programs were keyed and verified on six-hole paper tape by trained personnel in Whirlwind's tape preparation room, each tape identified by job, user, program and revision number. Listings were returned to the users and tapes filed in the room. When a user wished a test or production run, he or she filled out a brief performance request form specifying the paper tape or tapes to be run and any special instructions, though for the most part the entire specification was expected to be included in the tape(s) being run. Information needed for the analysis of program performance, beyond that generated by the program itself or routinely provided by the operator and the system, was specified on a "post-mortem request" tape to be run at the termination of failed program. By 1955, performance requests were often specified on a "director" tape which controlled the processing of a series of individual runs.

Thus, the files of user programs, data, and results were kept on paper tape and in printed or plotted form, produced by professional operators and filed manually by clerks. Assemblers, interpreters, utility programs, and post-mortems were kept on a single magnetic tape. They amounted to about 24K bytes for the entire Comprehensive System and 16K bytes for the Summer Session system. From tape, they were automatically copied to core or drum as required. Programs were assembled prior to each run using two other tapes for auxiliary storage in a two-pass system.

CONCLUSION

While the users of Whirlwind would certainly have been happy to have had today's facilities available to them, they would also surely recognize many of the logical capabilities of today's operating system in the system they used in 1955 and before.

ACKNOWLEDGEMENTS

The development of the Comprehensive System at M.I.T. paralleled that of other systems at the time and drew a considerable part of its inspiration from them, most notably from the Cambridge University group. Several of its leading lights, M. V. Wilkes, D. J. Wheeler, S. Gill and E. Mutch, participated in one or more Summer Sessions and shared many ideas with us. Those at Whirlwind who contributed ideas and working programs to the system included, in alphabetical order, D. N. Arden, S. Best, D. Combelic, M. S. Demurjian, H. H. Denman, J. T. Gilmore, J. M. Frankovich, I. Hazel, F. C. Helwig, E. S. Kopley and J. D. Porter (who took over direction of the group as I phased out of it).

REFERENCES

1. Redmond, Kent C., and Thomas M. Smith. *Project Whirlwind—The History of a Pioneer Computer* Bedford, Massachusetts: Digital Press, 1980.
2. Adams, Charles W. "Report R-233—The M.I.T. System of Automatic Coding: Comprehensive, Summer Session, and Algebraic—a Talk Delivered at the Symposium on Automatic Programming for Digital Computers, May 12, 1954," Cambridge, Massachusetts: Digital Computer Laboratory, M.I.T., 1954.

The North American 701 Monitor

by OWEN R. MOCK
Palos Verdes Estates, California

ABSTRACT

Although constrained by history, schedule, and hardware to triviality when compared to modern operating systems, the North American 701 Monitor was arguably the first operating system to be in operation. Installed in December 1955, the North American 701 Monitor was developed as a prototype monitor to extract more utilization from overburdened IBM 701's and pilot test the operating system concept prior to introduction of the General Motors/North American 704 monitor which was to follow. A historic separation of programmers from computer hardware combined with inadequate computer resources to establish the motivation and climate for the projected more efficient use of computer resources via a "monitor system." This paper presents an overview of the then contemporary North American Aviation operating philosophy, the IBM 701 hardware, the affected "system" software, and the resultant characteristics of the monitor system, and effect on the end user.

INTRODUCTION

Trying to recall programs that were written approximately 32 years ago is difficult enough. Trying to describe a system of programs whose hardware constraints, to say nothing of its goals and schedules, destine it to triviality by modern standards in an interesting manner, becomes a formidable task. It is hoped to add some interest by (1) being perhaps first, and also an immediate prototype predecessor to the North American-General Motors Operating System and subsequent Share Operating System, and (2) adding some comments on its historical perspective and general comments on the interaction between operating systems and hardware.

First of all, several of those whom I saw as pioneers should be mentioned. Dr. Derrick H. Lehmer talked me into going to the Nation Bureau of Standards Institute for Numerical Analysis at UCLA in 1951 despite my belief that computers would never amount to much until everyone could have one. Dr. Everett Yowell, in turn, arranged my opportunity to join North American Aviation when the Institute for Numerical Analysis closed in the summer of 1953.

But to me, those most immediately deserving of recognition were those people in management who created the early environment that led among other things to the foundation of SHARE. Somehow, management saw fit to encourage cooperation and experimentation at the time when it was most needed. With respect to what follows, credit belongs particularly to my immediate superiors Charlie Davis and Jack Strong, and to Frank Wagner of North American's engineering department. (The latter two were key figures among the founders of SHARE.)

Exemplary of the freedom that was given was that I was allowed during this period, to develop such strange things as: (1) a program patcher, which performed direct inline extension or shrinkage of code, (2) a loop generating subroutine which dynamically generated address modifying and limit testing code based on inline parameters, and (3) a multiprecision, variable length integer arithmetic interpretive system which could handle integers of up to 340 digits (divide never quite worked); all of which turned out to be dead ends.

A BACKGROUND OF REGIMENTATION

North American Aviation was rather unique in that computer operations grew up in the accounting department which was not as peculiar as it might seem. For most businesses, tabulating equipment was used almost exclusively for accounting. The first electronic calculators, the IBM 604 and subsequent Card Programmed Calculator (CPC, first delivered to North American in December, 1951), were basically punched card machines, and because of this reliance on cards it was felt desirable that their operation remain in Tabulating, a section of accounting.

For better or for worse, separation of operations from users had some far-reaching effects. Among other things, it resulted in a philosophy that users should not touch the machine; in fact, they were not even supposed to touch their punched card decks. It also resulted in a philosophy of strict accountability; even utility programmers (now called system programmers) were required to account for their machine time. The end result was a user regimentation that, at first blush, would appear to run counter to the freedom mentioned in the introduction but which facilitated the introduction of operating system concepts.

For the first 701, delivered October 10, 1953, a utility programming team was recruited and added to the operations staff. This team wrote an assembler (Ed Law), the usual square root and set of transcendental functions, the proverbial one card loader, decimal to binary conversion routines and vice versa, some simple I/O handlers, and a memory dump. In addition, a floating point interpretive system called DUAL, generously provided by the University of California at Los Alamos, was modified to operate with the above routines. Finally IBM's SPEEDCODE was added as a completely separate system. Again the philosophy was that the user was not to be bothered with any of these things so that he could concentrate on problem solving. In theory, he was only to provide key-punch forms and setup instructions, and everything else was to be done by operations.

DUAL was chosen because it permitted intermingling machine instructions with interpretive code. SPEEDCODE was chosen for its expected ease of use. Naturally, everything had to be renamed; DUAL was called DUET, SPEEDCODE was called SPEEDCO, and the system of programs encompassing DUET was called SPEEDEX although some preferred the terms "SLOWEX" and "SLOWCO" for the most likely of reasons.

Given the hardware constraints and state of the art, probably the key deficiency was the absence of a relocatable loader. The concept of a linking loader was yet to be developed. This meant that if a routine was to be executed from more than one place, it had to be reassembled for each instance. From this came the practice of premapping the utility programs, placing part of them at the beginning of memory and part of them at the end, leaving the middle as user space that began and ended at various places, depending upon which utility programs were to be employed at execution time.

Another important factor in the 701 environment was the rapid development of demand. Within 8 months from delivery, the 701 had already gone to two shifts. (701's were only rented and extra shift usage meant extra rent.) Within 13 months the 701 was on three shifts, and within 15 months time was rented on a Douglas Aircraft machine across the street. This intense demand resulted in a turn-around time of several days for jobs which would take only a few minutes, placing computer time at an extraordinary premium.

IBM 701 HARDWARE

It is worth taking the space to describe some characteristics of the IBM hardware, not for its own interest, but as to how it shapes any development of an operating system.

Original Hardware (October 1953)

Williams Tube memory, 2048 36-bit words (9k byte equivalent)
Four type 726 tapes with steel leaders
Four 2048 word drums
150 card per minute reader
150 line per minute printer
100 card per minute punch
No floating point arithmetic
No index registers
No memory protection
No interrupt mechanism
Machine cycle, 12 microseconds, with an add taking 5 cycles

Neither the Williams Tubes nor the 726 tapes were reliable, and the mounting mechanism of the tapes discouraged their usage even further. As a consequence, punched cards were still considered to be the only permanent storage medium.

Periquip Hardware (December 1955)

Six online 727 tape drives substituted for 726 drives
Offline 250 card per minute IBM 714 card to tape
Offline 150 line per minute IBM 717 tape to printer

It should be emphasized that the 714 and 717 were completely independent, in another room with no electronic connection to the 701 whatsoever.

SPEEDEX EXECUTION

The basic concept of SPEEDEX execution was that a user program was to be loaded onto a background of previously loaded system routines. All code was absolute and hence the only available loaders were absolute. The background routines were kept on a dedicated library tape. The first 256 words of main storage were dedicated to an execution control routine, including drum and tape handlers and a binary card loader. Beyond this, in various locations would be found:

A four-field decimal data card read routine
An 8-digit integer print routine
Fixed point elementary functions including square root
Duet, standard version
Duet, version A
Duet, version D

Duet was quite large and contained its own card read and print routines. Further routines existed at the end of main store. Since only absolute loading was possible, each routine had a different version for each address at which it was to execute. Library routines were accessed by record number so that library maintenance became quite complicated, trying to take into account both minimum tape travel and minimum disruption of pre-existing callers by changes of record numbers.

THE *PERIQUIP* DECISION

In the latter half of 1955, several events converged which led to the Periquip system. IBM announced the availability of 727 tapes on the IBM 701, as well as the 704, and of the 714 Card-to-Tape and 717 Tape-to-Printer. As it turned out, this equipment was welcome fallout from the IBM 702, the IBM business machine as opposed to scientific machine of the time that preceded the IBM 705. In addition, SHARE was born.

As a consequence of the formation of SHARE, General Motors approached North American about the possibility of jointly developing a monitor system for the IBM 704 that was scheduled for delivery in the summer of 1956. This system became the General Motors-North American Monitor that is the subject of another paper. At the same time, North American decided to develop a prototype monitor system for its second 701 that would have new 727 tapes and peripheral equipment. The purpose of this monitor system was two-fold: to mitigate the 701 demand crunch and to gain experience with the as yet untried concept of a monitor system. It was also decided to christen this system "Periquip."

PERIQUIP SYSTEM CHARACTERISTICS

The Periquip system was about the simplest possible batch processing system. Multiple jobs were placed on a single 727 tape that became a batch whose target duration was one hour. There was a small in core resident monitor and a single system library and control program tape that also acted as backup for the resident monitor. Output was stacked on an output tape that could be removed and replaced if necessary. Upon the completion of a batch, the input and remaining output tape were removed and replaced with the next batch, and the output tape was taken to the 717 to be printed. Note here that in contrast to most large modern systems, the term "batch" did indeed mean job batching.

Each job card contained, in addition to the programmer's name and accounting information, an estimate of maximum execution time and a hard maximum output line count. Following the job card normally would be a set of library call cards that would specify routines to be loaded from the system library tape. Then came a set of absolute octal cards that represented the program to be executed, and finally any data cards for the program. The program had to be loaded in octal because at that time the 714 card to tape was not capable of reading binary cards. (The inability to handle binary is still with us in some communication protocols.)

A job could be ended by the user program jumping to a specific entry point in the resident monitor, by an error in a standard subroutine, by a job exceeding its output line count, or by operator intervention. Operator intervention would occur if the program halted or if, in the operator's opinion, the program was caught in a loop or had substantially exceeded the programmer's estimated time. With luck, if intervention was necessary, the operator would first record the location counter and other relevant information and then would key in a jump to a particular address; this was the same entry point in the resident monitor as was used by programmers to take a memory dump and then transfer control to the next job. If this failed, he would load a three card program from the card reader, which would cause a dump and reload of the resident monitor.

Everything continued to have to be referenced by its absolute address. A library routine was referenced by the record number of its first record on the library tape. Actual entry to a library subroutine was performed by jumping to the absolute address of the routine although a transfer vector was employed to keep things from getting completely out of hand when the subroutine had to be reassembled.

SYSTEM INTRODUCTION

Considering that we are dealing with conversion from a manual operating system, the actual testing and conversion went rather smoothly. The new decimal conversion routines and the corresponding octal routines became both simpler and shorter than the routines they replaced. They so easily fit in the same space as their predecessors, and most importantly, their interfaces remained constant. Most of the other system functions had already been introduced, at least partially, in order to simplify and speed manual operation. The task was by no means trivial because one of the constraints was that user routines could not be moved, which led to a fair amount of nook and cranny programming. The author remembers one subsequent six-instruction routine, whose purpose now eludes him, that took six weeks to check out.

What was involved in conversion can best be illustrated by quoting from notes by Florence Anderson for a contemporary class in Engineering Computing:

"III. Program Considerations
A. Must conform to:
1. All instructions on octonary cards
2. No sense switches
. .
4. Must end on:
a. End of file condition for octonary or decimal card read
b. Transfer to location 102_{10} to start next job
5. No programmed stops—transfer to debug routine or memory print
6. do not use tapes 4,5,6
. .
D. P. E. routines
1. . . There are no binary card reading routines. The octonary card read routine is available in 4 different locations.
. .
3. Speedex and Duet print routines are available with a few changes. Errors cause transfer to 101_{10} (memory print). Estimate of pages printed is checked; if exceeded memory print.
4. No stops in program
. .
d. Programmer may change the instruction at 101_{10} to transfer to his own debug routine. Always transfer to 102_{10} afterwards."

IT WASN'T ALL THAT EASY!

First of all, SPEEDCODE renamed SPEEDCO, continued to be used outside of the system and there was always a user or two whose project was so important that they were above the system. Because of the demand crunch, a computerized priority system was instituted which may be of some interest. Each priority job was assigned a factor to be interpreted as a multiplier for that job's share of the computer. This was punched up on a schedule card together with the estimated maximum execution time and the time of job submission. The deck of active scheduled jobs was then run hourly, and an ordered priority schedule printed out (on line) which consisted of:

$$\text{Priority} = \text{PriorityFactor} * \text{CurrentWaitTime}/\text{ExecutionTime}$$

and the next batch of jobs was written to tape on the basis of this printout. This worked pretty well except for VIP (Very Important Project) jobs, which were invariably assigned a priority factor of 99.

Manual intervention was indeed a stumbling block; but this would not be surmounted in operating systems until there was an adequate hardware interrupt mechanism and adequate protection several hardware generations in the future. One nice by-product was that there was no such thing as a "system crash"; one could always blame the user, maintaining that he destroyed the monitor by either a wild store or a wild jump. Yes, there were system bugs, but the recovery from them was no different than from user bugs since they were indistinguishable to the operator.

PARTICIPANTS

For so small a system, the number of participants was rather large. This was because management endorsement, machine operation, and user cooperation played as big a role as the system itself. Participating in a variety of ways were Penny Barbe, Ray Berman, Don Breheim, Dale Hanks, Irwin Marshall, Kei Shimizu, Jack Strong, and Frank Wagner.

General Motors/North American Monitor for the IBM 704 computer

by ROBERT L. PATRICK
Rosamond, California

ABSTRACT

Pioneer Day papers are an attempt by the NCC Committee to document work of significance for the historical record. In that spirit, this paper relates some software work of 30 years ago.

Earlier work using an IBM 701 led to the pursuit of performance and thruput. Within that framework the concept of the tape-to-tape mode of operating an IBM 704 was developed. The progeny of this batch system are well known: SOS, IBSYS, and with the substitution of disk for tape, OS/360.

The roots of the General Motors/North American Aviation effort go back to 1954. At that time I was working for an aircraft foundry in Ft. Worth, Texas. Picture a bunch of miscellaneous college graduates (computer science hadn't been invented yet) trying to understand the physics of aircraft design, formulate mathematical design models, and program these solutions for a giant brain. Only 19 IBM 701s were manufactured. The Ft. Worth machine was serial #7. The 17th machine, which I will discuss later, was installed at General Motors in Detroit. The 701 was a .15 MIPS machine. It rented for about $23,750 a month, and filled a 40 foot by 40 foot room.

Architecturally, it was a single sequencing machine and could do only one thing at a time (cycle stealing channels hadn't been invented yet). Thus when a 701 addressed an input/output device, that's all it could do until the data transfer was completed. It was a batch machine and a typical configuration consisted of a 150 card-per-minute reader, a 100 card-per-minute punch, a 150 line-per-minute printer (48 characters), and an internal memory of 2,000 36-bit words. It also had four magnetic tapes whose transfer rate was 7.5 thousand characters-per-second, and a magnetic drum which held 2,000 words. The mean time to failure was about 30 minutes if you were lucky (see Figure 1).

Figure 1—IBM 701

The typical mode of operating was programmer present and at the operating console. When a programmer got ready for a test shot, he or she signed up on a FIFO list, much like the list at a crowded restaurant. The programmer then checked progress frequently to estimate when he would reach the top. When his time got close, he stood by with card deck in hand. When the previous person finished, ran out of allotted time or abruptly crashed, the next programmer rushed in, checked that the proper board was installed in the card reader, checked that the proper board was installed in the printer, checked that the proper board was installed on the punch, hung a magnetic tape (if he was going to use a master tape), punched in on a mechanical time clock, addressed the console, set some switches, loaded his punched card deck in the card reader, prayed the first card would not jam, and pressed the load button to invoke the bootstrap sequence.

If all went well, you could load a typical deck of about 300 cards and begin the execution of your first instruction about 5 minutes after entering the machine room. If only one person did all this set up and got going in five minutes, he bustled around the machine room like a whirling dervish (see Figure 2).

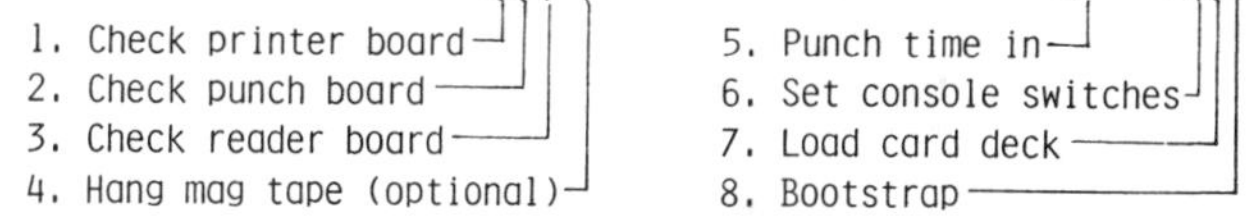

Figure 2—Typical 701 setup time phasing

Not always did things go smoothly. If a programmer was fumble-fingered, cards jammed, magnetic tapes would not read due to defective splices, printer boards or switches were incorrectly set up, and it took 10 minutes to get going; or worse—you lost your opportunity and the next guy took the machine when your time ran out. Usually the machine spent more time idle than computing. We programmers weren't paid very much and although the machine was fairly costly, its capacity was even a more precious commodity since there were only 17 in the whole world and only one in the entire state of Texas.

Now I had never heard of Henry Laurence Gantt, the father of industrial engineering, but if I had, this story would be a lot shorter. Seeing idle time on a precious resource caused several of us in various locations around the country to start a drive for efficiency that is still with us today. Informally we programmers started operating in teams so each programmer would have an assistant to help him get set up and going faster. That helped the fumble-fingered the most. We also gradually standardized on plug boards for the reader, printer, and punch to eliminate some of the board changing. We did some preventive maintenance on our card decks to reduce card jams and we tried to get programmer-operators better organized so they weren't so befuddled at the console (not entirely successful). All of this reduced the worst case idle time between runs, but the average productive use of the machine was still poor.

About this time, I was an obnoxious young hot shot and found a way to get my test shots in the idle time between other programmer's scheduled runs. I ran only with standard plug boards so I never changed any boards. I bootstrapped my programs from an unused magnetic tape instead of punched cards and this reduced my program loading time from about three minutes to ten seconds. Further, each input record loaded to a unique address so I could store the program on tape and overload patches through the card reader. I could get a full test shot in three minutes or less if my output did not exceed 150 lines of printing, (see Figure 3).

Now this may not sound like much in 1987, but I got a shot whenever I wanted just by squeezing in on the schedule. I was getting four and five shots a day when the others were lucky to get two. Furthermore, my total machine time was only 25 percent of what everyone else used.

Programming in the early 1950s could best be described as organized chaos. The typical programmer used assembly language, chose his favorite binary-to-decimal conversion routines from a library, figured out how to assemble and debug his programs as best he could from the primitive tools available, and at long last got a program checked out which may have been a work of art, but was always later than when the customer wanted results.

I was a premier user of an interpretive programming package, developed by John Backus and his colleagues at IBM, that was called the IBM 701 Speedcoding System. Speedcode was an integrated set of programs and provided packaged I/O, and a simplified three-address language with floating-point operands for programming. The purist programmers treated

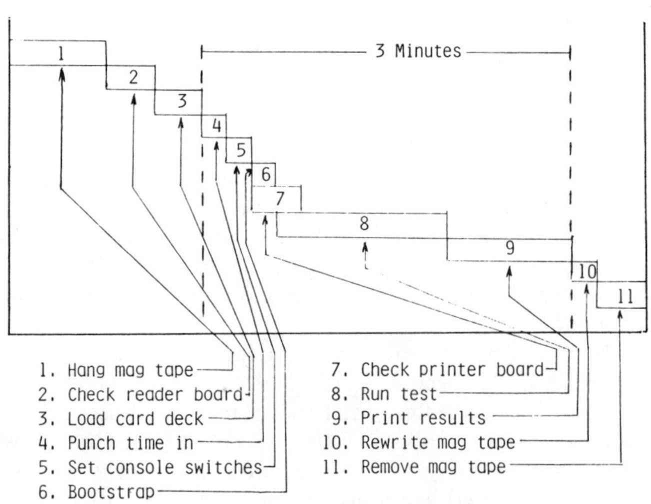

Figure 3—Speedcode debug time phasing

Speedcode with disdain, but I got a lot of work done and learned several lessons about machine room operation. Specifically:

1. Get the programmer off the console and out of the machine room.
2. Standardize on machine setups to eliminate setup steps.
3. Avoid reloading your whole job each time, maintain a magnetic tape copy, and update storage with a change deck.
4. The use of an integrated package of programs produced results much faster than with 100 percent custom programming and worked satisfactorily for all but the biggest compute-bound jobs.

In 1954, I got tired of defense applications and moved to General Motors Research in Detroit. They were just installing 701 serial #17, and I took Speedcode and my mode of operation with me. The results were much the same, even though my engineering applications then dealt with automobiles and automotive gas turbines.

In mid-1955, General Motors had an IBM 704 on order; George Ryckman was assigned to lead the team to plan for its installation and operation. I was on that team and played a role which today we would call architect. About that same time, the IBM user's group, SHARE, was being formed to allow the member installations to exchange programs and ideas for their mutual benefit. The third meeting of SHARE was held in Boston on November 10 and 11, 1955.

Prior to that meeting, General Motors published a description of an operating system for the IBM 704. There was a competing proposal from North American Aviation. After reviewing the system sketched by General Motors, the North American representatives decided to join with us, convinced us to make some modifications, and as a result we both got our operating systems for about 50 percent of the price, less than 50 percent of the elapsed time, and with much higher quality because of the talent available in the combined team.

The resulting operating system built upon my experience with the 701 and exploited the 704 hardware. The General Motors/North American Aviation effort was eventually used in about 20 of the IBM 704 installations. There were people associated with the system as developers or as users and improvers, who moved on to be participants in SOS, IBSYS, the Direct Couple for the 7094, OS/360, IMS/360, and JES.

Before proceeding with a discussion of the operating system we produced, let me momentarily digress and describe the IBM 704. The 704 was a grown up 701. It was faster, and the storage tube memories on the 701 had been discarded in favor of coincident-core memories on the 704. That simple expedient, coupled with the next generation of electronic technology, increased the mean-free error time to about eight hours.

The 704 instruction set was enhanced with some logic instructions and a set of binary floating-point arithmetic instructions. It had no built-in decimal capabilities. Internally the 704 was more than twice the speed of a 701.

In January 1957, the 704 installed at General Motors in Detroit had 8KW of core, four drums of 2KW each, eight mag tape units, and the same slow card reader, printer, and punch as had adorned the IBM 701. The base rent was $35,550 a month. Thus the available memory was greater, the speed was up, but the primary I/O equipment was the same. Further, the mainframe was still single sequencing (cycle-stealing channels didn't come along until the IBM 709), so one devoted 100 percent of the CPU to any input/output operation undertaken (see Figure 4). We recognized we had to change our mode of operation to achieve full benefit of the 704 over the 701.

IBM had realized that some large commercial accounts would have a lot of cards to read and had many checks to print. So they offered, as an extra cost option, three separate stand-alone devices to convert card images to magnetic tape images, to take tape images and print them, and to take tape images and punch cards. Since these were stand-alone, they were in some ways better than cycle-stealing channels as there was absolutely no interference to the processing being performed by the mainframe in the next room.

The following highlights of the operating system we developed were extracted from the 1955 SHARE proposal (referred to earlier) and a programmer's manual we found that was dated January 31, 1957. Thus fourteen months after the proposal, we put together a team, polished the design, implemented the system, and documented it. The following list contains the highlights of the joint General Motors/North American effort:

1. All input and all output were processed on the off-line card-to-tape equipment. These produced and received tapes containing files now known as SYSIN and SYSOUT. The mode of operation was then known as tape-to-tape since the reader-printer-punch attached to the mainframe were used only as extensions to the operator's console and for maintenance. They were not used for any production input or output.

2. The SYSIN tape contained a batch of independent jobs, and each job was identified by control cards whose functions are now provided by JCL. The sequence started with a job card which contained accounting information and the programmer's name. Each pack of cards that followed the job card contained header information which controlled its conversion from decimal to binary, and then its subsequent processing.

3. Although IBM provided plugboards in every reader, printer, and punch, we set up installation standards and figuratively welded them into the machine. Thus all the data reorganization was done by programming and not by board wiring. This standardized the setup and reduced the unproductive inter-job time from minutes to milliseconds.

Figure 4—IBM 704

4. We threw the programmers out of the machine room, hired professional computer operators, and standardized the communication between the programmer and the operator. The programmers caught on to the new mode of operation rather quickly since we instructed the operator to proceed to the next job when there was confusion or something didn't work out.

5. We gained programming efficiency through the use of standard decimal-to-binary/binary-to-decimal conversion routines and standard (built-in and integrated) debug tools. This reduced the programmer's effort since it did not require understanding the library routines. He merely had to write some job control statements to use them.

This had another important benefit to the programmer. The memories on these machines were relatively small, only 8KW. By providing all of the decimal-binary translation outside the programmer's domain, we provided an execution time environment that had binary input, computed in binary, and produced output in binary. This gave more usable space to the application than would have been possible for any but the most experienced programmers handling their own input and output, in customized fashion.

6. We augmented the IBM hardware with a custom designed, locally produced, binary time-of-day clock. Further, the system was programmed, just as modern operating systems are, to sample the clock whenever a job card was read for a new job, and to record the resources used during the run so proper accounting records could be maintained. Today we call these SMF records.

We even went a step further because we placed an advisory invoice on the trailing page of each printout so the programmer was aware of the resources used and the cost of those resources each time a run was made. We found the resulting self-discipline of great benefit since programmers naturally do more desk checking when a wasted shot at the machine costs more than a day's wages.

7. With the primitive control language we had on the SYSIN file, it was possible to assemble a program, load it into memory, present it with a data deck, and record the results of the assembly and the execution in a single pass on the machine. It was well into the 1960s before this "load-and-go philosophy" became generally popular.

8. Further, we designed the system, within limits, to be extensible so it was possible to add other language translators to the menu of input conversion routines. After I left the project, the other members of the system's team at General Motors added Fortran as an input translator so it was possible to compile and execute, in a single pass, canned library routines, assembly code, and Fortran programs.

The implementation of this system was largely dictated by the small core memory available and the speed of the I/O devices. As discussed earlier, the peripheral card reading equipment produced card images on tape. The data on these tapes was still decimal as no conversion had taken place. Further, the printer and the punch required decimal tape images as they too lacked any ability to convert. The 704 mainframe only had an 8KW core memory. Due to the small size of this memory and due to the large size of a general purpose decimal-to-binary/binary-to-decimal conversion routine, the system was conceived and implemented in three distinct processing phases (see Figure 5).

In the first phase, the binary coded decimal card images were read from tape, control cards were interpreted, and a binary file was created. Logically the binary file was the direct analog of the BCD image tape that had been created on the peripheral card reader. However, it was more compact and was in the native language (e.g., binary) of the CPU. A binary read program took only about 50 instructions. A decimal-to-binary conversion program took almost 2,000.

Similarly, each job during execution wrote a binary output file. Control statements, just like JCL, were imbedded in the output stream. These control statements caused the output translator to convert and format the binary stream properly, and subsequently, to include parameters on the decimal output file to control printer spacing, skips to the head of form, and insert separator cards between decks of punched card output. Again, to conserve memory and gain speed, the output translator was given the whole machine and conversion was optimized.

The resulting operating system had an input-translation phase which converted data from decimal to binary, and programs from source to object language (symbolic assembly language was initially available, soon after we added the then-new Fortran); an execution phase which was almost exclusively under the programmer's direct control; and an output translation phase which processed line printer output,

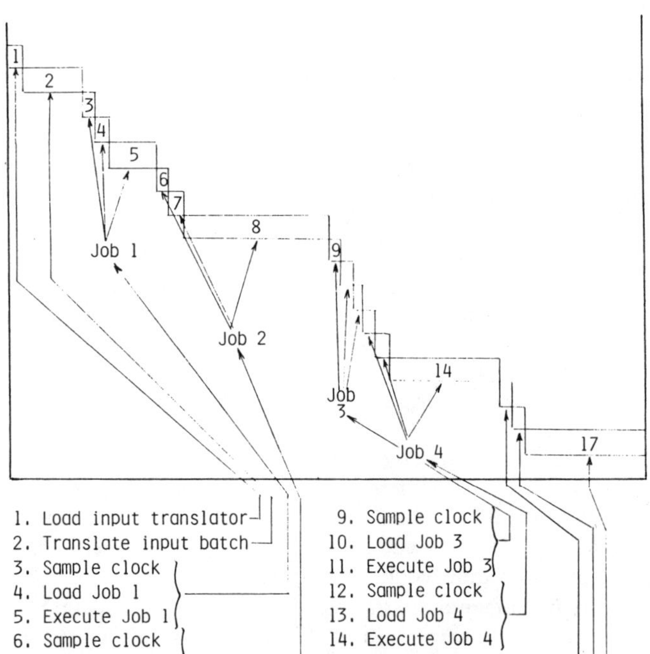

Figure 5—GMR/NAA Monitor time phasing

punched card output (both decimal and binary), and accounting records.

To recap, the advantages of the three-phase design were:

1. It provided the maximum amount of unencumbered memory to the application programmer during execution.
2. It was efficient since the conversion routines were bigger than the sub-files for individual jobs. The big conversion programs were loaded into memory only once per batch, and all of the little data files were passed by them, resulting in a smaller number of total cycles than if the large translator routines were fetched and executed at the beginning and end of each job.
3. By giving the translators the full machine during the conversion process, the translators could be made as large as is necessary to gain efficiency in execution and hence were optimized to be faster for the conversion tasks they had to do.

When the resulting code was written, 90 percent of the work was devoted to the input and the output translators, and only about 10 percent of the effort was devoted to supporting programmers during the execution phase.

When North American Aviation and General Motors Research decided in the Winter of 1955 to jointly develop the system, we split it right down the middle. North American developed the integrated programs that became the input-translation phase, and GM developed the output translator. In the Spring of 1956 GM extended the North American input translator to call Roy Nutt's symbolic assembly program (SAP) as an imbedded conversion subroutine during phase 1 input translation.

There was an intellectual disagreement concerning the services the operating system should provide to the programmers during phase 2 execution. At this point the software installed at North American and at General Motors was dissimilar. The software for phases 1 and 3 was identical at both locations, but we each had our own separate execution time facilities.

When we first started planning this system, we were concerned about protecting the execution-time facilities. The 704 had no limit registers or any other way to partition off and protect the operating system from the application programmers. These didn't come in the IBM world until the advent of System/360. Furthermore, we had only one class of instructions and every programmer had access to all of them. (The concept of privileged instructions for IBM computers also came about in 1964 with the System/360.) As it turned out, we needn't have worried on either count. Our application programmers were company-loyal and not mischievous. Most of them were delighted to have someone else worry about conversion translators and modes of operation. While we had a few application programs that ran away during execution and destroyed the operating system in low core, this was a relatively infrequent occurrence. I cannot remember a single instance where a programmer maliciously tampered with the operating system.

We were also worried about programmer acceptance of operating system standards. During the 701 days, programmers had unfettered access to all of the 701's hardware features. Some questioned whether programmers would fight the system since it denied them access to certain machine features (the operating system claimed a tape as a SYSRES device and the first 300 words of core during the execution phase). Perhaps it was because we installed the operating system when we installed the hardware and had no legacies to deal with, but in Detroit we had no serious attempts by headstrong programmers to read cards on-line, demand all of the tapes for their own personal use, or otherwise contravene the standard configuration we set up. This may have been partially due to our willingness to allow any programmer to violate the system constraints, but he was advised that if he did, his jobs would only run programmer present and only in the wee hours of the morning.

Of the direct contributors to this pioneering effort there were several. In the past 30 years many of us have moved several times. Recently some of the team has retired, others of us are still plugging away. Table I lists all of the original players with their original affiliations.

TABLE I—Contributors to the GMR/NAA Monitor

Individual	1955 Affiliation
Penny Barbe	NAA
Robert Christiansen	GMR
Jim Fishman	GMR
Dale Hanks	NAA
Don Harroff	GMR
Don Hart	GMR
Owen Mock	NAA
Bob Patrick	GMR
George Ryckman	GMR
Kei Shimizu	NAA
Frank Wagner	NAA

BESYS revisited

by R. E. DRUMMOND
AT&T Bell Laboratories
Holmdel, New Jersey

ABSTRACT

The origins and development of the BESYS family of operating systems are traced. Developed at AT&T Bell Laboratories in the late fifties, the system was used for over ten years to control and facilitate the use of the IBM 704-709X series of computers. Some of the novel operating system techniques created for the system and the people who produced them are chronicled.

INTRODUCTION

In the operating system sphere, Bell Labs is best known for UNIX.™* But before there was a UNIX operating system, there was an operating system called BESYS.** For over ten years BESYS was a mainstay for computing at the Labs and altogether served our users from late 1957 to early 1971.

The UNIX operating system has merited much attention in the literature. In contrast, BESYS is all but forgotten. A search of the available literature turned up a single one paragraph entry in *Encyclopedia of Computer Science and Technology* that mentioned BESYS.[1] Even the internal Bell Labs literature is scant when it comes to recording BESYS contributions. Once-common documents that described the system and how to use it have all but disappeared, having somehow escaped the document archives.

This paper rectifies that oversight and attempts to set the record straight about the development of BESYS.

THE PRE-BESYS PERIOD

Bell Labs has been involved with computers since the early 1930s. The computing establishment that gave rise to BESYS, however, consisted of a half dozen members of Bell Labs' Mathematics Research Center. In 1952, they acquired their first commercial computer: a small IBM Card Programmed Calculator.[2,3] This group included V. M. Wolontis and R. W. Hamming who, when IBM 650s were installed starting in 1955, developed the once popular problem oriented languages, L1 and L2.[4,5]

L1 and L2 extended the 650's capabilities by interpretively providing floating-point arithmetic, simplifying memory access, and supplying useful diagnostic information; thus enabling users to straightforwardly program the underlying machine. This encouraged users to program their own applications, allowing them to realize the right results faster and to benefit from the feedback provided by the programming experience. The essence of this "open shop" approach to computing was captured in a well known Hamming motto: "The purpose of computing is insight, not numbers."

The operation of the equipment itself, however, was "closed shop." Since 650 operations were not complex, users could set up their jobs to be run by professional operators. This permitted the machines to be run efficiently on an around-the-clock basis.

By mid-1957, to handle the growing computing workload and increasing complexity of applications, an IBM 704 was ordered to replace the 650s, and preparations for the new machine began that were in keeping with the philosophies that had evolved.

EARLY 704 ERA

The 704 had been announced in mid-1954, and the first one was in the field by the end of 1955.[6] So by mid-1957, many programming tools existed to facilitate its use. By then the SHARE 704 users group was two years old and was already an important source of programs developed by its members. Through SHARE, users built programming tool kits, I/O, and mathematics libraries enabling them to write, debug, and execute their own application programs using stable facilities. In addition, FORTRAN was about to make its debut.

Some of the more useful programs available through SHARE are shown in Table I. At that time, programs were written in SAP or FORTRAN. They were translated to binary machine level usually as card decks. These decks could be combined with those of previously translated I/O or mathematics routines and loaded into the computer using a tool like NY-RBL.

Execution, sometimes with a debugging tool like NY-SNAP, produced print or punch output. For large amounts of input or output, magnetic tapes usually came into play employing offline tape drives, printers, card readers, and punches where appropriate.

Characteristically, most tools were oriented to stand-alone use and only worked together through manual intervention by the user or a trained operator. Few operating systems existed or were in use at that time.

A definite mismatch was widely recognized between the 704's internal speed, the sluggishness of its on-line unit-record equipment, and the inherent slowness of manual operations associated with stand-alone use. Clearly a new mode of operation was required for the 704 if it was to be used in an effective and efficient way.

EMERGENCE OF BESYS

Soon after Bell Labs placed its first 704 order, G. H. Mealy and Gwen J. Hansen addressed the problem of using the machine by developing one of the earliest operating systems. Their solution was a system that provided:

*UNIX is a trademark of AT&T.

**The name BESYS has reportedly stood for BEll SYStem which although appropriate, is perhaps too grand. It actually is derived from a running together of BE and SYS. BE was the SHARE assigned installation code for Bell Telephone Laboratories, Murray Hill, NJ and SYS stood for system, which was indicative of the programming classification for BESYS. This was consistent with SHARE naming conventions for programs it distributes.

1. Flexible operator control of the hardware normally in a non-stop mode of operation
2. Efficient batch job processing usually in a tape-to-tape operating mode through use of off-line unit-record equipment
3. Effective user access to system facilities using control cards to minimize user-operator interaction
4. User program access to centralized I/O, system control, and elementary mathematical functions
5. Snapshot and post-mortem dump debugging facilities
6. Compatibility with the 650s by simulating the L1/L2 interpreters

TABLE I—Some SHARE programming tools. The installation codes shown in this table served to identify the tools' contributors. Thus, UA stood for United Aircraft; PK, IBM Poughkeepsie; NY, IBM New York; and so on.

SHARE Programming Tools		
Installation Code	Program ID	Functional Description
UA	SAP	Symbolic Assembly Program
PK	CSB 4	Card to Storage Binary (Loader)
NY	RBL 1	Relocatable Binary Loader
UA	CSH 2	Card to Storage Hollerith
UA	SPH 3	Storage to Printer Hollerith
UA	DBC 1	Decimal to Binary Conversion
UA	BDC 1	Binary to Decimal Conversion
NY	SNAP	SNAPshot dumper
NY	SNAQ	Snapshot Output Converter
UA	TAD 1	Tape And Drum utility
UA	TPH 2	Tape to Printer Hollerith
CE	650W	650 Wire Plugboard Simulator
CE	650S	650 Simulator
UA	STE 1	System Tape Editor
UA	LST 2	List Tape Converter

The initial system, BESYS-1, was in use by October 16, 1957.[7] It was designed for a 704 with drums, 8K 36-bit words of core memory, a full complement of tapes, and on-line/off-line unit-record equipment. The system was developed using facilities at the Esso Research Center. Ironically, it would never be used at Bell Labs because our original order changed before delivery to a drumless 704 with 32K words of memory. This change gave rise to BESYS-2.[8,9]

Both systems were essentially identical. They usurped the lowest 64 and highest 4K words of memory, a subset of the tape drives and the sense switches. In addition, BESYS-1 swapped a portion of the upper 4K memory to drum storage making it available for user program variable storage. The lowest 64 locations were reserved as a hardware communication area; the upper 4K locations were used for the core resident portion of the system. The complete system resided on tape and consisted of FORTRAN and most of the tools in Table I adapted to work in the BESYS environment as subsystems or integrated into the core resident portion of the system itself.

One specific aim of these changes was the removal of program stops when error conditions were detected. The stops were replaced by messages describing the condition and a standard recovery taken when possible. If operator action was required, the messages appeared on the on-line printer and a standard system stop occurred. This helped the operator distinguish random program stops from planned stops and contributed to the non-stop mode of operation.

BESYS OPERATIONS

Although much effort was devoted to reducing the involvement of operators in the processing of jobs, the operator still played a key role in the use of the machine. At the meta-system level, the operator was responsible for:

1. Starting the system
2. Batching jobs for system input
3. Assigning tape drives and mounting tapes
4. Responding to system error messages
5. Batching output for peripheral processing
6. Terminating jobs that stopped, looped, or exceeded job limits
7. Recovering from system failures or corruption

The heart of the system was the core resident portion. It contained the following:

1. System control program
2. Centralized I/O facilities
3. Comprehensive mathematical functions
4. Tables and buffers

The system control program functioned at several levels: (1) operator, (2) user, (3) program, and (4) hardware.

Operator Level

At the operator level, BESYS used the sense switches and the on-line printer as an interface to process a sequence of jobs. Jobs were presented to the system by the operator a "batch" at a time through the standard input stream. Normally, the medium was tape, and the system would sequence through the jobs in rapid succession. Each job was logged on the printer as it was encountered, permitting the operator to monitor the system's progress. The system also logged detected error conditions on the printer, sometimes soliciting an operator response. The printer could also be used by the operator to monitor the standard output stream. The operator used the sense switches to:

1. Select the standard input source: tape or on-line card reader
2. Alter normal sequencing of jobs in the standard input
3. Provide a go/no-go response to error conditions
4. Monitor output

User Level

At the user level, BESYS implemented a process that read user-provided control cards from the standard input and interpreted their contents to determine the system functions to exercise. The control cards looked just like SAP statements and consisted of an optional location field followed by an operation field and possibly a variable number of operands. The operation field specified the system function. The location and operand fields were passed to that function for further interpretation.

On initial entry, the control card processor searched the standard input for a JOB card. Once found, the system initialized itself to process the incoming job. It then read the next control card and performed the specified function. These functions included:

1. Invoking sub-systems like SAP and FORTRAN
2. Loading object programs
3. Patching loaded programs
4. Accumulating snapshot dump requests
5. Communicating to the operator via the printer

Control card processing would continue until a TRA card was encountered. The TRA function would complete any unfinished business associated with program loading, plant any accumulated snapshot dump requests and TRAnsfer control of the machine to the user's program.

Following is an example of a job that would have caused BESYS to do a FORTRAN compilation with test.

```
      JOB account-number, programmer-name
      FOR
(FORTRAN source program statements)
      LOD 4
      TRA
(Data cards for program test)
```

The JOB card signified the start of the job and identified the user in terms of an account number and programmer name. The FOR card invoked the FORTRAN compiler which would have processed the following source program leaving the resulting object program on tape 4. The LOD card loaded the object program from tape 4 into memory. Finally, the TRA card started the loaded program's execution.

Program Level

At the program level, BESYS provided many services. Primarily, they consisted of: I/O routines, snapshot dump routines, system control routines, and, initially, the common elementary mathematics routines. Nearly all the facilities normally available to the FORTRAN programmer were present in the core-resident portion of the system. The rationale for this was that the SAP programmer could also make use of them, and, since most programs would use them, the memory they occupied was not wasted. Also, the time saved by not having to load them repeatedly, contributed to over-all system efficiency.

Eventually, introduction of FORTRAN II and development of a program linking capability for the loader weakened this argument, making it reasonable to purge the mathematics routines from the resident portion of the system. This also proved to be a necessity because, as BESYS matured, free space within the system's 4K region became a critical resource.

Once control transferred to the user's program, overall control became tenuous. There was no hardware facility that enabled the system to constrain the user's program; their relation to one another was peer-to-peer. Hence, the system was at the user's mercy. Only honor and social pressure bound the user to conventions established by the system, and only the operator's sensitivity to how the system was behaving remained as the effective means to limit damage when things went awry.

Although the peer-to-peer relationship represented a potentially critical integrity exposure, in practice it did not prove to be a devastating factor. Because jobs were processed one at a time, the user that violated the system usually stood to suffer the most. Nevertheless, it was a weakness that forced a greater dependence on the operator than desired.

At least two facilities were provided for programs to return control to the system. The first, RETURN, simply returned control to the control card processor initiating a search for the next valid control card and resumption of control card processing. This facility made multi-step jobs possible. The second, ENDJOB, initiated end-of-job processing. Any post-mortem dump requests were taken, the snapshot converter was invoked, miscellaneous end-of-job housekeeping performed, and, finally, the control card processor was reentered to search for the next valid JOB card.

Hardware Level

At the hardware level, BESYS had to deal only with floating-point traps. Facilities were provided that examined the floating-point "spills" and either produced appropriate diagnostic messages or honored alternative actions specified by the user through use of ALT control cards.

SYSTEM ACCOUNTING

The 704 had neither a time of day clock nor a timer to simulate one; hence, usage accounting was crude. A time card accompanied each job submitted to the system. It served to:

1. Identify the user who submitted the job
2. Provide job run time limits and output estimates
3. Specify special handling requirements such as tape IDs and their logical tape drive assignment or paper and card stock to use for peripheral equipment

The card or the information it contained was also used by operations to: (1) schedule jobs, (2) fetch and set up tapes, (3) set up peripheral equipment, (4) feedback written remarks from operators, and (5) log time on and off the system using a manual time-clock.

Eventually, usage accounting was improved through use of an electro-mechanical time-of-day clock tied to the on-line printer. Accounting information was then punched on-line into cards as part of the ENDJOB housekeeping function.

BESYS DISTRIBUTION

True to its origins, BESYS 1 and 2 were submitted to SHARE for distribution and were also made available to several external installations directly. Reportedly BESYS was used by many installations,[10] but no records remain on which ones they were. Only faint recollections suggest they included The Esso Research Center, Mobile Oil Corporation, and The Shell Oil Company.

THE BESYS-2 SUCCESSORS

G. H. Mealy left Bell Labs for the Rand Corporation in 1959 just as plans were being formulated to develop BESYS-3, the first of a series of successors to BESYS-2. G. J. Hansen and the author continued this effort.

BESYS-3

BESYS-3 was a port of BESYS-2 to the IBM 7090. The major efforts involved revamping system I/O facilities, replacing SAP with FAP and upgrading FORTRAN from the 704 to the 709X version. It was placed into service in July, 1960.

In the process of porting, BESYS received a general face lifting. New control functions were added; others were dropped because their function had become obsolete or was done in some other way. Some control cards felt the effects of human engineering. The LOD control card for invoking the loader, for example, became the LOAD control card. The so-called Yum-Yum cards*** of NY-SNAP vintage were renamed and reformatted and came out as SNAP and COREPM.

Upgrading FORTRAN was no trivial task but in general it was straightforward. Replacing SAP by FAP, on the other hand, was more complex. By 1959, what started out as UA-SAP under BESYS had been significantly extended, and although FAP shared the same ancestry, it lacked these extensions. The most important extension was a conditional and recursive macro facility developed by D. E. Eastwood and M. D. McIlroy.[11]

Since FAP addressed the new facilities provided by the 709X hardware and was already in use on that hardware, our SAP extensions were ported to FAP; in effect, merging the best of both assemblers. The result became widely known as BE-Macro-FAP and eventually became the basis for IBM's IBSYS assembler: MAP.

Although the 704 BESYS environment encouraged using centralized I/O facilities, the peer-to-peer relationship of system and user programs enabled sophisticated users to start their own I/O directly and exploit the CPU-centered I/O copy-logic to process data on the fly as it was transmitted to tape, the CPU, and core. The architecture of the 709X machines, however, separated the data transmission function from the CPU by using independent channels. This provided the potential for a high level of concurrency if programmed properly. In addition, the channels could signal the occurrence of major I/O events by interrupting the normal sequential processing of the CPU.

Fully realizing the concurrency potential required the development of a sophisticated set of interrupt driven I/O routines. Even though only a simple buffering strategy was employed initially using such an approach,**** the implementation technique virtually precluded coexistence with user written I/O routines. Thus, users were forced to use the system's centralized I/O facilities.

This had two effects: (1) the user level I/O facilities had to be beefed up and (2) the amount of memory required by the resident system increased sharply. This led to the controversial decision to double the system area of memory from 4K to 8K, even though the maximum memory of 32K remained the same for the 709X machines.

Some arguments proposed, not unreasonably, that the 4K limit on system area size be preserved by purging from the resident system all the higher level FORTRAN based I/O

***So called because the handwritten words "Yum-Yum Cards" were scrawled across the top of a SHARE program write-up of NY-SNAP, presumably by G. J. Mealy, that was circulated within Bell Labs during the early 704 days. All the NY-SNAP cards were of the form Y- - where '—' stood for some condition imposed on the dump request. For instance, YUN—dump UNconditionally, YPL—dump if the accumulator was PLus, YPM—provide a Post-Mortem dump, etc. They were presumably good to feed to the system when debugging, whence Yum-Yum!

****Apparently BESYS-3 was an early user of interrupt driven I/O. This was based on our testing experience at several different 709 sites. Each time we tested at a new site we had to have jumpers changed in the Data Synchronizers to activate their Data Channel Trap feature.

*****Except for the type information, the blocking scheme was equivalent to what is currently called "Variable Block Span Format" in IBM's OS/370.

routines just as the elementary mathematics routines had been purged under BESYS-2. From a public relations point of view this would have looked good for the system, but from the user's perspective it was really a trade-off—user space for system space. Thus, although it would have been a challenge to live within the original 4K size, as an expedient the additional memory was taken for system use. Time would show that as the system continued to develop there would be no problem in using all that additional space.

A new and important dimension to computer output was introduced with BESYS-3 when C. F. Pease developed a basic software package to generate tapes that could drive a Stromberg-Carlson 4020 microfilm printer. This device was capable of producing high quality graphics. It enabled users to visualize their data, providing them with new insight. Soon after its introduction, it was even used to produce computer-generated movies.

One continuing goal of BESYS was to improve the quality of feedback to users about their programs. Along these lines, V. A. Vyssotsky in 1961 conceived and implemented a preprocessor to FORTRAN that analyzed source programs looking for use of variables before their initialization and sections of code that could not be reached. Typically, these problems went undetected by the compiler, yet frequently produced subtle and sometimes mysterious results at execution time. This improvement to FORTRAN was welcomed by our users but was treated with indifference when offered to IBM.

BESYS-4

Once the conversion to BESYS-3 was completed, thoughts turned to how the system could be made more efficient, how the operator interface could be improved, and how the system could be made more robust.[12]

Buffered and Blocked I/O

System efficiency was given a boost by moving from the simple buffered I/O strategy to one that was completely general, permitting read-aheads and write-behinds to an arbitrary depth. There was also a move away from unit record processing to a generalized blocking scheme employing logical records of arbitrary length and containing indications about the type of information being handled.***** Blocking effectively increased tape capacity and significantly improved data transfer rates.

The blocking format was designed with IBM's 1401 in mind so that the 1401s could process tapes used for the standard I/O streams. The logical record type enabled both print and punched output to be merged into the same stream along with job accounting information reducing the number of dedicated on-line tapes and eliminating the need for an on-line punch. User data tapes could also be dumped when necessary using the 1401s.

Unless the user took some deliberate action, all I/O was automatically blocked and buffered in a transparent fashion. Even the unused area of user programming space was automatically used for buffers. From the user's perspective, all I/O was done on a logical record basis without regard to detailed questions of hardware efficiency; that was deemed to be the system's job.

Hardware Extensions

To attack some of the major problems of operating the equipment and controlling the flow of work to and from the system as well as provide a high-speed data connection to the system, G. L. Baldwin and H. S. McDonald collaborated to build equipment that interfaced to the 709X systems using the Direct Data Feature. This equipment provided the following facilities:

1. Interval timer
2. Time-of-day clock
3. Day-of-year calendar
4. Operator's display panel
5. Tape control system
6. High speed data link

Interval timer

The interval timer eliminated the need for the operator to monitor the running time of jobs streaming through the system. The user now entered the estimated maximum run time to the nearest one hundredth of an hour on the JOB card and the operating system automatically cut the job if it was exceeded. A visual analog display of the amount of execution time remaining for the job on the system was provided to assist the operator with scheduling.

Clock and calendar

The clock and calendar were useful in providing accurate information for accounting and other time stamping applications. The clock provided user programs with the ability to measure time with full millisecond accuracy.

Operator's display panel

The operator's display panel consisted of five system status indicators, two with integrated push buttons and a programmable speaker. Four of the indicators reflected major system states: FAP, FOR, RUN, and SYS. The fifth indicator reflected the HOLD/RELEASE state of the interval timer. The RUN indicator was also a button. When lit, depressing it reset the interval timer and thereby normally terminated the job in progress. Using the button associated with the HOLD/RELEASE indicator, the operator could exercise a manual override of the interval timer. The speaker was driven by a flip-flop and was normally used by the system to produce an audible tone alerting the operator when some condition required manual intervention.

Tape control system

The tape control system provided BESYS with almost the same capabilities as the operator to control tape drives within the computing center. Each tape drive was provided with a control panel that displayed the unit's status and which the operator used to enter reel numbers, select unit addresses, switch drives on- or off-line, and set special status information. Except for entering reel numbers, the operator could also perform the same operations from a centralized console. Any change made by the operator using these facilities caused a manual entry latch to be set. This, in turn, caused the system to update its internal tape-drive-state table.

The operator still had to mount (taking into account a user specified channel), identify, and unmount tapes for the system, but from that point on the system did the rest, namely:

1. Read tape reel numbers entered by the operator
2. Switch the drives on- or off-line
3. Assign or sense unit addresses on drives
4. Ready or unready drives
5. Sense status indicators set by the operator

Drives mounted with private tapes were always placed in a reserve state. This distinguished them from drives that could be used for system or scratch purposes. The reserve state was also used with batched output tapes as an operator request for the system to close out the tape and queue it for peripheral processing. The next tape would then be automatically selected, switched on-line, and readied for use by subsequent jobs—all in a matter of seconds. Similarly, at the end of a batched input tape, the system would switch to a new one. The selection criteria were based on a unit address convention followed by the operator. The operator would be prompted only when a suitable successor couldn't be found.

The user conveyed non-system tape requirements for a job using MYTAPE control cards. For a given logical unit, they specified the tapes to use by reel number (multi-reel tapes were accommodated) and whether the tapes would be used for input, output, or scratch. Input tapes were file-protected and marked read-only to the system I/O routines. The tape control system proved to be an effective tool and significantly improved tape handling and the flow of work.

High-speed data link

The high-speed data link connected BESYS to a Packard Bell 250 computer located in a remote laboratory. Users within that laboratory could request the interjection of a job into the current job stream to process data transmitted through the data link.

Other monitor aides

Several RPQs were added to the 709X hardware to improve system robustness. One was a trap on halt instructions. Another was a crude form of memory protection that was used to protect BESYS from vagrant stores and, under the right conditions, was also used to protect buffer pools set up in user areas. Both improvements enhanced the system's control and reduced the monitoring role of the operator but did not alter the peer-to-peer relationship enjoyed by the knowledgeable user.

BESYS-4 went into operation in April, 1962.

BESYS-5

Like most of its predecessors, the production of BESYS-5 was motivated by hardware changes. On the surface, support was introduced for the CPU extensions associated with the IBM 7094 and for the IBM 1301 Disk Storage Facility. Internally, however, the changes called for major revisions of the system's I/O routines to cope with the 1301s and for wide spread changes to handle the new instructions that were present on the 7094.[13]

Support for the 1301s produced the biggest changes to the system. These changes had some good aspects and at least one unavoidable one. The good ones included moving from a tape resident system to one that resided on disk and, for users, sequential and random access to temporary files on disk. The unavoidable was that the changes required more space than was available in the 8K system area. This forced us to restructure that area and to use a storage overlay technique. This was palatable only because the system was now disk-resident.

Up to this point, system maintenance was done by the system itself, using a modified version of the system tape editor UA-STE. As an expedient, maintenance was done by switching to the IBSYS Editor. This was accomplished by incorporating a slightly modified IBSYS as a special purpose subsystem under BESYS.

The user was provided with I/O facilities at the FORTRAN and FAP levels to randomly access records within a file. Also, all the I/O facilities formerly used to access tapes were now made capable of sequentially accessing files on disk. This was a prelude to accessing user files stored on disk that would eventually be added to the system.

Facilities were introduced to make timer-cuts and floating-point traps more flexible. Exits could be set up to user code when these events occurred. For timer-cuts, if a timer exit was requested, a 10-second time extension would be granted and a one shot exit invoked. The exit procedure could wrap up processing and then go to ENDJOB. If for some reason the extension also expired, the job would simply be cut. For floating-point traps, any user-provided exit would simply override normal system handling. In addition, the user could request dumps conditioned on floating-point traps.

BESYS-5 was installed in May 1963. After the normal shakedown period, development work resumed aimed at fulfilling disk support as well as providing additional facilities of an innovative nature. However, as a result of the trauma of running out of space in the system area of memory and resorting to the overlay scheme, the development effort split in two. One effort, unofficially dubbed BESYS-6, since it was going to be the "next" system, set out to replace the fixed overlay scheme with a dynamic relocatable approach. The other effort, eventually called BESYS-7, continued the BESYS-5 approach concentrating on completing the promised disk support.

BESYS-6

The intent of the so-called BESYS-6 system was to organize the 8K system area of memory so that it consisted of a static nucleus of minimal size and a dynamic area into which relocatable portions of the system would be dynamically loaded as dictated by a job's processing. There was never any doubt that this was an ambitious approach that had a certain aesthetic appeal. That the associated effort would ever produce a production quality system, however, was in doubt.

Several practical factors were working against this approach. Foremost was performance. BESYS-5 had set a de facto performance level that would be difficult to beat. The overlay scheme was reasonably thought out and was designed to be optimal with respect to the way jobs normally used the system. The dynamic approach inherently had a higher overhead having to deal with module relocation and core fragmentation.

There would be no pending hardware upgrades to boost performance that could be traded for the increased overhead, and there was no hardware assist that could be used to reduce the overhead. The handwriting was on the wall for the 709X machines; attention had already shifted to the next generation of machines.

Finally, the promised upgrades for the disk support were ready and in demand. They would be offered in an edition of BESYS called BESYS-7.

BESYS-7

BESYS-7 was put into service in May, 1964. It delivered the promised additional disk storage support, support for private libraries, a user facility for input source switching, and some rudimentary terminal support.

User Disk Storage

When BESYS-5 was introduced, disk storage space was divided into three categories: permanent, semi-permanent, and temporary. The permanent space was used for system residence, and the temporary space was available for use by users for scratch files. With BESYS-7, provision was made to allocate semi-permanent space to users. Space from the semi-permanent category, called a key area, was allocated to a user on application to the computer center, and a name, called a key, was assigned to access it.

A facility called REVISE enabled users to manage their key areas and to dynamically create, name, and allocate the space to files. Such files could be opened using their key and file names and accessed using any system I/O routine.

As rudimentary as this file system was, it proved to be immensely popular. And surprisingly for a random access facility, it was primarily used to store many modest-sized sequential files. Development groups that used specialized sets of tools found the file system particularly effective because it permitted the tools to be centralized, made readily available to their users, and easy to maintain.

Source Switching and Private Libraries

Two system facilities added to the effectiveness of the disk file system. The first was a standard source switching capability, and the second was the ability to maintain and use private libraries of relocatable subroutines. Source switching could be performed at the control card or program level. It enabled users to redirect the system's standard input to any file. Almost overnight, drawers of job decks quietly slipped into the file system and suddenly cards took a step towards obsolescence. Private libraries that could be searched by the system's loader abetted this shift and made the life of developers of specialized tools even easier.

Experimental Terminals

In 1964, an experimental PB-250-based intelligent graphics terminal, developed by E. N. Pinson, and several typewriter-like terminals with local buffer storage were linked to the 709X systems and made to "interact" with the system at the job level. Although they showed that users could interact directly with the system, the job processing nature of the system precluded the type of interaction taken for granted today.

The End of The Line

BESYS-7 was the last of the systems we produced for the 709X machines. With the next generation hardware waiting in the wings, the pace of system development dwindled. Attention turned to the development of Multics and developments in the TSS/360 and OS/360 world. Optimistically, it was believed that one or the other of these systems would assume the work load being handled by BESYS.

By 1967, this optimism faded as it became clear that such a step would not be cost-effective. The investment in existing software was too great, and the conversion costs were too high for a flash cut to work. Instead a proposal by the author to emulate BESYS-7 on the System/360 as a means of smoothing the transition to the next generation machines and spreading out the conversion costs, gained favor.[14]

BE90 EMULATOR FOR BESYS-7

In 1967, the proposal to emulate BESYS-7 turned to action. A team led by the author and including F. T. Grampp and eventually G. J. Hansen was formed to act on it.

IBM had already produced an emulator for the 709X machines, called EM90. However, it did not support disk storage devices and, therefore, was not suitable for BESYS-7 emulation. Our approach was to develop an emulator, called BE90, by combining EM90's CPU emulation modules with new routines designed to meet BESYS-7's I/O requirements. In addition, direct interfaces to BESYS-7 and ASP were developed so that a mixture of BESYS and OS jobs could be processed within the same OS/360-ASP environment.

BESYS-7 itself was streamlined slightly, dropping most of the code supporting the Tape Control System in favor of set up information supplied by ASP. All other BESYS functions were supported and no user job needed modification.

BE90 was put into service in March, 1968, and within a month the plug was pulled on two 7094s. The last of the 709X machines would be retired from Bell Labs in March, 1969, and BESYS would continue to be used under emulation until February, 1971.

THE LAST CURTAIN CALL

One of the last programs that BESYS would ever run involved a humanitarian effort to help a boy being treated for Hodgkin's disease. K. Knowlton, a Bell Labs pioneer in computer graphics, had helped develop a technique for generating movies visualizing the treatment of deep body cancer by radiation. Since the computer programs for that purpose only ran under BESYS at the time, the system was fired up one more time under BE90 to process the patient's data. The results produced would determine the proper radiation doses and what vital organs and other parts of the body should get the radiation.[15]

One couldn't have asked for a more fitting end to BESYS's long and distinguished record of service.

CONCLUDING REMARKS

BESYS contributions are hard to quantify. Certainly it helped thousands of scientists and engineers gain more insight into their work as well as provide them the means to obtain the results they required. The author is pleased to have been a principal contributor to the development of BESYS-3 through BESYS-7.

Unlike IBM's IBSYS and OS, it didn't attempt to be all things to all people. Instead, it took a series of machines that had potential but were complex and difficult to use and provided a system that transformed them into efficient and effective tools.

Some like to say that BESYS influenced UNIX; but in practice, no more than L1 and L2 influenced BESYS. For their time, they are all good systems that marched off at right angles to one another sharing only the common bond and spirit of the people that work in the environment established by Bell Labs.

REFERENCES

1. *Encyclopedia of Computer Science and Technology,* Vol. 3, New York: Marcel Dekker, p. 210.
2. Holbrook, Bernard D. and W. Stanley Brown. "A History of Computing Research at Bell Laboratories (1937–1975)." *Computing Science Technical Report No. 99,* Bell Laboratories, 1982, p. 15.
3. Wolontis, V. M. *Bell Laboratories Record,* 52 (1974) 1, p. 18.
4. Wolontis, V. M. "A Complete Floating-Decimal Interpretive System for the IBM 650 Magnetic Drum Calculator." *IBM Technical Newsletter,* No. 11, March 1956.
5. Hamming, R. W. and R. A. Weiss, "General Purpose System." unpublished internal memorandum, Bell Laboratories, September 14, 1956.
6. McLaughlin, Richard A. "The IBM 704: 36-Bit FLoating-Point Money Maker." *Datamation,* 21 (1975) 8, p. 45.
7. Mealy, G. H. "704 Input-Output System: BE SYS 1." unpublished internal memorandum, Bell Laboratories, October 16, 1957.
8. Mealy, G. H. "704 Input-Output System—BE SYS 1 and 2." unpublished internal memorandum, Bell Laboratories, February 13, 1958.
9. Hansen, G. J., W. L. Mammel, and G. H. Mealy. "704 Input-Output and Monitor system—BE SYS 2." unpublished internal memorandum, Bell Laboratories, May 22, 1959.
10. Holbrook, B. D. and W. S. Brown. "Bell Laboratories and the Computer from the Late 30's to the Middle 60's." unpublished internal memorandum, Bell Laboratories, June 25, 1975, p. 54.
11. Eastwood, D. E. and M. D. McIlroy. "Macro Compiler Modification of SAP." unpublished internal memorandum, Bell Laboratories, September, 1959.
12. Drummond, R. E. and G. J. Hansen. "BE-SYS-4 Release Description." unpublished internal information bulletin, Bell Laboratories, February, 1962.
13. Cutler, M. R. "General Description of BESYS5." unpublished internal memorandum, Bell Laboratories, February 18, 1964.
14. Drummond, R. E. "Emulation of BESYS-7 on The SYSTEM/360, Model 65." unpublished internal memorandum, Bell Laboratories, April 3, 1967.
15. "Movies Help Radiation Treatment." *Bell Labs News,* May 21, 1971.

FMS: The IBM FORTRAN Monitor System

by RAY A. LARNER
IBM Corporation
Boulder, Colorado

ABSTRACT

This paper is a short history of the IBM FORTRAN Monitor System (FMS) and its follow-ons, which provided a popular early "work horse" operating system for the IBM 704/9/90 computer systems FORTRAN users beginning at the end of 1959.

The events and environment leading up to this sytem are explored. This system was developed through an ad hoc cooperative effort by members of the user group SHARE, and the IBM FORTRAN compiler group, as an interim operating system solution pending a more general planned and funded system. While there was controversy about the wisdom of distributing the system, it became widely used, and contributed to an evolutionary set of operating environments.

Fueled by dramatic growth in the popularity of FORTRAN, and some useful features of FORTRAN inter-program linkage, the system, and descendants of it, became standard for most IBM 704/9/90 series accounts throughout the 1960s.

BACKGROUND . . . 1956–1959

The Introduction of FORTRAN

In 1957, IBM's John Backus and his small FORTRAN group made available the first FORTRAN compiler, for the IBM 704 computer system. They had devised both the language and the compiler, and the reception by the user community was extremely positive. For the first time, there was a capability for "non programmers" to program these machines in a practical way. The language's emphasis was on engineering and scientific usage, and much sophistication had been put into producing object programs that were efficient for these applications.

In 1958, the same group produced FORTRAN II, which extended the original system's capabilities by allowing separately compiled FORTRAN programs to be linked together at load time, with symbolic linkage and data sharing. This extension was, in the author's opinion, a cornerstone to the practical acceptance of FORTRAN, and led to the expansion of the FORTRAN system into an early operating system.

FORTRAN Operation

At this time, there was no generally available operating system for FORTRAN users. It was the norm for a specific job to have uncontested control of the computer system, starting from a machine reset state, and ending with a program halt. The FORTRAN compiler behaved in this fashion, as did a FORTRAN object program. A FORTRAN object program could be composed of multiple program segments, each the result of an independent compilation. To run a FORTRAN object program job, a special loader (the BSS loader, for Binary Symbolic Segment loader) furnished with the FORTRAN system, was boot-strapped into the computer. The BSS loader loaded multiple relocatable segments into computer memory, assigning locations as it did so, both for programs and data. Hence, the BSS loader was acting as a main memory manager for that job. After loading the programs, it passed control to one of them (called the Main Program). When the program completed, the machine came to a halt, and the machine operator would reset the machine to run whatever the next job happened to be.

SHARE/IBM Operating System Strategy

Within SHARE (the user group for this line of computers) there was a cooperative effort among several of the more experienced members, and IBM, to define and implement a standard operating system called SOS (SHARE Operating System). SOS was meant to provide a machine control system to automatically sequence jobs without operator intervention, and to provide comprehensive development and debugging tools. This effort, however, was begun in parallel with the development and acceptance of FORTRAN, and there were some incompatibilities, both in concept and in detail, between SOS and FORTRAN.

Increasing Customer Usage of FORTRAN

Meanwhile, FORTRAN usage by many SHARE users began to increase dramatically. This was especially true with companies that were new users of these computers, and had little or no invested inventory of application software. It was claimed that development of engineering simulation and data reduction applications could be completed an order of magnitude faster than with conventional machine language (or symbolic machine language) approaches. FORTRAN contributed to the emergence of the "open shop," wherein engineers from outside the computer shop were allowed to write their own FORTRAN programs to solve their own engineering problems. Typically, these programmers were not trained in machine language programming, which was restricted to "closed shop" personnel.

Some of these heavy FORTRAN users began to devise machine room procedures around FORTRAN, and some revised the FORTRAN system provided by IBM to provide more efficient job-to-job transitions. Jobs were "stacked" onto an input tape using off-line peripheral equipment, and by local rules, the data written as output by jobs was written sequentially onto preassigned output tapes for subsequent off line printing and card punching. Some wrote "monitors," that provided transition from job to job without machine halts. These were, of course, practical solutions designed around the FORTRAN system, usually without regard to the concepts under development for SOS.

The North American 709 FORTRAN Load and Go System

One of these users was North American Aviation. Their Rocketdyne division computer center had devised such a monitor system known as the North American Load and Go system. This system allowed a single job to consist of one or more compilations, followed by immediate execution of the compiled job, and then automatic sequencing to the next job. Any or all of the job could have been compiled earlier, in which case the object program (in BSS form) was included with the input. North American Rocketdyne had made a number of revisions to the compiler and to the BSS loader to make this system.

In addition, they added a loading and execution time concept that was not in FORTRAN. This was a concept of "chain links." Multiple FORTRAN programs, each of which was a full memory load, could be successively executed, in any order, with the programs sharing data in memory. When one chain link completed, it invoked another chain link. The monitor would load the next chain link into memory (overlaying the previous one, except for common data variables) and pass control to it. Any chain link could be invoked an arbitrary number of times. This was an important function, because in those days main memory was very limited (a maximum of 32K words), and many engineering applications required much more than was available. Chain links were a much more efficient way to overcome this problem than dividing the application into multiple independent jobs.

The SHARE Subcommittee Report

In March of 1959, a special subcommittee of the SHARE FORTRAN Standards and Evaluation Committee met in New York with members of the IBM FORTRAN group. The subcommittee was chaired by James Fishman of General Motors Research Laboratories. Charles (Chuck) Bortek represented North American, who had proposed to the committee in February to make the North American 709 FORTRAN Load and Go System available to SHARE, assuming IBM would generalize, distribute, and maintain the system. The purpose of the subcommittee was to evaluate that system, and to make recommendations to the parent committee "concerning whether IBM should be directed to distribute and maintain this system for all 709 FORTRAN users."

The subcommittee, in a report to the SHARE FORTRAN Committee dated April 10, 1959, published the following conclusions:

"1) There is an immediate need and a future need for a 709 Fortran operating system
2) This immediate need may be met by the distribution and maintenance of the North American Load and Go System,* NA 308.9, but containing the modifications listed in the addendum to this report, as a part of 709 Fortran
3) The question of operating Fortran within the SOS System should be reviewed by Share and IBM.
* This name is North American's, and not that of the subcommittee."

The addendum listed 12 areas for which there were to be modifications made by IBM. These were not detailed specifications, but rather suggested an "approach that will insure no additional difficulty for installations whose prior experience or new plans makes use of the North American System without modification unacceptable, and should allow future expansion in the direction of a single overall operator." (The term "operator" was used to mean operating system, or monitor; that is, a computer program taking over some of the traditional tasks of the computer operator.)

The report went on to express puzzlement over "the proper place of SOS in relation to Fortran," and concern over whether "SOS will be efficient for Fortran users, since much of the design philosophy of SOS was based upon need for the correcting of coding errors, which Fortran does not produce. . . . " Additional concerns about SOS/FORTRAN convergence were expressed, and a requirement was given for an assembler to produce relocatable output, "since relocatable information is implicitly a present adjunct to the operation of Fortran II." This was a reference to the ability, with FORTRAN, to independently compile relocatable subroutines that could subsequently be included in different FORTRAN program executions, by means of the BSS loader.

The author's records are somewhat blurred with respect to official SHARE acceptance, or lack thereof, of this recommendation. They do include a few long and thoughtful letters, pro and con. On the con side, some thought that each installation had its own unique requirements, and that standardizing would be counterproductive, and would divert IBM's FORTRAN system programming resources from other important requirements. Of course, the fact that this system would be parochial to FORTRAN, and not usable for other application, was a major concern. SOS boosters, of course, wanted FORTRAN to run as a part of SOS.

For IBM's part, they expressed willingness to proceed with the work, but on a very limited basis. IBM did have, after all, a department developing SOS, which was still the recognized SHARE operating system, and it was not considered the mission of the FORTRAN group to develop operating systems. In fact, the assignment to accomplish this was given to the author, as a short-term, part-time task. The "IBM 709 FORTRAN Monitor System" was distributed to SHARE members around Christmas, 1959.

FMS HISTORY . . . 1960–1962

The IBM 709 FORTRAN Monitor System initially distributed to SHARE members was extended beyond the North American system, in that an assembler, called FAP (for FORTRAN Assembly Program) was included with the system. This assembler was provided to IBM for this purpose by the Western Data Processing Center (University of California in Los Angeles), along with an excellent manual. This FAP was based, to the author's recollection, on an assembler developed earlier by Bell Laboratories, as a part of their own monitor, BESYS. FAP produced relocatable output in BSS format, so FAP program segments (subroutines) could be easily mixed and matched with those produced by the FORTRAN compiler.

In addition, modifications that North American had made to the compiler itself were removed, and the necessary monitor functions were isolated in monitor modules themselves, so that the compiler could be used in a conventional mode (non monitored) by customers who desired to do so. Monitor functions were isolated and documented with a view toward installation customizing, or incorporation into their own monitor. Areas were made available in monitor modules for installations to install their own extensions, primarily for accounting purposes. Various enhancements in usability and flexibility, as requested in the subcommittee report, were made. Apart from the inclusion of FAP, however, the major functions were essentially those of the North American System.

Monitor Operation

Because main memory was so limited, the monitor modules were not present during compilations, assemblies, and object program execution. (An exception was that certain monitor linkage functions were packaged as optional library subroutines loaded with object programs.) The compiler and assembler were essentially "unaware" of the presence of the monitor. At the completion of a compilation or assembly, the compiler or assembler simply passed control to the next program (record) on the system tape. This was done in the same manner that control was passed between phases within compilation or assembly—via a tiny program in lower memory called "1 to CS." This program was only a few instructions long; it simply loaded the system program at the current system tape position into memory and passed control to it. In addition, a few words of memory with "1 to CS" were reserved by the monitor for job status, and for use by individual installations for accounting information.

Thus, the monitor modules were strategically placed on the system tape, to be brought in only on transition between job steps.

Job definition was controlled by control card images on the input tape. At the beginning of each job there was a "sign-on" card. Installations could customize the information on the sign on card, and could add logic to the monitor module that processed it, to perform accounting functions (e.g., billing by department for machine usage).

After the sign-on card were all the input data for the job, separated by appropriate control cards interpreted by the monitor. This could include FORTRAN source programs, FAP source programs, object programs (in BSS relocatable format), and input data for the execution phase of the object program. Execution phases were optional; that is, the job could consist of all compilations and assemblies. Similarly, the job could be execution only, or could be a mixture of compilations and/or assemblies followed by an execution phase.

When all compilations and assemblies (if any) for a job were completed, the monitor would load the (relocatable) segments of the job, load all library routines required by the job, and pass control to the main program of the job. When the program completed, the monitor would regain control and process the next job.

If the job was a "chain" job, the monitor would "load" each chain link, resolving all relocatable references, and write the "loaded" chain link to tape, with proper identification, and begin processing the next chain link within the job. Each chain link was like a "job" in itself, in that it could contain a mixture of compilations and/or assemblies and relocatable object code segments.

During an execution phase, selective or complete dumping of program and/or data areas could be performed via monitor library routines.

Source Language Debugging

In 1961, source language debugging capability was added to the monitor. This work was done by a select group of SHARE members, headed by Bill Heffner, then of General Electric, and integrated into the system by IBM. Source language debugging was a natural outgrowth of the BSS architecture. Adding symbol tables to BSS "decks" for internal variables, as well as already existing symbol tables for external names, was done in the compiler assembly phase, on option. This provided a platform for run-time monitor routines that performed snapshots of requested variables, (using source program symbols and indices). This feature had been long demanded by users and was a welcome addition.

Acceptance by SHARE

Up to the time the initial distribution of FMS was made, there was considerable reluctance within SHARE to formally endorse it (it was never officially endorsed, to the author's knowledge). At the February, 1960 SHARE meeting, it was duly noted that the distribution had occurred, but there had been such little experience with the system at that time that there was little discussion of it (or at least within the author's records). By the time of the next semiannual meeting, however, correspondence and minutes indicate that FMS was a "taken for granted" standard part of the FORTRAN environment, and polls indicated that FMS was almost universally in use. Lobbying for enhancements to the monitor became as commonplace as lobbying for compiler enhancements.

In 1961, a resolution was passed to remove the capability for non-monitored operation. User questionnaires indicated that a vast majority of overall 709 and 7090 usage was in FORTRAN, and that 76 percent of the installations used the FORTRAN Monitor System distributed by IBM. A few of the more progressive installations had made the FORTRAN monitor system a subsystem under the control of a "master monitor," that could also invoke other monitors for non-FORTRAN applications.

Incremental performance and functional improvements were made to FMS, including its integration into "IBSYS" (an IBM "master monitor") in 1962.

FMS INTEGRATION AND EVOLUTION . . . 1962 ON

IBSYS

Once FMS was in wide usage, IBM realized that it must develop and generalize operating systems including FMS functions. In 1962, IBM introduced a "master monitor" (IBSYS) that included FMS as a subsystem, along with Commercial Translator (IBM's entry into Business Oriented Languages), a buffered Input/Output Control System (7090 IOCS), and additional applications, such as tape sort and report generation. Additional subsystems were added over time. Provisions were made for optional FORTRAN usage of IOCS, to trade main memory for increased Input/Output performance.

IBSYS provided a number of services, including centralized I/O, dynamic device and channel allocation, centralized accounting, and uninterrupted flow between the various "subsystems." In this environment, FMS still performed basically the same functions as before, but could coexist more easily with other software packages. In addition, by channeling I/O through IBSYS, the support of disk storage (the IBM 1301) and new magnetic tape architecture was readily accomplished.

IBJOB

In 1963, IBM made FORTRAN IV (a new FORTRAN compiler) available. A new Monitor System, called IBJOB, was used with FORTRAN IV. In IBJOB, more software systems, including non-FORTAN languages and shared common run-time linkage and relocation architecture, and a more generalized program overlay structure, organized along tree structure concepts was available across this spectrum. IBJOB in turn ran under IBSYS, and so could coexist with the FORTRAN II FMS subsystem at that level, along with other subsystems. FORTRAN IV, and the IBJOB monitor, in accordance with agreements between IBM and SHARE, sacrificed compatibility with FORTRAN II and FMS, in exchange for language and operational improvements. FORTRAN II FMS continued to be distributed and maintained, therefore, to support existing FORTRAN II and FMS applications. Many SHARE members who purchased IBM's S/360 systems in the late 1960s continued to run these new systems in 7000 series emulation mode for several years, continuing to operate with FMS, IBJOB, IBSYS, and/or their own monitor systems and subsystems.

RETROSPECT

The FORTRAN Monitor System, together with its follow-on, IBJOB, and complementary system, IBSYS, served practical roles as "workhorse" systems for IBM's 704/9/90 series FORTRAN users throughout the 1960s decade. Their features (some of which were derived from FORTRAN II linkage concepts) laid foundations for the incorporation of similar features (now taken for granted) in subsequent operating systems. For example:

1. The Binary Symbolic Segment relocatable object program architecture concepts are still used in modern operating systems, as are the source language debugging aids built on them; the IBJOB extensions to this for automatic overlays during execution (replacing the FMS chain link concept) were carried into IBM System/360 operating systems until the advent of virtual memory hardware/software systems.
2. The concatenation of batch job steps in FMS has been carried forward and refined in all major modern operating systems.
3. The concepts of I/O resource allocation and control introduced by IBSYS are still present in modern operating systems.

These were important steps in the evolution of operating systems, and helped provide a productive application environment for emerging large system computer users in this period. The major impetus in the growth of these systems came from the users, through the good communication of the SHARE organization. The author is glad to have been a part of this early segment of operating systems history.

SMALL BUSINESS DAY

SHELDON GOLDBERG
S. Goldberg and Associates
Morton Grove, Illinois

The Small Business Day sessions offer a complete automation seminar for small business owners or managers contemplating installation or upgrade of a computer system. Learn what a computer can do for your business and how to maximize return on investment for your computer system. You need to know about automation as a solution for your business problems if you want to stay in business. The Small Business seminar tells you why you should automate, helps you decide what to automate, and explains how to proceed so you can begin immediately.

The first session features practical advice on how to find the resources you need as you define your automation needs. It also explains how to get financial assistance for funding computer hardware, software, and consulting services. Other sessions arm you with the facts you need to be an informed buyer. The sessions strip computer automation of its technical armor by describing it in practical small business user terms. Learn what steps to take and how to proceed in a manner that keeps you in control.

The final session addresses specific needs for specific industries, focusing on requirements for real estate offices, medical and dental practices, restaurants, hotel/motel operations, distributors, and small manufacturers. The session provides advice on how to get the competitive edge in your industry and how to avoid the pitfalls that have left many small business owners wondering where they went wrong. The complete four-session seminar provides scores of practical tips for getting the most from your automation plans, streamlining your computerization, and reducing your automation costs.

1987 NATIONAL COMPUTER CONFERENCE COMMITTEES

PROGRAM COMMITTEE

Chair
Margaret K. Butler
Argonne National Laboratory
Argonne, IL

Vice Chair
Alan Hirsch
Amoco Corporation
Chicago, IL

Administrative Assistant
Joan Murphy
Cass Junior High School
Darien, IL

Robert L. Ashenhurst
The University of Chicago
Chicago, IL

Martin L. Bariff
Illinois Institute of Technology
Chicago, IL

Richard Barnier
Digital Equipment Corporation
Rolling Meadows, IL

Judy Bennett
IBM Corporation
Chicago, IL

Hal Berghel
University of Arkansas
Fayetteville, AR

Barbara Campbell
Governor's Commission on Science and Technology
Chicago, IL

Carl K. Chang
University of Illinois at Chicago
Chicago, IL

Robert Clark
Boeing Computer Services
Seattle, WA

Joseph E. Collins
Data Processing Management Association
Park Ridge, IL

Charles Curran
Allan-Bradley
Milwaukee, WI

Jack Dongarra
Argonne National Laboratory
Argonne, IL

S. Krishna Dronamraju
AT&T Information Systems
Naperville, IL

Martha Evens
Illinois Institute of Technology
Chicago, IL

David Foster
LaSalle National Bank
Chicago, IL

Sheldon Goldberg
S. Goldberg & Associates
Morton Grove, IL

Scott Humphrey
Britton Lee, Inc.
Los Gatos, CA

Julie Hurd
The University of Chicago
Chicago, IL

Jie-Yong Juang
Northwestern University
Evanston, IL

Evelyn Marsh
Sears
Chicago, IL

Jorge Nocedal
Northwestern University
Evanston, IL

Eugene Norris
George Mason University
Fairfax, VA

Sandra Reed
Northern Illinois University
DeKalb, IL

George Ryckman
General Motors, Retired
Grosse Pointe, MI

Alan Sobel
Lucitron, Inc.
Northbrook, IL

Sandra Taylor
Britton Lee, Inc.
Los Gatos, CA

George B. Trubow
John Marshall Law School
Chicago, IL

Robert Vonderohe
The University of Chicago
Chicago, IL

David Weber
Argonne National Laboratory
Argonne, IL

Conrad Weisert
Information Disciplines
Chicago, IL

1987 NATIONAL COMPUTER CONFERENCE STEERING COMMITTEE

General Chair
John Brown
AT&T Information Systems
Naperville, IL

Vice Chair
Richard B. Wise
Sargent & Lundy Engineers
Chicago, IL

Program Chair
Margaret K. Butler
Argonne National Laboratory
Argonne, IL

Professional Development Seminars Chair
C. Robert Carlson
Illinois Institute of Technology
Chicago, IL

Pioneer Day Chair
George Ryckman
General Motors, Retired
Grosse Pointe, MI

Promotions Chair
Roger Halligan
Halligan & Associates, Inc.
Chicago, IL

Finance Chair
Marjorie Benson
University of Chicago
Chicago, IL

Operations Chair
Mary W. Owen
SPSS Inc.
Chicago, IL

Human Services
Shirley A. Baird
Milestone Systems, Inc.
Downers Grove, IL

Special Activities
M. Mildred Wyatt
Wyatt Communications
Chicago, IL

Secretary
David Jacobsohn
Chicago, IL

Advisor
Rolland B. Arndt
Lakeland, MN

Advisor
Albert K. Hawkes
Sargent & Lundy Engineers
Chicago, IL

Micro Mouse Chair
Susan Rosenbaum
Strategic Planning and Mechanization Specialist
Plainfield, NJ

NATIONAL COMPUTER CONFERENCE BOARD/AFIPS CONFERENCE BOARD

Chairman and DPMA Representative
Carroll Lewis
Commercial Data Corporation
Memphis, TN

Treasurer and AFIPS Representative
Seymour Wolfson
Wayne State University
Detroit, MI

Secretary and AFIPS Representative
Robert E. Blue
E COMP-COMM
Indialantic, FL

AFIPS Representative
Rolland B. Arndt
Lakeland, MN

AFIPS Representative
Jack Moshman
Moshman Associates, Inc.
Bethesda, MD

ACM Representative
Bertram Herzog
Boulder, CO

IEEE-CS Representative
Stanley Winkler
Bethesda, MD

SCS Representative
Carl W. Malstrom
North Carolina State University
Raleigh, NC

Ex Officio Members

ACM President
Paul W. Abrahams
Deerfield, MA

DPMA President
Robert A. Hoadley
City of Raleigh
Raleigh, NC

IEEE-CS President
Roy Russo
IBM Corporation
Yorktown Heights, NY

SCS President
Ralph Huntsinger
California State University
Chico, CA

AFIPS Executive Director
John Gilbert
AFIPS
Reston, VA

AMERICAN FEDERATION OF INFORMATION PROCESSING SOCIETIES, INC. (AFIPS)

OFFICERS

BOARD OF DIRECTORS

AUTHOR INDEX